For Mama Wes

$weet Jone$
THE
Pimp

Pimp C's Trill Life Story

(You Ain't Gotz To Like It
But You Gotz To Respect ME)

UGK's **Bun B** and **Pimp C** in Houston, 1999.
Photo: Deron Neblett

"Lil Wayne, Drake, I see it in all of [today's artists]. I see a piece of Pimp C in all of 'em. I truly do … Pimp C was soul, blues, and funk all rolled up in one." – Sleepy Brown

"UGK is the soul of Southern Hip-Hop." – Sway Calloway of MTV News, *Sama'an Ashrawi's All-Star Tribute to UGK*

"It's amazing to me how some of the greatest rappers of our generation pay homage to [Pimp C] almost on a daily [basis]." – Lloyd

"Pimp C was one of the creators or godfathers of this whole [Southern rap] scene. A lot of us got our whole style and swagger from Pimp." – Chamillionare, *Raw Report* DVD

"A hundred years from now, people are gonna look at UGK as one of the most innovative rap duos of all time. Not just sixteen bars, these are genius compositions in music … People are gonna look back and study [UGK] because it's not just some regular-ass rap shit. That's *music*." – Mac Miller, *Sama'an Ashrawi's All-Star Tribute to UGK*

"[Pimp C's death] is a great loss to the Southern Hip-Hop movement. Let the legacy of Pimp C live on." – Rick Ross, AllHipHop

"[Pimp C produced] some of the most funkiest vintage country rap tunes you ever heard. If you go back and get the CDs and read the credits, you'll see some of your favorites were produced by Pimp C … His talent went a long way as an MC and as a producer. A lot of people don't know that he made damn near all the beats on the old UGK albums. He gave Texas its sound." – Big Boi of OutKast, MTV News

"UGK is the church meets the streets." – Jazze Pha

"[UGK] inspired a lot of people in the streets – a lot of people that don't have nothing – to get out and get something." – Young Buck

"When you heard [Pimp C] rhyme, you heard his soul pour through your speakers because he spoke of nothing but the truth about the world as he saw it. He taught us that we never have to adhere to the music industry's standards in order to feel accepted and respected."
– Ludacris, AllHipHop

"Music was all Pimp [C] ever wanted to do. UGK was more his dream than mine, and I'm just happy that it came true for him." – Bun B, Madd Hatta radio interview

"[UGK] laid the foundation for the South and they never really got their credit … UGK was Jay-Z to us." – David Banner, MTV News

"They stayed true even when the world wasn't on it … Stay original and stay true to yourself. That's UGK. Bun B and Pimp C." – Kendrick Lamar, *Sama'an Ashrawi's All-Star Tribute to UGK*

"For some [artists], the genius is not realized originally. It takes a minute to be able to grasp the genius of someone. And I think that [UGK is] that kind of group … You cannot have a conversation about the greats of Hip-Hop and not include UGK … I could personally teach a class on the relevance of UGK in American music history." – Joi Gilliam

"It's the strangest connection. It's weird how your life takes you different places. I never woulda thought that I would feel as close as I do to somebody like Pimp C ... I feel really blessed to have met him and known him, especially because I never would've even heard his music [otherwise] ... [It's] like a whole world was opened up to me. I never would've gone to Port Arthur ... it's now a warm place in my heart."

— Anne-Marie Stripling, former Director of Video Promotion, Jive Records

TABLE OF CONTENTS

"I am grateful to all those people who said no. It is because of them I did it myself." – Wayne W. Dyer

_____

"Thank you so much for overlooking us and teaching us how to grind and how to sell our own shit and how to make our own relationships ... Thank you very much for overlooking the South [and] putting us in a position where we had to learn how to do it ourselves. We appreciate that very much. Thank you. I will laugh all the way to the bank." – Pitbull, _OZONE_ Magazine, January 2004

To order, send $25 plus $4 shipping and handling to:
Shreveport Ave Inc
PO Box 250009
Atlanta, GA 30325

For more information, visit us online at:
www.pimpcbook.com
www.shreveportave.com
Instagram: @pimpcbook
Twitter: @pimpcbook

Book design by Julia Beverly

ISBN: 978-0-692-46127-3

FOREWORD
by Todd "Too $hort" Shaw

Thursday, December 13, 2007
Port Arthur, Texas

I was with Scarface and Bun B and I couldn't believe I was looking at Pimp C in a fuckin' casket.

Bun B broke down in a real way, and what he said was exactly what I was thinking. I'm thinking: *This cannot be Chad. I can't believe this shit.* It won't settle, it won't set in. And when Bun really cried real tears, it wasn't the tears of a homie, it was the tears of a brother. And I could not share those tears with him at that moment because I knew that the bond they had was way deeper than any brother or friend either one of them ever had. Me and 'Face, we went over there and gave Bun a hug.

Every time I mourn Chad, that's the moment I'm mourning. I couldn't do that with Bun at that moment. I'm pretty sure he had a lot of moments where he had to let go. But that moment that I shared with him, to this day, whenever I have those moments – and it comes to me often – I have these 'Chad moments' where I just stop and think, *I had a real friend.* I lost a real fuckin' friend. Not these rappers I hang around and these muthafuckers that are always like, "$hort, $hort, $hort!" but I had *a real fuckin' friend.* And when I think about the loss of him, it always comes back to that moment: me, Scarface, sitting in that room, his body's right there, and Bun's trying to be strong. Bun was being real strong that day and being real responsible and real grown, but in that moment he could not control those tears. He could not hold 'em back.

When I cry and I think about Chad, it's like Bun is crying with me and Scarface is sitting next to me, and I just miss my homie. I'm so glad I was there to see him at a moment where he was laughing and being Pimp C and being himself right before he passed.

"Anytime you met Pimp C there was a story. If you met him three times, you had three stories to tell." – Bun B, HoustonSoReal, December 2007

"Hip-Hop is really an art form that comes from hardship and translating hardships into success ... [When you make] any piece of art, you just kind of do it the best you can and you throw it out there and see what happens. People get inspired by your art and they take it wherever it is going to go ... If you aim it and say, 'It has to be positive,' you will fucking dilute and destroy the story. So you have to make a raw piece of work and hope that people understand the artistry in it." – Ice-T, Collider.com, September 2012

October 2010
Atlanta, Georgia

"Nobody's ever won a Pulitzer Prize by keeping everybody happy," Bun B told me.

I was on the phone, pacing the sidewalk outside a Midtown Atlanta restaurant. I'd just presented Bun with an idea that had been brewing in my head for months: to write a book on Chad "Pimp C" Butler, his partner in the rap group UGK, who had passed three years earlier. I'd heard the family was divided after his death, with problems between his mother and his wife, and wondered if Bun thought it would be a good idea.

As the publisher and editor of *OZONE*, the premiere Southern rap magazine, I knew how much my readership idolized Pimp C. I felt privileged to consider him a friend and was stunned by his death, which left me feeling completely deflated. His fans, too, were crushed. In the South, he was held in the same regard as a Tupac Shakur or Notorious B.I.G., but with his passing, I felt that he hadn't received the level of recognition he deserved. And the more I thought about it, no one was more uniquely positioned to tell his story than I was. I scrolled through my BlackBerry: "U the only media person i talk 2!" he'd once texted me.

Books have been taking me on exciting adventures all around the world long before I ever got to go in real life, transporting me through time and making history come alive in ways that dry textbooks never could. I loved biographies and non-fiction books – *Catch Me If You Can, Into Thin Air, Random Family, Conspiracy of Fools, Catch a Fire: The Life of Bob Marley*, just to name a few – the ones that made me feel like I was *there*. I appreciated the writers who were able to make their era come alive for me to experience, and always had the vague notion that I should one day pass that gift along.

One of the basic tenets of responsible journalism is that you must keep a distance from your subjects in order to maintain your objectivity. Although I've never been one to follow the rules in the first place, as a 19-year-old white girl launching a Hip-Hop magazine, it quickly became clear that this philosophy would not work in my environment.

Over the years, I reached a point where some of the most respected figures in the industry welcomed me into their homes as a friend, calling me all hours of the day just to talk. The line between journalist and friend started to get blurry. I didn't realize it was happening until it was too late: I'd started out intending to cover the story and unintentionally become part of the story.

Nowhere did this become clearer than in examining my relationship with Pimp C, one of the most interesting people I've ever met. Throughout the unlikely journey of me, a missionary's kid, being mentored by a parolee named "Pimp C," a genuine friendship and professional respect blossomed. I'd appreciated his candor and insight and been entertained by his antics, but didn't truly realize what we'd lost until he was gone.

Based on my own experiences with Pimp in the two years prior to his death, I suspected his life was a hell of a story. The excitement of seeing my name in print in those first few issues of *OZONE* had long since passed, and I was ready for the next challenge. After my first sit-down with Pimp C's mother, who was as enthusiastic about the project as I was and could vividly recall detailed stories from twenty years earlier, I knew I *had* to write this book.

I began researching and conducting interviews all over the country, which turned into an adventure of its own. I found myself interviewing a pimp at his Atlanta home which apparently doubled as a bondage porn set; filling out a fake application to go undercover at a Las Vegas escort service (codename: Natasha). In Los Angeles, Snoop Dogg exhaled smoke into Bishop Don "Magic" Juan's mouth mere inches from my face ("blowing shotgun"), a visual which may have traumatized me for life. I yawned as the clock ticked past 4 AM in a Port Arthur recording studio, where an entertaining group of Pimp C's former classmates described their PCP-induced hallucinations. A psychic offered to connect me with Pimp C's spirit so I could interview him about his death; a jeweler offered to get my mouth fitted for a grill. (I declined both offers.) I got an interesting visit from the FBI and an angry phone call from a Texas Parole Board supervisor.

Suffice it to say, Pimp C led an interesting life and had plenty of fascinating characters in it. And the reoccurring theme in all their stories was that not only did they love Pimp C because of his unique rap style and brilliant production techniques, but on a very personal level, he sparked something within them that made them want to be better; to find greatness within themselves.

"People cared about Pimp because Pimp cared … Pimp C, whether you agreed with him or not, was passionate about what he did. He gave a damn about what he did," Bun summarized in a 2008 interview with the *Village Voice*. "If there's one thing Pimp C does, it's give a damn. He's not lighthearted or easygoing about anything he ever cared about. It was passion involved in everything that he was a part of, extreme passion. There was no middle ground."

Chad Butler was a talented musician and a complex man, embodying a multitude of contradictions. He had weaknesses and strengths and he made mistakes, sometimes with severe consequences. He was only human. But the legend of Pimp C is what he inspired in all of *us*.

Armed with three years of research, I finally began writing – not to "keep everybody happy," as Bun said – but to do what Pimp would do: tell the truth. Hope you enjoy the journey as much as I did.

AUTHOR'S NOTE

This book is not officially authorized by the Estate of Chad Butler and has no affiliation with his wife, Chinara Butler. However, it was written with the blessing and support of his mother, Weslyn "Mama Wes" Monroe, who also served as his manager for more than a decade. At her request, a portion of the proceeds will be donated to his three children directly, not through the Estate.

This is a true story, based on hundreds of hours of interviews with more than 250 of Pimp C's friends, family members, and collaborators, as well as 2,000 other documented sources. (See the Acknowledgments on page 687 and the Appendix on page 708 for a full listing.) Everyone who played a significant role in his life and the events discussed in this book was contacted and given the opportunity to be interviewed. Although there are inherent challenges in documenting someone's life posthumously, great effort was made to maintain the integrity and accuracy of the project.

At times, recollections differed, so written transcripts or documentation trumps memory whenever possible. Any conflicting information is noted in the footnotes. Unless otherwise indicated, all quotes are from interviews with the author.

Chad Butler was a man of many characters and many aliases, so the names Chad, Pimp C, Pimp, and "C," as his mother called him, are used interchangeably throughout the book. In general, he is referred to as "Pimp" or "Pimp C" when he is in character.

All of the dialogue comes from a credible source. If available, a direct transcript from an interview or an audio recording was used. When a transcript was not available, dialogue was recreated from participants' memories. Most of the dialogue between Chad and his mother is based on her recollection, which she asserts is "pretty verbatim."

CHAPTER 1

"[There] wouldn't be no Pimp [C] if it wasn't for his Mama custom-building him. She customized him and raised him, so all those different gifts he had, she had a major role in that ... Matter of fact, I'm almost thinking about doing an album with Mama [Wes], because you know Mama will spit it just as raw as Pimp spit it."
– J. Prince, Damage Control Radio, December 2008

"I had lost three [unborn] children before C [was born], and I lost one afterwards. So he was destined to be." – Mama Wes

February 2008
Port Arthur, Texas

"So how did he die?" Mama Wes asked. She was settled in her favorite chair in the kitchen, bracing herself for the difficult but necessary conversation.

There was a long pause over the phone. "I don't know," came the voice on the other end of the line.

His words hung in the air. After a lengthy silence, he repeated himself, speaking every word slowly for emphasis: "I… don't… know… how your son died."

Mama Wes was speechless; she thought she'd prepared herself for every possibility, but she wasn't ready for *this*. "So, you're just telling me…" her voice trailing off, "you just… *don't know?*"

"I'm sorry, but yes," he sighed, his tone one of sincerity. "I don't know."

If you're gonna tell me something, tell me he died of a drug overdose, she thought. *Tell me that he did himself. Tell me anything. Just tell me something.*

As if reading her mind, he continued, "I want you to know that he did not die of an overdose. There was not enough of…" his voice drifted off, searching for the right words, "any of these things that people may suggest… in his system to have killed him."*

Forty-three years earlier, Weslyn Jacob, a shy freshman at the University of Southwestern Louisiana in Lafayette, wound her way through the college lunchroom.** Carefully balancing her lunch tray, she planned to gulp down a few bites and rush across campus to her next class. She'd just settled in at an empty table when a football player slammed his tray down. Towering above, he informed her, "You can't sit here."

"Well, I just…" Weslyn blurted out, surprised at his aggressiveness. "I gotta eat my lunch so I can get going, 'cause I got this class…"

He interrupted, loudly: "You can't eat here, because I'm not going to eat with no *niggers*."

(*While Mama Wes vividly recalls this conversation with someone from the Los Angeles County coroner's office, she was not able to recall the name of the person who contacted her. The investigator handling the case was Jerry McKibben, who says he does not recall speaking to Chad's mother. McKibben says their records indicate that the Assistant Chief Coroner contacted Mama Wes on February 4, 2008, to inform her of the official cause of death. He says she may have been contacted by someone prior to this date while the cause of death was still pending.)
(**Today it is known as the University of Louisiana at Lafayette.)

His stance attracted a crowd, gathering behind him for support. Weslyn, slim and petite with a smooth caramel complexion, was determined not to be intimidated. She stayed seated and finished every bite of her meal.

The incident earned Weslyn a meeting with the university's Dean of Women, who reprimanded her for not being more ladylike. (The player was dismissed from the football team.) "A lady would have just moved to another table," Dean Ross advised her.

"I wasn't a 'lady,' I was a '*nigger*,'" Weslyn retorted.

Weslyn had always been close to her father Wesley, and it was her first inkling that she'd inherited his outspoken nature. Her name, Weslyn, was a compromise; she was an only child, and her father had hoped for a boy to carry on the family name.* Wesley, who had a taste for flashy clothes and jewelry, owned a funeral home, a pool hall, and a nightclub in their hometown of Crowley, Louisiana.

Officially, schools had been desegregated since the Supreme Court's landmark 1954 decision in *Brown v. Board of Education*, but Weslyn and all the other black kids in Crowley attended the black high school, H.C. Ross, where her mother taught Home Economics.

College was the first time Weslyn experienced overt racism, from which she'd mostly been isolated in rural Crowley. She found the Civil Rights movement exhilarating; change was sweeping the country. She participated in sit-ins and fought for a spot in the new air-conditioned dorms, a luxury not usually afforded the few black students on campus.

Her high-school sweetheart Charleston Butler was several hours away attending Grambling University near Shreveport. Charleston was an excellent singer and trumpet player whom she'd met in the high school band. She thought he was cute and more mature than the other boys. Under her parents' strict guidance, their dates usually consisted of little more than driving around the city in Charleston's car or watching a movie.

They planned to marry after graduation, but moved the date up when Charleston was drafted into the Army. Their wedding, held May 13, 1967, was an extravagant affair at Morning Star Missionary Baptist Church in Crowley followed by an elaborate reception.

Charleston, who played trumpet for soul singers like Solomon Burke and Barbara Lynn, was also touring with Otis Redding as a relief singer, entertaining the crowd during intermissions. Forced to relinquish his position when he departed for Vietnam, Charleston introduced a good friend to take his place in the Bar-Kays, the band backing Redding. Six months later, Charleston's friend perished when Redding's plane plummeted into the frigid waters of Wisconsin's Lake Monona.**

"I don't think [Charleston] will ever get over the fact that he had recommended his best buddy to take his place," Weslyn says.

In January 1968, Weslyn graduated from college with a double major in English (Liberal Arts) and History, and a minor in Psychology. A temporary substitute teaching job led to an assignment as a fourth-grade teacher in the tiny rural town of Iota, Louisiana.

Weslyn was one of only two black schoolteachers in the district during their first year of desegregation, and was considered such a rarity that locals would sometimes pass by the building and gaze through the open windows (the schoolhouse was not air-conditioned) just to get

(*Many years later, when Weslyn was in her mid-30s, she learned that she had a teenage half-brother named Wesley Jacob Jr.; they were 23 years apart.)
(**The only survivor of the plane crash was trumpet player Ben Cauley. The members of The Bar-Kays who died were Jimmy King, Ronnie Caldwell, Matthew Kelly, Phalon Jones, and Carl Cunningham, along with Redding and the pilot, Richard Fraser. It is unclear which group member was the one recommended by Charleston. The only other member of the group who survived was bass player James Alexander. Since the plane had limited seating, each member of the Bar-Kays took turns flying commercial, and the day of the crash happened to be Alexander's turn. When Alexander's son was born a year later, he named him Phalon in memory of his best friend and Bar-Kays bandmate Phalon Jones. His son Phalon Alexander is now known as rap producer Jazze Pha.)

a glimpse of her. "They just hadn't been accustomed to [seeing] black people, but I really never encountered any racial prejudice among the parents there," she recalls.

The Victnam War seemed distant from the Louisiana countryside, and Weslyn had only a vague understanding of what her husband was facing. "I didn't really understand the significance and the danger of [Vietnam] until after he came home," she says. Charleston was summoned back home after one year to care for his ailing father. He served briefly as a drill sergeant at nearby Fort Polk, keeping food on the table by playing the trumpet at local nightclubs.

But Charleston had changed dramatically since his return from combat, and Weslyn found it hard to connect with her new husband. "I don't think he ever really came back from Vietnam," she says. "He had real issues, [but] he would not deal with the fact that there was something wrong with him."

In early 1970, Charleston and Weslyn headed to Port Arthur, Texas, to visit some relatives. Port Arthur, along with nearby Beaumont and Orange, formed an area collectively known as the Golden Triangle. (At night, the sky lights up with flares from the refineries emitting chemicals and flammable gas.) The area's population explosion began in 1901 with the discovery of the Lucas Geyser. Spindletop, the most productive oil well in the world, was gushing more than 100,000 barrels a day, leading to the Texas Oil Boom and turning the United States into one of the world's leading oil producers.

Weslyn's uncle was the head of personnel at the Gulf Oil refinery and boasted about his ample salary with benefits. Nearly everyone in the city worked for the refineries in some form. Charleston wasn't sure what he was going to do with a degree in music education anyway, and decided to take a job with Gulf Oil instead of returning to college. Weslyn didn't expect him to last long at manual labor. "He was not the kind to get his hands dirty, okay?" she laughs.

But Charleston was soon promoted to supervisor, and Weslyn landed a job as a librarian at Stephen F. Austin School in nearby Port Acres. Interracial violence was such a problem at the newly integrated school that the soda machine had to be removed because students were using the glass Pepsi bottles as weapons. "It was tit-for-tat," Weslyn recalls. "They had some black girls and some white girls who could fight like you ain't never seen no dudes fight."

Now that he had a steady paycheck, Charleston appeared to be losing interest in playing the trumpet. A stint with a local rock band called The Five Rednecks was short-lived. ("What are they going to call themselves now, Five Rednecks and One Nigger?" Weslyn wanted to know.)

In March 1973 the Butlers bought their first house on 13th Street in east Port Arthur. (The downpayment on the $9,800.00 property was $10.00, with monthly payments of $76.05.) Weslyn soon learned she was pregnant. Three previous pregnancies had led to miscarriages and rendered her seriously ill; concerned doctors warned that she might die.

This time, she was relieved to find her pregnancy progressing normally. So normal, in fact, that she became the first pregnant woman in the school district to continue working. The policy previously requiring pregnant women to resign had just been changed.

Sonogram technology hadn't yet been developed, so the baby's gender was unknown. Weslyn desperately prayed for a baby girl, wearing pink throughout her pregnancy in the hopes that it would affect the outcome. She wanted her daughter to have the same initials as her husband, C.L., so the baby's name was to be Charlesea Leanette Butler: Charlesea in the hopes that Charleston would grow attached to the baby, and Leanette in remembrance of a cousin who'd died of leukemia.

Weslyn was so sure the baby was a girl that she hadn't even thought of a boy's name. She was a sponsor for the school's cheerleading squad, and the girls were excited about the new baby. Weslyn assigned them the task of selecting a boy's name with the initials C.L.

For a group of adolescent girls, the obvious choice for a namesake was a handsome television star. Thirty-something actor Chad Everett (real name: Raymon Cramton) played the role of heartthrob Dr. Joe Gannon on the CBS drama *Medical Center*. Meanwhile, the girls' favorite sitcom was NBC's *Sanford & Son*, on which actor Demond Wilson played the son Lamont. It was decided that if the child were a boy, his name would be Chad Lamont Butler.

Shortly after Thanksgiving 1973, Weslyn and her friends gathered at a relative's home in Crowley. Their "stork shower" was considered prestigious enough to warrant coverage in the local newspaper, the *Crowley Post-Herald*.

With the baby's gender still unknown, shower decorations included pink and blue roses, and guests ate blue mints and sipped pink punch. Next to Weslyn's chair of honor was a baby bassinet covered in blue, with tiny pink bows adorning the long skirt. She appointed her childhood friend and college roommate Brenda Harmon as godmother.

The baby was due on January 29, 1974, so Weslyn planned to work until January 12 before taking maternity leave. On the chilly, overcast Saturday after Christmas 1973, Weslyn headed out to Walgreens looking for clearance specials. She scoured the aisles for half-priced holiday decorations and the biggest Christmas tree available, hoping to be prepared for the baby's first Christmas. It was there that her water broke.

At 11:37 PM that night, December 29, 1973, Chad Lamont Butler entered the world a month early, weighing just five-and-a-half pounds. Since there were concerns about the premature baby's health, he was rushed into an incubator before Weslyn could see him.

"It's a boy," the doctor told her after the newborn was taken away by medical staff.

Weslyn loved dark-skinned men like her father, so there was only one thing she wanted to know: "Is he black?"

Having been assured by the doctor that her child was indeed "black," Weslyn drifted off to sleep dreaming visions of her "pretty chocolate child." The next day, as she lay in bed recovering, Weslyn was shocked when the nurse arrived with a pale, screaming infant. The baby was shaking, crying so furiously his skin had turned bright red, his black hair thick and matted.

"That's not my baby," Weslyn said firmly. "The doctor told me he was a black baby."

The nurse assured her it was the right child. The boy was sickly and had a birth defect; his feet were turned in slightly, tilted at an awkward angle. Doctors kept him in the hospital for two weeks before allowing his mother to take him home. She watched him peacefully drift off to sleep at 2:30 PM. *A perfect sleeping baby,* she thought.

"At 12:03 AM, this nigga woke up," she laughs. "That was the first night of his life at home, and he kicked and played all night until 5:30 [in the morning]. He wasn't crying, he was just *up*, entertaining himself."

Six weeks later, Weslyn went back to work, leaving the boy in the care of her mother Grandma Bessie. Bessie called the school one afternoon to inform her that there was "something wrong with [her] child."

Her heart pounding in her chest, Weslyn panicked. "What's wrong!? Call the doctor!"

Grandma Bessie was calm. "Now, I don't mean that," she explained. "[But] there is something wrong with him. I think he's off ... he just doesn't act like an ordinary baby."

They quickly discovered that music was the secret to keeping the baby quiet. He wouldn't sleep unless there was music playing. He interrupted a relative's wedding, howling when a soloist sang off-key.

At six months old, doctors outfitted his legs with bars to straighten his feet. After four months, the bars came off and he learned how to walk. Chad was lactose intolerant and had to be propped up at night to sleep due to a serious digestive problem. He had his tonsils removed and struggled through nine bouts of pneumonia, the last of which nearly killed him. He had

Stork Shower Hostesses

Mrs. Charleston Butler, seated, was honored with a stork shower by her hostesses, who stand around her and her gifts, on Sunday, November 25, at 3:00 p.m. Left to right are Mrs. Eva Grace Syria, Mrs. Pearl Holmes, the honoree, Mrs. Butler, and Mrs. Gladys Butler, in whose home the shower was held. Missing from the picture are two of the hostesses, Mrs. Josephine Charles and Mrs. Cozette Wilson. (POST HERALD PHOTO)

Shower Honoree

Mrs. Charleston Butler, the former Weslyn Jacob, of Port Arthur, Texas, formerly of Crowley, was honored with a stork shower in the home of Mrs. Gladys Butler on Sunday, November 25, at 3:00 p.m.

Hostesses for the event besides Mrs. Butler, were Mrs. Eva Grace Syria, Mrs. Pearl Holmes, Mrs. Josephine Charles, and Mrs. Cozette Wilson.

Using the color theme of pink and blue, the hostesses chose to decorate the refreshment table with a white cloth decorated with turquoise baby carriages and pink flowers trimmed in green. The centerpiece was a turquoise umbrella covering miniature baby dolls sitting on green fern. A crystal punch service graced one end of the table.

The white shower confection was trimmed with pink and blue roses and baby booties. Refreshments of cake, pink punch, mints in blue and pink and coffee was served to the guests.

The honoree's chair was placed by a baby bassinet covered in blue with tiny pink bows on the long skirt where guests placed their gifts.

Honoree

Mrs. Charleston Butler, on the right, of Port Arthur, formerly of Crowley, is shown with her mother, Mrs. Bessie S. Jacob, left, at the home of Mrs. Gladys Butler as she was honored with a stork shower Sunday, November 25, at 3:00 p.m. Mrs. Butler is the former Weslyn Jacob. (POST HERALD PHOTO)

poor eyesight and caught a serious case of pink eye, which rendered him legally blind and unable to see more than a few feet in front of him. Other kids teased him about his wandering eye.

His mother signed him up for swimming lessons, flag football, and basketball at the local YMCA, but he didn't seem to enjoy sports. He couldn't spend much time outside due to his severe allergies, complicated by the poor air quality in Port Arthur, one of the nation's most polluted communities.* Medication and vitamins didn't seem to help.

He'd quickly tire of the neighborhood kids who came over to play. Birthday parties would come to an abrupt end; thirty minutes in, he would scowl at the other children and tell them, "Time for y'all to go home."

He preferred to pass the time inside alone, hovering over a toy orange record player which his mother had purchased for $5.95. Weslyn, cooking dinner one day, watched him stare intently at a Michael Jackson album which he had been playing nonstop on repeat all day. *There's something wrong with this child,* she thought.

"The child was always strange," Weslyn recalled later on Damage Control Radio, laughing, "I knew he was 'special' when he was three [years old], but I didn't really know what the 'special' meant, 'cause I thought the nigga was crazy."

Charleston and Weslyn purchased three parcels of land on the south side of Port Arthur in an area known as Alvesta for ten dollars apiece. When a relative in Houston passed and left Weslyn an inheritance, she used the funds to build a 2,270 square foot home on the land on Shreveport Ave., which would include a large den with a pool table and a formal dining room.

Designed to entertain guests, it was the perfect place for family gatherings. Charleston, known to relatives as "Baby Joe," still pulled out his trumpet to entertain visitors, while Chad banged on his father's drum set. Chad's aunt had given him an organ for Christmas, one of his favorite toys. He referred to the black keys as "sad keys" and the white keys as "happy keys" because of the way the sounds made him feel. As he explained in *Scratch* Magazine, "I feared music at that time so I would stay away from the black keys 'cause they were sad to me."

He frequently poked through his father's jukebox, which came with 45s pre-installed from acts like B.B. King, James Brown, Marvin Gaye, Ray Charles, Jimmy Smith, Jimmy McGriff, the Isley Brothers, and The Ohio Players. "I was getting [exposed to] records that normal people might not get to hear, like the deep jazz records and real blues records," Chad told *FADER*, explaining that his father "always surrounded [him] with music" despite being forced to put his "hopes and dreams [of being] a professional musician" on the "back burner."

Weslyn and her son were nearly inseparable, and in her opinion, Charleston resented the child because she doted on him so much. "Everything that I did revolved around [Chad]," she remembers. "His dad really never paid much attention to him. I wouldn't say he didn't like C, he just … I don't know whether he was jealous of C. C was always my everything."

Charleston was stoic by nature and seemed to be growing more and more emotionally distant. He suffered from terrible nightmares, remnants of the war. They lost another child to a miscarriage. Weslyn hoped the new house would bring their family closer together, but it had the opposite effect. Charleston preferred living in the city near his friends, and the suburbs didn't suit him. "He really didn't like the house, he didn't want the house, and I guess that made him more unhappy," Weslyn recalls.

Weslyn picked her eight-year-old son up from school one day and explained that they were going to go stay with Uncle Joe and Aunt Bea for a little while. In July 1981 Weslyn and Charleston agreed on what she recalls as "a very cordial divorce." Weslyn would keep the home on Shreveport Ave. and raise Chad with the help of $400 monthly child support checks from

(*Port Arthur is located in an area dubbed "The Cancer Belt" by *Texas Monthly* for its high cancer rates related to chemicals emitted by the local refineries. Port Arthur also has extremely high rates of respiratory disease and childhood asthma.)

Charleston's Gulf Oil salary.

Although Chad appeared unbothered by the divorce, his mother believed he was just putting forth a brave face. "He dreamed to make it well," she says. "He took it as well as he pretended to, because he was a master of disguise."

Now a single woman in her mid-30s, Weslyn didn't know how to adjust socially. She'd been married to her high school sweetheart for 15 years and didn't have much experience dating. The nightclub scene didn't interest her, but even if she managed to find a babysitter for a night out on the town, she spent half the night worrying about Chad.

"One night it happened: I was out at a party, and he got sick," she recalls. "After that, I didn't go out [anymore] … It was too stressful."

Weslyn gave up on dating. Love would have to find her.

———————————

One Friday afternoon during the spring of 1982, Weslyn and eight-year-old Chad were outside in their front yard when one of her co-workers happened to drive by. His name was Norward Monroe, but friends called him "Bill" or just "Monroe."

Monroe, in his early 40s, was a strong man with a solid physique who loved the outdoors. He owned a small ranch in the area, where he raised horses and wrestled cattle. He'd recently been promoted to Assistant Principal at Stephen F. Austin School, but was best known for his previous position as a band director. Like Charleston, Monroe was also a talented trumpet player. A musician at heart, he seemed to sense a kindred spirit in Chad.

After Monroe pulled off, Chad tugged on his mother's shirt. "Mama, what's that man's name?" he asked.

"Monroe," she told him.

"He likes you," Chad said softly.

"Come on, baby," Weslyn laughed.

"No, Mama, he likes you," Chad insisted. "I can tell. He likes you."

She decided to play along. "Well, do you like him?"

"Uh huh," Chad nodded. "He just gave me five dollars."

Back at work the following Monday, Weslyn sought out the Assistant Principal. "My little boy really liked you," she laughed. "He said you okay, you gave him five dollars."

Chad was correct: Monroe did like Weslyn. In fact, Monroe himself was in the midst of a divorce from his wife of 16 years. A romance blossomed slowly. "I was really wondering whether I wanted to be anybody's wife," Weslyn says. "I cared for him, I loved him a lot, but I just wasn't sure that I wanted that kind of commitment again."

It was Monroe's connection with Chad that convinced Weslyn to give marriage a second chance. "Bill was a musician, and they're different. He was passionate, you know? I loved the way he loved C," she says.

When Weslyn sat her son down to tell him she'd decided to remarry, a concerned look crossed his face. "Is it Bill?" Chad asked.

When Weslyn replied that yes, it was Bill, the worried expression on Chad's face cleared. "Oh, goody," he smiled.

Mr. Norwood Monroe
Assistant Principal

Weslyn Butler (Librarian) "I expect all students to put forth their very best effort even when the going gets rough."

Clockwise from left, in 1976, 1983, and 1978: Chad's mother **Weslyn Butler** and future stepfather **Norward "Bill" Monroe** (incorrectly spelled Norwood) around the time they met at Stephen F. Austin School near Port Arthur.
Courtesy of Stephen F. Austin School

Below: An undated photo of the new **Mr. and Mrs. Monroe**.
Courtesy of Weslyn Monroe

CHAPTER 2

"I heard Run-DMC's first album in December 1983, and ever since that day, I've been bit by the rap bug." – Pimp C, *OZONE* Magazine, August 2007

———————

"Everybody in the eighties was tryin' to rap. I don't know why we [were the ones who] got good." – Pimp C, *Murder Dog* Magazine, 2001

December 1983
Crowley, Louisiana

"Two years ago, a friend of mine / Asked me to say some emcee rhymes / So I said this rhyme I'm about to say..." Chad Butler leaned in, entranced by the sound of Run's voice on "Sucker MCs" coming through the speakers. It was his 10th birthday, and he was spending the Christmas holidays at his grandmother's house in Crowley. The boy next door, Shannon Holmes, had found Run-DMC's self-titled debut album under his Christmas tree and let Chad borrow it overnight to dub it onto a cassette. "I fell in love with Run and from then on I knew I was gonna fuck with [rap], in some way shape or form," Chad told journalist Andrew Nosnitsky.

Everyone in Crowley knew Chad's grandmother, Miss Bessie. Her house on 4th Street bordered Duson Park, where locals gathered every weekend to barbecue. But when Chad came to visit, instead of running around playing football with the other kids, he could usually be found holed up at his friend Larry "NcGai" Wiltz's house a few blocks away experimenting with music. NcGai's father, a local gospel musician, didn't mind letting the boys play with his expensive equipment. With the discovery of rap music, their experimentation took a new turn.

"This dude Run made me want to rap, man," Chad told *FADER*. "I started taking notice and researching rap and doing my homework finding out the origin of Hip-Hop music and where it came from ... I couldn't rap at the time but I knew it was something I wanted to do, so I started trying. That's what really sparked my interest ... I was captivated by Run's style, I wanted to *be* the man. As a kid, when somebody got that kinda influence over a child ... you know how strong that can be."

———————

The following summer, an 11-year-old kid named Bernard Freeman moved from Houston to Port Arthur with his mother Ester. The youngest of four boys, he'd been given the nickname "Bunny Rabbit." His mother, a private nurse, kept a strict household: Bernard was required to iron his pants every morning before school and serve as an usher at church every Sunday.

The Freemans had relatives in town, but to Bernard, the move seemed like a step backwards. It came at a tumultuous time in his life, as his mother and alcoholic father were going through a divorce. They'd raised him on blues and Creole music, soulful tunes mourning lost love by artists like Bobby "Blue" Bland, Z.Z. Hill, Solomon Burke, and Step Rideau, so he turned to music to cope. Starting over in Port Arthur was a disappointment, but also a fresh start.

Bernard knew of Chad Butler, even if he didn't know him personally. Everybody knew Chad's mother Mrs. Monroe, the lovable-but-tough local librarian known as "Mama Wes."

In the fall of 1985, Mama Wes decided it was time for Chad to learn about the real world. She pulled him out of the quiet Central Baptist Accelerated School and sent him to what she considered the "ghetto middle school," Woodrow Wilson Junior High, for sixth grade.

Chad impressed teachers with his polite mannerisms, addressing them as "ma'am" and "sir." "He stood out because you could tell he was very well taken care of," his social studies teacher Susana Valdes told the *Houston Press*. "A lot of the students that I had were from the projects, and you could tell the difference between them and Chad." Unfortunately, he was ill-prepared to deal with bullies, often arriving home in tears after being robbed of his history folder, his math tablet, or even his backpack.

Band class was his only solace. He rode to school every day with Monroe, who had relinquished his position as Assistant Principal at Stephen F. Austin to return to the job he loved as the assistant band director at Woodrow. The first chair at trumpet was Adrian "Donny" Young, a troublemaker who was repeating the eighth grade. Donny and Chad hit it off immediately.

Thanks to the band's "no pass, no play" rule, students who didn't pass their courses were dismissed. Chad had mastered the trumpet, so he was often assigned to fill in playing other instruments like the trombone, the flugelhorns, or even the challenging French horn. (The only instrument he didn't like was the flute, which made him "get head dizzy" and "want to pass out.")

Chad wasn't the only one inspired by Run-DMC; everyone at Woodrow seemed to have dreams of rap stardom. Donny's brother Willie Young, a.k.a. "MC D," was one of the first rappers in Port Arthur. Chad confided in his new friend that he wanted to become a rapper too.

"Mama, I'm going to make a record," he told his mother one day after school.

One afternoon Chad passed by a popular seventh grader in the hallway on his way to band practice. Chad's red Kangol hat and confident demeanor caught the attention of Mitchell Queen Jr., who was headed to football practice. Mitch was wearing a Kangol hat too, which were tough to find in Port Arthur. They caught each other's eye, noted their similar wardrobe, and nodded at each other.

Mitch stopped when he noticed the Gucci logo on the side of Chad's prescription glasses. *Gucci glasses, too?* he thought. *Damn. He gotta be a rapper.*

"Hey, man, you an emcee?" Mitch asked.

Chad nodded. He knew Mitch was "MQJ" of the Hardy Boys, a local rap group which had generated some interest at talent shows. Chad invited Mitch to stop by the band room, where he played "I'm Fresh," a track he'd created with a rudimentary drum machine.

The beat was basic, sure, but Mitch was blown away. The Hardy Boys didn't know how to make beats, they simply rapped over instrumentals from other rappers' songs. As it turned out, Chad's mother was good friends with Mitch's father, Mitchell Queen Sr. The two boys became inseparable.

The Hardy Boys' de facto leader was a popular eighth grader named Nahala Johnson, an all-around star athlete and linebacker on the football team. Nahala went by the nickname "Boomer Schooner" (later, "Mr. Boomtown," a nod to Port Arthur itself, referencing the 1901 oil rush). Boomer was gaining a little notoriety around town with his record "No-Z Girl."

A mutual friend told Boomer that Monroe's son wanted to meet him. Boomer laughed; some little band geek? He'd seen him around school, a chubby kid with glasses.

"He got a lot of equipment at his crib," the friend said.

Equipment? Now Boomer was interested. He agreed to stop by Chad's house and was amazed at his setup. "Damn, bro, where you get this beat machine from?" he asked. "Where you get this keyboard from?"

Relatives never had to ask Chad what he wanted for Christmas. Every year it was a new piece of equipment. He experimented with DJing, digging through his father's 45s and crates of vinyl. He had a growing vinyl collection of his own, starting with his early childhood acquisitions like Rick James' *Street Songs* and Prince's *1999*.

Chad and Boomer experimented with remixing an explicit song Mitch and Boomer had originally done called "Let Me Cum Inside," improvising a hook over a catchy beat with heavy bass ("let me cum inside, I really wanna rock, girl / I really wanna ride, let me cum inside"), with Chad laughing maniacally over the instrumental outro.

One afternoon, Mama Wes picked 13-year-old Chad up from his eighth grade classes at Woodrow. He was silent and introspective the whole ride home, absorbed in his own thoughts, and retreated to his bedroom as Mama Wes started cooking dinner.

An hour later, Chad sat down at the kitchen table. Clearly, something heavy was weighing on his mind. "Mama?"

"Yeah, what's up?" she asked. "Something wrong, huh?"

"Yeah," he nodded. "Something's wrong with me, Mama. I think I need to go see somebody."

Concerned, Mama Wes scheduled an appointment for Chad to meet with a child psychologist in Beaumont. But when they arrived at her office the following week, Chad was combative. "He was another person, and he was hostile," remembers Mama Wes. "He wouldn't cooperate."

On the drive back home, the shy child returned. "Mama, I'm sorry," Chad said softly.

"You sorry about what?"

"I didn't give it a chance," he admitted.

"Well, I don't think that was really you."

"Yeah," he sighed. "But that was the *other* me."

Several follow-up sessions proved unsuccessful, and the therapist was at a loss to determine what was wrong. "Either [she] was not the right person to deal with him, or she just didn't have the expertise," Mama Wes says. "C was a master of disguise, and if he didn't want to let you in, you weren't going to get in … He never bonded with her."

Mama Wes couldn't figure out what was bothering him either. "There's just something wrong, Mama," he'd say helplessly. "I'm not the same all the time." She concluded he was just going through puberty and struggling with the public school transition; it would probably pass.

Mitch and Chad wanted to form a group with Boomer, but Boomer was losing interest in rap. His goal was to get out of Port Arthur, and a football scholarship seemed like the fastest way out. Boomer was headed to California to stay with his older sister over the summer of 1988, where he could practice football in the moderate temperatures.

Boomer, known for his arrogance, commented that the group wouldn't be able to do anything without him anyway. Chad and Mitch said nothing, but the callous remark hung in their heads long after he'd departed for California. "Man, we going to prove to Boomer ass we can do this shit without him," Chad grumbled. Mitch suggested that "Mission Impossible" would be an appropriate name for the group.

They spent the summer of 1988 working on more than thirty songs for the Mission Impossible demo tape.* For help with the recording process, the boys approached Dorie Dorsey. Dorie, three years older than Chad, had christened himself DJ DMD (Disc Master D) and was known for DJing all the local teen dances in the area. DMD was a self-described nerd, a smart kid with an impressive collection of music equipment. He modeled his style after East Coast rap like LL Cool J and Eric B. & Rakim. His crew, the Fresh Four, had experimented with breakdancing and graffiti and sold cassette tapes locally.

"When we recorded things with DMD, all our songs would come out a lot clearer and had a lot less error," Mitch explains. "We needed somebody that knew about engineering and sound

(*Recollections vary as to what year the Mission Impossible demo was recorded. Based on DJ DMD's record "Here's A Story," it seems most likely that the year was 1988.)

better than we did."

"[DMD had] access to a little bit more studio equipment than the rest of us. He was a DJ and he was good at it," Chad told journalist Andrew Nosnitsky. "And at that time, rap was really dependent on the DJ. He could scratch, he could mix real good and he could program drums a little bit, but he couldn't play no keyboards." Where DMD was lacking musically, Chad could fill in the gaps.

DMD produced an uptempo track for their introductory record "Mission Impossible." In band class, Chad sometimes referred to himself as "Charming C" (he'd even recorded a short ditty over an amateur beat, proclaiming himself "Charming C, the lovah, fo' you!") but, for Mission Impossible, dubbed himself "MC C" and introduced the group:

You see, a true emcee is versatile
The kind of brother that can change your style
Get wild and buck and still know how to chill
The kind of brother that can ill at will
Write a love song that's sweet as can be
And still maintain and be a rough emcee
Now that's me, a brother so unstoppable
The summertime Mission Impossible

He also dropped some basic rhymes on "Get On Up," which featured a sped-up sample of James Brown's "Get Up I Feel Like Being A Sex Machine" on the hook:

We got Mitch and C and Dangerous D
Examples of brothers that can rock the beat
Mission Impossible has to be sweet
Yo, I don't eat spam, I don't like spam
'Cause I like butter
You know, I'm a black brother

When Boomer returned from California, Chad and Mitch relished the moment when they played the Mission Impossible demo for him. He complimented them on the tape, apparently oblivious to the fact that they'd done it to prove him wrong. "I don't think he meant [his comment] to be arrogant," Mitch says. "[We had to] prove it to ourselves that we could do it."

DMD would unofficially become the third member of Mission Impossible, and along with Mitch and Chad, formed a growing conglomerate dubbed the "DMI Posse." (The name, which Mitch says was his idea, stood for "Dangerous Music Incorporated," but the informal entity wasn't actually incorporated. "That just lets you know we were thinking big," says DMD.)

Inspired by UTFO's popular record "Roxanne Roxanne," DMI held auditions for a female rapper and selected Kristi Floyd. Kristi was a popular cheerleader from Thomas Jefferson High, the homecoming queen voted "Miss Personality" for Senior Superlatives. Under the moniker KLC (Kristi Lynn Cool), she recorded a song called "Supa Soul Sista'" derived from Heatwave's 1976 funk record of the same title:

That's why they call me a pimp female
KLC's the name, and boys are my game
[...] When I drop my raps, it's not just me
It's usually Mission Impossible with KLC

Other additions to the crew included Boomer, Lee "Master" Harmason, Evander "Boonie" Cade a.k.a. "MC Bash," Darrell "Q-Tip" Zenon, and two dancers, David "Step" Broussard and Roderick "Tattoo" Randle. The idea was that one person from the DMI camp would blow up, leading the way for everyone else to follow.

The DMI Posse took a group photo at the Port Arthur seawall along the Intracoastal Waterway (the levee which protects the city from storm surges) and compiled a 22-track demo titled

Rap In It's Rawest Form. It began with the DMD solo track "Here's A Story," three solid minutes of DMD rapping over an uptempo beat:

[...] Well we'll start the story off, it's in this place called P.A.T.
Deep in the east side, as a matter of fact
It was the year of '88, the month was May
When we come across some guy, MQJ
He and his homie MC C were jacked
They need to hit the clubs where the people packed
They walked into the club and on the wheels was me
The master of the disc, DMD
Strollin' up to me at a medium pace
I checked out the grin that was on their face
They came to a halt and in their eyes I saw green
For money that is, 'cause I'm a stupid dope fiend
You're talkin' 'bout money so my hand moved faster
Then walkin' on stage came my homie Lee Master
I told him 'bout it, he said, "Okay"
He was down if I was down, 'cause I'm his DJ
I then kept rolling so we set up dates
A time for us to talk, and make some demo tapes
And out of our first session I soon discovered
That the DMI crew would be some stupid dope brothers
[...] DMI Posse remaining on top
A prime example of pure Hip-Hop
[...] Stay out the way, don't try to get the glory
DMI's on a mission, and that's the end of this story

Copies of the DMI demo circulated around town or at school, where the boys sold them for $5 or sometimes negotiated if a prospective buyer only had $2 lunch money. They improvised multi-track recording in DMD's mother's garage, hooking up four to six cassette decks and recording one instrument at a time.

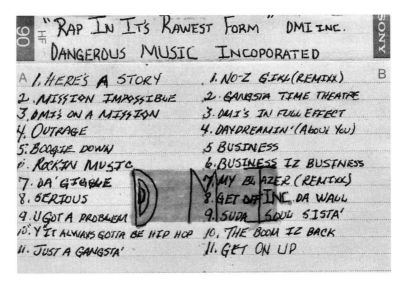

Above: **DMI's demo tape** *Rap In It's Rawest Form.*
Courtesy of Mitchell Queen Jr.

DMD had initially been amused by the young trumpet player with a jheri curl asking for help making beats, but grew to respect Chad's talent and innovative methods. "Ideas that he would come up with ... were way ahead of the game, way ahead of what everybody [else] was doing," DMD says.

Chad was one of the first people in the city to get a multi-track recording device, and DMI's base of operations gradually shifted to Mama Wes' house on Shreveport Ave. During a group meeting in Mama Wes' living room, a vote was held and it was decided that Q-Tip, an albino who sported a flat-top, would be the lead artist from the camp. He could dance *and* rap, and was therefore considered the most marketable.

While everyone agreed on the idea of DMI in theory, the logistics became more complicated: who was going to put up the money, for one?

Around the time the DMI Posse formed, Monroe retired from the Port Arthur school system. His daughter Ursula was a few years older than Chad, and adjusting to their blended family had taken some time. Chad enjoyed being the only child, and initially didn't like sharing his mother's affections with Monroe and Ursula. "Chad's an only child ... Everybody spoiled him, so he was accustomed to getting his way," says his friend NcGai. "That kinda shaped who he was."

Eventually, Chad adjusted to the younger brother role, even tormenting his sister's would-be suitors. "When guys came to see her, he was horrible," Mama Wes laughs. Chad refused to allow anyone to date his sister, sticking chewing gum on their chair before they sat down, or crying hysterically until they agreed to let him tag along on their date to the movies.

The family saved money every year for a long summer vacation, heading to places like the Cayman Islands, Hollywood, Disney World, or Las Vegas. Monroe wasn't normally a gambler but had a knack for hitting it big at the casinos, landing a $10,000 jackpot on one trip which launched an impromptu shopping spree for Mama Wes and the kids.

Mitch, who slept over at Chad's house often, considered Mama Wes his "second mom." One night, the 14-year-old boys planned to go to a party, which Mama Wes learned was "in the hood." She shut down their plans, sending Chad into a temper tantrum.

Mama Wes had been cleaning, and was up on a ladder preparing to hang a painting. She summoned Chad and informed him, "If you ever think you are going to tell em where you *are* or *are not* going, we gonna have to get together," shaking the hammer for emphasis.*

After sulking around the house, Chad and Mitch settled on plan B. Mitch was only a year older than Chad, but could pass for an adult with his solid physique and goatee. They snuck out and managed to come up with a 12-pack of Miller Genuine Draft. Mama Wes watched silently as they returned, trying to conceal the case of beer. But the beer was warm, and had them vomiting throughout the night. Early the next morning, satisfied that they'd learned their lesson, Mama Wes cheerfully whipped up some bacon and eggs and smiled at the nauseated boys.

Another youth who came by often was Chad's classmate Tim Hampton. Tim's mother struggled with drug addiction and alcoholism, and he'd been shuttled between family members and foster care homes since he was a baby.

By the time Tim and Chad started ninth grade at Lincoln High School, Tim's mother had cleaned up her life and was working as an elementary school bus driver. At 8 AM on the morning of November 3, 1988, she dropped off her students and headed back to the bus storage barn. En route, she passed a 10-year-old boy on a bicycle who was apparently skipping school. She

(*As an adult, Chad liked to tell exaggerated versions of this story. "That lil' lady crazy," he would joke of his mother. "One time she tried to hit me with a hammer.")

stopped and ordered him on the bus. Presumably afraid he was going to get in trouble, the boy produced his parents' .22 caliber handgun from his backpack and shot Tim's mother twice in the back of her head.*

Fifteen-year-old Tim was pulled out of class. "Timothy, let me explain to you what just happened," the principal told him quietly as his aunt and grandmother arrived. He spent the next 12 days in the ICU waiting room, surrounded by family members and media covering the sensational story which made headlines across the country.

Tim's only lifeline was the pay phone on the waiting room wall; Chad called daily to see how he was doing, offering to do his homework so he wouldn't fall too far behind. Despite doctors' best efforts, Tim's mother passed away at 40 years old. Chad offered him a place to stay. Mama Wes was touched when Tim told her that Chad was the only person who had said something to him that made sense. "I'll be your mother from now on," she promised, taking him in as her informally adopted son.

Monroe, now retired, spent most of his time helping Chad learn how to make music. "No other adult would ever work on it with him," says Mama Wes. "At the time, I didn't [take him seriously]. But [Monroe] did."

He frequently brought home new equipment, lying to his wife about how much it cost. "[He] gave C any and everything he wanted," Mama Wes says. "He would shower him with all sorts of musical [equipment] because that's what he was into, and he was just glad that C was into it [too]."

The house on Shreveport Ave. soon became the hangout spot for all the local boys with rap dreams, liked Chad's neighbor Ron Forrest. "They would sit here for like, days, just doing music. That was annoying as hell," recalls Ron's younger sister Ronda. "If I'd come in [his bedroom] it's like ten of [his friends] laid out and the track that's playing, they'd play the shit for hours, this one song."

Regularly, Chad and Monroe would stay up throughout the night, spending countless hours on the tedious process of manually synchronizing the track to the vocals. The thumping bass from the speakers often woke Mama Wes in the bedroom next door.

She would look at the alarm clock set for 6 AM and lie awake in bed thinking, *Jesus, give me strength,* as Chad and Monroe went over "the same fucking eight lines over and over and over and over again." Monroe was a perfectionist, and Mama Wes could often hear him drilling Chad through the bedroom wall.

"Almost?" Chad would ask.

"Nope, nope. Not quite," Monroe would tell him. "It's an eighth of a beat off."

This would continue for weeks. Mama Wes considered it a victory if they completed their task by 4 AM. *This is two hours of good sleep,* she'd think as she rolled out of bed to go to work.

(*The shooter's name was never released. The boy was only charged with aggravated assault in juvenile court, where the maximum sentence he could receive would be assignment to the Texas Youth Council until age 21. "In 1988 you didn't hear about kids toting guns, so basically, nobody knew what to do," says Tim Hampton, of his mother's murderer. "He was psychologically evaluated and then placed in detention for a short amount of time, [but] we were never contacted by the state prosecutors to [tell us] what happened to him. We don't know to this day.")

CHAPTER 3

"In Port Arthur, there was no Hip-Hop scene. The 'Hip-Hop scene' was Pimp C's bedroom." – Bun B, Sway in the Morning

———————

"When I heard the first person say 'muthafucker' on a record [it] fucked me up. I said, 'Oooh, shit, we 'bout to start cussin' on these muthafuckin' records' ... Next thing you know, I had a 2 Live Crew record ... When me and Bun started making these records, we were 16 or 17, so we *were* the kids. [Once] we got older everybody was like, '[Your music is] fuckin' up the kids!' Shit, I *was* the kids. *You* fucked *me* up!" – Pimp C, AllHipHop, 2007

Fall 1988
Port Arthur, Texas

When the freshmen at the predominantly black Lincoln High School were asked what they wanted to be when they grew up, Chad Butler announced that he was going to become a rapper, prompting laughter throughout the classroom. Many of his peers considered him strange. "Really, they ain't talk to dude," remembers classmate Daniel Thomas. "They thought he was weird."

Chad was most comfortable in choir, where his teacher Marjorie Cole considered him a great student and a talented singer. She'd often catch him "zoned out" in class, his mind clearly drifting, and summon him back to reality.

Often, he was writing rhymes, scribbling with a pencil on scraps of paper. Mrs. Cole approached him as class ended one day. "Let me see what you wrote today," she prodded.

Chad blushed, shielding the notepad with his hand. "Naw, you gotta see the clean version," he told her. "You can't see this."

———————

One afternoon in Coach Lamb's math class, Isreal Kight happened across a tablet. He skimmed through the pages and recognized the format: these were *raps*.

Kight, a troubled kid from Florida, had just been sent to Port Arthur to live with his father. He was still bitter towards the man for abandoning the family when he was a child. Kight's father was living above his means; he had a job and was always outfitted in fresh gear, but the refrigerator was usually empty. When Kight got in an argument with his father, he went to stay at his older friend Donny Young's house.

Donny had always dreamed of being rich, and when the crack cocaine epidemic hit, it seemed like the perfect opportunity to make some money. At 17, Donny drove to Houston and bought his first ounce of cocaine from Lil Troy (who was using the proceeds to launch his record label Short Stop Records) and brought it back to Port Arthur. "I was *the* nigga with the work ... I was one of the first niggas who started slangin' cocaine," Donny brags.

In downtown Port Arthur, the two-block stretch on the corner of Seventh Street and Texas Ave. was known as "Short Texas," the center of activity in the city's underworld. All hours of the day, Short Texas was lined with hundreds of people, mostly small-time hustlers selling crack cocaine or junkies looking to buy. Hole-in-the-wall nightclubs like Lane's and the Celebrity lined both sides of the street alongside gambling shacks, pool halls, and Freeman's Liquor Store. Crowds of people gathered to shoot dice in front of a small convenience store called Roscoe's, while a street peddler sold hamburgers and the older men lounged at Mooney's Café. At 2 AM, a preacher would often emerge on his soapbox, condemning all the sinners.

Short Texas even had its own terminology; it was here that the word "trill" emerged, a combination of "true" and "real."* "The old players wouldn't let nobody young come up here," Block, a Short Texas hustler, recalls. "You had to be a part of some kind of clique just to even stand up here."

Donny took Kight to Short Texas and showed him how to sell crack. "[Short Texas] was like a little community with a lot going on," Kight recalls. "I was hustling [just] to try to put some food in my stomach." As he waited for customers, he started rapping just to pass the time.

Kight was surprised to learn that the explicit lyrics in the tablet belonged to his classmate Chad Butler. He'd pegged the kid as a nerd. He returned it and mentioned that he rapped, too.

At some point, Chad had heard Run-DMC's "Here We Go (Live at the Funhouse)," and his mouth dropped when Run rapped, "Now if you say you heard my rhymes we gonna have to fight / 'Cause I just made the muthafuckers up last night."

Ooooooh, shit, Chad thought. *We 'bout to start cussin' on these muthafuckin' [records].*

"[That] fucked me up," Chad later told AllHipHop. "The next thing you know, I had a 2 Live Crew record."

Chad invited Kight to come by his house and listen to some music, where he played a track called "Dick Sucker" for him. The hook was an amateur attempt at mimicking a female moaning, apparently by speeding up his own vocals.** Chad rapped:

It's something 'bout how I rock on the microphone
It makes girlies wanna come suck me on my bone
There are girls everywhere that you go
Some are good, some are bad, and some are hoes
But not the kind of hoes digging in the yard
But the kind of hoes who come and make yo' dick hard
Now when you find one and you think you wanna fuck her
First find out if she's a dick sucker

The second verse told the tale of MC C's rendezvous with an older married woman in Beaumont:

I met this hoe in BM Texas
She took me to her house and she gave me sex
I bust that pussy 'til the shit was dripping
*I put her in the rabbit and the bitch started trippin'****
She pulled my dick out and she started to suck
And that's about the time I bust my nuts
The cum was drippin' all down her chin
And the bitch asked me if she could do it again
Right about that time her husband called from L.A.

(*Many people in Port Arthur credit Ezra "Spoon E Gee" Melancon as the originator of the term "trill." Melancon, who is now a preacher in Dallas, declined to comment.)
(**Chad later recorded a revamped version of "Dick Sucker," which featured samples of comedian Rudy Ray Moore on the hook. On the remixed version, the first verse ended with a few lines criticizing the "old men" who admonished him for "cussin' like that": "Don't criticize the words that I say / I hear the same damn shit in school every day / And when you hear this song you better say I'm right / 'Cause yo' daughter just sucked my dick last night.")
(***The rabbit is a sex position.)

He said he couldn't come home for a couple of days
She said, "That's cool, and I'll be okay"
And then I took his pussy away
How did I do it? He just can't see
Because I was only 15 and she's hittin' 23
See, women like a brother who can fuck all night
Who can keep the dick hard and shit up tight
Don't bust yo' nuts and then go to sleep
'Cause if you do, MC C will be fuckin' yo' freak

Perhaps anticipating reactions to the record, which certainly sounded like a page out of Too $hort's *Freaky Tales*, he rapped on the third verse:
The niggas who talk about the pussy they get
Usually ain't really gettin' shit
And the niggas who think they girl's wrapped up
That's usually the one that C's gonna fuck
All you punk muthafuckers tryin' to talk that crap
'Cause you say I'm tryin' to make some Too $hort rap?
But $hort is in Oakland and I'm in P-A-T
I been rockin' like this before I knew of Short-D
[...] My message to you, don't be no dumb fucker
And don't pimp a hoe unless she's a dick sucker

Beyond the Too $hort-styled "Dick Sucker," Chad showed his versatility, experimenting with R&B on "Turn Down the Lights," a smooth slow jam, and "My Place," which featured Chad singing on the hook and rapping on the verses. Chad and Mitch collaborated on another funky slow jam on which Chad rapped, "Me being in love is kind of absurd, word ... Yo, I never thought that this would happen to me."

Kight was especially impressed with the amusing record "Jenny Don't Wanna Say No," which featured Chad wooing a female who was resisting his advances. "Jenny don't wanna say no to me / So why you keep on fighting me?" he sang, promising to take her to "ecstasy." "Jenny is telling you to go ahead / But you act like you're so scared."

On the second verse, Chad clarified that "Jenny" was not the girl's name but rather a nickname for the part of her body that he hoped to introduce to "baby Jimmy." By the end of the song, Chad suggested they should "let Jenny and Jimmy play" ("c'mon baby, what d'ya say?" he whispered).

During the summer of 1989, Bernard Freeman was stuck in summer school. A classmate, football player Sylvester Vital, was an aspiring rapper, and Bernard wasn't impressed. He was introduced to Mitchell Queen through a mutual friend and conversation turned to rap; Bernard knew Mitch was in a group that was making some noise around town. "Fucking Sylvester Vital is rapping," Bernard complained. "Who the fuck said he could rap? That shit ain't even tight."

When Bernard told Sylvester to his face that his raps weren't "tight," Sylvester challenged him, "Well, shit. Come by the studio if you think you can do better."

Sylvester's friend Freddy Johnson's parents' house was one of four homes in Port Arthur which had recording equipment (Chad, DJ DMD, and DMD's cousins Wesley and Avery Harris were the others), mostly basic setups consisting of nothing more than a keyboard, a four-track recorder, and a basic Doctor Rhythm drum machine.

Freddy, inspired by the DMI demo, had linked up with his cousin Randy and Sylvester to form IMG (Innovative Music Group). Out of curiosity, Bernard came by Freddy's house to hear what they were working on.

Man, I could do better than that, Bernard thought. He took the beat home and wrote verses to it, the most intricate rhymes he could dream up. Titled "Lyrical Onslaught," he would later come to view it as "very, very, very terrible," but at the time, it was better than anyone else in the group, most of whom were unable to rap on beat.

Bernard struggled to come up with a rap name. (As Freddy recalls it, his first name was Shadow Storm.) He experimented with Bun B Chill, Bun B Ice, and Bun Beata, variations on his childhood nickname Bunny Rabbit, before deciding on Bunny B. When a classmate, Sherran Thomas, laughed it off ("naw, Bunny B, that shit ain't tight") he finally settled on just Bun B.

Freddy (sometimes known as 'Rick, short for Fredrick) was the only one who could even come close to matching Bernard's rap skills, and the two started recording together. "Bun was way ahead of his time [even] when he was in his teens," Freddy recalls. "When I first met Bun, he was way ahead of most rappers that were already established."

Bun splurged on a microphone from Radio Shack, but most of their recordings never made it beyond their immediate circle of friends. "We weren't even confident enough … to go anywhere and play that shit," Bun says.

Bun aspired to write socially-conscious raps, modeling himself after KRS-One, Chuck D, Daddy-O, and Brother J. He admired their intellect and conviction. His debate instructor told him he had a unique voice and advised that if he talked slower, he could get his point across more clearly, a suggestion which he carried into his rap endeavors. He and his classmate Jelon Jackson (who rapped as "Die Hard") started digging through the school lost-and-found to find empty notebooks, and Bun became a prolific writer, churning out 10 pages of lyrics a day.

When Freddy's track machine broke, the group wasn't able to record for a few weeks. Bun got the impression that Freddy's interest in rap was waning, so he started hanging out with a local DJ who lived nearby, Daniel "DJ Bird" Grogan.

DJ Bird, a few years older than Bun, had spent months washing cars to buy a coveted pair of thousand-dollar Technics 1200 turntables. Bird and his partner Maurlon "DJ Marly Marl" Banks also had an extensive vinyl collection and let Bun borrow instrumentals like Sir Mix-A-Lot's "Posse on Broadway" so he could practice rhyming.

Maurlon, a small-time crack dealer, had a spot at the rundown Gants Apartments, the unofficial hangout spot for the guys to bring girls. It wasn't uncommon to find a dozen people at the apartment, selling drugs downstairs and playing around with the turntables upstairs.

Meanwhile, Chad was starting his first summer job at Wendy's.* His mother gave him a ride to work and tried not to giggle at his fast-food uniform. "He even had the little hat," she remembers. "He looked like a damn fool."

Chad didn't get along with the manager, and as the new kid, he was assigned the worst jobs: frying greasy french fries, stocking the freezer. Three weeks in, Mama Wes came to pick him up and saw him on a ladder outside in the sweltering July heat, cleaning the building's exterior lights. He stumbled towards the car, exhausted.

"You look terrible," she observed.

"I think I have a fever," he complained.

She felt his forehead. "I think you do too."

Chad spent the next day at the doctor's office and asked his mother to wake him up the following day in time for his 2 PM shift.

Knowing that her son's pride wouldn't let him quit, Mama Wes simply didn't wake him up. When he finally found his way into the kitchen around 4 PM, he looked at the clock. "Oooh, I guess I'm late for work," he commented. "They probably gon' fire me."

"She probably will," agreed Mama Wes. "[Your boss] doesn't like your monkey ass anyway."

She watched as Chad called his boss, apologizing for oversleeping. "C, baby, I just really

---

(*Mama Wes isn't exactly sure which year Chad worked at Wendy's. Freddy Johnson recalls Chad working at Whattaburger and quitting after the first day because he was asked to clean toilets. It isn't clear if these were two separate jobs.)

don't think that's yo' job," she told him gently after he hung up the phone.

"You probably right, Mama," Chad agreed. He never went back to Wendy's, and told friends he'd quit "once [he] seen how they make the chili."

Monroe and Mama Wes had formed a company called N&W Vending (Norward & Wes) which serviced vending machines in the area. Monroe assigned a few machines to Chad; the job suited him better than Wendy's since he could serve as his own boss, and always had a pocket full of one-dollar bills and a Crown Royal bag full of quarters. It also meant that Mama Wes' house was always stashed full of honey buns, donuts, cookies, pies, potato chips, Danish rolls, and M&Ms, making it an even more attractive hangout spot for the local kids.

While Bun spent his time fine-tuning his vocals and writing pages upon pages of lyrics, Chad was absorbed in the music, trying to soak it all in. "I didn't understand how [rappers were] making that shit sound the way it was sounding," he explained.

"We didn't have sense enough to know that everybody didn't write they own raps, so we wrote our own because we thought everybody wrote theirs," Chad told journalist Andrew Nosnitsky. "We didn't have sense enough to know that they had people called 'producers' that actually make the music, so we made our own music because we didn't know no better … Shit, we thought everybody made their own beats, ya dig?"

He experimented with a lot of new equipment, which he would later describe as "mediocre shit": Mattell Synsonics Drums, a Casio SK-1 sampler, a Roland 626, an Alesis HR-6 drum machine, a Korg drum machine. He was thrilled when he came home from school one day to find a package sitting on the doorstep which contained an Ensoniq ASR-10 keyboard.

He'd share equipment with friends, giving his neighbor Ron Forrest his old Roland board when he upgraded to an EPS Ensonic Plus. He was the second person in Port Arthur to get a Roland R-8 drum machine, the only piece of equipment he refused to share. "That was Chad's baby," says DJ DMD. "He wouldn't let nobody play with [the Roland R-8] 'cause that was his signature … He knew that drum machine backwards and forward. He could do anything with that drum machine."

Chad listened to all the rap music he could get his hands on, trying to mimic their techniques. One of the cassette tapes he came across featured a mock newspaper on the cover titled *5th Ward Chronicle* with the headline, "Ghetto Boys Making Trouble." He flipped the tape over and was shocked to see an address for a record label in Houston, Texas. It was his first inkling that a record deal might really be attainable. *Goddamn,* Chad thought. *Shiiit. We can do it too.*

———

Houston's rise as a Hip-Hop hotbed could largely be credited to the efforts of two men: Steve Fournier and James Prince.* Fournier, a white kid from Chicago, moved to Houston as a teenager and felt something akin to a religious experience the first time he heard rap music. "It was almost like getting saved," he told the *Houston Chronicle.* "Something in my mind clicked."

Throughout the eighties, Fournier tirelessly campaigned for more rap music to be played on Houston radio stations as he DJed at local nightclubs like Strut's Discotheque and Boomerang's. All the opposition he encountered only motivated him: club owners who didn't want "too many blacks" in their clubs, New Yorkers who stereotyped Houston as "a big cow town," or redneck police officers who frequently raided his nightclubs. He even appeared on the local Channel 8 news for a highly publicized debate with Houston's chief of police, who objected to "gangsta rap" being played in the city.

In 1985 Fournier launched the Rap Pool of America, the first of its kind, where DJs throughout the country paid a fee to get vinyl from major record labels. "The idea that such an

(*The birth of Houston's Hip-Hop scene extends well beyond the scope of this book. For more reading on this topic see the book *Houston Rap.*)

institution would be run by a white man in Texas makes many brothers here in the Apple bristle, as if Fournier's efforts were an affront to the black roots of rap," music critic Nelson George wrote. "Fournier feels that's simply New York chauvinism."*

The following year Fournier launched a bi-weekly newsletter called *The Rap Connection* with LL Cool J on the cover. "Houston seems an unlikely place for a rap newsletter, but local DJ Steve Fournier says the city is a major Hip-Hop market," *Billboard* reported in March 1986.

At the annual New Music Seminar in New York, Fournier linked with influential DJs like Red Alert and Magic Mike and connected with record label executives. He brought artists like Eazy-E and N.W.A, Sir Mix-A-Lot, and De La Soul to Houston, and was eventually recruited by Russell Simmons and Lyor Cohen as a regional rep for Def Jam Records. Impressed with Cohen's new hi-tech toy (a Motorola StarTAC flip phone), Fournier accepted the job.

But Fournier's most enduring creation would be the weekly Rap Attack battles at the Rhinestone Wrangler, an enormously popular barn-sized nightclub on the south side which played nothing but rap music five nights a week. Every Sunday night from 2 AM until 5 AM, emcees went head-to-head, first in a lyrical contest and ending with the popular "ranking" contests, where opponents tossed out "yo' mama" insults and found creative ways to diss each other.

Popular emcees who emerged from the ranking contests included K-Rino, Romeo Poet, and Royal Flush, but the king was boxer Willie Dennis a.k.a. "Willie D," who won thirteen weeks in a row until police forced the club to shut down.** (He recalls defeating Vanilla Ice at least four times.) "I won so much … the competition stopped comin'," Willie D recalled later in the book *Houston Rap*, adding, "People would come up to me and tell me they lost they job because they stayed [all night] … to see the contest."

Steve Fournier was standing outside the Rhinestone Wrangler one night when he noticed a Mercedes-Benz convertible with the top down slowly looping in circles through the parking lot. "Anybody that had a Mercedes back then … [you] thought they were [a] millionaire or something," Fournier laughs.

Curious, Fournier caught a glimpse of the man inside, who was wearing a big gold chain. As the car approached the entrance, Fournier was informed that "Lil J" wanted to meet him. James "Lil J" Smith, a local entrepreneur who was in the car business, was launching a record label. He introduced himself and gave Fournier a 12" vinyl of his group the Ghetto Boys' single "Car Freak," handling it as if it were a precious diamond. "*Maaaan*, this is my record," he explained. "My first record. *Please* play it for me."

James Prince né James Smith was born into poverty in Houston's rough Fifth Ward.*** He spent most of his childhood dreaming up ways to make money, cutting yards and working on any other spare jobs he could find. "I wanted to break that poverty curse," he told *Complex*. "I was seven or eight years old and a lot of [other kids] were thinking about playing but I was thinking about how to get a dollar."

He worked briefly as a bank teller and found that he had a knack for networking, building relationships with local businessmen and athletes. He opened a car lot called Smith Auto Sales on the corner of 12th and Shepherd in north Houston. Shepherd Drive was lined with used car dealerships, but Prince's connections and ambition set him apart. He specialized in exotic used cars, convincing wealthy friends to let him sell their luxury vehicles on consignment.

As the story went, the Ghetto Boys' tale began when Prince came home from work on his lunch break one day and saw his younger brother, 19-year-old Thelton Polk, hanging out with a

---

(*New York City was often referred to as "the Big Apple.")
(**There were two Rhinestone Wranglers. The first was on the south side of Houston; after it closed, J. Prince reopened a new Rhinestone Wrangler on the north side.)
(***In 1996, James Smith changed his name to James Prince. The *Dallas Morning News* reported that he had changed his name to match that of his biological father, Earnest Prince III. In this book, he is consistently referred to as James Prince. Prince declined to be interviewed.)

couple younger teenagers, Oscar "Raheem" Ceres and Keith "Sire Juke Box" Rogers, who were cutting school. Prince and Thelton were close, only a year apart. Thelton was an aspiring rapper who went by the name "Sir Rap-A-Lot" (he later changed his name to K9). Prince offered the boys a deal, hoping to keep his brother out of the streets: if they stayed in school, he'd finance their rap dreams.

Thelton enrolled in college and Prince launched Rap-A-Lot Records. The idea of a rap record label based in Houston seemed farfetched, and some doubted Prince's vision, which only served as motivation. "That shit used to fire [me] up," he said later on the *Paper Chasers* documentary. "[People said], 'This can't be done.' I said, 'Okay.' That was inspiring, you know, that was gas on my fire."

The Ghetto Boys were initially a duo: Sir Rap-A-Lot and Juke Box. "I fell in love with the name [the Ghetto Boys] first," Prince told NPR. "I felt there were ghettos all over the world and I thought that it was a name that I could replenish over and over again."

Their first record "Car Freak" was a lighthearted comedic tune ("See, if you're walking down the street, there's no conversation / The girl wants a man with some damn transportation"). When Juke Box didn't show up for the scheduled recording session, Prince told Raheem, who had actually written the verse, to "go in there and spit 'Box's part."

With Prince mostly distracted by his other business ventures, the Ghetto Boys' sound and style were largely shaped by the three boys, who were heavily influenced by East Coast rap. They styled themselves after Run-DMC, posing for the cover of "Car Freak" in white FILA track suits and dookie rope chains.

"Car Freak" picked up a little momentum, but it wasn't a hit. "They was just happy to have their voices be on wax," Prince told *Complex*. "Houston, believe it or not, was a hard nut to crack back then. Just because you put out a record, everybody didn't embrace you."

One person unimpressed with "Car Freak" was Collins Leysath, a.k.a. "DJ Ready Red," who had just moved to town from New Jersey. (He'd jokingly sing the hook as "Corn Flakes, Corn Flakes.") At a Rhinestone Wrangler DJ battle, he showed off the techniques he'd learned in the Bronx – cutting breaks back and forth, scratching, and blending – and was approached by Juke Box and J. Prince's right-hand man NC Trahan. The Ghetto Boys were looking for a DJ.

DJ Ready Red joined the group in the midst of recording their album *Makin' Trouble*, and invited a friend named Johnny C to join the group when Sir Rap-A-Lot got arrested and Raheem decided to go solo.

Makin' Trouble achieved moderate success, but Prince was busy with more profitable ventures. When money started running short, he decided to take control of the label and relocate their headquarters to New York. He stopped by Def Jam Records, where executive Lyor Cohen showed him checks from LL Cool J and Run-DMC album sales.

Whoa... It's some money in this shit! Prince realized.

But five months passed, and still, nothing was happening. Finally, Prince had an epiphany. *Goddamn*, he realized. *We trying to be somebody else.* He gathered his staff and informed them that they were moving back to Houston to "finish [his] Ghetto Boy mission." He had a new strategy in mind.

Prince envisioned a darker, grittier Ghetto Boys; he wanted to show the world the things he'd experienced growing up in the Fifth Ward. But the group members weren't feeling the new direction. "They felt like my lyrics, the subject matter that I wanted them to write about was too deep," Prince told NPR. So he sought out new members, like Rap Attack rankin' king Willie D and Richard "Bushwick Bill" Shaw (at the time known as "Little Billy"), a Jamaican midget who could break dance, as the group's dancer and hype man. Prince pushed Bushwick Bill to become a rapper, asking Willie D to write his lyrics and teach him how to rap.

Finally, the missing link came in the form of Brad Jordan. Jordan, a diagnosed manic-depressive, had spent most of his childhood in and out of psychiatric hospitals. He'd attempted suicide four times and started experimenting with drugs at age eight with a schizophrenic uncle.

Raised on the south side of Houston, Jordan described himself as two different people. "It's been like that since I was born," he told the *Houston Chronicle*. "One person is up and happy and the other is down and depressed. I was born into a manic-depressive state of mind." Music became the outlet for all the conflict in his mind.

Dubbing himself "DJ Akshen," he dropped his first song called "Big Tyme" at age 16 and started working with Nigerian producer John "Bido" Okuribido. Bido produced a record called "Scarface," which sampled an Al Pacino line from the popular 1983 movie *Scarface*, and was released on vinyl by Lil Troy's Short Stop Records.*

"Everybody knew who Scarface was and nobody knew who [DJ Akshen] was," he later told *Complex*. "They would still say, 'Which one of y'all is Scarface?' and I would have to say, 'That's me, man.'"

Steve Fournier brought a copy of "Scarface" to J. Prince, who was blown away. *Whoa – this is my other Ghetto Boy!* Prince thought.

Prince arranged for his brother Thelton to battle Scarface at DJ Ready Red's house for their position in the group. The battle wasn't even close; Scarface, the clear winner, became the third and final Geto Boy.** "Whether [my brother] gave ... me [his blessing] or not, it was the right thing to do, business-wise," Prince told *Complex* Magazine.***

When Scarface, Willie D, and Bushwick Bill arrived at the studio to record the Geto Boys' 1989 album *Grip It! On That Other Level*, it was the first time they'd met. "That's why the album is so raw," Bushwick Bill explained on *Yo! MTV Raps*.

DJ Ready Red departed the group, accusing Rap-A-Lot of financial mismanagement (he later fell into a deep depression and cocaine addiction, which he has discussed at length in interviews). Critics have called him the "underappreciated architect" of the Geto Boys' early work. "Ready Red was so far ahead of his time ... nobody appreciated what he did until he was gone," Scarface told AllHipHop.

But DJ Ready Red wasn't the only Rap-A-Lot artist who claimed he wasn't receiving royalties. Word was spreading that many of the label's artists were unhappy. Aside from the Geto Boys, the label had signed many other artists who weren't getting recognition. Rap-A-Lot didn't have a publicity department and didn't put much money into marketing their projects.

Most artists were so thrilled at the opportunity to sign a record deal that they'd never even read the contract terms. Prince was known as a shrewd businessman who often joked, "I don't love money. But I like it so much it's hard to tell the difference."

"Niggas was just happy to get a record deal, so whatever was in the contract, who gave a fuck?" Scarface told journalist Matt Sonzala. "I had a record coming out. That's how I felt about it." Other Rap-A-Lot artists like D-A of the Blac Monks complained that their contracts amounted to "indentured servitude."

Rap-A-Lot's reputation became something like the Mafia, accompanied by an aura of fear. Once you were in, you couldn't get out without repercussions. "A lot of [artists] who left Rap-A-Lot [were victims to] home invasions; they got pistol whipped and got their equipment took back," DJ Ready Red claimed in an interview with HipHopDX.

Still, Rap-A-Lot was the only record label in Texas. Chad and Mitch had heard all the ru-

(*Lil Troy says that Scarface – then DJ Akshen – was signed to his Short Stop label, but Scarface denies that he was ever officially signed. Former Rap-A-Lot in-house producer Doug King recalls a meeting between J. Prince and Lil Troy at his apartment, which doubled as a recording studio. "Whatever [the deal was] Troy signed over Scarface [to Rap-A-Lot]," Doug says. "At the time, Scarface wasn't the monster success story that he is now ... James [Prince] wanted him. He made Troy an offer that Troy couldn't refuse ... I'm sure Troy regrets [that now].")
(**The spelling of the group's name was changed to "Geto Boys" at the suggestion of producer Rick Rubin.)
(***Thelton Polk a.k.a. Sir Rap-A-Lot's musical aspirations were derailed by his legal troubles in the late 80s. In July 1990, at age 24, he was sentenced to 20 years in prison for burglary of a habitation. In September 2000, a toothbrush with a razor attached to the end of it was found in his cell at the Estelle Unit. Thelton claimed it was planted there by a racist white correctional officer who had been taunting him after seeing pictures he received from a white woman. A judge sided with the officer, adding four more years to his sentence for possession of a deadly weapon. Shortly after he was paroled, he was arrested again in 2014 for aggravated robbery.)

mors, but decided to submit a demo tape anyway just to see if they'd get a response.* Chad was stunned when he came home from school one day and Monroe informed him that there was a message from Rap-A-Lot on the answering machine. Chad and Mitch didn't return the call. "We wasn't really trying to get with them, because we knew that they were doing their artists bad," Mitch recalls.

One afternoon, 15-year-old Chad came home from school with a wooden board from shop class, with "Pimp C" burned into it. "How you like this name, Mama?" he asked.

"*Pimp?!*"

"Yeah, you like that name?"

She shrugged. She wasn't offended by the term; besides, she thought Chad would probably change his mind tomorrow. "If that's what you want," she told him. "It don't matter to me one way or the other."

Chad asked Monroe what he thought. Monroe, always supportive, was unlikely to shoot down any of Chad's ideas. "Yeah, man, that'd be catchy right now," Monroe nodded.

"Originally [my name] had nothing to do with prostitution or pimpin' women," Chad told *OZONE*. "To me it was about pimpin' the pen. That's why I started using the word." Still, Chad was fascinated with the pimp lifestyle, watching movies like *The Mack* and *Dolemite* and reading books like Iceberg Slim's *Pimp: The Story of My Life.*

When 1989's *Grip It! On That Other Level* dropped, the first Geto Boys album featuring the new lineup of Scarface, Willie D, and Bushwick Bill, Chad was impressed with Scarface's lyricism and inspired by Willie D's bold country style. But he was convinced that a portion of their record "Scarface" was stolen from a track on the demo he submitted. (It's not clear which song he believed was stolen.) He played it for all his friends, complaining, "Man, this is my shit."

His neighbor Ron Forrest wasn't convinced. "I mean, it kinda sound like it, but it kinda don't," he shrugged. "Man, anybody could've sampled that," another friend pointed out.

Mitch had written two verses for a song called "Underground King" and brought it to Chad while they were recording at Avery and Wesley Harris' home studio. Trying to keep pace with the uptempo beat, derived from Clyde Stubblefield's famous drum breaks on James Brown's "Funky Drummer," Chad used the opportunity to vent:

I'm serving suckas with a quickness

[...] But a nigga's on my shit list

[...[But who is this I'm dissing?

[...] I'm in the six figures, nigga, and getting bigger

And getting better with time

*I'm 16, you're 24, and you still can't rhyme***

The 'Scarface' bass belongs to me

*Originally Pimp C, but somehow now it's GB****

But I got something to tell you, G

R-A-P-A-L-O-T ain't shit to me

[...] My name is Pimp C, and I'm the Underground King

(*Recollections vary as to how Chad submitted the demo; some recall him sending a demo to the label's headquarters, while others believe he gave the tape to Scarface or someone in his entourage at a local show. It's possible he did both.)

(**It's unclear who Chad was referring to here. In the context of the song, which mentions Rap-A-Lot, it could possibly have been a shot at J. Prince, although Chad always spoke respectfully of the rising mogul. At the time the song was recorded, Prince likely would have been 25 or 26 years old, not 24.)

(***"GB" refers to the Geto Boys. Scarface, who says he was completely unaware of Pimp C's accusation, denies that the bassline or any element of the record, which was produced by John Bido, was taken from a Pimp C record.)

CHAPTER 4

"We was trying to get in where we fit in. We was really trying to take on other people's characteristics so that we could get in the game and achieve something and really have a position in this thing. We didn't realize that being ourselves was gonna be the ticket." – Pimp C, *The Final Chapter* DVD

"I made my first record when I was 16 years old. Let me tell you something, man: Don't let nobody tell you [that] you can't chase your dream."
– Pimp C interview with J. Xavier, November 2007

Fall 1989
Port Arthur, Texas

Over at Thomas Jefferson High School, the mostly white school across town, Bernard "Bun B" Freeman was starting his junior year in the fall of 1989. An honor student in the advanced placement Summit program, Bun had been tested at a genius-level IQ and caught a bus to Lincoln High every day for accelerated learning classes. He had so much time to goof off that he'd earned a reputation as the class clown. "School was relatively easy for me ... I learned very early that school was pretty much just memorization and regurgitation," Bun recalls. "I was just bored more than anything, and that's kind of how I ended up giving all my time over to music."

Mitch was also in the Summit program. During their five-minute breaks between classes, Mitch and Bun would meet in the bathroom and listen to rap on contraband Walkmans which the principal had warned them not to bring to school anymore.

Rap music was hard to find, and exclusivity was half the fun. It was like belonging to a secret club; they dubbed copies for each other and traded tapes like baseball cards. "It was all about who had the shit first," Chad told *OZONE*, explaining, "Songs didn't hit every city at the same time ... I might have had a song on my tape that the next muthafucker didn't have on his, and vice versa, and we'd swap songs."

Chad would skim through vinyl at Sound Exchange in Houston or scour the shelves at Ted's Record Store in Port Arthur. "That's when rap and Hip-Hop music was fun, when it was like collecting tennis shoes," he said. "It wouldn't be no fun if it was mass-marketed and everybody could get everything ... that's what made rap music fun for us."

The nearby radio station 102.1 featured a three-hour Hip-Hop mixshow on Friday nights, and the boys used a hanger as an improvised antenna to get better reception so they could tape the show. They'd trade freestyles and album leaks, mailing tapes to friends and cousins in other parts of the country. "We would try to buy things we knew nobody in Port Arthur would have, so that when we traded, the trade was worth something," Mitch told *Texas Monthly*.

Bun had an extensive tape collection: Whodini, Biz Markie, EPMD and the Juice Crew, Craig G, Masta Ace, the Geto Boys, Public Enemy, Big Daddy Kane, Run-DMC, Kool G Rap, Rakim, KRS-One, the X-Clan, Ed O.G., Daddy-O, Def Jef, EST and Three Times Dope, Steady B, Cool C, and the Hilltop Hustlers. He had an impressive memory and could recite entire verses after just one listen.

Bun traveled more than his classmates, frequently visiting his father in Houston. His older cousins and brothers, who went to high school with popular Hip-Hop DJ Lester "Sir" Pace, would sometimes let him tag along to concerts at the Rhinestone Wrangler. Every trip he taped the Hip-Hop program on Houston's college radio station KSJM and came back to Port Arthur with tracks like C.I.A.'s "Illegal" (with Ice Cube) or the World Class Wreckin Cru's "Surgery" (with Dr. Dre). Bun soon became known as the guy with all the exclusive new music.

Like Bun, Chad was listening to everything he could find. Every time he visited relatives in Louisiana, he returned with bounce music or Gregory D tapes. (He and NcGai were endlessly amused by the photo on the back cover of Public Enemy's debut album *Yo! Bum Rush the Show*, which appeared to have been taken in the parking lot of a McDonald's.) He admired Dr. Dre's production style, and liked a wide variety of music including Too $hort, Schooly D, T La Rock, Eazy E, the D.O.C., Ice-T, and Rodney-O. He modeled his style after Big Daddy Kane, a "fly pimp player type nigga [who could] still whoop your ass."

The idea that Hip-Hop was regional – that Southern fans shouldn't like East Coast rap – never crossed their minds. "I assume[d] everybody listened to all the same stuff because there really wasn't room to differentiate," Bun told *Murder Dog*. "Everything was new, you know?"

Through Mitch, dubs of many of Bun's tapes ended up in Chad's hands and vice versa, but they rarely communicated. "Why your boy be so closed off?" Bun asked Mitch one day.

"Oh, he cool, he cool," Mitch assured him.

Bun found himself both intrigued and offended by Chad's swagger. *Man, this dude really think he doing something, this guy really think he live,* Bun thought, watching Chad pass by in the school hallway one afternoon wearing a mustard yellow Oak Tree suit with jewelry and a pair of Adidas sneakers. He knew Chad and Mitch had a rap group, and Chad was really living the part.

Still, Bun couldn't help but admit the whole outfit looked kinda fly. He stole another glance after Chad passed by. *Man, he look just like boys on TV be looking like. How he do that in Port Arthur?* Bun wondered.

Chad didn't know Bun that well, but had him pegged as just a big-talker, always name-dropping and bragging about some rappers he'd met. *This nigga lying,* Chad would think. *This nigga don't know nobody.* "I didn't really fuck with that nigga," Chad told *Murder Dog*. "The nigga would always come around, he always had all the tapes early. He was like a rap fanatic. I thought he was tellin' lies all the time."

"We were absolutely yin and yang," Bun agrees. "We didn't really know each other and we didn't really feel like we had anything in common. He thought I was full of shit, I thought he was full of shit."

Their simmering tension finally came to a head at a local football game, when Chad overheard Bun bragging about some rappers he'd met at an Eazy E concert in Houston. "Nigga, stop lying," Chad scoffed. "You don't know them dudes."

Bun pulled out a Polaroid picture of Ice Cube, Scarface, Juke Box of the Ghetto Boys, and MC Ren, which silenced Chad, but he wasn't completely convinced. *So where you at?* he thought sarcastically. *I bet you're takin' the picture, huh?**

Regardless, the Polaroid broke the ice, and Chad and Bun struck up a conversation if only for Mitch's sake. By the end of the game, Bun realized he'd pegged this kid all wrong. "You know, you aiight, cat," he told Chad, nodding his approval. Chad nodded back.

(*Bun and Chad both recounted their football game encounter in later interviews, with slight variations. In some versions of the story, the Polaroid was a picture of Bun and Eazy E. In others, it was a picture of Bun with Scarface and Ice Cube.)

At the end of the 1989 football season, the band director Mr. Pitre asked Chad, now a sophomore, to write a song for the football team and perform it at their end-of-season banquet. The track, "It's All The Way Live," was the highlight of the evening. Chad rapped:

I got a phone call from Mr. P
He said, "Make me a rhyme and a Hip-Hop beat"
I said, "What would be the subject of this Hip-Hop rhyme?"
He said "Football," I said, "Okay, fine"
[...] Place to place, town to town
The Lincoln Bumblebees sure do get down
Like when I'm on the mic I do get hype
The bees of P.A. cannot be stopped
Now Eagles can fly and Yellow Jackets can sting*
But like Coke, the Bumblebees are The Real Thing
Whether football or basket, band or scholastic
Lincoln High School always has the right package

Chad beamed as his peers rewarded him with a rousing ovation. "He put a lot of thought into doing that song," Mitch recalls. "It came over real well. I'll never forget the reaction that he got. The whole football team … was really, really hyped about it."

Mama Wes, applauding louder than anyone else, understood the significance of the moment. Throughout all the school activities and local talent shows, Chad had always been second to the older and more established DJ DMD. Now that DMD had graduated, Chad had finally earned the respect of his peers.

Chad and Mitch continued recording, experimenting with their style. Chad produced a solo MQJ record called "Nowhere to Hide," talking over the outro, "Aw, yeah, I gotta grab my nuts on that one, G! *Yeeaaah!* All the pussy ain't yours, nigga. I want some pussy, nigga! This is Pimp C!" before bursting into a bout of maniacal laughter.

"Hard Muthafucker" was another East Coast-style record, the hook a combination of West Coast rap group Duck Sick's DJ Quik diss "Compton's Most Wanted" over a sample from Soul II Soul's popular record "Back To Life."

Chad didn't realize Monroe had been paying such close attention to all the experimentation he'd been doing until he offered some unsolicited advice. "You know the problem with that rap shit?" Monroe told Chad. "The problem with that shit is that it's noise."

The teenager immediately turned defensive. "What you mean, it's 'noise'?"

"Naw, listen to what I'm telling you, boy," Monroe told him. "That shit is noise, ain't no music in that shit. You put some music in that shit and you might be able to get paid. You know how to read music … Get that noise out of there [and] make some music."

Chad was silent, thinking of The Bomb Squad and Public Enemy tracks he had on repeat, which were filled with sound effects and samples. Maybe Monroe was right; it *was* noisy. He'd already noticed that Dr. Dre and Too $hort were adding basslines to their music.

"Put some music in that shit, boy, and you gonna win," Monroe nodded.

Chad spent hours mulling over his stepfather's suggestion, digging through his vinyl collection of old school soul and funk records looking for samples. He pulled his childhood organ out of the closet and dusted it off.

He was also blossoming into a talented singer; he'd just set a state record as the youngest student to achieve a Division 1 rating on a classical solo. He'd blown away the audience with his rendition of Eddie Kendrick's first tenor on the Temptations' "Silent Night" during the school

---

(*The Lincoln High mascot was the Bumblebees, while the Eagles and Yellow Jackets were the mascots of the other two high schools in the area, Stephen F. Austin and Thomas Jefferson.)

Christmas concert. He and Mitch often traveled for choir competitions, perfecting Italian sonnets and Negro spirituals.

Monroe's mother adored Chad and arranged for the teenager to sing a "tea" at her Methodist church in Beaumont, a position usually reserved for professional singers. Accompanying him on the piano was his choir teacher Mrs. Cole, an accomplished pianist who was such a staple at the high school that yearbook staff used the same photo of her every year.

Through Mrs. Cole, the Lincoln High choir received an invitation to sing with Stephen F. Austin University's choir. The event put them on the radar of a concert production company called Mid-America which was organizing a performance at Carnegie Hall in New York City. Led by conductor Dr. Hugh Sanders of the Baylor University School of Music, the Sanders Chorus would include 350 exceptional high school choir students from more than seven states.

There was only one obstacle: they needed to raise $35,000, which seemed like an astronomical figure. Mama Wes, who was president of the Booster Club, took the lead on organizing car washes and bake sales. She begged the *Port Arthur News* to run a story soliciting donations and convinced local churches and oil refineries to chip in. The kids sold Lincoln Bumblebee watches and bagged newspapers for the post office. Mama Wes bought bags of candy and took Chad and Mitch to Crowley, where Chad's grandmother sent them door-to-door and called ahead to all her friends, insisting they buy at least five.

When Mama Wes organized a teen dance at the Sacred Heart as a fundraiser for the Carnegie trip, 19-year-old DJ Akshen/Scarface of the Geto Boys happened to be in town "on another mission." He'd been hustling small quantities of crack cocaine out of Port Arthur's Long's Projects, and when he heard about the dance, assumed it would be a good opportunity to meet some of the local ladies (YMA's, or "young men abusers," as he called them).

Mama Wes and Mitch's mother Margie were manning the entrance near the end of the night when a group of three approached the table: two boys in their late teens, one wearing a long black trenchcoat, and a midget.

"Five dollars," Mama Wes told them.

The midget produced a hundred dollar bill. "You got change for this?"

Chad, who apparently had forgiven the Geto Boys for "Scarface," rushed through the crowd and breathlessly asked his mother, "Mama, you made them pay? That's the Geto Boys!"

The Geto Boys trio walked straight towards the DJ booth, where DJ DMD was playing Afro Rican's "Give It All You Got (Doggie Style)." DMD's mouth dropped as DJ Akshen indicated that he wanted to get on the turntables. DMD handed over the headphones. After Akshen/Scarface found his place on the record, he took the headphones off and scratched the record furiously. DMD, Mitch, and Chad watched, impressed.

"That was the funniest thing," Mama Wes recalls. "I thought C and Mitch were gonna piss on themselves, they were so excited. I thought C and Mitch were going to have a stroke."

Still, DJ DMD was losing interest in rap, reflecting the general attitude in Port Arthur. "He said he wasn't gonna do no more rapping," Chad recalled on *The Final Chapter* DVD. "It was kinda like rapping wasn't cool no more, that wasn't the thing to do."

DMD had mailed out packages with DMI's *Rap In It's Rawest Form* demo to major record labels, but the only artist who had elicited any response was Lee Master, a popular athlete with clever wordplay. DMD decided he would rather focus on Lee instead of Mission Impossible.

Donny Young, who still spent most of his day hustling on Short Texas, passed by Lincoln High one day as school let out. He found Chad in the band room nearly in tears. "What the fuck is wrong with you?" Donny asked.

"Man, nigga Dorie left," Chad mumbled bitterly. DMD had decided to move to Houston.

Upset at DMD's abrupt departure, Chad and Mitch decided they needed a new name.

"We probably would have kept the name [Mission Impossible], but because it was affiliated with what Dorie [DMD] was doing, and it hurt so much for him to leave the group and not even really tell us what he was gonna do, we just decided to eradicate the name," Mitch explains.

Late one night, Mitch was sitting on the edge of the bed in his bedroom listening to music when the name of the song they'd done popped in his head: "Underground King."

He ran to the kitchen and dialed Mama Wes' phone number on his parents' rotary phone.

"Underground Kingz," Mitch blurted out as soon as Chad answered.

"What?"

"Underground Kingz! That oughta be our name."

It was a routine morning in the library when Mama Wes hoisted a heavy cast-iron overhead projector into its slot on a five-foot tall cart. The leg of the cart broke, sending the heavy apparatus smashing down onto her right foot, clad in open-toe sandals.

Mama Wes was already recovering from a car accident and could barely walk for months. Her foot remained swollen, stiff, and red, and even a light touch brought severe, burning pain. She was diagnosed with RSD (Reflex Sympathetic Dystrophy, today known as Complex Regional Pain Syndrome or CRPS), a rare incurable condition caused by nerve damage.

But even with a swollen foot, Mama Wes was determined not to miss the trip to New York. Monroe bought her a wheelchair and her mother Bessie donated a pair of crutches. She set aside some funds from their last and final fundraiser to get souvenirs for Chad and Mitch.

Mrs. Cole checked the weather conditions daily in New York and wrote the forecast on the board in her classroom. Chad and the other students weren't looking forward to the cold and rainy winter weather, which they weren't accustomed to in the warm, humid Port Arthur climate.

The *Port Arthur News* and news cameras from the local Channel 6 waited at Lincoln High before dawn on April 7, 1990, as 25 students and 11 adults gathered to load up on the chartered bus. "My Mama sold everything but pussy to get us over there," Chad remarked to one female reporter, ignoring his mother's glare.

"Kids ready for NY," read the headline in the *Port Arthur News* that morning, describing their "months of rehearsal and fund raising and a flurry of last-minute packing." After a layover in St. Louis they touched down at New York's LaGuardia Airport on Saturday afternoon and watched the landscape of towering skyscrapers come into view. ("Everything you have ever heard or read about drivers in New York is true," the group later reported in a letter to sponsors. "They might not even stop when the light changes. We never saw any speed limit signs.")

Chad and Mitch were entranced by it all: the atmosphere, the traffic, the crowds of people, the Empire State Building. Street vendors crowded the sidewalks. Mama Wes felt claustrophobic. "Everything was [close] together, just squashed up together," she remembers. "That was the hardest thing for us to adjust to."

After they checked into the Penta Hotel across from Madison Square Garden, the group saw the appropriately titled Broadway musical *Mama, I Want To Sing*. Chad and Mitch were sharing a room, and, as always, looking for ways to get in trouble. Mitch walked to a liquor store across the street to pick up a cheap beer called Little Kings Cream Ale (tagline: "It's Good To Be King"), which they only drank because it had "Kings" in the name.

The Penta Hotel was dated, and the group was in for a surprise the next morning when they learned the hotel had no hot water. After three hours of rehearsals they took the subway to Harlem for a tour of the Apollo Theater and sat through a filming of *Showtime at the Apollo*. Over lunch at Sylvia's Restaurant in Harlem, they happened to run into KRS-One affiliate Just-Ice, who signed autographs. Chad was silent on the subway, absorbing the whole experience.

On Monday afternoon, Mama Wes counted up their funds and realized they had enough

left to splurge. Her armpits sore from hobbling on crutches, she gathered Chad and Mitch. "Come on, y'all push me in the wheelchair," she told them. They headed to Chinatown and picked up some cheap Kangols and tennis shoes.

Their last stop was a jewelry store in Manhattan, where Mama Wes bought Chad a $700 hollow gold dookie rope chain with a Gucci emblem. She chipped in $50 so Mitch could get a $500 chain, too; the jeweler, feeling sympathetic, gave him a dollar sign piece for free. "Look, it's a bunch of muggers out here, and they know when they see tourists," Mama Wes warned as they exited, insisting that the boys conceal the jewelry boxes inside their trenchcoats.

The next night, April 10, was the big concert at Carnegie Hall, the opportunity of a lifetime. (They had dinner before the concert at the Hard Rock Café and were disappointed to learn that they'd just missed LL Cool J.) The crowd rewarded their rendition of Brahms and an Italian sonnet with a lengthy standing ovation.

But the highlight of the night came after the concert, when the 350 choir students and their chaperones were treated to a two-hour cruise on the Hudson River, floating through a thick fog in eerie silence until the Statue of Liberty appeared through the mist.

The group was greeted at Lincoln High as hometown heroes when they arrived the following evening. (When the kids' initial flight out of New York was delayed, upset parents bombarded TWA Airlines with calls and convinced them to hold the connecting flight in St. Louis.) The next day at school, Chad and Mitch met outside the band room like they did every morning, this time sporting their "Live from Carnegie Hall" t-shirts and gold dookie rope chains. Chad, sporting a high-top fade, wore his favorite jacket, his father's camouflage army fatigues with the name BUTLER. With their new jewelry, it was as if a transformation had taken place: the Underground Kingz looked like a real rap group.

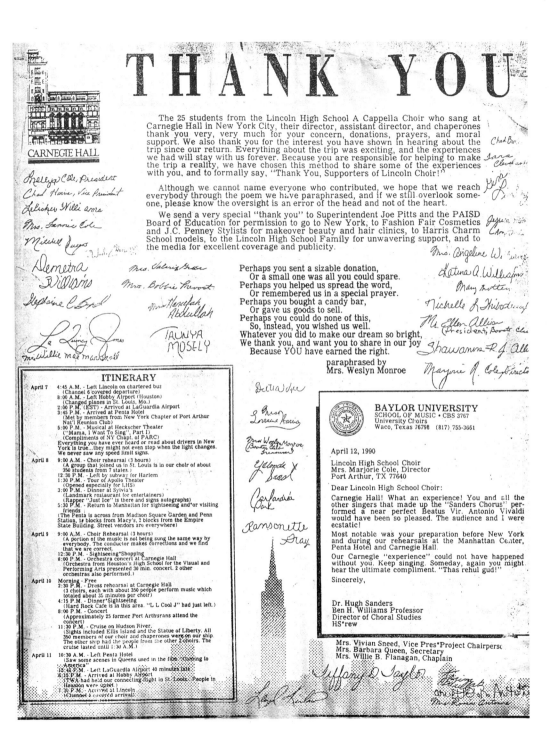

Above: **The Lincoln High School A Cappella Choir** itinerary and recap of their April 1990 performance at Carnegie Hall in New York City. (**Chad Butler's signature** is visible in the top right corner.)
Courtesy of Weslyn Monroe

As Chad and Bun started warming up to each other, Bun started coming by the house. "In Port Arthur … there was no Hip-Hop scene," Bun recalled later in a radio interview with Sway. "The 'Hip-Hop scene' was Pimp C's bedroom."

"I'm gonna make a record," Chad told him one day. Bun was intrigued by the idea; he'd formed a group called PA Militia with Jelon Jackson and earned a reputation as one of the best battle rappers in town.

Bun, Mitch, Jelon, and D-A of the Blac Monks headed out to Beaumont one night for a Geto Boys concert, where they battled some local rappers in the bathroom of the Connections Skating Rink. "That was the first night [me and Jelon] actually felt like rappers," Bun recalls. Their confidence, aided by their matching Starter jackets, was short-lived; Scarface came in the bathroom to join them and shut everyone down with one rhyme.

In time, Chad realized that DMD's departure actually worked to his advantage. "When Boomtown quit and DMD quit, that left me … I was the last one left to make beats," Chad told journalist Andrew Nosnitsky, adding, "I still was in high school, but I could scratch, I could play keyboards, [and] I had watched DMD loop them records with that turntable … Anybody in the town that was trying to get into the rap shit, they had to come to me."

Bun and Jelon needed beats for PA Militia, so they came to Chad for help. "You know the PA Militia is down with C. All my boys down with C!" Chad howled on the outro to one track before bursting into absurd laughter, a hallmark of his production at the time. "This is a Pimp C production, and I'm outta here, *hoes!*"

Bun and Chad were mutually impressed with each other's talents. "[He was the] best singer, best producer, best writer I had ever seen," Bun told *Mass Appeal*. Likewise, Chad realized that even though Bun was a relative newcomer, he was already "the coldest [rapper]" in the area.

By late 1990, with Mitch, Bun, and Jelon spending so much time at Chad's house, there was talk of combining the Underground Kingz and PA Militia into one group. They agreed on the name Four Black Ministers: "4BM." ("It sounds crazy now, but it was a crazy time in Hip-Hop," Chad admitted later on *The Final Chapter* DVD.)

Reggae music was extremely popular in Houston, and 4BM's concept was to lay hardcore gangsta rap verses over reggae-infused beats. (A primary example was "Cocaine In The Back of the Ride," which sampled Bob Marley.) Chad would create a beat and turn it over to the other three group members, often with a concept and a hook already in place. 4BM recorded a handful of tracks, including the stand-your-ground anthem "Dicks Hang Low (When The 4 Stand Stout)" with Bun on the hook and the braggadocio tune "Shit on Our Toe," which Mitch considered their best work.

The reggae-infused-rap sound didn't quite catch on, but it was a step in the right direction. DJ Bird had started working with the group, too. "[DJ] Bird was a big inspiration when it came to our sound," Mitch says. "At first we did a lot of uptempo music … because we grew up listening to a lot of East Coast stuff … [but] once we figured out that slowing everything down and articulating ourselves better was [sounding] better … we started sticking to that."

"We was trying to get in where we fit in," Chad explained on *The Final Chapter* DVD. "We was really trying to take on other people's characteristics so that we could get in this game and achieve something … and have a position in this thing. We didn't realize that being ourselves was gonna be the ticket."

The last song Chad and Mitch had recorded as Mission Impossible, which also featured Bun, was "Tell Me Something Good," a lengthy track built around a sample from Rufus and Chaka Khan's song of the same name.

On the first of five verses of oddly varying lengths, Chad took shots at an older classmate named Johnnie Remo. Remo was known around town as the local bully, always seeking a confrontation. "[He was] just an idiot," says Donny Young. "Like, you could cuss his ass out real bad, intelligently, he'll be like, 'What the fuck that nigga said?' and be ready to fight 'cause he didn't understand the shit. Like, that's how stupid he is."

Thanks to the movie *Colors*, gang influence was starting to creep in the city, and Remo was known to sport a Raiders jacket and start a fight at the slightest provocation. Chad rapped:

> *Let me tell you 'bout something that hurts me*
> *Why when I go out I gotta see violence and tragedy?*
> *Man, if you gotta come out and fight*
> *Stay at your damn house and stop fuckin' up my night*
> *A nigga's gotta be a nigga*
> *But why you hide behind the shades and a goddamn trigger?*
> *(I know why) You see your ass can't pull no hoes*
> *So you hide behind the Raiders and you try to act bold*
> *But it's a fake, you can't fool C*
> *You play a gangsta role 'cause you can't get no pussy*
> *Part-time, fake, wouldn't step in the hood*
> *I know some niggas that could tell you something good*

By the end of the song, Chad predicted that this "brother that was living fast" would "realize he's a stupid ass" once he found himself "locked down 'cause he couldn't control his trigger finger."*

As Isreal Kight recalls it, Remo was furious and confronted Chad over the song, threatening to "whoop his ass." In the end, mutual friends intervened and cooler heads prevailed. Remo agreed to leave Chad alone and Chad agreed to change the lyrics. Besides, "Tell Me Something Good" didn't fit with 4BM's rap-infused-reggae theme, so Chad set the song to the side.

Bun knew he could be a straight-A student, valedictorian even, if he cared enough to try, but school wasn't challenging enough to motivate him to put forth the effort. By the last semester of his senior year, he was just doing enough to maintain an 88 average so he could stay in the Business Professionals of America (BPA) program. BPA organized field trips where the kids had free time to sneak off and drink alcohol, smoke weed, and play poker.

Drama class was one of the few things that held his attention; he excelled in several plays, like *A Raisin in the Sun*. "You got a lot of foolishness in you, but it's not bad foolishness," his drama teacher told him.

With graduation fast approaching, Bun was getting a lot of pressure from all directions to decide on a career path. He'd always known he was smart – savvy enough to be a lawyer, articulate enough to be a preacher – but none of these options seemed intriguing. "I really had no aspirations to *be* anything," he recalls.

(*Johnnie Remo did not respond to interview requests. Although it is not known which incident Chad was referring to in this song, Remo actually *did* end up "locked down 'cause he couldn't control his trigger finger." After Lincoln High's football team faced off against Thomas Jefferson in the annual Yellow Jacket Classic, Remo got in a fight at the local McDonald's which turned into a parking lot shoot-out. Bun later referenced the incident on UGK's "Family Affair." Then, late on the night of October 21, 1990, Remo, whom friends described as very drunk and "acting crazy," drove slowly past the Celebrity Lounge on Short Texas. With his window rolled down, he fired several shots wildly out of the window, shouting, "You all are going to respect me!" The bullets struck two men who happened to be in the wrong place at the wrong time. One of them, Aaron Jacobs, died of a single gunshot wound to the head and Remo was charged with his murder. When the case eventually came to trial in February 1993, Remo testified in his own defense, choking back tears and admitting he'd been "drunk and stupid" and would "bring the young fella back" if he could. A jury convicted Remo on a lesser charge of involuntary manslaughter and he was sentenced to ten years in prison. In the car with Remo during the shooting was a good friend of Bun B's named Donald Buckner. Several years later, Buckner was jumped during a fight at Long's Projects and attacked with a lead pipe and glass bottle. His younger brother Stephen Jackson, a local basketball standout, was rushed to his bedside. Buckner passed away; his brother Stephen Jackson went on to play in the NBA and remains a friend to UGK.)

His three older brothers Rodney Jr., Robert, and Johnny had been in and out of prison for most of their lives. "I watched all three of my brothers break my mother's heart, and I just felt like I didn't want to do that shit," Bun remembers.

Fuck it, he decided. *I'm just going to go graduate and I'm going to go to college, so she can have one kid that she can brag on.*

Bun's friend Freddy Johnson walked out of drama class one day and happened to glance at the trash can outside the doorway. At the top of the heap was a notebook he'd recognize anywhere: Bun's rap notebook, filled with rhymes. He rescued the tablet and called Bun when he got home from school. "What's the deal?" he asked. "Why your shit in the trash like that?"

"Man, I'm givin' up," Bun said, sounding discouraged. "I don't wanna do this no more."

"Man, this is not something you just throw away," Freddy argued. "You a *rapper.*"

Bun and a drama classmate named Nolan Davis got drunk one day and decided it would be funny to pretend they were signing up for the Navy. They filled out all the paperwork to accept the G.I. Bill program with a $10,800 scholarship, but refused to take the oath. "As long as we don't do the oath, we are not in the [Navy]," Bun reasoned.

Dodging increasingly aggressive phone calls from the Navy recruiter, Bun realized they needed a way out. As two of the standout students in drama class, Bun and Nolan agreed to accept $4,000 drama scholarships to San Jacinto College North/Texas A&M to get rid of the incensed Navy recruiter. ("That Navy dude was madder than a muthafucker," Bun recalls.)

Another scholarship offer came in from Xavier University. Amoco offered a four-year scholarship to Lamar University, leading to a guaranteed entry-level position at Amoco. Bun's mother, who hoped her son would become a teacher, bragged to friends that her youngest, clearly brilliant, would be the first in the family to attend college.

But by his 18th birthday in March 1991, Bun was having a change of heart. While he lacked conviction about his future, which seemed filled only with vague ideas, Chad was the exact opposite. Chad knew exactly what he wanted to do: he was going to make a record. Everyone else had a Plan B, something to fall back on in case music didn't work out, but not Chad. Bun found himself drawn to his friend's confidence and determination.

As graduation approached, Bun reasoned that if he was smart enough to get a college scholarship *this* summer, he'd be smart enough to get a college scholarship *next* summer, too. He decided he'd try rap for one year, and if something didn't happen by the summer of 1992, he'd go to college and make his mother proud.

Bun told his disappointed senior counselor he'd decided to turn down all the scholarship offers and told his mother he was "gonna go rap with Chad." His mother was furious. "I knew it! You hanging with that boy, that boy's gonna be the death of you!" she predicted. "Nobody from Port Arthur makes music. Get this out your mind. All these [college scholarships] and you just going [to rap]?! You not going to do nothing with yourself!"

All the adults in Bun's life scolded him for letting them down. "You have a real opportunity to do something [with your life] and you're a sharp kid," he heard often. "I don't know why you got caught up in this rap shit."

Ultimately, the opposition only gave Bun the extra motivation he needed. "It was all about proving my parents wrong, and you can totally understand the tenacity of a teenager trying to prove his parents wrong," he recalls. "[I gave] 151 percent. I was like, I *got* to make it now, otherwise they're right. And I'm not going to give them that [satisfaction]."

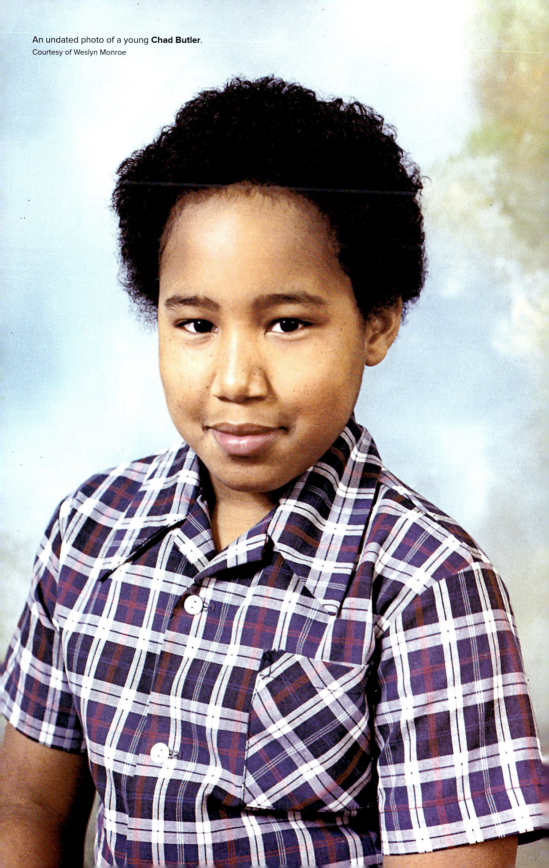

An undated photo of a young **Chad Butler**.
Courtesy of Weslyn Monroe

Above: An undated photo of Chad's mother, **Weslyn Monroe,** otherwise known as **"Mama Wes."**

Courtesy of Weslyn Monroe

Mama Wes' house on **Shreveport Ave.** in Port Arthur, pictured in 2013, was UGK's unofficial base of operations and home to many key moments in the group's history, like the "Use Me Up" video shoot and *The Southern Way* release party.

Photos: Julia Beverly

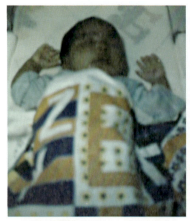

Clockwise from left: undated photos of **Chad** as a child; attempts to interest him in **YMCA basketball and football** were unsuccessful, but he did enjoy **swimming**.

Courtesy of Weslyn Monroe

Above: An early Polaroid of **Chad Butler as "C.L.B."**
Below: **Chad and his mother.**
Courtesy of Weslyn Monroe

Family vacations in the late 1980s with the newly blended Monroe family. *Clockwise from above:* **Chad** with his stepsister **Ursula** and mother **Weslyn**; **Monroe, Ursula,** and **Chad** on a beach vacation; **Ursula** and **Chad** on the Hollywood Walk of Fame; **Mama Wes, Ursula, Chad,** and his grandmother **Bessie** in the Cayman Islands**; Mama Wes, Chad,** and **Ursula** in the Cayman Islands.

Courtesy of Weslyn Monroe

THE LAND OF THE TRILL
1988 Port Arthur, Texas

BOOMTOWN   MQJ   PIMP C

LEE MASTER   BOONIE LOC

DJ DMD

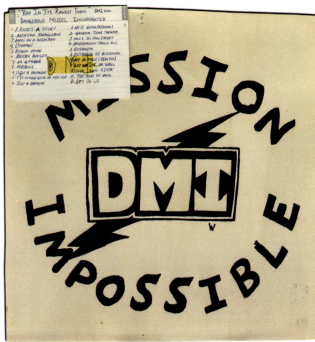

Above: The **DMI Posse** at the Port Arthur seawall in 1988: **Roderick "Tattoo" Randle, Lee "Master" Harmason, Nahala "Boomtown" Johnson, Mitchell "MQJ" Queen Jr., Dorie "DJ DMD" Dorsey, Kristi "KLC" Floyd, Chad "Pimp C" Butler** (at the time, "MC C"), **Darrell "Q-Tip" Zenon, Evander "Boonie" Cade a.k.a. "MC Bash,"** and **David "Step" Broussard.**
Left: The original **Mission Impossible/ DMI** logo and demo tracklisting.
Below: The original **Underground King** logo, drawn by Wesley Harris.
Courtesy of Mitchell Queen Jr.

Above: **Chad** and his stepfather **Norward "Bill" Monroe**.
Right: **Mama Wes** on crutches, along with other choir chaperones, accompanying Chad and the Lincoln High School choir to Carnegie Hall in 1990.

Courtesy of Weslyn Monroe

16-year-old **Chad Butler** preparing for Carnegie Hall in April 1990.
Courtesy of Weslyn Monroe

Chad with **Sonja Gipson** at a Lincoln High School dance (the Bumblebees were the school's mascot).
Courtesy of Weslyn Monroe

An undated high school photo of **Chad.**
Courtesy of Weslyn Monroe

Above: **Big Tyme Recordz'** booth in King's Flea Market, pictured in 2011.
Photo: Julia Beverly

Left: **Russell Washington** pictured on the back of Point Blank's album.

Below: The cassette insert of UGK's Big Tyme Recordz debut, ***The Southern Way***.
Courtesy of Mitchell Queen Jr.

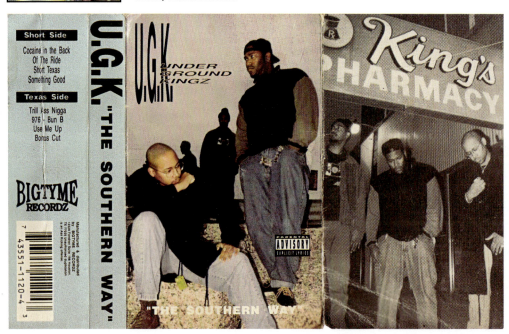

CHAPTER 5

"Half of the battle with anything is believing that you can do it."
– Pimp C, *Scratch* Magazine, Mar/Apr 2007

———————

"Whenever I sit back and think about the dumb shit I did, I honestly cannot believe I got the fuck away. I know guys who are gone [to prison] forever who did the same dumb shit I was doing. I was literally on the highway, with cocaine on the dashboard, car on cruise, with my feet out the window, smoking a blunt. Begging a state trooper to take me away for the rest of my fucking life."
– Bun B, *Believer* Magazine, March 2006

May 1991
Houston, Texas

Maurlon Banks' clunky blue Dodge Malibu with tinted windows and low-profile tires rumbled up to King's Flea Market on the south side of Houston. Out stepped Maurlon, Ron Forrest, two girls, and Chad, who was on a mission to pick up some "cheap man's jewelry."*

Big Tyme Recordz, a small booth which sold vinyl and cassettes, sported a booming sound system which carried throughout the entire flea market. The owner, Russell Washington, was a stocky former college football player in his early 20s.

Business was booming, and Russell and his wife were saving money to launch a record label. Russell didn't know much about the music business, but figured the first step would be to find an artist. He posted a sign outside the store: "Looking for artists to produce a record."

Chad had a demo tape in his pocket with a handful of records, including "Tell Me Something Good," "Use Me Up," and "Cocaine in the Back of the Ride." "I always walked around with a demo tape in my pocket 'cause I didn't know who I was gonna meet," he told journalist Andrew Nosnitsky.

He passed by Big Tyme's booth, wondering how his tape would sound in the large sound system. He stopped short at the sign outside the booth: *"Looking for Artists"?!?!*

"Shit, I had been walkin around with my tape in my pocket so long till the writin had come off that muthafucker," Chad later told *Murder Dog*. He asked the woman in the booth, Russell's wife, about the sign. "Let me go get my husband," she said.

Russell was impressed, eying Chad curiously as the tape played. This quiet kid, barely 17, had produced all this himself? Still, he had an aura about him, a star quality.

Chad was nervous, his heart sinking. Over the big sound system, it didn't sound nearly as good as he'd hoped. "I don't know how he heard any potential in that tape," Chad told *Murder Dog*. "But the nigga said he wanted to put us up in the studio."

As the demo finished playing, Russell nodded his approval. "Damn, y'all made that shit?" he said. "That shit sound nice." He kept the demo tape and rode around listening to it for weeks, convinced these boys were onto something. "I believed in it from the minute I heard it," Russell says. "I loved that demo."

(*In later descriptions of this event, Chad downplayed Maurlon's involvement after the two had a falling out. Maurlon, who feels slighted by his omission from UGK history, says he brought Chad to the flea market to introduce him to Big Tyme.)

Back in Port Arthur, Bun's mother was furiously reviewing a $700 phone bill. Bun and Freddy liked to call promotional 1-888 numbers where fans could listen to portions of an artists' album before deciding to buy it. They charged by the minute, and Bun had been listening to entire albums, like LL Cool J's *Walking with a Panther*.

On May 28, 1991, the day of Bun's graduation, his mother and new stepfather Vincent Taylor told him if he wasn't going to college, he had one week to get out of their house. "They didn't think that I was mature enough to go out into the world and make my way as a man," Bun said later on Damage Control Radio, explaining, "They were like, 'Well, we gonna kick him out and take his car and take everything from him, and that'll make him come back around.' But it only made me more determined. Because all it was saying to me was: *You don't believe in me.*"

No one believed rap was a viable career path. At the joint graduation ceremony for Lincoln and Thomas Jefferson High, the guest speaker, Grambling University president Dr. Joseph Johnson, encouraged graduates like Bun and Mitch to become scientists and engineers. "We don't need any more rappers, we don't need any more dancers, we don't need any more athletes. We already have a monopoly on those," he said.

Bun was unfazed. Another speaker was G.W. Bailey, an actor from Port Arthur who appeared in the *Police Academy* movies. Bun realized that like Janis Joplin and others who'd "made it" from the small town, Bailey had to leave Port Arthur to achieve fame before the town respected him. Bun hitched a ride to Houston after the ceremony with his only brother who wasn't in prison and moved in with his father, which he would come to consider "one of the best/worst decisions I ever made in my life."

"The raw realities of life kind of crashed down on me after I moved out of my mom's cushy house where food was cooked every day," Bun explains. The morning after graduation, his father woke him at sunrise to work for his landscaping company. From 7 AM to 7 PM every day, Bun toiled under the hot Texas sun, cutting lawns, tearing shingles off roofs, and laying fresh tar. *Is this what you wanted to do?* Bun asked himself, sweat pouring off his forehead. *Suffering for my art?*

When Chad rounded up the crew in Port Arthur and excitedly explained that Russell wanted to put them in the studio, everyone wasn't quite so enthusiastic. Mitch was already committed to a football scholarship at Prairie View A&M University two hours away. Jelon, whom Chad thought was "flaky," was now a senior at Thomas Jefferson and wanted to focus on football too, hoping he could land an athletic scholarship like Mitch.* They all believed rap and school couldn't co-exist: you had to choose one or the other. "I think [we were] severely underestimating ourselves at the time," Bun admitted on Damage Control Radio.

Chad was devastated at the thought of losing Mitch. Mama Wes and Monroe approached Mitch's parents, offering to pay for Mitch to go to Lamar University so he could stay in Port Arthur. Mitch's father, Mitchell Queen Sr., considered the suggestion. "Well, he won't have anything to get around [town] in," he pondered.

"I'll buy him a car," Monroe blurted out. Mama Wes glared at him: *Nigga, what?* As they drove off, she demanded, "Where the fuck are we going to get all the money to do this?"

"We [can] do it, I'm telling you," Monroe insisted. "I believe in him."

Amidst all the doubters, Monroe was the only adult who saw Chad's vision. "Bill [Monroe] really did. He believed," says Mama Wes. "No other old person believed."

But Monroe's attempts didn't stop Mitch from leaving. Mitch's father declined the generous offer. He had missed his opportunity to become a big football star, and Mitch was fulfilling *his* dream, too.

It was a sad day in Port Arthur when Mitch departed for Prairie View. Chad cried incon-

---

(*Although pursuing a football career was perceived as a safer bet than rap, the truth is, the odds of succeeding in either were slim. According to 2014 statistics from recruit757.com, for every 1,000 high school seniors who play football, only one will make it to the NFL and only half of those lucky 0.1% will last longer than three years in the league.)

solably and refused to get out of bed. "I thought the child was gonna have a massive coronary," Mama Wes recalls.

She tried to cheer him up, suggesting, "Why don't you just do it yourself?" Chad had his heart set on a duo; his mother got the impression he was afraid to try it solo.

A few days later, Chad told his mother he'd found a new partner. "He's in this other group, but I think he's gonna come with me," he explained. Chad didn't consider himself a very good rapper, and told his mother that this new kid Bun B was better than he was. "I know [I can't rap]," he explained. "That's why I gotta say crazy stuff."

With only two members left in the group, the Four Black Ministers name didn't make sense. Russell liked the name Underground Kingz, so Chad called Mitch at Prairie View and asked if they could use the name. Mitch gave his blessing and agreed that Bun, the best rapper of the crew, was the best person to replace him. Plus, Bun's deep baritone was a good match for Chad's high-pitched tenor.

"Half of the battle with anything is believing that you can do it," Chad told journalist Andrew Nosnitsky. "[Mitch and Jelon] didn't believe that they could be rappers or that they could make money or that it was serious. So when time came for them to do other careers … they took them opportunities. And I can't blame them for taking it. But me and Bun stuck with the shit. So when we looked up one day it wasn't nothing [left] but me and him."

Pimp C and Bun B, the new Underground Kingz, would become the first group to sign with Big Tyme Recordz, inking their signatures on a simple one-paragraph handwritten contract.

———————

Watching the Geto Boys' ascent in the latter half of 1991 convinced Chad and Bun they were headed in the right direction. "Geto Boys was a different group to niggas in Texas than anywhere else, 'cause them niggas was local," Chad told *Murder Dog*. "They really paved the way for us to know that we could go and make a record."

Although J. Prince was the most visible owner of Rap-A-Lot, he had a business partner named Cliff Blodget, and theirs was an unlikely pairing. Cliff, a white guy from the Seattle area, was an electrical engineer and a computer whiz with a passion for music. He had developed some proprietary recording equipment while attending college in Oregon. He'd married a black woman from Houston, who happened to be a cousin of Prince's wife, and moved to Texas with her.

As they were developing Rap-A-Lot, Cliff summoned some of his former classmates from the Northwest. Among them was a pale redhead named Karl Stephenson, a quiet computer nerd who slept in the studio and spent every waking hour working with DJ Ready Red on the Geto Boys' album.*

Cliff also reached out to two former classmates named Doug King and Aaron Brauch. Their joint computer software venture had just failed, and they agreed to move to Houston and work with the burgeoning label.

The unlikely merger between black men from Houston's Fifth Ward and a group of white Northwestern computer programmers was facilitated by Prince's co-sign. (As Doug recalls it, some of the Rap-A-Lot crew initially suspected Cliff of being an undercover police officer.)

"J. Prince was definitely somebody that you're gonna respect … [because] he was a man that was gonna work harder than everybody else, [and] was gonna put the right people in the same room and make that shit happen," says Pierre "Born 2wice" Maddox, an early Rap-A-Lot artist.

Although they came from different backgrounds, Cliff and Prince both shared a strong work ethic and what Doug recalls as "a multi-faceted talent for making stuff happen" with "sheer determination." Together, Doug says, they all possessed a "maniac vision that [they] were gonna make a record company." Instead of sending their artists to expensive recording studios in New

(*Karl Stephenson would later co-write and co-produce Beck's massive hit record "Loser.")

York or Los Angeles, Rap-A-Lot improvised. They came up with innovative ideas and outfitted local apartments with inexpensive equipment, giving their artists and producers all the time they needed and a substantial amount of creative freedom.

Doug became an in-house music producer, working with Rap-A-Lot acts like Def IV, Ganksta N-I-P, 2 Bad Brothers, and Too Much Trouble. When Prince signed Scarface, he asked Doug to create some demo tracks for Scarface's solo debut. Late one night in the studio, someone came across the vinyl for the *Tough Guys* soundtrack which included Isaac Hayes' "Hung Up On Me Baby." The sample would form the basis for the record "Mind Playing Tricks On Me." (Both Doug King and Scarface claim credit for producing the track. Most likely it was a collaborative effort.)

Doug didn't think much of the record. "It was just another song to me," he recalls. But J. Prince, who planned on making the Geto Boys his star group, thought they were onto something. He'd pull up to local DJs, play the track for them in his car, and ask for their opinion.

"James didn't particularly have an ear for music, but what James did do really well was, he would take stuff around and he'd play it for everybody, and he'd watch and listen," Doug says. "James is a pretty smart guy … At some point he wanted to be a [music] producer, but I think he was smart enough to back off and say, 'I'm gonna see what everybody else thinks.' And he didn't let his ego get in the way."

Prince decided to use the song for the Geto Boys' third album, asking Willie D and Bushwick Bill to add verses. His employees trusted him, admiring his uncanny intuition. "He seems to have a feel for what's getting ready to happen before it happens … he acts like someone who's been in the business for 20 years," Rap-A-Lot's Mel Smith told the *Houston Chronicle*.

While Bun was shooting pool one night in his father's garage, the radio announcer introduced the Geto Boys' new record "Mind Playing Tricks On Me." Bun listened in rapt attention, enthusiastically proclaiming it the greatest rap sample he'd ever heard and calling everyone he knew to see if they'd heard it too.

Around the same time, Chad heard Scarface's single "Mr. Scarface" from his solo album *Mr. Scarface is Back* on the radio as he was driving to DJ Bird's house in Port Arthur. *This shit is jammin' like a muthafucker,* Chad thought, reaching to turn up the volume, upset he couldn't record it. *Damn, I should've been at my boombox.*

Seeing the Geto Boys' "Mind Playing Tricks On Me" exploding nationwide gave UGK the extra motivation they needed. Chad had come to the conclusion that emulating East Coast rappers would never work with his high-pitched voice. *I can't help but be country,* he thought.

"I figured out … I couldn't talk like New York [rappers], so I stopped trying to do it and I stopped trying to rap like them," he told *FADER*. He also realized that he was going to have to do most of the production himself. "I was going to producers trying to buy the song but I couldn't get what I needed out of 'em," he said. "I would go to 'em and tell 'em: look, sample this record and sample this and put this together … and they would try to bring my ideas out of my head and put it onto the tape but they couldn't quite get it."

Chad sampled a loop from Marvin Gaye's "Inner City Blues" for "Trill Ass Nigga," the same way he'd borrowed from Bill Withers' "Use Me" for "Use Me Up," adding organs and twangy guitar riffs. He came up with most of the beats and concepts at home. The house on Shreveport Ave. morphed into a studio, a hotel, and a restaurant, with teenagers coming in and out all hours of the day. Monroe wasn't happy about the constant stream of visitors, but Mama Wes didn't mind. "The house was built to be used," she says. "I felt like I was just cooking and feeding niggas all day and all night. And I had a ball; I loved it. I enjoyed being a part of all that madness."

Chad and his friends started piling in his white Honda Accord (nicknamed "The Cigarette," because, as the joke went, it was always smoking) to go record at Houston's Sunrise Studios. This arrangement didn't last long because the owner didn't care for rap music. UGK finally found a home at Houston studio Track Designs, which was owned by an eccentric foreign couple, Asian-American Shetoro Henderson and his African girlfriend Bernie Bismark.

The recording process was slow and painstaking. When recording to two-inch reels, it was difficult to stop and re-start vocals in the middle of a verse ("punching in"). To save time and money, Bun got in the habit of spitting his entire verse the whole way through in one take. "It drove us to perfection, because … we didn't have the money to sit in the studio all day," Bun told *Murder Dog.*

Russell felt that "Tell Me Something Good" was UGK's best song, but the group didn't want to piss off Johnnie Remo. Irritated at having to redo the vocals, Chad decided to go for shock value, using the most explicit lyrics he could dream up. He began the record chanting: "One muthafucker, two muthafuckers, three muthafuckers, four!"

"[Pimp] was like, if he's gotta redo it, he's just gonna do it like a joke," Russell recalls.

By late 1991, Russell was running out of money, and UGK's debut *The Southern Way* was nowhere near completion. He'd planned to spend around $6,000 on the project but they'd already exceeded that budget. "The studios were fuckin' us out of our money, the producers were fuckin' us out of our money, givin' us trash, and when we looked around we didn't have no more money," Chad told journalist Andrew Nosnitsky.

Neither of the boys had much cash flow. Mama Wes' credit card was maxed out; she'd handed it over so her son could book a hotel in Houston instead of driving back to Port Arthur exhausted every morning at daybreak. Bun, now working at Russell's record shop, didn't even have a car. Russell picked him up every day in his modest Ford Tempo and paid him fifty dollars to man the counter, pocket change which Bun spent mostly on weed and dice games.

It was clear they wouldn't be able to finish the project without a large chunk of cash to pay Shetoro for studio time. And there was one guaranteed way to make a quick chunk of cash: sell cocaine. "[Russell didn't have any] more money, [so he] came to us and said, 'What you wanna do – we either gonna stop recording or we gonna sell this goddamn dope and keep going to the studio every weekend?'" Chad told journalist Andrew Nosnitsky. "We didn't have no choice, so we started hustling."

According to Chad, he and Bun agreed to take the risk in exchange for ownership in the label. (Chad later said that Russell agreed to a three-way split for ownership of Big Tyme Recordz and they shook hands on the deal. Russell denied he had ever agreed to a partnership.)

Bun is understandably vague about the source of the initial "cash investment" that launched this illegal venture. Although things didn't go smoothly the first run, they soon settled into a two-a-day routine. Every morning at 6 AM, Bun, apparently using someone else's car, would "go to the place and get the thing" (a kilogram of cocaine) and drive it to Port Arthur. By early afternoon, once they'd sold out, Bun would drive back to Houston, pick up another kilo, return to Port Arthur, sell out by midnight, and repeat the process the following day. "It was ridiculous how fast the shit was selling, how much money we were making," Bun recalls.

"Everybody had a job to do," Chad told journalist Andrew Nosnitsky. "Bun was in transportation, I was in packaging. The other motherfucker was in delivery." (Although Chad did not specify who "the other motherfucker" was, Maurlon Banks says he was the distribution arm of the operation, a claim which others substantiate. Maurlon was under the impression that Russell was the one supplying the product.)

Bun's friend Freddy, who lived across the street from one of Maurlon's crack houses in Port Arthur, was surprised to see Bun pulling up one day. "Bun, what y'all doing over there?" Freddy called out as he walked across the street.

Bun gestured towards the package of cocaine on the dashboard. "Man, I had to bring this work back to get this album going," he said.

Freddy asked why he hadn't put it in the trunk, out of sight. "Nah, why hide it?" Bun shrugged. "I sat it right there on the dashboard so I'll know where it is."

Bun later admitted in *Believer* Magazine, "Whenever I sit back and think about the dumb shit I did, I honestly cannot believe I got the fuck away. I know guys who are gone [to prison] forever who did the same dumb shit I was doing. I was literally on the highway, with cocaine on the dashboard, car on cruise, with my feet out the window, smoking a blunt. Begging a state trooper to take me away for the rest of my fucking life."

The whole crew got involved in the venture, with Chad acting more as the coordinator of the whole operation rather than a hand-to-hand distributor. Although it wasn't often he got his hands dirty, he and Bun would later recall one memorable night when the two were posted up on the trunk of an abandoned car waiting for customers.

Chad, still halfheartedly attending high school, was struggling with his Algebra II/Trigonometry homework. "When [Bun] left, my tutor was gone," Chad told *The Source*. "My motivator was missing. School wasn't shit to me." Like his mother, Chad was skilled in reading and writing, but math wasn't his forte.

A dope fiend wandered over to the two, who were hovering over Chad's textbook, illuminated by the street light above. He popped open a case to reveal a small derringer pistol and asked if they wanted to buy it.

"Say, man, get the fuck away from us," Chad told him. "We don't want nothing but money."

The fiend caught a glimpse of the Algebra textbook. "Nigga, what kind of dope men do homework?" he asked, howling with laughter.

All the money the boys made went into the recording fund, and neither of them intended to turn drug-dealing into a career. Chad viewed it as "a stepping stone."

"Anytime I got my hands dirty … it was to get some money to go to a studio," Chad said. "We never bought no cars or none of that shit [off of illegal drug sales,]" he added in an *OZONE* interview. "We hustled our way into the record business, 'cause we wanted to be rappers, and we didn't have nobody to finance us. We hustled, and at the end of the week, we took the money and went to the studio and gave it to the studio man."

Still, they couldn't shake their conscience. "As young cats in the street we understand that you make the hard choices and you're not proud of them, and you worry about how these things are going to affect what happens to you in the afterlife," Bun admitted in *Texas Monthly*. "[We wondered], is God really going to allow [us] to go to heaven?"

Plus, there were more immediate concerns. During one apparent altercation with a rival drug dealer, Chad left Port Arthur and hid out in Crowley to escape a potentially dangerous situation. "There was a short stint where he tried to live that life and it came to an abrupt halt rather quickly," his friend NcGai recalls.

Bun managed to avoid the state troopers, but he did get hit with a possession of a controlled substance charge which he chalked up to bad luck: being in the wrong place at the wrong time with someone else's drugs.* Still, the close call made Bun rethink things. *I'm gonna have to stop fucking around in the streets, 'cause this shit is not working for me,* he thought. *We gonna have to figure out something different.*

During one stop at Big Tyme, Bun and Pimp met Ganksta N-I-P, a south side Houston rapper who had just inked a deal with Rap-A-Lot, and they expressed a mutual appreciation for each other's work. Ganksta N-I-P was in the process of recording his debut album *South Park Psycho* and gave UGK three tracks as a preview, which earned him a shout out when they rerecorded "Cocaine in the Back of the Ride." ("Brought the Caddy across the pier and kicked it to Ganksta N-I-P.")

But it was Chad's opening line which was most memorable: "Pimp C, bitch! So what the fuck is up?" It was decided that "Cocaine in the Back of the Ride" would be the first track, their introduction to the world. "That really set the tone for everything," Bun said in a radio interview with Madd Hatta. "[When] you heard those first three words, that really lets you know every-

---

(*Bun has spoken on this arrest in several interviews but the details of the charges are unclear. There is no record of this arrest in Texas, and state-wide arrest records in Louisiana are not available to the public.)

thing you need to know about the group."

Bun also linked up with rapper Born 2wice and sampled a line from his record "This Is a Test" to create the hook of "Short Texas." The Port Arthur dope-dealing strip had become so infamous that locals liked to joke that they'd attended The University of Short Texas; they even pressed up t-shirts with the mascot, two brawling junkies known as the Fighting Fiends.

Chad's friend Donny Young initially didn't mind when outsiders started coming to Short Texas to sell drugs. After a while, though, things had gotten out of control, and Donny and his friends were tired of out-of-towners infringing on their turf.

One day, an arrogant Houston drug dealer pulled up in front of Lane's Lounge on Short Texas in a white Cadillac. "They figured they're from the big city [and could] come out here and run everything," recalls Chad's cousin Edgar Walker Jr. Instead, the unnamed drug dealer was confronted by Donny Young's crew. "[We] beat him up and took [his fake chain] from him [and] sent him on his way," a local hustler named Block recalls. Chad recapped the incident on "Short Texas":

Ask the last nigga [who] brought his fuckin' ass down
Tryin' to sell that fuckin' dope he bought in H-Town
Couldn't sell in Houston, so I guess he figured
I'ma go to Port Arthur and run them fuckin' niggas

"The only untruth about 'Short Texas' is when he says 'we,'" explains Mama Wes. "'*We*' had nothing to do with that … But that was a true story."

For the second verse on "Short Texas," Chad recruited his former classmate Isreal Kight, who had adopted "Bluelite" as his rap moniker.* (According to Kight, other hustlers on the block advised him against it.) Kight did the record anyway, never thinking the song would reach beyond the neighborhood. "I seen it as an opportunity to kinda clown around on a song," he recalls. "To be honest with you … I didn't think they were gonna sell records." He even mentioned an undercover police officer who worked Short Texas by name: "Cops finding my stash, yo, what could the worst be? / Durisseau going undercover, then turning dirty."**

The actual extent of Chad's involvement in the drug game during this timeframe is unclear, complicated by his own contradictory statements. "I used to take risks up and down the mutha-fuckin' highway," he boasted in an *OZONE* interview. "I was on the goddamn highway, I-10, riding up and down that bitch trying to get money to go to the studio to put these records out!"

But in the same interview, he implied that he'd left the drug game long behind, asking rhetorically, "You think if I really was still selling drugs I would get on a muthafuckin' record and make a song like 'Cocaine in the Back of the Ride' and ride up the highway with dope!? You dumb muthafuckers!"

For the most part, Chad and Bun viewed themselves as narrators, the voice of their community. "While I was … talking about it, you had people who really was doing this stuff," Chad said. "Rappers ain't got time to really be doing all these [illegal] thangs 'cause we in the studio rapping … The lifestyle I'm rapping about is the lifestyle that these brothers was actually living."

Once UGK completed *The Southern Way*, Russell tried to find somewhere that could manufacture cassettes. He also found a print shop, but they'd never done cassette inserts before. Russell and Bun took them a copy of a cassette tape from the shop (WC and the Maad Circle's *Ain't a Damn Thang Changed*) to use as a template.

Chad loved to wear jewelry, expensive Bally sneakers, and suede trenchcoats, and viewed the group's image as a crucial part of their presentation. Bun, on the other hand, was perfectly comfortable on stage in a cheap t-shirt and flip-flops. He'd also started growing out his hair in

(*He has also used the spelling Bloolight.)
(**The actual name of the officer on the record is hard to decipher. When asked how to spell the officer's name, Kight responds, "Just P-I-G, I don't know." When the song did blow up, Durisseau obviously was not amused, making Kight a target of local law enforcement.)

honor of their reggae-rap theme, and Chad told him he had to cut off his inch-long dreadlocks before the album cover shoot.

Bun was offended. "What my hair got to do with this shit?"

"Shave that damn thing, boy. That don't look good. Them hoes ain't gonna like you," Chad told him.

The issue of Bun's hair became the group's first argument. A vote was held with Chad, Bun, Russell, and Bird, who had officially become the group's DJ and third member. It was decided 3-1 that Bun would cut his hair.

Bun asked his friend Steven Webb, a sophomore in the journalism program at Lincoln High, to do the photo shoot. The newly clean-shaven Bun, accompanied by Chad, Bird, and a few friends like Ron Forrest, went by Short Texas and several other key locations around Port Arthur, snapping photos.

When they got the photos back, UGK settled on a shot they liked from the seawall, but there was one extra person in the back of the photo. "Why the hell you in the damn picture, nigga?" Chad asked Ron Forrest. "What you sneak in the picture for?"

"Man, the photographer told me to stand there!" Ron insisted. "I ain't sneak in the mutha-fuckin' picture!"

Chad shook his head. "Fuck it," he shrugged. Bun and Russell took the photo to the print shop, where the proprietor added a blue background and text. There was only one problem: with only one font in limited sizes, there wasn't enough room for "Underground Kingz" on the cover. He suggested they could abbreviate it: "U.G.K."?* (There also wasn't enough room for "Tell Me Something Good," which was listed only as "Something Good.")

Once they got the 5,000 printed inserts, cassettes, and plastic cases, they had to assemble everything by hand, a multi-step process which Bun remembers as "a fucking mess." Finally, they sent the tapes off to be shrink-wrapped. Russell also pressed up 12" vinyl copies of "Tell Me Something Good" as their lead single with "Short Texas" on the B-side ("Unauthorized duplication is an Ass Kicking offense," it read).

In early January 1992, DJ Reggie Reg, co-host of a Houston radio show with DJ Greg Street, stopped by Big Tyme Recordz at the flea market. While he browsed through stacks of new vinyl, Russell and Bun played a few UGK records for him. Reggie Reg cocked his head to the side as "Tell Me Something Good" came on.

"Yo, that's a jam," Reggie commented. "Y'all got a radio edit?"

Russell and Bun looked at each other; the need for a clean version hadn't even occurred to them. Reggie was in the midst of radio contest called Houston Home Jams; the artist who received the most votes would win a production deal and studio time with a company called BPM.

The group headed back to the studio and delivered an edited version to DJ Reggie Reg on the last day of the two-week contest. "Tell Me Something Good" blew away the competition. The station announced UGK as the big winner and played their record all weekend. Russell and Bun, riding in the car together when they heard the song on the radio for the first time, beat enthusiastically on the roof.

Around the same time Bun and Russell were premiering "Tell Me Something Good" for Reggie Reg at the flea market, BPM's founder, Doug King, was in a nearby parking lot staring down the barrel of a shotgun. Its owner, Nikki "Fatal T" Proctor, poised her finger on the trigger and twisted her face into a menacing scowl.

Doug stared intently into the viewfinder of his camera, snapping a few more photos. Fatal T readjusted her pose, glancing at her rap partner Imani "MC Bytch" Chyle as a patrol car pulled up outside BPM's studio/warehouse. Apparently, their photo shoot had attracted attention from

---

(*Russell Washington believes this was the reason the group adopted the moniker "UGK," but Mitchell Queen says they had used the abbreviation ever since the group's inception. On "Hard Muthafucker," one of their early high school records, Chad complained about the "weak-ass, punk-ass, lyin' muthafuckers ... talk[ing] shit on UGK.")

Above: **Pimp C, DJ Bird,** and **Bun B** pose on the Port Arthur seawall for UGK's first cover shoot. (**Ron Forrest** is in the background.) Photo: Steven Webb

neighbors uncomfortable with seeing two young black women toting pistols.

The officer, reporting that he "observed what appeared to be a gang with firearms," patted down the threesome. Doug, wary of all the "shady characters" coming in and out of his studio, was carrying a small pistol himself and was carted off to jail.

J. Prince saw Doug as an in-house Rap-A-Lot producer, but Doug had grown tired of waiting for assignments and decided to start his own production company (BPM) with Born 2wice. He soon sensed he'd made a wrong turn. "[Prince] was very possessive of everybody," Doug recalls. "You're either down with James [Prince] or you're not. You're either in or you're out."

When Born 2wice relocated to the West Coast, Doug started working with a smooth talker from Lafayette named Byron Hill. Born 2wice hadn't been impressed with Byron, who seemed like just a "grandiose talker," a "slick muthafucker" always bragging about things he'd done.

Byron's ambition and confidence attracted Doug, but there were plenty of red flags. Byron had done some work with Rap-A-Lot and apparently left on bad terms. (There were rumors he had stolen money, although details are elusive.) "Don't mess with that guy," Doug was warned.

Doug brushed off all the warnings, glossing over the problematic aspects of Byron's personality. "[Byron] had this belief that things would work, and such a conviction, and I appreciated that," Doug recalls. "Byron was really confident in that way, and he made some business deals for us that were pretty ballsy." Byron became Doug's new business partner in BPM, and arranged to market the company by running radio ads and promotions like the Houston Home Jams.

It was a winning formula. Bolstered by Doug's credibility from his work with the Geto Boys, BPM churned out demo tapes for local aspiring rappers for $200-300 apiece. MC Bytch was one of those artists. She and her rap partner Fatal T, as "2 Aggrivated," aimed to become the first female hardcore rap group.

While the girls were in the studio working on their demo with Doug, Byron Hill talked them into a management deal with his company Houserocker Inc. MC Bytch thought it would be a good move because they wouldn't have to pay for studio time anymore. Byron started shopping the group around to record labels. Tommy Boy Records and Eazy E's Ruthless Records expressed interest, and within a month, 2 Aggrivated landed a deal with Profile.

The girls didn't ask too many questions when Byron asked them to sign lengthy contracts. They were just happy to get customized Profile Records jackets, some pocket change, and free dinner. According to MC Bytch, they never realized Byron had accepted a $50,000 advance from Profile on their behalf.* "We had no clue," she says. "He was wining and dining us and giving us clothes." They assumed they'd get paid after the album was finished.

———————

The Houston Home Jams contest was for unsigned acts, so when BPM learned that UGK was already signed to Big Tyme, the radio host announced that UGK had been disqualified and automatically forfeited the contest. Outraged listeners, already hooked on "Tell Me Something Good," flooded the station with requests. The Box relented and continued playing the record.

"For probably a month we had a hot record on the radio in rotation with no product to sell," Bun told *Murder Dog*. "It was a big issue because it was basically against policy to promote a record that wasn't available for retail, but the demand was so high they had to play it. They were risking losing listeners [if they didn't]."

Russell, his business partner Eddie Coleman, and Bun took the track to other influential radio personalities like "Jammin'" Jimmy Olson and Mean Green.** Olson premiered some new

(*Byron Hill declined to be interviewed. Although Doug wasn't involved in the specifics of 2 Aggrivated's deal with Profile, he thinks it is quite possible that Byron did pocket their $50,000 advance. "He would do stuff like that … he [probably] justified it as necessary [to get the] artists what they needed," Doug says. "He was very controlling; I could see him taking an advance and holding it [for] travel [expenses]. He had no money. He had no source of income.")

(**Olson, a veteran of Houston radio, recalls premiering the record during a Kiss It or Diss It program at KISS 98.5, but Russell Washington and others believe he was at Majic 102 at the time. Olson also co-founded 97.9 The Box in April 1991.)

UGK tracks and put "Tell Me Something Good" in heavy rotation.

Bun also took a copy of the test vinyl for "Tell Me Something Good" to a local DJ he'd met at Houston's Club New Jack. Born Robert Earl Davis Jr., he'd earned the nickname "DJ Screw" for his habit of scratching vinyl records he classified as "bullshit" with a screw so that no one else could play them.

Screw had dropped out of high school and spent most of his time in his room, listening to music and playing around with the pitch control on his turntables. Other Houston DJs like Darryl Scott and Michael Price had experimented with slowed-down mixtapes, but it was Screw who wholly embraced the style.

"Tell Me Something Good" quickly became inescapable. The tune was played nonstop on local radio stations. The record's explosion even took them by surprise. "Pimp always knew that he was gonna make music, and he was always dreaming of becoming a star," Bun says. "[But] I don't think we realized how quick and how simple it was gonna be … Overnight, we were famous. We were the biggest group in Houston."

UGK started getting calls from Houston promoters like Steve Fournier and Captain Jack, who booked them to perform at nightclubs they weren't even old enough to get into. Chad used the proceeds from their first paid show to buy his mother a cocker spaniel named Brandy, christening her "the original UGK bitch."

While the Geto Boys seemed larger than life, UGK were somehow more relatable. For kids all across Houston, "Tell Me Something Good" planted the idea that rap was something *they* could do, too. Ten-year-old Paul Slayton was intrigued by the record. *His voice is so… Texas,* 11-year-old Stayve Thomas thought.

Joseph McVey, a high school freshman who had just turned 15, could barely afford to keep a roof over his head, much less purchase cassette tapes. Every afternoon on the way to basketball practice, he listened to the radio on a beat-up old Walkman. Pimp C's rhyme on "Tell Me Something Good" gave him the same feeling he'd had the first time he saw someone in his neighborhood exchange a small baggie of crack cocaine for cash. *Damn, I need to get me some of that shit so I can get me some money, too,* he'd thought. (Stayve Thomas, Paul Slayton, and Joseph McVey would later make their mark on the Houston rap scene themselves as Slim Thug, Paul Wall, and Z-Ro, respectively.)

The record also caught J. Prince's attention. To him, UGK was the epitome of everything he'd hoped to accomplish by revamping the Geto Boys. "We had to run New Yorkers out of this town," Prince explained on *The Final Chapter* DVD. "We had to blaze a trail, man, 'cause we was serious about everybody respecting us … They was trying to make us feel like [because] we were country, we couldn't be nobody."

J. Prince left several messages for Russell Washington trying to schedule a meeting. Russell, who viewed Prince as a threat to his own rap mogul aspirations, wasn't pleased about Prince pursuing his artists. When Prince started relaying messages through mutual friends like radio personality Mean Green, Russell sent a message back: "Tell J. don't be asking about my artists."

Chad was upset when he learned that Russell was dodging J. Prince. "You just can't do that. You have to call him," Chad urged. "You have to call him, at least sit with him and be a man and tell him, 'No.' Don't avoid him or nothing like that, that's gonna send the wrong impression."

Bun agreed, "Yeah man, you gotta show these dudes [at Rap-A-Lot] some respect."

Russell returned J. Prince's call, thanking him for the offer but declining to meet. There was nothing to discuss, he explained, because he didn't want to sell his group.

Above (L-R): Chad and UGK co-founder **Mitchell Queen Jr.** (Senior, Lincoln HS 1991) were inspired to record their first demo tape when upperclassman **Nahala "Boomer Schooner" Johnson** (Senior, Lincoln HS 1990) said they couldn't do it without him. He later directed several Pimp C videos (as "Mr. Boomtown"). **Daniel "DJ Bird" Grogan** (Sophomore, Lincoln HS 1987) would later become UGK's official DJ and third member. On the first version of "Tell Me Something Good," Chad dissed local bully **Johnnie Remo** (Sophomore, Lincoln HS 1987).

Above (L-R): **Bernard Freeman** (Sophomore, Thomas Jefferson HS 1989) around the time he adopted the moniker "Bun B." Bun started rapping to prove that classmate (and aspiring rapper) **Sylvester Vital** (Senior, Lincoln HS 1991) was "whack." Before joining Chad in UGK, Bun rapped with **Fredrick "Freddy Dub" Johnson** (Senior, Lincoln HS 1991) and formed the group PA Militia with **Jelon Jackson** (Senior, Thomas Jefferson HS 1992).

Above (L-R): **Dorie "DJ DMD" Dorsey** (Sophomore, Lincoln HS 1987) was one of the first rapper/producers in the Port Arthur area. He formed the DMI collective with Mitch and Chad, which included rappers like **Lee "Master" Harmason** (Senior, Lincoln HS 1991), **Evander "Boonie" Cade IV** (Freshman, SFA 1986), and **Darrell "Q-Tip" Zenon** (Junior, Lincoln HS 1984).

Above (L-R): Popular cheerleader **Kristi Floyd** (Senior, Thomas Jefferson HS 1989) rapped as "KLC" in the DMI posse; she and Chad later dated. Other women in Chad's life included high school sweetheart **Lalionee Russell** (Senior, Lincoln HS 1992) and **Nitacha Broussard** (Junior, SFA 1991), the mother of his oldest son. Nitacha's brother **Riley "Scoobie" Broussard** (Senior, SFA 1991) didn't mind being known as "Pimp C's baby mama brotha."

Above (L-R): Chad's friends and neighbors **Ron "Crumz" Forrest** (Senior, Lincoln HS 1992) of the Good-Fellaz and his sister **Ronda Forrest** (Sophomore, Lincoln HS 1990). Mama Wes unofficially adopted Chad's friend **Tim Hampton** (Sophomore, Lincoln HS 1990) when his mother was killed; Chad's cousin **Edgar Walker Jr.** (Sophomore, Lincoln HS 1987) would later become a valuable member of the Pimp C entourage.

Above (L-R): Many of UGK's early records depicted the lifestyle of Port Arthur hustlers like **Donald "D-Ray" Graham** (Sophomore, Lincoln HS 1991), whose car is pictured on the cover of UGK's *Super Tight*; **Ezra "Spoon E Gee" Melancon** (Junior, Lincoln HS 1987) who is credited by many as the original creator of the world "Trill"; and **Maurlon "DJ Marly Marl" Banks** (Junior, Lincoln HS 1987), who drove Chad to the flea market when UGK signed their first record deal with Big Tyme Recordz. NBA player Stephen Jackson's brother **Donald Bucker** (Junior, Thomas Jefferson HS 1988), a friend of Bun B's, was killed in Port Arthur's Long's Projects.

Above (L-R): Chad's influential choir teacher **Marjorie Cole** (Lincoln HS 1987); Chad's childhood friend **Langston Adams** (Sophomore, Lincoln HS 1990) later became an attorney and defended a man who disrupted a Pimp C video shoot; **Avery "Averexx" Harris** (Freshman, Lincoln HS 1987) and his brother **Wesley "Beat Master Wes" Harris** (Senior, Lincoln HS 1992) were two of the early rap producers in Port Arthur.

Above (L-R): Bun later lamented the loss of classmates **Terraine Box** (Freshman, Thomas Jefferson HS 1988) and **Charles "Chuckie" Fregia** on UGK's "One Day." Bun's friend **Joseph "JB" Melancon** (Junior, Thomas Jefferson HS 1991); **Dawn Nico** (8th grade, SFA 1990), a girlfriend of Bun B's in the early days of UGK.

Below: Chad and his high school girlfriend **Lalionee Russell** at Lincoln High School's 1990 Homecoming dance.
Courtesy of Lincoln High School

Left: **Mitchell Queen Jr.'s** signing with Prairie View A&M University's football squad, pictured here in Lincoln High's 1990-1991 yearbook, was big news.

Below Left: Popular cheerleader **Kristi "KLC" Floyd** became the first female rapper in the DMI Posse and later, Chad's girlfriend.

Courtesy of The Portal to Texas History

Right: **Bernard "Bun B" Freeman's** graduation announcement from the *Port Arthur News*, May 1991.

Courtesy of the *Port Arthur News*

BERNARD JAMES
FREEMAN

"There [was] no blueprint. Not at all. This [UGK] shit wasn't supposed to go this far. We figured we'd give it a try and see what happens and then get back to the real world. It just kept going."
– Bun B, *Houston Chronicle,* February 2008

"The fact that people thought [his rap career] wouldn't work was what made [Chad] wanna do it more. That's the kind of person he was: If you really wanted him to do something, tell him he couldn't do it, and he was gonna make sure it happened. And it did." – Mama Wes, *Trill Spill* TV

Early 1992
Port Arthur, Texas

Chad sighed, shifting restlessly in his wooden desk in Ms. Mitchell's second period English IV class. Frustrated with the assignment, an open-book test on the Shakespearean play *Macbeth*, he abruptly slammed his book shut. "Fuck this," he mumbled.

Chad had already been contemplating dropping out of school. UGK was getting booked for shows steadily every weekend, taking small dates for $500 a night. Now that Bun had graduated, it was tough for Chad to find the motivation to drag himself to school on Monday morning after a long weekend of performances.

He walked out of English class and never returned to Lincoln High School. It was a decision he later regretted; he admitted he'd been "a damn fool" for dropping out a few months away from graduation. "That hurt my mom that she didn't get to see me walk across that stage," he told *The Source.*

His relatives in Louisiana, many of whom were educators themselves, were shocked. "The idea that he was not gonna be a high school graduate was something that no one had ever really considered as a possibility," says his godmother Brenda Harmon. "It was just kind of understood: you finish high school and you go to college. That's just what you *do.*"

Even though Mama Wes didn't agree with her son's decision, she reasoned that he was young enough to chase his dreams; if it didn't work out, he had plenty of time to find another career. "One thing that I believe: whatever your dream is, you should pursue it," she told *Trill Spill* TV. "Even if you fail at it, you tried. But if you never try, you'll never know."

Besides, Mama Wes knew that trying to stop him wouldn't work anyway. "The fact that people thought [his rap career] wouldn't work was what made [Chad] wanna do it more," she added. "That's the kind of person he was: If you really wanted him to do something, tell him he couldn't do it, and he was gonna make sure it happened."

Chad's father wasn't quite so open-minded. Although he'd always supported Chad's musical aspirations, he saw it as a hobby, not a full-time career, and was worried that his son was headed in the wrong direction. "Nigga, you dropped out of school. You made me buy you that leather Raiders jacket. I found out that's some gang shit," Chad's father told him angrily. "Nigga, you ain't my son. You come talk to me when you ready to go back to school."

"My father wanted better things for me in life than he had when he was coming up … and he didn't see this [rap] shit as no stable career for me," Chad told journalist Andrew Nosnitsky. "He wanted to see me go to college and do some better things than he was able to do in life. So my old man was not with this shit. He couldn't see that this shit was gonna win. And frankly, I can't blame him."

In early February, UGK held a release party for *The Southern Way* at the only venue which seemed appropriate: the house on Shreveport Ave. Mama Wes and Monroe retreated to their bedroom for the night, telling Chad and Bun, "Y'all just have at it."

The house was swarming with teenagers; it seemed like the whole town was there. *The Southern Way* played all night. The climax came when Bun and Chad stood up on chairs in front of the TV in the living room to create a makeshift stage, performing without microphones.

The only blemish on the night was when a friend of Ron and Kight's got in a fistfight which spilled out into the front yard. Chad jumped over the hedges on his way outside, insisting they take the fight further down the street. "Hey man, we'll never be able to do this again!" he yelled.

As the night wore on, one of Chad's friends, a 16-year-old girl named Nitacha Broussard, grew tired of the crowds and ducked off in his bedroom to watch a movie. Nitacha was two years younger than Chad and had never seen him in a romantic light. She knew him as the shy, nerdy kid with a jheri curl from middle school choir practice, and didn't care for this arrogant new "Pimp C" character bragging about being "the 69 King."

"That's when Pimp C was born," she recalls. "I could not stand that man." Still, she was proud of Chad for his persistence. Where everyone else had given up, he'd always kept going, and the release party was his triumph. "That was the guy I knew," Nitacha recalls. "He never stopped, never quit, no matter what."

Chad had just broken up with his high school sweetheart Lalionee, upset that she'd been spotted with another guy while he was away at a show in Louisiana. Lalionee, voted Choir Sweetheart, wasn't into rap and was embarrassed by her boyfriend's explicit tunes. ("Why are you writing that?" she'd complain. "Everybody's gonna think you're talking about me.")

The night would mark the beginning of Chad and Nitacha's transition from a friendship into a relationship. Mama Wes had never been too impressed with Lalionee, whom she considered "lazy" and "trifling," but loved Nitacha. *My God, he finally got a pretty one,* Mama Wes thought, practically falling all over herself to accommodate the girl.

Nitacha's family, however, wasn't too excited about this new development. They didn't approve of Chad, not only because he was a rapper, but because he was two years older than Nitacha. And Nitacha's older brother Riley "Scoobie" Broussard knew Chad well enough to know that he wasn't the type of guy you wanted messing with your sister.

The Southern Way, a six-song EP, was officially released on February 11, 1992.* Bun didn't even bother giving his mother a copy, knowing that after hearing the first three words ("Pimp C, bitch!") she would eject it with a stern, "I don't want to hear this mess." She had no concept of the momentum UGK was building and remained convinced that her son was a drug dealer. (She was only halfway right: Bun estimates that at the time of *The Southern Way*'s release, half of his income was from drug sales.) But Chad's father was becoming a believer, and co-signed the project in his own way. "Hey, man, let me get one of them [UGK] t-shirts," he told Chad.

Russell and his partner Eddie hit the road, dropping off copies of *The Southern Way* on consignment at record stores throughout Texas and Louisiana. "Russ was a hard worker, and he was a go-getter, and he was going to touch everybody he needed to get it done," says Mama Wes. "In the beginning, Russ was the only person that would even [look at] those kids. He saw their talent … He recognized it, and he jumped on it."

One of those stores was Peaches Records in New Orleans' French Quarter, the oldest

(*Some records list the release date as February 21.)

mom-and-pop record store in the country. Working at Peaches was a young woman named Mia Young, who also rapped under the moniker Mia X. She had gained local notoriety as a teenager with her bounce record "Da Payback."

"Tell Me Something Good" was the hottest song at the New Orleans' project jams, and *The Southern Way* was selling out at Peaches. Mia X and UGK soon met through mutual friends. She arranged for her concert promoter boyfriend Warren Mayes to book the group for a show in New Orleans. Mia and Chad, both Capricorns, clicked immediately, and he started coming by Peaches whenever he was in the area to restock tapes.

Bun was also doing his part to move units in the flea market. When Big Tyme customers asked about new releases, Bun got a kick out of recommending UGK without telling them he was in the group. "We got this shit, some new cats," Bun would say, popping in the cassette tape to give them a preview. It was never a hard sell.

One customer came back a week later with his copy of *The Southern Way*, squinting at the cover. Bun, sitting behind the counter, suppressed a smile as the customer asked incredulously, "Is this *you* on this muthafucker?"

The Southern Way was selling well at the Big Tyme booth, and Russell assumed the company where he purchased records, Southwest Wholesale, would be willing to distribute it. But Southwest was actually not a distributor but a "one-stop," a middleman between major distributors and small mom-and-pop stores.

Southwest's Vice President and co-owner, Robert Guillerman, was approached by one of his employees, who asked, "One of our customers, Russell, he wants to know if we could distribute [an album for him]."

"We don't do that," Guillerman responded. Southwest's business model had been working fine for the past 16 years, and he saw no reason to change. Guillerman viewed distribution as too risky. He'd heard of scams where artists would convince a retailer to purchase large quantities of their record, enabling them to collect payment from the distributor. (At the time, there was no SoundScan, and no way to verify sales numbers.) Months later, when the retailer returned all the unsold product, the distributor would be forced to give a full refund.

Guillerman was hesitant, but his staff was insistent. They considered Russell a good client.

Russell finally got a call from his Southwest rep, who informed him that they would distribute one hundred copies of the album. Russell's heart sank. *Only a hundred?**

"I sold like a thousand in the store," he protested.

When the first hundred copies were snatched up immediately by retailers, Guillerman was shocked. He hated rap music. He listened to the tape with a few of his employees, trying to understand the appeal. "That's the worst thing I've ever heard," he said, shaking his head. "If y'all say this is a favor to Russell, we'll keep carrying it."

Southwest asked for a hundred more copies. Then five hundred. So many retailers wanted to stock *The Southern Way* that Guillerman was convinced it was a scam. He arranged a meeting with Russell, whose quiet, sincere demeanor settled Guillerman's nerves. "The record kept getting hotter and [we] kept on ordering more and more, and then finally it got to the point where Russell couldn't keep up with supply," Guillerman says. He offered to help with manufacturing.

The record's growth was reflected on the charts in Southwest's newsletter *The Informant*, which reached more than a thousand retailers every week. Russell came home one night to find an unsolicited record contract in his fax machine from rapper Sir Mix-A-Lot's label, Nastymix Records, offering UGK a $15,000 record deal. Russell knew they'd easily make more than that through Southwest; he ignored the offer.

By April, Southwest was calling every three or four days to order 5,000 more copies, and Big Tyme was struggling to keep up with the demand. When rap/pop sensation Kris Kross'

(*Guillerman remembers their first purchase as 25 copies, while Russell believes it was 100.)

debut *Totally Krossed Out* (which went on to sell four million copies) failed to knock UGK from the #1 slot on Houston and Dallas retail sales charts, music industry executives took note. "They wanted to know who the fuck was selling all these records," Bun recalls.

Russell hired a local attorney named Warren Fitzgerald to write up a more formal contract. On April 14, 1992, Chad and Bun signed a five year, five album agreement with Big Tyme Recordz. UGK would receive 25% of the wholesale price (after Big Tyme deducted 10% for packaging costs) and Russell would also serve as the group's manager.

———————

Over at Prairie View, Mitch was staying busy on campus, but football wasn't going very well. The Prairie View A&M Panthers had once been a powerhouse in the 50s and 60s, but by the time Mitch arrived, they were what ESPN calls "the worst college football team of all time."*

In mid-April, Mitch was one of nearly 200,000 people flocking to Galveston for Kappa Weekend. Throngs of visitors spent hours cruising along the ocean, backing up traffic for miles and generally irritating the locals.

Mitch smiled the first time a car rolled past blasting "Tell Me Something Good." Then another one. And another one. And another one. Mitch shook his head in awe. "It's over," he said, to no one in particular. The Underground Kingz had made it.

———————

The Geto Boys' success proved that the combination of street-oriented rhymes and graphic shock-value was a winning formula. Rap-A-Lot paired two Louisiana natives, Chris "3-2" Barriere (sometimes referred to as Lord 3-2 or Mr. 3-2) and Michael "Big Mike" Barnett to form a group called The Convicts and assigned them controversial song topics.

Rap-A-Lot was connected to a new West Coast label called Death Row, and executives decided that The Convicts should, appropriately, be on Death Row. The group was sent to California, where they were put up in condos not far from Death Row's Hollywood studios.

Death Row artist Calvin Broadus, better known as "Snoop Doggy Dogg," lived an hour away in Long Beach. "Big Mike, cuz, you need to let me stay here with you," Snoop told him one day when he stopped by The Convicts' condo. "It be hard to get people to come get me and then bring me all the way back home."

Big Mike shrugged. "You can stay here. I ain't trippin."

Snoop became a permanent fixture on The Convicts' couch; he picked up on some of 3-2's lingo, like his habit of referring to everyone as "big baby." On a trip back to Houston, Big Mike had picked up a copy of *The Southern Way* and played it constantly on their karaoke machine, which functioned as a boombox.

"Who is that, cuz?" Snoop asked.

"This UGK, mane, they from Texas," Big Mike told him.

Snoop didn't know much about the South. He had family in Mississippi, but had only visited once and considered it "countrier than a muthafucker." As he left the condo later that day, he paused. "Big Mike, man, let me hold that tape," he asked.

"Which tape, man?" Mike asked.

"The one where he say, 'she scratched me on my *boooty*,'" Snoop said, imitating Pimp's Southern drawl.

"Oh, you talking about the UGK tape?" Mike laughed.

"Yeah, man, I love that shit," Snoop said. "Let me hold that right quick. I'ma leave something for you in the tape deck."*

(*The Panthers lost every game and scored a *total* of 48 points all season, while their opponents averaged 56 points per game. Between 1989 and 1998 the Panthers set a Division I-AA record by losing 80 games in a row. Mitch's scholarship also didn't turn out as planned. "Everybody that signed letters of intent from Port Arthur had fake letters," Mitch says. "All of them. To this day, I can't explain it … It was all messed up.")

Snoop stopped by his friend Ricardo "Kurupt" Brown's house and popped UGK in the tape deck. "Man, you gotta hear these cats."

By late April 1992, *The Southern Way* had sold 40,000 units.** Bun pored over sales charts, noting that they'd sold 115 copies in New York. Intrigued, he wondered aloud if it would be possible to go to New York and find those 115 people.

On West 25th Street in Manhattan, Jive Records' CEO and President Barry Weiss was reading the latest copy of *Radio & Records*. A straightforward, no-bullshit graduate of Cornell Business School, Weiss had gained a reputation as a shrewd businessman, a talent he'd likely inherited from his father. Hy Weiss, a Romanian immigrant who founded a successful record label in the 1950s, was credited as the creator of "payola" and was known for his aggressive promotional tactics like the "$50 handshake."***

The younger Weiss, who usually sported Argyle socks with boat shoes and Dockers pants, relied on his staff to keep him in tune with the Hip-Hop world. He had a large network of contacts at one-stops, distributors, and independent record stores. He scoured industry publications like *Radio & Records* religiously, noting anything out of the ordinary. If 50 copies of a record sold at a retail store in Tuscaloosa, Alabama, he'd circle the listing and hand it to his Director of A&R, Sophia Chang. "Call them and find out what's going on," he'd say.

Jive, a subsidiary of London-based Zomba Records, was the largest independent label in the world. They'd had some success with rap group Whodini in the 80s, and now that rap was becoming a real phenomenon, they were building a solid roster which included Spice 1, Too $hort, DJ Jazzy Jeff and the Fresh Prince, and KRS-One. (Weiss ignored critics who told him not to sign R. Kelly, telling him the Chicago singer was "nothing but an Aaron Hall ripoff.") A Tribe Called Quest's sophomore album on Jive, *The Low End Theory*, was receiving critical acclaim.

Jive specialized in finding regional acts. "It was incredibly forward-thinking of Barry [Weiss] to recognize that the market was going to expand beyond the [East] Coast," says Sophia Chang, who considered her boss brilliant and thorough.

Signing acts which were already selling units regionally meant Jive wouldn't have to spend as much money on artist development and promotion. "Jive likes to find acts that already have a fanbase built that they can just put out there and give 'em a push," Bun told *Murder Dog*.

Weiss skimmed the airplay charts for KBXX The Box in Houston and noticed "Tell Me Something Good." He'd never heard of a group called UGK. He reached out to the station's music director Greg Head to inquire about the record. He also called Robert Guillerman at Southwest, asking if this UGK thing was "legit."

"Yeah, it's totally legit," Guillerman assured him.

Retail stores in Texas told Weiss that UGK's cassette was flying off the shelves – in fact, they were having problems keeping it in stock, because it was taking Big Tyme a long time to manufacture product. Jive's regional rep Greg Powell assured Weiss that UGK's movement was real, and Sophia Chang thought the group would be a good acquisition.

Weiss had previously launched an unsuccessful bid to sign the Geto Boys. "Jive wanted to make money," Chad told *Murder Dog*. "Jive was lookin at that Geto Boys success and they wanted a Geto Boys. They wanted to sign some niggaz from down here that [were] blowin up."

One Thursday morning in late April, the phone rang at Big Tyme as Bun was opening the

---

(*Snoop kept his promise, leaving the debut album from 1960s soul group Enchantment in Big Mike's tape deck. "I [never] got the opportunity to tell Pimp that [story], that Snoop was digging on they shit way back when," says Big Mike. "I wound up falling in love with Enchantment.")

(**In later interviews, Chad said they sold 70,000 copies of *The Southern Way*. Russell and Guillerman believe the figure was 41,000.)

(***"Why waste time going out with someone you don't like, and sit down and feast with them when you can't stand them?" Hy Weiss was quoted as saying. "Just give them the money and let them play the fucking record.")

store. It was Sir Mix-A-Lot's record label, calling to raise their offer to $25,000. Russell declined.

A few hours later, Select Records called and offered $40,000. Calls came in all day Thursday and Friday; Priority Records offered even more money. Polygram Records topped that offer. As the bidding war escalated, the number kept rising.

Late on Friday afternoon, Bun fielded a call from Def Jam Records, arguably the hottest rap record label. "Hold on a second," he said, trying to conceal the excitement in his voice as he handed the phone to Russell.

Oh shit, Bun thought. *This is gonna be the shit.*

Russell tried to maintain his composure when the Def Jam caller offered $200,000 for UGK. "We'll think about it," he said nonchalantly.

"Going to bed on Friday night knowing that Def Jam just offered you $200,000 … there was no feeling like it," recalls Bun B. He spent the weekend bragging to anyone who would listen, "Def Jam wanna fuck with us, so, you know, we probably gonna fuck with [them]."

But as Saturday and Sunday passed and the phone didn't ring at all, Chad and Bun's enthusiasm started to wane. It never occurred to them that record labels were closed on the weekend. *Maybe we fucked this up,* Bun thought. *Maybe we played hardball too hard.* What if they'd missed their chance?

By Sunday night, it was agreed: they'd sign with the next label that called.

———————

The first caller on Monday morning was Jive Records, offering to fly the group to New York to sign a record deal for $150,000. Afraid they would lose the opportunity if they continued trying to escalate the bidding war, the group agreed.*

Jive sent Russell the contract, and Guillerman asked an attorney friend, Steve Shelby, to look over it. Record label contracts were naturally skewed in the labels' favor, especially with rap music, which was seen as a passing fad. As Guillerman remembers it, Shelby reviewed the contract and warned Russell, "Y'all are going to be their slaves."

Guillerman advised Russell that if he stayed independent, he could make more money. Still, it was a risk; there was always the chance that another opportunity like this might not come along again. And even though the product was selling, Russell hadn't received any money yet. Major retailers had up to 90 days to pay, but in the meantime, Russell still had to continue manufacturing product. $150,000 sounded enticing.

"Russell should have known not to [sign with Jive]," says Guillerman. "I would have told Pimp and Bun the same thing. It's the same thing that happens with every one of [these artists]. They try and try to get a major label interested, and they have no interest at all. But then they get something that is a little bit hot and all of a sudden they get the attention [and] they always go with the first [offer]. As soon as somebody says, 'We like you,' [they say], 'Where do I sign?' They sign their life away. Every one of them."

Russell told Guillerman that he didn't really have control of the group, and at the end of the day, it was UGK's choice. Russell, Chad, and a few friends congregated at Bun's house to make the final decision. Chad was excited about the potential perks; the label had already promised to send them on tour with Too $hort. The decision was made: they would go to Jive.

"We didn't know what we was doin'," Chad admitted later in *Murder Dog*. "We was some sheep getting ready for the slaughter."

(*"Oh, man, if I could go back…" Bun sighs. "We didn't even get the best deal out of Jive. We could have gotten much more money out of Jive.")

CHAPTER 7

"[UGK] seemed fearless. [The rap game] was still kind of like the Wild West ... You [had to get] out there and ... you kicked and clawed and scratched until you made a name for yourself, and they did. They did it, [and] they did it *their* way ... There was very little compromise." – Sophia Chang, former Jive Records A&R

"The business part [of the music game] is exhausting, man. You gotta look at the whole game like it's just full of fuckin' snakes, which it is."
– Scarface, HoustonSoReal, December 2004

Wednesday, April 29, 1992
Port Arthur, Texas

As the brutal Rodney King riots exploded throughout South Central Los Angeles, some 1,600 miles away in Port Arthur, a different scene was unfolding. It was near midnight when a caravan of cars pulled up to Mama Wes' home on Shreveport Ave.

Chad opened the door as more than a dozen men from Rap-A-Lot piled into the living room, then retreated to his bedroom with Bun. The two boys peeked out into the hallway, silently watching the proceedings. "They were some scared lil' niggas," Mama Wes laughs.

Mama Wes, accustomed to visitors, was still in a rust-colored business suit and short heels from her daily errands and greeted the men politely. "It was a whole bunch of black guys in here, and I was not frightened," she recalls. "My attitude [was], this [house] is *my* bitch, you know? Every month, them people [at the mortgage company] want *me* to send them some money."

One man informed her that James Smith (a.k.a. James Prince) wanted to speak with her. The name meant nothing to Mama Wes. "Who is James Smith?" she asked.

"That would be me," said the man perched on the edge of the living room sofa.

"Well, how can I help you this evening?" she asked.

"We came to sign these boys," he said firmly.

"That's not going to be possible, because they've made a commitment. They're going to Jive," she said, deliberately neglecting to mention that they were literally *going to Jive* to finalize the deal in a few hours.

"But we want them," Prince said.

Mama Wes, determined to keep this a "very short conversation," replied in a firm tone which made it clear there would be no further discussion: "I know one thing: C is my son, and he can't sign. The answer is 'no.'"

An awkward silence filled the room as the men exchanged nervous glances. It wasn't often that J. Prince took "no" for an answer.

Mama Wes' foot injury had gone from bad to worse; it remained stiff and difficult to move more than a year after the projector accident, and doctors had refused to clear her to go back to work. She loved her job, but had already logged more than 25 years in the Port Arthur school system and reluctantly settled on a good retirement plan. Now, she spent most of her time cooking so she'd be ready when Chad's friends came over. There were three full meals waiting in the freezer, and she knew exactly what to say to a group of men to ease the tension.

"Y'all hungry?" she asked. "Because I can get something up right quick."

It was almost 2 AM when Mama Wes sent the Rap-A-Lot entourage on their way with full stomachs. She walked them outside, calling after them, "Y'all be blessed!"

The night would mark the beginning of a mutual respect and twenty year friendship between J. Prince and Mama Wes, the woman bold enough to tell him "no."

———————

As Mama Wes recalls it, Chad and Bun didn't emerge until the Rap-A-Lot posse departed. Humming with adrenaline and energy, no one felt like sleeping. They finished packing and headed out to Houston around 4 AM to catch their early flight to New York. (Chad was still young enough to qualify for a discounted youth ticket.)

The group touched down in New York at noon on April 30, where there was a car waiting for them. Chad, clad in jeans, a polo shirt, and some new red Nikes, had been quietly staring out the window the whole trip, lost in thought. Bun was the exact opposite, excitedly chatting nonstop. He called friends back home from the Radisson Empire Hotel on Columbus Circle, bragging about the view from his room.

The following day, Bun, Chad, Mama Wes, Russell, and his attorney went to Jive Records' small, cramped headquarters for a lengthy meeting. (DJ Bird, who thought Russell didn't like him, wasn't invited.) Mama Wes knew they were in over their heads. "We didn't know shit about shit," she remembers. "[Chad and Bun] were just thrilled to have the deal … [And] they didn't have anything to worry about … They didn't have any responsibilities."

When UGK arrived, Barry Weiss was still tied up in another meeting and asked Jeff Sledge, the head of Rap Promotions, to accommodate the group. Jeff, friendly and talkative, welcomed them into the conference room, making small talk about the weather. It didn't seem like they had much in common until the conversation turned to music. "We [all] had a straight love for this music and this culture," Jeff recalls. "These guys were listening to records that most people from the South, I didn't think would listen to."

Jeff clicked with Bun, but couldn't get a read on Chad, who seemed quiet and pensive. Bun, a film fanatic, also found a kindred spirit in A&R Sophia Chang.* Sophia was impressed with the boys' youthful intelligence and enterprising spirit. "[They] seemed fearless," she recalls. "[The rap game] was still kind of like the Wild West … You [had to get] out there and you made a name for yourself, you kicked and clawed and scratched until you made a name for yourself, and they did. They did it, [and] they did it their way … There was very little compromise."

Barry Weiss eventually joined the meeting, and his pitch to UGK was simple: "You guys are the shit, and I really believe in you, and I think your music is dope. We can blow you up and make you a national group."

Although Jive was technically an independent label and much smaller than true "major" labels like Warner Bros., EMI, Universal, Elektra, Atlantic, and Capitol, to UGK, Jive *was* major. Major labels had bigger budgets than Jive, but most had no idea how to market a rap act.

It wasn't unusual for Weiss, who was very hands-on, to personally sign new acts. He'd landed R. Kelly in the midst of a bidding war by acting quickly and decisively, and was far more accessible to his staff than executives at major labels. "To me, one of the most compelling things about our company was Barry [Weiss]," says Sophia Chang. "[Jive] was a phenomenally nimble label … [Barry] could turn that company on a dime … To me, that was part of the genius of him, was how he ran that company and could be really fast to make decisions."

Weiss was impressed with the boys, and he loved their balance: Chad's Southern drawl,

---

(*After Sophia Chang departed Jive in January 1993, she was instrumental in signing the Wu-Tang Clan to Loud Records. She also became their unofficial Japanese importer, introducing them to old karate movies and films like John Woo's *The Killer*, which was referenced on the "7th Chamber" skit on the *Enter the Wu-Tang (36 Chambers)* album. "Yo Meth, where my *Killer* tape at, God? … Where the fuck is my tape at?" Raekwon demands.)

Bun's lyrical intelligence. "I thought they were amazing," he recalls. "I thought they were amazing in the same way that Too $hort was amazing. They had their own [sound]."

Weiss believed UGK's sound had the potential to reach a mainstream international audience. "[Chad was creating] such well-produced, melodic records [that were] so musical compared to [other rap records that were] out at the time," Weiss says. "That was what ultimately gave me the confidence that we could break them big and sell them outside of Texas."

Jive's lengthy contract had made Russell realize how little he understood about the music business, so he'd hired Austin-based attorney Frances J. Jones to negotiate on their behalf. "We thought we were slick when we signed our deal," Bun told NPR Radio. "We hired an attorney that previously worked for the label, so we thought she would have taken this inside information and used it to our advantage."

It didn't quite work out that way; the attorney appeared more motivated to maintain her relationship with Jive than fight for her new clients. (She did ensure that the contract included a provision by which she would be paid $2,000 every time UGK released an album.)

"[All rap artists'] contracts were blatantly unfair," says Wendy Day, a consultant familiar with record label contracts at the time. "Rap was new, and skewed to be disposable music. Nobody at the labels really thought it was gonna last, so they didn't really treat rap artists with the same respect that they did country or rock [musicians]."

An artist like Too $hort, Wendy notes, was able to negotiate a better contract with Jive because he had already sold tens of thousands of units. UGK and Big Tyme didn't yet understand how to leverage their independent success to their advantage.*

After Russell signed the paperwork, Chad and Bun excused themselves and stepped out into the hallway so they could celebrate without appearing unprofessional. *We did it!* they told each other in hushed tones. *We just did this shit!*

For Chad, the thought of being labelmates with Too $hort was sufficient incentive to sign with Jive, and Bun felt the same way about KRS-One. And there, coming down the hallway, was the man himself: KRS-One. He nodded as he passed. "Yo, we UGK, we from Texas," Bun told him. "We up here signing this contract...."

KRS-One interrupted, a concerned look on his face. "Did y'all sign already?"

"Yeah, we just signed," Bun said, gesturing towards the conference room.

He shook his head and sighed. "Good luck."

Chad and Bun looked at each other as KRS-One continued on down the hallway. *What the fuck was that about?* they wondered.

"We were happy for about 15 minutes and then ... reality set in," Bun told journalist Matt Sonzala. "We never even had the chance to be disillusioned about having a record deal. We regretted it right after signing."

But to Mama Wes, most of the trip felt like a surreal dream sequence. Bun, Chad, and Russell returned to Houston flush with cash, more money than they'd ever imagined. The $150,000 was an advance: $125,000 to produce UGK's album and $25,000 for Big Tyme to develop other acts.

Russell felt he'd been generous and transparent by bringing his artists along to sign, even though it was technically *his* deal. It was at this point Russell made what he considers his "biggest mistake." He hadn't yet been paid by Southwest for the 41,000 units they'd sold independently, but knew roughly how much they would receive.

Instead of only giving Bun and Chad their portion of the Jive advance, Russell says, he included their cut of *The Southern Way* in one lump sum, instructing Jive's attorneys to make the

(*Bay Area rapper E-40 was also being courted by Rap-A-Lot and Jive Records around the time UGK signed their deal. Since he had already sold nearly 200,000 units independently, E-40 was able to negotiate for an unprecedented distribution deal with Jive in which he would keep 75% of the proceeds. "They said they would never do a deal like that again," E-40 says.)
(**Russell believes Chad and Bun each received $32,000, while Bun thinks it was around $50,000. Adjusted for inflation, $32,000 in 1992 is roughly the equivalent of $54,500 in 2015.)

RECORDING CONTRACT

This Agreement is entered into between **BIG TYME RECORDZ**, referred to as "Company," with offices at 12329 Fondren, #198, and U.G.K., referred to as "Artist."

Exclusive Recording Services

1. Company agrees to employ Artist to make recordings, and Artist agrees to record exclusively on Company's label for a period of five (5) years from the date of execution of this Agreement. During the period in which this Agreement remains in effect, Artist shall make a minimum of one (1) master recordings of previously unrecorded material and material that has not been recorded at a "live" or "in concert" performance, which Artist shall select and/or compose. Artist shall complete one master recording of at least 35 minutes duration every year during the term of this Agreement. Company shall have final rights of approval on all material to be recorded by Artist under this Agreement. During the term of this Agreement, Artist shall not make or participate in the making of any recordings other than on the Company's label, unless Company expressly approves of that participation in a signed writing. Except for poduction by Pimp C Production.

Above: A portion of UGK's April 1992 contract with **Big Tyme Recordz**.

Below: A portion of UGK's May 1992 contract (technically, Big Tyme's contract) with **Jive Records**.

THIS AGREEMENT is made as of May 1, 1992 between ZOMBA RECORDING CORPORATION of 137-139 West 25th Street, New York, NY 10001 (hereinafter called "Zomba", "we" or "us"), and Russel Washington d/b/a BIGTYME RECORDZ of 12329 Fondren, Suite 198, Houston, Texas 77035 (hereinafter called "you").

1. SERVICES

1.01   During the Term, you will cause Chad L. Butler p/k/a "Pimp C" and Bernard J. Freeman p/k/a "Bun B", collectively p/k/a "Underground Kings" (the "Artist") to render Performances exclusively for us for the Territory, to the best of the Artist's ability, for the purpose of recording Masters, which you will cause to be produced and you will Deliver to us in accordance with the provisions of this agreement.

2. TERM

2.01   The Term will consist of an initial contract period ("First Contract Period") and each of the renewal contract periods ("Contract Periods") for which we will have exercised the options herein provided. We will have four (4) separate and successive irrevocable options, each to extend the Term for a further Contract Period. The second contract period will be called the "Second Contract Period", the third Contract Period will be called the "Third Contract Period", and so on.

2.02   The First Contract Period will commence upon the date hereof and will continue until the later of:

(a)   The date twelve (12) months from the date hereof; or

checks to Bun and Chad payable for $32,000 each.** This gave UGK the impression that all the money they received came from Jive, and none from Big Tyme.*

Bun blew through his check in a week, going to the ATM every day just to have cash in his pocket. First stop was nightclub Jamaica Jamaica, where he and two friends bought a dozen $60 bottles of Moët and got "pissy drunk," offering drinks to everyone in the club. "We had all this champagne and nobody to drink it with," he recalls. "We were just … doing what everybody else is doing and sitting there looking like idiots."

"[I] sat on the stage and thought I was doing it, mane," Bun said on Damage Control Radio. Blinded by the lump sum, he didn't care that this check was supposed to cover all his day-to-day expenses through the end of the year as they recorded their album.

A bit of a packrat, Bun spent nearly $20,000 of the advance on guns, just in case someone tried to rob him or Russell. "I just wanted guns," he shrugs. "I just had a fucking old apartment full of [sawed-off] shotguns. I thought that was the coolest shit in the world, to just sit in my house and saw shotguns."

Afraid that Chad was going to waste all his money too, Mama Wes insisted he purchase a house and helped him look at several properties on the east side of Port Arthur. He put down a $10,000 deposit on a $22,900 four-bedroom home on San Jacinto Ave., with Mama Wes and Monroe co-signing the mortgage. "The Cigarette" was on its last legs, so Chad bought a new white Honda Prelude and splurged on some jewelry with the leftover cash.

Two weeks after the boys inked their record deal, promoter Captain Jack brought them to perform in Houston, introducing them as "Jive recording artists Bun B and Pimp C! UGK!" Chad's eyes widened at the official announcement.

Initially, most people in Port Arthur weren't aware that UGK had signed a record deal. "They ain't really doing nothing," scoffed some jealous peers. But Chad's cousin Dwayne Diamond, a local DJ and promoter, recognized the potential and approached Mama Wes about putting together a concert.

On Saturday, May 23, 1992, while Chad's former classmates at Lincoln High were prepping for graduation, a line was wrapped around the building at Duke's Social Club (better known by its previous name, Antoine's Auditorium), a historic venue which had once housed James Brown. The Memorial Weekend Jam would be UGK's first show in Port Arthur. (Tickets were $8 pre-sale and $10 at the door.)

Dwayne was older than Chad, and liked to brag that he'd once changed his diapers. He pulled Chad to the side in the dressing room and told him, "Look, cuz, you know you can't go out there and do all that cursing. There's a lot of kids in here."

Chad readily agreed, then kicked off their performance with a loud, "We in this bitch!" shooting a smile in his cousin's direction.

But although he presented an arrogant persona on stage, Chad remained introverted and didn't like performing. Bun loved being recognized by strangers, but all the attention bothered Chad, who got upset when he was flagged down by fans at the mall. His mother gently told him that his days of peaceful anonymity were gone. "Your life is changed now," she told him. "You will never be able to do that again, baby."

———————

UGK's first major out-of-state show came when Mississippi promoter Kavin Stokes happened to come across *The Southern Way* and called the number on the back of the cassette tape.

(*According to figures provided by Guillerman and Russell, *The Southern Way* sold approximately 41,000 copies independently at $5 each, since it was only an EP and not a full CD, and Big Tyme received $3.75 per unit. At these numbers, Big Tyme would have received $153,750, of which approximately 10% went towards manufacturing and packaging. Thus, UGK's payment for *The Southern Way* would have been around $17,297 each to Chad and Bun.)

D & D ENTERTAINMENT
proudly presents
The Memorial Weekend Jam
FEATURING BIGTYME RECORDZ

U.G.K UNDER GROUND KINGZ

LIVE IN CONCERT
with

smash hit
"Tell Me Something Good"
also "Short Texas" and
new release "Use Me Up"

Also Special Guest and D & D's M-C Domino, M.y.P. and Sir Pleaz ON THE BOX

Duke's Social Club

TICKET OUTLETS:
In Beaumont
B.J.'s Record Store Washington @ 4th
In Port Arthur
Alvin's Hair Care Across from Judices on 7th
Musicworld 2600 Gulfway
Raymond's Barber & Beauty 148 7th

Saturday, May 23, 1992
8:00 til Midnight

548 Houston Ave.
Port Arthur

Pre-Sale
$ 8.00
At Door
$10.00

For more info:
call 721-4242
or 983-6703

Above: UGK's first concert in Port Arthur.
Courtesy of Mitchell Queen Jr.

He arranged to bring the group to Club Underground in Jackson, MS for $2,500.*

A local weed dealer, Freddie "Smoke D" Southwell, was a fan of UGK and was developing an artist of his own named Black. He dropped off a care package for Stokes to give UGK, which contained Black's demo tape and a sack of weed.

Smoke D typically avoided Club Underground because of the heavy police presence. ("The Feds raided the club while we were there performing," Bun recalls. "It was the craziest shit we had ever seen.") But Stokes insisted that Smoke come by. A bodyguard led Smoke through VIP and out the back door to a white limousine, which contained Bun, Pimp, and three girls. *They must want some weed,* Smoke thought, preparing to make a sale.

Chad didn't want weed – Stokes had passed along a second cassette tape of a song Smoke D had freestyled as a joke, called "The Pimp Mack Hustle." Smoke D started laughing when Chad popped it in the limo's tape deck. Chad was impressed enough with Smoke's rap skills to ask for his contact information.

Calls for shows started coming in from small towns all over Louisiana and Texas. There wasn't much money to be made in those cities, where even the largest nightclubs could only hold 400 or 500 people, but Chad and Bun knew that if they could touch people in those markets, they'd have a fan for life.

Occasionally the turnout wasn't what they expected, like one early show where there were only seven people in attendance, including the club owner and promoter. Bun found a payphone backstage and called Mama Wes, complaining, "Mama, they got seven niggas [here]." She instructed the group to "rap [their] ass off" regardless, and they did.

Promoter Warren Mayes brought the group back to New Orleans for his popular $5 Con-

(*Stokes says he first brought UGK to Jackson to perform at Club Volcano, but both Bun and Smoke D believe it was Club Underground.)

cert Series. Strawberries, a huge nightclub in Lafayette, would become another UGK staple, where promoter Bobby Caillier booked the group consistently.

Working the so-called "chitlin' circuit" put UGK in contact with a wide variety of people. Backstage at a show in North Memphis, they met a local rap group named Three 6 Mafia. Chad also met an up-and-coming rapper at a show in Lake Charles who would become a good friend; Brodrick Smith was an angry 16-year-old using the moniker KillEmAll, but Chad dubbed him "Young Smitty" after a character in an Iceberg Slim book.

By keeping their show price affordable, UGK gained a faithful client base of promoters who would book the group consistently for years to come. "I never lost with those guys," says Houston promoter Captain Jack. "Never. They might be the only group I can actually put my hand on a Bible and say, 'I never lost money with UGK.'"

They'd promised Houston radio pioneer Jammin' Jimmy Olson a free show in exchange for putting "Tell Me Something Good" in heavy rotation; UGK kept their word, and the building was packed. "They were constantly doing shows at a fair price, and that's why they were doing it for so long," Olson says. "They always did a phenomenal show … they never, ever, ever disappointed the crowd. Everybody always left there wanting more."

As promised, Jive sent UGK out on Too $hort's *Shorty the Pimp* tour in the fall of 1992. Chad told Too $hort his album *Born to Mack* helped inspire him to become a rapper. "We had a big brother/little brother relationship developing from the start," Too $hort recalls.

One of the opening acts was Profile Records' Ron C, whose record "Trendsetter" was huge in Texas. Chad was impressed with his elaborate stage show, which involved his hype man Bo-Bo Luchiano (real name: Elliott Kennedy) dressed as an escaped convict with an Afro wig and a Jason hockey mask (from the horror movie *Friday the 13th*), brandishing a chainsaw. Bo-Bo was much more effective at getting the crowd involved than UGK's backup dancers, QT and Jamie. Backstage in Ron C's dressing room at the Lafayette tour stop, Chad and Bo-Bo exchanged numbers.

When UGK came to Dallas, Chad invited Bo-Bo to come by Dallas Sound Lab and drop a verse on their record "Welcome to Texas," which also featured DJ Bird and Ron C. Chad and Bo-Bo stepped out to get some weed, and when they returned, Ron C had already filled Bo-Bo's slot with his younger brother Ganksta C.*

Chad, pissed off, pulled Bo-Bo to the side and asked how much Ron C was paying him. Bo-Bo's pay was $175 per show; Chad laughed at the figure. "I tell you what," he said. "If this dude ever screw you over, you got a job being the hype man for UGK."

UGK maintained a grueling travel schedule, often performing five nights in a row or doing two shows in one night. "Those guys were really, really, really ambitious, and they wanted it," Mama Wes recalls. "They were willing to go out there and do it."

But even though they were working consistently, the reality was that funds were still tight. The advance from Jive was long gone and the small-town shows didn't always cover their expenses. Mama Wes was often the group's investor, letting the boys borrow her Astro van and handing them cash for gas and food. More than once, they'd run out of gas as they exited State Highway 73 down the street from Mama Wes' house. "These niggas would eat all the gas money up … and then they'd make poor Bun push the car back," Mama Wes recalls.

Wardrobe was also an issue. Chad, Bun, and Bird wanted to dress alike in all black, but coordinating outfits was difficult on a limited budget. (Plus, Chad refused to wear the same clothes twice.) They went shopping for some cheap options and came across Dickies work pants. "That's how we started wearing Dickies, because I couldn't afford anything else," says Mama Wes. The outfits were so cheap she picked up a few for herself and Monroe to wear while they restocked their vending machines.

(*Jive released "Welcome to Texas" under the shortened title "Texas" as the B-side on the vinyl for the second single "Use Me Up," but the track was cut from *Too Hard to Swallow*.)

"Mind Playing Tricks On Me" exploded nationwide, established the Geto Boys as a major act and Rap-A-Lot as the premiere Southern rap label. The song hit #23 on the *Billboard* Hot 100 and crossed over to pop radio, even generating spins on New York radio stations. Critics called it "a perfect song"; *The Source* Magazine labeled it 1991's "Single of the Year." Their album *Grip It! On That Other Level* sold 500,000 copies independently.

Rap-A-Lot assigned the task of producing the video to Doug King's BPM. Doug and his new partner Byron Hill didn't have any experience with video production, so they practiced with a low-budget video, Willie D's "Bald Headed Hoes," as a test run. Doug was tired of boring, predictable rap videos, and hoped to create something more cinematic. He hired an artist to draw up a storyboard and bring "Mind Playing Tricks On Me" to life as a mini-movie.

Byron proved to be adept at logistics, coordinating details and delegating tasks to production assistants. "Byron had a big role in making that video happen … [but] he almost destroyed it," Doug recalls. "[Byron] felt threatened by the director [Richard Hunt] … he really didn't know how to be a leader. He was always paranoid of other people."

Doug and Byron hadn't anticipated the video shoot would draw such a large crowd, and they were ill-prepared for crowd control and restroom facilities. The three-day shoot deteriorated into near-anarchy, but they managed to pull it together and "Mind Playing Tricks on Me" would come to be recognized as a groundbreaking video.

Officially, Doug King was the producer; Byron Hill had not even been paid for his contributions. But Byron used his experience from "Mind Playing Tricks on Me" as his pitch to Jive, offering to produce UGK's "Tell Me Something Good" video.

Jive approved a video budget (according to Russell, $79,000) and presumably cut a check to Byron Hill, as producer, for that amount. Byron then reached out to an established video director named R. Scott Budge. As Budge recalls it, Byron told him the budget was only $35,000, well below his usual rate. Budge agreed, on the condition that he would receive a co-producer credit.

For unknown reasons, Byron decided to shoot in Dallas, although UGK and Jive both preferred Houston. In the sweltering summer heat, UGK filmed at a variety of locations throughout the city. Between scenes, Chad and Bun headed out to grab something to eat. Outside the restaurant was a young hustler offering a variety of bootleg cassette tapes for sale. Chad paused when he saw a bootleg copy of *The Southern Way*. "Let me see that," he barked.

As the kid handed over the tape with a Xeroxed copy of the cover, recognition struck and the color drained from his face. Chad handed the cassette back, shaking his head. "Man, that shit foul," DJ Bird told the embarrassed bootlegger.

The "Tell Me Something Good" video shoot would mark the beginning of the end of UGK's relationship with Big Tyme's Russell Washington. Russell didn't drink or smoke, but he had one vice, and her name was Sunshine. Entranced with his newfound money and fame, Russell's attention was focused on his stripper mistress and he seemed to have lost his vision for UGK's burgeoning career. Bun and Chad, still teenagers, viewed Russell as "their OG," but he himself was only 23 and hampered by youthful inexperience.

Chad spent most of the day grumbling about all the "hoe ass shit" Russell was doing. In particular, Russell used the funds which Jive had earmarked for UGK's wardrobe and per diem to take Sunshine on a fancy dinner and shopping spree. "I don't know if he thought [Chad and Bun] wouldn't find that out, but … he made some terrible mistakes at that video [shoot]," says Mama Wes. "I don't think he was being malicious. I think he got caught up in the glitz and the glamour."

In Russell's opinion, the problems originated with Byron Hill. "I had no idea the video [producer] would be chirping in my group's ear all day telling them I'm wrong and I don't know what I'm doing," Russell says. "That was my first time meeting him, and for the next two years, all I did was curse him out on the phone."

Even though Byron was, as Bun recalls, "a black guy that talked like a white guy" and "was talking good English," something about him didn't sit right with Mama Wes. His entire family was from Lafayette, Louisiana (coincidentally, Chad's godmother Brenda Harmon was one of his high school teachers), but he came across like a slick New York hustler. "I have a problem with people that talk too fast," says Mama Wes. She advised the boys to take their time before making any hasty decisions.

"[Byron] convinced us that we needed to leave [Big Tyme] and let him manage us," Bun later told NPR. "He talked the good talk. He was an incredible conversationalist, and he sold the dream to us, lock, stock, and barrel."

From the beginning, UGK had considered hiring another manager. It was a conflict of interest for Russell to serve as both the group's manager and the CEO of their record label. Still, Russell was surprised Bun didn't fight harder on his behalf. He'd thought they were friends; this was the same kid he'd picked up every day for work. "I would have thought [Bun] would have been my boy," says Russell. "But Pimp was a pretty dominant force … in their group."

On August 20, 1992, Bun and Chad, still teenagers, signed a nine-page management contract with Byron Hill. The contract granted Byron Hill 20% of their income and the right to extend the term of the contract at his own discretion. The contract also granted Byron the Power of Attorney and the right to take out life insurance policies on Chad and Bun ("with Manager being the sole beneficiary … in an amount to be determined by Manager").

Although wildly unfair to the artist, the contract was industry standard at the time, based on a template created by powerful law firm Grubman Indursky. Crucially, the contract did not allow the artist to fire their manager (aside from giving written "notice of such breach," which the manager would have sixty days to "cure"). There were no requirements Byron had to achieve, no minimum income he needed to procure for the group in order to maintain his position.

The "Tell Me Something Good" video was never released. "It was a $79,000 waste of money," Russell says. "Byron ran away with all the money."*

According to R. Scott Budge, the morning after the video shoot, Byron Hill was nowhere to be found and hotel staff were looking for him to settle a $1,400 bill. Budge and his production crew had received half of their fee upfront, but never received the second half. Russell Washington fielded dozens of calls from cameramen, grips, and production assistants complaining that they'd never been paid. The Director of Photography threatened Jive with a lawsuit if they released the video without paying the crew.

Bun and Chad, it appears, assumed the video was a failure on Jive's part. The only person in position to question Jive about the fact that the video never aired was their new manager: Byron Hill. No one at the label was really sure what had happened, and fans didn't understand why UGK wasn't on television, either.

In the midst of trying to complete UGK's "official" debut album, *Too Hard to Swallow*, it appears that the video shoot drama slipped past unnoticed. Jive, eager to capitalize off the momentum of "Tell Me Something Good," hoped to get an album in stores immediately. Russell had pulled *The Southern Way* off shelves, hoping to revamp those six songs for their Jive debut.

There was one major problem: Chad, just 18 years old, was a young producer whose entire craft was built on sampling. Nearly every song he submitted, Jive rejected by saying they couldn't clear the sample. Many older musicians were hesitant to clear samples of their music because rap music was perceived as a gimmick, plus, it wasn't very profitable.

(*Director R. Scott Budge posted the video on YouTube some 15 years later, which he says was the first time it was viewed publicly. According to numbers provided by Russell Washington and R. Scott Budge, it appears that Byron Hill pocketed more than $60,000 from UGK's "Tell Me Something Good" video budget, the same way he allegedly pocketed 2 Aggrivated's $50,000 Profile Records advance. Jive employees were not able to confirm the actual figures, but Jeff Sledge says the tale is likely accurate. "That story definitely is pretty true," Jeff says. "Byron was just like a slimy, slimy cat, man." There are indications that Byron had financial difficulties at the time; the IRS filed a tax lien against him a few months after the video shoot.)

Chad believed that Jive *could* clear the samples but simply didn't want to pay for them. Removing the samples, he felt, would destroy the whole essence of the song. "Once we got into [recording] the [*Too Hard to Swallow*] album, it just wasn't fun no more," Russell says.

"Tell Me Something Good," for example, had to be redone because it contained an unauthorized sample of The Isley Brothers' "Summer Breeze." At Jive's request, Chad and Bun modified their verses to something a bit more palatable for the general public. ("Bet it feels funny when ya doin' 69 / Knowin' that ya sippin' on all my jimmy wine / And when ya get a kiss, do you feel bad / Knowin' that ya swallowed all the skeeter that I had?")

"Use Me Up" also had to be censored. "I don't think I have to explain the difference between a girl who makes you hot potato pie and a girl who *tastes like* hot potato pie," complained journalist Andrew Nosnitsky.

Jive rejected at least six more songs UGK submitted for the album, deeming them too controversial or explicit. One was "Pregnant Pussy," a horrorcore-inspired tune which one critic called "the most hilarious and beautifully vulgar rap song ever recorded." "Mutha Ain't Mine," although tame in comparison to "Pregnant Pussy," covered the gruesome topic of coat hanger abortions.*

Chad would later credit their mindset on these records to the ignorance of youth. "The attitude that a 16 or 17 year old has is a different attitude than a 30-something year-old man," he told *Thick* Magazine. "We didn't have no kids, we didn't give a damn … [we were] kids expressin' … what was on our mind. It was kinda a rebellion type of thing, when kids want to get off on their own and feel their nuts … We said a whole bunch of shit for shock value."

And in retrospect, Chad found the censorship amusing. "When me and Bun started making these records we were 16 or 17, so we *were* the kids at one time making records," he told AllHipHop. "Then we got older and everybody was like, 'You're fuckin' up the kids.' I *was* the kids. *You* fucked *me* up!"

As Chad tried to salvage their records without the original samples, Barry Weiss grew impatient with his "non-stop tweaking." "He was very intense when it came to his music," Mama Wes told *XXL*. "If it wasn't absolutely perfect, he wouldn't deal with it. He was a musical genius, and you know, geniuses are always a little strange."

"He was brilliant, but he was mad," Weiss agrees. "He was a little nutty, and he couldn't finish the album." Jive's goal was to make money, not achieve artistic perfection, and executives feared they would lose fans' attention if they didn't get a product in stores immediately.

Complicating matters was the chain of command: Jive's contract was with Big Tyme, so Russell was responsible for finishing the album, but Chad and Russell were barely on speaking terms. "It was a lotta miscommunication between us and the label," Bun told *Murder Dog*.

Bun, afraid they would lose the deal if they didn't complete the project, even tried his hand at production. He brought an aspiring female rapper from Port Arthur, Kim "Infinity" Broussard (no relation to Nitacha and Riley) to the studio to spar with him on "Cramping My Style."

"We ultimately ended up finishing the record without Pimp C's involvement … I could not get Pimp C to get the damn thing finished, so I basically just took matters into my own hands," Barry Weiss recalls.

Russell and Weiss turned the project over to the studio owners Shetoro and Bernie, who replayed portions of the songs which had previously contained samples. For example, when Jive couldn't or wouldn't clear the Marvin and Steve Miller loops Chad used on "Cocaine in the Back of the Ride," Shetoro and Bernie replayed it. (A critic would later slam Shetoro's "garbage ass drum machines" and Bernie's "crappy keyboard style.") Of the six songs on *The Southern Way*, only "Short Texas" remained intact on *Too Hard to Swallow*.*

(*"I'm not a big fan of that song ['Pregnant Pussy']," Bun admitted in a 2014 interview. Russell bought the masters for "Pregnant Pussy" and "Muthafucka Ain't Mine" back from Jive for $15,000 each. "They charged me for my own songs," Russell sighs. He released them independently on a five-track EP titled *Banned*. "They Took Our Samples, They Took Our Hardness," the cover complained.)

Chad was still a young, shy, inexperienced producer who didn't know how the recording process was supposed to work. "Bernie and Shetoro literally pushed them around," says Mama Wes. "I think they just really wanted the money [for finishing the project]. Russell, bless his heart, was probably well-intentioned, but he didn't know what the hell he was doing either."

In an interview with *Thick* Magazine, Chad complained bitterly that Shetoro and Bernie had taken "all the soul outta the music" and destroyed the project's "integrity." "They thought they was some muthafuckin' producers," he told journalist Andrew Nosnitsky. "[Jive] let them muthafuckers change our music and paid them under the table to do it. And they gave 'em production credit on the shit. Ain't that a bitch?"

When *Too Hard to Swallow* was finally released on November 10, 1992, the finished product was drastically different from Chad's artistic vision. For this, Chad blamed Russell. "That's where the rift came between me and Pimp," Russell says. "I want[ed] to live up to my commitment to [Jive], to get the record in on time, [so we could] get paid."

"Russell had made some changes to the record … without our permission," Chad told *Murder Dog*. "So by that time the relationship had disintegrated."

They'd expected their major label debut to be their big moment of triumph, but the victory felt hollow. "I wasn't even in the studio when they was fucking with them records … In my opinion, that shit is garbage. I don't even listen to that [album]," Chad told journalist Andrew Nosnitsky. Even the album cover was beyond their control; Jive selected a photo and used it without their input.

"*Too Hard to Swallow* was not done by UGK," says Mama Wes. "Shetoro and Bernie fucked it up. UGK didn't do that album. Shetoro and Bernie did."

In Chad's opinion, the only "savior" of the album was a new track called "Pocket Full of Stones." As the story went, Chad and Bun were catching a ride from Port Arthur to Houston for a recording session, and in the backseat of their friend's car was a drug dealer acquaintance they knew only as "D." When a police car happened to pull behind them, D became visibly agitated, complaining, "*Maaaan*, slow this car down. If the goddamn law pull us over, I'm runnin.'"

Chad looked at Bun. "Man, whassup with yo' man?" he asked.

"*Shiiiit*…. We got a trunk full of guns, and a pocket full of stones," D said.

Chad started laughing, and the phrase stuck in his head. He borrowed the string and bass from Eugene McDaniels' "Freedom Death Dance" and added a jazzy horn sample to create the beat for "Pocket Full of Stones." They took the track to Houston recording studio Digital Services, where engineer Roger Tausz laid the bassline using a handpainted violin bass guitar he'd just picked up in Galveston.

Initially, Bun didn't want to rap on "Pocket Full of Stones" because the slow-tempo beat didn't give him the opportunity to show off his lyrical abilities. (He had the same complaint about "Feel Like I'm the One That's Doing Dope," which would remain a Pimp C solo record.) He finally agreed to drop a verse about crack cocaine, "the devil's love potion." Chad rapped about buying his first kilo of cocaine "from [his] baby mama brotha," a line which most people assumed was a reference to Nitacha's brother Riley.**

At Jive, Jeff Sledge wasn't completely on board with the UGK project until he heard "Pocket Full of Stones." Like Chad, he considered it the standout track on *Too Hard to Swallow*. Even New Yorkers liked the tune, and it seemed universal enough to take them nationwide. Jive arranged for a remixed version of the track to appear on the upcoming *Menace II Society* soundtrack.

(*Jive similarly butchered E-40's debut album *Federal* and his group The Click's record *Down & Dirty* when they signed E-40's Sick Wit It imprint and reissued both albums.)

(**Although Riley certainly enjoyed the notoriety of being Pimp C's "baby mama brotha," most of Chad's friends say the infamous line wasn't actually true. In fact, it was recorded several months before Nitacha learned she was pregnant. Isreal Kight claims that Chad borrowed the line from a Port Arthur street hustler, the same way he'd presented the story on "Short Texas" as his own. When Mama Wes heard the record, she recalls asking Chad, "Who are you talking about?" to which he replied with a laugh, "You know, Mama, everything ain't true. You gotta come up with some things that rhyme.")

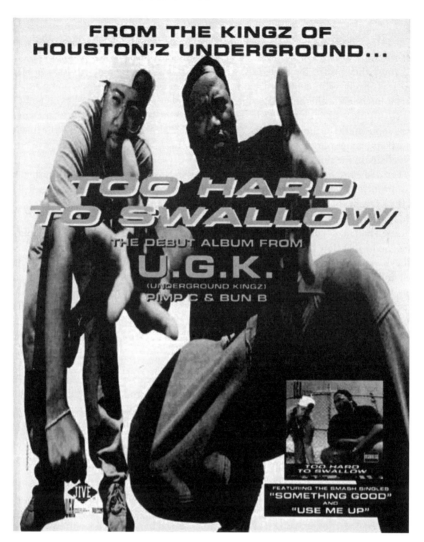

Above: A 1992 advertisement for UGK's Jive Records debut, *Too Hard to Swallow*.

Above: An early **Pimp C business card**.
Courtesy of Mitchell Queen Jr.

CHAPTER 8

"Everybody around me in my age group [was] affected by crack. Either you sold it, or you knew someone that did it, or you lived in a neighborhood that was changing because of it." – Killer Mike

---

"[There's] always been this intertwined [relationship] between Hip-Hop and gangstas: those that tell the gangsta's life, and those that live it. [Pimp and Bun] felt like they was just as [much a] part of the hustle game as everybody else. And so they had a great level of respect for people who was in the streets."
– Merrick Young

After *Too Hard to Swallow*, the relationship between UGK and Russell rapidly deteriorated. Russell divorced his wife for his stripper girlfriend Sunshine; Chad complained that Russell was too busy "trickin' at Foxxy's [Cabaret] and shit" to be focused on UGK's career. "He will never admit it, but he was just all fucked up with Sunshine," says Mama Wes. "Sunshine must have had some gold hangin' off that pussy."

Russell splurged on a large office for the Big Tyme record label, setting up shop on the ninth floor of one of the Arena Towers in southwest Houston. "He fooled himself when UGK hit," says Mama Wes. "He thought he was gonna be [a mogul] … and he might've been, if he had taken some good advice."

Russell's large, expensive desk and office furnishings didn't sit well with the group. "He didn't need all that," says Mama Wes. "He wasn't at that level, and he didn't really need to be spending that kind of money … They didn't like that."

Chad told *Starvyn* Magazine he'd stopped by Russell's office one day and noticed a $75,000 check from Southwest Wholesale, from which he believed the group had never received their share. (According to Russell, he had already advanced the group their percentage of the Southwest check when they received the Jive advance.)* UGK took their complaints to Robert Guillerman at Southwest Wholesale, who told them there was nothing he could do – his contract was with Big Tyme, and Big Tyme was responsible for distributing funds to the artist.

The more they argued, Russell started adding ridiculous clauses to UGK's contract, like a "cursing clause" so the group would be fined hundreds of dollars every time they cursed at him. "Pimp wasn't getting any money, 'cause Pimp was straight cussing him the fuck out," Bun says.

Bun still worked at the record shop, and Chad didn't like the way Russell was treating him. "This nigga [Russell] started talking like he was our boss," Chad told journalist Andrew Nosnitsky. "[We were] like, 'Nigga we all sold crack to get this goddamn record done, what the fuck is you talking about? You fitta give us this little percentage over here and you fittin' to take the largest [percentage] when we all risked our motherfucking lives to put this shit together?' That was the breaking point with us and Russell. We all hustled to put that shit down and we felt like we all should've had ownership."

After one show at Cocomo's on the north side of Houston, Chad was nearly in tears after yet another financial dispute. "Man, I just can't believe this shit," he told Ron Forrest. "It's like

---

(*Russell Washington says he always paid UGK what they were owed and denies any financial mismanagement, but admits he "should have tried harder to communicate with [Chad].")

I'm in a circle and everybody got a fuckin' knife tryin' to stab me in the fuckin' back ... my [friends] stealing from me, bitch ass Russ stealing from me..."

Things came to a head in Austin, when Chad confronted Russell over some money. As they argued, Russell pushed Chad with enough force to break down a door at the Red Roof Inn. Although she knew Chad was "probably being an asshole," Mama Wes considered it "unforgivable" that Russell had laid hands on her son, and Monroe was livid. Mama Wes scheduled a meeting at Russell's office, hoping they could keep things civil.

The meeting didn't go well, to put it mildly. Chad quickly got fed up with Russell "talkin' sporty" and Mama Wes asked the boys to wait outside. As Monroe tried to reason with Russell, he leaned back arrogantly in his large, plush office chair, making it clear that he wasn't interested in negotiating. Monroe's temper flared and he threatened to throw Russell out of the ninth-floor window. "I got everybody to leave, because I could see that it was gonna get violent very, very quickly," Mama Wes recalls.

Jive approved a modest video budget to shoot a video for UGK's second single, "Use Me Up," in which Chad played the role of a man completely infatuated with his girlfriend. It was one of the first major happenings in Port Arthur since UGK signed their record deal, and throngs of locals came out as police blocked off the bridge to nearby Pleasure Island.

The base of operations for the two-day shoot was Mama Wes' house, where her bedroom, living room, and dining room were used as props. She whipped up turkey, rice, sweet potato pies, cornbread dressing, and gumbo for the crew.

Ever since their run-in with KRS-One in the hallway at Jive, Chad and Bun had started to suspect that maybe this whole record deal thing wasn't what they thought it was going to be. Reality was starting to set in: they had a successful single and an album in stores, but they weren't receiving any royalty checks.

Chad had even more reason to be concerned: he was about to become a father. On his 19th birthday, Nitacha, who was still in high school, told him she was pregnant. Mama Wes came home one day to find Nitacha asleep on the couch, her belongings piled on top of the pool table. Monroe explained that Nitacha had stormed out of her parents' house after an argument over Chad.

"Baby, get your stuff and put it in the room," Mama Wes gently told Nitacha when she awoke.

Eventually, Nitacha moved in with Chad at the San Jac house, but the undefined nature of their relationship caused problems. Chad was also dating Kristi Floyd, who was attending college at Dillard University in New Orleans. Kristi, several years older than Chad, had been hesitant when he first called, remembering him as the shy, timid band geek from DMI. Chad's friends were impressed that he'd managed to snag Kristi, whom they saw as out of his league. Not only was she beautiful and popular, but her father was the local judge.

Mama Wes loved Kristi; they belonged to the same sorority (Alpha Kappa Alpha) and shopped together for pink-and-green sorority clothes. She thought Chad and Kristi made a cute couple. (Kristi's father, who envisioned his daughter settling down with an attorney or a doctor, was less enthusiastic about the pairing.)

Kristi was in a singing group called Joy and often accompanied Chad to shows, where she was stunned by the women blatantly throwing themselves at him. "Kristi loved C dearly, and I really do believe that C truthfully did love that little girl ... but they had issues," says Mama Wes.

In Mama Wes' opinion, the "issues" were mostly because their strong personalities clashed, and Chad found Kristi intimidating. "Kristi is nobody's fool, and if you tell her something stupid she's gonna tell you, you know?" says Mama Wes. "That sometimes frightened C, 'cause she could go head to head with him. She could whip his ass too, and he knew that. She's a little thang but she was fiery."

During a college break, Kristi came back to Port Arthur for a visit and Chad admitted he had a baby on the way. Kristi, who thought they were dating exclusively, was stunned. As Kristi recalls it, Chad tried to downplay his relationship with Nitacha to keep both women in his life, which led to an uncomfortable confrontation with a very pregnant Nitacha at the San Jac house.

Both women, young and in love, had no idea how to handle the situation. "I just felt like I was left out of the loop," recalls Kristi. "It was really weird." Eventually, it was Kristi who backed off, but she and Chad would remain friends.

Nitacha, who was pregnant and working at Jack N The Box to help pay the bills, was infuriated by the way Chad blatantly flaunted his other women. Women called all hours of the day; she found panties in the house which didn't belong to her. She came home from work one night to find Chad cuddling on the couch with another woman; unsure what to do, she retreated to her bedroom and cried. "Some of those females were so disrespectful," she recalls. "It was bad … real bold shit."

Chad was still a supportive partner, rubbing Nitacha's belly and massaging her feet and ankles throughout her pregnancy, but she was disgusted by his new rap persona and terribly embarrassed by the notoriety of "Pregnant Pussy" around town. (The song likely was recorded several months before she got pregnant.) "He was really feeling the 'Pimp C' thing … and [I wasn't] feeling that dude," she remembers. "I don't know that dude."

Now that he had a family to support, Chad was worried about his unstable financial situation. "Man, I don't want to fuck this up," he confided in Bun. "I can't fuck this up, man." He wondered aloud if they'd gone from a "shitty deal" with Big Tyme straight into a "shitty deal" with Jive. "We need to know what's in that contract," he said.

Bun's finances weren't much better; he'd become too recognizable to keep working at the record shop. When UGK was invited to participate in the parade during Port Arthur's first Mardi Gras of Southeast Texas in February 1993, there was one problem: they didn't have anything to wear. Mama Wes took them shopping. "They was broke as hell," she recalls.

They piled in Chad's friend Donald "D-Ray" Graham's candy-painted 1983 Buick Park Avenue on the afternoon of February 21, rolling down Procter Street to the fairgrounds while some 30,000 spectators waved.

Chad glad-handed the crowd, a fake smile plastered across his face while muttering some self-depreciating humor only loud enough for D-Ray, Bird, and Bun to hear: "Look at all these muthafuckers sitting up here. Y'all know y'all ain't got shit. If I collect from all of y'all, y'all ain't got a dollar and fifty cents in your pocket. U-G-fuckin'-K, you broke ass muthafuckers!"

"Make him stop, Mama!" Bird shouted, howling with laughter as they spotted her in the crowd alongside the parade route. "Make him stop!"

On February 28, 1993, one week after the Mardi Gras parade, Mama Wes and Monroe were making their usual vending machine rounds. Monroe stood up abruptly as he restocked one of the machines, looking slightly dazed. "I don't feel good," he said, his voice wavering.

They happened to be across the street from the hospital. Mama Wes looked at him closely, disturbed to note that his dark brown skin was taking on a slightly purplish hue. "Let's run into the emergency room," she suggested.

Monroe spent the next ten days in the hospital as doctors struggled to determine the cause of his sudden illness. As the days dragged by with no improvement, Mama Wes called Monroe's daughter Ursula and suggested she should come home from college for a visit.

On March 10, Chad and Ursula came by the hospital. Neither of them had realized his condition was so serious. Chad emerged from the hospital room, his face pale. "Mama, I'ma take Ursula to get something to eat," he said, adding softly, "He ain't gonna make it."

"Oh, baby, don't…" Mama Wes consoled him. "Don't say that."

"You was right, man," Chad told Monroe that night by his bedside, thanking him for the suggestion to put music in his rap, which he considered "the best advice I ever got."

"That was one of the best things he coulda told me," Chad would later conclude. "It worked … that's where I get the organ influence, the live bass and the live guitar and the real acoustic pianos … That's [how] I make music, 'cause I always remember what he told me."

53-year-old Norward "Bill" Monroe died at 6:30 AM the next morning. The cause of death was never determined. The loss struck Chad particularly hard, not only because of the love they shared as a father and son, but the fact that Monroe had taught him nearly everything he knew about music. More than anything, Chad wanted Monroe to see him succeed.

"Didn't know until you died how much you meant to me," Chad would rap more than a decade later in a dedication to Monroe on "I Miss You."*

As they laid Monroe to rest on March 13, Chad vowed it would be the last time he attended a funeral. "[Chad] became overwhelmed with death when Bill [Monroe] died, and [that feeling] never left," says Mama Wes.

There had been a little buzz around Port Arthur when the boys signed their deal, but as the months passed, enthusiasm for the group started to wane. It was during this time of discouragement that Chad and Bun, sitting on Mama Wes' couch, eagerly flipped through a rap magazine to read the first review of *Too Hard to Swallow*.

The harsh review ridiculed UGK, mocking the group by saying that they sounded like a skit on *Hee Haw*, a country-themed hillbilly variety show on CBS.** Chad, who hadn't yet fully embraced the idea of being "country," burst into tears.

"That just really crushed them," Mama Wes remembers. "That shit made me mad because it hurt them. It really did … I was so mad at those people … if it wouldn't have hurt [UGK's future coverage], I would've called and cussed them out."

But even though Chad wasn't proud of it and critics were cruel, *Too Hard to Swallow* was having an impact across the country. In Atlanta, two high school seniors named Andre "3000" Benjamin and Antwan "Big Boi" Patton were cutting class, riding around Greenbriar Mall blasting UGK. "They were so real and blunt and honest with it," Big Boi told MTV years later after their group OutKast became international superstars.

The tape also reached several other Atlantans with rap dreams, like 21-year-old Willie Knighton and 18-year-old Michael Render, who would later become a part of the rising Dungeon Family collective as Khujo Goodie and Killer Mike. It was the album cover that first caught their attention: these were some regular-looking guys, a chubby kid and a kid with glasses. If these regular guys could be rappers, so could they.

"*Too Hard to Swallow* literally was a history moment in my life," Killer Mike told filmmaker Sama'an Ashrawi. "For me, in the South, it gave us a group that was comparable to any group from any other region, and they was saying player shit from a Southern perspective."

But it was the inclusion of "Pocket Full of Stones" on the *Menace II Society* soundtrack

---

(*In time, they were able to find some wry humor in the situation. "If I knew that Bill [Monroe] was gonna pass away in just a few months, I woulda let him throw [Russell] out that damn window," Chad would say.)

(**Mama Wes believes the insulting review appeared in *The Source* Magazine, and Chad held a grudge against the publication his entire life because of it. "[C] never forgave *The Source* for that," says Mama Wes. "He hated them with a passion, because they just crushed [UGK] at a time when they really needed the lift … It really turned him off on [doing interviews for] magazines, period." However, Chad's anger towards *The Source* may have been misplaced. Former *Source* music editor Reginald Dennis scoured their back issues from the early 1990s and was unable to locate any review for *The Southern Way* or *Too Hard to Swallow*, although Jive did run a full-page black-and-white ad for the release. "I would have to conclude that [the 'Hee Haw' comments] might be misremembered when it comes to their publication in *The Source*," Dennis writes, explaining that quotes from upstart magazines like *The Bomb, Rap Sheet*, and *Rap Pages* were often incorrectly attributed to *The Source*, as it was the most prominent rap publication at the time.)

which marked UGK's big break, the turning point in their career. The movie itself set trends: braids, white tees. Everywhere UGK performed, they saw fans in the audience emulating the movie's villain O-Dog, portrayed by actor Larenz Tate. The movie's soundtrack sold 500,000 copies and Chad and Bun received gold plaques.

Jive sent UGK advance clips from the movie and a copy of the script before it was released. "You couldn't beat that shit," Bun remembers. "The only bragging right we had better than that was … the fact that me and Pimp were the only two people in Port Arthur with Sky Pagers." They flew to Los Angeles for the star-studded movie premiere, which was also attended by Too $hort and the Geto Boys.

On a deeper level, the song reflected the grimy reality of street hustlers all across the country. The crack cocaine epidemic was ravishing the nation, and small towns like Port Arthur were hit the hardest. "['Pocket Full of Stones'] was definitely about experiences that [Chad and Bun] saw firsthand," says Mitchell Queen. "That's what was going on [in Port Arthur] at that point in time. Everybody and they mama was trying to be out there hustling. The refineries were closing down. It wasn't a lot of work out there anymore."

UGK's music was vastly different from the pop-friendly rap music topping charts at the time. "[Vanilla Ice and MC Hammer] were huge, but what they were rapping about wasn't relevant where *I* was," says Killer Mike. "Everybody around me in my age group [was] affected by crack. Either you sold it, or you knew someone that did it, or you lived in a neighborhood that was changing because of it. [For me], it was all of the above."

Killer Mike listened to UGK every day as he hustled small baggies of crack cocaine; their music was what he considered "a religious experience." It became an anthem for hustlers all across the country, like Jay Jenkins south of Atlanta, who later reinvented himself as the rapper Young Jeezy. "We *had* [a 'Pocket Full of Stones'] then, homie," Young Jeezy said later. "It wasn't nothing like getting up in the morning, standing on the block and listening to 'Pocket Full of Stones.' Like, that was just your music for the day."

Teenage hustlers weren't thinking about the potential consequences or the impact the drug would have on their community. "We didn't know [crack cocaine] was an epidemic," Young Jeezy said on the *ATL Rise* documentary. "We just thought it was the new thing. We didn't know it was going to destroy families and destroy neighborhoods, we just saw the money and the potential … so if you're a young kid and you're coming home from school, and you're serving a couple fiends so you could make sure you got Jordans for next week, what's wrong with that?"

In the same way "Tell Me Something Good" inspired Texas youth, "Pocket Full of Stones" reached kids all across the country – 10-year-old Dwayne Carter in New Orleans, Louisiana (Lil Wayne); 12-year-old David Brown in Nashville, Tennessee (Young Buck); 17-year-old William Roberts II in Miami, Florida (Rick Ross) – planting the idea that maybe *they* could rap, too. "Pimp's voice is so distinctive," Lil Wayne said later. "Even though I probably heard a billion songs at that age, I knew his voice from that one time."

In New Orleans, Byron Thomas, who DJ'ed under the name Mannie Fresh, was one of many enamored by "Pocket Full of Stones." *Damn, dude, these are some real country Southern muthafuckers,* he thought.

Mannie admired the way Pimp programmed his drums to match up with the bass lines. *Damn, that shit's kinda catchy,* he thought. *His 808 drums follow whatever the music is doing. That shit is fantastic.* It was Mannie's first inkling that he might want to experiment with production himself.*

He connected with UGK when they performed at Strawberries in Lafayette to a packed house which included NBA superstar rookie Shaquille O'Neal. The group stopped by the DJ booth and exchanged contact information with Mannie, promising to stay in touch.

(*Mannie Fresh says he mimicked Pimp C's production techniques a decade later when creating "Still Fly" for the Big Tymers, the Cash Money rap group he formed with the label's co-CEO Birdman. "['Still Fly'] was based on some shit I heard from Pimp," Mannie says. "[I asked myself], 'How can I [add] my element to what [he's] done?'")

However, "Pocket Full of Stones" wasn't roundly applauded. Pastors attending the Southern Baptist Leadership Conference in Dallas spoke out against the song. But for those who criticized the duo for glorifying the hustler's lifestyle, Bun felt they were missing the real message.

"People who don't really understand the music … [only] listen to the hook of the song," Bun told Austin's KLRU TV. "But if you listen to the [verses], the person in the song starts out as a guy on the corner selling drugs, he actually moves up in the drug game, makes a lot of money, loses everything and goes to jail. Because he didn't give himself an opportunity to learn anything else about the world … he comes out of jail and he has no education, no job experience, nothing else to do but go right back to selling drugs. It's just an endless cycle."

"We're trying to expose the cycle," Bun added. "You think you're gonna beat the game, but you're really just going to end up stuck in it forever if you hustle without a plan."

———

By July 1993, "Pocket Full of Stones" was everywhere, and *Too Hard to Swallow* had sold nearly 250,000 units. "Local rap thriving on independent labels," read the headline in the *Houston Chronicle,* citing Big Tyme as a local success story.

Thanks to UGK, Southwest Wholesale was now a full-fledged distributor attributing 85% of their revenue to rap music. "[Southwest has] been a big part of helping us keep going," Russell told the *Houston Chronicle.* "They go out and get our money for us."

———

J. Prince drove straight to Port Arthur in a brand new Lexus when he heard "Pocket Full of Stones." "I knew it was gonna be something real big," he said later on Damage Control Radio. "I just wanted to be a part of it."*

With Scarface along for the ride, Prince pulled up to the San Jac house and got acquainted with Chad. "I was excited because this nigga was a legend in the South already," Chad recalled on the *Pimpalation* DVD, adding, "I was ecstatic about him being a fan of our music."

Chad was into cars and was especially impressed with Prince's new acquisition. "Shit, take that muthafucker," Prince told him, dangling the car key. "You can have it. Come over to Rap-A-Lot and you can have that muthafucker. I'll get a ride home."

It was a tempting offer, but Chad declined. Prince, like Chad, was nocturnal, and their informal meeting lasted until dawn. Chad called Bun after Prince departed, excitedly recapping the Rap-A-Lot offer. "What did you say?" Bun asked.

"Man, I just told him, you know, I don't want to go over to your team and be number ten when I'm already number one over here," Chad explained.

"That was it?" Bun asked.

"Yeah," Chad said. "It was gangsta."

"What was he in, a Benz?"

"Naw, nigga, he was in a Lexus."

"A Lexus?! Jesus Christ, he drove a Lexus to Port Arthur?" Bun asked.

"Yeah, man," Chad said. "These dudes are so rich."

———

(*Recollections vary as to the timeframe and the specifics of this visit. Bun believes it was a yellow Ferrari, but J. Prince and Scarface recall driving there in a Lexus. It's possible there was more than one visit.)

CHAPTER 9

"If death had a taste, [fry] would be it." – Anonymous fry smoker, Erowid.org

_____

"People do a lot of dumb shit trying to fit in."
– Bun B, Rhapsody.com, March 2008

Throughout 1993 the San Jac house would become UGK's base of operations as they set to work recording their second Jive album. One side of the house was reserved for Chad's growing family, Nitacha and their son Chad Lamont Butler II, who arrived in August. The two bedrooms on the other side were were usually occupied by any number of friends who passed through to smoke weed, make music, and crash on the sofa.

When UGK complained that they weren't receiving royalties from _Too Hard to Swallow_, Jive executives explained that technically, there was nothing they could fix because UGK was signed to Big Tyme, not Jive. With growing problems between Big Tyme and UGK, Russell reluctantly agreed to renegotiate their deal. "Once the money gets involved, everybody wants to get rid of the middleman," Russell sighs.

Originally, under Big Tyme's production deal, Big Tyme received 14 points off the album, or 14% of the retail price _after_ Jive deducted all recoupable expenses. Russell agreed to renegotiate the contract so that Big Tyme and UGK would each receive seven points directly from Jive.

As an advance for _Super Tight_, Jive sent Russell $50,000 and UGK $50,000. UGK used their half to purchase equipment for the San Jac house, but it wasn't exactly a "home studio." "[Chad] didn't build a studio, [he just had] equipment," Bun recalls. "You used to have to walk over this shit … he had keyboards and rack mounts and shit all over the fucking house." A piano and a large Hammond B-3 organ with a Leslie speaker took up most of the room in the cramped den.

Chad considered it "selfish" to do all the production himself, but when they tried to buy beats from other producers, he said, "niggas kept fuckin' us out of our money." He decided it would be wiser to invest in keyboards and drum machines and make the beats himself, even though he was a bit insecure about his production skills. "I've always considered myself just to be decent. Not great," he told _Too Real For TV_. "I'm a decent producer, and I'm a character. I'm not no hell of a rapper, I'm a character. But I got something to talk about."

The den/studio was also known as the "weed room," a man cave of sorts where women were forbidden. The walls were plastered with posters of Bob Marley, the Geto Boys, and UGK's _The Southern Way_ and _Too Hard to Swallow_. The small refrigerator was always stocked with a pound of weed, and guests were instructed to help themselves. In theory, at least, weed smoke would be confined to that one room. ("They used the studio as a weed room, but honestly and truly I couldn't tell the difference [from the rest of the house]," Mama Wes laughs.)

The studio walls lacked soundproofing, so Chad designated one of the bathrooms as the vocal booth due to the relatively good acoustics. "Don't shit in the front bathroom, because we're doing vocals today," Bun would call out. DJ Bird would often ignore his instructions and use the studio bathroom anyway, forcing Bun to smoke strong weed or spray air freshener to try to clear the stench as he faced the toilet, pulling the microphone close.

Chad had become extremely protective of his music after the Bernie and Shetoro fiasco, determined to maintain as much control as possible over the recording process. "Just don't touch my shit," he'd say.

"[*Too Hard to Swallow*] was a real learning experience ... [which] molded the way C would behave with his music from then on," says Mama Wes. "I really doubt whether he would've been as picky about things had that not gone down the way it did on the first one."

The concept for their second album *Super Tight* was to blend UGK's two favorite movies. "The player side leaned more towards Pimp, which was *The Mack*, and [the] gangsta side that leaned more towards *Scarface*, which is more for me," Bun explained on Damage Control Radio.

They settled into a routine: Chad would make a beat and present it to Bun, usually with a hook or concept already in place. He often sang the hooks himself out of necessity. "A lot of times in the studio we didn't have nobody to sing on the hooks ... I didn't have no money to pay no singer, so I had to sing 'em," he told journalist Andrew Nosnitsky.

After they decided the structure of the song and how many verses or bars each would contribute, they'd write their lyrics separately. "Once we decided the direction of the record, there was no more communication," Bun says. Because the two were so different, the result was the same topic discussed from completely opposing viewpoints. "[We never] looked at everything in the same way, and even if we did, we weren't going to say it the same way," Bun explains.

"Bun raps, and then I explain it to 'em," Chad would summarize.

Their recording method functioned so that even when they were mad at each other, they could still create. Their opposing personalities inevitably clashed. "They would get in arguments all the time," remembers Freddy Johnson. "Sometimes, they wouldn't even speak to each other until it was time to [record] the music."

The house was always filled with visitors, mostly aspiring rappers who passed by to hear what Chad was working on. His friend Leroy White became their in-house engineer. Ron Forrest's sister Ronda worked the closing shift at the nearby McDonald's, where employees tossed out all the leftover food at midnight. Every night without fail, Chad would pull up at 12:01 AM, usually with a few people stuffed into his tiny white Honda Prelude.

"What you got, Lil' Forrest?" he'd ask.*

Among the frequent houseguests were Smoke D and Young Smitty, who planned to form a group called the B.U.D. Bros. Chad had been working on a record called "Front, Back & Side to Side," using samples from The Meters' "Rigor Mortis" and Eazy E-'s "Boyz-N-The-Hood" remix. Critics later described it as "the perfect summer cruising track," "the purest example of the UGK method in action ... one of the most perfect Hip-Hop beats of all time."

When they went to New Orleans to record the vocals, Chad brought Smoke D, who dropped a memorable verse introducing himself as "a country-ass, gold-teeth, chicken-eatin' mack" with plans to "take your bitch to [his] crib and throw a party on that pussy."

Jive pressed up vinyl for the record, which landed on the soundtrack to *A Low Down Dirty Shame*, and *The Source* lauded the single in their December 1994 issue as a welcome "lighthearted" tune from UGK instead of their usual "gritty crime & drug scene tales."

Things at Death Row had come to a halt for The Convicts, with the label focused on Dr. Dre's *The Chronic*. When Big Mike got a call inviting him to replace Willie D for the Geto Boys' album *Till Death Do Us Part*, he returned to Houston and Mr. 3-2 soon followed.

Big Mike was also recording his solo album *Somethin' Serious* and connected with Pimp C, who invited him to come by the San Jac house and listen to some tracks. Mike's father was an accomplished jazz musician in New Orleans' French Quarter, and he and Pimp soon found that they shared common musical interests.

(*Ronda laughs, "I gave away so much food they closed down that McDonald's.")

Mike spent a week sleeping on the couch at the San Jac house, and the beat Pimp created specifically for him, "Havin' Thangs," would become the standout track on his album. "Pretty much everything about Pimp C's production brilliance is contained in this beat," rap critic Brandon Soderberg later wrote. Big Mike planned to sing the hook, but when he heard Chad's soulful demo vocals, decided to leave it on the record.

Bun, who wasn't at the house during the creation of "Havin' Thangs," couldn't believe Chad had given the track away. "That's the greatest song in the world! What's wrong with you?" Bun said. "Y'all didn't even let a nigga rap on that shit? Man, that's cold."

"Havin' Thangs" also landed on the *Dangerous Minds* soundtrack, although it was overshadowed by Coolio's massive hit record "Gangsta's Paradise." The video shoot was one of Chad's first opportunities to appear on camera, but most fans didn't even realize that this youth in a Polo shirt and glasses was the creative force behind UGK.

Officially, DJ Bird had always been the third member of UGK, but as they started recording *Super Tight* there was talk of adding a third rapper to the group. Smoke D was in consideration, as was Mr. 3-2, who was staying at the San Jac house for weeks at a time. 3-2 and Big Mike were both renowned for their off-the-dome freestyle abilities.

Bun had always admired The Convicts' rap skills, taking cues from Big Mike's aggressive lyricism and 3-2's humorous wordplay, and he enjoyed the challenge of rapping alongside them. "Chad would make beats and we would all sit in the room and literally just rap for hours," Bun says. "That's literally all we used to do. Just sit in the room and rap for hours."

While 3-2 was recording with the group, they spent several months traveling back and forth to Dallas Sound Lab. "I always had high expectations for UGK. I think that's why I spent so much money in the studio on them albums," Chad said later. "I took the extra time to put special shit in them songs that cost a little bit more money than the record label [wanted to spend]. I used to run up budgets real high … come post up in Dallas for three months at a time, recording. Jive didn't like that but they had to respect it when I sent 'em the product."

Sadly, many of these songs would never be released, mostly due to clearance issues. During one marathon session, they recorded "Pussy Got Me Dizzy," "Stoned Junkee," "Ménage à Trois," and "Weed Weed," but only two would be cleared for *Super Tight*.

"Ménage à Trois" was a seven-minute long solo Pimp C slow jam. In it, Pimp invites Tracy, a friend from school with "light brown eyes and a big round booty," to come by his house with her friend Stacy, who's "hot potato" he had always dreamed of getting "wet." When the two ladies arrive at his doorstep at 9:59 PM, he has everything in place for a weed-and-liquor-fueled threesome and some Al Green playing on the stereo.

Immediately, one of the girls grabs his "jimmy" and Pimp is soon "getting' licked" and "livin' like an old player from the funky old school." After christening the entire house ("we did it on the table, we did it on the rug / I went to take a shower, they was freakin' in the tub") they all "came at the same time" as the song comes to an end.

Pimp hoped to release "Ménage à Trois" as their first single, but the record was based on a sample of soul singer Angela Winbush, who wouldn't clear it.

"Weed Weed" was a slow, laidback track featuring Bun rapping with a mock Jamaican accent and singing marijuana's praises on the hypnotic, catchy hook, along with verses from Mr. 3-2 and Mitchell Queen. On the extended outro, Pimp broke into an impromptu rendition of the Red Hot Chili Peppers' "Give It Away," and then proclaimed, "3-2 is in the fuckin' house, Big Bun is in the muthafuckin' house, Leroy is in the muthafuckin' house, my nigga Mitch is in the house. And that's for all you ol' fake ass niggas, yeah, come in and sit on my couch talkin' about you wanna be down with me, nigga … Everybody wanna be a rapper…"

"Eat a big 'ol dick," someone in the studio chimed in.

The record sampled the Isley Brothers, who were in the midst of litigation over the rights to their music. It was impossible to clear the sample, which was an integral part of the song, so

"Weed Weed" was pulled from the album. Another Bun B solo record called "Smooth Slangin'" was based on the Isley Brothers' "Smooth Sailing," which also had to be pulled. "I knew when I did ['Smooth Slangin'] that song was probably never gonna come out," Bun said on Damage Control Radio. "I think it was obvious that the Isley Brothers [weren't] gonna [clear that]. But it just had to be done. It had to be written and it had to be rapped, even if it never came out."

Other tracks which were cut from the album included "Mack The Knife" featuring Tim Smooth, "Here They Come," "Rat-Tat-Tat," and "'93 Mac." UGK made copies of some tracks from the *Super Tight* sessions on black Maxell tapes and passed it out to their friends. "Weed Weed," the undisputed standout, would remain what Bun calls "a hidden classic."

Chad was a huge fan of influential New Orleans funk band The Meters; he'd based his trademark organ style on their keyboardist Art Neville and admired the group's guitarist/song-writer Leo Nocentelli. Instead of just sampling the group, as dozens of other Hip-Hop acts had already done, Chad wanted to have a live musician replay their samples.

"He was trying to find someone to recreate the sound but he couldn't find anybody he felt was doing it justice," Bun told *Pitchfork*. Chad eventually got in touch with Nocentelli himself through a mutual friend and hired him to come to Port Arthur, where Nocentelli was flattered by Chad's near-hero worship. "[The] immense respect [he had] for The Meters was almost un-heard of," Nocentelli says. "[Being] in my company, me being in the same room [as him] was like a big thing to him. I couldn't believe it."

Nocentelli was impressed with Chad's thorough knowledge of The Meters' catalogue and "unique way of thinking." "His thing was funk, but it was like … mysterious. If it wasn't abstract and kinda out of the mainstream, he wouldn't record it," Nocentelli recalls. "He had a certain way he wanted to represent himself and the sound, and he didn't venture from it that much." Chad also called on other prominent New Orleans musicians, like keyboard player David Tork-anowsky and bass player Chris Severin.

"[Legendary musicians usually] do not give themselves or their intellectual properties over to the younger generation, especially the Hip-Hop generation [because] a lot of times they as-sume [there's] a lack of knowledge," Bun told *Pitchfork*. "… [but] Pimp was very good at letting people know that he understood their sound and their music, had a great respect for their cata-logue, and wasn't trying to rape their catalogue, was trying to create something unique through what they had created."

Another artist Chad admired was rapper Rick Royal, whose group Royal Flush had been one of the first groups signed to Rap-A-Lot in the late 80s. (Bun considered them "the dopest rap group that ever came out.") Rick Royal's record "I Never Made 20," a vulnerable, honest record written from the perspective of a black teenager who feared he would never make it past age nineteen, struck a nerve with Chad. "[The song is] really a reflection of the paranoia that young black men feel," Bun told AllHipHop. "[That] was Pimp's favorite rap song. Period."

Rick Royal had changed the name of the group to Ukfe Uye (Pig Latin for "fuck you," or, as Rick liked to call it, Nig Latin) and inked a deal with Epic Records. His home on the north side of Houston, dubbed "The Tilt," became the hangout spot for many Texas rappers including Chad and Bun. "[Rick] was like the leader of the pack, so to speak," says Lichelle "Bo$$" Laws, a female rapper signed to Def Jam who was dating Rick. "It was a hundred thousand rappers over there [at his house] every day."

The whole crew became known as The ORG (Original Righteous Gangstas, among other acronyms), an informal rap collective which Rick saw as an umbrella organization to launch other artists' careers.

"Mounting police pressure on cocaine traffickers has drug abusers turning to a bizarre alternative for a high – smoking marijuana cigarettes laced with embalming fluid," the *Houston Chronicle* reported. Adventurous weed smokers were dipping their blunts in "embalming fluid," a liquid Scarface describes as "fuckin' piss green … [like] hazardous material … nuclear waste." But many users were unaware that the "embalming fluid" actually contained PCP, a powerful hallucinogenic known to cause frightening "out of body" experiences.

It wasn't a new idea; PCP-laced weed had been around since the 1970s. On the West Coast, PCP-laced cigarettes known as "sherm" were popular. It had different names all over the country: "dank" (Kansas City), "hydro" (New York), "wet" (Philadelphia); "happy sticks" (Chicago); "illy" (Connecticut).

When the trend hit Houston in the early 90s, it was known as "fry," "amp," "water," "form-aldehyde," "wet," or simply "dip." (Urine samples from drug suspects in Texas showed that PCP use quadrupled throughout 1993 and 1994.) Users described the taste of fry as something akin to rubbing alcohol, nail polish remover, gasoline, or a Sharpie marker. "I would actually say if death had a taste, that would be it," one fry smoker reported on Erowid.org.

Smoking fry could cause hallucinations so vivid that users became completely discon-nected from reality. Some described feeling like they were in a mirage. Users saw themselves in an alternate universe, envisioning things that weren't there and believing they were invincible; feeling powerful enough to uproot a tree or tear down a skyscraper.

Between Big Mike, 3-2, and Chad's friend/engineer Leroy White, all avid fry smokers, there was always a bottle of dip at the San Jac house. ("You can ask Leroy White, we ain't scared of no water," Pimp rapped later on "Deep in the Game.") While weed was Chad's drug of choice, he wasn't much of a fry smoker. "I smoked my first blunt with 3-2 … might've [smoked] my first fry stick with Big Mike," he reminisced in *Thick* Magazine.

Fry was what Bun B refers to as a "mood-intensifying drug." "If you get fried with an ag-gressive attitude, then you become very aggressive," Bun explains. "Chad's one and only time that I can remember him smoking fry, he was very nervous about doing it. Therefore, when he became high, he was extremely paranoid and he thought he was going to die."

Chad mentioned the drug to his mother. "It's shit that make you act crazy," he explained. She had never been concerned about weed, but was adamantly opposed to him experimenting with "that crazy stuff," especially when she started noticing Leroy White and 3-2's erratic behav-ior. ("I used to smoke fry, wasn't scared to die / Every day when I woke up I wanted to get high / My Mama came and got me from that devil dope," Chad rapped later on "My Angel.")

Bun took to the drug more than Chad, passing most of his time smoking fry while listening to Ganksta N-I-P.* Cocaine and heroin were too hardcore for his taste, but he'd experimented with Xanax, ambien, mushrooms, and ecstasy, which were easily available for purchase at Dallas nightclubs. ("Like, 'Give [me] two tabs [of ecstasy] and two Heinekens," he says.)

"I [smoked fry] a lot," Bun admits. "I thought that was what made me a good rapper. Artists sometimes get that confused … People went through it with heroin, they went through it with cocaine, with marijuana, and all these things we thought to make people's minds more expan-sive. [I thought,] 'I need this dope to be this great artist.'"

When asked about his production techniques in late 1993, Scarface told *Rap Pages* he would create a track and then take it to his partners for the finishing touches. "I'll go to [John] Bido and get the chronic, Joe's got the Swisher Sweets paper, and when you get to me, I got the embalming fluid, and that's what tops it all off," Scarface explained.

Fry was popular, easy to find, and cheap, offering high profit margins for drug dealers. "It's just like with any other drug," says Big Mike. "Why does anybody get high? It's for the escape … from your everyday cycle, your everyday routine … that's why people get high."

(*Today, Bun says he keeps Ganksta N-I-P music in his phone to "remind [him] to not fucking ever do amp [fry] again." Pimp would later brag on the record "Massacre," a Lil Troy diss, that he'd "smoked dip with Ganksta N-I-P" to insinuate that he was better connected on the south side of Houston than Troy.)

Big Mike told Chad he should meet Roderick "Smit-D" Smith, an up-and-coming rapper who belonged to Scarface's Facemob crew. Smit-D pulled up to Rick Royal's house The Tilt one day and recognized Chad sitting outside in his small white Prelude.

Chad extended a hand as Smit approached the car. "You Smit, right?" he asked. "Been wanting to meet you, boy, you live."

"Yeah, man, Mike told me to fuck witcha," Smit-D said.

"Man, let me let you hear what I'm on right now," Chad said, gesturing for Smit to climb in the car. Smit hesitated. An athlete who excelled at football and basketball, Smit managed to squeeze his solid 6'5" frame into the tiny Prelude. He winced, his shins pressed up against the dashboard in the cramped space, as Chad played some new tracks from *Super Tight* for him.

A few days later, there was a knock at the front door of the apartment Smit-D shared with his girlfriend and their two young children in southwest Houston. His girlfriend had just left for work, and Smit opened the door to find 3-2, Big Mike, Bun, Chad, and DJ Bird. They'd just picked up some dip and needed a place to hang out and smoke.

Smit had never smoked fry before, but felt obligated to join them. Besides, he felt safe in the comfort of his own home. The six of them spent the entire day smoking fry, lazily lounging on Smit-D's sectional and watching TV. As the day wore on, Smit muted the TV so they could listen to some music. Their minds hazy from the effects of the drug, they watched in a stupor as the TV hosts soundlessly introduced a block of Mary J. Blige videos.

After watching Mary J. Blige on the screen for what seemed like an eternity, 3-2 stood abruptly and confronted the large television, standing close enough to the screen that his nose nearly touched.

3-2 finally turned around, tears falling from his eyes. "Mane, Mary J. is dead," he proclaimed, sadness in his voice. Before long, everyone in the room was crying.

When their drug-induced haze finally lifted, one by one, they realized that Mary J. Blige was *not* dead; BET was just airing a segment of her videos. Smit-D tactfully told everyone they had to leave shortly before his girlfriend was due home from work. They left the rest of the fry sticks in the freezer to marinate.

Two days later, Chad called Smit-D. "Man, I just found my way home," he said. "I been trying to find my way home for like a day and a half."

UGK would soon record "I Left It Wet For You," which had a double meaning. While Chad boasted, "What a nigga tryin' to say is, *shiiiiit*, niggas be straight up fuckin' your gal, fool," Bun bragged, "Getting fried like that dip, I'm full of that dank and ready to trip."

"My nigga 3-2 came down with the water / A dip, dip, nigga trip, trip ya fried," Chad rapped. "What's up, Smit?" he asked on the outro. ("He's really talking about the dip sticks we left in the freezer," Smit-D explains.)

Fry references were abundant on *Super Tight*; on "Stoned Junkee," Mr. 3-2 rapped:
And I'm still rollin' a fattie but I'm dippin' that bitch in that water
And makin' me a wet daddy, the green monster
[...] Every day I find myself full of that fuckin' embalming fluid
Yeah, so you can certify me as a fiend
And if you smoke dip, fool, you know what I mean
Now let me lean to the muthafuckin' left
Start walkin' fast and get my blast by my goddamn self
That's how it go, movin' slow in the south
A stone cold junkee with some drugs in his mouth
High 'til I die, and fry is all it takes

Although 3-2 would remain on several tracks from *Super Tight* and Bun considered him "an incredible artist," UGK ultimately decided not to add any more members to the group. They were concerned it would change the group dynamic, plus, 3-2's drug use often made him erratic and unreliable.

"Smoking that fry, man, that's the best high I ever had," Scarface says. "I liked it too much … so I quit … Anything you like too much you gotta stop, or it'll hurt you … I just realized [that] this shit makes me feel *too* fuckin' good. It had to be something wrong with it."

Smoking fry was something like a game of Russian roulette. "[Dealers would] cook embalming fluid and [then] cut it, so you have to know exactly what you're doing," Bun B says. "And [even] the people who could cook it good … still had bad batches."

It wasn't uncommon to see a fry smoker who'd gotten ahold of a bad batch running down the street completely naked. (In a study commissioned by the Texas Commission on Alcohol and Drug Abuse, 20% of fry smokers admitted to such behavior.) "When you see guys that are butt-naked in the grocery store with a knife and it takes ten cops to pull them down … this is the power of the drug," Bun explains.

"People do a lot of dumb shit trying to fit in," Bun said in an interview with Rhapsody. "I ain't used to pictures coming up off the paintings and walking around the room … When I was smoking water [formaldehyde], that first hit feels good and it's a nice little rush. But then you take that second hit and you get that wash-over, and you know that you're in that world and not coming out no time soon."

It didn't take long to realize that this cool new drug was pretty dangerous. Long-term fry smokers could be seen muttering to themselves, dirty and disheveled with poor hygiene. "Niggas smoke too much fry, and I tell 'em that shit / But you can't stop no junkie nigga 'til he ready to quit," Pimp rapped on the 5th Ward Boyz' record "Swing Wide."*

"The [fry] trend couldn't sustain itself because of the violent nature of the drug – it's prone to giving folks hallucinations, violent outbursts and unexplainable rages," writer Jesse Washington noted in the *Houston Press*. "In short, fry doesn't make you cool. So along came syrup."

Since the early 90s, DJ Screw's slowed-down mixtapes had become so popular that friends started coming by his father's apartment with special requests. One of Screw's early clients was Quincy "Q-Dawg" Evans, a well-known hustler from the south side.

Quincy would ride around South Acres in his 1969 Impala, blasting Screw's mixtapes through his customized sound system. Before long, everybody wanted a Screw tape. In nearby Cloverland, the tapes caught the attention of Courtney "C-Note" Smith, a teenager who passed his time hustling on Botany Lane with a handful of friends. *I can actually rap over them slow beats,* C-Note thought.

C-Note asked Quincy to introduce him to Screw and bought some mixtapes to play in his car. "Hey, would it be okay if I tried to rap on one my tapes?" he asked.

Pretty soon, everybody wanted to rap on their own tapes. Screw started shouting out local neighborhoods; customers requested tapes for special occasions like birthdays or even funerals. Screw's growing mixtape business drew so much noise and traffic that unamused landlords forced his father to move four times until Screw finally moved into his own house at 7678 Greenstone in southeast Houston.

In early 1994, Bun stopped by DJ Screw's house and was surprised to see a gate up around the property. The steady stream of traffic had been growing, and visitors now had to be buzzed in through the gate before encountering several massive guard dogs.

Screw opened the door, sipping from a pint-sized prescription bottle. Bun shot him a

(*Over time, the drug had serious effects on several members of the UGK camp. "I used to get fried with people who are now in mental asylums and will never get out because they have lost all sense of reality," Bun admits. His friend Joseph "JB" Melonson, a local barber who worked alongside Jelon Jackson, apparently suffered a mental breakdown after smoking a bad batch of fry and has never recovered. Another frequent fry smoker was Chad's friend and in-house engineer Leroy White. "I don't think even Leroy understands how that shit actually just switched him from a real person into someone else," says Mama Wes. "And he never stopped. I don't think he ever has." Leroy is currently serving a ten-year prison sentence in Port Arthur for assault.)

strange look. "What's wrong? You sick or something, nigga?" he asked.

"Naw, this is syrup," Screw drawled. "This is what we doin' right now."

Bun had never heard the term before. "Syrup? Let me in. What is this shit?"

"This is promethazine-codeine cough syrup," Screw explained. "You drink it and it slows you down. It chills you out."

Inside, rapper Big Mello and a local street hustler named Kenny Bell were rinsing out dozens of four-ounce jars of Gerber baby food. "What the fuck is y'all doing with baby bottles?" Bun asked, his curiosity piqued. He opened the freezer, which was stacked full of baby food jars.

"That's how you sell the syrup," Screw explained. Users liked to purchase syrup in four ounce increments, and cheap Gerber baby food jars were the ideal size.

Sipping codeine-promethazine cough syrup to get high had been a trend in Houston as far back as the 1960s, when it could be purchased over the counter at any pharmacy without a prescription. ("Sippin' lean ain't no thang of the past," Pimp C later rapped on "Let Me See It.")

Cough syrup was perceived as "safer" than illegal drugs because it was prescribed by a doctor. Users drank it straight out of the bottle, or ignored the blatant warnings on the label and mixed it with alcohol like cheap Boone's Farm Wine. Combining alcohol and codeine was a dangerous mixture which could lead to blackouts, and the practice became known as "leanin'."

For two decades, Houston's popular folk singer/country artist Townes Van Zandt built a career of singing codeine's praises. Known to drink a quarter-pint of codeine every day, Van Zandt loved Robitussin DM cough syrup so much he gave it a nickname ("Delta Mama"), a theme song ("Delta Mama Blues," by the Delta Mama Boys), and named his pet parakeet after the pharmacy where he bought the drug. The first song he ever wrote, 1968's "Waitin' Around to Die," was a mournful dedication to codeine:

Now I'm out of prison
I got me a friend at last
He don't steal or cheat or lie
His name's codeine, he's the nicest thing I've seen
An' together we're gonna wait around and die

Bun tried some syrup from Screw's stash, smoked a fry stick, and passed out at a friend's house. He would later recap the day on Beanie Sigel's record "Purple Rain":

Way back in '94, when Screw still had his gate up
He called me over to his house and he poured me an eight up
I asked him what it was, he said, "Bun, get your weight up,
This is lean, them white folks call it promethazine
But shit, we gon' call it drank, dawg, 'cause that's what we be doin' to it
Now take this Big Red and pour about a two into it."
I said, "Twos and eights, what the fuck is you trippin' on?"
He said, "Man, that's the ounces of cough syrup that you sippin' on."
He poured it, I sipped it, then I sipped some mo'
I fired up a green monster and I hit that hoe
Started relaxing, shit, and to my surprise
I was nodding off looking at the back of my eyes
They tried to wake me up, but shit, I just kept yawnin'
I fell out in my chair and woke up the next morning
God bless my nigga 'cause since then I've been spoiled
On my white muddy cup of Texas tea, that oil

CHAPTER 10

"We took [Mama Wes'] living room and made it a lounge. We took her kitchen and made it a cafeteria. And in our own moment of audacity, we took her life from her and made her our manager. And that's when everything changed."
– Bun B

"It was just me, C, and Bun against the world, 'cause everybody thought all of us was nuts." – Mama Wes

October 1993

The day before a scheduled UGK performance at the Bomb Factory in Dallas, Mama Wes got a call from Byron Hill with some bad news: UGK's road manager Drake Jolivette couldn't make it to the show. He and his brother Eric had to turn themselves in to a federal prison.*

The Jolivette brothers, three years apart, were from Opelousas, Louisiana. They'd been out on bond for a year and a half, accused of playing a minor role in a drug organization which had allegedly moved 200 kilograms of cocaine between Houston and Lafayette. After testifying against their superiors, the Jolivettes admitted to providing their "residence for the storage and safe keeping of the cocaine" and were sentenced to 21 months.

Mama Wes couldn't believe Byron's poor judgment; surely, he'd known this was coming. "He had that nigga going out on the road with these kids, and he *knew* that fool was going to the Feds," she says. She wasn't comfortable with the idea of her 19-year-old son making the trip to Dallas alone. Of course, he'd be accompanied by Bun, DJ Bird, and their driver/friend Leroy White, but with no responsible adult in the crew, she worried what might happen if something went wrong.

Byron certainly wasn't going to go. Still on bad terms with Rap-A-Lot, he rarely showed his face. He liked to coordinate things by phone from a safe distance, as if operating by remote control. On the rare occasion UGK did see him in person, he struck them as paranoid and evasive, refusing to even take pictures with the group.**

With no one else available on short notice to serve as the group's road manager, Mama Wes decided she would do it. It had already been a bizarre six months. She'd just had the wires removed from her jaws and was learning how to talk again after a nearly fatal car accident. She'd been forced into retirement and lost her husband. Why not?

Now a retired widow with a brand new lease on life, Mama Wes would later come to see the tragic yet timely events of 1993 as divine intervention.

When they arrived at the Bomb Factory for soundcheck, Mama Wes scanned the empty floor in front of the stage. She'd left her closet full of business suits, sorority clothes, and high heels at home, opting instead for the comfortable pairs of Dickies work pants she wore on her

---

(*The brothers, both named John Jolivette, went by their middle names. They were released from federal custody in April 1995. Attempts to reach them for comment were unsuccessful.)
(**As previously noted, Byron Hill declined to be interviewed. His statements and actions as described in this book are from others' recollections.)

vending machine runs. Attending rap concerts was so far out of her element she had no idea fans stood up during the show. "When are they gonna get the club ready?" she asked Bun.

"Mama, it's ready," Bun told her.

"Well, no, it's not," she said, confused. "Where are the tables and chairs?"

The only thing she knew about being a road manager was the most important task: get the money. In a cash business with very little regulation, this wasn't always as easy as it sounded, and things sometimes turned ugly. "It got tense in a lot of back rooms … fists got balled up, sticks and bottles got grabbed, blue steel got cocked … it's been some very, very tense situations," Bun said on Damage Control Radio.

The club owner had paid a $2,500 deposit, 50% of UGK's show fee. While the boys waited in the limo late that night, Mama Wes went inside to pick up the $2,500 back-end and modest $200 travel fee to compensate them for the five-hour drive from Port Arthur to Dallas. Inside the nightclub office, the club owner was holding a conversation with a handful of security guards and Greg Street, a popular DJ from Dallas radio station K104.*

"I came to get the paper," Mama Wes announced.

The club owner handed over a stack of cash. Mama Wes counted the $2,500 in front of him. "You know the transpo was $200," she said.

"I'm not gonna pay that, 'cause y'all was late by ten minutes," he responded.

"Well, you not gonna see UGK then," retorted Mama Wes. "That was yo' limo out there who picked us up late, so deal with it, baby."

As more words were exchanged, the conversation grew heated. Greg Street, a worried look crossing his face, stepped between the two. Finally, the club owner pulled out a handful of bills and threw them derisively in Mama Wes' direction. The bills floated to the floor, falling in disarray at her feet.

Every eye in the office turned towards Mama Wes. The retired librarian, a petite grandmother in her late 40s who'd recently lost her husband, stood alone surrounded by a dozen men double her size. She was terrified, but knew better than to let it show.

A hush fell over the room, aside from the dim bass from the nightclub speakers thumping through the walls. She locked eyes with the club owner, desperately hoping he couldn't see her knees trembling inside her Dickies and silently praying that her voice wouldn't quiver.

"When you find a bitch to pick that money up," she stated firmly, pausing for emphasis, "You let me know."

Mama Wes turned towards the exit, blocked by four oversized security guards.

"They didn't know how scared I was," Mama Wes recalls. "But I kept walking, and they just parted like the Red Sea."

Greg Street picked up the $200 off the floor and ran outside, following Mama Wes to the limo. She made him wait outside, eying him suspiciously. *Who the hell is this nigga?* she wondered.

"Some nigga here say his name Greg Road or something?" she told Bun as she climbed in the limo. "I don't know who the nigga is."

Bun peeked outside. "Mama, that's Greg Street!"

The name meant nothing to Mama Wes. "So?"

Greg had history with the group, ever since he'd been DJing in Houston when "Tell Me Something Good" started to blow up. He climbed in the limo and everyone had a good laugh over the brief skirmish with the club owner. Chad quietly chastised his mother, his tone one of slight embarrassment. "Mama, that ain't what you supposed to do," he said.

"Well, honey, I didn't know," she responded, as only a mother could.

But any doubt Mama Wes had about her new career path dissipated the moment the show

(*Mama Wes doesn't recall his name, and isn't sure if he was the club owner or a promoter.)

began. She'd been to a handful of shows before, but had never seen anything like this. Bun ran out on stage as the crowd chanted, "UGK! UGK! UGK!"

"What you gonna do?" Chad asked his mother, mic in hand.

"I don't know, honey," she said. "What am I supposed to do?"

"I gotta go, Mama," he said, preparing to run out on stage.

"I guess I'll follow you, nigga," she shrugged. She found a spot behind the DJ booth with DJ Bird. Unsure what to do, she put one hand in the air and waved it from side to side. Watching their command of the stage and the crowd's reaction in the hot, sweaty nightclub was her first inkling that the group was destined for greatness. *Those kids have something,* she thought.

"They were magic," she said later on Damage Control Radio. "I had two magical babies who were very magical when they hit that stage." Her mind flashed back to her teenage son's prediction: "I'ma make a record." No one had really believed him then, but she was awed by the realization that he'd really done it.

After the show, Mama Wes looked at her son. "C? I don't believe this shit," she said.

"Mama, I told ya," he smiled.

"You did," she nodded. "You really did."

Although supportive of the group, Mama Wes didn't yet understand the music. She didn't like the explicit content on *Too Hard to Swallow*, but felt it was important to let them develop their own voice. "I didn't like that album, but [I knew] the children were trying to say something," she says.

She started listening to rap music, trying to understand why her son found it so intriguing. *If I don't ever understand what they're doing, then I'll never be able to support them,* she reasoned. She couldn't get into the "East Coast crap," but quickly caught on by listening to her son's Too $hort tapes.

Months passed, and it became clear Byron had no intention of hiring another road manager. "He would always wait until Friday [before a show], late morning, and call [me] with the rush act," says Mama Wes. "He knew I wasn't gonna let them go by themselves … so I'd always end up having to do it."

The group already suspected Byron was overcharging promoters and pocketing the extra money. "[Byron] really didn't seem like he had those guys' best interest at hand," says Mississippi promoter Kavin Stokes. "[He] just wanted to benefit and those boys put in all the work."

"Everybody in the group [could] see what he was doing," says DJ Bird. "He was a crook." After their experiences with Russell, Chad was especially wary. "When you're young … trying to get in the business, you don't know people [are] trying to take advantage of you," adds DJ Bird. "C wasn't the type to try to take advantage of nobody."

Byron's aggressive, controlling nature irritated Chad, and they clashed often. "You know, *you* work for *us*," Chad would snap when Byron tried to give him orders. "*We* gon' tell you what *we* want you to do."

MC Bytch was growing similarly disillusioned with Byron. 2 Aggrivated's album still wasn't finished, and producers wouldn't work with them anymore because Byron hadn't paid them. One producer asked if they'd gotten their advance. The girls looked at each other. "No, what advance?"

"Man, y'all need to check y'all contracts," he suggested.

With the future of their Profile Records deal looking shaky, 2 Aggrivated confronted Byron. "[Our album] was gonna fail because Byron wasn't delivering the product [and] he had spent all the advance money," says MC Bytch.

Byron assured them he had a plan. "I have this group, UGK," he explained. "I'm gonna send you down there [to Port Arthur] to work with them." MC Bytch, already a fan of "Pocket Full of Stones," was excited about the opportunity.

Byron dropped 2 Aggrivated off at the San Jac house. "[Chad's] house was like the hangout for all the rappers in Port Arthur," MC Bytch recalls. "They looked up to him and Bun B like they were gods." They ended up staying for a week, mostly because Byron hadn't arranged transportation for them to return to Houston. MC Bytch didn't mind; she had a slight crush on Chad and flirted with him whenever Nitacha was out of earshot.

Eventually, the conversation turned to Byron Hill. "Yo, Bytch," Chad said. "You know, I think he fuckin' y'all." Chad explained that he'd recently learned the "Tell Me Something Good" video hadn't come out due to Byron's apparent financial mismanagement. "Byron was messing over everybody," MC Bytch recalls. "He was taking the money and spending it on *his* lifestyle, on *his* needs, sending it home to his wife in Louisiana."

Mama Wes became more than just a road manager: she cooked dinner, she did laundry. "[I was] their nurse and their doctor and their psychiatrist and [gave them] advice on love lost. I wiped asses, all that," she joked on Damage Control Radio. "I would stand on that stage on a Friday or a Saturday night and see them do what they did [so] I could work another week 24/7, because they were so energizing."

Most of all, she was their motivational speaker, the force behind UGK when things got tough. "Quitting is not in our vocabulary," she'd tell the boys. "No matter how bad it gets, quitting is not in our vocabulary. Roll forward."

"It became a family affair," Chad told *Scratch* Magazine. Even baby Chad Jr. traveled to the shows. He generally stayed in the room with a babysitter, but at Prairie View A&M's homecoming, his father brought him out on stage and performed with the child in his arms.

Mama Wes didn't scold the boys for smoking weed, entertaining groupies, or cursing; hell, she'd probably curse right back at them. "[Mama Wes] was always cool," says Too $hort. "She was always like everybody's Mama." If Chad and Bun stepped too far out of line, she wasn't above embarrassing them, loudly calling them by their childhood nicknames "Chaddyboo" and "Bunny Rabbit."

During one stop in Baton Rouge, Chad's childhood friend NcGai was stunned to see Chad casually conversing with his mother with a blunt stuck behind his ear. "It's cool," Chad explained. "When we on the road, she's my manager, not my mom."

"My Mama's never done drugs, but she's not a square," Chad told the *Dallas Morning News.* "Everything I can do in the dark, I can do in the light in front of my Mama. She's got a Master's degree in English and she was a teacher, but when she got into this rap thing, she learned fast. Now, you can't pull nothing over on her."

Occasionally, Mama Wes even served as UGK's groupie coordinator. "Who that for?" she asked her son quietly after one Dallas show, observing a girl who'd followed the group back to the hotel.

"Well, she would want it to be me, but I'm trying to help Bunny Rabbit today," Chad told her.

"Something about her don't feel right," Mama Wes observed.

"I know," Chad laughed. "That's why I'm gonna put her on Bunny Rabbit."

Although Chad and Bun admitted to being some "wild young teenagers," Chad rated their sexcapades as mild by rapper standards. "[We] ain't never been butt naked in no room together with no hoes, pulling no orgy type shit or doing none of that hoe ass type shit," Chad said on *The Final Chapter* DVD, adding, "Nigga, if you in a room naked with some other niggas and some broads … That shit is gay … Me and [Bun] got nothing but respect for each other. We ain't never pulled no trains, we ain't no muthafuckin' freaks … we don't desire to do no shit like that."

The Dallas groupie turned out to be what Chad referred to as "one of them *Fatal Attraction* hoes," and for weeks after their brief encounter, she called Mama Wes' house daily asking for Bun. "She *stalked* that boy," Mama Wes laughs. "That girl used to call here every damn day, because they would give them hoes *my* number."

―――――――――――――

While Chad grew silent and withdrawn before performances, Bun was usually so nervous he talked constantly until he inevitably threw up. It became something like a pre-show ritual. Sometimes he'd make it to the bathroom in time, but sometimes he didn't. In the limo on the way to the venue, Chad would joke to his mother, "Put that boy by the window and keep your hand on the button."

Bun's mother still wasn't convinced her son was a rapper, but Mama Wes' involvement made her a bit more comfortable. "She took them all in like they were hers," she told the *Port Arthur News*. "I loved her for that."

Mama Wes adopted Bun as one of her own, considering him "one of my little protégés." When a *Murder Dog* interviewer erroneously asked Bun how his mother had become the group's manager, he didn't correct them, simply answering, "She kinda felt like everybody else … didn't have our best interest at heart. So she took [the management role] upon herself and I love her for that. She didn't have to do that. But if you ask her she'll tell you it's the only option she had left."

Those long road trips in the early days of UGK, Mama Wes felt, brought them together for life. "We were all together at times when the going was rough," she says. "It was me, C, and Bun against the world, 'cause everybody thought all of us was nuts. We've been through a lot. We have a special bond."

As UGK's show schedule picked up, Mama Wes no longer had the time or desire to maintain N&W Vending. "[Mama Wes] had an extremely profitable company and she let it go to spend a lot of money [on us]," Bun told radio host Madd Hatta. "[Her son] needed help, he didn't have anybody else to turn to, [and] she was there for him."

"I lost paper because I really should've done it differently and sold it properly, but I just walked away from it," she admits. "Honestly, [the boys] were way more important to me than [the vending machine business] was."

Her peers didn't understand her decision to get involved with a rap group. Her sorority sisters thought she was crazy; one told her she was disgracing the sorority by wearing her pink and green AKA clothes on UGK road trips.

Mama Wes was approached one day by a local woman while grocery shopping at Johnnie Alford's in Port Arthur. "I just cannot believe it," the woman said.

"Excuse me?" Mama Wes asked.

"I just *cannot* believe it," she repeated. "I heard your son's album the other day. My son had it. And I have never in my life heard anyone say '*beeeyotch*' like that!"

"No, that must have been Too $hort," Mama Wes quipped.

The reference was lost on the woman. She shook her head, scolding, "Your son has the filthiest mouth I've ever heard!"

"He was cussing?" Mama Wes asked, with feigned concern. "I saw your son the other day in the cut, on 7th Street, cussing for free and being a d-boy. When your son makes as much money cussing as mine do, holla at ya' girl."

CHAPTER 11

"DJ DMD tried to make Chad kill Isreal Kight. But Chad wasn't no killer, and Kight wasn't no thief." – Boonie

---

"Every nigga of that era from P.A. – other than C and Bun – feel like they was overlooked. Let me tell you something: Nobody in this little city had any aspirations to be anything in the music industry until C and Bun came along. To this day, everybody [in Port Arthur] thinks they are a great rapper, a great R&B singer, probably a fuckin' dancer ... It was a one in a million chance that [UGK] would come out of here and get anything going. H-Town, this ain't. Dallas, this ain't. Atlanta, it ain't. This is a little [city of] 50,000 people." – Mama Wes

UGK's growing success stirred up plenty of emotions in the small community of Port Arthur. Many congratulated the group, but inevitably, there were others who harbored resentment and envied their position.

One group waiting for their shot at fame and fortune was the Good-Fellaz, a duo consisting of Chad's childhood neighbor Ron "Crumz" Forrest and former classmate Isreal "Bluelite" Kight. Kight was upset because he hadn't been paid for his verse on "Short Texas," but it wasn't really about the money.* Mostly, he felt he hadn't received his share of the spotlight.

In Kight's opinion, he'd done more for UGK than just drop a verse – he'd given them credibility. "['Short Texas'] gave them street cred for people to even start buying they music in Port Arthur," Kight says. "Even when the song blew up, I was still in the streets ... [but] Chad and Bun ... they not really from the streets." ("We had to get permission from somebody to come out here [to Short Texas]," Chad admitted.)

Since UGK's rap career was taking off, Kight thought they should help the Good-Fellaz land a record deal too, and Ron was feeling left out because Chad had stopped hanging out with him. "We was always trying to figure out ... why didn't Chad come back and holla at us?" Ron recalls. "Why didn't he include us in what he was doing?"

Mutual friends felt that Kight was expecting too much of Chad. "Really, Kight was just jealous. That's all it was," says Donny Young.

The Good-Fellaz were introduced to a friend's wealthy aunt, who agreed to put up a modest budget to release their debut album *Illegal*. The Good-Fellaz' raps were gritty and grimy, set over dark, moody beats. On their biggest record "Pharmacy," they bragged of selling weed, heroin, and "anything that make you feel good" to a client base which included "doctors and lawyers." But their records lacked the musical quality of Chad's production. Neither of them knew how to produce, so the Good-Fellaz turned to DMD.

While DMD had technical skills, he didn't have Chad's creativity. Chad laughed when he heard the work in progress, saying that DMD was trying too hard to emulate UGK. "Man, y'all whole record sound like 'Pocket Full of Stones,'" Chad told the Good-Fellaz.

According to Kight, Chad agreed to produce their album with no money upfront, partly

---

(*Payment was technically Big Tyme's responsibility, not UGK's. "Russ told [Kight] he was supposed to get paid, so really his beef wasn't with Chad, his beef was with Russ," says Ron Forrest.)

to compensate Kight for his contribution to "Short Texas." When they were ready to go to the studio and record vocals, the Good-Fellaz' investor paid for studio time at Houston's Digital Services. But Kight says that Chad was nowhere to be found on the day of the scheduled recording, and the session had to be cancelled.

Kight, known for his short temper, was furious that Chad had caused them to lose money and look bad in front of their investor. When no one answered the door at the San Jac house, Kight kicked it in and took the floppy discs from Chad's Ensoniq ASR-10 keyboard.*

Kight took the stolen floppy discs to producer Rob Quest a.k.a. Blind Rob of the Odd Squad, a Rap-A-Lot group which included Devin the Dude. Rob was literally blind, but his lack of eyesight enhanced his ear for music. His home studio in Houston's Third Ward was lined with posters of beautiful scantily-clad women from *JET* Beauties of the Week and 2 Live Crew posters. (Chad, who stopped by occasionally, had once asked Rob why he had posters on the wall that he couldn't see. "They're for you," Rob laughed.)

When Kight explained where the discs came from, Rob was hesitant to get involved. "Aw, man, that's wild," Rob told him. "I can't do nothing with it, but let's see … I wanna hear what he produced for y'all."

Blind Rob was unable to recover the beats; the discs, apparently corrupt, returned error messages. Kight's temper cooled, believing that a technical malfunction was to blame, but he still felt disrespected that Chad had skipped out on the studio session.

According to DJ Bird, the reason Chad didn't go to the session was because the Good-Fellaz hadn't paid him. "We was doing bad, y'know? [Chad] ain't have no money," Bird recalls. "We was already struggling with Jive. They put us on hold, trying to starve us."

"There was no money in rap," Bun said on Damage Control Radio. "People don't really realize there was nothing for me and Pimp to get in the early days but recognition."

Between the occasional show money, Nitacha's meager fast-food wages, and Mama Wes' contributions, Chad was managing to stay afloat. But Bun's financial situation was so dire he took a delivery job at soul food restaurant RBJ's. Deliveries were a challenge because his run-down, bulky Cadillac could only drive forward, not in reverse. "I had literally the number one record in the city and was delivering soul food dinners," Bun recalled later on NPR. "We were making absolutely no money from the record company."

All in all, it wasn't a bad gig; Bun got free meals, loading up daily on pork chops, red beans and rice, cornbread, macaroni and cheese, and sweet potato pies. "Boy, we was eating heavy from RBJ's," Mama Wes recalls.

The job also gave Bun the opportunity to make extra money on the side selling weed. The typical customer, too lazy to drive a couple miles to pick up a plate, was already a pothead. Unbeknownst to the owners of the establishment, Bun started offering an informal two-for-one special. "I'd bring you like, a pork chop dinner and a dime bag, if that's what you wanted," Bun recalled in *Mass Appeal*.

Chad, obviously, was not motivated to do any more work for the Good-Fellaz after Kight kicked in his door. Chad and Kight avoided each other.

Sunrise Records in Beaumont was a popular spot for aspiring rappers and beatmakers to dig through old 45s, looking for soul samples. On one trip to Sunrise, Ron and Kight selected a sample from George Clinton's band the Funkadelics' "What Is Soul."

Ron tried his hand at production, but was limited with his rudimentary equipment. There were only a handful of producers in town, so the Good-Fellaz again turned to DJ DMD, asking him to create a beat using the sample.

(*Kight says he only took the discs labeled "Good-Fellaz," but according to Bo-Bo Luchiano, Chad was upset because Kight also stole a number of tracks intended for UGK's *Super Tight*.)

Chad dissed Big Tyme's Russell Washington on "Return," which would become the opening track on *Super Tight*. Jive was apparently so concerned about their potential liability for slander that they trimmed the song down from five minutes to two. But Chad still got his point across in the the first verse:

Mr. Big Man, Mr. Big Tyme, give me what's mine
Instead of buying cars for a bitch named Sunshine
Give me what's mine, give me what's mine
Before it come down to triggers

The song deeply hurt Russell, who coped by listening to self-help audio books. When one suggested he should take his most negative moment and turn it into a positive, he decided to adopt the name "Mr. Big Man, Mr. Big Tyme," using it as the intro on the DVDs he produced.

As things deteriorated with UGK, Russell turned his focus towards his artist Reginald "Point Blank" Gilliland. (Chad accused Russell of using Jive funds designated for UGK to record Point Blank's Big Tyme debut.)

Point Blank had once been on good terms with UGK; the record "Cut U 'N ½" on his debut *Prone to Bad Dreams* was a leftover Pimp C-produced track from *Too Hard to Swallow*. But as animosity grew between UGK and Russell, Point Blank sided with Russell.

In 1994, Big Tyme released Point Blank's second album *Mad At The World*, which included at the end of his liner notes: "Oh yeah I forgot U.G.... Naw fuck dem niggaz they sold out record company like some 2 bit hoes (Got big headed but ain't got a damn dime)." On "Forgive But Don't Forget," which featured Russell on the hook, Point Blank rapped:

I know a couple more hoes live in P.A. and they go by the name of UGK
Supposed to be down with Big Tyme but they ain't
Trying to get out of they contracts but they cain't
And Big Russ getting tired of this shit, tell 'em Russ

At the height of the bad blood between UGK and Russell, Houston promoter Captain Jack booked the group for a show at Boomerang's, a huge nightclub on the south side. Russell frequented Boomerang's, and called Captain Jack the night before the show to tell him he was planning to come. "We not with 'em anymore, but I still like them guys," Russell said. "Tell those guys not to diss us at the show."

Captain Jack, unaware of the drama, didn't understand why Russell was calling. "Diss you? Why should they diss you?" he asked.

"Just make sure that Pimp C and them don't diss us, man," said Russell. "This is our backyard over here in South Park. As long as they don't diss us, we'll sit back and watch the show and everything will be cool. I guarantee."

A confused Captain Jack never mentioned the conversation to UGK. But the group was already halfway expecting war, arriving at the club with an unusually large entourage. "They had half of fuckin' P.A. on the stage that night," Mama Wes recalls.

In the middle of the show, the DJ threw on Point Blank's record and then brought it to a screeching halt as Pimp C commanded, "Take that shit off." As Pimp transitioned into "Return," the record dissing Russell, Point Blank lunged towards the stage and grabbed a large wooden 2" x 4" off one of the barricades. Point Blank, a towering 6'5", rushed towards Pimp, swinging wildly. Russell, who walked with a limp due to an injury, trailed behind, yelling at Captain Jack over the din of the crowd, "I told you not to let them dudes diss us, man!" The ruckus brought the show to a complete stop as everyone ran for the exits.

Point Blank was also at war with DJ DMD, but the two didn't even know each other. DJ DMD had formed a group called Point Blank and signed with a Houston record label, and both claimed they'd had the name first. DMD's group started calling themselves the Original Point

Blank, while Big Tyme's Point Blank was dubbed "SPC Point Blank" due to his affiliation with South Park Coalition ("I hope you didn't get confused / When those punk ass Port Arthur niggas tried to step in my shoes," he rapped on Ganksta N-I-P's "Fuck You.")

The investors funding DMD's group were deep in the drug game, planning to use the record label to wash their illegal proceeds. "That's how every label got started unfortunately, with street money," DMD said later in *Houston Rap*, remembering, "I saw FBI agents bust open my door and they raided my record company's clique ... Here I am with DEA agents with shotguns in the back of my head, thinkin' that I'm some part of [a] dope ring."

With the record label owners facing federal drug charges, DJ DMD moved back to Port Arthur to manage a record store his family had purchased called Music World. Chad and Bun were finishing up *Super Tight* and still needed a few more records, so DMD submitted a beat CD.

Chad selected three tracks he liked; the first was the one DMD created for the Good-Fellaz using the Funkadelics sample. DMD explained that the beat was for Kight, but he hadn't paid for it yet. Chad, still angry at Kight for breaking into his house, bought the beat and flew DMD to Dallas to record the song.*

DMD says he had no idea there were problems brewing. "I didn't realize Chad was gonna take a beat he knew [Kight] wanted and rap about [Kight] on the same beat," DMD says. "When I got [to Dallas], I found out they [were] turning it into a diss song ... Maybe that's why Chad wanted the beat in the first place, just to spite him."

Bun had written a verse for DMD, taking shots at Big Tyme's Point Blank: "How you gon' diss me with a clique full of hoe niggas?" The track, "Three Sixteens," would become the closing track on *Super Tight*, and UGK selected two more DMD beats to complete the album.

The first, "It's Supposed to Bubble," contained a sample of Pleasure's "Thoughts of Old Flames." (The hook, "that's Dom Perignon, it's supposed to bubble" was borrowed from Whodini's "Echo Scratch.") Chad called in guitarist Leo Nocentelli, bass player Chris Severin, and keyboard player David Torkanowsky to replay portions of the track.

To the world, "It's Supposed to Bubble" was a bottle-poppin' champagne celebration. But those in the know in Port Arthur understood that it was an ode to smoking fry. Locally, "Dom Perignon" was a slang term for the bottle of dip, otherwise known as the "green monster" for its radioactive-green hue. After the fry stick was dipped in the "green monster," it was placed on a sheet of foil paper in the freezer. "When you put it in the freezer, the shit start bubbling up," explains Port Arthur rapper Hezeleo. "That's your Dom Perignon bubbling."

Mainstream listeners never caught the reference – a decade later, the *New York Times* described the song as one where "Pimp C claimed he was forsaking syrup in favor of Dom Perignon." (DMD says he had no idea the song had a double meaning. "I'm a nerd ... I thought it was about champagne," he says.)

"Pass that dip and it's gon' be alright / Soon as I get fried tonight," Bun rapped. On his verse, Chad rhymed:

Well I'm Pimp C, bitch, I'm smoking big fat dank
I don't fuck around no mo' with that goddamn drank
But every time I get with my nigga Big Mike
We go and get a bottle of that Dom on ice
I got that green monster, baby, can you buy that?
Plus I got Swisher Sweet for days, you wanna try that?
We roll 'em up so big and fat they look like ball bats
I live in P-A-T, the east side, nigga, San Jac

The third DJ DMD-produced track, "High Till I Die," featured Bo-Bo Luchiano and Big

(*According to Kight, DMD never gave them the time or opportunity to complete the transaction. Kight claims they had already paid DMD around $12,000 to produce five songs for their EP, and by the time he brought DMD the $3,000 he'd requested for the beat, DMD had already sold it to Pimp C. DMD denies this, saying he'd agreed to do the project for mere "pennies," and they had only paid him a thousand dollars total.)

Mike.* It was included on some early advance copies of the album but cut at the last minute when Jive couldn't (or wouldn't) clear its George Benson sample. On his verse, Chad explained why he needed mind-altering substances "to keep [his] mind right":

I gotta worry about the laws tryin' to take my life
It seem like every bitch I fuck, they wanna be my wife
So I smoke a lot of pot to keep my head cool
'Cause if I don't I might just get in my Caddy and act a fool

Jive and UGK couldn't agree on which record to release as a single. While UGK thought "Front, Back & Side to Side" was their strongest record, Jive preferred "It's Supposed to Bubble." "They wouldn't let us pick the song," says Mama Wes. "We knew what the hit was."

Jive made the decision to go with "It's Supposed to Bubble" and arranged to send the group to Atlanta's Freaknik in April 1994 to shoot the video.** When the bus pulled up to the San Jac house at 5 AM, everyone was drinking and smoking, excitedly buzzing about the upcoming trip. Mitch, DJ Bird, D-Ray, Port Arthur rapper Superb Herb, Freddy Johnson, and Bo-Bo Luchiano, who was now touring with UGK as their hype man, piled in and they headed out in the pre-dawn darkness.

Chad called for everyone's attention as the bus pulled off, explaining apologetically that, at the bus driver/owner's request, there would be no smoking on the bus. Everyone agreed reluctantly and Chad returned to the front with his mother and the driver.

Two hours later, they pulled off at a rest stop on I-10 near the Atchafalaya Basin swampland of Southern Louisiana. Most of the crew were passed out asleep, but Bo-Bo went to use the restroom. When he emerged and the bus was gone, he chuckled. *They must be playing with me,* he thought.

But as the minutes ticked by, Bo-Bo realized this was not a joke. Worse, he had no idea where he was, and no way to contact anyone on the bus. Thirty minutes later – after Bo-Bo, in a panic, had called 911 from a pay phone trying to determine his location – the bus pulled back up, with Chad apologizing profusely.

It was nearly a twelve hour drive to Atlanta, and as the hours dragged by, the bus full of smokers started getting antsy. It didn't help that one of them had a suitcase full of weed. Eventually, someone figured out how to crank open the small air vent at the top of the bus, and suggested that if they blew the smoke out the air vent, no one would notice.

Before long, their supposedly discreet smoking session turned into what Freddy Johnson recalls as a full-on "Cheech and Chong Fest," and the scent wafted towards the front of the bus. Chad burst through the door and exploded when he saw everyone passing around blunts. "Man, what the hell are y'all doing!?" he hissed. "Y'all about to get our ass kicked off of here! Man, put that shit up!"

As they neared the Atlanta city limit, traffic was backed up for miles with long lines of colorful Cadillacs and rimmed-up Benzes. "The freeway and the exits were at a standstill," Bun told *VIBE* Magazine. "So, I got out of the car and literally walked down the freeway, down the exit ramp, and into downtown ... When I got out of the car people were drinking and dancing because everybody was there to party, they were pumped up and ready to go but they couldn't get to the party. So, they were like fuck it. We're going to party right here and right now."***

Freaknik began innocently enough: in 1982, it was a small picnic at Atlanta's Piedmont Park for Spelman and Morris Brown students. Attendance multiplied every year, and by the 90s

(*Big Mike, relieved that the song never came out, says his conscience was starting to bother him and he has since stopped rapping about drugs to avoid being a negative influence on listeners. "I had a guilt trip ... I really don't wanna glorify getting high," he says.)
(**Bun B has stated in interviews that the video for "It's Supposed to Bubble" was filmed during '93 Freaknik, but it seems more likely that it was 1994.)
(***In this interview, it was unclear if Bun was referring to arriving at Freaknik for the "It's Supposed to Bubble" video shoot, or a different year.)

it was an out-of-control street party drawing wild crowds of more than 200,000. "For the most part Freaknik was a fun and enjoyable environment but … the city of Atlanta was not really ready for the traffic … the drinking and smoking in public places, the nudity. It was a lot," Bun told *VIBE*.

"[There were girls] naked on top of vans, dancing and stuff," Bun recalled. "The madness and the traffic was unlike anything I've ever seen … One guy had a van of girls and the pulled up to the corner and he put the girls on the top of the van and then if you wanted to see the girls naked, you had to give money. Once he got 'x' amount of money the girls would get naked on the van and they'd dance around … If you had a disposable camera … or maybe if you were lucky enough to have a camcorder [you could film it]."

Surprisingly, the raucous Freaknik festivities were mostly absent from UGK's video, which consisted of nothing more than the guys playing dominoes and rapping in an abandoned lot.

After UGK had returned from Freaknik, Isreal Kight and Ron Forrest walked into Music World in Port Arthur one stormy summer evening and were surprised to see the store unusually crowded. DMD had called them to come by and listen to some tracks for their album. *Damn, why is everybody in here?* Ron wondered.*

DMD started playing a track, which Ron recognized as the Funkadelics sample they'd found at Sunrise. He looked at Kight, who was bobbing his head. "Yeah, this is jammin', Dorie," Ron told DMD, nodding.

Kight and Ron looked at each other in surprise when Bun's voice came over the beat. They'd thought it was an instrumental for them to use. "Kight, is that the same track that we went to Sunrise and got?" Ron asked.

"Fuck yeah," Kight said, heated. He turned to DMD. "What the fuck is up with that shit?"

"Aw, man, I…" DMD chuckled. "I went 'head and sold the beat to Chad and them." As the track continued, Pimp C's unmistakable voice came through the speakers:

Some muthafuckas think they can go with me
But most of them niggas just some hoes to me
I got a lotta niggas that's down with me
But too many niggas like to clown with me
They act like they know me, but they really don't
They ask me to come kick it, but they know I won't
[…] Tryin' to be a gangsta, but nigga you's a fool
And tryin' to kick it with me, like me and y'all cool

To make it clear who he was dissing, Chad finished with a reference to Kight's break-in:

But nigga, let's see if you can deal with that chrome
I shoulda popped yo' ass when you broke into my home
But bitch niggas steal, and G niggas mack
And busta ass niggas gettin' bullets in they back
And that's a muthafuckin fact!

Kight bolted for the door. Ron scrambled after him, but he was already gone. It was pouring rain and Kight had ridden there with him. *Where the fuck this dude went?* Ron wondered.

Ron finally drove off and spotted Kight walking down 10th Street in the rain, his face twisted into a mean mug. "Kight, where you going?" Ron called out, pulling alongside him.

(*The story as described here is recalled by Ron, Kight, and several others affiliated with their camp. DJ DMD's recollection of this event is far different from others. Most people believe DMD played the "Three Sixteens" track intentionally for Kight and Ron to stir up drama, which DMD denies. In DMD's version, he wasn't even sure if "Three Sixteens" would make the album. According to DMD, the Good-Fellaz crew heard the song on *Super Tight* the day it was released and came to Music World to confront him. "[I] didn't really get a lot of time to explain [because] they was so mad, and they immediately left my record shop," says DMD.)

"Chill, dawg. Just c'mon. Get in the car."

"Fuck that shit," Kight growled. "Let me go talk to this dude."

"C'mon, dawg," Ron argued. "Calm down, man. If you wanna be on some battle rap shit we could do it that way."

"Naw, fuck that shit!" Kight yelled back. "I'm a real ass nigga. I just wanna go talk to this nigga and let him know we could square off in the grass if we want to. That's what homeboys do! But homeboys don't do this shit on a record talking about you 'shoulda shot me' and all this other bullshit!"

Ron, who didn't really think Kight would walk the full two miles to Chad's house in the rain, decided to go home and give his friend time to cool down.

Some thirty minutes later, Kight was standing on the porch at the San Jac house, trying to calm down and get his temper under control. He halfway wondered if this was some kind of joke – back when they were on good terms, Chad had joked that they should diss each other as a publicity stunt.

"I walked all the way over there [because] I had to calm down," Kight recalls. "I [didn't] want him to think I'm comin' over to his house to fuck him up." But Chad had already received a phone call from DJ DMD warning him that Kight was on the way over, and he was out for blood.

Kight pounded on the door. Nitacha cracked it open, baby Chad Jr. cradled in her arms. (Kight claims Nitacha greeted him with a rude, "Yeah, nigga, they in the studio," while others say Kight shoved the door open, knocking Nitacha and the infant to the floor.)

Chad was in the studio room a.k.a. the weed room, sitting on the couch waiting for Kight with a small pistol. "*What*?! You gonna pull a *gun* on me?" Kight yelled in disbelief as he stormed in. As Kight lunged towards him, Chad let off several shots. "We [were] all standing there lucky we didn't get shot, because C was just shooting [haphazardly]," DJ Bird recalls. "[Chad] was trying to scare [Kight] off. He wasn't trying to kill him."

As Bird, Bun, and Bun's friend Joseph "JB" Melancon dove for cover, Kight swung on Chad. Chad pulled the trigger again from close range; the bullet grazed Kight's side, but he barely noticed. The two punched each other, brawling on the sofa.

In the ensuing tussle, Kight wrestled the pistol away. ("I just started beating his ass," Kight claims. "I had him on the sofa. I was choking him out, beating him up, punching him … I got the gun and pistol-whipped him, then I put the gun to his head." DJ Bird says Kight is exaggerating the extent of the beating, but he did manage to get control of the gun.)

Kight rammed the pistol into Chad's head and pulled the trigger.

Nothing happened. The bullet, jammed in the chamber, refused to budge. Bun dove forward, tackling Kight and knocking the disabled weapon to the ground. Kight shoved a thumb into Bun's throat and pushed him off. Kight fled as Chad shouted that he was going to kill him.

Kight ran four blocks in the dark before he felt a pain in his side; he glanced down and noticed blood on his shirt. *Damn*, he thought. *Fuck.* The rain had subsided; he pulled his shirt up to get a better look at his wounded stomach under the glare of the street light.

He stumbled down the street towards McDonald's, where Ron's sister Ronda Forrest was working. "Fool, you bleeding!" Ronda exclaimed as Kight staggered in.

After he was released from the hospital Kight went to the police station, where a detective laid out the evidence he'd collected at the San Jac house: shell casings, pictures, and statements

(*Chad never spoke on the record about the Kight incident, so this account is based on others' recollections. The date when it occurred is unknown. Superb Herb recalls reading a newspaper article about the shooting, but a scan of 1994 articles in the *Port Arthur News* reveals nothing. Mama Wes says she urged the responding detective, who had once been a student of hers, to keep the situation quiet. The Port Arthur Police Department, which only retains documents for ten years, could not locate any record of this incident in a 2014 search.)

from the witnesses.* Kight, who was already on probation, hated police and refused to cooperate. "Hey, man, I ain't gonna do your job for you," he sulked. "I ain't got nothing to say. I mean, I got shot. Been a rough day for me."*

Neither Chad nor Kight wanted to press charges, but authorities decided to charge Chad with Aggravated Assault. "The only memory in my mind of Kight is that he cost me $5,000," recalls Mama Wes. She hired an attorney to represent Chad in court, where Kight was a no-show. "That fucker couldn't show up because he had too many damn warrants," says Mama Wes.

With the "victim" unwilling to cooperate, the charges were dropped. Although there were no legal consequences, the incident divided the community, pitting the most popular rappers in Port Arthur against Kight's clique of Short Texas hustlers. "It just left such a bitter situation," recalls local producer Avery Harris. "It's just something that went too far. Somebody could've ended up dead."

Kight's friend John "J-Will" Williams III, a stocky guy with street credibility, was infamous around town. "[J-Will] was a beast," Kight says. "He done beat so many people [in] Port Arthur … [and] when he beat somebody up, he beat 'em up to [the point] where they eyes [would] roll in the back of they head."

One night J-Will and his crew ran into Bun at the BV, a popular nightclub around the corner from RBJ's soul food restaurant, and exacted revenge for the Kight shooting.** "They had [Bun] hiding under a table in the club," recalls Lee Master. "Pimp wouldn't make himself available after the incident with Kight, so Bun had to suffer the consequences."

Bun might have been suffering the consequences of his affiliation with Chad, but he was also reaping the blessings. At a music industry event, Bun ran into Bad Boy Records' Craig Mack and The Notorious B.I.G. a.k.a. Biggie Smalls. Everyone swarmed Craig Mack, who had the hottest record in the country with "Flava in Your Ear." But Bun went straight for Biggie Smalls, expressing his admiration for his lyrical abilities.

"Yo, Biggie, you're a bad muthafucker," Bun told him.

Biggie nodded. "I heard your shit too, I know who you are."

"No shit?" Bun asked.

"Yeah, 'Pocket Full of Stones' is my shit," Biggie said.

Wow, Bun thought.

"I didn't honestly believe I was a rapper, like a *real fucking rapper*, probably until I met Biggie [Smalls] and Biggie knew who I was," Bun told *Believer* Magazine.

———

On Sunday, June 19, 1994, exactly one week after the bodies of OJ Simpson's wife Nicole Brown Simpson and Ronald Goldman were found in a gruesome murder scene in front of Nicole's California condo, newspapers across the country featured extensive coverage of the infamous slow-speed Ford Bronco chase. In Mississippi, buried amidst the *Jackson Clarion-Ledger's* coverage of OJ Simpson turning himself in to police was a headline on the front page of the local section: "4 killed in double shootings."

"Police have issued an arrest warrant for a man wanted in the second double homicide committed in Jackson this week," it read. "Police spokesman Lee Vance said an arrest warrant has been issued, but he would not name the suspect because he 'is still at large, and we need to get him locked up.'"

Shortly before the Kight shooting, Smoke D had gone back to Mississippi, where UGK's

(*Kight appeared to find humor in the incident in retrospect. Years later, when Screwed Up Click rapper C-Note was working on his *Third Coast Born* album, Kight happened to stop by the studio. "Man, Pimp C, I know that's your people. He shot me before," Kight told C-Note nonchalantly when they were introduced.)
(**Bun later reminisced about "BV's on Sunday night" on the record "Family Affair.")

"Front, Back & Side to Side" was already getting heavy radio play. He was surprised to find that he was already a local celebrity.

Smoke's younger brother Rance, always a bit of a troublemaker, got in a heated argument with a group of local guys over a pickup basketball game. The situation had never been resolved, and Smoke was afraid that if he went back to Texas, his brother would be in danger. Smoke received word that the men who had problems with his brother wanted to squash things, and invited him to come by a small party to talk things over.

Suspecting it was a setup, Smoke brought a friend with him. They pulled up to the apartment past midnight on the night of Friday, June 17, 1994. Before he got out of the car, Smoke hesitated, then reached for his pistol.

While details are sketchy, an argument broke out inside the apartment which quickly turned violent. (Some witnesses said the argument was over a marijuana sale.) Smoke struck an intimidating figure, standing a solid 6'5" and heavyset with a gleaming gold tooth. Smoke would later claim he was jumped by a man named Tony Anderson and several others. Although Tony was a much smaller man, Smoke says he feared for his life. "It was a situation where it was either him or me," Smoke says.

Smoke shot both Tony and his cousin, a 20-year-old woman named Shanine Body, at point-blank range. Local news reports described it as "an execution-style double slaying." The murders came as a shock to many in the small community, where Smoke D and his family were well-respected. Sixteen friends and family members signed an appearance bond agreeing to pay the State of Mississippi $100,000 if Smoke didn't show up to court, with five families offering up their homes as bond.

At trial, Smoke took the stand in his own defense and broke down in tears, testifying that he'd acted in self-defense. Facing life in prison, Smoke accepted a last-minute plea bargain as the jury was deliberating and was sentenced to 20 years for manslaughter.

After Sophia Chang departed Jive, UGK was assigned to a rookie A&R named Joe Thomas. Joe had no concept of UGK's popularity until he came to Port Arthur for a visit. "It was a real eye opener for me, because in New York, no one knew who UGK was," Joe recalls. He was surprised to learn that Chad was not only rapping, but producing all the tracks and singing the background vocals.

Even with Russell out of the equation, UGK's relationship with Jive was still strained. Communication was a constant issue, and Joe, who had been on the receiving end of several of Chad's angry rants, started to understand his frustration. "The record label is [all the] way in New York, so the only way [Chad] could talk to [us] was on the phone," Joe says. "He was so frustrated with the record company." Cell phones weren't yet common, so Chad had to call long distance during office hours and hope to catch someone at their desk just to have a conversation.

On top of that, Byron Hill insisted that all decisions regarding UGK be filtered through him. "It was hard trying to market a project … [where we] never really got to talk to them directly," says Cheryl Brown-Marks, UGK's product manager at the time. "He was the liaison." Byron struck her as a loud-talker, the type who would resort to threats of violence if things didn't go his way. "He was one of those guys [who] you couldn't just have a meeting [without it being] … drama-filled," Cheryl recalls.

Jive called in Los-Angeles based photographer Shawn Mortensen to shoot the *Super Tight* cover. Mortensen was responsible for iconic rap photos like Tupac wearing a straightjacket on the cover of *VIBE* Magazine, the Notorious B.I.G. with a red leather suit and a cane, and Dr. Dre on the cover of *The Source* with a gun to his head. UGK posed in front of D-Ray's Buick which they'd debuted in the Mardi Gras parade. The graphic designer added *UGK 4LF* on the license plate, a nod to Pimp's line on "Front, Back & Side to Side" ("UGK-1 on my muthafuckin' plates").

UGK's A&R Joe Thomas had been confused by the group's constant references to "sweets" until he realized they were referring to Swisher Sweets blunt wrappers. (On the East Coast, smokers used Phillies Blunts or White Owl cigarillos.) Chad came up with the idea to use the Swisher Sweets shield-shaped logo, slightly modified so they wouldn't face any legal repercussions, to create UGK's logo for the *Super Tight* cover.*

After UGK turned in *Super Tight*, Russell got a letter from Jive notifying him that Big Tyme was being removed from the contract. Barry Weiss stopped taking his phone calls.**

"Jive, being true to their name, [had] a clause in the contract that said if you don't want to deliver for your original label [Big Tyme Recordz] no more you can take the option to cut out the middle man," Chad told journalist Andrew Nosnitsky. "[So] we exercised our option and got him up out of there. 'Cause there was a lot of money that wasn't being accounted for. And goddamit we wanted some of it. We felt like we should've had ownership in Big Tyme."

Russell couldn't understand why UGK still wanted to eliminate him after he'd already agreed to renegotiate their contract on more favorable terms, especially because it wouldn't benefit them financially; according to Russell, they gained no points on the album by removing him. "That was the part that stung," Russell says. "[They] were willing to *lose* money to get rid of me, [and] I believed when nobody believed."

Big Tyme filed a lawsuit; UGK countersued. Chad became even more vocal, speaking out against Russell in interviews. "Big Tyme stole money from UGK … I'm not gonna say no names, but the people over there stole money," he told *N-The-Biz* newsletter. "Anyway we got a new deal with Jive Recordz direct. NO MORE BIG TYME RECORDS … eliminating the shiff in '94."

When *Super Tight* was released on August 30, 1994, the line at DMD's Music World was wrapped around the corner, even though most locals already had a dubbed bootleg copy. Bun viewed the finished product as "a middle finger to the music industry," raw and uncut, much like the environment in which it was created.

The album broke into the *Billboard* Hot 200, peaking at #95. Their first major album review appeared in the October 1994 issue of *The Source*, where writer J-Mill awarded *Super Tight* 3.5 mics. "While the UGK'z never stray too far from a slow-paced flow that is highlighted by their strong southern accents, it is nice to hear them mix things up by varying their rhyme patterns and adding more complexity to their basic lyrical structure," he concluded.

Ultimately, Chad was disappointed with the response to *Super Tight*. During one late-night weed smoking session, he broke down the album track-by-track and expressed his frustration with the album's reception. For example, he wondered why their sarcastic police anthem "Protect and Serve" hadn't attracted the same level of attention as Ice-T's "Cop Killer."*** "He was kinda upset by how that album was received," Freddy Johnson says. "It's like the ultimate album. It's dope. But he couldn't wrap his mind around why it wasn't as successful as it shoulda been."

The video for "It's Supposed to Bubble" didn't get much play outside of local outlets like Houston's Street Flava TV. "[Jive] didn't have a department for [music] videos back then, so you always got forwarded over to somebody else who had no answers," recalls Street Flava's Pam Harris. "They weren't really supportive."

The television at the San Jac house was always tuned to music videos on MTV or BET, but it seemed like the only acts featured were from New York. "[Chad] was always commenting about how we could never get the video play," remembers UGK's hype man Bo-Bo Luchiano. "People wasn't giving us our just due."

(*The title was shortened from its original title: *Super Tight... P.A. Niggaz Worldwide.* "I'm fried, P.A. nigga worldwide," Bun rapped on "Three Sixteens." DJ DMD later used a similar subtitle for his album *Twenty Two: P.A. World Wide.*)
(**This wasn't an unusual move for Jive. Most of their artists, like Too $hort, R. Kelly, and Will Smith, had already been signed to smaller independent labels first. "Jive would seek them out, and then if they weren't happy with the way their business was going, Jive would work out a deal with the label," says Jeff Sledge. "That was Jive's way of doing business.")
(***Jive censored a line on "Protect & Serve" where Chad referred to a police officer by name; some say Chad also took a shot at Kight on this record, rapping, "You got sugar in your nuts just like them Good[-Fellaz] niggas.")

CHAPTER 12

"At one time, the East [Coast] was very hostile towards us. After buying all their records for so many years, it was like a slap in the face. After trying to be accepted for so long, we turned our backs. [We decided,] we don't wanna be accepted now. We've got our own thing down here. We don't wanna listen to you, and we don't care if you don't wanna listen to us. We're gonna do our own records and sell our own records to our own people. That's the attitude that created country rap tunes." – Pimp C, *OZONE* Magazine, May 2005

"This ain't no muthafuckin' Hip-Hop records. These [are] country rap tunes. So you can separate us from the rest." – Pimp C, UGK's "Let Me See It"

During one trip to Atlanta for a Greg Street event, Bun, Chad, and Mama Wes pulled up to a small house in Lakewood which belonged to Rico Wade's mother. The basement, nicknamed the Dungeon for its dark, dank atmosphere and dirt floor, was home to production trio Organized Noize and their growing Dungeon Family.

Organized Noize, which included Rico Wade, Patrick "Sleepy" Brown, and Ray Murray, could trace its origins back to the late 80s, but they hadn't started perfecting their own sound until the early 90s. "Sleepy's the funk, Rico's the rock, I'm the Hip-Hop," Ray explains. "We thrive off of each other."

Like UGK, Organized Noize was digging through crates of old soul records and incorporating live instruments into their tracks. Sleepy Brown felt like he was meeting his musical twin. (Sleepy's father was a vocalist/trombonist in the 70s funk band Brick, and he'd grown up hanging around backstage, learning to play instruments by ear.) "It just blew me away because he was so *funky*," Sleepy says. "Pimp was just soul, blues, and funk all rolled up in one."

Chad also clicked with Cameron Gipp a.k.a. "Big Gipp" of the Goodie Mob. "It was good [timing] when they came, 'cause they got to meet everybody at they rawest," Big Gipp says. "We were the first ones to really introduce them to the Atlanta music scene ... we was all family at that time. We was young, inspired, and trying to break all the rules of music together."

Gipp tagged along to a UGK show and couldn't believe Chad's mother was really their road manager. "His Mama was out there driving, at the wheel of the Cadillac, and picking up the money," Gipp recalls. "I just thought that shit was *so* gangsta."

Among those sleeping on the floor at the Dungeon were Big Boi and Andre 3000, whose mothers were not thrilled about their teenage sons spending all their time smoking weed in a dark basement. ("I hang with Rico Wade 'cause the Dungeon is where the funk's at, boy," Big Boi rapped on OutKast's "Git Up, Git Out.")

Like Chad, Andre 3000 had initially been imitating East Coast acts like Das EFX and Redman, rapping loudly and mimicking their accents. When Rico Wade heard him in the recording booth one day having a normal conversation, something clicked. "That's it. Right there," Rico told him. "Your normal voice is your rap voice."

OutKast's 1994 debut *Southernplayalisticadillacmuzik* focused on live instrumentation and sampling. OutKast would lead the way for the Dungeon Family to take over Atlanta, bringing soul to a music scene which had once been dominated by booty music.

"I met Bun and Pimp C very early in our career," Andre 3000 told *XXL*. "When we first arrived on the scene, I think there was a Southern kinship unspoken … I was happy to see how welcoming they were to us, the new guys, and they really kinda ushered us in."

Even before he became "Pimp C," Chad was always cognizant of the fact that Southern rappers were viewed as outsiders, subpar, a few notches below their East Coast peers. ("I ain't from [Queensbridge] or the South side Bronx / But I got the kind of rhymes to give the people what they want," he'd rapped in high school.)

In the early days of Hip-Hop, New Yorkers made their feelings clear towards rappers from other parts of the country. The Geto Boys were booed while performing records like "Gangsta of Love," "Let a Hoe be a Hoe," and "Mind of a Lunatic" in front of two thousand people at the Lyric Theater during the 1989/1990 New Music Seminar, their first New York show.

"They didn't comprehend a new era of Hip-Hop called gangsta rap," says Bushwick Bill. "They said we were disrespecting our black queens; we didn't have to curse."

A year later the Geto Boys were vindicated on the Public Enemy tour, performing "Mind Playing Tricks on Me" to a packed house at Madison Square Garden. But the sting still remained. "That's what I base my whole fuckin' life on," Scarface told *OZONE* twenty years later. "They was *not* fuckin' with us. We sold records all over the fuckin' country and New York made a mockery of it. They fuckin' booed the Geto Boys in New York."

UGK had only gone to New York a few times, rarely venturing beyond Jive's Manhattan offices. During one trip in the mid-90s, they decided to explore the city and hailed a cab. "Man, let's go to Harlem," Chad suggested.

Bun could hear a warning from Big Gipp ringing in his ears: *Be careful in New York, man. They don't like us out there.*

They cautiously picked up some Jamaican food and a sack of weed, then stopped by a nearby barbershop to get a haircut. Bun halfway expected to get robbed. But once they explained that they were UGK from the *Menace II Society* soundtrack, they were greeted with respect. Love, even. As they stood on the street corner smoking a blunt, Bun couldn't help but laugh. *We just standing on 145th, smoking weed, eating Jamaican food… being, like, from Port Arthur, Texas.*

UGK had connected with New York-based producer Lorenzo Dechalus, better known as Lord Jamar of Brand Nubian, at a show in St. Louis. "We could respect each other's art forms … the music is what brought us together," Chad said. Lord Jamar was a huge fan of "Pocket Full of Stones and had incorporated some Pimp C production techniques while recording Brand Nubian's 1994 album *Everything is Everything*. "I was real interested [in the way that] people outside New York were using live instruments within their music," Lord Jamar explains.

He'd always been more open-minded than his New York counterparts, passing around copies of Ice Cube's *Amerikkka's Most Wanted* and OutKast's debut *Southernplayalisticadillacmuzik*. "A lot of people from New York didn't understand [Southern rap]," says Lord Jamar. "We were real arrogant with our 'Hip-Hop started here' [attitude]. We didn't really believe people from other regions were even gonna do it, to be honest."

Lord Jamar became UGK's unofficial ambassador in New York, helping them get into nightclubs and find the best spots to buy weed. Jive labelmate Keith Murray was another friend to the group.* "People [in New York] would see us together and that would fuck them up," Chad told *OZONE*. "They were wondering, how the fuck is this nigga from Texas hangin' with the gods?"**

(*UGK, Keith Murray, and Lord Jamar's friendship led to an impromptu collaboration called "Live Wires Connect" which landed on 1996's *Don't Be a Menace to South Central While Drinking Your Juice in the Hood* soundtrack. The record also included Rick Royal on the third verse, who was credited as "CoCo Budda" because his record label Sony was demanding a high clearance fee for his appearance on the record. "Major labels be getting in the way of family business," Rick says.)
(**Lord Jamar belonged to the Five-Percent Nation, an organization which branched off from the Nation of Islam. Five Percenters view themselves as their own gods.)

When the group was in town, they often stopped by Lord Jamar's Brooklyn apartment at 560 State Street. On one occasion, they passed by a man in the hallway exiting the duplex at 10C, his New York Yankees hat cocked to the side. They acknowledged each other as a courtesy.

"Oh, that's Jay-Z right there," Lord Jamar commented as the man, Shawn Carter, disappeared down the hallway. Lord Jamar told UGK that he was in the process of recording an album. That album, 1996's *Reasonable Doubt*, would launch Jay-Z to superstardom.

———————

Another group involved with Rick Royal's The ORG was the MDDL FNGZ (originally called Full House). The three group members - Charles "Pep C" Young, Anthony Bowser a.k.a. "B.A.N.D.I.T." (Black Azz Nigga Down In Texas), and Sean Wee - were also roommates.* Pep struck up a conversation with a classmate at Texas Southern University, Leslie "DJ Peace" Blair, and brought him in as the group's DJ.

Pep had known Smit-D of The ORG since high school, and as things were souring between Smit and the mother of his two children, Pep let Smit start camping out indefinitely on the MDDL FNGZ' living room couch. But over time, Smit's negative attitude wore on Pep. After one heated argument, Pep slept with a knife at his bedside. "Watch that boy, man," he warned his roommates. "Something ain't right."

The next morning, Pep decided he'd had enough. *I'm not finna be uncomfortable in my own house,* he thought. When he told Smit it was time to go, Smit landed at DJ Peace's apartment.

On the night of Friday, October 21, 1994, Smit went to his former girlfriend's house hoping to see his young son and daughter, but it was past 11 PM and she refused to let him in.

Four hours later, two men pulled up to a Circle K gas station 25 miles down I-69 from DJ Peace's apartment. They bought a $1 bottle of Sprite, drank it, and asked to buy $1 worth of gas. Angry when the clerk refused to sell gas in an illegal container, they went to a nearby Chevron.

Peace was scheduled to leave at 7 AM to drive to Corpus Christi with another rapper he was working with, Lamont "Precise" Lewis. Precise and his manager paged him several times to confirm if he was ready to leave; when no response came, they went by his apartment but there was no answer. His new black Honda Accord with rims wasn't in the parking lot.

It was Texas State University's homecoming weekend, but Pep C and the MDDL FNGZ were at home; they didn't have any money or transportation. That evening, Smit-D called to invite him to the homecoming concert. "Hey, man, c'mon," he urged. "Bun and them performing."

"How we gon' get there?" Pep asked.

"I got Peace car."

Pep C couldn't believe it; Peace never let anybody drive his car. "Peace left you his car!? Where Peace at?"

"Man, he gone out of town with them girls," Smit said. Pep had heard that Peace was working with a female R&B trio called Tha Truth!, who were signed to Erick Sermon's label. Smit said Peace would be gone for a few weeks doing a promo tour with the group.

Homecoming concerts had become a staple of UGK's annual income: Prairie View A&M, Texas Southern University, Southern University, and Grambling University called every year.** For Texas Southern's annual homecoming concert, UGK was booked alongside Brand Nubian, the Odd Squad, and Seeds of Soul, and the night started with a friendly debate between UGK

(*Later additions to the MDDL FNGZ included Kilo, Bam, and a towering 6'9" man named Michael Grisby. As a small-time dope dealer he'd been known as "Money" until a Jamaican crack fiend commented in his thick accent, "You's a big munn." The name stuck; Big Munn would become part of the MDDL FNGZ and later, a UGK bodyguard.)

(**The only drawback to homecoming shows was that school officials insisted they perform the clean version of their songs. Chad would argue that they were "depriving the kids" who wanted to hear the original version.)

and Brand Nubian over who should close out the show.

Brand Nubian wanted UGK to close out in their hometown, while UGK preferred to defer to Brand Nubian. "That was our way of letting them know we had a lot of respect for the gods," Bun explained on Damage Control Radio.

Backstage, UGK was joined by Smit-D and the MDDL FNGZ; blunts were passed. After Smit-D walked away, Chad remarked, "*Maaan*, that nigga smell like death. That nigga smell like a different type of smoke."

If Smit did smell different, Pep and Bandit of the MDDL FNGZ hadn't noticed. Inspired after seeing Bun and Pimp on stage, they readily agreed when Smit invited them to come over to Peace's apartment after the show and work on some music.

"Shiiiit, he left his equipment there?" Pep asked.

"Yeah, man, them girls got him all new stuff," Smit said. "They got him all new turntables and everythang."

DJ Peace had recently moved in to a new apartment in the same complex, so Pep didn't notice that his prized possession, the centerpiece of his comfortable living room, was missing. The 8" x 10" white Flokita rug made of authentic lamb wool had been a gift from his father from a family vacation to Greece.

Smit-D made himself comfortable in the kitchen, whipping up a late-night dinner. "Peace done let you up in here, cooking his food and spinning records on his goddamn turntables?" Bandit joked, his tone one of disbelief.

After tinkering with Peace's keyboard and turntables, Pep and Bandit eventually passed out. Around 5 AM, Pep was roused by a noise and glanced over to see Smit-D with a rag, wiping down furniture. Pep yawned. "Man, what are you doing?" he mumbled.

"Aw, man, just cleaning," Smit said. "You know, if that boy Peace come back, mane, [and] stuff dirty, he gon' be trippin', man. He let me stay here, so I'm just cleaning up."

Pep nodded drowsily. *You ain't clean up when you stayed with me, but if you done changed…* he thought, drifting back to sleep with a satisfied smile across his face. Maybe he'd taught Smit a valuable lesson by putting him out of the MDDL FNGZ's apartment.

Later that afternoon a young couple and their six-year-old daughter pulled off rural Ricefield Road in Rosenberg to shoot off a BB gun. Not far from the road, on an old dirt driveway, they stopped short when they saw a badly burned corpse covered in a charred white rug.

Police arrived on the scene, making a casting of the partial FILA shoeprint next to the body and a nearby tire tread. Scattered around the body were partially burned yearbooks. Through the yearbooks, police were able to determine that the victim was Leslie "DJ Peace" Blair. They arrived at his apartment, where Smit-D was cleaning and rearranging furniture, and his worried girlfriend Tina Byrd was looking for him. Both were asked to come in for questioning.

Police discovered that the rear hatchback of Peace's Honda had significant bloodstains; inside the apartment, there was substantial blood spatter all over the living room walls and ceiling. Detectives believed Peace had been bludgeoned with a claw hammer at least fourteen times. There was a large blood stain under the entertainment center, which had been moved from its original location.

More blood stains were found throughout the upstairs bathroom, where it appeared the killer had attempted to clean himself up. And in the bedroom was a pair of FILA sneakers which matched the shoeprint found next to the body.

Smit-D insisted he'd last seen DJ Peace at 5:30 AM when he left the house, giving him the keys to his apartment and his car. He insisted that he couldn't have been the killer because he'd spent the day at TSU Homecoming with Pep and Bandit. After his interview, Smit-D was formally charged with first-degree murder.*

Bandit and Pep soon found themselves in a holding cell as suspected accomplices to the crime. Police showed them photos of Peace's disfigured, badly burned body and grilled them for information. Pep realized that Smit had insisted on going to the UGK concert to have an alibi for the weekend. "It all started making sense," Bandit recalls.**

As Chad's rap career was taking off, his new persona was taking a toll on his home life. While he was a tender, supportive father with his young son, his relationship with Nitacha was falling apart. "Chad was awesome," Nitacha says. "Pimp C, on the other hand, was a muthafucker. You know, he was hard to handle … 'Pimp C' killed us. He killed our relationship."

Not only was there a steady stream of other women, but Chad dedicated all his time to music, often staying up all night recording. "It drove me freaking nuts," Nitacha says. "[Music] was his other love. It was his other woman. Besides the bitches, that was the other woman."

"She was a pretty lil' thang," Mama Wes says of Nitacha. "I think she really did love C, if you can love somebody at [18], and C really cared a lot for her. I think he probably even loved her, but he was [young] and that peer pressure, influence from people around him … [it] got to him."

Despite their problems as a young couple, friends felt that their love was genuine. One of those friends was Nitacha's 17-year-old cousin Dawn Nico, who had been sleeping with Bun. "Bun and I was always back and forth but we admired what Nitacha and Chad had," Dawn says.

Over the summer of 1994, Dawn learned that she was pregnant with a son. According to

(*In an interview, Smit-D is vague when asked about the reason he was arrested. "[The ORG's] spirituality and beliefs clashed with mine," he says. "They turned on me pretty bad and that led me to going to prison." He suggests that Rick Royal was jealous of him and challenged him to "show us what you're made of.")

(**Many of Smit-D's friends were convinced of his innocence until his FUBU tennis shoes which matched the prints found by the body were presented at trial. "Peace was known to have a smart-ass mouth and pop off, but nobody [was] gonna hit Peace, 'cause Peace was a lil' nigga. You'd just let that shit slide," says Big Munn of the MDDL FNGZ. "I just think [Smit] was out of his mind," theorizes Bandit. "He snapped. He was on fry or water or whatever and he just snapped." Smit-D denies that he was a regular fry smoker, saying that his experience smoking with 3-2, Big Mike, and UGK was his first and only "wet experience." After Smit-D was convicted of the murder, he changed his story, telling his attorney that he was now willing to reveal the killer's true identity. His appeal was declined and he was sentenced to 25 years in prison.)

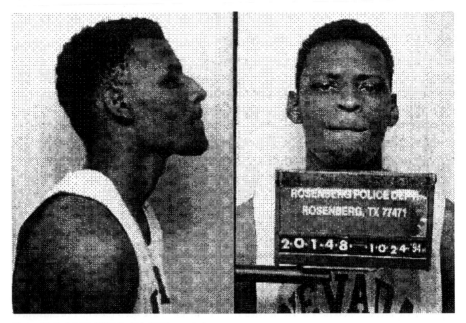

Above: **Roderick "Smit-D" Smith's** 1994 mugshot.

Dawn, when her mother threatened to send Bun to jail for statutory rape, she lied and had another man sign the birth certificate to protect him.*

Around the fall of 1994, Nitacha moved out. Mama Wes attributed the demise of the relationship to their youth. Chad, still just 20 years old, was enjoying his new life as a star. "He wasn't [mature enough] to handle his job, his career, and his family [at the same time]," Nitacha says. "We were both just babies."

In Mama Wes' opinion, Nitacha left hoping Chad would beg her to come back. "And he didn't," says Mama Wes. "I'm not sure he shouldn't have, I'm just saying he didn't."

Chad wasn't used to coming home to an empty house. Late one evening after they'd returned to Port Arthur from an out-of-town trip, Chad called his mother.

"Mama?" he asked.

"Yeah?"

"Man, I don't like this shit."

"What's wrong?"

Chad explained that it was too quiet. "All I hear is the air conditioner running."

"[His son] Chaddyboo was really, really, really important to him," Mama Wes says. "He really missed that little booger ... C had a lot of regrets, I think, after [he and Nitacha] split. And I really do feel like it was his fault."

Nitacha later filed for child support and alimony, claiming that their living situation constituted a common-law marriage. In Texas, a common-law marriage or "informal marriage" occurs when "the man and woman agreed to be married and after the agreement they lived together in this state as husband and wife and represented to others that they were married."

Chad didn't go to court and was ordered to pay $1,100 a month in child support. Because Nitacha had not used the San Jac house as her primary mailing address, her request for alimony was denied. Chad would later rap on "Ain't That A Bitch":

The next thing you know the bitch got you in court
Tryin' to get your paper, callin' it 'child support'
Takin' half of yo' shit, talkin' 'bout a divorce
If you don't know then game, then here's a crash course
*They say you lived with the bitch, so you common-law married***

Bun and Chad had become friends with Charles Moore Jr., better known as "Mike Mo," the weed man on campus at Lamar University in nearby Beaumont. Chad came by the school often to visit some females.

Mike, who considered himself a "wholesome drug dealer," was selling weed to get through

(*Dawn's son Aaron was born in March 1995. Six months later she married the other man, Dwayne Brisco, a former classmate of Bun's. Dawn says that she was forced to reveal the truth about Aaron's paternity when she was diagnosed with laryngeal cancer in 2006. "My only request to Bun was [to] let me die with dignity," she says. "That means if I did die – and I fought like hell to live ... at least let Aaron go to the proper place [to live with him] and he said no." Dawn overcame cancer. Dawn says her son, who graduated from high school in 2013, inherited Bun's high IQ. Others are skeptical. "C always said that wasn't Bun's child, so I don't know," laughs Mama Wes. "Bird and C used to laugh about that child all the time." Since she listed another man on the birth certificate, Dawn cannot force Bun to take a paternity test unless she files for paternity fraud. "She's so crazy ... she wanna be known as Bun B baby mama for everything in the world, man," says Donny Young. "And it's all for child support. That's all that is ... She takes it to the extreme, man. She schemes on money." Still, the consensus among mutual friends is that if Bun wasn't the father, he would've taken a paternity test to silence her. "Bun is a good politician as far as public appearances [and his] public persona, but his personal life is just an image ... If you ever mention my name to him, he won't even discuss it," Dawn says. "But there's a child that looks exactly like him and that's smart as a whip like him, that's suffering because [of it]." Bun B did not comment when asked about Dawn Nico and his alleged son.)
(**Chad also thanked his mother for supporting him through the "false divorce" on "My Angel.")

college after his track scholarship ended. His uncle, a major drug dealer in Houston, had fronted him his first stash of weed. "I kind of got in the [drug-dealing] game with a silver spoon in my mouth," Mike Mo says. "He would come through [with] 100 pounds."

At his uncle's suggestion, he rented an apartment to stash his weed. It was strategically located in Atascocita, which led directly into Beaumont on US-90. It was a good way to avoid the heavily-policed areas of I-10 which Chad referred to as "the muthafuckin' cocaine pipeline."

On April 13, 1995, Mike Mo's Honda Civic was pulled over in nearby Anahuac with more than five pounds of weed. Police pressured him to give up information on his suppliers. Still a rookie in the game and unsure what to do, he turned to UGK for advice. As he gave them the rundown on his situation, Chad laughed out loud.

Mike was slightly offended; it wasn't a joking matter. "Why you laughing?" he asked.

"Man, you don't know what you supposed to do?" Chad asked. "Dawg, what you trying to do and who you trying to be in the world, and the circles you trying to move in, there is no choice. You have to go to jail. You can't tell. You can't snitch."

"Don't ever tell on anybody," Bun advised him. "Go do your time, and when you come back, bro, you gonna have so much love, man. Do *not* tell."*

"I didn't tell because of what Bun B told me," Mike says. "Bun B told me some real shit. That saved my life."

———————

Shortly after Mike's arrest, Chad went to Atlanta for Freaknik. Sleepy picked him up in his red XL Benz convertible and the two cruised around Piedmont Park, music booming through the system. OutKast's debut album had gone gold and received critical acclaim; the Dungeon Family was reaching the mainstream. Chad confided that he was getting discouraged; he couldn't understand why UGK wasn't seeing the same level of success.

"Dude, you gotta understand, Underground Kingz is the biggest 'hood group right now," Sleepy told him. "I know you not seeing the benefits, but you will soon."

As if on cue, a group of girls recognized Pimp and ran over to the car. He was soon surrounded by fans. Sleepy laughed, shooting him a meaningful glance. *See?!?*

A few months later OutKast headed to New York for the 1995 Source Awards, where they were nominated for New Artist of the Year. The awards were dominated by The Notorious B.I.G., and tension hung thick in the air all night between the East Coast and the West Coast.

Death Row rap mogul Suge Knight famously took shots at Bad Boy Records impresario Sean "Diddy" Combs, inviting artists who were tired of their "executive producer trying to be all in the videos, all on the record, dancing" should "come to Death Row!" (Many would later pinpoint this moment as the spark which lit the fuse of the East Coast/West Coast war which led to the death of Death Row and Bad Boy's flagship artists, Tupac Shakur and Biggie Smalls.)

But the surprise of the night came when female rap group Salt 'N Pepa announced OutKast as the winner for New Artist of the Year over Brooklyn rap group Smif-N-Wessun. Boos rang out throughout the crowd as Big Boi and Andre 3000 approached the podium.

After a few words from Big Boi, Andre leaned in towards the mic. "Yeah, first of all… we wanna thank God, dead serious, 'cause if it weren't for him… we wouldn't be here," he said. He paused, his voice growing stronger. "But it's like this, though: I'm tired of folks, y'know… the closed-minded folks. It's like we got a demo and tape and don't nobody wanna hear it. But it's like, the South got somethin' to say. That's all I got to say."**

(*Mike pled guilty to a lesser charge of "failure to pay marijuana tax" and was sentenced to 10 years of probation. Years later Pimp C referenced Mike Mo's predicament on "Rock 2 Rock," rapping, "I'm puttin' fresh coke on the corner … I-10 … Gotta take shit slow through that Anahuac!")
(**The audio of this speech appears on OutKast's "Chonkyfire" from their album *Aquemini*.)

The South got somethin' to say. Those six words resonated with every Southerner who had felt the sting of East Coast arrogance. OutKast and the Dungeon Family departed New York with new resolve, fed up with New York's attitude. "We were *all* OutKasts," explains Ray Murray. "[OutKast] wasn't [just] a group, it was *all* of us. That's what we identified with." That included UGK, whom Big Boi considered "an extended part of our Dungeon Family."

It was a pivotal moment that helped launch the Southern rap movement. (Andre's brief-but-effective speech also helped push OutKast's debut to platinum.) "I think that's what started a fire in a lot of the Southern youth," Big Boi told *XXL*.

"It finally gave [us] a clear-cut incision from 'New York wannabeism,'" Killer Mike explained on the *ATL Rise* documentary. "It was a great thing that [OutKast was] handled in that way, because it finally cut the umbilical cord [and we decided], 'We don't have to impress you. We don't have to be influenced by you' … It made us fierce about our own identity."

UGK and the Dungeon Family were on a mutual mission to earn respect for the South, and the 1995 Source Awards brought them closer to other like-minded individuals. "Pimp was there at [a] point in time … that helped us all see that this is a unified fight," explains Ray Murray.

From that point forward, the focus in the South turned to developing their own style, their own sound, their own culture. "I don't know if *we* knew it was actually a movement," ponders MJG of fellow groundbreaking Southern rap group 8Ball & MJG. "We were too much of a part of the movement to actually *see* the movement. We was like, on the inside looking out."

Chad and Bun were mostly offended because they had always supported music from all over the country, but felt that their music didn't get the same respect from the East Coast. "[Chad and Bun] are probably the biggest Hip-Hop fans I ever worked with," says Jive's Jeff Sledge. "Like, they knew every song, every release, they listened to *everything*: North, South, East, West."

"If it wasn't for us, them niggas wouldn't have been able to take no Fresh Fest tour," Chad said on the *Will Hustle* DVD. "They wouldn't have been selling all those goddamn records they sold in the 80s if it wasn't for the South and the Midwest."*

Chad was especially offended by something he'd heard KRS-One say about Southern rap that left him feeling "alienated" from the Hip-Hop community. (It's not clear exactly what KRS-One said.) He vowed not to listen to KRS-One anymore. "I heard KRS-One tell us we wasn't 'Hip-Hop' for so long, I had to start saying, 'You goddamn right. We ain't,'" he told *OZONE*.

"They shitted on us for so long," he continued. "After a person rejects you for so long and keeps telling you [that] you're not ['real Hip-Hop'], eventually you're gonna decide that they're right. You're right … we don't want to be a part of your movement."

Rather than trying to fit in where they were clearly not wanted, Chad made a conscious decision to separate himself from New York rap. "UGK, bitch, representing that South," he would later proclaim on the end of "Let Me See It." "And, this ain't no muthafuckin' Hip-Hop records. These country rap tunes. So you can separate us from the rest. Like I told you before on the last one."** He defined "country rap tunes" as a "hybrid," a musical cousin of New York rap. "It ain't gangsta music – as white folks call it. I call it real nigga blues," he told *On Tha Real* Magazine.

"I don't give a fuck about [the state of] Hip-Hop 'cause I ain't never made none of that shit," he said on the *Will Hustle* DVD. "Them niggas [up North] been saying we wasn't 'real Hip-Hop' since the beginning of time. They said we wasn't 'real Hip-Hop' 'cause we don't have no trains or no backpacks and one leg of our pants ain't rolled up to our knee … So after a muthafucker tells you something for so long and lets you know they don't want you, after a while, a nigga don't wanna be down with you bitch ass niggas no more. We got our own shit down here."

(*The 1984 Fresh Fest, featuring Run-DMC, Kurtis Blow, and Whodini, was Hip-Hop's first big tour, grossing $3.5 million.)
(**It was on 1999's "Belts to Match" that Pimp C first announced, "Down here, we ain't makin' Hip-Hop songs, know what I'm sayin'? We make country rap tunes so, uh, separate us from the rest, ya heard what I'm talkin' 'bout?")

CHAPTER 13

"Byron [Hill] always did and always will keep a very low profile, because it's too many people that wanna kill him, okay? He has a lot of enemies." – Mama Wes

---

"[Byron Hill is the] textbook definition of a sociopath. He had a certain amount of charisma and he could motivate people, and he was very smart. But he was amoral." – Doug King

UGK didn't receive any money from Jive after the release of *Super Tight*, and their royalty statements showed that the label had recouped hefty expenses out of their album sales. UGK believed Byron had "looted" their advance by charging Jive for fictional or inflated expenses, purportedly for their *Super Tight* recording budget, and pocketing the money. Plus, Chad didn't really have a clear understanding of how the financials worked – every time he used a sample, Jive had to pay out a publishing royalty and mechanical royalty on UGK's behalf.

Russell found it ironic that the group had left him for Byron Hill. "[Byron knew] how to steal," Russell says. "He knew a lot of tricks. Man, he knew more tricks than me." Even Bun admitted they'd "ended up jumping out of the frying pan into the fire."

"The manager I had wasn't shit, the nigga stole everything and snorted coke like a bitch," Chad later rapped (on "My Angel"). Mama Wes had never seen Byron using cocaine, but says, "He had a horrible alcohol problem. He drank all day, every day."

Mama Wes didn't think Byron believed in the group anyway. "Well, that's probably as far as they're gonna go, because they're still screaming, 'P.A., P.A.,'" he told her when *Super Tight* dropped. Their relationship deteriorated to the point where Chad pulled a pistol on Byron during an argument.

"It was a confrontation with UGK and Byron," remembers MC Bytch. "They wanted to beat him down … it was gonna be real ugly. So Byron disappeared because Pimp C and they boys was really ready to take it to the streets."

"Byron always did and always will keep a very low profile, because it's too many people that wanna kill him, okay?" says Mama Wes. "He has a lot of enemies."

"You will *never*," she adds, repeating for emphasis, "You will never, *ever* see Byron… not if he sees you first."

Most of UGK's friends and collaborators had never even heard of Byron; they thought Mama Wes *was* the manager. She called all their regular promoter clients to make sure they didn't send Byron any more money on UGK's behalf. "Hey, baby," she'd greet them. "I'm out here on the road with my baby. You can deal with me now."

Maintaining cash flow between albums proved to be a challenge, and as their show schedule started slowing down after *Super Tight*, UGK was looking for other ways to supplement their income. When a promoter called Mama Wes' house to ask if Bun was available "to do 16," referring to a 16-bar verse, she readily agreed even though she had no idea what that meant.

Bun's features and Chad's production would become their main source of income. One of the first groups to reach out was the X-Mob, from the small town of Lake Charles, Louisiana. The three members (E-Vicious, Bundy, and Slice) were working on their second album *Ghetto*

Mail.

Bundy and E-Vicious connected with Pimp C through a girl who had dealings with all three of them. "It wasn't no serious [relationship], just one of those running-behind-rapper females," laughs Vicious. "She was looking good. She told me she was messing with Pimp but I didn't believe her."

When the X-Mob got on the phone with Pimp, he said he'd heard of the group but they needed some better beats. "How soon can you get to Port Arthur?" he asked.

Pimp created the beat for X-Mob's "Watcha Gone Do" after a quick session in which he told them that "something old, something new, something borrowed, and something blue" were the elements required for a hit record. "When he'd unplug them headphones, you'd be amazed what's coming out," Bundy of the X-Mob recalls. "He was magical on that board."

Bundy also appreciated Pimp's straightforward nature. "If it ain't jammin', [Pimp's] gonna tell you," says Bundy, adding, "Pimp taught me a lot. He made me love – *really, really love* – music, and really made me believe that I can rap and I can be somebody."

"It's a damn shame that there aren't more collaborations between Pimp and X-Mob available, since his production aesthetic fits them like a glove," a music critic noted on TheTrillConnection.com.

UGK had practically laid the blueprint for hustlers-turned-rappers, and they started to get calls from drug dealers throughout the South who were all hoping to make it big in the rap game. "[Drug dealers] are some of the few people that can even afford studio time," notes Chad's friend Mike Mo. "Being [in] the music business is a luxury business."

One such call came from Merrick "Money McNasty" Young of Starvin' Artists Entertainment. Merrick and his producer cousin, Raymond "Mo B. Dick" Poole, were from a tiny section of Southern Louisiana called Siracusaville, population 422.

When Mo B. Dick departed for college at Wichita State in Kansas, Merrick took control of the label. Merrick was a major drug trafficker using the proceeds to fund his rap group, Critical Condition, which included himself, Will Chill, and Tech. Impressed by the beats Pimp C had done for the X-Mob, Merrick got in touch with Pimp and came by the San Jac house.

Merrick considered music his "escape away from the streets," and while he was intrigued with Chad's musical talents, he believed Chad was also intrigued with his lifestyle. "[There's] always been this intertwined [relationship] between Hip-Hop and gangstas," says Merrick. "Those that tell the gangsta's life, and those that live it."

Even though Bun and Chad had left their brief drug-dealing careers in the past, they still empathized with those who were still in the game. "They felt like they was just as [much a] part of the hustle game as everybody else," says Merrick. "And so they had a great level of respect for people who was in the streets."

Merrick brought Chad to Dallas to produce five tracks on Critical Condition's second album *CC Water Bound*: "Bout 2 Go Down," "Hood Card," "Playa Haters," "4 Real Nigga Posse," and "Creepin'." (Chad also dropped vocals on "Creepin'" and "Bout 2 Go Down" alongside Bun.)

Production for the other half of the album was handled by Mo B. Dick. He took a break from classes at Wichita State to come down to Dallas to work with Chad, whom he considered not only a "grade A professional" but a "world class comedian." Both talented singers, they shared an appreciation for soul music (Mo B. Dick later released an R&B project called *Gangsta Harmony*) and quickly found that they had great musical chemistry.

Shortly after the Critical Condition studio session, Mo B. Dick happened to stop by a Dallas nightclub. He didn't know that Percy Miller, his second cousin whom he hadn't seen in years, was scheduled to do a promotional show that night as his new alter ego "Master P."*

Raised in the crime-infested Calliope projects in New Orleans, Master P had been deter-

---

(*Merrick and Master P were also distant cousins. "Everybody up and down I-10 [in] that whole area [of Louisiana is] pretty much kin," laughs Mo B. Dick.)

mined to make it out of the 'hood ever since his younger brother Kevin was killed. He thought basketball would be his way out. He practiced obsessively and landed a scholarship at the University of Houston, where a knee injury sidelined his career before it could begin.

When his grandfather died in the late 80s, Master P received $10,000.* He moved to Richmond, California to be closer to his mother, and used the funds to open a record shop called No Limit Records. Eventually he shut down the store and hit the road with his third CD, *The Ghetto's Tryin' to Kill Me*, selling more than 100,000 copies out of the trunk. The following year, he sold 200,000 copies of *99 Ways to Die* and landed a distribution deal with Priority Records.

When they reconnected in Dallas, Master P invited Mo B. Dick to fly out to California to work on his No Limit compilation, *Down South Hustlers: Bouncin' and Swingin'*. Mo B. Dick suggested they should get UGK on the album. "You know 'em or something?" Master P asked.

Mo B. Dick explained that he'd just worked with them on the Critical Condition project. "If you can get in contact with 'em, we'll fly 'em out," Master P said.

Two days later, UGK arrived in San Francisco. Starting with a bass line created by Mo B. Dick, Pimp C added some drums to create the beat for "Playaz From the South."

Master P also flew out Louisiana producer Craig "KLC" Lawson, putting him up in a Richmond apartment with Mo B. Dick while they worked on P's album *Ice Cream Man*. The two decided to form a production team called Beats by the Pound.

"[No Limit was] pretty much a lot of mergers," explains Mo B. Dick. "[What] P did was, he took a lot of people who were doing their own thing and then consolidated [them] under his company and created this big ol' movement."

Master P had a vision. "I'm growing something," he'd tell new recruits. "Either you believe or you don't."

———————————

Shortly after UGK returned from California, in August 1995, Mama Wes was sitting by the bar at the Hawthorne Inn in southwest Houston. A man scooped up a handful of corn dogs from the table of appetizers laid out for happy hour. As he passed Mama Wes' table, she joked, "They could be fattening."

Millard Roher, a disabled Air Force veteran starting his life over from scratch, was in no mood for jokes. He'd struggled with mental health issues ever since his traumatic experiences during the Vietnam War, which included picking up a helmet after a helicopter crash to find the pilot's severed head inside. He'd just moved to Houston from Washington D.C. after a divorce, aiming to start fresh and get his life together. He was depressed, lounging around the hotel bar because he didn't have enough money to go out.

"I think I could afford it," Millard snapped back, referring to his skinny frame, before returning to the bar. As he sat down, he saw a vision of his father, who had been dead for eight years. "Son, I didn't raise you like that," his father said. "Now go apologize to that woman."

After the initial shock of seeing his father wore off, Millard finished his drink and decided his father was right. He walked back to Mama Wes' table. "Look, I apologize for being so nasty, but I just have a lot on my mind," he said.

She gestured towards an empty chair. "Well, have a seat. Tell me about yourself."

"I'm just trying to get my life started over again," he explained. "I'm just going through some changes, you know?"

She nodded.

"What are you doing?" Millard asked.

"I'm managing my sons," she said. "They're rap musicians."

(*Conflicting accounts state that it was either an inheritance or a settlement from a negligence claim filed against the hospital where his grandfather died.)

Mama Wes invited Millard to come grocery shopping with her so she could whip up some dinner for the guys after they returned from the studio. The two soon became a couple, and Millard would become affectionately known as "Pops."

Byron Hill had convinced his partner in BPM, Doug King, to come with him to Atlanta, a move which Doug believed was mostly to get him away from Rap-A-Lot. "In some ways, it's the same thing an abusive husband would do to their wife," Doug says. "They isolate them, they rip them out of some place where their support is, and then they call the shots."

The more time they spent together, the more concerned Doug became with the dark side of Byron's character. "He was a master orchestrator [and] manipulator … [but] I thought I had him under control," Doug says. "I thought I knew what I was doing with him."

"He was definitely somebody that plays a chess game with people," Doug says, adding, "He was very paranoid, too. I realized that anybody that is always paranoid of other people and is always concerned about other people lying [is] very good at it [themselves]. He was always worried about other people and their lies and their manipulations, because that's what he was good at. So he was always planning."

From Doug's perspective, Byron's entire life was consumed with analyzing and predicting other people's decisions. He had an uncanny knack for understanding others' motivations and predicting how they would react in potential scenarios.

Against Byron's wishes, Doug returned to Houston for a month to smooth over some personal problems with his child's mother. Alarmed when Byron ceased communication, Doug drove back to Atlanta in a U-Haul to pick up his studio equipment.

Doug's apartment, which he'd leased in his name, was empty. The landlord shrugged, saying, "He moved out." Byron had completely vanished, along with all of Doug's studio equipment, gold plaques, paperwork, and contracts. Doug broke down in tears. He would never hear from Byron Hill again.

In Doug's opinion, Byron perfectly embodied the symptoms of a sociopath as defined by Professor Robert Hare's *Psychopathy Checklist*: glib and superficial charm, grandiose self-worth, pathological lying, conning and manipulativeness, lack of remorse or guilt, callousness and lack of empathy, parasitic lifestyle, lack of realistic long-term goals, criminal versatility, and the failure to accept responsibility for their own actions.

While UGK (likely unaware of Doug King's predicament) thought Byron's issues were related to drug and alcohol abuse, Doug believed Byron was fully in control of his actions but simply unable to distinguish right from wrong. "He's a textbook definition of a sociopath," Doug says. "He had a certain amount of charisma and he could motivate people, and he was very smart. But he was amoral."

"If you look up ['sociopath'] in the dictionary, that's [Byron]," Doug adds. "He had no concern about [how] his actions [affected] other people … I thought he was a good partner until I realized he was 100% in it for himself."

"After we figured out that [Byron Hill] was a worse person to be in business with than Russell Washington, we started separating [from] him and got with Jive [directly]," Bun says. When Byron reached out to Jive in the fall of 1995 to discuss some UGK business, he was told that Mama Wes was now the group's manager.

Byron faxed an angry letter to Bun on October 3, 1995, accusing him of breaching their management agreement. "I have been informed that you (and/or Chad Butler) have communicated to employees of [Jive] that you have 'fired' us as your manager without any reason whatsoever," Byron wrote. "However we have never been notified by you of any purported breach by us of the [Management] Agreement." The letter also alleged that Bun owed Byron commissions on features he'd done for Cash Money Records and other independent labels.

Bun was unbothered by the October 3rd fax; in fact, he was in the midst of an unprecedented 90-minute freestyle at DJ Bird's house (a.k.a. "The Ghetto Palace"). Bun's unstoppable freestyle, inspired by the "not guilty" verdict in the O.J. Simpson murder case, was dubbed the "Free OJ Tape."*

Byron faxed a similar letter to Chad, claiming he was owed 20% commission on Chad's production fee for Big Mike's "Havin' Thangs" and other side production, plus 20% of the advance Jive had given UGK to purchase equipment.

MC Bytch had sought out an entertainment attorney, who was very familiar with Byron Hill's schemes, to get her out of her management contract. Byron Hill never responded to her termination letter. But UGK didn't hire an attorney; they simply ignored Byron Hill's letters and set to work on their new album.

With Russell Washington and Byron Hill out of the picture, the advance for the next album *Ridin' Dirty* was the first time UGK had received any substantial amount of money from Jive. Jive brought the group to New York to record and then flew them to Chicago with their A&R Joe Thomas and several live musicians.

After three weeks recording at Jive's Battery Studios in Chicago, Bun and Chad arrived back in Port Arthur late one night and stopped by Mama Wes' house. As they debuted the tracks for her in the den, she was silently horrified.

By now, Mama Wes had developed a taste for rap music, and it didn't sound anything like the quality of work she'd come to expect from UGK. She'd become one of Chad's greatest critics, hoping not to discourage him, but push him to do his best work. She knew if a track was "jammin'" or not, and this was not it.

No one uttered a word; Chad was quiet and downcast, staring at his feet. Unsure how to tell them the truth, Mama Wes found an excuse to retreat to the kitchen.

"Mama don't like it," Bun commented quietly.

When she returned, Chad observed that she wasn't "doing that with [her] head," bobbing along with the beat like she normally did. "It's not good, is it," he said flatly.

She shook her head. "No. It's boo-boo."

There was a long silence. "I know what's wrong," Chad said. "We gotta be home to record. We gotta be in Texas."

Mama Wes nodded. "Well, that could be it."

"Well, Mama, what we gonna do?" Bun asked. Jive wasn't going to be happy that they'd wasted a large chunk of their recording budget.

She couldn't hold back anymore. "That shit is so bad," she admitted. "It's *so* bad. That's the worst shit I ever heard in my life."

(*The "Free OJ Tape," which has never been released, remains with Mitchell Queen Jr. for safekeeping.)

CHAPTER 14

"Our life is slowed down [in the South] so we don't miss nothing. When shit gets moving too fast you miss everything. Shit's slowed down here so we see it all."
– Scarface, *OZONE* Magazine, May 2010

––––––––––

"Screw tapes was like our radio station ... to be on a Screw tape, that was like having a hit song on the radio." – Dat Boy Grace

UGK scrapped most of the work they'd done in Chicago and started from scratch. With the realization that their music needed to reflect Texas, they didn't need to look far for inspiration. The center of Houston's bubbling rap scene was their friend DJ Screw's house.

Screw, a friendly, agreeable type of guy, never had problems with anyone. But the first time he'd met Pimp C in the flea market, Pimp's attitude rubbed him the wrong way. "Good ol' C," Screw chuckled when a journalist asked him for Pimp's number. "Man, when I first met him, I thought he was an asshole. I met him at Big Tyme and he was just talking so much shit ... C knew he was gonna be big. He wasn't big at that time. I don't really like people just talking big about themselves. But man, once me and C just sat down and talked, man, I'll do anything for that muthafucker."

Ever since he'd put up the gate around his house, Screw's popularity had exploded. By 1995, he was practically a household name in Houston. The line to buy tapes was so long that he started setting business hours. At 7 PM, the gate would open, signifying that he was open for business. At his height, Screw was going through a pack of 120 tapes every day.

"He was what you call one man independent ... it was just him," Lil Randy of the SUC said in *Houston Rap*. "He would sit there and copy all those tapes by himself ... put the labels on the front and the back of each tape and write on each tape." He'd handwrite the title – *South Side Still Holdin', Down South Hustlers, Syrup Sippers, Jammin' Screw, Syrup and Soda* – along with his pager number, 713-289-1026.

Police, convinced the long lines were for something other than music, raided his house and tore the place apart looking for a nonexistent drug stash. Screw proudly pinned the search warrant on the wall above his turntables. He was still somewhat awed by his notoriety; after all, he'd really never made any effort to market or promote himself. The rarity and exclusivity of the tapes increased their perceived value.

"Lotta people look at me like I'm a star or something [but] I don't see that," he told *Murder Dog*. "I'm just a regular person, it's just a lotta people know my name. I don't consider myself no superstar or nothing."

If the line was long to buy Screw tapes, competition was even fiercer to record a Screw tape. At Screw's house, anyone could become a rapper, and everyone wanted their shot. "Making a Screw tape is some major shit," Lil Keke told *VICE*. "Making a Screw tape is damn near making an album. You've got to make a list [of the songs you want] and turn it in to Screw and he'll call you, [or] he might not never call you. So getting to his house and getting in is going to be a major thing."

Screw recording sessions were impromptu, spur-of-the-moment occurrences which usually started out as a loose gathering of friends hanging out and getting high late at night. "With Screw, your days turned into nights and your nights turned into days," filmmaker TJ Watford recalled in *Texas Monthly*.

Screw tapes became the soundtrack to the city, turning local street hustlers like Pat Lemmon (the "drank man") and car aficionado Corey Blount into larger-than-life legends. Many Screw fans belonged to car clubs called SLAB clicks (A SLAB was a car, but not just any car: it had to be Slow, Loud, And Banging) like Red Line or Blue Over Grey. (Red cars were affiliated with the South side and blue cars with the North, but the colors were not gang-affiliated.)

Screw tapes introduced SLAB click terms like "tippin'" (the car dropped so low it tilts to one side), "swangin' and bangin'" (swerving in your car from side to side), "elbows and vogues" (rim and tires), and "on the slab" (the car dropped down so low that it scrapes the concrete) to the popular lexicon.

As the voice of the streets, Screw viewed it as his responsibility to help expose local talent. "[On the] East Coast, they got a lotta studios, radio stations, [and] TV stations … [but] down here, all we got [is] one Rap station," he told *Murder Dog*. "Really two – we got 97.9 The Box and we got the radio station SCREW … I try to help everybody [and play] shit you don't hear on the radio."

Screw, known for his generosity, encouraged his friends to get out of the streets. He gave them opportunities to make money off Screw tapes instead of selling drugs. "I'm just tryin' to get everybody off the streets, mane, get 'em [into] something legal, 'cause these [police] out here, they ain't playing. They really wanna lock us all up," he said on the *Ghetto Dreams* documentary. "But when we got something positive and we making money and we reaching and teaching people, can't nothing go wrong."

Screw had dabbled in rap himself and planned to put out a Screwed Up Click (SUC a.k.a. Soldiers United for Cash) album which would also feature him rapping. Initially, he envisioned the Screwed Up Click as a group: Screw tape favorites Lil Keke, Fat Pat, and himself. (Later additions included Big Pokey, Hawk, Lil O, Big Moe, Trae, Z-Ro, and Lil Flip.)

But while Screw was arguably a creative genius, he had little interest in running a business. He'd never even opened a bank account and paid for everything with hundred dollar bills. Although he often complained about bootleggers duplicating his tapes, he'd never set up a more efficient distribution system.

Owners of large retail stores like Austin's Musicmania grew tired of driving in Houston and waiting in line to buy Screw tapes, so they started buying from bootleggers instead. "People would say to me, 'You're screwing Screw,'" James Cooper of Musicmania told *Texas Monthly*. "Well, I'd told him I'd buy from him. He wasn't interested in being a businessman. He could never get it together. He could have made a fortune."

Russell Washington recruited Screw to do a Big Tyme compilation called *All Screwed Up*, which moved 20,000 units. Seeing an opportunity, Russell asked Screw if he would be interested in releasing an actual album. (In a *Murder Dog* interview, Screw was careful to clarify that he had "done work" with Big Tyme but was not signed to the label.) Russell considered Screw music "an acquired taste" and was hopeful that he could help it spread beyond the South.

Retail stores were thrilled when Southwest announced plans to release DJ Screw's first Big Tyme album, *3 N Tha Mornin': Pt. 1*, generating an unprecedented 80,000 pre-orders. But when Russell turned in the finished product, Southwest's Robert Guillerman was horrified to realize that every song was an unauthorized sample of a major label artist. Obtaining clearances, even if it were possible, would cost a fortune. They agreed on a compromise: Southwest would pay an advance for Screw to do a second version using local artists.

It took more than a year to create *3 'N The Mornin': Pt. 2*; Screw, a perfectionist, spent hours upon hours perfecting the tape. "He was a true artist," Russell Washington told *Texas Monthly*. "He cared about the minutest of details. The scratches had to be just right. He told me that every song on that tape told a story."

Russell viewed the project as his own redemption, a chance to sooth his bruised ego and prove that his success with UGK hadn't been a fluke. It was Big Tyme's second opportunity to put all their promotional ideas and groundwork behind a solid album. Russell and his team hit the streets and the project sold nearly 100,000 copies independently.

3 'N The Mornin': Pt. 2 marked the first time Houston's drug slang and car culture reached an audience outside the city. The standout track was Lil Keke's "Pimp The Pen," which sampled UGK's "Pocket Full of Stones."

Initially, Screw said his slowed-down style of music was inspired by marijuana. "When you smoke weed, you really don't be doing a whole lot of ripping and running," he told *Rap Pages*. "[I was] in the crib mixing, you know, getting high … I started messing with the pitch adjusters on the turntables and slowed it all the way down. I thought the music sounded better like that. It stuck with me, because when you smoking weed listening to music, you can't bob your head to nothing fast."

But by 1995, codeine-promethazine cough syrup was taking over. Someone came up with the idea to mix it with soda; they'd pour a few ounces of purple syrup into a big bottle of soda, shake it up, and then pour it over the ice in a Styrofoam cup. When the perspiration covered the outside of the cup, they'd stick it in a second Styrofoam cup. "We got grandmothers and uncles that drink it straight," says rapper Lil Flip. "They actually think we playing by diluting it with soda."

This launched an experimental phase in which syrup sippers debated which soda was the best mixer. After trying all the name-brand sodas, someone stumbled on an off-brand called Nehi. As word spread that Nehi's blue cream soda was the best mixer, there was a mad rush on the handful of convenience stores in town that carried it.

"Oh my God, I remember I had to take Screw to go get some Nehi," Bun laughs. "It took us three stores." Screw, who also had an affinity for orange soda, started churning out tapes with titles like *Sippin' Codeine, Syrup and Soda,* and *CODINE FIEN.*

Although plenty of Screw tape rhymes revolved around drugs and car culture, there was often a deeper message. "Screw would speak to you through the turntable," says Tosin, who runs the fan site thescrewshop.com, told *Texas Monthly*. "[For example], say one of his friends died. He'd play certain songs with an RIP feel, keep doing it over and over, chopping words to make a point. It's like he knew what you were going through by the way he was playing."

"'Cause I play my music slow, people think you gotta get high, get fucked up, do drugs, just to listen to my music," Screw told *Murder Dog*. "It ain't like that at all. Or [they think] that I just do drugs all day, that's why my music's slow. It ain't all about that … You don't gotta get high to listen to my music. It ain't no worship the devil music. [Some] people think you worshippin' the devil when the music drags. It ain't about that. I'm just bringin' it to you in a different style where you can hear everything and feel everything. Give you something to ride to."

Still, the correlation between drugs and Screw music was inescapable. The liner notes of his album *3 'N the Morning* instructed listeners to "get with your click and go to that other level by sippin' syrup, gin, etc., smoke chronic indo, cess, bud, or whatever gets you to that other level."

"Drugs and pop music have always been intertwined … but Screw's dying-battery style just begged to be filtered through an altered consciousness," writer Jesse Washington noted in the *Houston Press*. "Screw was indeed a great DJ … but what [he] will always be remembered for is dragging down the speed of a record until folks swore he had created a whole new song. Often those folks were high. And if they weren't, they wondered what they were missing."

Ridin' Dirty, modeled after a Screw tape, would mark a transition in both UGK's style and sound. They drew heavily from Houston's popular car culture, referencing swangin' and elbows and "diamonds up against the wood" and other popular Screw tape references, using slower beats to mimic the sound.

But trying to explain the Screw lifestyle to out-of-towners was like speaking a foreign language. During a meeting with Jive, UGK tried to explain the importance of doing a Screwed version of their upcoming album, popping in an underground Screwed version of Mary J. Blige's album. Jive's Joe Thomas and Jeff Sledge looked at each other with blank stares as the slowed-down tape played. "What is this?" Joe laughed.

The Convicts' Mr. 3-2 was in the process of getting released from his Rap-A-Lot contract, leaving some of the music from his planned solo album *The Wicked Buddah Baby* in limbo. One of these tracks, "One Day," produced by DJ Boss and Original E of the group OG Style, utilized a sample of the Isley Brothers' "Ain't I Been Good to You?"* The hook, sung by Ronnie Spencer, sounded eerily like Ronald Isley.

"What are you going to do with this song, Three?" Chad asked when he heard the track. 3-2 had no solid plans, so they agreed on a price.**

Chad redid the beat, adding a guitar riff, a thick bassline, programmed shakers, tambourines and 808 drums. But when he brought it to Bun, Bun didn't want to rap on it. He preferred aggressive, uptempo tracks, and didn't like the idea of redoing the song.

Chad argued that it was important for UGK to have balance in their music. By sharing some part of themselves, showing vulnerability, they could connect with listeners. "That's a hit record," he insisted.

"I don't wanna rap over somebody else's version," Bun complained. "We make our own songs."

"Man, [3-2] don't wanna do that song," Chad told him. "That's a hit record. If he gonna throw it away, we might as well take it. He don't see it, but Bun B, I'm telling you, if we do this record we gon' shut these boys down. This is a hit record."

With Bun hesitant to record to the slow-tempo track, Chad invited Screw tape superstar Lil Keke to drop a verse. On the night of December 4, 1995, Chad and Screw pulled up to Lil Keke's apartment to pick him up. En route to the studio, they planned to stop by Carrington's, a popular pool hall/nightclub. They pulled up to a Stop-N-Go around the corner to pick up some Swisher Sweets, Styrofoam cups, and soda. Lil Keke stepped around the corner to the restroom.

Parked next to Chad's rented Cadillac was a black Ford Taurus, in which two men – David Routt and Troy Bennings – were smoking a blunt.*** On the other side of the Taurus was an undercover police officer, Hector Gonzalez, on the lookout for possible drug transactions. He smelled marijuana and radioed for an arrest unit to move in. Two police cars came screeching into the parking lot, lights flashing, and surrounded both vehicles.

Lil Keke, coming back from the restroom, stopped abruptly at the sight of police lights and ducked back around the corner, afraid they were looking for him. He was already on probation for cocaine possession and knew he'd failed a drug test.

Chad, clad in a black t-shirt and brown Dickies, hastily put out his blunt in the center console's ashtray, but it was too late. DJ Screw, pulled from the backseat in his Dallas Cowboys jersey, had three marijuana-filled Swisher Sweets on him. Chad and Screw were carted off to the County Jail. "One Day" would have to wait.****

(*An early Good-Fellaz track called "Selling Wax," produced by DJ DMD, was based on the same sample. Kight was convinced Chad stole their idea as retaliation for the shooting incident, although there is no indication that this is true.)
(**UGK also gave 3-2 a track called "You Wanna Ride," originally intended for *Ridin' Dirty*, which was used on his album *The Wicked Buddah Baby*.)
(***It's unclear if Routt and Bennings were accompanying Pimp C & co. or were complete strangers.)
(****Chad and Screw were each sentenced to spend 48 hours in the County Jail and had to pay a small fine. Lil Keke went back to jail a few weeks later and would never appear on "One Day." Shortly after his release, he hit big with his own single "South Side.")

Chad and Screw bonded out within 48 hours, and their bailbondsman Travis "Mugz" Cains turned out to be a fan. Styrofoam cup in hand, he asked them to pose with him for a Polaroid. They made light of the situation, telling Mugz a (likely exaggerated) version of the story, in which a police car pulled them over en route to the club. As Screw told it, the officer banged on the window and Chad cracked it open, blowing weed smoke in the officer's face.*

The day after Chad and Screw bonded out, UGK's hype man Bo-Bo Luchiano headed off to work at Sears on a dreary Friday in Dallas. A slight rain had been falling all day as thick clouds blanketed the city in a dull gray. He'd returned to Dallas for his son Luke's fifth birthday party and decided to stay for a few months, hoping to spend more time with him before heading back out on the road with UGK.

Luke lived with his mother Darlene and her parents, the Woodsons, not far from Dallas' Love Field airport. Mr. Woodson was a retired brick mason who had turned their one-story brick home into a two-story, adding three bedrooms upstairs to accommodate their growing family. Darlene's sister Yolanda moved in with her five-year-old and newborn twins, in addition to two of the Woodson's older grandchildren.

With temperatures expected to dip into the twenties, the Woodsons were in for the night and decided to cozy up to the fireplace. Their artificial Christmas tree, pleasantly decorated, was resting on the raised brick hearth. With the four youngest children upstairs getting ready for bed and the rest of the family out for the night, the Woodsons sparked a match in the fireplace and briefly stepped out of the room.

They rushed back into the den minutes later to find it engulfed in thick smoke, flames racing up the wood paneling and devouring the Christmas tree. The winding iron staircase in the corner, the only way to get upstairs, was scalding hot.

They rushed outside, screaming for help. A neighbor called 911 while two others helped Mr. Woodson attempt to break through a window. The elderly Woodson cut his leg on broken glass as fire trucks arrived. Some firefighters rushed inside while others restrained 52-year-old Mrs. Woodson, who was trying to run back into the house to save her grandchildren.

Firefighters could not ascend the blazing hot iron staircase; it took them nearly an hour to extinguish the blaze, during which time the roof collapsed. By the time they'd fought through the heat, smoke, and flames to get upstairs, it was too late. Through the haze they saw the remnants of three charred bodies huddled on top of each other; a fourth lay deceased on the bed.

"We couldn't help them. There was just too much fire. It was too hot," firefighter Lt. Frank Gamez somberly told the *Dallas Morning News*. "We all said a prayer for them, and then we came back down. We were all silent. You know, we have kids of our own."

The Woodsons were devastated by the loss of four of their grandchildren; Mrs. Woodson was inconsolable, screaming hysterically. It was one of the deadliest fires in Dallas history.**

Late that night, Bo-Bo called Chad from his parents' house, choking back tears. Chad was not only sympathetic but began sobbing himself, likely thinking of his own two-year-old Chaddyboo. "He cried just as much as I did," Bo-Bo remembers. Touched by sudden inspiration, Chad hit the studio a few days later and rapped:

> My world a trip, you can ask Bun B, bitch, I ain't no liar
> My man Bo-Bo just lost his baby in a house fire
> And when I got on my knees that night to pray
> I asked God, "Why you let these killers live and take my homeboy's son away?"
> Man, if you got kids, show 'em you love 'em, 'cause God just might call 'em home
> 'Cause one day they here and baby the next day they're gone

Chad also referenced his friend since middle school, Donny Young, and Donte Cole, an-

(*If this did happen, it is not mentioned in the police report.)
(**It was originally thought that the fire was caused by "an artificial Christmas tree placed too near a roaring fire," but investigators later determined that faulty electrical wiring was most likely the culprit.)

other friend from Port Arthur, who had both been sentenced to lengthy prison terms ("They gave my nigga Donny 40, Donte 19"). Details about Donte's case are scarce, but he was known for his wild behavior, nicknamed "O-Dog" after Larenz Tate's character in *Menace II Society* and sporting a tattoo of the Chuckie doll with a machine gun and the words "Wanna Play?" across his forearm.

Donny Young had already escaped prison time for stabbing someone and spent six months on the run. In March 1993 he was caught selling two ounces of cocaine and sentenced to 10 years of adjudicated probation, which meant that if he violated, he would be sentenced on the original charge of delivering a controlled substance: 5 to 99 years, regardless of the amount.

After pissing off his probation officer with his flashy jewelry and arrogant attitude, Donny was arrested again in August 1994 for driving with a suspended license. At his next court hearing, Donny's probation officer passed a note to the judge which read, "[Donny] Young is spoiled rotten and can't stand to suffer the consequences. He needs extensive prison time." The judge obliged, sentencing Donny to 40 years in prison.**

After hearing the nearly-finished version of "One Day," Bun had second thoughts about the record. Everyone who heard it seemed to connect with the message. "Different people were just talking about what the record meant to them, and I started understanding what [Chad] saw in it," Bun said later in an interview with Madd Hatta.

On a more personal level, he could relate; he'd recently lost two friends in separate incidents. The first was Charles "Chuckie" Fregia, a former Lincoln High basketball player. While Chad's living situation was stable, Bun hopped around from place to place, crashing on the couch at Ronda Forrest's apartment in Houston before he ended up at Donny Young's place on the north side. Bun, Donny, D-Ray, and some other friends often hung out at Chuckie's nearby apartment.

One weekend in mid-August 1994, Bun and the whole crew drove back to Port Arthur. Chuckie drove separately and stopped at his mother's house in Beaumont. He planned to meet up with the group later that night at the club.

As they headed out that night, they kept calling Chuckie, who had apparently fallen asleep. "Man, I'm on my way," he mumbled. "I'm coming." En route, Chuckie fell asleep at the wheel and drove into a water-filled ditch, where he drowned at just 19 years old. "That just fucked the whole clique up," remembers Donny Young.

In April 1995, Bun's friend Terraine Box, a former classmate at Thomas Jefferson, was killed during an argument over a $5 dice game in nearby Orange, Texas. Bun spoke on the losses on "One Day":

I saw [Box] once before he died, wish it was twice, mane
[...] When we lost [Chuckie], I knew the world was comin' to an end
And I had to quit lettin' that devil push me to sin
My brother been in the pen for damn near 10
But now it look like when he come out, man, I'm goin' in
So shit, I walk around with my mind blown in my own fuckin' zone
'Cause one day you're here, the next day you're gone

Bo-Bo sadly relinquished his position as UGK's hype man, opting to stay in Dallas and provide support to his son's mother, who was having a rough time dealing with the loss. Besides, he wasn't in the mood to be out on tour partying. "When my little boy died, it threw me for a loop," he says. "I miss him. I think about that boy every day."

(*According to NBA player Stephen Jackson, a mutual friend, both men have calmed down after spending time in prison. Donte Cole was paroled in 2005. "[Donte's] a wild one," Jackson says. "He did every bit of his time but he ain't really changed too much ... he's a little smarter. [Donny] changed his life completely." As of 2015, Donny Young still has 26 years remaining on his parole term. He loves to cook and says his only regret is being unable to travel to other countries to experience their cuisine.)

Although Bo-Bo appreciated Chad's gesture on "One Day," over the years to follow he grew weary of fielding the inevitable question from UGK fans. They'd ask, "That wouldn't be you that [Pimp C] was talking about on that song?"

"Yeah, that's me," he'd nod, dreading the next question.

"Well, what happened?" they'd prompt.

Jive released "One Day" as a single, with the clean version of UGK's new record "Fuck My Car" ("Ride My Car") on the B-side. Everyone, of all ages and backgrounds, could relate to "One Day." Chad's older relatives were glad there was finally a UGK song they could appreciate. "'One Day' really don't sound like it's rap, it sounds like it's my era – Frankie Beverly and Maze – the music is more like a ballad," says Chad's older cousin Stephanie Starring, who loved embarrassing her teenage daughter by riding through the neighborhood with "One Day" blasting loudly.

Shortly after their arrest, Chad stopped by Screw's house while Screw was recording a tape called *3-4 Action*. When the mic was passed to Chad, Screw threw on Whodini's "Friends," one of his favorite tracks. Screw mostly liked the song because of its message. Although he was laid-back and would hang out with anybody, it took a special type of person to be invited into his inner circle. "Kinda hard to pick your friends," he told *Murder Dog*. "You gotta see a person's heart. When I look at a person I study them hard."

Chad reminisced on their arrest ("me and DJ Screw, locked in the clank") and bragged that they'd been "down since '92." He freestyled about "eatin' gravy and rice" before telling the story of an unknown associate who'd been caught trafficking cocaine:

The nigga started snitchin', got caught on I-10
And put all the niggas that he knew in the pen
Now all of the niggas in the town, they say,
"How could this muthafucker just treat us this way?"
Snitch ass nigga told on the whole clique
And now niggas wanna chop off his dick
I couldn't understand, I thought they was men
But these is the bitches that we call friends

Bun spent a lot of time hanging out at Screw's house on Greystone, usually getting high rather than actually rapping. One night, Chad and Bun stopped by Screw's house, where Big Mello, Kenny Bell, and a few others were lounging on folding chairs. Eventually, the suggestion was made that UGK was long overdue for a Screw tape.

"There was no forethought about making that tape," Bun told journalist Maurice Garland. "All we knew was that we wanted to rap on some of our favorite beats … it was just about having fun."

Screw asked who they wanted to have featured on their tape. Lil Keke and Big Pokey were fan favorites, but Chad requested a relative unknown named Charles "Macc" Grace. Grace, once a stellar athlete on track for a promising career in major league baseball, had been sidetracked by injury. Now a small-time hustler and Crip affiliate, he'd appeared on a dozen Screw tapes. Ever since Screw remarked, "Man, dat boy went off!" after one of his most impressive freestyling sessions, people thought his name was Dat Boy Grace.

"We need Dat Boy over here," Chad remarked. Screw called Grace, who was riding around with some friends. "Whatever you doing, stop, and get over here. Pimp and Bun requested you," Screw told him.

"Yeah?" Grace was surprised.

"How long it gonna take you to get to my house? Man, c'mon," Screw urged him. "Stop whatever you doing. Don't make no stops, just come straight to us."

Grace did make one stop. Parties at Screw's house were B.Y.O.P.: Bring Your Own Pint. "My way to show respect and homage [to UGK] was to come with all the party favors," he recalls. "I showed up with pints and the best of the 'dro and pills." When he pulled up around 9 PM, the party was already in motion.

Someone made a Jack N The Box run to pick up food for everybody, and the group hung out in the garage, sippin' lean, shooting pool, and smoking weed until the wee hours of the morning. When the mood was finally right, everyone gathered in the wood-paneled room which served as Screw's lounge/recording studio. He stood along the wall with his two turntables, his back to the room as he sifted through vinyl. As Screw kicked off the mix, he challenged them to try to make it through the whole tape without stopping. "If you mess up, we're gonna have to start over," he told them. "So don't mess up."

"I'm not even gonna tell y'all what beats are gonna come on," he added. "I'm just gonna be mixing, y'all pass the mic. Nobody gonna know what track gonna come on next, y'all just gotta go." Screw kicked it off with UGK's new vinyl for "Fuck My Car."

"What's up, world?" Bun began. "It's that big Bun B, representing P.A., and they bangin' Screw." He passed the mic to Pimp, who started rapping an improvised remix to their own song: "You wanna be seen flippin' with a superstar, but you ain't kickin' it with me, you wanna sip my barre."*

Pimp and Bun shouted out their friends back in Port Arthur as the blunts and Styrofoam cups were passed around freely. Screw dropped some classic West Coast instrumentals from WC, Ice Cube, Tha Dogg Pound, Lady of Rage, Mack 10, and Ant Banks.

"The boy C rollin' joints, Screw mixin' it up," Bun observed. "I think that boy want that old school!"

Screw threw on an old school slow jam for Pimp, who launched an impromptu commercial for Screw. "A lot of niggas think anybody can' muthafuckin' do this!" Pimp said. "After standing right here on this mic, man, talkin' to y'all, can't nobody do what Screw doin'! STOP! All y'all out there doin' it, just STOP! Right now!"

Grace rapped about dropping out of school and passed the mic to Pimp, who drawled, "*Maaaan*, I dropped out too, dawg."

"I know y'all felt that boy, just like y'all felt that boy Biggie," DJ Screw intoned after Pimp was done freestyling to Biggie's "Juicy" beat, adding, "Dat Boy Grace on the lean."

By 5 AM as the freestyle session drew to a close, Grace's homeboys were asleep, passed out around the room in various states of disarray. While Bun and Al-D lounged on a battered couch playing NBA Live, Screw went to work on the B-Side, blending some of his favorite songs with a list provided by Chad and Bun which included Tupac, B-Legit, and Westside Connection.

The tape raised Dat Boy Grace's profile in the streets, putting him on the same level as Lil Keke and other Screw stars. "It was just a real good look for me 'cause at the time, Screw tapes was like our radio station," Grace explains. "It was doing more for local artists than 97.9 [The Box] was at the time. So for me to be on a Screw tape, that was like having a hit song on the radio."**

<hr>

(*"Barre" is another slang term for lean or syrup.)
(**At the time, the *Ridin' Dirty* Screw tape was never mass-produced or sold in any large quantity. It is now available from screweduprecords.com as *Chapter 182: Ridin' Dirty* in the Diary of the Originator series. Grace's rap career ultimately was stalled by his legal troubles. Shortly after recording the tape he was arrested for possession of a small amount of cocaine, a violation of his probation on a similar charge, and sentenced to a year in jail. He later served federal time for possessing a weapon as a convicted felon.)

CHAPTER 15

"Ridin' Dirty was the best [album] we made, hands down."
– Pimp C, *On Tha Real* Magazine, April 2005

———————

"Ridin' Dirty represents Texas rap in its rawest and purest form."
– Chamillionaire, *OZONE* Magazine, June 2006

Hoping to give *Ridin' Dirty* a cohesive feel, Chad reached out to Rick Royal and offered to pay him to oversee the project. He liked the way Rick sequenced his albums with creative skits and interludes. Rick was flattered, but didn't understand why Pimp would want to put that responsibility in his hands. "I admire UGK as a group, so I didn't feel like I should put my stamp [on] it," Rick says, admitting, "I dropped the ball."

Plan B was to use dialogue from *The Mack*, laid over the beat to "7th Street," for the album's intro and skits. ("I'm true to this, not new to this!") But the idea had to be scrapped when Jive couldn't, or wouldn't, clear the samples from the movie.

Since he'd reluctantly agreed to do the slow-tempo "One Day," Bun begged Chad to create a hard, uptempo beat for him. "I want a song that I can go off to," he explained. All the hours he'd spent freestyling with 3-2 and Big Mike had improved his flow. "People were telling me [I was getting better]," Bun told *Believer*. "That was the only fucking clue I had. Everybody was like, 'Man, you killing it.'"

Chad obliged with the uptempo track for "Murder" and kicked things off with, "I'm still Pimp C bitch, so what the fuck is up? Puttin' powder on the street 'cause I got big fuckin' nuts!"*

Even though Bun had been up all night partying, he was up for the challenge. He wrote his verse on the spot, fell asleep on the control panel, and was awakened when it was time to drop his vocals. Still sleepy, he made it through the first 16 bars and then uncharacteristically flubbed a line. The engineer was using a new digital program called ProTools, and assured Bun that he could just punch in and complete the verse where he'd left off.

But even though it *could* be done, Bun felt like he'd be cheating if he didn't rap the entire verse without stopping. "I wanted to spit it all the way through so that when the a capellas were made available, people could [hear] that there were no breaks," he explains. He knocked out the 32 bars in one take. "After I did that record, I went to sleep," Bun told *Believer*. "That song put me to sleep. Because it was that demanding."

UGK set to work at Houston's Digital Studios, where the owner, John Moran, a white man in his 40s, was more open-minded than his peers when it came to rap music. ("Kids love horrifying their elders," he told *Texas Monthly*. "My pet theory is that it's protest music. Economy's

---

(*"In the span of two bars, Pimp provided examples of five of the reasons why our elders (more than likely) collective hate rap music," music critic Buhizzle observed. "First, he introduced himself – on how many Beatles' songs did John Lennon say his own name? Second, he insults his listener – likely a listener who just spent money to support Pimp's cause ... Third, he drops the F-bomb, with another one coming mere seconds later. Fourth, he glorifies drug dealing, by attributing the cause of his trade to the size of testicles ... which leads perfectly into number five – he speaks candidly about his genitals. Most rappers not named Todd Shaw would need at least a full song to evoke all of these reactions out of their listeners.")

doing good, stock market is setting records, yet a good third of black men under 28 are doing or have done jail time.")

Chad called in Corey "Funkafangez" Stoot, a versatile musician who had gained a reputation around town as the "wah wah man" for his funky guitar and bass riffs. If there was a sample they were having trouble clearing – Isaac Hayes or the Isley Brothers, for example – Chad would ask Funkafangez to replay it, maybe with a slight twist. Funkafangez added his funky touch to "One Day," "Diamonds & Wood," and "Hi Life."*

For the most part, UGK studio sessions were serious business. Studio time cost $125 an hour or more, and even if Jive was cutting the check, it was still coming out of their budget. "They were all pros," remembers Roger Tausz, their engineer at Digital Services. "Business came first … it was their money they were spending, ultimately, and they knew it. So it wasn't totally regimented, but there was little time wasted."

However, that didn't mean they were sober; Chad was convinced that drugs helped him make better music. "At one time I couldn't live without marijuana in my system, which was always my drug of choice," he later told *OZONE.*

Ridin' Dirty showcased Chad's vulnerability on tracks like "Hi-Life." (His cousins Amy "Dee Dee" Mossenberg and Edgar Walker Jr., who was working on an oil rig, got shout-outs: "Now Dee Dee getting married, and Edgar on the boat.") After his grandmother lectured him about missing church, he rapped:

I'm tired of living fucked up, tired of living bad
Tired of hearing grandma telling me, "When you gonna go to church, Chad?"
Now I'm trying to live up to the image that she would want me to be
But I got one foot in the streets, and every week I flip a key

With Chad and Nitacha separated, Riley often served as the neutral liaison to transport Chad Jr. when the two of them were on bad terms. One afternoon at the San Jac house, Chad was headed out to Houston to record and planned to bring Chad Jr. with him. Nitacha, who was mad at him, objected to him taking the boy. The conversation grew heated, and Nitacha called her father. By the time Mama Wes arrived, police were on the scene trying to calm everyone down.

After the police drove off, Mama Wes shook her head. "You don't make Chad mad when he's going to the studio," she warned Nitacha and her father. "It's not a good idea, because he gonna make a song about you. If he'll put his grandma in a song, what you think he gonna do to you?"

Chad was headed to the studio to record vocals for "Diamonds Up Against That Wood," a track he'd created using a sample from .380's "Elbows Swangin'" off of DJ Screw's *3 'N The Mornin' Pt. 2.* (The track also sampled Bootsy Collins' "Munchies For Your Love" and incorporated some of the riffs played by live musicians like Leo Nocentelli during their Chicago trip.)

He used the opportunity to vent, referencing Nitacha ("I got a baby, but his mama act like he ain't mine / Wicked women, using children to live on / Wanna hurt and try to hate, 'cause she know the thrill is gone") and her father ("Niggas talk a lot of shit in a safe place / I know 'cause he can't look me eye-to-eye when he in my face").

After things had calmed down, Chad called Nitacha to warn her about the record. "We were going through our problems at the time, so I just want to apologize to you upfront, before the album comes out," he told her.

"He puts our lives on [the records], you know?" Nitacha says. "And this is the city I gotta live in, so this is how these people [in Port Arthur] are thinking about me. [They think] I'm the bad guy." Tired of comments from mutual acquaintances, Nitacha decided not to speak on their

---

(*"UGK put me on the map," says Funkafangez. Thanks in part to the exposure he gained from *Ridin' Dirty*, Funkafangez spent the next few years working with Mannie Fresh and Cash Money Records, making significant contributions to Juvenile's 1998 classic *400 Degreez* and the Big Tymers' 1998 debut *How You Luv That.*)

relationship anymore. "If you want to know about me, go buy the album," she'd tell them.

Smoke D, serving out his 20-year manslaughter sentence in a Mississippi prison, managed to smuggle in a digital recorder. (He declines to explain how he accomplished this.) He sent it home with instructions to mail audio tapes to UGK. "The only reason I did that was to let them know that I was okay," Smoke D explains.

Chad had been listening to Smoke D's tapes every day on the way to the studio. ("Man, I got to holla at my nigga Smoke D that's locked in the pen," he rapped over the "Juicy" beat on DJ Screw's *Ridin' Dirty* tape. "See, he sending me tapes and tell me what's going down / He tell me that niggas is locked down and ready to clown.") After his ideas to use Rick Royal's skits and *The Mack* dialogue had fallen through, he realized that the soundtrack for the album had been in his tape deck the whole time.

Chad took snippets from Smoke's tapes to create skits throughout the album. "Live from the muthafuckin' pen, nigga," Smoke's husky voice announced on the intro. A memorable line from a Mexican inmate would form the soundbite for the beginning of "Murder."

"Dawg, it's real up in here. Niggas will kill you if you fuck up, y'know what I'm saying?" Smoke reported on the intro to "Hi-Life." "They shoot all kinds of game. I'm just thankful the Lord blessed me that I can see it a hundred miles away."

"Everything started coming together … it seemed like God was playing on our time," Chad reflected later in *OZONE*.

To complete the record, UGK settled in at Skip Holman's home studio in Katy, a suburb on the west side of Houston. Producer N.O. Joe, who had contributed the track for "Fuck My Car," would become an integral part of the recording process. He and Chad were both perfectionists with an affinity for live instrumentation, and functioned almost as a production team. "Where he would leave off, I would catch on, and vice versa," says N.O. Joe.

Another sample Chad was able to salvage from the Chicago sessions was a portion of jazz musician Wes Montgomery's "Angel," which he used for "Ridin' Dirty." "[That song] was one that he had been wanting to interpolate for years, but he wasn't really sure if people were gonna understand him fucking with Wes Montgomery['s music]," Bun recalls.*

N.O. Joe also encouraged Chad to develop his singing voice, teaching him new techniques to stack his vocals. Kristi Floyd, who had remained a good friend, was flattered when Chad invited her to the studio to record background vocals with him for "Pinky Ring."

Mama Wes remained one of UGK's harshest critics. One day, after she suggested one of the records could use some more fine-tuning, Chad laughed. "Hey, Mama, hol' up," he said. "You're talking to *The Pimp*."

"So?" she smiled. "I'm *The Pimp's* Mama. And you need to go back and fix that."

Chad told his mother he was thinking about moving to Atlanta. Bun had just returned to Houston after six months in Atlanta. Mama Wes, knowing her son's short attention span, didn't take his comments very seriously. "Okay, well, whatever you want to do," she said absentmindedly.

"I think it would be a good business decision," Chad thought aloud. He liked the Dungeon

<hr>

(*Several records which were cut from *Ridin' Dirty* eventually landed on other projects. Using a sample of Danish synthpop duo Laid Back's record "White Horse," Chad created a track called "Black Horse (My Bitch)." It remained as a bonus track on the cassette version of the album, but was replaced on the CD by "You Don't Know Me" and later ended up on the MDDL FNGZ debut *TROUBLE* under the title "My Bitch." "Family Affair" appeared on Cash Money's *Baller Blockin'* Soundtrack, "Hi Side" landed on E-40's *Southwest Riders* compilation, and "The Southern Sound," minus its original sample, was later reused for the interludes on UGK's *4 Life*. While UGK was in the studio with N.O. Joe they also recorded several tracks for N.O. Joe's planned solo album, which was never released. "Time" would later be repurposed for The *Sweet James Jones Stories*, while "Bump & Grill" later ended up on *Dirty Money*.)

Family's movement, and he had friends there already, like Big Gipp and Too $hort, who had just relocated from the West Coast.

"Well, if you think it would be a good business decision, try it out," she suggested.

Chad was quiet for a minute. "How far is it?"

"Well, I think it's 12 hours," she said. "Don't you remember when we went up there? It took us 12 hours to get there."

Atlanta was quickly becoming a music mecca. Annual events like Freaknik and the Jack the Rapper music conference brought thousands to the city. Jack the Rapper had been partly responsible for breaking acts like MC Hammer, Kris Kross, New Kids on the Block, and TLC.*

Even the mayor, Bill Campbell, was a self-described "child of the Motown era" who attended local artists' listening parties and made a bid, albeit unsuccessful, to bring the Grammy Awards to the city. With the 1996 Olympics approaching, Atlanta was in the international spotlight. ("The whole country thinking that my city is the big lick for '96," Big Gipp rapped on OutKast's "Git Up, Git Out.")

"They got the whole town just buzzin' with music," Too $hort told *The Source*, explaining his decision to move to Atlanta. "I got to keep my Oakland roots but I'm gonna try to tap in on some of this shit. [Atlanta] is up and coming." ("I went to the Freaknik, shit turned me out / Came back for Jack the Rapper, bought me a house," Too $hort rapped on "That's Why.")**

Mama Wes had forgotten about their Atlanta conversation when Chad called a few days later to tell her he was breaking down the studio equipment.

"For what?" she asked.

"I'm going to ATL," he said.

"Oh, yeah? Well, okay, where you gonna get a truck?" Mama Wes asked. She still didn't believe him. "Look, I tell you what. I'm on my way over there."

When Mama Wes arrived at the San Jac house, she was surprised to see her son winding up cords from the studio. As he was packing, he got a call from Master P.

With the success of "Playaz From the South," Master P had apparently realized that Chad and Mo B. Dick's production chemistry was a winning formula. Master P was planning to drive from New Orleans to Houston and wanted to pass through Port Arthur to get a track from Chad for his upcoming album *Ice Cream Man*. He'd spent several nights on the couch at the San Jac house already, often pulling up in an old Cadillac with smoke pouring out of the exhaust pipe.

Chad halted the studio packing and started experimenting with some ideas for the record. By the time Master P, his right-hand man Anthony "Boz" Boswell, and Mo B. Dick pulled up at the San Jac house, Chad had already laid a bassline and was creating a drum pattern on his trusty Roland R-8 drum machine, using an 808 drum and experimenting with a hand-clap as a snare. "See if you can do something with this," he said, turning it over to Mo B. Dick.

Mo B. Dick went to work on his keyboard, adding tenderoni chords and "the whistle," a

(*Too $hort recalls performing at an impressive Jive showcase at Jack the Rapper which also featured UGK, KRS-One, and several other Jive acts, likely in 1993. "That was a big day for me," Too $hort says. "I always kept thinking, this would be a major tour, the Jive Records tour, but [either] Jive did not want that comradery to happen or they did not see the value in sending their artists out on a tour." Unfortunately, the 1993 Jack the Rapper event was marred by violence between the Death Row camp and Uncle Luke Records, which had just released a Death Row diss record called "Cowards of Compton." There were reports of gunshots, and news reports described Uncle Luke leading "his 'posse' on a rampage of overturning and throwing furniture, which in turn set off a series of fights leading to several arrests." Recalls Wendy Day, who coordinated some of the event's panels, "A free-for-all broke out in the lobby on the escalators. Guys even threw a [Coca-Cola vending] machine off one of the lobby balconies trying to hit [Uncle] Luke's crew. [It was a] miracle no one died." When the Marriott Marquis refused to allow the event back the following year, Jack the Rapper relocated to Orlando. It attempted to return to Atlanta in 1995, but had lost its appeal with music industry executives.)

(**Jive and Too $hort were in the process of staging a faux "retirement," complete with a press conference, to promote his album *Gettin' It (Album Number Ten)*. "[I had released] 10 albums, six platinum and four gold. It was a mathematical thing. I was turning 30 years old," Too $hort told *Complex*. "It was all a fucking hoax, the whole shit - from the start. I never retired. I was under contract with Jive. I was planning on making the next album. I wanted the money and I needed the money. There was no fucking retirement.")

signature sound he and KLC had created on the Ensoniq ASR-10 sampling keyboard. As they created the beat, Master P bobbed his head and came up with an idea for the hook: "Don't make me break 'em *off* somethin'!" Bun, who had written his verse quickly, was busy with his head buried in a medical book about pills.

Chad had already started dismantling some of the equipment and taken down some of the padding around the vocal booth, so he brought Master P in the bathroom to record vocals. It made perfect sense to Mo B. Dick. ("In the bathroom, you get this natural reverb," he explains.) They put a mattress in the bathtub as padding and ran cables from the bathroom to the ADATs in the bedroom.

When Chad started recording, Master P had just inhaled on a blunt and coughed sharply before freestyling most of his verse. "Boy, we 'bout to fill they muthafuckin' head up with this ghetto dope," he said. "Tryin' to break these hoes off something. Got my niggas Bun B, Pimp C … UGK done hooked up with Master P, we 'bout to bring this shit 'cross the borders, ya heard me? From Texas to New Orleans."

A few hours later, the song was complete. The coughing at the beginning of the track would stay. "We did a lot of [No Limit] stuff just off the cuff, original," says Boz. "That's why I think people felt our music."

The beat for "Break 'Em Off Something," slightly reminiscent of a song Chad had produced for the X-Mob titled "Mob or Die," was one of the first times he'd used double-time hi-hats. The technique would later become a staple of Southern rap. "When I took a handclap out of my 808 and made it into the snare drum and played the hi-hat double time … I wasn't settin' out to make no statement," he told *FADER*. "I was [just] trying to make a good record for Master P … that's all we ever set out to do, is [do] the best we could do that [day] and be a little bit better than we was the day before."

Once UGK's album was complete, the packaging for *Ridin' Dirty* was turned over to their product manager in New York, Cheryl Brown-Marks. Ideally, Cheryl was the point person responsible for coordinating everything between the artist and the label, but she found her job difficult because she had little communication with the group. "[Even after Byron was] out of the picture, they weren't easy to work with," Cheryl says.

While Chad had some supporters at Jive, he hadn't endeared himself to many of the staffers. He often complained bitterly, blaming them for UGK's "sharecropper's contract." "I don't think he helped the situation," says Freddy Johnson. "[When] those Jive reps would call, he would be going off on those people … like he was talking to a stepchild."

On one occasion, the phone rang at the San Jac house. Chad picked it up and, without saying hello, launched into a slew of obscenities before slamming down the receiver. The phone rang again and Pimp slammed the receiver down again without word. Donny Young stared at him, mouth agape. "Who the fuck is that?" he asked.

"Man, them bitches at Jive Records," Chad told him. "Them hoes ain't wanna pay me my muthafuckin' money, so I don't wanna talk to 'em." (As Donny recalls it, this phone call was the inspiration for Pimp C's line on "Murder": "I ain't rappin' shit 'til my money in my hand.")

Bun was known at Jive as the nice guy, the articulate one who could hold a decent conversation. "I don't know that artists really realize this, [but] being a nice person in life, particularly as an artist, gets you a really long fucking way … because most of us are overworked and underpaid," says UGK's former A&R Sophia Chang. "We've only got so much bandwidth, and for the person that's gonna actually be kind to us and extend niceties and be grateful and be gracious with us, we are going to go way further for that person than we are for somebody that's a dick."

At a meeting in New York to sketch out plans for the *Ridin' Dirty* cover shoot, Chad expressed irritation with their previous cover, where Jive had simply put UGK "in some damn Dickies." He insisted, "We want *real* clothes."

Mama Wes considered their product manager Cheryl a "pushy bitch" and didn't like her condescending attitude towards Chad. "Don't let that girl push her way into coming to Texas, I'm telling you," she warned a Jive staffer as they departed. "When she gets to Texas, she's gonna be way out of her element. And I'm telling you, C is not gonna hold back. Not in Texas."

Jive sent Cheryl to Texas anyway. On a Saturday afternoon, Chad and Bun met up with her and art director Nick Gamma at Houston's Galleria Mall. The plan was to find some clothes for UGK to wear for the *Ridin' Dirty* cover shoot. Predictably, there had already been a debate over the wardrobe budget, with UGK expecting more than Jive was willing to spend.

As they strolled through the mall, Chad picked out various items and instructed Cheryl to pay for everything. Finally, Cheryl stopped. "Okay, hold on," she said. "We're buying a whole bunch of things, but we need to buy complete outfits. Let's stop and just look at everything that we bought so far, just so we can kinda gauge what we have."

In Cheryl's opinion, she was being logical and reasonable, but her tone didn't sit well with Chad. As the argument grew heated, Cheryl snatched an expensive Versace shirt out of Bun's hands and raised her voice, yelling at him. Bun didn't react, but Chad snapped back in his partner's defense. Chad cussed her out, called her a bitch, and threatened to "get [a female] to beat [her] ass."

"You can't come down here from New York, thinking you gonna tell me what to do!" Chad yelled.

"What does me being from New York have to do with any of it?" she yelled back. Finally, she screamed, "I'm not doing this!" and stormed off.

Mama Wes, who was in Port Arthur, was slightly amused when she got the phone call informing her that Chad had called Cheryl "several kinds of bitches." "In a way, I wasn't really upset that C had attacked her, because I knew that shit was gonna happen," Mama Wes says. "I had warned them not to send her ... and I felt like she had done something to provoke it."

Along with DJ Bird, she drove out to Houston to try to smooth things over. The incident didn't surprise Bird either. "It didn't take you long to piss C off," Bird laughs. "[If] C cool with you he'll be your best friend, but man, if you piss him off, he'll go live on you."

While they were en route to Houston, Mama Wes got a call from a concerned Barry Weiss. "Wes, Wes, Wes, how near are you to there right now?" he asked.

Mama Wes was always amused by New Yorkers who seemed to think that getting from Port Arthur to Houston was as easy as walking a few Manhattan city blocks. "I'm only about a half hour out," she told Weiss. "But, you know what you all think about Texas."

"Oh, Wes, what are we going to do?" he sighed. "Do you think Chad is gonna hit her?"

"Barry, Chad's not gonna hit that bitch!" Mama Wes scoffed. "It ain't that serious, he knows better than that. But I told them not to send Ugmo [Cheryl] over here. She was not the right person. What I suggest you do, is get that ugly bitch out of Texas fo' something happen."

Cheryl was already boarding a flight back to New York, to the relief of everyone involved, and UGK was headed to DJ Screw's house to meet the photographer Keith Bardin. They posed with Screw in front of his turntables; the test copy of the "Tell Me Something Good" vinyl Bun had given him nearly five years earlier hung on the wall behind them.

As word spread that UGK was doing a photo shoot at DJ Screw's house, the place was soon packed with friends, affiliates, and aspiring rappers. "It was cool for me, 'cause I got a chance to see how major [record labels] work," says C-Note of the Botany Boys. "I always wanted to do those type of things that they were doing but didn't know how to do it, you know what I mean? And so I was kinda in the learning mode."

Parked outside Screw's house was C-Note's brand-new Suburban, fully customized with leather seats, a woodgrain steering wheel, and $10,000 Brabus rims known as "blades." Chad and Bun snapped some photos in the Suburban, which would end up on the cover. "It kinda [fit]

Pimp C working out of his makeshift studio at the San Jac house during the recording of *Super Tight*.
Courtesy of Weslyn Monroe

Above: UGK's ***Super Tight*** **cover shoot** in Port Arthur.
Photo: Shawn Mortensen

Below, Right: In October 1993, Chad's mother **Mama Wes** took over as the group's road manager.
Courtesy of Weslyn Monroe

SHOWS AND PRODUCTION

UGK, INC.

UGK
Underground Kingz

Wes Monroe
Manager

5048 Shreveport Ave.
Port Arthur, Texas 77640

409-982-0141 Home
409-726-5759 Pager
409-982-7441 Fax

Above: **Pimp C** in a scene from UGK's "Use Me Up" video, December 1992.
Courtesy of Mitchell Queen Jr.

Below: **Bun B**, UGK's dancers **QT** and **Jamie, Too $hort, Bo-Bo Luchiano,** and a guest on the Lafayette tour stop of Too $hort's *Shorty the Pimp* tour, 1992.
Courtesy of Bo-Bo Luchiano

Smoke D *(far right)* and a few friends at the San Jac house, 1993.
Courtesy of Weslyn Monroe

Left (L-R): The Good-Fellaz **Ron "Crumz" Forrest** and **Isreal "Bluelite" Kight** on the cover of their debut album *Illegal*.
Courtesy of Ronda Forrest

Above: **Mitchell Queen Jr.** *(far left)* and **DJ Bird** *(far right)* lounging with a few friends at the San Jac house.
Below: **Bun B** *(blue shirt)*, **DJ Bird** *(in the Orlando Magic hat)* and friends having an impromptu celebration at the San Jac house after the release of *Too Hard to Swallow.*
Courtesy of Weslyn Monroe

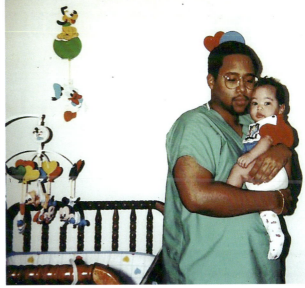

Above (L-R): **Nitacha** as a junior in high school, around the time she and Chad started dating; **Chad** and their son **Chad Jr.** in 1993.

Courtesy of Riley Broussard

Right: **Bun B** and **DJ Bird** on the road for an early UGK show.

Below: **Chad** experimenting with a team of live musicians at the San Jac house during the recording of *Super Tight*.

Courtesy of Weslyn Monroe

The Dallas Morning News

Texas' Leading Newspaper   © 1995, The Dallas Morning News   Dallas, Texas, Saturday, December 9, 1995   8 Sections   HF   • • •   50 Ce

Spy damage severe, CIA chief says

Ames' betrayal aided Yeltsin, Deutch states

By James Risen
Los Angeles Times

WASHINGTON — Russian President Boris Yeltsin continued to reap the benefits of Aldrich Ames' treason against the United States long after the collapse of the Soviet Union by making it difficult for the United States to figure out the Russian leader's intentions on critical foreign policy issues, CIA Director John Deutch revealed Friday.

Offering newly declassified information from the CIA's internal damage assessment on the Ames spy scandal, Mr. Deutch disclosed that Mr. Ames' betrayal complicated the nation's ability to predict Mr. Yeltsin's intentions on such issues as nuclear proliferation and Moscow's role in other former Soviet republics.

The CIA director also said America suffered from a diminished ability to understand the extent of the decline of Russian military technology in the late 1980s and early 1990s and had a harder time grasping the

4 children die in Dallas house fire

Heat repels grandfather, other rescuer

By Robert Ingrassia and Jody Sowell
Staff Writers of The Dallas Morning News

Fire that apparently spread from a fireplace ripped through a Love Field-area house Friday night, killing four young children who had huddled upstairs to escape the smoke and flames, authorities said.

Intense heat repelled the children's grandfather, two neighbors and firefighters who tried to rescue the children from the burning house, neighbors and officials said.

"We couldn't help them. There was just too much fire," said firefighter Lt. Frank Gamez, who discovered the dead children in an upstairs family room. "It was too hot. Damn, it was too hot."

Through the heat, smoke and flames, they saw three bodies huddled on top of each other and a fourth on a bed, he said.

"We all said a prayer for them, and then we came back down," said. "We were all silent. You know we have kids of our own."

The fire ranks among the deadliest in recent Dallas history, o

Please see 4 YOUNG on Page 11A

A Dallas firefighter works Friday night in the remains of a house in the 5900 block of Wren Way, near Love Field. Four children, ages 1 to 6, died trapped in an upstairs room. It took firefighters an hour to extinguish the blaze, which apparently started accidentally in a downstairs fireplace and spread rapidly.

The Dallas Morning News: Juan Thompson

When UGK's friend and hype man **Bo-Bo Luchiano** lost his son **Luke** *(right)* in one of the deadliest house fires in Dallas history *(above)*, Chad memorialized the tragedy on UGK's record "One Day."
Courtesy of Bo-Bo Luchiano

Below: **Chad** and his own son **Chad Jr.**
Courtesy of Riley Broussard

Above: **UGK** at an in-store signing for *Ridin' Dirty*.
Left: **DJ Bird** at Mama Wes' house with the *Ridin' Dirty* gold plaque.

Courtesy of Weslyn Monroe

Clockwise from below: **C-Note** of the **Botany Boys** and his **Suburban** which was used for the *Ridin' Dirty* cover shoot; Charles Grace a.k.a. **Dat Boy Grace**; a **Screw tape**.

Dat Boy Grace photo by Peter Beste

Above: **Bun B, DJ Screw,** and **Pimp C** shooting the *Ridin' Dirty* album cover at DJ Screw's house, 1996.
Photo: Keith Bardin

Below: **Pimp C** and **DJ Screw** with bailbondsman **Travis "Mugz" Cains** *(center)* after their 1995 marijuana arrest.
Courtesy of Mugz

the whole vibe of *Ridin' Dirty*, the whole album," explains C-Note. (The Botany Boys were also photographed in a mock carjacking which appeared on the inside cover.) The group gathered at N.O. Joe's plush home in Katy for the rest of the shoot, with Mitchell Queen, DJ Bird, and Leroy White making cameo appearances.

Chad and Bun were immensely proud of their creation. "*Ridin' Dirty* was the best [album] we made, hands down," Chad told *On Tha Real* Magazine. Even the fact that Jive changed the titles of his two favorite songs ("Diamonds Up Against That Wood" and "High Life" became "Diamonds & Wood" and "Hi-Life" on the album's tracklisting) didn't dim his enthusiasm.*

"*Ridin' Dirty* was the first true, full representation of UGK," Bun says. "Musically, lyrically, artwork, [everything]." There was a sense that things were about to change. "Up until this point I was just rapping and runnin the streets," Bun said. "Not that [the previous albums] weren't good … But we all knew this one was different."

Everyone who had worked on the project sensed it was a masterpiece. But when *Ridin' Dirty* was actually released, the moment seemed anti-climactic. "There was no promotion on it whatsoever … It was disappointing to me [because] we put so much into that record," says N.O. Joe.

But even with no radio single, no video, and hardly any promotion, the album hit #2 on the *Billboard* charts and sold 67,200 copies in its first week. On the SoundScan charts, it outsold pop star Celine Dion, country singer LeAnn Rimes, and The Fugees' masterpiece *The Score*. The album would go on to sell nearly 850,000 copies, earning UGK their first gold plaque.

"Street credibility is something you can't buy," Chad told *OZONE*. "Of course we'd like to go triple platinum, but would I trade that for my fan base of 500,000 or 800,000 people? No, I wouldn't. It's all about pleasing your fan base."

Over in Mississippi, prison officials were not pleased to learn that one of their inmates appeared on the album. They tore apart Smoke D's cell and probed him (literally, he admits, "like an alien") trying to figure out how he had managed to record the audio. Stumped, officers finally left him alone. In Smoke's opinion, they were more impressed with his ingenuity than angry.

A few weeks after *Ridin' Dirty* dropped, Scarface was in the studio with Tupac Shakur collaborating on "Smile" and passed along a copy of UGK's album. Tupac was impressed, especially with "One Day," which struck home because he'd just lost two of his cousins. "Yo, I don't know who these cats is," Tupac told EDI of his group The Outlawz. "'Face just gave me this album, [and] these cats talkin' 'bout what we talkin' 'bout, these cats gonna be down with us."

The potential Tupac/UGK collaboration would never come to fruition. Two weeks later, on the night of September 7, Tupac was shot after leaving a boxing match at the MGM Grand in Las Vegas.

The following week, UGK was in Los Angeles attending Bay Area rapper Richie Rich's release party for his Def Jam debut *Seasoned Veteran*. In the hotel lobby, UGK ran into Method Man of the Wu-Tang Clan, who enthusiastically greeted them with a "Pocket full of *stooooones!*" In the van en route to the release party, the festive mood died when the radio station announced that Tupac Shakur had passed away in a Las Vegas hospital.

———————

At the hotel in Los Angeles, Mama Wes was cooking some gumbo when a knock came at the door. Irritated at the interruption, she washed her hands and peered through the peephole. She squinted; the man looked a lot like rapper-turned-actor Ice-T.

Naaah, she thought as she opened the door. *Couldn't be.*

"You must be Mama," Ice-T said.

(*In a 2006 interview with Rapz.de, Chad said he considered "Diamonds Up Against That Wood" his greatest creation.)

She nodded, still shocked. "Yeah. And can I assume you are who you look like?"

"Yeah," he laughed. "I came to see your son."

"Which one?"

"They're both yours?"

She laughed, invited him in, and called Chad. "How close are you?" she asked, not wanting to ruin the surprise. "You have company ... And I really do think you wanna see this company."

"Is she cute?" Chad asked.

"I wouldn't say that."

"Mama, who is it?"

"Just c'mon."

Chad and Ice-T had previously been introduced by mutual friend Born 2wice and bonded over their common love of Iceberg Slim. "We had that light-skinned nigga connection," Ice-T jokes. "When light-skin niggas connect, it's always fly."

It was the first time Mama Wes had ever seen her son starstruck. Ice-T, who had branched off into acting, was encouraging Chad to pursue similar opportunities. "Look, don't limit yourself to this [rap] game," Ice-T suggested. "You're talented. You're a natural. I'll help you."

"Ice-T took me under his wing ... he showed me the game," Chad told WordofSouth.com.

"I was like an L.A. ambassador," Ice-T explains. "L.A. is a very interesting place. You gotta almost have a pass to be there. I have a lot of street connections ... so I would come and say, 'Yo, everything's good' ... just kinda lay out the land, because L.A. is a very dangerous place."

When Jive arranged for UGK to do a promotional tour for *Ridin' Dirty*, Bun invited a woman he'd met in Houston, Chalvalier "Queenie" Caldwell, to one of the first shows in Lake Charles. Queenie wasn't a fan of the group, but was impressed enough with Bun to drive down with a few friends.

Among them was a woman named Angie Turner, whose attractive grey outfit and matching boots immediately caught Mama Wes' attention when the group met downstairs at the hotel to head out for the show. "Who is that one right there?" she asked Chad, nodding towards Angie. "Who does she belong to? She don't look like she fit in with the rest of these hoes."

"That's mine right there," Chad nodded. "She came here with me, Mama."

Mama Wes introduced herself to Angie and caught a whiff of perfume. "Oooh, you smell so fresh!" she gushed. She usually didn't like Chad's girlfriends, but decided to make an exception for Angie and invited the woman to ride with her. The two women, both Sagittariuses who shared a birth week, hit it off immediately.

Chad wasn't happy that Jive had arranged for them to do 50 shows for free, especially because shows were their main source of income. But despite Chad's reluctance, the promo tour brought the group in contact with many key people they might not have met otherwise, such as DJ C-Wiz in Nashville. They also reconnected with Brian "Biz" Hunter, a local hustler who had invested money in a previous Nashville UGK show.

Biz, tall and flashy with dreadlocks, was a UGK fan with access to plenty of top-quality weed and plenty of money. The source of Biz's funding was a major drug dealing operation led by Waymond "Big Dog" Fletcher. UGK's street-oriented music inevitably attracted hustlers everywhere they went, and Chad was selective about the ones he allowed in his circle. "Dog and Biz was some guys he really, really had a lot of respect for," says Chad's friend Young Smitty. Chad liked to joke that Big Dog had so much money he had to pay someone to flip the bundles of cash in his warehouse to make sure the ink didn't rot the money at the bottom.

After the *Ridin' Dirty* promo tour, Big Dog and his crew came out to see UGK perform in Birmingham. The huge nightclub was packed, but UGK was still at the hotel waiting for the promoter to bring their money. Biz, who overheard a heated phone conversation between Mama

Wes and the promoter, reported back to Big Dog, "The dude don't wanna pay Mama."

Chad was upset that his mother had allowed Biz to overhear the conversation. "Mama, you don't say that to killers and thugs," he warned.

"Well, C, let's try to do it the easy way first," Mama Wes suggested. "Let's go over there and see if we can get the paper."

At the club, Mama Wes went inside the office to try to reason with the promoter, but emerged empty-handed. "Did you get it?" one of Dog's enforcers asked. When she said no, Big Dog peeled off thousands of dollars from his own pocket and handed it to Mama Wes.

"They were going to [pay us to perform] and then take it out of [the promoter's] ass," Mama Wes laughs. "I'm just there to do the show and get the paper, [so] I don't give a damn where it come from. I know we had bills due next week and I needed to get them bills paid … frankly I didn't give a damn what happened to [the promoter], because he didn't wanna pay my baby."

Mama Wes returned to the limousine where Chad and Bun were waiting, unaware of the drama taking place inside. "You got the paper, Mama?" Chad asked.

"Yes," she answered, neglecting to mention the source of the funds. *Well, it's not a lie,* she thought. *I do have the paper. That's a fact.*

But when Biz explained the situation, Chad was concerned. "Mama, you can't do that," he warned his mother. "Now you gonna be responsible for that nigga's death tonight."

"Not me," she shrugged. "He's gonna be responsible for his own death."

UGK rocked the club, made a hasty stop at the hotel to grab their luggage, and drove straight through the night until they were safely back home in Port Arthur. "All I can tell you is that they did a hell of a show, and we got the hell up out of there," laughs Mama Wes. "So if you want me to tell you what happened [after the show], I don't know, and I don't want to know."

"[My] Mama loves killers and thugs," Chad liked to brag. "That's her friends, she will call them in a heartbeat … if you did her wrong, they're coming after you."

CHAPTER 16

"[Pimp C] was a character. I feel like it'll never be nobody like him [again] because ... the world will never be in the same condition it was in when we came up." – Big Gipp

———————

"Whenever Bun and Pimp came to town, it was like your cousins came to visit. It was like extended musical family across the world ... [There was] so much love and so much creativity ... [They were] just trying to make their mark and do their part to change the world, and it was all pure and honest. And that's why I think that the ripple effects of it can still be felt now, because of the genuine nature in which everything was created, and the genuine love that was shared by all of us." – Joi Gilliam

Late 1996
Atlanta, Georgia

Chad moved into his first place in Atlanta sight unseen, which turned out to be a small one-room apartment on top of a junk-filled garage. Mama Wes came to visit and was not impressed with the place, which she considered "dead in the hood" near the Atlanta airport.

Scurrying up the wooden steps one day with several bags full of groceries, Mama Wes spotted a tall, lanky 18-year-old outside the house two doors down. Tauheed Epps was a standout basketball player headed to Alabama State University on an athletic scholarship. She waved; he waved back.*

The Atlanta winters proved to be much colder than Port Arthur, and by late 1996, Chad was miserable. He called his mother late one night while lying in bed buried under his electric blanket. A heavy sleet was coming down outside, nearly snowing in the frigid temperatures.

"Mama. What you doing?" he asked.

"Trying to stay warm."

"Me too," he said. "I got the blanket on and I got the heat on, but you know how many air holes they got in here?"

"Yeah, baby, I imagine they do."

"But that's not why I'm calling you."

"Well, why you calling me?"

"Well, they got this rat," Chad explained. "And he's over there, Mama, you know where the sofa is, and the coffee table? He's on the other side of the coffee table."

"Okay, what is he doing?"

"Looking at me," he said. "And I hit on the coffee table, and he just put his head to the side. And I hit on it again, and he still didn't move."

———————

(*Tauheed Epps wouldn't formally meet the friendly woman until nearly fifteen years later. By that time, he had reinvented himself as a rapper – first as Tity Boi of Playaz Circle, a group signed to Ludacris' DTP label which toured with Lil Wayne off the strength of their collaborative single "Duffle Bag Boyz," and then as the rapper 2 Chainz – never knowing that Pimp C had once been his neighbor.)

"Well, I think you need to move around," she advised. "'Cause evidently, he ain't gonna move. He ain't scared of you."

"Hol' up, Mama, hol' up," Chad said dramatically. He then called out in the background, "What did you say?"

There was a long pause.

"Who are you talking to?" Mama Wes asked.

"The rat, Mama."

"Well, what did the rat say?" she responded, without skipping a beat.

"The rat said, 'Cut the heat up, muthafucker, I'm cold!'" Chad laughed.

"Oh my God," she sighed. "C, get out of there."

UGK's show schedule had been slow, so leaving wasn't even an option. "Man, I ain't got no paper, Mama. I can't go nowhere," Chad sighed.

The following weekend Mama Wes drove up to Atlanta for a UGK show in Decatur with Greg Street, and to Huntsville, Alabama, the following night. Mama Wes and Chad headed back to Atlanta with their half of the show money. The weather was still gloomy, and after the three hour drive, they arrived back at the garage apartment to find that the heater wasn't functioning because the landlord hadn't paid the gas bill.

Mama Wes reached for the loaf of bread on top of the refrigerator to make some sandwiches. The bread collapsed; the rat had eaten clear through the middle, leaving only the crust around the edges with a hole through the center. "Oh, no," Mama Wes gasped, horrified. "The rats ate the bread."

Chad shrugged as if this were a regular occurrence. "Oh, yeah," he nodded. "He do that." In their absence, the rat had also torn cleanly through one of Chad's down pillows. "I'm not staying here," Mama Wes said firmly.

They gathered some clothing and essentials and used the weekend's show money to book rooms at a nearby Ramada Inn. But Monday morning came and the outlook wasn't any brighter. With a steady rain falling and gloomy, dark clouds hovering outside, Mama Wes rose with the morning newspaper and skimmed through the rental classifieds. After seeing two listings in Mableton that looked promising, she called Too $hort and asked him where Mableton was.

$hort laughed. "It's nothing but a whole bunch of crackers out there. You're gonna have a whole bunch of bad neighbors."

While Chad slept, Mama Wes headed out to Mableton, a suburb on the west side of Atlanta. The builder, David Wilson, greeted her to show two brand-new houses on a cul-de-sac. Only one was complete, but Mama Wes preferred the design of the unfinished three bedroom at 605 Jenmarie Drive. The 1,200 square foot home had an outdoor deck, a split-level basement which was the perfect size for a recording studio, and a "cute" kitchen.

She called Chad and woke him up. "I think I found somewhere. I need you to come out here and see which one of them you like, 'cause I'm looking at two."

"I don't care. Just get it," Chad mumbled.

Wilson warned that the property wasn't ready for move-in. The carpets hadn't been laid yet in the upstairs bedrooms and some of the appliances weren't functional. "Look, I need a place to stay *today*," Mama Wes explained.

"It's early enough in the day [that] we can get the carpet down," Wilson thought out loud.

"We don't have a place to stay tonight, sir," she told him. "And if pay you, then I don't have any hotel money." It was true. UGK usually covered their own travel expenses, and ever since they'd run out of gas two blocks away from the venue in a small town in Texas, Mama Wes insisted on setting aside travel money for the next show in advance. They had just enough money left over from the weekend's shows to put down a payment on the house.

He was confused. "Well, where are you staying now?"

She gave him the whole story: the garage apartment, the rats, the Ramada. Wilson agreed to have the property ready by the end of the day and Mama Wes signed the lease on the spot.

Too $hort was right: the white residents of this Mableton neighborhood weren't happy to see black people moving in, especially not *rappers*. "Oh, God, there were some terrible people out there," recalls Mama Wes. "They did not like seeing these *niggas* coming along."

Chad set up his recording equipment in the basement, and the Mableton house came to life with activity. Frequent visitors included Too $hort, Big Gipp, and Sleepy Brown. Guests would pull up to the house in customized cars with enormous rims, music blasting loudly and the bass pounding through the trunk.

Their presence was a clear source of irritation for the elderly white woman who lived across the street, and Mama Wes decided that "killing her with kindness" would be the best policy. She woke up early every morning to fix herself a cup of coffee, which she sipped on the front porch in her rocking chair, a gift from Chad. Often, the highlight of her day was waving as the elderly woman glared at her from across the street. "Good morning! How you doing? Did you sleep well?" Mama Wes would call out.

Shortly after Chad moved to Mableton, he stopped by Atlanta rim shop Peachtree Motoring with his friend Biz from Nashville. Biz's younger cousin, 23-year-old Lanika, happened to pass by the shop and recognized Biz's truck.

Lanika pulled over and poked her head in the truck, where she was surprised to see a light-skinned man in a t-shirt and some khakis. "Where's my cousin?" she asked.

Chad smiled at her. "I don't know, but who are you?"

They flirted; Lanika was pretty and flashy, with jewelry and plenty of cash. Chad admired her drop-top '96 Cadillac El Dorado; she also had a convertible 5.0 Mustang, both black and outfitted with black-on-black rims.

Lanika's lifestyle was being funded by her drug-dealer boyfriend back in Nashville, Terrell "T" McMurry, but she was instantly attracted to her new friend's swagger and laid-back demeanor.* Chad, admiring her "pretty legs," announced that he was going to call her "Red" and invited her to come by the house. Later that night, Lanika was surprised to see two gold plaques on the fireplace mantle for Big Mike's *Somethin' Serious* and the *Menace II Society* soundtrack. She realized she'd hit the jackpot when a friend explained that "Pimp C" was the guy from Master P's "Break 'Em Off Something."

As Lanika remembers it, their first night together was such a success that she never left. She proved to be a good housekeeper, keeping the Mableton house neat and clean despite the revolving door of rappers and producers coming through.

When UGK's show schedule started getting hectic off the strength of *Ridin' Dirty*, there had been talk of bringing in another road manager to lighten Mama Wes' load. "I really wasn't ready to have my load lightened, because honestly, I just didn't trust anybody with them like that," says Mama Wes. "I'd rather be there and do it myself."

DJ Greg Street, one of UGK's early supporters, had relocated to Atlanta to work with radio station V103. He mentioned the opportunity to Hashim Nzinga, a friend from Dallas who had just moved to town with his brother, a first round draft pick for the Atlanta Falcons.

Hashim wasn't much of a rap fan, so en route to Chad's Mableton home, Greg briefed him on UGK. "[Pimp C] needs a road manager who's disciplined and who understands security, 'cause Pimp get himself in a lot of dangerous situations," Greg explained. Based on Greg's description, Hashim envisioned a fearless drug dealer like Al Pacino in the movie *Scarface*.

Mama Wes greeted Greg and Hashim with some coffee and they held an informal interview. A mild-mannered Chad, who had just woken up, came downstairs in a robe and house shoes, groggily rubbing sleep from his eyes. After a brief conversation, Hashim was impressed

---

(*When Cash Money shot Juvenile's breakthrough video for "Ha" in 1999, it was Terrell "T" McMurry who provided the yellow Ferrari and a blue Jaguar as props.)

with his intelligence, introspection, and calm demeanor.

Chad took a break from the conversation and stepped into the kitchen to make a cup of hot chocolate for his son Chad Jr., who was visiting for the summer. Hashim leaned over to Greg and asked when he was going to meet Pimp C.

Mama Wes was impressed with Hashim, who introduced himself as the National Spokesman of the New Black Panther Party and was clearly well-versed in black history.* "[Chad] was already a revolutionary," Hashim says. "He was revolutionary [in his own way]."

Dr. Khallid Muhammad, the controversial leader of the New Black Panther Party who had recently survived an assassination attempt, clearly understood the importance of working with the rap community to get the NBPP's message to the public. Snippets of his lectures had already appeared on Hip-Hop records like Tupac's "White Man's World," Ice Cube's "White Cave Bitch," and Public Enemy's "Night of the Living Baseheads."

Chad and Mama Wes invited Hashim to come out to UGK's show that night at Atlanta's Club 559. Prior to aligning himself with the New Black Panther Party and adopting the name Hashim Nzinga, Hashim was a used car salesman named Steve Washington. He still had some connections at a car dealership and had a fleet of Navigators. He arranged for Byron Amos, a driver who was also a community activist, to drive them to the club.

Byron, a huge UGK fan, was stunned when he saw his passengers for the night emerging from the Mableton house. He tried to wipe the smile from his face as Chad, Bun and the rest of the crew climbed in the back seat.

But when their driver introduced himself, Chad was less than enthusiastic. "*Byron*!?!?" he yelled. "Get that muthafucker out of here!" Chad told Byron Amos that if he wanted to work with UGK he would need to change his name, instead anointing him "Big B." He spent the rest of the drive complaining about their "scandalous" ex-manager Byron Hill.

Until that point, UGK's road crew had literally been a family operation, with Pops now serving as Mama Wes' assistant/driver. Mama Wes was very lenient with promoters, often lowering UGK's show price for small markets. One contract for a 1997 show in San Antonio read: "Full Price Agreed Upon: at least $5,000 Depending on Crowd." They only charged $350-$600 for transportation "depending on how far" to cover the cost of gas. ("Travel expenses is not an issue now," she wrote on one contract. "Let's see how you do on your show.")

Mama Wes was concerned about making sure that the promoter made money too, because when the promoter made money – as Stokes, Captain Jack, Bobby Caillier, and other promoters did every time they brought the group to the market – they would bring UGK back again, guaranteeing future income. UGK even occasionally agreed to do door splits with good clients, accepting half of the money collected at the door as payment instead of a flat fee. This was risky for the artist, because there was a chance they'd take a loss if the promoter was dishonest or didn't promote the show properly.

Hashim came on board as the group's road manager, hoping to adopt more stringent business practices and security techniques so they could travel more efficiently and safely. He brought in new security guards from the Fruit of Islam. "We really took our [security] detail seriously," says Byron Amos, who doubled as security. "It was never just a bunch of goons hanging around."

Bringing in new crew members meant replacing some of the tasks that had previously been handled by Pops, Bird, Leroy White, and Mr. Freddy, one UGK's first security guards. It didn't help that Hashim was getting paid more than anyone else, which stirred up resentment in the crew.

(*The New Black Panther Party has no affiliation with the original Black Panthers of the 1960s and 1970s. Members of the original panthers denounced the NBPP as a "black racist hate group" and obtained an injunction against founder Aaron Michaels preventing him from using the original Panther name or logo, although it was never enforced.)

"We was a happy lil' family … everything was going good until Hashim Nzinga and them stepped into the picture [and] caused confusion," Pops says. "Hashim pushed us all out. He totally disrupted the family."

"We got rid of a lot of the dead weight and people that was in the way," Hashim shrugs. "There's a place for friends and there's a place for business."

Lanika, who considered it "love at first sight" when she met Chad, neglected to mention that she was also involved with rap producer Jazze Pha. One day, Jazze Pha pulled up to Patchwerk Studios with rapper MC Breed, where he was surprised to see Lanika's convertible parked outside.

Inside, Pimp C, wearing a mink coat over a wifebeater, seemed to be agitated. He greeted MC Breed enthusiastically and continued talking, telling the handful of people in the studio about his new woman and her drop-top Cadillac. The more Pimp talked, the more certain Jazze Pha became that he was talking about Lanika. Still, Jazze barely knew Pimp, certainly not well enough to call him out in front of a group of people. He hesitated, unsure how Pimp might react if he pulled him to the side.

Around this time, Lil Jon and the East Side Boyz' record "Shawty Freak a Lil' Sumthin'" dropped, getting heavy airplay on Atlanta radio stations. The record featured Jazze Pha on the hook, enticing a female to "freak a lil' somethin'." On the outro, Jazze cooed, "in my drop-top Caddy, baby," which Lanika believed was a reference to her. Lanika came clean and told Chad she'd been messing around with Jazze Pha.

Chad, furious that Jazze hadn't told him directly, called and demanded, "Nigga, what's up with you and this bitch, man?"

Jazze tried to calm him down. "Hey, dawg, look… Naw, Pimp, it wasn't like that."

"Yeah, nigga," Chad spat before angrily hanging up the phone. "We gon' holla."

Jazze didn't want to leave things on bad terms and reached out to Hashim, a mutual friend, to try to schedule a meeting. The following day, while Jazze was getting his car detailed at a Buckhead car wash, Chad and Hashim pulled up in Lanika's Cadillac.

Hashim laid a hand on Jazze's shoulder. "Man, Jazze's a good man," Hashim told Chad. "I know this guy. He's a real guy, he gonna tell you the truth. He gonna let you know what's happening."

Jazze and Chad stepped off to the side to talk privately. Jazze explained that he considered Lanika a friend with benefits, not his girlfriend. "Man, I been dealing with this girl," he admitted. "I didn't wanna put her out there because I don't know what y'all got, but I'm not dealing with her right now."

"Man, she live in my house!" Chad yelled, heated. "She stay at my house, nigga! That's her car right there!"

"I *know* that's her car," Jazze said.

"Well, how come, nigga, you ain't come and tell me?" Chad demanded.

"I know, man… I meant to tell you," Jazze said. "But you was talking about the chick and it looked like, you know, I didn't want to bring it up and badmouth [her]. I didn't want rain on your parade at that moment."

Chad sighed. "Man, Jazze, tell me what's up, man," he barked. "Is you talking to the bitch or what, man? What's going on, tell me? Give me the lowdown on the bitch."

Jazze enjoyed Lanika's company but also sensed she had some groupie tendencies, and didn't think her interest in either of them was sincere. At the risk of sounding like a hater, he decided to keep his opinion to himself. "Like, here it is, man," Jazze explained. "Like, we was talking, and we ain't talking no more."

As Jazze recalls it, Lanika was thrilled to have two men fighting over her. "She thought it was funny," Jazze says. "She's 'hood, so she liked all that drama shit. That would bring him closer to her, you know, 'cause don't nobody want nobody that nobody [else] wants."

After six months at the Mableton house, Lanika's excitement at dating a rap star had waned. Chad was a homebody, preferring to stay home watching old movies like *The Mack* and eating gumbo when he wasn't in the studio. UGK's show schedule was sporadic and Chad's finances were shaky. Lanika was used to the fast life, hitting the club scene and partying with drug dealers who always had plenty of money to throw around.

Eventually, she left, but she and Chad would remain friends for many years. The situation had the unintended effect of bringing Jazze and Pimp closer. They ended up in the studio together, where Jazze was producing several tracks for MC Breed's album *It's All Good*. Pimp dropped a verse on "Rule No. 1" alongside Kurupt. (The hook: "Rule number one, bitches ain't shit, so why even trip off a bitch that eat dick?")

Ironically, the next woman who came in Chad's life also came through Jazze Pha.* Jazze had met Sonji Mickey, a local singer, on a party boat at Lake Lanier with MC Breed and Keith Sweat. Strong and outspoken, Sonji wasn't the type of woman who was easily impressed by celebrities.

"There's something authentic about [Sonji]," says Jazze Pha. "She's got that mama/sister/auntie/friend [vibe]. Beautiful personality, loves God, but she's still got a street mentality." Sonji had done hooks and features for local artists and sang background vocals for artists like Too $hort, MC Breed, and Erick Sermon.

Chad met Sonji through Jazze Pha and the two soon became an item; Sonji moved into the Mableton house. Sonji was raised in the church but still had a sharp mouth. "I come from a generation of 'muthafucka this' and 'muthafucker that' and that's exactly what might come out of my mouth at any time," she admitted later. "I'm a Christian, I am, but God is still working on me. He's still working on my mouth. I pray about it all the time."

Sonji loved to prepare hearty meals for guests, but also knew when to be harsh when necessary. "Y'all muthafuckers get in there and clean that shit up," she would yell at messy visitors who came by the home studio. "Y'all ain't gonna disrespect this man's house."

Through Too $hort, Chad met Kool Ace, an Atlanta pimp embarking on a rap career. "[Kool Ace] and Chad got a lot of the same demons and a lot of the same angels, on a spiritual level," says songwriter Big Zak, who sat in on their studio sessions. "They both were ahead of they time … [They were] good dudes at heart, legends, hustlers, and leaders … They really respected the [pimp] culture, the dress, the attire, the gators, the minks … [and they had] the gift of gab to go with it."

The three met up at Too $hort's studio in the appropriately-named Atlanta suburb of Oakland City, where they recorded "Pimpin' Ain't No Illusion" with the help of guitar player Charles Pettiway. Musicians appreciated working with Chad because unlike most rappers, he treated them as equals. He was one of them. "He had a lot of respect for musicians, and he had a swag about him," says Charles Pettiway.

Through Too $hort, Pimp met a lot of other real-life pimps, like Ohio's Calvin "Good Game" Winbush. "When I [first chose the name] Pimp C, I was talking about pimping an ink pen … later, as my career went on and on, I kept meeting P.I.s," Chad told *OZONE*. "They took

(*Jazze Pha describes his relationship with Sonji as "play brother and sister." Several of Chad's friends were under the impression that their relationship was not so platonic and that Jazze was slightly jealous of Chad for once again stealing his woman. Sonji declined to be interviewed.)

it upon themselves to give me the game … and I started slowly but surely putting a lil' bit of the pimp game in my rhymes."

One of them, Sir Captain, pulled Chad aside at Too $hort's studio and asked him not to "mis-pimp with this shit." He explained, "You and $hort, y'all be right on with your pimpin', then you go off talking about freaking and sticking your dick in a bitch mouth."

Alongside the gold plaques on the mantle of Chad's Mableton home were a stack of Iceberg Slim books, including the bestseller *Pimp: The Story of My Life*, *Death Wish*, *Mama Black Widow*, and *The Naked Soul of Iceberg Slim*. Chad, who had been infatuated with the Iceberg Slim books since childhood, started referring to himself with the alter ego "Sweet Jones," a character from *Pimp*. (Later, "Sweet James Jones," a reference to J. Prince. "I put the James with it to be a tribute to The King James Prince," Chad told *On Tha Real* Magazine).

Being in Atlanta also brought Chad closer to the Dungeon Family. By now, Rico Wade had upgraded, moving into a large three-story home. The basement, the new "Dungeon," was lined with platinum plaques from OutKast, TLC, En Vogue, and Ludacris.

The Dungeon Family was at the center of everything happening in Atlanta: it was Rico Wade who introduced Tionne "T-Boz" Watkins to Lisa "Left Eye" Lopes of TLC and produced their massive 1995 record "Waterfalls." When executive L.A. Reid discovered a teenage singer from Tennessee named Usher Raymond, the Dungeon was one of his first stops, asking Rico for some beats. "It was like a big creative camp," Organized Noize producer Ray Murray remembers.

Sleepy Brown also had a large home studio, and Chad spent a lot of time there working with him on his project *Sleepy's Theme*. "[Pimp C] was one of my favorite producers to watch because he was so into it," Sleepy remembers. "He could make that [drum machine] turn into a choir. It was insane."

"Pimp and Sleepy are the same. It's all funk and soul," says Organized Noize's Ray Murray. "Their technique of creating is very similar."

"He was the best brother I ever had because he understood me," Sleepy adds. "That's why we did so well with *Sleepy's Theme*, because musically we were on the same tip."

Big Gipp was dating Joi Gilliam, the daughter of a popular NFL quarterback who was a talented genre-bending singer in her own right. Her brand of R&B/funk/rock/soul would be one of the first dubbed "neo-soul."

Chad and Joi, who both considered themselves musical purists and "funk connoisseurs," clicked instantly. "If he don't fuck with you, you'll never *know* him. But if he fuck with you, you'll get to meet all the characters; all the people that encompassed Pimp C," says Big Gipp. Pimp and Joi spent hours analyzing music; both were adamant about making the type of music they wanted to make, not the type of music that would sell. Pimp encouraged Joi to dabble in production herself.

"Whenever Bun and Pimp came to town, it was like your cousins came to visit," says Joi, of the Dungeon Family's attitude towards UGK. "It was like extended musical family across the world… [There was] so much love and so much creativity … [They were] just trying to make their mark and do their part to change the world, and it was all pure and honest. And that's why I think that the ripple effects of it can still be felt now, because of the genuine nature in which everything was created, and the genuine love that was shared by all of us."

The musical comradery between UGK and the Dungeon Family, Big Gipp felt, was a once-in-a-lifetime occurrence. "[Pimp C] was a character," he says. "I feel like it'll never be nobody [else] like him, because… the world will never be in the same condition it was in when we came up."

CHAPTER 17

"Houston rappers couldn't beat the system, so they created their own."
— *Texas Monthly,* August 1998

"[C-Murder's 'Akickdoe!'] showed me that [Pimp C] wasn't a selfish [producer].
That was a big-ass record that he could've done by himself." — KLC

Fall 1997
Houston, Texas

Master P's "Break 'Em Off Something" had exploded, cementing his position as a rising force in Southern rap and establishing Pimp C as a top-notch producer. But although the two men were valuable to each other as business associates, their personalities clashed. Master P was accustomed to ordering people around, but Chad was not one to take orders. "From the beginning … they was kind of like oil and water," Mama Wes says. "They really didn't mix very well."

In the fall of 1997, Mama Wes was at Pops' townhouse, which functioned as UGK's base of operations in Houston, when she got a call early one morning from Master P. His younger brother Corey "C-Murder" Miller was wrapping up his debut album *Life or Death* and wanted UGK on the project. Artists outside the No Limit roster were rarely featured, but UGK was an exception. Master P wanted them to come to Baton Rouge immediately.

Chad was already committed to a studio session that night with an upstart Houston rapper. The indie label had been courting him for several weeks, taking him to dinner to get acquainted with their artist and paying a 50% deposit for his $10,000 production fee. "Well, we can't do it because C's got a project," Mama Wes explained. "He's gotta be in the studio at 6." She suggested they could come the following day.

Master P told her to cancel Chad's previous commitment. "Their shit ain't gonna get played. Mine is," P said.

Mama Wes didn't like his tone. "Their money is just as green as yours is, so you either want [UGK] tomorrow or you don't want them at all," she said.

Master P snapped back with something that Mama Wes interpreted as a threat. "Well, fuck you then," she retorted. "We won't come at all." She hung up.

This wasn't the first time they'd had a heated conversation; Mama Wes was accustomed to P's temper and expected he would call back later after he'd calmed down. But she didn't realize that Chad, who was coming downstairs, overheard the end of the conversation.

"Who's that you talking to?" Chad asked.

"That was just some business," she said, trying to downplay it. "It was P. But it's no problem. He'll call back."

Master P did call back, but Chad was so irritated with P's attitude towards his mother that he didn't want to go. "We need the paper, so let's hustle up and go," Mama Wes told him. She and Bun picked Chad up early the next morning after he'd been up all night in the studio.

When Mama Wes filled Bun in on the situation with Master P, Bun sighed. "Oh, man, y'all at it again?"

"[Master] P never knew how to talk to people," Mama Wes says. "That was not one of his strong [points]. That would piss C off, and they would go back and forth."

It was true that Master P was willing to pay more money than the indie artist and his song would reach a wider audience, but Chad knew how it felt to be young and struggling. "That [local artist] had paid his hard-earned money, and that was way more valuable to [Chad] than Master P's money, because P had way more money than that little boy had," Mama Wes explains. "[Chad] wasn't going to just drop him and run off and do something with somebody else."

When they arrived in Baton Rouge, Chad was more standoffish than usual. Even though they'd clashed, Mama Wes greeted Master P with a smile. His record "Make 'Em Say Uhh!" was getting heavy airplay, and she liked to tease him about the catchphrase, which Pops referred to as his "toilet sound."

"Hey, boy, you gonna do that toilet stuff again tonight?" Mama Wes joked.

The small No Limit office consisted of just four rooms, and the studio was barely big enough for three or four people. The Beats by the Pound production team – Mo B. Dick, KLC, and new additions Craig B and O'Dell Vickers – had been churning out most of the No Limit tracks.

Chad started working on a rough structure for a beat for C-Murder and turned to Mo B. Dick. "C'mon, Dick," he said. "What you hear on that bitch?" Mo B. Dick created a rock guitar bassline on his Kurzweil keyboard. Chad turned to KLC, who was known for his powerful drums. "KL, man, get on this muthafucker, mane," Chad encouraged him. "Put somethin' on it, man. Let me hear what you got."

The finished product, "Akickdoe!", was what Mo B. Dick calls the only "full-fledged Beats by the Pound/Pimp C production." "['Akickdoe!'] showed me that [Pimp C] wasn't a selfish [producer]," says KLC. "That was a big-ass record that he could've done by himself."* KLC also picked up some unique engineering tricks from Chad, ways to give the vocals "more life."

Not only was Chad unselfish about sharing production credits (and potential publishing checks), but he was unselfish about giving away his sounds. Chad gave his drum sounds to Craig B, who shared them with the rest of Beats by the Pound. "That's like giving up yo' secret ingredients," explains KLC. "A lot of producers have [the same] keyboards [which come with the same sounds] so it's pretty much your drums that separate you from everybody else."

In the studio observing the recording process was 21-year-old New Orleans rapper Richard "Fiend" Jones. Fiend had caught the label's attention with his independent project on Big Boy Records and was now working on his No Limit debut, *There's One In Every Family*.

Fiend had first met UGK when he was a young teenager hanging out with his cousin DJ Lil Daddy; his mother had given him permission to pursue rap early. ("Go get this out of your system," she'd said. "I don't wanna hear nothing about this [rap music] when you get older.") He and Chad also had something in common: the women they were dating in Baton Rouge were sisters, and they'd sometimes cross paths late at night at the ladies' apartment, lounging on the couch watching television together.

The following day, Chad and Bun returned and laid verses for Fiend's "Slangin'," produced by KLC and O'Dell. For Fiend, the entire process was a learning experience. Not only were they creating music, but a business transaction was taking place. Money was exchanging hands. It excited him to realize that rap was really a viable career.

———

A few weeks later, Chad was back in Port Arthur catching up with his friend D-Ray. One of the biggest drug dealers in the area, D-Ray had always been into cars (it was his Buick which

———

(*C-Murder's *Life or Death* dropped in March 1998 and went platinum, hitting #3 on the *Billboard* charts. Pimp and Bun were the only artists outside the No Limit roster featured on the project.)

appeared on the cover of *Super Tight*), and his recent purchase of a brand new Lexus had earned him both the admiration of his peers and unwanted attention from law enforcement. D-Ray felt his days were numbered and told Chad he needed to find a legal hustle.

D-Ray was also having problems with one of his friends, Damon Giron, who seemed to be growing more unhinged. D-Ray decided to move after Damon, in a fry-induced rage, threatened to kill him and tried to set his house on fire.

Chad suggested D-Ray should come to Atlanta with him. Maybe he could find a new direction in life, or help Chad somehow with his music career. They talked it over at Mama Wes' house the day before Chad planned to drive back to Atlanta.

"I'm tired of the game, Mama," D-Ray reflected.

Mama Wes nodded. "Well, I think you oughta be."

Chad decided to extend his visit one more day. Later that night, on September 30, Mama Wes got a call saying there had been a shootout at D-Ray's house on Ft. Worth Ave. The caller reported that D-Ray was wounded and another man was dead.

Chad rushed to St. Mary's Hospital, where he learned that the opposite was true. D-Ray, a 23-year-old father of four, was dead.*

Chad took the news hard, feeling that he'd failed his friend by not helping him in time. "Damn, one more day and he would've been out of here," he sighed. He got a cross with "in memory of my nigga D-Ray" tattooed on the inside of his right arm.

———————

UGK headed out to Killeen, Texas two months later for a show alongside a slew of opening acts who were all staying at the same hotel. A haze of marijuana smoke hung in the hallway and an irritated hotel guest called police to complain. As the headliner, UGK was the last act to leave for the venue. When police arrived, an officer knocked on the door to Chad's room, calling out, "What is that I smell, sir?"

In the story as Chad loved to tell it, he cracked the door open with the safety chain on and peeked out. "I don't know what you smell," he told the officer. "I know I'm eatin' beef jerky, so maybe that's what you smell."

Next door, Bun allowed officers to enter despite the pile of weed next to his bathroom sink. He was promptly handcuffed and carted off to jail. As Chad and Mama Wes tried to figure out what to do, the show promoter called apologizing, saying that a fight had broken out at the venue. Mama Wes agreed to reschedule, neglecting to mention Bun's arrest.**

"Damn, Mama, we got lucky on that one, didn't we," Chad laughed. "Hey, you got the paper?"

"I got the paper!" she smiled. After encountering one too many shiesty promoters, UGK now insisted that promoters bring payment to the hotel in advance. It certainly wasn't the first time a show had been cancelled due to fistfights, gunplay, or shiesty promoters who didn't have the rest of their money. "I used to go to all the UGK shows and [only] 50% of them would happen, literally," recalls journalist Matt Sonzala.

———————

Many Southern rappers had come to the same conclusion as Pimp C: major labels didn't

———

(*The other man, Frank Arceneaux, survived gunshot wounds in both legs. Damon Giron turned himself in the following day and confessed to D-Ray's murder. A psychiatrist was asked to evaluate his sanity. At trial it was suggested that he was legally insane and/or under the influence of drugs at the time of the shooting. In January 1999, he was sentenced to life in prison. On appeal, he was re-sentenced to 35 years. His scheduled release date is September 2032, but he became eligible for parole in April 2015.)

(**As Mama Wes recalls it, when the whole crew trekked to sleepy Belton, Texas, for Bun's July 1998 court date, Pops and DJ Bird discovered a brown paper bag in the courthouse restroom which contained nearly $800 in small bills. They used the proceeds for a hearty dinner on the drive back to Port Arthur. The marijuana charge resulted in Bun spending three days in jail and paying a small fine. Bun spent the three days reflecting on all the friends he'd lost to prison or the grave, resolving to "chill out from here on.")

take them as seriously as their East Coast counterparts, but maybe it didn't matter. Instead of trying to get a record deal, they focused on selling albums independently in their own region.

This mentality worked for Texas rappers because they had a solid distribution outlet. Southwest Wholesale's Robert Guillerman had initially been hesitant to branch off into distribution, but the success of UGK's *The Southern Way* – which brought Southwest a $50,000 profit in three short months – convinced him otherwise.

Other one-stops didn't have the time or patience to deal with upstart indie rap labels, which they considered a headache. But although Guillerman didn't like rap music, he was fascinated by the entrepreneurial spirit of the business. "These kids can make a [rap] record in their garage [and] succeed nationally … that is what is kind of exciting about it," he marvels.

Texas Monthly concluded that it was mostly Guillerman's "willingness to show prospective clients the ropes, giving them a packet that outlines such essentials as bar codes, packaging, and label identification" which helped Southwest grow into a distribution powerhouse throughout the mid-90s.

"The rap guys have a better sense of how to market than the other genres do," Guillerman told *Texas Monthly*. "They're willing to pour their profits back into promotion. They really are trying to do it themselves. There's a movement to not … sign with a big label. They've figured out the economics. If they're going to sell 20,000 units a major label is not going to be happy with that. But if they do it themselves, well, 20,000 units can be $150,000 in their pocket."

It wasn't hard to sell 20,000 units in Texas alone. "It's kinda like Texas is its own fuckin' country, man," Houston rapper Slim Thug said in *Houston Rap*. "This state so big, and there's so many cities in it, that we really don't have to go outside of Texas to be successful."

Independent labels also had an advantage because they were more agile. "James Prince [at Rap-A-Lot] can make a decision on a single for one of his artists today, and it'll be on the street next week. [At] a major label, it'd take a month just to make the decision and another month or two before it's in the stores," Destiny's Child manager Matthew Knowles told *Texas Monthly*.

Many of the Southwest-distributed rap albums had covers created by Pen & Pixel Graphics, a design company known for their over-the-top imagery: stacks of cash, sparkling diamonds, enormous Hummers, and big-booty females all crammed into outrageous compositions. Pen & Pixel was a direct spin-off from Rap-A-Lot, launched by brothers Aaron and Shawn Brauch, who had come down to Texas as part of the Cliff Blodget faction. (Prince bought Cliff Blodget out in 1993, and he and most of his friends departed the label. Doug King, still trying to recover after Byron Hill disappeared with all his equipment, also worked out of the Pen & Pixel offices.)

Like Southwest, Pen & Pixel assisted new artists with learning the business: how to get incorporated, how to write a business plan. Southwest even took things a step further, functioning almost like a major label. Once a client had established themselves – Gangsta N-I-P or Suave House, for example – Southwest often paid a six-figure advance in exchange for distribution rights. They had in-house publicists and paid for marketing and promotions at retail stores. Plus, Southwest didn't require exclusivity, so their artists were still free to sign lucrative major label deals.

There was now a clear blueprint for rap entrepreneurs to follow which hadn't existed prior to UGK. "Houston rappers couldn't beat the system, so they created their own," *Texas Monthly* noted.

At its height, Southwest Wholesale was distributing more than 1,500 independent labels (with creative names such as On The Run Records, Legal Dope Records, Stankface Records, Hung Jury Records, Limp-A-Lot Records, Mo' Cheez Records, Money Green Records, Inmate Records, and Verbally Diseased Records) and servicing more than 1,400 retail outlets nationwide, boasting record profits while their competitors were going bankrupt.

In a *Houston Business Journal* profile, Guillerman's partner Richard Powers credited the company's growth to their decision to distribute independent rap labels – a decision inspired, in part, by UGK.

DJ Screw's camp the Screwed Up Click was also experiencing tremendous growth. Aside from Lil Keke, the rapper showing the most potential from the SUC was Patrick "Fat Pat" Hawkins. With his deep baritone voice, charismatic stage presence, and the timing of a stand-up comedian, Fat Pat had become a local superstar. As his record "Tops Drop" exploded, hitting #5 on the *Billboard* rap charts, Fat Pat was poised to be the first from the SUC to break through on a national level.

Before rap, Pat was already known in Houston for a different type of hustle. "We were in the dope game, tryin' to feed our families," Screw admitted in *Murder Dog*. "But it ain't like what people think, out there robbin', jackin'. We weren't with that. Just hustlin', tryin' to make ends meet, feed our families."

One of Fat Pat's street counterparts was Kenneth "Weasel" Watson, a young and flashy Austin-based concert promoter who had just been released from prison on federal cocaine charges. Weasel came by Screw's house while Fat Pat was recording a tape called *It's All Good* to celebrate his 27th birthday. "Weasel in this

Have you seen Weasel?

Warrants have been filed for the murder of Patrick "Fat Pat" Hawkins in Houston, Texas 180th District Court for the arrest of Kenneth "Weasel" Watson

Black Male mid 20s 160 pounds 5'8" recently seen in the Houston and Austin, Texas areas.
A Second unidentified suspect is also wanted.
reward for any information leading to the arrest and conviction of Kenneth "Weasel" Watson and his accomplice is offered.
Please contact (713) 222-TIPS

Above: A flyer requesting information on **Fat Pat's alleged killer.** Courtesy of Wickett Crickett

bitch," Pat announced as Screw threw on the instrumental to Biggie's "Kick In The Door."

Shortly after that, in early January 1998, Fat Pat, DJ Screw and the SUC camp rolled out in a fleet of Suburbans and Expeditions to do a show at Dessau Music Hall in Austin. The show, a favor for Weasel, was seen as a good opportunity to promote Fat Pat's upcoming album *Ghetto Dreams*, which already had a huge buzz in the area.

Getting paid for shows was a new concept. "At that time we hadn't even put out an album yet, [our buzz] was strictly off of Screw tapes," says SUC rapper KayK of the group DEA. "We was still young, so somebody paying us to rap, that was something new to us."

At the show, DJ Screw kicked things off with the instrumental to Nas and Lauryn Hill's "If I Ruled the World (Imagine That)," for a Big Moe and ESG freestyle. Next up was Al-D, Shorty Mack, and A.C.T.; then DJ Screw threw on the instrumental to Biggie's "Juicy" as Fat Pat hit the stage, kicking his lyrics from "Body Rock." He ran through the rest of his hits: "3rd Coast," "Tops Drop," and "Jammin' Screw" to an enthusiastic crowd.

After a quick intermission for Screw to sell some tapes, Austin locals clamored for the mic during a free-for-all freestyle session. Once Fat Pat was back on stage, Screw dropped one of his favorite tracks, Whodini's "Friends." "I done flipped the game, put blades on a diesel / Got real live with my nigga fuckin' Weasel," Fat Pat rapped.

A few weeks after the Austin show, Screw opened Screwed-Up Records and Tapes on Houston's Cullen Blvd. Screw and Fat Pat were upset when they heard that Weasel was selling tapes of the show, which they'd done for free, without sharing the proceeds. "Come to find out the dude who we done the show with named Weasel video taped and audio taped the show without tellin' us," Screw told *Murder Dog*.*

(*Some have claimed that DJ Screw also sold grey Maxell tapes with audio from the Austin show labeled simply *THE CONCERT*. Allegedly, the tape was discontinued due to the unfortunate events which followed.)

When Screw confronted Weasel about selling tapes, he denied the accusation. "Don't mess with that cat," Screw told Fat Pat. "We got plenty more shows we can do."

Early on February 3, 1998, the day before Fat Pat's album *Ghetto Dreams* was scheduled to drop, Weasel called Pat to say that he had some money for him as compensation for the show. Shortly after noon, Fat Pat and his cousin Kenneth "Snoop" Franklin Jr. and two other friends pulled up to Weasel's girlfriend Casandra's apartment complex in southwest Houston. While the others waited in the car, Fat Pat went inside to meet with Weasel alone.*

Fifteen minutes later, Snoop spotted Weasel and another man running out of the complex. Already concerned because Pat had been gone so long, Snoop circled the parking lot and eventually called police. Firemen pried open the locked door to apartment 2409, where they found Fat Pat dead on the floor with four bullets in his body.

Word spread throughout the city, cell phones ringing with cries of, "They killed Pat! They killed P.A.T.!" Within an hour the apartment complex resembled a sorrowful block party, cars outfitted with "swangaz" circling slowly, bumping Fat Pat's Screw tape freestyles. Grown men sobbed openly; females huddled together for comfort.

As for motive, rumor held that Weasel had just been robbed and suspected Fat Pat of involvement. "[Weasel] was a flashy dude, liked to flash what he got," DJ Screw told *Murder Dog*. "Some kinda way he got robbed … [and] he thought Fat Pat had something to do with it."

Fat Pat's close friend Corey Blount sobbed uncontrollably on Lil Keke's shoulder as Pat was laid to rest on February 7, while unsympathetic federal agents snapped photos.**

On the north side of Houston, problems were brewing between Big Mike and Rap-A-Lot over finances and contract negotiations. Two weeks after Fat Pat's murder, bullets blasted through Big Mike's living room in the middle of the night. He believed Rap-A-Lot was responsible. After another altercation at a local nightclub, Mike decided to go on the offensive.

On the afternoon of February 19, 1998, Big Mike attempted to set fire to a Rap-A-Lot recording studio in northwest Houston, resulting in $5,000 worth of damage. He was arrested the following day for arson.***

Many assumed that Big Mike had been under the influence of drugs to attempt such a blatant crime, which he denies. "Just for the record, whatever happened [that day], I wasn't out of my mind, ya feel me?" he says. "I wasn't doing it for some kind of stupid reason … It was really self-defense, if you ask me."

While Texas rappers were making a lot of money independently, UGK still wasn't getting any royalty checks. Chad couldn't understand how it was possible that *Ridin' Dirty*, which had sold more than 500,000 units with practically no promotion, wasn't profitable. Mama Wes frequently debated Jive's Director of Royalties, Lenny SooHoo. In response to a set of complicated royalty statements, Mama Wes faxed a handwritten letter to Barry Weiss.

"I must tell you honestly… I have never in my entire life been more disappointed by anyone as I am with you at this moment," she wrote. "I received your fax and frankly, it was a damn insult. Please don't underestimate my intelligence anymore."

(*Kenneth "Weasel" Watson declined to be interviewed.)
(**Blount, two relatives, and six other people had already been named in a sealed federal indictment filed a month before Fat Pat's death. Blount was accused of masterminding a Continuing Criminal Enterprise, but friends say he was only guilty of being too flamboyant. "He never got caught with any drugs red-handed," SUC rapper Mike-D told *Houston Rap*. "It was the lifestyle he lived – everybody portrayed him as bein', you know, this big drug dealer, but really he was just … flashy, [living] that flashy life." Blount was convicted of CCE, which carries a mandatory life sentence. Several appeals were unsuccessful.)
(***A jury found Big Mike guilty and he was sentenced to seven years of probation and ordered to pay $7,000 in restitution. After his probation was revoked due to two minor arrests, he was sentenced to seven years in prison. He was paroled in April 2004 and released from parole in December 2007.)

Apparently, Weiss had made reference to Scarface when discussing the promotional costs that Jive recouped from UGK's sales revenue. "How in the world can you compare us to Scarface!!" Mama Wes wrote. "That was not even a sane comparison … Scarface has had … all kinds of promotion and videos too. When we were on tour with *Super Tight*, he was doing release parties with life size standups & posters at record stores + venues. We have never had that."

"Your royalty statement is a joke," she wrote. "I assure you that money that I see put out for promotion has not been spent to promote us … I do not want any more of our funds being spent … Let us pay for our studio time [and] our promotion, our everything. Just give us the money we are asking and we will bill you as you have billed us for the last (5) years."

"What I want to know is what will it take to get us off Jive," she finished. "Give me a price. I know that everyone has a price … What do you want to let us go?"

Chad was already tossing around the idea. According to Critical Condition's Merrick Young in Louisiana, there were tentative conversations about the possibility of him putting up $500,000 to buy UGK out of their Jive contract. Then, Merrick, who was a distant cousin of Master P's, planned to cut a deal with No Limit to release UGK's albums through their Priority distribution deal. "[We were] just flirting with the idea," Merrick says. "That boy wanted to be so free from Jive it was ridiculous."

The discussion came to an abrupt end when Merrick was arrested on federal drug charges. He was at the center of a major drug investigation titled Operation Rap Crack, due to his side ventures in the rap game. He was accused of running a Continuing Criminal Enterprise, a charge which carries a mandatory life sentence. Sixteen others, including his brother and several Critical Condition affiliates, were also charged.

In February 1998, Merrick was one of the first to plead guilty, agreeing to testify against his suppliers and co-defendants. While Merrick was in jail, he called Chad several times at Mama Wes' house. After one call, Chad hung up the phone, shaking his head. "Sound like that nigga trying to set somebody up," he remarked.

On April 2, less than two months after Merrick's plea agreement was reached, the FBI met with a confidential source in Lafayette, believed to be Merrick Young, who told them that Chad was a major drug trafficker in the Port Arthur area.* The source believed Chad had already "been indicted or arrested on Federal narcotics charges somewhere in Louisiana."**

Merrick became the government's star witness in at least three other trials. His original sentence of 292 months (more than 24 years) was reduced to 17.5 years in return for his testimony.*** His Houston-based drug supplier John Cotton was sentenced to life in prison and forfeited $12 million dollars in assets. In total, more than 50 people were convicted in connection with Operation Rap Crack.

After a year in Mableton Chad had decided it was time for something bigger; he and his girlfriend Sonji moved into a large red brick house on Bridlegate Way, around the corner from Greg Street. (Although it was commonly referred to as the "Stone Mountain house," it was technically located in the Atlanta suburb of Lithonia, now Snellville.)

Chad became even more reclusive at the Stone Mountain house, preferring to spend days

(*Large portions of the transcript from this FBI interrogation are redacted. The source's name is also redacted. The source is described as someone who began working with UGK in 1995, the same year Merrick recruited UGK to appear on Critical Condition's first album. Merrick acknowledges that he was being held in Lafayette Parish in April 1998, the time and place when the FBI interview took place. Merrick also acknowledges discussing Pimp C with the FBI, but says it was "just general protocol if you are under federal indictment" for agents to "go through your phone and ask about everybody." Merrick says he never had any illegal dealings with Pimp C and never considered him a drug trafficker. "Me and C, all the business we had done was music, 100% legit," he says.)

(**The idea that Chad was pulled over in Louisiana with drugs in the 90s but managed to somehow avoid prosecution seems to be a persistent but unverified rumor. FBI documents indicate that there was no record of Chad being arrested in Louisiana.)

(***In July 2008, when the federal government enacted new guidelines for crack cocaine offenses, Merrick's sentence was further reduced to 14 years. He was released from federal custody in August 2009 after serving 11.5 years.)

FEDERAL BUREAU OF INVESTIGATION

04/07/98

Date of transcription

In this manner he became associated with the
UNDERGROUND KINGS or UGK in 1995. UGK had been signed with JIVE
RECORDS and had nation wide connections to known groups, who were
introduced to _____ UGK consisted of two artists, CHAD BUTLER
aka PIMP C _____ During this time period
_____ The proceeds of which were concealed within the
record proceeds. _____ believes that CHAD BUTLER has been
indicted or arrested on Federal narcotics charges somewhere in
Louisiana.

CHAD BUTLER aka PIMP C of UGK dealt with _____
_____ in narcotics transactions in the Port
Arthur area of Texas. The prices paid for crack cocaine in Port
Arthur are comparable to the going price in Louisiana and higher
profits for Houston based distributors.

Investigation on 04/02/98 at Lafayette Parish La.

File # 92D-HO-31652-13   Date dictated 04/07/98

by _____

This document contains neither recommendations nor conclusions of the FBI. It is the property of the FBI and is loaned to your agency;
it and its contents are not to be distributed outside your agency.

Above: In 1998, **an FBI informant,** likely Merrick Young, alleged that Pimp C was a major cocaine trafficker.

or even weeks inside working on music. "If you live with Chad, you gon' be in the house," recalls Young Smitty, who stayed there frequently. "[But] the house is so entertaining."

Visitors stopped by often: Big Gipp, Erick Sermon, Queen Latifah. "I don't know if you wanna [write] this about the Queen, but the Queen smoked some kush with us," remembers Smitty. Regular mediocre weed, which Chad referred to as "swag," was not permitted in the house – only high-quality kush.

A caravan of Suburbans once pulled up, and Cash Money Records' CEO Birdman emerged. He and Chad talked business over plates of shrimp linguini and glasses of champagne while his up-and-coming group the Hot Boys wandered around the house. Juvenile, loud and boisterous, kept everyone entertained, while Lil Wayne sat quietly on the staircase.

Another aspiring artist who stopped by Chad's house with a demo tape was Atlanta radio personality Chris "Lova Lova" Bridges, who was reinventing himself as the rapper "Ludacris." Chad told him he was talented but he was rapping too fast. "Man, I like that shit," Pimp said. "But I'm gonna have to go and Screw this music and listen to it over again."

Other frequent visitors included Chad's friends from Nashville, Big Dog and Biz, whom he'd apparently introduced to a drug connect in Texas. Their couriers made regular trips to Texas, where they purchased kilograms of cocaine for $16,000 and transported them back to Atlanta or Nashville, where they could be resold for $23,000 - $27,000 at a hefty profit.

While the actual extent of Chad's involvement in these transactions is unclear, it was around this time that he started using cocaine. Many considered Biz a bad influence.

On one trip to Atlanta, Dog and Biz brought a teenage rapper named David "Young Buck" Brown, a high school dropout hustling dime bags of weed and crack cocaine on the Nashville streets. Biz thought Young Buck had potential and wanted Chad to help develop him as an artist. They hung out in Chad's garage smoking weed, where Bird threw on some beats for Young Buck to freestyle over. *This dude is cold!* Bird thought.

On the morning of June 15, 1998, Waymond "Big Dog" Fletcher was discovered dead at age 27 on a Nashville sidewalk with multiple gunshot wounds. Authorities suspected the shooting was drug-related. Chad memorialized his friend with a tattoo, a cross with the name "Big Dog" across it, on his left arm.*

The following day, June 16, would have been Tupac Shakur's 27th birthday. Chad had enacted a Tupac shrine at the Stone Mountain house, a glass table in the living room decorated with Tupac pictures and memorabilia.

Although Chad had never met Tupac personally, he admired him and had been deeply affected by his passing. "I don't want to say it was a fascination, but after Tupac died, [Chad] started thinking about mortality," Bun told the *Houston Chronicle*.

(*Nearly a decade later, on the XVII record "True Story," Pimp implied that Terrell "T" McMurry, a Nashville hustler and Lanika's ex-boyfriend, was responsible for Big Dog's murder. "The bitch killed Dog 'cause he was fuckin' his hoe / Same time, T was fuckin' Dog wife / Shot him in the back 'cause he's a bitch for life," Pimp rapped. The man actually charged with the murder was 21-year-old Kevin Perry, whose father lived at the apartment near the sidewalk where Big Dog was found. Perry was convicted on a lesser charge of voluntary manslaughter and sentenced to four years.)

CHAPTER 18

"Gimme thirty thousand and I'll serve you some heat /
I'll write your rhymes, sang the hook, and I'll make you a beat."
— Pimp C, UGK's "Life Is 2009"

"UGK and Pastor Troy were really strong influences on the way David Banner
represents the South. When Pimp C said, 'We don't do Hip-Hop music, we do
country rap tunes,' and when Pastor Troy said he ain't worried about the rest of
the world because as long as he's got [Georgia], he's cool; that kind of mentality
really changed the way that I do music. I had always felt that way in my heart;
but when Pimp C and Pastor Troy said it [it made sense]."
— David Banner, *OZONE* Magazine, January 2008

Wednesday, July 1, 1998
Jackson, Mississippi

Brad "Kamikaze" Franklin winced as the apartment door creaked shut, hoping the sound
didn't wake his girlfriend and two-year-old asleep in the early morning hours. He slung a duffle
bag over his shoulder and walked down the staircase to the dusty green Nissan idling below.

Inside the car, Lavell Crump nervously scanned the street behind him in the rearview
mirror, absentmindedly fingering the pistol resting on his grey sweatpants. Another pistol was
lodged under the driver's seat. He had been dreaming of fame, of a life beyond Mississippi, for as
long as he could remember. His *Real World* audition tape hadn't succeeded in landing him a spot
on MTV, but rap music had now captured his attention. He'd been up all night hovering over a
beat machine, and his face betrayed his exhaustion. He'd earned the nickname "David Banner"
for his propensity to transform instantly from mild-mannered Southern gentleman to raging
Incredible Hulk at any perceived threat.

They both knew there was a chance the rundown car wouldn't make it to Atlanta, but it was
their only option. They'd run both of their vehicles into the ground chasing their rap dreams,
hitting nightclubs and recording studios in nearby Birmingham, Mobile, Memphis, and New
Orleans. Banner's car had literally been through hell and high water, its coat of paint dull and
dirty after being submerged during flooding in Baton Rouge. Thieves had also broken into the
waterlogged four-door and stolen the stereo.

The six-hour trek from Jackson to Atlanta was routine for them, but this trip was special,
and Banner wasn't about to let some petty thievery ruin their road trip ritual. A notoriously
hazardous driver, he flattened the gas pedal and nudged the steering wheel with his knees up the
entrance ramp to I-20 as he leaned into the backseat, pressing "play" on a large square battery-
powered boombox.

"We listened to *Ridin' Dirty* the whole way to Atlanta," Kamikaze recalls. "That was one of
our favorite albums, UGK was one of our favorite groups, and that day was a dream come true.
We were going to Atlanta to work with Pimp C."

Banner and Kamikaze, who first met in 1995 during an impromptu freestyle session backstage at a DJ Quik concert, formed a duo called Crooked Lettaz in honor of their beloved state of Mississippi. In many ways their pairing reflected that of Pimp C and Bun B: Banner was the charismatic, soulful producer with a country twang, while Kamikaze delivered complicated, calculated wordplay.

Throughout history, Mississippi had always been associated with images of racism and poverty. In 1955, 14-year-old Emmett Till was brutally murdered in Mississippi for allegedly whistling at a white woman. The two white men who killed him bragged about the crime in a magazine interview after they were acquitted. The 1988 movie *Mississippi Burning* helped solidify the perception of Mississippi as a constant racial battleground.

Both men aimed to help Mississippi rise above its legacy of racial injustices and earn respect in the Hip-Hop world. "The South was going through [an] identity crisis," says Kamikaze. "Me and Banner always went into situations with a chip on our shoulder because we were from the South, because we were from Mississippi ... We felt like [we had] to prove ourselves."

Both men were intelligent and educated; Banner was elected SGA president at Southern University in Baton Rouge, while Kamikaze majored in Mass Communications at Jackson State. When Kamikaze graduated, he was one of only a handful of African-Americans who landed a coveted job writing for the Associated Press. But his heart wasn't in it. Stuck with the 4 PM to midnight shift, he spent most of his time utilizing the AP's resources – long distance calling, a FedEx account – as a cost-effective way to send out Crooked Lettaz' demos. "It was like having my own free Kinko's," he laughs.

At the time, few media outlets covered rap music. The only one that really mattered was *The Source* Magazine. Their column *Unsigned Hype* profiled a new Hip-Hop act every month and had helped Mobb Deep, DMX, and Common land record deals.

The Notorious B.I.G. was highlighted in the column in 1992, two years before he dominated the rap world with his 4x platinum debut album *Ready to Die*. It had been easy for him to get their attention. "Me and my DJ 50 Grand was in the basement makin' tapes. He was cutting back-to-back instrumentals and I was just rhyming over the top of 'em. I gave my tape to Matty C at *The Source* for their *Unsigned Hype* section," Biggie told *Represent* Magazine. "Matty met [Bad Boy's Sean] "Puffy" [Combs] in a club, gave him my tape and that's it."

Southern rappers didn't have those same luxuries; they weren't going to bump into influential magazine journalists or aspiring record executives at a local nightclub. When Banner suggested submitting their demo for *Unsigned Hype*, Kamikaze was skeptical. "Man, them cats ain't gonna feel what we're doing in the South," he argued. "We're from Mississippi. They're going to throw our demo in the trash."

It was true that *The Source,* launched by Harvard University roommates David Mays and Jon Shecter as a one-page newsletter in the late 1980s, had initially been consumed with East Coast rap. As the publication grew, new employees like music editor Reginald Dennis realized the importance of expanding their coverage nationwide.

The Source not only covered music, but also civil rights issues and current events that affected the Hip-Hop community. In 1994, a *Source* writer came down to Mississippi to do a story about a black man who had been lynched. While in the area, he was so impressed with the rising music scene that he profiled a local group called The Ragabumpkins for *Unsigned Hype* and began working on a larger piece about Mississippi rap.

Tensions were high at *The Source* offices due to co-owner Dave Mays' controversial relationship with Boston rapper Raymond "Benzino" Scott. Allegedly, Benzino had been furious when OutKast's debut was granted a 4.5 mic rating by the publication and threatened to start "puttin' niggas in bodybags" if his group The Almighty RSO didn't get at least 4.

The Source had a firm policy that if an artist threatened a staffer, they would no longer even be mentioned in the publication. When editors refused to cover The Almighty RSO, Dave slipped in a three-page story without telling them. Co-owner James Bernard faxed an open letter to Dave Mays to *The Source's* contact list, demanding that he resign from the publication.

"You violated basic tenets of objective journalism when you made a unilateral decision to place a three-page article about the group that you manage, the Almighty RSO, in the magazine," Bernard wrote. "You did this knowing full well that every editor on staff objects to giving coverage to a group whose leader has threatened to assault or kill at least two of our editors."

Instead of resigning, Dave Mays changed the locks at *The Source* office. The writer working on the Mississippi piece was one of many who departed with James Bernard, co-owner Jon Shecter, and music editor Reginald Dennis.* The story on The Ragabumpkins appeared in *Unsigned Hype*, but the piece on Mississippi rap would never run.

Despite the internal turmoil at *The Source,* aspiring rappers like Banner and Kamikaze still viewed an *Unsigned Hype* feature as the Holy Grail; getting noticed by *The Source* would surely lead to a record deal. One slow evening at the AP office, Kamikaze was brainstorming. *These cats at* The Source *get hundreds of faxes and demos every day,* he thought, wondering how he could catch their attention and make sure their demo didn't get tossed aside.

Finally, inspiration struck. He penned "CROOKED LETTAZ IS COMING!" on a blank sheet of paper in large block letters and called *The Source* and asked for their fax number. He faxed it more than 30 times over several days and then FedExed their demo, penning "CROOKED LETTAZ" all over the envelope.

He continued the fax campaign a dozen more times: "CROOKED LETTAZ DEMO WILL BE IN YOUR OFFICE TOMORROW. UNSIGNED HYPE!"

Eventually, a response came via fax. "Please stop faxing! We received your package."

When the June 1996 issue of *The Source* dropped, David Banner and Kamikaze (a.k.a. "MC Vel and Mr. Sho-Nuff") were featured in *Unsigned Hype*. Writer Selwyn Seyfu Hinds lauded them as "solid," "diverse," and "refreshing," quoting Banner's verse on "Questions": "So why y'all frontin' on the South / Come and get some / Ask your scared ass parents where you from."

Unsigned Hype led to features in other upstart magazines like *Beat Down* and *Rap Pages*. Eventually, Crooked Lettaz landed a record deal with Penalty Records. While recording their debut album, their A&R Greg "Mayhem" Taylor asked Banner who they wanted to work with. The answer was easy: Pimp C.

Penalty was located on the same block as Jive's New York offices, so Mayhem walked down the street to get a contact number for Pimp C. He was amused to find that the person on the other end of the line was his mother, quoting a $10,000 production fee.

David Banner, Kamikaze, and their A&R Mayhem exchanged nervous glances as they arrived at Chad's Stone Mountain house, unsure what to expect in such an intimate setting. They expected to go straight to work, but instead, Chad told them to make themselves at home and pulled out a gallon of Hennessy.

Apparently in a talkative mood, Chad started by sharing his unsolicited opinion on some recent albums. Banner and Kamikaze sat in rapt attention, hanging on every word. Chad loved to analyze other producers' work. "I see what he was trying to do, but he couldn't do it," Chad would say, demonstrating an improvised remix to the beat. "He almost got there."

"Y'all know that muthafucker 8Ball?" Chad asked abruptly, shooting them a sharp look. "That muthafucker's a hoe."

(*After the split Reginald Dennis and James Bernard launched *XXL* Magazine, *The Source's* main competitor.)

Kamikaze and David Banner hesitated. They glanced at each other, unsure what to say, but Chad continued without waiting for a response. "Well, I don't give a fuck if you *do* know that nigga. He *had* to be talking about me, because I'm the only cat from Texas that he know named C, and I was selling dope."

Chad had just heard 8Ball's solo album *Lost*, and was offended by the song "My Homeboys Girlfriend." It began:

> *My nigga C, he from Texas, I'm from Tennessee*
> *We do our thang, with them thangs, makin' currency*

8Ball's rhyme went on to tell the tale of meeting Angela, "the woman that was C's fiancé" who was "fine" and "dressed to kill." By the end of the second verse, his "homeboy's girlfriend" was cooking him an early morning breakfast "half-naked" and then she was:

> *All in my lap, on my early mornin' hard dick*
> *Grindin' on it, pullin' it, before I knew it, suckin' it*
> *Ended up fuckin' it*
> *I guess I'm a weak man*

Chad suspected 8Ball's record was a slug in his direction, but said he didn't want to retaliate until he was sure. 8Ball had come by the townhouse in Houston a few times, wolfing down an enormous plate of Mama Wes' homecooked Southern food. Chad continued ranting about all the "slick talk" and "sneak dissing" in the rap game, wondering why 8Ball had never said anything to him directly if a problem existed.*

Conversation turned to production. Fed up with Jive, Chad had turned his focus towards independent features and tracks. Chad shared one of his favorite analogies: record labels were pimps, and rappers were hoes.

Kamikaze got the impression that Pimp C was testing them, making sure he could connect with them before they worked together. Signaling that it was time to get to work, Pimp finally stood up. "You know what? Y'all some real ass niggas. I dig y'all." Kamikaze and Banner looked at each other; for Pimp C to label them a "real nigga" felt like the ultimate validation.

Mama Wes has observed this initiation process many times. Bun would do features for anyone who paid. But Chad liked to examine the artist first, and the vibe he got from them would determine how much effort he put into their project.

To Mama Wes, there was something different about these aspiring rappers. Not only were they intelligent and articulate, but it was something about the way they responded to Chad. They were *listening* to him; they looked up to him. *Daaaamn*, she thought. *What's up with that?*

As he settled in front of his Ensoniq ASR-10 sampling keyboard, Pimp explained that he'd recently gone to a Run-DMC show in Atlanta and left feeling inspired. He played the introductory rift from Run-DMC's "Rock Box" on his keyboard.**

"I don't know if we should use that. Didn't Tela just do it?" Banner said, referring to Memphis rapper Tela's record "Twisted."

"Don't even worry about that," Pimp assured them. "I'm gonna freak it. Nobody's even going to hear [the similarity]. Just trust me."

While toying with the beat, Pimp said he'd often heard people refer to UGK as the Run-DMC of the South. And as much as he loved the group, he couldn't accept the comparison.

(*Chad later confronted 8Ball, who said "My Homeboy's Girlfriend" was an invented story about a fictitious man named "C"; Chad accepted the denial and his temper cooled. He would later describe 8Ball & MJG as "one of the greatest groups of the South" in an *OZONE* interview. According to 8Ball's manager Duprano, the record was "a mixture of fiction and nonfiction," but the man 8Ball was actually referring to was strip club owner Phil Liase, who was later gunned down in his Bentley in Houston in 2013.)

(**Pimp C borrowed from Run-DMC for several other songs recorded around this time. He used a variation of Reverend Run's "There ain't enough room … first serve basis" line from "Sucker MC's" on UGK's "Take it Off," and adapted Run's "They got me rockin' on the microphone" on Too $hort's "All About It," rapping, "$hort got me rockin' on the microphone.")

"Nah, you can't compare me to DJ Run. He was first! He was the predecessor. They're the fore-fathers of rap music," Pimp said, as he transformed the "Rock Box" intro into a smooth, funky track titled "Get Crunk."

Mama Wes sent everyone off with a homecooked meal, the perfect end to a productive day.* Blasting the beat on the way back to their hotel with Pimp's words still marinating in their minds, Kamikaze and David Banner wrote their verses. While Kamikaze reflected on their small-town similarities ("It's like Pimp say, it's hatin' goin' on in P.A. / But shit, them same hatin' niggas is on them streets where I stay") Banner recapped Pimp's advice:

Sweet [James Jones] done analyzed the game, now he taught me the shit
I got some golds in my mouth, platinum game I spit
Pimp [C] done told me, "'Vell, these niggas ain't nothin' but hoes
You make most of your cheese off production and shows"

Back at the house, Mama Wes was cleaning up the kitchen when she heard Chad laugh out loud in the living room. "What the hell you laughing at?" she asked, poking her head into the next room.

Chad, lounging on the couch, gestured towards the TV where a commercial for Pruden-tial Insurance Company was playing. "When Prudential talks, everybody listens," the powerful voiceover intoned.

"That's the way they are. They listen when I talk," Chad laughed. Like Mama Wes, he'd been impressed by the admiration and respect in Crooked Lettaz' eyes. He still considered himself a newcomer, and an almost imperceptible switch had occurred: he was no longer just a student of the game, but a teacher.

"It was so many little milestones, so many little hills that you'd cross, and you'd [think], 'Damn, I never thought I'd see that happen,'" says Mama Wes. To her, this moment represented one of those small victories. "That was something that was real, real special to C, to see himself gain respect," she adds.

Crooked Lettaz and Pimp C met up at Doppler Studios the next day to record their vo-cals. Pimp laced the intro to "Get Crunk" with his trademark ad-libs, bragging on his "sixty-four dollar cologne, bitch."

By the end of the session, Banner felt like Pimp had warmed up to them. "Until he really knew you, he was Pimp C. It wasn't until he really got to know you and really trusted you that you'd meet Chad," Banner says.

"We were really green at the time," Banner adds, laughing. "He spent a couple days with us in Atlanta and really put us up on game. He really didn't have to do all that; he coulda just took our money."**

As the Crooked Lettaz session came to an end, Too $hort stopped by Doppler. $hort loved being in the studio with Pimp C. They made a good team; $hort would provide the weed and al-cohol and call some girls to create a party atmosphere, while Pimp directed the music. "Me, I go with the flow," Too $hort says. "He loved to bang on the machines and be in charge of the studio and orchestrate the session … I [liked] making songs with Chad because he was very adamant about how he wanted to structure the song."

(*Mayhem and Kamikaze don't remember Mama Wes being at the house when they came by. Mama Wes recalls watching Chad's interaction with a duo of intelligent young rappers, but isn't entirely sure that it was Crooked Lettaz.)
(**"Get Crunk" would prove to be the standout track on Crooked Lettaz' 1999 album Grey Skies, even though their label chose a different record as a single. "Get Crunk" spread regionally with no push and helped establish Crooked Lettaz throughout the South. Critics welcomed the project for its fresh new sound and substance. "A million wack Pimp Trick Gangster Click type albums will come out this year, but dope groups like Crooked Lettaz on independent labels will go un-heard and unnoticed, unless you do your service to the Hip-Hop nation and buy a copy of this album [and] play it LOUDLY every chance you get," concluded music critic Steve "Flash" Juon.)

Too $hort's decision to move to Atlanta had been what he considered a "career booster." Being in Atlanta put him in touch with people from all over the country and gave him the opportunity to collaborate with a lot of artists he might not have otherwise met: Lil Jon, Lil Kim, JT Money, Jazze Pha, Erick Sermon, and Redman. He'd picked up a lot of new recording techniques and ideas in his new environment; plus, Atlanta's strip clubs proved to be "the best goddamn A&R in the world," giving him insight into which records would work best in the clubs. In the same way, Chad's Atlanta move was opening up him up to a whole new world of possibilities.

Several of Too $hort and Pimp C's collaborations from the Atlanta years would land on soundtracks and other compilations, like "It's Alright" (from the *Dangerous Ground* soundtrack) and "Jus' a Playa" (from the *Obstacles* soundtrack). The two spent so much time together that they developed their own private jokes. They commonly greeted each other with a "smoke somethin'" in lieu of "what's up," and Pimp started ad-libbing it on his records as a shout-out to Too $hort.

"When I hear ['smoke somethin' on a Pimp C record] … it means something to me that I don't think it means to anybody else," Too $hort says.

Chad still harbored anger towards Big Tyme's Russell Washington, and one issue of contention involved an early 90s concert at Dallas water park Wet N Wild. The concert promoter, K-Rude, was a friend of Russell's, and Chad believed that K-Rude and Russell had collaborated to avoid paying UGK their proper fee.

K-Rude's investor was Ron Robinson, a Dallas hustler whose name carried weight in the streets. In the mid-90s, Ron was in talks with UGK's hype man Bo-Bo Luchiano about investing in his rap career. Bo-Bo arranged for Chad to come to town and do a beat with the understanding that Ron would pay for it. Ron booked him a room but never showed up to pay for the track, which would become Bo-Bo's record "Bitch Get Up Off Me."

In the summer of 1998, Chad was in Dallas for a show and called Bo-Bo the next day, asking him to come by the hotel room with some weed. Chad's recording equipment was laid out in a large suite, where Bo-Bo was shocked to see Ron Robinson, bobbing his head to the beat.

Chad, loud and boisterous, was ranting about K-Rude. "K-Rude down with them fuck boys," he said, referring to Big Tyme. "K-Rude a fuck boy too! He owe me money."

Ron looked uncomfortable. "Man, you can't just talk about my homeboy like that."

Chad ignored him. "Fuck him!"

Bo-Bo pulled Chad into the bedroom so they could talk privately. As soon as they were out of sight, Chad burst out laughing. "I got this nigga mad!" he chuckled.

"That's the dude who threw the concert at Wet N Wild with K-Rude," Bo-Bo told him quietly. "That's the dude that didn't pay you the money [for the] beat."

"I *know* that's K-Rude homeboy! That's why I been fuckin' with him about K-Rude all night!" Chad laughed. "He in there mad right now!"

Bo-Bo wasn't laughing; he'd known Ron since junior high school. Ron had worked for the U.S. postal service until his mail truck flipped over in a bad car accident; thanks to life-saving brain surgery, Ron now had a thick scar all the way from the back of his head to the front. Ever since the accident, Ron hadn't been quite the same. "C, leave that dude alone," Bo-Bo warned. "He crazy."

Again, Chad's business with Ron ended on a bad note. Unsure if he liked the beats, Ron wanted Chad to do a few more for him to choose from for the compilation album he was funding. They agreed to reconvene at a later time, but Chad was pissed off. He called Bo-Bo after Ron left, fuming. "I never had somebody tell me my beats wasn't jammin'! Ever!" Chad complained.

Legal proceedings for Big Tyme's lawsuit against UGK had dragged along slowly for years.

A week before the case was finally scheduled for trial, Bun and Chad halted the case by filing notice of bankruptcy. (It appears that they never actually followed through with the bankruptcy filing.)

Russell still kept in touch with Mama Wes even while their respective entities were in litigation. They were cordial enough that Russell paid UGK to appear on PSK-13's 1997 album *Born Bad?* Pimp produced the track, "Like Yesterday," which drew comparisons to "One Day."

By July 1998, Russell had racked up more than $85,000 in legal fees and decided it was useless to stay at war with Jive; they had deep enough pockets to stall him forever. Plus, he was tired of fighting. Without telling his attorney, Russell drove to Mama Wes' house in Port Arthur for a settlement negotiation with Bun and a Jive representative while Chad called in from Atlanta.

According to Russell, an agreement was reached in which Jive would cover $60,000 of his attorney's fees and pay him $35,000 cash. Russell had deliberately used samples from Jive artists like Too $hort and R. Kelly on Big Tyme projects over the years, knowing they wouldn't sue him because he could easily countersue. As part of the settlement agreement, Big Tyme would be released from any liability for those samples. UGK would also turn over six songs (four new songs and two remixes), which Russell could release on an album titled *Banned featuring UGK*.*

Russell's attorney, who didn't learn about the settlement until after the fact, considered it a terrible deal, but Russell was happy to be able to finally walk away from the whole ordeal with $35,000. He went to Atlanta to visit Chad, where they spent a week working on some music and finally squashed their personal issues over dinner. Like Mama Wes, Chad didn't believe Russell's actions had been malicious. "Mama, the boy had pussy in his eyes," Chad concluded.

"Russell's a good nigga, he just got fucked up," Chad told *Murder Dog*. "That money fucked him up. He'll get it back, [but] first he'll have to do some soul searchin though."

———————

UGK's friend Big Munn of the MDDL FNGZ, who had started traveling with the group as a security guard, had been sent to prison to serve a short sentence for drug charges from the early 90s. On the long bus ride to be processed for release, he heard the radio for the first time in months, where the local station kept playing a song with an annoyingly repetitive chorus: "*UGHHHHH*! Na Na Na Na!"

"What the fuck is this shit?" Munn thought aloud.

"That's Master P," someone told him. "Master P and that nigga Mystikal."

Master P? That dude who used to be sleeping on the couch at the San Jac house? Munn thought. *What the fuck went on while I was locked up… these niggas blew the fuck up?*

Master P and No Limit had indeed "blown the fuck up," thanks to Master P's work ethic and, in part, the Pimp C creations "Playaz From the South" and "Break 'Em Off Something." Master P had proven to be a genius at marketing and branding, using non-traditional, inexpensive marketing techniques and a simple formula to churn out albums.

"The [No Limit] tank wasn't just a logo, [Master P] really ran his company like an army," says Wendy Day, who helped No Limit negotiate an unprecedented distribution deal with Priority. "He was the General. He had Beats by the Pound cranking out hit after hit. All they did was stay in the studio and just crank out music … they were putting out a new record every six weeks. That was incredible. It was almost like an assembly line."

While UGK was only receiving around 7% of the sales revenue from Jive *after* all expenses were recouped, Master P's distribution deal with Priority allowed him to retain ownership of his masters *plus* 80% of the proceeds. Master P already had leverage because he was moving units in

(*Russell says he had 50,000 pre-orders for the album but UGK never turned in the songs. After their settlement agreement, he was offended by a UGK interview in *Murder Dog* where they discussed their departure from Big Tyme. Upset that the magazine hadn't reached out to get his side of the story, Russell mailed them a copy of the settlement agreement and complained that he had never received the songs as promised. *Murder Dog* printed his response.)

the streets, plus, Priority saw the deal as low-risk. "Priority didn't really see the value in owning his masters ... [they didn't think] his music would become classic," says Wendy Day.

In 1998, thanks to their assembly-line approach, No Limit released 23 albums; 15 of them went gold or platinum, bringing in revenue of more than $200 million. Master P, who had been sleeping on Pimp C's couch less than two years earlier, was now a multi-millionaire and a bonafide music mogul. Film companies were throwing millions at him to star and produce in new movies, thanks to the success of his independent films *I'm Bout It* and *I Got the Hook Up* (UGK was featured on both soundtracks). He was launching a sports agency and building a $7.8 million dollar studio complex, where he planned to enact a gold-plated tank at the entrance.

Chad and Master P had never really seen eye-to-eye, and Chad got the sense that success was changing him. "Once [Master P] popped [off] it was like he didn't know Chad no more," says Young Smitty. "Chad didn't respect that."

More importantly, Master P was getting the look that Chad felt UGK deserved. Master P's success was all the more impressive considering the fact that he wasn't a very good rapper, and other artists on the label, like his brother Vyshonne Miller a.k.a. "Silkk the Shocker," could barely even rap on beat.

When the New Black Panther Party needed funding for their Million Youth March, Hashim convinced Chad to arrange for him to meet with Master P. While the NBPP claimed the goal of the march was to demand free education and reparations for the youth, New York City's mayor Rudolph Giuliani considered the proposed event a "hate march" and denied their permit application. (The NBPP's national chairman Dr. Khallid Muhammad, who was organizing the march, called his former mentor Louis Farrakhan a "hypocrite" for allowing whites to attend the Million Man March.) A federal appeals court overturned Giuliani's ruling and the permit was granted.

According to Hashim, Master P donated $100,000 to cover the costs of the outdoor staging, lighting, and sound system, on the condition that his involvement with the controversial event would remain anonymous.* "If it wasn't for [Master P's donation] we couldn't have did the Million Youth March," says Hashim.**

Pimp C was featured on "I Miss My Homies," the lead single from Master P's 1997 album *Ghetto D*, which sold 761,000 the first week of its release. The video came on MTV one day when Pimp was at Too $hort's Dangerous Studios in Atlanta, working on a track called "All About It" for $hort's *Nationwide: Independence Day* compilation. Shot mostly with a fish-eye lens, the expensive video featured swooping shots of Master P walking alone through the desert seeing an angel; dressed in a white suit in front of a church full of people holding lit candles.

Pimp glared at the television. "Man, this is some bullshit. Them muthafuckers at Jive, they ain't respecting us," he complained. "This is how a muthafucker is *supposed* to be looking, man. We ain't gonna never go platinum until they give us a platinum look." It was hard for him to accept the fact that a mediocre rapper like Master P – spurred by his business savvy and marketing ingenuity – could get big-budget videos, while Jive seemed to be halfheartedly stringing UGK along on a shoestring budget.

(*The $100,000 figure was not confirmed by anyone in the No Limit camp. "Master P did make a sizable donation [so] that the march would become a reality," says Houston activist Quanell X, who was also involved with organizing the march.)
(**The Million Youth March took place in New York on September 5, 1998, and newspapers estimated that the 6,000 - 10,000 attendees were surrounded by 3,000 NYPD officers. Dr. Muhammad waited until 20 minutes before the march permit expired to approach the podium. As he surveyed the crowd and saw the heavy police presence - which included sharpshooters, a riot squad, and helicopters circling overhead - he instructed followers to "look these bastards in the eyes, and if anyone attacks you... beat the hell out of them... the no-good bastards! ... If they attack you, take their goddamn guns from them and use their guns on them!" Scuffles broke out as police aggressively forced the crowd to disperse, leaving 16 police officers and 12 attendees injured. As the *New York Times* reported it, Muhammad himself "vanished in a puff of anti-Semitic exhaust." A grand jury recommended that Muhammad should be formally charged with inciting a riot.)

CHAPTER 19

"I don't give a fuck if they don't like me on the East Coast. I don't give a damn if the record company don't like it. I don't give a fuck, and that's my attitude towards the game: If I don't eat, you ain't gonna eat off me."
– Pimp C, *OZONE* Magazine, April 2007

"I loved [Chad]. I thought he was an absolute madman, but I loved every fiber of his body. He had a rough exterior, but underneath it all, he had a big heart. [He] was really just a good person who was – as many artists are – just frustrated [trying] to get his voice heard." – Barry Weiss, former CEO, Jive Records

By the late 90s, UGK's relationship with Jive had deteriorated into one big tug-of-war. "C got vengeful and they did too," says Mama Wes. "They did as many rotten things to us as we did to them. That's a fact."

Chad refused to turn over any more songs to Jive until they paid him royalties he believed he was owed. Besides, he was making more money producing on the side. Like many artists, he'd grown to hate the music business, but still loved the music. "I never saw [his problems with Jive] affect his ability to create," says Joi Gilliam. "If anything, whatever frustrations he had, I would see him take it out on a track ... [that was] his redemption ... Just put it on wax."

Despite the popularity of *Ridin' Dirty*, UGK remained a mostly underground phenomenon. "[Since] we were [selling units] ... we didn't understand why the shit wasn't translating to magazines and TV," Bun recalls. There weren't many media outlets in Texas, and nationally, the only publication giving UGK significant coverage was *Murder Dog*.

Journalist Matt Sonzala knew UGK was a big deal in Texas, but didn't realize how far the music had spread until he started traveling as a freelance writer for *Murder Dog*, interviewing underground rappers in small towns all over the country. No matter where he went, the answer to one of his standard interview questions – "who are you influenced by?" – was *always* UGK. "It shocked me," Matt says. "UGK didn't have videos on MTV [or] songs on the radio."

But when Matt pitched the idea to do a story on UGK to an editor at a major New York-based Hip-Hop magazine, he was met with apathy. "Nobody cares about UGK," he was told.

UGK blamed their lack of media coverage on Jive's failure to promote them, which wasn't entirely fair. "UGK didn't always make it super easy for people to interview them, either," says Matt Sonzala.

"We were kinda mad at the media because nobody ever did anything on us, but then we realized we're kinda hard to find," Bun admitted, when asked by *Murder Dog's* editor Black Dog Bone why the group didn't do interviews. They'd never even realized they needed a publicist.

Another editor, Vanessa Satten at New York-based *XXL* Magazine, heard that Pimp C was difficult. She didn't understand why UGK wouldn't want the publicity. She reached out to Mama Wes, who told her that UGK would only do an interview if they were featured on the cover, a suggestion which Vanessa found outrageous. "[They were] too regional," she explains. Vanessa, accustomed to dealing with publicists who understood music business politics, felt out of her element trying to negotiate with a rapper's mother.

In a *Murder Dog* interview, Pimp explained his aversion to speaking to the media. "If we're gonna do an interview with somebody I would like it to be a magazine that will write what we really say and not twist it up," he said. "I feel like y'all gonna take what we got to say and bring it across to the people ... Magazines like *The Source* [are] supposed to be the voice of the street. But these labels can just go in there and buy 'em a four or a five [mic album review]. That shit ain't right. I think *Murder Dog* is real, 'cause you write what the artists really say."

For his part, Bun was tired of seeing the same "gumbo funk Southern fried" descriptions pigeonholing every Southern release. "I had never seen anything overly flattering about Southern artists [written] in the Hip-Hop media, so I had the attitude, like, 'They're probably gonna shit on us anyway, so I don't see the point in doing it,'" he recalls.

When they did get coverage, Bun was the spokesman on the group's behalf, and his intelligence earned them the attention of OGs like Public Enemy frontman Chuck D. "His statements and his interviews were really sharp," Chuck D told filmmaker Sama'an Ashrawi. "He was able to back up ... what they were doing lyrically and musically with some concise words."

One of UGK's biggest issues with Jive was their video shoot budgets, or lack thereof. "There just wasn't a respect for the [Southern] region or for the talent from the region," Bun told *The Source*. "They had all these excuses to not do anything for us and yet you had [other artists] who weren't selling half of what we were selling getting two or three videos." As Mama Wes recalls it, Barry Weiss told her that the Jive staff didn't think Chad and Bun were "video-friendly," a term which left her livid.

While other artists were getting $150,000 or $200,000 video budgets, Bun says Jive would only spend a paltry $50,000 or $60,000 on UGK, passing them off to unknown directors to shoot in less-than-ideal locations. The videos UGK envisioned, featuring luxury cars in exotic settings, cost more money than Jive was willing to spend.

In the past, UGK had agreed to shoot sub-standard videos with small budgets, like "Use Me Up," which only received minimal play. Outside of MTV and BET, there were few outlets where consumers could watch music videos, so it seemed pointless to shoot a video unless it would be up to major networks' quality standards.

UGK's first video with a substantial budget came when Jive placed their record "Take It Off" on the soundtrack to the movie *The Corruptor*. (Jive and New Line Cinema each contributed $50,000 for the video, which was shot in San Francisco's Chinatown with director Brian Luvar.) Bun, who was a film buff and a huge fan of *The Corruptor*'s director James Foley, was thrilled about the opportunity. Bun envisioned himself branching off into a future career writing screenplays, with Pimp acting and scoring the films.

Jive didn't need to spend a lot of money promoting UGK projects because the albums practically sold themselves, a fact which even Jive employees could sense. "They didn't have to say it, because you could see how much [more] attention was paid to other projects," says UGK's former A&R Joe Thomas. In his opinion, acts like KRS-One and A Tribe Called Quest were clearly a higher priority, and their budgets reflected it.

From a business perspective, Chad understood. "We sell 500,000 albums every time we drop and they don't have to spend any money on videos or promotion or anything," he told *OZONE*. "Our album [*Ridin' Dirty* almost] went platinum with no video. If you were a businessperson, would you let that go? Or would you try to hold onto it and capitalize off it? It's not personal, it's business."

"[Chad's beef with Jive] was always [about] money," says Jeff Sledge. "He didn't like the contract that they were under and he always felt like we should give them more money ... it was always a very adversarial relationship between him and Jive, always."

Frustrated that they still had never received a royalty check, during an interview with Houston radio station The Box, UGK told fans that they were broke because of the "crazy contract" they had with their record label and their former management. "You can perpetrate whatever kinda fraud you want on TV or in magazines, but the people in the street, you can't hide from them … We always told people we ain't rich," Bun told *Murder Dog*.

It wasn't exactly true that they were "broke." Their lifestyle had improved, actually, but all their money was coming from their shows and outside features and production, not from Jive. Still, their failure to educate themselves about the business had been part of the problem. "We knew exactly how to make music [but] we had no idea how to sell it and profit off of it," Bun told NPR. "So other people … ended up making a lot more money than we did off of our music."

"The game is to try to get all the music they can from you and then break your spirit at the same time before you learn the game," Bun told journalist Matt Sonzala. "That's the whole thing, to get as much music as they can up out you before you educate yourself about the business. And once you do educate yourself about the business, hopefully you're not viable anymore."

"A record company would love for every artist to be a one hit wonder," he continued. "They really would. They talk about nurturing artists and catalog and all that, but their dream would be to get a three million selling [debut] out of every artist they sign and then they would fall off and they could just drop them and then sign somebody else. That's their dream … that's why they want to sign [young teenagers], people who know less and less about the industry."

As UGK became more vocal about their issues with the label, Jive was understandably even less motivated to set up interviews for the group. Writers and editors who contacted the label were frequently rebuffed.

Jive staffers preferred dealing with Bun, who was clearly the group's voice of reason. "Chad didn't really have a sensible mind of reasoning of his own. He was very irrational," says Too $hort. Still, it was understood that at the end of the day, Chad was the one calling the shots.

"[With] Bun, I could at least have somewhat of a rational conversation," says Jeff Sledge. "[But] Bun would play the back[ground] a lot, 'cause Bun was a team player. Even if Bun didn't necessarily agree with some of Chad's actions – [sometimes] Chad would do something fucking looney tunes – I think Bun deep down always knew [that] one thing Chad was *not* was selfish … Even though he would be over the top and crazy sometimes and wrong sometimes, he was doing it for UGK. He wasn't doing it for himself."

Sometimes, it was intentional: Chad and Bun developed a good cop/bad cop routine when dealing with Jive. "Me and Pimp never walked into a room [for a] negotiation where we weren't on the same page," says Bun.

The approach was simple: Chad would rant, rave, curse, and make demands. Exasperated, the Jive reps would throw up their hands in frustration. "I can't talk to this guy," they'd mutter, and then turn to Bun, who would articulate Chad's basic sentiment in a far more calm, eloquent manner. It usually worked.

Chad made an exception on one occasion when Jive flew him to New York and were courting him for a project. They'd laid out a shrimp buffet for the noon meeting in an effort to impress him. Chad decided it was time to show his "intelligent side," and he spent the meeting sitting at the conference table calmly conversing with Barry Weiss and taking notes on a small notepad from his attaché case. Staffers, accustomed to him screaming and cussing, were awestruck. After they left, Chad joked that he'd "really yanked Barry's dick."

In a different meeting, Barry Weiss recalls a "very disgruntled" Chad demanding health care benefits. "I want a Jive Records Blue Cross/Blue Shield card. I wanna be on the medical plan!" Chad yelled.

Damn, that's a new one, Weiss thought. *I never heard an artist ask to be on the medical plan.*

"I'm an employee here," Chad reasoned. "I'm an artist, I'm an employee. If I'm an employee I should be getting benefits like the regular employees got. I got kids too."

"It was at that moment I just fell in love with this guy," Barry Weiss recalls. "He was such a character … but incredibly frustrating at the same time … I loved the dude. I thought he was an absolute madman, but I loved every fiber of his body. He had a rough exterior, but underneath it all, he had a big heart. [He] was really just a good person who was – as many artists are – just frustrated [trying] to get his voice heard."

UGK believed that most of their struggles with Jive were due to the label's lack of respect for acts outside of New York. "[Jive] never knew how popular Too $hort and UGK was," Too $hort told *Murder Dog*. "Living in New York it never sunk in … The way people would fall out if they saw me, Pimp C or Bun B [in the South or the West Coast] wouldn't happen in New York, so it never registered to them that they had a roster of mega stars."

Even when Jive did try to develop ideas for marketing and promotion, their ideas were met with skepticism by UGK. "They did not know how to market us … they didn't [have] the right personnel to know how to market a hardcore Southern rap group," says Mama Wes. "The success that UGK [had] … [was] basically us beating the pavement. We did it for ourselves."

Weiss dismisses the idea that UGK was discriminated against. "Every artist feels that they're never getting their just dessert, that they're never getting enough promotion and stuff put behind them," he says. "But we worked really hard on their records, and they weren't typical radio records, but they were culturally significant records."

With most artists, an A&R might give creative input, suggesting alterations to the music. But not with UGK. "[As an A&R,] you didn't [manage Chad creatively]," laughs Jeff Sledge. "You didn't. You couldn't do that with Chad."

Jeff Sledge appreciated dealing with Chad in that respect because he knew exactly how he wanted his music to sound. "The best rap artists [are] like that," Jeff says. "[Chad] was like that, $hort was definitely like that. These guys know their audience. Chad knew what people wanted from UGK."

Although UGK typically dealt with Jeff Sledge or Barry Weiss, the Senior VP of A&R at the label was Jeff Fenster. Fenster was not a fan of Southern rap and did not find Chad's artistic quirks endearing. Chad's conversations with Weiss or Fenster frequently devolved into cussing and screaming matches. While Weiss wasn't one to take such things personally, Fenster was, and often retaliated by refusing to take UGK's phone calls.

The geographic distance contributed to miscommunication; UGK didn't have the benefit of popping up at Jive's office for a face-to-face conversation or bumping into them at a local nightclub. And even when they did come to an agreement, the label didn't always follow through. "It's about proximity: out of sight, out of mind," Bun told NPR. "They'll tell me anything over the phone and then nothing happens 'cause I'm not in their face."

Frequently, these exchanges only hardened Chad's resolve. "I don't give a fuck if they don't like me on the East Coast," he told *OZONE*. "I don't give a damn if the record company don't like it. I don't give a fuck, and that's my attitude towards the game: If I don't eat, you ain't gonna eat off me."

UGK's acrimonious relationship with the label caused them to miss other opportunities, like the Sprite Voltron commercials. A marketing firm for the soda conglomerate polled Hip-Hop fans throughout the country asking who they would like to see appear in a commercial. In the South, UGK was the overwhelming response. (Artists selected from other regions included Common, Fat Joe, and Redman.) But when Sprite's marketing reps reached out to Jive, they were told that UGK was too hard to deal with and preferred to stay underground. Sprite filmed the commercial with the second choice, Goodie Mob, instead.*

With the success of OutKast and Goodie Mob, the Dungeon Family's Rico Wade had earned a reputation not only for his creativity but his business savvy. Tall, slim, and charismatic, Rico knew how to communicate with label executives. "Rico was the front [man]," says Sleepy Brown. "He was the voice [of the Organized Noize production team]. He would go into meet-

---

(*UGK would not learn about this slight until more than a decade later, when Bun happened to meet the former Sprite marketing representative.)

ings and [business] people loved Rico."

Chad was convinced they needed Rico on their team, someone who understood the business and could speak on their behalf. "You gotta talk to them people," Chad urged. "We just want somebody to be able to talk for us that don't sell us out."

Rico didn't know if he was worthy of the praise Chad was lavishing on him, and didn't think he could manage UGK properly while his hands were full with other projects.* But Chad wouldn't take no for an answer, sometimes calling Rico on three-way with Jive executives. "I couldn't turn him down," Rico laughs. "He Deebo'ed me. I couldn't *not* help; [he] was family."**

Although Rico ultimately declined to manage the group, he didn't mind sharing some advice and had a clear understanding of the issues between Jive and UGK. In his opinion, Jive was treating UGK as an independent label, but they weren't equipped to function as such. Most of the other artists on Jive outside of New York were self-contained entities, like E-40's Sick Wid It Records, which handled the bulk of their own marketing and promotions.

"[Jive] was treating them like they [were their] own company," explains Rico Wade. "[Jive] was treating them like businesspeople, [but] they were acting like amateurs [with] the business. That's why [Chad] wanted me involved ... Jive [would] just give them a lump sum [but do] no promotion, no videos, nothing, just [tell them], 'Here go some money; do everything yourself.' And they [weren't] organized."

The difference was that UGK had only received a small fraction of the amount E-40 had received for his label deal but they were still expected to function as an independent. From Rico's perspective, UGK's original Big Tyme deal was similar to the situation he'd placed OutKast in under L.A. Reid's Arista. In this analogy, Russell Washington was UGK's L.A. Reid, and Rico felt that the dissolution of the relationship with Russell – coupled with Russell's inexperience in the music business – was the major cause of UGK's problems.

Through their conversations with Rico Wade, Too $hort, E-40, Scarface, and J. Prince, UGK gained a much better understanding of publishing, publicity, and other aspects of the music business. In late 1998, they brought Wendy Day on board as a consultant to renegotiate a better deal with Jive.

Wendy, who had helped negotiate No Limit's distribution deal, had gained a reputation as a woman who could get things done. A white woman from the suburbs with a background in corporate marketing, Wendy understood how to communicate with record label executives but was also passionate about fighting for fairness on the artists' behalf. She'd formed the Rap Coalition on 1992, a non-profit "artist advocacy group" designed to prevent artists from being exploited. She'd become an expert at contract negotiation, often helping artists get out of bad contracts or renegotiate for better deals.

When Wendy first met UGK in the mid-90s while they both were in Ohio for a radio concert, Mama Wes instructed her to stop by Chad's hotel room. He greeted her at the door in nothing but a pair of plain grey boxer shorts and invited her to "come on in."

She hesitantly followed him in the room, nervously blurting out the fact that UGK's "Murder" and "Pinky Ring" were her two favorite songs. As if he'd known her forever, Chad, still in his boxers, casually shared some studio memories from their "Murder" session with N.O. Joe. Shocked that this perfect stranger was so open and accommodating, the moment would become what Wendy recalls as one of her "fondest Hip-Hop memories."

"It's always cool to meet your heroes, and nine times out of ten, they're assholes," Wendy

---

(*In 1997, Rico Wade had signed a $20 million dollar joint venture deal with Jimmy Iovine's Interscope Records to distribute Organized Noize Records. The deal eventually fell apart. Some say that most of the funds advanced were squandered on Kilo Ali, one of the label's first signings. Spiraling out of control due to drug addiction, Kilo Ali ended up in prison for arson and cocaine possession. Sleepy Brown used Interscope funds to fund his debut *The Vinyl Room*, which featured Pimp C, and released it himself when the label wasn't showing enough interest. As the story went, Jimmy Iovine was furious and cut off Organized Records' funding, and other projects like Lil Will's *Betta Days*, which also featured Pimp C, would never be released.)

(**A reference to Deebo, the neighborhood bully from the popular movie *Friday*.)

recalls. "He wasn't. And that just made it that much sweeter."

Wendy often saw blatantly unfair record label contracts, but in reviewing UGK's contract with Jive (which was so complicated she hired a lawyer to "translate" it), she felt that the label wasn't wholly at fault. "[UGK's] expectations were very unrealistic for a New York record label that was notoriously cheap to begin with," Wendy explains. "Jive just didn't spend money the way other labels did ... They thought that Jive would just open up the checkbook and let them spend millions of dollars without clocking where the money goes, [which is] really unrealistic."

"[Barry Weiss] is very savvy ... and he's great at what he does," adds Wendy. "But I could see where artists [would get frustrated with him because] he always made very sharp, astute business decisions ... [but] artists want unlimited spending."

Wendy also concurred with Rico Wade's assessment that Jive was treating them like an independent label, mostly because Jive didn't have the resources in the South to properly market the group. "[Jive's] artists [from outside New York] kinda had to fend for themselves," Wendy says. "[Too] $hort and E-40 were artists who delivered finished albums, got a check, and kept it moving... $hort was always Barry Weiss' favorite artist, because $hort understood business."

"[UGK] had a battle going with Jive," Too $hort says. "I never had that battle. Their battle was [that] they had other people in their business [and] they wanted to get their money right. They always felt they weren't getting the proper respect or the proper push."

"After speaking to people that worked for the label, I didn't think that the relationship could be repaired," Wendy recalls. "Everybody was kind of angry and bitter [at UGK] except for Jeff Sledge." She advised UGK that it would be best for them to leave the label. But Chad preferred to stay at Jive and asked Wendy to focus her efforts on trying to renegotiate a better deal.

Chad also wanted to start his own label, UGK Records, with distribution through Jive. As Chad originally envisioned it, UGK Records would be a partnership between Chad and Bun, designed to release UGK's own records. However, Bun had little interest in running a record label or developing new talent, so Chad suggested bringing in Big Gipp as his partner. Gipp would function as a figurehead to ease Chad's strained relationship with Jive.

Wendy put together a proposal and arranged to meet with Barry Weiss. Weiss, already impressed with her track record, was eager to get her involved with something at Jive.

Around January 1999, Wendy arrived at Chad's Manhattan hotel room the morning of the Jive meeting and was shocked to see singer R. Kelly's manager Barry Hankerson.* Wendy, who had heard nothing but negative things about Hankerson, considered him "the scourge of the music industry." She'd heard that R. Kelly, also a Jive artist, was preparing to fire Hankerson. Bringing him into the situation, she felt, would only make things worse.

Upset, Wendy pulled Chad to the side and asked why Barry Hankerson was there. As she recalls it, Chad said he'd borrowed a significant amount of money from Hankerson (around $30,000) and he was now acting as the group's manager.

Although Wendy felt that UGK could benefit from new management, she didn't think Barry Hankerson was the right one to fill that role. "I love [Mama] Wes, and I think she tried really hard [as UGK's manager], but I think that it was really hard to manage Pimp, just 'cause he's all over the place and he didn't really listen," says Wendy Day. "She was also not a veteran of the music industry. She was an outsider, a schoolteacher her whole life ... it was a really hard job, and she wasn't taken seriously. Some people took her seriously, but Jive sure didn't."

Unlike Wendy, UGK believed that bringing Hankerson into the situation would *help* their relationship with Jive. "We realized that it was going to be too long and complicated to try to break ties with Jive, so it was a matter of making the relationship work ... which is why we brought in Barry Hankerson," says Bun.

(*Hankerson parlayed his relationship with R. Kelly into a distribution deal for his label Blackground, which released a breakthrough debut album for his 15-year-old niece Aaliyah in 1994, selling three million copies. The same year, Aaliyah's age was allegedly falsified on a marriage certificate when she wed the 28-year-old R. Kelly; the marriage was later annulled.)

A heated discussion broke out in the hotel room. As Wendy recalls it, Hankerson announced that he was now acting as the group's manager, and they no longer wanted to renegotiate their deal with Jive. Wendy, who had spent months trying to renegotiate, was furious. "We had already discussed that months earlier and had [decided to] move forward with [renegotiating] the deal, so for him to come in at the eleventh hour really made us all look like assholes in the meeting," Wendy says.

During the meeting with Jive's Barry Weiss and Jeff Sledge, there was confusion on both sides of the table. Hankerson walked out halfway through, signaling that he was not interested in renegotiating anything. Barry Weiss threw his hands up. "Wow, this is … This is a circus. This is ridiculous," Weiss said, exasperated. "When you guys figure out what you want to do, call me. In fact, don't call me. Have a lawyer call me. Let's do this professionally."

"There was too many chefs in the pot," Bun admits. "[We] realized again, ultimately, we kind of had to start taking things into our own hand."

Wendy, who had come to consider Chad a friend, was livid because he didn't seem concerned that he'd wasted months of her time. A follow-up phone conversation turned into a screaming match. "Eat a dick," she snapped, and hung up.

UGK and Hankerson soon parted ways also. "His management style didn't mesh with UGK … his personality and Pimp's personality [clashed]," Bun says. "Both of them were very alpha males, and it's hard to have a situation when you got two alpha males trying to work together."

"I really think they should've listened to [Wendy Day] instead of Barry [Hankerson]," Mama Wes says in retrospect.

———————

Throughout all the behind-the-scenes drama, it had been years since *Ridin' Dirty,* and UGK fans were desperate for new material. Underground bootleg mixtapes of unknown origin, like *The Lost Tracks, Unreleased Trill Ass Shit,* and *Kingz 4 Life* began circulating; many assumed they were leaks of their next album.

During their *Ridin' Dirty* promo run, UGK met a Nashville DJ named C-Wiz who was a diehard fan of the group. They'd never seriously considered his pleas to do a UGK mixtape until they reached an impasse with Jive. It didn't look like they were going to come to an agreement anytime soon, so why not get some music out to the fans in the meantime?

C-Wiz was thrilled when Pimp C called to invite him to Atlanta. "As a big fan of UGK, to [get to] spend the night at Pimp C's house, that was amazing," he recalls. Pimp gave him tracks such as the a capella vocals from "Pocket Full of Stones" and "Murder," and a remix he'd produced for "One Day" which sampled Rodney O and Joe Cooley's "Everlasting Bass" and The Isley Brothers "Summer Breeze."

"Jive rejected it, man!" Pimp told him, of the "One Day" remix. "But you could have it, Wiz!" The only thing DJ C-Wiz really wanted that Pimp couldn't give him was the a capella and instrumental for "Break 'Em Off Something" – in fact, Pimp said it didn't exist.*

A month and a half later, DJ C-Wiz came back to Atlanta with the finished mixtape, his name plastered on the cover. He planned to give UGK the tape and let them distribute it, hoping it would raise his profile as a DJ.

"Naw, man, look, we gonna make some money off of this," Pimp told him. "[But] you need to take your name off it, because I don't want Jive to act a fool on you." Pimp suggested that UGK would pay to press up 5,000 copies; C-Wiz would keep 1,500, which he could sell hand-to-hand anywhere except Texas.

C-Wiz agreed, redesigning the cover with only a huge UGK logo and the words "TRILL AZZ MIXEZ" beneath it in stenciled yellow letters. The mixtape spread quickly throughout the South and Midwest. The fact that no one seemed to know where it came from only added to its

(*As DJ C-Wiz recalls it, Pimp C told him that they'd recorded the song using equipment purchased by Jive from the *Ridin' Dirty* budget and erased everything afterwards to eliminate the evidence.)

mystique; its scarcity and the fact that it wasn't easily available from major retailers only raised its demand. C-Wiz's blends of a capella UGK vocals with classic beats like Tupac's "Hail Mary" and Lil Keke's "Southside" helped set a new standard for underground mixtapes.

The standout track on *Trill Azz Mixez* was "Top Notch Hoes," which many fans thought was a new Pimp C solo record. DJs and music critics labeled it "the epitome of country rap tunes." But it was actually a combination of two records Pimp had done for independent artists. The hook, the beat, and the last verse were originally created for a Miami trio called 3re Tha Hardaway.* DJ C-Wiz combined this with two verses Pimp did for Patchwerk Recordings' artist Meen Green's record "Deep In The Game."

On "Deep In The Game," Pimp C took shots at Philadelphia Hip-Hop band The Roots. He believed their satirical video "What They Do," which featured actors filling in on the drums and guitar in place of actual musicians, was a Too $hort diss.

"[The Roots' video] was a diss to me and a bunch of other artists who were slapping a guitar player in the video," Too $hort says. "But in my case, it was totally on the [video] editor, it wasn't on the musician. I never had a fake guitar player. It was mostly Shortly B, he could play his ass off … we always had real musicians in the studio."

While $hort considered it merely a misunderstanding, Chad wasn't so quick to let it go. "I saw yo' video, nigga, sound like you dissing my friends," he rapped on "Deep In The Game."

Bun sighed, never eager to go to war with anyone. "Exactly! That's what it *'sounds'* like, you don't really know," Bun reminded him. Chad got more specific at the end of the verse, repeating the chorus to The Roots' "What They Do":

Bitch nigga get some nuts, bitch nigga say my name
We ain't got no time to be guessin' and playin' no pussy-ass games
'What they do, what they do,' niggas was corny as fuck
*You gets no play in that Texas, yo' shit don't bump in the trunk***

"He thought they were shooting at Too $hort … and you know how close they were. Pimp was always taking up other people's battles," Bun told journalist Maurice Garland. But the subliminal mention on the underground record apparently never became widespread enough to cause any damage. "[The Roots] probably never knew Pimp was dissing them," Bun theorizes.

Trill Azz Mixez was in short supply. UGK and DJ C-Wiz continued pressing up sets of 5,000 copies or more, which sold out quickly.*** "Everywhere we went, people wanted it," Bun said. "We'd never have enough copies of it." In total, DJ C-Wiz estimates they sold around 40,000 copies for at least $8 each, translating to a handsome profit for everyone involved, but more importantly, getting music out to the starving fans.

The success of the project seemed to surprise even Pimp C. "[DJ C-Wiz] helped us understand the scope of our spread," Bun says. "Doing that tape with him is the reason why we [started putting] the UGK logo big as hell on all of our CDs."

Jive wasn't bothered by the underground sales of *Trill Azz Mixez*; most likely, they were too busy to notice. Something else was happening at the label in the spring of 1999: Too $hort's eighth album *Can't Stay Away* was at number five on the charts, but topping that were two other Jive releases: the Backstreet Boys' *Millennium* and Britney Spears' debut *…Baby One More Time*.

(*3re Tha Hardaway's debut album *Undaconstruction*, released in 1999 on Dead Serious Records, included the original "Top Notch Hoes" and three other Pimp C beats: "Spooked," "Affiliation," and "Headcrack." The latter two beats were re-used with new verses on their 2001 album *D.S. Foundation*.)
(**On this song, Pimp also improvised the "pop ya pussy if you don't give a fuck" line from Crooked Lettaz' "Get Crunk" and rapped, "Fuck BET, 'cause they ain't down with the South." The BET diss was edited out of Meen Green's record "Deep In The Game" but left intact on the *Trill Azz Mixez* version of "Top Notch Hoes.")
(***Pimp had feared Jive would sue DJ C-Wiz if his name was on the tape, but promised he would make sure everyone knew who did it. Pimp kept his word, connecting C-Wiz with Three 6 Mafia. C-Wiz's 2003 collaboration with Project Pat, *The Appeal*, was one of the first mixtapes to chart on *Billboard*, selling more than 100,000 copies independently.)

They soon signed 'N Sync, another pop boy band molded after the Backstreet Boys.

The Backstreet Boys, Britney Spears, and 'N Sync would become the three best-selling acts in the label's history as Jive dominated the teen-pop era of the late 1990s. Their multi-platinum worldwide success transformed Jive's parent company Zomba into the most profitable record company in the world, with a reported $1 billion in sales and $300 million in profits.

Rap acts, even those which consistently sold well like Too $hort and UGK, couldn't compete. "[Jive] dropped us like pancakes after they got ahold of Britney [Spears], 'N Sync and [the] Backstreet Boys," Too $hort told the *San Francisco Chronicle*. "If you didn't sell a million copies the first week out, they didn't want to take your phone call."

"They turned a blind eye and a deaf ear on urban music at that time," agrees E-40. "That's when things started going down the drain for the urban department [at Jive]."

Too $hort couldn't understand why Jive wasn't taking advantage of this massive windfall to put marketing dollars behind their Hip-Hop acts. "They said 'fuck rap,'" he recalls. "It's amazing how you could be the hottest rap label one year and then end up with Britney Spears."

In the spring of 1999, after one particularly heated exchange with Jive, Mama Wes skimmed through the mail one morning at their Houston townhouse. In it was a 1099 IRS form for "miscellaneous income," several months past the January 31 deadline for tax reporting. In it, Jive Records' parent entity Zomba reported that they'd paid Chad Butler $10,990,034.00 in 1998.

Mama Wes stared at the form in disbelief and showed it to Pops. They were both stunned; there was no way Chad had received anywhere near a million dollars, and certainly not *eleven million*.* Pops joked that Chad was never going to believe them. They were already overdue for a trip to Atlanta, so they hit the road the following day. Chad skimmed over the offensive paperwork and laughed. "Mama, I can't even write that amount of money," he said, tossing it aside. "Hey, if they want the money, tell 'em come get it out my ass. Fuck it."

Math had never been Chad or Mama Wes' strength. Chad refused to write checks and had never even learned how to balance a checkbook. "He didn't want to keep up with his money because he didn't want to know when he didn't have none," laughs Mama Wes. The group was already behind in their tax reporting, since several years of paperwork and receipts had vanished in the hands of Byron Hill. Bun was having IRS problems, too. "[Byron Hill] withheld all of our legal paperwork as well as tax paperwork so we ended up in the red with the IRS, with no way to rectify it because he had all the receipts, all the paperwork," Bun said.

The incorrect tax form only compounded Chad's existing problems. The IRS, now incorrectly believing that Chad had made more than *eleven million dollars* in 1998, calculated that he now owed $4,707,341.00 in taxes on the fictitious income.

Mama Wes believed the culprit was Dan Zucker, Jive's Vice President of Business Affairs. "Dan didn't like C [and] he didn't like me," she says. "I can never prove this, but I think he intentionally did that fake [IRS form] … He only sent that to C, 'cause of course C was the hellraiser … I think that little muthafucker did that on purpose."

Mama Wes believed the erroneous tax form was intentional, because Bun had not received a similar form. Chad and Bun's payments from Jive were always equal, and payments could not be released to one of them without the other receiving the same amount. "[Since they were a] group … it has to be even at all times, otherwise it fucks up the accounting," explains Jeff Sledge.

Mama Wes confronted Barry Weiss about the IRS form. "I don't think Barry was aware [Dan Zucker] did it [until] I told him," she recalls. "I could tell because he was shocked … [but] Barry covered for him. I think I knew Barry well enough to know when he was covering – and bullshitting. He was covering for that little fucker."

(*Chad's actual income for 1998 was $177,219 of self-employment income, resulting in a tax liability of $61,092. Bun and Chad would both use the IRS drama as rhyme material in later records. "The IRS say I owe 'em nine million…. [took] my Mama shit, my grandmamma and daddy too," Chad later rapped on "Still Ridin' Dirty." On "The Story," Bun B rapped, "IRS hitting us with axes: Pimp, you owe seven figures, Bun, you owe six.")

CHAPTER 20

"[Chad] could do his best work when he was pissed off." — Mama Wes

———————

"[Pimp] C just had this [thing where] if he felt like you wasn't doing your people right … he had a problem towards you. He felt like [Master] P didn't do his people right … His lashing out was just when he felt people was being treated wrong. That was his pet peeve in life." — Merrick Young

Monday, April 12, 1999
Atlanta, Georgia

Chad, his girlfriend Sonji, and Hashim pulled up to Patchwerk Studios, a small yellow house near Georgia Tech.* They walked down the purple hallway lined with plaques from Usher and TLC, discussing *The Temptations,* a two-part mini-series which had recently aired on NBC.

Their engineer for the night, Dale "Rambro" Ramsey, was behind the console hooking up the DA-88 machines Chad requested for his session. Rambro, an older man with long dread-locks, looked younger than his 45 years. He'd signed to Motown when Chad was in kindergarten and contributed vocals to The Temptations' 1980 Christmas album. He'd landed at Patchwerk after touring Europe with 'N Sync.

"*Yeaaaah,* that David Ruffin, he uh, slapped Tammi Terrell," Chad chuckled in his distinctive drawl as they stepped in the studio.

Rambro, still behind the console, laughed out loud.

"Who in here?" Chad said sharply.

Rambro stood up so they could see him. "Rambro, your engineer for the night."

Chad's voice softened. "Why you was laughing?" he asked.

"It didn't happen like that for real," Rambro said.**

"How you know?" Chad asked.

"I used to play with The Temptations," Rambro said matter-of-factly.

"*You* used to play with The Temptations!?" Chad exclaimed in disbelief.

As the group departed the studio past midnight, Chad turned to Hashim. "That nigga Rambro? I want him on our team," he said. "Whatever it take. Get him."

Chad spent the next two nights at Patchwerk with Rambro, and later that week, asked if he could help pick out equipment for his home studio. (The Stone Mountain house had narrowly escaped tragedy when five-year-old Chad Jr. lit a large box of his father's shoes in the garage on fire and nearly burned down the house.) Chad had some basic studio equipment, like a Mackie console and some DA-88 digital eight-track recorders, set up in the living room.

As they rode out to the Guitar Center together, Chad laid out his creative vision. "He had all these crazy concepts … they were great, but [I'd] never heard a *rapper* talking like this," Ram-

---

(*The studio, originally launched by the Atlanta Falcons' Bob Whitfield in 1994 to help his friend Ras Kass' rap career, became a staple of Atlanta's music scene. Post-NFL, Bob Whitfield achieved pop culture notoriety when his ex-wife Sheree Whitfield appeared as a castmember on Bravo's hit reality TV show *The Real Housewives of Atlanta.*)

(**"A lot of [*The Temptations* movie] is true, [but] the timeline was a little off for entertainment value," says Rambro.)

bro recalls. "[I've] worked with people like Stevie Wonder, Earth Wind and Fire, Marvin Gaye, [and] The Temptations … and I hold everyone to that [artistic] standard and no one ever gets there [except] this kid Chad Butler."

At Rambro's suggestion, Chad picked up a Roland 16-track digital recorder and a few microphones. Chad was impressed with Rambro's background – he was not only an engineer and producer who could sing, but knew how to play the saxophone, flute, and synthesizer. "Man, I've been looking for you a long time," Chad told Rambro, explaining that he needed an Atlanta engineer.

UGK appeared on Master P's 1998 album *MP Da Last Don*, touted as his "retirement" album, which debuted at #1 on the *Billboard* charts and sold more than 3 million copies. By 1999, though, there were signs that the empire was starting to crumble.

For one, Master P had turned his attention away from No Limit and was instead focused on his dream of playing for an NBA team. (He tried out for the Charlotte Hornets and attended the Toronto Raptors' training camp, but was waived by both teams.) He was also shooting a pilot for an MTV show. With so many distractions, Master P was no longer accessible to No Limit artists, and any issues they had were relayed through a middleman, leading to plenty of miscommunication. "The artists were disgruntled," says Wendy Day. "Even C-Murder wanted to leave, and when your own brother wants to leave your label, it's kind of a sign that the end is near."

"[Master P] … didn't pay his artists properly," she adds. "He was sort of giving them trinkets. He would give them down payments for cars and houses but the guys couldn't really keep up the payments."

"That's all I ever heard people complain about [at No Limit] was that P didn't pay nobody," agrees Mystikal's photographer King Yella. "He'd always give them some upfront money [but not on the back-end]."*

"[Master P] controlled everything," Wendy Day adds. "Show money: it wasn't a Master P or a Fiend show, it was a No Limit show. So you'd have to book the entire camp to come through. He would get a chunk of money and then he would choose how that money was divided up. Because he was the biggest star, he would get the largest share of the income. Fiend might have the biggest hit record of the time, but Master P was still getting the biggest check from the show."

Among the disgruntled acts at the label was Beats by the Pound, the four-man production team responsible for over 800 No Limit songs.** Under their direction, No Limit had sold more than 50 million units (a staggering 26 million records in 1998 alone, more than any other rap label). And according to Beats by the Pound, they had never signed a contract.

Master P was trying to push Beats by the Pound into signing contracts, but KLC didn't like the terms. As No Limit artist Mr. Serv-On recalls it, Master P was on a speakerphone call with his attorney, not realizing that Beats by the Pound was also on the line. "[If] they don't wanna sign [the contract], fuck 'em!" P commented.

Needless to say, Beats by the Pound was offended – especially KLC, who was responsible for many of the label's biggest hits, like "Bout It, Bout It" and "Down 4 My Niggaz." Master P didn't apologize for the comment, and Beats by the Pound left, changing their name to the Medicine Men.

KLC felt that Master P had made a huge mistake by letting the production team go. "He knows in his heart that he needs us," KLC told Down-South.com. "I don't give a fuck how you put it. Once people get used to hearing [rappers] on certain [types of beats], that's what they expect … No Limit became bigger than just the artist or the company, it had a certain sound that people liked. Once you have that certain sound and people get accustom[ed] to hearing that

---

(*Anthony "Boz" Boswell, No Limit's Vice President of Operations, disagrees. "If you ask any artist on No Limit, one thing they can never say is that we ain't pay 'em," he says. "Everybody had houses and cars before they even put an album out.")
(**Master P considered Carlos "C-Los" Stephens, a producer who was working with No Limit artists Tre 8 and Skull Duggery, the unofficial fifth member of Beats by the Pound.)

shit, you can't fuckin' break it."*

An advertisement in the CD booklet for Mystikal's 1998 Jive album *Ghetto Fabulous* promised fans that UGK's *Dirty Money* album was coming on April 13, 1999. They'd now pushed the date back to November 1999 and time was running short to turn in the album, so Bun came to Atlanta over the summer of 1999 so they could record.

Bun and Chad rarely lived in the same city, and only saw each other when it was time for shows or recording sessions. "Pimp and I learned very early on that we were very different people and we didn't need to be around each other every day," Bun says. "All we were gonna do was argue, because we didn't have the same point of view about much of anything besides music."

Many understood that the distance was precisely the reason the group worked. "It's better when [a group isn't] friends [because] they become a team instead of having all the emotional baggage of friends," says Wendy Day. "Everybody has a job to do, and everybody's good at what they do, and they play their own roles, whereas with a friend, the lines are more blurred."

Jive decided to release "Pimpin' Ain't No Illusion" on vinyl as the lead single, and needed a record for the B side. UGK came up with "Belts to Match," which featured Young Smitty and Sonji singing on the hook.

During the "Belts to Match" session, Hashim reached out to a graphic designer and illustrator he'd met a few months earlier, Kevin "Mr. Soul" Harp, and invited him to come by the house. Mr. Soul's goal was to become the "creative savior of the music business," and, as a fan of UGK, the idea of being able to contribute to their movement was exhilarating. "[UGK was] at war with Jive and Pimp didn't wanna deliver no music," Mr. Soul recalls. "So a lot of [the designs] that we did was based on his concept of putting out his own music."

Byron Amos, who had been spending a lot of time with UGK serving as their driver, was also at the house. He traveled with them on the weekends for shows, but music was just a side gig – his focus was on non-profit organizations, plus, holding down his day job at the City Council.

It was past midnight by the time UGK wrapped "Belts to Match," which needed to get to Jive immediately to meet a deadline for inclusion on *The Wood* soundtrack. After a stop at local nightclub, Byron dropped everyone off at the Stone Mountain house. Chad asked him to take the DAT tape to the airport to be air-lifted same-day Delta Dash to Jive.

Byron headed down Rockbridge Rd.; by the time he hit the 285 freeway, it was past 5 AM, and he realized he hadn't slept in 24 hours. He started to doze off, jolted awake by the blaring horn of a tractor-trailer passing just inches from his window.

Byron slapped himself to wake up. *I dodged a bullet,* he thought, as he pulled off the Riverdale exit. *I need to wake up.*

He made it to Delta Dash and dropped off the precious cargo. As he turned back towards

(*Beats by the Pound's departure led directly to No Limit's demise. In October 2000, Beats by the Pound sued Master P. The same month, he signed an amended contract with Priority, giving them the right to acquire ownership of the No Limit catalog if they didn't recoup millions of dollars in advances. Beats by the Pound claimed they were owed more than $10 million dollars in royalties for their contributions to more than 30 No Limit albums, saying they only had a handshake agreement which entitled them to 50% of all royalties. No Limit countersued, claiming that Beats by the Pound was in breach of a contract which entitled them to less than 1% of the royalties. KLC claimed they had never signed any contracts and his alleged signature was a forgery. By March 2001, with the value of the No Limit brand plummeting, Priority calculated that they had overpaid No Limit more than *$47 million dollars* and exercised their option to retain ownership of the No Limit catalog, valued at $40 million. Beats by the Pound then sued Priority over copyright issues related to the catalog. No Limit litigation would drag on for over 10 years. It was finally determined that Beats by the Pound were the rightful owners of the No Limit catalog, which Master P had once considered his most valuable asset. "Those are the bank," Master P had once told *Fortune* of his masters. "If you don't own, then you are owned." Master P agreed to repay Priority for the millions in advances they had paid out; when he defaulted on the payment terms, a judgment was issued against him. As of April 2011, Master P was still indebted in the amount of $35,440,611.44 to Priority and other creditors. "Honestly … [we had] a five-year long run, and we basically monopolized the whole urban market and really changed the game," Mo B. Dick says of No Limit's collapse. "We had our run; it ran its course. In order for Hip-Hop to evolve, we had to move out the way. We could stay and point fingers [at each other] but I think ultimately … it just ran its course." Today, all four Beats by the Pound producers still receive royalty checks when No Limit songs are sampled. Kanye West's "Blood On The Leaves," for example, samples C-Murder's "Down For My Niggaz.")

his modest Mazda Millenia, he was stunned to see a deep gash across the side of the vehicle all the way from the front to the back wheel. His brush with death had been closer than he thought.

Aside from "Belts to Match," Chad refused to release full songs to Jive. "Snippet that shit, Ram," he'd say. "They ain't getting no whole songs from me. Just give 'em a little piece of it. Give 'em like fifty-nine seconds or something. Give 'em verse one and half of the hook."

Chad was upset that Jive wasn't giving him the resources he needed to bring his vision to life. Their pop acts had massive recording budgets, and Chad wanted access to the same caliber of musicians. While other Hip-Hop acts were mainly using samples, Chad wanted to expand his production into a whole orchestra with live strings and horns, which could easily total $30,000 - $70,000 per song.

Rambro reached out to Jive A&R Stephanie Tudor and tried to convince her to approve a bigger budget for UGK, reminding her that they'd done similar projects for R. Kelly. "Jive didn't wanna do that for UGK," Rambro says. "[Their attitude] was kinda like: 'You're not R. Kelly.'"

Meanwhile, 29-year-old Master P was being trailed by a *Fortune* Magazine reporter profiling him as "the most intriguing executive in the music business." *Fortune* estimated he was worth $361 million, naming him one of the 40 Richest Under 40.

Chad knew of Beats by the Pound's departure; he was still on good terms with C-Murder, Fiend, Mia X, and other No Limit artists who were on the verge of leaving the label. "C just had this [thing where] if he felt like you wasn't doing your people right, just in general, then he had a problem towards you," recalls Merrick Young. "He felt like P didn't do his people right."

Chad had an issue with Master P too, although the specific reason is unclear. There had been discussions about Master P using his connections at Priority to get UGK out of their Jive contract. But he was only willing to get UGK out of their deal if they would sign to No Limit, and Chad didn't want to sign to No Limit. (According to No Limit's Boz, they had done a similar deal when they bought Mystikal out of his Jive contract through Big Boy Records.)

Although Master P always paid UGK upfront, around $10,000 per track, there had been an agreement for P to purchase some equipment for Chad on the backend (either a drum machine or some DA-88 digital recorders) as additional compensation for "Break 'Em Off Something."

Chad also felt that he wasn't getting the recognition he deserved for his contributions.* Another point of contention was a record that UGK had done for No Limit (probably "Meal Ticket," featuring 8Ball & MJG, which appeared on the soundtrack for *I'm Bout It*) which Jive wanted to use on *Dirty Money,* but No Limit refused to release.

Chad was also irritated that Master P had kept his involvement with the Million Youth March a secret. Frustrated that P wasn't taking his calls, Chad stopped by the No Limit studio while he was in Baton Rouge, hoping to confront him about their issues and the money or equipment he believed he was owed. Chad was told that Master P wasn't there, but saw his wife bringing in a plate of food. Convinced that P was avoiding him, Chad was furious.

Chad finally got Master P on the phone while he was at Greg Street's radio show at Atlanta's V103. He put Master P on speakerphone and demanded to know why he hadn't sent the equipment as promised. "Man, I told you I'm playing basketball and I can't answer all yo' calls," Master P told him. "I'm busy, man!"

While cracks were forming in the No Limit empire, fellow Louisiana-based label Cash

---

(*Rumor held that Pimp C was upset because Master P added Beats by the Pound's name to the production credits on several songs, but according to Mo B. Dick, that is incorrect. "A lot of people speculate, who weren't there, and make theoretical assumptions … [but] that wasn't the case," Mo B. Dick says. According to Mo B. Dick, the credits were listed correctly: Mo B. Dick and Pimp C co-produced "Playaz From the South" and "Break 'Em Off," and Pimp collaborated with Beats by the Pound members KLC and Craig B on C-Murder's "Akickdoe!")

Money Records was vying for their spot. "Master P did something nobody's done in music out of New Orleans. He mastered it, and he got one of the best contracts ever, and he went all the way with it," notes UGK's road manager Hashim. "Master P made millions of dollars right out of them projects in New Orleans, and Baby and them [at Cash Money] watched it, and then they repeated what he did. And you can't be an icon and not expect to get followed, especially if it worked."

Like No Limit, Cash Money started out independent, churning out more than 30 records in six years and selling between 5,000 and 25,000 units of each. In August 1997, Penalty Records offered Cash Money a $75,000 deal for their artist Juvenile. They declined.

The brothers who owned the label, Bryan "Birdman" Williams (a.k.a. "Baby") and Ronald "Slim" Williams, heard about Wendy Day's involvement with the groundbreaking No Limit/Priority deal and asked her to negotiate a similar deal for them. Wendy helped them develop marketing strategies and began shopping them to major labels as they continued releasing successful indie projects from Juvenile, B.G., and the Hot Boys.

Rumors of No Limit's internal conflict was spreading. "Master P had gone off to play basketball and No Limit wasn't that strong," Wendy remembers. "The perception was they were falling off." Wendy used this perception to their advantage in her sales pitch.

"These guys [at Cash Money] are going to take the place of No Limit Records," Wendy boasted to major labels. "They're filling that lane, which is going to be wide open in a minute." Universal Records bit, signing Cash Money in March 1998 to an unprecedented distribution deal worth $30 million; magazines called it "the best deal in [the] history of black music." Cash Money would receive a $2 million dollar advance every year for three years and receive 80% of the revenue.*

Cash Money had three of the hottest singles of 1999, ushering in the so-called "bling bling" era of rap with Juvenile's "Back That Azz Up," the Hot Boys' "I Need A Hot Girl," and B.G.'s "Bling Bling." The label's co-owner Birdman formed a group called the Big Tymers with their in-house producer Mannie Fresh, which he told HipHopDX was modeled after UGK. "We followed them," Birdman said. "We looked up to Bun and Pimp. We formed our whole group around them niggas."

Hip-Hop was quickly becoming big business. Jay-Z's "Hard Knock Life" tour with DMX, Redman, and Method Man grossed $13.7 million in 1999. With Cash Money dominating the airwaves, a Houston-based promoter named Darryl "D.A." Austin reached out to them to organize an arena tour.

When Miami rapper JT Money pulled out as the opening act, Darryl called UGK. They readily agreed to join the tour, which would also feature Too $hort. UGK had done some shows with Darryl before, but Chad didn't particularly like him and would sometimes pretend to forget his name. "Hey, David!" he'd say, when Darryl called. "You don't have no work for a nigga? 'Cause you know you need to pay me!"

When Rambro came by the Stone Mountain house one evening, Chad told him they were heading out on the Cash Money tour in a week and wanted to make use of everything he'd learned touring with 'N Sync. "I know you was out there with them white boys, I know you know how to get that shit," Chad told him. "I need a bus, and I need pyrotechnics."

"*Next week*?!" Rambro laughed and shook his head. "None of that shit ain't gonna happen … You ain't getting no bus, and you ain't getting no pyrotechnics in a week … You have to have the fire marshall's [approval]. All that stuff has to be designed. You have to have a fire marshal

(*Wendy Day says she spent nine months working with Cash Money to secure their deal, but once they signed, refused to pay her percentage. She was forced to sue them and was evicted in the meantime. "I lost everything I owned, working with Cash Money. I don't even have a baby picture of myself anymore," she says, adding, "I don't think [Cash Money CEOs Birdman and Slim] are good human beings. But I think that they're great businessmen.")

license in every city."

"All I know is, you go to a concert and they be blowing up shit," Chad laughed. "I want that."

Rambro shook his head. "Ain't gonna happen on this tour."

"You gotta come on the road with us," Chad told him. "I want my music [during the show] to sound just like it does in the studio."

Rambro had already done more than his fair share of traveling. He'd just spent months touring Asia and Europe with 'N Sync and was happy to be at home with his family. He quoted Chad an astronomical daily rate, fully expecting he would decline.

Chad considered the figure. "*Shiiiit*, that's all you want?" he said.

Rambro thought fast. "Plus per diem," he added.

UGK's technical requirements were almost laughably simple: two speakers, three cordless mics, and a DAT player. Rambro agreed to come on the road as UGK's audio engineer to step up the sound quality of their live performances. UGK had also recruited Louisiana-based Demetrius "DJ Dolby D" Charles as their tour DJ.

DJ Bird had become Chad's dedicated personal assistant, a goofball with a boyish, selfless humility who would literally do everything Chad told him to do, to the extent that Chad sometimes had to clarify he was joking. ("If C told Bird to go climb up on top of the house and jump off, that's what he was gonna do," laughs Mama Wes.)

Bird was also the unofficial hoe wrangler; if a woman in the crowd caught Chad's eye, he'd shoot Bird a knowing glance. "Him and Bird was good at that. I think Bird and [Chad] had a connection," laughs Dolby D. "He'll tell Bird, 'Say Bird, grab her,' and he'll [bring] her [backstage]."

Hashim's recruits Byron Amos and Carlos "Lo" Moreland would serve as drivers/security on the tour, along with Big Munn of the MDDL FNGZ. And although Hashim was officially the tour manager, everyone knew Mama Wes was still the real backbone of the team. "We couldn't get Mama off the road," laughs Hashim.

Having Mama Wes on the road meant homecooked gumbo nearly every night, but it also created an additional security concern. "Anytime your mother's there and you're talking about rap [music, it's a security risk]," says Hashim. "But Mama was a soldier, and we understood it. She was just gonna take the risk."

While Chad Jr. was out of school during the summer he often came to shows, too; Chad brought a keyboard for him to play with to keep him busy. Traveling with both a rap group and a toddler presented unique challenges. On one occasion, Mama Wes walked in Chad's hotel room to find him smoking weed, as his young son bounced around the room in a hazy cloud of smoke.

Chad Jr. was unusually rambunctious the rest of the day, prompting Mama Wes to lay down the law. "Just don't do that," she told Chad. "That's where I draw the line. What they do when they're of age, okay. But don't smoke on them kids like that!"

The whole crew gathered in Houston for the opening night of the tour on July 2, 1999.* Darryl had slated Too $hort to perform before UGK, but Chad refused. "Hell naw, $hort is a legend," he said. "$hort don't open up for us. We open for him." After a short debate, it was decided that the lineup would be opener Ginuwine, UGK, Too $hort, and then Cash Money.

The Houston show at the Astro Arena went off without a hitch. But things got off to a bad start the next day when the truck carrying the sound equipment broke down en route to Dallas and arrived late. There had been an apparent miscommunication between Darryl and UGK on their Dallas set time. (Some thought Chad deliberately showed up late because he wanted to perform last; others believe Darryl gave them the wrong time to avoid paying their fee. "[Darryl] was acting like a broad that whole trip," says Big Munn.) Halfway through Too $hort's set, UGK hadn't even left the hotel yet.

(*Recollections are somewhat shaky as to the exact order in which these events occurred, and in which city. The confusion was probably compounded by the fact that the tour routing was changed several times in the weeks prior to the event. The dates listed here are from MTV News articles about the tour.)

By the time UGK finally arrived, Cash Money's set was ending with the last notes of "Back That Azz Up" and more than 5,000 fans were heading for the exits. Rambro, who had arrived separately and been waiting all night at the sound console with UGK's show DAT, was confused. He was climbing down when a voice boomed over the loudspeakers: "Don't leave your seats now. UGK's in the house!"

Rambro scrambled back to the console and turned on UGK's mics. "Young Pimp and Bun is in the *houuuuse*!" Pimp announced from backstage. With the opening notes of "Return," the mass exit came to a screeching halt. Fans reversed course, streaming back into the arena. "It all started with a 'Pimp C, bitch, so what the fuck is up?!" Pimp spat, making his grand appearance. The energy was palpable; the arena came to life.

The Cash Money crew turned back towards the stage, watching UGK's show in rapt attention. Mannie Fresh watched the crowd in amazement as UGK ran through tracks from *Ridin' Dirty*. *Damn, y'all following is so nuts*, he thought, admiring Pimp's arrogant swagger. "I've seen maybe 20 UGK performances, and every time the shit has been crazy. To hear a crowd know every song and every word, that's nuts to me," Mannie says.

Too $hort was also impressed with their growth. "Every time I'd see them, their show would get better and better," he told MTV News. "I just used to listen to their song selection and how they could take their fans [on a journey] … You're talking about a group that had no singles, that had no video, and they're ripping every crowd they see. The crowd knows every word … [and they're] loving every second of it."

The crowd of thousands was on their feet for UGK's entire 30-minute set, screaming along with every word to every song. No one was more stunned than Rambro, who was realizing for the first time how popular his new employer really was.

Rambro worried that UGK's Dallas performance might actually be *too* good: over three decades of touring with acts like The Isley Brothers, he'd learned that the opening act should never outshine the headliner. "They turned the whole place out," he says. "Their show was more well-received than Cash Money."

"In certain cities [the lineup] worked with Cash Money being the headliner, but [in] certain cities … [there] wasn't nothing left for them niggas to do when Bun and Pimp got off the stage," agrees Big Munn. "It was crazy."

As UGK headed to Mobile the following weekend, the tour promoter Darryl Austin got a call from Master P. He had previously done a huge show with Master P at the Compaq Center in Houston, and rumor held that he'd made a million dollars.

Master P was planning to kick off the No Limit Army Tour in August, featuring himself and Snoop Dogg as the headliners. Apparently, Master P had been hearing about UGK's impressive performance in Dallas and was upset that they were aligning themselves with his direct competitor.

Master P told Darryl to take UGK off the Cash Money tour, suggesting they could work together on the No Limit tour. It was more of an order than a suggestion. Mama Wes, who had been on the receiving end of calls like this, knew how Master P operated. "He just thought when he spoke, you were supposed to just jump," she recalls.

Darryl relayed the message to UGK that Master P wanted them off the tour. (It's unclear if they performed that night in Mobile.) The next morning, July 10, as they piled into their vehicles for the four hour drive to Birmingham, Chad was upset and emotional. He spent much of the trip wondering aloud why Master P was trying to take food out of their mouths. Didn't he know they had families to feed, too? He was making millions – why didn't he want UGK to eat?

That evening at the hotel in Birmingham, Mama Wes was busy cooking when Master P called. Since her hands were full, she put him on speakerphone. "I don't remember what [he was calling about, or] how it started," she says. "Master P is a pushy muthafucker, and he wanted C to do something."

When Mama Wes told him they'd have to see if they could work it out, P launched into a curse-filled rant. Rambro, who overheard the whole conversation, walked next door to Pimp's room and told him Master P was cursing at his mother.*

Mama Wes didn't like Master P's condescending tone, but she wasn't offended by his words. Pimp stormed into the room, furious. Mama Wes tried to calm her son down. "[P] wasn't really cursing [at] me, he was just cursing," she insisted.

When they headed out to Birmingham's Fairpark Arena for the show that night, Pimp was still sulking. After Eve and the Ruff Ryders and Too $hort performed, the opening notes of UGK's set rang out throughout the crowd of nearly 5,000 people.

"Ram, stop my muthafuckin' music!" Pimp declared as he took the stage. "Stop my mutha-fuckin' music!" Rambro cut off the show tape and a hush fell over the crowd.

"Yeah! What up, everybody!?" Pimp barked. "Y'all know that muthafuckin' Master P, that damn No Limit? That fuck nigga tried to cancel our show in Birmingham. He called my pro-moter and told him to take UGK and Cash Money off this damn Block 2 Block Tour and make it a No Limit tour!"

The crowd rumbled in surprise. "Now, this old ass nigga cussed my mama," Pimp contin-ued. "I feel like he takin' money out of my baby mouth. So all them hoe ass movies he made, all that hoe ass music he does, I want y'all to boycott that shit. Don't buy nothing else that Master P make. And on the count of three, I want y'all to say, 'FUCK NO LIMIT!'"**

The crowd didn't even hesitate. "When Pimp C talked, people listened," laughs Mama Wes. Adds Houston promoter Captain Jack, "When you got [so] many people that love you and love your music and [you've] got the power of the mic like [Pimp C] had, he could pretty much get the people to say anything."

"ONE! TWO! THREE!" Pimp yelled.

"FUCK NO LIMIT!" the crowd screamed.

"One more time!" Pimp encouraged. "ONE! TWO! THREE!"

"FUCK NO LIMIT!" the crowd screamed, even louder this time.

"When I say FUCK, you say Master P! FUCK!"

"MASTER P!"

"FUCK!"

"MASTER P!"

Bun attempted to continue on with their set as usual, saying nothing to cosign Pimp's state-ments about No Limit. But even though he didn't want war, he still supported his partner. "Ev-ery time I grabbed my nuts, [Bun] supported me," Pimp told *The Source*. "I used to be wrong sometimes. He'll tell me later, 'Man, you was trippin'.' But in front of muthafuckers, that nigga would ride with me."

The show was already running behind schedule and there was an 11 PM curfew. It was nearly 10:50 by the time Cash Money hit the stage for their hour-long set, wildly swinging towels to kick off the first song.

At 11 PM sharp, the fire marshal and an entourage of police officers pulled the plug on the whole production. The bass blaring from the huge speakers was quickly reduced to a faint muffle from the small on-stage monitors. As the lights flickered on and the crowd realized the show had abruptly come to an end, chairs started flying through the air and a full-on riot broke out. "Get your stuff! We're leaving!" Hashim yelled over the din, trying to round everyone up as people stampeded towards the exits.

As everyone rushed Pimp to the vehicles out back, Byron Amos spotted six-year-old Chad

(*"I regret that for the rest of my life, that I had that phone on speaker," Mama Wes laughs. Some people recall this speak-erphone conversation taking place before the Birmingham show, while others believe it took place the following night in Memphis. Mama Wes' recollection of the exact timeline is hazy. It seems likely that there may have been two separate conversations.)

(**Pimp C's on-stage rant about No Limit as described here is not a direct quote but rather paraphrased from others' recol-lections of the event.)

Jr. wandering into the crowd. Everyone had assumed the child, who normally stayed at the hotel during shows, was safe in the car or was in someone else's care.

Byron Amos ran after Chad Jr. and brought him back safely to Chad's hotel room. Relieved and impressed with Byron's extra effort, Chad joked that he was now willing to overlook the fact that his name was "Byron" and officially hired him as his security guard.

Master P, of course, heard about the Birmingham show. The following evening as UGK arrived in Memphis, there was another heated speakerphone conversation between Mama Wes and Master P. Apparently, P had called to find out why Pimp was dissing him. No Limit Vice President Tevester Scott was also on the line.

Everyone's hotel rooms were on the same floor and most had their doors propped open as they prepared to head out; as the heated conversation continued, the whole crew gathered in Mama Wes' room as Master P and Tevester blurted out threats. (Byron Amos recalls Tevester promising Pimp they'd "kill you and yo' mama" and Carlos Moreland believes Master P threatened to "put his foot up [Mama Wes'] ass.")

Pimp, who came in the room just in time to hear the tail end of the conversation, leaned in towards the phone. "Fuck you, nigga," he spat.

"That was the end of the peace negotiations," laughs Byron Amos. Instead of the scheduled performance at the Pyramid in Memphis, UGK drove back to Atlanta. Rumors spread that UGK had pulled out of the tour because Master P had a hundred people wearing No Limit shirts in the front row.

The following week, the Cash Money tour hit Shreveport, Louisiana.* Even though Louisiana was No Limit territory, UGK had a lot of support in the state. When Master P's "Break 'Em Off Something" came on, one of the last songs in UGK's set list, Chad instructed DJ Dolby D to bring the record to a screeching halt. "That's not that nigga's song," Pimp proclaimed. "That's *my* fuckin' song."

"*I* sold you that song. If it wasn't for me, you wouldn't have had no hits!" Pimp continued, addressing Master P. He announced that he was "taking [my] song back" and again led the crowd in a chant of "FUCK NO LIMIT! FUCK NO LIMIT!"

When they pulled up to the Cajun Dome in Lafayette the next night, a radio personality from the local station who happened to be wearing a No Limit t-shirt greeted them at the entrance. Security jumped out of UGK's van and pulled pistols on the man, who quickly backed away with a terrified look on his face.

"Who are you!?" Byron Amos barked. "You with No Limit!?"

"No! No!" the man insisted. "I'm with the radio station!"

Pimp, sullen and standoffish, stayed in the vehicle. Everyone knew he was in a mood and backed away to give him some space. Pimp had asked Carlos Moreland to get him a bulletproof vest. As Carlos remembers it, Pimp stripped off his shirt when it was time to go on stage and, wearing only the blue collared bulletproof vest, emerged yelling, "FUCK NO LIMIT! FUCK MASTER P!" to a stunned crowd.

Although the tour was initially slated to continue through the end of August with stops in more than 10 other cities, UGK came off the road and many of the dates were cancelled.

Rambro believed that "tour politics," not Master P, was ultimately responsible for UGK's removal. "If you're upstaging the headliners, you get kicked off the tour. That's the bottom line," Rambro says. "And it has nothing to do with the rivalry between the acts … it was no rivalry between UGK and Cash Money … it's just how the audience perceives an opening act. If they feel [the opening act is hotter than the headliner] you'd get dismissed."

(*The Block 2 Block tour was scheduled for Shreveport's Hirsch Memorial Coliseum on July 16. Some entourage members believe UGK's participation in the tour ended after Memphis the previous weekend, but others clearly recall the Shreveport show.)

Master P was not only fending off Cash Money's rise, but he had another challenger in Atlanta: up-and-coming rapper Micah Troy, better known as "Pastor Troy." Pastor Troy didn't know Master P; he'd simply selected him as a target because aiming at the biggest name in the rap game would help generate buzz for his own project. For the intro to his record "No Mo' Play in GA," Pastor Troy staged a fake phone call to the "No Limit Records studio" declaring war.

The gimmick worked; by the summer of 1999, "No Mo' Play in GA" was huge in Atlanta. When Pimp stopped by Atlanta's V103 for a radio interview with Greg Street, Pimp asked Greg to call Pastor Troy to come down to the station. Now that they had a common enemy, it only made sense for them to become allies.

"He was ready to bomb [on Master P]," recalls Pastor Troy. "We were just gonna make some music and vent our frustrations." Pimp wanted to feature Pastor Troy on his solo album for a Master P diss record called "You Ain't Pac."*

As Pastor Troy recalls it, Pimp took him out in the hallway at the radio station and played an audio recording of Mama Wes cussing out Master P, possibly from the Memphis call. In the call, Master P sounded as if he couldn't understand why Pimp was angry with him. "'Cause you ain't *real*, P! You got to be fair, P!" Mama Wes snapped. "You got to look in the mirror. You know you ain't *real*, you don't sell no drugs! You know you ain't no real [drug dealer] … You need to stop lying to these damn people!"

Pastor Troy and Pimp shared a good laugh over the recording. "Mama was just outtalking [Master P]," Pastor Troy recalls. "She [was] just going off." Although Pastor Troy had no real problem with Master P, he understood why Pimp did. From his perspective, Pimp's contributions to No Limit had been an essential part of their success.

"Behind the scenes… this [rap] shit here, it's a real sensitive game," Pastor Troy explains. "People just wanna be treated with respect. Don't give me $10,000 and make a *million* dollars off of me, ya feel me? That shit might make somebody mad."

UGK was back in Dallas on August 22 to perform at the outdoor Hot Fest '99 alongside Too $hort and the Geto Boys (and, as the *Dallas Morning News* reported, an opening act from Atlanta called "Little Johnny and the Eastside Boys"). The following day, Chad made arrangements to meet Bo-Bo Luchiano and Ron Robinson at a studio in North Dallas to finish up the beats he'd agreed to redo.**

From the lobby, the studio parking lot was visible through a large window. Chad watched as another car pulled up; the man who stepped out was K-Rude, the Dallas promoter who owed him money. Furious, Chad turned to Ron. "Man, you done invited [K-Rude]? I'm supposed to be working for *you*, and you bring a dude that you know I'm into it with?"

As K-Rude stormed out of the car, cursing, Chad left.

The following night, Chad met up with Bo-Bo at a different studio called The Kitchen to finish Bo-Bo's record "Bitch Get Up Off Me." Ron Robinson showed up uninvited and told Chad he needed to talk to him.

"I'm not finna talk to you about nothing," Chad snapped. "The shit is over. You put my life in danger by bringing K-Rude to the studio. I'm over here working for *you*!"

(*Pimp also planned to collaborate with Bun B and Three 6 Mafia for a record called "Break 'Em Off 2002," which likely would have included some shots at Master P. "Break 'Em Off 2002" and the "You Ain't Pac" record with Pastor Troy never materialized, but Pastor Troy did end up in the studio with Pimp C and Too $hort to collaborate on E-40's record "Doin' the Fool." Looking around the studio at the rap legends, Pastor Troy recalls, was the first time he realized he was a "muthafuckin' real rapper.")

(**Bo-Bo believes this incident happened around this timeframe but it is not clear if it was while Chad was in town for the Hot Fest or a different event.)

As they argued, Biz, who had been traveling with Chad acting as security, stepped into the small restroom to the left of the studio entrance. The sound of a Mac-11 machine gun being cocked back echoed off the bathroom's square porcelain tiles and resonated throughout the studio. Everyone glanced at each other uneasily.

Ron threw his hands up. "Oh, aiiight," he said, retreating backwards. "Aiight."

An uneasy feeling washed over Bo-Bo as Ron departed. He glanced around the room. "Listen, let's go home," Bo-Bo insisted. "Let's leave. Right now."

The studio owner J.P. agreed. "Yeah, man, that dude is crazy," J.P. nodded. "Y'all need to just leave, because he ain't finna take that lightly. You cocking a *gun* on him?!?"

Everyone rushed outside and piled into the Navigator. Bo-Bo was in such a hurry he hopped a curb while exiting the parking lot. As they sped down the street, an old-school big-body Benz crept by, heading slowly towards the studio with its lights off, presumably preparing for a shoot-out. Bo-Bo slammed down the gas pedal.

A few days later, Chad called Bo-Bo. "Man, this dude done sent a hitman down here to kill me!" he reported. "He went to go ask J. [Prince] for permission to kill me, and Lil' J an' them kidnapped the dude."

Apparently, Ron Robinson had hired a Houston-based hitman to kill Chad. Out of respect for Prince, the hitman reached out to him first requesting permission. Prince explained that he had business in progress with Chad and wasn't going to let someone mess up his money.

"J. was like, 'Hell naw. Who paid you to do that? Get that nigga on the phone,'" Pimp told *The Source*. "J. told [Ron Robinson], 'Get over here and talk to me. If you ain't here by this time, I don't wanna talk no more.'" Prince brought the three men together for a sit-down and brokered a peace treaty between Ron, Chad, and the would-be hitman.

There was one upside to all the turmoil with No Limit and Ron Robinson: it inspired Chad to record. "I liked it 'cause the music was so *angry*," recalls DJ Dolby D. "*Angry* songs, and they was *jammin'*, man."

"He could do his best work when he was pissed off," agrees Mama Wes. Many of the diss records recorded during this timeframe, including a collaboration with Beats by the Pound airing out their own issues with No Limit, would never be released. But Pimp immortalized the Ron Robinson drama on a track called "Play Hard":*

I went to Dallas and some bitches tried to test me
But my nuts too big to let a pussy nigga check me
[...] I told you, nigga, I don't fuck with no K-Rude
When I was young that nigga fucked me out some paper, dude
But to call him to the studio, that was the cross
But bitch, you almost got your homeboy broke off
[...] The next night I'm at The Kitchen makin' hits and ends
I see some niggas drivin' funny in a square-like Benz
And showin' up it was the bitch that put me in the cross
The first line in my mind was to pick him off
I said, "Fuck him, let's don't do him yet, let's let him talk"
But if that bitch go for his pistol, we gon' kill him off
I told that girl it's Rap-A-Lot Mafia life, bitch
And whatever you try, it's gonna be repercussions and consequence
[...] Yo' niggas weak so you called Houston for the hit

(*"Play Hard" wasn't released until several years later on Lil Boosie and Webbie's 2003 album *Ghetto Stories*, with the shit-talking outro removed. It was also included on Pimp's 2005 album *The Sweet James Jones Stories* under the alternate title "I Know U Strapped.")

But didn't know that we got gangsta niggas all over this bitch
So now you bitches got to deal with the King [J. Prince], hoe
'Cause you done crossed me three times, we just can't let that go

Although most fans thought the entire record was a No Limit diss, Chad didn't reference Master P until the last four bars:

And to that phony Tupac that threatened my precious Mama
You a bitch for life, you gonna feel the drama
They gon' be flying you to the center for the gunshot trauma
You can get hit in your Bentley or your purple Impala (bitch)

"Fuck No Limit Records!" he added on the outro. "You can eat a dick, ol' Tupac wannabe-ass nigga. Grave-stealin' ass nigga. Get yo' brains blew out on your dashboard, bitch. You ain't no gangsta, nigga. You a bitch … You should've known not to fuck with me."

Above: A portion of Pimp C's handwritten lyrics from **"Hogg in the Game,"** another record from the late 90s in which he dissed Master P: "Bitch you ain't had a hit since I sold you 'Break 'Em Off.'"
Courtesy of Weslyn Monroe

CHAPTER 21

"I really wrote [my verse on 'Big Pimpin"] being sarcastic. [I thought,] if this is gonna be the biggest song of my career I'm finna talk about sippin' syrup, I'm finna talk about everything we do [in Texas]: grippin' the grain [and] choppin' on blades." — Pimp C, HoustonSoReal, March 2005

"It was like a fuckin' act of Congress to get that nigga to rap on that goddamn song." — Big Munn

DJ Bird, flipping through a rap magazine at a Houston barbershop, came across an interview which quoted Jay-Z saying that UGK was one of his favorite groups. Bird showed the magazine to Chad, who was next to him getting a cut. "Dang, C, Jay-Z cutting for us, man," Bird marveled. "Man, that's an honor."

Even though Jay-Z was arguably the biggest pop star in the world, Chad wasn't too impressed. He'd known for years that they were on Jay-Z's radar. In the mid-90s, UGK's A&R, Joe Thomas, told Chad that an up-and-coming music executive named Irv Gotti told him that Jay-Z liked UGK. Chad merely nodded. "That's cool."

While many New York rappers were apathetic to music from outside their region, Jay-Z sought out material from groups like UGK, the Geto Boys, and The Convicts. Jive's Jeff Sledge frequently fielded phone calls from Jay-Z's assistant. "Yo, I lost the *Ridin' Dirty* album," Jay would say as he came on the line. "Can you just messenger me over another one? I need it for my car."

"Jay-Z is a massive UGK fan," says Jeff Sledge. "He knew [their albums] backwards and forwards. Like, he was a *fan* fan."

While recording his 1997 album *In My Lifetime, Vol. 1*, Jay-Z tried to recruit Scarface to drop a verse on "Real Niggaz." When Scarface didn't jump on the opportunity, Jay-Z got in touch with Too $hort instead. On the follow-up, 1998's *Vol. 2... Hard Knock Life*, Jay-Z asked Too $hort to do the hook for "A Week Ago." He also wanted Pimp C to drop a verse.

Too $hort had been trying to get both Scarface and Pimp C to come up to New York; he recognized that New York rappers were opening up to the idea of working with artists from the rest of the country, and he was regularly picking up $30,000, $40,000, or even $50,000 checks for features. He wanted his friends to have those same opportunities, but trying to convince them, he says, was "like punching brick walls."

When Too $hort reached out to Pimp C with the opportunity to drop a verse on "A Week Ago," the rap world was embroiled in the East Coast/West Coast battle. The Notorious B.I.G. had just been gunned down in Los Angeles less than a year earlier, in an unsolved murder rumored to be retaliation for the murder of Tupac Shakur.

"I ain't workin' with nobody that don't fuck with Tupac," Pimp told Too $hort. "That nigga [Jay-Z] don't fuck with Tupac. Fuck anybody who ever said 'Fuck Tupac.' Fuck 'em."

The fact that Jay-Z had never actually said "fuck Tupac" was a moot point; he was affiliated with Biggie, affiliated with the East Coast, and that was enough for Pimp. As Too $hort recalls it, Pimp had done a "six degrees of separation" and calculated that "Jay-Z was connected to the 'Fuck Tupac' movement some kinda way." Not wanting to be the bearer of bad news, Too $hort apparently never relayed these sentiments back to Jay-Z

In Atlanta, Chad was working with Melvin "Big Mel" Vernell Jr., a Baton Rouge-based entrepreneur hoping to start a record label called Trill Entertainment. "They were buying production from me, and they came to me and offered me a piece of the company," Chad told *OZONE*. "I would've been a fool not to take it." Young Smitty would be their first artist.

In September 1999, Chad packed up his studio equipment and headed back to Houston, apparently tired of the Stone Mountain house. (He didn't bother telling anyone his plans, and when Mama Wes asked Byron Amos to move the furniture out, the power had been off for two weeks leaving a refrigerator full of spoiled food.) He stopped at Mel's house in Baton Rouge to spend a week recording Smitty along with Dallas-bred producer Steve Below, who impressed Chad enough to earn exclusive training on his secret weapon, the Roland R-8 drum machine.

But with the album nearly complete, Smitty backed out of the record deal, apparently because they weren't seeing eye-to-eye on the financial terms. Smitty says he was concerned about Trill Entertainment's "shaky infrastructure."

While Chad's initial instinct was to try to hold onto his artist, a conversation with J. Prince gave him a new perspective. Prince explained that if a woman tried to leave him, he'd simply let her go. "When a bitch leave me to be with another nigga, her value goes down, know what I'm saying?" Prince told him.

To Chad, the analogy made perfect sense. "When a nigga wanna go, I'm gonna let him go," he told WordofSouth.com. "[Because] when a muthafucker fuck with the real, and then go fuck with the fake, a nigga depreciate a whole lot." Chad released Smitty with the understanding that he would retain ownership of all the beats, rhymes, and hooks he'd done for Smitty's project.*

"What happened with a lot of people that [C] would want to help [was that] niggas didn't want to work, they just wanted to ride his dick," says Mama Wes. "He wanted a nigga to put in work like *he* put in work ... [And] just like C got bored with hoes, he got bored with niggas, too."

After things fell through with Smitty, Mel brought Pimp another artist, 16-year-old Torrence "Lil Boosie" Hatch. Chad was impressed with Boosie's energy, talent, and knack for writing catchy hooks and singles. "The lil' dude was on fire," Chad told *OZONE*. "He was rappin' it and living it ... I was real wild, so to see someone on the same crazy vibe, it was attractive to me." Most of the material Chad and Steve Below had been developing for Smitty would end up being repurposed for Lil Boosie, such as "I Smoke Blunts," built around a Tupac sample.

Although Chad had been living with Sonji in Atlanta, he'd been dealing with Angie in Houston ever since they met on the *Ridin' Dirty* tour. "Chad had different lives," Rambro laughs. "Chad had an Atlanta life, and then Chad had a Houston life."

In Mama Wes' opinion, Sonji had become too clingy. "I think he really cared for her a lot [in the beginning]," says Mama Wes. "[But] she was a lot older than C, and I think she kinda mothered him too much." Plus, Chad was living the life of a rap star. Sonji tried launching a solo music career of her own, beginning with her first single criticizing the men who "go out and stay out all night, and half the next day / And expect us to be home when you get there."

While Mama Wes believed Sonji was "psychotic and bipolar and schizophrenic," others say she was only perceived as "crazy" because she wouldn't accept Chad's lifestyle. "Sonji was crazier than a muthafucker," says Big Munn. "She was 'crazy' like, she wasn't gonna put up with none of that [cheating] bullshit."

Bun was often accompanied by Queenie on the road, but Chad wasn't in the habit of bring-

---

(*Smitty finally released his debut album *Takin' Over* on Imperial Records in 2001. The only remnant of his Atlanta days was "What Up My Boy," featuring UGK, 3re Tha Hardaway, and PSK-13, produced by Steve Below. Pimp C and Young Smitty remained cordial and later mended their relationship. "He realized his error," Pimp told WordofSouth.com. "Any man that can come to me and say they made a mistake, I'm willing to listen to that. I don't hold grudges.")

ing his women to shows, where there was no shortage of women. "Man, I ain't carrying no sand to the beach," Chad would say. "Is you a fool, Bun? Everywhere you go, you got *her* with you."

"We liked [Sonji] but it was always some drama with [Chad's] woman around," recalls DJ Dolby D. One such incident was in Birmingham, where Sonji showed up at their hotel uninvited early one morning after a show. Chad, in bed with another woman, refused to answer the door and summoned hotel security. "She banged on that door so [hard] she broke her foot," Dolby recalls. "She was at the next show in crutches."

Angie considered her relationship with Chad a "special friendship," not a romance. Mama Wes appreciated Angie for her level-headed stability. Angie, six years older than Chad, was a hard-working woman who owned a beauty shop and was attending nursing school. Rap shows didn't interest her much, but she and Queenie sometimes came on the road with UGK, leaving their children home in the care of an older cousin. While the group hit the clubs, Angie could usually be found in the hotel room ironing Chad's clothes and babysitting Chad Jr.

As Mama Wes saw it, Angie was one of the few people strong enough to stand up to Chad. While Chad was surrounded by "yes men," Angie wasn't afraid to tell him "no," and tried to steer him away from his growing drug habits. "Angie was his voice of reason; his stability," says Mama Wes. "She didn't take no shit off of C … so whenever he was acting crazy he avoided her."

Angie tried to keep her emotions under control, knowing she wasn't the only one. Chad was usually honest with her about the steady stream of women coming in and out of his life. But when Angie and Bun's girlfriend Queenie heard that UGK had a show in Dallas and they hadn't been invited, they decided to find out why.

"Let's drive down," Queenie suggested. When they arrived at the club, Angie spotted Chad in the VIP section getting a little too friendly with some other women. She caused a scene and stormed outside; the night ended in a huge blow-up.

The incident convinced Angie that their friendship could never go to the next level. "We got serious in conversation, but I could never imagine a monogamous relationship, knowing him," she says. It was the only time she'd let jealousy get the best of her, and promised herself it would be the last.

"We gonna do it [one day]," Chad told her once, explaining that he planned to get married when he was 30. "We gonna get married."

Angie, who didn't believe he was capable of being faithful to one woman, told him it could never work. She felt that any woman who chose to marry him would have to accept his infidelity. "No we not, because you cannot do it," she told him. "You cannot do it the way I want you to do it … I want all or nothing. I'm not gonna marry you and knowingly allow you [to cheat]."

After the big blow-up in Dallas, Angie went back to Houston and was shocked to learn that she was pregnant. She already had two boys and two girls from a previous relationship and wasn't planning on adding any more to the fold. She told Chad that they needed to talk. "Well, I have some good news and I have some bad news," she began.

"What?!?" he said, in response to the news. "No, come on. Stop playing."

"I'm serious," she said.

"Oh, man," Chad reflected. "What are you gonna do?"

She corrected him. "What are *we* gonna do?"

"You wouldn't [keep] it if it wasn't me," Chad said.

"Probably not," she agreed. "But it *is* you."

Shortly after his conversation with Angie, Chad was in a van with Bun and a few other members of the crew headed out of town for a show when Bun's phone rang. Bun glanced at it suspiciously; the incoming caller ID read "private number."

Bun hesitated. "Yeah, who this?" he answered.

"This is Jay-Z," came the voice on the other end of the line.

True to form, Bun's deep monotone voice betrayed no emotion. "I don't know who this is, but quit playing on my phone." He hung up.

Bun's phone rang again, this time from an unblocked number. "Yo, family," the caller said. This time, the voice sounded familiar. Jay-Z explained that he wanted to feature UGK on his upcoming album *Vol. 3… Life and Times of S. Carter.*

Bun covered the receiver with his hand. "Yo, I think this is Jay-Z on my phone," he said.

"What he want?" Chad asked.

"Y'know, he wanna do a song," Bun said.

"Well, tell him to send it," Chad said. "We'll see."

A few days later, Bun received a FedEx box. Chad was in the studio putting the finishing touches on "Wood Wheel," a track he'd produced for a Rap-A-Lot double-disc compilation called *J. Prince Presents: R.N.D.S. (Realest Niggas Down South).* (It was an extended version of the intro from the Geto Boys' *Till Death Do Us Part.)* He popped in the Jay-Z track expectantly. "I wanted to do some hardcore *Reasonable Doubt* shit," he told journalist Matt Sonzala. "[I thought] we [were] finna do some gangsta shit."

Chad was proud of "Wood Wheel," of the "slab music" they'd been making, so it was a shock when a "happy-go-lucky tune" came pouring through the speakers. What the hell was this? A *pop* record? They'd spent years building a fanbase off street credibility; how would this sound to their fans?

"This got a lotta flutes, man," Chad said as the track played. "I don't know about them flutes." By the time the instrumental finished playing, Chad's face was twisted into a scowl. "I'm not doing it," he said.

"*Maaaan*, you want me to rap to that shit, Pee Wee?" Chad said, calling Bun by his nickname used only by UGK's inner circle. "Maaaan, nigga, they gon' laugh at us. I don't think that's the type of shit we need to be on. How is Texas muthafuckers gonna look at us?"

"Imagine hearing that beat … after you've been rapping hardcore shit all night," Chad said later. "To my ears, it was sabotage."

"Ram, man, Jay sent me this track," he told his Atlanta engineer Rambro over the phone. "Tim did the beat, man. Jay shoulda let me do the beat. He gave him 100 stacks for it. I coulda did that shit for sixty. The track is boo-boo … It got a whistle in there, sounds like [the country-themed variety show] Mayberry R.F.D."

"Timbaland shouldn't have done that to Jay," Chad vented to Mitchell Queen. "Timbaland shouldn't have sold that man that beat. He know that wasn't his best shit. That's terrible."

Chad refused to do the record and flew to Atlanta the next day. "He walked out on the song," Mama Wes told Hashim by phone. "He won't do it. He say he ain't gonna fuck up his career with that funny-ass beat … He wanna send it back to Jay-Z."

"Naw, Mama, give us a shot at it," Hashim said. "Send the song. Overnight the song to Patchwerk. Tell Rambro to set up a session."

To Bun, whether he liked the beat or not was irrelevant because he understood the significance of doing a song with Jay-Z. It would automatically propel them "into a totally different media bracket." As he told Rhapsody.com, "All I know is, Jay-Z calls me and wants me to do a song. So I don't care what the content of the record is."

Bun approached features as if it were a competition, a technical exercise, and he was excited about the challenge of rapping alongside Jay-Z. He headed out to New York solo to record the track. He was nervous, believing that his performance alongside Jay-Z could either solidify or destroy his rap legacy.

"I was totally intimidated before I even got to the booth," Bun told *Believer* Magazine. "I probably took that song ["Big Pimpin'"] a whole lot more seriously than Jay-Z. Because that was a lackadaisical, laid-back party track, and I attacked it."

Bun relaxed a bit when he heard Jay-Z's verse, on which Jay bragged of keeping a rotation of women who could be disposed of at any time "'cause I don't fucking need 'em."*

He's playing with it, Bun thought. He wrote his verse in twenty minutes, first deciding on a rhyme pattern, then filling in the words. Once in the booth, Bun was determined to get through the whole 28 bars (nearly double the average 16-bar verse) without stopping to take a breath. "I wouldn't dare punch in mixed company," he told *Believer*. "I maintained my integrity to the fullest in them days."

───────────

Back in Atlanta, Chad heard the nearly-completed record with Jay-Z's verse, Bun's verse, and the hook, but still couldn't get past how much he hated the "corny" beat. (Jay-Z wanted Pimp to do the hook, but Bun did it instead.) "If it hadn't been for the beat, I think it would've been easier to corral him into doing it," says Mama Wes.

"He wanted to produce it," agrees Wendy Day. "He felt like Jay-Z was using him to be embraced by the South. [But I told him] he should do it because it was Jay-Z, and it [would take] him to another level."

"On a personal level … I understood why Pimp didn't wanna do the song," says journalist Matt Sonzala. "He was like, 'Man, nobody wanted us before, fuck 'em,' y'know?" Agrees Big Munn, "He didn't have a problem with Jay-Z [but] Pimp's whole thang was, 'I pay respect to New York niggas, but New York niggas don't pay respect to us.'"

Bun tried to appeal to Chad's baser instincts, pointing out the obvious financial benefits. "This is *Jay-Z*," Bun told Chad, exasperated. "Everybody loves him. He just did 'Hard Knock Life.' Everybody is going to go out and buy his next album. He could sneeze, cough, or fart on the record – it's going to sell a million-plus off the top, why wouldn't we at least get a song on that record?"

Barry Weiss and Jeff Sledge tried to talk him into it, too; they couldn't understand his resistance. "Dude, you *gotta* do this," Jeff Sledge insisted. "It's a great opportunity."

"Fuck that," Chad said. "I don't think we need Jay-Z … we good." Jay-Z personally called numerous times. "If you don't do it for yourself, just do it for me," he said, promising it would be the biggest record of their career. That was precisely the problem: Chad didn't *want* a big record, which might turn UGK into "pop stars."

Bun and Mama Wes enlisted the help of mutual friends like Big Gipp, Too $hort, and Jazze Pha, begging them to convince Chad to do the record. "I just want people to respect us for what *we* do," Chad told Big Gipp. "I don't wanna feel like we gotta go and do records with everybody for people to respect how we do it [down South]."

"It was like a fuckin' act of Congress to get that nigga to rap on that goddamn song," remembers Big Munn. After being bombarded from all directions, Chad finally had enough. "I'm gonna go do this bullshit," he told Mama Wes. "Just leave me alone."

On October 31, 1999, Chad was napping at an Atlanta hotel with Sonji when he got a call from Hashim's friend Malik Zulu Shabazz.** Shabazz, an attorney based out of Washington D.C., worked closely with the New Black Panther Party and served as a mentor of sorts for Chad. "Malik had a way of talking that was highly intelligent [and he could] really get you to thinking," says Mama Wes. "He had that ability."

Chad and Malik often had in-depth discussions. Beyond his rhymes about cocaine, codeine, and women, Malik could see that Chad was a man of intelligence, and hoped to help him develop into a positive voice for his community. "Most artists do not want to consistently

---

(*More than a decade later, as he looked at his "Big Pimpin'" verse in print for *Decoded*, his book collaboration with dream hampton, Jay-Z said he was embarrassed to revisit the misogynistic attitude of his youth. "I can't believe I said that. And kept saying it," he told *The Wall Street Journal*. "What kind of animal would say this sort of thing? Reading it is really harsh.")
(**Chad said that Malik Zulu Shabazz was "very instrumental in that song coming about" and that it was his phone call which ultimately convinced him to do the record. "[Malik] might have been the last person to talk to [Chad about the 'Big Pimpin'] record," says Mama Wes. "But *everybody* was on C about that. He did have a great deal of respect for Malik and his opinions. I do too … I really have a lot of respect for his knowledge, his expertise, [and] his professionalism as a lawyer.")

promote drug-dealing, booty-shaking, and otherwise – for lack of a better word – 'nigga activity,'" Malik says. "Many artists would like to say more positive things [and] lead their people in a better way but there are wicked label executives [and] a hidden hand behind the scenes that is manipulating the black artists to be an agent of destruction of its own people, and sometimes, of its own selves."

"Brother C, I think you need to come down to the studio," Malik said in his deep, commanding voice. "You need to do this song with Jay-Z. That song is a hit."

Chad reiterated his belief that Jay-Z was somehow connected to Tupac's death. "I'm not fucking with them niggas," he said. Malik countered by telling him that history has to heal itself, and Tupac wouldn't want him to turn down a huge opportunity on his behalf.

Later that afternoon, Chad finally pulled up at Patchwerk Studios' new location on Hemphill Ave., where Rambro was waiting for him in the PWR 995 studio room (now known as Studio B), named in honor of their original location at 995 McMillan Street.

Chad still wasn't fully convinced, so Malik and Hashim launched a compelling argument. Not only would it benefit his career and expose him to a wider audience, Malik explained, but it was the perfect way to send a message to Jive. The record was going to get heavy radio play in New York, and Jive wouldn't be able to stop it even if they wanted to.

"Send the man a message," Malik encouraged him. "Send Jive a message."

A woman in the studio bobbed her head enthusiastically to the beat, and Chad looked at her curiously. "You like this?" he asked.

She smiled. "Yeah, I like it!"

"Ram, what do you think?" Chad asked his engineer. "You the only OG in the room, what do you think?"

"Well, I agree with you about the beat," Rambro said. "But on the other hand, Jay-Z's really coming up, and I think we need this type of shit with UGK."

They got on the phone with Jay-Z's team and ironed out some details; Chad agreed to do the verse for $60,000 upfront ("and a bunch of Rocawear clothes"). Part of his hesitation was that he felt out of his league rapping alongside Bun B and Jay-Z. "I couldn't figure out how to rap on the song," he told journalist Matt Sonzala. "I couldn't get into the rap contest Bun and Jay was having, 'cause I can't rap like that. I'm not a lyricist."

Chad's phone rang; it happened to be Big Gipp. "Hey, man, let me ask you something," Chad said. "Can I use your style on this song?"

Gipp laughed. "What is you talking about?"

"Gimme permission to use your style right quick, man," Chad said.

Gipp had no idea what he was talking about. "Yeah, go on ahead and do it."

Using Gipp's technique, which he felt was the best fit for the beat, Chad decided that if they were going to *make* him rap, he would give them an exaggerated slice of Texas life, the most country verse he could dream up.

"I really wrote it being sarcastic," he told Matt Sonzala. "If this is gonna be the biggest song of my career I'm finna talk about sippin' syrup, I'm finna talk about everything we do [in Texas]: grippin' the grain [and] choppin' on blades." Within minutes, he scrawled down his verse:

Smokin' out, pourin' up, keeping lean up in my cup
All my cars got leather and wood, in my 'hood we call it buck
Everybody wanna ball, holla at broads at the mall
If he up, watch him fall, nigga I can't fuck with y'all
If I wasn't rappin', baby, I would still be ridin' Mercedes
Comin' down and sippin' daily, no record 'til whitey pay me
(Uhh) Now what y'all know 'bout them Texas boys?
Comin' down in candy toys, smokin' weed and talkin' noise?

PATCHWERK
RECORDING STUDIOS

Session Report

Date 10-31-99

Studio PWR 995

Engineer DALE "KAMBEO" RAMSEY

Assitant

Client Def Jam Records

Artist JAY-Z featuring UGK

Producer Timbaland

Time

Confirmed Start Time 3pm   Time Out 11³⁰ pm

Project	Start	Stop	Duration
Project	Start	Stop	Duration
Project	Start	Stop	Duration
Project	Start	Stop	Duration
Project	Start	Stop	Duration

Total Hours

Tape Used

Two Inch

Adat

DA 88 3

Cassette 3 (30min)

Dat 3

Diskette

ZipDisk

Rentals

Project Description

Vocal Session "Big Pimpin" Belly Dance

Rough Ref Mix

He quickly knocked out the eight bars, running through the verse twice, and emerged from the booth shaking his head in exasperation. "Let's go, man," he told his crew.

His message to Jive ("no record 'til whitey pay me") didn't offend Barry Weiss. "I never take this stuff personally, to be honest with you, on behalf of the company or [myself]," Weiss says. When it came up briefly in conversation with Mama Wes, he merely chuckled, "That's Chad for ya." As Mama Wes explains it, "[Barry Weiss is] not overly sensitive or vengeful. He definitely does not hold a grudge, because he and C would cuss each other out all the time … [and] basically it was C doing the cussing."

As for the rest of the verse, Pimp C's staunch representation of Texas made him a hero back home. "Pimp C [was] really strict about his roots in Texas," says Lil Keke. "He represented that shit hard … that's one thing I respect about Pimp. No matter what he did or what songs he did with Jay-Z or Master P, he kept it Texas. He gon' rep Texas, he gon' talk about candy [paint], he gon' talk about drank … because it's his roots. He ain't never get to New York and start being something he wasn't."

Shortly after the "Big Pimpin'" session, Chad moved into his new house in the Atlanta suburb of Alpharetta. For the first time, it was one befitting of a rap star; friends referred to the home, with a pink stucco exterior atop a hill, as the "mini-mansion." A few doors down was R&B superstar Keith Sweat; the basement included a large theatre room and space for Chad to set up his studio. The large kitchen, perfect for Mama Wes to whip up her famous gumbo, featured dark cherry red wood paneling and black granite countertops. A gold chandelier hung above the curved staircase.

Although Mama Wes loved the Alpharetta house, it soon became apparent that C – or the "C-ster," as they began calling him – didn't plan to hire any help to keep the large home clean, even with its steady rotation of guests. "He thought I *was* the help, and that bitch had five bathrooms," she laughs.

Back in Houston, Bun had moved in with the MDDL FNGZ at their new house, dubbed The Manjah. Several members of the group came to stay at Chad's house in Atlanta for a few days, hoping to get some free beats for the next project due to their affiliation with Bun.

Kilo of the MDDL FNGZ, a young up-and-comer, felt privileged to be welcomed into Chad's home. As he got dressed one morning listening to some R&B music, Chad walked by and poked his head in the room, commenting on the singer.

"*Maaan*, you jam that?" Chad asked, shaking his head. "Let me tell you something about that nigga, man. That nigga wear makeup. That nigga have eyeliner. I know 'cause I been fuckin' with him and he's a mark, mane. The music industry is so crowded with homosexuals, man. Most of yo' favorite rappers and singers are fags. They getting a bowl of sausage, y'know what I'm sayin'?"

Later that day, the group congregated in the basement. Everyone was silent, bobbing their head as Chad played some beats. Finally, he asked, "So which one y'all want?"

"Man, all that shit jammin'," one of the MDDL FNGZ said, then paused, adding, "But we was waiting for that *one*."

Chad took off his glasses and squinted at the group.

He done pissed Pimp off, mane, Kilo thought.

"I don't know what the fuck you talkin' 'bout," Chad spat, offended. "This shit *jammin'*."

The group stayed for three more days. Chad was cordial, funny even, dancing around the house and cooking them a steak dinner, but there would be no more music. "We ain't hear *no* more beats the rest of the time we was there," laughs Kilo.

A few weeks after the "Big Pimpin'" session, Rambro's phone rang. "Hello, Dale?" a woman's voice said. "I have Jay for you."

Rambro, surprised at the use of his government name, drew a blank. *Jay? Jay who?*

When Jay-Z's unmistakable voice came through on the other end of the line, it clicked. "I heard you're the one that convinced Chad to do the song," Jay said. "We're getting ready to do the video, and we're going to Trinidad. You think he'll come?"

Rambro didn't even hesitate. "Nope. He doesn't like to leave the country."

"You think he would come to Miami?" Jay asked.

"Yeah, he'll go to Miami."

"This is what I want you to do," Jay said. "Since he didn't do the full 16 [bars], I want you to edit the song so I could backdoor him, and when we do the video, I'll do another verse."

Rambro extended the end of the instrumental and sent it back; Jay added another verse at the end of the record. Rumors spread that Jay had added another verse because he'd been upstaged on his own record.

Bun told Rhapsody.com that Jay added another verse "to even up the publishing." But Bun's statement was actually incorrect: UGK was only paid a flat fee. "We did that song work for hire, so we didn't get no publishing," Pimp said later.*

"That was a big mistake [that we didn't get publishing]," nods Mama Wes. "I'm gonna be honest with you: I don't even know how that happened."

When Jeff Sledge heard the finished version of the record with Chad's vocals, he was elated and called Chad to congratulate him. "You killed it! [But] why did you only do [eight] bars?"

"Man, fuck Jay-Z, man," Chad grumbled. "I ain't giving him 16 [bars]. I'm only giving him [eight]."

Despite Chad's reluctance, when "Big Pimpin'" dropped around Christmas 1999, it took UGK nationwide. "There's no way to downplay it at all. It really was [a turning point]," Bun told *Murder Dog.* "For the markets that we already had, this was a victory for people who had been down with UGK for years."

Even Jay-Z's camp wasn't expecting "Big Pimpin'" to blow up; it was initially intended to break ground for his next single "Things That You Do" with Mariah Carey. And it was Pimp C's eight bars that fans enthusiastically screamed word for word at every show.

"Jay-Z has always been ahead of the curve," Chad told AllHipHop. "It's like he's got a vision of what's about to happen. He saw that eventually the torch was gonna get passed to the South."

With "Big Pimpin'" taking off, Jive pushed back the *Dirty Money* release date, hoping to find the best way to capitalize off the song's momentum. In an interview with *Murder Dog,* Chad explained that his vision for the album was to "bring some consciousness to this Rap shit, instead of always rappin about bitches and cars and shit."

"Everybody's rappin about their watches and rings. It's fucked up right now," he complained. "Rap is in a state of emergency. I listen to Rap all day long. I try to watch BET, but they play the same shit over and over again. I listen to niggaz rap, all they talkin about is fuckin bitches, how many watches they got and all this ol' shit … It was a time where a nigga wouldn't wear no watch unless it was a real Rolex with real diamonds. Now these boys just put a science project on their wrist. A chandelier, a Geneva with a Rolex face on it. And they spend a gang of money on it."

"Me and Bun B bout to talk about some real life shit," he concluded. "I got some homeboys doin 40 years in the penn. Fuck!"

(*Jay-Z, Timbaland, and UGK were sued in 2005 by an Egyptian man who owned the copyright to "Khosara Khosara," the song sampled for "Big Pimpin'." UGK's attorney successfully argued that because UGK was only paid a flat fee to contribute vocals under a work-for-hire agreement, they did not have any liability. UGK settled their portion of the lawsuit for $5,000. The case against Jay-Z is still ongoing and scheduled for trial in October 2015.)

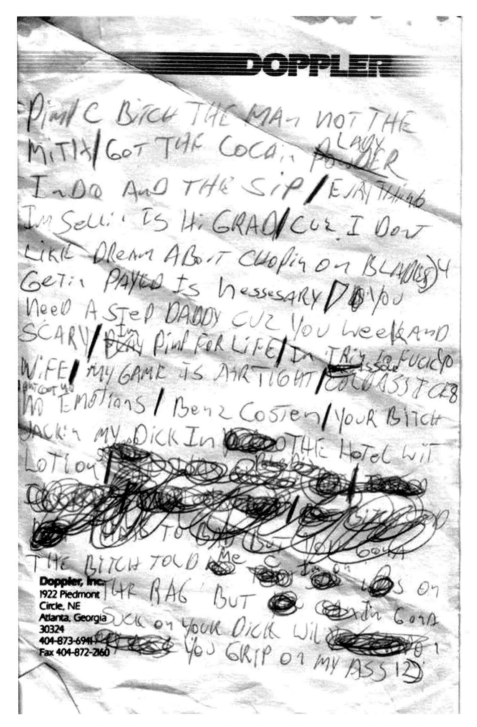

Above: A portion of Pimp C's handwritten lyrics from **"Down Here,"** which appeared on 1 Gud Cide's *Contradictions* album.

Courtesy of Weslyn Monroe

CHAPTER 22

"[The 'Big Pimpin' video is] the beginning of the imagery leading the music, and really his presentation to the world. Like, this is who PImp C *is*." – Bun B

———

"TV ain't got no temperature." – Pimp C

Wednesday, January 26, 2000
Atlanta, Georgia

UGK's former manager Byron Hill pulled up to an Atlanta courthouse, navigating the sludge-covered streets. The city was still recovering from a paralyzing ice storm. Temperatures had dipped below freezing in Atlanta for several days, and the city wasn't equipped for severe winter weather. Icy roadways led to fatal accidents and knocked out power to more than half a million homes.

It had been more than four years since UGK cut ties with Byron Hill, but now that "Big Pimpin'" was exploding at radio, Byron decided he was owed a portion of the proceeds. On January 26, 2000, he filed a lawsuit in Atlanta claiming that since he had never been formally fired, he was entitled to 20% of the group's income since 1995.

All those long days on the road traveling for shows, all Bun's indie features, all the sleepless nights in the studio Chad spent fine-tuning beats, Byron believed he deserved 20 cents of every dollar. He also sued Mama Wes for interfering with his management agreement by "expressly undertaking [management] responsibilities." (In the lawsuit, Byron referred to himself as the "president of Nomad, Inc." a corporation which didn't exist. He registered it a week later.)

The ice storm came at a particularly bad time as the city of Atlanta prepared to host Super Bowl XXXIV. "Millions of Americans tuning in for the biggest TV event of the year saw a gray, frozen city," the *Atlanta Journal-Constitution* reported. One radio station gave away a Super Bowl ticket to a diehard fan who swam across the frozen fountain at Underground Atlanta.

On January 30, the morning of the Super Bowl, temperatures finally crept above freezing, melting most of the ice which had accumulated on roads, trees, and power lines during the miserable week. But some slick spots still remained on bridges, overpasses, and hills, like the driveway to Chad's Alpharetta home. J. Prince and the Rap-A-Lot crew managed to make it safely to Atlanta, but couldn't make it up the hill. They parked their entourage of vehicles at the bottom, slipping and sliding their way up the icy driveway.

Also on the road to Atlanta for the Super Bowl were DJ Paul and Juicy J of Three 6 Mafia, a rising Memphis rap group which had been talking with UGK about collaborating. Yellow cough syrup was a popular underground drug in Memphis, sometimes known as "snot" due to its color and runny texture. Purple syrup, which was more visually appealing, cheaper, and mixed better with soda, was also getting popular in Memphis thanks mostly to Texas rap music. (Chad actually preferred yellow syrup.) DJ Paul wanted to do a record about syrup for their upcoming album *When the Smoke Clears: Sixty 6, Sixty 1,* and it would only make sense to collaborate with someone from Texas.

About two hours into the drive, near the Mississippi/Alabama border, Three 6 Mafia's Navigator hit a slick icy spot on a bridge and spun out of control into oncoming traffic. An 18-wheeler flew past, missing the truck by mere inches as the driver tried to gain control.

DJ Paul saw his life flashing before his eyes in slow motion. As the truck skidded to a halt near a grassy median, the driver struggled to coax the engine back to life as another 18-wheeler swerved out of their path. DJ Paul and Juicy J dove out of the backseat into a pool of mud and ice alongside the freeway.

Another 18-wheeler passed, trying to slam on its brakes which were all but useless on the ice. "GET THE FUCK OUT!" DJ Paul screamed at the driver as horns blared. "GET OUT OF THAT MUTHAFUCKIN' TRUCK, MAN!" The driver revved the Navigator's engine just in time and skidded out of the way, missing the truck by a few feet.

Thoroughly shaken but unharmed, Three 6 Mafia and their driver gathered their composure and plodded on slowly the rest of the journey. As they neared the Atlanta area, DJ Paul realized he'd lost his Skytel two-way pager with Pimp C's contact information when he dove out of the vehicle.

Through a mutual friend at the radio station, they managed to locate the Alpharetta house. The driveway was still iced over, so getting Three 6 Mafia up to the house was an ordeal. Chad tossed them a long rope, anchored by Bun holding on to a tree at the top. "We had to form a chain with us and Bun B to pull each other up," DJ Paul recalls.

Finally inside, the guys feasted on a hearty meal prepared by Sonji and spent the rest of the day watching the Super Bowl and recording.* When Three 6 Mafia drove back to Memphis the following day, most of the iced-over roads had thawed out. DJ Paul spotted deep skid marks alongside the bridge where their terrifying incident had occurred and asked the driver to pull over. There he found his Skytel pager, coated in mud but still functional.

Three 6 Mafia planned to release a different song as their first single, reasoning that "Sippin' On Some Syrup" would be too controversial for mainstream radio. "We were kind of nervous," recalls Juicy J. "We thought nobody was going to play it because of what it was talking about. But really, nobody knew what Sizzurp was."

A few weeks after they got back to Memphis, Three 6 Mafia went to meet with their label head, Loud Records' Steve Rifkind, at an upscale steak house. Joining them was a Memphis radio program director, who told them, "Man, that 'Sippin' On Sizzurp' song, that's the one. That's the song. That song is a hit."

A month after the Super Bowl, UGK was scheduled to perform in Dallas, where things were still tense because of the Ron Robinson altercation. Even though J. Prince had defused the situation, Chad had no intention of giving Ron his money back. "Fuck that shit," Chad would grumble. "That nigga disrespected me, fuck that. I ain't givin' that nigga his money back."

The show promoter, James Price, was a mainstay in Dallas area nightclubs.** Bo-Bo Luchiano alerted the group to an advertisement where Price was using UGK's name to promote a different event the week before. Mama Wes told Price that they expected to be compensated for the unauthorized use of their name.

On February 27, UGK arrived in Dallas for the scheduled show at Park Avenue nightclub.

(*The St. Louis Rams held on to a 23-16 lead to defeat the Tennessee Titans, who were stopped one yard short of a touchdown as time expired. The ice didn't stop the post-game festivities, and Baltimore Ravens linebacker Ray Lewis was one of many athletes who went out to party that night in Atlanta's popular Buckhead district. A fight broke out as he left a nightclub, and in the aftermath, two men died of stab wounds. Lewis and two of his friends were arrested on murder charges. The *Atlanta Journal-Constitution* later wrote that "the ugly incident profoundly altered Atlanta's landscape" by pushing "city leaders to tame Buckhead's wild party scene." Neighborhood groups urged the City Council to push back the alcohol serving cut-off time from 4 AM until 2 AM. Lewis, who spent more than a million dollars in legal fees, pled guilty to a misdemeanor charge in exchange for testifying against his friends. He was sentenced to probation but the incident would continue to follow him throughout his professional career. Both of the other men, who claimed they acted in self-defense, were acquitted.)

(**James Price, not to be confused with James Prince of Rap-A-Lot, was unable to be reached for comment.)

1) I'm TRILL WORKin THE WEEK /
PIMP NOT A SIMP
2) Keep THes DoPe Fine HieR THAN
A GooD YeaR KciP
3) WE EAT So mANy SHRIP WE GOT
I Dien Poison'c /
4) FUck yieem MAKi ie SiC wiT ALL
THAT / Pinci. AnD BARGAinin
5) You SAY You A LLess I Aut BeLivin
THAT SHiT / GoT THe FuNy Geniin
WATCH WiT THE Rolex KiT
TAKE THAT MuNKY SHiT OFF /
You EmBARisin US / I Got RoO
PReni TWAZ in THiK ORAn6 AnD YeLLow
TUS /
HiDRoCobon / HANDz FRee Fone /
84 DRove / on THEm BLADz 2c InCHCReme
IF You GoT 16 You CAN GeT A BizeRO
In CHoCKin on THAT DoSHA GweeT
AnD SiPin on Some SizeRP

Above: Pimp C's handwritten lyrics from his verse on **Three 6 Mafia's "Sippin' On Some Syrup."**
Courtesy of Weslyn Monroe

Bo-Bo Luchiano, who had a song buzzing locally and was slated as the opening act, was one of the first to arrive at the club. As he stepped out of his car, he was approached by a man wearing a large cowboy hat. "Hey, I'm looking for these two guys," the man said, holding out individual pictures of Chad and Bun. "Have you seen 'em?"

Bo-Bo eyed him suspiciously. "They're not here."

UGK pulled up in their customized van, outfitted with a 32" TV, while Bo-Bo was on stage. Hashim had ended the group's practice of traveling in limousines, which were difficult to maneuver in the case of an emergency. The group went inside to collect the back end of their show money, around $10,000, from James Price.

Out back, the man in the cowboy hat approached the driver's side of the van, asking Pops if he was with UGK. He produced a badge and explained that he was a federal marshal looking for Chad Butler and Bernard Freeman.

Rap-A-Lot's Anzel "Red Boy" Jennings, who had started working with the group in a management/security capacity, thought the marshal was trying to arrest them. Meanwhile, Bo-Bo had just stepped off stage and rushed to find Chad and Bun, who were upstairs in the nightclub's office. "Man, it's a constable here looking for y'all," Bo-Bo warned them, out of breath, as Red Boy arrived.

Chad was already irritated with James Price. "I didn't wanna do the shit no way," he said.

"Let's go." The whole entourage made a hasty dash for the exit.

As they piled into the van, the marshal tried to shove a stack of paperwork in Chad's hands. He was a process server hired by Byron Hill to serve them with his lawsuit. "Man, we don't want them muthafuckin' papers," Chad yelled. "Get that shit out my muthafuckin' face!"

They slammed the van doors shut. "Pops, take off!" Chad yelled. "Go! Go!"

Pops slammed down the gas pedal and the van roared off. Red Boy was right behind them, the federal marshal trailing closely. Pops had only been to Dallas a few times and had no idea where he was going. "Drive this muthafucker, Pops! Drive it!" Chad urged.

Red Boy blocked the marshal at a stop sign, giving Pops time to make a U-turn and speed off, finally finding the entrance to the freeway. By now, everyone in the van was enjoying the excitement of the high-speed chase. "*Driiive* this muthafucker, Pops!" Chad crowed. "*Drive* this muthafucker! Pop, you a *driiivin'* muthafucker!"

Once they'd lost the marshal, Pops dropped Chad and Bun off at a different hotel and headed back to the Anatole to gather everyone's luggage. Mama Wes suggested they could use the incident as inspiration for song called "Drive This Muthafucker!"

Back at Park Avenue, James Price was furious that UGK had dashed off, especially since he'd already paid their full fee. Assuming they'd left to spite him because of their financial dispute, he took to the stage himself and yelled, "Fuck UGK!" on the microphone. Price told the crowd that UGK left because the club didn't have the champagne they'd requested. He announced that if anyone wanted a refund, they could find UGK at the Hotel Anatole, and gave out Bun and Chad's room numbers.

The crowd was in an uproar; some heard there was a hit out on Pimp C, while others heard that the Feds were at the club looking for them. Both of those rumors had truth to them: among those waiting for UGK to take the stage were several of Ron Robinson's armed street soldiers. The men exchanged glances and headed for the Hotel Anatole, where they were spotted banging on the door to Chad's room, now vacant, with pistols. Ironically, Byron Hill may have indirectly saved Chad's life.

Downstairs at the Anatole, Pops was dragging out the last of the luggage when the federal marshal, exasperated, tried to hand him the stack of paperwork.

The following day, James Price called in to Dallas radio station K104 to defend his reputation, accusing UGK of breaching their contract. Chad, who believed Price had deliberately put him in danger, was furious. "James Price let a bunch of Ron's people in the club with pistols, and [Chad] thought that as soon as [he] walked on the stage … [he] was gonna get shot in the club," remembers Bo-Bo Luchiano. "That's what C's perception of it was."

Chad responded to Price's accusations on Greg Street's Dallas radio show, launching an expletive-filled rant. He told Price that if he wanted his money back, he could come to Houston and get it in blood. "You know where to find me!" he barked. "I'm down with Rap-A-Lot Mafia!"

Ever since the Cash Money tour, Chad had aligned himself with Rap-A-Lot for protection, relying on Prince to get them out of tough situations – for example, when dozens of men in No-Limit t-shirts were waiting in the parking lot outside their hotel in Mobile, Alabama. All it took was a phone call and the crowd dissipated. "That nigga [J. Prince] been our guardian for a long time," Chad told *The Source*. "He has stopped a lot of shit from going down."

———

Bun flew to Trinidad to film the "Big Pimpin'" video with Jay-Z during the island's annual Carnival festival on March 6 and 7, 2000. But Chad refused to go, which Jive executives interpreted as just an extension of his refusal to do the song in the first place.

The more likely explanation was that Chad didn't want to admit he was terrified to fly overseas. "I ain't gonna be over no water that long, Mama," he told his mother. Jeff Sledge tried to reason with him: if he could fly to Los Angeles, why couldn't he fly to Trinidad?

"Chad just had certain beliefs, and he was a very stubborn guy," says Rambro. "Certain things, he just wasn't gonna do."

Fortunately, Def Jam had allotted more than a million dollars for the shoot and arranged for Chad's scene to be filmed in Miami. For their first real big budget video, Chad knew the visual was crucial. Jermaine Dupri had recently purchased a blue Mercedes-Benz CL600, which wasn't even available yet for purchase, and Chad had his heart set on the car.

Through his connections at a car dealership, Hashim tracked down an Atlanta doctor who had already pre-ordered the Benz and convinced him to let Chad buy it. "We made him an offer he couldn't refuse," Hashim says.

Chad called Jeff Sledge at Jive, a fellow car aficionado. "Yo, I gotta have this car for the video," Chad told him. "I need that car." Jeff knew immediately which car he meant. Chad explained that he had a connect to get it and all he needed was around $60,000.

"Dude, what are you saying?" Jeff asked.

"You gotta figure out a way to get me some money, Jeff, so I can get this car for the video," Chad said. "I gotta have something nobody else has."

Chad's friend Biz overheard the conversation. Biz, who apparently had inherited Big Dog's drug empire after he died, spent a lot of time shuttling back and forth between Nashville and Atlanta. He was dabbling in the music business and often crashed at Chad's house, and vice versa. (They'd grown so close that Chad once woke up at Biz's house and, realizing he hadn't packed any clean underwear, borrowed a pair of boxers from Biz's room.)

Biz volunteered to loan Chad the money. "Hey, I'll give you 80," he said, explaining that he needed to get back to Nashville anyway.

Chad thought about it and pulled DJ Bird to the side. "Look, man, I need you to go get this money for me," Chad told him. "Just drop Biz back home and he gonna give you the money."

Bird and Biz headed out in a gray Suburban for the four hour drive, reaching Nashville after 1 AM. Bird sat in the SUV idling outside a sketchy-looking house while Biz ran inside and emerged with two hefty garbage bags.

"Count the money," Biz said, shoving the bags in Bird's direction. Bird pulled out a stack of bills: tens, twenties, fifties, and hundreds. His mouth dropped. "*What*!? You telling me you want me to count *eighty thousand dollars?* You ain't got no money machine?" Bird asked.

"Nah, not here," Biz said.

"Man, I ain't counting all that damn money in that shit," Bird told him. "Just give me the muthafuckin' two garbage bags so I can hit the road."

Bird popped a No-Doz caffeine tablet to keep himself awake and made the overnight trek back to Atlanta solo, sweating bullets and biting his fingernails. He was careful not to go even one mile over the speed limit, envisioning what would happen if police pulled him over. *Boy, them laws stop me...* he worried.

Bird caught himself drifting off into a dream, picturing himself at a traffic stop. "What in the fuck is all this damn money comin' from!?" the officer demanded, putting him in cuffs. "What you doing transporting money!?"

Bird shook his head and popped another No-Doz.

Back in Alpharetta, Chad was worried too. He'd been unsuccessfully trying to call Bird for hours, not realizing that Bird's cheap cell phone didn't work outside of the metro Atlanta area. When Bird finally pulled up to the house near dawn, Chad was waiting for him on the living room couch. He embraced Bird and kissed him on the cheek for dramatic effect. "Bird, man, I love you, man," Chad said, reaching for the garbage bags.

Bird collapsed on the couch from exhaustion while Chad called Hashim to come to the house. Hashim and his brother helped count the cash, stacking it in piles all over the living room floor. As Bird recalls it, the total was around $60,000, not $80,000 as promised. Chad called Biz, who admitted he had no idea how much money there was in the garbage bags.

———————

Jeff Sledge had reluctantly approached Barry Weiss with Chad's request for an advance. As it turned out, UGK had a publishing check coming soon, and Barry agreed to issue an advance of $60,000 each to Chad and Bun. The funds would be wired to Chad's account immediately so he could purchase the car in time for the video.*

Chad got the silver Mercedes-Benz the day before the video shoot. Late that night, he and his crew drove over to Too $hort's house in southwest Atlanta, where $hort was loading up his black Porsche 911. $hort admired Chad's new car; Chad bragged that he'd gotten Jive to shell out the money.**

With several other vehicles in the procession, they headed out overnight on the 10-hour drive to Miami.*** En route, "Big Pimpin'" came on the radio repeatedly. "We looked pretty good riding up and down the highway in our lil' caravan," Too $hort recalls. "The mission was all about the video shoot."

Things got off to a bad start when the group arrived on South Beach and checked into the National Hotel on Collins. There was nothing wrong with the hotel, but Chad was livid when he learned that Jay-Z was staying at a different hotel, which he assumed was much nicer.

Chad was pissed enough to drive over to the five-star hotel where Jay-Z and his crew were occupying most of the top floor and demanded to know why they'd been booked at a different hotel. Jay-Z offered to get him a room there, which defused Chad's temper.

When Pimp C pulled up to the video shoot later that day, he parked his new Benz alongside UGK's trailer. On the other side was Jay-Z's trailer, where an enormous bodyguard emerged, barking, "You can't park that car there."

Someone ran to grab Bun, who was watching some girls in bikinis getting oiled up for the shoot. "Man, come get your boy," Bun was told. "They got him hemmed up in the trailer."

As a heated argument ensued, Pimp popped the trunk and told Pops to get his pistol. Jay's business partner Damon Dash finally overheard the commotion and came outside to call off the bodyguard, who didn't know who Pimp was. Mama Wes crowned the bodyguard "a king-sized asshole" and told him he needed "an attitude adjustment."

Once they'd cleared up the misunderstanding, Damon Dash tried to ease the tension, apologizing for the drama and inviting everyone to party in their trailer. Before long, it was filled with video models, but Jay still hadn't made his appearance. "Why won't *he* come in here?" Pimp muttered dryly.

When Jay finally did make his appearance, he struck Pimp as standoffish. Still in a sour mood, Pimp stepped outside and called Big Gipp, who understood his sentiments towards Jay-Z. "*Maaaan*, I don't *like* this nigga, man," Pimp told Gipp.

To Gipp and Pimp C, it was more about what Jay-Z represented than him personally. They both were bitter towards the way New York artists were held in higher regard. "I take it as a slap in the face when I see kids coming up, praising Jay-Z and these other cats," Gipp told *VIBE*. "Back in the day, they wouldn't even talk to Southern rappers. They praise Jay-Z and to me, Jay-Z ain't never said anything besides how to sell dope."

"[Pimp] never liked Jay-Z. He *never* liked that cat," says Big Gipp. "He always felt like, 'Man, he a fuck nigga, man.'" (In Mama Wes' opinion, Chad actually had a lot of respect for Jay-Z, but didn't want to let it show. "C felt like he had some kind of persona to live up to," she says.)

(*It isn't clear how much Chad actually paid for the car, and if it was purchased with the cash from Nashville, the funds from Jive, or, most likely, some combination of both. It seems that Chad used the leftover funds to party excessively in Miami.)
(**As his labelmate, Too $hort was very familiar with UGK's battle with the label. "Tell them muthafuckers at Jive to quit trippin'," Too $hort told Pimp C on the outro to their record "It's Alright" from the *Dangerous Ground* soundtrack.)
(***As Jeff Sledge recalls it, Chad insisted that Jive also pay to have the car shipped to Miami. Most of Chad's friends remember him driving it down from Atlanta.)

Although Mama Wes liked Jay-Z personally, she resented the condescending attitude from the rest of his crew; one asked why she wasn't wearing cowboy boots. "Jay's people kind of had this attitude that we were a bunch of Texas hicks," she recalls.

Pimp was still heated and Bun tried to calm things down, reminding him why they were here: this was business. "If it wasn't for Bun, that [video shoot] wouldn't have even went down," Pimp would later say privately.

But publicly, Pimp never had anything negative to say about Jay-Z or his Roc-A-Fella label. "It's a good thing to see young blacks getting rich like that together and staying unified," he told AllHipHop. He told them Jay had smiled at him in the midst of the video shoot, laughing, "See, family, I told you. I told you this shit was gonna be the biggest record."

Even if the elder Chad wasn't too impressed with Jay-Z, his son Chad Jr. was, but tried to play it cool. He'd met some of his father's other rap friends, but Jay-Z was a real superstar. "I never got too starstruck," Chad Jr. explains. "I always felt like it would detract away from the aura of my dad ... I felt like he would seem cooler if his kid [wasn't starstruck]."

The shoot was an elaborate affair; craft services, catering, makeup artists, wardrobe, staffers everywhere. Def Jam spent a rumored $15,000 renting out a mansion on the beach; MTV cameras swooped around capturing it all for their *Making the Video* behind-the-scenes segment.

"We up to $1.4 million [spent on this video] and I ain't seen no aerial shots," Jay-Z kept shouting on set, to no one in particular. "There's supposed to be a helicopter flying over shooting footage. I ain't seen it. I need my money back."

Pimp C apparently found a passive-aggressive way to get back at Jay-Z for any perceived slight when he bumped into video girl Gloria Velez in the hotel elevator and invited her for a ride in his new Benz.

Gloria, the hottest video girl at the time, was in high demand. Pimp, wearing a mink coat, set up his scene using the silver Benz as a prop as Gloria danced on him. Bun, sweating profusely in the Miami spring heat, looked at Pimp and laughed. "How can you stand out there and rap in a mink coat?" he asked.

The thought crossed his mind to take it off, but he decided to stick with his artistic vision. "Man," Pimp replied, "TV ain't got no temperature."

Bun understood. The mink coat with no shirt, the exclusive luxury car, the girl: this was the image of "Pimp C" Chad wanted the world to see. "That's the beginning of the imagery leading the music, and really his presentation to the world. Like, this is who Pimp C *is*," Bun explains. "If you listened to the music, you're like, 'Yep, that's exactly what I expected him to look like.'"

After shooting their scene, Pimp C and Gloria disappeared together and were inseparable for the rest of the weekend. "Those guys were all mad at him 'cause he scooped her and they wanted to get with her," says Jeff Sledge, who didn't actually attend the shoot but heard about it afterwards. "All those guys was mad because they didn't get a chance to get with Gloria."*

The perception, whether true or not, was that Pimp had stolen Jay-Z's girl. "Really, Jay had picked her for [his scene], and C just wasn't having that," says Mama Wes. "[C] started shooting his part before Jay got over there, and then it was too late."

Pimp C wasn't one for on-set debauchery. "I ain't never walked on no video set and seen a whole bunch of freakin' and shit going on," he told *OZONE*. "I ain't never seen that kind of shit but I've heard niggas talk about it. I ain't seen no niggas getting head in the back of the [video shoot] trailer. I'm sure it happens, but ... it takes a certain caliber of nigga to even get down like that. So, I've never seen it personally or participated in no shit like that."

Behind closed doors at the hotel, though, was fair game. Once he and Gloria were finished, Pimp C asked Bird to give her a ride home in his Benz, then called Gipp to brag about their

(*Too $hort disagrees on this point, saying there were so many girls on the set that it wasn't necessary for anyone to be fighting over one. Gloria Velez declined to be interviewed. "She doesn't wanna relive those days," theorizes Jeff Sledge. "She's settled down and all that [so] she don't wanna talk about it.")

sexcapades. ("It was always pimpin', man," Gipp laughs. "She liked it everywhere. [He] gave her a little tutti frutti.")

While Pimp was tied up with Gloria, Bun was already committed for the weekend with his girlfriend. Pimp couldn't understand why Bun brought Queenie to a video shoot on South Beach. "You don't need to bring no sand to the beach," he'd lectured his partner. "Already got enough sand on the beach, mane."

Chad's old friend from Port Arthur, Nahala "Boomer" Johnson, whose condescending comment had inspired Chad and Mitch to create the Mission Impossible demo, was now an aspiring filmmaker tagging along to the video shoot. Watching a director like Hype Williams at work (assisted by Benny Boom and Little X, who would go on to build impressive resumés themselves) was a dream come true. "Mr. Boomtown," as he was now known, was soaking it all in and enjoying the eye candy. "That was the first time I seen that many goddamn girls in bikinis," he recalls. "It was the craziest video [set] I have ever been [on]."

On set, Chad regaled onlookers with the story of the Kight shooting, embellishing a bit for entertainment purposes. Boomtown told Chad he was going Hollywood, a comment which sparked an argument. Chad reminded him of that summer more than a decade ago, when Boomtown had headed off to play football and predicted that Chad and Mitch would never make it in rap. Boomtown's football career hadn't panned out, but now here they were, on the set of Chad's video.

"You still the same way, [on] that ol' bullshit, man," Chad said, shaking his head. "You was all about that football shit when we were trying to do a group."

Boomtown laughed. He'd long ago forgotten the incident, but for Chad it was obviously still a sore spot. "Pimp always felt like he had to prove something to [his peers in] Port Arthur," says Mr. Boomtown. "Because [when] he was young … dudes looked down on him. He was just a little band kid."

During the shoot, Bun had a conversation with Def Jam Records' executive Lyor Cohen, who expressed interest in bringing UGK over to Def Jam alongside Jay-Z. "How much longer do you guys have with Jive?" Cohen asked.

"Well, we've still got two more albums left," Bun said.

"So you've been over there with a five album deal? You could've turned those albums in [over the last] five years. But how long have you been over there?" Cohen asked.

"Right now, eight years," Bun sighed. "And we've still got two more albums."

"Why don't you just turn in those two more albums and go on with your life?" Cohen suggested.

Bun couldn't think of a good answer. Cohen was right; they could've been done with Jive already and moved on.*

By the end of the day, the shoot had turned into a full-on party. Damon Dash, who had just smoked weed for the first time and was extremely drunk, was spraying champagne on the video models as Little X followed them into the ocean filming. *I need to go to more Dame Dash and Jay-Z video shoots, 'cause this muthafuckin' video shoot is a party,* Too $hort thought.

After a quick trip to Los Angeles, UGK came back to Miami to shoot Three 6 Mafia's "Sippin' On Some Syrup" video, where the party continued. DJ Bird kept an eye on Chad Jr. swimming in the hotel pool while Mama Wes cooked red beans, rice, and gumbo in her hotel room.

After dinner, UGK went out for a raucous evening on South Beach with Three 6 Mafia. "Me

(*Barry Weiss agrees it was it frustrating that UGK didn't produce more material. "[We had our] ups and downs, obviously, like any marriage [or] partnership, but at the end of the day, I think we had a really good relationship, particularly given the volatility of Chad's personality," Weiss says. "[His] personality really stopped him from having a more consistent flow of records. [UGK] should've had twice the amount of albums put out in that time period.")

and Pimp got in the Mercedes and we rode off and fucked off," recalls DJ Paul. "Shit, man, it was a blast." The night was so wild, in fact, that the video shoot the next morning almost didn't happen. "I woke up with this crazy hangover," recalls Juicy J. "I couldn't even move."

John "Dr. Teeth" Tucker, a producer for BET's *Rap City: The Basement*, happened to be in Miami vacationing with his girlfriend. *Rap City* was filmed in Washington D.C., and like many East Coast media outlets, only had mild interest in covering Southern rap.

When *Trill Azz Mixez* came out, Dr. Teeth, who had gone to college at Texas Southern University, lobbied his boss to let him spend a week in Houston filming a story on UGK, DJ Screw, and the growing Texas movement. Bun hosted the segment, but couldn't convince Pimp to do an interview.

Even without Pimp's cooperation, the program *Under Houston* was a big success, marking the first time DJ Screw appeared on BET. "It was the first time that *Rap City* ever went that deep in the underground to expose another culture," says Dr. Teeth.

Dr. Teeth came by the set of "Sippin' on Some Syrup" on Ocean Drive, where Pimp C was sitting in his Mercedes smoking a blunt. Pimp had seen the *Under Houston* program and motioned for Dr. Teeth and his girlfriend to get in the car.

Through Jeff Sledge, Dr. Teeth had heard about their struggle to convince Pimp to do "Big Pimpin'." "They're saying that you didn't want to do the thing with Jay-Z, and then I was trying to get you to do the stuff for BET..." he began.

Pimp explained that he was fed up with the business side of the music industry and he felt like everyone, especially Jive, was trying to use him. He seemed especially bitter that Jive didn't think they looked good enough to be in videos; he had to be on someone else's song, using someone else's budget, like Sony's Three 6 Mafia or Def Jam's Jay-Z, to appear on television.

The conversation helped Dr. Teeth understand why Chad had declined to appear on the program. "He felt like his music was bigger than the way [Jive] was treating it, and he was just at a point in his career where he just didn't give a fuck," remembers Dr. Teeth. "He was going to do it *his* way, he was going to protect his brand the way he saw it, and doing media [interviews] wasn't [as] important to him as getting the truest form of his music out."

CHAPTER 23

"[Chad's bipolar disorder] was his greatest enemy and his greatest friend."
– Mama Wes

"[The] real reason why [Chad] created all those characters was because he did not want people to know the real C. The real Chad was very, very quiet, very unassuming, very sensitive, and he had a lot of fears. And he didn't want anybody to know that side of him ... He definitely didn't like to share it, but C was also a very, very quiet, very bashful kind of person, so he had to create those characters so he could be who he wanted to be ... He would create a character so that he could behave [like a gangsta or a pimp]. Chad Lamont Butler could never do that, so he had to create a character who could." – Mama Wes

Saturday, April 15, 2000
Stone Mountain, Georgia

Chad's silver Mercedes, trailed by two vans, snaked through the packed parking lot and past the long line outside Atrium Nightclub on the east side of Atlanta. It was April 2000, and the city had finally managed to stifle the raucous annual anarchy of Freaknik.

Earlier that day, the *Atlanta Journal-Constitution* happily reported that "the [100,000+] college students who clogged Atlanta's streets with party-mobiles for most of the past decade" were instead "sunning themselves on the beaches of Galveston, Texas." UGK was scheduled to perform for a radio event alongside rapper Fat Joe as Freaknik fizzled out for good.

As the group pulled up at the rear entrance, a security guard announced that he was going to search everyone and reached towards Mama Wes, grabbing her roughly and pushing her up against the wall as he frisked her. As many years as she'd been on the road with the group, Mama Wes had never been patted down. It was even specified in their rider that UGK would "not be patted-down or searched before entering [the] building" because "it is degrading."

Chad went ballistic when he saw the burly security guard manhandling his mother. "Search us!?" he yelled, raising his shirt to display the two pistols stuck in his waistband. "I got what you're looking for right here, fuck boy!"

Oh shit, thought Byron Amos, who was accompanying Chad as his bodyguard. Byron wished someone had warned him that Chad was in one of his moods.

Several police officers outside heard the commotion and ran towards the back entrance, one radioing over his walkie-talkie for backup. Byron grabbed Chad's .38mm and 9mm, rushing him back towards his car. Chad and Sonji hopped back in the Mercedes and hauled out of the parking lot. Within seconds, the nightclub was surrounded by flashing lights; police, already on edge during Freaknik weekend, surrounded the vans with their weapons drawn. Byron, who had a license for his own weapons but not Chad's, was arrested for disorderly conduct and carrying a concealed weapon.

Byron spent a week in the DeKalb County Jail and Chad hired him an attorney. The charges were eventually dropped, but Byron had to scrap his tentative plans to run for City Council, knowing the arrest would be tough to explain.

The incident solidified Byron Amos' place in the camp. Mama Wes liked having him around because he was good at diffusing potentially volatile situations. She considered him firm and level-headed, and Chad respected his calm, professional demeanor. "Byron [Amos] was real good for C [because] he could settle C down ... he would listen to Byron," says Mama Wes.

For years, Chad's Jekyll-and-Hyde mood swings had baffled even his closest friends. It was frustrating for people like Jeff Sledge, who never knew what to expect from him. When Jeff flew down to Atlanta, Chad enthusiastically volunteered to pick him up from the airport, proud to show off a new maroon Mercedes-Benz S-Class. After a productive trip, Jeff headed back to New York with a glowing report.

The next trip, Chad didn't offer to pick him up. Jeff rented a car and pulled up to the Alpharetta house around noon, where Mama Wes greeted him warmly. Jeff waited at the house until midnight and Chad never even came downstairs. *This is more than just sleeping,* Jeff thought. He returned to New York empty-handed and discouraged, convinced the rumors of Chad's escalating drug use must be true.

By all accounts, Chad's drug use was getting out of control by the spring of 2000. It didn't help that he'd been spending a lot of time with Biz; not only did Biz indulge himself, but he had a nearly endless supply of cocaine and was always willing to give Chad whatever he wanted. "His [drug] intake was just crazy," says Hashim. "I didn't like and didn't respect [Biz, and he] kept plenty of [drugs] around [C]."*

Mama Wes felt that Hashim's reasons for not liking Biz were more self-serving. "Hashim didn't like Biz [because] Hashim always wanted to be in C's ear," says Mama Wes. "So for Hashim, Biz may have been a threat."

Many in the camp didn't like Hashim, labeling him a con artist hiding behind a religious façade. "I don't trust [Hashim] as far as i could throw him," says security guard Carlos Moreland.

Although he was well-connected and always seemed to have hook-ups on cars and houses, Hashim usually had an ulterior motive. He'd convinced Chad to invest in his Fantasy Car Rental venture, purchasing expensive Benzes, Range Rovers, Lexuses and Navigators. In theory, at least, these cars would be rented out to paying customers, but in reality, Chad was paying for all of them, often with unnecessary customizations like expensive rims, tinted windows, or Playstations.

"Fuckin' Hashim got me buying all these damn cars and shit," Chad would complain. Pops, who hated Hashim and considered him a "hoe ass muthafucker" and a "total jackass," couldn't understand why Mama Wes trusted him. "Don't y'all understand that this dude is robbing y'all blind!?" he would ask.

When Hashim and his wife were planning a trip to Cancun with Malik Zulu Shabazz and his girlfriend, they invited Chad and Sonji to accompany them. It was the first time Chad had ever flown over water, and it was a challenge to convince him to board the flight. According to Hashim, he intended for the trip to be a mini-intervention where he could pull Chad to the side and have a serious talk with him about his cocaine and codeine use.

Mama Wes laughs off Hashim's claim that he held an "intervention," saying that the expenses for the Cancun trip came out of Chad's pocket. "[Hashim] just wanted to take his wife to Cancun, and do it at somebody else's expense," she says. "As far as I'm concerned, Hashim didn't do anything to either perpetuate [Chad's drug use] or curb it."

Angie, who was pregnant, was concerned when someone sent her a picture that supposedly showed Chad doing a line of cocaine at a video shoot. She'd never seen him do anything except smoke weed, and when she confronted him about the allegation, he brushed it off, telling her, "They just hating."

(*Biz's brother T-Roy disagrees. "A person can't make [another] person do nothing," he says. "It's a choice.")

Chad did start being a little more discreet about his drug use, sometimes using an inhaler to ingest cocaine during performances. "I snorted more cocaine than most of these [rap] niggas ever sold in the fuckin' [drug] game," he said years later.

DJ Bird was often the one stuck with the task of trying to get Chad out of the house. "He'd be so high he don't wanna move, he don't wanna go do the shows," Bird remembers. "I ain't going nowhere," Chad would mumble. "Fuck that shit." His constant mood swings were not only affecting his income, but the whole group – if Chad didn't go, no one got paid.

But while others thought Chad had a serious drug problem, Mama Wes believed his drug use was only a symptom of his struggle to cope with his mental health issues. Chad would often push himself to the limit, recording for hours on end and leading to an inevitable crash. Exhaustion led to depression, and when depression hit, it was severe.

"He suffered from depression terribly bad," says Mama Wes. "I would venture to say that C was depressed 80% of the time. But he was also a master of disguise, and sometimes you wouldn't really see it because he [handled] everything internally … [If] he didn't really want anybody to know, he would just disappear."

On one occasion, Chad was scheduled for a public appearance, but was feeling so down that his mother knew he wouldn't be able to do it. She invented a story on his behalf and called to reschedule as Chad sat and watched her talk on the phone.

"Thank you, Mama," he mumbled when she hung up. "*Maaan,* I just shouldn't be like this."

"Why, 'cause you *The Piiimp?*" his mother asked. In her opinion, Chad had a problem accepting the idea that he, as a black man, a rapper, was in need of mental health care. "[There's] a kind of a stigma … niggas don't see shrinks," says Mama Wes. "That's [perceived as] a 'white boy sickness.' Nobody wants to deal with the fact that a black man could be depressed."

When Chad was depressed, it wasn't unusual for him to sleep for as long as 48 hours. He would emerge from these mini-comas re-energized, ready to be "Pimp C" again and often bursting with creativity.

His mood swings reached a point where he confided in his mother that they were severely disrupting his life. She arranged for him to see a new therapist, who diagnosed him as bipolar. Bipolar disorder is characterized by two extremes: mania and depression. It wasn't unusual for someone suffering from bipolar disorder to abuse drugs or alcohol to try to control their moods, as Chad did, often creating a vicious cycle. While there was no cure for bipolar disorder, its symptoms could be eased with medication.

Finally having a diagnosis, an explanation, a name for the problem which had haunted him for years was somehow comforting. Mama Wes realized that being bipolar was part of what made him brilliant and unique. "I think [Chad's bipolar disorder] was his greatest enemy, and his greatest friend," she says. "And [I know] that sounds crazy, but I do."

It was the manic side of his disorder which drove him to create; he wouldn't be the same without it. The music was also his escape, the way he coped with depression, and Mama Wes' greatest fear was what might happen if he ever lost that outlet. "I was always afraid that if he ever hit a dry spot, [where] he couldn't [create music], that it would take him out, it would destroy him," she says. "Because the couple of times that I saw him where his creativity wasn't quite up to par, he couldn't handle that."

The more she researched bipolar disorder, Mama Wes realized the symptoms had been clear ever since Chad first asked to see a therapist at age 13. At the time, the symptoms of bipolar disorder weren't widely known.

"C had an addictive personality," adds Mama Wes. "There are people who are prone to be addicted, and you can tell that by the force with which they do everything. Like, C couldn't just write a song. It had to be a *perfect* song. He couldn't just make a beat, he had to keep [going] until he thought it was perfect [and then he] might wake up in the morning and think it was trash. He had that part of his personality, and I think all of that makes for lots of kinds of addictions."

She believed that whatever it was which drove him to experiment with cocaine and other drugs was the same impulse that kept him in the studio for hours at a time, obsessively listening to the same track repeatedly, tweaking each instrument to perfection.

Chad readily accepted the bipolar label, sometimes making a joke of it. "I'm a legal psychotic! They say I'm bipolar! Give me my pill and my check to go with it!" he would rant. He'd use it as an excuse if Jive was trying to talk him into something he didn't want to do. "Now, you know I'm bipolar and schizo, too," he'd say with a straight face, looking at his mother for support. "Ain't that right, Mama?"

Chad told his mother he believed he also had symptoms of schizophrenia, a severe brain disorder. Schizophrenia typically develops in a person's late teens or early twenties, and symptoms sometimes manifest themselves in subtle ways.

Mama Wes believed Chad's multiple personalities were a symptom of his schizophrenia (contrary to popular belief, schizophrenia and multiple personality disorder are actually considered two unrelated disorders). In her opinion, his multiple personalities also functioned as a protective shield.

"[The] real reason why he created all those characters was because he did not want people to know the real C," Mama Wes explains. "The real Chad was very, very quiet, very unassuming, very sensitive, and he had a lot of fears. And he didn't want anybody to know that side of him … He definitely didn't like to share it, but C was also a very, very quiet, very bashful kind of person, so he had to create those characters so he could be who he wanted to be."

Chad had once attempted to explain his alter egos to his childhood friend NcGai, describing "Pimp C" as an escape from the restrictions of reality. "He told me … Pimp C was that person inside of him," NcGai says. "[There were] always things he wanted to do and things he wanted to be; that was Pimp C, [but] *he* was Chad … They were two separate people."

"He would create a character so that he could behave [like a gangsta or a pimp]," agrees Mama Wes. "Chad Lamont Butler could never do that, so he had to create a character who could."

Mama Wes understood why he'd invented each of the characters. The pimp, Sweet James Jones, was simply because he liked to be controversial. (James Jones was a separate personality; calm but conniving, a shrewd character modeled after Rap-A-Lot's James Prince.) Percy Mack, another personality, was a gangsta. "He was always fascinated by the psyche of gangsters," says Mama Wes. "He studied [them] really in depth … He liked to get into [people's] heads, and he was pretty successful at doing that."

Those closest to Chad understood that Chad, C, Pimp C, James Jones, Sweet James Jones, Percy Mack, Tony Snow, Jack Tripper, and all his other personas were distinctly different people. Mama Wes was fascinated with them all. "I liked [the] Pimp C [character] because he was funny," she says. "And he *was* all those people."

Childhood friends and family members had a hard time reconciling the loud, brash "Pimp C" persona with the shy, quiet boy they'd known as a youth. While Chad the man valued his privacy and tried to shield his children from the public, Pimp C loved the attention.

Mama Wes could distinguish between his personalities, which could change in an instant, by his demeanor or the tone of his voice. Sometimes when he called, he'd save her the trouble of guessing and introduce himself ("This is Pimp," "This is C," or, "What's up Mama, Sweet James Jones comin' atcha"). Even Chad and C were two different people; Chad (or "Chaddyboo") was the shy child who'd call his mother with a gentle, "Hey, my lil' mama, this your baby boy." (Mama Wes had always affectionately referred to Chad as "Chaddyboo" until Chad Jr. arrived and inherited the nickname.)

If Bun or J. Prince needed to talk to Chad about something important, they'd call Mama Wes first. "I gotta call that boy," they'd say. "Should I talk to him today?"

"I don't think so," Mama Wes would advise. "[He's] James Jones today."

In 2000, a rap duo named The YoungBloodz were picking up momentum in Atlanta with their records "U-Way" and "85," featuring OutKast's Big Boi. Group member Sean Paul, who wore his long hair in a braid, had a slow laid-back country drawl reminiscent of Pimp C. His partner J-Bo's rap voice sounded so much like Khujo Goodie that Khujo's father nearly couldn't tell the difference when he heard a YoungBloodz song on the radio.

The YoungBloodz were a part of the informal coalition called the Attic Crew, which also included Noontime Records' rap group Jim Crow. Pimp C stopped by Jazze Pha's Noontime Studios late one night in a bad mood, saying he had some things to get off his chest. "Man, gimme a track," he instructed Jazze, heading straight for the vocal booth. "Gimme that track right there. Load that up."

Pimp spent nearly thirty minutes in the booth, unleashing a lengthy freestyle. Jazze kept looping the track; Pimp's rant eventually turned to Master P. *Damn, why you going so hard on everybody?* Jazze Pha wondered.

By this time, the session had attracted a small crowd. Cutty, a member of Jim Crow, was one of several onlookers in the studio bobbing their head to the beat. When Pimp started rapping about that "fuck nigga Sean Paul," Jazze froze.

Cutty stared at Jazze. "Man, what the fuck? You let that nigga talk like that about your boy?"

Jazze cut the beat off. "Man, what the fuck was that?" he asked Pimp.

"He trying to rap like me," Pimp spat. "He trying to sound like me. You could never, *ever* be Pimp C."

Cutty walked outside on his cell phone; Jazze knew he was calling for reinforcements. Worried that the studio was about to turn into a battleground, Jazze told Pimp they needed to wrap things up. "Hey, we gotta make a move," he said.

While it's unclear exactly what sparked Pimp's anger (some say Sean Paul had made a statement during a radio interview which Pimp incorrectly interpreted as a diss), he was mostly upset because he felt Sean Paul was biting his style.* "When you're one of the first people to pioneer something, you don't ever really get the credit you deserve," says DJ Greg Street. "Other people come behind you [and] emulate some of the stuff you do. I think that in the beginning, [Pimp] was kind of irritated by that."

As they say, imitation is the sincerest form of flattery, and most of Pimp's friends felt that he should simply take it as a compliment. But they couldn't say he was wrong. "[Sean Paul] *was* trying to sound like him," agrees Rico Wade. "That's how much influence Pimp had." The way Rico saw it, the fact that young rappers were emulating Pimp C instead of East Coast rappers was a positive thing: it meant that the South was in the rap game to stay.

The next day, Pimp C stopped by V103 to do an interview on Greg Street's radio show. Pimp again dissed Sean Paul on the air before heading out to Atlanta nightclub The Garage, where Greg was holding an event with Scarface, Too $hort, and Three 6 Mafia. During Too $hort's segment, Greg brought Pimp C on stage to do his verse on "Big Pimpin."

Pimp held the crowd in rapt attention, explaining that he was sick of people imitating him. He asked if The YoungBloodz were in the building. "Where is this muthafucker named Sean Paul at, he sounding like me?" Pimp demanded. "And this other nigga J-Bo, sounding like Khujo? Where is this nigga at?"

Nervous laughter and murmurs broke out in the audience. "Man, Sean Paul rap like me again, I'm gon' cut his ponytail off," Pimp announced. "If you see that muthafucker Sean Paul, you tell that muthafucker I'll fuck him in the ass with a broomstick."

The YoungBloodz weren't there, but the crowd was filled with his friends and associates from the Dungeon Family and the Attic Crew. "Man, get your mans," one told Too $hort.

Sean Paul's friend Pretty Ken of the Attic Crew had already heard about Pimp's statement

---

(*Sean Paul, whose government name is Sean Paul Joseph, says he has no idea what set Pimp off. "To this day, I don't know what happened," he says. He denies that he was intentionally trying to sound like Pimp. "Everything I do is original," he says. "I talk just like how I rap, man … I don't even have no rap name. My name [is] Sean Paul, that's my real name. I'm not a character.")

and was busy rallying the troops to head over to The Garage.* Atlanta DJ Lil Jon leaned over towards Hashim. "You better get [Pimp] outta here," Jon suggested.

By the time Sean Paul, Pretty Ken, and several dozen men stormed into the dressing rooms, Pimp C was already gone. DJ Paul, like most onlookers backstage, was baffled. "I don't know what the fuck that situation was about," he says. Sean Paul and Pretty Ken were confused, too. They'd even stopped by Pimp's Mableton house once to listen to some beats and thought they were on good terms.

Others didn't find the outburst unusual. "Pimp was [just] like that," shrugs Kool Ace. "Pimp would wake up every three or four months and just go off on everybody."

Rico Wade was one of many who tried to intercede and make sure the situation didn't explode. He considered both Sean Paul and Pimp C family, and didn't want division in their midst. "That's like Dungeon Family little cousin," Rico told Pimp. "He don't mean no harm."

Another Dungeon Family member with ties to Pimp C was Kawan "KP" Prather, one-third of the group Parental Advisory. Their early 90s debut *Ghetto Street Funk* was one of the first projects produced by Organized Noize. Pimp dropped a verse alongside Big Gipp for Parental Advisory's 1998 record "Dope Stories," but KP was in the process of transitioning from a rapper to an executive.

KP landed a job at LaFace Records, where he had his own imprint, Ghet-O-Vision Entertainment. His first signee was a rapper from Atlanta's Bankhead housing projects named Clifford "Tip" Harris, who changed his name to "T.I." to avoid any confusion with his new labelmate Q-Tip of A Tribe Called Quest.

Despite his small frame, T.I. had a brash, cocky attitude developed from his years of hustling on the streets. He'd started cutting school when he was just twelve years old to sell crack, until groups like UGK helped inspire him to switch up his hustle and pursue the rap game. He'd been a fan since *Too Hard to Swallow*. "The young T.I., he reminded you of what the young Pimp was," says Big Gipp. "He got [his] attitude and swag [from] Pimp."

KP had 19-year-old T.I. in the studio working on his debut album *I'm Serious* and arranged for him to be one of the opening acts at a UGK concert in Atlanta. Backstage, T.I. and his P$C crew approached UGK's dressing room. Pimp, wearing a red mink coat, waved them off. "We good back here," he said.

"Naw, man, I'm on the show with y'all -" T.I. began, trying to introduce himself. Pimp cut him off. "I don't give a fuck," he snapped as he closed the dressing room door.

Most of T.I.'s crew were heavily armed, and KP sensed imminent disaster. He pulled T.I. to the side to calm him down before edging his way into Pimp's dressing room. Tactfully, KP reminded Pimp how it felt to be young and struggling.

"You've been through it yourself," KP told Pimp. "You can't do people like that if you want to set an example. So now the example you setting is for him to be a dickhead to somebody."

"*Maaan*, you know what, KP?" Pimp drawled. "You are absolutely right. Tell that young man to come back on in here."

With "Big Pimpin'" dominating radio and "Sippin' on Some Syrup" heavy in the streets, UGK's star power was at an all-time high during the summer of 2000. Calls came pouring in for shows – and not the meager $4,000 or $5,000 shows they'd been doing for years. Offers were coming in for $12,500, $15,000, even $20,000 or more.

The "Big Pimpin'" video had finally given Pimp the "look" he wanted. And ever since Barry Weiss told Mama Wes that Jive staffers didn't consider UGK "video-friendly," she'd been eagerly awaiting the day she could prove them wrong. She savored the moment, calling Barry to ask if

(*Nearly everyone interviewed about this event, including Sean Paul, recalls Pretty Ken being a central character in the drama, but Pretty Ken claims he has no recollection of the incident.)

he'd seen the "Big Pimpin'" video yet. "Hey, looks like they 'video-friendly,' huh?" she smiled.

In addition to solidifying Pimp's image with the public, the video also boosted his confidence as a performer. "I think he felt secure [in being Pimp C] after he did those two successful videos," says Mama Wes. "At first, he didn't really feel that secure [playing that character]. And C liked doing what he knew he could do [well]."

For many people in New York or Los Angeles, when they saw the video, it finally clicked: this was that underground group they'd always heard about but never seen. Brand Nubian's Lord Jamar no longer had to explain to his New York friends who Bun B and Pimp C were. It made people all over the country take note of UGK: up-and-coming producers like Pharrell Williams in Virginia, and aspiring young rappers like a 13-year-old Compton teenager named Kendrick Lamar Duckworth.

The record even convinced Bun's mother, who had always thought her son was a drug dealer, that he actually *was* a rapper. Far removed from the music industry, she had never understood why he was struggling financially if he was a successful musician. Finally seeing him on TV made her a believer.

"Big Pimpin'" also put Pimp C on the radar of the pimp community, real pimps like Matthew "Knowledge Born" Thompkins on the East Coast, whose stable of prostitutes were enamored by the video and assumed Pimp C was an actual pimp. At Sharpstown Mall in Houston, Pimp's mink coat and matching mink shoes caught the attention of "Pimpin'" Ken Ivey, who had been featured in the 1998 film *Pimps Up, Hoes Down*.

"[The idea of] being a pimp is kind of intriguing to men," says Pimp's friend Mike Mo. "It was kind of a dynamic relationship with [Pimpin'] Ken and Pimp. They was both intrigued by each other's work."

"[Pimp C] taught me a little bit about the rap game," Pimpin' Ken explained on the *Too Real For TV* DVD. "I was learning the rapping and I was teaching them the pimping, and the game was merging, man. We was taking it to another level."

Regardless of how Pimp C or his friends felt about Jay-Z personally, they couldn't deny he'd handed them a huge opportunity. "When Jay fucked with UGK, it really took them to another level where other people started looking at them and respecting them," says Big Gipp. Other New York artists, who had previously been apathetic to the movement taking place in the South, soon followed Jay-Z's lead and started reaching out to Southern acts for features.

Producer Mannie Fresh viewed it as validation for everyone in the South who had done it *their* way. "[UGK's success] was like a victory for everybody [that] knew Pimp C or UGK," Mannie says. "[We admired the fact that] his dude [Pimp C] ain't apologetic for nothing, he's just going to say it how it comes out [instead of] trying to correct [his] words and sound New Yorkish."

Pimp later complimented Jay-Z for his foresight. "We played our part, but that's his record," he said. "Jay-Z is very smart. The man knows how to put singles together, he knows what's gonna sell before it sells and that's a talent that a lot of artists don't have. By him bringing us in … he was really giving us a meal ticket and a blessing."

Of course, it wasn't entirely a philanthropic gesture on Jay-Z's part; the collaboration benefited both of them. "Being on a song with Jay-Z did a lot for UGK … but people never talk about the fact that Jay-Z being on a song with UGK [helped] Jay-Z too in the South," notes journalist Matt Sonzala.

"[Jay-Z] saw a way to help us and at the same time help himself," Pimp C told AllHipHop. "You've got to understand that a lot of people who would never buy a Jay-Z album bought a Jay-Z album off the strength of that record."

In a feature for *Texas Monthly*, Destiny's Child manager Matthew Knowles explained that collaborations between rap artists, in general, was a smart business move. "You've got your market, and I've got mine," he said. "We bring those together, we both win. In corporate America, that's called a merger."

In June 2000, Jay-Z invited UGK to make a guest appearance during his headlining set at Hot 97's Summer Jam, arguably New York's biggest music event of the year. Roc-A-Fella rapper Beanie Sigel, thrilled to see UGK backstage, flagged down Pimp C. Beanie was from Philadelphia, where gangstas had been sipping cough syrup to get high since the 1960s. He'd started sipping at eight years old, watching his uncle nodding off and scratching himself absentmindedly in his grandmother's kitchen.

"Yo, Pimp C, I always wanted to meet you!" Beanie Sigel told him excitedly. "Yo, we be doing that shit in Philly too! I didn't even know it had spread. We be sipping that syrup in Philly, too, hell yeah. I be getting it in."

Bad Boy Records' CEO Sean "Puff Daddy" Combs pulled Bun to the side. Bad Boy had just signed Tony Thompson, the Texas-bred lead singer of R&B group Hi-Five.

"Yo, what's up with you Texas niggas?" Puff Daddy asked.

"What you mean?" Bun laughed. "What's up with you Harlem niggas?"

"Naw, naw," Puff Daddy backtracked. "I'm sayin', though … I just signed your man Tony from Hi-Five [and] he took all the pills in my medicine cabinet. He drank my cough syrup."

When UGK hit the stage with Jay-Z, the crowd went crazy for "Big Pimpin." Jive's Jeff Sledge, watching in amazement, felt that it was a turning point for the group to finally gain the recognition they deserved in New York.

Suddenly, for the first time in their career, UGK was a hot commodity at Jive, but it was a bittersweet victory. "[Jive] didn't move until Jay-Z called," Bun told journalist Matt Sonzala.

"[Jive had] the desire to take UGK to the next level at that time," Pimp agreed in an interview with *XXL*. "Never before or after."

But now that UGK had the label's attention, they couldn't agree on what direction to go creatively. To Jive, the plan was simple: "Big Pimpin' Pt. 2." They wanted to repeat the same formula: get another Timbaland track, ask Jay-Z to return the favor by dropping a verse, and have Hype Williams shoot a video.

It had been four long years since *Ridin' Dirty*, and the last thing UGK wanted to do was return with a radio-friendly pop record and risk losing their diehard fans. They preferred to stick with their country rap tunes formula which they'd perfected on *Ridin' Dirty*. UGK felt that instead of spending money on a Timbaland beat and Jay-Z feature, Jive should put those funds behind *their* creative vision.

Barry Weiss was baffled at Chad's resistance. "They were such kings of the underground they didn't wanna be *overground*. It's almost like [Chad] was scared of big success. It was kinda strange, you know?" muses Weiss. "After 'Big Pimpin,' I thought, *now it's time*. They were so poised to be humungous, ginormous, one of the greatest – because they were *that* good – and I couldn't get a damn record out of them."

"Pimp didn't wanna go to another level," agrees Hashim. "I think he had liked being that lil' guy in the middle." Others felt that while Chad wanted recognition, it was bittersweet that it had to come through Jay-Z: he wanted to be recognized on *his* terms, for *his* music. "That's all Pimp ever wanted for them, to get the notoriety," says Rico Wade. "He wanted what OutKast had … he just hated for it to come through [Jay-Z]."

Although they were adamantly opposed to the label's idea to repeat the Timbaland/Jay-Z formula, Bun and Chad didn't present a better suggestion, either. "We didn't have an alternative plan for [what] the label was saying," Bun told *VIBE*. "We didn't have an alternative marketing strategy."

Ultimately, the golden opportunity to follow-up the buzz from "Big Pimpin'" would largely go to waste. "We as a team weren't really ready to capitalize on everything that we got from the song," Bun admitted.

CHAPTER 24

"I think that [Master P incident] scared C way worse than he would ever admit. I think that made him realize how vulnerable he really was ... it just scared the shit out of him." – Mama Wes

———————

"We lived in the streets [so] we lived by street rules ... If you do something, just be ready for the consequences ... that's the reality of all situations. As far as I'm concerned we squared whatever it was up and we handled our misunderstandings ... After that time and place we never heard about [Pimp C dissing No Limit] again." – Anthony "Boz" Boswell, Vice President of Operations, No Limit Records

July 2000
Stafford, Texas

Late one night as a key clicked in the lock of Chad's room at the Marriott Residence Inn, he and his female companion looked up in surprise. The door flung open and five men, their faces covered with black ski masks, rushed into the room. The woman grabbed the nearest thing she could find – the hotel coffeepot – and threw it at them, but she was quickly subdued.

One man, gripping a knife in his hand, threw Chad onto the bed and held the knife to his throat. His hand, mere inches from Chad's face, was covered in cutoff workout gloves with the "No Limit" logo. Four men held Chad down on the bed as the fifth man shoved a pistol in his mouth and told him he'd better stop dissing No Limit.

After a severe pistol-whipping, his assailant removed his mask so Chad could get a good look at his attacker. It was Master P. The other four men were likely his right-hand man Boz, his bodyguards Kirt Hankton and Tony, and his cousin Jimmie Keller, who had joined No Limit as an A&R after spending eight years in prison for manslaughter.* Jimmie was known for his hot temper and short fuse, a loose cannon who had once jumped over a Waffle House counter and knocked out the cook for taking too long preparing his food.

Before they left, Master P commented that if it was any consolation, he wasn't the only one – they'd just launched a similar attack on No Limit rapper Mystikal.**

DJ Bird and Leroy White, who were on their way to pick up Big Mike for Pimp C's scheduled studio session at N.O. Joe's Platinum Sounds in nearby Stafford, got a call from Rambro at the hotel. They rushed back to find Chad with a black eye, his hotel room torn apart. "He was like, stunned," DJ Bird remembers. "He really didn't wanna say too much about the situation

(*Pimp C never spoke on the record about the alleged hotel room beating. The story as told here is based on several of his friends' recollections of his description of the incident. Master P declined to comment on the alleged hotel run-in; as for their "beef," he simply says, "I always kept it 100 with him." According to Jimmie Keller's ex-fiancé Mia X, Keller later admitted that he was one of the men who participated in the beating. Keller is now deceased. Boz declined to confirm or deny if he was there. Some No Limit affiliates heard that the other two men accompanying Master P were his bodyguards Kirt Hankton and Tony. Tony's full name is not known, and Kirt Hankton was unable to be reached for comment.)
(**As DJ Bird recalls it, Chad said Master P bragged that he had cut off Mystikal's braids. Rumors were circulating that the Mystikal beatdown was retribution either for trying to leave No Limit or allegedly sleeping with C-Murder's girlfriend, singer Monica.)

because it just happened. C was kinda quiet, trying to get over it."

Rambro called Mama Wes, who was asleep back in Port Arthur. "Chad's been hurt," he told her. Her mind flashed to a car accident; visions of twisted metal everywhere. *"Hurt!?"* she said, panicking. When she learned what had happened, Mama Wes was furious that Jive booked his rooms at the Residence Inn in Stafford (near Sugar Land, where Master P had recently purchased a house) instead of downtown at the usual location.*

Mama Wes called Red Boy, who had been at their townhouse earlier that day. Red Boy wondered aloud why Chad hadn't called him when he left. "I told him to tell me when he moved," he sighed.**

To Mama Wes, Red Boy's offhand remark spoke volumes. She knew how Rap-A-Lot operated – or "R-A-L," as she liked to call them – and clearly, they'd been anticipating something like this. "[The conversation with Red Boy] led me to believe that they knew [Master] P was after C," she says. "I think that J. [Prince] knew that C was in imminent danger and he didn't tell him. That's why C wasn't supposed to move without telling Red Boy; they didn't want that to happen. What they wanted was the [Rap-A-Lot] goon squad to be there and [squash] the whole situation … [but] it backfired."

Hashim, as head of Pimp C's security detail, got the same impression. "In the real world … there's made men out here. And if you cross a made man's path, he's [gonna] do one of two things: he'll either get you assassinated, or he'll get permission to touch you and let you know he can touch you," explains Hashim. "I believe Master P got permission to touch Pimp, but don't kill him, and don't hurt him too bad … [And] there's only one person who could give that kind of permission."

As Mama Wes recalls it, Red Boy convinced Chad to go to the hospital, where it was determined that he had a concussion and several fractured ribs. One of his eyes was swollen shut. "[They] beat him damn near to death," Mama Wes says.

How Master P located Chad remains a mystery. Mama Wes believed that someone either followed Chad from the townhouse or recognized one of his vehicles. Master P knew that Chad always stayed at Residence Inns and could have heard that he was recording in the area. Chad and DJ Bird suspected that the hotel clerk summoned Master P, while others wondered if Chad's unidentified lady friend set him up.

In a story which later circulated around the No Limit offices, Master P happened to be staying at the same hotel because he had an early flight to catch and the hotel clerk commented, "Oh, y'all all staying here?" mentioning that Pimp C had just checked in. The clerk, either a No Limit fan or easily bribed, handed over a key to Pimp's room.***

"I think you know the story already," Master P's right-hand man Boz laughs when asked to explain what happened that night, declining to confirm or deny the hotel pistol-whipping tale. He is similarly coy when asked how they might have located Pimp C, simply commenting, "There's an old saying that goes, 'What goes around comes around … Two mountains may never meet, but two men always will.'"

"We lived in the streets [so] we lived by street rules … If you do something, just be ready for the consequences … that's the reality of all situations," Boz adds. "As far as I'm concerned … we handled our misunderstandings … After that time and place we never heard about [Pimp C

(*Master P's four-bedroom, six-bathroom home in a gated community in Sugar Land was outfitted with an arcade, a recording studio, a movie theatre, game room, aquarium, basketball court, and a pool. The home was featured in February 2002 as the #1 Teen Celeb Crib for Master P's son Lil Romeo's episode of MTV's *Teen Cribs*. In it, 12-year-old Lil Romeo, who wasn't even old enough to drive, showed off a customized Mercedes-Benz with 20" rims.)

(**Anzel "Int'l Red" Jennings, or "Red Boy," who is now Bun B's manager, declined to be interviewed. Most of his statements and actions as described in this book are from Mama Wes' recollection.)

(***Later, in some dramatic retellings of the story, Chad said that Master P kicked his door in, but those who were present at the hotel that night believe he used a room key.)

dissing No Limit] again."

As Houston party host Wickett Crickett recalls it, J. Prince was at Houston strip club Score's Cabaret with boxer Floyd Mayweather when he got a call informing him that something had happened between Master P and Pimp C. "J. [Prince] was always trying to defuse any beef, any problem that was going on … he was the one always bringing everybody together," says Wickett Crickett.

The following day, J. Prince told Mama Wes things were being handled. "I called that nigga [Master P]," she recalls him saying. "I told him he probably needs to move around, because there's too many people that love that boy [C]."

Master P soon relocated to the West Coast. "When [Pimp C] got J. Prince [and] them involved, that's why [Master] P left the South," Big Gipp observed. "Ain't been back since."

For many in Chad's crew, their thoughts immediately turned to retaliation. Byron Amos, who tended to be the most level-headed, tried to calm everyone down. But ultimately, it was Chad who made the decision to fall back. "Look, I ran my mouth," he admitted. "P and me got into it, and whatever happened, happened … Leave that shit alone. Let's move on."

N.O. Joe had been waiting at the studio and called Mama Wes a few days later to find out what was going on. "The guys still coming to the studio?" he asked.

Mama Wes told him what had happened and said they'd reschedule in a few days. But Chad was already on a flight back to Atlanta nursing bruises and a swollen black eye. Mama Wes felt that he wanted to hide out while his bruises healed to salvage what was left of his pride.

About two weeks before the Master P incident, on June 15, Angie had given birth to a son, naming him Dahcorey or just "Corey." She dropped by the townhouse one Sunday afternoon after church so Mama Wes and Pops could meet the baby. At dusk, Chad called from Atlanta, in a silly mood. "Mommy, what you doing?" he asked.

"I'm sitting down."

"What are you sitting down for? You're never sitting down. You feeling okay? You go to church today?"

"Yes, I went to church today, and I feel fine," she answered.

"Well, why you sitting down?"

"I'm tired. I've been playing with a little baby boy all afternoon."

"Who's little baby boy?"

"A young lady named Angela, that you know very, very well."

Chad suddenly got quiet. "Oh yeah? What he look like?"

"Remember that picture that I had in Chaddyboo's crib after he was born?"

"Yeah."

"Kinda looks like that picture."

"A lil' red nigga?"

"Mmmhmm," confirmed Mama Wes.

"Did you like playing with him?"

"Yeah, I like playing with him."

"What did you feel?" Chad asked.

"I feel like I wanna play with him again," Mama Wes said. "I told his mama to drop him off in the morning."

There was a brief silence. "I'm coming home," Chad announced.

Two days later, Chad came back to Houston to meet his son. He picked the baby up and cradled him in his arms. "Hmm," he said. "Yeah, Mama … it feels right."

He gently rocked the boy back and forth. "Now, this ain't Chaddyboo," he continued, a sly grin crossing his face. "See, this nigga right here, yeah … we're gonna have to make a rapper out of him. I already hear it … he has my talent."

Plans to resume recording for *Dirty Money* were indefinitely delayed; in the months following the hotel incident, Chad became reclusive and withdrawn. "He lost his inspiration," says Mama Wes. "He was strange [during that time]. He was pissed … He was really hurt that [Master P] would do that. He felt like, 'If you want to come at me, come at me one-on-one … don't come at me with niggas holding me down.'"

"Anytime I've ever seen a man get jumped … it changes them drastically," agrees Young Smitty. "It changes a man … It changed Chad." New security procedures were implemented in the UGK camp, and they were now accompanied by Rap-A-Lot security. Everyone was tense and on edge; DJ Dolby D was reprimanded for getting "out of the circle" for making a solo late-night Waffle House run after a show.

Chad started carrying a pistol with him everywhere he went, sometimes sleeping with a Glock resting on his chest. "I think that scared C way worse than he would ever admit," Mama Wes says. "I think that made him realize how vulnerable he really was … it just scared the shit out of him … C was not accustomed to getting knocked around … I think that was pretty traumatic for him."

Of course, Rap-A-Lot protection came with strings attached. J. Prince was a businessman who didn't give away his valuable resources without getting something in return. He had seen potential in UGK from the beginning, and now he could offer something Jive couldn't.

The Master P drama would cement Pimp C's ties to Rap-A-Lot. For years, J. Prince had always been there, so Pimp decided it was time to make it official. "When thangs would go wrong and I'd have problems, [he would] sometimes be the last resort," Pimp said on the *Pimpalation* DVD. "I had to use that goddamn number, and I called him, and the man wasn't making no money off me. We wasn't even affiliated."

Bun was already starting to feel that Mama Wes' management position was compromising her motherly responsibilities. Plus, she didn't have a clear understanding of clearances, royalties, and other intricacies of the music business.

"Pimp and I both made [the decision] that Mama Wes wasn't going to manage us anymore," Bun says. "The reality was that we were finding ourselves in positions where we didn't agree with some of the decisions that management wanted to make, and basically it was putting a son at odds with his mother. I felt that our business relationship wasn't worth fucking up their personal relationship."

Pimp C and Bun signed a co-management agreement with Mama Wes and J. Prince. Although Mama Wes would still be actively involved with booking shows, J. Prince would now bring his business savvy and his muscle to the equation. Prince and Chad also agreed to form a record label together, a 50/50 joint venture called Wood Wheel Records.

News of the Master P pistol-whipping spread, but with no one ever officially confirming the story, it remained little more than a rumor. Bun deflected questions to his partner. When asked by MVRemix what had "really happened that night Master P had Pimp C beat up in that hotel room," Bun replied, "It's kind of hard to say because I wasn't really there … you'd probably have to ask Pimp C or Master P about that."

When Pimp's angry verses about Ron Robinson on "Play Hard" (a.k.a. "I Know U Strapped") were released, some fans assumed he was referring to the rumored Master P altercation. The story of the hired hitman and the Master P beef became intertwined into one larger-than-life tale; rumor held that Master P had called J. Prince and asked for permission to kill Pimp C.*

(*In 2011 the *Houston Press* dismissed the story that Master P "kidnapped Pimp, took him to a motel, pistol whipped him, then called J. Prince and asked for permission to kill him" as one of "The Most Ridiculous Houston Rap Rumors Ever," adding that "none of it has ever been confirmed by anybody with proper knowledge of the situation.")

Chad and Bun had perhaps assumed that, like Russell Washington, Byron Hill would grow weary of their legal battle and leave them alone. They didn't really understand the court system, and didn't have money to spend on attorney's fees. "C [and] Bun weren't really gung-ho about fighting [Byron]," Mama Wes says. "They thought he'd probably just go away. And he didn't."

In an Atlanta courtroom, Byron claimed that he had served UGK in Dallas and requested a default judgment since they had not filed an answer. Byron claimed he was owed 20% of the group's income from 1996 through the end of 1999, which he estimated as $2,070,000 in royalties from their three Jive albums, $1,610,000 for side features and production, and $1,365,000 for shows. With no one there to dispute Byron's version of the story, a judge granted him a judgment of $1,009,000 plus interest and $3,823.74 in attorney's fees.

After learning of the judgment against them, UGK hired an Atlanta-based attorney, Tanya Mitchell-Graham, to attempt to reopen the case. She argued that they had never been personally served and the Dallas marshal had only succeeded in giving the paperwork to Pops, who was not legally "an authorized agent of the Underground Kingz."

Byron argued that he had gone to "extraordinary lengths" to serve the "ever-evasive Defendants" who were trying to avoid "the inevitable entry of Judgment against them." The judge sided with UGK and dismissed the case, questioning its placement in a federal courtroom.

But the dismissal of his lawsuit only encouraged Byron Hill to try again; he filed another lawsuit in Atlanta in October 2000 and sent a process server to N.O. Joe's studio during a scheduled recording session. UGK wasn't there, but the man left a FedEx package with a copy of the lawsuit. (N.O. Joe would later assert in an affidavit that the package vanished and he could "only assume the cleaning crew disposed of it.")

In the fall of 2000, Jay-Z was trailed by cameras for *MTV Diary* as he guided his Mercedes-Benz around Brooklyn. "I'm somewhat of a loner," he admitted. "I like, ride around in the car by myself just thinking about different things." With his seat reclining comfortably, he drove over the Brooklyn Bridge bobbing his head to "Pocket Full of Stones." "Wood Wheel" blasted as he pulled up to grab a pair of white Nike Jordan 6's from a local shoe store, en route to his old 'hood, Marcy Projects.

A month later Jay-Z brought UGK out as a special guest when he performed at Houston's Reliant Hall for the 2000 Los Magnificos car show. "We always been blessed to have a large fanbase in the South," Pimp C told *South Coast Live* TV backstage. "It was just a matter of time before somebody was gonna take us to MTV. Jay-Z did that and opened the door and kicked it in. I'm just loving it."

Although Crooked Lettaz' debut album *Grey Skies* was critically acclaimed, it didn't sell many units. Pimp C's contribution on "Get Crunk" was the standout track on the album. Crooked Lettaz felt they were being overlooked at Penalty Records, which was focusing most of its efforts on promoting New York rappers Capone-N-Noreaga.

Penalty Records folded not long after Crooked Lettaz' album dropped, and the group was absorbed into their distributor Tommy Boy. As the group languished, David Banner grew more and more frustrated. He'd left a few messages at Mama Wes' house hoping they could shoot a video with Pimp for "Get Crunk," but they went overlooked in the rush of attention from "Big Pimpin'."

Banner decided to follow Pimp's advice and stick with production as the best way to make money. He'd worked with Pastor Troy, T.I., Devin the Dude, and Fiend, and finally broke through with Trick Daddy's "Thug Holiday." One afternoon, while sifting through a stack of CDs at a friend's house, he came across a promo CD with the a capella and instrumental versions of UGK's "Take It Off." He drove around for several days listening to Pimp C's a capella

Chad shopping in Atlanta in 1997.
Courtesy of Lanika

Shortly after he moved to Atlanta, Chad met **Lanika** *(above, in her drop-top Cadillac)*, who caused some drama between him and producer Jazze Pha.

Courtesy of Lanika

Lanika was connected to several Nashville drug dealers, including her cousin **Brian "Biz" Hunter** *(above left)*, his partner **Waymond "Big Dog" Fletcher** *(above right)*, **Terrell "T" McMurry** *(below left)*, and **Askia "Priest" Covington** *(below right)*. Pimp C later recapped his dealings with these men on the XVII record "True Story."

Above and left: **Chad** in his Mableton home in 1997.
Courtesy of Lanika

Below: **Chad** celebrating **Chad Jr.'s** birthday in the late 1990s.
Courtesy of Nitacha Broussard.

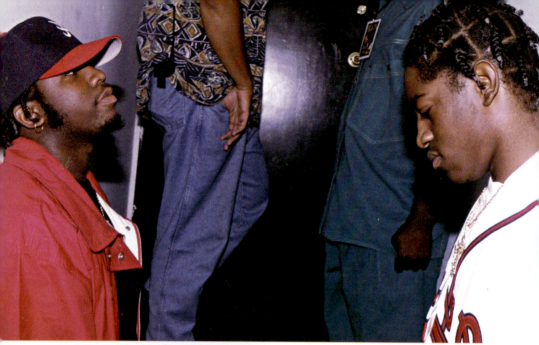

Living in Atlanta in the late 1990s brought Pimp C closer to his "musical cousins" Organized Noize and the Dungeon Family, which included **OutKast** *(above)* and the **Goodie Mob** *(below)*.

Photos: J Lash

Left (L-R): **Pimp C, Khujo Goodie, Vicious** and **Bundy** of the **X-Mob**, guest, and **Big Gipp** of the **Goodie Mob.**

The Atlanta years, clockwise from above: **Sonji Mickey**; **Rambro** at Patchwerk Studios, where "Big Pimpin'" was recorded; **David Banner** and **Kamikaze** of **Crooked Lettaz**; **E-40, Pimp C, Bun B, Jeff Sledge,** E-40's manager **Chaz Hayes,** and **B-Legit** in the studio; **Byron Amos** after his arrest at the Atrium Nightclub; **Mama Wes** and **Pops**; **Hashim Nzinga** and **Malik Zulu Shabazz.**

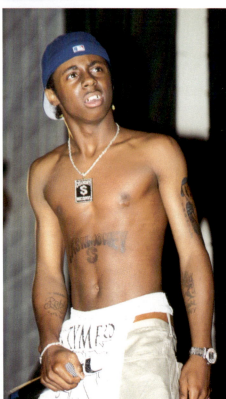

Cash Money Records around the time UGK toured with them on their 1999 Block 2 Block Tour. *Clockwise from below:* **B.G., Birdman,** and **Lil Wayne**; **Lil Wayne**; **Young Buck** and **Mannie Fresh**.
Photos: King Yella

Below: **Wendy Day** and **Mannie Fresh**.
Photo: Rick Edwards

Above: **Juvenile** on the set of his video shoot for "Ha," backed by the other Hot Boys **Turk** and **Lil Wayne**. **Bun B** and **Birdman** are seated inside the car.
Below: **B.G., Lil Wayne, Birdman, Bun B, Juvenile, Turk,** and guest.
Photos: King Yella

Ice melting on the driveway to **Chad's Alpharetta home** after an ice storm during the 2000 Super Bowl weekend. Three 6 Mafia's "Sippin' On Some Syrup" was recorded here.
Courtesy of Weslyn Monroe

Chad pulling up to the National Hotel on South Beach in his **brand new Mercedes-Benz** for the "Big Pimpin'" video shoot, March 2000.

Courtesy of Weslyn Monroe

Chad Jr. in Miami, March 2000 *(clockwise from above)*: getting dap from **DJ Paul** of **Three 6 Mafia** on the set of "Sippin' On Some Syrup"; clowning around at the hotel with Daddy; "driving" Daddy's car; visiting South Beach.
Courtesy of Weslyn Monroe

Bun B, Jay-Z, and **Pimp C** on the set of "Big Pimpin'" in Miami, March 2000

Clockwise from left: **Bun B** and some ladies on South Beach during the "Big Pimpin'" video shoot; **Chad** lounging with an unidentified lady friend; Jive Records' CEO **Barry Weiss** pictured with **Jay-Z** in 2003; video vixen **Gloria Velez**.

UGK photos courtesy of Weslyn Monroe
Barry Weiss/Jay-Z photo by James Devaney/Getty Images
Gloria Velez photo by J Lash

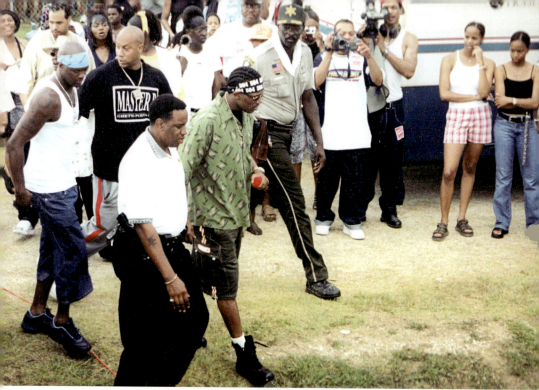

Pimp C had an altercation with No Limit CEO **Master P** *(above)* at this Houston area **Residence Inn** *(below left)* in July 2000. It is believed that Master P was accompanied by his right-hand man **Anthony "Boz" Boswell** *(below)*, his cousin **Jimmie Keller** *(pictured at right)*, and his bodyguards **Kirt Hankton** *(at left in the blue bandanna)* and **Tony** *(at left in the black "Master P" shirt)*.

No Limit photos by King Yella
Residence Inn photo by Julia Beverly

(L-R) No Limit's **Percy "Master P" Miller** pictured in the late 90s with his cousin **Jimmie Keller** and his brothers **Corey "C-Murder" Miller** and **Vyshonne "Silkk the Shocker" Miller.**
Photo: King Yella

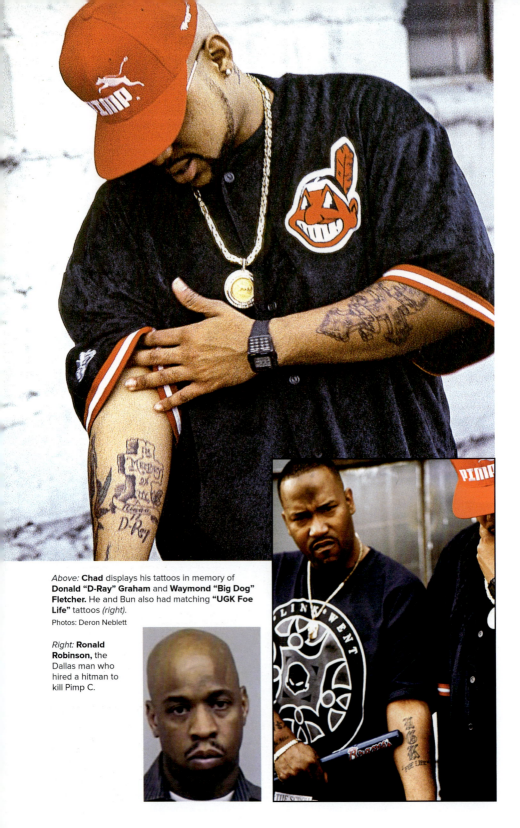

Above: **Chad** displays his tattoos in memory of **Donald "D-Ray" Graham** and **Waymond "Big Dog" Fletcher**. He and Bun also had matching **"UGK Foe Life"** tattoos *(right)*.

Photos: Deron Neblett

Right: **Ronald Robinson,** the Dallas man who hired a hitman to kill Pimp C.

Pimp C's altercations with Master P and Ron Robinson brought him closer to Rap-A-Lot. He is pictured with **Bun B** *(above)* wearing a Rap-A-Lot chain.

Right: **Pimp C** performing in Baton Rouge in the late 1990s.
Photos: King Yella

Below: Chad's son **Corey,** born in June 2000.
Courtesy of Angie Crooks

Above: **DJ Screw** working on *3 N tha Mornin'* at Samplified Digital Recording Studio, 1996. Courtesy of Big DeMo
Below: DJ Screw's father Robert Earl Davis Sr. a.k.a. **"Papa Screw"** after his son passed. Photo: Peter Beste

verse on repeat. Something about the line "make them gu'ls get down on the flo'" kept speaking to him. He built a beat around the sample, creating a quick track in fifteen minutes. Unsure if he liked it, he set the beat aside.

Several months after the Master P incident, Chad still wasn't inspired to record. Jive, concerned about the lack of output and the fact that UGK had once again missed their *Dirty Money* deadline, started putting pressure on the group to produce. Mama Wes explained the situation to Barry Weiss and asked him to give Chad some time to recuperate.

"He was still in a lot of pain and his head wasn't really right to do music," Mama Wes recalls, adding, "[It] was such a bad time for that to have happened, because it really pushed [*Dirty Money*] way, way off track again. That was the hardest album to get done."

When Chad finally did get back to work, another incident halted the recording process. Biz had loaned Chad the money for the Benz with the understanding that it would be repaid, but they'd never agreed on specific payment terms. Chad didn't have the money, and suggested that Biz could drive the Benz; after all, he'd paid for it. As DJ Bird remembers it, Biz got pissed off when he tried to take the car for a few days and Sonji stopped him.

A few weeks later, Biz appeared at the Alpharetta house early one morning. DJ Bird let Biz in the house and then went back to sleep.

By the time Chad woke up later that day, Biz was gone, and the studio downstairs was cleared out. Biz had gone back to Nashville with Chad's unreleased DAT tapes of music he'd been developing for *Dirty Money*.

Bird apologized profusely, but Chad remained calm. "*Shiiiiit*, that ain't shit," Chad mumbled. "He got my music, he ain't never gonna get my money. That ain't nothin' but a thang. I could always do more music. He can have that shit."

CHAPTER 25

"When Screw died, a lot of people didn't want to admit this, but we were all drug addicts. We didn't want to face the reality that we would have to stop." – Pimp C, *Beaumont Enterprise*, November 2005

"When Screw passed, I kinda made excuses. I said it was other things that killed him, just the whole lifestyle. That's part of being a drug addict. You make excuses and try to validate what you're doing. But at the same time, in the back of my mind I was always thinking, 'What if I go to sleep right now and don't wake up?' That's a scary thought." – Paul Wall, *OZONE* Magazine, April 2010

While Chad was living in Atlanta, DJ DMD linked up with a group of Port Arthur hustlers, including Chandrea Celestine and John "J-Will" Williams III, to launch Inner Soul Records. They signed some of the former DMI artists, like Lee Master and Boonie Loc, and dropped DMD's 1997 album *Eleven* with the Pimp C-assisted "Candy."

But it wasn't until 1998's "25 Lighters" that DMD's career finally started to take off. Although DMD took credit for producing the record, most say it was actually created by Marlan Rico Lee, a talented but eccentric engineer. And Isreal Kight, who was close to Inner Soul's co-owner J-Will, claims he wrote DMD's verse but wasn't credited for it.

DMD admitted to the *Beaumont Enterprise* that he "didn't even know what '25 Lighters' meant." The phrase, borrowed from the rapper MJG, referred to an easy container for crack sales. DMD took some old unused vocals from Lil Keke and Fat Pat, placed them on a demo version of "25 Lighters," and dropped it off at a Houston radio station. Within days, the song was in heavy rotation, spurred by its catchy hook and the significance of the record due to Fat Pat's recent passing.

Thanks to "25 Lighters," DMD's second album *Twenty-Two: P.A. World Wide* sold more than 50,000 copies independently in four short months and sparked major labels' interest. Mama Wes tried to offer some advice, sharing some of the mistakes they'd made when "Tell Me Something Good" blew up, but was rebuffed. "We tried to help [DMD] so he wouldn't do all the stupid wrong things we did, but he was a smart ass," she recalls.

Inner Soul signed a deal with Elektra Records to re-release the record nationally and the album went gold. They received a $500,000 advance and used nearly half of it to build Hiroshima, the only state-of the-art recording studio in Port Arthur.

"I thought all my dreams were coming true, [but] the whole time I [was] just getting knee deep in stuff that I shouldn't have gotten into," DMD admitted later. "It was a huge moment, and I wasn't mentally or spiritually prepared for it," he told the *Houston Chronicle*. "I was a clean-cut kid, but when Hip-Hop took that hard turn, I became enraptured by it. I wanted to be a gangster. Everybody was thugging, and so that's what I did. And I started to believe my own lies. I got wrapped up in a lifestyle and couldn't get out."

The rest of the Inner Soul Clique didn't like what success was doing to DMD either. Even those who had known him since childhood started to see him as selfish, arrogant, and greedy. "DMD has an ego out of this world ... DMD got the big head," says engineer Marlan Rico Lee.

"He thinks he's the shit. He does. And he will fuck you if he has to. He's got some good in him, but if he can see an opportunity to run around you and get [to] the gold, he's gonna take it. He's gonna put a banana peel [to stop you] and run in front of you." By the time DMD started recording for his third album *Thirty-Three: Live From Hiroshima*, he wasn't even on speaking terms with most of the Inner Soul artists.

It was in the midst of this turmoil that Chad started spending a lot of time back in Port Arthur and recording at Hiroshima. He started knocking out several records a day for his planned solo album, which he envisioned as a double album titled *PIMP: The Sweet Jones Story*. Among them was the standout track "I'm a Hustler," produced by DeJuan "D Stone" Durisseau.

Chad jokingly referred to D Stone and his brother Kehinde "KD" Durisseau as the Stone Boyz, comparing them to the Neptunes production duo. The Stone Boyz didn't even have a car and were impressed that Chad came to pick them up in his Navigator. "We [felt] like, 'Damn, we *that* special, rolling with C?'" remembers KD. "He was very humble ... he'd pull out the Pimp C character [for the public] but [with] the people he did deal with, he didn't act like no superstar."

When he wasn't recording at Hiroshima, Pimp was at his friend Mike Mo's home studio in Houston. Mike had been in and out of jail, and, hoping to keep his younger brother Cory Mo out of the streets, bought some cheap equipment to put in their mother's two-car garage and dubbed it M.A.D. Studios (Money At the Door).

By late 2000, Hiroshima had become one of the most popular hangout spots in Port Arthur. DMD's marriage was falling apart, mostly because of his affair with a woman named Ashanta. Ashanta and her friend Chinara Jackson often came by to hang out at the studio. When Inner Soul artist Boonie Loc needed a female to play the role of his weed-smoking side chick for a skit leading into "My Baby Mama" on his 2000 album *Dahellwitcha*, Chinara filled the part.

Chad came by the studio one day and asked Riley Broussard who the girl in the short skirt was. "That's that girl, she used to be real big," Riley told him. "She used to live right next door to James Bessard."

Chad narrowed his eyes, thinking; James Bessard was a Lincoln High classmate who sang with him in the choir. "I don't remember her," he said.

Chinara and Chad had briefly attended the same elementary school, but they hadn't seen each other in years. As children, Chad's neighbors Ron and Ronda Forrest were often dragged by their grandmother to visit an aunt who was Chinara's neighbor. Ron overheard enough of his grandmother's conversations to understand that the girl "didn't have an easy life." Chinara and Ronda would often sit together on the swing outside talking about "girly stuff" until Chinara's strict stepfather would summon her back inside with a hard Jamaican accent. There were whispers of abuse. "I think her stepdad used to beat her," Ronda recalls.

Chinara and her older brother Chama both attended Thomas Jefferson, where they were a few years behind Bun. Chinara had lost a lot of weight since her high school days as an overweight teen, and she'd caught Chad's attention at Hiroshima.

As a teenager, DMD had jokingly been known as the "Preacher," always lecturing his friends about the dangers of drugs and alcohol. But as his rap career took off, he'd fallen into many of the same traps. He was going through a fifth of Hennessy and two packs of Newports a day, popping ecstasy pills in an attempt to escape reality.

"[When] you get [a] lil' bit of success in this business, everything gets thrown your way. Anything you can imagine comes your way, and if you aren't prepared for it, you can get overcome by it," says DJ DMD. "I was no different than anybody else. [When] my record started selling, [it] gave me the world on a platter."

Chad didn't like ecstasy, which he described as "some punk ass shit" which gives you an "unnatural high." He tried it once and had a bad experience. "[Ecstasy] made me feel like I was on a trip that I couldn't control," he told *OZONE*. "I couldn't come down… [it] made me sweat [and] made me feel fucked up … I don't like to be out of control."

He did, however, like cocaine, and had convinced himself that he needed to be high to be creative. "Indulging in drugs … actually does something to your [mind], it sends you places that you wouldn't even think about going if you wasn't [high]," says Lee Master. "You lose something technically, but creatively, you gain a lot."

"When I did snort cocaine, I'll do it in front of you and anybody else, if I feel like snorting some right then," Chad later told WordofSouth.com. "'Cause I wasn't 'shamed of it … if you a powder head … it's gonna eventually come to the light, so you might as well put it all out [in the open like the movie] *Scarface*, like a player. If you got to hide to do it, you fucked up, man."

DMD allegedly walked in on Chad one day in the studio bathroom with a bloody toilet tissue to his nose. Through Ashanta and Chinara, word eventually reached Chad that DMD was gossiping about his drug habits. Furious that DMD was "pillow talking" about his cocaine use, Chad cussed DMD out and vowed never to record at Hiroshima again.*

Drugs were also taking a toll on DJ Screw. He'd stopped smoking weed, telling *Murder Dog* he was "burnt out" on the habit, but still lived an extremely unhealthy lifestyle. Screw went days without sleeping and ate nothing but fried chicken. He sipped syrup constantly. Between his poor eating habits and the syrup slowing his metabolism, Screw's once-small frame was now bloated to more than 200 pounds.

There had been indications for a while that he wasn't in good health. In December 1999, while DJing in San Marcos, Texas, stunned fans watched as Screw collapsed behind the turn-tables. His productivity was also dwindling; he'd churned out thousands of tapes throughout the nineties but only released a dozen in 1999.

Some felt that Screw was struggling under the immense pressure brought on by his success. Every aspiring rapper saw Screw as their savior, and he didn't have the heart to let them down. "It's stressful when you have over 100 people pulling you in different ways all the time, and they looking for you to be Superman," says SUC rapper KayK. Screw literally dedicated his entire life to music, leaving no time to exercise or address health concerns.

In August 2000, filmmakers TJ Watford and Ariel Santschi interviewed Screw for a documentary called *Soldiers United for Cash*. Screw, who had been up for three days recording, looked disheveled; he was smoking cigarettes that appeared wet, as if they'd been dipped in something. "Screw didn't seem to have any direction," Watford recalled later in *Texas Monthly*. "He was talking in circles. I thought I saw a dead man walking."**

Less than a month later, Screw was arrested for possession of PCP. Smoking PCP-laced cigarettes or blunts while drinking syrup, according to fellow drug aficionado Lee Master, is an "immaculate combination" because the two drugs balance each other out. "It's perfect," he says. "That's what Screw was on: drankin' drank and one cigarette [dipped in embalming fluid with PCP] is the marriage of a lifetime."

About a month after his arrest, in October 2000, Screw came by Mama Wes and Pops' townhouse in Houston. He and Chad went upstairs to work on some music while Mama Wes whipped up greens and cornbread in the kitchen.

"Something smells good," Screw commented as he came back downstairs.

"You probably don't fool with country food, you one of them H-Town boys," she joked.

Screw looked back at Chad, descending the staircase. "Tell her, mane," he laughed.

"Man, he from the country, Mama," Chad told her. "This nigga from the country. He wanna

---

(*DMD denies gossiping about Chad's drug use. "Some people in the studio saw [him doing cocaine, but] I didn't personally see it [and] I never saw his nose bloody," says DJ DMD. "All I saw was [drug] paraphernalia … it hurt my heart.")
(**In Screw's second interview for the documentary two months later, which would be his last, he appeared healthier and far more coherent.)

tell everybody he's from H-Town, but he ain't from H-Town, Mama. He's from the country."*

They all laughed as Screw hovered over the stove admiring the greens Mama Wes had prepared. "Do cornbread go with that?" he asked.

Mama Wes liked Screw, but his jittery demeanor over dinner struck her as odd. "Screw was paranoid," she remembers. "I picked that up just on his movements, his behavior … how he sat. His body language was jumpy."

She adopted a motherly tone, telling Screw he should take better care of himself. She could tell he was high, but that wasn't what concerned her – it was his skin tone. The darkened hue reminded her of her father when he was a cardiac patient.

After Screw left, Mama Wes commented that he must have some kind of heart problem. In fact, Screw's friends and family say he had already suffered two mild strokes and a heart attack, and was ignoring his doctor's orders to stop drinking and smoking.

A few weeks later in mid-November, Chad was back in Atlanta when he got a call from Mama Wes. She'd received some bad news: DJ Bird's father had just passed. Bird was out at the store running some errands. When Bird got back to the Alpharetta house, Chad approached him with a heavy sigh. "I need you to take a ride with me back to Port Arthur," he said.

Bird shrugged. "Okay."

They grabbed a few things and loaded up the car. Chad lit a blunt and passed it to Bird. As they hit the highway, Chad, tears flowing, gently broke the news.

Bird asked Chad to stay for the funeral, but Chad respectfully declined. It was nothing personal, but he'd made a promise to himself after Monroe died. "I just don't go to funerals, bro," Chad explained, before heading back to Atlanta. "I just can't."

At 8 AM the next morning, November 16, 2000, DJ Screw's cousin Christopher Cooley found Screw fully dressed on the bathroom floor of the Southwest Houston warehouse he was in the process of building into a recording studio. Screw was dead at just 29 years old, clutching an ice-cream wrapper in his hand.

DJ Bird was at Mama Wes' house when she heard the sad news. "You break it down to C, Bird," she said, reaching for the telephone. She told him it was only right since Chad had done the same for him.

"C, Bird need to talk to you," she said, handing over the receiver.

"C, man…" Bird began. "Um… Screw just died, man."

"*What!?*" Chad said.

"Screw just died, man," Bird repeated. "They found Screw in his bathroom."

"*No, Bird, no!*" Chad yelled repeatedly. "Man, yo' dad just died, man. Now *Screw* dead!?"

Houstonians were devastated by the loss of DJ Screw. Chad didn't attend the services, where he was listed as an honorary pallbearer, but paid his respects by adding an "R.I.P. DJ SCREW" tattoo on his left bicep.

Tests revealed that Screw's blood contained "toxic levels of codeine" as well as promethazine, PCP (phencyclidine), and Valium (a benzodiazepine). The coroner concluded that Screw's death was caused by an accidental "codeine overdose with mixed drug intoxication."

News reports attributing Screw's death to a "codeine overdose" were met with anger and disbelief. Fans wanted to remember him as a great DJ, not a drug addict. Many flat-out refused to believe it. SUC members attributed his death to his overall unhealthy lifestyle. "We say [Screw] died of an overdose of work," says Dat Boy Grace.

Others pointed to another possible contributing factor: Screw's autopsy revealed that he had an enlarged heart, weighing 450 grams (the average human heart is between 200 and 425 grams) and a condition known as "ventricular hypertrophy," often caused by untreated high blood pressure or other heart problems.

Regardless, with DJ Screw's passing, the connection between codeine and Texas music would be permanently forged. And while his death should have been a wake-up call for syrup sippers, in reality, it had little effect.

"I've always been a big defender of syrup," Houston rapper Paul Wall admits. "Even when Screw passed, I kinda made excuses. I said it was other things that killed him, just the whole lifestyle. That's part of being a drug addict. You make excuses and try to validate what you're doing. But at the same time, in the back of my mind I was always thinking, 'What if I go to sleep right now and don't wake up?' That's a scary thought."

"Screw was my friend," Chad later told the *Beaumont Enterprise*. "We got too far out there with the drugs, all of us did. We were regular syrup drinkers … When Screw died, a lot of people didn't want to admit this, but we were all drug addicts. We didn't want to face the reality that we would have to stop."

A few weeks after Screw's death, UGK had a show in Atlanta. As they headed back to the Alpharetta house, Chad asked Mama Wes what time they were leaving to go back to Texas. "Well, babe, I didn't think you were leaving," she said, surprised.

"I am," he said. "I'm going back. I'm tired of these ATL trees, these stupid-lookin' niggas, and it's too damn cold."

Mama Wes believed his real motivation for leaving Atlanta was to get away from Sonji. Their relationship had deteriorated to the point of physical violence. During one particularly intense episode, Sonji called police. "I don't hit no women," Chad told *OZONE*. "The only broad I ever hit was broads that hit me first."

Chad had never really recovered from Monroe's sudden death, and back home in Texas as the reality of Screw's death sank in, he considered it a crushing blow. "When [DJ Screw] died … a part of me died too," he told *On Tha Real* Magazine.

For a man already battling severe depression and substance abuse, the back-to-back losses were almost too much to bear. Screw's death brought Chad's mind far too close to the uncomfortable idea of his own mortality. D-Ray, Big Dog, DJ Bird's father, DJ Screw... Chad felt like everyone around him was dying. Overwhelmed by this sense of what he described as "total destruction," Chad dropped to his knees at his bedside one night and pleaded with God for help.

His prayer was simple, earnest and sincere: *"Don't let me die."*

CHAPTER 26

"I was quiet, [kept] to myself, before [UGK]. Rap brang problems to me. Every step of the way, it's somebody tryin' to fuck you in this game."
– Pimp C, *XXL* Magazine, March 2006

"[I] did four years on an Aggravated Assault [charge] where I didn't even pull my pistol. A bitch and four other people was fucking with me and I showed 'em my muthafuckin' pistol." – Pimp C, *OZONE* Magazine, July 2007

Saturday, December 16, 2000
Houston, Texas*

One month after DJ Screw died, Chad eased his black Lincoln Navigator into a handicapped space near the entrance to Sharpstown Mall. As he climbed out of the car, Chad stuck a 9mm pistol in the waistband of his blue jeans. Since the Master P incident, he'd never gone anywhere without it.

Mama Wes, who was out running some errands, was irritated that Chad hadn't taken DJ Bird with him. Bird, back at the townhouse, didn't like the fact that he'd gone to the mall alone either, but Chad had been doing that a lot lately. He had his eye on a woman who worked at one of the mall kiosks.

Chad was often "in character," perhaps feeling pressure to live up to the persona he embodied on "Big Pimpin'." While the fans, particularly in Texas, viewed him as some kind of superhero, those who really knew him were concerned. Jeff Sledge was worried because Chad had become "extremely volatile … probably the most volatile" he'd ever been.

"Look at the nigga in the mink. I know him from somewhere," 18-year-old Chaka Prince told her older friend Lakita Hulett. She gestured towards the escalators, where a man in a flashy mink coat was talking on his cell phone. Suddenly, it clicked; she'd seen him in a music video. "That's Pimp C," Chaka said.

Lakita Hulett spent a lot of time in shopping malls. Back in July 1996, three weeks before UGK's *Ridin' Dirty* dropped, Lakita, then 20 years old, and her friend Sharonnie Brown were spotted on closed circuit cameras in the junior department of Foley's department store (now Macy's) at Houston's Willowbrook Mall. Lakita tried to slip a $78 denim Guess dress on under her clothes, while Sharonnie tucked a $45 pair of pink Polo tennis shoes into her purse.

Both women were arrested for theft and transported to the County Jail when they walked out of the store with the stolen merchandise. Lakita knew the routine – she was already on probation for a similar November 1994 theft charge. Her actual date of birth was 10/22/75, but she told police it was 10/22/76, presumably in an attempt to disguise her criminal history. Once it

(*Between police reports, affidavits, and interviews, there are more than 15 different written accounts of the incident that took place at Sharpstown Mall. Taking all these accounts into consideration, this is the most likely description of the events that occurred that day. Numerous attempts to reach Lakita Hulett for an interview were unsuccessful.)

was discovered that she had five outstanding city warrants, Lakita spent 10 days in jail.

A year and a half later, Lakita and Sharonnie were spotted on security cameras at the *same store*, this time walking out with two blue $129.99 Motorola pagers. They were again stopped at the exit by the same security guard who had apprehended them back in 1996. Lakita again gave the responding police officer an incorrect date of birth (10/22/79) and spent two days in jail.

———————

After they spotted Pimp C at Sharpstown, 25-year-old Lakita, Chaka, and two of their friends, Shameka Hawkins and a man named Donya "Dooley" Anderson, headed towards Jarman's Shoe Store so Dooley could try on some shoes. Still on the phone, Chad happened to walk past Jarman's on his way to a nearby record store, where he spotted an advertisement for Born 2wice's new album *Pimp* in the window.

Since departing Houston for the West Coast, Born 2wice had become close friends with Ice-T and was living at his mansion on Sunset Plaza Drive at the top of the Hollywood Hills. Hanging out with Ice-T, Born 2wice says, you were bound to get "overloaded [with] game," and he'd put it all on a record.

The title *Pimp*, of course, was based on Iceberg Slim's novel. Chad had already commissioned Mr. Soul to start working on the artwork for his solo debut *PIMP: The Sweet Jones Story*. Even though Born 2wice was a friend, he was upset he'd used the idea first. He went inside the store to buy it, but the clerk told him it wasn't available.

Disappointed, Chad walked back towards Jarman Shoe Store, where he greeted the store manager Kevin Nesby with a handshake; Nesby always took care of him when he stopped by. Still talking on the phone, Chad picked up a new set of Timberland boots near the cash register and asked for a size 11.

Lakita, inside the store browsing the shoe racks, leaned towards her friend Chaka. "Don't pay him no mind," she instructed. "Act like you don't know him."

Dooley and another male friend were at the register paying for their shoes when Lakita approached. She'd already gotten into a short spat with the store clerk, who wouldn't allow her to exchange some shoes.

Making conversation, the store clerk gestured towards Chad and asked the ladies if they knew who he was.

"No," Lakita snapped.

"This is Pimp C," the manager Nesby told her. "You don't know Pimp C?"

"Who the fuck is Pimp C?" Lakita snorted.

"The guy from UGK," Nesby said.

"Oh! I don't listen to them ol' pussy ass niggas," Lakita said, her voice rising.

Chad, who had his back turned to the other customers, heard the remark behind him. "Hey man, let me call you back," he told Bun.

Chad hung up the phone and turned around to face Lakita. "Hey man, uh, why you gotta talk that shit with my name in ya mouth?" he asked. "You must don't watch videos."

"You never heard of 'Big Pimpin' with Jay-Z?" Nesby chimed in.

"Fuck Pimp C," Lakita said. "I don't know no Pimp C or UGK."

Chad's demeanor, which had first been lighthearted, quickly turned dark. "Bitch, you don't know UGK? You must have been in jail or something," he snapped, loudly.

"It ain't like you muthafuckin' Master P," Lakita snapped back, louder.

At the mention of Master P, Chad lost his temper and let loose with a flurry of obscenities. Nesby rushed out from behind the cash register and stood between the two as they hurled insults at each other. He faced Chad and grabbed both of his arms. "Calm down," Nesby told him.

"She isn't worth it."

Shameka was already outside and Dooley, who had finished paying for his shoes, tried to get his friends to leave. "Let's go," he insisted. As Lakita and her friends started backing away, still yelling insults in Chad's direction, Chad stepped towards her.

Lakita, who stood 5'9" and 160 pounds, wasn't a small woman, and as she reached inside her purse, Chad thought she was reaching for a weapon. Instinctively, he lifted his jacket to show her that he had one, too. "Freeze, don't move no' mo'," he snapped.

Chad glanced at the two men with Lakita. Dooley, who'd seen the pistol tucked in Chad's waistband, threw his hands up to indicate surrender. "Man, we don't want it," he said.

"I don't want it either, man," Chad said. "Y'all need to back up out this store. This not funny no more."

As they left the store, headed in different directions, Chad spit one last "bitch!" and "hoe!" at Lakita.

On her way out, Lakita passed by a police officer at the security desk. He first looked skeptical when Lakita told him that a man had pulled a gun on her. She started yelling, louder, insisting that a man had put a gun in her side and threatened to kill her. The officer put out an alert over the radio for an armed suspect in a mink coat. Another officer nearby spotted Chad leaving out of the North exit and both officers took off running.

A customer who had observed the exchange shook his head at Lakita, telling her it was some "hoe ass shit" to tell the police. Nesby was also upset with Lakita. Didn't she know Pimp was down with the Mafia? He didn't want any problems with Rap-A-Lot.

In the parking lot, Chad was soon surrounded by eight police officers, all circling his vehicle with their weapons drawn and barking out commands. Chad ignored their orders to get on the ground and show his hands, instead opening the driver's side door.

He'd barely gotten his right foot inside when two officers rushed him and forced him to the ground. "After the cop handcuffed me, four more officers came running up and slammed me down to the ground," Chad told *F.E.D.S.* Magazine. "They started kicking me and hitting me." Police slammed his head against the car door and pushed his head onto the concrete.

The police report acknowledged that Chad was wrestled to the ground with "much resistance," claiming that he had become "aggressive and combative" and that "only the force necessary" was used to subdue him.

As police brought Chad back inside in handcuffs, Lakita was exiting the mall. "I'm gonna fucking kill you, bitch!" Chad yelled after her. He was growing more and more irate, and as police struggled to contain him, they smashed his head against a glass doorway, which knocked him nearly unconscious. They finally managed to drag him into the mall's security office.

With Chad in custody and nearly incapacitated, police took statements from Lakita and her friends. Lakita's last name was spelled incorrectly ("Hullett" instead of "Hulett"), which was likely intentional, given her documented history of giving police incorrect information to avoid revealing her own criminal past.

Lakita told police she wanted to press charges, claiming that Chad stuck a gun in her side and threatened, "I will shoot you … I will kill you hoe and will slap you hoe." Her friend Chaka also claimed that Chad threatened, "Bitch, I'll shoot you," before pulling out the gun and sticking it in Lakita's side. According to the police report, Dooley said that Chad pulled a pistol on his "little sister" Lakita and "called [her] all kinds of bitches and hoes."*

Lakita's friend Shameka, however, told police she had never seen Chad pull out a gun. The store manager Kevin Nesby also disputed Lakita's version, telling police that Lakita started the whole argument by "talking very ghetto" while "Pimp C was just staying calm."

(*Dooley later claimed he had never made these statements and the police report did not accurately reflect what he'd said.)

Nesby said he was standing between Chad and Lakita throughout the whole argument and Chad had never pulled out a gun, although it was possible she had seen it in his belt line. Nesby said he would be willing to go to court and testify on Chad's behalf. "If she had not jumped on the man, this would [have] never started," Nesby said.

The police report also claimed that Chad had a "prior arrest record for dangerous drugs and assault."*

When he finally regained consciousness inside the security office, Chad's head was throbbing. He opened his eyes to see a small wrinkled plastic baggie with less than a gram of cocaine dangling in his face. "What is this?" the officer holding it demanded.**

Even in his groggy state, Chad hadn't lost his sharp tongue. "I don't know, 'cause that can't be mine," Chad said. "If it was mine, it would be in a big ol' Crown Royal bag." He did acknowledge that the quarter-ounce of marijuana belonged to him.

Chad looked around the security office and glared at Officer Matheny, who had wrestled him to the ground in the parking lot. "I'm gonna remember you, white boy," he spat. He asked to file a formal complaint about the parking lot altercation.***

Back at the townhouse, Mama Wes grew uneasy when hours passed by and Chad hadn't returned. She finally got a call from Bun, who informed her that Chad was going to jail. Red Boy, who had become her trusted right-hand man, rushed to Sharpstown, but Chad was already en route to Ben Taub Hospital.

According to Mama Wes, Chad passed out again at the hospital, but police wouldn't allow the emergency room doctor to do a CAT scan. "I kid you not, C was black, like all over his body," says Mama Wes. "The kidney area, the ribs, I saw this [myself]. His neck, his head. He was a mess."

Chad was transported to the Central Jail and charged with Aggravated Assault with a Deadly Weapon. "They said that was an assault 'cause I showed them my pistol," he told journalist Matt Sonzala. "They call [that] Aggravated Assault, but … there was no bodily injury and it actually was not an assault. In the State of Texas, if a person fears for they life and you have a weapon, that's classified as Aggravated Assault."

Mama Wes believed the severity of the charges was more a result of his parking lot altercation with police than the initial argument with Lakita. "He never touched her, he never got that close to her," says Mama Wes. "But then he started raising hell with [the police], and that's how he got that [Aggravated Assault] charge."

Chad posted $10,000 bond at 6 AM the next morning. When he finally made it back to the townhouse, DJ Bird asked, "What happened, man!?"

"The broad say something about 'Fuck Pimp C, I'm down with Master P,' y'know," Chad explained.

Mama Wes got a sinking feeling in her stomach. "I just knew, somehow, it wasn't going to turn out good," she remembers. "It was just all downhill for a long time from there."

(*It is not clear what prior charges they were referring to; charges had never actually been filed in the Isreal Kight shooting. His only known arrest was the misdemeanor marijuana charge in 1995. It is not clear if he was ever actually charged in the domestic violence incident with Sonji.)

(**Chad never denied using cocaine, but, according to Mama Wes, the plastic baggie was planted by police. He preferred to carry his cocaine in a Crown Royal bag. "When I saw it, a little wrinkled up baggie … [I knew] that wasn't his," says Mama Wes. "That wasn't his style." Chad also told DJ Bird the drugs weren't his. In future legal proceedings, however, he didn't fight the cocaine charge.)

(***In response to an open records request, Harris County either could not locate or would not release the complaint Chad filed against the officers.)

No-01 Disposition-ARRESTED /CHARGED   HPD-no-00000000
     Name: Last-BUTLER   First-CHAD   Middle-
     Address-3737 HILLCROFT;HOUSTON,TX 77036
     Race-B Sex-M Age-26-00 Hispanic-N Date of birth-12/29/73
     Height-510 To-   Weight-200 To-
     Hair: Color-BLACK   Type-KINKY   Length-SHORT
     Complexion-LIGHT   Facial hair-   MUSTACHE AND BEARD
     Speech/Accent-   Eye color-BROWN
Dress-COAT SHORT BRO/JEANS BLU
     Weapon used-PISTOL
Misc-GA ID# 0000000085,GA ADDRESS 605 JENMARIE DR MABELTON GA. 30059

INTRODUCTION:
     OFFICER E.K. DAVIS PR.████████ AND J.A CORBIN PR ████████ WHILE WORKING AN
APPROVED EXTRA JOB AT SHARPSTOWN MALL IN THE 7500 BLOCK OF BELLAIRE. OFFICER
DAVIS AND CORBIN WERE ADVISED BY THE COMPLAINANT THAT THE SUSPECT HAD A GUN, AND
THAT HE HAD PLACED IT IN HER SIDE AND THREATENED TO KILL HER. OFFICER DAVIS
AND CORBIN PROCEEDED TO LOOK FOR THE SUSPECT IN THE MAIN MALL AREA AND PUT OUT
A DESCRIPTION AND ADVISED OTHER MALL UNITS THAT THE SUSPECT HAS A GUN.

COMPLAINANT#1
     COMP-#01, STATE OF TEXAS
     COMP-#01, STATE OF TEXAS WILL BE THE MAIN COMPLAINANT IN THIS CASE.

COMPLAINANT#2:
     COMP-#02, HULLETT,LAKITA A BF025 ███████████
     COMP-#02, HULLETT,LAKITA A BF025 STATED IN HER WRITTEN STATEMENT, THAT SHE
WAS IN JARMAN SHOE STORE IN SHARPSTOWN MALL. COMP-#02, HULLETT,LAKITA A BF025
STATES THE SUSPECT,SUSP-#01, BUTLER,CHAD BM026 , TOLD HER HE WAS PIMP C A RAPPER
WITH VGK AND DID I HEAR OF HIM, AND THE COMPLAINANT STATED SHE SAID,"NO". THE
COMPLAINANT STATED THAT THE SUSPECT CALLED HER A "BITCH" AND THEY BEGAN TO
EXCHANGE WORDS. THE COMPLAINANT STATES THE SUSPECT THEN STATED THAT IF SHE DID
NOT STOP SPEAKING TO HIM ,"I WILL SHOOT YOU.", AND PULLED OUT A GUN AND STUCK

IN MY SIDE AND STATED, " I WILL KILL YOU HOE AND WILL SLAP YOU HOE", AND PUT
HIS GUN BACK IN HIS SIDE AND KEPT CURSING AND WALKED OFF. THE COMPLAINANT
STATED SHE WOULD PRESS CHARGES AGAINST THE SUSPECT.

REPORTEE:
  MALL SECURITY.

WITNESS#1:
     WITN-#01, HAWKINS,SHAMEKA BF023/ ██████████
     WITN-#01, HAWKINS,SHAMEKA BF023 STATED SHE HEARD THE SUSPECT CALL HER A
BITCH AND YOU DONT KNOW ME AND I AM THE MAN. THE WITNESS STATES SHE DID NOT
SEE THE SUSPECT PULL OUT A GUN AND POINT IT AT THE COMPLAINANT.

WITNESS#2:
     WITN-#02, ANDERSON,DONYA BM025 ██████████
     WITN-#02, ANDERSON,DONYA BM025 STATED THAT HE SAW PIMP C PULL HIS .9 MM OR
.380 BLACK GUN ON MY LITTLE SISTER LAKITA HULLETT. HE ALSO STATES THAT THE
SUSPECT, SUSP-#01, BUTLER,CHAD BM026 , CALLED ALL KINDS OF BITCHES AND HOES.
  WITNESS#3:
     WITN-#03, PRINCE,CHAKA BF018 / ██████████
     WITN-#03, PRINCE,CHAKA BF018 STATED WHEN THEY WALKED IN TO THE STORE MY
COUSIN R.A SAID DONT PAY HIM NO MIND, AND I DIDN'T SO WE WENT TO THE REGISTER
SO DOOLEY COULD BUY HIM SOME SHOES. SHE STATES PIMP C COMES INTO THE STORE
WHILE THEY WERE AT THE REGISTER, AND STATED TO THE MAN BEHIND THE REGISTER,
"WHO IS VGK AND PIMP C ?", AND," BITCH YOU DON'T KNOW VGK ?" , BITCH YOU MUST
HAVE BEEN IN JAIL OR SOMTHING.". THE WITNESS STATES THAT THE SUSPECT,SUSP-#01,
BUTLER,CHAD BM026 , RAISED UP HIS SHIRT AND SAID,"BITCH, I'LL SHOOT YOU.", AND
HE PULLED OUT THE GUN AND STUCK IN HER SIDE AND AND SHE KEPT WALKING.

WITNESS#4
     WITN-#04, NESBY,KEVIN D BM034 / ██████████
     WITN-#04, NESBY,KEVIN D BM034 STATED THAT HE AND PIMP C WAS TALKING ABOUT
SHOES, AND TOLD THE CUSTOMER THIS WAS PIMP C. THE WITNESS STATES THE CUSTOMER
SAID ," WHO THE FUCK IS PIMP C.". THE WITNESS STATED HE SAID THE GUY FROM UGK.
THE WITNESS STATES SHE THEN SAID ,"I DONT LISTEN TO NO UGK AND NO PIMP C". AND
THE COMPLAINANT STATES HE SAID YOU NEVER HEARD OF BIG PIMPIN WITH JAYZ. HE
STATES THE FEMALE STARTED TALKING VERY GETTHO, AND SAID, "FUCK RAP MUSIC.". THE
WITNESS STATED UNTIL THIS POINT PIMP C WAS JUST STAYING CALM. HE STATES THE
SUSPECT THE STATED ,"YOU MUST DON'T WATCH VIDEOS.".
     THE WITNESS STATES NO GUN WAS EVER PULLED IN HIS STORE, BECAUSE HE WAS
STANDING BETWEEN PIMP C AND THE LADY. HE ALSO STATES SHE MUST HAVE SEEN IT IN
HIS BELT LINE. THE WITNESS ALSO STATES HE WAS WILLING TO GO TO COURT AND
TESTIFY , BECAUSE IF SHE HAD NOT JUMPED ON THE MAN THIS WOULD NEVER STARTED.

Above: Portions of the **Houston Police Department incident report** from Chad's arrest at Sharpstown Mall.

CHAPTER 27

"That's what we known for down here in Texas, baby. We lock your ass up down here and have ya locked up for a long time." — Lil Keke

---

"That was a terrible thing that [Chad] had to do that time. He had to do four years behind nothing, you know?" — Scarface

There's never a good time to get arrested, but Chad's timing was particularly bad. Texas had just spent 10 years and three *billion* dollars building the largest prison industrial complex in history. Tens of thousands of empty prison beds had generated millions of dollars for private entrepreneurs who had significant incentive to fill them and keep the money flowing.

Even Andy Collins, the former executive director of the Texas Department of Criminal Justice (TDCJ) who oversaw the construction of a staggering *43 new prisons in 18 months* in the mid-1990s, admitted it was "the stupidest thing the State of Texas has ever done." This was, of course, after he ensured that his friends and business partners were guaranteed multi-million dollar TDCJ contracts, and resigned from the job to operate a private prison, which would bring him far more money than his $120,000 annual TDCJ salary.*

When Andy Collins was promoted to executive director of TDCJ in April 1994, Texas had 65 prisons housing 72,000 inmates. Crime hysteria was at an all-time high thanks to the crack cocaine epidemic. "The public was absolutely hoodwinked into thinking that the only way the crime problem could ever be solved was prosecution and incarceration," Collins later told *Texas Monthly*. "[We were] taking juveniles and feeding them directly into the system. I mean, look who was behind it all. Prosecutors, cops, politicians — all of them with a self-serving agenda. [The media] did as much as anyone to build all those prisons because they fanned the flames of public hysteria … crime had become entertainment. Turn on the TV. *Cops. Rescue 911.*"

Ever since the landmark class-action lawsuit filed by inmate David Ruiz in 1972, Texas prisons had been under pressure to solve their overcrowding problems. In 1994, two state bonds were issued for prison construction. And Andy Collins, considered incompetent by many of his former peers, suddenly had access to billions of dollars to build prisons.

"All of a sudden, the gloomy prison business was the hottest thing going," writer Robert Draper noted in *Texas Monthly*. "Money grabbers poured in from all over North America to get in on the action. Private-prison operators reaped more profits in Texas than anywhere else in the nation. Construction firms and subcontractors raked in hundreds of millions of dollars. Vendors great and small … The Texas prison expansion became a feeding frenzy."

By December 1995, when Collins resigned, TDCJ had doubled their inmate capacity from

---

(*After Collins resigned, the FBI investigated the "sweetheart contracts" he handed out during his tenure at TDCJ. Most notable was the VitaPro scandal. Collins approved a $33.7 million dollar contract for VitaPro, a soybean-based powder fed to Texas inmates as a meat substitute. It was later discovered that he was making money on the side as a VitaPro "consultant." Collins himself referred to the powder, which could stretch 10 hamburger patties into 15, as "dog food." Collins' business partner Pat Graham was also arrested in a bizarre FBI sting in which he accepted a $150,000 bribe as a downpayment towards a $750,000 fee to have a Texas inmate released and pardoned. In 2001 Collins was found guilty on federal charges of bribery, money laundering and conspiracy, but his conviction was overturned by an appeals court in 2005.)

72,000 to more than 140,000. The state filled many of those beds by manipulating the parole board: they simply stopped granting parole. TDCJ absorbed the Board of Pardons and Paroles (BPP), which had previously been a separate entity, and parole rates dropped from 85% to 16%.

Prison had become such big business that the goal was no longer to keep people *out* of prison, but to make sure the prisons were profitable. Incarceration had become an industry of its own. "Just as New York dominates finance and California the film industry, Texas reigns supreme in the punishment business," writer Robert Perkinson noted in his book *Texas Tough*.*

Meanwhile, street hustlers, trying to get by day-to-day, were largely unaware of these political and economic forces at work. "Prison is big business, man," Screwed Up Click affiliate Mike D noted in the book *Houston Rap*. "[We were still doing] … what we do out here [in these streets] … not even bein' mindful of what the government has in store for us."

Texas lawmakers blamed the inmates themselves, not economic factors, parole board manipulation, or extreme sentencing, for the exploding inmate population. "It's disappointing that so many human beings have done something to get themselves locked up," state Senator John Whitmore, chairman of the Senate Criminal Justice Committee, told Dallas-area newspaper the *Star-Telegram*.

But mass incarceration was a national problem, not just a Texas problem. America's incarceration rate had remained remarkably stable until the 1970s, when everything changed with the enactment of New York's infamous Rockefeller Drug Laws, imposing lengthy sentences on low-level drug dealers. Federal parole was eliminated in the 1980s and Congress established mandatory sentencing guidelines, taking power away from judges and handing it to prosecutors.

Between 1980 and 2000, the number of people under the control of the criminal justice system in the United States tripled from 2 million to 6 million. The United States' incarceration rate was a staggering 682 per 100,000 people, second only to Russia (685) and far higher than the global average of 125. (In Texas, the rate was an astronomical 1,035.)

For black men, the rate was 3,109, four times greater than it was during apartheid in South Africa, the most openly racist society in the world. This came as no surprise, since in Texas, the prison system was created directly from a need to control a certain segment of the population after slavery was outlawed.

"The system of mass incarceration works to trap African Americans in a virtual (and literal) cage," writes legal scholar Michelle Alexander. "If mass incarceration is considered as a system of social control – specifically, racial control – then the system is a fantastic success."

Texas' incarceration spree reached its height in the summer of 2000, just a few months before Chad's arrest. TDCJ inmates were typically assigned a six-digit identification number, but in July 2000, they ran out of six-digit numbers and officially created prisoner number 1,000,000.

Texas' criminal justice population (including people on parole or probation) exceeded the entire population of Vermont, Wyoming, or Alaska, with a full 5% of the adult population (1 in 20 people) under TDCJ's control. For black men between age 21 and 29, the percentage was 29%, or one out of three.

Put simply, Texas in the year 2000 was *the worst time and place in history* for anyone – *especially* a 26-year-old black man – to find himself in a courtroom.

———————

J. Prince referred Chad to Robert Jones, a black attorney who impressed Mama Wes with his knowledge and professionalism. Jones' plan, as Mama Wes recalls it, was to stall for time,

———————————————————————

(*America's mass incarceration problem extends well beyond the scope of this book. For further reading, *Texas Tough: The Rise of America's Prison Empire* is a good place to start.)

Texans Under Criminal Justice Control, 1999, Race Estimates

	Black Men (over age 18)	Young Black Men (age 21-29)
Prison	60,329	18,078
Jail	23,831	7,006
Parole	28,718	8,443
Probation	67,236	19,767
Total:	180,114	53,294
African American Male Population	752,281	183,496
Percentage Under Criminal Justice Control	24%	29%

The African American Incarceration Rate in Texas is 7 times higher than that of whites.

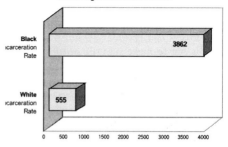

U.S. Incarceration Rate, 1880-2008

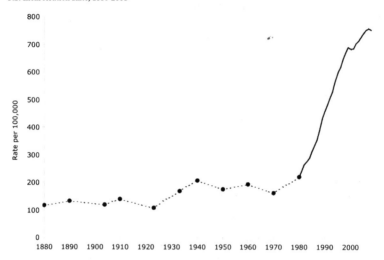

Incarceration Rate per 100,000 in OECD Countries (Most Recent Year, 2008-2009)

Country	Rate
Iceland	44
Japan	63
Denmark	66
Finland	67
Norway	70
Sweden	74
Switzerland	76
Ireland	85
Germany	90
Italy	92
Belgium	94
France	96
South Korea	97
Austria	99
Netherlands	100
Portugal	104
Greece	109
Canada	116
Australia	134
Slovakia	151
Hungary	152
England and Wales	153
Luxembourg	155
Turkey	161
Spain	162
New Zealand	197
Czech Republic	206
Mexico	209
Poland	224
United States	753

Rate per 100,000

Charts from the Justice Policy Institute's 2000 study **"Texas Tough? An Analysis of Incarceration and Crime Trends in the Lone Star State"** and the Center for Economic and Policy Research's 2010 study **"The High Budgetary Cost of Incarceration"** give a good look at the extent of the mass incarceration problem in the United States, especially in Texas.

using legal tactics to postpone the hearings and ultimately plead out to a lesser charge. But Chad had his mind set on going to trial.

During Chad's first court appearance on January 9, 2001, he stepped outside for a quick consultation with his attorney. Mama Wes, sitting in the courtroom, saw the district attorney watching Chad exit. He turned to his assistant with a smile. "I'ma catch this lil' rapper boy," she overheard him saying. "Oh, I'ma have fun getting him!"*

"[The D.A.] was arrogant. I really don't think he cared [if I heard him]," says Mama Wes. "You know … the justice system is a farce. Everybody knows that."

Chad wasn't helping the situation; his demeanor was sullen and angry in court. He carried himself with an attitude and kept his head down, rarely looking up at the judge. He wore a mink coat and tinted prescription glasses. The judge ordered him to remove the glasses, and he sat through the hearing unable to see more than a few feet in front of him.

"[Chad] didn't act 'nice' in court," admits Mama Wes. "He had that arrogance about him."

"C could've avoided jail, but he thought he was badder than the judge," agrees Pops. "He thought his Mama could get him out of any [trouble] he got into."

Chad privately referred to the district attorney, a thin man with bad acne scars and effeminate mannerisms, as a "rail-faced faggot." Most of Chad's friends were under the impression that he'd said this *in court*. "[I heard] he went in there talking that bullshit to the judge and the judge gave him the max," says Big Gipp.

According to Mama Wes, he'd never actually called the district attorney a "faggot" to his face. "I would've knocked the teeth right out of his mouth if he said [that in court]," she says.**

Bun was angry about Chad's arrest; the timing couldn't have been worse. UGK was at the highest point in their career, poised to drop a project on the heels of "Big Pimpin'." It had even earned them a Grammy nomination (for Best Rap Performance by a Duo or Group).***

"We had more eyes looking at us and what we were about to do than we ever had before in our career … [it] just ended up getting sidetracked," Bun told journalist Matt Sonzala.

Beyond his immediate circle, most of Chad's friends and associates didn't know what had actually happened at the mall. There were a lot of rumors and misinformation, but for the most part, friends tried to keep a supportive attitude rather than pressing him for details. Chad only shared the story with a select few, but everyone could agree on one thing. "Pimp, you got to slow down," DJ Paul of Three 6 Mafia advised him. "Shit like this, that's unnecessary."

Chad hadn't been back to Atlanta since the last blowup with Sonji, and now that he'd caught a case in Texas, it was clear he had no intention of returning to the Alpharetta house. Plus, he told friends he was tired of his landlord, Stephanie Gowdy, always pressing him for more money. (According to Gowdy, Chad was months behind in his rent.)

After Chad's first court date, Mama Wes asked Byron Amos to pack up the Alpharetta house. Byron had learned his lesson with the Stone Mountain move, so this time he hired a moving company to load Chad's furniture and personal effects into a 24-foot U-Haul with an attached trailer. He made the drive alone, rolling out of Atlanta at noon on January 12. Byron had never driven past New Orleans, and as night fell, the freeway got smaller and smaller. He was nervous as he passed over long, narrow bridges in the middle of Louisiana swampland, the overloaded U-Haul bouncing and swerving unpredictably.

(*The District Attorney's possible motivation for wanting to "get" Chad is discussed in detail in the following chapter.)
(**Mama Wes hated the district attorney as much as Chad did. "[Chad] never had an outburst [in court], no, but was [the district attorney] a faggot? Yes. He was a faggot … a lil' skinny, ugly, rail-faced alcoholic … horrible lil' fucker," laughs Mama Wes, adding for clarification, "[I don't mean] 'a gay person.' I like gay people. [But] he was a *faggot* … he was so overbearingly gay [like a woman]. And I just hope I never see that little fucker ever again.")
(***Neither Jay-Z nor UGK attended the 2001 Grammy Awards. Jay-Z had previously announced that he was boycotting the Grammys because they didn't understand rap. The award for Best Rap Performance by a Duo or Group went to Dr. Dre and Eminem's "Forgot About Dre.")

Mama Wes gave him directions to the townhouse in Houston, joking, "[If] you get off on the wrong exit, get your ass back on as soon as you can. [If] you get off in the [Fifth] Ward we'll never see you again."

Byron made it safely, and as he finished unloading the U-Haul, Mama Wes got a panicked phone call from the landlord Stephanie Gowdy. There had been a massive explosion and the Alpharetta house was going up in a sea of flames and smoke.

Mama Wes' immediate reaction was to call Chad and tell him that Sonji had burned down the house. Most of Chad's friends, too, were convinced Sonji was responsible. But when Sonji met with local authorities, she had an alibi: video footage showed her on the red carpet of the Stellar Awards, a Gospel music event in Atlanta, when the blaze began.*

Chad's mood swings had become wildly unpredictable. "There were times when he would have every reason to be up, and [his mood would] be down, and then there were times that he would have every reason to be down, and he was up," says Mama Wes.

One afternoon Chad came to his mother's house moping around slowly, asking if she could make some sweet corn and sausage in red gravy. Mama Wes knew what that meant: he planned to hibernate for several days.

"C, I think you really need to try the therapy thing again," she suggested. "Your [moods are] swinging too much now."

Just as she'd suspected, Chad went into hibernation mode. A few days later, when he was feeling a bit better, the topic came up again. They were having a lighthearted conversation when Mama Wes joked, "C, you know you're nuts, and you really need to go see somebody?"

Chad laughed so hard tears came from his eyes. Mama Wes was laughing, too, and then her expression turned somber. "Baby, I'm serious," she said. "Your ass is crazy."

He stopped laughing. "I am, ain't I, Mama?"

"You are," she nodded.

"I just don't…" he mumbled. "Ordinary people just don't do the crazy shit I do."

"No," she agreed.

"You think you know somebody?"

"Yeah," Mama Wes said. "You know what? I think you will find this lil' guy funny, and while you're laughing at him, you might be able to get into it."

Chad skipped his February 28 court date, forfeiting his $10,000 bond. But he did show up for an appointment the next day with his mother's therapist, Victor Fermo Jr. (His mother suffered from depression and lingering injuries from her near-fatal car accident.) He admitted to using cocaine as recently as 10 days ago, but felt that his main problem was depression, complicated by the stress of dealing with his legal troubles.

Fermo wrote a note recommending that Chad be admitted into the drug rehabilitation program at Beaumont Neurological Hospital to treat his "drug dependence, mainly cocaine, also marijuana and codeine."

"He know me pretty damn good," Chad told his mother after the session. "He really told me some stuff. He was right on target."

"So you like him?" asked Mama Wes.

"Yeah," Chad said. "I think he's nuts, but I like him."

Chad was finally starting to deal with his mental health issues, but four days after his first session with Fermo, a warrant was issued for his arrest because of the missed court date. He was

(*According to the homeowner Stephanie Gowdy, the cause of the fire was never determined. The home at 2285 Hopewell Plantation burned to the ground. The land was sold to a property developer and the house was rebuilt. In a 2014 records search, neither the City of Alpharetta nor Fulton County were able to locate any records related to the fire. Records are only maintained for 10 years.)

also receiving threatening letters from the IRS regarding his alleged seven-figure tax debt. Darryl Austin, the Cash Money tour promoter, referred him to a man named Eddie Floyd to help get his financial affairs in order.

Chad had initially planned to hire Prince's attorney Robert Jones, but at Eddie Floyd's insistence, he hired an attorney named Greg Glass and turned himself in to the County Jail.

When two men strode into the Harris County Jail a week later, outfitted in military-style uniforms consisting of black boots, black pants, a black shirt with New Black Panther Party patches, and black berets, their presence attracted considerable attention. The men, believed to be Hashim Nzinga and Malik Zulu Shabazz, announced they were there to visit Chad Butler.*

A month earlier, the leader of the New Black Panther Party, Dr. Khallid Muhammad, died in Atlanta at age 53 in poor health. It was agreed that Shabazz would succeed Dr. Muhammad as leader of the organization, appointing Hashim the National Chief of Staff. They didn't trust doctor's conclusions that Muhammad's death was the result of a cerebral hemorrhage, even going so far as to confiscate bodily fluids from Dr. Muhammad's bathroom and saving them in a "secret location" for testing. Hashim penned a 25-page "Official Death Report" which criticized Muhammad's wife, suggesting she may have killed him "acting on the instructions of influential Jews" and accusing certain NBPP members of being "agent[s] working for the devil."

The NBPP, convinced the government was responsible for Dr. Muhammad's death, considered the FBI their enemy, and the feeling was certainly mutual. The FBI considered the NBPP a terrorist organization and was investigating several NBPP members for alleged firearms violations, counterfeit identification documents, and fraud.

On March 20, the Harris County Sheriff's Department informed the FBI's Houston bureau of Chad's visit from the NBPP members. Two days later, the Houston FBI bureau sent a memo to their Atlanta office, which was heading the NBPP investigation. Attached to the memo were copies of both visitors' driver's licenses and the police report from Chad's Sharpstown arrest.

"Butler, a rapper with ties to Rap-A-Lot Records is currently being held in Harris County Jail on aggravated assault and possession of a controlled substances charges," the FBI memo read. "Both charges occurred during an incident at a local shopping mall where BUTLER allegedly pointed a gun at a female customer and threatened to kill her after the two started arguing."

"The subject of conversation between Butler [and the two NBPP members who visited him] is unknown," the memo concluded.

Shortly after the FBI was notified that "a rapper with ties to Rap-A-Lot Records" was being held in the Harris County Jail, Chad got a visit from men he called "special prosecutors."**

They offered him an easy way out of jail: all they wanted was some information about James Prince.

"We don't want you, Chad Butler," he was informed. "We really want James Prince. Just tell us something about James Prince and we'll let you go."

Chad said nothing. *Fuck you,* he thought.

(*In FBI documents, the NBPP visitors' names are redacted. Hashim recalls visiting Chad in the County Jail around this time accompanied by Shabazz.)

(**Although the exact date of Chad's alleged visit from the "special prosecutors" is not known, in interviews he implied that it was shortly before his April 25, 2001 court date. The FBI was notified of his incarceration on March 20 and he bonded out on March 27, so it seems likely that the visit took place between March 20 and 27. Also, it is interesting to note that at Chad's March 27 court appearance, he was represented by one of Prince's attorneys, Kent Schaffer. A Freedom of Information Act request filed with the FBI does not reveal evidence of this meeting, but that doesn't necessarily mean it didn't happen. In fact, there are eight wholly redacted pages of Chad Butler-related documents which the FBI refuses to release, making it seem all the more plausible that it *did* occur. The visit was one of the few things Chad didn't share with his mother, likely for her own protection. "We did not discuss [the 'special prosecutors'] … [I think] he wanted me to know as little as possible about that for safety reasons … [But] I think that happened. Yeah, I do," says Mama Wes. Chad told AllHipHop, "I went to the penitentiary because I wouldn't tell on someone." He added in *VIBE*, "I wouldn't snitch, so they nailed me.")

(Rev. 08-28-2000)

FEDERAL BUREAU OF INVESTIGATION

Precedence: ROUTINE   Date: 03/22/2001

To: Atlanta   Attn: DT Supervisor

From: Houston
       CT-2
       Contact: SA

Approved By:

Drafted By:

Case ID #: 266A-AT-86895 (Pending)

b6
b7C

Title:

ET AL;
FIREARMS VIOLATIONS;
COUNTERFEIT IDENTIFICATION DOCUMENTS;
FRAUD;
DT

Synopsis: Houston provides Atlanta with information reference captioned subject.

Enclosure(s): Copy of driver's license for [   ] and [   ] and Houston Police Department report.

Details: On 03/20/2001, Houston received the enclosed information from Harris County Sheriff's Department, Houston, Texas. The information advised NBPP members [   ] [   ] both dressed in standard NBPP uniforms, visited CHAD LAMON BUTLER, an inmate incarcerated in Harris County Jail, Houston, Texas.

b6
b7C

     BUTLER, a rapper with ties to Rap-A-Lot Records is currently being held in Harris County Jail on aggravated assault and possession of a controlled substances charges. Both charges occurred during an incident at a local shopping mall where BUTLER allegedly pointed a gun at a female customer and threatened to kill her after the two started arguing. The details of the offense are described on the enclosed report.

     The subject of conversation between BUTLER, [   ] and [   ] is unknown.

b6
b7C

Above: An **internal FBI memo** alerting investigators of Chad's visit from New Black Panther Party members at the Harris County Jail.

CHAPTER 28

"Don't for one second get it fucked up. J. Prince is a real gangster. He ain't no TV [gangsta] or a muthafucker that's hiding behind a desk talking that shit. He is the true living definition of what a gangster is ... That's why the Feds was watching us all." – Scarface, *Complex* Magazine, January 2013

"James [Prince] is ... really easy to underestimate. He talks slow, he's very countrified, but something is going on inside his mind that's pretty incredible. He wouldn't have the string of successes that he's had otherwise."
– Doug King, former Rap-A-Lot in-house producer

Friday, February 27, 1987
Sierra Blanca, Texas

Back when Chad Butler was just a seventh-grader going through puberty, a brand new Chevrolet El Camino pulled up to a United States Border Patrol checkpoint on Interstate 10 in the desolate, windy expanse of West Texas. The town of Sierra Blanca was so tiny it didn't even have a stoplight, but the checkpoint, 30 miles from the Mexican border, had a reputation as one of the toughest in the country.**

The checkpoint utilized drug-sniffing dogs, which could detect contraband from more than ten feet away. Even when smugglers got creative – concealing drugs inside factory-sealed jars of jalapeño peppers, for example, or stuffing marijuana inside the car's battery hoping the acid would conceal the smell – the dogs would squat, signaling to Border Patrol agents that the vehicle smelled suspicious. In most cases, the search would only turn up small amounts of marijuana, but occasionally, agents hit pay dirt.***

In the El Camino, which was coming from Los Angeles headed east towards Houston, Border Patrol agents discovered a hidden compartment which contained 76 kilograms of cocaine. Kilos were selling for around $13,000, making the cocaine shipment worth nearly a million dollars.****

The driver, Anthony Price, was arrested. His passenger Daryl Prince carried a business card identifying him as a salesman for Smith Auto Sales in Houston. The El Camino had Texas dealer license plates registered to James A. Smith Auto Sales; Smith was Daryl Prince's cousin.*****

(*Editor's Note: This chapter takes a brief detour. Pimp C's story resumes with Chapter 29 on page 279.)
(**In recent years, Sierra Blanca – dubbed "the checkpoint of no return" by *The Hollywood Reporter* – has become infamous as the place where Snoop Dogg, Nelly, Willie Nelson, Devin the Dude, and other touring musicians have been arrested on drug-related charges.)
(***Roughly 2,500 people are arrested at this checkpoint every year, and about 2,000 of those are for small amounts of marijuana. The city doesn't have the resources to prosecute them all, so most people are allowed to pay a $527 misdemeanor fine in lieu of going to court, generating more than a million dollars of revenue for the city every year. Occasionally, the marijuana arrests help authorities find criminals wanted on more serious charges. "Every pothead isn't a bad guy," deputy chief patrol agent Carry Huffman told *Texas Monthly* in 2013. "But every bad guy is a pothead.")
(****Adjusting for inflation, roughly $1.8 million in 2015 dollars.)
(*****As previously noted, James Smith changed his name to James Prince in 1996 and is consistently referred to as Prince throughout this book. Prince declined to be interviewed. His quotes and the events described in this chapter are taken largely from transcripts of Congressional hearings. Prince has said that his battle with the DEA is one of many stories he recounts in his upcoming memoir, *Boss: Power, Money, & Respect.*)

Daryl Prince was released from custody when it was decided there was insufficient evidence to prove he was aware of the cocaine hidden in the vehicle. The El Camino driver, Anthony Price, was sentenced to 21 years on federal cocaine charges.*

The incident obviously put James Prince né James Smith on the radar of both local and federal authorities, who believed he was the mastermind behind the whole operation. As Rap-A-Lot Records exploded on the scene in the late 80s and early 90s with their "gangsta rap" success, it only raised Prince's profile with law enforcement.

Tensions were already high between the police and the urban community in the wake of Ice-T's inflammatory record "Cop Killer." Plus, Rap-A-Lot was embroiled in controversy over the Geto Boys' self-titled album, essentially a re-release of *Grip It! On That Other Level*. Their distributor, Geffen, refused to distribute the project due to its "violent, sexist, racist and indecent" content.

But Prince realized that the controversy was a blessing in disguise; it was exactly what they needed to break into video and radio, which were largely monopolized by major labels. "[Before that] none of the majors wanted to look at me," Prince told *Complex*. "So I had to create something that would cause controversy and get publicity in order to sell records. We became masters at that."

During a bizarre suicide attempt (which he later attributed to the fact that he'd been drinking pure-grain alcohol) the Geto Boys' Bushwick Bill shot himself in the eye. "Fame will make you crazy," he told MTV News. But the Geto Boys' 1991 album *We Can't Be Stopped* was ready to be sent off for manufacturing, so Prince and his partner Cliff took Scarface and Willie D to the hospital and pulled Bushwick Bill out of his room for an impromptu photo shoot in the hallway with his gruesome eye socket exposed.**

Fueled by their massive single "Mind Playing Tricks on Me" and the controversial, eye-catching cover, the Geto Boys crossed over to pop stations and *We Can't Be Stopped* went platinum.

By 1992, Prince was arguably overseeing the largest independent black-owned record label in the country (the only other label vying for the title was Luther Campbell's Miami-based Luke Records), pulling in an estimated $15 million per year in revenue. Prince's name had generated enough interest that the DEA opened a case file on him, but agent Michael Statlander couldn't find anything solid enough to charge him with a crime.

In May 1992, Prince had a run-in with a Houston police officer named B.J. Raymond at a local restaurant. It was the fourth time Prince had been detained by HPD, but each time, the charges were dismissed for lack of evidence.

Office Raymond, who claimed that Prince was carrying a small derringer pistol in his pocket, arrested him and charged him with unlawful possession of a firearm. Once they went before a judge, however, the case was dismissed. Prince's attorney David Dudley told the *Houston Chronicle* that "the judge found [that] the officer lacked credibility."

Eight months after they faced off in court on the pistol charge, Prince had another run-in with Officer Raymond, who pulled him over late on the night of Saturday, January 9, 1993, driving a luxury car with RAPALOT vanity dealer plates. (Raymond claimed he pulled the vehicle over because it was swerving and he suspected the driver was drunk.)

When Officer Raymond discovered that Prince had an open warrant for speeding, he

(*Anthony Price was released from federal prison on August 11, 2006. He was credited as an A&R on Scarface's 2007 Rap-A-Lot album *M.A.D.E.* as well as Devin the Dude's 2008 album *Hi Life*.)

(**Although the image was a flash of marketing genius, Bushwick Bill was disturbed by the fact that album sales were apparently more important than his health. "It still hurts me to look at that cover because that was a personal thing I went through," he said in an interview for *Check the Technique: Liner Notes for Hip-Hop Junkies*. "I still feel the pain from the fact that I've got a bullet in my brain. To see that picture only brings it back more so. I think it was pretty wrong for them to do it, even though I went along with the program at first. I really didn't understand why that picture was so important for them, important enough to take the IV out of my arm and endanger my life by taking the patch off my eye. I could have been blinded for life. And 'Face was against it the whole time. That's why he has that look in his eye in those pictures.")

placed him in handcuffs. After several hours of waiting, Prince was transferred to another squad car with two younger officers. "Why don't you all take me to jail, let me pay for the ticket or do something?" Prince asked, frustrated.

Prince was allegedly told that Officer Raymond was awaiting instructions from the DEA. When Raymond finally returned, he retrieved a small white pill from the squad car where Prince had previously been seated, claiming it was ecstasy.

Man, I know they're not trying to put that drug on me, Prince thought.

He was finally transported to a police station to pay for the speeding ticket. He was then transported downtown and arrested for drug possession (according to the police report, the pill was not Ecstasy but Mandrax, an illegal depressant).*

"I found that real strange," Prince said. "I don't smoke drugs. I don't do any type of drugs."

The following morning, Prince posted bail and voluntarily took two drug tests and a lie detector test. The lie detector revealed he was telling the truth when he said he did not know how the pill got in his car, and the drug tests showed no traces of drugs or alcohol.

Prince told local news media he'd been "setup" by "a trigger-happy, racist cop," accusing Raymond of planting the pill in his car and announcing his plans to file a complaint with HPD's internal affairs division. His attorney called the arrest "plain and simple harassment" and said Prince was being targeted because his artists' records "address things like police corruption." Nearly a hundred of Prince's supporters protested in front of the Houston police station, carrying "No Justice No Peace" signs.

"He fits a profile," Rap-A-Lot attorney Kim Harris told the *Houston Chronicle*. "He's black, he's 28 years old, and he's got a lot of money. People see that he's got all these cars, and they think, 'That guy must be dealing dope.'" She said police only had a problem with Prince because he made money off of "this sort of music that they regard as offensive or dirty."

After Prince's public statements, the DEA backed off. Prince used these real-life experiences as material for the Geto Boys' 1993 album *Till Death Do Us Part*. Although he'd never aspired to become a rapper, the Geto Boys were Prince's creation, and largely, his voice.** On the intro, he proclaimed:

There's a lot of people mad about our success, such as the DEA, IRS, and other wicked people in high places. When I was growing up people used to tell me how dirty the system was, but I refused to be controlled by an ungodly system, so now they mad and I'ma tell you why. I was born in the ghetto but I didn't allow myself to be systemized by the welfare system, poverty that they try to handicap us with in the ghetto. I work my ass off, I pull brothers off the street and together we [built] a multi-million dollar record company in a few years … [They say] those guys at Rap-A-Lot must be doing something wrong, because it's no way a group of niggas from the ghetto could run a multi-million dollar business. It's all a conspiracy against ghetto boys all over the world … So keep supporting Rap-A-lot, 'cause the only kind of dope we're selling is dope CDs and cassettes.

But even Rap-A-Lot's cofounder Cliff Blodget was questioning if gangsta rap was becoming part of the problem rather than the solution. "In 1987, there was a definite message that the general public badly needed to hear about what was happening in the inner city – the drug situ-

---

(*The pill was later determined to be Valium, a legal prescription drug. The drug charges were dismissed. While Prince was being arrested, UGK and Scarface were wrapping up a concert in Shreveport, Louisiana. Pimp and Bun headed back to the hotel, but Scarface and his crew went across the street to the Waffle House. While they were inside, someone stormed the restaurant and shot at them, striking Scarface in the leg. His bodyguard Rodolfo "Rudy" Sanders rushed outside in pursuit of the shooter. An off-duty police officer moonlighting as a security guard at the restaurant ordered Sanders to drop his gun; when he didn't, the officer shot him in the back and killed him. Scarface later rapped about the incident on his record "Now I Feel Ya," saying, "They shot my longtime partner Rudy in cold blood … It ain't no justifiable homicide, you never gave a warning, you straight up shot him from behind.")

(**Prince did rap on one version of the Geto Boys' 1992 promotional single, "Damn It Feels Good To Be A Gangsta," which didn't gain popularity until years later when it was included on the soundtrack to the 1999 movie *Office Space*. Prince also helped write the controversial Geto Boys' record "Crooked Officer," threatening to put a crooked officer's "ass in a coffin.")

ation, the degradation … [but] now, not too many people are still unaware that we've got some kind of problem," Cliff Blodget told the *Houston Chronicle* in 1993.

"Hard-core rap … is a symptom of a problem, not the cause of the problem," he added. "It's like analyzing a scab. The bigger issue is what made the wound … what purpose does the music serve? Is it digging the hole deeper, or is it communicating that there is still a problem here? It's almost like a cry for help."

Not only was Cliff struggling with his conscience, but he and Prince were having creative differences. Since both men were highly independent thinkers accustomed to doing things their way, the dual power structure of the company was becoming an issue. Plus, Cliff wanted to branch off into other genres of music, while Prince felt strongly about sticking with Rap-A-Lot's brand of hardcore rap. In February 1993, Prince bought out his partner and the two split amicably.

Ultimately, all the controversy surrounding Rap-A-Lot only amounted to free publicity, piquing fans' interest and putting more money in Prince's pocket. "Whether it's real or rumor, [Prince's] gangsta image hasn't done anything to hurt sales of Rap-A-Lot artists," noted the *Houston Chronicle*.

The Geto Boys' album *Till Death Do us Part* went gold. Not only did Rap-A-Lot's blueprint become the foundation for other independent labels like Suave House, No Limit, and Cash Money, but the perception of Prince as an outlaw set the tone for many other Southern rappers and entrepreneurs.

Shortly before UGK's *Super Tight* dropped, on the afternoon of July 7, 1994, two young Colombian men waited at the Interstate Motor Lodge just off I-10 in east Houston. They were expecting a buyer coming to purchase 5-10 kilograms of cocaine. The Colombians didn't know that the "buyer" was actually a federal informant wearing a wire. More than a dozen officers were nearby, ready to make an arrest as soon as the drug transaction was complete.

But there was a twist: the Colombians weren't actually planning to sell cocaine to the informant. They were planning to rob him. When the informant arrived, the Narcotics Task Force listened intently to the conversation taking place in Room 101 and it became clear things weren't going as planned. To protect their informant's safety, officers decided to rush the room. In the ensuing struggle, one of the Colombians was shot in the head and the other was killed.

The officer who fired the fatal bullet was Jack Schumacher, a DEA Agent in his early 40s who had been in law enforcement since the late 1970s. Officers at the scene told press that the shooting was justified, describing it as a "cut and dried" case of an officer acting in self-defense.

Even so, Schumacher seemed to have a knack for putting himself in these types of situations. He admitted that the Colombian was at least the ninth person he'd shot and sixth person he'd killed while on duty, although he claimed, "It's not something I care to keep track of."

Even though it had been years since the only drug bust even tenuously tied to Prince, and it was well-documented that Rap-A-Lot was selling millions of records, the DEA appeared convinced that Prince's money was illegitimate.

Between 1994 and 1997, DEA and IRS agents raided at least two car dealerships and a brokerage firm to confiscate records related to Prince and Rap-A-Lot, but couldn't find evidence of anything illegal. A broker professed that "anyone who had any accounting skills would be able to research the trail of funds [in Rap-A-Lot's accounts] and know that they were honestly earned and not illegally obtained." The IRS reviewed paperwork and informed the DEA that there were "no IRS violations there."

Rap-A-Lot certainly wasn't the only rap label drawing federal scrutiny. The FBI was also investigating Death Row Records for suspected "links to street gangs" and "drug trafficking, money laundering and violent acts." It was believed that incarcerated drug dealer Michael "Harry O" Harris had financed Death Row. In a lengthy *Los Angeles Times* feature, Harris not only claimed he'd provided the start-up money for Death Row, but also claimed he'd given Prince a significant sum (rumored to be $200,000) to launch Rap-A-Lot.

The Ghetto Boys' 1988 single "Be Down" did open with a shout-out to "Harry-O," and Death Row and Rap-A-Lot did have ties dating back to the early 90s (as evidenced by the collaborations between Rap-A-Lot's The Convicts and Death Row artists, but Prince dismissed Harris as "a pathological lying snitch" and denied his claims of ownership.

"He must be working with the Feds trying to bring down black-owned companies," Prince told the *Los Angeles Times*. "I started Rap-A-Lot with my own money."

When Ernest Howard arrived in March 1997 as the Special Agent in Charge of the DEA's Houston Field Office, the Prince/Rap-A-Lot file was still stagnant. A year later, Jack Schumacher, the agent with the dubious distinction of having killed at least six people in the line of duty, completed an assignment and needed a new project. Howard asked Schumacher to "actively pursue and target the alleged drug related activities of Mr. [Prince] and his Rap-A-Lot enterprise" to determine if the case was still viable.*

The Houston Police Department was also interested because they believed Prince had "corrupted" several of their officers. In October 1998, Schumacher formed a joint task force with seven Houston police officers from Sergeant Williams Stephens' Narcotics Squad. They believed that a RICO charge (racketeering), basically the ultimate "guilt by association," would be the best angle to pursue against Prince. A RICO charge would essentially mean that Prince was responsible for everything Rap-A-Lot employees or associates did.

Many Rap-A-Lot employees were ex-convicts; some argued that Prince was just giving a chance to people who didn't get many opportunities. "We took people off the street and gave them careers," Rap-A-Lot's Tony "Big Chief" Randle told the *Houston Chronicle*. "We found talented people who never had a chance. We've got people here who definitely would be in jail if they weren't here."

Two of those people were Steve "Cash" McCarter and Edward "Spook" Russell. Cash, who was responsible for making sure artists showed up on time to record, had previous convictions for burglary, robbery, assault, and drug dealing. Spook served as Rap-A-Lot's part-time promotions director, but the DEA considered him the "COO" or "assistant CEO" of the label. The DEA also labeled Spook a "career criminal" since he had been to prison twice for robbery and drug charges.**

Armed with government funds and resources, Schumacher and the joint task force went to work setting up elaborate sting operations to ensnare Rap-A-Lot affiliates and, they hoped, eventually put enough pressure on someone who had information on Prince. There were two ways to motivate people: one was money, and the DEA regularly spent up to $35 million dollars per year on confidential informants. The other angle was to find someone who was already facing significant prison time and had no choice but to cooperate.

"The government's snitch system is predicated on the draconian mandatory minimum sentences Congress has attached to federal drug sentences and the fact that parole has been abolished from the federal system," observed journalist Scott Hensen, who writes extensively on the criminal justice system on his blog Grits for Breakfast. "When you give a man… twenty years without parole he gets desperate. He's supposed to."

(*The original DEA code name for the Prince investigation was "Smash Cookies," although agents rarely used this title.)
(**Schumacher had done extensive research on Rap-A-Lot and referred to it as a well-organized hierarchy, often referencing their "organizational flow chart." The DEA considered both Cash and Spook "upper management" because they had offices on the same floor as Prince.)

The Rap-A-Lot complex on Governors Circle, commonly referred to as The Compound, operated on an unusual schedule; Prince liked to work at night and rappers liked to record late, so the building buzzed with activity 24/7. RAL didn't know that the DEA and HPD had teamed up to launch a full-on investigation, but by the fall of 1998, it was pretty clear that *something* was going on.

As employees and visitors departed The Compound, they were frequently pulled over by police for alleged traffic violations and searched illegally. Police asked if they'd purchased drugs at the RAL compound. Sometimes, threats were issued. "We're going to send James to hell," police told one visitor.

On Thursday January 7, 1999, RAL's promotions director Spook got a call on his office line at The Compound. "Rap-A-Lot," he answered.

The caller was a woman he knew named Phyllis Conner. Phyllis told Spook she'd stumbled across an opportunity to make some money. Some people she knew from Louisiana were headed to Houston to buy cocaine. They'd likely be carrying a large sum of cash, and it was the perfect opportunity to rob them.

Spook clearly didn't know that just yesterday, Phyllis was in a federal courtroom in Louisiana for a pretrial hearing. She'd been arrested six months earlier in New Orleans with two kilograms of cocaine, and was set to go on trial in two weeks. DEA agents were listening in on the call.

Later that day, the DEA sent Phyllis to the Rap-A-Lot compound to meet with Spook in person, wearing a wire. They went over the robbery plan. By phone later that night, Spook told Phyllis to get him the location and he'd have fellow Rap-A-Lot employee Cash "handle it."

Shortly before 11 PM, Phyllis called Spook and told him the "money and food" was inside an ice cooler in Room 339 at the LaQuinta Inn. She said she would get the targets out of the room and leave a spare copy of the room key on the rear tire of her vehicle in the parking lot.

While DEA agents listened to Phyllis and Spook's conversation, HPD Sergeant Stephens packed an ice cooler with six kilograms of cocaine and $90,000 of government cash.

Police watched as Cash and Spook pulled into the LaQuinta parking lot in a black Volvo, circling slowly and inspecting the surroundings. A few minutes later, two other men pulled in behind them in a maroon Camaro. With Cash and Spook acting as a lookout, the other men retrieved the room key and removed the ice cooler from Room 339. They placed it in the back of the Camaro and followed the Volvo out of the parking lot.

Both vehicles were promptly pulled over, and Schumacher retrieved the government's cocaine and money. All four men were charged with federal drug conspiracy charges that could put them in prison for life. Cash's bond was set at $1 million.

Schumacher, elated at the success of his sting operation, hoped he could get Cash or Spook to give them some damaging information on Prince in exchange for a lighter sentence.

The next day, one week after the sting operation, Phyllis Conner was back in a federal courtroom in Louisiana finalizing a sealed plea agreement. Her trial was cancelled and she was released again on bond.*

Obviously, Phyllis Conner was no longer welcome at the Rap-A-Lot compound. The DEA heard there was a price on her head, and threats had been made by someone known to drive the Rap-A-Lot company van. ("We are still paying for her safety," the DEA's Howard wrote more

(*Phyllis Conner's sentencing was pushed back *nine* times over the next three years and there is no record of her ever appearing before a judge for sentencing. There is also no record of her serving any federal time. Her case apparently vanished in exchange for her cooperation.)

than a year later.)

As the Rap-A-Lot van pulled off from a nightclub three weeks after the sting operation, it was pulled over by HPD patrol car and directed to a dark area on the side of the road. A second car pulled up with DEA agents Schumacher and Scott dressed in plainclothes.

Nothing illegal was found in the van, but the three men inside were detained and taken to a DEA facility, where they were strip searched. The DEA agents ridiculed them, calling them Prince's slaves, and asked if they were aware that Rap-A-Lot was just a front for drug dealing and gang activity.

One of the Rap-A-Lot employees, Christopher Simon, was wearing an 18-karat gold chain with a "5th Ward Circle" piece. DEA agent Scott ripped it off his neck, laughing at him for wearing it, and then slapped him in the face with it. He then put the necklace on himself. Schumacher allegedly punched Simon in the stomach and slapped around the other two men, leaving one with an abrasion on his chin.

The driver was given a traffic ticket for "failure to signal when changing lanes" and all three men were released. Scott tossed Simon's $1,200 necklace in his desk drawer. "[We thought] they were the ones trying to kill our [confidential source]," Howard later wrote, defending their decision to bring the men in for questioning. "When it was determined that they were not the subjects, they were not processed."

Scarface, enjoying the fruits of his success, had settled into a two-story five-bedroom home on a lake in northwest Houston. His house became the popular hangout spot where friends often stopped by to barbecue on the back porch, play dominoes, or shoot dice in the garage.

Among them was a childhood friend named George Simmons, who went by "Spooney G" or just "G," and an old friend named Ronnie Carboni, a used car salesman who always had some good weed.

Scarface was considering some renovations to his property at 12618 Waterside Way, calling around inquiring on the cost of adding a Spanish tile roof. One day, Carboni mentioned he was launching a construction business. "Let me do that roof for you," Carboni offered. "I won't charge you [full price], y'know, it's really a $60,000 job [but] I'll only charge you $45,000."

Scarface briefly wondered how Carboni knew about the roof, but it sounded like a good deal. They reached an agreement where Scarface would pay for the supplies needed and pay Carboni something minimal on the side for labor.

Carboni always had access to good weed because he had been buying it wholesale and transporting it to Detroit for nearly a decade. Scarface didn't know that Carboni and five other men were under a federal indictment, accused of running a large-scale criminal organization.

In May 1998, Carboni pled guilty. With his lengthy criminal history (aggravated robbery, forgery, theft, drug charges and more), federal law required that he serve a minimum of 188 months (more than 15 years) in prison. But when Carboni appeared before a judge in October 1998 (the same month the DEA/HPD Rap-A-Lot task force was formed), he was only sentenced to 54 months, less than one-third of the required time, and ordered to pay a $250,000 fine.

"This sentence is the result of a 5K1.1 departure," his paperwork stated. The 5K1.1 rule allows that if "the defendant has provided substantial assistance in the investigation or prosecution of another person who has committed an offense, the court may depart from the guidelines" by decreasing it up to 75%.

Carboni's sentencing paperwork also contained an unusual provision. Instead of being taken into custody immediately, Carboni wouldn't have to turn himself in until February 1, 1999. (A judge later extended this deadline until June 15, 1999.) It appears that this seven-month reprieve gave Carboni time to fulfill promises he'd made to the government as part of his sealed plea agreement.

From the beginning, Carboni's offer to do Scarface's roof seemed shaky. First, when Scarface wrote a check to the supply store for the first set of materials, Carboni was upset it wasn't written to him personally, and tried to get him to rewrite the check. Scarface refused. As the days went by, Carboni didn't seem motivated to actually work on the roof; he'd stop by, but spent most of his time hanging around smoking weed.

One day, Carboni stopped by to show Scarface some tile samples. He was accompanied by another white man sporting long, light brown hair. Carboni introduced him as a fellow roofing contractor, but in reality, he was an undercover police officer named Rodney Glendening.

While he was there, Carboni mentioned he had pounds of high-grade marijuana for sale, and asked if Scarface was interested in buying weed, or maybe trading for cocaine.

Carboni's request caught Scarface completely off guard. "Hell naw," he said, giving him a strange look. "I don't even fuck around like that … Man, I don't fuck with no muthafuckin' dope. I make music, dawg."

As it turned out, though, Scarface *did* know somebody looking to buy some weed. His homeboy George had always been the neighborhood hustler, sometimes selling dime bags of weed. George came by one day to smoke a blunt with Scarface and commented on the good quality of the weed, which he'd gotten from Carboni.

"Where did that kill come from?" George inquired.

When Scarface eventually introduced Carboni to George as an old friend looking to buy some weed, Carboni kept redirecting the conversation to cocaine. "[We] told them that I didn't mess around with no crack or cocaine," George recalls. "[They said] if I could find somebody [with cocaine] they would give me a sweet deal on some weed."

George, who was already on probation for a previous drug charge, worked at a local store called First Choice Music. Carboni and the undercover officer Glendening started coming by the shop, producing large stacks of cash and pressing George to find them some crack cocaine.

"Wave [a lot of] money around in a nigga's face who ain't used to having no money and you'll see a man do some strange shit, alright?" Scarface reflects.

George's younger cousin Byron Harris had just gotten off parole for a previous cocaine charge, and his mother had been begging him to help find his cousin a job. George started picking his cousin up and bringing him by the shop to help detail cars and run miscellaneous errands. Harris eventually met up with Glendening in the parking lot of a nearby restaurant, selling him eight ounces of crack cocaine for $4,500.

The following week, Glendening called George at the shop and asked to buy two more ounces of crack. When George said he wanted to buy 100 pounds of weed, Glendening asked if a portion of it should be delivered to Scarface. George paused at the odd question and replied that *no*, all the weed would be delivered to *him*.

At noon on March 12, Harris again met with Glendening ("against my judgment," says George) and sold him 44 grams of crack for $1,000. While he was waiting for Harris to arrive, Glendening called the record shop looking for him. "I think he's on his way," George said. (This phone call would later be cited as evidence of George's involvement in the conspiracy.)

Meanwhile, Scarface hadn't heard from Carboni in weeks, and he was wondering what was going on with his roof. Finally, Carboni came by the house. "Yeah, man, that stuff you gave me, that was like some Peruvian flake," he commented. "That was some good high grade coke."

Scarface stared at him. "Naw, bro, that's just some good weed," he said. "We just smoke good weed."

"G, man, watch that white boy," Scarface warned George later. "He *gotta* be the police."

Scarface was growing increasingly suspicious that his phone line was tapped. He'd been hearing nearly imperceptible clicks in the background. He got ahold of a device which turned either green (clear) or red (alert) if it detected a bug. It flashed red. Someone was listening.*

On the morning of April 26, Glendening again called the music shop and made arrangements to buy more crack cocaine from Byron Harris. When Harris arrived at their usual meeting place to sell 227 grams of crack for $6,000, he was promptly arrested.

Meanwhile, Jack Schumacher and the rest of the DEA/HPD task force convened at Scarface's home in northwest Houston with a search warrant. No one was home, but the back door was unlocked. They scoured the house and came up with nothing but a glass jar with less than two ounces of weed, just enough for one fat blunt.

"It wasn't shit in there for them to get," Scarface snorts. "They [couldn't] even take my fuckin' firearm [because] I'm not a felon."

When Scarface came home that evening, he was arrested for possession of marijuana. Schumacher took pride in bragging that he had "personally" arrested Brad Jordan (alias "Scare Face," as it read on the police report).

Shortly after Scarface's arrest, newspapers reported that a Rap-A-Lot associate was arrested for trying to barter a moving van once owned by Prince for six kilograms of cocaine.

Frustrated with all the negative media attention, Prince told *Link* Magazine, "I pay millions of dollars in taxes each year. I don't know why they assume something illegal is happening within my company. They want to destroy me because I'm young, black and rich, and did it against all odds."

Prince's public statements only encouraged the DEA to turn up the heat. During the summer of 1999, while Pimp C was proudly proclaiming his affiliation with the "Rap-A-Lot Mafia" on the Cash Money tour, the HPD/DEA task force focused solely on Rap-A-Lot. They dedicated their entire summer to Prince, logging more than 3,700 hours investigating him.

Late one night in June 1999, a month and a half after Scarface's arrest, Prince pulled out of the Rap-A-Lot complex and was immediately pulled over on the freeway. The officer instructed him to pull off at the next exit and park at the McDonald's.

As Prince exited the freeway, he saw the McDonald's, which was closed for the night. In its dark parking lot was a green Jeep Cherokee and an older-model burgundy Cutlass. Something didn't feel right. "I was a little leery about pulling in the dark," he said. "[Especially since] some of my friends that was in the Rap-A-Lot van had pulled [over] in the dark and got jumped on."

Prince passed the entrance to the McDonald's and stopped at the red light. The officer pulled alongside him and yelled, "Pull over! I told you to pull over at the McDonald's! Pull fuckin' over!"

Prince pointed across the street to the Shell gas station, which was well lit. "I'm going to pull over here, at the Shell," he gestured, pulling off as the light turned green. He parked and reached for his wallet, intending to pull out his driver's license, but the officer seemed uninterested in identification. Instead, he asked, "Where are your guns?"

"How you know I have guns?" Prince asked. He was an excellent marksman and did, in fact, have two licensed weapons in the vehicle. "What are you stopping me for?"

"You were swerving," the officer said.**

Prince climbed out of the vehicle and pointed towards the floor mat. "My guns is under the floor mat," he said.

The officer, who seemed to be killing time, instead began searching the back seat. Eventu-

---

(*In retrospect, Scarface believes his phone had been tapped for a long time, and that was the reason Carboni knew he was looking to have his roof done. He believes the offer to do his roof was merely a ruse to get closer to him and have a paper trail of money being exchanged.)

(**"This is the lie they tell when they want to stop you and do something to you," Prince said later. "The world know I don't drink or smoke.")

ally, the Cutlass and the green Jeep Cherokee in the McDonald's parking lot drove over to the Shell station. The driver of the Cutlass emerged and had a brief conversation with the officer (Prince would later recognize the man as DEA agent Chad Scott) while the Cherokee circled the gas station.*

The officer asked Prince how much money he had in his pocket. "Man, you need to borrow some money?" Prince quipped. "Why you asking me about my money?"

Clearly not amused, the officer told Prince to wait. "I'm gonna give you a warning and I'm gonna let you go," he said.

The officer returned to his vehicle and came back with a warning ticket, written to James Smith. But Prince had never been asked for identification.

"How do you know my name is James Smith?" he asked.

"Well, you look like..." the officer looked uncertain, stuttering. "Well, you look like James."

"Okay. Well, I understand what time it is," Prince said.

Why was they trying to pull me in that car? Prince kept asking himself. When he arrived safely home, he retrieved his weapons and ammunition from the car. Almost as an afterthought, he counted the bullets. There was one missing.

Man, they took my bullet. What the hell? he wondered.

Why would they take his bullet? What purpose did it serve? The question bothered Prince for weeks. He couldn't come up with any solid answer, but clearly, whatever they had planned for him, it wasn't good.

"That led to me doing a lot of things as far as protecting myself," Prince told *Complex*. "And shining the spotlight on them to let people know [what was happening]. It put me in [a] position where I [had] to protect myself."

Through his attorney, Prince hired a private investigator, who learned that Jack Schumacher was leading the DEA/HPD investigation and had a lengthy history of killing people in the line of duty. The investigator requested copies of Schumacher's internal affairs files with the state and HPD. (He also filed a request with the DEA asking for an accounting of all the taxpayer dollars that had been spent investigating Prince.) The hunter was becoming the hunted, and as Prince was fond of saying, "Every good hunter studies his prey."

Prince's investigator interviewed some of Schumacher's former colleagues, who believed that "in most cases, Mr. Schumacher has created the situation that resulted in the use of deadly force." Another explained that "in Mr. Schumacher's sting operations, he always leaves an open end to the end of his investigation, which always results in somewhat of a confrontation... [sometimes] resulting in the loss of life of his target subject." There had been other instances where the target of Schumacher's investigations turned up dead under strange circumstances.

As Prince's private investigator continued asking around about Schumacher, a strange burglary took place at the home of the investigator's son. Someone broke in, defecated on the living room floor, and stole nothing but his wife's panties.

On July 8, 1999, Spook and Cash's trial began, putting Prince and Schumacher in the same room for the first time. Their interaction wasn't without its humorous moments; Prince held the door open for an elderly lady leaving the courtroom and allowed Schumacher to exit, too. "Gee, you are being very nice today," Schumacher commented.

Schumacher believed that Prince's mere presence in the courtroom was evidence of his own involvement. Prince's perspective was different. "I was in court [because] I wanted to know what had happened," Prince said. "These are guys that worked for me, and I really wanted to

---

(*According to Scarface, Schumacher drove a green Jeep Cherokee. Schumacher later claimed that he "personally had not ever known of Mr. Prince being stopped.")

know what in the hell they was doing."

Cash and Spook were both found guilty of conspiracy and possession of more than five kilograms of cocaine and sentenced to 20 years in federal prison. Both men immediately appealed the ruling and asked for a new trial.

Spook's motion for a new trial was denied.* But in Cash's case, prosecutors had made a serious error. They raided his home six days after the LaQuinta sting and found a shotgun in his closet, adding weapons charges so they would be able to introduce his criminal history to the jury. Judge Nancy F. Atlas agreed with Cash's complaint that the prosecution's strategic move may have "corrupted the jury's verdict." Combined with "the weakness of the evidence of [Cash's] knowledge of the contents of the cooler," Judge Atlas overturned Cash's conviction and ordered a new trial.

The ruling deflated the DEA, who believed Cash was their best chance to "get" Prince. "We really need[ed] [Cash] to roll over [on Prince]," Schumacher admitted.**

The only other link the DEA had to Rap-A-Lot, through Scarface, was even shakier. Even though George Simmons was not present at any of the drug transactions handled by his cousin Byron Harris, he was charged with possession with intent to distribute crack cocaine. A DEA affidavit filed in Byron's case mentioned Scarface repeatedly, claiming that he had introduced George to his "cocaine supplier," a claim which Scarface and George both adamantly deny. The real target was clear: "[Scarface] is a recording artist for the Rap-A-Lot Recording label," the affidavit read. George claims that the affidavit was largely embellished.***

The DEA hoped to file charges against Scarface and pressure him into giving up information on Prince, but prosecutors felt there wasn't enough evidence. "We could not convince [the U.S. Attorney's office] to indict Brad Jordan, AKA 'Scarface', even though I strongly believe we had him tied in solidly on a federal drug conspiracy charge," Schumacher's DEA supervisor James B. Nims complained. "This was devastating to the case as we felt that Brad Jordan could have provided us with important leads and information regarding Mr. [Prince]."

Now, Scarface understood why Carboni had been so insistent that the check should be written to him personally instead of the roofing supply store. "[The DEA] tried to make up a story and say I introduced my pa'tna to the dope man and they were transacting business for me," Scarface says. "[They were] trying to make it [seem] like I was the kingpin funding these projects, and all they wanted was a check with my name on that muthafucker payable to [their] informant. No sir. I ain't no muthafuckin' rat and never will be."****

"They were trying to get [George] to roll over on me to try to get me to roll over on J. [Prince]," Scarface told *Complex*. "But that plot failed."

(*Spook, who is now in his 50s, is scheduled to be released from federal prison in June 2016.)

(**Cash was also facing separate charges in an unrelated November 1998 incident. He was accused of enlisting the help of a crooked HPD officer, Cedrick Rodgers, to rob a man who was trying to buy two kilograms of cocaine for $30,000. The conspiracy was not discovered until his accomplice, Randy Lewis, was arrested on unrelated federal charges in Beaumont and confessed. Rodgers was convicted of conspiracy to violate another person's civil rights and sentenced to 41 months in prison. In Cash's first trial, the jury couldn't reach a decision. The second trial was also declared a mistrial because of alleged threats against the testifying witnesses and members of the jury. Coupled with the charges from the LaQuinta incident, Cash's legal proceedings dragged on for several years, and he remained in prison for much of this time. In May 2003 he agreed to a plea agreement in which the cocaine charges were dismissed and he pled guilty to being a felon in possession of a firearm. He did not have to serve any additional time; he was sentenced to three years of probation, plus the time he had already served.)

(***Pimp C didn't place too much stock in federal affidavits. "If you read nigga's affidavits, that shit says anything," he grumbled in *OZONE*. "Muthafuckers will write anything in that shit.")

(****Curiously, on the night of the LaQuinta arrests, Schumacher claimed Spook had a check from Prince for $10,000 in his possession. Presumably, the DEA's aim was to have a paper trail connecting their informants to Rap-A-Lot. Carboni got four more months shaved off his sentence for the "substantial assistance" he'd provided, bringing his sentence down to 50 months. He was released from federal custody on December 20, 2002.)

George Simmons was sentenced to 20 years, while Byron Harris, who testified against him, only got six. According to George, Byron portrayed himself as a helpless drug addict who was only delivering product for his cousin. "[Byron] did everything he could to put those charges against me," George says. "I got 20 years for keeping my mouth shut, plain and simple."*

When he received the private investigator's report detailing Schumacher's history of violence, Prince became convinced that his life was in danger. "This is what I believe. They put a hit man on me," he told *Complex*. "[It's] highly unusual for an officer to have to use his gun and kill that many people."

Prince decided it was time to go on the offensive. Fortunately, he had friends in high places. Congresswoman Maxine Waters was a powerful yet controversial Democrat, an outspoken critic of racial profiling. Her husband had grown up in Houston's Fifth Ward, and they were good friends with the Prince family.

Prince reached out to Waters to explain that he was being pursued by an overzealous DEA agent named Jack Schumacher and feared for his life. Waters had just received a similar complaint about Schumacher in a letter from Lemuel "Bucky" Bond III, a convicted drug trafficker serving a 27-year sentence. Schumacher was one of the investigators who worked Bond's case and testified against him in court. In his letter to Waters, Bond too complained that Schumacher was too quick to resort to gunplay.**

"If you don't have anything to hide, come to Washington to file a report," Waters suggested. She called the United States Attorney General Janet Reno, complaining that the DEA was "picking on" Prince. Reno called Donnie Marshall, the new Administrator of the DEA, and asked him to investigate the allegation that a prominent black businessman was being harassed by a DEA agent with a history of killing his targets.

After the unusual call from Janet Reno, Administrator Marshall asked Howard in the Houston office to send over some information on the Rap-A-Lot case. Howard emailed a three-page briefing, which concluded, "The Houston Field Division remains convinced that James [Prince] is a viable target for a criminal prosecution. The recent arrests [in the LaQuinta sting] have reportedly unnerved [Prince], who has decided to go on the offensive."

To follow up, Congresswoman Maxine Waters faxed a letter marked "Urgent!" to Attorney General Janet Reno on August 20. It read, in part:

Mr. James Prince, owner of Rap-A-Lot Records, believes his life to be in danger at the hands of rogue officers from the Drug Enforcement Agency (DEA) in Houston, Texas. James Prince is a 34 year-old, African-American entrepreneur who has created a very successful business producing and managing rap artists. It is my understanding that Mr. Prince has amassed sizeable assets from his business which is operating out of Houston, Texas. Mr. Prince believes that he is being harassed and intimidated by the DEA officials in his hometown of Houston because of their assumption regarding the legitimacy of his business finances …

He alleges that he has been subjected to racial slurs, the illegal search of his automobile, and that his customers and workers are stopped and questioned without provocation by the DEA. Mr. Prince also has raised concerns about the interference in his right to travel, and he has been stopped numerous times on dark stretches of Texas highways. Simply put, Mr. Prince believes strongly that the Department of Justice must intercede into the questionable practices of the DEA and provide him with the necessary protection to ensure that his life and livelihood are not subjected to ongoing harassment and intimidation.

(*Scarface commended the El Camino driver Anthony "Ant" Price, Edward "Spook" Russell, and George "Spooney G" Simmons for "keeping [their] mouth shut" on the Geto Boys' 2005 record "G-Code," rapping, "I got love for you Ant, you a real nigga, Spook / My nigga Spoonie Gee, I can only name a few." In June 2011, the U.S. Sentencing Commission adjusted the sentencing guidelines for crack cocaine convictions, and George Simmons was able to get his 20-year sentence slightly reduced. He is scheduled to be released in October 2016, after serving more than 17 years.)

(**Schumacher admitted involvement in at least 12 gunfights during his 27-year law enforcement career.)

Congress of the United States
House of Representatives
Washington, DC 20515-0535

August 20, 1999

Ms. Janet F. Reno
Attorney General
U.S. Department of Justice
Constitution Avenue & 10th Street, N.W.
Washington, D.C. 20530

Dear Attorney General Reno:

Pursuant to our telephone conversation this morning, I am writing to request your assistance on what I believe to be an urgent matter. Mr. James Prince, owner of Rap-A-Lot Records, believes his life to be in danger at the hands of rogue officers from the Drug Enforcement Agency (DEA) in Houston, Texas.

James Prince is a 34 year-old, African-American entrepreneur who has created a very successful business producing and managing rap artists. It is my understanding that Mr. Prince has amassed sizeable assets from his business which is operating out of Houston, Texas. Mr Prince believes that he is being harassed and intimidated by the DEA officials in his hometown of Houston because of their assumption regarding the legitimacy of his business finances.

Mr. Prince alleges that the DEA has accused him of earning the profits from his business illegally. In addition, he alleges that he has been subjected to racial slurs, the illegal search of his automobile, and that his customers and workers are stopped and questioned without provocation by the DEA. Mr. Prince also has raised concerns about the interference in his right to travel, and he has been stopped numerous times on dark stretches of Texas highways. Simply put, Mr. Prince believes strongly that the Department of Justice must intercede into the questionable practices of the DEA and provide him with the necessary protection to ensure that his life and livelihood are not subjected to ongoing harassment and intimidation.

Attorney General Reno, Mr Prince has contacted me out of desperation. While in Houston, Texas, I had the opportunity to visit Mr. Prince's buildings and I spoke to his workers.

After listening to Mr. Prince's concerns, and that of his customers, I suggested that he document his torments at the hands of the DEA agents and send it to you for your perusal. Please understand that Mr. Prince has asked me to assist him because of my work surrounding the intelligence community, police harassment and brutality, and the reported incidents of "driving while black/brown."

I am often contacted by African Americans who feel helpless when confronted with the incidents as described by Mr. Prince. The harrowing details of Mr. Prince's allegations and my reputation in vigorously pursuing such matters warrants that I assist him to the best of my capabilities. Will you please give this matter your immediate attention? I anxiously await your response.

Sincerely,

Maxine Waters
Member of Congress

Reno forwarded the letter to Marshall, and his immediate impression was that it didn't sound credible at all. "Dark stretches of Texas highways"? He'd been expecting more detailed, specific allegations. Still, the accusation that a man's life was "in danger at the hands of rogue officers" was too serious to ignore.

Marshall instructed Felix Jimenez, the Chief Inspector for the DEA's internal affairs division, to arrange an interview with Prince. Through Congresswoman Waters, Prince informed the DEA that he was in fear for his life and would only be willing to meet with them at Congresswoman Waters' office. "Rather than forego the opportunity to hear what his actual allegations were … we very reluctantly accepted those conditions," Marshall said later.

The government is not normally known for its speed or efficiency, but just four days after Waters' letter was sent to the Attorney General, Prince met with three DEA representatives in Congresswoman Waters' Washington D.C. office. (Normally, the DEA never had direct contact with Congress, and it was unprecedented for an interview like this to take place in a Congressional office.) During a transcribed interview, Prince detailed the recent harassment and traffic stops and explained that he was in fear for his life.

The DEA's investigator Jimenez pointed out that Prince did not really know if the DEA was orchestrating the traffic stops. "Let's talk about facts … What [has the] DEA done wrong, so we can investigate?" Inspector Jimenez asked.

"Well, my biggest concern is I don't want to be dead before that happens," Prince responded. "If you could tell me why [DEA Agent] Chad Scott and whoever else would be over there [at McDonald's] waiting for me in the dark, then maybe I could feel better about just being comfortable to drive in the streets and feel like no harm would come my way."

Clearly frustrated as they neared the end of the interview, Jimenez told Prince he hadn't provided enough specific information. "Mr. Prince, tell me what [Schumacher] is doing to intimidate you," Jimenez asked. "Maybe we didn't ask the question right or something."

"I'm aware of this guy being a killer, first of all," Prince said. "[He has] killed a lot of people … I just have no idea why they wanted me to pull in the dark [at the McDonald's]."

"We will take a look at the situation. I just want to put it on the record that we feel that the information provided by Mr. Prince is insufficient at this point," Jimenez said. "It does not pinpoint any civil rights violation. [There are no alleged] specific acts of wrongdoing of DEA agents … it's very generic information."

"You're kind of focusing on me directly versus Rap-A-Lot the company," Prince explained. "I think a lot of this [harassment] is happening to the company directly … a lot of these things are taking place to a lot of employees or different people affiliated with the company … [They're] trying to … destroy the company."

"From my understanding from everybody I encounter, I am the target," Prince said. "They're actually attacking [Spook] and … [other people] affiliated with me and basically pressuring them and offering them all type of deals to lie on me."

At the conclusion of the interview, Prince gave Jimenez a copy of his private investigator's report, which detailed the claim of physical abuse and the stolen necklace during the traffic stop of the Rap-A-Lot wrapped van. Jimenez decided to open an internal investigation regarding those two specific allegations.

"I thought we would very quickly disprove those [two allegations] and [it] would be over with," the DEA's Administrator Marshall said later. Howard, the agent in charge of the Houston DEA office, didn't believe it was true either, but both men realized that Prince had put the DEA in a terrible position.

"[I was concerned] that Maxine Waters had characterized Jack Schumacher as a killer cop, as a rogue cop … [If Schumacher] goes out into the Fifth Ward now and gets into a life-threatening situation and has to kill Mr. Prince or some of the other defendants in here, he's going to be automatically assumed guilty," Marshall said.

DEA investigators went to Houston, where they learned that Simon's gold chain was indeed sitting in Chad Scott's desk drawer; improper handling of potential evidence amounted to theft. Marshall was also disturbed to learn that the agents had not filed the required paperwork when taking the three Rap-A-Lot employees into custody.

One DEA agent, Marty Fanning, confirmed that Schumacher had "slapped around" the Rap-A-Lot suspects, kicking their feet out from under them as they were up against the wall being searched. (Fanning was being investigated himself because of a separate incident with Schumacher and was fired shortly thereafter.)

The Rap-A-Lot task force had dragged on for nearly a year, and the Houston Police Department needed their narcotics team back at headquarters for regular duty. Without the federal government's blessing, HPD simply couldn't afford to continue setting up stings. "To buy the kind of narcotics and do the kind of work we need to do in order to infiltrate this organization, it's very difficult," explained HPD Sergeant Stephens. "We don't have the buy money [to purchase narcotics]. We can't pay the informants like the Federal Government can."

Without DEA funding, HPD officers wouldn't have been able to leave $90,000 cash at the LaQuinta, nor would Carboni have been able to flash money to entice George.

One morning in late September 1999, Howard came downstairs from his sixth floor office of the DEA's Houston bureau and approached Schumacher. The team of agents and HPD officers from the joint task force gathered around him.

Howard told the group of a dozen men that the case was being shut down for "political reasons" and there would be no more undercover work or surveillance operations until the internal investigation was complete. The men looked at each other in frustration, muttering amongst themselves. *Why?*

Howard was frustrated too, but didn't want to answer questions from demoralized troops. He looked at his watch pointedly. "As of 10:21 this morning, we're shutting it down," he said firmly, before heading back upstairs to his office.

The agents continued grumbling after Howard went back upstairs. "It was like somebody had kicked us in the stomach," Schumacher said later. Schumacher, who was still convinced that Rap-A-Lot was selling 5-15 kilograms of cocaine a week, assumed that Congresswoman Waters had somehow shut down the case.

Five months later, on March 9 and 10, 2000, DEA management from Houston and Washington D.C. convened at a DEA conference in McAllen, Texas. As Howard and several colleagues sat down for dinner, the Prince/Schumacher situation came up.

R.C. Gamble, who had taken over the ongoing internal investigation, was surprised to learn that Schumacher had been promoted and was now supervising the group responsible for the Rap-A-Lot investigation. For one, it was a conflict of interest for Schumacher to be overseeing agents who were being interviewed about his behavior.

Plus, everyone understood that Schumacher was now a liability. If he were to get involved in another violent shooting, both he and the DEA would be perceived as guilty no matter the circumstances. It was agreed that Schumacher should be reassigned and the confiscated necklace should be returned to the Rap-A-Lot employee Simon. "Let's get together on this on Monday," Mercado, the Deputy Administrator from the D.C. office, suggested as the conversation drew to a close.

Two days later, on March 12, Prince went to church like he did every Sunday. He was good friends with Dr. Ralph Douglas West, the pastor of Brookhollow Baptist Church (otherwise known as The Church Without Walls), and had recently donated more than a million dollars to the church to build a new chapel.

The Vice President of the United States, Al Gore, who was in town on other business, also happened to be in attendance. Prince normally lingered after Sunday morning services, but this week, he rushed out. "My intuition had me feeling kinda funny that day," he recalled. "I didn't feel like all those people with black glasses on was there for Al Gore."

One of those men with black glasses on was Ralph Chaison, an HPD officer who had worked on the DEA task force and was assigned to extra security detail for Gore's visit. Rumors spread; supposedly, Gore had been spotted having a private meeting with Prince and the church's pastor. A "confidential source" told Jack Schumacher that Prince made a donation of $200,000 to Vice President Gore.*

To Prince it was merely a coincidence that he happened to be in the same place at the same time as Gore, but high-ranking DEA officials viewed it as a personal insult. Howard thought it was too much of a coincidence that Gore attended services at a church where Prince had donated a million dollars.

"[Prince] was at the church with the Vice President. To me, that was him slapping me in the face, saying ha-ha. Here I am. You can't touch me," Howard said later. He wrote bitterly in an email to Schumacher's supervisor Nims, "James was there Sunday with the VP at church. He undoubtedly had a picture session as well."

Back in the office on Monday, Howard couldn't get in touch with his superiors in Washington D.C. and fired off a frustrated email which ended, "I have decided that the Houston Division will curtail any enforcement action against [Rap-A-Lot]… it's over and we are closing our case on PRINCE."

In a follow-up email the next day, he assured superiors that he would "terminate all active investigation of Rap-A-Lot," complaining that they were "bow[ing] down" to the "political pressure." Later that day, a memo was sent out reassigning Schumacher to a desk job, the supreme insult for any investigator.

For Schumacher, who wasn't privy to the management conversations, the timing seemed too coincidental. Already angry because Waters' inquiry had halted the investigation, he believed Gore's visit was the reason for his reassignment. A retired military friend of Schumacher's fired off an irate letter to Texas Republican Senators Kay Hutchinson and Phil Gramm, accusing Prince of making "a mockery of our political system."

The allegation that political pressure from a prominent Democrat forced the DEA to shut down the investigation of an alleged drug kingpin reached Indiana Republican Congressman Dan Burton. Burton, the Chairman of the House Committee on Government Reform, emailed DEA Administrator Marshall informing him that they would be doing an "oversight investigation" into the Rap-A-Lot situation.

The situation had largely died down until late September 2000, when Scarface's sixth solo album *The Last of a Dying Breed* was reviewed by major publications. On "Look Me In My Eyes," he rapped, "I can't get no peace, 'cause Schumacher's been chasin' me / Tryin' to set me up, bustin' down my streets / Lockin' up my dawg, to see if he can catch me / But I don't sell no dope… Fuck the DEA / Fuck the undercover that lock me up for weed."

On "Gangsta Shit," Scarface bragged that he "can't be stopped, not even by a badge," later adding, "there ain't enough bullshit in the United States to stop this Rap-A-Lot Mafia shit."

(*Schumacher wouldn't reveal his source but later admitted it was "third-hand information, hearsay information that has not been corroborated … from a confidential informant." Prince's publicist Phyllis Pollack told MTV that the rumors of a link between Prince and Gore were "kind of silly." Prince, who wasn't even registered to vote, said it was "not true at all" that he had donated money to Gore. Some pointed out that the link wasn't just unlikely but laughable; Al's wife Tipper Gore was an outspoken opponent of "gangsta rap" labels like Rap-A-Lot. It was later established that there was no record of any contributions from James Prince or Rap-A-Lot to Vice President Gore or the Democratic National Committee. "We found no political action committee with the word 'rap' in its name," dryly reported one Congressman.)

As Scarface's new records circulated, someone – likely Schumacher or someone close to him – leaked DEA documents about the case to Lee Hancock from the *Dallas Morning News*.

"A federal drug investigation of a Houston rap recording label and its associates was frozen after a prominent California congresswoman intervened on behalf of the label's founder with top Clinton administration officials, case investigators say," Hancock's article on October 2, 2000 began. "This week, the record label Rap-A-Lot plans to release a CD in which one of its best-selling artists taunts the Drug Enforcement Administration and talks of killing agency informants … [Scarface] brags of the 'Rap-A-Lot mafia's' ability to derail an investigation and drug agents' careers."

Prince responded by issuing a statement to the *Dallas Morning News*, accusing the DEA of using "Gestapo-type methods" and "criminal tactics" in their investigation.

"Over at least a 12-year period, law enforcement officials have investigated me and subpoenaed my financial records on at least two occasions. After such extensive review, they have found nothing inappropriate and can only produce innuendo and propaganda," Prince said. "If this is not another investigation motivated by racial profiling, then what kind of investigation is it? Many companies have former employees who were involved in illegal activities. Should their actions condemn the entire company?"

"I ask people to use their common sense. I have more money than I can spend in my lifetime, so I have no motivation to be affiliated with drugs," Prince said. "The facts, which law enforcement agencies well know, are that I pay millions of dollars in taxes each year and have contributed millions to numerous community and charitable organizations… I am living right, and I have no fear of extreme elements or of any investigation. I know that God is for me and no evil can stand against me; this includes rogue officers of the DEA, FBI, HPD, [and] IRS."

The ongoing news coverage spread throughout the country. Although the connection between Gore and Rap-A-Lot would prove to be completely unfounded, it made for eye-catching news headlines, especially in light of the upcoming 2000 presidential elections. Republicans and conservative news outlets jumped on the opportunity to link Gore to an alleged drug kingpin. *The Washington Times* described Prince as a "Houston rapper" who had "offered $1 million to the Gore campaign" and "met with Mr. Gore at a Houston church" to shut down the case.

After more than a year, the DEA's internal affairs division concluded their investigation. Chad Scott was reprimanded for his failure to follow proper DEA procedures regarding the confiscated necklace. Since Marty Fanning, the only DEA agent who confirmed the physical abuse allegations against Schumacher, had been fired, his testimony was considered not credible. Schumacher was cleared of all charges.

Meanwhile, Republican Dan Burton had learned of the March emails where Howard referenced "political pressure" as the reason for shutting down the case and threatened to subpoena the emails if the DEA wouldn't provide them voluntarily. Howard and the DEA were now on the defensive, forced to explain their actions to Congress. Howard argued that the "political pressure" he mentioned was a reference to Prince himself, a man who "played the game to the max."

Attorney General Reno and DEA Administrator Marshall asked the Office of the Inspector General to investigate allegations that the DEA had improperly closed a criminal investigation due to political pressure. Now, the government was spending all its resources and manpower on not one but *two* investigations *of itself*, instead of investigating Rap-A-Lot.

When DEA officials refused to cooperate with Congress, Burton subpoenaed them to testify before his Committee on Government Reform. Hearings were held on the morning of December 6, 2000 in Washington D.C. The only people eager to testify were Schumacher and his HPD task force officers William Stephens, Larry Jean Allen, and Ralph Chaison, who were frustrated that all the work they'd put in amounted to nothing. They'd picked up a copy of *JET* Magazine to read on the flight to Washington and were especially irritated to see that Scarface's

Last of a Dying Breed was at the top of the charts.

Ohio Congressman Steven LaTourette asked about Scarface's CD during the hearings. "I don't remember seeing any of his hits at the local music store in Ohio," he said sarcastically. "Is this something that I can buy on Amazon.com? How would I get ahold of this CD?"

LaTourette asked if the officers could "be so kind to … get their hands on their timeless classic by Brad 'Scarface' Jordan" to submit it for the record. A staffer volunteered to go pick up the album; in the ultimate ironic twist, Congress purchased a copy of Scarface's *Last of a Dying Breed* and played it during the hearing.

Scarface's angry vocals resonated throughout the high ceilings of the wood-paneled hearing room: "Do you think I'm crazy? Schumacher's been chasing me. Fuck [the] DEA!"

A few Congressmen chuckled as the song drew to an end. "Do you really find it that funny?" asked Burton. "I don't find it funny at all, and that's number 6 or 7 on the charts? My God."

"This guy, this artist, Mr. Whatever-his-name-is, feels confident making a threat record, threatening the confidential informant's life … and kids, teenagers, young people in Houston are listening to it," snarled Congressman LaTourette. "And now … the [rap] stars say it's okay to diss the DEA and threaten the lives of confidential informants."

"I think it shows what a vicious bunch of thugs that we were dealing with here," the DEA's Marshall agreed. "I wish that those kind of lyrics were a crime."

Burton had prefaced the hearings by saying they would not presume Prince guilty, but repeatedly implied otherwise. Prince was referred to as "Mr. Big" or "the big Kahuna," someone who was "down in the Houston area … poisoning their children with cocaine." Congressmen often referred to the 76 kilos of cocaine found in the 1987 drug bust, nearly 14 years earlier.

Although it was repeatedly mentioned that Scarface's album was on top of music charts, the idea that Rap-A-Lot was making a lot of money legitimately off music (and probably didn't need to be selling drugs) seemed foreign to Congress. Congressmen repeatedly mocked Prince and Scarface for claiming there was a conspiracy against them, apparently oblivious to the irony that the entire hearing *was about a conspiracy against them.**

Writer Cedric Muhammad concluded that the DEA's Rap-A-Lot investigation was "full of lessons for the Hip-Hop community." The *Houston Press* dubbed it the "Best Black-and-White Soap Opera" of the year, concluding that Prince "enjoys the limelight but not the microscope."

Not only was the case a stunning example of government inefficiency, but it painted Prince as a brilliant strategist. His unexpectedly overt move put the DEA on the defensive, effectively halting their investigation. He had successfully divided and conquered the federal government in a massive game of chess.

Nine days after the Congressional hearings, Chad Butler was arrested at Sharpstown Mall. Three weeks later he had his first court appearance, walking straight into the waiting arms of District Attorney Craig Goodhart. While Prince publicly outsmarted and embarrassed the DEA and local law enforcement, Goodhart had been working closely with Jack Schumacher, anxiously awaiting the day they could prosecute someone from Rap-A-Lot.**

(*Two weeks before the hearings, Scarface's album was reviewed in the *The Washington Post*. In it, writer Richard Harrington ironically dismissed "the CIA/FBI name-checking" on "Conspiracy Theory" and "Look in My Eyes" as merely a product of "Scarface's legendary paranoia.")
(**On the intro to Scarface's 2008 album *Emeritus*, Prince accused the District Attorney Craig Goodhart of having an "obsession with destroying [him].")

CHAPTER 29

"[Chad's case] was the biggest mockery of justice. Where we made our fatal mistake was not going to trial." – Mama Wes

––––––––––––

"You've got to reap what you sow. You've got to pay for what you do. And you know what? I was an animal for a long time. I wasn't nice. I hurt people's feelings, and I could see it. I was going to be the bad guy if I had to. Fuck you if you don't like me. You can like Bun you ain't gotta like me. [My attitude was,] fuck you, pay me! [If] you do enough of that, it's going to come back on you. It's karma. I got back what I put into it." – Pimp C, *XXL* Magazine, March 2006

Wednesday, April 25, 2001
Houston, Texas

Chad found himself back in court a month after he bonded out, facing off against the Harris County District Attorney's office, led by Craig Goodhart, who had a clear motive to put him behind bars regardless of the circumstances of his case. He had to make a decision: either go to trial or plead guilty to aggravated assault.

Chad was confident that the case against him had "no merit," but, describing it as a "personal vendetta against me and my organization," he didn't believe he could get a fair trial. Based on his Rap-A-Lot affiliation, the timing of his case, and his visit from the "special prosecutors" four weeks earlier – not to mention Texas' prison industrial complex mentality – Chad knew that the odds were heavily stacked against him.

What he *didn't* know was significant, too. When a staffer at Greg Glass' law firm ran Lakita Hulett's name through the Harris County criminal records search (spelling her last name "Hulett" as it was incorrectly listed on the police report) the response was: "No records found – Please try again." Due to the misspelling, whether intentional or unintentional, Chad and his attorney didn't know that his accuser had a lengthy criminal history, which could easily cast doubt on her credibility if they went to trial.

Greg Glass' investigator Renee Huggins had just finished interviewing witnesses at 9:45 PM the night before the hearing, so it was unlikely that Chad had been briefed on their statements, which had many inconsistencies. For example, Lakita's friend Shameka initially told police she had never seen Chad with a gun. But when the investigator spoke with both Lakita and Shameka on a three-way call, Shameka claimed she'd seen Chad pull out a gun, stick it in Lakita's side, and say, "I'll shoot y'all. Y'all don't know me."

Lakita's story had changed, too. In the new version, she'd caught Chad's eye in the main area of the mall, and he had been following her around trying talk to her. She said he'd become angry because she wasn't paying attention to him.

Lakita's friend Chaka admitted that Lakita knew exactly who Chad was and had been deliberately trying to antagonize him. The only person whose story hadn't changed was the store manager Kevin Nesby, who echoed his previous claim that he'd been standing between Chad and Lakita the entire time and never saw a gun. Chad didn't know that witnesses like Nesby were willing to testify on his behalf.

At the hearing, Greg Glass told Chad he thought they should go to trial; he felt they had a good chance of winning the case. He was also worried that if Chad pled guilty, he wouldn't be able to fulfill all the terms of probation.

Because there was a "deadly weapon" involved, the case was considered a "3G" offense. A judge could not give regular probation for a 3G offense, only "deferred adjudication" probation. With deferred adjudication, if Chad violated the terms of his probation, he would be sentenced on the original charge and would have to serve half of his time before being eligible for parole.

The judge overseeing Chad's case, Judge Jeannine Barr, was what some attorneys described as a "prosecutor in a robe," known for sending probationers to prison for minor technical violations (for example, being late to a probation meeting due to a flat tire). Although Barr described herself as "a fair trial judge" who wasn't "afraid to make tough decisions when necessary … [or] temper justice with mercy when appropriate," she had spent nine years as a prosecutor before becoming a judge, and many felt she still thought like one.

For Glass, going to trial clearly was the best option, but Chad wasn't so sure. "[Chad] was insistent that he knew best and that there were things about his case and being a rap artist that I didn't know," Glass later wrote. "I asked him to tell me what those things were, but he refused."

During the hearing, the judge allowed Chad, his mother, and Greg Glass to step into a small room alongside the courtroom to go over their options. Chad was tired of dealing with the whole situation. "Mama, you decide," he said quietly.

Mama Wes did a lot for her son, but she knew she had to draw the line somewhere. "I can't make that decision for you," she said. "All I will say is that you know you're not guilty of what you were charged with."

She looked at Greg Glass and asked, "What do you think his chances are, his chances of beating it [if we go to trial]?"

"I would never say 100%, because there's always a possibility," Glass said thoughtfully. "But I would give it 90%."

"There you go, C," Mama Wes said, looking back at her son. "It's your decision. But you know you're not guilty."

There was a long silence. "Yeah, but a lot of guys get life [sentences], and they're not guilty," Chad finally said.

Mama Wes nodded. "That's true too."

Chad silently weighed his options and decided to accept the plea bargain. In it, he would plead no contest to Aggravated Assault with a Deadly Weapon and Possession of a Controlled Substance and receive four years of probation.*

On probation, he would be required to do 120 hours of community service (minimum 4 hours per week), pay a $1,000 fine and $10 a month in court costs, and submit to random drug testing. He also couldn't travel beyond Houston and Port Arthur without written permission. Chad's court paperwork instructed him to report to probation on "the 25th of each month."

For community service, Chad was assigned to work at HPD's Mounted Patrol Facility, where he literally handled shit, cleaning out the horses' stalls. Chad was surprised to find that he actually enjoyed working there and became friendly with some of the people at the facility, who understood his schedule and allowed him to come whenever it was convenient.

Mama Wes and Red Boy encouraged him to do as many hours as he could and finish his community service early; that way, he wouldn't have to worry about it anymore, and it would look good for his probation. "Go on and knock that community service out of the way and pay that paper," Red Boy told Chad. "That's all they want anyway."

(*In 2001, there were 443,682 adults on probation in Texas, roughly equivalent to the entire population of Atlanta. Nationwide, the number of adults on probation in the U.S. was approaching a staggering 4 million.)

No one was very optimistic about Chad's chances of successfully completing four years of probation, least of all Chad. "I knew I was gonna violate it because the system is set up down here [in Texas] to where 90-95% of the people who take this type of probation violate it," he told journalist Matt Sonzala. "But … I had it in my head that … [if] you violate … they usually give you the time you had left on probation."

His attorney had tried to explain otherwise, but Chad still incorrectly believed that even if he violated during his four years of probation, he would only have to serve out the remainder of the four year term in prison.

But at least it was a step forward; he no longer had the uncertainty of the case hanging over his head. They were making progress with Jive, too. UGK refused to turn in any more music until their contract was renegotiated, and a week after Chad's hearing, they finally came to an agreement. Under the terms of the revised contract, UGK would submit the masters for *Dirty Money*, within ten days. After that, they would owe Jive one more album, and J. Prince would be the Executive Producer of both albums.

The revised agreement gave UGK a slightly better royalty rate, and more money to shoot videos. Still, Jive hadn't budged much. "UGK was never well-liked at Jive, and they kept bringing in 'managers' that Jive disliked even more. This contract illustrates that," says Wendy Day. "They gave up very little to the group or to Pimp C that [an artist] can usually negotiate with a label."

The new contract also allowed for a Pimp C solo album to be released through Jive. He would receive a $500,000 recording budget, and could keep whatever he didn't spend on recording as an advance. However, the $500,000 was not only recoupable from his solo album's sales, but also from his half of UGK's royalties.*

Most importantly, though, the revised agreement gave Chad more freedom to appear on other projects outside of Jive. Specifically, he and Prince planned to release an album on their joint venture Wood Wheel Records. Jive agreed that Chad and Bun could appear on up to three songs from the Wood Wheel album, but only one could be released as a single.

Rap-A-Lot was also negotiating with Jive for a possible distribution deal which would include a new Geto Boys album. Assuming the deal went through, Jive would permit Chad to appear on the album as a member of the Geto Boys.**

Although the financial terms hadn't changed significantly, Chad liked the new deal because it gave him freedom to release music outside of Jive when they weren't seeing eye-to-eye. "I got a side artist agreement with James Prince where I [can] drop as many projects as I like over there [with him]," he told *OZONE*. "I get as many release dates as I want [with him] … and I'm gonna continue to drop records with James no matter what goes on with any of these other record labels."

Meanwhile, Lakita Hulett was becoming even bolder with her boosting excursions. Two weeks after Chad pled guilty, she was caught walking out of a store in the Houston suburb of Humble with a hefty load of stolen merchandise (six pairs of pants, eight shirts, six shorts, and six jumpsuits) and charged with felony theft.

———————

With the success of "Big Pimpin'," life had started to imitate art, and Mama Wes was slightly amused by her son's habit of "changing hoes like he changed drawers." She stopped paying attention to his girlfriends, referring to all of them as "baby" after she accidentally called one of them by the wrong name. She made a conscious decision to stop bonding with the women rather than face the inevitable disappointment when he moved on to the next.

(*"This is not standard, and somewhat [unfair] since they know Pimp C is the driving force in sales for UGK," notes Wendy Day. Wendy hadn't spoken to Chad since their argument over Barry Hankerson, and wasn't involved in renegotiating the deal.)
(**According to Scarface, this version of the Geto Boys would've included Scarface, Pimp C, and Rap-A-Lot's DMG. The only person presumably not too happy about this idea was Bun.)

At their Houston townhouse, Chad had the upstairs floor while Mama Wes and Pops lived downstairs. Chad's floor, which had an entrance on each side, seemed to be a constant revolving door of women. Mama Wes loved to tease him about his playboy lifestyle. "One of these times you're not gonna get Hoe A out of Door A before Hoe B walks in Door B, and then you're gonna be in the middle of that sucker," she'd joke.

Mama Wes wasn't paying attention when Chad brought a woman to a UGK show in Houston, assuming she was just "another hoe." At Chad's instruction, the girl trailed Mama Wes throughout the nightclub so closely that J. Prince couldn't resist pulling her aside to ask, "Who's that shadow you got?"

Mama Wes was surprised the next morning when she recognized the girl at the townhouse getting dressed as the same one from the show the night before ("it wasn't usually that way," she laughs).

After seeing the same face come and go a few more times, Mama Wes learned that the girl, Chinara, was the daughter of Normia Jackson, a Port Arthur woman she despised. Normia was once close friends with Mama Wes' neighbor Linda, who was Chinara's godmother. After Linda and Normia suffered a falling-out, Linda often came by Mama Wes' house to vent about Normia. Based on what she'd heard, Mama Wes considered Normia "a crazy evil old bitch."

"Normia just is not a very good person," says Mama Wes. "She took care of old men [as their caretaker] and [she would] swindle them out of their money and property."

Mama Wes was livid with the realization that her son was dating the Jacksons' daughter. "He was well aware that I did not like that family," says Mama Wes.*

One day, back in Port Arthur, Chad stopped by his mother's house with the Jacksons' daughter in tow. "Hey, Mama," he greeted her. "Chinara wanna show you her picture."

Chinara sat down at the kitchen table. Mama Wes, prepping dinner, dried off her hands on a dish towel and joined them. She looked at a small black-and-white printout of a sonogram, not comprehending what she was looking at.

"Okay, where the damn pictures at?" she asked.

"Mama, that's my little girl," Chad told her, explaining that Chinara was pregnant with their daughter.

Over in Atlanta, Byron Hill told a judge he had served UGK with the new lawsuit at N.O. Joe's studio and more than four months had passed with no response. Judge Craig Schwall granted him a default judgment for $3 million dollars, an apparently arbitrary figure.

As soon as they learned of the judgment, Bun and Chad both signed affidavits claiming they had never been served with the lawsuit. After another hearing, the judge overturned Byron's $3 million judgment, ruling it invalid, and ordered that Byron should have to prove the amount of his alleged damages. But UGK's attorney didn't send over the paperwork for the judge to sign until a month later. The judge never signed the order overturning Byron's judgment and the attorney failed to follow up.

On May 24, 2001, the probation office called to ask why Chad wasn't there. Chad was confused; his probation paperwork clearly said May 25th. He went in the following day with his paperwork showing that the date was incorrect, and his probation officer Bruce Alan Shaw assured him that their mistake wouldn't be held against him.

(*Chinara declined to be interviewed. The interactions between Mama Wes and Chinara described in this book are from Mama Wes' perspective.)

On his next two visits on June 28 and July 19, he was asked to pee in a cup.

Both drug tests were positive for marijuana. On September 6, 2001, the State of Texas officially filed a motion to adjudicate guilt (a probation violation) against Chad Butler because of the failed drug tests and his May 24 "failure to report."

Mama Wes was upset when she learned of the failed drug tests. She had a candid conversation with her son, in which Chad admitted that he simply didn't *want* to stop doing drugs. Although marijuana was arguably less serious than cocaine or codeine, it was actually worse while he was on probation because the drug lingered in his system far longer. In Mama Wes' opinion, he hadn't really considered the consequences and thought he was smart enough to beat the system.

On September 21, Chad didn't show up for a scheduled meeting with his probation officer, and on September 25, he turned himself in and spent the night in the County Jail. Eddie Floyd bonded him out again the next morning.

With Greg Glass serving as Chad's attorney, Eddie Floyd, who had introduced the two men, was somewhat involved in Chad's case. Eddie kept telling Mama Wes that more money was needed to fix the IRS situation, and she continued paying, even borrowing some money from Chad's grandmother. In total, more than $150,000 had been deposited into Eddie Floyd's account.

Around this time, with the IRS still hounding Chad for money, Mama Wes learned that not much had changed with his tax situation. During a meeting with Greg Glass, Chad confronted Eddie Floyd, demanding, "What about this tax shit you supposed to be handling?"

The meeting devolved into a heated argument, and through it all, Greg Glass never volunteered a key piece of information: the only reason he knew Eddie Floyd was because he'd represented him in a theft case involving a sizable amount of money.* In fact, less than a year earlier, Glass had visited Eddie Floyd in jail.

A decade earlier, Eddie Floyd worked at The Leschaco Group, a global corporation which coordinates transportation logistics. Between September 21 and October 30, 1992, six Leschaco company checks were written totaling $76,312.73 to the vaguely named entity American Federal Financial Services.

When accounting noticed the discrepancy, their attorney frantically filed for a temporary restraining order to freeze the bank account where the unauthorized checks had been deposited. "American Federal Financial Services" turned out to be a d/b/a registered by a Houston woman named Debra Senegal just 10 days before the first fraudulent check was issued.

Fortunately for Leschaco, the thieves hadn't spent all the money yet. The $44,240.44 still remaining in the bank account was returned to the company and criminal charges were filed against Eddie Floyd and Debra Senegal. Senegal was acquitted, but Floyd was sentenced to 10 years of probation (and presumably, fired).

Now that he'd already forfeited his chance to have a trial, Chad came to the sinking realization that Eddie Floyd, who was actively involved in his case (and possibly Greg Glass, too) might gain more from his incarceration than his freedom. If Floyd had pocketed the money and Chad went to prison, it would increase his chances of getting away with a six-figure theft.

———

During an October 12 hearing, prosecutors offered to reinstate Chad's probation if he spent 30 days in jail, and Chad agreed. Judge Barr was out for the day, with Judge Woody Densen presiding in her place. The District Attorney handed the judge a Motion to Dismiss which was erroneously written to dismiss the *entire case* instead of the probation violation. Judge Densen signed the dismissal sheet stating that after Chad served 30 days in jail, the entire case would be

(*Glass later defended himself, saying that he believed Chad was aware of the previous case he had handled for Eddie.)

dismissed.

The conditions of reinstating his probation were also amended to require that Chad attend drug treatment classes. After he'd spent two months in an outpatient drug program, Chad had another session with his therapist, in which he discussed his struggles with bipolar disorder. "He has [a] mood problem," his therapist Victor Fermo wrote. "He gets manic and depressed. When he is manic, he gets into buying spree, like he would buy cars, and then when he is depressed he would sell them. He has a lot of energy and racing thoughts when he is manic. When depressed, he has no [interest] in doing anything. He just be sleeping and keeping to himself."

Above: A **Motion to Dismiss** filed in Chad's case in October 2001. This apparent mistake on the state's behalf would not be discovered for several years.

While Chad was in the session with Fermo, his "victim" Lakita Hulett was in court for yet another theft charge. This time, she'd run off with more than $1,500 worth of stolen goods and was also charged with trespassing and evading arrest. She was sentenced to 30 days in jail plus two years of probation.

Two days later, as Lakita was getting settled at the Harris County Jail, Chad turned himself in to begin serving his 30 days. Mama Wes wrote him a letter of encouragement. "You can make it," she wrote. "I don't know how you are doing with the drug problem, but I do know it is a problem. Don't deny that, Chad. I love you and we can get through anything."

"You have to feel castrated by this probation shit + community service shit. That's not you, but for now you have to do it," she added. "Baby, the only way to get back on track is to work. You have to try, and it probably won't work right away, but it will work eventually. You can work

---

	103	Department of the Treasury - Internal Revenue Service		
Form 668 (Y)(c) (Rev. October 2000)		**Notice of Federal Tax Lien**		

Area SMALL BUSINESS/SELF EMPLOYED AREA #10 Lien Unit Phone (713) 209-3825	Serial Number 760175752	For Optional Use by Recording Office

As provided by section 6321, 6322, and 6323 of the Internal Revenue Code, we are giving a notice that taxes (including interest and penalties) have been assessed against the following-named taxpayer. We have made a demand for payment of this liability, but it remains unpaid. Therefore, there is a lien in favor of the United States on all property and rights to property belonging to this taxpayer for the amount of these taxes, and additional penalties, interest, and costs that may accrue.

Name of Taxpayer CHAD L BUTLER

Residence   5048 SHREVEPORT AVE
              PORT ARTHUR, TX 77640-2541

IMPORTANT RELEASE INFORMATION: For each assessment listed below, unless notice of the lien is refiled by the date given in column (e), this notice shall, on the day following such date, operate as a certificate of release as defined in IRC 6325(a)

Kind of Tax (a)	Tax Period Ending (b)	Identifying Number (c)	Date of Assessment (d)	Last Day for Refiling (e)	Unpaid Balance of Assessment (f)
1040	12/31/1998	449-55-8148	02/19/2001	03/21/2011	7286836.87
1040	12/31/1999	449-55-8148	02/19/2001	03/21/2011	8724.42

Place of Filing COUNTY CLERK - PERSONAL PROPERTY Jefferson COUNTY BEAUMONT, TX 77700	Total $ 7295561.29

This notice was prepared and signed at _____ Houston, TX _____ , on this,

the _____ 07th _____ day of _____ November _____ , _____ 2001 _____

Above: The $7 million dollar **Federal Tax Lien** filed against Chad in 2001 as a result of the erroneous Jive filing.

without drugs. You can be in control."

"I don't know what other problems you have," the letter concluded. "But if you want to talk, Mama will take care of everything."

The false 1099 form had never been corrected, so the IRS still believed Chad had made $11 million dollars in 1998. The payments Chad believed he was making through Eddie Floyd had never reached the IRS. On November 7, while Chad was sitting in the Harris County Jail, the IRS filed a tax lien against him for $7,286,836.87 and began scooping up any of his assets they could find, including incoming publishing checks.

Between posting bond three times, paying attorney's fees and court fees, and the fact that Chad hadn't been able to travel, significantly decreasing his income, his funds were drained.

The San Jac house was in foreclosure, but Mama Wes managed to scrape together the money to save it. "Don't tell me I can't do anything," she wrote Chad. "When the heat is off, money talks and bullshit walks."

After five years of problems with Jive, drama with Master P, Biz holding the DAT tapes hostage, IRS threats, debates over masters with N.O. Joe, Byron Hill's lawsuit, Big Tyme's settlement, and countless other distractions and delays, not the least of which was Chad's legal situation, *Dirty Money* was finally released on November 13, 2001, while Chad was in jail.

Two and a half years had passed since the original scheduled release date, and the buzz generated by the Jay-Z and Three 6 Mafia features was gone. But even with Pimp absent and virtually no marketing or promotion, *Dirty Money* landed at #2 on the *Billboard* charts, topped only by pop superstar Michael Jackson's *Invincible*.

The album would go on to sell half a million copies, but still fell short of *Ridin' Dirty*'s sales figures. As a whole, the album felt less cohesive than their previous efforts. Some critics, like *XXL*'s Brendan Frederick, would later summarize it as "indecisive."

"*Dirty Money* is a good album, [but] I can't sit here and honestly say I feel it's a *great* album," Bun admitted later in an interview for Jeff Sledge's *Shop Talk*. "[It was a] time period where we were in a very funny place business-wise, [and] musically as a group."

Although it certainly contained some new classics ("Let Me See It," "Like A Pimp," "Choppin' Blades"), many of the songs on *Dirty Money* had already leaked out or been released on other projects. The original single, "Pimpin' Ain't No Illusion," had been circulating for two years. "Take It Off," from *The Corruptor* soundtrack, and "Wood Wheel," from the *RNDS* Rap-A-Lot compilation, were both several years old.*

Chad hadn't given final approval on the project, and it contained some oddities, like the fact that "Ain't That A Bitch" was inexplicably censored on both the explicit and clean versions of the album.** Even the cover artwork wasn't what Chad wanted; he'd had Mr. Soul design a different cover. "We should have used [the design you did]," he wrote Mr. Soul.

On November 18, 2001, Chad came home from the Harris County Jail, barely able to walk. He'd been bitten by a spider, likely, a brown recluse.*** The antibiotics given to him by jail of-

---

(*Another unofficial, underground bootleg CD titled *Some Mo' Trill Azz Mixez* dropped around this time. Although some people assumed DJ C-Wiz was responsible, he didn't have anything to do with the release, which was not nearly as impressive as *Trill Azz Mixez* and failed to achieve the same level of notoriety as the original. It is unclear who put out this tape. The cover artwork seemed intentionally vague, crediting "Tha Streetz Of Tha Mutha Fuckin' South" as the executive producer and "Port Arthur Entertainment" as the copyright owner.)

(**The editing was reportedly due to a sample clearance issue with the estate of Johnny "Guitar" Watson. Another unconfirmed rumor about the song appears to have originated on a semi-official UGK fan site, where site administrator DRod posted that the track had been edited before it even got to Jive "because the daughter of the 'editor' didn't like the word 'bitch' in the track.")

(***Brown recluse spiders were a documented problem in Texas jails. In January 2000 the Galveston County Jail had to send in an exterminator "swat team" after more than 33 inmates were bitten by brown recluse spiders. Their bites are rarely fatal and sometimes go undetected for several days, but if left untreated, can become serious. "[They are] not particularly painful at first," says John Jackman, a professor at Texas A&M University. "You get a reddened area a few days later and that winds up as a red ring. The skin will die in that area and you wind up with an open wound that oozes. It takes a long time to heal and may cause scar tissue.")

ficials didn't help much. He showed his mother an enormous black hole the size of a small pancake on his inner thigh.* "Oh, my God!" she gasped, insisting he go to a hospital.

Chad refused. It was late at night, and he was exhausted, just glad to be home. Mama Wes sought out some home remedies and got some Epsom salts to draw the venom out of the wound. "[I] kept putting presses on it all night until [it exploded]," she remembers, shaking her head in disgust. "It was like a volcano erupting. It was horrible. It was *horrible*."

Over in Mississippi, Smoke D was granted parole in December 2001 after serving more than six years of his 20-year manslaughter sentence. On his way out, he crossed paths with an incoming inmate, a man he'd known on the streets only by the nickname Cuzzo. Cuzzo, a major drug trafficker, offered Smoke a job. While he was locked up, Cuzzo needed someone to transport his product.

Smoke declined, mostly because he didn't like the idea of working for someone else. He'd be taking all of the risk but only receiving a tiny share of the profits. Besides, after seeing the response from "Front, Back & Side to Side," he'd already made up his mind to leave the streets behind and pursue a career in rap. Thanks to his notoriety off the *Ridin' Dirty* interludes, he had a real shot at making legitimate money in the rap game.

After his 30 days in jail, Chad's probation was transferred to officer Bobby Santiago in the Baytown office, which was closer to Port Arthur. On November 21, with Chad still recovering from the spider bite, Mama Wes drove him through a thunderstorm to make it to Baytown with 15 minutes to spare. He waited in a lengthy line, only to be handed paperwork to fill out. By the time he finished, he was two minutes past the 15-minute grace period and was marked absent.

"Be sure they know that you were there on time," Mama Wes suggested when he was finally called in to meet his new probation officer.

He went to see Santiago again on December 13, who told him that his original community service assignment at the horse barn was no longer available. He was still required to do four hours of community service a week, and Chad was a week behind. (Mama Wes blamed herself "for not just ramrodding him" and forcing him to fulfill his community service obligations.) He was given a new community service assignment and instructed to be there on December 15.

Chad didn't do his community service on December 15; instead, he went to the hospital for the unexpected birth of his daughter, Christian Lan'ae Butler. Like her father, she arrived a month early.

"I got a daughter!" Chad reported in a call to Rambro, elated.

Chad, Chinara, and baby Christian settled in at Mama Wes' house, where they had been staying while Pops and Mama Wes relocated to the townhouse in Houston. Mama Wes drove over from Houston, excited to meet her new granddaughter and thrilled that the girl had arrived just three days after her own birthday.

The new baby was born sickly and proved to be a handful, but everyone was so caught up in the excitement that Chad's legal troubles and community service requirements were momentarily forgotten.

(*Do not Google image search "brown recluse spider bite.")

CHAPTER 30

"[Going to prison] perpetuates a myth and it gives you street credibility, like it's a notch on your belt. But that's a misconception. Truth be told, when you go to prison, you lose. Your kids lose. Your family loses. You lose time that you can never get back." – Pimp C, *Dallas Morning News*, February 2006

"If you got people locked up, mane, send 'em some bread. Send 'em some pictures. Write 'em a letter. If you ain't got no bread, write 'em and tell 'em [that] if you had some you would send it to 'em. Stop being a bitch. It ain't never too late to stop being a bitch." – Pimp C, *Tha Buzz* TV, 2007

Friday, January 25, 2002
Houston, Texas

Bun called Bo-Bo Luchiano from the courthouse. "They keeping him," he said, choking back a sob.

"They took him to jail, Jeff," Mama Wes told Jeff Sledge, her voice breaking.

Up in New York, Jive was mostly unaware of the seriousness of Chad's legal situation. "We honestly weren't expecting him to go to *jail*," recalls Jeff Sledge.

While UGK was in the midst of planning a 30-day tour and two video shoots (for "Look At Me" and Bo-Bo Luchiano's "Bitch Get Up Off Me"), the state of Texas had filed a second probation violation against Chad, who owed $40 in supervision fees and $180 in court costs, and had "failed to perform community service at the court ordered rate."

The crew, which could no longer depend on consistent show money, mostly scattered. Chad's mistakes were costing a lot of people. DJ Bird took a full-time job working security at a plant in Port Arthur, and Big Munn was driving trucks. Dolby D went back to doing radio full-time to support his three kids.

Bun, who couldn't imagine his life without Chad, had an emotional breakdown. "I was lost as a muthafucker," he admitted on the *Pimpalation* DVD.

He couldn't see how anything positive could come from the situation, and was angry at Chad for ruining everything they'd built. He turned to alcohol to cope, downing a fifth of liquor every day. "I'm a bad drunk," he admits. "I was a shitty mess, just mentally fucked up," he told *XXL*. "I'd get mad at [Queenie]. I'd be fuckin' punching holes in the wall. I probably knocked six windshields out of the truck."

Late one night, Queenie and Angie found Bun drunk and depressed, walking down a railroad track acting crazy. They had to pull him off the tracks and take him home. "Nobody wanted to get in my way at that time," Bun told the *Houston Press*. "I [took] my frustrations out in all the wrong ways."

Friends tried to be optimistic, but privately, many felt that Chad could benefit from a time-out. "I think him going to prison was probably the best thing for him at that time," says Sleepy

Brown. "He was really turning into the character that he was portraying."

"At the time I think he needed to go to jail," agrees Big Gipp. "He was stupid with that shit. I was talking to him the whole time he was going through that [probation] bullshit and instead of goddamn handling his business and doing what he was supposed to do, he was [doing cocaine]. He was all the way into his Tony Snow shit."

Even aside from his drug use, many felt that Chad was putting himself at risk and some time away might actually save his life. "Chad was wild," says Nitacha. "Somebody would have *shot* Chad [if he hadn't gone to prison]."

As Mama Wes recalls it, Jay-Z performed in Houston shortly after Chad went back to the County Jail. "I want you to give it up for my brother Pimp C," he instructed the crowd of thousands. "And I want you to holler so loud he can hear you in the County [Jail]!"*

He led the crowd in a chant: *Free Pimp C! Free Pimp C! Free Pimp C!*

He actually was the first person to do that," says Mama Wes. "He started that, and from then on, all you heard was 'Free Pimp C!'" Homemade "Free Pimp C" t-shirts started popping up everywhere. Mama Wes had never been a fan of Jay-Z's music, but while Chad was away, she grew to appreciate and respect him as a friend. He often called just to see how she was doing. "I don't like your shit, but you alright with Mama," she told him once, laughing.

With Chad gone, Chinara and Christian moved back into Chinara's mother's house. Mama Wes was disappointed she hadn't gotten to spend much time with her granddaughter. But Pops, who considered Chinara "filthy," was glad to see her gone.

One day, Mama Wes passed by the San Jac house to pick something up. Leroy White, his girlfriend Shelly, his group Ovadose, and a few others were living there in Chad's absence. ("It was always a bunch of people in there that shouldn't have been there, in my opinion," says Mama Wes.) Chinara and Leroy were friends, and Mama Wes noticed Chinara's car outside.

They weren't expecting Mama Wes. "When I walked in the back door … it was so smoky in there you couldn't even see them niggas," she recalled. "And they were high as fuck off that wet."

Mama Wes had been around enough to recognize the unmistakable chemical-laden stench of fry. She was livid that her granddaughter, a premature baby just six weeks old, was in the smoke-filled house.

"[Fry smells] loud, and it'll get you high if you start smelling it [secondhand, because] the contact off it is so strong," explains Freddy Johnson, who always tried to avoid the San Jac house when there were fry smokers around.

Mama Wes was furious, but as she recalls it, Chinara was in no condition to have a serious conversation. "I didn't see [Chinara] smoking it, [but] she was in the house and she couldn't even talk," Mama Wes recalls. "[She was] mumbling."

Shaking with anger, but feeling helpless, Mama Wes went outside to calm down. She sat alone in her car and cried. *What the hell do I do?* she wondered. *Do I take the baby?*

Mama Wes decided it would be best to address the situation at a later time, but when she attempted to have a serious conversation about the topic, concluding with, "I just wish you wouldn't do that shit with her [around]," Chinara brushed it off, saying dismissively, "Aw, she couldn't get [high off] it."

People in Texas avoided fry smokers not only because of the lingering stench but because of their unpredictable behavior. On the night of Wednesday, March 13, 2002, Darrell "Pharoah" Burton came home to his mother's small apartment in southwest Houston. Pharoah was a member of the five-man rap group Street Military which had enjoyed underground success in

(*Jay-Z was on probation himself for a third-degree assault charge related to an incident where he allegedly stabbed record promoter Lance "Un" Rivera during Q-Tip's December 1999 listening party. He pled guilty and was sentenced to three years of probation rather than risk a potential 15-year sentence if he went to trial and lost.)

Houston since the early 90s.

Pharoah was already on parole for previous drug charges, and he had a fry-smoking habit. His mother wasn't home, but he was upset to see her friend Gloria Caldwell on the couch. The two began arguing.

"Look, I don't have time for this today," she snapped back. "Leave me alone, boy."

Pharoah, who had been smoking fry, was in no mood for her attitude. He snatched her off the couch, threw her on the kitchen floor, tied her hands behind her back with his necklace, and whipped out a small Swiss army knife. For several hours, Pharoah assaulted and stabbed Gloria with the Swiss Army knife and a household hammer, covering her face with a blanket. He also tore the house apart, throwing the TV on the floor and blocking the door with the loveseat.

It was nearly 1 AM by the time Pharoah's mother and her friend Karl arrived at the downstairs apartment and heard screaming inside. As they tried to jack open the door, blocked by the loveseat, they saw Pharoah holding a knife and hammer as Gloria, covered in a blanket, writhed and screamed. Blood was pouring from both ears. Her face was bloody and disfigured, her forehead and lip swollen and covered in dried blood.

Pharoah's mother stared at him, stunned. "Why did you do this?!" she demanded.

"What? I didn't do nothing to her," Pharoah said blankly, as his mother rushed him outside. When she refused to let him back inside, Pharoah smashed the front window with a hammer. As the glass shattered, his mother called the police.

Karl went outside, yelling, "Why did you do that to that lady? [At your] mama's house?" As Karl reached for the knife and hammer, Pharoah took a swipe at him and cut his finger, then took off running as the sound of approaching sirens grew louder. Gloria was rushed to the emergency room as police arrived to survey the damage.

When Pharoah returned to the apartment shortly after 4 AM that night, his mother alerted police as instructed. He was arrested and charged with Aggravated Assault with a Deadly Weapon, the same charge as Pimp C. Police delivered Pharoah to the County Jail, where he was placed in the same tank as Chad, along with two dozen other men on bunk beds.*

In a hearing on March 28, 2002, the state agreed to reinstate Chad's probation if he first attended Substance Abuse Felony Punishment (SAFP), a six month drug rehab program.

At the Harris County Jail, SAFP was reputed to be the only thing worse than prison. "[I wouldn't even] put my worst enemy through [SAFP]," one SAFP inmate told the blog Grits for Breakfast. "I would kill myself before I would ever go back there," said another, who referred to SAFP as "Hell on Earth." Another compared it to living out scenes from *The Diary of Ann Frank*. "Prison is a breeze in comparison to the physical, emotional and psychological warfare going on in [SAFP]," reported another.

In theory, SAFP was a way to rehabilitate offenders with drug and alcohol problems instead of adding to Texas' already overcrowded prison population. It was a "therapeutic community" based on a controversial 1970s drug treatment program called Synanon.**

But, one former SAFP inmate told the *Austin Chronicle*, "What actually goes on at SAFP is nothing like what the officials and lawmakers think or pretend to think goes on there. The horrible abuse I and so many others endured there was in no way healing or therapeutic."

"We need prisons," Chad told HipHop2Nite. "But let's stop playing games like prison is to

---

(*Pharoah was the exception to the rule. The majority of the inmates at the County Jail were there for non-violent offenses. Roughly half of them were charged with drug offenses of less than a gram. When asked to explain the incident that led to his incarceration, Pharoah writes, "I left an incompetent individual down and out on luck outraged by rejection. It escalated to something real ugly that could've been prevent[ed] if tha desperate spirit wouldn't have surfaced." In another interview for the book *Houston Rap*, he says he's being "held on a bullshit charge" and was "defend-n myself at a life threaten-n time.")
(**Synanon later became known as the Church of Synanon and was criticized as a cult. One of the main components of the Synanon experience was the "Game," a form of group therapy in which members were encouraged to humiliate each other and expose each other's weaknesses. Later studies determined Synanon's controversial methods to be psychologically damaging and ineffective.)

rehabilitate … Let's stop acting like you really trying to help these people be productive citizens and put 'em back in the community when you know that's not what it's for. It's there to hurt people and break up families … and in the state of Texas it's a money thang, it's a cash cow."

Most of the SAFP facilities were run by the Gateway Foundation, a private non-profit organization based in Chicago. Gateway, one of the largest providers of substance abuse treatment services in the United States, boasted annual revenues of $60 million. A large chunk of that revenue came from the State of Texas, which granted them a five-year contract worth $38 million.

But Gateway's hefty contract only covered their "counseling" services. Texas was still responsible for inmates' housing, food, and clothing. And there was a serious flaw in this design: Gateway also was not responsible for covering the cost of inmates' health care.

Gateway's usual response was simply to ignore those who needed medical care, even those with serious conditions like HIV, hepatitis C, epilepsy, or diabetes. TDCJ medical staff were overheard saying that they wouldn't service SAFP inmates "unless they are literally dying." Sometimes even that wasn't enough; SAFP inmates reported seeing a woman die of pneumonia right in front of them. Physical contact was forbidden. "[We] were told to keep our eyes front, while someone lay frothing at the mouth beside us," recalled one inmate.

No medication was permitted in SAFP, even for pregnant women or people suffering from seizures, bipolar disorder, or schizophrenia. Anti-depressants were not allowed. The running joke was that even patients lucky enough to see someone in the medical department would merely be sent away with instructions to drink "miracle water."

More than 20% of the inmates in the Harris County Jail, including Chad Butler, were taking psychiatric medication. (TDCJ is the largest mental health care provider in the world.) Chad had already heard of SAFP's terrible reputation, and once he learned that they wouldn't allow him to continue taking his bipolar medication (mood-stabilizing drugs like Zaprexal, Paxil, and Elivil), he refused to go.

He'd tried to stop taking his medication in the past, in an effort to prove to himself that he didn't need it, but fell right back into a deep, hopeless pit of depression. "He was absolutely petrified about not being on his [bipolar] meds," Mama Wes says. "Really, in all sincerity, C couldn't really function off of those meds."

Chad still believed that even if he violated his probation, he would only have to serve out the rest of the four year term in prison. He could go to SAFP without the benefit of his bipolar medications keeping him levelheaded and sane, or remain in the County Jail in relative comfort and take his chances in court. He chose the latter.

On April 2, a few days after the hearing in which he was assigned to SAFP, Chad wrote a letter to the judge which illustrated how little he understood about the legal proceedings. "I wish to withdraw my plea and take the time (3 year's) that I was offerd on 3/28/02," it read. "I feel that I can not make it on probation. So rather than me coming back in front of you later, I would like to do my time and be finished with everything. Thank you very kindly."

The response he received read simply, "You need to contact your attorney on this request."

Out in the free world, smoking PCP (or "fry" or "wet") was still mostly an underground phenomenon. On April 10, 2002, less than a month after Pharoah's PCP-induced crime, the drug was thrust into the national spotlight when 6'7" Antron "Big Lurch" Singleton walked through South Central Los Angeles in broad daylight completely naked, staring at the sky and barking like a dog. His hands, face, chest, and neck were covered in blood. Big Lurch was a Dallas-born rapper best known for his record "Texas Boy," on which he rapped about getting "high off of formaldehyde."

In a nearby apartment, police discovered a gruesome scene containing the bloody, disfigured body of 21-year-old Tynisha Ysais. She'd been a mother of two with a wide, vibrant smile and dimples. Ysais was the girlfriend of Lurch's roommate Thomas Moore, who admitted he'd

863827
863828

Jw/14/994
Jw/14/995
4/2/02

"DEAR JUDGE BARR (182 COURT)"
I WISH TO WITHDRAW MY PLEA AND TAKE
THE TIME (3 years) THAT I WAS OFFERD ON
3/28/02. I FeeL THAT I CAN noT MAKE
IT on ProBATion. So RATHER THAN ME
Coming BACK InFront OF You LATER, I
WOULD LiKE To Do MY TIME AnD Be FiNiSHED
WITH EveryTHinG.
THANK You Very KinDLEY

CHAD L. BUTLER
SPn 01501058/8B3

smoked PCP with Lurch the night before. Big Lurch had apparently broken her neck and jaw, fractured one of her eye sockets, hacked her open with a three-inch paring knife, removed her right lung, and chewed on her intestines. Lurch was arrested and taken to a psych ward, where a medical examination found blood and flesh that didn't belong to him in his stomach.

During a televised interview from jail, a visibly disheveled Big Lurch told interviewer Geraldo Rivera he had no recollection of the murder. "All I can remember [is that] the world was finna end, and I had to find the devil and kill the devil before the world ended. That's the last thought I had," Lurch said. "The next thing I remember is waking up in a room by myself."

"Any kids out there that's using [PCP] I would say, please, I would beg them [to stop] before something that they can't control happens," Big Lurch concluded.

Lurch's catalog included collaborations with Jive rappers Too $hort, E-40, and Mystikal, and the subsequent media frenzy focused on the bizarre crime's connection to Hip-Hop. "I don't think this fits anyone's rap persona," Hip-Hop activist Davey D, who had worked with Lurch, told BET.com. "PCP is capable of taking anyone out of their mind. This is bigger than Hip-Hop."*

In May, a third and final motion to adjudicate guilt was filed against Chad due to his refusal to attend SAFP. He would spend the summer in the Harris County Jail along with some 12,000 other inmates, waiting to see a judge.

(*Big Lurch pled not guilty by reason of insanity. His lawyer claimed he had been in a PCP-induced insanity at the time of the crime, but prosecutors pointed out a state law under which a defendant cannot plead insanity if the mental illness is caused by drug use. The jury found him guilty during their lunch break and he was sentenced to two consecutive life sentences without the possibility of parole. He is serving his sentence in solitary confinement at California State Prison in Lancaster, California. A 2011 documentary *Rhyme and Punishment* suggests that he is innocent. Although he remembers nothing that happened that day, Big Lurch doesn't believe he was the murderer. He has an unlikely ally: the victim's mother, Carolyn Stinson. Stinson believes that Lurch's trial was unfair and suspects the real killer was her daughter's boyfriend, who already had a history of domestic violence.)

All things considered, the County Jail wasn't so bad. Inmates had television and phone access, and some of the officers worked second jobs at local nightclubs, so it wasn't hard to relay messages to friends on the outside or stay up to date on local happenings. Chad had an ally in Pam Harris of Street Flava TV, who was always available to make three-way calls for him.

Chad called his mother three times a day and frequently talked to other artists like Three 6 Mafia's DJ Paul and Juicy J. "He always acted like he was in a good mood, like he was in a fucking hotel or something," laughs DJ Paul.

Juicy J's older brother Patrick Houston, better known as the rapper Project Pat, was one of Chad's favorite rappers. His single "Chickenhead" had been taking off when he was arrested during a Memphis traffic stop for having two revolvers. Since he was already on parole for aggravated robbery, Project Pat had been sentenced to four years in federal prison and was serving out his time in nearby Beaumont.

With Project Pat behind bars, his record label Sony didn't bother doing much promotion for his 2002 album *Layin' Da Smack Down*. The lead single, "Choose U," was produced by Three 6 Mafia using a sample of Willie Hutch's record "I Choose You" from *The Mack* soundtrack.

"Choose U" only got minimal radio play, but Chad heard it while he was in the County Jail and called Three 6 Mafia. "When I get out, I'm coming straight to your house," he told them. "I want you to get me that instrumental, that same instrumental that y'all used in that Project Pat record. I want that instrumental with the same hook, keep everything the same."

Three 6 Mafia, Young Smitty, and others kept money on Chad's books, and he was generous, often sharing commissary snacks with others who weren't as fortunate. His friends Mike and Cory Mo came to visit and were glad to see him sober and clear-headed, teasing him about his shaved face and the weight he was starting to put on. ("We have to cut our hair short and keep our face cut bald or they don't feed us," Chad complained in a letter to *VICE*.)

Angie brought Corey to visit and, as a courtesy, told Chad that she had rekindled a relationship with a former high school boyfriend. Things were getting serious, but Chad still kept calling collect. Angie's boyfriend would scowl and hand her the phone: "This your baby daddy."

When Mama Wes told eight-year-old Chad Jr. that his father was going to be away for a while, he didn't yet realize the implication. Their first visit was tough; Chad Jr. didn't know how to handle seeing his father behind a glass, dressed in county orange. "The first time seeing your dad in prison ... it has a different impact on you," he says.

Bun had finally cleared his head by "reconnecting with God" and was ready to get back to work. "I had to get down on my knees and have a long talk with God because the situation ... was something I couldn't handle [alone]," he said on the *Pimpalation* DVD.

When Bun came to visit, Chad tried to prepare him for the idea that he was going to be gone for a while. "You gonna have to do this solo album," he said. "If you don't, we outta here."

Bun refused to listen. "Naw, you coming home," he insisted.

After Chad had been in jail for five months, Biz decided to visit, apparently hoping to squash their beef over the loaned money and hostage DAT tapes. He called Mama Wes to tell her he was driving down from Nashville to Port Arthur on the way to Houston. "You gonna cook something, Mama?" he asked.

"Of course I am, baby, if you coming," she replied.

She called back later that night to see if Biz had headed out yet on the 12-hour drive. "You on the road?" she asked.

"Nah, Mama." Biz said he was feeling sleepy. "It'll probably be about 12 [midnight]."

"No, Biz, c'mon now," she said. "Get on that road now. You told me you were coming, and you know I know how long that takes ... come on, baby."

Biz decided to stay in town another day because he had some business to handle. He'd invested $7,500 in Hardy Lawncare, a Nashville start-up owned by Carlos Hardy and Charles Carter. As an investor, Biz expected to receive a share of the company's income. Carlos, who resented Biz' involvement, didn't seem to be taking the financial obligation seriously. (Plus, all three men were former drug dealers, who were sometimes in for a rude awakening when investing their money into legitimate ventures with much thinner profit margins.)

At some point, a heated argument ensued and Biz threatened Carlos and his family. To settle things, it was agreed that Hardy Lawncare would reimburse Biz's $7,500, but they were having trouble coming up with the money. Biz had just learned that the check Carlos gave him for $1,600 bounced; Biz thought he'd put a stop payment on the check. Infuriated, Biz wanted his money before he left town.

The following morning, June 6, 2002, Biz called Carlos and Charles asking about his money. The two men were headed to a landscaping job along with Carlos' older cousin, a woman named Atlanta "Kita" Hardy.

Charles managed to come up with $750, which he reasoned would be enough to calm Biz down. They arranged to meet at his mother's duplex on 16th Avenue. When Biz pulled up around 1:30 PM, he left his black Monte Carlo running in the driveway, music blasting from the stereo. He hopped out of the car in a sleeveless white t-shirt, leaving his 9mm in the trunk.

Inside, Charles gave Biz the cash. "[The] conversation between you and [Carlos], you know, let that die," Charles suggested. Biz started talking loudly, raising his voice so that Carlos could hear him from outside.

Carlos came inside, angrily telling Biz he wanted him "out of the business." As the argument continued, Kita followed her cousin inside.

"Who is this bitch?!" Biz yelled, motioning towards Kita, irritated that she was inserting herself in their conversation. "I don't want this bitch in here!"

It was the wrong thing to say to the six-foot-tall Kita, who was already on parole with a lengthy criminal history. She pulled out a pistol and pointed it at Biz.

Biz started to back up, looking at Charles and asking for help. Charles stepped between the two of them. "It ain't gotta go down like this," Charles told Kita, trying to calm her down.

"Move," Kita told Charles. "Get out of the way."

Kita reached around Charles and fired at Biz from less than two feet away. As the shot rang out, Charles and Biz both fell to the ground. Charles crawled towards the door in a panic and ran outside as several more shots rang out. Biz screamed in agony. As Biz lay dying, Kita dug through the pockets of his jean shorts to see if there was any money in them, leaving him face down in his white underwear with his jean shorts pulled down to his ankles. The Hardy cousins emerged from the duplex together, laughing as they left.

A neighbor called police, who arrived to find 32-year-old Brian "Biz" Hunter face down in a pool of blood, his body riddled with eight bullet wounds.* "Had [Biz] left [Nashville] when I told him to leave, he wouldn't have gotten killed," sighs Mama Wes.

Shortly after Biz's death, his girlfriend reached out to Leroy White and DJ Bird inviting them to come pick up the box of Pimp C's unreleased music from their basement.**

In July 2002, Lakita Hulett filed a lawsuit against Genesco, Inc., the owner of the Jarman

(*Most likely, all eight of these shots were fired by Kita. The murder weapons were never found, but it was later determined that the bullets that killed Biz came from two different guns. Kita Hardy and Carlos Hardy were both charged with first-degree murder, but at trial, it was disputed whether Carlos Hardy had a gun or not. Carlos Hardy and Charles Carter both testified that Kita had two handguns and was the only one responsible for the murder. The trial divided the family, with relatives on each side testifying against the other. A jury found both Carlos and Kita guilty of second-degree murder. The court considered Kita a career violent offender and sentenced her to 60 years with no eligibility for parole, in addition to finishing the sentence she was already serving for other crimes. Carlos Hardy was sentenced to 25 years with no eligibility for parole, in addition to the six years he had left on prior drug charges.)

(**No one retrieved it; sadly, the box was later discarded by a family member who didn't realize its significance.)

shoe store at Sharpstown Mall. In her version of the incident, "an employee of Jarman Shoe Stores invited Chad Butler aka Pimp C into the store, knowing him to be a dangerous individual, who was in possession of both controlled substances and weapons. While at the store, Chad Butler assaulted [Lakita] by pulling a gun on her. Mr. Butler threatened on numerous occasions to kill [Lakita], and Jarman's store employee encouraged said behavior, failed to call security, or take any other steps reasonably designed to provide safe premises for [Lakita] to shop."

Lakita claimed that as a result of Jarman Shoe Stores' negligence, she had suffered "extreme emotional trauma" and endured "anxiety, pain, and illness." Her lawsuit asked to be compensated for her "reasonable and necessary medical care" for unspecified injuries and the "mental anguish" she'd experienced.

Genesco demanded a jury trial, and the case was ultimately dismissed.*

With Chad's upcoming court date, Mama Wes spent much of the summer in Judge Jeannine Barr's courtroom, observing her handling of other cases. In Mama Wes' opinion, Barr seemed like "an evil man-hating bitch" who "took out all of her frustrations in the courtroom."

If Jeannine Barr was angry at men, she had reason to be. A few years earlier, she'd been sitting in a courtroom herself. A writer from the *Houston Press* observed her "wearing [an] expressionless mask" as she sat silently behind the "pale, pinched" and "mirthless" face of her husband. Judge Jim Barr was being disciplined for making inappropriate sexual remarks towards female prosecutors in his courtroom, among other complaints.

Jim Barr had always considered himself a jokester, but others said he was simply a "mean-spirited prick." He was known to use profanity and often referred to three female prosecutors he worked with as "the all-babe court." His favorite joke was to beckon them towards the bench, quipping, "I just wanted to see if I could make you come with one finger." He'd also told a defense attorney to "go screw himself" and threatened a prosecutor, "I feel like coming across the bench and slapping the crap out of you."

The last straw was when Jim Barr ordered a sheriff's deputy arrested and jailed overnight with a $150,000 bond just to prove a point, an abuse of power which infuriated the sheriff's department. It was determined that Jim Barr's conduct "not only diminishes his dignity, but also the public's respect for the judiciary of the State of Texas" and he was removed from office.

With scandal swirling around her husband's name, Jeannine Barr refused to even pose for photos with him. "I have my own political career to consider," she said, declining when a photographer attempted to snap a photo of the two of them together.

By the end of the summer, Mama Wes concluded that Judge Barr's favorite sentence was the maximum allowed by law. "I sat in her court[room] a lot, whether C was in there or not, 'cause I was seeing where her head was [at]," explains Mama Wes. "[I] researched her. If the maximum was 50 [years], that's what your ass was getting. That was one mean woman."

(*It is not clear if Lakita received a cash settlement. Calls and emails to Genesco requesting comment were not returned. While Chad was in the County Jail, police tracked down a murderer through a phone number registered to Lakita Hulett. The local paper noted that numbers for two other "young men with extensive criminal records had been registered to her … as well." Chad was an acquaintance of Lakita's boyfriend Elijah "Ghetto" Joubert, whom he called "Wild Child." When Ghetto robbed a convenience store near the Sharpstown Mall in December 2002 and made off with $6,487, an innocent man named Desmond Haye was charged with the crime due to lazy police work and a faulty eyewitness. Haye, who had been working two jobs to support his wife and young daughter, lost his job and his house while he spent 11 months in jail awaiting trial with Judge Jeannine Barr, the same judge handling Chad's case. While Haye sat in prison, Ghetto was arrested two more times, posted bond, and then tried to rob an Ace America Cash Express with two accomplices. When the clerk, a woman who had just returned from maternity leave, alerted police, Ghetto and his friends killed both her and the responding police officer. Ghetto was found guilty of murder and sentenced to death. He has admitted to participating in the robbery but denied that he was the shooter. The Supreme Court denied his appeal. In a letter from Death Row, he declined to be interviewed.)

CHAPTER 31

"[Chad Butler] gets released, he screws up over and over and over again. He gets released on bond, he screws up. He gets released, he smokes dope, he doesn't do his community service ... He took a gun into a mall with his cocaine and pulled it on a girl ... He's dangerous. No one can guarantee you that the next time ... he's not going to pull a gun on that girl in the shoe store or somebody else. No one can. No one can say anything to guarantee us that. He needs to be in prison where we are safe." – Assistant District Attorney Lance Long, closing arguments in Chad's sentencing hearing

---

"I ain't gonna lie, [being in] jail is nothing to glamorize. I done been a couple times, learned my lesson, bumped my head here and there. But that [time in a tank with Pimp C] was the best time I ever had in jail."
– Sylvester "Vesto" Bullard

Monday, August 5, 2002
Houston, Texas

On his 244th day in the County Jail, Chad and his new attorney Ross Lavin faced off against Assistant District Attorney Lance Long in Judge Jeannine Barr's courtroom to discuss his third probation violation.

By this time, the facts of what had actually happened at Sharpstown Mall were irrelevant. Because he had pled guilty, the question wasn't whether he'd committed the crime but how long he should be punished for it. "That was the biggest mockery of justice," says Mama Wes. "I think where we made our fatal mistake with that whole thing was not going to trial."

The state began by stating their case for the probation violation: he had failed to report on several occasions, hadn't kept up with his community service hours, and owed court fees. He had tested positive twice for marijuana. But the final straw was his refusal to participate in SAFP.

Chad admitted that these things were true and gave up his right to have a formal hearing. He would now be sentenced on the original charge of Aggravated Assault with a Deadly Weapon, a second-degree felony punishable by up to 20 years in prison.*

Chad's attorney Ross Lavin introduced Robert Outten, a substance abuse counselor who had met with Chad several times, to make recommendations on his sentence.

"You're familiar with Mr. Butler's profession, is that correct?" Lavin asked Outten.

"Yes, I am."

"And is that type of profession conducive to staying clean and sober?"

(*In at least 22 states, "serious physical injury" or "great bodily harm" must occur for someone to be charged with assault. But in Texas, a person can be charged with assault simply for "intentionally or knowingly threaten[ing] another [person] with imminent bodily injury." The charge may be escalated to Aggravated Assault if the person "uses or exhibits a deadly weapon during the commission of the assault." Aggravated Assault is a second-degree felony in Texas, falling into the same category as Murder of Sudden Passion, Manslaughter, Indecency With a Child by sexual contact, Sexual Assault, Robbery, and Arson. A second-degree felony in Texas is punishable by 2-20 years of imprisonment and up to $10,000 in fines. Besides Texas, only two other states – Georgia and Arizona – allow for penalties of up to 20 years in a situation where no bodily injury has occurred.)

"No, it isn't."

Outten explained that Chad's frame of mind had changed during his seven months in the county jail. "I think he's finally realizing he does have a serious problem," said Outten. "The medications are helping. The mental attitude, mental status from the first time I [saw] him to the last time I [saw] him was completely different … I really feel he still needs treatment."

Outten said he had researched several possible treatment centers for Chad, specializing in patients with a "dual diagnosis" (someone with both a drug addiction and a mental illness) where he would be allowed to continue taking his bipolar medication. Outten recommended that Chad should be sent somewhere away from Houston so that he could have a "change of scenery" and not "fall back into the same pattern."

"Why should the Court not just send him to prison for 10 or 15 years?" Lavin asked.

"Basically, I think he's salvageable," said Outten. "I have gone to court a lot of times where I testified against people that were on probation and just needed to go to prison, there were no other options left. I don't think we have exhausted all of the options … with Mr. Butler before he's incarcerated."

On cross-examination for the State, Long suggested that Chad could go to a treatment center after completing his prison sentence. Outten balked when asked the specifics of Chad's drug use, citing "client confidentiality," but Judge Barr ordered him to answer and explain "why you think he's appropriate for the [SAFP] Program."

Outten said Chad had been smoking marijuana for a decade and had used cocaine "extensively" as well as prescription medications like valium.

"And this [drug use] was all going on for a length of time prior to him pulling a gun on a girl in a record store?" Long asked.

"Yes."

"Prior to the defendant committing that offense, and I say that because he has entered a plea of guilty to the underlying offense that he's on probation for, he was able to maintain and establish a career, was he not?"

"Yes."

"May not have been a career that you thought he hung around the best people, he earned a living, didn't he?"

"Yes."

"He earned quite a good living, didn't he?"

"Yes, as far as I know."

"Did the defendant ever discuss with you the facts of the underlying offense?"

"No."

"Have you been made aware of the fact that what he's on probation for is pulling a gun on a girl in a record store because she said she didn't know who he was?"

"Yes."

"And at the time after he did that he was arrested, they found the gun and the cocaine on him?"

"Yes."

"I think you would have to agree with me that's an extremely serious offense?"

"Yes, sir."

"And I think you would also have to agree with me that the defendant was given one chance when he got deferred rather than went to prison at the time, he was given a second chance by the Court?"

"Yes, he was."

"And after he tested positive for marijuana he was given another chance by not being revoked at that point in time?"

"Yes, he was."

"And the last time he had a motion he was given another chance because he wasn't sent to prison at that point in time either?"

"Yes."

"You talked about [the fact] that you think that the defendant is capable of being saved."

"Yes, I do."

"Wouldn't you agree with me [that] it's not just about the defendant after a while?"

"I understand that, however, most of these behaviors were under the influence of drugs. The career, the profession he was in basically advocates that type of behavior."

"I guess my next question is: Can you guarantee this Court, if she puts him back on probation, that he won't do it?"

"You know I can't."

"You can't guarantee he won't shoot a girl in a record store..."

"Well, that depends. I could pretty much give you very, very good odds if he's not... using drugs and alcohol that probably wouldn't happen..."

"Can you guarantee the Court he won't use drugs and alcohol again?"

"No."

Judge Barr instructed Chad to raise his right hand. "You do solemnly swear any testimony you give in this case will be the truth, the whole truth, and nothing but the truth, so help you God?"

"Yes, Your Honor."

Chad's attorney Lavin began by telling Chad that he was facing "20 years in the penitentiary," noting that "this Judge has the power to do basically whatever she wants." He then prompted Chad to explain why he had refused to participate in SAFP.

"When you agreed to go to [SAFP], did you think you had to go off your medicines?" Lavin asked.

"No, sir."

"Did you mean any disrespect to this Court?"

"No, sir."

"To the assistant district attorney?"

"No, sir."

"Do you think it's a fair assessment that you kind of messed up on that last chance?"

"Yes, sir."

"If you had to do it over again would you have gone off your medicines?"

"No, sir."

"Tell the Judge why you wouldn't have gone off your medicines?"

"My medicines keep me stable, Your Honor. When I say stable, I mean not in a manic state or a depressed type of state. And in a depressed state I mean – I'm sure you're familiar with depression. I'm not very productive [when I'm depressed]. When I'm on my medication I'm stable."

Chad's attorney admitted that in prior hearings, Chad had "perhaps come into court and was disrespectful or was laughing or perhaps condescending to an assistant district attorney." He asked Chad if he had anything to say.

"If I disrespected the Court in any way I would like to apologize to you, Your Honor, and to you, also," Chad said, nodding towards the assistant district attorney.

"Let's talk about the underlying offense," the assistant district attorney Lance Long said during cross-examination. "What were you thinking when you pulled a gun on a girl?"

"It wasn't one person, sir. It was a group of five people, two males and three females. And it wasn't a record store, it was a shoe store, and we had words. She made a ... what I took to be a gang type statement and reached into her purse. At that time I overreacted and pulled my weapon."

"Were you high at the time you did it or not?"

"No, sir."

"So you can't say that the drugs made you do it because you weren't high at the time, right?"

"I'd been using drugs for a period of time, sir."

"But at the time it happened you weren't under the influence of drugs."

"I wasn't taking any drugs at the time it happened. I was in the shopping mall, sir."

"And you brought a gun into a shopping mall, didn't you?"

"Yes, sir."

"Along with some cocaine?"

"Yes, sir."

"And you weren't sent to prison for those problems, were you?"

"No, sir."

"Given a chance, right?"

"Yes, sir."

"And then you went and smoked some more marijuana while you were on bond – actually, I think you tested positive one or two times, right?"

"Yes, sir."

"And you knew you could go to jail if you kept smoking marijuana while out on bond, didn't you?"

"Yes, sir."

"Decided to do it anyway?"

"Yes, sir."

"After you pled guilty you tested positive for marijuana again, didn't you?"

"Yes, sir."

"And I entered into an agreement to let you do just 30 days in jail to hope you would learn a lesson, that was it, wasn't it?"

"Yes sir, you did."

"You knew you could have gone to prison at that point in time, didn't you?"

"Yes, sir."

"And after everybody goes out of their way to give you yet another chance you smoke marijuana again, didn't you?"

"No, sir. Both of those offenses … had already happened before I came and [served] the 30 days."

"Oh, I am sorry … You stopped doing your community service, right, as ordered by the Court, that was what you did wrong, wasn't it?"

"Yes, sir, it is."

"Would it be safe to say that the entire time that you were on [probation], the only thing that mattered was you and your career?"

"No, sir."

"I mean, you were upset that you couldn't travel to certain places for your career, weren't you?"

"No, sir."

"You never were upset about that."

"No, sir."

"Then why didn't you report like you were supposed to?"

"I did report. I was marked as being late when I got to the place where – both times was the first time I went to the facility. I was going to a probation office on the southwest side of Houston at first. After I got out of jail, I was staying in Port Arthur, so they changed it to Baytown. Both of those times were the first time I reported and … I was marked absent because I was late. Actually, the second time I was sitting in the lobby filling out my paperwork and that was my mistake."

"Wait. You missed your very first appointment, you never showed up, they had to call you on May 24, 2001, didn't they?"

"No, sir. I had a different date on my paperwork and I think it will show it. I had the day – the day that was wrote on my paperwork was a Friday, and the lady called me on Thursday and I had the paperwork to show that it was a different date on my paperwork. And actually, the probation officer told me that that wouldn't be marked on my record, but it was, sir."

"Did you ever call this Court or the probation officer assigned to this Court to tell them the problems you had with giving up your medications after being – agreeing to go to [SAFP], within a day or two after?"

"No, sir, but I did write a letter to the Court and I did write a personal letter to the judge."

"When did you do that?"

"The first letter I wrote was a day or so after I had signed for the [SAFP] program and found out that they didn't have a place where I could get my medication. And after I got a response I was denied that motion, so I wrote a personal letter to the Judge explaining to her what was going on with my life and apologizing for disrespecting the Court and asking if there was another option besides me having to come off my psychotropic medication."

"How long have you been using drugs?"

"Approximately 10 years."

"What drugs have you abused in the past?"

"Valium, cocaine, marijuana, PCP."

"After December 2001, after you got out of jail you never went back to do any of your community service, did you?"

"No, sir. And the reason being –"

"I understand. I didn't ask you – I remember you said you had a spider bite and you were sick."

"And I was on medication prescribed to me by the Harris County [Jail] people before I left."

"The question again, though, is: You never did any [community service], sir, after you were released the last time?"

"No, sir, I didn't."

"Your Honor, everything that I have heard from Mr. Butler is consistent with him being a drug addict," Chad's attorney Lavin said in his closing argument. "That's what drug addicts do. They use drugs … Everything that Mr. Butler did is consistent with the problem that he's got for which he's asking help. He needs to go to a treatment center."

"I think the problem with that argument, it's just about him, him, him," Mr. Long countered in the State's closing argument. "It's about time to focus on the rest [of] us … He gets released, he screws up over and over and over again. He gets released on bond, he screws up. He gets released, he smokes dope, he doesn't do his community service. Person after person has come in here and we have treated him differently than anybody else."

"He took a gun into a mall with his cocaine and pulled it on a girl," Long said. "He pled guilty, he was given a break. He's come back here, this is his third time. It's not about him anymore. I think he's blown all [his] chances … People don't get that many chances. They shouldn't."

"He's dangerous," Long concluded. "No one can guarantee you that the next time … he's not going to pull a gun on that girl in the shoe store or somebody else. No one can. No one can say anything to guarantee us that. He needs to be in prison where we are safe."

"Do you have anything else to say before I sentence you?" Judge Barr asked Chad.

"No, Your Honor."

"Having nothing to say, it's the order of this Court that you, Chad Butler, having been found guilty … [shall] be delivered by the sheriff of Harris County, Texas, to the director of the Texas Department of Criminal Justice … where you will be confined for a period of eight years."

Chad's face remained blank and expressionless. He said nothing.

"Good luck to you," Judge Barr said, signaling the conclusion of the hearing at 9:50 AM.

As fate would have it, after the sentencing, Mama Wes found herself alone in the elevator with Judge Barr. The door closed and a few seconds of awkward silence passed before the judge looked at Mama Wes and cleared her throat. "When I walked in, I had my mind set to give him 20," Judge Barr said. "And something moved me."

The bell rang signaling the elevator's arrival at its destination. "Well, even though I personally can't say I like it, I am glad something moved you," Mama Wes answered thoughtfully as the elevator doors parted.

The following day, Mama Wes mailed a 10-page handwritten letter to the judge. She first explained her background as a retired schoolteacher on disability and requested that Chad be sent to a nearby facility in Beaumont so that she, and his three young children, could easily visit. "The nine year old is a boy (honor student) who has always been very close to his daddy and even though seeing his daddy in prison may not be the best … it is still better than nothing because he misses his daddy very much … we are all trying very hard to keep some kind of a family unit together," she wrote.

After asking that the rest of her letter "not be held against my son," she begged the judge to reconsider "the extenuating circumstances," explaining that he was mentally ill and had developed a drug problem. "I am in no way condoning his actions … [but] when my son entered the mall stupidly carrying a weapon, he had reasons to fear for his own life," she wrote, explaining that only five months earlier he'd been "beaten, kicked, and had a large caliber gun stuck in his mouth" in his hotel room. Chad, she wrote, had "felt honestly that he was only protecting himself" at the mall.

Mama Wes argued that there were explanations for most of the technical violations – the missed probation meetings, the community service he'd missed due to the spider bite and his daughter's birth. "Judge Barr, I am not asking for pity," she wrote. "My son does need mental help and drug rehabilitation, but prison is not going to help that … he is not a danger to society … he is simply a young man who needs a lot of professional help."

"I beg you, please … give my son one last chance," she wrote. "I know … [I may be] as crazy as he is to ask this of you … but my father always taught me that if you don't ask, you never receive."

Mama Wes finished the letter by asking to meet with the judge in person. "I am fighting for my son's life, my life, and a decent life for my grandchildren," she wrote. "My son is not a hardened criminal and I don't [want] him to become one in that place."

Judge Barr never responded; the district clerk filed the letter away with a notation at the bottom: "Court informed of request. Out of court's jurisdiction."

"Damn, Mama, I never should've [taken probation]…" Chad told his mother the next time she came to visit him at the County Jail.

"I know," she nodded. "You remember when we were standing in that room? I told you – it's your decision."

"I think if he had known that he was gonna get [eight years in prison] he might've opted for [SAFP] instead," reflects Mama Wes.

"Thinking back on it, I really can't tell you what our mindset was back then," she adds. "But, he should have gone to trial. Had he gone to trial, he would have been exonerated … the [accuser] had a [lengthy criminal] record … and she never showed up for any of the [hearings] anyway, because, you know, people with warrants don't want to go to [a courtroom]."

"It was ignorance on our part; inexperience," Mama Wes concludes. "We really didn't know [what to do]. C had never been in a position [like] that before; we should have gone to trial … It was a matter of us not really understanding a lot about [the legal system]. Actually, I'll charge it up to our stupidity."

Chad was still hopeful that with an appeal, he could get a new trial. "The latest news regarding Pimp C's verdict was to be posted here, but I've been asked not to share that information at this time," webmaster DRod posted on UGK's unofficial Geocities fan site. "Aside from the 'rumors' … the process IS NOT over yet."

Once it was clear that Pimp C would be gone for a while, Jive's CEO Barry Weiss was skeptical that Bun B could carry on the UGK legacy alone. "I understood, from Barry's point of view, Pimp did the production [and] Pimp was more the heart of the group," Bun B admits. "Pimp's gone, [and I] obviously don't make music, so how [could I] keep this thing going [by myself]?"

Incarceration was viewed as a career killer. Tupac Shakur was the only rapper who had managed to emerge from prison as a bigger superstar than he was when he left.* Typically when an artist was gone from public view, their fanbase languished, fickle listeners moving on to the next hot artist.

There was a clause in UGK's contract which allowed that if one member went to jail or died, they had the option to replace the group member. Weiss reached out to Bun and suggested they could exercise that option; perhaps they could bring in Mr. 3-2 to replace Pimp C?

Typically in their dealings with Jive, Pimp played "bad cop," while Bun was the more reasonable "good cop." But with Pimp gone, there was no one else to say "no," and Bun found himself stepping into a more aggressive role. Upset, Bun refused to even entertain the idea of replacing Pimp.

"What's wrong with you?" Bun demanded, telling Weiss he was out of line. "The shit ain't over!" He said he wasn't interested in replacing Pimp, and suggested that he could do a solo album to keep the momentum going.**

Weiss didn't have much interest in a Bun B solo project, but told him he wouldn't have a problem with him doing it on another label. The solo album could still benefit Jive financially in the long run by keeping the UGK brand relevant.

While Weiss was not optimistic about Bun B's chances at solo success, Bun already had a believer in J. Prince. Less than three weeks after Chad's sentencing, Bun signed a one album solo deal with Rap-A-Lot, with an option for two more.

To Bun, Rap-A-Lot was the only logical place to go. After everything they'd been through with Russell Washington, Byron Hill, and Jive, J. Prince had always been there. "There was a lot that we really didn't understand about the dynamics of the music industry," Bun said on KLRU TV. "We were very lucky to have someone like James Prince [as a mentor]."

Although Bun had never wanted to be a solo artist and really wasn't sure if he could do it alone, he felt that the circumstances left him with no other option. "I was adamant about trying to leave something there for [Pimp] when he came back home," he explained on Jeff Sledge's *Shop Talk*. "I know a lot of dudes that have nothing to do with the music [business], they [go to jail] and whatever [business] they had going dies when they leave, and they come home and it's not there anymore. So I just wanted him to have at least some kind of decent, fair shot."

Besides, it was not only the "trill" thing for Bun to do, but also necessary for his own family's survival. "[My income] was much lower [at that time], because people felt like, 'This is not [really] UGK. We're not gonna pay you for that,'" Bun adds. "It [was] a hard time to really kinda build it back up."

Bills still had to be paid, so after he'd made it through the rough spot, Bun forced himself

---

(*In February 1995, Tupac began serving a 1.5 year – 4.5 year sentence for a controversial sexual assault charge. A month later, his album *Me Against The World* debuted at #1 on the charts, selling 2.5 million copies. After his 1996 release, he signed to Death Row Records and released *All Eyez on Me*, which sold over six million copies.)

(**Bun described his furor with Weiss' suggestion in a 2013 interview with Jeff Sledge's *Shop Talk*. However, his statement appears to be contradicted by a letter he sent to Jive on August 21, 2002, a few weeks after Chad's sentencing. "This is to serve as notice that Chad Butler ceases to be an actively performing Member of [UGK]. Moreover, we will promptly designate a Replacement Member for such Leaving Member," it states. It is possible the document may have been a legal strategy, as it went on to "request an advance of $250,000 against the Recording Fund for the Fifth Album.")

to get back to work. His first solo show was in Arlington, Texas. Bun had always been a nervous wreck before shows, and now with Chad gone, it was even harder. He dedicated the event to his partner. "This gonna be for Pimp," he announced. "Y'all gonna rep with me for Pimp."

On the road, Bun was frequently approached by fans who weren't sure what was going on with UGK. They'd ask if the group had broken up, or inquire, "What's up with Pimp?"

Tired of giving everyone the same answer, Bun had a t-shirt pressed up with a picture of Pimp C's face and "Free Pimp C" across the top, "UGK 4 Life" across the bottom.

He focused on marketing the UGK brand and polished himself as the group's spokesman, surprising rap reporters with his intellect and ability to articulate. Writers loved Bun; calling him "open and accommodating" and gushing that he was "universally acknowledged as the best interview in Hip-Hop."

A month after Chad's sentencing, his attorney Ross Lavin filed a motion for a new trial, claiming that Chad was now a "changed man" willing to attend SAFP, and that "the last nine months in the Harris County Jail actually did him some good." His attorney suggested Chad could do community service to "spread the good news of the Gospel" and "an anti-drug campaign aimed specifically at the young people that [Chad] has the ability to reach through his musical profession." He also offered that Chad could "wash pots and pans at the Salvation Army for whatever length of time the court deems appropriate."

Sylvester "Vesto" Bullard, a youngster with braids, was an aspiring rapper who had met Pimp during a studio session with DJ Screw's brother Al-D. Like Pimp, Vesto had been in and out of jail the past few years fighting a case (which he claims were "some trumped up charges") and attending probation meetings and drug classes. He'd violated a few times for minor charges like driving on a suspended license or possession of marijuana, and now, he'd been caught again with a couple grams of cocaine and charged with possession of a controlled substance.

Since they'd met at the recording studio and hit it off, Vesto had tried calling Pimp a few times. He hadn't heard back for several months and didn't understand why. *Damn, it went from us communicating to now everything went dry,* he thought. *I know he's not acting funny with me 'cause we was on some cool, straight, real nigga shit.*

When he was escorted into the AB3 tank at the Harris County Jail, Vesto stopped short, a grin crossing his face as he saw several faces he recognized. There was Pharoah from Street Military and a few other "street comrades," and there, sitting over in the corner, was Pimp C.

"Damn, boy, this where you been?" Vesto laughed.

"Man, look," Pimp smiled. "You see me, don't you?"

Chad passed most of the time reading books and writing song lyrics. Once he'd completed ten songs, he'd put them in an envelope and mail them home to his mother. In total, he estimated he wrote 300 songs in the County Jail.

At night, during rack time, when radios and televisions were turned off, inmates would often gather around one of the bunks and remove the top mattress, placing their food and drinks on the flat metal. They'd go around in a cypher, kicking verses to keep each other entertained, or coming up with song ideas.

Pharoah was the go-to guy for the soundtrack; he'd pound on his chest and provide a beat, using his fist as the drum and his knuckles as the snare. He, Chad, and Vesto would take turns dropping rhymes, while the rest of the inmates crowded around watching the free live show.

Being in jail hadn't dimmed Pharoah's rap ethic, either, and he compiled entire songs in written form in a tablet. Chad told Pharoah he was the first person he'd ever seen with a full-length album in a writing tablet. ("That meant a lot to me on tha organized tip," Pharoah says.)

Pimp C and Vesto's "Legend in Texas" and Pharoah and Pimp C's "Screenz Down" were two standout songs which emerged from these sessions, although they would never come to fruition as actual records. As Vesto recalls it, Pimp C's greatest creation at the County Jail was a humorous diss record titled "You Got Dropped," ridiculing rappers who had lost their record deal.

Aside from impromptu freestyle sessions, there were other benefits to being in a cell with Pimp C. He got mail every day, which often included pictures of parties or girls which he shared with the rest of his cellmates. Correctional officers brought them a tub of ice daily so they could stay cool. "We was the only muthafuckers that had ice," remembers Vesto. "Having ice, man, that was unheard of."

"That's probably the only time I remember going to jail and actually having a good time up in that muthafucker," laughs Vesto. "I have never had a better time in jail [than] when I was in there with him."

Female officers loved Chad, and often found reasons to pass by his tank for a glimpse. "These people [working at the County Jail] were UGK *fans*, man," says Vesto. "The trustees was treating him good. The female officers ... they would only hate on him when those male officers were around. But when those male officers weren't around, the female officers wanted autographs, man ... It was funny ... They was giving us extra shit, extra food, whatever we needed."

But not everyone was a fan. At count time, some officers made it a point not to show Chad any special treatment. "*Shiiit*, you ain't 'Big Pimpin'' now, huh?" one sneered as he reached Chad, taunting him and hoping for a reaction. "Why you ain't call Jay-Z to get you out?"

"Harris County Jail was the rawest thing I went through," Chad said on the *Cheddar* DVD. "The laws [are] breaking [inmates'] arms and [they] had hit squads and they was acting bad."*

"While you're in that county jail, you still have hope. You still have fight in you," explains Vesto. "You have hope of trying to get out of there ... [Your lawyer] is coming and you're still communicating with the free world."

The main challenge in the County Jail was fighting boredom and finding ways to pass the time. Inmates were only allowed to leave the tank for one hour a day for recreation; even meals were delivered to the tank. The only way to get out was to have a visitor.

Chad had no shortage of visitors. Knowing that others weren't as fortunate, Chad would sometimes get on the phones and work his magic, making arrangements for groups of women to come so that his friends could get a visit, too. "Look here, mane," Chad would announce in the tank. "If y'all ain't got no visits this week, I got you covered." He'd jot down the inmates' identification code numbers and nod.

On the given day, groups of women would arrive together at the Harris County Jail visitation room, turning heads in full makeup and trendy outfits. Frequently, they were strippers whom Chad had befriended, bringing along a few of their friends from the strip club.

"Them women look like they [was] from Hollywood or some shit," laughs Vesto, who was the beneficiary of several of these blind-date style visits. "It was player ... We'd just sit there and [talk]. Hell yeah. We trying to get out that damn tank. We been sitting in that damn tank all day."

And in the County Jail, there was always the chance you'd be home soon. "Look, I'm finna be getting out in a minute, lil mama," Vesto would pitch as the visit drew to a close, hoping to exchange numbers. "So *shiiiit*, can we meet [again]?"

When they didn't have visitors, if Chad was feeling talkative, he'd entertain his cellmates with stories or give them advice on the music business, explaining that it wasn't necessary to spend money on expensive producers or recording studios.

"Look, do you know where I recorded ['Break 'Em Off']?" Chad told Vesto. "I recorded it in the shower in my bathroom."

"Damn, I thought y'all recorded that shit in big studios," Vesto said.

(*Correctional officers in Texas are often referred to as "laws.")

"Hell naw," Chad said. "I recorded that shit in my bathroom, standing with half the damn mic where the shower at."

He often griped about the way his relationship had soured with Master P, whom he referred to as "Bastard P."

"He [felt that] how P [treated] him was fucked up," remembers Vesto. "Some of their business moves, he was trying to put [Pimp] on the back burner, but when they needed a hard-hittin' [track], they was the first niggas he came to fuck with. [Pimp] said he fucked with 'em, them niggas was cool at first, but as time passed and that money started coming in … he wasn't treating them the same way."

Chad also regaled his cellmates with stories from the "Big Pimpin'" video shoot, telling them about the video girls ("[Gloria Velez] was a live muthafucker … Some of 'em was some real live go-getters!"), the hotel accommodations ("What the fuck? Y'all got us in this cheap-ass motel but Jay-Z downtown in a goddamn high rise? I wasn't feeling that shit, man. Put us in the same spot!"), and the vibe he'd picked up from Jay himself. "It was his video, [but] we supposed to be doing it together. That man wasn't even – he'll just go shoot a scene or something – but [he] wasn't hands-on right there with [us]," Chad complained.

An officer passed by the tank one day and tossed in a copy of the *Houston Chronicle*. "I got *City and State*," Vesto called out.

One by one, each section got passed around, and the classified ads which no one wanted were tossed onto the table. Somebody glanced at an advertisement for Circuit City. "Damn, Pimp," he remarked. "*Shiiiit*, nigga. You got a new album out?"

Chad was relaxing on his bunk reading a book. "Man, stop fuckin around, man," he said. "Ain't nobody told me shit."

The inmate held up the Circuit City ad, which prominently displayed the cover for a new UGK album called *Side Hustles*. In disbelief, Chad hopped off his bunk. "Man, I'll be damned," he muttered, shaking his head. "Man, what the hell is this right here? What the fuck?"

Jive released *Side Hustles* on September 24, 2002, apparently without any input from UGK. The album was a collection of miscellaneous tracks, alongside Scarface, Too $hort, 8Ball, and E-40, which had already been released on other compilations or soundtracks.

Bun wasn't happy about *Side Hustles* either. "It was something [Jive] tried to put together right quick," he told MTV News. "They were sitting on a few songs that they had already paid for and they felt they were sitting around on the product, so why not reissue it and make some clean cash?"

Bun's primary concern was that the album's packaging was misleading. "It's not top-quality UGK," he said. "Not to say the songs aren't top quality, because everything we do is top notch, but I think [Jive is] giving people the impression that this is the fifth album by UGK. This [isn't] what Pimp and I sat down and put down to present to the public."

He also assured fans that Pimp's legal situation would soon be over. "Hopefully we'll have him home in the next couple of months … so we can put together that fifth album that people need to hear, the right way," Bun said.

On October 18, Judge Jeannine Barr reviewed Chad's motion for a new trial, which included affidavits from Chad, his mother, his father Charleston, Pops, and other friends like Pam Harris stating that Chad was unable to function without his bipolar medication. Chad claimed he had been "depressed, irritated, disoriented, and confused" at the sentencing hearing because "the jail people" had refused to give him his medication.

"When I entered my plea … I did not understand what my lawyer was trying to explain to me," he wrote. "I did not understand that I was pleading to eight years in TDC. I certainly do not remember being given my options. If I had been given those options, I would have chosen to go to a hearing before pleading to eight years in TDC." Judge Barr denied the motion.

Over in Atlanta, more than a year had passed since UGK's attorney sent over the order for Judge Schwall to sign ensuring that Byron Hill's $3,000,000 judgment would be overturned. UGK's attorneys were not particularly motivated to make sure this was completed, since they hadn't been paid. With their invoice outstanding for a year and their primary client sitting in the county jail, they withdrew from the case.

With UGK now defenseless, Byron requested a new hearing. With no one present to contest Byron's claim Judge Schwall again signed a $3,000,000 judgment against UGK. When Mama Wes found out about the judgment, she hired a new attorney and filed to reopen the case.

Pharoah's day in court for the PCP-induced stabbing finally came two days before the 2002 Thanksgiving holiday. Vesto was standing in line waiting for his turn before the judge when Pharoah passed him on the way out of the courtroom. "Man, whassup, you putting up a fight? It's still on?" Vesto asked, inquiring how things were going in his case.*

"Naw, man. It's over," Pharoah responded calmly. "How you doing? You alright?"

"Yeah, I'm alright," Vesto nodded, surprised at Pharoah's demeanor. "It's over? What you mean? What they gonna do with you?"

"Just signed for 50 [years]," Pharoah said matter-of-factly.**

50?!? Vesto stared at Pharoah, speechless. *Man, I wouldn't even be talking right now. 50!? Man, damn.*

Word quickly spread about Pharoah's extreme sentence. For Chad, seeing a friend his own age (Pharoah and Chad were a month apart) get 50 years made eight years sound relatively easy. Chad tried to be optimistic. "My time ain't shit," he told *On Tha Real* Magazine. "I'm blessed to have a single digit number to do, so I ain't complainin' or feelin' sorry for myself."

Back in Port Arthur, things were falling apart at Inner Soul Records. DJ DMD found himself divorced and alone, depressed and miserable. One of his business partners, Chandrea Celestine, was serving time on federal drug charges, and he knew his other partner J Will would end up there too if he didn't stop dabbling in the streets. "These guys were doing all this hustling … to help my career," DMD says. "[I decided] I can't have that on my conscience no more."

DMD left Port Arthur abruptly. "All I knew was, I was not gonna make it if I kept living the way I was living," he said. "So … I just disappeared." He didn't tell anyone he was leaving or take time to fix any loose ends. Hiroshima soon fell apart, and Inner Soul Records effectively disbanded. "As far as I know, the studio [was left] in shambles," he admits. "[The] equipment got sold."

Needless to say, everyone didn't understand his sudden, abrupt departure. "When I left Port Arthur, I left to try to better my life," says DJ DMD. "A lot of people didn't like that, because a lot of people was banking on me being the one to save their lil' ol' careers."

Nitacha's brother Riley, who always had a knack for being the middleman, apparently approached DMD with a way to make some money, suggesting that he could arrange a meeting with J. Prince. "I don't know how [Riley] always gets in the middle of things, but he does," says

(*As Vesto remembers it, he spent nine months in the tank at the Harris County Jail with Pimp C and Pharoah. Harris County records seem to indicate that it was a much shorter timeframe: Vesto was arrested on September 17, 2002, and bonded out two weeks later on September 30. It is not clear if he returned. Vesto distinctly recalls being present at Pharoah's November 2002 sentencing hearing.)

(**"I've never seen a person take 50 years like [Pharoah]," Vesto says. "He took that time like a G." Pharoah is still incarcerated with a release date of 2052; he will not be eligible for parole until March 2027. Pharoah explains his calm demeanor in a letter from the Coffield Unit, where he is currently housed: "Due to the fact that I'm an undaground celebrity I disciplined myself to reflect positively to the onez that I have influence on by remain-n calm afta receive-n a 50 year sentence. On the outside I was live but on tha inside I waz actually hurt-n from tha cruel and unusual punishment.")

former Inner Soul engineer Marlan Rico Lee. "[Riley] was always in [Chad's] business," adds DJ DMD. "[He was] somebody who just wanted to be down, you know?"

In any case, the meeting between DMD and J. Prince would become somewhat of Port Arthur folklore. As Lee Master tells it, DMD went to the Rap-A-Lot compound in Houston against J Will's wishes to have a "garage sale" with Pimp C's leftover music. The tracks included "I'm A Hustler," "On Them Dubbs," "Get My Money," "Young Prostitute," and "Young Ghetto Starz."

As the story went, Prince greeted DMD in his trademark Texas drawl: "Yeaaaaah, I hear you've got some music. Let me hear what you've got." DMD inserted a CD of Pimp C tracks and Prince bobbed his head in approval before dismissing DMD with a simple, "Alright. Get the fuck outta here."

DMD's crew arrived for the tail end of the meeting and were shocked when DMD departed, leaving the tapes behind. "Apparently … somebody [in our group] thought that we was gon' get some money," says DJ DMD, adding, "These guys … started saying that I had a secret deal going on with Rap-A-Lot to get paid … but I ain't get no money from Rap-A-Lot."

J. Will and D Stone, who produced some of the beats, were angry at DMD for handing them over to Rap-A-Lot. DMD told them he was only turning over Chad's vocals, and if Rap-A-Lot wanted to use the accompanying track, they would pay for it later.*

"[The word on the street was that DJ DMD] went over there [to Rap-A-Lot] tryin' to sell shit, and they just *took* it," says Isreal Kight. "I don't know that for a fact … but I believe it, 'cause he already had a history of doing that type of shit. [DJ DMD] has no loyalty."

Rap-A-Lot also obtained the vocals from Chad's impromptu freestyle sessions at Mike Mo's studio. Mike says he received a letter from Chad instructing him to release the music, but others say Rap-A-Lot simply pressured Mike into turning over the tracks without Chad's permission. (Chad later denied sending the letter and Mike was unable to locate it. "[In prison] that's a lot of mental trauma," Mike says. "I think he didn't really remember telling me [to send his music].")

On February 15, 2003, Riley mailed Chad a letter, scrawled on the back of a Jive 8x10 press image of UGK. "I heard you were upset at me for giving your music to Red-Boy @ Rap-A-Lot but I kept telling folks that is what I was told to do," Riley wrote. "I called J Prince and Bun B to find out what the deal was … [they told me] everything was O.K. [and] not to worry about if I did the right thing because 'Business is Business.'"

"I do not need something like this to haunt me for the rest of my days, I did what you asked … I need to know I did the Right thing," Riley wrote, signing off, "Your Baby Momma Brotha."

Mama Wes didn't know exactly how Chad's music ended up in Rap-A-Lot's hands for free, but she didn't think too highly of any of the men involved.

"My best guess is somewhere between [the engineer] Avery [Harris] and [Riley]," she says. "It could've been any of them, because Mike Mo is a pussy, but he always was … Avery, I don't care what he says [now], he did not like C [then]. He had a jealousy thing going on with C way back to high school. [Riley] just likes to be important, y'know. It could've been any of them, or all of them together."

"I just look at them and laugh, because I'm like, what the fuck does it matter [now]?" says Mama Wes. "Y'all know what y'all did."

(*DMD insists that he only "relinquished the vocals to Lil' J himself in his office" at Chad's request. DMD says there was a "dark period" in his relationship with Chad, who had made threats against him and his family if he didn't turn over the material to Rap-A-Lot. "Apparently he was trying to do a deal with Rap-A-Lot and … someone gave him the impression that I wouldn't turn over [his] vocals," says DJ DMD. "He thought I was holding up his project.")

CHAPTER 32

"They (the State of Texas) have my body on lock but my mind is free. For many years I had allowed my mind to be intraped by thinking with a negative nigga mentality. I am happy to say that those chains don't hold me anymore. I'm getin up on game right now. Not street game or music game but 'life game.' The game of life!!! The way we play it will effect what our legacy will be when our body life is over. It will also determen what our after life will be like."
— Pimp C's letter to Kevin "Mr. Soul" Harp, October 2003

"Every day [in prison] it's a constant struggle to hold [onto] your mind and keep your sanity." — Pimp C, HipHop2Nite TV

December 2002

Shortly before Christmas 2002, Chad was shipped off to the Garza West transfer facility in south Texas to begin serving his TDCJ time. The realization that he was in *prison* finally struck. "When you [are] thrown in a position like that, it really puts some perspective in your life," he said later on the *Pimpalation* DVD. "It really shows you what's important. You need to get your priorities in line. It'll show you who's who that's around you."

Even though there had been rumors about his legal situation, fans were surprised to hear of Pimp C's lengthy prison sentence. With *Dirty Money* out, and plenty of ways to communicate with the outside world from the County Jail, many hadn't yet noticed his absence.

After seeing Chad in the County Jail, Bun didn't think he could handle a prison visit. The emotions were too raw. "When he got sent off to prison, that shit just hurt a lot … and I had a lot of personal reflection and time that I had to take to figure out what I was gonna do with myself," Bun says.

Plus, Bun was angry with Chad. "He had responsibilities and he didn't take care of them, and because of it, other people suffered," Bun says. "It wasn't like he made [just] one mistake … he made a mistake, and he made another one and another one, and it was just a chain of events that could have been avoided."

"I fucked up the group," Chad admitted in *XXL*. "I fucked up our show money. I fucked up our guest appearance money. I fucked up our money coming from the record label … He had a right to be angry."

But Bun's anger was directed as much at himself as it was at Chad because he felt partly responsible. *That's your little brother, you should have been able to do something,* he chastised himself. He'd known that Chad wasn't in a good place mentally and was headed for self-destruction, but he hadn't done everything he could've to prevent something like this from happening.

"It's hard being Pimp C, and I don't think a lot of people understood that," Bun told *XXL*. "People don't understand how many people told Pimp, 'You can't do it, you're too short, too small, you wear glasses. You can't be a fuckin' rapper.' I won't knock that man, that's a self-made fuckin' man right there. Sometimes I wonder if the distance I kept between us maybe played a part in that shit. There's definitely guilt in my heart. I know he wouldn't blame me at all, though. He's a self-made man, never blame nobody for nothing. Nobody really understood him ... nobody went through it but me and him."

There was at least one bright spot: In January 2003, after four long years, Jive corrected Chad's erroneous 1099 form. The fictitious $10,990,034 additional income was removed, bringing his actual 1998 income down to the original $177,219.00 and reducing his $4,707,341.00 tax debt to a far more manageable $61,092.00.

After a long fight, Crooked Lettaz had finally been granted a release from Tommy Boy Records and David Banner and Kamikaze split amicably to pursue solo careers. Banner couldn't afford to pay artists for features, so he worked out a barter system, trading beats for verses and eventually compiling enough material to drop an album titled *Firewater Boyz Volume 1*.

Houston rapper Lil Flip reached out when he needed tracks for his *Undaground Legend* album Banner, who had been living out of his red Astro van, drove down to Houston and dropped a verse on Flip's record "What Y'all Wanna Do." He also came across the track he'd produced more than two years earlier with Pimp C's voice sampled on the hook. Flip dropped a verse, and Banner titled it "Like A Pimp," a nod to UGK.

Banner had originally intended "Might Getcha" with Lil Jon to be his lead single, but it was "Like A Pimp" which took off, getting heavy play first in Atlanta nightclubs and spreading quickly at radio. The record's explosion sparked a major label bidding war and Banner inked a $10 million dollar five-album deal with executive Steve Rifkind's new SRC imprint through Universal Records. The Pimp C-assisted "Like A Pimp" would become the lead single for David Banner's major label debut *Mississippi: The Album*. "Like Pimp C before him, David Banner's greatest strength lies not in his energy, but his truth," journalist Andrew Nosnitsky wrote.

Through it all, Banner reminded himself that the man who had helped make it all possible was sitting in a Texas prison. "A lot of times when rappers go to jail, the love [from the fans and friends] isn't there anymore. [His voice] changed my life, and I felt like I owed [Pimp C] something," Banner says.

Banner and Pimp C had a mutual friend in Wendy Day. Wendy hadn't spoken to Chad since their falling-out over the Barry Hankerson/Jive situation, but her heart softened when she read an interview with him in *Murder Dog*. Sympathetic to his current situation, she extended an olive branch by mailing him a card with a brief note and some books to read.

Chad wrote back, apologizing for the way their friendship had deteriorated, and the two began exchanging letters regularly. Through Wendy, Banner wrote Chad a letter and put some money on his books. Many of their letters discussed production techniques; Chad was curious about some of the newer equipment, so Banner sent pictures with a written tutorial. "He's gritty and grimy, and he don't mind sampling a record," Chad told *OZONE*, of Banner's production. "Sampling records [is] what this music game was based on. We can't stop using break beat records in our songs [or] we'll lose the essence of what this music is about."

Southwest Wholesale's distribution business flourished throughout the late 1990s. They reached their height in the year 2000 with revenue topping $100 million as they sold more than a million albums from Houston-based independent rappers following the formula pioneered by UGK. "We specialize in Southern rap," co-owner Richard Powers told *Billboard*.

But only 25% of the company's revenue came from the distribution side. They still made the bulk of their money as a one-stop, a middleman between major distributors and small retail stores, and one-stops were getting squeezed out of the business. It wasn't economical for mom-and-pop stores to purchase an album from a middleman like Southwest for around $10.75 and try to resell it for a meager profit, when a consumer could purchase that same album at Best Buy for $9.99.

Although Robert Guillerman was the most visible partner of the company, he only owned 15%. The other 85% belonged to Richard Powers, who ran the San Antonio warehouse and handled most of their one-stop business.

Periodically, a major distributor like Universal would issue a list of records that were no longer being manufactured. One-stops and retail outlets were then required to recall those records and turn them over to a company which is referred to as a "cut out" business. The "cut out" business marks the unsold CDs by drilling a hole in the corner of the case or "burning" them with a thin wire which marks a circle in the corner of the CD, indicating that it can no longer be returned to the manufacturer for a refund.

Clients like Southwest could return any unsold album in the Universal catalog for a $9 credit as long as it wasn't marked as a "cut out." As a one-stop, Southwest had a lot of leeway with returns, because retail stores could return product through them even if they'd purchased it somewhere else. For example, if Southwest purchased 10 copies of an album and returned 50 copies for credit, it wouldn't necessarily raise a red flag.

But *this* was too much to be a coincidence. A Universal employee stumbled across an oddity: Southwest was returning huge batches of product – 300, 400, even 500 copies of a record – of which they had never even purchased *one* copy.

When this was brought to the attention of Universal executive Jim Urie, he sent a representative to see Richard Powers at Southwest's San Antonio warehouse. Powers apologized, saying they'd come across some cheap product but it wouldn't happen again.

A few months later, it did happen again. Some insiders suspected that Southwest was manufacturing counterfeit copies of Universal product for about 30 cents each and returning them for huge illegal profits. A former Universal executive familiar with the Southwest account (who asked not to be identified) says it was more likely they were actually purchasing cheap "cut-out" product which hadn't yet been marked for around $1 each and then returning it directly to Universal for an easy profit of $8 each. (Either way, Guillerman says he had no involvement with Powers' scheme, which he calls "a big mistake.")

After they were caught the second time, word came down from Universal executives that the company would no longer do business with Southwest Wholesale. Southwest could not purchase any more product, nor return unsold product. The situation was turned over to the legal department for a possible lawsuit.*

With its recent purchase of Polygram, Universal had become the largest music company in the world. Losing Southwest as a client wouldn't hurt Universal, but losing Universal would be devastating for Southwest. Universal also alerted all the other major music distributors (WEA, Columbia, and RCA) of the apparent scam. All the product sitting in Southwest's massive Boeing 747 airline hangar-sized warehouses was now basically worthless.

After the Universal fiasco, it was decided that Richard Powers had to go. With a $150,000 bank loan and the help of three private investors, Guillerman bought out Powers' share of Southwest. He briefly considered opening a new distribution company and starting fresh, but his pride wouldn't let him. "I wanted to hang in there and save [Southwest]," he says.

In January 2002, Guillerman took over as Southwest's president. He laid off about 75 of the company's 250 employees, announcing that they were phasing out their one-stop operation and focusing on distributing independent labels – the part of the business which, prior to UGK, Guillerman had considered too risky.

But it was too late to stop the bleeding. In 2002 Southwest's annual revenue dropped 33%. Not only were revenues declining, but Southwest was embroiled in a flood of lawsuits, generally

(*A Universal executive confirms that they were considering legal action, but it is not clear if a lawsuit was ever actually filed against Southwest. Manufacturing counterfeit copies of Universal product would be a serious federal offense, but it is not clear if there was enough evidence to prove it.)

relating to ownership of the music on the CDs they were distributing (Suave House, Bizzy Bone, Khia, and others).

Southwest was hemorrhaging money paying out legal fees, and when Wherehouse Music, one of their largest retail outlets, filed bankruptcy in January 2003, it was the final nail in the coffin. (Wherehouse owed Southwest $568,000.) Despite insisting to *Billboard* that the company was not on the verge of bankruptcy, Guillerman was forced to lay off the rest of the staff.

When Southwest closed their doors for good on February 3, 2003, they owed nearly $2 million to WEA, and more than a million dollars each to EMI, Sony, and BMG. While major labels could afford to absorb a million dollar loss, independent labels couldn't. Wendy Day, who was managing Chicago rapper Twista, estimates that he was owed more than $1.6 million. Houston labels like Beltway 8 Records estimated losses of more than $150,000.

While Guillerman insisted the whole situation was "beyond [his] control," as the face of the company, he bore the brunt of most artists' anger. "Robert Guillerman went bankrupt with all our money," Big Tyme rapper Point Blank summarizes bitterly. "That's all I remember about that."

Prior to Southwest's collapse, Texas artists didn't have much incentive to seek out major label deals. "We were so spoiled in Texas, selling 20,000 and 30,000 [units just] in the city [of Houston]," says Lil Keke. "It's easy for us to get rich right here … It was a blessing and a curse at the same time. We don't have to have radio and TV to survive."

"It was a sad day, man," says Mike Moe of Beltway 8 Records.* "Southwest was actually the distribution company that built Houston [rap]. When it fell apart … the majors were like, 'Ok, here's [our] opportunity' like vultures to go down there and scoop them up." With their main distribution outlet gone, Texas rappers started considering major label offers.

On the same day Southwest Wholesale closed its doors, Byron Hill filed for Chapter 13 bankruptcy. It was clearly a strategic move; the following day, a hearing was scheduled in which a judge would likely overturn his judgment against UGK. By filing bankruptcy, the case would be put on hold, effectively freezing his $3,000,000 judgment for the alleged damages he'd never proven in court.

Chapter 13 bankruptcy cases were lengthy proceedings which could drag on for years. Mama Wes breathed a sigh of relief, hoping the Byron Hill saga was finally over.

———

Garza was a five-hour drive from Port Arthur, but Mama Wes made the trek faithfully; in the TDCJ system, immediate family members were allowed to have contact visits instead of impersonal visits behind a glass wall. When she couldn't make the drive, she wrote letters. On March 17, 2003, she wrote:

I know it has been a couple of weeks since I wrote to you. There are a number of reasons for my delay. I guess the 1st reason is that I have been a little bit depressed. I do miss you so very much. Despite our usual Mama + son problems, we have always been really close and it does get hard for me sometimes. I also worry about you a lot even though you tell me not to. And I really like to write to you when I am upbeat because I want you to keep yourself up. So today is really a pretty good day, so here goes.

I still have Corey and though he is a sweet little boy, he keeps you on your toes. He is sleeping, he takes a nap at 1:30 P.M. and usually sleeps from 2-4 hours. When he wakes up, he'll go to the park. [Pops] tries to take him every day that it doesn't rain. They met [Chad Jr.] + [Nitacha's daughter] Emoni there the other day. They had a good time. He doesn't want to go home yet. He has to behave here, but he likes being here.

[Pops] takes a lot of time with him and I try to be sure he eats right because he eats too much

(*Not to be confused with Pimp C's friend/engineer Mike Mo.)

PIMP C'S TRILL LIFE STORY **311**

junk in Houston because he rules them pretty good. I took him to Great-Granny last week. She really enjoyed him. She hadn't seen him in a while, she thinks he's really smart. He is, too, and Angie does a good job with teaching him a lot of things. He can dress himself, even if he can't get his shoes on the right foot yet. (smile). He poo-poos in the toilet all the time now, but he still doesn't' have t-t all the way. He gets busy and he just won't stop. But he's doing better. He talks about you a lot and he loves to look at your picture.

Chad had always intended to get married when he was 30. "If a muthafucker is 30 and still not married, he must be gay," he often said. "I think any successful man over 30 years old that's not married needs to be askin' [himself] a question about why he's not," he told *OZONE*.

By now, it was pretty clear he would be spending his 30th birthday behind bars. Plus, he was getting pressure from several different directions. According to Mama Wes, Chinara's mother was advising her daughter to stop bringing baby Christian to visit. "He's gonna have to marry you, or he won't see this baby until he gets out," Chinara's mother allegedly told her.*

Chad brought up the topic during one visit with his mother. "Mama," he asked. "Would it look better for me if, uh … if I was a family man? Think I could get out sooner or something like that?"

"I don't know," she said thoughtfully.

"Well, them people keep coming up here bugging me," he said, apparently referring to Chinara and her mother. "They said it would look better if I was a married man; a family man."

Nitacha had little respect for any of the other women in Chad's life. As far as she was concerned, their love, born of youthful innocence, was more pure and valid than any others who might have come around after he became a star. "There is not a woman Chad has ever been involved with that I have ever respected," Nitacha laughs. "As far as I'm concerned, any female Chad was involved with are bitches … skanks, hoes, tramps, skeezers, chickenheads, and sluts."

Still, she had moved on, marrying a man named Terry Hasan who was also the father of her daughter. Nitacha and Chad still kept in touch for Chad Jr.'s sake. Chad was always pleased to see his son's good report cards, marveling that he'd turned out so smart despite having two high school dropouts as parents. "Boy, he's gonna be the first one [to graduate]," Chad would say.

When Chad heard that Nitacha and her husband were headed for a divorce, he asked if she would marry him. (Nitacha was under the impression that Chad was convinced marriage would somehow help him get his time cut.) Nitacha, who was still trying to work things out with her husband, declined.

Mama Wes frequently brought Corey to visit, but Angie, now engaged, had stopped coming out of respect for her fiancé. When Chad asked Angie to marry him, she declined, afraid to leave a secure situation for something so uncertain. She didn't believe Chad would ever settle down or be faithful to one woman.

When Mama Wes heard about the proposal from a mutual friend, she asked Chad during a visit, "C, did you ask Angie to marry you?"

"Yep, she turned me down," he confirmed, grumbling about Angie's fiancé. "I tried to talk her into it. She gonna be sorry. She don't like that ol' black ass [nigga]."**

Meanwhile, Chinara and Christian came every weekend with Mama Wes. "We went [to visit] faithfully," Chinara told *XXL*. "He didn't have weekends without visits, no matter where he was … [When your man is in jail] you're in jail, too. It's torture … you can see him, but you have to talk to him from a window. You have a newborn kid. We're watching him, showing him she can walk."

(*"That's a fact," says Mama Wes. "I *heard* her mama say that.")
(**This account of Chad's marriage proposals is recounted separately by Nitacha and Angie and confirmed by Mama Wes.)

On March 15, 2003, Bun's 30th birthday, he married his longtime girlfriend Chalvalier "Queenie" Caldwell. (Pops and Mama Wes had also made it official the previous year, marrying with a small ceremony at their church in Port Arthur.) A month later, on Easter Sunday, Chad and Chinara married.

Mama Wes didn't learn of the wedding until after the fact. "I'm gonna marry that one, Mama," Chad had told her a thousand times before, but she'd never believed he would actually do it. She disapproved of the union, and not just because of Chinara. "I didn't think C should marry anybody, because C wasn't the marrying type," says Mama Wes. "He got bored easily."*

Wendy Day wasn't surprised to hear that he'd gotten married. "When guys are in prison, they see … who is really there for them, and who's not. She was really there for him, and I think he was grateful for that," says Wendy. "She loved him through his bid, and most women don't. You know, that separates the women from the girls. It's hard to stay with a man through a bid. You gotta deal with a lot of emotional tangles and bullshit and disappointment, and it's very one-sided."

Texas law required that county jails maintain temperatures between 65 and 85 degrees, but there was no such law for state prisons. Only 21 of the 111 TDCJ prisons were air-conditioned. Older units, which were built before air-conditioning on former slave plantations, were specifically designed for maximum ventilation. But newer units, like Garza West, which was built during the 1994 prison-building spree, were thrown together with no such foresight.

In the summer, temperatures regularly hit triple digits, and the heat index could reach a sweltering 134 degrees. Men who were already obese or battling heart disease were at serious risk for a heat stroke. Sometimes, the heat was so intense inmates found it hard to breathe.

Some cell blocks had industrial fans, and miniature electric fans could be purchased at the commissary for $22, but these were minor fixes. Inmates resorted to walking around with wet towels on their heads, or throwing soda cans to break the windows for extra ventilation.

Guards had it even worse, working 13 hour shifts in the brutal heat while wearing uniforms and bulletproof vests, sweat pouring down their faces. The heat kept everyone on edge, but Chad mostly stayed to himself to avoid getting caught up in any unnecessary trouble.

Mean Green, a well-known Houston DJ and radio personality, had been a part of the UGK family since the early days. His son Yakeen Green, otherwise known as "Lil Green," was four years younger than Chad. At 19, he'd been accused of robbery and in and out of prison ever since.

Around Valentine's Day 2003, he'd allegedly threatened the mother of his child with a razor blade. She promptly filed for a restraining order and child support while Green went back to court. Even with prior assault and robbery convictions, Lil' Green was only sentenced to two years for Aggravated Assault with a Deadly Weapon, the same charge for which Chad received eight.

Lil Green arrived at Garza West in April 2003. At dinner one day at the chow hall, he introduced himself. "Man, I done heard a lot about you," Chad laughed.

"Shoot, man, it's an honor and a pleasure to finally meet you," Lil Green told him. "I hate to be meeting like this."

(*At this point, Mama Wes stops the interview and makes me promise never to become "no nigga's third choice for a wife." However, if it had been Angie, Mama Wes would have approved. "I could still beat her ass for not marrying him," Mama Wes jokes.)

COUNTY OF   JEFFERSON

To Any Person Authorized by the Laws of the State of Texas
To Celebrate The Rites of Matrimony in the State of Texas.

GREETING:

YOU ARE HEREBY AUTHORIZED TO CONDUCT THE

Between   **CHAD LAMONT BUTLER**

and   **CHINARA KUSHANA JACKSON**

and make due return to the Clerk of the County Court of Jefferson County, Texas, within thirty days thereafter certifying your action under this License.

Witness my official signature and seal of office at __04:40__ *o'clock* __p__ .m. *this the* __8 th__ *day of* __April__ , A.D. 20 __03__

By __Belinda Scoggin__   *Sandy Walker*
     Deputy   *Clerk of the County Court, Jefferson County, Texas*

I hereby certify that at __3__ *o'clock* __p__ .m. *on the* __29th__ *day of* __APRIL__ A.D. 20 __03__ *I united in Marriage the parties abovenamed. Witness my hand this the date last above written.*

NAME OF PROXY:
CHRISTOPHER ALPOUGH

WAIVER OF 72 HOUR WAITING PERIOD

____ GRANTED

_____
JUDGE PRESIDING

Robert T. Morgan, Jr.
SIGNATURE OF PERSON OFFICIATING

ROBERT T. MORGAN, JR., JUSTICE OF THE PEACE, PCT. TWO
TITLE/PRINTED NAME

525 LAKESHORE DRIVE, PORT ARTHUR, TEXAS
ADDRESS

JEFFERSON
COUNTY IN WHICH MARRIAGE PERFORMED

Returned, filed for record, and duly recorded this the __6th__ *day of* __MAY__ A.D. 2003 *in the Marriage Records of Jefferson County, Texas.*

By __Mary Godina__   *Sandy Walker*
     MARY GODINA   *Deputy*   *Clerk of the County Court, Jefferson County, Texas*

The marriage ceremony may not take place during a 72-hour period immediately following the issuance of the marriage license unless an applicant is a member of the armed forces of the United States and is on active duty or a district court order is obtained. Sec. 6.110, V.T.C.A. Family Code.

A marriage is voidable and subject to annulment if the marriage ceremony takes place in violation of Section 6.110, V.T.C.A. Family Code.

☑ Section 2.009(c)(4) and 2.010 Family Code complied with

Marriage License will expire at the end of the 30th Day following the date of issuance.

Person Conducting Ceremony Must Return This License To:

SANDY WALKER, County Clerk
Jefferson County
Beaumont, Texas 77704

Above: Chad married **Chinara Jackson,** the mother of his daughter Christian, in April 2003 while he was incarcerated.

Chad and Lil Green were both assigned to work as S.S.I.s, a janitorial job which had its benefits. "I was able to move around more freely than the average inmates do," Chad said. It was also a humbling job, where they were often required to clean toilets. They reported for their eight-hour shift at 2 PM, cleaning the 60-man dorms, the guard station, the barbershop, and mopping the front hallways. "[You'd] hope to God it ain't a thousand degrees in there, 'cause it's so hot, and you only get one cup of ice every three or four hours." remembers Lil Green.

One day, after they'd spent the better part of the afternoon sweating and cleaning toilets, they lounged in the shade against a wall outside. Chad laughed to himself, as if he'd thought of something funny. Lil Green glanced at him. "What's up?"

"Everybody thinks that me and Bun are just the richest down South rappers there are, and that we have all this money stashed away and stacked on top of each other," Chad chuckled, struck by the sudden irony.

Lil Green stared at him in surprise. Like everybody else, he thought Pimp and Bun were rich beyond their wildest dreams.

Chad laughed and shook his head. "Mane, we ain't even break even," he said. He explained that even when they did receive advance money from Jive, he'd poured it back into the project, because creating timeless music was more important to him than making money.

Chad was correct: UGK had never received a royalty check from Jive because the group never recouped. In fact, UGK owed Jive more than $1.3 million, and the debt was only growing while Chad was in prison. (For example, between January and June 1994, UGK record sales generated revenue of $27,992, but $47,742 was paid out for samples and producer fees, pushing UGK even further in debt.)

Jive didn't mind having an artist indebted to them for $1.3 million. In fact, that's exactly how record label contracts are designed, according to Wendy Day. It was a form of control. "No artist ever recoups, keeping them permanently indebted to the label," Wendy says. "Like indentured servants." (Rare exceptions are major crossover superstars like Eminem.)

Even if UGK did manage to recoup the $1.3 million and start receiving royalty checks, Chad's half would be mailed directly to the IRS towards the tax lien initially created by Jive's false income tax reporting.

While Lil Green stayed at Garza to serve out the rest of his term, Chad was transferred to the Dominguez Unit in San Antonio. Before they parted ways, they promised each other they'd never come back to prison.*

Chad's attitude had improved significantly by the time he arrived at Dominguez, and he decided he might as well make the most of his time by signing up to get his GED. It would look good when he came up for parole, plus, the schoolhouse was the only building at Dominguez which had air-conditioning and a radio. Most importantly, he knew he'd disappointed his family when he dropped out of school and felt he owed it to them to finish.

The open dorm he shared with 57 other inmates did have two televisions, but he tried to avoid the "one-eyed devils," preferring to spend most of his time in the library, where he "fell in love with reading."

"I'm taking this shit one day at a time," he wrote *On Tha Real* Magazine. "I have good days & f'ed up days like everybody else … I ain't cryin' & dyin' in this muthafucker & we ain't sittin' around here all sad 24/7 either. We laugh, we read, we go to work, we go to church … we just can't go home right now!"

He concluded that there were two different types of people in prison, and made up his mind not to become complacent. "You got folks that made prison they home and they have accepted that this [is] where they gonna be and they gonna live it to the fullest, and you got the other people that are every day trying to get home and get back to they family," he told his cousin

(*The exact timing of Chad's transfer to Dominguez is unclear, but it was likely between May and September 2003. Lil Green was denied parole because his victim protested. He served his entire two year sentence and was released in February 2005. It appears that he kept his promise and has avoided trouble since then with the exception of a minor marijuana charge.)

10/2/03
10:42 PM

"DEAR KEVIN"

WHATS THE DEAL MAN, IT WAS GOOD TO HERE
FROM YOU MY FRIEND. SORRY IT TOOK ME A MIN
TO HIT YOU BACK. I HAD RUN OUT OF STAMPS, SO
I HAD TO WAIT TELL I WENT TO THE STORE (COMMISARY).
OFF TOP, I LOVE THE BLACK ANGEL. I GOT
THE ONE YOU SENT HANGIN UP OVER MY HEAD
ON TOP OF MY BUNK. SHE PROTECTS ME AT NIGHT
AND SHE HAS BEN BRINGING ME GOOD LUCK (ON THE REAL).
PLEASE, SEND ME MORE AS YOU WORK ON THEM.
I HOPE EVERYTHING IS GOOD ON YOUR SIDE. ME,
IM DOING FINE TO TELL YOU THE TRUTH. I KNOW
THAT SOUNDS CRAZY, HOW CAN I BE DOIN FINE
LOCKED UP YOU MIGHT SAY? WELL, ILL TELL YOU.
SEE THEY (THE STATE OF TEXAS) HAVE MY BODY ON
LOCK BUT MY MIND IS FREE. FOR MANY YEARS I
HAD ALOWED MY MIND TO BE INTRAPED ~~WITH~~ BY
THINKING WITH A NEGATIVE NIGGA MENTALITY. I AM
HAPPY TO SAY THAT THOSE CHAINS DON'T HOLD ME
ANYMORE. IM GETIN UP ON GAME RIGHT NOW. NOT
STREET GAME OR MUSIC GAME BUT "LIFE GAME".
THE GAME OF LIFE!!! THE WAY WE PLAY IT WILL
EFFECT WHAT OUR LEGACY WILL BE WHEN OUR
BODY LIFE IS OVER. IT WILL ALSO DETERMEN
WHAT ~~WILL~~ OUR AFTER LIFE WILL BE LIKE!!!
YOU DIG...

YeA MAN, Iv Ben PimPin THE SHiT OUT OF MY PEN
Too. Im PUTin ALoT OF InFo In MY SonGS. Im TRYin
To TAKE IT BACK To WHEn RAP MUSiC WAS MoRe LiKE
THE nEWS (89-93 ERA). Now ITs ALL WWF, FAKE AND
NeGATive FAR AS MY EARS CAn See. THAT 50¢
SHiT I HeRe on THE RADio AnT ALL WHAT I THOUGHT
IT WoULD BE. MABE I SHOULD HeRe THE ALBUM
BeFoRe I JUDGE HiM?

   LiKE I ToLD BRo H, MY HeALTH Is GooD (GoT To LooSe 20 PounD)
MY MinD Is SHARP, AnD I FeeD MY BRAin DAILY. Im
In SCHOOL GeTin MY G.E.D RiGHT now. I TAKE THE
TeST In DEC, THEn I CAn START MY CoLLEGE
CouRSes. THAT SHiT Is FREE, So Im GoNA GeT
IT!!! THE SCHOOL HouSe Is THE onLY PLACE HeRe
WiTH A RADio. I Don't GeT To See AnY ViDio's, So I
Keep UP BY ReADinG WHATs Goin on In MAGA2ins.
I Won't LiE To You, I CRY Some TiMES, BUT I
SMiAL MoRE THAn AnYTHinG. I Miss MY KiDS AnD
MY FAMiLY BUT GoD AnT GoNA PUT MoRE on ME THAn
I CAn HANDEL. THiS Is onLY A TeST, AnD I WiLL
PASS IT. I Don't Know WHEn, BUT I WiLL Be Home
one DAY. Sooner THAn You THink. I'll HoLLA
P.S./ SenD ME THAT
PiCTuRe OF ME In THE
MinK, IF You GoT IT.
I neeD To MAKE Some CopY's
For MY FAn MAiL FrienDs!!!

Tony Montana
OUT ATLANTA
PeRcY MACK's
MiLLionA
AKA "$WEET"
JoNE$

Dwayne Diamond.

He had plenty of time to think about the businesses he wanted to launch; he planned to form UGK Records with Bun as well as his own Pimp $tick Recording$. He wrote Tim Hampton about other planned ventures, which included real estate investments and Butler Trucking Company (dump trucks, 18-wheelers, and flatbeds) to provide "good paying jobs (with benifets)" for his friends.

———————

At Patchwerk Studios in Atlanta, Mr. Soul bumped into Sonji, who was laying out a feast she'd prepared for a studio session. Sonji was renowned for her culinary skills, and for Mr. Soul, the homecooked meal brought back memories of meetings at Chad's house. Mr. Soul mailed him a letter with some words of encouragement and an illustration he'd done of a "black angel" which was tattooed on his shoulder.

Chad liked the drawing so much he hung it above his bunk in cell B5-16. Late on October 2, 2003, he wrote back to thank him for the angel ("she protects me at night and she has been bringing me good luck" and request books and magazines ("something my soul can feed on") and pictures of him in a mink coat to include when responding to fan mail. He wrote:

I'm doing fine to tell you the truth. I know that sounds crazy, how can I be doin fine locked up you might say? Well, I'll tell you. See they (the State of Texas) have my body on lock but my mind is free. For many years I had allowed my mind to be intraped by thinking with a negative nigga mentality. I am happy to say that those chains don't hold me anymore. I'm getin up on game right now. Not street game or music game but "life game." The game of life!!! The way we play it will effect what our legacy will be when our body life is over. It will also determen what our after life will be like!! You dig …

Iv ben pimpin the shit out of my pen too. Im putin a lot of info in my songs. Im tryin to take it back to when rap music was more like the news (89-93 era). Now it's all WWF, fake and negative far as my ears can see. That 50 Cent shit I here on the radio ant all what I thought it would be. Mabe I should here the album before I judge him?

… I won't lie to you, I cry some times, but I smial more than anything. I miss my kids and my family but God aint gona put more on me than I can handel. This is only a test, and I will pass it. I don't know when, but I will be home one day. Sooner than you think.

True to form, Chad signed off on his letters with different names depending on which character he was at the moment: "Pimp," "C," "C.L.B.," or "$ir Sweet Jone$." This one was signed with four: "Pimp aka $weet Jone$," "Tony Montana out [of] Atlanta," and "Percy Mack Million$."

———————

Byron Hill didn't file required paperwork in his bankruptcy case. When his case was quietly dismissed in September 2003, he never notified the court as required to reschedule the hearing in the UGK case to reevaluate the questionable $3,000,000 judgment.

In November 2003, Byron was arrested in Atlanta during an apparent domestic dispute and charged with Aggravated Assault, False Imprisonment, Battery, Interfering with a 911 Phone Call, Obstruction of a Police Officer, and two counts of Cruelty to Children. (He was sentenced to two years of probation and 40 hours of community service.) Six months later, he lost his Alpharetta home to foreclosure.

———————

By late 2003, Mama Wes says, it was clear that their dealings with Eddie Floyd had turned into "such a nightmare." When Eddie ceased communication, Darryl Austin hired a CPA firm to investigate Chad's tax situation. After uncovering Eddie's previous theft case, they learned that he was not a licensed CPA and the IRS had not received any payments on Chad's behalf.

Apparently, all the checks Mama Wes had written to "Eddie Floyd, CPA," since December

2000, totaling somewhere between $100,000 and $250,000, had been deposited in his personal account. The CPA firm suggested filing criminal charges.

Meanwhile, the IRS was confiscating Chad's assets. "[The IRS] damn near ruined me … [they] took damn near every fuckin' thing I had," sighs Mama Wes. "They took my money, they took my mama's property, [and] they took his daddy's shit, 'cause we had C's name on everything. They cleaned out every damn account I had. They took *everything.*"

"Anything that I spent on C, anything that I gave C, I have no regrets," she says. "But when the [IRS] came in and just took my shit – I got a problem with that, because that was our little nest egg for old age. It just cleaned us the fuck out."

When Darryl couldn't locate Eddie Floyd, he contacted Eddie's wife Stephanie at work and explained that Eddie would be facing major criminal fraud charges and prison time if he didn't make immediate arrangements to return the money. A few days later, Mama Wes got a strange phone call from a woman claiming to be an FBI agent. (Darryl believed the caller was really Eddie Floyd's partner-in-crime from his previous theft case, Debra Senegal.) This was followed by a faxed letter from "P. Mac & Associates" to Weslyn Monroe which read:

Thank you for your cooperation with the ongoing investigation. However, serious allegations against you have been brought to our attention. Conspiracy to commit bank fraud, bank fraud, wire fraud, conspiracy to commit the crime of filing false 1040 tax returns, filing false 1040 tax returns, conspiracy to commit tax evasion, tax evasion, conspiracy to commit mail fraud, mail fraud and conspiracy to commit the crime of making a false statement on a loan application.

It concluded, "we will be in touch with you in the near future," listing only the phone number to the main switchboard of the Houston FBI office. Apparently intended to scare Mama Wes, the letter also listed the government names of 15 people "cc'ed" on the correspondence, including Chad, Darryl Austin, Pam Harris, Mama Wes' mother, and Bun B, Greg Street, J. Prince, and Red Boy.

When Darryl finally got in touch with Eddie, Eddie claimed he had turned over Chad's money to an attorney named Rhett Buck. But Rhett Buck had never heard of Eddie Floyd. Darryl reached out to Harris County's Major Fraud division to discuss filing criminal charges. Theft of over $200,000 was a First Degree Felony, punishable by five years to life in prison.

Darryl was also taking the lead on finding a way to get Chad home, possibly because he felt guilty for introducing him to Eddie Floyd.* Or, as Mama Wes thought, he was "trying to put himself in a nice [management] position for when [C] got out."

Darryl found an attorney who agreed to file an appeal for $25,000. "Congratulations, My brother," he wrote Chad. "God has shown favour upon thee and I can guarantee you will be free shortly." He explained that producer N.O. Joe, radio personality Madd Hatta, and and others had pledged to contribute $5,000 apiece. "It's a done deal. You will be on the ground soon. Don't forget me I've sacrificed greatly that you might be free."

Some of Chad's unfinished vocals and song concepts (much of the same material which had ended up at Rap-A-Lot) had been scraped together for an underground album called *Sweet James Jones: Live From the Harris County Jail.* Darryl hoped to cover the difference from sales of the album, which was released on March 26, 2004.

Chad hated the cover, which featured a cartoon-like illustration of him. The CD insert included snippets from the police report of the Sharpstown incident, with Kevin Nesby and Shameka Hawkins denying Chad had ever pulled a gun on Lakita. The insert also included his prison mailing address and Mama Wes' contact information, asking fans to send donations to help him "fight the richest state in the union."

Some of the vocals came from impromptu freestyle sessions he'd done in the studio behind

(*Darryl Austin declined to be interviewed. Judging from his letters to Chad, he felt unappreciated for his efforts.)

Weslyn B. Monroe
5048 Shreveport
Port Arthur, TX 77640

February 23, 2004

VIA FAX: 281-565-1408

Eddie Floyd
P.O. Box 56447
Houston, TX 77256

Re: Chad Butler

Dear Mr. Floyd:

    I have made and or authorized deposits dated December, 2000 to January, 2004 to Bank of America, account #2667016314, Houston, TX 77252-2518 totaling $250,000. This entire amount, paid at my direction and on Chad Butler's behalf, is to be paid to a qualified Tax Attorney and immediately to the Internal Revenue Service.

    If I may be of further assistance, please call me at (409) 982-1744.

    Best regards.

Sincerely Yours,

Weslyn B. Monroe

Cc: E. Rhett Buck

Above: An alleged con man named **Eddie Floyd** was never prosecuted for posing as a certified accountant and allegedly stealing six figures from Pimp C. He is pictured *(below)* in an unrelated 1992 mugshot.

Below: UGK's former manager **Byron Hill** pictured after a November 2003 domestic violence arrest in Atlanta.

Jelon Jackson's barbershop in Port Arthur. "It sounded like somebody put him in a conjugal visit room with a keyboard," laughs Lee Master. But some people appreciated the album's raw, unfinished feel. Standout tracks included "Hustler," "Comin' Up," Sixteen Five," "Very Thin Line," and "Where the Dollas At (In My Pocket, You Bitch)," featuring Lil Boosie.

Darryl informed Chad that he was bringing the attorney to the Dominguez Unit for a visit. "Please cooperate this is very important," Darryl wrote. "The lawyer has already been informed by me that you are crazy and is nervous about meeting you. Don't cuss him out and try to be accommodating."

"Please try to remember all conversations, meetings between you and Eddie, especially those involving Greg Glass," Darryl added. "If Glass knew that Eddie was stealing from you and didn't disclose to you that he was Eddie's lawyer in the theft case, that's textbook conflict of interest and would be grounds to overturn your conviction."

To distance himself from the growing Eddie Floyd mess, Darryl sent Chad information on the criminal charges they planned to file along with a letter titled "Eddie the Thief." He also included a copy of a letter he'd sent Eddie, in which he accused Eddie of "creat[ing] fictional characters" and "falsify[ing] documents to take advantage of people."

"You acted alone deceived and misrepresented these people and diverted funds designated for the IRS to your bank account … you know I had no knowledge of your stealing money from them yet when caught you try to implicate me," Darryl wrote Eddie, adding, "You have a cocaine problem and your whole existence is a lie." Darryl accused Eddie of conspiring with Greg Glass to convince Chad "into accepting probation … to conceal your theft." His letter concluded on a melodramatic note:

I was your friend for nearly a decade and you took advantage of me through your intricate web of deceit and lies. I would have helped you get treatment for your dependency on cocaine. I don't like you but I don't want you to spend 20 years on-lock either but it's your choice … I had charge to the game the money you beat me for but when Wes called me and told me about the money you stole from them, I felt guilty because I brought you to them … You are obviously a very sick person and in need of psychiatric and drug treatment and I hope you will get help before it's too late.

You think Wes is bluffing about filing charges but she isn't and unfortunately once she does, it's out of her hands. At 10:00 AM, on Monday morning charges will be filed with the Major Fraud division of the District Atty.'s office and later the Criminal Investigations unit of the IRS. I know you will try to hurt me and retaliate against me in some way but God is my shepherd, I shall not want … and No weapon formed against me shall prosper. I know you are an atheist but embrace God and your family they want to help you. Please stay out of my life forever and don't wait until it's too late to save yourself.

It was signed, "A friend betrayed."

But Mama Wes *was* bluffing – she never pressed charges against Eddie Floyd because it simply wasn't a priority. "Eddie Floyd took us all to the fuckin' cleaners," she says. "Honestly, around that time I didn't give a lovely fuck about no money. All I cared about was C."

She stressed over the loss during a visit. "Mama, stop worrying about that [money]," Chad told her. "That shit is gone. I can get some more. Don't cry about that. We didn't know."

She felt silly for falling prey to Eddie's scam, but soon found out he'd run scams on others, too. "This fucker was good," she sighs. "I just felt so stupid. I'm a better judge of people than that."

Chad's prison time was draining Mama Wes both financially and emotionally. "I think that [situation] took at least 15 years off of me," she says. The ordeal brought her closer to Jive's Jeff Sledge, who called almost daily to see how she was doing. "She just needed somebody to talk to," Jeff recalls. "We would just talk [about life]."

In March 2004, Chad's mugshot was featured prominently on the cover of *The Source* Magazine alongside other incarcerated rappers like Mystikal, Shyne, and C-Murder. "Hip-Hop BEHIND BARS: Are Rappers the New Target of America's Criminal Justice System?" it read.

He wasn't happy about the cover, which wasn't the way he wanted to present himself to the public. The mugshot, he told Wendy Day, was taken at his "low point." "I can't trip cuz anybody can get it off the [internet]," he told *On Tha Real* Magazine. "[But] I feel they should have got at me before they ran it."

The accompanying interview had been done a year earlier for *F.E.D.S.* Magazine while he was at Garza, and he didn't like the fact that *The Source* had repurposed it for their cover story without contacting him.* "A lot has changed with me since then," he told *On Tha Real* Magazine.

Darryl wrote Chad in April saying that no one had come through on their pledge to contribute towards attorney's fees. He'd borrowed $25,000 on Chad's behalf from an entity identified only as "the Chinks" to be paid back at the staggering interest rate of 10% ($2,500) per week. "I had no choice," Darryl wrote.

He'd obtained signed affidavits from two of the Sharpstown witnesses, Dooley and Chaka, which contradicted the original police report.** "[When I told police that] 'Pimp C' pull[ed] out a gun and stuck it in Lakita's side that statement was not true," Chaka admitted. "I made that statement … just to help my friend [Lakita] who was angry with 'Pimp C.' I did not see 'Pimp C' pull out a gun and point it at anyone."

Darryl wrote a press release titled "New Evidence could free jailed rapper Pimp C of UGK: Habitual thief lies to keep Pimp C of UGK in prison," which included copies of Lakita's lengthy criminal record. The press release also included this blurb; apparently, Darryl hoped to publicly pressure Jive into paying for legal fees:

Pimp C is [also] fighting the IRS as a result of an erroneous tax bill created by Jive Records falsely claiming he was paid $11 million for tax year 1998. Jive has negligently taken over 4 years to correct this injustice. This IRS tax liability allowed a crooked accountant [to steal] over $80,000 … Jive has not contributed one dime to Pimp C defense despite numerous pleadings for assistance. Jive has released two albums since the incarceration, 'Side Hustles', and 'Best of UGK' without paying anything to the group. Jive has shown no interest in Pimp C's case and has repeatedly refused to consider a loan to pay for his legal defense while paying nearly $350,000 for Mystikal, convicted of gang rape, and far more for R.Kelly, who is charged with statutory rape. Apparently, Jive will only help their artist if they rape someone.***

Jive was wary of paying legal fees because they'd heard all these stories before. "There's always these lawyers that are like, 'Oh, if you just give me this [much money], I can get [your artist] out,'" explains Jeff Sledge.

In any case, the pressure worked. A week after the press release went out, Darryl convinced Jive to send $10,000 towards Chad's legal fees. Mama Wes faxed over her bank info with a handwritten note to Jive's Dan Zucker: "Thank you very kindly, and although the $10,000 is not sufficient to solve our problems, it is indeed more than we had."

The same day, Darryl also received $2,880 from Gonzales Music Wholesale for sales of the *Live from Harris County Jail* album. But with the astronomical interest rate he'd agreed to from "the Chinks," nearly all of that money went to interest.

"I have resisted writing because I wanted something positive to tell you," Darryl wrote Chad on May 14. The bad news, he explained, was that even with the money from Jive, he still needed $22,000 more. But he had good news, too: "If you agree to this loan from Quanell X I can

---

(*The publisher of *F.E.D.S.* – Finally Every Dimension of the Streets – was also an editor at *The Source*.)
(**The third witness Shameka Hawkins also filed an affidavit, which is missing from Chad's file in the Harris County District Clerk's office.)
(***It is not known if Jive paid attorney's fees for Mystikal and R. Kelly, as Darryl Austin claimed.)

have you home in about two months max … The only thing stopping your freedom is money $22,000 as of today."

Quanell Evans, otherwise known as Quanell X, was a childhood friend of Scarface's who also considered J. Prince a mentor. He'd worked with the New Black Panther Party during the controversial Million Youth March, but had since branched off to form his own organization and considered himself a "community activist."*

The proposed $22,000 loan would come at a high price. Chad would have to sign a promissory note agreeing to repay double that amount, $44,000, within six months of his release. (Quanell X says the exorbitant interest rate was Chad's idea.)

"Nobody would help him because he was considered to be [high risk]," says Quanell X. "He was dealing with a lot of internal demons … They couldn't get money from anywhere else because nobody would loan Pimp C money … he, at that time, had a reputation of not being stable-minded, not being focused, and his behavior had burned many bridges."

Quanell was initially hesitant to loan a large sum of money to someone with a reputation as a loose cannon, but after a lengthy talk with Chad on a guard's cell phone, was impressed with his lucidity. "He was clear-minded … and you could tell that the brother was highly intelligent," Quanell says. "As long as he was sober, he was a very brilliant, highly intelligent young man."

He agreed to loan Chad the money, and attorney Troy J. Wilson set to work preparing the appeal. In it, Wilson argued that Chad's attorney Greg Glass had not only "failed to do any investigation, file any motions, [or] interview any witnesses" but had failed to "disclose a … conflict of interest" involving his relationship with Eddie Floyd.

"Despite Mr. Glass' awareness that Mr. Floyd was being accused of stealing approximately $100,000 from [Chad], Glass continued to represent both without disclosing to [Chad] his representation of Mr. Floyd," Wilson wrote. "[Chad] has a strong belief … that [Floyd] had an interest and desire to see [Chad] go to prison as long as possible to cover up his theft. Had Mr. Glass revealed his multiple representation … [Chad] would have changed [attorneys]."

———

San Antonio was brutally hot, and it wasn't uncommon for inmates to die of heat stroke. When the summer of 2004 rolled around, Chad didn't like his job assignment. He purchased a bottle of Windex from the commissary and visited the warden's office – in the air-conditioned visitation complex – with his bottle of Windex and a roll of paper towels. Rumor held that the warden was a UGK fan and didn't mind Chad's presence.

Mama Wes came to visit every weekend, but Chad was inevitably late. He preferred to wait until the last minute to take a shower and get fresh for his visitors. "He had to get all spiffy, he couldn't come in just the regular [clothes]," says Mama Wes. "[His clothes] had to be white, white, white, and [he had to] have his new shoes on and his dark glasses and the whole nine yards. He had to be *Pimp*."

One weekend, Mama Wes had been waiting for an unusually long time, so she ambled over to the desk and asked the clerk if something was wrong. "I been waiting for my son a long time, and a whole bunch of people have come, y'know, come out, since I got here," she began.

"[Are] you 'Mama'?" the clerk asked.

(*Quanell X's work as an "activist" was later called into question in a series of investigative reports by Houston's KHOU Channel 11. Several people alleged that when they approached Quanell X seeking help for injustice or police brutality, he charged hefty fees for investigative services which were never performed. Quanell X's non-profit organization also failed to file required paperwork revealing their annual income. Other community activists considered his methods unorthodox. "I don't call him an activist, I call him an entrepreneur," said Lecia Brooks, an activist who runs the Civil Rights Memorial at the Southern Poverty Law Center. "[If] you're a community leader during the press conference and you're an entrepreneur when someone comes to you for help, it's very unfortunate." Quanell defends his entrepreneurial ventures, arguing, "Where is it written that an activist should be poor? Where is it written that in order to stand up for our people, without fear, without compromise, that you gotta be piss-poor [and] raggedy? … The poorer you are, the more legitimate you are? That's foolishness.")

"Yeah," Mama Wes confirmed.

"Ol' Windex will be here in a minute," the clerk chuckled.

"No, no," Mama Wes said, confused. "I'm waiting for Butler."

"Yeah, Windex will be here in a minute," the clerk repeated.

When Chad finally made his grand appearance in clean linens, Mama Wes couldn't resist greeting him with, "Whassup, Windex?"

"How you know 'bout that?" he asked.

"I gotta know what the Windex is about."

Chad explained how he'd been able to stay out of the heat.*

It was during this time at Dominguez that Chad often reported "seeing" Tupac, who had been dead since 1996. He brought it up again later in the visit. "Yeah, talked to 'Pac again last night," he commented casually.

"For real?" Mama Wes asked, expecting him to laugh, or at least crack a smile, but he didn't.

"Yeah," he paused, his tone serious. "You don't believe me, do you, Mama."

She thought for a moment. "I find it hard."

"You believe I can reach him?" Chad asked.

"I believe…" her voice trailed off. "If you believe you can reach him, that's all that's important."

Bun had never taken their issues with Jive as personally as Chad, but he didn't like the fact that Jive had released both *Side Hustles* and a greatest hits album titled *The Best of UGK* while Chad was incarcerated. He hired an attorney to file a lawsuit against Jive and their parent company Zomba, arguing that the terms of their deal - five albums and one greatest hits - had been fulfilled.

On July 7, 2004, both parties agreed to a settlement agreement which clarified the terms of Pimp and Bun's solo albums. Jive would still receive 50-75 cents off each of their solo albums sold, and Pimp and Bun could appear on each others' projects as long as it wasn't marketed as a single or referenced as a "UGK" song. It was agreed that Side Hustles didn't count towards UGK's contract. With Chad's release date still unknown, Jive wanted the option to release UGK's fifth album or pass. If they opted to release it, UGK would receive $350,000 recording budget.

While digging through Chad's case file, Darryl came across the Order to Dismiss which the sit-in judge Woody Densen had erroneously signed back in October 2001. It stated that after Chad served his 30 days in the County Jail, the entire case was dismissed. Darryl believed it was a loophole that could set him free.

"You are truly blessed that I found this dismissal order," Darryl wrote Chad. He added, "I have enclosed a management agreement which is the same as what you had before, please sign it so that I can have the authority to go get your money Jive has stolen from you and to get their ass to pay for the $11 million 1099 they sent you that started this mess."

Darryl had been presenting himself Pimp C's manager as far back as the Cash Money tour, although there had never been any formal agreement. With the letter, Darryl included a standard management agreement granting him 20% commission. "I will consult with you on moves that I make prior to making them," he wrote. "I won't fuck you and you can fire me if you don't like the job I'm doing."

Since the Byron Hill fiasco, Chad had been wary about signing a management deal with anyone, and he didn't like the way Darryl was using the appeal as leverage to pressure him into

---

(*"He loved to tell this story [about the Windex]," remembers Mama Wes. "Damn, I hate he didn't make the song. He was gonna make a song about that bottle of Windex.")

management. Chad never signed the agreement.

Chad's appeal put his former attorney Greg Glass in the position of having to defend himself against his former client. Glass submitted the original interviews that had been done with the witnesses, which Chad had never seen, and argued that his representation of Eddie Floyd was not a conflict of interest.

A judge denied Chad's appeal, noting his numerous probation violations and concluding that he had "failed to demonstrate that his conviction was improperly obtained."

Chad received letters daily at mail call, often from fans, and he made it a point to try to write everyone back. Most were elated to get a response from their idol, and some became regular penpals. He offered relationship advice to a fan in New Orleans, Ansel Augustine, who wrote that he was going through a hard time after a breakup.

"You got to go thru sumthin to get to your blessing," Chad wrote. "God gona make sho you read[y] before he just drop the right person into your life. Just cas you was 'in love' don't mean that was 'the right woman' for you … [and] as for your homi getin wit yo old girl, a nigger ain't to be trusted and all you realy got is your family when the shit go's down and the chipz fall."

Another penpal was Heather Johnson, an out-of-control white teenager from Dallas. Heather had fallen into the wrong crowd in high school, developing a bad cocaine habit, and was on probation for a fraud charge. She'd briefly met Chad at a UGK show and started writing him while he was in the County Jail.

Initially, Chad was drawn to her wild side, making plans to "get high as a muthafucker" with her once he was released. But as the months wore on, his attitude noticeably shifted, and Heather came to consider him like an older brother. He told her to get out of the streets and get her life together, and sometimes offered dating advice: "Don't settle for scrap iron when you should be fuckin' with platinum."

Even though Chad was trying to steer her in the right direction, Heather wasn't taking her probation seriously. After failing three drug tests, she was sent to the County Jail in Beaumont. She felt like her parents had abandoned her, and was elated when Chad suggested she should reach out to his mother.

The two women began corresponding and hit it off immediately; Heather considered Mama Wes a substitute mother. She believed Chad and Mama Wes had come into her life for a reason. "It's one of those relationships that you rarely find in life," she says. "You really can't explain it, but you know that you two are supposed to be in each other's lives. God put us in each other's lives … [it was] a total blessing."

On August 17, 2004, Heather was sent to SAFP, where most of the women were far from hardened criminals. Most, like Heather, had committed minor crimes and were struggling with drug addiction. There were nurses, attorneys, even wealthy suburban moms, many of whom had become addicted to prescription opiates. Some women had been charged for something as minor as picking up the phone and relaying a message to their drug dealer boyfriend, or calling in a refill on prescription cough syrup. Others had already turned their lives around and were doing time for minor charges from years ago.

SAFP, Heather says, was even worse than she'd heard. "The whole idea [of SAFP] was to break you down and build you back up," Heather says. "So they take away every ounce of pride and dignity and self-respect that you have and throw it out the window."

Inmates were forced to learn coordinated dance routines, singing nursery rhymes like "Old MacDonald Had a Farm" over and over for hours. They would march in sync while singing, "*Freeeeee wooooooorrrrrld! Freeeeee woorrrrrrld!* I'm gonna get to the *freeeeeee world!*" or other ridiculous tunes like, "Mama, Mama, look at me / I'm in a program called SAFP / I used to drive a little Ford / Now I'm cruisin' with the Lord!"

SAFP came with a lengthy rule book, and inmates were under incredible pressure to report each other for violating the rules. "[SAFP] is a drama factory," one former inmate wrote on the blog Grits for Breakfast. "[The counselors] try to play mind games [and] turn you against each other."

The most dreaded punishment was the "tighthouse," where inmates were required to sit motionless in hard plastic chairs from 4:30 AM until 8 PM for days, weeks, or even months on end.* "It was living hell," Heather says. "It's crazy shit. Crazy shit. I couldn't wait to get out of there."

After six months, Heather was released to a halfway house. "I can't believe you did that shit," Chad wrote. "People in here would rather die before they go do that shit. They would rather do all their time than go to SAFP."

Chad told Heather that he wanted her come work with them once he was released. It was rare that Mama Wes got along with a female, so Chad knew she must be something special. "I want you to be on the team," he wrote. "My Mama loves you."**

———————————

Contrary to popular belief, says Houston rapper Z-Ro, it actually wasn't easy to stay sober in prison, especially for a high-profile inmate. Two months into his prison stint for drug-related charges in 2004, Z-Ro was approached by an overly exuberant correctional officer. "Man, what you need?" the officer asked him.

Z-Ro eyed the officer warily. *Man, I need you to leave me the fuck alone. I don't know what the fuck you tryna do,* his expression read.

The officer discreetly produced a bag of Xanax pills. "Man, I got these handlebars…"

"No shit?" Z-Ro leaned over to get a closer look. "Man, I ain't been high in like, mutha-fuckin' seventy days, man. Give me three. How much they is?"

"Man, they for *you,*" he offered. "I'm here for you, man."

"That's how it starts," Z-Ro sighs. "They hit you with that ol' 'I'm your dope dealer and this is your first free hit' type shit … before you know it, you're fucked up … If you got celebrity status you can get what the fuck you want. It's a trap."

Chad was approached with similar offers, but he knew better. "They ain't finna set me up for the okie doke," he'd told Lil Green after declining an offer at Garza West. "That's another five years right there."

"I [saw] every type of drug imaginable in prison, right there in my face," Chad told *OZONE* later. "Anything you want is in jail. Muthafuckers will give it to you just to knock you off your game."

With Heather preparing to leave the halfway house and Chad coming up for parole soon, they exchanged a few final letters. Now both sober, they made a pact not to let each other slip back into cocaine use in the free world. "We gotta be watchful of the snakes, because the snakes are out there and they're gonna try to get us," Chad wrote.

(*Descriptions of the "tighthouse" are from SAFP inmates who were not necessarily in the same unit as Heather Johnson. The *Austin Chronicle* ran a series of articles in 2008 about the alleged "psychological and physical abuse" taking place in SAFP, specifically in the womens' units. Gateway management disputed many of the womens' allegations.)
(**Chad's statements here from his letters to Heather are paraphrased from her recollection, not exact quotes.)

CHAPTER 33

"This is divine intervention right here. I'm not in [prison] just because. So when it's supposed to be over, then it'll be over and I'll go home."
— Pimp C, HoustonSoReal, March 2005

"The broads is bopped up [at Darrington]. They [got] they fingernails done, they got they hair whipped, and they choosing." — Pimp C, *Cheddar* DVD

November 2004

The news that Pimp C would be spending the weekend at the Darrington Unit in Rosharon in transit was the most exciting thing that had happened there all year. Darrington had earned the nickname "Chocolate City" and a reputation as one of the toughest, wildest farms in TDCJ, and an officer's meeting was held to coordinate logistics for his arrival.*

A high-profile inmate like Chad in transit was considered a security risk, and prison officials tried to place him in protective custody. "I had to sign papers [to decline it]," Chad told *Cheddar* DVD. "They was just doing that for they own protection. They wasn't really concerned about me or my well-being, they was just trying to cover [their] ass in case something went down and I got hurt."

He declined not only because he felt it was dishonorable, but because he didn't think he could handle doing time in solitary confinement without the company of other people. "I [did all my time in general] population ... living with the niggas," he told *OZONE*. "'Cause the niggas, I'm they hero 'cause I'm 100%. I was more scared of the guards than I was of niggas, 'cause the guards was the enemy."

But even as a part of the general population, Chad was still red-flagged as a security threat. "If they red flag you, that means you're a security threat, like, you could fuck their bitches [or get] the officers [to bring you] phones, DVD players, whatever," explains Smit-D.**

Smit-D was at the Darrington Unit serving out his sentence for the 1994 murder of DJ Peace.*** He commanded fellow inmates' respect not only because of his Facemob affiliation but his large, imposing physique. He was well-connected and had a good relationship with the officers at the unit, who were very familiar with his rap group The Outfit.

The Outfit included Smit, two men nicknamed Psych and Pike, and John Singleton, a Muslim man who went by the name Shabazz or "Baz." Baz, a tall, slender man in his mid-30s, had been in prison for most of his adult life. Accused of being the ringleader in a string of Rolex robberies which terrorized the Houston area in the late 80s and early 90s, Baz was now serving

---

(*In the 1994 movie *Jason's Lyric*, featuring Jada Pinkett Smith and Naughty By Nature's Anthony "Treach" Criss, the scene where actor Bokeem Woodbine's character Joshua Alexander emerges from prison was filmed at the Darrington Unit.)

(**TDCJ struggled to attract quality employees both because of the location of the prisons and the low pay. The starting salary for a correctional officer as around $18,924, far below the national average, which meant they were only taking home $300 a week. Inmates, who were only allowed one five-minute collect phone call every three months, were often able to bribe officers to bring in cell phones and other contraband.)

(***Smit-D had successfully filed an appeal in which he was resentenced to 17 years instead of 25 years.)

out a 50-year sentence for aggravated robbery.*

Baz, who was Muslim, had devised an ingenious way to hold rap concerts. He was responsible for organizing the unit's Islamic services, and argued that by law, he needed to have access to the same equipment as other religions. The Christian services held regularly at the unit used drums, guitars, speakers, monitors, and mixing boards.

According to Baz, Islamic services weren't subject to the same restrictions as the Christian services. He started doing spoken word sessions about black history during the weekly Islamic services. Baz asked producers like Odd Squad's Blind Rob to mail in CDs with instrumentals, and convinced officers to let the contraband slip past. The Islamic services soon turned into a full-on rap concert under the guise of religion, with 300 inmates regularly packing the church house for these unofficial concerts.

The female guards at Darrington let Chad know that if there was anything he needed – *anything* at all – he could get it. "The broads is bopped up [at Darrington]," Chad told *Cheddar* DVD. "They [got] they fingernails done, they got they hair whipped, and they choosing."**

One Darrington guard in particular, Ms. Brown, seemed to have taken a liking to Chad. "Pimp had one of the female officers when he hit the farm already going crazy for him," Smit-D laughs. "He had already won."

Because Chad was flagged as a security risk, food was delivered to him so he wouldn't mingle with the rest of the inmates in the chow hall. Baz, who worked in the kitchen, put together a tray with heaping portions of hot dogs, chicken, and beans for Ms. Brown to deliver.

For the most part, Chad avoided getting too close to the correctional officers or taking any unnecessary risks. "I wasn't tryin' to catch no bossy lady hoes or tryin' to put no bitch on my team," he said on the *Pimpalation* DVD. "I ain't need nobody to bring me no cigarettes or no tobacco 'cause it wasn't nothing but a way for me to get in trouble and lose my [chance at] parole."

Chad, like every other inmate in the TDCJ system, had heard about The Outfit's concerts. As he was getting settled, he asked an officer to send for Smit-D.

A sergeant poked his head in Smit's cell. "Say man, Pimp C wanna see you."

"Really?!" Smit-D said in disbelief.

As the sergeant escorted Smit – or "Facemob," as he was known – upstairs to the fourth tier, hundreds of inmates swarmed against the windows, pounding frantically to get his attention. It was "count time," where any movement would normally be restricted, so they knew something major was happening.

"Facemob! Get me in there, Facemob!" they begged. "Pimp!? Man, Pimp C over there, man!?"

Smit finally reached the dayroom, which had been cleared out for Pimp C's arrival. "Who you want to come over here?" the Sergeant asked.

A few minutes later, Chad entered the day room. The two men greeted each other warmly, and both started laughing as they recalled the last time they'd hung out together.

"Man, you remember?" Chad asked.

"Yeah, '*Mary J dead*,'" Smit-D said, reminiscing on Mr. 3-2's drug-induced outburst and laughing so hard tears started streaming from his eyes.

Smit had heard the rumors about the Master P pistol-whipping, and when he brought up the topic, Chad started laughing. "Yeah, man, P beat me up pretty bad, man."

(*Baz admits being involved in some of the robberies, but denies that he was the ringleader. He says he was charged for several crimes in which he was not involved at all.)

(**A "bopper" is popular Texas slang for a groupie-type female who likes to hang out with rap stars and celebrities.)

The MDDL FNGZ had heard that Smit had sent a letter of apology to DJ Peace's parents. Without getting too specific, Smit apologized to Chad for coming to UGK's show on the night of DJ Peace's murder. "It was a mistake I made," he admitted of his case. "One mistake, I'm gone."

Conversation turned to spirituality. Here, in this place, even a murderer could be a friend, a confidant, a therapist. Chad was close to tears as Smit talked about the "Free Pimp C" movement. "You don't know what Bun done for you," Smit told him. "This man got you *ready*. Like, you finna have millions, bro."

Through prison word-of-mouth, Smit had incorrectly heard that Chad was arrested for carrying a cup of lean through the mall. "Man, what it do with the drank?" Smit asked, his expression turning serious.

Pimp shook his head. "I'm addicted, Smit," he said quietly. "I'm addicted."

"Chad, man, you ain't drank in three years, man," Smit said. "How the hell you gon' be addicted, man?"

"Man, I'm addicted, man," Pimp repeated.

"For real, mane!? For real, Chad!?" Smit said. "C'mon, man, look where we at. For real. I been down for damn near 10 years. I'm telling you, man, Bun got you ready. Go home, get that money!"

Chad nodded. "I'm with God, man. I'm a Christian."

"You sure, man?" Smit stared at him. "'Cause you wouldn't be talking about that drank if you was sure of that."

The mood lightened as The Outfit arrived in the day room. Smit encouraged Baz, Pike, and Psych to let Chad hear something. Someone pounded out a beat on one of the round tables and they took turns freestyling in a cypher, the energy flowing as everyone wanted to impress Pimp C. Chad had never been much of a freestyler, but he enjoyed the show, watching everyone spit and bobbing his head along with the improvised beat. When they finished, Chad nodded his approval. "Man, y'all live, man," he said. "I like y'all, man. Outfit, yeah?"

"Yeah, that's the name of our group, The Outfit," Baz nodded.

Chad leaned back. "I'ma let y'all hear something, mane," he said. "I'm on this here."

Instead of a rap, he started singing: "Swing down, sweet chariot, stop and let me ride!"*

"That's some George Clinton," Pimp explained, laughing at their blank expressions. "Man, I fuck with y'all, man." He showed The Outfit a letter he'd just received from David Banner. "I'ma get David Banner to fuck with y'all, too, man," he said.

Chad had a pen and pad with him, and throughout the session, he scribbled down ideas on his notepad. As they'd been talking, the inmates who passed by the day room shouted at him through the chicken-wired windows to get his attention, some rapping lines from their favorite UGK songs and banging on the windows to improvise a beat.

The energy at the Darrington Unit was so explosive it sparked Chad's creativity, inspiring him to write nine songs in the three days he was there.

Chad had been without radio access for months. The following day, November 14, Smit-D sent over a care package with commissary snacks, soap and deodorant, and a radio with instructions to tune into DJ Michael Watts' Sunday night mixshow.

"I wanna hit Brad [Scarface] & J [Prince] & let them know you straight, so let me know what it do!" Smit-D wrote. "I'm pray'n for you and yours bro! I GOT MUCH LOVE FOR YOU, BUN & BIRD, C!!!"

He assured Chad that if he ever had any problems, all he had to do was say the word and it

(*Chad was singing from the Parliament Funkadelic record "Mothership Connection," which was adapted from a classic slave spiritual. Fat Pat had also improvised a version of the song for the hook of the Southside Playaz' record "Swang Down," which appeared on a classic 1998 Screw tape.)

would be handled. "My handle [is] still the same," he wrote, including a PO Box address. "You can't put yo prison # on none of the letters! When you hit me I'm a hitcha right back. Right Back! If you need anything holla at me. If you hit a farm and anybody plex with you, ask me in the letter if I know who it is & I'm a get the picture and get right on it!!! Believe Me C, I'm a get right on it!!! KEEP YOU A CASE OF WATER TOO BRO!!! No B/S on that! Oh, don't make reference to being locked up in your letters. Use 'that boy' (ex.)… 'They done got that boy on Dominguez Unit!' You feel me?"

"I apologize for coming to ya'll show that night under them circumstances!" he continued, referring to the 1994 TSU Homecoming weekend when DJ Peace was killed. "You look good bro! In a minute it'z gone be bigger than you ever imagined. GET. READY. Mentally, Physically, Spiritually and Emotionally!!!"

Chad departed the Darrington Unit on November 17, 2004. Things on the outside were in motion, too; parole attorney Lori K. Redmond was preparing a letter with instructions on hiring her to handle his parole hearing. Redmond was a referral from Chad's friend Donny Young; with her help, Donny had been granted parole in 1999 after serving just five years of his 40-year sentence referenced on UGK's "One Day."*

Chad's next stop was at the quiet Byrd Unit in Huntsville, a huge letdown after the explosive energy of Darrington. "It's so dead and boring in Huntsville … [I had] no motivation [to write]," he told *Cheddar* DVD.

"Different environments will make you create different type of material," he told his cousin Dwayne Diamond. "[In] some environments, you can't create at all. I hit some units where I couldn't write any songs."

(*Donny was back in prison since he had been arrested in 2003 with several pounds of marijuana, but gave Redmond rave reviews and told Chad he planned to hire her again.)

CHAPTER 34

"Folks are actually living out life sentences right here in front of us … We see a lot of deaths, but not from killings. These people are just old or they sick, and they die. I had never been around this much death before out there in the world … I'm seeing how your whole life can get taken away from you in this place … I've got a different outlook on life now from being here. For me, it's put my life in perspective. This ain't where you wanna die."
— Pimp C, South Coast Live TV

"When everybody rallied around me and was spittin' the 'Free Pimp C' shit … I didn't expect [that] to happen … them people out there hollering that shit and me reading that shit in the magazines is what kept me level and grounded."
— Pimp C, *Thick* Magazine

December 2004

In early December 2004, Chad was shipped off to the C.T. Terrell Unit 30 miles south of Houston. It was closer to Port Arthur and easier for family to visit, but he initially hated the transfer. The Terrell Unit (previously Ramsey III) was what Chad considered "an old school prison," built on a farm acquired by the Texas prison system in 1908.

He corresponded regularly with his childhood friend Tim Hampton, who had worked as a correctional officer and understood the TDCJ system. "My lawyer that filed my [appeal] has flaked out on me," Chad wrote in a letter to Tim. "The man who brought me to him [Darryl Austin] tried to force me into a management deal. After I wouldn't get down he got at the lawyer (they are friends) and now he won't return my letters or my peoples phone calls."

Chad still had a copy of the 2001 Dismissal Sheet, an angle he thought was worth pursuing. He sent a copy of it to Langston Adams, another childhood friend who was an attorney in Port Arthur. Chad told Tim he planned to turn his case over to Langston, someone he could trust.

"What do you think about all of this?" Chad asked. "Do you think Im working with something? Man Im sorry to lay all this stuff on you but I need some help cuz Im not suppose to be in this shit hole." He wanted Tim to help him get "shipped off this bullshit as unit," explaining:

I cant take it no more. First off it's a snitch unit and I ain't no snitch. Next they got me in a dorm with sick old people (herd a law lady call it the nursing home) and I ain't old or sick. Then they give me some old bullshit ass job at 5:30 AM that I ain't fit to do man. Plus they (the staff) don't know how to talk to people and Im just about to go off next time somebody try to handle me. I ain't had no problem wit no inmates but niggahz hate behind my back and long as they don't bring it to my face Im cool. I get alot of luv and respect from people too (in my face).

All in all it's shity over here and I want to move around to a convict unit where there is a respect level (and 2 man cell's. Man I just did 3 years in open dorm's and I want my own space) … sorry for writing you cryin like a lil bitch but Im tryin not to blow my cool in this MFKA!

Terrell actually *was* a medical unit, essentially a prison nursing home. (When asked why he was transferred to a medical unit, Mama Wes laughs, "'Cause he was nuts! Why else!?") During her first visit, Mama Wes had been waiting the better part of an hour, and every inmate she saw was unable to walk on their own power. Every time a man in a wheelchair, a man using a walker, or a man babbling incoherently hobbled into the visiting room, Mama Wes' panic grew.

She wasn't normally one to cry in public, but when Chad finally emerged looking perfectly healthy, she couldn't stop the tears falling from her eyes. Chad was in good spirits, wearing a brand new set of whites starched and lined with sharp creases.

He laughed and embraced his mother. "Mama, you sick?" he asked, concerned.

"Oh, my God, baby, it's so good to see ya," she said, wiping away her tears. "Let me look at you." She touched his head, inspecting him closely to make sure he wasn't sick.

"Oh, Mama, I would've come out sooner if I knew you was gonna be crying," he chuckled.

Once he got settled, Chad realized Terrell wasn't so bad after all. He described the minimum-security unit as "laid back," rating it a "2" on a 1-10 scale of "how raw it can get" in the TDCJ system. During their first visit, the guard even allowed Chad and his mother to go outside for a pleasant walk in the clear, crisp December air.

"Compared to other units, this place is like Disneyland," Chad told journalist Matt Sonzala. "This place is alright." Still, the energy at Terrell was bleak; more than half of the men there were serving lengthy sentences of 20-40 years and were largely resigned to their fate.*

Chad landed a coveted job in the kitchen, where he didn't have to report to work until 2 PM. He'd skip the 4 AM breakfast and 10 AM lunch, sleeping in until noon and then rousing himself with a cup of coffee or instant cappuccino before reporting for duty. His job was to serve dinner to inmates coming through the chow line.

One day, an elderly inmate who was in the early stages of Alzheimer's disease picked up his tray, but was confused and disoriented by the time he reached the end of the chow line. He didn't understand where he was or why he was in prison. Another inmate had to step in and carry his tray. The moment struck Chad as profound.

At Terrell, aging inmates often died of a stroke or brain aneurysm. "Folks are actually living out life sentences right here in front of us," Chad said during a rare televised interview from the unit with South Coast Live TV. "We see a lot of deaths, but not from killings. These people are just old or they sick, and they die. And I had never been around this much death before out there in the world … I'm seeing how your whole life can get taken away from you in this place … I've got a different outlook on life now from being here. For me, it's put my life in perspective. This ain't where you wanna die."**

Chad was placed in a 52-man open dorm, with cubicles for a bit of privacy. "It's a big room," he told *XXL*. "No stacked bunks, just bottom bunks. When you in a [two-man] cell you feel caged up. In this environment you can walk around. I can go from one place to the other. It's a little bit more freedom."

He still avoided the television, but radios were allowed at Terrell. His first commissary purchase was a $13.60 clock radio. Terrell was close enough to pick up signals from Houston radio stations, giving him the opportunity to catch up on everything that had been happening in the outside world.

During the year and a half Chad spent at Dominguez with virtually no access to music, a lot was happening in the rap game. For one, Mel had soldiered on with Trill Entertainment, teaming up with a new partner named Marcus "Turk" Roach and signing another young Baton Rouge rapper named Webbie. "[Chad] didn't like people to just sit around and wait for him to

---

(*As of December 2012 there are 1,616 inmates at Terrell, more than half of whom are serving a sentence of 20-40 years or more. 21% are serving sentences for Burglary, 18% for DWI, 15% for Indecency with a Child, and 13% for Aggravated Sex Assault with a Child.)

(**During the year 2005 while Pimp C was at the Terrell Unit, 351 inmates died in Texas prisons state-wide. Heart disease, cancer, liver disease, AIDS-related diseases, and other illnesses were the most common causes.)

do stuff for them," Trill producer Steve Below explains. "[He wanted you to] go get your own shit … [and] if he saw you trying to help yourself, he was willing to help you."

Trill Entertainment released Lil Boosie and Webbie's joint project *Ghetto Stories* in 2003, which included several leftover Pimp C tracks, like "Finger Fuckin," originally intended for Pimp's solo album. (Pimp had apparently also given the beat to his friend Pimpin' Ken, who used it for his group The Boss Pimps' album *Pimpin' Off Top*.) Other tracks included "In My Pocket," originally developed for Young Smitty, and "Play Hard," Pimp's record venting about Ron Robinson and Master P (the No Limit disses were removed from the outro).

Webbie and Boosie followed up with *Gangsta Musik* in the summer of 2004, selling 22,000 units independently. Boosie was just 20 and Webbie 19, and their growing buzz caught the attention of major record labels.

Chad, who considered Webbie "very valuable" and appreciated his work ethic, kept up with their progress by reading magazine articles, ripping out a page from *XXL's* Show & Prove feature. In it, Boosie predicted, "When Pimp comes home, major labels will [be offering us] more money than they coming with now."

Chad still considered himself a silent partner in the label. "Tell me what Mel + Turk need to do wit Trill Ent," he wrote in a letter to Wendy Day. "They will do what I ask. You are right we ain't as close as they may want you to think but I can get at em."

Houston's bubbling music scene was on the verge of exploding. Many of the second generation of Houston rappers originated with the Swisha House camp, formed by DJ Michael "5000" Watts and OG Ron C in 1997 as the North side equivalent of DJ Screw's SUC. As Screw's production had tapered down prior to his death, they'd stepped up to fill the growing demand.

Watts took things a step beyond Screw's do-it-yourself ethos, using ProTools and digital CD mixing for better sound quality. "Watts was the only one who came close to rivaling Screw himself," writer Roni Sarig observed in the *Houston Press*. "And Watt's success helped preserve the music and legend of Screw for people who didn't catch on to slowed-down music until after Screw's death."

SUC members argued that Watts couldn't technically call his music "Screwed & Chopped" if Screw didn't do it. After Watts was quoted in *Murder Dog* saying that he'd taken Screw music to a whole new level, Screw's brother Al-D and the SUC's Z-Ro dropped a Watts diss record.*

Regardless, Watts became known as a worldwide ambassador for Screwed & Chopped music, and major labels started recruiting him to create slowed-down versions of their artists' albums. (His version of 8Ball & MJG's 2000 album *Space Age 4 Eva* was the first major label Screwed & Chopped release.)

UGK had tried to convince Jive to release a Chopped & Screwed version of *Ridin' Dirty* in 1996, but at the time, the label didn't understand. "We were a couple years ahead of our time," Bun told *OZONE*. "Back when we first started talking about Screw music and blades and all that shit down here, it was still a local thing."

Jive, finally understanding that this was a way they could generate album sales with hardly any expense, dropped an album titled *Jive Records Presents: UGK Chopped & Screwed* in December 2004. It included a solid selection of UGK classics ("Something Good," "One Day," "Pocket Full of Stones") and newer tracks from *Dirty Money* ("Let Me See It," "Take It Off"). But instead of Michael Watts or OG Ron C, Jive turned over the project to a rookie named named DJ 007. Fans and critics were unimpressed, and the *New York Times* called the album a "transparent effort to squeeze a bit more money out of the UGK catalog."

"DO NOT BUY THIS ALBUM," one reviewer named R. Allred wrote. "Jive records has Fucked over UGK for years and years, and this is another attempt to swindle the pockets of the

(*"Screwed and chopped by who? Probably never met the man," Z-Ro rapped on "Screw Did That." "5,000 Watts of skills? Naw, 5,000 pounds of trash / Watch what you say in the magazines, ol' fat-ass nigga / Instead of nibblin' off my nigga's cheese, ol' rat-ass nigga / I call it like I see it, and I can't be nothin' but real / I guess they can't originate, so they do nothin' but steal.")

greatest rap group of all time. Jive knows that they can't make any more money from them and now that the rest of the nation is finally giving them their credit, Jive is trying to capitalize on that profit. If you want to hear UGK Screwed the way it should be. Get a SCREW TAPE."

Chad learned of the Chopped & Screwed album when a friend mailed him a print out of the tracklisting with a post-it note attached that read, "Just found this on a website didn't know if you knew about it??"

Michael Watts and OG Ron C's 1999 Swisha House compilation album *The Day Hell Broke Loose* highlighted several young Houston rappers, up-and-comer Slim Thug and a duo named Paul Wall and Camilean (later, "Chamillionaire").

Childhood friends Chamillionaire and Paul Wall modeled their group after UGK. "Chamillionaire had a deeper voice and I had a more high pitched voice," Paul explains. "We kind of tried to have the same kind of chemistry [Pimp and Bun] had."

They, along with other rising Houston rappers, considered UGK one of their greatest influences. "[UGK] made me wanna rap," Slim Thug said. "[UGK] made it cool to be gangsta and to rep Texas ... they're the epitome of rawness," Chamillionaire agreed on the *Pimpalation* DVD.

While Chad was passing the time in TDCJ, Houston was on the verge of bursting onto the national Hip-Hop landscape. MTV News called it "a musical renaissance." Many popular underground artists who had previously relied on Southwest Wholesale for distribution were snatched up by major record labels.

Houston rapper Lil Flip, who had been toiling on the underground since his 2000 album *The Leprechaun*, dropped two platinum albums on Sony. After a major label bidding war Slim Thug signed with Jimmy Iovine's Geffen/Interscope. (Fans were less than impressed with the result after Iovine paired him with Virginia production duo The Neptunes, a vast departure from the Texas sound they knew and loved.)

After selling 150,000 units independently (on Madd Hatta's label Paid in Full) of their 2002 debut *Get Ya Mind Correct*, Paul Wall and Chamillionaire went through a bitter breakup. Chamillionaire inked a lucrative deal with Universal Records for his solo album *The Sound of Revenge*.

Todd Moscowitz, President of the newly formed Asylum Records, sought out Rap-A-Lot and Swisha House and signed them to distribution deals through Atlantic/Warner Bros. Paul Wall's major label debut *The People's Champ* (described by one reviewer as "a beginner's course on Houston Hip-Hop") was the first Houston rap album to debut at #1 on the *Billboard* charts.

But the biggest breakthrough was Swisha House newcomer Mike Jones, whose massive hit "Still Tippin'" incorporated elements of Screw music and also featured memorable verses from Paul Wall and Slim Thug.* The hook sampled a late 90s Slim Thug freestyle from a Michael Watts mixtape, on which he drawled in his low baritone about "tippin' on fo'fo's, wrapped in fo' Vogues," a reference to 44-spoke rims and Vogue white-wall tires.

Mike Jones, who rapped using his real name, was best known for his gimmicky marketing techniques, repeating his name and giving out his phone number (the catchy 281-330-8004) on records. "[Some people felt like] he wasn't payin' dues," Salih Williams, who produced "Still Tippin'," said in *Houston Rap*. "But he had the right song at the right time and he had a new energy, he had a nice little gimmick and he could sell." Propelled by "Still Tippin'," Mike Jones' debut album *Who Is Mike Jones?* sold 180,000 copies in its first week and landed at #3 on the *Billboard* charts.

By 2005, Houston was on top of the rap game. "We've been doing this same sound for years," Paul Wall told MTV News. "We ain't changed up our blueprint ... The world is just tired of the same old, same old [sound, and] they're ready for something new."

(*There were two versions of "Still Tippin'." The first featured Mike Jones, Chamillionaire, and Slim Thug, and appeared on the 2004 Swisha House/Rap-A-Lot compilation *The Day After Hell Broke Loose*. After Chamillionaire and Swisha House fell out, he was replaced on the song by Paul Wall for the new version, which was used as the lead single for Mike Jones' debut.)

All the attention on Texas brought renewed interest in UGK as one of the pioneers of the scene. "There was an infatuation with Houston, with the sound, with what we were doing – the lifestyle, the cars … we all were selling Houston," Bun said in the book *Houston Rap*.

The new generation of artists, many of whom were raised on UGK's music, all wanted to work with the group. With Pimp unavailable, all those opportunities came to Bun, who recorded dozens of features. A blog called Government Names released a list of the "Top 30 Bun B Features of the Year" from 2004, noting that "every rapper with a microphone and a checkbook got [Bun B] on a track." Notable features included "Ova Here" for rising trap star Jay "Young Jeezy" Jenkins and "As the World Turns" for a then-unknown rapper named Curtis "50 Cent" Jackson. And nearly every verse ended with a "Free Pimp C."

"Bun rose to the occasion," says producer Mannie Fresh. "The South missed the shit out of [Pimp when he] was in jail, [Bun] ripped everybody's song … I don't really even think Bun knew how important that was, because it put him on the map … it made him a household name. It pretty much resurrected UGK while [Pimp] was in jail … he kept dude alive."

The movement also gained traction because Pimp C's incarceration was widely perceived as an injustice. Unlike Mystikal (forced his hairstylist to perform oral sex on him, on camera, for allegedly stealing money) and Shyne (incarcerated for a nightclub shooting which injured three people), who appeared to have committed actual crimes, fans didn't understand why Pimp C was in prison at all. "Pimp C was not a danger to society. That's the bottom line," says Willie D.

"I think people were able to recognize that maybe for what I was charged [with] … [the prosecution] didn't quite play fair," Chad said in an interview with Dwayne Diamond. "They tried to make an example out of me because of the position I was in with the music. Instead of Chad Butler going on trial, rap music as a whole went on trial."

"People out here are smart … [they wondered], 'Why is Pimp in prison for eight years for some bullshit?'" he told HipHop2Nite.

With Houston in the national spotlight, "Free Pimp C" became the city's unofficial motto. Bun could be seen sporting "Free Pimp C" t-shirts at all his shows and in videos alongside T.I., Slim Thug, and Young Buck. "It seems like that boy's entire wardrobe consists of shirts with my face on it," Chad joked. ("I got the world screamin' 'Free Pimp C,'" Bun later rapped on "Free.")

"Bun singlehandedly kept his legacy alive," says Willie D. "Everybody just started saying ['Free Pimp C']. Everybody just kind of jumped on the bandwagon."

"Every time [Bun] said C's name in a song or an interview, that helped Bun as much as it helped C," Too $hort added in *OZONE*. "[At first] folks thought [Bun] couldn't make it without Pimp C. Bun is a better lyricist, but Pimp had that swagger. By Bun doing all those guest appearances on other rapper's songs, he not only saved both of their careers but also elevated them to a level they'd never been on before."

Chad credited the "Free Pimp C" movement with not only elevating his rap career but helping him through the day-to-day struggle of prison life. "Maybe, at one time, I motivated [the new rappers] to do what they doing now," he told MTV. "But right now, being where I'm at, those guys are motivating me to keep going."

"When everybody rallied around me and was spittin' the 'Free Pimp C' shit … I didn't expect [that] to happen," he told *Thick* Magazine. "[I] had never seen nothin' like that happen for anybody else."

"I'ma tell you something, man," he continued. "Some of them days in that place … them people out there hollering that shit and me reading that shit in the magazines is what kept me level and grounded. It kept me from just … going along with prison life and making that shit my home. It's easy to just say, fuck it, and go along with that shit and just make yourself as comfortable as you can. When [you're] 'comfortable,' that means you start actually living your life in that motherfucka and trying to get the most outta prison. In some ways that can be a mistake. Once you get that attitude, you stop trying to get out, man."

CHAPTER 35

"It just hurts my stomach to think that some dudes were sitting around producing my songs and taking freestyle raps and making songs out of them. It's kind of strange. It's like I'm dead, but I'm not dead. Like they trying to make a post-mortem album." – Pimp C, Yahoo.com, March 2005

———————

"I feel like I got put on the shelf, preserved, so I could come back and do something positive. Maybe I will be in a position where I can prosper when I get out. I'm not going to challenge it, I'm just gonna take it for what it's worth. If 'Pac hadn't got out [of jail], he might still be alive today. Maybe there was a worse fate out there awaiting me."
– Pimp C, *OZONE* Magazine, May 2005

With all eyes on Houston and a new Rap-A-Lot distribution deal through Asylum/Atlantic/Warner, J. Prince felt the timing was perfect to drop a Pimp C album. He'd put money on Chad's books and stayed in touch with Chad regularly, and proposed the idea during a visit.

Although the circumstances, creatively, were far from ideal, Chad had to be realistic: he needed the money. "I still had some paper left, we was blessed, but it'll knock a hole in your pocket when you just sitting down and ain't [no money] coming in," he told *Cheddar* DVD.

"Rap-A-Lot is droppin a solo album on me soon," Chad wrote in a letter to Wendy Day. "We have no paper work. In some ways that's good and in other ways it's a bad thing."

"C let [J. Prince] do that [album, but] as far as that contract [for that album] … *I* know that wasn't C's signature [and] *J* knows that wasn't C's signature," nods Mama Wes, her lips pursed tightly. "And that's all we gonna say about that."

Rap-A-Lot turned over the vocals from Pimp's incomplete songs (most of which had already been released on *Live From Harris County*) to several producers, including Mike Dean and Cory Mo, to see who could come up with the best track. The files also landed in the hands of New Orleans-based producer Danny Kartel (sometimes incorrectly spelled Dani), who had gotten his big break with Soulja Slim's posthumous hit "Slow Motion."* Danny considered Pimp C his primary production influence; he and Soulja Slim had spent hours cruising the city together, enormous speakers blasting UGK tracks for inspiration. "[We] kinda wanted to mold ourselves after [Pimp] or let that sound influence us a bit," Danny says.

Danny's beats were selected for Pimp C's "U Belong 2 Me" and "A Thin Line," both featuring Devin the Dude. Rap-A-Lot added verses from their artists Trae and Z-Ro on songs like "Young Ghetto Stars" and changed some titles ("Sixteen Five" became "Swang Down/10 a Key"). Highlights included the lead single "Hogg In The Game" (which included some shots at Master P), "Comin' Up" featuring Lil Flip, and "I'm a Hustler," one of the Hiroshima tracks DMD had

(*Soulja Slim was murdered in November 2003 and "Slow Motion" came out on Juvenile's March 2004 album *Juve the Great*. Chad believed that Soulja Slim's death was a hit. "Some of these rap niggas will pay people to kill you, pay people to kill their artists," he told *The Source*. "That shit that happened to Soulja Slim … wasn't no random shit – straight business." Others say Soulja Slim had more enemies in the streets than the music business. "[He was] a gangsta … he didn't back down from anything," says Danny Kartel.)

Dear Ms DAY
   THANK You For THE Book AND I GoT your LeTTer
ALSo. Tell Me WHAT MEL + TURK neeD To
Do WiT TRILL EnT. THEY WiLL Do WHAT I ASK.
You ARE RiGHT We AinT AS CLoSe AS THEY
MAY WANT You To THink BUT I CAn GeT AT
EM.
   On MY SHiT! RAP-A-LoT Is DROPPin A SoLo
ALBUM On Me Soon (03/01/05 Is THE DATE I
tterD). We HAVE No PAPER Work. In Some
WAYS THATS GooD AnD In OTHER WAYs ITs
A BAD THinG. ALL I KnoW Is THAT Im
Gona Do WHAT You TeLL Me To Do On MY
ReTURn. I CouLD Be Home In AS ERUy AS
10 MonTHS. We STiLL OWe Jive one RecorD.
BUn Is SiGneD To R-A-L AS A SoLo ARTisT
FAR AS I KnoW? He Don't GeT AT Me MUCH
AnD I AinT MAD AT Him (JUST HURT).
I neeD A PUBLiciST AnD Some ReaL MAnAGEMenT
RiGHT Now. Don't KnoW WHo To HoLA AT ABouT IT?
   Im ABouT To WriTe MR CRUMP AnD THAnK Him
For EveryTHinG. He And A DUDE nAME MiRicaL
From ATL ARE THE Only ARTisT THAT HAVE GoT
AT Me THis HoLe TRip. I AinT MAD ABouT THAT
ETHER.
   So Look OUT THis Is MY neW LocaTion IF You
AinT KnoW By Now. HiT Me BACK IF you HAVE Any
IDEAz On WHAT I SHouLD Do oR JUST To LeT Me
KnoW You GoT MY LeTTer It's GooD...

PS/I See U
MoVeD Down
SoUTH! How
U LiKE IT?

turned over to Rap-A-Lot. The producer, D Stone, was upset that no one contacted him to pay for the track. He called Mama Wes, who told him Chad didn't have anything to do with the album.

On the softer side was Chad's dedication to his mother called "My Angel (Tribute to Momma)," which Bun called "the most sincere gangster record you've heard in your life." But for the most part, Bun kept his distance from the project. "I only brought myself into the fold of Pimp C-related stuff when he asked me to," Bun explains.

The only record featuring Bun was "I'sa Playa," also featuring Twista, which had been recorded nearly a decade earlier for N.O. Joe's album. When N.O. Joe's project was scrapped, Twista included it on his 2000 compilation *Adrenaline Rush* under the title "Time."* For *The Sweet James Jones Stories*, Rap-A-Lot renamed the track and added a catchy, melodic hook from Z-Ro. "It's worth a whole lot more with [Z-Ro] on that hook than it was before," Chad told journalist Matt Sonzala.

On March 1, 2005, *The Sweet James Jones Stories* debuted at #3 on the *Billboard* rap charts, despite poor reviews labeling it "sloppy, amateurish" and "a bit dated." Chad had only heard two of the songs (on the radio) and barely recognized them as his own.

In the past, a common complaint from Rap-A-Lot artists was that the label didn't put enough money into marketing and promotions. In fact, Rap-A-Lot didn't even have a publicity department. But under their new deal through Asylum/Warner, things were about to change. Officials at the Terrell Unit generally liked Chad, and TDCJ officials granted him permission to do interviews in support of the project, a press junket of sorts coordinated by Asylum.

One interview request came from MTV News, which was sending a team that included host Sway Calloway out to Houston to film a segment called *My Block: Houston*. Bun picked them up when they landed at the airport and proved to be a courteous host.

At the prison, Sway was impressed with Chad's calm introspection. Chad struck him as "almost like a little Malcolm X," nothing like he'd expected.

"If I could rewind and change what happened with the situation that put me here, yeah, I would," Chad admitted during the MTV News segment with Sway. "[But] I have to make the best of what's going on right now. I'm using this time instead of letting this time use me."

Another journalist granted permission to interview Chad was Matt Sonzala.** Matt, who was much closer to Bun than Pimp, convinced Bun to ride out to the Terrell Unit with him on March 20 for the scheduled interview. The idea was that he would present Bun as his "assistant" and manage to snap a photo of UGK together, separated only by a glass partition. But as they pulled up to the Terrell Unit, it seemed as though Bun was having second thoughts. He announced that he'd forgotten to bring his ID.

Matt stared at him in disbelief. *Dude, bullshit. You forgot your ID?*

Matt assumed Bun was hesitating because of the possibility that it would get Chad in trouble. C-Murder, in a New Orleans jail awaiting his second trial, had been granted permission to do interviews with *Court TV* and a local cable-access show.*** He used the opportunity to film a music video for "Y'all Heard of Me," which didn't amuse the Jefferson Parish Sheriff Harry Lee. "He will not make another video while he's in my jail," Lee promised *Billboard*.

The previous year, T.I. had pulled a similar stunt at the Fulton County Jail in Atlanta. Somehow, an inmate managed to slip out through an employee exit while T.I. was shooting a video

---

(*The song also appeared as "Something Going Wrong" on a few underground UGK bootlegs like *The Lost Tracks*.)

(**Quotes from Matt Sonzala's interview with Pimp C ran in *The Source* Magazine's July 2005 article "Locked & Loaded," and he posted the Q&A in its entirety on his blog HoustonSoReal.blogspot.com.)

(***In January 2002, a 16-year-old named Steve Thomas was shot and killed at a nightclub outside New Orleans. Witness accounts varied, but in the fall of 2003, C-Murder was convicted of second-degree murder by an all-white jury; the charge carried an automatic life sentence. His conviction was overturned the following year when a judge ruled that prosecutors had withheld information about some of the witnesses' criminal history. The decision was reversed by an appeals court and then went to the Louisiana Supreme Court.)

intro for his Hot 107.9 Birthday Bash performance. Although authorities insisted the two incidents were unrelated, they'd been thoroughly embarrassed by the headlines plastering *USA Today* the following morning: "Inmate escapes jail while rap video filmed."

Bun and Matt certainly didn't want to risk pissing off the very people who held the power over Chad's freedom. But as he walked inside alone, Matt wondered if the more likely explanation was that Bun wasn't sure how his partner would react to seeing him.

Publicly, Bun said all the right things. "Niggas be hurting [in prison], and it's not just for commissary – [it's] for human contact," he told *The Source*. "[Anybody] can write a letter, buy a disposable camera and take pictures. Sometimes that's all it takes to get them [through]."

The media and the public loved the feel-good narrative of the "Free Pimp C" movement, the faithful partner holding things down for his brother. But it wasn't entirely true. In fact, the reality was that Pimp hadn't heard from Bun in two and a half years.

"I'm just not a good letter writer," Bun shrugs. "What am I gonna write him in a letter and tell him? That I love him, that I miss him? He knows that. There wasn't any information on what's going on in the streets that he [didn't] already know ... [he had] other opportunities and means of getting information."

Bun didn't visit, either; Mama Wes overheard him saying that it was just too far to drive. "I was never really comfortable with seeing him in prison," Bun admits. His excuse was that he didn't want to occupy space on Chad's visitor's list, which was limited to 10 people and one visit per weekend.

"I love Bun dearly, but Bun is lying," says Mama Wes. "Bun didn't *wanna* go see C; that's the truth of the matter."

"What Bun did with the whole 'Free Pimp C movement' [was] a good thing in the street's eyes, to keep the [UGK] fire lit ... to the public," says Tim Hampton. "Bun held it down in the street's eyes, but everybody was not in the streets."

Most of Chad's family and friends believed that Bun was pocketing the proceeds from the "Free Pimp C" t-shirts, a notion which Bun disputes. "That was always a misconception ... I have never made any money off of 'Free Pimp C' [merchandise]," Bun says. "I only *wore* Pimp C t-shirts. I never *sold* t-shirts. I never made some for other people. [When I saw] people everywhere making them and selling them ... at first I got real offended ... because people were making money off my brother's name. [But] it's kind of like a catch 22, because at the same time, it's getting the message out there, and people are only buying them to show support."*

"I thought [the 'Free Pimp C' campaign] was a big cash cow for his family," says Russell Washington, who recalls seeing the merchandise at chain stores like Foot Locker. "If the family didn't get a big chunk of all that money, then somebody made a lot of money."

Mutual friends understood that there was more going on beneath the surface. "I don't respect some of the things that Bun didn't do for Pimp, but at the same time, it's some things Pimp didn't do for Bun," says Born 2wice.

"When Chad went to jail, he left Bun by hisself," adds Donny Young. "So he was mad at that shit, right? So he did all the necessary work and 'Free Pimp C' shit, but he was mad!"

Chad often vented to Wendy Day in letters. "[Bun] don't get at me much," he wrote, adding, "I ain't mad at him (just hurt)."

But his disappointment with Bun remained private. Publicly, he lauded his partner's support. "It's like he took everything on his shoulders and held me up," Chad told the *Beaumont Enterprise*. "I'll ride or die with him at any cost, right or wrong, for richer or for poorer ... I

(*According to Bun, the only licensed t-shirts were a collaboration with Algierz. "It was great knowing I wasn't forgotten about, but at the same time, a bunch of that stuff was not licensed," Chad told the *Dallas Morning News*. "They used my likeness without permission." Chad said he planned to pursue legal action against people who had sold unauthorized Pimp C merchandise, but it was unclear how he would locate those people.)

wouldn't trade this man for nobody or nothing on this small planet," he told *XXL*.

He also shouldered the blame. "Part of that was my fault," Chad told *XXL*. "For a long time, he wasn't on my visitor's list. You can't have but 10 people on your list. I knew the man wasn't trying to come to no prison anyway. So I wasn't going to ask for him to come down here. [But] I knew what he was doing. He was working. He was doing the best thing he could do for us. And I understood that. I knew that. He was on the grind every day. I knew how to reach him. He knew how to reach me. What was there to talk about?"

Besides, Bun wasn't the only one absent. "[You] got all these entourage [members] and these so-called homeboys talking about they're gonna ride to the end, [but] as soon as you get in trouble them dudes gonna be blowing in the wind," Chad told Dwayne Diamond. "You go to prison and you see how many of these dudes gonna ride with you and gonna put money on your books and gonna come see you. You know who gonna be there? Your mama."

As Bun waited in the car outside the Terrell Unit, Chad told Matt Sonzala his version of the Sharpstown incident for the first time on the record:

I'm in a mall, I'm by myself, I'm in a store and I got a cell phone up to my ear. I tell the manager, "I need this pair of shoes" and I got my back turned. There's a group of five people, three girls and two guys. I hear a conversation going on behind me. One of the girls ask the girl behind the counter, "Who's that?" And the girl proceeds to tell her, oh that's Pimp C whoop de whoo, this and that, gets to naming some songs. So real loudly and real belligerently the broad goes, "Oh! I don't listen to them old pussy ass niggas." Like that, right? So uh, I'm on the phone with Bun at the time [and] I tell him, "Hey man, lemme call you back."

So I hang up and I turn around and when I see them broads, I asked her, I said, "Hey man, uh, why you gotta talk my name with that shit in ya mouth?" You know what I'm sayin'? So me and the broad, we get in a little argument but it's really funny. People laughin', you know what I'm sayin'? She crackin' on me, I'm crackin' on her, and in the process I got the best of her.

So the broad was like uh, "Yeah nigga, I got your bitch, this such and such street," and she reached off in her jacket and when she did that I lifted up my jacket and showed her the thang. So when I showed her the thang I said, look, I said, "Freeze, don't move no mo'." And I look over at the two dudes and I say, "Mane, don't even try it," and the dude put his hands up and said, "Man, we don't want it." And I tell them, "I don't want it either, man." I look back at the broad and I say, "Y'all need to back up out this store, this not funny no more."

That's the incident that led to me getting locked up here. I ended up getting charged with aggravated assault for that. They said that was an assault 'cause I showed them my pistol.

"Are you happy that [your solo] record is out?" Sonzala asked.

"I mean..." Chad paused. "What do you mean, 'happy'?"

"In one sense it can keep your name alive and it's a hot record; people like it," Sonzala said. "You might not be able to reap the benefits now, but can you see the big picture and what this coming out can do for you in the future? How do you feel about that?"

"I'm gonna be honest with you," Chad answered. "I don't like the idea of other people producing songs with my lyrics ... I'm a producer first, remember that, and we have a certain standard, I feel. Can't nobody do me like I can do me. So naw ... other people sitting around playing with my freestyle verses and trying to make songs out of them, naw, that's not a very charming idea. But now, on the flip side, it's good to hear another record out. It's good to know that somebody still cares and ... some money is getting generated while I'm just sitting here."

Even though he hadn't even heard the album, he told the Associated Press that he'd approved the project because he trusted J. Prince. "James Prince is like my godfather and I respect him as a businessman," Chad said. "[He] found a way to generate some capital."

Still, he resented the fact that the album was perceived as his solo debut, since it certainly wasn't his best work. "That shit wasn't no solo album," he told *FADER*. "It was a good way to make some money right quick, but it wasn't no *album*."

Rapper releases hit album from prison

By Kristie Rieken
The Associated Press

ROSHARON — From the seclusion of his prison cell in rural southeast Texas, Pimp C said he had little reason to celebrate the release of his first solo album.

He could barely stand listening to his own songs: The music coming from the radio didn't sound like his work at all.

"It just hurts my stomach to think that some dudes were sitting around producing my songs and taking freestyle raps and making songs out of them," Pimp C, half of the celebrated southern rap duo Underground Kingz or UGK, told The Associated Press in a March jailhouse interview. "It's kind of strange. It's like I'm dead but I'm not dead. Like they trying to make a post-mortem album."

"The Sweet James Jones Stories" was created from a series of freestyle raps he did years ago that Houston-based Rap-A-Lot Records turned into the 14-track album. Even without his support or any of the usual hype that accompanies an album release, Pimp C's record sits at No. 8 on Billboard magazine's latest list of top rap albums.

Pimp C, whose real name is Chad Butler, said he hasn't heard the album, which debuted at No. 3 on the rap

Lottery Results

Pick 3
March 26, day: **2-2-3**
March 26, night: **3-7-9**

Cash 5
March 26: **37-36-13-8-12**

Lotto Texas
March 26: **35-34-20-1-29**
Bonus number: **13**

Texas Two Step
March 24: **11-24-25-27**
Bonus number: **25**

Mega Millions
March 25: **11-18-19-45-49**
Megaplier number (x4): **2**

AP/DAVID J. PHILLIP

Rapper Pimp C, whose real name is Chad Butler, is shown during a jailhouse interview at the Terrell Unit of the Texas Department of Criminal Justice near Rosharon this month. He has been imprisoned since January 2002 after violating probation by falling behind on the community service requirement of an aggravated assault plea stemming from a dispute with a woman in a mall.

charts, and he barely recognized the two songs he caught on the radio as his own.

"I'm not talking down on the producers that worked on the record, but can't nobody do me like I do me," he said. "Had I been out there, none of that stuff would have made it to the record."

It's the rapper's first solo album after selling well over 1 million records since 1992 from five major-label releases with UGK.

But then he fell behind on the community service required after he pleaded no contest to aggravated assault. He was charged after brandishing a gun during an argument with a woman at a mall. He began an eight-year sentence in January 2002 and will be eligible for parole in December.

Stripped of the accoutrements that fame and wealth bring, he's not the royalty he was as Pimp C, the underground king. But inmate No. 1136592, with the easy laugh and endless, "Yes, Ma'am's," comes across as far more of a gentleman.

The album, like those during his days with UGK, is full of brash tales about money, cars and women, sprinkled with drug references and delivered with profanity-

laced lyrics in his rich southern drawl. Rap-A-Lot records released the album under their new distribution deal with Asylum and the Warner Music Group.

In a visiting room at the Texas Department of Criminal Justice's Terrell Unit, about 35 miles south of Houston in rural Rosharon, Pimp C is introspective while discussing his lifelong love of music.

Pimp C, 31, can trace his interest in music back to his childhood days in Port Arthur — the South Texas coastal town that Janis Joplin also called home — where his family owned a jukebox that played blues, rock 'n' roll, jazz and country.

"That's how I came up listening to everything," he said. "Music don't have no color or no face. It's a universal language. I think being exposed to all that kind of stuff influences the way I make records."

His route to rapping had an interesting twist, though.

Pimp C studied classical music in high school and his choir traveled Carnegie Hall to perform an Italian sonnet. He became the first student in Port Arthur to receive a Division I rating on a tenor solo at the University Inter-

scholastic League choir competition.

Pimp C met UGK partner Bun B in junior high school, when Bun was bused to Pimp C's school for accelerated learning classes.

A single, "Tell Me Something Good," off their first independent album "The Southern Way," accidentally got mixed into a contest on a Houston radio station and sold out the next day. Calls from major record labels quickly followed.

UGK signed with Jive Records before Pimp C's 18th birthday. He dropped out of high school as a senior to focus on his music career, but has since earned his G.E.D.

Pimp C spends his days serving food in the prison cafeteria and his nights reading books and writing songs — he's penned more than 2,000 since his incarceration.

The roughest part of prison, he said, is being away from family, which includes two sons, 11 and 4, and a 3-year-old girl. His daughter was less than a month old when he went to jail.

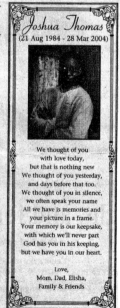

Joshua Thomas
(21 Aug 1984 - 28 Mar 2004)

We thought of you
with love today,
but that is nothing new
We thought of you yesterday,
and days before that too.
We thought of you in silence,
we often speak your name
All we have is memories and
your picture in a frame.
Your memory is our keepsake,
with which we'll never part
God has you in his keeping,
but we have you in our heart.

Love,
Mom, Dad, Elisha,
Family & Friends

Above: An **Associated Press feature** on Chad, March 2005.

As one of the journalists recruited by Asylum Records to interview Pimp C as part of their promotional campaign for his Rap-A-Lot album, I found myself speeding down the freeway south of Houston in a bright orange wrapped OZONE/CRUNK Energy Drink truck on March 21, 2005. It was a gorgeous spring afternoon, puffy clouds dotting the clear blue sky as I pulled onto a rural road in Rosharon.

I'd been sheltered and homeschooled throughout most of my childhood and finally left home at 17, eager to explore the world. While studying computer science at the University of Central Florida in Orlando I landed a corporate IT job at an architectural firm with a full salary and benefits, but was quickly bored. I couldn't envision myself sitting at the same desk from 9-5 every day for the rest of my life.

Looking for some excitement, I started experimenting with photography, shooting model comp cards and album covers for aspiring local rappers. I started covering local nightclubs and concerts, coming home regularly at 3 or 4 AM and struggling to stay awake the following morning during 8 AM board meetings in the silent hum of the conference room.

About a month after I'd mentally clocked out of the job, I was officially fired and swore I'd never work for anyone again. I fell into publishing almost by accident, initially intending it as a way to display my photography. My calls to publications like *XXL* and *The Source,* inquiring about photography and design opportunities, were never returned. After a brief stint as co-owner of Mert Deezine's *Orlando Source* Magazine, I branched off on my own and launched *OZONE* Magazine in May 2002.

We started distributing the magazine by hand, first in Orlando, then dropping off a box or two in nearby cities like Tampa and Miami. We started getting calls and emails from DJs, rappers, and promoters asking for a box to distribute in their city. By 2005, *OZONE*'s coverage had expanded to the entire Southeast region of the country and we were making monthly runs to drop off boxes of magazines in nearly every city from Orlando to Houston and back. And our timing was impeccable; not only was Houston experiencing a "musical renaissance," but rappers all over the South were breaking through on a national level.

It was 1996 when I'd first been entranced by Hip-Hop, starting with OutKast's *ATLiens* and Tupac's *Makaveli* album, but UGK wasn't on my radar at the time. I was still playing catch-up, and didn't know much about Pimp C. I relied on others, like our music editor DJ Wally Sparks and journalist Matt Sonzala, to fill me in. Matt and Wally had briefed me the previous night with some Pimp C questions.

As I parked at the Terrell Unit, I stuck my video camera in the center console of the truck and then paused. I heard the voice of my old boss, Jim Flynn, who always told me: "Ask forgiveness, not permission." I hadn't requested permission to film the interview, but no one had told me I *couldn't*, either.

I approached the guard booth, video camera in hand. He said nothing about the camera, simply handing me a sign-in sheet. I skimmed the list: James Prince, *XXL* Magazine's Vanessa Satten.

"Butler again, huh?" the guard asked dryly.

My impression on entering the waiting area was that it was a bizarre setup. Inmates were secured inside a large glass cage and visitors sat down outside the cage. "It was just a weird jail," recalls Vanessa Satten. "The jail, the whole vibe, it was weird. If you told me we were in 1964 and there were people outside picking cotton, I wouldn't have been surprised ... everything about it was surreal."

In a rectangular room was a large glass enclosure, light streaming in from the afternoon sunshine. Chad emerged in the empty waiting room wearing a standard TDC white jumpsuit and a black rosary with a cross.

I'd started sending him monthly copies of the magazine in preparation for our visit. I'd barely settled in on the hard wooden chair when he asked sharply, "Who owns this magazine?"

He sounded mad. *Shit.* Were we getting off to a bad start already? I couldn't think of anything negative or controversial we'd printed about UGK. "Me. I do," I said.

"*You* own it?" he asked incredulously.

"Yeah," I nodded.

He seemed to relax, the mood lightening. "Yeah, it's good," he said, his voice softening. "I like it, man."

The man on the other side of the glass was nothing like I'd envisioned "Pimp C" to be. He was mellow and softspoken, speaking slowly and taking time to think before he answered my questions. His quiet demeanor was almost unnerving.

Midway through our interview, I still wasn't sure *why* he was in prison; eight years for a probation violation over an argument at a shopping mall sounded extreme. I wondered if I was missing something. "It seems like you're doing a lot of time for a somewhat minor offense," I said cautiously. "Do you think if you had a different lawyer, or more money or something, your situation could have been handled differently?"

He sighed. "I had a whole bunch of money. I had the best lawyer. There was nothing they could do," he said. "I was real frustrated at that time, you know? I was spending my own money to get out. It isn't a money thing. If it's in your plan and it's supposed to happen, then it's gonna happen. You can't even try to stop it."

I nodded.

"I feel like I got put on the shelf, preserved, so I could come back and do something positive," he continue, speaking slowly. "Maybe I will be in a position where I can prosper when I get out. I'm not going to challenge it, I'm just gonna take it for what it's worth. If 'Pac hadn't got out [of jail], he might still be alive today. Maybe there was a worse fate out there awaiting me. Feel me?"

He'd made a similar statement in his interview the previous day with Matt Sonzala. "Maybe [prison is] helping me more than I know it is," he'd mused. "Maybe if I would have been out there I might not be alive right now. I might have crashed a Benz full of syrup and weed and killed myself, then y'all [would] be wearing RIP Pimp C shirts instead of Free Pimp C shirts."

"Has your relationship with Bun B changed at all due to your situation?" I asked.

Chad cocked his head to the side. "In what way?" he asked.

"I guess, personally," I said. "I mean, he's kind of had to step up to keep your name out [there]."

"He's kind of in the position of being the mother and the father," Chad agreed. "So he's carrying the weight of UGK on his back. He ain't have to do that. He could've just as easily pushed me out of the way and focused on just himself. He ain't have to keep focusing on me, he ain't have to get out there and wear them shirts and keep hollerin' 'Free Pimp C.' He's under a tremendous amount of pressure, so I appreciate that."

As I drove off, something he'd said kept resonating:

At one time, the East [Coast] was very hostile towards us. They were like, 'That ain't real Hip-Hop that y'all are doing, so we don't wanna hear y'all. We don' care how many records you sell, it's not real.' After buying all [their] records for so many years, it was like a slap in the face to us. If we ain't from New York City, we don't got the right to rap? We don't wear backpacks so we can't make records? So, after trying to be accepted for so long and never being accepted, we turned our backs … We don't wanna be accepted [by you] now. We've got our own thing down here. We don't wanna listen to you, and we don't care if you don't wanna listen to us. We're gonna do our own records and sell our own records to our own people.

I departed feeling like I had a new ally, a comrade at war. Pimp C's attitude struck a chord; it was exactly how I'd been feeling but hadn't yet been able to articulate: if you don't want me to be a part of what you're doing up there, I'll do it my own way down here.

I'd spent years trying to figure out how to get "in" the music game, how to become a photographer, but was always treated like an outsider at industry events. It wasn't so much hate as it was ignorance, the simple assumption that we didn't exist; didn't matter.

As I traveled city to city throughout the South, watching virtually unknown artists perform to packed crowds rapping along with every word, I was usually the only photographer or journalist in sight. I couldn't believe no one else was covering this. I rarely met anyone who worked for major magazines; I was under the impression that they spent their day in a cubicle somewhere in a skyscraper in New York, completely out of touch with what was happening out here in the field.

As *OZONE* gradually gained attention from major record labels, they seemed fascinated, marveling at our "grassroots" efforts in marketing meetings. To me, it was only natural. How could you possibly cover what was happening in the community if you weren't actually *there*?

I'd watched many other Southern artists reach the same conclusion as Pimp C: if New York wasn't going to accept them, they'd do it their own way. As a result, by the time Southern rappers finally broke through nationally, they'd already spent years on the underground circuit perfecting their craft and building up a fan base.

A movement was growing, not only in Texas, but all throughout the South. "These New York labels are so fucked right now," Miami rapper Pitbull told me during a 2004 *OZONE* interview. "Thank you so much for overlooking us and teaching us how to grind and how to sell your own shit and how to make our own relationships. It's ridiculous, really, 'cause you go up there [to New York] sometimes and they don't wanna show nobody love. Thank you very much to the labels for overlooking the South, teaching us, putting us in a position where we had to learn how to do it ourselves. We appreciate that very much. Thank you. I will laugh all the way to the bank."

The video footage from the prison made me a hero at my next stop, in Jackson, Mississippi, where a crowd of people gathered around the *OZONE* truck at a local car wash to watch Pimp C on my small handheld camcorder.

I didn't know it at the time, but my visit had left quite an impression too. When Mama Wes came to visit the following weekend, Chad told her about his interview with "dat gu'l" from *OZONE* and suggested we should meet.

A female? Oh, no, thought Mama Wes. She despised feminine, frilly, women trying to make it in the business world. The cutthroat music business was no place for a woman, Mama Wes thought, and most of them didn't know what they were getting themselves into. "I don't wanna meet that bitch," Mama Wes said.

Chad knew exactly what she meant. "Oh, no, Mama. You're just like her."

"I am?" she asked.

"Yeah, she a bitch just like you," he laughed. "She ain't one of them."

Chad was also visited by several mainstream media outlets, like the *Beaumont Enterprise,* which grilled him about his lyrics "filled with images of violence, drugs and misogyny."

"We were these angry kids," Chad explained. "Our friends were getting killed, getting locked-up. The police were harassing us. We were trying to say the most shocking things that we could say because we wanted to rebel against the establishment ... [but] stuff I said at 17, I don't say at 31."

"My mind was sick, street sick, from being out there," he admitted. "I had all kind of vices ... my body was poisoned."

He was also visited for a filmed segment with Fox 26 News anchor Isiah Carey, who asked if he felt guilty for his crime. "For leaving my kids, of course," Chad said. "Of course I [feel guilty]. Wouldn't you? Yeah, *I've* put me here. *I* allowed for this situation to happen where these people could get me caught up in this system."

Conversation turned to the rising Houston Hip-Hop movement. "It's a blessing," Chad said. "Mike Jones keeps screaming my name. Lil Flip is screaming my name. Paul Wall is screaming my name."

At home in Houston, Paul Wall stared at the TV in disbelief. *Damn, man,* he thought. *He said my name!*

Paul, who looked up to Bun like an older brother, had recorded a Texas tribute song called "They Don't Know" which included a sample of Pimp C yelling, "Texas, muthafucker, that's where I stay!" (from "Murder") on the hook. He'd heard about Pimp C's volatile temper and wasn't sure how he would react to the song.

"When he come out, you think he gonna be mad at me?" Paul asked Bun, seeking some words of reassurance. "He ain't gonna be talking shit about me or nothing, is he?"

Bun merely shrugged and deadpanned, "Shit, I don't know. He might come out talking shit about *me.*"

After the noncommittal reply, Paul decided to write Pimp and introduce himself as a fan. ("I would want people to write me a letter [if I were in prison], you know?" he laughs.) Paul nervously rewrote the letter four times, making sure everything was spelled correctly and his handwriting was crystal clear.

Pimp wrote back suggesting that Paul should reach out to Mama Wes. "Give her a call, I think she would like to talk to you," he wrote.

Too $hort wasn't a big letter-writer either, but felt he had to make sure Pimp C knew he wasn't forgotten. "A lot of times when my homies get locked down, I feel like a couple of words from the 'dog always brings good vibes," $hort says. He dropped him a three page letter with some "real homie shit, some funny shit, some you-got-something-to-look-forward-to-when-you-get-home type shit." Killer Mike, a new addition to the Dungeon Family who had been profoundly impacted by UGK's early material, also sent a letter offering some words of encouragement, explaining, "You're my fuckin' hero."

As Pimp C's address circulated in magazines like *OZONE*, fan mail came in from UGK supporters all over the world. Prison officials looked the other way when women of all races mailed him sexy pictures, some catering to Chad's fetish for "hairy pussy" which he often rapped about. One letter from an unidentified woman included a print out of the lyrics to Marvin Gaye's song "I Want You" with a post-it note attached ("I Love You Chad!!") and a picture of him onstage thrusting his pelvis with the words "won't be long!"

Raven in Hawaii admired his mugshot in *The Source*, suggesting he should grow his goatee back and offering to ship some chocolate-covered macadamia nuts as a souvenir. J'Vonda, a woman serving in the military in Iraq, sent pictures of herself in a red velvet catsuit ("I'm sure you love big asses so here's a pic of me and my big ass!"). Stephanie, a mother of three who identified herself as "a country ass white girl from Alabama," promised to "fuckin' frame it" if he wrote back, adding that she played UGK loudly in her "cracker ass community" to "make sure they hear yall all the time … weather they like it or not."

The letters ranged from the lighthearted to the heavy. "My [daughter's] father passed away earlier this year, and yesterday I sat in my living room and listened to 'One day' on my discman," wrote Lars, a woman from Norway. "[My daughter] was just laying with her head on my shoulder (not knowing what I was listening to) and at the part where your saying 'one day you here and baby the next day your gone', she started crying, as if she knew what you was saying. I felt I had to tell you how your music has travelled from Port Arthur, Texas, to Bergen, Norway, and how it touches people so far away."

While Smoke D spent six years in prison in Mississippi, it was his dream of coming home to work with UGK that helped him get through. His crew, the Hustle Squad, were also banking on the idea that once Pimp came home, Smoke D was going to become a star and bring the whole camp along for the ride. They all viewed it as a huge setback when Pimp C had gone to prison just a few short weeks after Smoke's release.

Smoke became good friends with David Banner, who was already a fan based on his affiliation with UGK. Smoke appeared on Banner's debut album *Mississippi*. Smoke also became good friends with Jaro Vacek, a talented photographer who had come to Mississippi as a foreign exchange student from the Czech Republic.

Smoke and Jaro became inseparable, bonding over their common love of marijuana and traveling throughout the South as Smoke tried to relaunch his rap career. He was hopeful that when Pimp returned, he could make enough money doing music to stop hustling. "I felt like once Pimp got home, I could totally get the streets off of me [and] I wouldn't have to be involved in none of that," Smoke explains.

Jaro couldn't understand why Smoke didn't seem in much of a hurry to release music. His father tapped into some family funds to launch a label called God, Family, Music Entertainment (GFE) and invested in wrapped vans and billboards, but they had no product to sell.

"Smoke, what are you waiting on?" Jaro asked him one day. "You have the buzz, everybody's just looking at you everywhere we go. Why we ain't having no shows and making releases?"

Smoke shrugged. "I'm just waiting for Pimp to get out, and we gonna go hard."

A few weeks after Smoke appeared wearing a "Free Pimp C" t-shirt in David Banner's "Ain't Got Nothing" video, he rode to Houston with a friend named Stan Shepherd, known around Jackson as "Hot Boy." Stan had a record label called Ball or Fall and had recruited Smoke to drop three verses for $3,000.

As they passed through Port Arthur, they stopped by Mama Wes' house for a homecooked dinner. Smoke was a frequent visitor, often staying for three or four days. But this trip, Mama Wes sensed something was off. She'd never met Stan before and didn't like his vibe. She tried to convince Smoke to stay for a few days.

"No, Mama, I'm going to do this music," he told her as Stan waited in the car to pull off.

"I ain't convinced of that," she said disapprovingly. "You can tell *yo'* mama and *yo'* daddy that, but now you talking to Mama. I ain't convinced that's what you going to H-Town for. So all I can tell you is, 'be careful,' but I really wish you'd stay."

A few days later, on May 17, 2005, Stan picked Smoke up in a brand new rimmed-up Mercedes-Benz CLK 600. Smoke discreetly inspected the trunk as he dropped his duffle bag inside. When they stopped back at Mama Wes' house, she recognized the new car immediately and knew they were up to something. She intercepted them in the driveway. "Smoke, please get out of that car," she demanded. "Please get out of that car and stay with Mama a few days."

He declined. "I don't have no clothes."

"That's a terrible excuse," Mama Wes said. She'd fed and clothed dozens of houseguests over the years, all the way from baby Chaddyboo to UGK's enormous bodyguard Big Munn. "Smoke, you know I got every size drawers that any man has ever worn in this house. I've got every size Dickies any nigga ever wore, and they're all fresh and clean."

"Aw, Mama," Smoke said, exhaling a cloud of smoke and flicking ashes from his blunt onto the driveway. "Don't worry about it."

"And why are you smoking?" she demanded. *This fool, a black man, a convicted felon, plans to drive down the Louisiana freeway in a brand new Benz with rims, smoking weed?*

"Why don't you stay? I'll call your wife," she offered. "She'll believe me. She's gonna believe Mama. She knows Mama ain't gonna do nothing but feed you."*

Stan and Smoke hit the highway instead. The Benz was pulled over less than 100 miles down I-10, just outside Jennings, Louisiana. The officer, who claimed they'd been following too closely behind an 18-wheeler, separated the two men and asked where they were coming from. Stan, who thought he would look suspiciously like a drug trafficker if he said he was coming from Houston, lied and said he was coming from Lake Charles. Smoke told the truth.

With these conflicting stories, police grew suspicious and called in a drug-sniffing dog. In the trunk, police discovered a hidden compartment with 15 kilograms of cocaine. And inside Smoke D's duffle bag was a two-shot Dellinger pistol, which he was prohibited from carrying as a convicted felon.

"I had a gun because … I would go somewhere and do a rap for somebody and get $6,000 – $7,000 [cash]," Smoke explains. "I'm 315 pounds; nobody gonna fight me, y'know? They're gonna *shoot* me."

Both Stan and Smoke agree on one point: the drugs didn't belong to Smoke. "[Smoke] wasn't gonna make a dollar off of this deal," Stan says. "From my understanding, he didn't sell drugs no more. He was rapping." According to Smoke, the drugs actually belonged to Cuzzo, the incarcerated drug dealer who had once offered him the transportation job. Smoke says he didn't know that the job had been offered to Stan after he declined.

Regardless, both men were charged and appeared the next morning before a judge. Stan's bond was set at $150,000, while Smoke, as a convicted felon, had to post $250,000 bond. (Stan says he put up the money to bond both of them out; Smoke believes the funds actually came from Cuzzo.)

On her visit the following weekend to see Chad at the Terrell Unit, Mama Wes shifted uncomfortably in the stiff wooden chair in the visiting room, telling her son about Smoke's predicament.

Jennings, where the men had been arrested, was in Jefferson Davis Parish.** Mama Wes was from neighboring Acadia Parish, and considered Jefferson Davis Parish the absolute worst place in the country for a black male (*especially* a convicted felon who had previously murdered a woman at point-blank range) to be caught with a trunk full of drugs and weapons. She couldn't believe he'd been so foolish.

"It was dumb! It was just dumb," she told Chad. "That's Jeff Davis Parish! He's going to jail. The minimum is going to be 20 [years]. Ten automatic, just for the guns."

Chad thought aloud, wondering how he could help Smoke, but his mother advised him not to get involved. "Please don't fool with that," she begged. "Please don't get into that. It won't do any good." She advised him to stay focused on his own situation; someone else's legal troubles was the last thing he needed to be worried about.

(*While Mama Wes recalls Smoke and Stan passing by her house shortly before their arrest, Stan believes it happened on a different trip. Smoke's recollection of the incident is vague.)
(*Louisiana is divided into parishes instead of counties due to its Catholic heritage. Smoke and Stan were arrested in Jefferson Davis Parish, named after the Civil War-era politician who served as the President of the Confederate States while the South attempted to secede from the United States in the 1860s.)

CHAPTER 36

"I was writing rhymes in there but really on my day-to-day I was concentrating on prison life and how to make it to the next day. I wasn't thinking about all that [rap] shit. Late at night, yeah, I dreamed of what it'd be like to get back. But ... it's a day to day mental struggle to stay sane in that place and to stay afloat and don't go under and be able to ride the wave." – Pimp C

"I figured out [that prison time] added to my life, but I didn't figure it out until the last minute. [I had said a] prayer, [which] went like this: 'Don't let me die.' I seen everybody dying around me and it was total destruction, and the only way to save me from death was to hide me. And I didn't figure it out until the last year [of my time]. But I turned a negative into a positive." – Pimp C

In June 2005, Chad Butler's file was one of some 6,000 pulled by the Texas Board of Pardons and Paroles for consideration.* His father had paid the $1,500 fee to hire Lori Redmond, the parole attorney recommended by Donny Young.

During Cognitive Intervention class one afternoon in June, Chad wrote a letter to Wendy Day, asking if she had a contact on Jay-Z. "Did you see the MTV shit I was on? What u think? *Source* inteview? *XXL*?" he wrote.** He also asked for advice on seeking a distribution deal. "I can't rap forever for other MTHFKS Wendy!" he wrote. "We owe Jive one more album then what do I do? Bun don't want to have shit! He's happy just rappin on other niggahs records but I want a record lable! I want to be well respected as a biz man (as well as a producer and rapper)! Am I movin to fast or what?" His letter continued:

What I want is a record lable (a respected lable not just a name plate)! Whatz up with David Banners album? I ain't herd nothing on the radio yet! I like the Snow Man (Young Jeezie or Geezie I can't spell shit yet)! His shit is hot! They on the radio sayin them Trill Ville boys are down wit Rap-A-Lot down here! Have they lost there minds are is the shit not true! When I see James (he comes to see me) Ill ask him what it do! I think Bun signed as a solo artist with them? For the record I am not on Rap-A-Lot as a solo artist or anything else Wendy! I know better than to sign anymore shit with anyone!"***

(*More than 72,000 inmates were considered in 2005 and only 19,061 were approved, for an overall approval rating of 26%. It was the sixth straight year the Texas Board of Pardons & Paroles charted well below their expected approval rating of 40%. In 2006, the Sunset Advisory Commission, an entity created by Texas lawmakers to "eliminate waste, duplication, and inefficiency in government agencies" issued a highly critical report of the inefficient Parole Board. The report pointed out that the Parole Board's low release numbers were costing the state millions of dollars. In 2003, the average cost to incarcerate an inmate in Texas was $41.64 per day in a state-operated facility. A later study by the Vera Institute of Justice estimated that the cost was actually as much as 34% higher. Based on these figures, it is reasonable to assume that the State of Texas spent more than $81,464 to keep Chad Butler incarcerated.)

(**XXL's July 2005 issue included a feature on incarcerated rappers like C-Murder and Pimp C, using the interview Vanessa Satten did when she visited in March.)

(***Chad was critical of Atlanta-based rap group Trillville both for their name and their "crunk" style of music, which he felt they'd bit from Three 6 Mafia. In an interview with *On Tha Real*, Chad said he didn't approve of the group's name because Port Arthur was "the real Trillville." He added, "We the original trill niggas – we made that word, trill. That's a Port Arthur thing. All these other niggas that's talking about being trill is playing with themselves." Trillville member Don P had signed a side deal with Rap-A-Lot for his group Trilltown Mafia, which was recording at Houston's Studio 7303 while Chad was at Terrell. In a later interview with WordofSouth.com, Chad clarified that he had "nothing against those [Trillville] boys" and wanted to "see them prosper" but felt that they should give proper credit to UGK and Port Arthur for coining the term.)

But Im makin it Wendy! I got this shit beat! At one point (in 2002) I didnt think I was going to make it! That picture of me on that Source cover was at my low point! But I gripped my nuts and got my head right! Now after this I know I can do and have anything I want! And what I want is a record lable (a respected lable not just a name plate)!

Whatz up with David Banners album? I aint herd nothin on the RADIO yet!

I like the Snow Man (Young Jeezie or Geezie I cant spell shit yet ☺)! His shit is hot! They on the radio sayin them Trill Ville Boys are down wit Rap-A-Lot down here! Have they lost there minds are is the shit not true? When I see James (He comes to see me) Ill ask him what it do! I think Bun signed as a solo artist with them? For the record I am not on Rap-A-Lot as a solo artist or anything else Wendy! I know better than to sign anymore shit with anyone!

Anyway, Get back to me when you have some time to white ☮

C.L.B

Above: A portion of **Chad's letter to Wendy Day** from the Terrell Unit in Rosharon, June 2005.
Courtesy of Wendy Day

By summer, the heat at Terrell was unbearable. "It's hot like a MTHFKA down here," he wrote Wendy. "You'd wake up in the morning and find a man who died in his sleep because he overheated," he told *OZONE*. "It gets hotter than a muthafucker down here ... they've got people living in that hot ass shit with no real form of ventilation."

"They've got fans, but it's too hot down here for that shit," he added. "These muthafuckers won't spring for some type of cooling system. I ain't sayin' that niggas are supposed to be laying up in the shade, but damn, you've gotta keep that shit from getting past 85 or 90 degrees. With all the money that the state of Texas is making off these prisons, they won't even cool it off. They keeping us like cattle."*

By July, Chad had a new job as a library clerk. Being "surrounded by radios and books" in the air-conditioned library was a dream job compared to the other options. He'd inherited his mother's love of the library and felt right at home. The job was easy; he'd spent an hour cleaning up and organizing books and have the rest of the day to read.

"[If] you wanna hide something from black folks, they say you can put it in a book. I don't believe that, 'cause I done read four libraries full of books," he said later on "Livin' This Life." His favorites included Niccolò Machiavelli's *The Prince*, Milton William Cooper's *Behold a Pale Horse*, Sun Tzu's *The Art of War,* and Steven Sora's *Secret Societies of America: From the Knights Templar to Skull and Bones.*

Wendy Day sent him a copy of the *48 Laws of Power*, which they discussed at length in letters. ("If you want to read about how to protect yourself from deception go get the book '48 Laws of Power,'" Chad suggested in a letter to a fan. "It will help you re-co when people are runnin 'Game' on any level.") "A lot of people in Hip-Hop really like the *48 Laws of Power*," the author Robert Greene noted on CNBC. "The music industry has to be perhaps the most Machiavellian environment that there is and [rappers] find the advice very helpful."

Another favorite was Fredric Dannen's *Hit Men: Power Brokers and Fast Money Inside the Music Business*, a book explaining how the music industry was designed to financially benefit record label owners, not artists. Chad saw parallels between the music industry and the pimp game, which was solely designed to benefit the pimp.

He'd return to his dorm around 9 PM after things had cooled off and entertain himself with thriller novels by his favorite author, James Patterson. He also enjoyed novels by J. California Cooper, Teri Woods, and Sister Souljah.

Wendy Day also sent *Confessions of a Video Vixen*, a controversial book by Karrine "Superhead" Steffans documenting her years of sexcapades with high-profile celebrities. "This broud SuperHead™ is off the chain! I wounder if all them niggahz knew they was messing with the same girl? This rap game is a trip!" Chad wrote Wendy, adding, "PS / Im glad I didn't end up in the book!"

When he wasn't reading, he was writing or listening to music, scribbling down song ideas and lyrics on scraps of paper. "I keep a little piece of paper by me, and when I hear [an] old-school song that I might wanna sample, I write the title and the group down. If I don't know, I just write out how the hook sounds [and] I'll go find the record when I get out," he told *XXL*.

Prior to his arrival at the Terrell Unit, he'd already written close to 2,000 songs. He didn't anticipate that they would all become actual records, but viewed it as a necessary process to maintain his creativity. "I was trying to keep my skills up and stay polished in what I do, because it's easy to get away from the art form," he told Dwayne Diamond.

He found it a challenge to spell out his production ideas on paper. "I never produced like this before," he told *XXL*. "Hopefully, when I get home and I read this stuff, it don't sound like gibberish and maybe I can still capture the ideas." Without access to musical instruments, he resorted to notes for songs he wanted to sample, like Marvin Gaye's "I Heard It Through the Grapevine" ("string loop after verse"), Earth, Wind and Fire's "Can't Hide Love" ("sing the virse

(*In 2013, inmate advocacy groups were outraged when it was revealed that TDCJ spent $750,000 on climate-controlled "swine buildings" to keep pigs cool as they awaited being slaughtered for inmates' dinner. "They serve that dirty-ass swine five days a week," Chad complained in *XXL*.)

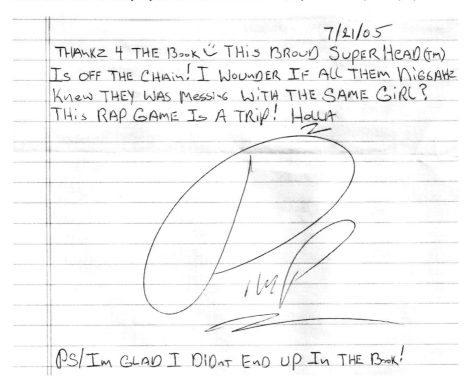

7/21/05

THANKZ 4 THE Book & THis BROaD SupER HEAD (TM)
Is OFF THE CHain! I WOuNDER IF ALL THEM NiGGAHz
Knew THEY WAS Messing WiTH THE SAME GiRL?
THis RAP GAME Is A TRip! HoLLA

PS/Im GLAD I DIDnT EnD uP In THE Book!

re play music"), Rick James' "Ghetto Life" ("play new bass"), Marvin Gaye's "Sexual Healing" ("redo song with him in the hook"), or The Isley Brothers "That Lady" ("speed up or replay bass line").

He planned to sample portions of various songs, like the break of Sade's "Smooth Operator," the horn from the end of Stevie Wonder's "I Wish," the piano from The Lovin' Spoonful's "Summer in the City," the organ from Harold Melvin & the Bluenotes "Wake Up Everybody," the intro from the Bee Gees' "Night Fever" and Sheryl Crow's "My Favorite Mistake." (Chad apparently didn't know Sheryl's name, referring to her only as the "white girl artist."

"It's kind of wild to read production ideas on paper," he told *OZONE*. "If something pops in your head at two or three in the morning, you don't wanna lose it."

On the back of an envelope he paraphrased a Public Enemy song ("they say that I'ma criminal – don't believe the hype") and jotted down a line from T.I.'s "Motivation" ("kant even look me in my eyez / put yo face down / Im out of jail now what u got to say now").

After picking up some lotion, cotton swabs, aloe cream, toothpaste, deodorant, refried beans, beef pot roast stew, and sausage summer beef from the commissary, he scribbled some Young Jeezy lyrics ("I got real clientel / we ain't brakin down shit we don't need no scale" and "He worth a mill on the low / cuz the weatha man say it's a light chance of snow") and a nod to the Notorious B.I.G.'s 1995 hit "Player's Anthem" ("How you livin sweet jones? Im suroundid by criminal / shisty individualz") on the receipt. It was covered with production ideas, along with a list of "Album title ideas":

$weet Jone$ Greatist Hit
$weet Jone$ (Biggi$t Score)
Reveng of $weet Jone$

When the IRS sent an ominous notice informing Chad that he still owed $291,889.89 in taxes for 2000 and 2001, he turned it upside down and wrote a song on it called "More Bounce":

Sport Polo Horses / Fuck Hilfigur*
[…] Got a boat load of dope nigga sellin waight
These other pussy niggahz out here is fake
[…] I got the best deal on a hole key
Fuck the Mexican you can do it wit me
I let the bird fly for ten-5
You pay fifteen my bitch a take the ride
And drop that chicken right at yo dow

Sometimes, he used more traditional writing material, counting out bars on yellow lined sheets. "Im home now no mo sellin free Pimp shirts and hat I'm back," read one line from a song titled "Gripin The Gran." There was "Pimp" (which would sample the bass line from Grover Washington Jr.'s "Let It Flow"), which began:

Too $hort is a mfkn Pimp
Pimpin Ken is a mtfkn pimp
Cool Ace is a mtfkn pimp
Jayz is a mtfk he's a mthfkn Pimp
Good Game, Ice T, Snoop Dogg, Don Juan, Ice Duck
Sweet Jones I'm A Mthfkin Pimp to my heart
Check game and my name I been a pimp from the start / start
I'm shittn on the pot / wild them other niggaz fart

Another planned song titled "Jason Grant (Bitch)" (a reference to a 1979 novel published by Holloway House, the home of Iceberg Slim) would sample Leon Haywood's 1975 hit "I Want'a Do Something Freaky To You":

I'm Pimp C Bitch
But don't take that shit wrong
Thatz just the way I like to start off my songz
I bet yo pussy is long and them hairz is to
A young niggah wana freak off wit you
I can make u squirt when I go in yo but
I make u cum like u got 2 nutz

There was an ode to a prostitute titled "Pimptential":

The bitch got pimptential / yu can see it on her face
Everybody stop when she walk up in the place /
Style she got grace / she was born a pro
Could have modelled for a stow / but she chose to hoe /
Sunshin sleet or snow / she jumpin out cadilac dow
Leave the scratch on the dresser and leave the heater on the flow

And a marijuana tribute titled "Mary Jane":

I wit her in the evnin luvin her at night
My California bitch make a nigga feel right
We ridin in the rover got my eyez real tight
Got my hi beamz on and I'm flyin like a kight
She like to get around I ain't mad at the girl
If you got the money right you can have her in yo world
When you see the pussy cat itz fuzzy like a squerl

(*A line from "Choppin' Blades" on *Dirty Money*.)

MARY JANE

I WIT HER I.. THE EVNIN LUVIN HER AT NIGHT/
MY CALIFNIA BITCH MAKE A NIGGA FEEL RIGHT/
WE RIDIN IN THE R~VER GOT MY EYEZ REAL TIGHT/
4 GOT MY HI BEAMZ ON AND IN FLYIN LIKE A KIGHT/
SHE LIKE TO GET AROUND I AINT MAD AT THE GIRL/
IF YOU GOT THE MONEY RIGHT YOU CAN HAVE HER IN YO WORLD/
WHEN YOU SEE THE PUSSY CAT ITZ FUZZY LIKE A SQUERL/
8 FIRST TIME YOU GET TO HIT/YOU GONA LICK ON THE PEARL/
SHE GO BOTH WAYZ/THE WOMEN LUV HER TOO/
YOU OUTA SEE THE THINGZ SHE BE TELLIN EM TO DO/
SHE MAKE EM TAKE OFF THEY CLOTHZ/GET XSPOSED
12 AND WANTA GET DOWN ON THE MTHFKN FLOWZ/
SOME CALL HER A GANGTTA SOME CALL HER KILLA/
BUT IF YOU FREAK WIT HE ONES YOU GOTZ TO FEEL HER/
I BEN DOWN WIT HE SCENCE 91/
THE WOMAN GREEN THAN A BITCH BUT MAN SHE BIG FUN/

LEON HAYWOOD/ 20TH CENTURY RECORDS
I WANA DO SOMTHIN FREAKY TO YOU
"JASON GRANT" (BITCH)

IM PIMP C BITCH/BUT DONT TAKE THAT SHIT WRONG/THATE JUST
THE WAY I LIKE TO START OFF MY SONGZ/ I BET YO PUSSY IS LONG
AND THEM HAIRZ IS TO / A YOUNG NIGGAH WANA FREAK OFF WIT YOU /
I MAKE U SQUERT WHEN I GO IN YO BUT/ I MAKE U
CUM LIKE U GOT 2 NUTZ/
IS YOU DOWN OL WHAT/ I CAN TELL THAT U IS / I NEED A
BIG FINE WOMAN I DONT PLAY WIT NO KIDZ/AND I DONT NEED
TO FUCK AROUND MAKEN TAPES LIKE KELLEY/ SO LET ME GET U
WHERE WE GOIN SO I CAN JAM WIT YO JELLY/
LET ME PUT IT IN YO BELLY/ BUST ON YO STOMIK/BUT I
AINT PULLIN OUT MY JONES TELL U TELL ME U COMIN/
I AINT GONA GIVE U MY HEAD AND IT AINT CUZ I AINT DONE
IT/ IT JUST AINT TIME FOR THAT YET/ BUT IM GONA SEE
WHAT IT DO/ YOUNG BITCH/ IM GONA GET FREAKY WIT U/

Above: **Song ideas** from the Terrell Unit, 2005. Courtesy of Weslyn Monroe

GROVER WASHINGTON (LET THE BASS GO) Dol Re-PLAY   "Pimp"   10:22 pm
5/27/05

Too SHoRT Is A MFKy Pimp/ PimPin KEn Is A MTFKy
Pimp/ Cool ACE Is A MTFKy Pimp/ JAYz Is A MTFKi/
He's A MTHFKy Pimp/
Good GAME Is A MTHFKy Pimp / Snoop Dogg Is A MTJEKy   LATER ICE-T
Pimp/ Don JuAn Is A MUTHFKy Pimp/ ICE DUCK Is A
MUTH / He's A MUTHAFUCKn Pimp/
 Sweet Jones Im A MTHFKin Pimp To MY Heart/
CHeak My GAME And MY nAME I Been A Pimp From THE
START/ START
Im SHittn on THE PoT/ wild THEm OTHER niggaz FART/
Got Mo MACK In MY BRAin THAn THEY Got SHiT AT   OPm
WAL MART/④
And I Been Down BY LAw Sence THE AGE oF 16/
Come From PoRT ARTHUR TexAs We sip CoLD phonitHHzin/
WATCH THAT HoE SwiTcH Hot ASS/ UnDER CADDY Hi
Beamz/ Now WATCH THAT TRICK GeTin SUcked
UnDER 5 inch ScReenz /⑧
You THink IT Stop IT Aint Gona Stop/ Been Goin
on Sence THE Beginin oF Time / Some niggaz
Pimpin WiT THEy Gulz Some niggaz Pimpz WiT THese
RHYMES/ Some niggaz THink/ THAT THEy Pimpiy/ THEy
onLY Pimpin In THEy MinD/ He MiGHT noT Be A
TRUE one YET/ BUT I Aint Gona nok Him Cuz   MACK
He TRyin/⑫
And Pimpz Go UP And BRown Come Down/ I Got BiG
Rockz OFF In MY CRown/ BUT I Dont wHole IT on
MY HeAD/ I Keep IT on A CHAin AnD IT HAnG Down/

Above: Handwritten lyrics for a song idea called **"Pimp"** from the Terrell Unit, May 2005.
Courtesy of Weslyn Monroe

To my Nutz/ He Got THAT CUT/ I GOT THAT YOU'LL
NeveR WIP/ THATz WHY MY PHoNe IT ALWAYS BUZZin
WiN Im GUIDiN THE MUTHA SHIP/
Sweet JoNes Is A MUTHAFUCKiN PimP/ PeRCY MACK He's
A MUTHAFUCKiN PimP/ JoHN Ross Is A MUTHAFUCKiN PimP/
PimP C He's A MUTH/ He's A MUTHAFKN PimP/
Osun B Is A MTHFK PimP/ MJG Is A MTH FKn PimP/
BX6OBALL Is A MTFKn PimP/ BiG BLACK Is A MUTHA/
SHE's A MUTHFKn PimP/
TRicke TRick AT niGHT Time/ TRicke TRick In DAY/
THE oNly THiNG ScARe A MACK Is wHeN He AiNT
NoTHiN To SAY/ THAT BiTcH GoNA Be A Hoe NewTHeR
WiT You or RUN AWAY/ So NiGGA U Need To sToP
TRYiN To SAVE THE BiTcH EVERY DAY/ THAT TRAMP/
DoNt LUV U/ THAT FLUZZY LUV To ScRew/ So sToP
TRYiN To PreDicT WHAT THAT ProstiTUT GoNA Do/
So Let He HAVE HeR WAY/ Let HeR FReaK OFF EVERY DAY/
Let THE BiTcH EAT uP DickE UNTell SHe Suck HeR
LifE AWAY/ IF SHE ReAl THAN SHe GoNA LAST IF
SHe FRAWD THiAN SHe GoNA FALL/ BUT EITHeR WAY
Im GoNA DRiVe CADPiLOcz AND BALL AT EVERY MALL/
NiGGA Yo SWiP CoULD Be LoNG or NiGGA Yo DicK
CAN Be SMALL/ IT ReAly DoNT MATTeR LoNG AS
Yo CoversaTioN STRoNG/ CUZ Im GoNA Tell U
THis/ AND I AiNt GeT IT oUT No BookZ/
SiR CAPTAN ToLD Me PiMPiN AiNt GoT SHiT To
Do WiT LookZ/ IF U PreTTY U CAN CATcH EM
BUT ITz Yo MoUTH THATz GoT To HoLD EM/ CUZ THE
GAME Is IN No BRAiN NiGGA ITz NoT oFF IN Yo ScROTUM/

First time you get to hit you gona lick on the pearl
She go both wayz the women luv her too
You outa see the thingz she be tellin em to do
[...] I ben down wit [her] scence 91
The woman green than a bitch but man she big fun

Chad wasn't the sentimental type and usually didn't keep his handwritten lyrics. "The only other time I ever had tablets full of rhymes was when me and Bun went to high school, 'cause we didn't have no records yet," he told *XXL*. "After the first record, all our songs were wrote in the studio. [We'd] go in the booth, we spit it, we tear the paper, throw it away. So I never actually had tablets of rhymes." Concerned his writings could get lost, he'd mail them home 10 at a time to Mama Wes or Chinara, who stuffed them in a Neiman Marcus bag.

"I [also] didn't wanna keep my rhymes on me 'cause they'll come put a bogus case on me and lock me up, [and] when I come back all my rhymes [are] gone," he said on the *Pimpalation* DVD. "Or [they could] go in my rhymes [and] they see me rappin' about hustling or doing something, and [they'll] say, 'Oh, this [is] what you wanna do when you get out? [They could] Xerox that shit and put it in my file, [so that] when [the] parole [board] open my shit they reading rap songs."

But song ideas were just a way to pass the time. "I was writing rhymes in there but really on my day-to-day I was concentrating on prison life and how to make it to the next day," he said. "I wasn't thinking about all that [rap] shit. Late at night, yeah, I dreamed of what it'd be like to get back. But ... it's a day to day mental struggle to stay sane in that place and to stay afloat and don't go under and be able to ride the wave."

―――――――――

In mid-July 2005, Bun came to visit for the first time in nearly three years. "He's good, doing his solo album right now!" Chad wrote in a letter to Donny Young. "I had not got to see him scence I left Harris County Jail [in 2002]! He's workin hard right now!"

Bun had been at Houston's Studio 7303 working with producers like Mannie Fresh, Jazze Pha, Lil Jon, and Salih Williams on his solo album. For the first time in his career, recording felt like *work*. Bun realized how lucky he'd been for the past decade, having "the easiest fuckin' job in the world – show up and rap to Pimp C tracks."

"It feels real fucked up rapping without Pimp. You have no idea," Bun told *XXL*. "I don't feel as creative. What I do right now ... this is 9-to-5 type shit ... A UGK album was never work to me. [But] this is labor."

The album was filled with Pimp C references, especially on the triumphant "Draped Up (H-Town Remix)," which borrowed its hook from Lil Keke's "Pimp Tha Pen" freestyle on DJ Screw's *3 'N Tha Mornin' Pt. 2* and featured literally every rapper in Houston.* "Please free Pimp C," begged Lil Keke. "Tell Pimp hold his head," chimed in Lil Flip.

The only record featuring Pimp C was the lead single "Get Throwed," produced by Mr. Lee. Pimp and Mr. Lee had spent some time in the studio together in the late 90s while working on Scarface's platinum double album *My Homies*. Mr. Lee had some leftover Pimp C vocals on a Roland vocal machine and managed to extract them using a software program called Digital Performer. "Pimp was so far ahead of his time you could go back ten years and listen to stuff that he rapped and put it on beats today and it'll be relevant right now," Mr. Lee notes.

The record also featured Z-Ro on the hook; Bun made some calls to arrange for Jay-Z, who had recently "retired," to drop a verse. Bun strategically placed Jay-Z's verse last to ensure that radio DJs would play the whole song. When Bun recruited rising rap star Young Jeezy to drop a verse on "Keep Pushin'," Jeezy heard the incomplete version of "Get Throwed" with Jay-Z and volunteered to drop a verse on that, too.

(*Russell Washington was irritated that Bun didn't request a clearance for the sample. "You found it on a gold record [released by Big Tyme] and didn't even call me and ask me for permission?" Russell says incredulously.)

Mama Wes and Chinara made the trip faithfully to the Terrell Unit with the kids every weekend. "It's a hell of a thang raising your kids from a penitentiary cell," Chad said. "That's some hell of a shit trying to concentrate and trying to raise your babies through letters … That's some cold shit."

Chad Jr., initially weary of the long drives, now looked forward to seeing his father every weekend. Being able to embrace him, even if he was wearing a white jumpsuit, was certainly better than peering at him through a glass in the ugly orange County Jail uniforms. "[He was always] being strong," Chad Jr. recalls. "[I] didn't see any weaknesses [in him], and as long as he wasn't being weak, I wasn't either."

Most of all, Chad felt guilty for leaving when his daughter was just a baby. "It's hard because she only knows me in prison," he told the Associated Press. "She don't know no better."

"[My son Corey] was like a year old when I left," Chad told WordofSouth.com. "But he's not a square either, he know what the fuck went on. [My kids] know who their father is, and they know that people hate on us, because they out there living it too. Ya know what I'm saying, folks is gonna hate, because anything they don't understand, anything they can't control, they gonna hate it. So my kids take a lot of slack because of me."

Chad had never been very athletic, and during rec time while other inmates were playing basketball or lifting weights, he could usually be found reading a book and eating commissary snacks. Spending all day in the kitchen didn't help, and being in the library kept him sedentary throughout the summer. He'd gained nearly a hundred pounds during his incarceration.

During one visit, Mama Wes was disturbed to notice him doze off as he talked to his kids. She came alone the following weekend to try to figure out what was going on. "Are you like, 'not there' sometimes?" she asked.

Chad admitted that he'd been having trouble sleeping at night and sometimes caught himself dozing off in the daytime. His symptoms sounded familiar; Mama Wes had a friend whose overweight husband had recently been diagnosed with severe sleep apnea. She suspected Chad's extra weight was causing the problem. "I'm gonna do some more research," she said. "But it sounds like sleep apnea problems that you're having."

Parole attorney Lori Redmond came to visit Chad in mid-September and was optimistic about his chances at parole, estimating his chances at 85-90%. Still, he tried not too get too excited about the possibility. "It's an 'if,'" he'd told MTV. "I don't want to concentrate on the 'if.'"

"If it's my time to go [home] then I'm gonna go," he told Matt Sonzala. "If there's still something [here] I need to see, then I'm gonna stay here to see it. This is divine intervention right here. I'm not in [prison] just because. So when it's supposed to be over, then it'll be over and I'll go home."

Chad's scheduled interview with the parole board caseworker was delayed due to the fast-approaching Hurricane Rita. As dawn broke on the morning of September 21, he was one of thousands of inmates cuffed in leg irons and escorted onto white buses, where they spent hours in traffic with thousands of other evacuees fleeing the incoming Category 5 hurricane. Residents were understandably cautious after seeing the widespread destruction caused by Hurricane Katrina just three weeks earlier in New Orleans.* The National Hurricane Center predicted a 20-foot storm surge over the Texas coast, along with dangerous winds, heavy rain, and possibly tornadoes.

Prior to the storm, Chad had been getting discouraged with his music. "I done ran out of things to write about," he'd told the *Beaumont Enterprise*. "A lot of rappers go to prison and they

(*Nearly two million evacuees from New Orleans settled in Houston in the wake of Hurricane Katrina, causing the city's population to grow 10% nearly overnight.)

> IF Pimp C Aint produce It THEn THE SHit Aint TRill
> And IF Sweet Jones Aint white It THEn THE SHit Aint Real
> I Got PLATinuM on My NECK It WoRTH A 100 GRAnD!
> RockZ on My WRisT My Pistol Close AT HAnD
> Im A SeLF MADE MillionaR FRom RYMES AnD BeaTZ
> NEVER Been To No AWARDS BUT STILL We THE SHit
> on THE STReetz
> You SAY You Never HeRD OF Me Well I CAn See
> How Its TRUE
> Wild Y'all WAS WATcHin MTV We WAS BAnGin on
> ScReW
> We THE UnDERGROunD Kings Its not Just A nAME,
> We FifTEEN Years In It And We STill In THE GAME
> I Done Been To THE Pen STAYED   CAME BACK
> AnD THE DAY I TouchED Down I BousHT A
> BRAnD nEW LACK A XLR WiTH A BLowD out
> ToP Cuz Aint Really Nothin LiKE DRiVEn A DRop
> I BoustT MAMA A STS AnD My GRAnDMAMA Too
> Now Tell Me WHAT THE FUCK WAS I SupposTo Do

Rita Flood 9/24/05

come out and write songs about prison [but] I haven't seen anything that's fly enough to write about in here." But all the movement seemed to spark Chad's creativity; he jotted down ideas for several records, with the notation "Rita flood" in the margins:

> *If Pimp C ain't produce it then the shit ain't trill*
> *And if Sweet Jones ain't write it then the shit ain't real*
> *[…] The day I touched down I bought a brand new Lack*
> *A XLR with a blowd out top*
> *Cuz ain't really nothing like driven a drop*
> *I bought mama a STS and my grandmamma too*

Mama Wes, who had no idea where Chad had been relocated and was "worried to death" about him, was in the midst of evacuating Port Arthur with Chinara and Christian in tow. "It was horrible," she recalls. "My worst nightmare."

Hurricane Rita made landfall on September 24 with a direct hit on the Port Arthur seawall. Many downtown homes and businesses were destroyed, with significant damage throughout the rest of the city.* The house on Shreveport Ave. remained intact, but Mama Wes spent several weeks at a Houston Residence Inn while the power was out.

When authorities notified residents that they could return during daylight hours to re-

(*FOX News correspondent Geraldo Rivera filmed a dramatic segment in downtown Port Arthur, displaying empty streets and rows of abandoned buildings. "Look at what Rita did to this town! It's gone. Just gone!" he yelled, apparently not realizing that the area had been nearly a ghost town since the oil industry slipped into a decline in the 1970s.)

trieve their belongings, Mama Wes found 100 pounds of spoiled shrimp stashed in the garage. "As I was throwing away my money, I was really sad," she recalls. "C cried when I told him about the shrimp I threw away."

Chad's father, who waited out the storm in Louisiana, returned to Port Arthur to find significant damage to the house on 13th Street. The carport was gone; while climbing on the roof to inspect the damage, he fell and landed on his left knee but managed to avoid serious injury. "You got to know how to fall (smile)," he wrote Chad.

Another song Chad wrote shortly after the Rita evacuation, titled "Trillest of the Trill," borrowed from his verse on Crooked Lettaz' "Get Crunk":

I'm the trillest of the trill
You the fakist of the fake
Pussy ass niggaz in the club tryin to playa hate
Wild I'm standing hear drapped in diamonds
I'm down wit made niggaz them choppin on blade niggaz

The following day he jotted down two pages of lyrics for a song titled "What The Fuck Im Suppos To Do," which included the following:

Cuz I'm a choose luva
Under cover
*Never poke wit out my rubber**

Four days after Hurricane Rita hit, a Hummer H2 was pulled over with a broken tail light near the airport in Jackson, Mississippi. The driver, a tall man named Larry with dreadlocks described as "unkempt" in the police report, produced a badge. He claimed he was a police officer from the tiny town of Winstonville, Mississippi.

Lieutenant Johnson with the Pearl Police Department, concluding that something "seemed strange" about the situation, radioed for backup. The Chief of Police in Winstonville said he didn't know Larry, but Larry insisted that the mayor of Winstonville, Milton Tutwiler, had personally given him a badge.**

In the passenger seat was a Mexican man named Daniel Hernandez. Police searched the vehicle and found more more than $20,000 stashed in the center console, as well as a brown leather bag in the backseat which contained a set of digital scales and marijuana residue. Both men were arrested and charged with conspiracy.

Bun's *Trill* album, featuring an all-star cast of guest appearances including T.I. and Ludacris, landed atop the charts. "When the *Trill* album came out, it was like my album came out that day," Chad told *OZONE*. "It was like I had a breath of fresh air blowed into my career."

Since their initial correspondence, Chad and Paul Wall had become regular penpals. Paul had connected with Mama Wes and stepped into a father figure role for Chad Jr. and Corey, taking them to the mall, McDonald's, or the swimming pool whenever he was in town. "Paul Wall has been there [for the boys] in every way," says Mama Wes. "Financially, physically … he was the most physical presence when C was in jail."

(*These lyrics would later be modified and repurposed for UGK's "Int'l Player's Anthem (I Choose You).")
(*The mayor of Winstonville, Milton Tutwiler, would later confirm that he had deputized Larry but failed to notify the Chief of Police. Tutwiler himself was already under investigation by federal authorities for fraud. Tutwiler had requested a $1.3 million dollar federal grant to build a chemical plant in the city and was accused of creating "false invoices billing for work … which had not actually been performed" from electrical/construction companies which did not exist to defraud the government of more than $500,000. Tutwiler allegedly used the funds to cover his gambling debts. Tutwiler was convicted and sentenced to 63 months in federal prison but died of cancer while the ruling was under appeal.)

Paul wore a "Free Pimp C" t-shirt in the video for his single "Sittin' Sideways," but television networks edited it out when it aired. "Got yo letter and my mom (and kids) told me how you got at em! Thank you for givin a fuck man!" Chad wrote Paul one evening from the library. "Yeah, I saw you had my face on yo shirt in yo video (even thou they blerd it out itz the thought that you tryid)!"*

"It's good to see you boyz getin play from EVERY direction right now!" he added. "It was harder for Bun + I back in 91 to get folkz in New York and Cali and the Mid West to open up to our music (cuz they just didnt understand). Now the spot light is on yall boyz, so don't drop the ball and get stuck in one style homie!"

"Itz goin down soon as I hit the streetz!" the letter concluded. "Like Dre 3000 sead 'The South got sumpthin 2 say!'"

On October 8, after hearing Paul's feature on rising Chicago rapper Kanye West's record "Drive Slow," Chad penned another letter to Paul:

Man you got doors open up so wide for you, all you can do is win! All this shit (rap shit) is yourz for the takin man! Remember itz 80% bullshitin and frountin; 10% talent and 10% pro-mo! If they think you the shit thatz what you are! Never get it twisted and start believing yo own bullshit (thinking you the shit)! Never play con on yoself always remember who you are but con the world that Paul Wall is the best thing scence sliced bread! The bigger you become the more humble you have to become! Thatz good game from me to you (no charge)!

O.K., yea I herd the "Drive Slow" and I like it! I like the fact that he got luv for the South (didn't know)! That beat is a old sample but he took it and played it a new way! I luv when MTH-FKZ take old shit and flip it to some new shit! Thatz what this rap is all about man! Please tell Mr West he getz nuff respect from U.G.K and boyz locked up feelin him!

As the letter continued, Chad, who was taking a course on STDs to become a certified health educator, abruptly changed topics:**

Yea, so I know you on the road right? And you fuckin wit some bad bitchez every night right? Just remember this! You are to valuable to be givin yo dick away to them hoez (for FREE)! And even if a hoe pay you to fuck, thatz revers prostitution unless she yo hoe and you pimpin on her! (Never let this game fall out yo head)! So what is a player to do? Stay ice cold as much as you can! When you do get hot be a choosse lover and if you can fly somebody you know about in to the city you going to be at to freak off with! (do that)

Fuckin wit strange pussy is like brushing yo teeth with another niggahz tooth brush! And if you just cant control yo nutz man ask the bitch some questions! Do she have herpies, HIV, HPV, (HAV, HBV, HCV, HDV, all OF THE A TO D ARE HEPITITUSS)? How many times she had the claps? Yea, don't be shy wit a hoe! If the bitch get mad or clam up just tell her ("Look Im just tryin to protect myself Lil Mama, you should be glad Im taking the time and you should want to know the same info about me")! Im giving it to you uncut man cuz itz real! A rubber don't protect you from herpies homie!

... I wouldnt even talk about this stuff with you if I didn't feel like you was a good dude! Im not fit to let no funky hoe ass bitch steal my dick when I get home BABY! I realy got my head on production right now man! I only did our beatz for the most part but I want to spread out! Get down wit the young dudes thatz comin up! Help boyz overstand that it ain't just about the 808 drum!

(*Mama Wes credits Chad's spelling to his elementary school teacher. "C couldn't spell, because she [emphasized] phonics, phonics, phonics," laughs Mama Wes. "He spelled phonetically for the rest of his life.")
(**Pimp C had always been a safe sex advocate in his own way. "Pimp C wanna live / Have you had your test? Are you H-I-positive?" he rapped as a teenager on "Tell Me Something Good." In 1995 he doled out some advice on "Satisfied" alongside underground Dallas rapper Kottonmouth: "See a bitch can suck your dick and she can squeeze your balls / But you don't really know what's coming down those pussy walls / It could be steaming, nigga, it could be VD / She could be fucking a nigga that used to fuck a bitch that used to fuck with Eazy [E]!" He followed that up on *Ridin' Dirty's* "Hi-Life" with "In 1996 niggas is dying from laying in that ass / First Magic Johnson got it, then Eazy-E died ... I wish that I could tell you I wore a rubber every time / But if I told you that, nigga, you know that I'd be lying.")

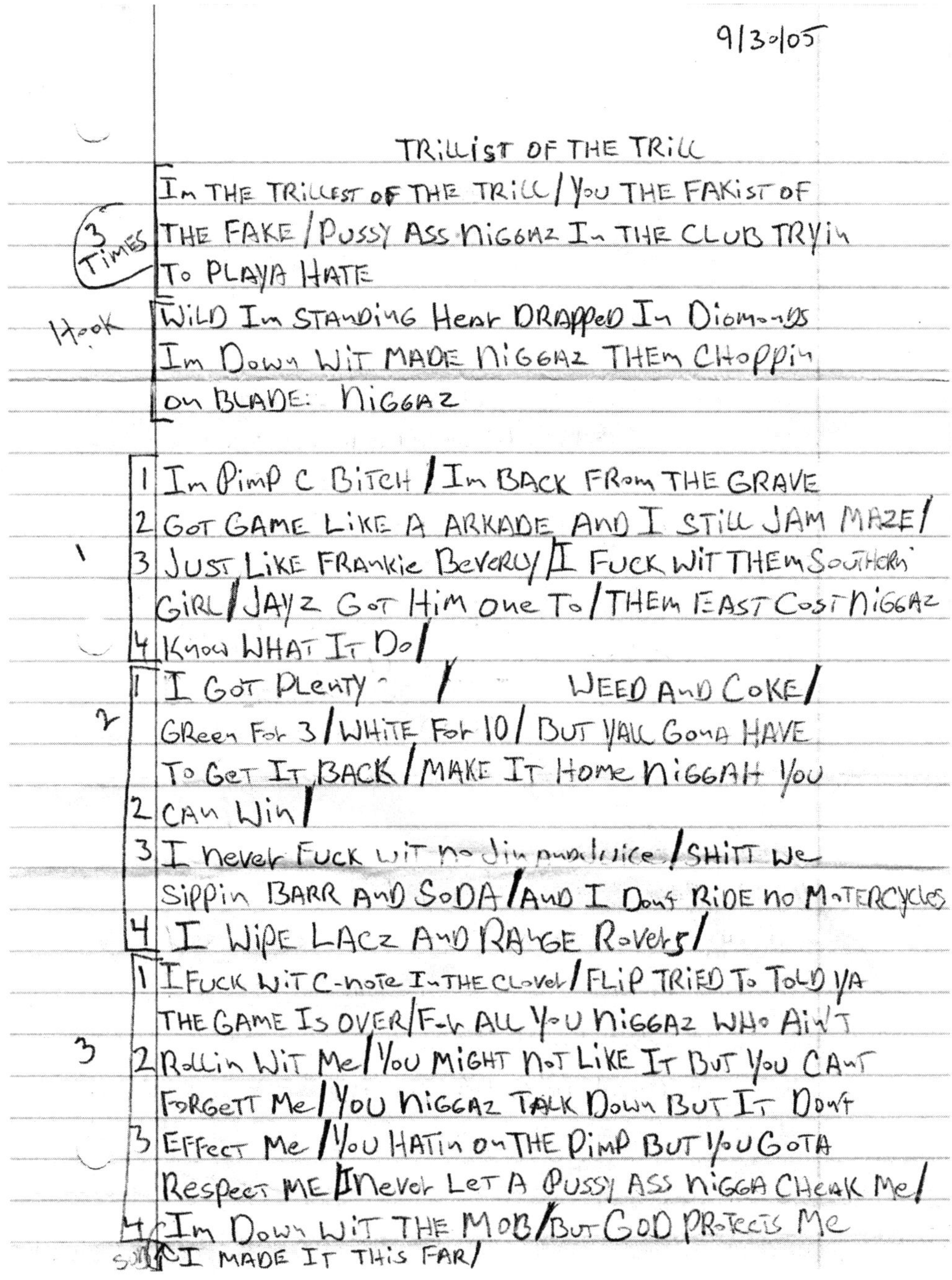

9/30/05

TRILLIST OF THE TRILL

Im THE TRILLEST OF THE TRILL / You THE FAKIST OF

(3 TIMES) THE FAKE / Pussy Ass niggaz In THE CLUB TRyin
To PLAYA HATE

Hook WILD Im STANDING Hear DRApped In Diomonds
Im Down WiT MADE niggaz THEM CHoppin
on BLADE: niggaz

1 | Im Pimp C BiTCH / Im BACK FRom THE GRAVE
2 | GoT GAME LiKE A ARKADE AND I STiLL JAM MAZE /
1 ⟍ 3 | JUST LiKE FRankie Beverly / I FUCK WiT THEM Southern
Girl / JAyz GoT Him one To / THEM EAST CosT niggaz
4 | Know WHAT IT Do /

2 1 | I GoT PLenTy   WEED AND CoKE /
GReen For 3 / WHiTE For 10 / BUT yall Gona HAVE
To GeT IT BACK / MAKE IT Home niggAH you
2 | CAn Win /
3 | I never FUCK wit no jim purdujice / SHiTT we
Sippin BARR AND SoDA / AND I Dont RiDE no MoTERCycles
4 | I WiPE LACz AND RANGE Rovers /

3 1 | I FUCK WiT C-noTe In THE CLovel / FLiP TRiED To ToLD ya
THE GAME Is OVER / F-h ALL You niggaz WHo Ain'T
2 | Rollin WiT Me / You MiGHT noT LiKE IT BUT You CanT
ForGeTT Me / You niggaz TALK Down BUT IT Dont
3 | EFFecT Me / You HATin on THE Pimp BUT you GoTA
RespecT ME I never LeT A Pussy Ass nigga CheAk Me /
4 | Im Down WiT THE MOB / BUT GoD PRoTecTs Me
SonG I MADE IT THiS FAR /

Above: Pimp C lyrics for a song idea titled **"Trillist of the Trill"** from the Terrell Unit, September 2005.
Courtesy of Weslyn Monroe

R.I.P
"DJ"
Screw
I MISS YOU
HOMIE (4 TRUE)
9/16/05
1:11 AM

C-MURDER HOLD YO HEAD UP!

"MYSTIKAL" IT'S ALMOST OVER BABY!

"JAY-Z" We Ready To Come To THE "ROC" So Get AT Yo FAM ASAP

"FAROU" I'M NOT OVER I'M COMIN GET YOU SOON AS I Get FREE BABY

Hello WORLD (ITz STiLL U.G.K 4 LiFE)

As I SET IN THis FUNKY ROTTEN MTHFKA ALL
I CAN THiNK OF Is How "HoT" I AM RiGHT Now! NoT
JUST THE FACT THAT IT'z "HoT" IN TEXAS AND AiNT
No WAY FoR US To COOL OFF IN THiS ROTTEN MTHFKA!
BUT RiGHT Now MY NAME Is "HoT" LiKE FiRE
THANKz To BUN-B AND THE REST WHO Keep SCREAMiN
"FREE PiMP C" AT EVERY CHANCE THEY GET!
I'M THANKFULL FoR ALL WHO Keep MY NAME OUT
THERE (FoR TRUTH)! ALL THE LUV Is GRAVY To ME
BUT AT THE SAME TiME LUV BREEDz HATE!
I'M A YOUNG "HoT" RED MTHFKA (A STREET FLAM)
AND CUz OF THis FACT ITz ALoT OF HATiN
ASS NiGGAHz THAT DoN'T LiKE ME AND WHAT
I STAND FoR! SoME IN GREY AND ALoT IN
WHiTE! WELL NEWS FLASH : I HATE YoU
BiTCH ASS NiGGAHz Too! ALREADY...
So To THE 30% THAT GoT LUV FoR $WEET JONE$!
THANK YoU! To THE 40% THATz GLAD IT'S ME
AND NoT THEM oN LoCK! I FEEL YoU! AND To THE
30% THAT ARE HAPPY I'M HERE AND WOULD LiKE To SEE
ME STAY! IT AiNT GoNA HAPPEN BiTCH! $iR
ILL SEE YoU oN THE SLAB ☮
         MUTHAFUCKERZ

"BUN-B" Keep BUSiN THEM NiGGAHz AS oN THEY OWN SONGS!!! IT IS SHoEN WHoTTiME BABY

"Project PAT HoLA AT Yo BoY

DA NiGGAz WoRD UP JOE

$WEET JONE$

Above: Pimp C's letter to fans for **OZONE Magazine's "Prison Diaries,"** September 2005.
Courtesy of *OZONE* Magazine

Chad at the Terrell Unit, March 2005.
Photo: Julia Beverly

Above: Chad's "victim" **Lakita Hulett** had a lengthy history of shoplifting arrests.

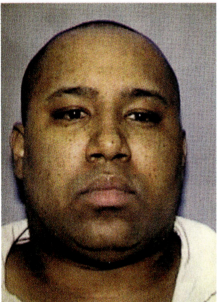

Chad was not happy about the inclusion of **his mug-shot** *(left)* on the **cover of *The Source*** *(below left)*. "That picture of me on that *Source* cover was at my low point!" he wrote in a letter to Wendy Day.

Below: Chad hung this **illustration of a "black angel,"** drawn by Mr. Soul, above his bunk at the Dominguez Unit in San Antonio.

Courtesy of Mr. Soul

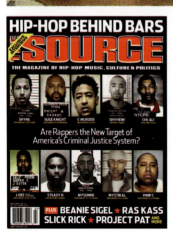

The DEA used **Phyllis Conner** *(left)* and **Ronald Carboni** *(right)* to help them ensnare *(below, L-R)* Rap-A-Lot employees **Edward "Spook" Russell** and **Stevon "Cash" McCarter**, as well as Scarface's friend **George "Spoonie Gee" Simmons** and his cousin **Byron Harris** in their investigation of **J. Prince** and **Rap-A-Lot Records**. Pimp C said he was approached by federal agents with similar offers while he was being held at the Harris County Jail.

J. Prince in Miami in the late 1990s.
Photo: J Lash

Pimp C and **Bun B** in July 2001, in the midst of Pimp's legal troubles.
Photo: Pam Francis/Getty Images

At the Harris County Jail, two of Chad's cellmates included fellow Houston rappers **Sylvester "Vesto" Bullard** *(below left)* and **Darrell "Pharoah" Burton** *(below right)* of Street Military.

Two other men Chad befriended in prison included radio personality Mean Green's son **Yakeen Green aka "Lil Green"** *(left)* at the Dominguez Unit and **John "Baz" Singleton** *(right)* of rap group The Outfit at the Darrington Unit.

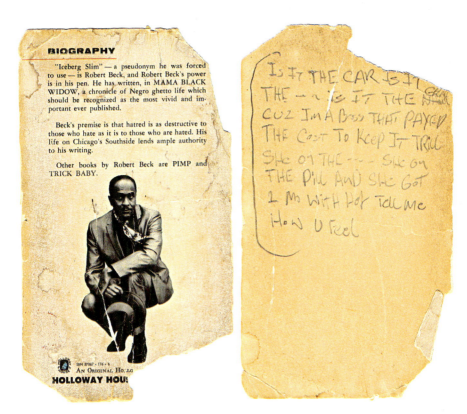

Above: Chad's handwritten lyrics on the back cover of an **Iceberg Slim book**. Courtesy of Weslyn Monroe
Below: **Mama Wes** taking the boys (Angie's son **Elijah** and Chad's sons **Chad Jr.** and **Corey**) to visit Chad at the Harris County Jail, 2002. Courtesy of Angie Crooks

10/8/05
9:40 PM

PAUL WALL
WHAT IT REAL-E IS YOUNG HOMIE!
GOT YO LETTER! MAN YOU GOT DOORS OPEN
UP SO WIDE FOR YOU, ALL YOU CAN DO IS WIN!
ALL THIS SHIT (RAP SHIT) IS YOURZ FOR THE TAKIN
MAN! REMEMBER ITZ 80% BULLSHITIN AND FRONTIN;
10% TALENT AND 10% PRO-MO! IF THEY THINK
YOU THE SHIT THATZ WHAT YOU ARE! NEVER GET
IT TWISTED AND START BELEAVING YO OWN BULLSHIT
(THINKING YOU THE SHIT)! NEVER PLAY CON ON YO SELF.
ALWAYS REMEMBER WHO YOU ARE BUT CON THE WORLD
THAT PAUL WALL IS THE BEST THING SCENCE SLICED
BREAD! THE BIGGER YOU BECOME THE MORE HUMBLE
YOU HAVE T> BECOME! THATZ GOOD GAME FROM ME
TO YOU (NO CHARGE)!
   O.K., YEA I HEAD THE "DRIVE SLOW" AND I LIKE
IT! I LIKE THE FACT THAT HE GOT LUV FOR THE
SOUTH (DIDN'T KNOW)! THAT BEAT IS A OLD SAMPLE
BUT HE TOOK IT AND PLAYED IT A NEW WAY! I
LUV WHEN MTHFKZ TAKE OLD SHIT AND FLIP IT TO
SOME NEW SHIT! THATZ WHAT THIS RAP IS ALL ABOUT
MAN! PLEASE TELL MR WEST HE GETZ NUFF RESPECT
FROM U.G.K AND BOYZ LOCKED UP FEELIN HIM!
   YEA, SO I KNOW YOU ON THE ROAD RIGHT? AND YOU
FUCKIN WIT SOME BAD BITCHEZ EVERY NIGHT RIGHT?
JUST REMEMBER THIS! YOU ARE TO VALUABLE TO BE
GIVIN YO DICK AWAY TO THEM HOEZ (FOR FREE)! AND
EVEN IF A HOE PAY YOU TO FUCK, THATZ REVERS PROSTITUTION
UNLESS SHE YO HOE AND YOU PIMPIN ON HER! NEVER LET
THIS GAME FALL OUT YO HEAD)! SO WHAT IS A PLAYER TO
DO? STAY ICE COLD AS MUCH AS YOU CAN! WHEN YOU DO
GET HOT BE A CHOOSSE LOVER AND IF YOU CAN FLY
SOMEBODY YOU KNOW ABOUT IN TO THE CITY YOU GOING
TO BE AT TO FREAK OFF WITH! (DO THAT)

Fuckin Wit Strange Pussy Is Like Brushing
Yo Teeth With Another Niggahz Tooth Brush!
And If You Just Cant Control Yo Nutz Man
Ask The Bitch Some Questions! Do She Have
Herpies, Hiv, HPV, (HAV, HBV, HCV, HDV, all of the A to D
Are Hepititus)? How Many Times She Had The Claps?
Yea, Dont Be Shy Wit A Hoe! Befor You Buy A Dog
Dont You Make Sho It Aint Sick? Well Do The Same
Wit A Hoe! If The Bitch Get Mad or Clam Up
Just Tell Her "(Look Im Just Tryin To Protect Myself
Lil Mama, You Should Be Glad Im Taking The Time And You
Should Want To Know The Same Info About Me")!
Im Giving It To You Uncut Man Cuz Itz Real!
A Rubber Don't Protect You From Herpies Homie!
    O.K, I Wouldnt Even Talk About This Stuff
With You If I Didnt Feel Like You Was A Good
Dude! Im Not Fit To Let No Funky Hoe Ass Bitch
Steal My Dick When I Get Home Baby! I Really
Got My Head On Production Right Now Man! I only
Did Our Beatz For The Most Part But I Want To
Spread Out! Get Down Wit The Young Dudes
Thatz Comin Up! Help Boyz Overstand That It
Aint Just About The 808 Drum! What About The
TR-909 or The 303? It Aint Just About The Moog
And The B-3. Im The First Niggah To Fuck Wit
The B-3 In A Rap Song! I Was Just Trying To
Do Somthing New! I Was Fuckin Wit The TR-808
Cuz Everybody Else Had Left It Alone For The
Most Part. Itz About Bringing New Shit To The
Table (But Whatz Old Is Whatz New)! Now Every Song
On The Radio Got A 808 Clap (As The Snar) And A
808 Kick Drum And The Hi-Hat Playin Trippl Time!
So Whatz Next? If You Think Ahead (Realy Reach Back
To The Past) You Can Beat Everybody To The Next
Movement!

Above: A Jive Records promotional photo for UGK's ***Dirty Money***.
Courtesy of Jive Records

Left: A proposed cover for ***Dirty Money*** designed by Mr. Soul.
Courtesy of Mr. Soul

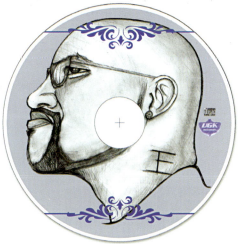

[Handwritten proposed tracklisting]

1 INTRO
*PLAYHARD ****
*FALLIN IN LOVE AGAIN / ***
*YOU AIN'T PAC / FEATURING PASTER TROY ***
*SAY MY NAME (FEATURING BUN B OF U.G.K ****
BIG DOGIN
FUCKIN WIT MY DIAMONDZ ON ***
*PIMP (OF THE YEAR) **
ALL MY CARS LEATHER + WOOD
GETO 4 LIFE (FEATURING BUN B OF U.G.K
LIVIN THIS LIFE (LORD ITS SO HARD) FEATURING BIG GIPP
OF THE GOODIE MOBS
SOUTHSIDE PART II — BONUS CUT
BRACK EM OFF 2002 BONUS CUT (FEATURIN THE
3-6 MAFIA
14 OUTRO   AND U.G.K
1 SHATERD DREAMS ****   (THE TRILL ASS 6 NIGGA
2 DON'T LOOK ANY FURTHER (PART I) ****
3 HOT STUFF **
4 FANTISY LIFE (YOU DON'T KNOW) ***
5 HAIRY HOLE ***
6 SHE NEVER LEFT (WHAT YOU TALKIN BOUT)
7 IN YOUR MOUTH *
8 GET MY PAPER TOGETHER
9 HEAVEN
10 THATZ WHAT I'M
11 GON OUT THAT
12 MAKE YOU WANT
13 SHAKE IT SHAKE

Chad wrote this proposed tracklisting for his **planned solo album *PIMP: The Sweet Jones Story***, which would've been a double album, around the year 2000. (Some songs listed were just ideas.) He also asked Mr. Soul to begin designing album packaging; the **proposed CD design** is pictured above.

A slightly edited version of "Play Hard" appeared on Trill Entertainment's *Ghetto Stories* and later on *The Sweet James Stories* under the title "I Know U Strapped." "Fallin' in Love Again" appeared on Sleepy Brown's *The Vinyl Room*. "You Ain't Pac," the proposed Master P diss record with Pastor Troy, never materialized. (Some have theorized that "Break 'Em Off 2002" would also have been a Master P diss record.) "Fuckin Wit My Diamondz On" later ended up being used twice, for Boosie and Webbie's "Finger Fuckin'" and Pimpin' Ken's "Diamonds On." "Livin This Life (Lord Its So Hard)" would presumably have been an extended version of Goodie Mob's "Free" interlude; Pimp later used this idea on the *Underground Kingz* double CD as "Living This Life." "Heaven" and "Shattered Dreams" also appeared on the double CD.

Photo and CD cover courtesy of Mr. Soul; Tracklisting courtesy of Weslyn Monroe

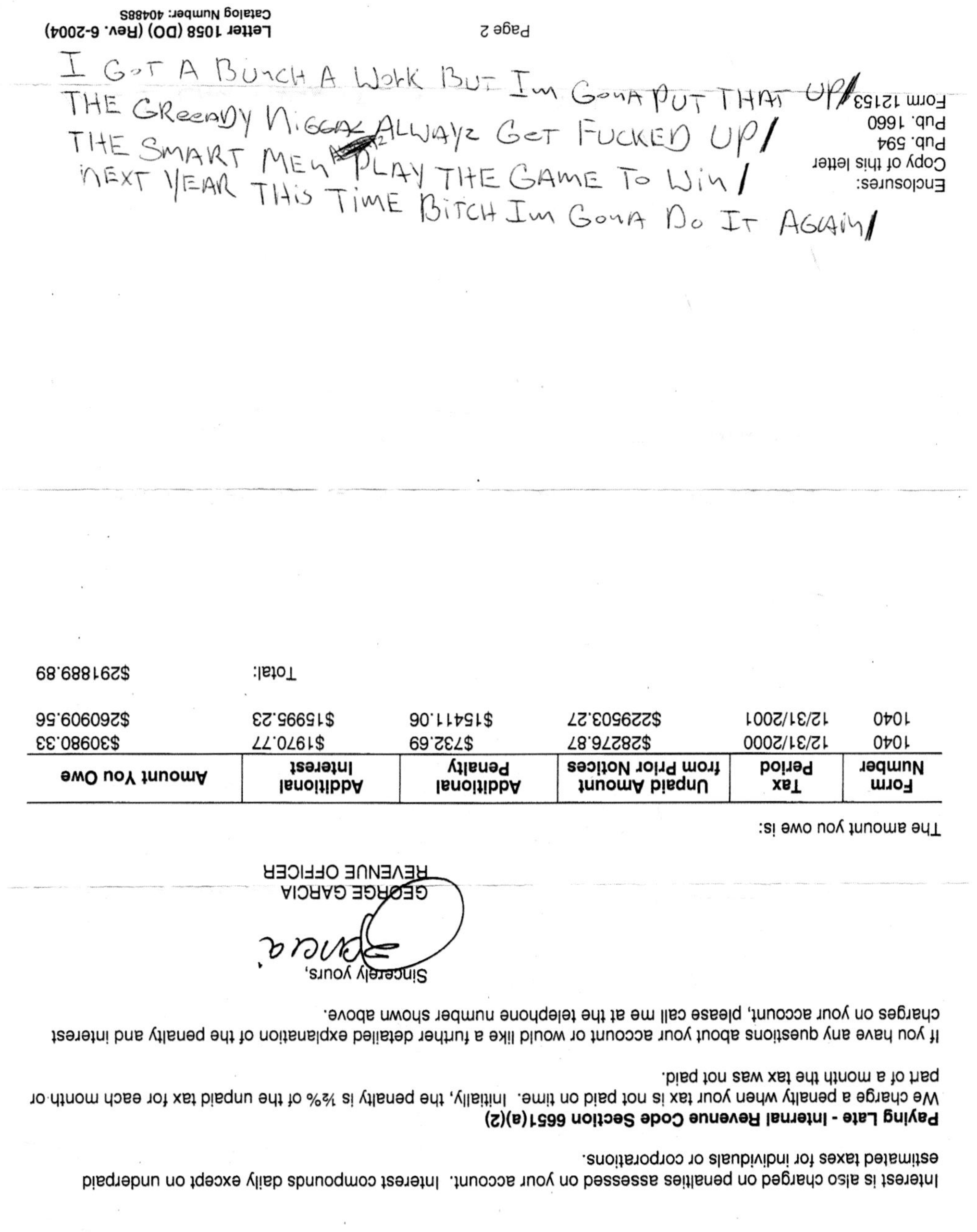

Interest is also charged on penalties assessed on your account. Interest compounds daily except on underpaid estimated taxes for individuals or corporations.

Paying Late - Internal Revenue Code Section 6651(a)(2)
We charge a penalty when your tax is not paid on time. Initially, the penalty is ½% of the unpaid tax for each month or part of a month the tax was not paid.

If you have any questions about your account or would like a further detailed explanation of the penalty and interest charges on your account, please call me at the telephone number shown above.

Sincerely yours,

GEORGE GARCIA
REVENUE OFFICER

The amount you owe is:

Form Number	Tax Period	Unpaid Amount from Prior Notices	Additional Penalty	Additional Interest	Amount You Owe
1040	12/31/2000	$28276.87	$732.69	$1970.77	$30980.33
1040	12/31/2001	$229503.27	$15411.06	$15995.23	$260909.56

Total: $291889.89

Enclosures:
Copy of this letter
Pub. 594
Pub. 1660
Form 12153

I GOT A BUNCH A WORK BUT IM GONA PUT THAT UP/
THE GREEDY NIGGAZ ALWAYZ GET FUCKED UP/
THE SMART MEN PLAY THE GAME TO WIN/
NEXT YEAR THIS TIME BITCH IM GONA DO IT AGAIN/

Page 2

Letter 1058 (DO) (Rev. 6-2004)
Catalog Number: 40488S

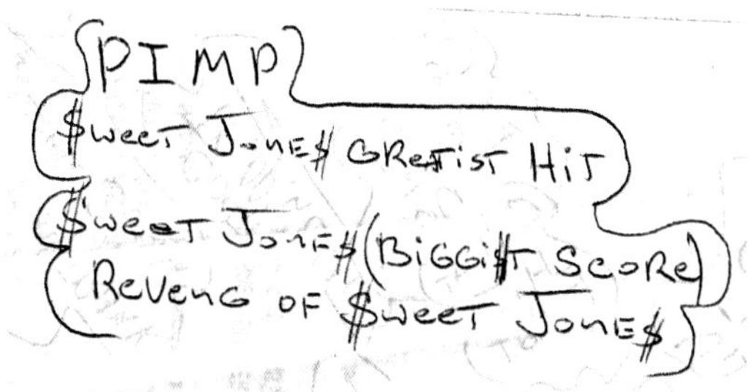
PIMP
$WEET JONE$ GREATIST HIT
$WEET JONE$ (BIGGI$T SCORE)
REVENG OF $WEET JONE$

While incarcerated, Chad wrote lyrics and production ideas on any scrap of paper available, like **magazine subscription cards** *(left)*, **IRS notices** *(above)*, or even **a commissary receipt** *(following page)*.

Courtesy of Weslyn Monroe

(Im So X-SIGHTED
(POINTER SISTERZ)
RE-PLAY

STEVIE WONDER
I WISH THEM
DAYZ WOULD COME
BACK ONCE MORE
(HORN SAMPLE
AT EWD OF S

Re-PLAY
TS ITA
CRIME
SADE

Date: 12/31/04
Time: 12:34:47
Page: 1

Begin Spend Limit: $75.00
Spend Limit

I THINK
ABOUT US

Is THERE ANYONE
OUT THERE CUZ
ITZ GETIN HARDER
AND HARDER TO
BREATHE

I GOT REAL
CLIENTEL/WE AIN'T
BRAKIN DOWN SHIT
WE DON'T NEED NO
SCALE

$640.23
Ext.Amt   Class

$73.40 REGU
$72.50 ????
$71.65 REGU
$70.90 REGU
$69.95 REGU
$68.95 REGU
$66.95 HYSN
$66.00 REGU
$61.60 REGU
$60.10 REGU
$59.10 REGU
$57.60 REGU
$54.60

1.60
.90
.85
.75
.95
1.00
2.00
.95
4.40
1.50
1.00
1.50

THAT PLAY HAS
NO NAME

Sample
Intro
MELODY
YOU GET
THE BEST
OF MY LOVE

ONE IS
THE
LONLIEST
#

"BEETMS"
ALL THE LONLY
PEOPLE

YOU LIVE
I'M A
CRIMINAL
ISY

I NOT GONNA
CRY

HOTEL CALI
LIVE
SAMPLE AT END

MARY BLIGE
Sample

SMOOTH
OPERATOR
SAMPLE BRAK
SADE COTTON

Sample
WHEN A
WOMAN FED
UP

Location:
Purchaser: CHAD
ID Number: 011365-2
Item Number,

Sample
Rachel Ferret

SAMPLE
THE
PAIN

HOW CAN
I EAZ
THE

Comm: Down
GIFFING MAIN

I KISS-U
IS ALL
THAT
I BEEN
THINK
OF

WE DON'T
NEED NO
SCALE

TOTAL

HE WORTH A MILL OUT H LOW/COL THE WEATHA MAN SAY ITS ALL.6HT CHANCE OF SNOW

IN THE BACK

****

"DANCE ALL NIGHT" (YOU CAN CALL IT WHAT U WANT TO WHAT IS THIS G6ole THAT MAKES U MOVE SOME PEOPLE CALL IT FUNK

DIONIC

WHAT THE H...

UNTEC THE B... OF THE PRINCE ... LOOP...

FREAK OF THE WEEK

SAMPLE AT THE END

ONE NATION

GRAPEVINE MARVIN ... SKATE...

MAKE U ...

Date: 12/31/04
Time: ...
Page: ...

Begin Spend Limit $640.00
Spend Limit $5.00

Class Ext.Amt
REGU $52.40
REGU $5.80

$26.20
$1.23
$614.03
Ending Spend Limit $48.00

OFFENDER THUMBPRINT
NO EXCHANGES!!!

Yes Michael ...

YOU ARE/MY STAR SHIP/COME TAKE ME UP TO NIGHT/AND DON'T BE LATE

(COMODORS) FLY AWAY ZOOM

LUV COME DOWN ... MAKE ME POP MY TRUNK AND COME ... POP MY TRUNK

Commissary Purchase Receipt

Beginning Account Balance
Unit Price Quantity
1.10   2
.90   4

Transaction Total: 36
...ded in above ...
Ending Account Balance: $614.03

Purchase: RIDER, TRUNK
ID Number: ...
Gatekeeper: FS...
Local Code...PB 21 01 Chaplain...

09935 ... SAUSAGE-SUMMER/PIECE
00313 BEEF POT ROAS(STR-POUCH

POP WHAT? YOU GO ON HOE

(RAY PARKER (RADIO) IT'S YOUR NIGHT TO BURN DOWN FINAL!!!

(GHETO LIFE (BRAKE SAMP PLAY NEW BASS)

WHERZ THE BLAC LIKE ENROLE

TRIPPLOW

CURTIS ...

CROSBY STEAL2 AND NASH

TI REET GREAT

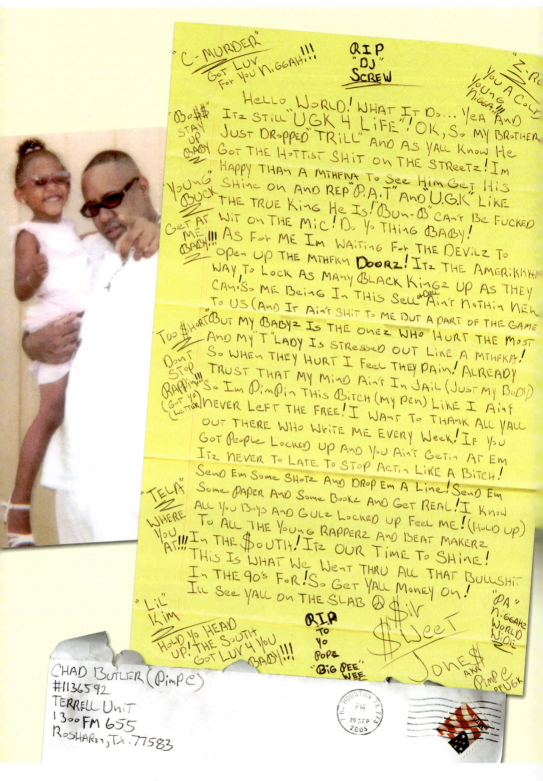

Above: Chad gets a family visit from **Chad Jr., Mama Wes, Christian,** and **Chinara**.
Below: **Mama Wes** married **Millard "Pops" Roher** while Chad was incarcerated.
Courtesy of Weslyn Monroe

The **"Free Pimp C"** movement. *Clockwise from above:* **Bun B** and **David Banner** on the set of Young Buck's "Let Me In" video shoot in Nashville, 2004; **Paul Wall** on the set of his "Sittin' Sidewayz" video shoot in Houston, 2005; **J. Prince** at the 2005 Los Magnificos car show in Houston; **Smoke D** and **Kamikaze** of Crooked Lettaz on the set of David Banner's "Ain't Got Nothing" video shoot in Los Angeles, 2005.

Photos: Julia Beverly

Born 2wice, who had just spent more than a year in a Texas prison himself, sent Chad pictures of some girls and a print-out of an email with a quick note from Ice-T. "I ain't to much herd from them [other] niggahz out there," Chad wrote in a letter back to Born 2wice. "Out of sight out of mind I guess? But I aint mad at nobody 2wice! They just showin what they realy are! Shit I only saw Bun one time (this year) scence I left the county jail in 2002! I overstand niggahz out there tryin to get it so I don't trip! Plus the man keepin my name (our name) alive!"

"The rap niggahz I herd from are Too $hort, Paul Wall, David Banner, Killer Mike, Daz, DJ X Large, Wicked Crickit, Chingo Bling, you, and Ice!" he added. "Pimpin Kin got at me too! But a lot of other [rappers] screamin my name so Im blessed to not be forgotin!"

"It was a handful of rappers who wrote me when I was locked up, and it wasn't the ones I thought was gonna write me," Chad said later. "Before I got locked up I never wrote no letter either!" he admitted in his letter to Born 2wice. "I got my head together and I can thank TDC for part of that! Im just waiting for my touch down time baby! ... Im drug free and ready to get $!!!"

On a Tuesday afternoon in November, Mama Wes and Chinara headed out to the Angleton Parole Board office, a large, official-looking building not far from the Terrell Unit. Chad's parole attorney Lori Redmond (whom Mama Wes complimented as a "tough bitch") had arranged for them to meet with the Parole Board's lead voter on Chad's behalf. After the lead voter made a decision, Chad's file would be passed along to two other parole commissioners for review. If two out of three voted for release, parole would be granted.

Although Mama Wes and Chinara had spent a lot of time together traveling to visit Chad, they'd never developed a close bond. "I never liked that girl, I ain't gonna lie to you," Mama Wes says. "All she ever told me was how pretty she was and what a great movie star she was gonna be."

Chinara's smoking habits continued to be a point of contention. "[Chinara] would ride around [in] the car with [Christian] and Chris would be high as a kite!" Mama Wes says. On one occasion, Mama Wes met Chinara at a Wal-Mart, intending to bring the toddler inside for a toy-shopping spree. But according to Mama Wes, Christian emerged from the car reeking of marijuana. *I can't take this baby in this Wal-Mart,* she thought.

Mama Wes was also concerned because she'd heard rumors that Chinara's drug use was much more serious than recreational weed smoking. "To be perfectly honest ... I never even pursued [the rumors], because frankly, I didn't wanna know," says Mama Wes. "I frankly don't know [what type of drugs, but] she's got major drug issues. I don't know what it is, but the girl is *always* high."

Today was one of those days: in Mama Wes' opinion, Chinara had arrived for the meeting with the parole board visibly under the influence. Mama Wes was already nervous, knowing it was highly unusual for an inmate to be granted parole during their first year of eligibility.

As they met with the lead voter – a stern, intimidating woman whom Mama Wes describes as "the meanest fucker" – Mama Wes grimaced as Chinara continued talking, volunteering unnecessary information. *Be quiet! Shut the fuck up!* she thought in frustration, kicking Chinara under the table.

Lori Redmond faced the lead voter to begin her presentation on Chad's behalf. "A wise man once said, 'In spite of all mankind's mistakes, messes, and mishaps, one thing in his favor is the ability to learn from them,'" she started. "Chad Butler whole-heartedly agrees with that statement. He is a good man. Not a perfect man, but a good man just the same."

She attributed Chad's problems with the law to his "emotional immaturity and failure to get his priorities in order," adding that he "accepts full responsibility for his actions" and "believes that this time in TDC has afforded him an opportunity to mature spiritually and emotionally."

She added, "For Chad, disappointing his family has been the worst punishment of all."

After a standard line of questioning, the lead voter skimmed through some paperwork. Chad didn't have any strikes on his record and had managed to avoid trouble while he was incarcerated. He had a respectable job as a library clerk. In his file were letters from Tim Hampton and Langston Adams, childhood friends who were also familiar with the legal system, praising Chad's character.

"Well, it is usually my standard for them to have taken GED courses," the lead voter said, as she skimmed through Chad's file.

"He did that. The certificate's right here," said Ms. Redmond.

"Well, I would really want him to take Cognitive Intervention."

Ms. Redmond nodded. "Certificate's right here."

And on it went. Finally, the lead voter asked, "What *didn't* he take?"

"Nothing," Ms. Redmond smiled. "He's taken everything that we had to offer." She finished her presentation by pointing out the fact that Chad had a stable place to live, the support of his family and friends, and job opportunities.

"Chad Butler is human and he makes mistakes … [but] despite the nature of his offense, I do not believe he is a violent person," she concluded. "When you review his file, I ask that you look beyond the surface of this case. I believe you will see a man who has finally arrived at a place of emotional maturity. In talking with Chad it was obvious that he is genuinely tired of his former lifestyle … [he is] a man who is ashamed of his actions, and only wants a chance to prove to himself, his family and friends that he is capable of being a law abiding citizen."*

Chinara and Mama Wes were asked to step outside. As Mama Wes recalls it, once they were out of earshot, she turned to Chinara, fuming. "Why would you smoke that shit before coming here!?" she demanded. "Why the hell would you do that?! We trying to get C out of jail and you, his wife, is sitting up here high as fuck. Jesus! Don't volunteer no damn information. Answer what they ask you and shut the fuck up, and don't spurt out ignorance! And when you high, you don't want to draw attention to your face! You don't want nobody to look at you! Your pupils dilated as a muthafucker! I'm trying to keep them people from seeing this!"

Mama Wes' phone rang with a call from her mother's doctor. Her mother Bessie, now 89 years old, had recently been diagnosed with a brain tumor.

"I trust that you are praying because God answers prayers," Grandma Bessie had written Chad a month earlier. "Remember I love you + will do anything for you … There is a brighter day ahead." Mama Wes visited her in Crowley often and kept Chad updated on Granny's status. "She is doing great Chad," she'd written. "She'll probably outlive us."

After a brief delay, Ms. Redmond summoned the ladies back inside. "Well, I probably shouldn't tell you all this, but I will," the lead voter told them. "There are three members on the parole board. And my vote will be yes."

Mama Wes was ecstatic. "Do you have any idea how soon he might be released?!"

The lead voter skimmed the calendar, explaining that it could take up to six months. "We'll set March the 21st as his release date," she said.

"C is an only grandchild, because I'm an only child, and he's my only child … [My mom] has a brain tumor," Mama Wes said. "I would like for her to be able to see him, and be cognizant."

"When was she diagnosed?" the lead voter asked.

"About three months ago."

(*For her efforts, Chad's parole attorney earned a shout-out on Trae tha Truth's "Swang" remix: "Since Lori Redmond freed The Pimp, it's goin' down in Houston.")

"Can you prove that?"

"I'll call the doctor back right now."

"No, that's not necessary." The lead voter flipped through the calendar. "We might be able to move it up to January."

"My birthday is December 12th," Mama Wes smiled, offering an exaggerated grin and batting her eyelashes. "[Or] his little girl's birthday is December 15th."

"No, we've got too many people in there. They're not gonna be able to get him in [that soon]," the lead voter replied. She paused as she glanced through his file. "Oh, his birthday is December 29th? We're gonna try for that date."

After the parole meeting Mama Wes drove back east towards Louisiana to return to her ailing mother's bedside. While she navigated rush hour traffic, her cell phone rang with a Houston number she didn't recognize. "Mama!" the voice said.

"Who is this!?" she demanded. "Look here, I really don't feel like playing with no muthafucker right now. I'm in traffic."

"Mama, it's me!" he insisted. "C!"

"Boy, what are you doing on a phone!? You know you not supposed to be on no telephone," she fussed.*

Chad, calling from a female guard's cell phone, knew it was the day of the scheduled parole meeting. "Mama, what happened!?" he asked eagerly.

"She said yes, but you know there's two more [parole commissioners]," she told him. "It's gotta be two out of three."

"But she said yes!? She the head of that shit, ain't she!?" Chad said excitedly, then letting loose with a loud, "*Yeaaaaaahhhh!!!!*"

On November 30, 2005, the Parole Board officially voted to grant Chad Butler parole, concluding that the length of time he had served was sufficient for his crime.

Two days later Matt Sonzala wrote a blog post titled "PIMP C FREEEEE!!!!!!!" on his blog HoustonSoReal. "It's Official. Pimp C has been granted parole," it read. "Let's hope the man can be home with his family for Christmas … You heard it here first."

The news was soon confirmed by the Associated Press and spread to other news outlets like MSNBC and MTV News. "He's been approved for parole and should be home in the next 60 days," Bun told radio host Charlamagne Tha God. "It's definitely a blessing, it's a beautiful thing. I hope that everybody will be able to burn the 'Free Pimp C' shirts real soon and [start] throwing those ['Free Pimp C'] caps away. Then we can start rocking the 'Welcome Back Pimp C.'"

A post on AllHipHop about Pimp C's imminent return caught the attention of Bad Boy Entertainment A&R Conrad Dimanche, who wrote to offer a solo record deal. "Holla at me if this is something that you would at all be interested in so that I can try to set a meeting with you and Diddy," Dimanche wrote.

Chad didn't like the idea of signing to someone else's label; he wanted to have his own. "If I ever fuck around like that again [and sign a record deal] the man I would want to be signed with is Jay-Z," he told *On Tha Real* Magazine.

Besides, he had other priorities in mind. As Bun was doing radio interviews confirming his upcoming release, Chad was filling out student loan applications for the University of Hous-

(*According to other inmates who were at the Terrell Unit around this time, it was easy to get access to cell phones or smuggle other contraband into the prison. A man identifying himself as El-Haqq wrote in a web forum alleging that corruption at the unit "would have been obvious to anyone who cared to look." He added, "No one was in charge. The unit was on automatic. You could not tell the officers from the inmates … The culprit, is women officers. In my humble opinion, WOMEN don't belong in [an] all male environment. This is not a single unit issue, it is a statewide pandemic." Three years after Chad departed Terrell, the unit was the subject of a major corruption investigation which found that guards were having sex with inmates and accepting cash to smuggle tobacco, drugs, and cell phones into the prison. In the subsequent uproar, the warden was forced to resign.)

ton and Texas Southern University. He tore a page from *Forbes* Magazine listing the wealthiest people in the world, noting the ones who'd made their fortune off Wal-Mart. He also stopped by the law library and picked up paperwork to register a new corporation and apply to have his criminal history expunged.

———————

As Chad prepared to re-enter the world with a brand new outlook on life, not much had changed with his "victim" Lakita Hulett. In fact, on the evening of December 14, 30-year-old Lakita was exactly where she'd been 10 years earlier: shoplifting in the fitting room of the Foley's Department Store at the Willowbrook Mall.

Two loss prevention officers recognized her from her previous shoplifting excursions and Lakita was arrested after walking out of the store with $261.99 worth of clothing. But police were more interested in the contents of her purse, which included a stolen Bank of America debit card, four stolen drivers' licenses, and more than a dozen gift cards (Saks Fifth Avenue, Neiman Marcus, Nordstrom, Sears, and more) which they suspected were obtained illegally.* Lakita was charged with felony theft and sentenced to four months in the County Jail.

———————

Mama Wes came to visit the weekend before Christmas. "Look, you only got one more week here, so I'm not gonna come next week," she told Chad. She planned to spend the Christmas holidays in Crowley with her mother, who had just been released from the hospital in a wheelchair.

Chad nodded. He'd just had a visit with J. Prince to discuss his career plans. "Man, when you get home, don't worry about shit," Prince had told him.

"When I come home, I wanna take like six weeks, and let's just chill and get our thoughts together," Chad told his mother. "I can't think in this bitch right. That's what we gonna do. I already talked to James, he got my back. He gon' take care of everything so we don't have to worry [for] like six weeks."

Before she left, Mama Wes addressed something weighing heavily on her mind. She'd always accepted her son's vices, knowing that it would be futile to try to change him. But it was time to draw the line. She told him that if she ever suspected he was doing drugs again, she would turn him in. "I'd rather have you alive locked up than dead, and that's what's gonna happen if you keep that shit up," she warned.

As the days ticked by slowly, Chad reached the same conclusion as many of his friends: in some ways, prison had helped him. "Maybe [the Sharpstown incident was] a trumped-up charge, but the truth is, I did a whole lot of wrong stuff, and eventually, it gets you," he told the *Beaumont Enterprise*. "I don't blame anybody for me being here. I created an atmosphere where either I was going to hurt somebody or somebody was going to hurt me."

"You've got to reap what you sow. You've got to pay for what you do," he added in *XXL*. "And you know what? I was an animal for a long time. I wasn't nice. I hurt people's feelings … It's karma. I got back what I put into it."

At some point, he had an epiphany, thinking back to the earnest prayer he'd said by his bedside shortly before the Sharpstown incident: *"Don't let me die."* Maybe prison was God's answer.

"I figured out [that prison time] added to my life, but I didn't figure it out until the last minute … the only way to save me from death was to hide me," he would later reflect.

———

*(*On a more amusing note, Lakita was also carrying three prescription medications which are primarily used to treat irritable bowel syndrome, urinary tract infections, and vaginal infections.)*

CHAPTER 37

"For Chad Butler, [going to prison] was a bad thing. But for the rapper, the character, the Pimp C myth, yeah, it was cool. Yeah, Pimp went to prison, did his time in population, didn't tell on nobody and came home ... everybody likes that kind of story." – Pimp C, *OZONE* Magazine, February 2007

"How can a nigga come home from the pen for four years, ain't got no album out, [and be] out here drivin' all these [Bentleys] and doin' it like this? I *got* to have God on my side, mane, 'cause it ain't nothin' else that could do these thangs." – Pimp C, *Too Real For TV* DVD

On December 29, 2005, Chad's 32nd birthday, he was transferred to the Huntsville Unit to be processed for release. The oldest state prison in Texas, the Huntsville Unit (also known as the Walls Unit) was located in Huntsville, about an hour north of Houston, where inmates accounted for about 30% of the city's population.*

While Chad spent his last night behind bars, Bun was performing at a Houston nightclub. Along with his crew (his wife Queenie, Red Boy, who was now managing him, and his road manager Eric "Bone" York), he drove out to Huntsville after the show. There was no need to go home – Bun was too excited to sleep anyway, and since prisoners were sometimes released at 6 or 7 AM, he wanted to make sure he was there when Chad walked out of the gate.

A few days before the scheduled release, Matt Sonzala forwarded me a text message with the address and date of Pimp's scheduled release. If *OZONE* was going to serve as the South's voice, I felt a responsibility to make sure we covered everything that was of interest to Southern rap fans, and Pimp C's release was certainly one of them. I felt that we'd had a great interview at the Terrell Unit, but wasn't sure if he'd want me to come, and there wasn't time to write and ask.

I had never attended someone's prison release, much less a celebrity, and had no idea what the setting might be. Would there be a group of media outlets with cameras crowding around him, or would I be the only one, awkwardly intruding on a private family moment?

Like most people, I assumed that Bun and Chad talked frequently, so I reached out to Bun and asked if he thought I should come. His reply was vague and noncommittal. Unsure what to do, I weighed the options: If I didn't go, and it turned out that Pimp did want *OZONE* there covering it, it would be a once-in-a-lifetime missed opportunity. If I did go, and he didn't want to take any pictures, I'd have wasted a few hundred dollars and few hours of my time. I decided the best-case scenario outweighed the risk of the worst-case scenario: I'd attend, but fall back and observe the situation before pulling out my camera.

The big moment was almost anticlimactic. Around 11:30 AM, several dozen men emerged

(*Five years later, when the warden of the Huntsville Unit retired, he was replaced by a black warden named James Jones.)

at the top of a concrete stairwell at the far end of the Huntsville Unit. A uniformed guard watched as they made their way down the stairs.

When Chad finally came into view near the end of the procession, he broke into a smile, seeing his family waiting below in the parking lot. Wearing a patterned button-down shirt over a white thermal and blue jeans, he carried his red mesh commissary bag in one hand, and in the other, a framed plastic-wrapped pencil drawing of Bun B wearing a "Free Pimp C" hat, a gift from a fellow inmate.

He greeted his sons first, leaning over to hug six-year-old Corey. After he'd had a moment with his sons, Bun and Red Boy greeted Chad, handing him a phone so he could talk briefly to J. Prince.

Everyone backed away as Chad embraced his mother on the sidewalk, giving them space. They rocked from side to side, his hand on her head holding her in a tight embrace. After holding one another for a lengthy amount of time, Chad kissed his mother on the cheek.

Bun, who had called Big Gipp, passed his Sprint Nextel chirp phone to Chad. After speaking to Gipp, Chad examined the phone carefully, impressed with the "chirp" function. Bun had always been amused by Chad's "weird infatuation with cell phones."

After talking with Gipp, Chad wanted to go straight to studio. Bun insisted that he go home first, spend some time with his family, take a hot bath, and eat a warm meal. "That's why I worked like that, so you wouldn't have to do all that hustling when you came out," Bun told him. "The studio isn't going anywhere."

Chad posed for a few pictures in front of the brick Huntsville Unit, the clock at the top of the building stuck at 12:55. Before climbing into his own vehicle, he gazed over the barbed wire fence, where second-story inmates in TDCJ whites were waving down on him with both hands. "We freed Pimp C! We're coming to free you next!" Bun yelled loudly as Chad and his mother climbed into an SUV.

"It's kinda beyond words," Bun told *OZONE* when asked to describe his emotions that day. "There's no real way to explain that kind of feeling … I never really had to anticipate anything like that. There's very few things in life I've ever really wanted [that much]."

Before they pulled off around noon, Bun leaned into the SUV and handed Chad a brown paper bag filled with several thousand dollars in tens and twenties. It was the back-end of his show money from the night before. With Chinara driving, Mama Wes in the passenger seat, and the kids in the backseat with Chad, they pulled off from the prison. They had the radio on and the DJ at The Box started screaming, "The Pimp is Free! The Pimp is Free!"

Mama Wes caught her son's eye in the rearview mirror. "Hey, Mama, turn that up," he said. She turned up the radio.

"What they say?" he asked.

"They're saying the Pimp is free."

Chad hadn't yet grasped the idea that he was now a bonafide celebrity. "They know I'm free?" he asked in disbelief.

"C, I've been trying to convince you for two months," his mother replied. "You're huge right now, baby. You're huge."

The DJ launched into a Pimp C set, running through all his verses. As they reached the highway, Mama Wes remembered the phone. Chad had always been infatuated with cell phones and had been talking about the Motorola RAZR, for months. Mama Wes got the hint and bought him one, programmed with a Louisiana number.

"Oh!" she said, handing over the box. "I got you a birthday gift."

"Oh, a RAZR?!!" he inspected it excitedly. "Can you charge it?"

"Yes, it's charged," Mama Wes told him.

"Damn, I don't have no numbers," Chad thought aloud.

"I put every number in it that I could think of," Mama Wes replied.

"You got the radio in there?"

"I do."

Pimp called the radio station 97.9 The Box and did a quick phone interview. Next, he called his Grandma Bessie in Louisiana and Tim Hampton in Florida. "Yeah, man, I'm home," he told Tim.

"Oh, man, congratulations. How's it feel?" Tim asked.

"Well, you know, it feels good," Chad replied. "Man, I got a lot of people around me, but uh… I'm gonna call you tonight when I get home and [I'm] relaxing."

Tim laughed, knowing he was in high demand. "Chad, you gonna be busy as hell."

"Oh, no, man," Chad said. "Shit, I ain't gonna be doing nothing but just chilling at the house."

Tim realized Chad wasn't aware of his celebrity status yet. "You have no idea. You gonna be busy as hell," Tim said. "Just hit me later."

As they approached the Houston city limits, Chad spotted a McDonald's and asked them to pull over and get some food. He was unprepared for the reaction; people swarmed around him at the McDonald's and in the parking lot. He was silent most of the ride back to Port Arthur, still processing his newfound fame.

"All those 'Free Pimp C' T-shirts and baseball caps can be put away," *USA Today* announced.

Paul Wall got a text from his sister: "The t-shirt worked. Pimp C's out of jail." Pimp C's incarceration had turned him into a martyr of sorts, a representative of something bigger than himself. "The whole jail experience kind of made him an even bigger legend, because everybody was screaming 'Free Pimp C,'" explains Paul Wall. "Every artist, big or small, everybody [was] united. It was a unified front … a cause [to rally behind]."

Meanwhile, I loaded up the pictures of UGK reunited, stamped with the OZONE logo, and emailed them out to media outlets with the help of a Verizon wireless broadband card. I'd only made it halfway back to Houston when Bun B texted me remarking how fast I was.

OZONE music editor DJ Wally Sparks blasted it off with the subject line, "OZONE MAGAZINE: Exclusive Photo of Pimp C & Bun B TOGETHER AGAIN!" Other media outlets and websites quickly reposted it. "Damn, Julia Beverly is on her game, your boy just got out at like noon," read the caption on website nahright.com.

"im happy pimp c is finally out but yo what is half the south gonna rap about now? most of their bars end with free the pimp," asked one commenter. "it breaks my heart to see how much we care about people that commit crimes and go away for 5 years and its this whole big event and celebration, when somebody's brother just graduated from college and we could care less," griped another "Htown chick."

"They still look like two old men from the club though," said one commenter. Another was more rude: "FUCK PIMP C! …THIS ASSHOLE WENT TO PRISON FOR NOT COMPLETING HIS DAMN COMMUNITY SERVICE! HONESTLY, HOW HARD IS IT TO PICK SHIT UP OFF THE SIDE OF THE FREEWAY? I WOULD MUCH RATHER DO THAT AND GO HOME AND CHILL WITH A FEMALE THAN SPEND THE NEXT 4 BEHIND BARS SURROUND[ED] BY OTHER LONELY ASS NIGGAS."

"i can't believe ya'll mutha fuckas hatin on pimp c," wrote another. "pimp c is a fuckin don from h-town, all you faggots bumpin that mike jones bullshit. he's the reason there is a fuckin' mike jones. I kant believe this disrespect, ya'll dont know nothin bout that shit. UGK FOR LIFE."

———————

When they pulled up to Mama Wes' house, Chad headed straight for the shower, but couldn't find anything to wear. Most of his old clothes were either the wrong size or out of style. "Baby, you can't wear none of these clothes around here," Mama Wes told him. "I did get you some super, super big Dickies, and you might be able to wear that … I got you a big t-shirt, why don't you put that on and go to the mall?"

Although most media coverage had been dominated by footage of Hurricane Katrina in New Orleans, other cities along the coastline like Port Arthur had suffered extensive damage in the wake of Hurricane Rita. Mama Wes' home was one of many in the area with a blue FEMA tarp still covering the roof.

Driving through his beloved hometown, Chad was shocked to see the extent of the damage from Hurricane Rita. Some landmarks were completely gone, while others were now abandoned due to widespread flooding. "A lot of shit is tore up around here," he said. "Some stores I've been going to ever since I can remember … they don't exist no more."

Chad picked up some clothes and cologne at one of the few stores in the Central Mall that was open and passed by Mitch's house to catch up on old times. He spent most of his afternoon on the phone, doing radio interviews with longtime UGK associates like Bo-Bo Luchiano in Dallas and Mean Green in Houston, who got his son Lil Green on the line so they could reminisce on their days cleaning toilets together at Garza West.

Back at Mama Wes' house, Chad was getting a haircut and visiting with his cousin Ed when the phone rang. "C, you want to take this," Mama Wes said quietly, holding her hand over the receiver. "It's Jay."

Chad thought she was referring to J. Prince. "I already talked to him," he said.

"No, Jay-Z," Mama Wes replied.

Chad thought it was a prank caller; he'd seen pictures of Jay-Z and Beyonce vacationing on a yacht. "Oh, Mama, that nigga out on the ocean," Chad laughed. "Don't you know he always be on the water at Christmas time? He don't come back 'til -"

"Well, they got phones on there, because it's him," she insisted.

"Man, stop playing," Chad laughed. "That's somebody playing with me."

Chad took the receiver into the game room for some privacy. It was, in fact, the real Jay-Z, and the two men had a lengthy conversation. An hour later Chad emerged from the game room, programming Jay-Z's number into his new RAZR.

Part of Chad's conversation with Jay-Z involved his irritation with the media presence (me) at at his release. "He [wanted] that to be a very private moment," says Mama Wes. He also complained to Wendy Day, who told him he was "fortunate to have somebody give a shit and show up."

I later learned that Rap-A-Lot had declined FOX News, BET, and MTV News, who all wanted to send news cameras to cover his release. "This is a business," Chad told me later. "I would rather sell my story than give it away to these folks for free … Rather than just giving away the game, I would rather just do a DVD. Let people get the story like that instead of giving the game away. The game is still to be sold." (The footage shot by Omar Wilson for Rap-A-Lot at the prison appeared on the *Pimpalation* DVD.)

Shortly after the call from Jay-Z came a call from Master P, who was no longer the rap powerhouse he'd been in the late 90s. (On his *ReMix Classics* album released on Koch in 2005, he'd removed Pimp C's verse from "I Miss My Homies.")

Chad again retreated to the game room. If he aspired to become the new spokesman for unity among Southern rappers, he knew he had to start by squashing his own beefs.

According to Master P, Chad attributed his previous behavior to drug abuse and apologized for his role in instigating the drama. "He was a great artist, [but] the drug situation turned his life to where people thought that it was a [beef] between me and him," says Master P. "When he got out of jail, he explained to me that it was just … the drugs [he was doing] had him out

[of] his mind... [So] we forgave each other and moved on."*

Chad also didn't like the fact that Master P was at odds with his blood brother, C-Murder, and encouraged P to repair the relationship. "[Master P is] not a very nice guy ... and he's selfish," says Mama Wes. "And C didn't like that. And C did try to talk to P about [reconciling with C-Murder] but he didn't get anywhere with that."**

Chad came back to the kitchen after their conversation with a broad smile. "[We] reconciled our differences," Chad told WordofSouth.com. "We had sat down like real men and came to this conclusion that that shit was stupid. We can make way more money together on each other's side than we can going to war." Chad told his mother that he planned to reunite with Master P and record "Break 'Em Off Something Pt. 2."

Mama Wes wasn't quite so forgiving; she was having a hard time erasing the image of her poor baby's swollen face after the hotel incident. "You know, I'll do business with anybody, but when it comes to him, I can't," she told Chad. "I can't do it because I can't give up my mama role. I'm still your mama. In most cases I can separate the mama and the manager, but in this case – I never did trust that sucker."

"If he could just say, 'Hell, I fucked up,' [we could] move on from there... but the truth of the matter is, he won't admit that he did anything," Mama Wes says. "So ... [my attitude is,] 'fuck you.'"

"Personally, I have a lot of respect for [Master] P as a businessman," she continues. "[But] I have very little respect for P as a person. And that didn't just happen after the hotel incident. I felt that way about him before ... as a businessman, I think he's excellent. As a human being, I think he sucks."

The Master P incident had helped Chad realize how powerful his words could be. "Eventually if you diss somebody man, you gonna have to smell they cologne, you gonna have to see 'em," he told WordofSouth.com. "That's why I'm very careful about what I say. I'm very careful about what comes out [of] my mouth."

Mama Wes prepared a hearty welcome home meal, but the spicy seasoning didn't sit well with Chad's stomach and made him sick. "I was so used to eating that bullshit they cooked in [prison], my body still ain't used to eating real food," he told *OZONE*.

———————

Late that evening, Bun arrived at Mama Wes' house. For the first time in years, he found himself able to relax. He came bounding in, a wide grin across his face.

Mama Wes had never had the heart to tell her son that during the four years he'd been gone, Bun had never come by the house. She'd only seen him once when she took the kids to his show in Houston. It was information she chose not to share, knowing it would only hurt him. But Edgar the Dog barked furiously and nearly attacked Bun as he came through the garage entrance.***

Mama Wes always let Edgar 'meet' friends and family so he'd be familiar with their scent. Chad, sitting on the living room couch, clearly understood the implication. "Edgar don't know

(*Although Master P doesn't acknowledge that the hotel incident ever happened, he does recall speaking with Chad after his release from prison and squashing their beef.)
(**On "Came 2 Da Can," his 2014 collaboration with Lil Boosie, C-Murder raps, "I used to love my own brother, but I don't love him no mo' / Don't want to hug him no mo', 'cause there's a limit fo' sho'.")
(***The mutt was sometimes referred to as "Edgar the Dog" to avoid any confusion with Chad's cousin Edgar the Human. Chad generally refused to have pets because he'd been devastated as a teenager when the family dog died. Mama Wes was of the opinion that the dog died from eating too much of the vending machine candy which Chad, Mitch, and their friends left lying around the house. "Fuck a pet, man," Chad joked during an interview with Jaro Vacek. "You know why? Them hoes die, man, and I be sad than a muthafucker. Hell no, man ... I got a fish tank in my new house; I'm finna get some fish. I can't take it. [If] my muthafuckin' dog died I'd be sad then a muthafucker.")

you, you ain't been here," he mumbled quietly, his face twisting into disappointment. His mother shot him a warning glance: *now isn't the time.*

It was a time for celebration, not anger or accusations. Chad pushed the thought aside and greeted his partner warmly. "We been through a lotta shit together," he told *The Source.* "We done laughed, cried [and hurt] people together. We done fought the IRS, went to war with Jive, walked up in their office and told them, 'Man, fuck you. We takin' the DATs, bitch. We don't give a fuck if you [shelve] us. We'll go back to sellin' dope. We'll blow this mu'fucka up.'"

Chad told Bun he was ready to get back to work and get in the studio – right now. Bun wanted him to take a little time with his family and get readjusted first. "Dog, you can relax," Bun chuckled. "Everything is waiting for you. Whenever you ready, it's ready for you."

"Overall, it was just like a weight lifted off of you," recalls Chad Jr. "Just knowing that you're gonna be able to see him in the next few hours, and you can just call him whenever and say, 'What's up?'"

Later that night, Herbert "Hezeleo" Mouton stopped by, a Port Arthur rapper who had become a part of Mama Wes' inner circle while Chad was incarcerated, providing emotional support and helping her out with miscellaneous errands. Hezeleo mentioned that he was on the way to Beaumont to perform as an opening act on Chamillionaire's show.

"Chamillionaire, the nigga [who] be with Paul Wall?" Chad asked. He'd seen Chamillionaire's red 1986 Cadillac Eldorado Biarritz in his "Turn It Up" music video and promised cellmates he would come home and get the car. (Chad rapped about a "Biarritz with a slantback ass" on "Let Me See It.")

"Yeah," Hezeleo nodded.

"Man, when you get by that nigga, tell him I want that muthafuckin' candy-red Cadillac," Chad said. "Matter fact, when you get by that nigga, call me."

"Say, man, Pimp wanna holla at you," Hezeleo told Chamillionaire later that night, handing him the phone backstage at the concert.

"He was telling me how much he loved [the car]," Chamillionaire remembers. "He didn't ask for it. But I was so much of a fan of UGK that I gave him the car. The deal was to tell people I sold it to him."

Sill accustomed to prison hours, Chad woke up early the following morning to find his two youngest children Corey and Christian – partners in crime who frequently found ways to get into trouble together – loudly parading around the house. During one visit he'd told Mama Wes and Chinara they were too hard on the kids, to which the ladies rolled their eyes. Now, he understood. Wearing nothing but boxer shorts, Chad wandered into the kitchen where Mama Wes was preparing breakfast.

"What's wrong with these lil' muthafuckers?" he grumbled, wiping the sleep from his eyes.

"Don't call my grandchildren 'lil muthafuckers,'" Mama Wes laughed. "Now you're gonna have to move around, with them big white drawers on."

"Man, they're making all that noise and I'm trying to sleep," Chad complained. "My first morning home and these niggas making all that noise." He paused, then asked, "What you doing?"

"Making pancakes," Mama Wes said.

"I'll take three," he smiled.

The phone started ringing as soon as they finished breakfast. One of the first callers was Chad's prison penpal Heather Johnson, who had been released to a halfway house. "Is he out!?"

she asked Mama Wes excitedly.

Chad took the phone. "Yeah, man, we 'bout to do this." He made plans for Heather to move down to Port Arthur and join the team as Mama Wes' assistant.

Chad hit the studio the following day, on New Year's Eve, to record his verse for Bun's "Get Throwed" remix. The original record featured Jay-Z, and Bun hadn't planned to release it as a single because he knew Jay-Z wouldn't be available for the video. The song was picking up in the streets, so they decided to do a remixed version of the record and shoot a video.

Everyone was tense; the unspoken concern was that Chad's rap skills might have lost a step during his time away. But Chad didn't miss a beat.

Red Boy stepped outside to call Mama Wes, who was anxiously awaiting news of the session. "Mama!" Red yelled into the phone excitedly.

"You don't need to say no more," Mama Wes smiled.

"He got it!" Red assured her. "We'll be there in an hour or two."

Bun was almost as surprised as Chad at his newfound superstar status. "[He's] literally... more recognizable – more famous or more infamous, however you would like to put it – than he was before he went into prison," Bun marveled in the *Village Voice*. "[It's] almost unheard of."

"The Pimp C myth is a whole lot bigger than who you really are," Bun commented.

Chad laughed, understanding exactly what he meant. Although prison time was terrible for Chad Butler the man, it was great for Pimp C the rapper.

"Unfortunately negative things like [prison time] give us street credibility," Chad told *OZONE*. "You lose when you go to jail ... for Chad Butler, that was a bad thing ... But for the rapper, the character, the Pimp C myth, yeah, it was cool. Yeah, Pimp went to prison, did his time in population, didn't tell on nobody and came home ... everybody likes that kind of story."

In a way, Chad's honesty about his incarceration fit perfectly with UGK's ethos. It was one of the traits which separated them from other rappers: vulnerability. "One thing that people respect about UGK is that we were always so honest with them," Bun told journalist Matt Sonzala. "We let them know about our ups as well as our downs ... Pimp C did a crime, he had to go to prison, like everybody else. We're human. [He admitted,] 'It was my mistake, it wasn't anybody's fault and I'm paying for it.' He stood up as a man, he did his time in general population and he came home to respect, love and admiration."

But although he'd emerged a celebrity, Chad was careful to emphasize that prison wasn't something to be glorified. "It's not a party, it's not fun," he told MTV News. "Jail affected my whole family. My family got locked up. My group got locked up. I lost when I went to prison. That's something to be ashamed of, and that's not a badge of honor. My youngest son was eight years old when I went in. I came back and he's a teenager. I can't get them years back."

The day after New Year's, Mama Wes took Chad to the DMV to reinstate his driver's license and meet his parole officer, Ms. Sjolanda Brown. He had chosen to be paroled in Port Arthur, not Houston, which impressed some of the locals. "He came back even when he didn't have to," says his cousin Ed. "He always said the people here [in Port Arthur] were real warm and that he just felt welcome here."

Chad would be on parole until December 4, 2009, and during that time he was expected to "avoid persons or places of disreputable or harmful character." He wouldn't be able to travel outside the state of Texas without written permission.

But all things considered, he figured he was in a great position. "It coulda been a lot more restrictive than it is," Chad told *OZONE*. "I'm able to move around the state as I please, and in a couple months they'll let me move around the country. I'm in a really good position right now.

I'm blessed. I could have [an ankle] monitor on me, or I could have a long list of bullshit that they make me do every week. It's really not like that … it's pretty good."

While he was out running errands, there was one more item of business to handle. He'd been given a check for the remaining funds from his commissary account. Remembering David Banner, Paul Wall, and others who had generously put money on his books, Chad mailed the check to C-Murder.

"It wasn't enough money to help me on the streets, but it was enough money to help him where he was at," he explained later in an interview with Greg Street. "So I sent that to him. I didn't get no publicity or try to tell nobody about it, because it was genuine and from my heart, and I know how it is in that place."

From then on, Chad adopted the motto "commissary is very necessary," a very relevant topic in a state with such a high incarceration rate. Nearly everyone had a friend or relative in prison. "You might think your folks is mad at you 'cause you ain't been hollerin' at them," he said in an interview with Donna Garza. "But the bottom line is this: they not mad at you, they just hurt … send 'em a postcard."

"If you got folks that's locked up, you need to write them some letters and send some pictures and drop a couple dollars," he added in *OZONE*. "That shit goes a long way in there. If you ain't hollered at your people in years and they sittin' up there mad at you, holla at them anyway, 'cause they just wanna hear from you. Keep it real with your folks, man. It's never too late to stop acting like a bitch."

Within days of his release, Chad, accompanied by Mama Wes, Chad Jr., and Big Gipp, who had flown into town to welcome his friend home, met up with J. Prince and Red Boy at the Houston Bentley dealership. Chad tried several cars before settling on a silver Bentley with an orange leather interior. The salesman took him for a test drive as Prince, wearing a black "Free Pimp C" t-shirt, looked on.

Of course, the Bentley wasn't exactly a *gift*; it was a lease in Prince's name, and Chad would end up paying for it one way or another. The financial terms were something they'd agreed on privately as part of Chad's compensation for the *Sweet James Jones Stories* album and/or the upcoming *Pimpalation*.

"J. Prince is a great person, he's been very helpful … but J. Prince ain't just *giving* nobody a Bentley," smiles Bun B. "[J. Prince is] not the first label head to go and buy the artist a car. It's a lot easier to take you somewhere and sign for a car than actually getting money allocated from the company. It's a lot easier to give you possessions and stuff like that than cold cash. The reality is that you can get a $100,000 car without necessarily spending $100,000 cash. It makes it a lot easier financially."

After departing the Bentley dealership, the next stop was to see Prince's jeweler Emit at Exotic Diamonds, where Chad picked out two pinky rings, a bracelet, a watch, and a small chain with a cross pendant.*

He also spotted a praying hands piece which belonged to the singer R. Kelly, who had sent it to the shop to get some work done on it. "Hey, man, ask Robert if … it'll be alright for me to get a duplicate of that piece," he asked. Pimp would later recap the day on "Free":

(*Attempts to interview Emit were unsuccessful. Although Chad was initially complimentary, telling HipHopNews24-7, "Emit is dealing in quality, not quantity … he's really making some nice pieces," their relationship later deteriorated, apparently after Chad had a bad experience at Emit's shop. "Funky hoes don't know how to treat a nigga when he come to the sto' … eat a dick," Chad complained on the outro of his record "Down 4 Mine," adding in a light whisper, "Give me somethin' for free, bitch." He complained that Emit was "overchargin' a nigga." In a July 2007 interview for *OZONE* he said Emit "ain't no better than the rest of 'em," accusing him of charging a 300% markup, and instructing readers to "find you a muthafuckin' black jewel dealer, a muthafuckin' man of color, and let's start buying our rocks directly from muthafuckin' Africa" instead of spending money with Arabic men like Emit who "don't give a fuck about me and don't give a damn about my people.")

The boy Emit had me shining when I stepped out the do'
Thought I had enough, but James told him [to] gimme some more
And the same damn day I went to the Bentley lot
Off the showroom floor, I copped and splurged, that thang was hot

Still, Chad didn't want to be stereotyped as a typical rapper wasting his money on frivolous things. "They criticize us a lot for buying jewelry and shit when we get our first royalty check," he told *OZONE*. "But let me tell you my outlook on why we do this shit … Before we was brought over here to this country, we was kings and queens over there in Africa."

"When they brought us over here [in slavery] they made mutts out of us because they crossbred with our women, that's why we all got different skin tones," he continued. "But the African side of us … is yearning to get back to our roots… that's why we buying this shit. Wearing alligator shoes and suits and spending all this money on clothes and shit, buying $800 jeans and $1,200 jeans and $5,000 jeans … we just subconsciously trying to get back to our roots, 'cause in the motherland we was kings … Our language been took from us, our religion been took from us, everything that we believed in has been stripped from us, but the spirit still lives on and the blood of [our African ancestors] still pumping through our veins."

"So man, don't judge the young nigga that take his muthafuckin' advance and go buy a goddamn chain," he concluded.

Big Gipp, who felt like it might've been a good thing that Pimp had to sit down for a little while, admired his friend's new calm demeanor. "[Prison] gave him enough time to get a lot of the drugs out of his system and made him sit down from the life that he had," says Big Gipp. "He grew up very fast." Gipp felt like his friend had gotten caught up in the fast life, much like a young drug dealer or pimp with too much money and too much success at a young age.

Pimp C also stopped by 97.9 The Box, sporting a mink coat, to do an interview on Brandi Garcia and the Hollywood Boys' nightly mixshow. Michael Watts' mixshow on The Box had been a lifeline for him while he was incarcerated at the Terrell Unit, and he'd often tuned in to Brandi's Thursday night Cell Block Check-In segment.

Before he left, though, he did have a slight bone to pick with Brandi, who was new to the Houston area. He recalled an interview she'd done a few months prior, in which she mentioned that Bun was accompanied by his wife Queenie.

"Be careful with doing that," Pimp advised. "'Cause you never know [who the] rappers' actual wife is."

Brandi giggled, embarrassed. "Oh wow… did I break rapper code?"

At a local nightclub, Chad ran into his ex-girlfriend Kristi Floyd's cousin and got her number. Kristi, now married, had never quite forgiven Chad for their past issues. He evaded the question when Kristi asked if he was married.

"Heh heh," he chuckled. "Who told you that?"

He was also coy with the other women in his life. He stopped by to see Angie and Queenie, and, swallowing his pride, thanked Angie's husband for being a father figure to Corey while he was gone.

Angie had heard mention of Chad's "wife," but, not knowing that he was legally married, thought it was a figure of speech. When the topic came up in conversation, she laughed it off. "C, you not married," she said.

Chad was silent.

Shocked, she asked, "Did you get married?"

"I don't know where you got that from," he said.

"Well, you know, you can look up anything on the internet," she threatened. "Don't make me go to the web."

"I told you, it's hard out here for a young, single man in my tax bracket," he joked.

Angie couldn't understand why his marital status would be such a big secret. When he pulled off in his Bentley, Angie turned to Queenie. "Queenie, what kind of car [does] Chad have? It looks like a Chrysler."

"Fool, that's a Bentley," Queenie laughed.

Angie did a Google search to find out how much a Bentley cost. Seeing six figures, she called Chad. "Boy, have you lost your mind!?"

The situation between Pimp C and Sean Paul of the YoungBloodz had never come to a head, but never officially been resolved, either. At the 2004 Source Awards in Miami, the Young-Bloodz and Lil Jon accepted the Song of the Year Award for "Damn!" J. Prince was in the building too, appearing on stage with Source co-owners Dave Mays and Benzino and fellow industry heavyweights Russell Simmons and Suge Knight.

During an intermission, Sean Paul spotted J. Prince in the crowd and approached him to gauge the status of the Pimp C situation. "I respect J. Prince all my life anyway just for him being a businessman," says Sean Paul. "I like [to see people's] faces, man. I like to see what's going on. I don't like to just sit back and [let] shit hit me in the head, you know? I like to walk *towards* the tension."

From Prince's reaction, Sean Paul could tell that the situation had cooled down. They exchanged contact information and Sean Paul made it a point to visit Houston for some one-on-one time with Prince.

The A&R responsible for the YoungBloodz' hit "Damn!" was Mickey "MempHitz" Wright, a young executive at Jive Records. MempHitz was originally from Memphis, as his name might suggest, a diehard Southern rap fan who had grown up on UGK. MempHitz's first signing at Jive was Tallahassee native Faheem "T-Pain" Najm, a self-contained rapper/producer/singer. His sound was unique, different, and untested, and the selection was initially met with skepticism around the Jive offices.

T-Pain's debut album *Rapper Ternt Singa* dropped in December 2005, three weeks before Pimp C's release. His first two singles "I'm Sprung" and "I'm N Luv (Wit A Stripper)" exploded, establishing MempHitz' position as something of a wunderkind at Jive.

With Pimp C home, everyone at Jive was in high spirits and optimistic about the coming year. New employees like MempHitz were representative of the many changes that had taken place during Chad's four-year absence.

Hip-Hop was no longer seen as a passing fad, it was now a multi-billion dollar business. Southern rappers were no longer regarded as backwards and country but were in high demand at major labels. Jive was no longer staffed by condescending New Yorkers who looked down on Port Arthur, Texas. Now, in addition to having veterans like Barry Weiss and Jeff Sledge on their team, UGK would be supported by fresh young employees like A&R MempHitz and Ron Stewart in the mixshow department, many of whom were UGK fans.

Plus, UGK had stood the test of time, proving their fanbase would stick by them even during a lengthy hiatus. UGK were leaders of the movement which was now topping music charts, putting them in a much better position to negotiate. They had far more power than they did as teenage rookies in 1992.

UGK owed Jive one more album, and riding off the wave of the "Free Pimp C" movement, everyone understood the potential for their project. Also, Jive now had access to more money. Thanks to their massive worldwide pop success, Jive's parent company Zomba had been purchased by BMG for $2.84 billion, the largest-ever acquisition of an independent label with major-label distribution.

MempHitz was just one of several Jive employees who flew down to Houston within a week of Chad's release to welcome him home.

Jeff Sledge reached for an hor d'oeurve and turned around anxiously as the door to their lavish suite at the Four Seasons opened, but it was just the server. He glanced anxiously at Barry Weiss. The room was silent, Jive executives exchanging glances. This felt too familiar: here they were again, waiting for Pimp C.

Knowing that Jive considered him difficult and unreliable, Chad planned to impress them by arriving early. He and his mother departed Port Arthur two hours ahead of time to make the 90-mile drive to Houston. Hoping for a fresh start, he wanted to show that things would be different this time around.

It wasn't meant to be; a serious accident on I-10 held them up in traffic and by the time they arrived at the Four Seasons, everyone was already there, even Bun and Red Boy. Chad apologized profusely for his late arrival, but they didn't hold it against him. Everyone was just glad to have him home.

Jeff Sledge, one of the few original staffers left, was known to fight the hardest for UGK around the Jive offices. The support he'd shown Mama Wes while Chad was away solidified him as an ally in Chad's mind. "I feel good, man," Chad told Jeff. "I'm not going to mess with no crazy shit no more. My mind's clear, I'm sharp, man. I feel good. I want to try to cut down some of this weight [I gained], but I feel good."

"Chad changed so much better when he went to prison," says Jeff. "He was like a completely different person ... [he was] humble, nice, smiled all the time ... [his] personality had really evened out. He obviously did some soul searching."

Barry Weiss, too, was impressed with the all-new and improved Chad. In the late 90s, Weiss found Chad difficult to work with because of his volatile personality and drug use. "He was in a really bad state from drugs; he was really incoherent at times and not that lucid," recalls Weiss. "[But when he came home] he was in a great space. It was great to see how clearheaded he was."

They sipped champagne, ate hors d'oeuvres, and talked business. Chad was touched by the welcome home party, a nice gesture which showed good faith on Jive's behalf, and everyone departed the gathering in high spirits with eager anticipation for the coming year.

"Jive is 100% better – no, 200% better – than they were when I left," he told *OZONE* after the meeting. "They got a hell of a staff right now... They had some good ass ideas that surprised the fuck out of me. They really ain't trippin', and they talking good. Jive's got a hell of a machine right now. It's a different place than it was before I left."

While he was gone, he'd had time to reflect on the positive things that had come from their relationship with Jive: the inclusion of "Pocket Full of Stones" on the *Menace II Society* soundtrack, for example, or the *Ridin' Dirty* promo tour.

Bun tried to look on the bright side, too. "I learned more about the music industry bein' on Jive than I think I would've ever learned [on] any other label," he told *Murder Dog*, reflecting, "I'm glad that we never blew up before. I don't think we woulda been able to handle it. Now me and Pimp have really matured. We're takin' our success in stride. If we had got millions and shit, we probably wouldn't have it now. Maybe the name would be gone and the fame would be gone by goin' out blowin' a lotta money, doin' stupid shit."

Plus, the staff seemed as excited about the project as they were. "This time around I'm just hoping that everybody does their job," Chad told AllHipHop. "When we bring a project in that we've put our blood, sweat and tears into we just want them to step up and do their part – no more, no less."

After the suite party, MempHitz found himself in the elevator with his idol, Pimp C. During the meeting, Weiss introduced him to UGK as his up-and-coming star A&R who could help them with anything they needed. MempHitz tried to contain his enthusiasm, not wanting to seem too starstruck. He could recite the words to every UGK song by heart and couldn't believe he had the opportunity to work with them.

Pimp glanced over at MempHitz, who had tattooed his mantra, "DO WORK," in large block letters on his left arm. He smiled. "You the gangsta at Jive, huh?" Pimp joked. "You don't be doing all this bullshit they be doing?"

"I ain't no gangsta," Memphitz laughed. He paused. "Your music did that to me."

The moment stuck with Memphitz, who had always admired Pimp C's attitude and style. "He put something inside of me that made me like, *Fuck this corporate stuff*," he laughs. "I used to be trying to impress people at Jive, but Pimp had that attitude like, *Fuck em in they pussy!* So I was like, *Yeah, fuck 'em in they pussy!*"

CHAPTER 38

"I never said I was a pioneer. Other people kept saying that. If that's how they feel, good. I'd rather get my flowers while I'm still in it and still alive than when I'm dead and gone. That ain't for me to say. I don't go in the studio making records like I'm some type of dude on a pedestal or something any different from anybody else that's out here grinding, 'cause you're only as good as your last record." – Pimp C

"[Being on parole] you've got to stay focused every day on this [shit] ... because you've got one foot in prison and one foot out. I'm not gonna jinx myself and say it's gonna be easy. But I'm gonna put my best foot forward and stay creative and do the right thing. I don't smoke. I don't drink. I don't do no drugs. It's a new way of living. I'm out now, and I'm gonna take advantage of that blessing."
– Pimp C, *Dallas Morning News*, February 2006

Now that he looked the part, Pimp was ready to hit the studio with his jewelry and brand-new Bentley. He detailed his plans on the *Pimpalation* DVD: "I'm really gonna be home trying to do some family shit or in the studio trying to do three songs a night. Anything else don't make no sense. I ain't out here tryin' to be no freak. I ain't out here trying to have no ménage a trois… I don't drink, I don't smoke, I don't wanna kick it, [and] I don't want no friends."

"[If] you wasn't writing me in no penitentiary or coming to see me down there, I don't wanna see you now," he added. "Unless you got some money."

On the evening of Wednesday, January 4, 2006, Pimp arrived at Studio 7303 for his first recording session. Filmmaker Ariel "REL" Santschi of the *Pitch Control* DVD was on hand to document Chad's first few sessions. During the first week and a half, Pimp recorded the T-Pain "I'm In Luv (Wit' A Stripper)" remix, T.I.'s "Front, Back," Trae's "Swang" remix (which referenced Fat Pat's verse from DJ DMD's "25 Lighters"), E-40's "White Gurl," 8Ball & MJG's "Whatchu Gonna Do," Project Pat's "'Cause I'm A Playa," "Hood" for Big Gipp and Ali's Kinfolk album featuring Nelly; and five songs with Webbie and Boosie.

"Before I came home James told me that all these things was gonna be available to me when I touched down," Pimp said later on the *Too Real For TV* DVD. "The day I touched down I had like 25, 26 guest appearances between $17,500 and $20,000 a pop … I ran through them muthafuckers in a matter of three or four days." He was also working on ideas for his upcoming Rap-A-Lot project, a compilation tentatively titled *Pimp C & Friends*, and "I Don't Fuck Wit' U" and "Get Down" with Smoke D, whom he planned to release as one of the first artists on UGK Records.

Pimp ran into T-Mo Goodie at the studio and showed off his Bentley. "That's a blessing to be able to get out and shine," T-Mo observed. "That's a prisoner's dream, to get out of jail and shine like that and be able to get your Bentley and live good."

"How can a nigga come home from the pen for four years, ain't got no album out, out here drivin' all this shit, man, and doin' it like this?" Pimp reflected on the *Too Real For TV* DVD. "I got to have God on my side, mayne, 'cause it ain't nothing else that could do these thangs."

T.I. was in the midst of recording for his *King* album and had recruited Mannie Fresh to produce a revamped version of UGK's "Front, Back & Side to Side." Prior to Pimp's release, an early version of the track leaked out which featured only Bun (and T.I. on the outro talking about what he planned to do "when Pimp walk out that courthouse," followed by an obligatory "Free Pimp C!").

Pimp came home as they were mixing the record, and Mannie told T.I. the song wasn't complete without him. "You gotta have him say that 'never let hoe ass niggas ride' [on the hook]," Mannie told him. Former No Limit rapper Fiend was now an A&R for Atlantic Records and helped facilitate the deal, arranging for a hefty five-figure check to be cut. They met up at Studio 7303 and were able to share a laugh over the Master P hotel incident.

Pimp viewed his reconciliation with Master P as a template for other rappers to follow. "If me and P could make peace after the thangs we went through, I know anybody can have peace out here," he said later during a radio interview with DJ Greg Street.

"[Our beef] wasn't [just on records]," he added later in an interview with WordofSouth. com. "It was serious, people's lives was at stake ... so if me and P can put our differences aside after all the history we had together, these lil bitch ass rap niggas can do the same thing." He shouted out Master P and C-Murder on BET's *Rap City*; on Chamillionaire's "Ridin' Dirty," he rapped, "Just got off the phone with Master P."

Pimp hoped to do a record with C-Murder, Project Pat, and Mystikal, who was still incarcerated. Through C-Murder, he got a phone number on Mia X, who had bowed out of the rap game and dedicated her time to raising her children.

Mia hadn't talked to Chad since she heard about the hotel incident, and was nervous when she first got the call. Although her ex-fiancé Jimmie Keller had initially denied involvement in the hotel beating, she'd eventually learned that it was true, and worried that it would affect her relationship with Chad. "I was so blindsided by that incident, and it hurt me so bad, because I had really become friends with Chad and Bun over the years," Mia X says. "It really, really hurt my feelings when I found out that actually did happen."

In any case, Mia X's volatile relationship with Keller had long since ended. Keller married another woman in 2005. And Chad certainly wasn't the only person who had a physical altercation with Jimmie. "He done things [to people] all through the city, you know, and how you live is how you die," Mia X sighs. Two weeks before Chad was released from prison, Keller was killed in New Orleans.

"Chad, I don't even know what to say," Mia X began, when her old friend called. "I didn't know that [hotel incident] happened to you."

"Mia, don't worry about that," Chad said. "I already talked to [Master] P. And I know you had nothing to do with that."

"Me and this guy ... we ended up going out in a blaze of gunfire ... Jimmie [Keller] was the type that just fly off the handle," Mia explained apologetically. "Sometimes you really didn't know what he was gonna do. And he's dead [now]."

Pimp didn't want to dwell on the topic anymore; he told Mia it was good to know that his old friends still answered the phone when he called. He'd been trying to reach out to the crop of new rappers who played a part in the "Free Pimp C" movement, just to thank them for their support, but was surprised how hard it was just to get them on the phone. "People will give you, like, their assistant number [or] they manager number," he griped. He didn't like the rap industry's new impersonal way of doing business.

Pimp called Slim Thug, who happened to be out on the road with Killa Kyleon and his Boss Hogg Outlawz clique promoting their *Serve & Collect* project. Conversation turned to the growing beef between T.I. and Lil Flip. "You know, you gotta be careful what you say on these records, because real niggas gon' come see you," Pimp advised, relaying the Master P hotel room story.

"Man, you know that nigga P, man, that nigga P a real nigga," Pimp laughed. "P a real gangsta, mayne. I said some crazy shit to P and P came and whooped me and my bitch ass, man. I deserved that, mayne. After that, me and P, man, we was cool. We ain't got no more problems."

Pimp also smoothed things over with Sean Paul of the YoungBloodz on a three-way call with J. Prince. And through mutual friends, a sit-down was arranged between Pimp and Isreal Kight, who had spent the past twelve years wondering why Pimp had pulled a gun on him.

"[DJ DMD] called me and told me you was gonna kill me," Pimp explained. "He said you just had left his parents' music shop and you was coming over there to kill me." In retrospect, Kight blamed DMD for instigating the incident and they agreed to put the past behind them.

After a solid week of recording, Pimp started doing interviews. With an XXL writer and photographer in tow, Pimp revisited Short Texas, the old dope spot, which was now a quiet, abandoned street. Although Hurricane Rita had caused significant damage in Port Arthur, the area had already been in a steady decline and had one of the highest unemployment rates in the state. (Between 1980 and 2010, Port Arthur's population dropped 12%.) "Ain't like it used to be," Pimp commented, adding apparently without irony, "Just a couple of junkies out here now."

They stopped by a local barbershop, where Pimp checked in with a bunch of old friends. Many of them had been to prison themselves, and conversation revolved around their time behind bars. The moment struck a chord with XXL photographer Mike Schreiber.

"It was the exact same way that me and my friends [back in Long Island] would talk about college," recalls Schreiber. "For me, prison would be really the worst thing that ever happened to me, and I'm not saying it wasn't for him, but it didn't seem that way. It was just like a rite of passage ... the way they were speaking [about going to prison] was just so matter-of-fact, and almost in a fond way ... [as if it were] just part of the [Texas] lifestyle."

During our phone interview for *OZONE* a few days later, Pimp frequently referred to the Texas prison system as "modern day slavery" and said he felt a responsibility to draw attention to the problem, hoping to pressure "people in powerful positions" to come down to Texas and investigate unfair sentencing guidelines.

"It's some bullshit," he said. "You've got one man in prison who got two years for running over somebody in his car, and then the next man got 30 years for getting caught with some [cocaine]. Those numbers don't match."

"We could do a whole interview about what's wrong with the penile system in Texas ... We really need to get [investigative reporting television show] *60 Minutes* up inside the prison and really show the living conditions," he said. "It's common knowledge what's going on in Texas," he added in an interview with AllHipHop. "It's just that the powers that be are so strong down there that the media doesn't even really want to open up that can of worms."

"There ain't nothing gangsta about that shit, nothing fly about it," Pimp concluded. "People often ask me, 'Are you gonna rap about being in prison?' and I tell them that I didn't see nothing in there worth rapping about. I saw a bunch of men missing their families ... that shit is some painful shit, seeing folks that have done 15 years and got another 30 years to do. They're getting old and they're cut off from their families. It's really some sad shit."

Although Pimp had posed in front of the Huntsville Unit, he now had second thoughts about the photos. He invited me out to Houston to take some better pictures – now that he was outfitted with new jewelry and a Bentley – to print alongside his interview.

On January 19, Bun arranged for Sway to interview UGK at Rap-A-Lot's office for MTV News, displaying the wall full of plaques and the Rap-A-Lot logo embedded in the floor. (D-Solo and Pam Harris' Street Flava TV also got the interview Pimp had promised them while he was in prison.) Sway had been a mainstay at MTV for years and could claim the distinction of being the last person to interview both Tupac Shakur and Biggie Smalls before their untimely passing. Sway welcomed the chance to speak with these "iconic figures" who had become "Southern folk heroes" and "witness their dynamic in person after years of listening to their music."

"Watching him go in was a kind of pain that I can't really describe with words," Bun said.

"And watching him come out was a joy that you really can't describe with words, either."

I flew out to Houston later that afternoon to meet up with Pimp C at Studio 7303, where he was in the booth with Lil Flip, Pimpin' Ken, and Lil Keke, doing a prerecorded radio appearance for Lil Flip's new Clover G show on XM 66 Raw satellite radio. Pimp also dropped a verse on the remix to "U'z A Trick," the lead single from Lil Flip's fourth album *I Need Mine*.

"He had a whole trashcan full of raps," recalls Lil Flip. "He had so many verses lined up, [he'd be] like, 'Hold on, let me knock out this verse for such-and-such.' He would do his verse then tear the paper up and put it in the trash can." All in all, he'd churned out more than 32 features during his first few weeks home.

Lil Flip, who was sipping syrup from a double-cup of Styrofoam, offered Pimp a sip.

"Nah, I'm good," Pimp declined. He was in a good mood, cracking jokes in the studio. Lil Keke was entertained by this new, flamboyant Pimp; he'd remembered him as a quiet, introspective musician back in the Screw days.

"We wasn't making this kind of money before. [Before] Pimp went to jail, we were getting $2,000 – $3,000 a show," Lil Keke says. "Now when Pimp came home, we getting $10,000, $15,000, so look at the stars we are now: Slim Thugs and [Lil] Kekes and Z-Ros and Traes, we self-made stars. [So] when Pimp came home [he had] earrings and watches and chains and Bentleys and mink coats … This was the Pimp that he always wanted to be."

Also in the studio were Vicious and Bundy of the X-Mob. Their momentum had stopped back in 1997 when both men went to prison on unrelated drug charges. Vicious had been home for a few years, but Bundy was fresh out, and Pimp wanted to help give his old friends an opportunity, laying out his vision for UGK Records.

It would be an informal deal, Pimp explained; he didn't want to force them into signing contracts until he had something more solid to offer. "Straight up, man, I don't have the money to give y'all right now," he told them. "But y'all now I'm gonna get it. I'm not gonna sign y'all [to paperwork] in case somebody else come [along] and wanna sign y'all."

After doing a quick photo shoot with Pimp and his Bentley, we pulled off from Studio 7303. I hopped in the backseat and caught the tail end of a conversation Pimp was having with Pimpin' Ken, in the passenger seat, about his prison nuptials. "Yeah, I got her a ring," Pimp nodded. "She knows what it is."

My ears perked up, but that was the extent of their wedding conversation. Both as a woman and a journalist, I could barely contain my curiosity. That was it? This was how pimps discussed marriage?

Chad's friends and former classmates back in Port Arthur, who remembered Chinara as a chubby youngster, were mostly shocked when they learned that the two had married. Pearce Pegross, a Port Arthur athletic standout who went to high school with Chinara, was dumbfounded. *How in the fuck did they…* he wondered. *Where the fuck they met at?*

"Why would you be a famous dude and marry any chick from Port Arthur?" Pearce laughs. "Everybody [here] slept with everybody. [We're all] kin, you know?" Chad's childhood neighbor Ron Forrest felt like Chad could've done better. *Goddamn Chad, you muthafuckin' Pimp C.*

Ron's sister Ronda, who had been gone for a while and recently moved back to Port Arthur, was a little out of the loop and still catching up on the local gossip. "Nigga, who you got pregnant?" she teased Chad.

"Man, you know that gu'l, man, yo' homegal," Chad mumbled.

"Her!?" Ronda couldn't believe it. "That was you? For real!? *You* got her pregnant?"

"Maaaane," Chad said, drawing out every syllable. "What had happened was…"

"Nigga, shut up," Ronda laughed, changing the subject.

Boonie, who had been around in the beginning when Chad and Chinara first crossed paths at Hiroshima, was back in Port Arthur catching up with some old friends when "Pimp's wife" was mentioned in conversation.

"Pimp *married*?" Boonie laughed. "That's wild."

"Yeah, Pimp married Chinara," someone told him.

"Yeah? Chinara who?" Boonie asked.

"Man, Chinara. Your homegirl," came the response.

Boonie laughed wholeheartedly. "Boy, stop fuckin' playin'."

When he learned that it was really true, Boonie couldn't believe it. He reached out to Chad via text and he called him back. The two chatted about music and caught up on old times before Boonie finally brought up the topic.

"So you married Chinara, huh?" Boonie asked.

Chad started laughing and then changed the topic.

"That laugh could've meant a million thangs… [so] I left it [alone]," Boonie shrugs. "What the fuck else I'ma say?"

Shortly after he came home, Pimp called Scarface. "Where you at, mayne?" he asked. "Man, I gotta see that boy Brad, mayne. Where that boy Brad?"

"Man, I'm at Ray Cash video shoot," Scarface told him.

Ray Cash was a Cleveland rapper signed to Kawan Prather's Ghet-O-Vision imprint who had added a "Free Pimp C" ad-lib on his humorous record "Sex Appeal (Pimp In My Own Mind)." (KP recruited Pimp to drop a verse on the remix, which also featured T.I., Young Dro, and Project Pat. The remix was never officially released due to clearance issues, but circulated on some underground mixtapes.)

Ray Cash and Scarface were filming the video for "Bumpin' My Music" in Houston. Pimp made a grand entrance, pulling up on set outfitted in a mink coat in his brand new silver Bentley. "You gleamin' like a muthafucker," Scarface told him, laughing.

"When we seen each other, we couldn't do nothing but laugh," Scarface recalls. "'Cause he knew, just like I knew … we went through a lot of our shit in our careers, and we was coming of age … That was a terrible thing that he had to do that time [in prison]. He had to do four years behind nothing, you know? [And] I was glad to see my homeboy in the Bentley with the fur on, you know, that's some funny shit."

Before he left, Pimp turned to a few DJs on set from Houston radio station The Box. "What up, Agg?" Pimp asked, acknowledging DJ Aggravated. He turned his attention to DJ Rob G, who was wearing a 97.9 The Box hat. "What's yo' name?" he asked.

"Rob G."

Pimp didn't miss a beat. "Don't know you. You gotta do something to get yo' name out there," he said, then walked away, leaving Rob G speechless.

"Part of me wanted to say, 'Well, you've been in jail for four years,'" Rob G laughs. But he held his tongue and realized Pimp was right.

On January 26, Pimp gamely posed for the cover of *The Source*, wearing a black mink coat and a black Trill hat, but still harbored a grudge towards the magazine which he believed had dissed UGK's debut *The Southern Way* in the early 90s. ("I couldn't get on a *Source* cover 'til I went to prison," he griped later in an interview with *XXL*. "I had to go to prison to get on the cover of yo' funky-ass magazine?")

The following day he made an appearance at his "Welcome Home Party" at Club Blue in southwest Houston. Earlier in the night, they filmed scenes there to be used in the "Get Throwed" remix video.

Pimp walked on stage, his arm draped around Bun's shoulder, and raised his glass to the enthusiastic crowd. The DJ threw on "Pocket Full of Stones" and Pimp rapped along with the hook. Willie D, who was in the building, couldn't believe the crowd's response. "He was treated like a rock star," Willie D remembers. "He was way bigger than he ever was before he went in."

The following day, Pimp and Bun continued shooting scenes for the remixed version of Bun's "Get Throwed" video with Young Jeezy and Z-Ro. REL from the Pitch Control DVD was there filming all the behind-the-scenes footage for Rap-A-Lot, but other videographers were instructed to stop filming. Those who didn't were confronted by Jonathon Pete, an enormous 7'1", 400 pound man with an Afro whom Rap-A-Lot had recruited to act as Pimp's bodyguard.

As they wrapped one of the last scenes, Jeezy, wearing a "Mr. 17.5" t-shirt, slung his arms around Bun and Pimp and leaned down into a behind-the-scenes camera. "I came out here for my big homies, nigga!" Jeezy proclaimed in his trademark raspy voice. "UGK for life, nigga! Pimp C back on the muthafuckin' streets."

The next morning, Pimp and Bun joined T.I. on the set of his video for "Front Back." For the car-themed video, Pimp had his heart set on Chamillionaire's red Cadillac Biarritz. "Man, I need that car for my part," he told his cousin Ed.

Chamillionaire was another artist who, like David Banner, had achieved great financial success while Pimp C was incarcerated largely by building off the movement UGK created. Artists like David Banner, Paul Wall, and Chamillionaire felt a responsibility to show love back to UGK since they had been raised on their music.

"[The new generation of Southern rappers] came along on a foundation that was already built," Too $hort noted. "They didn't blaze the trail … they came down a path. [To] make a path, you gotta chop down some shit to get to it. UGK was one of them ones [who made the] sacrifice."

Bun pointed to Chamillionaire and UGK as a great example of Houston's music scene sustaining itself. "I think we helped to validate Houston's musical scene and I think Houston's music scene had to validate us," Bun told *VIBE*. "Say for example, UGK makes an album called *Ridin' Dirty* and Chamillionaire makes a song based on that movement called 'Ridin' Dirty.' It becomes a big song then he comes back and puts UGK on the remix. It's like UGK reaches a level of fame; Chamillionaire takes what we've done and builds on it, takes his thing to another level and then comes back and brings us and exposes us to the wider audience."

Off the strength of his single "Ridin' Dirty," produced by Play & Skillz, Chamillionaire had achieved international notoriety, and he'd always credited UGK with originally coining the term. "I stole that idea from [Pimp and Bun, and] I made millions off of that," Chamillionaire said. "I felt like, because of that, I owed everything to these guys."

Pimp had never asked for the Biarritz, only expressed his love for it, but Chamillionaire got the hint and wanted to give it to him, to repay him for the influence he'd had on his own career. Besides, he didn't drive it often. "He didn't ask for it," Chamillionaire says. "But I was so much of a fan of UGK that I gave him the car." They agreed that Pimp would tell people he bought it.*

As the camera crew wrapped the first clothing store scene for "Front Back," MTV's Sway sat down for a lengthy interview with Bun B, Pimp C, and J. Prince; the footage would later be used

(*According to Bun B, the transaction turned into a barter in which Pimp C gave Chamillionaire a verse and a beat in exchange for the car. Chamillionaire declined to be interviewed for this book but discussed the Biarritz exchange in a public UStream session. Despite their agreement, Pimp still told people that Chamillionaire gave him the car. "I can't lie, I can only keep it trill … I don't wanna be no liar," Chamillionaire recalled Pimp telling him. Pimp later referenced the car on UGK's "Chrome Plated Woman," rapping, "Chamillion' gave me the bitch, she was already a star / Now all these niggas wanna fuck my car.")

on several UGK documentaries. It was not often that J. Prince spoke on the record. "You got an hour and a half, maybe two hours of candid time with J. Prince," Bun B later told Sway. "That's not an easy thing. I don't think I've [ever] had two hours of candid time with J. Prince."

"When I came to visit you [at the Terrell Unit] we talked about what a lot of these dudes are rapping about these days, and how a lot of these dudes are glorifying being incarcerated and in prison," Sway noted. "They wear it like a badge of honor. I don't really understand that logic."

"When you're gone in a position like that it really puts a perspective on your life. It really shows you what's important," Pimp nodded. "It helps you get your priorities in line, and then it shows you who's who around you. We had a bunch of fairweather muthafuckers around us for a long time, and when the shit went down, a lot of niggas fell off and a lot of people stepped up to the plate that I didn't expect to. So I really got to see what side of the plate my bread was buttered on; really got to analyze life, and I learned I can get more bees and flies with honey than I can with vinegar."

"The real niggas that known anything about [prison] or have homeboys or family members that's been down there theyselves know it ain't nothing live about that shit," Pimp added. "The only person that would feed into that [glorification] would be a square or somebody from the outside looking in that don't know no better … Most of the niggas that be [saying] that shit, they ain't never been to the penitentiary. They [just] went to the state jail or SAFP or some shit."

Pimp told Sway that they were planning to release a self-titled UGK album through Jive. "Jive talking some good shit," Pimp admitted. "But, you know, they talking good shit because of the grinding and the work that Bun and J. Prince put in and that's cool, as long as they've got some paper. They wanna be able to get down with [our movement]."

"That [album] that J. [Prince] put together for me [while I was incarcerated] was a paper move, and you know, it served its purpose," Pimp said. "We got some bread, we generated some money while a nigga was sitting down, but you know, I'm gonna do a real solo album soon."

Pimp said he planned to do a group album with Too $hort called the Broad Playas and a group album with Webbie and Boosie called the V12 Boys on Trill Entertainment. He hoped to release Smoke D, the X-Mob, and Bo$$ on his own label, and also do an album with Z-Ro. "Me and J gonna have to sit down with him and … chop it up and figure out what's gonna make him smile," Pimp said. "'Cause a nigga like him…"

"That nigga don't smile too often," Prince interjected.

"Yeah, but I got something that'll make him smile," Pimp said. "We gonna sit down and get him right. He's very talented, one of the most talented youngstas in the fuckin' South in the game right now. The nigga produce, the nigga rap, the nigga sing his own hooks, and with me and him … me and him could do an album in four days."

While Sway conducted the lengthy on-camera interview with UGK and J. Prince, I rode over to the Sharpstown Mall with MempHitz, where he planned to get fitted for a grill at TV Jewelry.

Nelly's record "Grillz" was huge, and in Houston, Paul Wall and his business partner Johnny Dang, better known as "TV Johnny," were taking advantage of the high demand. Pimp had come by to get two sets, one filled with white diamonds and the other with white-and-blue diamonds. He bought a watch and got a TV Johnny watch pro bono.

"I love [it] whenever he stopped by," says TV Johnny. "Most artist when they stop by, they either buy jewelry or get something quick, they never pay attention [to] sit down and talk to you … [and] he's one of the only rappers [that] I never heard a customer talk bad about."

MempHitz sat down in the back room and TV Johnny mixed 3M putty in a plastic tray, handing it to him to bite into and make a mold of his teeth. MempHitz' BlackBerry, on the small table next to his chair, vibrated loudly. He gestured towards his phone as if I should pick it up. The incoming call was from Rawle, a mutual friend who managed the rapper Twista.

"Good afternoon, and thank you for calling MempHitz' phone," I announced in the most professional voice I could manage. "How may I be of service?"

There was a pause. "Uh… Is MempHitz there?"

I laughed and told Rawle who I was. "He's getting fitted for a grill. He'll call you back in a minute."

"Okay," Rawle said. "Just let him know that I got his message and we're in for the 'Stripper' remix." T-Pain's record "I'm In Luv With A Stripper," was blazing the charts, and MempHitz was putting together the remix.

We wrapped up with TV Johnny and headed out into the parking lot, the afternoon sun warm overhead. As I jumped in shotgun of MempHitz' rental SUV he explained his dilemma.

"I asked Pain who he wanted to have on the 'Stripper' remix, and he gave me a whole list: R Kelly, Too Short, Pimp C, Twista, MJG, Paul Wall…" MempHitz said, explaining that he'd been overeager and had reached out to all of them at the same time. The problem was, they all agreed to do it, even Pimp C, who'd been hesitant until he heard who else was involved. Now how was he going to fit everybody on one record?

"We damn near don't have room for T-Pain, and it's his song!" he half-joked.

"Just split it up and let everybody do half a verse," I suggested.

When MempHitz and I got back from Sharpstown, Sway was wrapping up his interview and everyone headed to the second location. It was an unusually windy day, and the group congregated on a blocked-off section of a quiet Houston freeway where Dr. Teeth's crew had set up mock I-10 and I-20 signs to represent Atlanta and Houston.

As I lounged in the passenger seat, a crew member brought Pimp two plates of food during the lunch break. He passed one to me. As T.I. approached the car, Pimp asked me to get in the backseat.

As I grabbed my camera and the plate of food and slid in the backseat, I accidentally tilted the plate sideways and a small handful of rice tumbled onto the plush bright orange leather interior. Panicked, I glanced up to make sure that Pimp hadn't seen my blunder before carefully scooping the rice back onto the plate. Fortunately, the leather looked untouched. I felt Ed looking at me and glanced over at him as he offered a reassuring smile.

In a tone of sincere admiration, T.I. welcomed Pimp home, his pronunciation proper. His conversation was peppered with "yes, sir." T.I.'s arrogant swagger was as much a part of his public persona as his rap skills, and I had never heard him sound so humble.

I stole a glance at Ed and the expression on his face was exactly what I was thinking: *T.I.?!? Starstruck!?* I halfway wanted to peek around the corner of the seat to check and see if this was the real T.I. or an imposter.

"With muthafuckers he respects, Tip is actually the most pleasant person in the whole world," laughs T.I.'s former A&R Kawan "KP" Prather. "If he has any respect for you, it's absolutely incredible just to sit and talk to him sometimes, because he turns on his intelligent shit, his I've-been-thinking-about-this-all-week-but-ain't-had-nobody-to-talk-to-about-it shit… Like, having in-depth conversations [with T.I.] about his views on family and all that, I'm [thinking,] *This nigga is awesome.*"

The conversation wasn't what I expected from two rappers: they began sharing investment ideas, discussing real estate. As the conversation became more personal, I started to feel like I shouldn't be there, intruding on their conversation. I mentally zoned out, focusing my attention on T.I.'s fingertips grasping the back of the leather headrest a few inches in front of me. The moment felt tender; historic, even.

When they were done talking and the video shoot resumed, it was back to business as usual. T.I. resumed his cocky swagger and emerged from the vehicle ready to film. I climbed back in Pimp's car, behind him this time, when it was time to head to the next location.

As we exited the freeway, Chamillionaire's brother Rasaq followed in the red Biarritz. The car was a show car, not really meant to be driven, and it crawled along at a snail's pace. A police car emerged behind us, its lights flashing.

A concerned look crossed Pimp's face as we pulled into the nearby gas station. When he saw the officer emerge from the police car behind us, he relaxed. "Oh, that's Rap-A-Lot police," he said dismissively, his eyes connecting with mine in the rear-view mirror with the most meaningful glance I'd ever seen.

The officer approached the driver's door with a wide smile and grasped Pimp C's hand. "Just wanted to say welcome home, Pimp," he beamed, inquiring where we were headed. "Follow me," he instructed, then led us through a handful of red lights with his lights flashing.

By the time we reached the third and final scene, night had fallen, and a *Cheddar* DVD camera on set panned to Slim Thug. "It was some fake-ass hoe-ass niggas on [your] DVD last time," Slim told the cameras, referring to Lil Flip. "Tell them ol' crumb-ass, cake-ass, bitch-ass niggas [to] suck a dick. Fliperachi, [you] gay ass nigga. You and your Clover gay-ass niggas, all you flower-wearin' bitch-ass niggas, suck a dick. I'm over here, Third Ward, in your 'hood. Where you at, bitch? Yeah. The Boss. I'm on the cover [of *Cheddar* DVD]. Where you at? Put your album out, mayne."

Chad's new mission was to bring peace and unity to Southern rappers, especially in Texas. "He became such a cooler elder statesman after he came out of jail," says KP. "He still had his [controversial] ways, but he was open to talk to new artists and give 'em game." In his new position, he knew he could be instrumental in bringing people together. "It's a lot of beef going on right now," he said. "They kinda mad at each other, and a lot of 'em don't even know why they mad. They can't even remember what it's all about."

Lil Keke, a staunch representative of the south side, had signed a deal with Swisha House on the north side, a moment he viewed as the official end of Houston's north vs. south beef. To symbolize the city's unity, he collaborated with Paul Wall on a record called "Chunk Up the Deuce."

The record initially featured Slim Thug, but they were having problems clearing his vocals through Interscope Records and needed someone to replace him. Paul Wall's manager T. Farris happened to bump into Pimp and he did the verse. The hook was borrowed from one of Lil Keke's early Screw tape freestyles.

Another record which utilized a sample from an old Lil Keke Screw tape freestyle was "Knockin' Doors Down." The record, produced for Myke Diesel, was initially intended as the lead single for P.O.P., the first artist released on Southern Empire, a record label owned by J. Prince's sons Jas Prince and J. Prince Jr.

Instead, J. Prince decided to use the track for Pimp C's upcoming compilation project, with a verse from P.O.P. Although Keke's original "knockin' doors down" line was a car reference, Pimp took the song to have a different meaning. "When he's talking about 'knocking doors down,' he's talking about knocking down the doors of bullshit, ignorance, and whatnot," Bun B explained on the *BEEF IV* DVD.

"Don't you fools realize that we can get a whole bunch of money together? … As much money as we having, as much business as we giving this Rolls Royce lot and this Cadillac lot and this BMW lot, what is you mad about?" Pimp asked. "We all living behind big gates, big ol' houses, having big jewels and getting paid to party?! We get paid to party! What is y'all mad about, man?"

Amidst rapidly changing technology and the frenetic pace of the music industry, it was tough for a woman nearly 60 to keep up. Mama Wes still conducted business with simple one-sheet contracts and handwritten letters via fax. While Pimp was in prison, Bun had assembled his own management team, with Red Boy overseeing things and Eric "Bone" York handing the day-to-day responsibilities on the road.

Chad decided it was time to seek out new management, taking some stress off Mama Wes and leaving her with more time to be a mother and grandmother. Bun and Pimp preferred to have separate management because they led separate lives and had so many individual projects outside of the group. Through a former classmate, Chad was introduced to Walter "Rick" Martin, a smooth-talking businessman based in Los Angeles.

Rick, a 35-year-old UC Berkeley graduate, owned a company called FM2 Radio which arranged worldwide syndication for popular DJs like Green Lantern and DJ Clue. He wanted to branch off into artist management. Pimp hired Rick as his business manager; Mama Wes would still serve as his personal manager, handling most of his show bookings and appearances.

After the Eddie Floyd fiasco, Pimp no longer felt comfortable having his mother handle all his finances, so Rick set him up with a California-based business management firm called Provident Financial.

Rick also called on an old friend, publicist Nancy Byron. Nancy, born and raised by a Jewish family in London, had recently relocated to Houston after working in Hollywood for 18 years. While working with Three 6 Mafia and the YoungBloodz she'd sought out Southern rap, discovering Chamillionaire and UGK in the process, and was so dedicated to wholly engrossing herself in the culture that she decided to try sippin' syrup.

"When people can dedicate entire albums to a subject, it kinda makes you want to try it," she admits. (After spending $120 on the drug which didn't do much except put her to sleep, Nancy was not impressed. "I don't get it," she says. "If you ask me, the whole city of Houston needs to snort a big line of coke. It's slow enough out here [already].")

In any case, Nancy was ecstatic when she got a phone call from Rick Martin out of the blue, announcing, "You're Pimp C's publicist." Martin arranged a conference call with Pimp, Nancy Byron, and his financial team to plot out the direction they wanted to go with his career.

The first objective was to build on the buzz created by the "Free Pimp C" movement and take advantage of the new attention to display Pimp's musical talents and draw in new fans. "Rick felt like he had a cultural icon on his hands … and was basically just strategizing how to make the most of that," says Nancy Byron.

From a business perspective, Rick also hoped to present Pimp as a reformed character, not the wild and crazy persona of the late 90s. Pimp wasn't so sure about that, but he did agree that his life needed to be more focused, more business-oriented, and more positive. The rest of Pimp's team wasn't sure if they trusted Rick, who struck them as a fast, slick talker.

In another order of business, Chad wanted to have his criminal record expunged. He planned to sue the state of Texas, the prisons where he was held, and his previous attorneys for botching his case. Rick connected Chad with Los Angeles-based attorney Craig Wormley, who dug through Chad's case files

After reviewing them, Wormley wasn't optimistic about getting his record expunged. "[There] wasn't a lot we could do because … there wasn't a trial," Wormley explains. "He took a deal, [and] when you take deals, you give up some of your rights." After weighing the costs of moving forward with a civil case, combined with the low probability of success, Chad decided against it, but he and Wormley became friends.

A week after the T.I. video shoot, I was scheduled to interview him for the cover of the May issue of *OZONE*, our four year anniversary, to promote his *King* album release. Inspired by the conversation with Pimp in his Bentley, the thought struck me – why not have Pimp interview him?

When I explained my idea to T.I.'s publicist Sydney Margetson, there was a long pause and a slight chuckle. "You really think we can get both of them the phone at the same time?"

Miraculously, we did get both rappers on the phone together at the scheduled time with no problems. In the same humble tone of admiration he'd had during their Bentley conversation, T.I. talked about his upcoming album as well as his profitable ventures outside rap, including New Finish Construction, Elite Auto Concierge, and his nightclub Crucial.

Other topics of conversation included T.I.'s war with Lil Flip. Pimp advised that he was "seeing niggas making too much money to be mad at anybody right now" but that it was okay to "agree to disagree."

Even though he was encouraging T.I. and Lil Flip to put their beef aside, Pimp let it be known he was supporting T.I. by recording an interlude for his album *King* (which included eight "nawtambouts" and four "muthafuckin's"). As he explained in an interview with AllHipHop, he didn't take any offense to T.I. crowning himself "King of the South."

"I don't think the kid meant no disrespect to anyone by saying that," said Pimp. "He meant that he was the king. As black males we have a fixation with things that are royal, like jewels for example, kings wear jewelry. Take the nice cars, for example, the kings had the nicest horses and carriages along with fine fabrics and nice homes ... I [can see how his statement] might have been misinterpreted and I could see how that would offend someone if they were insecure with themselves, [but] I know what he was saying and I support T.I."

Beefing over the title was silly, anyway, Pimp thought. "You niggas fighting over the King of the South?" he said later on the *Will Hustle* DVD. "Nigga, DJ Screw is the King of the South, bitch! And if he ain't, it's gotta be J. Prince."

J. Prince, in fact, had arranged for a sit-down for T.I. and Lil Flip, instructing them to "get your money and stay out of each other's way." As much flak as Prince had received from law enforcement, in certain situations he was more powerful than them, stepping in to mediate potentially dangerous situations.

"I was glad to hear that y'all sat down like men," Pimp told T.I. "That made me feel good, 'cause down here in the South, we don't need that bullshit. We need to be getting that paper. No negative shit, man. Let's talk about some more positive shit."

T.I. and Pimp commiserated about the challenges of balancing a family life and a rap career. "I know how [hard] it is on my children ... [especially] my oldest son," Pimp admitted. "I have three kids. I got a 12-year-old son, a five-year-old son, and a four-year-old daughter. For [my oldest son], everywhere he goes, he feels like he's representing me. This shit is a trip, 'cause when you in this shit, you ain't got no personal life no more. Muthafuckers feel like you ain't got no fears no more, so they say whatever. They take shots, and he feels like he gotta represent to the fullest 24 hours a day."

"Y'all changed a lot of niggas' lives and a lot of niggas' mindset," T.I. told Pimp. "You really put a lot of niggas up on game, man. That *Ridin' Dirty* shit was one of the greatest albums of all time."

"We was just some young country boys put in the position where we could prosper, and we did," Pimp reflected. "It was a bumpy ride, but I feel like it was for a reason."

"You know, I just got the rough cut of the video [for 'Front, Back'] back, Pimp," T.I. told him as the interview drew to a close.

"How we look?" Pimp asked.

"We lookin' like something, man," T.I. proudly affirmed. "We lookin' like something."

"You know, man, we need to lock down for seven days and do a whole album," Pimp C said thoughtfully. "That'll really fuck up the world."

"What are you sayin', man!?" T.I. laughed.

February 7, the day of the interview with T.I., happened to be also Chad's grandmother's 90th birthday. Chad's parole restricted him from traveling outside the state of Texas, but he'd developed a good relationship with his parole officer Sjolanda Brown.* Mama Wes reached out to Ms. Brown, explaining that Chad's grandmother was fighting brain cancer and requesting permission for him to travel to Crowley, Louisiana and visit her.

Ms. Brown approved the request, and they went to see his grandmother the following day. "He was Pimp that day … he was going around singing in the stores," recalls Mama Wes. "When he wanted to be seen, he would draw attention to himself, and he liked to do it by singing … And when we got to [my mother's house] and we walked in the door … he reverted back to little Chaddy. He became the kid again."

Radiation treatments had caused his grandmother to lose her hair, which saddened Chad. He ordered some recliners and furniture for Nanny Brenda to have delivered to the house to make her more comfortable.

On the way back to Port Arthur, Mama Wes thought aloud. "C, you can't just make money in Texas," she said. "You gotta go somewhere."

C was nervous about pushing his luck with the parole office. "Now, Mama, you gonna push [them] too far," he said.**

"No, baby, all she can say is 'no,'" Mama Wes insisted.

Mama Wes called Ms. Brown early the next morning and asked if Chad could travel for work out of state. "He can go anytime! For work!" Ms. Brown assured her. "Request it, just like you did for him to go see your mom," she explained.

Mama Wes' mind was already racing with promoters she could call, longtime friends and supporters who had always done well with UGK shows in the past. As soon as they hung up, Mama Wes started going through her Rolodex. Her first call went to Mississippi promoter Stokes, who had done dozens of UGK shows over the years. Stokes passed the word that Pimp C was available to travel, and by late afternoon, the phone was ringing constantly with show inquiries.

By February 15, things were really looking up; Chad received a $100,000 advance from Jive for the next UGK album and $30,000 from producer Deja "The Great" Johnson for two Brooke Valentine features ("he did both verses in like five minutes," Brooke told the *Houston Chronicle*). The same day, he drove his Bentley to Dallas to pick up $17,000 to host a party at downtown nightclub Purgatory, which was attended by several local rappers and Dallas Mavericks players.

While he was in town, he linked up with producer Steve Below and his former artist Young Smitty. He and Smitty had communicated while he was in prison and mended their issues. In an interview with website WordOfSouth.com, Pimp said that he was considering working with Young Smitty again and bringing him back into the UGK Records fold.

A *Dallas Morning News* reporter, Thor Christensen, came by the club to do a quick interview with Pimp, who expressed his disbelief at all the sudden media attention. (Pimp's bodyguard JT frisked the reporter, who noted in the morning paper that he was found to be "packing no heat.") "I left a G., and I came home an O.G., you know what I mean?" Pimp told the reporter. "I came home at Run-DMC status."

"After years in prison, how hard is it adjusting to the outside?" the reporter asked.

"Well, I came out of prison, and Bun B put a stack of money in one hand, my momma handed me a cellphone in the other, and I jumped into a brand-new Cadillac," Pimp said. "So it

(*A voicemail message left at Ms. Brown's Beaumont office requesting an interview was returned by an angry supervisor who informed me that TDCJ parole officers do not have personal relationships with their parolees. Others disagree, remembering Ms. Brown as "starstruck" – but a pleasant, yet firm woman who had a good working relationship with Chad – who became a friend to the family.)

(**When asked by German website Rapz.de when he would be performing in Europe, Pimp C looked at his watch before replying with a laugh, "I'll be off parole in 2009 … unless they can find it in they hearts – in they devilish hearts – to let me go a lil' bit early.")

was a little bit easier for me than for someone who comes out and starts from the bottom up."

"You're on parole 'til 2009," the reporter noted. "How hard will it be staying out of trouble?"

"It's like this, man: You've got to stay focused every day on this [shit] because you've got one foot in prison and one foot out," Pimp said. "I'm not gonna jinx myself and say it's gonna be easy. But I'm gonna put my best foot forward and stay creative and do the right thing. I don't smoke. I don't drink. I don't do no drugs. It's a new way of living. I'm out now, and I'm gonna take advantage of that blessing."

After being gently informed in Dallas that the Coogi sweater he was wearing was no longer in style, Pimp started consulting with Teresa, co-owner of Houston urban clothing store SF2, to help him get back caught up on the cutting edge of fashion. He often stopped by to pick up new gear, with Teresa serving as his informal stylist. "Lay out five outfits for me, and I'll be by to pick them up," he'd instruct her. "Don't make me look like a punk, T."

On one occasion, Pimp stopped by with a friend in tow who had just been released after a lengthy prison sentence, plopping down several thousand dollars on the counter. "Man, my homeboy is so far behind in the times, when he went to jail, FUBU jerseys were still hot," Pimp explained, eyeing some Artful Dodger jeans and allover-print hoodies. "I know he gonna be reluctant to [wear all these] colors and shit, but I need you to get him fly."

Late one night after a stop at SF2, Pimp pulled up to Cory Mo's new home studio in Acres Homes. Mike and Cory Mo's MAD Studios (Money At the Door) had become UGK's unofficial studio; Pimp and Bun knew they were welcome to stop by any time and the financial arrangements would get worked out later.

Mike and Cory were attempting to help Pimp get caught up on technology. He loved to wave his cell phone around and was starting to send texts and emails. But in the studio, he was accustomed to recording in analog onto two-inch reels, a time-consuming and cumbersome process.

Pimp finally relented and bought a MacBook, but refused to convert from his tried-and-true Roland R-8 drum machine to the newer MPCs which he considered some "pussy ass shit." "He had a bunch of old equipment … but the nigga just knew how to make that shit sound the way it was supposed to sound," recalls Cory Mo. "He hated computers and the digital world."

Steve-O, an engineer serving as an intern at MAD Studios, offered to go pick up some food. Pimp was in the mood for chicken, so Steve-O suggested KFC or popular Houston 'hood spot Frenchy's.

"Mane, don't bring me no Frenchy's, mane!" Pimp howled. "Frenchy's had me all up in the airport with the boo-boo's!"

Steve-O laughed as Pimp handed him three crisp $20 bills and asked him to pick up something from KFC which wouldn't cost more than $10. Steve-O hesitated, unsure if this was some sort of test. "Hey, Pimp, you know you gave me $60?" he asked.

"Yeah!" Pimp barked. "Go get you some gas, nigga!"

Mike Mo pulled up around 4 AM that night just as Pimp was leaving. "Hey, man, where you get them pants from?" Mike asked, admiring his new Red Monkey jeans.

"Shiiiit, man, you want 'em?" Pimp asked. "Man, I paid $800 for these." He peeled them off and handed them to Mike.

As Mike stood speechless, Pimp, wearing only a pair of white boxer shorts, hopped in his Bentley and sped off.

In mid-February 2007, the who's-who of the sports world and the music industry descended on Houston for the NBA's annual All-Star weekend. Chad took the opportunity to meet up with some old friends who were in town, collaborating with producer KLC at Studio 7303 on a few records and strolling through Sharpstown Mall to pick up a new grill with his ex-girlfriend Lanika, who was amused by his new celebrity status.

NBA player Stephen Jackson, perhaps the biggest celebrity from Port Arthur outside of Pimp and Bun, also dabbled in rap under the moniker Stak5. He'd snuck out of the house at age 16 and drove to Houston to see UGK perform at Chocolate Town for his first concert, an "incredible experience" which left a lasting impression. Several years after Chad departed Lincoln High, Jackson led the school to a state championship. He was drafted in the second round of the NBA draft and earned a championship ring with the San Antonio Spurs in 2003.

Now a top scorer for the Indiana Pacers, Jackson viewed All-Star weekend as the perfect opportunity to hold a launch party for his new record label. With Red Boy's help, he secured Bar Rio, a large Houston nightclub, to hold UGK's reunion concert on the night of February 19.

Jackson viewed the night as a triumph for the entire city of Port Arthur; UGK would perform with his roster as the opening act, and Mr. Boomtown would be on hand capturing all the footage. J. Prince and everyone else from Houston was there, ready to see UGK reunited on stage for the first time.

Pimp C made his grand entrance, pulling up at the back in his silver Bentley followed by a lengthy caravan, which included myself. As he approached the crowded back door, a throng of 40 people followed behind him. After a dispute with the towering security guards, a promoter emerged at the back door and said he would only let Pimp in. "Yo, you gotta let all my people in," Pimp argued. "I ain't going in until you let *all* my people in!"

A handful of us slid inside the door, cracked open about two feet. We could still hear Pimp outside yelling, calling the promoter a "pussy nigga" and a "fuck boy." Finally, he demanded, "Yo, how much we getting paid for this show!?"

Pimp pulled out a wad of cash and threw it in the promoter's face as his crew rushed the door and everyone followed him inside. Among the crew was Chamillionaire and MTV News reporter Shaheem Reid, who was amazed to see that everything he'd ever heard about Pimp C was true.

In a small, narrow hallway serving as Pimp's dressing room, he turned over the show CD to the sound man, put in his new grill, and changed into a fresh all-white Dickies outfit over a red-shirt, topped by a red leather Exclusive Game jacket customized with "UGK 4 Life." He adjusted a red Trill baseball cap on his head and carefully put on all his jewelry before finishing off the look with crisp black-and-white Jordans with red laces.

While Pimp was backstage perfecting his look, New Orleans rapper Choppa, who had a moderate hit with his record "Choppa Style," appeared on stage. (It was later said that Choppa had paid the club owner or promoter for a performance slot.)

Surprised, Jackson went backstage and asked Pimp how he wanted to handle the situation. "Man, you want me to get these muthafuckers off stage?" Jackson asked.

"Yeah, get them off stage," Pimp said.

Accompanied by his crew from Port Arthur, Jackson approached the stage, but Bun stopped him. "Jack, hold on a second," Bun said.

Jackson tried to restrain himself. "I'm pissed," he recalls. "I really wanna throw him off the stage."

Jackson wasn't the only one who was pissed. The fans were here to see UGK, not Choppa, and someone in the crowd tossed a handful of ice at Choppa. Choppa reacted by tossing a speaker into the crowd; his whole crew dove into the crowd pursuing the man who'd thrown the ice. The 6'6" Jackson tore off his shirt and dove into the crowd after Choppa.

The crowd scattered towards the exits and as the bloody melee spilled out of the club, police who were waiting outside instructed the club owner to turn on the lights and shut down the club. When Pimp learned what was happening, he finally emerged on stage but less than a hundred people were still in the club. They surrounded the stage and screamed enthusiastically as he appeared.

Pimp stood on stage holding a microphone with a cord, maintaining his composure but clearly irritated that things were not going as planned. With his enormous bodyguard JT towering beside himn, Pimp tapped on the small microphone repeatedly, but no sound came out. The crowd began booing, voicing their displeasure with whoever had turned off his mic. Pimp, anger plastered across his face, continued tapping on the mic.

Bun, who had been waiting in a separate backstage area, had left the venue as soon as someone told him the show was being canceled. He was already on the freeway headed home when he got a call. "B, where ya at?"

"Man, they said they were canceling!" Bun said.

"Shiiiit, Pimp on stage," the caller reported.

"No shit!?" Bun said, exiting the freeway to make a quick U-turn.

People like Shaheem Reid, who'd been anxiously awaiting their first UGK show, left disappointed. Mama Wes was upset waiting upstairs in the VIP section. "That night would've been so special," sighs Stephen Jackson. "Not only just for Port Arthur, but special, period, 'cause everybody wanted to see Pimp … it was just crazy."

The day after the failed Bar Rio show, Texas rappers convened at J. Prince's ranch, Prince Estates, deep in the country an hour west of the city for *The Source* Magazine's "A Great Day in Houston" cover shoot. In theory, it was a triumphant gathering celebrating Houston's reign at the top of the rap game, but in reality, it was close to 100 people who didn't necessarily like each other traipsing around in the mud on a cold, dreary afternoon.

"The whole day was kind of drama to begin with, because we had brought so many people together in one place that literally couldn't stand one another that the tension was palpable," laughs publicist Nancy Byron, who helped coordinate the shoot. "Everywhere you walked were like little pockets [of war]; it was like Afghanistan. You just had to laugh." Z-Ro even showed up wearing a bulletproof vest.

Nancy, who also worked with Chamillionaire and Trae, met Pimp at the shoot for the first time. Pimp was in a foul mood, unhappy about walking around in the mud in his clean tennis shoes. A golf cart was called to transport him. Pimp was wearing the red leather UGK jacket he hadn't been able to debut the night before.

Photographer Michael Blackwell got Bun and Pimp (cell phone in hand, as always) along with Chamillionaire, Slim Thug, Z-Ro, Lil Flip, J. Prince, Michael Watts, Mike Jones, and Scarface together for the cover. A photo for the inside cover pullout included DJ Michael Watts, SUC OGs Lil Keke, Hawk, and Lil O, and up-and-coming rappers Trae, Chingo Bling, and Short Dawg, among others.

"We've come a long way," Bun said, surveying the group.

"This some Hall of Fame shit right here," J. Prince added. "Y'all don't even know what you're standing on. You're on Holy Ground. You know, I never thought all you niggas would be out here on this land."

"Y'all make sure we put DJ Screw in this muthafucker," Prince added to one of *The Source* representatives.

Paul Wall, who wasn't on speaking terms with his former partner Chamillionaire and was also having problems with Lil Flip and Mike Jones, was a no-show, not wanting to be hypocritical. "I thought it was fraud," he says. "Everybody on the cover standing next to each other all had problems with each other. I felt like [if] I have a problem with certain people [and] certain people have problems with me, let's address those problems … not just ignore it … I don't want to stand on the front cover of the magazine next to these people that I don't like, and act like I do. I'd rather talk about the problems and then celebrate it by doing a photo shoot."*

Chamillionaire, who arrived with the red Cadillac Biarritz, felt differently. "It truly is a great day in Houston," he said, flashing a gold-grilled smile for the cameras.

Shooting at the ranch gave artists a glimpse of the true possibilities; Prince's expansive ranch, which stretched miles in every direction, was a business in itself, producing Black Angus cattle and bales of hay. He loved the serenity, listening to crickets and frogs and birds and the sounds of nature.

"I take my hat off to J. Prince. That's who I wanna be. I don't wanna be no rapper," says Slim Thug. "I'd rather be J. Prince and just sit back and be a businessman... To see him come up and [now he owns] a ranch which is like a thousand and something acres. That shit looks like a [whole] city... that's some player shit, man."

The Source's cover story, "Don't Mess With Texas: Why Houston's Reign Won't Stop," was penned by Matt Sonzala, who chose not to come to the ranch. Sonzala, who had developed a "love/hate relationship" with many Houston rappers, was disgusted by the inflating egos around town.

"[There was] a period of time [during Houston's rap explosion] where everybody had their heads so high up in the sky [I] just [felt] like, 'Dude, fuck you,'" Sonzala recalls. "The way everybody started acting, it was like, 'Dude, muthafuckers worked for this ... people put in work to make this happen and you idiots are acting like this?'"

On a commercial level, Mike Jones was arguably the most successful of the group – his debut *Who Is Mike Jones?* had already sold 1.3 million copies. But Jones didn't seem to realize that a large part of his success was based on timing: he'd come along at the right time and the right place to capitalize off the movement created by all those who'd come before him, and many of his peers were bothered by his arrogance.

"I'm the king of H-Town right now," he bragged in his *Source* interview with Carlton Wade. "The city wouldn't be on fire if it wasn't for Mike Jones. Since Jones blew up, [TV Johnny] the jewelry guy has blown up. The 84s have blown up. The candy paint blew up. H-Town ran 2005. Am I right or wrong?"

He also didn't give much credit to Swisha House ("I was the last dude to come to the House, and I was the most popular and the biggest-selling artist in Swisha House history. Nobody ever sold platinum at Swisha House before Mike Jones") and made it clear that he was striking out on his own. "My heart is with [my new record label] Ice Age," he said. "Where my heart is at is where I'm fully devoted. When you see me on TV, Ice Age gonna be on my piece and coming out my mouth. I ain't saying no other label or no other name."

Sonzala's article concluded that even if Houston's reign at the top of the rap game didn't last forever, they'd be alright. "As much attention as Houston is enjoying right now, its greatest artists have already learned to live quite nicely off their hustle," he finished. "If the attention wanes, they will simply go back to doing what they have always done. Houston has been a self-sufficient Hip-Hop city from day one – it's the main reason the city was able to explode. With or without the help of mainstream media, you can safely bet that all of its independently-minded hustlers will continue to thrive. For now, Houston is running this rap shit."

After a brief impromptu performance at DJ Dolby D's birthday party in Lafayette and knocking out a verse for Talib Kweli's "Country Cousins" at a discounted rate, Pimp headed down to Miami to shoot his scene for T-Pain's "I'm In Luv (Wit' A Stripper)" remix video shoot.

Too $hort arrived and was impressed with his friend's new calm demeanor; it was the first time he'd seen Pimp since his return. "Maaaan, I got a lot of letters, but I liked when I got that

(*According to Lil Flip, at least one brewing beef was squashed at *The Source* cover shoot when Z-Ro spoke with Michael Watts on behalf of the Screwed Up Click, which had been feeling disrespected by statements Watts made about DJ Screw.)

one [from you]," Pimp told Too $hort.

When Paul Wall arrived, Pimp couldn't resist teasing him. "Paul Wall was on that square shit writing me in jail," he joked. "Wasn't nobody else writing me. You were on that square shit, man."

During a brief intermission on set, a comedian approached Pimp C for a quick video interview, asking him, "You ever fell in love with a stripper?"

"I'm in love with a lifestyle, nawtalmbout?" Pimp responded. "I'm in love with nice things. Now if a stripper can help me get them thangs, then yeah, I'ma love her. I'ma love her as far as the paper love me."

When the comedian asked, "How did the South win?" it prompted a heavy pause.

"That's a loaded question," Pimp said. "Ask me what you're asking me?"

"You know, [the rap game has] been [in] the North for a long time," he said. "[Now there's] so many dudes coming out the South. And I heard them say we won."

"Well, thangs happen in cycles. It was inevitable that it was gonna come down here eventually and that we was gonna get the ball," Pimp said. "[Now] the question is how long we gonna keep it. We gotta step our rap game up because if we keep rapping about the same things and get stuck in a style, we ain't gonna have it much longer. It's gonna go somewhere else."

During the shoot, I introduced Pimp to Big L from U Digg Records, a huge UGK fan who ended up paying Pimp to come by the studio and drop a verse late that night. Pimp's verse, which landed on Young Stally's record "Diamond Grill" off his 2007 *Young and Flashy* debut, included nods to Big Boi and Killer Mike ("If you want some you can find me in the H-Town," in the same cadence as the hook of their hit record "Kryptonite"), and Too $hort's early hit "Life Is… Too Short" ("Didn't know if I wanted to rap or sell coke, 'cause niggas like me ain't never broke").*

One element of the rap game that was new to both Pimp and Bun was the internet. Rap-A-Lot had a young staffer named Chris McNutt create MySpace pages for Pimp and Bun in the fall of 2005 to promote Bun's album *Trill*, but Chad created his own page for $ir $weet Jone$, a single male Capricorn living in "THE GREAT STATE OF TEXAS."

A 2005 profile of blogger Byron Crawford in St. Louis' *Riverfront Times* newspaper labeled him "The Mad Blogger," depicting him as an overweight 24-year-old who spent 20 hours a day in the bedroom of his dirty apartment, filled with empty beer cans and baskets of dirty laundry, playing video games, watching porn, and blogging. Through satire, race-baiting, and headlines worded for optimum shock value ("J-Kwon beats his baby's mother" or "The Game was a gay stripper"), Crawford's website attracted close to 10,000 visitors a day.

The crowning achievement of Crawford's career thus far had been eliciting a response from Kanye West, after accusing him of stealing "Jesus walks" from rapper Rhymefest and suggested he should be disqualified from the Grammys. Crawford's numerous posts about Kanye included one comparing the "striking similarities" between Kanye and Nazi leader Adolf Hitler. Beneath another, titled "Let's Hunt and kill Kanye West's Mother," was a comment signed by Kanye's mother Donda West: "How painful it must be to be filled with so much hate."

(*At the video shoot, we did an impromptu photo shoot of Pimp in his white mink coat which was intended for a feature in *VIBE* Magazine. The day after the shoot I stayed in Miami to shoot Dre's "Chevy Ridin' High" and DJ Khaled's "Holla At Me" video shoot, then loaded all the images on my laptop and drove straight to Atlanta. I pulled up just in time to make it to T.I.'s *King* album release party at Visions. When I came out of the club at 3 AM, my door handle had been drilled through and everything in the car, including my laptop with the exclusive Pimp C photo shoot was gone, never to be seen again. I'd emailed one low-res photo to *VIBE* as a sample and was able to recover the image, which Pimp's graphic designer Mr. Soul recreated for the cover of this book. *VIBE* ended up using one of our photos from the Studio 7303 Bentley photo shoot instead for the article, which featured 10 words of advice from Pimp C, such as, "Just 'cause motherfuckers is related to you, that don't make them family.")

Crawford didn't care who he pissed off, mostly because he had nothing to lose. "What, is someone gonna sue me and take away my six-year-old computer?" he told the *Riverfront Times*. Even though other bloggers criticized Crawford's "relentless mean-spiritedness," his popularity led to a weekly blogging gig for *XXL* Magazine's website. (The column included a disclaimer that Crawford's "views very rarely, actually, never reflect those of *XXL* or its staff.")

On the April 3, 2006 installment of his blog, titled "Southerners quit yer bitchin'," Crawford declared that "the southern rap of today, both in its style of rappin' and especially its beats, bears very little relation to the Hip-Hop most of us grew up listening to."

He did correctly point out the hypocrisy of major record labels riding the wave of southern rap to which they'd previously been oblivious. "In 2006, southern rap is the style of rap music that the tall Israelis who run the music industry have decided to promote, to the detriment of all other styles of rap music," he complained, concluding that "fans of southern rap no longer have any legitimate claim that they're being discriminated against."

Clearly trolling for a response from the Southern rap fans that Crawford denounced as "the most annoying group of fans in Hip-Hop (other than, of course, women)," the piece likely wouldn't have garnished much attention had it not been for this blurb:

"And they all rallied around Pimp C as if he was Leonard Peltier or somebody, but come to find out he can hardly rap. Is everybody aware that he was locked up for pulling out a gun on a woman in a mall? … As far as I'm concerned, his ass should go back to jail."*

When Bun heard about the piece, he couldn't contain himself. "I let people say whatever [they want] about me, but he was so adamant about trying to tear down Pimp C's character. I just couldn't do it," Bun later told radio host Combat Jack. He posted a lengthy response on Crawford's blog post:

*Who the **** are you to sit behind you safe little cubicle and criticize who we are and what we do? For more than 20 years. Southern Artists and fans have faithfully supported any and all Hip-Hop that was offered. We accepetced everyone on their own merits, gave evryone a fair listen, and then spoke. In light of you comments and views, it occured to me that you haven't given near as much open mindedness to our music as we have to yours. The reasons I say yours is that it doesn't what type of music came out, we supported it, so we in no doubt supported whatever the **** you listen to. To think that all we know is what we do, or that we may know nothing at all is preposterous. If you're a paying member of Soundscan, you can see that ALL MUSIC SELLS IN THE SOUTH! 5 percenter? Bought it. Backpackers? Bought it. Black power, Wu-Tang, horrorcore, need I say more? Meanwhile, after 25 years of unconditionally holdin down all forms of rap/hiphop music, as soon as we even try to join a club we bought and help build the clubhouse for, they wanna deny us access. Well guess what you Elks lodge habitatin, Masters in Augusta wanna-be, finger-pointin behind the bushes, throwin a rock and runnin ass nigga, I just thought I'd tell you to take whatever preconcieved notions you have built up in your air and watertight cranium AND STICK IT IN YO PUSSY!*

*I guarentee you the TRUE FANS AND MAKERS OF HIP HOP JUST MIGHT DIFFER WITH YOU! I know this because I am friends with Cool Herc, Grandmaster Caz, Melle Mel, Big Daddy Kane, Kool G Rap and other extremely well known originators and creators of this artform. The problem now is the act of causing division and dissention amongst the fans by people whom are not in the know. You see, YOU may not like Laffy Taffy or DFB or whoever, and you know what, that's your GOD-given right. Hate all you want on the South, Southern rappers, or just Pimp C, since you brought him up. IT STILL WONT HELP WHOEVER YOU LIKE SELL ****! Talib Kweli: close friend of UGK. De La Soul: close friends of UGK. Kanye West, Common, Dead Prez, close firends of UGK. Jam Master Jay, 2 Pac, Biggie Smalls: ALL ****ING FANS OF UGK, and I dont say this from second hand conversation. These people told me this from their own mouths,* *yet you would have people believe otherwise. They could learn to be openminded about the music the listened and the regions the music was popular in, so it should come at no surprise these people went further thatn the average artists. Whatever alterior motive you may have is trying to bring down the Southern rise, it won't work. God kills hate with love.*

Oh yeah, by the way, as far as your comments on my brother and his reason for incarceration, he pulled a gun on a group of people thrreatening him in a mall. Only the girl went back and told the police, that's why it seems as if it was between only him and the girl. The problem is, misinformed people give misinformation and cause misfortune to the learing. I hate to call this the blind leading the blind, because by the look of your commment posts, they know what's up. So instead of just going to New York, screaming and ranting in White Nigga's office, I came to see you on your turf, because I'm no coward. I'm willing to come in your yard: care to come in mine? Right a rhyme, let;s see what you have the Hip-Hop community musically. Oh and make sure it's Grammy-nominated when you do it, because mine was. And while you're at it ask Nas, Jay-Z, Papoose, Camron,, Russell Simmons, 50 Cent, Fat Joe, Chino XL, Self Scientific, Cyrpess ill, Snoop Dogg, Ludacris or anybody else in this industry you like if Pimp C is wack. I bet they bark on you louder than I want to.

*God forbid you're in the wrong place and the wrong time like Pimp and have to spend 4 years of your life behind bars. You're a black man, so **** how educated and well read you are. You'll ride just like Pimp, and you'll be sorry about it, just like Pimp. The only difference: nobody's gonna wear a ****in t-shirt with yo face on it. Leave the South alone, becausse we're just tryin to eat. Quit bloggin and write a book if you got more goin on besides gossip and shootin slugs. Because after blogging has come and gone, and XXL is no longer on stands or online(which I would hate to see), UGK and our musical legacy will survive. Will your triflin rants sustain?*

Thrilled that his piece had not only drawn "retarded, misguided, emotional outbursts (filled with ridonkulous misspellings, ALL CAPS, and what have you)" from fans but from a pioneer of Southern rap, Crawford responded with a follow-up blog titled "Bun B quit yer bitchin,'" letting loose with even more vitrol.

"It could very well be the case that Bun B doesn't know how to read, and that one of his hoes read it for him (while Pimp C pointed a gun at her, natch) and then typed up his response," Crawford concluded.

As word spread that Bun B had "beef" with Byron Crawford, calls started coming in from the St. Louis area, where the blogger lived, offering to handle the situation. Bun assured them that it wasn't "that serious."

"I gotta be careful," Bun later told radio host Combat Jack, "Because if I really act like I'm angry, people are gonna move regardless whether I tell 'em to or not, and I don't want that on my conscience. We just gonna call you a bitch 'cause you a bitch, and keep it moving. Believe me, there were no points to get [by] putting your hands on Byron Crawford. You don't get no 'G' points for that."

Crawford followed up with another hateful blog rant labeling Pimp C a "violent, drug-addicted criminal," offering a completely hypothetical theory that Pimp was under the influence of PCP and suffering "illusions and hallucinations" when he was arrested at Sharpstown.

"For all we know, Pimp C could've been under the impression that he was being chased through the mall by a gang of angry leprechaun," Crawford concluded. "The bottom line is, that crazy motherfucker pulled out a gun on a woman, in a mall. That's why his dumb ass did five years in jail."

Taking a step back from his emotions, Bun realized that by responding, he'd actually helped Crawford. "I feel like he won, to be honest," Bun conceded later. "I have to give credit where credit is due, and that's his job to get under people's skin. He got a lot of points for that; for getting Bun B to respond. He got a reaction out of me; a real reaction. I was really upset about that."

"I hate that I even wasted any energy addressing him," Bun later admitted in an *OZONE* interview. "I'm not built for the comments section," he added in an interview with Combat Jack. "It's real raw and gritty and grimy in the comments section. Some of the worst people on the planet live and exist in the comment section. And they don't just live there, they thrive."

While Bun was bothered, Pimp shrugged it off. "He was just trying to get some airplay," he told *OZONE*. "He didn't really know anything about my case."

"I know they don't like me," Pimp added on the *Will Hustle* DVD. "They be all on the internet talking about The Pimp … hiding behind them muthafuckin' email addresses."

CHAPTER 39

"Smashed up the grey one, bought me a red."
– Pimp C, UGK's "Int'l Player's Anthem"

———————

"We can look at that glass half empty or we can look at it half full. If that kid
hadn't smashed into me, the guy behind him that was shooting at him might
have hit his mark ... If me smashing up that car saved that kid in the Impala's life,
well, it's worth it." – Pimp C, *In the Spotlight With Dwayne Diamond*

Nahala "Mr. Boomtown" Johnson sat in the director's chair, soaking it all in. His football career path hadn't panned out, but he'd fallen in love with film and directed several independent films. His old friend Chad Butler had given him his first big chance with a $80,000 budget for the "Pourin' Up" video off the *Pimpalation* album.

Ashlei Morrison, a soft-spoken Rap-A-Lot intern, knocked hesitantly on the door of Pimp C's trailer. Boomtown had instructed her to get Pimp ready for his call time, and she wondered why she'd been chosen for this particular task. Based on all the stories she'd heard, she was nervous about pissing him off. *Who am I?* she wondered. *He's gonna immediately go off on me.*

She decided a quick, blunt approach would work best: she planned to walk in the trailer, blurt out, "Boomtown wants you to be out in 30 minutes," then turn sharply and get out of Pimp's presence as quickly as possible.

Instead, Ashlei found that Chad was the exact opposite of what she'd been expecting. "That felt good ... to know that one of the so-say 'most difficult' artists in the industry didn't treat me that way," Ashlei recalls. "I'd seen him be the 'Pimp C' that he showed to everyone else, but I think that particular day, I was able to meet Chad."

As Ashlei left, a girl from the wardrobe department entered the trailer to bring Pimp C a box of Nikes. He pulled them out of the box and stared at them skeptically. "What the fuck?" he snapped. "This ain't no goddamn real Air Force Ones. What the fuck is this shit?"

He turned to Hezeleo. "Heze, look at these damn shoes," he said. "This ain't no goddamn real Air Force Ones, are they?"

Hezeleo looked at the shoes. "Naw, them shits ain't real Forces."

The shy wardrobe girl told Pimp that it wouldn't matter anyway. "We are not going to be filming your feet," she assured him.

Pimp threw the shoes to the ground. "Man, y'all burning up my budget on fake shoes," he said. "Somebody better go get me some muthafuckin' real Air Force Ones!"

Ashley, outside the trailer, heard Pimp yelling and cussing. *Wow, okay, I'm glad I went in when I did,* she thought.

In another trailer nearby was video model Esther Baxter. She was being paid $3,500 per day for her appearance, but apparently because of a dispute over her wardrobe and/or makeup, didn't appear in the video. Pimp, who felt that they'd gone out of their way to accommodate all her requests, grew irritated and railed at her in front of everyone on set.

"He cussed this girl out," remembers Bun's road manager Bone. "He cussed her out like that was one of his bitches … It fucked everybody up [because] we couldn't understand why [he] was [cussing her out] to that extent, you know?"

———————

Mama Wes got the sense that Chad had quickly grown tired of married life. "C got bored easily," she shrugs. "He was beginning to feel like he didn't wanna be in that situation. That shit was cool when he was in jail, he only saw her every three weeks or so, but [being married] … that just wasn't C."

"Once he got in the streets … I don't think [marriage] was something he was ready for," agrees Pimpin' Ken. "I think he might have made [that move] out of desperation … He probably loved her, too, but … I don't think he was ready for it."

Knowing that they didn't get along, Chad rarely mentioned his wife to Mama Wes, only referring to her occasionally as "yo' favorite bitch" or "the one you call bitch." One day, he passed by his mother's house, and as they sat at the kitchen table talking, a thought struck Mama Wes. She chuckled.

"Mama, why you laughing?" he asked. "You laughing at me?"

"I just looked at you, thinking, am I the only woman that you never get bored with?" she said.

"Why you say that?" he asked.

"Because you get bored very easily with the female gender," she said.

"I do, don't I?" he mulled.

"You do," she nodded. "You didn't answer my question."

"Yeah," he said. "I don't get bored with you, Mama."

"See, me? I would never be in relationship with you. If I wasn't your mama I probably wouldn't even like you," she joked.

Chad's close relationship with his mother contributed to the strain on his marriage. "I think it was a jealousy issue," Mama Wes says of Chinara. "You know, me and that baby [Chad] were just really close, and it was gonna always be like that, for ever and ever." Others viewed their situation as just a typical mother/daughter-in-law squabble.

One point of contention was the red mesh bag which Chad had brought home from prison. Mama Wes, tired of asking him to come pick it up from her house, delivered it to him one day at the San Jac house. As soon as she set it down, Chad picked it back up, walked outside, and put it right back in her trunk. "You keep this shit," he said. "I don't want nobody in my shit."

Chinara, who'd been watching the whole transaction, was offended. "You calling me no-body?" she complained.

"Take it like you want," Chad snapped back.

As the two began arguing, Mama Wes sighed and drove off, the red mesh bag full of "Chad's shit" intact in her trunk. "The reason why C wanted me to keep the bag is because it was private to him and he didn't want Chinara going through it," says Mama Wes. "That's basically it. Because it's girls' letters and [pictures] of girls' bootys and girls' titties … And not just that, [but] it was *his* stuff."

From Mama Wes' perspective, her son had a short attention span and had quickly gotten bored with Chinara, as he had with so many women before her. "He got bored [easily], and he didn't always like that in himself. He recognized it," she says. "He was kind of just set in his ways and he wanted to do stuff like he wanted to do it. That's just the way he was."

"Nothing lasted long with him," she says. "The only thing that I can truthfully say that lasted with C was those kids and his grandmother. He loved his grandmother. But anything else? Nothing lasted with C."

Chad had spent his whole life around strong, independent women, and had great admiration for self-sufficient women. Mama Wes believed that the way Chad treated the women in his life varied according to his perception of their strengths and weaknesses.

In Mama Wes' opinion, he had lost respect for Chinara. "His respect level was very special for strong women ... [but] he had a problem with anybody that he could really push around," she says. "He loved a good fight."

Others also viewed her as a pushover. "Chinara's a 'yes-bitch' ... If you told her to jump, [she'll] say, 'How high?'" agreed Nitacha's brother Riley. "[Chad's exes] Sonji and Nitacha would never do no shit like that ... If I tell my sister [Nitacha to] jump, she'd be like, 'Man, you crazy. I'll beat your muthafuckin' ass,' you know? Sonji was the same way. She'd be like, 'Muthafucker, *you* jump. See how far your fat ass can jump.'"

Shooting for the final day of the three-day "Pourin' Up" shoot resumed in Port Arthur on April 19, with Mr. Boomtown getting some extra footage of Pimp C riding around the city in Chamillionaire's red Cadillac Biarritz and performing in front of his Bentley on Short Texas. Pimp, already irritated, had been running around the set yelling, "Whoever that is talking on the megaphone, shut that hoe ass shit up! That's fucking off my concentration!"

In the trailer, Chinara asked when she was getting her cameo. He snapped back, "You'll be getting that in 2010, bitch," as he exited the trailer.

Mama Wes followed him outside. "C, I wish you wouldn't do that," she told him. "Number one, that's very ugly, and don't act like that in front of people."

"You don't like her anyway, Mama," he said.

"That's not the point. The point is, I don't like you acting like that. So don't do that. I've told you before. Please don't do that."

Pimp stormed back in the trailer. "My Mama done saved your ass again," he told Chinara.

Locals loved the fact that Pimp C had chosen to be paroled in Port Arthur. "[C] loved [Port Arthur]," Mama Wes told the *Houston Chronicle*. "When he came home [from prison] he chose to live here. And to be honest, I wasn't sure of it. But he was. This was his choice."

"[A lot of successful people from Port Arthur] don't give like you'd think they would give, or should be able to give," notes KD Durisseau. "But [Pimp C] gave more in a personal manner. He may not give donations of ten or twenty thousand [dollars] but he did reach out to the community, [where it] really matters."

The shoot wrapped shortly before 5 PM, giving Pimp enough time to make it to Houston for his scene in Brooke Valentine's "D-Girl (Dope Girl)" video. Mike Jones was also in a rush to get back to Houston for a Juvenile video shoot. Pimp, his bodyguard JT, and Truck's cousin Cleo pulled off in his silver Bentley, trailed by Mike Jones' black Bentley.

Among the fans and curious onlookers on set was Shawn Jones, better known as "Lil Shawn," a cousin of Chad's childhood friend Donny Young. Shawn had a lengthy criminal history, with more than 19 convictions for a variety of offenses. He'd just spent 30 days in jail for assault and been reprimanded by a local judge for filing "frivolous lawsuit[s]" against the district attorney, the police department, the State of Texas, and even the local hospital.

As he was leaving the video shoot, Shawn spotted Qualan Joseph, a man he'd had an altercation with the night before, climbing into a maroon Impala. Shawn and another friend jumped into his friend Joseph Smith's white Ford Explorer and took off in pursuit of the Impala.

Qualan Joseph later testified that as they pulled off, he saw Shawn hanging out of the window of the Explorer behind them with an SKS rifle. Qualan tore off down the street, the Explorer close behind. Shots rang out and the Impala's rear windshield shattered. Qualan slammed down the gas pedal, hitting 70 MPH in a quiet residential area of Port Arthur.

As the Impala and the SUV tore down Gulfway Drive in a hail of bullets, Chad was turning left into a gas station to fill up before making the drive to Houston. (The Bentley Flying Spur clocked in at a paltry 11/18 MPG.) As he turned left through the intersection of Scott and Gulfway, the bullet-riddled Impala tore through the red light and slammed into the rear driver's side of the Bentley.

Chad's Bentley happened to be accompanied by a police escort, which took off in pursuit of the Explorer and called for backup. The SUV roared down West 17th Street and stopped twice, allegedly so Shawn could toss out the SKS rifle and magazine clip, shell casings, and boxes of ammunition, all of which were later retrieved by police.*

Chad was dazed but uninjured, cursing at anyone within earshot. Cleo, in the backseat, had aggravated a previous shoulder injury. But it was JT who appeared the most seriously injured, requiring a team of paramedics to help lift his 7-foot, 4-inch frame onto a stretcher and into a waiting ambulance.

Hezeleo called Mama Wes, who had left the video shoot to run an errand in Beaumont. "Now, C's alright," he began. "Don't get excited."
Mama Wes froze, bracing for bad news.
"He's on his way to the hospital to get checked out, but it's gonna be okay, Mama."

Mama Wes rushed to the hospital, where doctors concluded that Chad had a concussion. He was released after being treated for minor injuries. Even though he was shaken up, he planned to still make the drive to Houston for the Brooke Valentine video, but Mama Wes was adamantly opposed to the idea. "Y'know, you gotta stay awake [to deal with the concussion]," she reminded him.
"Well, that'll be a good way for me to stay awake," he joked.
Mama Wes glared at him. "C, I will kill ya," she said.

Chad tried to be optimistic. "I just smashed the Bentley that J. [Prince] gave me," he told Wendy Day. "But I'm kind of glad 'cause I didn't like the color, and now I can get a color I like."
He reflected on the incident during an interview with his cousin's local television show, *In the Spotlight with Dwayne Diamond*. "We can look at that glass half empty or we can look at it half full. If that kid hadn't smashed into me, the guy behind him that was shooting at him might have hit his mark ... If me smashing up that car saved that kid in the Impala's life, well, it's worth it. Nobody in my car got seriously injured ... had we been in another type of car, we may not have been able to sustain that lick... [if they had] hit us directly in them doors, I might not be here talking to you ... [So] if smashing that car up saved that kid's life, so be it. That's how I look at it."
If nothing else, the accident served as great rap material, and Pimp referenced it on several records. "Smashed up the grey one, bought me a red," he would later rap on "Int'l Player's Anthem."
Chad was sore the next day, and at Mama Wes' insistence, waited an extra day before head-

(*Shawn Jones was not arrested until more than a year later for the shooting incident. He hired Chad's childhood friend Langston Adams as his defense attorney and pled not guilty to the charge of Aggravated Assault. Langston subpoenaed Chad 13 times asking him to testify on Shawn's behalf; Shawn hoped to cast doubt on the identity of the shooter. Chad, who didn't want to get involved, was understandably not eager to assist a man who endangered his life. Normally, if someone refused to respond to a subpoena, an attorney could have a warrant issued for their arrest, but Langston did not arrest Chad. At trial, Shawn insisted that he was not the shooter, despite the fact that his hands were covered in gunpowder residue and his fingerprints were on the ammunition boxes and the SKS rifle clip tossed from the SUV. The victims identified Shawn as the shooter and their testimony was corroborated by video filmed during the chase from one of the patrol cars. A jury found him guilty, and prosecutors called him "a chronic offender who has been a terror in the city of Port Arthur for years." Shawn Jones was sentenced to 70 years in prison and must serve at least 30 before he is eligible for parole.)

ing to Houston's Third Ward to shoot his part in Brooke Valentine's video with director Benny Boom. JT would spend the next two days in the hospital with a back injury.*

Late that night after the Brooke Valentine video, Joseph "Z-Ro" McVey was posted up in front of the entrance to Scores Cabaret, a small strip club in southwest Houston. As always, his face was fitted into a sullen expression, as if an angry black cloud were hanging over his head. A blue bandanna wrapped around his forehead identified him as a Crip. He had three days to turn himself in to prison on weapons charges.

Z-Ro shifted his weight uncomfortably, scanning his surroundings. He stared out into the parking lot. Somebody was looking for him; he was looking for them too, and hoped he'd find them first. The beef was gang-related; something he wasn't at liberty to discuss ("somebody did some shit they wasn't sanctioned to do and I had to handle that shit," he says vaguely).

He wore a bulletproof vest beneath his loose t-shirt. A pistol was gripped tight in his left hand; in his right hand, a bag containing $700 worth of weed already rolled up in some Swisher Sweets. He'd come prepared for a long night, with another pistol in his right pocket and another bag of weed in his left pocket.

The mission was threefold: "Before I blow [my enemy's] muthafuckin' head off, I'ma make some money out here," Z-Ro explains, of his thought process. "All these strippers want some weed before they get on stage. So I'm selling weed, I'm finna blow somebody's shit off they shoulders and try to get some pussy at the same time. So I ain't give a fuck. I gotta go to jail in three days anyway."

A friend of Pimp's was leaving the strip club and nodded at Z-Ro outside. Clearly, 'Ro was up to no good. Once out of earshot, the friend called Pimp C.

"Pimp, where you at?"

"Nigga, I'm on Westheimer, comin' down," he drawled.

"Say, mane. You know where 'Ro at? Your boy trippin'," the caller reported. "This nigga 'Ro is up here really out of line. This nigga looks like a war veteran, with a bag of weed and pistols and shit and a muthafuckin' Crip rag."

While Pimp's Bentley was in the shop for repairs, he was stuck driving a Suburban, which Mama Wes considered "a big ugly gas-guzzling bitch." ("I ain't buyin' no more Bentleys, mane, them hoes ain't got no good customer service over there. My shit be fucked up, they don't even give a nigga another car to drive, so fuck them hoes," Pimp complained on "Down 4 Mine," adding that his next vehicle would be an "apple red" Lamborghini Murcielago with "blowed out brains.")

A large SUV pulled into the parking lot and headed straight for Z-Ro, headlights closing in on him. *Shit,* Z-Ro thought. *Who is this?* There was nowhere to run or hide. He tried to stuff the pistol in his pocket but it wouldn't fit, not with the extra bag of weed. In the silence of the night air he heard the automatic window coming down.

"Say bitch, get in the back seat," he heard a muffled voice say inside the car.

He'd recognize that voice anywhere. "*Man…is this that nigga Pimp?*" Z-Ro laughed to himself, shaking his head. He still couldn't see inside the vehicle. A hand emerged from the driver's side window, the index finger beckoning, "Come here."

Damn, this is that nigga, dawg, Z-Ro thought. *Damn.* He was about to be in trouble.

Z-Ro walked over to the driver's side and reached for the handle to the back door.

(*Some believe JT was greatly exaggerating the extent of his injuries, hoping for an insurance payout. "He showed up here [at the police station] walking with a cane [after the shooting incident], but he was at the club the next night [walking] fine," laughs Port Arthur Police Detective Marcelo Molfino. "So, I don't know. I'm not a doctor.")

"Naw, nigga. Come get your ass in the front," the voice said. A woman in the passenger seat was climbing into the back.

"Hold up, man. What the fuck?" Z-Ro didn't like anybody talking to him like that, even if it *was* Pimp C. "Who the fuck are you talking to?"

"Man, get in the front," Pimp ordered again.

Z-Ro reluctantly settled in the passenger seat, his face still fixed in a mean mug.

"What the fuck is you doing out here?" Pimp demanded.

"Man, I ain't even tryin' to hear this shit," grumbled Z-Ro.

"Naw, you finna hear it," Pimp said.

Reluctantly, 'Ro let it all spill out.

"You trippin', dawg," Pimp told him. "You finna go to jail in three days? That shit is fuckin' with you like that? Like, nigga, you just got four years. Nigga, you been doing sets of twos and threes your whole life. This shit really fuckin' with you?" He held his hand out and motioned for Z-Ro to hand over his pistol, still gripped tight in his left hand.

"Man, I ain't finna give you my gun, dawg," Z-Ro said. "I'm really finna get out yo' car, 'cause somebody lookin' to kill me." He preferred to roll solo because he hated to get anyone else involved in his problems, and knew he was potentially putting Pimp and his female companion at risk.

"Go home," Pimp ordered. "I know you don't want me up here watching you, but I'm telling you, I'm not finna leave until you leave."

Z-Ro agreed to give up on the mission for the night and Pimp insisted on following him all the way home. "This nigga followed me to my crib and made sure I went in this muthafucker," Z-Ro recalls. "Like, he was just chaperoning a nigga."

Z-Ro had lost his mother at six years old and his father's absence had always been a sore spot. "I'ma be honest, I hated that nigga," Z-Ro says of his father. "So that's why I ain't really take too much [to having a father figure] … This nigga [Pimp] was like my daddy for real. This nigga actually gave me, like, a curfew."

Less than two weeks after the "Pourin' Up" video shoot, Pimp arranged to meet Mr. Boomtown at MAD Studios to take a look at the rough cut of the video. He called Cory Mo and told him he was on the way as soon as he picked up a friend from the airport.

When Pimp pulled up in the Bentley, Cory was thrilled to see that his surprise guest was one of his idols, Too $hort. Pimp and $hort had been talking about doing a group project on Jive called the Broad Playas for years, and Pimp estimated that they already had half a dozen songs for the project.

They knocked out a record called "Single Life" over a track produced by Jazze Pha and collaborated on another track titled "Made 4." Too $hort worried that they were giving out "too much game for these bitches," while Pimp suggested to a promiscuous woman that instead of "fuckin' for a dinner and a movie" she could be on his "DVD sellin' pussy on a disc."

Too $hort, who had just celebrated his 40th birthday, was impressed to see his friend "a much more mature and wiser man," sober and clearheaded. He didn't even smoke weed anymore. "I'm drug free," he told WordofSouth.com. "Drugs don't go with my program. I have no desire to put anything foreign in my body."

Still, that didn't stop them from reminiscing on their wild youth. "He would tell me stories about crazy shit we did back in the day that he remembered, and I'd tell him what I remembered," Too $hort says. "Other people in the room would be looking at us like we really were crazy."

Pimp also passed by Avery Harris' Trill Studios in Port Arthur to drop vocals for the

"Knockin' Doors Down" remix. Smoke D's friend Jaro came by late one night, hoping to interview Pimp for German rap publication Rapz.de. He waited patiently all night, but when he finally got Pimp in front of the camera, it was worth it for the humorous exchange.

Pimp laughed incredulously when Jaro requested his "personal recipe for purple lean."

"Recipe?!" Pimp laughed. "It's a pharmaceutical. You get promethazine with codeine cough syrup and you mix it in your favorite flavor soda. It's not very hard. Put some Jolly Ranchers in the cup and it's a done deal."

He paused, glancing around the room, and decided to clarify. "Hey, man, look. Just because I'm not indulging don't mean that I don't know how to do it. I done probably had enough for all you muthafuckers."

"Tell us some synonyms for syrup," Jaro asked.

"What is a muthafuckin' synonym?" Pimp laughed. "Man, I just got a GED in prison, what the fuck is you talking about? What is that, another word for 'drank'? Mane, you want me to give up the game, don't you. Naw, fuck that question, man. Next question."

"Which artist will break through in 2006?" Jaro asked.

"Tony Snow."

"Who's that?"

"You'll find out who he is later on." Pimp paused, then laughed. "He gon' blow, though."

"Is it somebody close to you?"

Pimp chuckled. "Oh, he's real close."

Tony Snow was a new personality Chad had invented while he was in prison, to add to his multitude of other personalities. "That nigga was crazy, man," laughs Big Munn. "He brought Tony [Snow] home from the pen. Tony wasn't around before, it was always Percy Mack, Sweet James Jones, [and] Jack Tripper."

On the south side of Houston, Fat Pat's brother John "Big Hawk" Hawkins was pulling up to a friend's house to play dominoes. He'd started rapping after his brother died but still held down his day job selling insurance at American General. His wife Meshah was always impressed by the way he balanced his rap career with his home life; just last week, he'd worked all day, performed late that night at Club Blue, and came home in the wee hours of the morning to change their youngest son's diapers and warm up his bottles.

"All these guys was out here just partying, going out of control. But he would get up … he would be with them, all night, and he would get up and go to work," Meshah said in the book *Houston Rap*. "And he would come home and do it all over again. I don't know how he did that. I don't know how he did it, but he did. He did. He got up every morning and went to work."

As Hawk got out of his car and walked towards the side entrance of the house, gunshots rang out. A neighbor saw a small white compact car with tinted windows speed off. Hawk, who was struck several times, died at the scene.*

Z-Ro, who had just been released from jail on an appeal bond, was in high spirits until he got the phone call. "Say mane," he was informed. "That nigga Hawk dead."

"Nah, nigga, you trippin'," Z-Ro said.

(*Hawk was laid to rest alongside his brother Fat Pat. His wife Meshah was confident that the police would do ballistics tests and forensic analysis to find out who had murdered her husband. "From looking at CSI and all these different [detective TV] shows, I mean, you feel like the process is very sophisticated … I really left the job in their hands," Meshah explained in the book *Houston Rap*. "I've never been through this in real life, so I don't know what to expect, you know?" In the end, though, police were just as baffled as Meshah, and a motive or suspect in Hawk's murder has never been identified. "It's been a scary, scary, scary experience for me because I don't know who would want to hurt him. He was just really a peaceful person. He never had beef with anyone," Meshah says.)

News of Hawk's murder was met with disbelief. Who would want to kill Hawk, one of the nicest rappers you'd ever meet? "Because he was a rapper there will be people who will take his death the wrong way," Bun admitted to the *Houston Chronicle*. "But he was a peaceful guy and a family man who had no beefs with anybody."

Chad sent his condolences to the family, calling the loss "unnecessary" and "dumb." "We losing the whole muthafuckin' Screwed Up Click. What the fuck goin' on?" he asked. "We gotta stop this violence, because it don't bring nothing but pain to our families."

On the morning of May 9, Z-Ro was among the many friends and family members of Hawk arriving to honor him at Mabrie Memorial Mortuary. Z-Ro was having problems with everybody: Lil Flip, Trae, Slim Thug, his record label. "I was ready to go to war," he admits. "I was going to war with anybody. I didn't give a fuck about nobody. [I felt like] everybody could kiss my ass with they tongue hanging out."

Chad had played "Knockin' Doors Down" for Z-Ro ("Slim Thug and Z-Ro, y'all still bullshittin' / Need to sit down, take a tour, there's too much money to be gettin'") and advised him that if they were "still trippin'," he would give them each a pair of boxing gloves so they could settle things at J. Prince's boxing gym.

Z-Ro cautiously approached the funeral home where a handful of people were scattered outside. He'd vowed not to attend any more funerals after watching his mother lowered into the ground as a child. He saw Slim Thug to his left; Trae over there to his right. He couldn't even pin-point his issues with Slim, he'd just been hearing through third parties that Slim had a problem with him. His issues with Trae ran far deeper; that was family.

As he approached, Z-Ro spotted a third man he had issues with and decided maybe he should just leave. *Fuck this shit,* he thought as he turned away, then paused, thinking of Hawk's wife. *I know Meshah gon' be mad like a muthafucker, but I ain't finna start nothing if a nigga slide up on me wrong … man, look … they better be lucky the police already here.*

It was too late; Z-Ro saw Slim Thug walking in his direction. His body tensed up. He nodded his head at Slim and attempted to sidestep him, hoping he would pass by.

Pimp C had been in Slim's ear, too, encouraging him to squash things with Z-Ro.

"Nah, bruh, hold up," Slim said, blocking his path. "This shit me and you got going on is some bullshit, dawg. Fuck this shit, man … We need to put this shit in the ground with big homie [Hawk]. Big homie would wanna see us getting money together, dawg."

Z-Ro stood silently, letting the words marinate for a minute. Finally, he spoke, his tone expressing his newfound respect for Slim. "Man, you know what dawg? You right, man," Z-Ro said. "My bad. I'm out of line."*

(*Z-Ro and Slim each recall the other man being the one who made the first move to squash the beef.)

CHAPTER 40

"I don't need the twenty year friendship from Pimp C with all those ups and downs – I'd rather hear the stories from other people. But the few times we met, I left with things that changed my life." – Killer Mike

---

"I'm glad that we never blew up before. I don't think we woulda been able to handle it. Now me and Pimp have really matured. We're takin' our success in stride. If we had got millions and shit, we probably wouldn't have it now. Maybe the name would be gone and the fame would be gone by goin' out blowin' a lotta money, doin' stupid shit."
– Bun B, *Murder Dog* Magazine, 1999

In mid-May 2006, Pimp C signed a modified contract with Rap-A-Lot and headed out to Atlanta. Production on the *Pimpalation* was in full swing at Patchwerk, where engineer Leslie Brathwaite was mixing and mastering Pimp's record "Honey," featuring Jody Breeze and Tela, "Cheat On Yo Man" featuring Mannie Fresh and female rapper Suga (affiliated with Rick Royal and Bo$$ in the early 90s), and "Put This On Your Mind," a record produced by Jazze Pha.

When songwriter Big Zak passed by Patchwerk and happened to hear the finished version of "Put This On Your Mind," he was stunned to hear his own voice alongside Big Gipp, Ali of the St. Lunatics, and Jazze Pha. The vocals he'd laid were only intended as demo vocals for Jazze to redo, but Pimp left him on the record. Big Zak rapped:

Chill up a shot of Patron, roll a blunt of the kush
I'm kinda old school, still like hair on the puss

Thrilled, Zak got Pimp's number from Jazze Pha and called to thank him for the opportunity. "Mane, that touched my heart," Pimp explained. "When you said that about 'hair on the puss,' it touched my heart, mane."

Zak laughed. "I ain't know that he felt so deeply about hairy pussy," he recalls.

UGK's scheduled show in Atlanta had to be cancelled when the promoter (Tennessee's Twin Entertainment) was $5,000 short on the backend. They'd also dropped the ball on promotion, and the turnout was light.* Chad headed back to Patchwerk to knock out a verse for Ludacris' "Do Your Time." (He had gone to considerable trouble to track down his engineer Rambro, who was in West Africa building a recording studio for the president of Gambia. "You know I'll find you anywhere on the planet," Chad joked when he finally reached him by phone.)

As Chad strolled through Patchwerk, the hallways lined with plaques, he noticed a Jay-Z plaque which bothered him. While he'd always acknowledged that Jay-Z handed them "a meal ticket and a blessing" by including them on "Big Pimpin'," he was bitter that they hadn't received any publishing off the song.

"I still ain't get no platinum plaque for that song yet," he complained. "So, right now what I'm trying to do, I'm trying to get my plaque. And my publishing. And I ain't saying it's Jay-Z's

---

(*UGK agreed to reschedule the show for a later date, but the promoter later sued them.)

fault, I'm saying that somewhere the ball was dropped. Partly on our end, a whole lot on Def Jam's end, but … let me get my plaque, man. 'Cause I go to the studio where it was recorded at and I see the plaque … how come I don't have one?"

It wasn't the first time Patchwerk's studio manager Curtis Daniel III had heard a complaint like this. Obtaining a plaque was a headache, and Curtis often spent considerable time and expense going through the process to obtain them.

Jay-Z actually *had* sent a plaque while Chad was in prison, an enormous piece celebrating more than 16 million albums sold on Roc-A-Fella Records. But it wasn't for Pimp; it was engraved to "MOMMA OF UGK." Chad had never noticed it hanging about his mother's living room television until they drove back to Port Arthur.

"Where you got that from?" he asked.

"It dropped from Heaven," Mama Wes joked.

"Why I ain't got one like that?" he complained. "Get that nigga on the phone."

Several weeks later, another plaque arrived at Chad's Oakmont home. "He did it with his own money, so hooray for Jay-Z," he told *OZONE*. "He's an outstanding citizen."

Around this time, Chad got a call from Stephen Starring, one of Mama Wes' cousins from Louisiana. Stephen, a former NFL wide receiver, had fathered a child in Boston while playing with the New England Patriots. He'd recently reconnected with his daughter Tara, who was now 17 and curious about her father's side of the family.

Tara had been infatuated with rap ever since childhood. While raiding her brother's CD collection looking for The LOX's *Money, Power & Respect*, she'd grabbed another CD which caught her eye: the red and yellow UGK logo on the front of *Ridin' Dirty*. Her mother soon confiscated the CD due to its explicit language, but the damage was already done. Tara soon gained a reputation around Boston as the "little 13-year-old yellow kid" who wasn't scared to join freestyle battles in the 'hood.

In an effort to bond with his daughter, Stephen told her that his cousin was a rapper too. Tara rolled her eyes, picturing an aspiring rapper at an open mic session. "He's with UGK," Stephen explained.

Tara didn't believe him until he called Chad on the phone. "Yo' daddy tells me you rap," Chad said.

Her mouth dropped open. "Yeah, I'm nice," she replied, in a sharp Boston accent. After hearing some of her material, they talked about her coming down to Port Arthur to become the first lady of UGK Records.

Surprised to learn that the new generation of Houston rappers were commanding higher performance fees than UGK, Chad decided to raise his show price. He'd also started to distance himself from JT after the Bentley accident; JT believed Chad should pay for his medical bills, but in Chad's opinion, JT was there of his own accord. Pimp brought back some of the old crew, like Byron Amos and Big Munn, and recruited Elliot Thomas to work security.

Chad's cousin Ed had been making good money working on an oil rig, but photography was his true passion. Impressed with his work, Chad invited Ed to come on the road as his personal assistant/photographer. Mike Mo, who came along as his sound engineer, gradually fell into the position of road manager.

Mama Wes no longer traveled to most of the shows, but still played a key role in coordinating things behind the scenes. "She don't do the road [management] no more, but she's my personal manager, which is a beautiful thing – having a family member that you can trust," Chad told the *Dallas Morning News*.

Pimp C hit the studio to finish up the *Pimpalation* project, which included tracks from Mike Dean, Jazze Pha, Cory Mo, Clay D, Mannie Fresh, and Salih Williams of Carnival Beats. J. Prince dropped one of his trademark intros ("Mama, yo' son is home, out of the slavemaster's system, and we about to act real bad, yeah, and make a bunch of money"). Pimp hoped to feature both Big Mike and 3-2 on "Havin' Thangs '06," a Convicts reunion on the follow up to "Havin' Thangs," but only Big Mike (who had been paroled on 2004 on the arson charges) showed up for the studio session.

Pimp tried, unsuccessfully, to get in touch with Jay-Z for the *Pimpalation*. "I would have loved to have gotten him on it but he is an extremely busy man right now … so maybe next project," he told *OZONE*.

On "I Miss You," Pimp showcased his vulnerability, penning an ode to his deceased Aunt Bea (who "wiped [his] tears away tryin' to explain why [his] life had to be this way" when his parents got divorced) and a dedication to his stepfather Monroe:

You showed me how to be the man that I was meant to be
Taught me how to play music and 'bout the melody
And to this day I remember what you was telling me
You told me, 'Son, most of this rap shit is just noise
But if you put some music in it, you'll get rich, boy'
That's why I stay up in the studio, up all night
I fuck with live musicians to get the groove right
Yeah I'm a rap star now, yeah, you could say that
'Cause now my walls is filled with gold and gray plaques
Doin' shows and videos and makin' big stacks
But if it would bring you back I would trade all that

Four of the tracks on the album ("Rock 4 Rock," "Gitcha Mind Right," "Bobby & Whitney," and "Overstand Me") were produced by Dallas producer Mr. Lee, who considered it an honor to be in the studio with one of his main production influences. "The studio was like a sacred place for him," recalls Mr. Lee. "He was serious about his music and critiquing [every little aspect of it] to the highest point."

On "Gitcha Mind Right," Pimp shot a slug at a young Houston rapper, 20-year-old Charleston Davis, who called himself Short Dawg. "Me and Short Dog go and smoke in the coupe," Pimp rapped, "I'm talkin' 'bout Too $hort, not that fake nigga."

Pimp felt that it was disrespectful for a new rapper to adopt Too $hort's nickname, but Short Dawg had actually earned the name when he was 4'9", the shortest player on his high school basketball team. He'd signed with Russell Simmons' label RSMG, and Pimp blamed Russell for not telling him to change his name. "His record label should have told him that wasn't no good name," Pimp said.

Pimp didn't know that Short Dawg and Too $hort had already had a conversation. Russell Simmons' label reached out, hoping to get the two on a song together. "It's just a little awkward to work with somebody that's jackin' you for your name," laughs Too $hort. Still, he was cordial, and the two went to dinner together, even posing together for pictures at an Atlanta pool party.

When Short Dawg heard about the Pimp C diss, he reached out to Bun in an attempt to find out what was going on.* He didn't hear back, and family members kept pressuring him to respond. One day, he happened to pass by Pimp C in his Bentley on I-10 in Houston and trailed him on the freeway for several miles, envisioning a confrontation. He had second thoughts when he remembered Pimp's affiliation with Rap-A-Lot.

"You can't be takin' other rapper's names that's friends of mine and thinking you gon' put

(*Coincidentally, Short Dawg was related to Bun B's wife Queenie, making Bun his step-uncle.)

out records with they name," Pimp had told me during an *OZONE* interview. "That's like some-body … saying they 'Sweet Jones' and putting out a record. You a clown … You from my state and you got my OG's name and you thinking you finna put some records out? You're not finna do that. [And $hort is] not going to say nothing about it, because he's too old school to get involved into anything like that. [But] I can say what I wanna say."

Before the interview went to print, he'd had second thoughts and asked me to remove the entire section. "i realy dont like the shit about short dawg!!!!!! please take the shit bout him and his name out this shit 4 me!!!!" he emailed me. "i was tripping giving him all that air time and some of that shit soundz like thretz!!! im on parole and i cant say shit like that even if i feel that way!! please fix it 4 me b 4 u go to press!!!!!! thankz."

Meanwhile, Smoke D and his co-defendant Stan were still out on bond for their Louisiana arrest. Smoke knew that Chad was hesitant to help him shop for a record deal while his freedom was uncertain, and tried to get him on the phone with Stan to explain their plan.

Initially, Stan and Smoke had agreed that Stan would claim responsibility for the drugs. They had time to coordinate their stories, a luxury usually not afforded co-defendants. But as things unfolded, their relationship deteriorated and both men believed the other was turning against him.

According to Stan, he paid Eddie Austin Jr. of Austin Law Firm a $30,000 retainer for his own case and a $20,000 retainer for Smoke D's case.* (Stan also claims that he paid his attorney an additional $50,000 under the table, which was supposed to ensure that the case would not be turned over to federal authorities.)

Stan complicated matters by getting arrested again not once, but *twice* in three days: first in Anahuac with four ounces of codeine and seven grams of marijuana, and again in Jefferson Davis Parish with four pints of codeine in an unpaid rental car which had been reported stolen. After his *third* arrest, bail was set at a million dollars. If he posted a million dollar bond, the case would be turned over to federal authorities. Stan decided he'd rather sit in jail than get caught up in the federal system, where he'd have to serve 85% of his time.

Smoke didn't trust Eddie Austin Jr. because he'd met him through Stan. Chad had planned for Smoke to be one of the first artists on UGK Records, so hoping to preserve Smoke's freedom, he reached out to his attorney friend Craig Wormley on Smoke's behalf.**

Wormley turned the case over to another California attorney named Chris Dombrows-ki.*** Dombrowski flew out to attend a hearing with Judge Wendell Miller, the only judge in the parish, and was taken aback by the unorthodox small-town Louisiana proceedings. "He said they were cutting deals in the [judge's] chambers, which is not what you normally do," recalls Wormley.

Dombrowski and Austin planned to put together a plea bargain which would ensure that Smoke would only have to do four or five years. Their plan would also put Smoke in a mini-mum-security prison where he could get more time shaved off his sentence for good behavior.

Shortly before Smoke's scheduled court date, he drove down to Port Arthur, this time ac-companied by his wife and his mother. While they ate dinner, Mama Wes stepped into the

(*Smoke D says that *he* was the one who paid Eddie Austin Jr., and that his fee of nearly $60,000 would ensure that he would only receive probation. Instead, Smoke says, Austin did absolutely nothing to prepare for his defense and showed up in court with nothing other than a rolled-up copy of *OZONE* Magazine, apparently to argue that Smoke was legitimately pursuing a career in the music business and not a drug dealer.)
(**There is debate over who actually paid for Smoke's attorney. Chad told his mother, Wendy Day, and numerous other people that he paid Craig Wormley's law firm $25,000 to defend Smoke. Wormley believes that is correct, but does not recall specifics. Smoke, however, says *he* was the one who paid, dipping into some relatives' savings to pay Dombrowski $25,000.)
(***Wormley and Dombrowski apparently parted on bad terms. When contacted by phone for comment, Dombrowski snapped, "If you're connected to Craig [Wormley], I have nothing to say," and hung up.)

kitchen and called her son to let him know his guests had arrived.

"C, they're here. What is it you need to talk to them about?" she asked.

"Mama, I'm gonna tell these people that the boy going to jail," he responded. "I just finished talking to the lawyer, and they'll try to cut it down to the least number of years that he can get."

She sighed. "C, there's no need for you to come over here," she told him quietly. "That's not gonna work, because I just finished talking to these people and all of these bo-bos sitting here thinking that this boy gonna walk. [They think] he's gonna get probation."

Twenty minutes later Chad came bounding through the side garage door into his mother's kitchen, a cell phone in each hand. He greeted his mother, who was washing dishes. Smoke D, his mother, and his wife were lounging in the living room, talking amongst themselves.

"Hey, how's everybody doing?!" Chad said enthusiastically, greeting his guests. "Mama, you cooked?"

"Yeah, everybody's eaten and everything," she answered.

"I wanna talk to everybody. Mama, you coming in here?" he called from the living room.

"No, y'all go ahead and talk," she called back. "I'm gonna clean the kitchen."

"Man, you know you're gonna have to do a little time," Chad began, looking at Smoke D. "Now this is what we're gonna try to do: get him the least number of years," turning towards his mother and wife. "The lawyer has a hook-up with somebody in the system."

For 19 solid minutes he preached uninterrupted, strolling back and forth in the living room with all the enthusiasm of a Baptist preacher giving a sermon on a Sunday morning, waving his cell phones in the air. ("He was so cute. I wish I had taped that," says Mama Wes, who was watching with amusement from the kitchen.)

His guests sat silently through the whole spiel. Once Chad was finished, he looked intently at his audience. "Now, anybody got any questions?"

Smoke D cleared his throat and spoke slowly in his husky baritone voice, "Well, yeah, man. You see, when they give me probation tomorrow…" His wife sat silently while his mother echoed his sentiments: "When we get back to Mississippi…"

That was all Chad needed to hear; they hadn't listened to a word he'd said. With one cell phone still in each hand, he shoved them both in the pockets of his Dickies and walked out of the living room without a word. "Holla at'cha later mama," he called after his mother, exiting through the kitchen into the garage. "Let's go to Waffle House after a while. I'm gone."

Twenty minutes later, after Chad's temper had cooled, he called his mother. "Mama," he asked, "Them crazy ass niggas still over at your house?"

"I told you not to come," she laughed. "I told you, I said, 'Don't give that lawyer no more money, 'cause he's not gonna listen to him.'"

On June 26, 2006, Smoke D appeared in court on the drugs and weapons charges. He knew that as a convicted felon, if he were convicted of carrying a firearm he would be sentenced to a mandatory 10 years in federal prison, with no chance of early release.

On the advice of his attorney, Smoke D agreed to a plea bargain in which the state would drop the gun charge if he agreed to testify against Stan on the drug charges. He was under the impression that his attorney could then negotiate for a sentence of less than 10 years state time, and he'd be home in less than five.

Stan, still sitting in jail, received paperwork indicating that if he chose to go to trial, Smoke D was scheduled to testify against him.

Back home in Jackson after the hearing, Smoke D met up with Jaro, who asked how things went in court. "Well, I entered a plea," Smoke told him. "They made me plead."

"Plead what?" Jaro asked.

"Plead guilty," Smoke shrugged. "That's all they want. And when they get what they want, they gonna give me what I want."

Jaro stared at him. "Damn, you just fucking shot yourself in the foot, man! Once you enter a plea they don't have to talk to you no more!"

"They tricked Smoke," Stan says in retrospect. "But… he kinda fell for it, too."

With the *Pimpalation* release fast approaching, the task of fielding media inquiries fell to Pimp C's publicist Nancy Byron. Pimp had always avoided interviews, preferring to let Bun handle things as the more tactful, articulate, and prompt group member. But the people wanted to hear from Pimp. The requests came flooding in: *RIDES* Magazine, *FADER*, *Black Men's* Magazine, *XXL* Magazine, *Streetz* Magazine, *XPOZ* Magazine.

Nancy loved Chad as a person but considered Pimp C a "god-awful client" whose inconsistencies were hurting UGK's brand. He showed up hours late for interviews and photo shoots, if he showed up at all. "You can't blow people off on a continuing basis and not have it affect [your professional] relationships," she notes.

After committing to a major feature for *Complex*, Pimp changed his mind on the day of the interview. An interview for *FADER* went unpublished because he didn't show up for the photo shoot. He was several hours late for a *XXL* photo shoot. "Pimp thought nothing of making [photographers] wait four hours, five hours, and he wouldn't be remotely apologetic when he arrived, either," says Nancy, recalling a *Mass Appeal* photo shoot which was delayed four hours. "He didn't mind making Bun wait either."

To a certain extent, Chad seemed to enjoy living up to the notoriously difficult Pimp C persona he had created. Nancy couldn't see any valid excuse for his inconsistencies. "[He'd be late] because he just didn't fucking feel like it," she says. "Pimp would always feel like he [didn't] owe anybody reasons for why he wouldn't want to do stuff."

In Too $hort's opinion, there were two possible reasons for Pimp's unreliability. "[Sometimes] it's like a tug of war between the schedule and reality," he says. "The schedule says you're gonna do all this shit in [one] day but the reality is, most of that shit [isn't] gonna get done."

"He was a human being. There's a lot of impossible scheduling and some shit that people just [don't understand]," agrees Mike Mo. "Everybody wants him to be Pimp C, but sometimes he ain't feel like doing that. [He'd think,] *Gimme a break, can I be Chad today?*"

Secondly, Chad was a man of principle. "He had a whole chip [on his shoulder] against the East Coast media," says Too $hort. "We all did. It wasn't about New York, it was about the Hip-Hop media in New York. [If an artist] made one local New York record, a record that's not even big in Texas or California, [they] were all over the magazines, because all the magazines [were] in New York. [But] you could be platinum outside of New York and you'd get like, way in the back, some little page."

Even though things were starting to change, he hadn't forgotten the discrimination of the past. "Pimp had this line," Too $hort adds. "He'd always had this line … he ain't crossin' this line, ever, and he was just firm about it. [If he said], 'I don't fuck with them,' [or], 'I'm not doing that,' he meant it."

While Pimp could be combative and difficult with other media outlets, he'd become a regular contributor to *OZONE*. After interviewing T.I. for our cover story, he reviewed Scarface's debut album *Mr. Scarface Is Back* for a feature titled 20 Essential Southern Albums. "I do interviews for people that cut for me and magazine folks that I like … when folks look out for us, we get down for them," he explained.

"*OZONE* was the first publication to really [base their] entire business model around supporting the South and opening people's eyes and exposing the South to bigger and wider markets," says Nancy Byron. "I'm sure he had a great deal of respect for that and obviously he liked you personally … that's why you got a better side of him than, say, *Complex* or *Rolling Stone*."

"Everybody recognizes what [*OZONE* did] for us [in the South]," agrees journalist Matt

Sonzala. "Everybody knows. Pimp knows ... We came from a time when there was nothing like that ... *Murder Dog* came along and changed the game completely for independents, but the majority of [Pimp's career] there was nothing. [When *OZONE*] came along, you could see how a lot of the other magazines shifted [their coverage of the South] when they saw your success. They didn't give us shit before."

On July 11, the day of the album release, Pimp appeared on the Madd Hatta Morning show on Houston's The Box, where he spoke on the South's prominence in the rap game. "When the rappers in [New York] neighborhoods was selling, we was buying they records," he pointed out. "So now that we got the ball, all of a sudden, [they say] 'Hip-Hop is dead'?"

"I told 'em a long time ago we wasn't making Hip-Hop records," Pimp said. "I remember back when KRS-One got on a record and said, basically, if you not from where we from, you not real Hip-Hop anyway. You know, that offended me, because I was a fan of the music. I'm still a fan of the music. I was buying everybody's records ... I know my Hip-Hop history ... At a certain stage in the game, we was getting vibes from the East that they didn't want us to be a part of what they was doing. We went off and started doing our own thang, and after a minute, I stopped trying to rap like them and be down with what they was doing [and] I coined the term 'country rap tunes.'"

"They just mad that they records not selling ... All these rappers crying [talking] about 'Hip-Hop is dead,' it's dead because y'all froze everybody out. And now we freezing y'all out," he added. "Get your mind on your money ... stop complaining. I'll see you on the charts ... Y'all [need to] stop crying, man. On that East [Coast] y'all been eating for years. It's time for us to eat ... If Hip-Hop is dead, it's y'all fault that Hip-Hop died."

DJ Screw's father Papa Screw stopped by Pimp's in-store signing for the *Pimpalation* at Music Depot in Houston's Greenspoint Mall. Michael Watts was recruited to do the Chopped & Screwed version, which he considered "an honor." *Pimpalation* was also released with the accompanying *Pimpalation: Return of the Trill* DVD, produced by Ariel "REL" Santschi for Rap-A-Lot.

On the DVD, Pimp explained that he had mixed feelings about his new "legendary" status. "We still rapping with these youngsters," he pointed out. "We ain't on no shelf somewhere collecting dust, we still out here going verse for verse and rhyme for rhyme with these niggas. You have to work with the new young artists, because you get energy from them."

"I never said I was a pioneer," he added later. "Other people kept sayin' that. If that's how they feel, good. I'd rather get my flowers while I'm still in it and still alive than when I'm dead and gone. That ain't for me to say. I don't go in the studio making records like I'm some type of dude on a pedestal ... 'cause you're only as good as your last record. My mama told me a rapper is only as good as his last show."

Pimp's feelings towards the media seemed justified when reviews came out of the *Pimpalation*. *XXL* Magazine criticized the project for its "very little substance" and "cliché subject matter," calling it "more like a glorified compilation than a true solo disc." Many other reviews didn't seem to understand that it was intended to be a compilation.

"You dumb muthafucker!" Pimp howled in an interview with *FADER*. "Don't you know it's a comp-u-lation? Can't you get 'compilation' from *Pimpalation*? Where do they *find* these people?"

"Any idiot can figure out 'compilation' from *Pimpalation*," he griped in *OZONE*. "This fool [who reviewed my album] really had no ties to the South and really doesn't know what we like down here ... Why did [a magazine] get somebody to rate a down South album that doesn't know anything about or history or doesn't know anything about our music down here?"

"Back in the day the people reviewing the albums was really fans of the music," Pimp complained. "[Now] you got dumb muthafuckers reviewing LPs." (He even suggested the negative publicity might a "deliberate plot by some people at Jive" to sabotage the record since it was released through Rap-A-Lot instead of Jive, adding, "I wouldn't put it past 'em.")

Still, it was true that the album was more rushed than previous UGK projects, with Pimp delegating tasks to other producers. Guitarist Funkafangez was slightly upset when he heard "Free," which utilized a Tom Petty sample instead of live instrumentation. "Why didn't you call me, man!?" he asked Pimp.

When AllHipHop asked why he'd chosen to release a compilation instead of a solo project, Pimp explained that it was less pressure that way. "[With UGK] we're so serious about our music that we never got to have a good time making music," he said. "I've never had a fun album in my career; everything was like giving birth to a baby – painstaking and such. I wanted to come out and do something I've never got to do."

Despite the critics, *Pimpalation* went gold. And if there was one thing all the reviewers agreed on, it was this: "No more solo joints," wrote SOHH.com. "We want a UGK album."

"Truth be told, I'm not excited about a solo career," Pimp told AllHipHop. "I'm in UGK. I don't even enjoy being onstage without Bun. If I look over to my left, or I look over to my right and he ain't there, the shit ain't right."

———————

In late July 2006, Pimp was back in Atlanta hosting a party at Visions. He linked up with rapper Killer Mike of the Dungeon Family, a longtime UGK fan, who had exchanged letters with him while he was incarcerated.

Killer Mike idolized Pimp, and some of their mutual friends, like Wendy Day and Bun B, urged him not to take things too personally. He understood what they were trying to tell him: "If you fortunate enough to ever have Pimp as an associate or a friend he is gonna be one of the best, closest friends you ever known, but at some point he is gonna cuss your muthafuckin' ass out," he summarizes.

The two linked up at Grindhouse Studios inside Big Boi's Purple Ribbon office, where Killer Mike explained that he had a limited budget but didn't want to lowball him. Pimp offered to do the verse for free because he appreciated the intellectual content of his music, which reminded him of the political Ice Cube or the soulful Goodie Mob of the 90s.

"I can't charge you," Pimp explained. "I'ma charge these other fools callin' me talkin' 'bout 'candy paint' and 'comin' down.' I'ma make *them* pay. I ain't got to get my money from you. Don't worry about it."

Killer Mike was flattered. "He wouldn't let me pay him for a verse because he considered me to be valuable to the Southern legacy," Killer Mike says. "And that isn't my ego saying that, that's him telling me."

Pimp knocked out not one but two free verses for Killer Mike, who was fascinated watching him in the studio. Instead of adding an effect to his vocals, for example, Pimp repeated his line while moving backwards in the booth ("gone… gone… gone… gone") to create a real echo.

"The two or three things he showed me are with me [forever] and they'll be passed on to another rapper," Killer Mike says. "I don't need the 20-year friendship from Pimp [with all] those ups and downs. I'd rather hear [those] stories from other people. But the few times we met I left with things that changed my life."

Pimp told Killer Mike that he was rooting for him, both because of his rap skills and because he was an underdog. "I know how that feels," Pimp told him. "Bun used to say, 'Pimp, boys ain't recognizing us. They ain't respectin' it.' And I used to tell him, 'Don't worry about it, 'cause where them boys who doing that bullshit gonna be 10, 20 years from now? Our music gonna last forever.'"

Also sitting in on the session was Killer Mike's girlfriend Shay, and after Pimp learned she was a diehard UGK fan, he told Mike, "Yeah, you need to marry her."

"I tell you what," Pimp instructed Shay. "[If] he out there in the streets, [if] he keep messing up, you call me, and we gonna get him together."

Across the street from Big Boi's Purple Ribbon office was OutKast's studio Stankonia, and next door, Zak's Studio, singer Lloyd and 8Ball were recording a song for a posthumous Tupac project. When Lloyd stepped outside, he saw Pimp exiting Stankonia.

"Hey, man, I'm working on 'Pac," Lloyd told him. "You should come in and just bless it."
Pimp did "bless it," with a raw, explicit verse that ended with:

Dick up in they ears, dick up in they nose
Ass, pussy, mouth, I'm finna fuck in every hole
Put it between they titties and between they toes
That's how a gushy gush out when ya bitch get chose

Although Tupac's verse wasn't much cleaner ("oh, come to Papi, I love it when it's wet and sloppy / In and out the mouthpiece until I cum, no one can stop me") Pimp's verse was a bit too much for Tupac's mother, Afeni Shakur, who was spearheading the project, and she decided not to use the verse.*

Another young ATLien Pimp hoped to meet was female rapper Diamond. He'd been impressed with her verse on Crime Mob's "Knuck If You Buck" and arranged to barter verses with her while he was in town. Her track, "Go To War," was built around a sample of Pimp C's voice from UGK's "Like A Pimp" ("If you wanna go to war, I'll take you to war").

Diamond had never recorded solo outside of the group, and was nervous how the other group members would feel if they found out she was recording with Pimp C without them. Plus, she was nervous about rapping in front of a legend.

When she confessed the reasons behind her hesitation, Pimp stopped the beat and told her a story about the "Big Pimpin'" video shoot. He recalled sweating profusely in the mink coat, the Florida sun beaming down, and Bun asking him if he was hot.

He'd briefly considered taking it off. *A nigga hot,* he'd thought. *I'm out here on the beach with all these beautiful women.* But he'd remained confident, stuck with his vision, and it had paid off. "If you look back at that video, you would never know that I was [thinking that]," he explained. "[And] when the video came out, that [mink coat] was one of the main things that everybody talked about … [They said,] 'I can't believe that nigga got on TV and he really did that shit.'"

In case she missed the point, Pimp explained, "It's all about the delivery. It's not what you say, it's *how* you say it. So you could be talking about something that ain't really hard, but if you say it to the point where there's conviction in your voice, your fans, people that listen to you and fuck with you, they gon' believe it. They gonna buy into it."

(*Pimp C and Tupac's verses from this song would later be used on Bun B's "Right Now.")

CHAPTER 41

"Once we started recording for *Underground Kingz*, we literally couldn't stop.
That's why it ended up being a double album."
– Bun B, *Village Voice,* March 2008

———————

"Time brings change, and it's been like four or five years since we had an album,
so of course we've got a different outlook on things. We're not gonna rap about
the same things at 30-something that we was rapping about at 16. We've got a
different approach. To run from change would be unnatural." – Pimp C

With *Pimpalation* in stores, Chad turned his attention towards the UGK album. They decided to title it simply *Underground Kingz*, as if to emphasize their fresh new start. Everyone understood that this was it: the pinnacle of UGK's success, the time for them to claim the throne. "This is our last chance to get it," Bun told *OZONE*. "If we don't get it on this run, after the whole Free Pimp C movement and the Houston movement, we'll never get it. There is no better set up for this. It's our time."

In retrospect, the things they'd argued with Jive over seemed petty; even though there were legitimate issues, Bun realized they'd made a mistake by allowing those arguments to stop the flow of their music. After sitting down for several years, Chad had come to the same conclusion. "We wasted a lot of time arguing about petty shit … [but] the people lose when we don't make … good music," Chad admitted. "Man, let's just … make music."

Now older and wiser, Chad and Bun both felt a responsibility to share their knowledge with listeners. "I know that time brings change, and it's been like four or five years since we had an album, so, of course we've got a different outlook on things now … we're not gonna rap about the same things at 30-something that we was rapping about at 16," Chad said. "To run from change would be unnatural."

He felt that there was a void in the rap game because artists were no longer speaking on political topics. "Niggas is real shallow right now," he complained on the *Will Hustle* DVD. "I think we gotta elevate our game down here. It's cool to rap about the cars and the jewels and thangs, but at some point, we got a responsibility to talk about some different things."

"When I didn't know no better, I had an excuse for making a shallow record, but now that I know I have a responsibility to tell what I know," he added in *OZONE*. "We gonna give [the listeners] what they want and what they need."

Chad and Bun had both come to understand that UGK represented something greater than themselves. "People really love and invest in this UGK shit … [because] we're the ones that made it for the cats that didn't," Bun told *XXL*. "Their hopes and dreams are aligned with ours … We still give a certain generation of niggas they vitality. They still live through us."

UGK had always touched on spirituality in their music with records like "One Day," and on their self-titled project, Chad hoped to explore these topics more in-depth. "We try to raise issues in our music: What does happen to the gangsters and the drug dealers when they die? Is there heaven for the real G's?" Chad told *OZONE*, adding, "Everybody that hustles [drugs] is not a bad person [and] everybody that's been involved in prostitution is not a bad person, on either side – the prostitute side or the pimp side. Everybody that's done bad things in life is not necessarily a bad person. It's never too late to change."

"So what happens to people that go on to the next life before they've completely made the transition from their negative lifestyle to where they want to be in life?" he asked rhetorically. "We're raising those types of issues on our album."

Things at the *OZONE* office in Orlando were hectic as we prepared for the first-ever OZONE Awards. Whether by fate or by circumstance, but certainly not much planning on our part, the night of August 6, 2006, would mark the first time Bun and Pimp appeared on stage together since Pimp's release from prison.

We'd lucked up with a last-minute performance by Ludacris, who was filming an episode of *MTV Diary*, and highlighted other rising stars like T-Pain and Yung Joc. The opening set, inspired by DJ Khaled's annual birthday bash, featured a medley of Miami rappers including newcomer Plies, O.G. Trick Daddy, rising pop star Pitbull, and Rick Ross, who had just hit big with his single "Hustlin'." The headliner, Lil Wayne, was in a tour bus out back awaiting his cue.

Bun had initially declined to perform, and I wasn't even sure if Pimp planned to attend. But midway through the show, there they were; the crowd of people backstage parted as Pimp and Bun snaked through, with the co-host David Banner introducing them as "my fuckin' favorite rap group of all time... U-G-muthafuckin'-K!"

The climax came with the triumphant ending of "Draped Up": "Back in the days all they ever did was doubt us," Bun rapped. "Now the South is in the house and they can't do nothing about us!"

Still, it was evident from Pimp and Bun's body language that it had been a while since they'd been on stage together. A fumbled embrace came off as awkward. When Pimp announced, "Let's go all the way back..." intending to a launch into "Pocket Full of Stones," he was interrupted by Young Jeezy running out on stage, his arm around Bun, rapping his verse to "Get Throwed" a capella.

After the show, Pimp, David Banner, and the *OZONE* crew were among the last to trickle out the side entrance. One of our clients had traded me a white BMW 745 with rims to drive for the weekend in exchange for an ad in the magazine. Even though Pimp's hotel was directly across the street, I knew someone of his status deserved personal service. He climbed in the passenger seat. Banner smiled, knowing it wasn't mine. "Nice car," he winked.

After a stop at the hotel so Pimp could change, we headed down the street to the Club at Firestone for the Atlantic Records-sponsored afterparty, with Webbie and 8Ball. Pimp reached for the stereo, which was playing Plies' popular underground mixtape. "Who is this?" he asked.

"This is the dude that just performed, Plies," I told him. "He opened the show."

Pimp nodded and bobbed his head along with the beat.

I hadn't slept for four days prior to the show, and the day after the event, I was knocked out cold until late afternoon. I woke up in a panic, worried that I'd overslept and hadn't been able to coordinate all the artists' transportation back to the airport. But my BlackBerry, which had hummed with calls and emails literally every 30 seconds for the past three days, showed zero missed calls or emails. For a brief moment, I wondered if it had all just been a dream.

A quick glance around the room, strewn with ticket stubs, wristbands, and all kinds of OZONE Awards flyers assured me that it had really happened. As it turned out, I'd been so engulfed in the OZONE Awards craziness that I'd forgotten to pay my phone bill and the line was disconnected. Once I paid the bill, a stream of encouraging emails and texts came pouring through from everyone from Bun B to Lil Jon ("heard your shit was big!").

It was several weeks before life returned to normal; when I finally saw the rough cut of the show, edited by MTV Jams for broadcast, I couldn't believe we'd actually pulled it off. I'd been so busy scrambling around backstage that it was the first time I'd seen most of the show.

When Young Jeezy presented UGK with the Living Legend Award, Bun accepted the award as Pimp stood silently by his side. After thanking "everybody in here that ever bought an album from UGK, Bun B, and Pimp," Bun said:

I wanna thank everybody out here that actually came to this shit, because I'ma be real and say what everybody ain't gonna say. I ain't know what this shit was gonna look like, and I really didn't know if I was gonna come. But I know Julia supported us when we didn't have a lot going on so I came out and supported her, man, and I'ma tell you what: I'm bringing a hundred trill niggas with me next year. And y'all better do the same. 'Cause this some South shit right here. Ain't nobody else gonna come together and put this shit together for us but us.

For us, by us. I replayed the clip four times. The OGs had officially cosigned *OZONE*. Wow.

———

In Port Arthur, when he wasn't at his mother's house, Chad was still staying at Chinara's apartment and he'd grown tired of hearing people laughing at his Bentley parked at an apartment complex. With his prior bankruptcy and IRS troubles, Chad's credit was in poor condition, but in the buoyant economy there was still a lender willing to issue him a mortgage – at the astronomical interest rate of 9.925%.* He selected a large gated home on Oakmont next to the local golf course.

———

"[A] source reporting on [a] gang/narcotics distribution network in the Baton Rouge area indicates that a major source of illegal drugs into the Baton Rouge area is an individual known as 'PIMP C', located in Houston, TX," read an August 15 memo circulating in the FBI's New Orleans office. "Searches for an individual by that name revealed Chad Butler is a rapper and part of a group known as Underground Kings or UGK. Chad Butler was believed to have been arrested on narcotics charges somewhere in Louisiana. Additionally, Butler was believed to deal narcotics in the Port Arthur area of Texas." Following up on the lead, the FBI sleuths Googled Chad and and printed out his Wikipedia page.**

———

In Houston, Chad and Bun convened at Mike and Cory Mo's MAD Studios, UGK's unofficial home studio, to start recording vocals for the UGK project. First and foremost, the brothers were fans, who recognized what a privilege it was to have a front-row seat to see a UGK album come to life.

With digital recording, ProTools, and steadily advancing recording technology, the recording process had become much smoother and even faster than before. "[Being in the studio with Pimp C] was always fun," Bun told *Murder Dog*. "We never argued about music!"

The first track they pulled up was produced by Mannie Fresh, which sampled the Isley Brothers' record "Here We Go Again."*** Bun couldn't help but be a little nervous. *We haven't done this together in, like, four years,* he thought. *Is it still gonna be like it was?*

(*Chad's lender Home123 Mortgage was a subsidiary of New Century, the largest U.S. provider of home loans for people with poor credit. 80% of New Century's business dealt with so-called "subprime loans"; they issued a staggering $51.6 billion dollars of subprime loans in 2006 when Chad purchased his home. The subprime mortgage market imploded in early 2007 due to mortgage defaults, and CNN called New Century "the poster-child for the meltdown." New Century was the subject of two criminal investigations and an SEC probe and, in debt more than $8.4 billion, was forced to file bankruptcy. The subprime mortgage collapse was a major cause of the U.S. recession and global financial crisis in 2008/2009.)
(**Wikipedia is a free internet-based resource where information can be submitted by anyone.)
(***Later, Mannie Fresh ran into singer Ron Isley in St. Louis and forwarded him the song. Isley readily agreed to sing over the demo vocals Chad had laid for the hook and sent the track back immediately. *Oh, wow, this is some fantastic shit,* Mannie Fresh thought. *He ain't send an invoice with it or nothing.* The track didn't make it on the *Underground Kingz* double album, but was later released under the title "The Pimp & The Bun" on *4 Life*.)

Chad and Bun wrote their rhymes separately and each took a turn in the booth spitting their lyrics. It fit together perfectly; clearly, UGK's chemistry was still intact even after four years apart. *Wow,* Bun thought. *Back in business.*

Next, Chad pulled up Kenny Lattimore's "Let's Straighten It Out," a song he'd been planning to sample for more than a decade. He'd produced the track for *Super Tight*, redone it for *Ridin' Dirty*, and once again for *Dirty Money*, and each time, to Bun's frustration, he'd abruptly cut off the drum machine without even saving the track. "No, not time yet," he'd say.

The record Chad envisioned, "Quit Hatin' the South," was a frustrated response to the animosity and apathy they'd felt coming from New York for years. But now, the tables had turned: New York rappers, their hometown style no longer in favor on radio station playlists, started to adopt Southern sound, slang, and style. Chad and Bun viewed it as karma.

Now that the South was on top, Chad was hearing the grumblings from disgruntled New Yorkers. "Being a Southern rapper now is as good as being a New York rapper [was] in '89–'90," Bun told *XXL*. "Even more so because of the profitability, the ability to make money off it."

While Bun's verse on "Quit Hatin' the South" was aimed at internet bloggers and commenters hiding behind a screenname, Pimp took things a step further, proclaiming that they should separate the "country rap tunes" from the rest of the "Hip-Hop records" in the store and see who could "sell out first."

"Keep talkin' that shit, I'ma send them young Gladiators to come get you too, pa'tna," Pimp proclaimed on the outro, a reference to Bun's bodyguard Nicholas "Truck" Brown, who always joked that he was in "gladiator mode" if he needed to rough somebody up.*

All things considered, though, Chad understood that New York's arrogance had been a blessing in disguise. "People started selling records in their own regions because they got tired of the abuse. We got tired of the abuse, and the Southern thing was regional for a long time," Pimp explained. "The Florida rappers were selling records in their region, we were selling records in our region, in Texas … [and] somewhere along the line, it popped, and the whole rest of the country caught on to it. So now it's our time to shine … You reap what you sow, and karma is a muthafucker."

At the same time, Chad wanted to make it clear he wasn't talking to *all* New Yorkers; he still considered Brand Nubian's Lord Jamar a friend, as well as Raekwon, DJ Kay Slay, and others. (To emphasize this point, he featured Big Daddy Kane and Kool G Rap on *Underground Kingz'* "Next Up," produced by Marley Marl.)

"Make no mistake … I'm not talking about everybody [in New York]," he clarified in *OZONE*. "I'm talking about the ones hating on the internet." On the *Will Hustle* DVD, he said it was only the broke New York rappers who were mad, because "the cost of living down here in Texas is good, mane."

"I don't hear the Dipset niggas crying … I don't hear Jay-Z crying," Chad pointed out. "But you know who crying though? Them bitch ass niggas that can't sell no records. They crying because they can't sell no records right now [but] Mike Jones got 15 cars and 22-carat diamonds in his ring."

Seeing Bun and Pimp together in the studio at the same time was a rare occurrence, but their chemistry was just as impressive as it was on the stage. "It was some real magic," remembers Cory Mo. Pimp explained his process on the *Pimpalation* DVD: "We write the rhymes [in the] studio, go in the booth, spit it, tear it up, and throw it in the garbage. Tell the nigga bring

(*Pimp's mention on "Quit Hatin' the South" inspired Truck to form a real entity called the Trill Gladiators. Originally a security company, it has now grown into what Truck describes as a "brotherhood," a fraternity of sorts which encompasses a wide variety of people including his high school friends and Bun's videographer Sama'an Ashrawi.)

the next track up. That's how we work." Cory Mo, who couldn't stand the thought of some Pimp C handwritten lyrics balled up in the trash, saved "Quit Hatin' the South" for safekeeping.

But although their joint studio session produced top-notch records, Chad and Bun felt that it was more efficient for them to work separately. Bun was a family man and an early riser, while Chad preferred to work vampire hours, so they fell into an arrangement which suited both of their schedules. Bun would arrive first thing in the morning, wearing house shoes and reading a newspaper, and get started on the UGK "day shift."

"He'd write verses so damn quick, it was ridiculous," Cory Mo recalls.

Bun would be done with the day's work and home by 6 PM, around the time Chad was just getting himself together to leave the house. It would often be past midnight by the time Chad arrived at the studio, holding down the UGK "night shift" until the sun came up the following morning.

"When I come in that night, I finish whatever it is Bun left for me to finish, and I start on something else," Chad explained. "He comes in, he'll finish whatever I left him, and he'll start on something else."

UGK's new round-the-clock recording schedule at first proved tough for their engineers. Inevitably, as soon as Mike Mo turned off the equipment after a long day in the studio with Bun, Chad would be on the line: "Smacky, open the gate!"

Cory was regularly awakened in the middle of the night by Chad blowing the horn outside. Blearly-eyed, he'd drag himself out to the gate to let Chad in and mumble, "Goddamn, nigga, it's five in the morning."

"We didn't get much sleep," remembers Mike Mo. "They thought that shit was funny … we'd be in [the studio] falling over [asleep] … but it was UGK, man. You can't even get mad at 'em. You were in there with the best … how you gonna get mad?"

After several exhausting weeks, the brothers worked out a routine: Mike would handle the day shift with Bun, and Cory would run the late night sessions with Chad. Mike had been pushing the limits of his psychology degree in an attempt to understand Chad and the two often clashed, but Cory's laid-back demeanor fit perfectly with Pimp.

Chad instructed Cory when to stack vocals and which effects to add on each track, often sharing mixing and mastering tips. "Some artists depend on the engineer to do everything … But Pimp, he told you what it was," says Cory Mo. "And it wasn't right until he said it was right."

In one session, Chad recorded some vocals for an intro, proclaiming that he was "back from the dead." He paused. "We gonna save that," he told Cory. "Hold on to that."

Bun didn't care what the schedule was as long as he could rap over some Pimp C beats. "It just felt good to me after so many years to rap on some Pimp C tracks, 'cause I hadn't done that in a while," Bun said. "I think people don't understand that UGK is just as important to me as it is to the people that buy the music. I be needing that UGK in my life, too."

As they had in the past, Jive largely left UGK to their own devices, preferring to let Pimp work his magic rather than try to force them to use certain producers or make a certain type of music. "One thing [Jive has] respected over the years is Pimp C's talent as a producer, I'll give 'em that. They just didn't wanna pay him for it," Bun told *OZONE*. "They never really told us now to make our music. They just won't let us promote it the way we want to promote it. We always bumped heads with them on promotion and shooting videos and sample clearances."

Even though UGK's relationship with Jive was far better than it had been in the past, sample clearances were still an issue. A track Cory Mo produced with an R. Kelly sample had to be scrapped when Jive couldn't clear it. Cory redid the beat without the sample, but it was less potent than the original and was cut from the album. "It broke my fuckin' heart," Cory says.

Pimp called Scarface at 4 AM one night asking for some beats. He came by the following night and put his own spin on a few classics, producing a remake of Too $hort's "Life Is… Too Short" and "Still Ridin' Dirty," on which he also dropped a verse. Chad sang an extended version of Goodie Mob's "Free" interlude for the hook of "Living This Life," produced by N.O. Joe.

Pimp was impressed to see Bun taking the initiative to come up with song concepts. "Bun grew a whole lot during the time I was away," he told *FADER*. "[He] grew in this business [and] got a hunger for it. It's more of a team effort than it was for years."

In keeping with their new grown-man perspective, they were sure to balance out records like "Two Types of Bitches" with records like "Real Women," a revamped version of Raheem DeVaughn's "Guess Who Loves You More" which also featured Talib Kweli.

"The nigga's name is Pimp C, so it's a lot of derogatory stuff about women coming out of the UGK file," Talib Kweli admitted in *XXL*. "[But] for Pimp C to have that balance, for him to be singing and crooning on that record and talking about what a woman means to him – it shows there were many facets to him that were not fully appreciated."

In reality, the relationship between the women in Chad's life was growing increasingly stressful. "[Chad] was extremely protective [of his mother], and I don't think Chinara understood his devotion to his mom," says Chad's godmother Brenda, who believed that Chinara perceived Mama Wes as some type of threat. "Bottom line, if Chad was gonna make a decision on anything, he was gonna pass it by his mom first ... so Chinara probably felt like she was never fully a part of the core of his life."

Mama Wes believed that Chinara's issues stemmed from jealousy. "No matter who she might be, I'm still C's mama and that's the way it is. And everybody in the world knows that C loved his Mama," says Mama Wes. "All of her issues are about jealousy, that's all it is ... and I can't do anything about that. I wish I could."

Chad didn't do much to try to repair the strained relations between his mother and his wife; if anything, he instigated it. When it came to making large purchases, he frequently deferred to his mother.

According to Mama Wes, Chad wanted his children to grow up in his childhood home on Shreveport Ave. He planned to add a fence around the large property and build a studio on the adjoining land, which they also owned. Chad told Chinara that he had purchased the Oakmont home with the intent of ultimately switching with his mother, and frequently asked Mama Wes to come over and approve new furniture and décor.

"I'd always say 'yes,' even if I didn't [like it], because I was really trying not to create problems," recalls Mama Wes, who sensed Chinara's irritation. "He bought that house [on Oakmont] because that was the house *I* wanted, not because that was the house *he* wanted."

Over at the Shreveport house, Pops and Mama Wes had a new houseguest, a white kid named Travis. Travis and Mama Wes had first connected in the late 90s, when Travis was hoping to interview Pimp C for his blog site. Chad wasn't sure how he felt about Travis spending so much time with his mother. "All I hear about you is, 'White Boy did this, White Boy did that,'" he complained. "I don't like people around my Mama."

Travis described himself as a "professional smart ass," but unofficially, he'd become Mama Wes' gofer, running errands for her and giving the kids rides back and forth from Houston to Beaumont. Travis came in handy in other ways, helping to arrange the two Brooke Valentine features for $15,000 each.

Chad and Bun were both prone to losing things, especially their music. "That's one thing I never did is keep music, 'cause I lose shit all the time," Bun admitted on Damage Control Radio. "I don't carry a wallet 'cause I'd lose a wallet." Travis, who was a music lover and also a bit of a packrat, started to take over where Mitchell Queen had left off as UGK's archivist, trying to keep track of all the unreleased hooks, beats, and other unfinished tracks.

While he was staying at Mama Wes' house, Travis helped her clean and organize the game room, which, between Hurricane Rita and years of accumulation, had morphed into a storage shed for miscellaneous items. In the process, he found close to 80 DAT tapes with a variety of old Pimp C material. Travis bagged them up and loaded them into Chad's red Bentley.

He headed back to Houston and got a call the following morning from Mama Wes. "C wants to know if you have any more copies of those DATs, because he's lost them," she said.

How the fuck did he lose 80 DATs? Travis wondered, shaking his head.

As they finished cleaning out the game room and came across 50 more DATs, Travis made a CD backup first before giving them to Chad. "Man, you can't just lose history," Travis told him.

"You're like Mitch, you like to keep shit," Chad laughed. "That's cool, 'cause I ain't keeping shit, but it may be handy."

One Wednesday night when he was in Port Arthur, Chad attended services with Mama Wes and Corey at United Christian Fellowship Church in nearby Port Neches. Mama Wes had been attending the non-denominational church since the late 1980s. She liked her pastor, John Morgan, a middle-aged white man with a laid-back, affable demeanor, for his non-traditional approach. The church catered to a wide variety of people from all races and backgrounds.

As they left the services, Chad seemed quiet and introspective. "Ma, hold up," he said softly. "May I ask you about something?"

"Sure. You want to ask something about the services?"

"No, about them people who was in there."

"What's wrong with them?"

"They always smile like that?" Chad asked. "When you walked in there, you went to grinning too."

She couldn't hide her amusement. "Yeah, I do."

"If I stay there I'll grin too?" he wanted to know.

"You probably will. You'll just start being a grinning fool too," Mama Wes laughed.

Chad wasn't sure if he was ready to become a "grinning fool" just yet, but he did visit the church several more times and started building a friendship with Pastor John Morgan. Morgan was a hearty eater who never hesitated to stop by Mama Wes' house for dinner. On one occasion, Mama Wes served dinner to a large group of men, not realizing that the rice cooker had shut off prematurely. Morgan helped himself to a generous portion of the mostly-uncooked rice and cleaned his plate, believing it was some new kind of "crunchy rice."

When she realized what had happened, Mama Wes told her son. Late that night, Chad called his mother, warning that she was going to be responsible for killing a preacher. "Mama, did you check on it?" he asked.

"Nah, C, John is a grown man. He knows," she replied.

"Man, looka here. That raw rice is going to swell up in him," Chad said. "He needs to go to the hospital."

John Morgan's apartment was not far from Chad's house. "You right down the street from him," Mama Wes said. "Just call him on the phone ... [tell him] you going to come and sit and look at him all night, while he snores and farts."

"Man, Mama, I don't want to call him. I might excite him," Chad said.

"I'm going to call him by nine or so," Mama Wes assured him.

At 9 AM the next morning, Mama Wes called John Morgan, who was perfectly fine and rather surprised at her concern.

"C, he's fine," Mama Wes assured Chad later that day when he woke up.

"Yeah, I prayed for him all night long," Chad replied. "I had to call up Jesus. I said, 'Jesus, please don't kill him.'"

All jokes aside, Pastor Morgan later struck up a conversation with Chad about spiritual matters and asked if he had accepted Jesus Christ as his Lord and Savior. It was a question Morgan often asked, not out of judgment or condescension, but of genuine interest and a way to spark up a conversation on spiritual topics. Chad assured him that he was a believer.

A few weeks later, Chad saw Morgan in traffic. He wasn't in his Bentley and was having a hard time getting the pastor's attention. Always the prankster, Chad couldn't resist the opportunity. He intentionally cut Morgan off, forcing him to slam on his brakes. Chad cackled with glee when Morgan responded with some ungodly hand gestures.

"I'm not confessing anything on record," Morgan laughs, but admits he may have used some "impure language which left something to be desired for a pastor."

Chad called his mother howling with laughter. "He gave me that middle finger, mama! I'm about to tell everybody!"

Morgan also had a penchant for forwarding email chains with off-color jokes. Mama Wes was on his mailing list and often passed them along to Chad, who took great pleasure in forwarding them with the tongue-in-cheek subject line "FROM OUR SPIRITUAL LEADER."

When UGK performed at the Montagne Center in nearby Beaumont with 8Ball & MJG, Morgan stopped by, leading both groups in prayer backstage. After the show, Chad introduced guests to Morgan as "my buddy John," proclaiming simply, "John came to be with me tonight."

Most fans assumed "John" was a record label executive. "They didn't know you was a preacher!" Chad howled after they left. Mama Wes joked that it would be a scandal if a pastor were spotted backstage at a rap show.

While Pastor Morgan's congregation accepted him hanging out with rappers, others in the community were not so open-minded. Morgan shrugged off the criticism. "Look who Jesus hung around," he says. "I try not to judge anybody, because none of us are perfect. If the spotlight was put on any of our lives, we would all come up looking pretty ugly."

After the Beaumont show, Chad headed to Georgia for a scheduled show in Macon. He normally flew out of the Houston area, which had two major airports, but ended up catching a flight back a day earlier than expected into the small regional airport in Beaumont.* He called his mother to ask for a ride. "Mama, can you lift me up?"

She smiled. "I'll cook something."

When they arrived at the Oakmont house, no one was home. As Mama Wes recalls it, Chinara wasn't expecting him home for another day and didn't know he had changed his schedule.

As they walked in the front door, Mama Wes began coughing uncontrollably, her eyes watering from a strong, smoky odor. Mama Wes knew the sickly sweet smell of marijuana and the chemical stench of fry, but this was something different entirely. Reasoning that she hadn't been at many shows lately and maybe was behind in the times, Mama Wes fanned the air in front of her nose, her eyes still watering. "Damn, that weed is strong!" she remarked.

There was a long pause as Chad frowned, shaking his head. "That ain't weed," he said.

"Oh," Mama Wes said quietly, the implication sinking in. "Well, you gotta open this place up. I can't stay in here. It's burning my eyes."

Mama Wes went to Wal-Mart to pick up some groceries for dinner, and by the time she returned, Chad had aired the place out thoroughly, with the fans and A/C blowing and the windows open, but the smell still lingered.

Later that night, Chad called his mother and implied that he was concerned about his wife. "Can you help her?" he asked.

Mama Wes wished she could, but really didn't know what to say. "Y'know…" she said, her voice trailing off. "That's not my area of expertise."

Although it was never explicitly stated, the conversation led Mama Wes to believe that Chinara was smoking crack.

(*Records indicate that Chad flew into the Beaumont airport on September 5, 2006, although it is not known if this was the same date this incident occurred. Mama Wes believes it was around this timeframe.)

CHAPTER 42

"The biggest pimps are the record labels and the biggest hoes are these mutha-fuckin' rap niggas. Rap niggas and entertainers are getting hoe'd more than any prostitute I've ever seen on any track or any bitch I've ever seen selling pussy. Muthafuckers get out here and do all the work and risk their lives, get shot, see their homeboys get shot, got to jail, all kinds of shit. Take all the risk and another muthafucker gets the lion's share of the money? Hey, mane, if that ain't pimpin', you tell me what is." – Pimp C, *OZONE* Magazine

---

"The record labels use the same tactics as pimps. A pimp will feed a girl every-thing she needs; give her the minimum necessities, just enough money to get by. He might give her $200 to her name and a basic place to live in, and clothing that she needs to look good enough to attract the attention and the type of cli-ents [he] wants. And if she complains or leaves ... they'll feed her a little bit more and give her incentives to make her stay and cloud her vision of how they're really fucking her [over] and just taking all of her money." – Jada

October 2006
Hollywood, California

The automatic glass doors at the entrance to The Mondrian hotel slid open late one Octo-ber night. Heads turned in Jada's direction as the petite, pretty brunette sailed through the all-white lobby, faster than seemed physically possible in a pair of stilettoes. Ignoring the obvious stares of admiration in her direction, Jada headed straight for the elevators.

Less than 20 minutes later, having completed the services for which she was hired, Jada popped back out of the elevator on the lobby level. A man called out to her, but she ignored him, walking faster towards the exit.

"Jada" wasn't her real name. Her driver's license identified her as Jennifer Finnerty, but that wasn't her real name, either. Clients knew her as "Tia," "Nina," or "Kayla." She flew all over the country entertaining clients of "V.I.P. Entertainment, LLC," a Las Vegas-based escort service, and today was just another day at work.

There was a lengthy list of rules which women in "the game" were expected to follow. Most importantly: don't make eye contact. Women were required to avert their eyes when they en-countered a pimp, or risk being "out of pocket" and suffer the consequences. Making eye contact with a pimp would indicate an invitation to approach. Judging from his clothing and demeanor, Jada assumed this man was a pimp.

Jada didn't exactly have a pimp, but Jamal, the owner of the escort service she worked for, was pretty close to it. His business model was different from most pimps; he had dozens of other girls working for him and rarely had the time or interest to keep tabs on them, so most likely, she wouldn't get in trouble for speaking to this man at the Mondrian. She just didn't want to. She already knew what he was going to say. Most pimps who approached her had nothing to offer;

they couldn't do anything for her except ruin her credit and take her money, so it was better to just stay out of their way.

But this man was persistent. "Hey! Where you going?" he said.

She walked faster towards the front door, still avoiding eye contact.

"Bitch, I ain't a pimp!" he called out after her, laughter in his tone. He'd realized why she was avoiding him. Jada, slightly offended that a total stranger had cursed at her, stopped walking and cautiously turned around. "I pimp the rap game," he told her, laughing. "I pimp the music." Now she was intrigued, and they struck up a real conversation. He introduced himself as Chad.

Even though she'd gone to college at the University of Houston, Jada wasn't much of a rap fan and was initially skeptical of Chad's claim that he was the rapper "Pimp C." She Googled the videos for "Big Pimpin'" and "Sippin' on Some Syrup," and, satisfied that the man wasn't an actual pimp, struck up a conversation.

As a teenager, Jada had been intrigued by the apparently glamorous life of pin-up girls she'd seen on the internet. While studying Biology in college, she worked as a health and sexuality educator at Planned Parenthood, giving speeches at schools and youth centers about STD awareness, abstinence, and birth control.

But even though she enjoyed the work, it didn't pay very well. She admired the professionally-designed escort websites with airbrushed pictures of girls like Amy Taylor and Ivanna DiCarlo. They looked like they made a lot of money.

"I wanted to make a lot of money," she shrugs. "I was greedy, I guess … I loved money."

A 19 she started stripping, changing her major from Biology to Art History to lessen her coursework. "I thought I was slick … it was just something on the side," she says. "[I thought,] 'I'm winning.'" She was making a lot of money for a college student, sometimes pulling in $2,000 a night at the strip club. But many of the strippers were making even more money offering blowjobs on the side.

Jada caught the eye of one frequent visitor, a wealthy man who owned the largest Cadillac dealership in Houston, who began paying her $1,500 or more just to hang out at his house. Finally, he propositioned her for sex, offering so much money that she couldn't turn it down. Their first encounter in a bubblebath was gentle, almost romantic.

The transition from stripper to prostitute came easily, especially since her first experience was a positive one. She soon started working for Andre "Dre" McDaniels, a former drug dealer who owned several brothels in the Houston area disguised as legitimate businesses: Total Pleasure, Taboo Modeling Studio, and the Paris of Katy spa.*

Soon, Jada was making as much as $17,000 a week escorting; her pimp Dre used the proceeds to buy her a townhouse. "There's a whole language to [the game]… [it's] another environment, it's another world," Too $hort explains on the documentary American Pimp. "But it's really all about money."

Jada knew there was a lot more money to be made escorting if she ventured beyond Houston. She spotted an advertisement seeking "upscale, classy, elite models" for a company called International V.I.P., which appeared to be a thinly veiled escort service. After going on a few calls for them, she flew to Las Vegas to meet Jamal, the owner of the service.

(*In August 2009, Andre "Dre" McDaniels was arrested on federal sex trafficking charges as part of Operation Total Exposure. The FBI's Innocence Lost Task Force accused him of recruiting underage prostitutes as young as 16. Four other men and one woman were also charged. The bust was a wake-up call for Jada, since McDaniels' co-defendant Kristen "Princess" Land was her first "wife-in-law." Land was sentenced to six years. McDaniels was sentenced to eight years on the original charges, plus six-and-a-half years for allegedly threatening the women and federal agents who testified against him. McDaniels is scheduled to be released in April 2022.)

Jamal, a tattoo-covered Egyptian who resembled the actor Vin Diesel, was raking in millions from his escort services and had just purchased a $2.6 million dollar home.* He wore expensive jewelry and was chauffeured around Las Vegas in a fleet of Rolls Royces. Jada had never met anyone so flashy and flamboyant. His walk-in closet was bigger than anything she'd ever seen on *MTV Cribs*, full of expensive designer clothes and Christian Louboutin shoes. His collection of exotic pets included a capuchin monkey, two bobcats, a python, and two serval cats, which he described as "cheetahs."**

This love of animals, Iceberg Slim told *The Black Collegian* in 1975, was common among pimps. "Every pimp I've ever known, even though he was a thorough monster to the human beings under his control, had a pet," Iceberg explained. "He always had a dog or something. Some of them had lions and cubs. I know niggers that had panthers … I know a pimp that killed a man that ran over his dog. That shows you the displaced humanism. It isn't that the pimp isn't human. He simply diverts his humanity from a woman and seeks substitute gratification in the form of a dog and so forth."

Jada dropped out of college and moved to Las Vegas, joining the small army of escorts servicing tourists. With over 50 girls actively escorting for International V.I.P. throughout the country, money came pouring into the company's bank account. Jamal developed a system to track deposits. Each girl was assigned an employee number: Jada began as employee number 7. If a client paid $2,000, Jada would deposit Jamal's 50% plus seven cents to identify the drop as her deposit: $1,000.07.

Jamal put up a website for Jada, who was going by the name "Tianna," listing her rates from $350 for a "half hour lunch break" to $3,000 for an "Overnight VIP Retreat" ("credit card charges will appear discreetly under my corporate name, which … will not indicate or give any suggestion of the nature of our transaction," it promised). Calls came pouring in, and Jada regularly made deposits of $1,000.07, $2,500.07, $4,000.07 and more.

Jamal had a reputation as one of the most successful pimps in Las Vegas, and once Chad found out who Jada was working for, he was intrigued, curious about how he ran his operation.

While most escort services in Las Vegas only took 20% of the girls' income, Jamal initially offered a 50/50 deal. The pimps of the 21st Century were nothing like the flamboyant, over-the-top pimps of the Blaxploitation movies; they dressed like rappers and presented prostitution to young women as a viable business opportunity. They promised to be a financial manager who would manage their money and help them save up to start their own business.

"Their whole [pitch] is [that] they're gonna give you a business and graduate you out [of] the game, within five years … every [pimp] tells you that," says Jada. "You wanna stick around [because] you think … 'They're saving up for my big business.'"

Pimp C didn't consider this type of arrangement, where the women were able to keep a percentage of their earnings, "real pimpin." Regardless, Jamal's business model had proven to be extremely profitable.

For an escort, choosing up with Jamal meant a life of relative safety and security. He owned properties and cars; you'd live in a luxury high-rise and a personal chauffer would deliver you to see clients in an expensive vehicle. His service catered to high-end clients, so there was low risk of danger.

After luring Jada in with the 50/50 arrangement, Jamal told her she needed to give up 70%

(*The "seven Rolls Royces outside" that Ray J bragged about during his infamous 2011 radio interview with The Breakfast Club belonged to Jamal. Jamal was referenced by Drake on his 2011 record "The Motto." Jamal also developed a strange Svengali-type relationship with pop star Justin Bieber, gifting him with a pet monkey named "Mally" which was infamously quarantined in Germany. The two even have matching tattoos. In 2014 Jamal appeared on the VH1 reality show *Love & Hip-Hop: Hollywood* as "Mally Mall," with some scenes filmed at his Las Vegas mansion. A week after the show first aired, his home and escort service were raided by FBI agents looking for evidence of human trafficking. As of May 2015, no charges related to the raid have been filed.)

(**Serval cats are African animals which resemble a cheetah with the head of a house cat.)

of her income to become a "priority girl," which meant more clients and more perks. Chad told Jada she was selling herself short and suggested she should invest in her own escort service or webcam business.

Shortly after they met, Chad flew Jada out to Houston. She wasn't concerned about the fact that he was married, and for the most part, his entourage stayed out of his personal business when they saw him with other women. Most friends, like Jaro, assumed Chinara had accepted Chad's "Snoop Dogg style of living."

"I didn't marry no square and I didn't marry a person that has false expectations about what I'm about and who I am ... she's not tryin' to change me into something different than I am," Chad told *OZONE*.

And although Chad's infidelities weren't exactly a secret, Chinara wasn't in a position to confront him about such things. If she tried, Chad would be quick to remind her who "pays the bills around this muthafucker."

Chad's friend Joi, who was still recuperating from a tough divorce from Big Gipp, understood the challenges of being married to a rapper all too well. "The rap game stole my man from me," she mourned on her 2006 record "Gravity." It was a tough balancing act for a rapper to maintain a home life and still fulfill the image of the character he portrayed on records.

"Rap culture definitely lends itself to a man never really growing up and never really having to be culpable for the things that he does," says Joi. "The titillation, the temptation, the starry eyes ... the desire to be able to compete, the desire to be able to accepted – meaning, selling millions of records. To be adored by millions of people. To have millions of dollars."

Joi believed the rap game was no different from other addictions. "It's a very seductive kind of world. It seduces you, it makes you wanna risk everything to be in it. It can become the most important thing ... to the detriment of themselves and [their families]."

Jada was initially skeptical of Chad's motives but soon came to consider him a genuine friend. "Maybe he felt like I needed him in my life," she says. "He was just there for me. He reminded me a lot of maybe like a father [figure] or a brother or a best friend ... [who] always respects you, lifts you, and motivates you."

Chad always compared the music business to prostitution, and here was someone who completely understood. "The biggest pimps are the record labels and the biggest hoes are these muthafuckin' rap niggas," he told *OZONE*. "Rap niggas and entertainers are getting hoe'd more than any prostitute I've ever seen on any track or any bitch I've ever seen selling pussy. Muthafuckers get out here and do all the work and risk their lives, get shot, see their homeboys get shot, go to jail, all kinds of shit. Take all the risk and another muthafucker gets the lion's share of the money? Hey, mane, if that ain't pimpin', you tell me what is."

Jada could relate, and the similarities became an endless topic of discussion. "The record labels use the same tactics as pimps," explains Jada. "A pimp will feed a girl everything she needs; give her the minimum necessities, just enough money to get by. He might give her $200 to her name and a basic place to live in, and clothing that she needs to look good enough to attract the attention and the type of clients [he] wants. And if she complains or leaves or complains about leaving, they'll feed her a little bit more and give her incentives to make her stay and cloud her vision of how they're really fucking her [over] and just taking all of her money."

But once the power shifts, the pimp is forced to renegotiate. "A girl will leave and [her pimp] will call her back to... offer her the house she wanted," says Jada. "That's just gonna buy them enough time until she realizes that she's being fucked again."

CHAPTER 43

"These record labels are inclined to keep us as dumb as possible. They know that if we get to communicating, putting our heads together, comparing notes ... it's a chance we could unionize, and they really don't want that. They don't want rappers united ... They want division, because divided they can conquer."
— Pimp C

———————

"Jive wants to go pop at all times, but I'm going to keep it hard. They got their agenda and I know what I've got to do for the streets. They can consider doing video shoots for the wrong song and send out the wrong song [to radio], but I don't have to show up to the video shoot. I don't have to support it. When I don't like what they're doing, I e-blast my own song out the radio stations. I've got relationships with enough people across the country to where I can damn near get records put in rotation on my own. So when I don't like what they do, I just go off and do my own thing." — Pimp C, *OZONE* Magazine

Tuesday, October 17, 2006
Houston, Texas

Pimp C pulled up in his red Bentley to day one of the two-day video shoot for "Knockin' Doors Down" dressed in a brown pin-striped suit, light brown shoes and a matching tie, and a black fedora hat. Behind-the-scenes cameras followed him making his grand entrance with his publicist Nancy Byron.

"[She] keep ya up on your shit, mane," he bragged of Nancy. "Even though I don't show up to half the shit she set up for me, she still the coldest in the game 'cause I ain't no magazine-type nigga, know what I'm talkin' 'bout? I'm out here on the slab for real."

"Oh, he show up, he just show up four or five hours late," Nancy chimed in. "So they hate him. By the time he gets there they don't wanna interview him anyway."

"I'm on Trill Time, though," Pimp explained. "Know what I'm talkin' about? Ya dig?"

"I love your crazy ass," Nancy said.

"I'm walking to this video shoot. I'm feeling funny in this suit, but, um, it's okay," Pimp said.

"You look like your daddy," Nancy noted.

"I feel like my daddy," Pimp said, before breaking into an impromptu rendition of "Free Ballin'" to the tune of Tom Petty's "Free Falling."

All the artists were asked to come decked out in a dark suit and jewelry. Bun arrived in an Armani Dior suit with a Gucci tie and matching Gucci shoes, topped off with a black baseball cap and a Ten Commandments piece on his chain.

J. Prince sported a brown fedora and his Rap-A-Lot chain, his phone clipped on the side of his belt and a pistol tucked in his waistband. His three eldest children were there, including his sons Jas and J. Prince Jr. The song originally belonged to P.O.P., an artist signed to Jas and Jr.'s label Southern Empire, and this would be their first video shoot.

"This is a once-in-a-lifetime thing," Trae tha Truth noted. "J. [Prince] got me in a hat and a suit." Lil Flip bought a black suit just for the occasion, but still arrived carrying his requisite Styrofoam cup. Mike Jones arrived in a black pin striped suit with a red tie, a black du-rag, and his enormous Ice Age chain.

DJ Screw's father, affectionately known among the rap community as Papa Screw, stopped by the set. "I'm a firm supporter of Pimp C, he's a very nice gentleman," Papa Screw commented, adding that he was "very happy to be amongst all these superstars." Even Pimp's cell phone provider, Sameer, who owned a shop in Port Arthur called Mobile Connections, was there. "My shit don't never go off, man," Pimp bragged, showing off his multiple cell phones. "[If you] fuck with Sprint, you owe them hoes two pennies they gon' cut your shit off, but with Sameer, man, [he] keep your shit rolling until you get your shit rolling."

The script for the video, written by J. Prince, involved the owner of a fictitious record label called Y-T Records (pronounced "whitey") who was angry to see his artists uniting. "I'm gonna break these guys up," the owner griped. "I'm telling you, they owe me money. Don't mess with Y-T's money."

Pimp believed the concept wasn't too far from reality. "Divide and conquer is the game that these record company people are playing with these kids … These record company people *want* division," Pimp told Dwayne Diamond. "[They] don't want us to come together and compare notes on a business tip to figure out what's going on with this paperwork [because] if they can keep us at each other's throats – you know, the best way to win the war is to divide the army."

"Record labels [know] that controversy sells … they fuel the fire," Bun agreed in *OZONE*. "They give [artists] room to do the dumb shit that they're doing … Real men are gonna have beef sometimes but a lot of this shit is petty and it coulda been talked about and discussed. But the people who make money off the records choose to let bullshit get big just so [albums] can sell."

"[For] these record company people, it's really important for them to keep the so-called beefs going on," Pimp added in an interview with Donna Garza. "And what happens is, [while our] people [are] out there getting hurt behind this stuff, these record company folks is up in their offices eating bagels with cream cheese on it."

In Pimp's opinion, there were only two reasons for real beef, and there was a simple solution for both. "Two things [will] make you get into it with a nigga, and that's money and a bitch," he told WordofSouth.com. "Show me the bitch, let's get the bitch in a room [and] let her tell who she fucked, when, and let's get it out in the open. Or tell me who owe who some money, and we gonna make the person who owe that money give 'em that money."

In one scene, Pimp C recreated his last visit with J. Prince before he was released from prison, removing his jewelry and replacing it with some rosary beads so it would look authentic.*

"What's up, homie?" Prince said, holding a phone as he talked to Pimp through the glass. He pressed his fist up against the window and Pimp reciprocated. "Tomorrow your big day, huh?" Prince asked.

"Yeah, man, it's been four years, man," Pimp nodded. "It's been a long journey."

"What's the plan?" Prince asked.

"You know, it's been a lot of division between these rappers, a conspiracy to keep everybody divided," Pimp said. "I wanna bring everybody together and have a meeting."

"Well, look here. Say no more. I'ma make it happen," Prince nodded.

In another scene at a CD duplication plant, all the artists sat at a roundtable in a dimly lit

<hr>

(*Pimp admitted that they were taking a little artistic license with the scene by staging the visit as the day before his release, when in reality, it was at least several days prior.)

room meeting with J. Prince as actors posing as SWAT team members kicked in the door and rushed in with their weapons drawn.

"[We're] having a meeting talking about the state of emergency that's going on in the rap game, and trying to bring everybody together," Pimp explained. "Now, as you can tell, the laws and the powers that be don't want this meeting to take place at all. They really don't want us talking to each other, and they don't want us to get together and squash it, 'cause the game is divide and conquer."

Chad had a real purpose in bringing all the artists together; he asked if I wanted to help organize a tour featuring all of the Houston artists. "[Next year] a nigga down here is not gonna be able to make a record about another nigga without sitting down and talking to him," he told WordofSouth.com. "We ain't finna have none of that hoe ass shit down here in the South, because you know what I wanna see? Next summer, I wanna see all of us take a tour together … we gonna go out on the road on about 20 tour buses … Niggas put your differences aside and get this money man. That's my vision."

Besides, for Chad, it was personal. "I'm proud of all the Houston rappers … the Mike Jones, the Paul Walls, the Lil Flips, the Slim Thugs, the Traes … when I see them out there selling all these records and going platinum, I'm proud of them because I know that all of the things that me and Bun went through in the 90s were not in vain," he told Dwayne Diamond.

Noticeably absent from the shoot were Paul Wall, Chamillionaire, and Slim Thug. "All the real niggas is here representing," J Prince told a behind-the-scenes camera. "All the niggas that's not here that I invited? Y'all know what time it is … [If you] could've been here and just chose to not make it, I'll visit y'all later on."

Although Paul Wall thought the overall concept was a good idea, he was hesitant about appearing in the video for the same reason he'd decided not to appear on *The Source* cover. "There's a time and a place to address things," he reasons. "[I thought we should] address the problems first and then celebrate it by shooting a video, not address the problems in the video and tape it at the same time."

Unlike some of the other petty beefs around Houston, Paul and Chamillionaire's issues were deep-rooted.* "The problems I had with Chamillionaire, it was very personal," says Paul Wall. "It wasn't just some industry shit or … a publicity stunt."

Because it was a sensitive topic, most of Paul and Chamillionaire's mutual friends avoided talking about it. By mentioning them in the song, though, Pimp C had put some pressure on them to work things out.

Chamillionaire, who viewed Pimp as a father figure, respected the fact that he'd called them out. Paul viewed it as "a real wake-up call," admitting, "As much as I tried to ignore [our issues, 'Knockin Doors Down'] kinda forced me to address it."**

In the script as Prince envisioned it, an informant was working with FBI and DEA agents, conspiring to give Pimp a life sentence. As they set up the following day for the courtroom scene, Prince sat down on the judge's bench, a pleased expression crossing his face. "I never sat in the judge seat," he commented. "It's kinda different. Can you imagine me being a Judge [in] downtown Houston?"

Prince leaned back comfortably and propped his dress shoes up on the desk as he reached for the Judge's gavel, pounding it emphatically. "Not guilty!" he joked.

As they set up to begin shooting, the man playing the "snitch" (inexplicably, the track's

---

(*Chamillionaire and Mike Jones had also exchanged a number of diss records, with Mike rapping "I'm getting deals offered to me for me by myself / Your deal disappeared quick soon as Paul Wall left" on "99 Problems" and Chamillionaire responding with an entire mixtape dissing Mike Jones.)

(**Eventually, Paul Wall and Chamillionaire did squash their beef and reunited for a 2010 tour. "[Pimp C] was a big part of me and Chamillionaire getting back together," Paul says.)

producer Myke Diesel) was seated with four white prosecutors, facing down Pimp C and his "attorney," while J. Prince watched from the first row of the courtroom gallery.

"Is it true you're part of the biggest mob family in Texas?!" the prosecutor demanded.

Pimp C shrugged.

"Then what are you here for?!" the prosecutor yelled. "C'mon, Pimp C, tell us!"

Pimp C, breaking character, burst into a fit of laugher. "I held it as long as I could, mane," he chuckled. "That's how they talk to us, though, in court."

Chad forgave Mr. 3-2 for his no-show on the *Pimpalation* project and give him another chance to feature on the *Underground Kingz* album. But again, 3-2 kept Chad waiting in the studio for hours and never arrived.

Still an avid fry-smoker, 3-2 had gained a reputation for being unreliable. He'd amassed a large collection of mugshots, eyes wild and hair in disarray, appearing to be in various states of "under the influence." He'd spent half of the past four months in jail after two back-to-back arrests for possession of a controlled substance and sometimes called Mama Wes' house in the middle of the night rambling incoherently.

A week after the "Knockin' Doors Down" video shoot, Pimp C was in Houston when he heard that Trae tha Truth was shooting a video for his Rap-A-Lot record "In The Hood," featuring Yung Joc. While Chinara waited in the car, Pimp stopped by to make a brief appearance.

In the crowd at the shoot, Pimp spotted Mr. 3-2, wearing a t-shirt with a picture of DJ Screw. Knowing that he was about to get cursed out over the missed studio session, Mr. 3-2 approached him apologetically. "Chuuuuuch!" 3-2 greeted him. "Chad, don't be mad at me!"

3-2 had gotten in a strange habit of talking like Dr. Seuss, so Pimp responded the same way. "I don't fuck with you no more, no I won't, no I won't!" Pimp told 3-2. "You'd better lose my number, yes I will, yes I will!"

After reprimanding him, Pimp, wearing a set of brown Dickies and a matching Trill hat, threw his arm around Mr. 3-2's shoulders and turned to me, the photographer on set, asking me to take a picture of the guy who taught him how to rap. I took the picture, unsure if he was serious – *this* disheveled guy, eyes heavy and glazed over, taught Pimp how to rap?

Pimp told someone else standing nearby that this was the man who taught him how to roll his first blunt. *That makes more sense,* I thought.

Pimp tried to leave, but was swarmed with people wanting to take pictures with him. As a crowd gathered, Pimp pulled out $15,000 cash and threw it on the hood of his car. "I'm gonna put all this money [on a bet that] nobody can out-rap Bun B," Pimp announced to the growing crowd, gesturing towards Bun. "This is the real muthafuckin' king of the South."

Bun grimaced; Chad often proclaimed that he would give $100,000 to anyone who could out-rap Bun, and he was always afraid someone might accept the challenge.

"I used to tell him, 'Don't say that,'" Bun told Madd Hatta. "[I didn't wanna be] in that position 'cause I didn't have the confidence … but at the same time, I wouldn't have backed down. And I sho' wouldn't have let [Pimp] lose that money … I don't think I ever would've been able to live that down."

Still, Bun knew that Pimp's unwavering belief in him was part of what enabled him to be great. "I know for a fact I wouldn't be the emcee that I am if [not for Pimp C]," Bun added. "I never had as much confidence in Bun B as he did."

Chad drove back to Port Arthur after the video shoot and stopped by Mama Wes' house. "Mama! 3-2 done smoked himself black!" he yelled as he came through the garage. "Three used to be a pretty red nigga like me! Now he smoked himself black!"

Chad recounted his strange conversation with 3-2 at the video shoot. "Man, Mama, I had to talk like him! He had me talking like I was Dr. Seuss! … Muthafuckers were looking at me like

I'm crazy!"

"People would be looking at you crazy because you *are* crazy," Mama Wes corrected him, laughing.

Chad shook his head. "Mama, now that I'm not smoking that shit that he's smoking, I could see that he's fucked up. I never saw that shit until now. Now when I'm clean and they smoking that shit … [I can see] he's fucked up."

———————

Two days after the video shoot, while Chad flew to Birmingham for a show at Club Red, a tentative tracklisting for UGK's next album leaked out online. They'd already accumulated more than 24 records and didn't anticipate stopping anytime soon. "The shit just kept getting better and better," Bun told *OZONE*. "We didn't feel a need to stop making music if the shit was jammin'. If it ain't broke, why fix it?"

"Once we started recording for *Underground Kingz*, we literally couldn't stop," Bun told the *Village Voice*. They decided to do a double album, which would allow them to experiment with some new ideas while still satisfying UGK's core fanbase with their traditional sound. Plus, Pimp liked the idea of doing a double album because each sale counted twice, pushing them closer to gold or platinum status.

Bun and Pimp approached Barry Weiss with the idea. "If you can bring me a double album with enough good music on a single album budget, I'll put it out," Weiss told them.

———————

Pimp asked Vicious of the X-Mob to fill the third verse on "Quit Hatin' the South." He had a knack for bringing out the best in the artists he worked with, sending them back to rewrite their verse if he didn't feel it was their best work. "That shit sound funny, man," he'd scowl, sending them back to the drawing board.

After two or three tries, though, Pimp still wasn't happy with Vicious' verse. "Willie D would be perfect for this song," someone in the studio remarked.

For Willie D, it was easy to summon the motivation to do the record. "[My verse] came from all the disrespect," he says. "If you go to [New York] … I think there's a lot of animosity for the South, period … a lot of people can't take the fact that we winning. They can't take the fact that Hip-Hop has grown to be not just an East Coast thing or a West Coast thing, but the South is really dominating Hip-Hop now."

Willie came by MAD Studios and recorded his verse with Cory Mo, who emailed it out to Pimp and Mike Mo in Los Angeles. "Boy, Willie D killed that bitch," Pimp told Cory Mo. He called Willie D howling with laughter. "'*Bitch, cut yo' fingers off?*'" he laughed, quoting one of Willie D's lines about internet haters. "Aw, man, that's the shit, man … That's the shit we were missing."

———————

For the first time, UGK had a large budget, and Pimp wanted to splurge on some tracks from other established producers. "That was a luxury for us," Pimp explained. "We ain't never had no budgets big enough to be able to buy no beats."

"Pimp always felt like he was being selfish [because] if I kept rapping to Pimp beats, I would never be able to evolve as an artist," Bun told *Pitchfork*. Pimp recruited high-powered producers Swizz Beatz and Lil Jon to produce a sonic landscape to challenge Bun's lyrical skills. He'd met both men during his Atlanta days and didn't mind paying their asking price, shelling out $70,000 to Swizz Beatz and a rumored $80,000 to Lil Jon.

"If a man quotes me a price and he feels like that's what he's worth, and [we] ain't had no prior commitments with each other, I'm not gonna try to jew him down and make him come down off his price," Pimp told *OZONE*. "I either want to buy what he's got to offer or I don't. I'm not gonna tell him to give me a different price. So if a nigga quoted me $80,000 and I wanted the song, I bought the song."

UGK got in the studio with Swizz Beatz in L.A. to record "Hit The Block," which also featured T.I. on a verse. Swizz Beatz had no idea Pimp C was such a comedian. "He was one of the funniest guys I ever met," recalled Swizz. "[He] had me on the floor [laughing] the whole time."*

It didn't take long to realize that UGK could only afford so many $70,000 and $80,000 beats, especially if they were going to do a double album. Pimp started working on some beats himself and reached out to several producers he'd been grooming, including Avery "Averexx" Harris in Port Arthur. An unfinished track Avery had been developing for a local R&B artist named Sonya Rose prompted Chad to stand up, throw his hat on the ground, and yell, "Man, hold the fuck up! *You* made that beat, mane!?"

Avery's track would form the basis for UGK's record "The Game Belongs To Me."

Chad was staying in New York handling some business on November 2nd when his attention was captured by the television. The episode of A&E's reality show *SWAT*, which had been filmed two months earlier, began with a 911 call shortly after 4 AM.**

"This is Dallas 911. What's going on there?" the 911 operator asked.

A woman could be heard in the background crying hysterically as a man calmly asked for an ambulance to be sent to room 405 at the Radisson Hotel near Dallas' Love airport.

"What happened over there?" the operator asked again.

No response; the woman continued crying in the background.

"Hello?" the operator asked.

Dialtone.

Police quickly arrived and approached the corner room at the end of the hallway, where a woman inside could be heard screaming for help. Officer Jeremy Borchardt tried to enter the room with a master key from the hotel, but it wouldn't open; it appeared to be barricaded shut.

"It's the Dallas Police," one officer called out, banging on the door.

Shots rang out through the door; Officer Borchardt was struck in the thigh and began bleeding profusely from a severed artery. "Oh, God!" the woman inside the room screamed. Seven more shots rang out. The other officers dove for cover, shouting, "Get down!" as they dragged Borchardt down the hall to the elevator, leaving a thick trail of blood along the carpet.

The SWAT team and a hostage negotiator, J.D. Byas, were called in. Byas raced from police headquarters to the hotel and a truck of SWAT officers pulled up, congregating in the hotel lobby where a trail of blood led out the sliding glass doors.

Byas worried aloud that they might have a possible murder/suicide on their hands, but told the cameras he was optimistic that they could "end this without any more bloodshed."

By now, police had learned the identity of the man who had barricaded himself in room 405. A mugshot of 37-year-old Ronald Robinson flashed across the screen.

Chad stared at the television. It was the Dallas man who had ordered a hit on him in 1999.

Around 6 AM on December 21, 2004, back when Chad was arriving at the Terrell Unit, a

---

(*Apparently, Pimp later soured on Swizz Beatz when he wouldn't turn over all the elements of the track. "I paid $70,000 for a beat from Swizz Beatz and dude won't send me my master," Pimp complained in *Thick* Magazine. "I don't want to sample your drums. Man, even if you do a song for $5,000, send me all my mixes.")

(**The episode of *SWAT* first aired on November 2; records indicate that Chad was in New York on this date. It is not known if he saw the episode on this date or during a later rerun.)

fight had broken out at Dallas strip club The Fare. Witnesses saw Ron Robinson run out to his truck, return with a pistol, and shoot 27-year-old Dominic "Capo" Patterson, a local rapper and father of six, point blank in the chest.

Capo died and Robinson fled to California. He eventually turned himself in and posted $50,000 bond; he had been free for more than a year awaiting trial. He planned to claim self-defense, but the murder investigation was bringing a lot of unwanted attention to his extravagant lifestyle. The IRS was curious to know how he was able to drive a Ferrari and purchase a six-figure home with cash, but had no verifiable source of income.

After a routine court hearing on Tuesday, August 29, 2006, Robinson had checked into the Radisson with an ex-girlfriend from Los Angeles.

———————

The hostage negotiator, Jake Byas, called Room 405.

"Hello?" Ron answered.

"Ron, hey. This is Jake, and I'm with the Dallas police department," he said calmly. "Tell me what's going on, guy."

Ron sighed. "I'll just come down, man… I'll just come down."

"You just wanna come down? Uh… will both of you be coming out?"

"Yes."

"Is she there that I can talk to her for a second?"

"Yeah, she's here."

"May I talk to her?"

"Hang on a sec."

A few seconds paused; a woman moaned, as if in pain.

"Are you there, dear?" Byas asked.

"Yes."

"Okay. Are you alright?"

"I'm okay," she said weakly.

"Okay. I understand that you and Ron are gonna come out in just a second?"

Ron came back on the line. "Call me in exactly five minutes, sir," he told Byas.

"I tell you what. Have her just go ahead and come on out," Byas asked.

"Call me in five minutes, sir," Ron repeated.

"But you're not gonna let her come out?"

Dialtone.

Five minutes later, Byas called the room again. "Ron?"

"Yes."

"You comin' out? We're a little worried about you there."

"Yes, sir. I'm coming out."

"Okay. Here's what you can do for me, alright? I'm gonna ensure your safety, but you gotta work with me, okay?"

"Okay."

"Alright. First of all, what I need for you to do is, if you have any weapons, I need for you to leave them inside the room."

"Right."

"Don't come out with any weapons, Ron, okay?"

"Okay, [I'll] make sure of that."

A tense hour passed as the sun began to rise; news helicopters circled above the hotel as a dozen SWAT team members waited in the dark fourth-floor hallway. During that hour, police learned that Ron Robinson had recently had alarming conversations with his pastor. He'd been considering suicide.

Finally, Byas called Room 405 again.

"Hello?" Ron answered.

"Ron?"

"Yes."

"You holding up okay?"

"Yeah, I'm holding up alright," Ron sighed. "Okay, this is what I'm 'bout to do. I'm gonna say a prayer and then I'm coming out. Just give me like three to five minutes. I'ma say my prayer and… call me back in exactly that and I'm coming."

"Tell you what. I'll stay on the phone with you and I'll be more than happy to listen to it."

"Nah, I have to do this," Ron declined. "I'll do this myself and then I'll come on out."

"Well, here – here's the problem with that, okay? It's not a bad plan, but the problem is, if you just walk out and I don't know that you're coming…"

Ron interrupted. "You got… You got, uh, paramedics now?"

"Yeah, certainly," Byas said out loud, as he silently scribbled on his notepad in large letters, "SUICIDE."

"Okay. Have a paramedic ready," Ron said.

"Have the paramedic ready?"

"Just bear with me just one second, Officer Jake."

"Okay, how much time do you want?"

Silence.

"Ron?" Byas asked.

Dialtone.

Up on the fourth floor, a half-dozen SWAT team members were still assembled in the darkened hallway when a gunshot rang out.

The SWAT team found the woman badly beaten, but still alive. She'd been shot in the leg and grazed by another bullet on her back. Ron's lifeless body lay on the floor of the hotel room with a gunshot wound to the head. The camera panned to the pistol resting in his limp hand.

As the 15-minute SWAT segment ended, Chad snapped a screenshot of Ron's televised mugshot on his phone and texted it to Bo-Bo Luchiano. "That dude was crazy for real, huh?" Chad's text read. "He was gonna kill me!"

———————

Meanwhile, the FBI was still keeping an eye on Pimp C. Memos were exchanged between their Houston office and New Orleans office. "Efforts to reveal Houston-based rapper CHAD BUTLER, AKA 'PIMP C' as a drug supplier/trafficker … were unsuccessful," concluded a memo from the Houston office.

On November 16, 2006, an FBI agent met with a detective from the Port Arthur Police Department. A memo from this meeting indicated that the PAPD was "currently investigating Butler and his associates for several violations, to include drug trafficking."*

———————

Pimp C had initially assured fans that the UGK album would be out no later than October. Jive originally scheduled the release for November, then pushed it back until December 12, then December 19. But with the release date quickly approaching and no hit record, everyone was getting nervous. "They were rushing the record out for the fourth quarter… to balance out their books," Pimp complained in the *Houston Chronicle*. "They were going to throw the record out there whether they had a hit single or not."

Although UGK wasn't as dependent on radio as other artists, radio was still viewed as an

———

(*In response to an open records request, the Port Arthur Police Department denies the existence of any records relating to an investigation on Chad Butler.)

Document Title: LEAD COVERED.

Approval Date: 11/27/2006
Classification: SN

Contents:

Precedence: ROUTINE Date: 11/27/2006

To: New Orleans Attn: SA [   ]
Houston Attn: FIG

From: Houston
Beaumont Resident Agency
Contact: [   ]

Approved By: [   ]

Drafted By: [   ]

Case ID #: [   ] (Pending)
[   ] (Pending)

Title: [   ]
ET AL;
VIOLENT CRIME;
INTELLIGENCE ANALYST PRODUCTION –
CRIMINAL

Synopsis: Lead Covered.

Reference: [   ]

Enclosure(s): Voluntary statement and criminal history of
[   ]

Details: On November 16, 2006, Special Agent (SA) [   ]
met with Detective [   ] Port Arthur Police Department
(PAPD), Port Arthur, Texas. During the meeting SA [   ] was
informed that PAPD was familiar with Chad Butler, date of birth
(DOB) December 29, 1973, a.k.a. Pimp-C. Based on information
received from Detective [   ] PAPD is currently investigating
Butler and his associates for several violations, to include drug
trafficking. Detective [   ] stated that the Chad Butler SA
[   ] was inquiring about is the same Chad Butler that PADP is
investigating and aware of, based on the name, DOB, and the
connection to Underground Kings (UGK).

Detective [   ] stated that recently [   ]
[   ] was involved in [   ] allegedly
[   ] took place at
a known location where narcotics trafficking is believed to be
occurring. The incident is still under investigation.

Detective [   ] stated that a current check revealed
that Butler has a residence located at [   ]
Texas. He also list a residence at [   ]
Arthur, Texas. The residence located at [   ] is in
[   ] believes [   ] may be residing [   ] at the
location.

Detective [   ] and the PAPD are willing to share all
information involving the investigation against Butler [   ]
[   ] can be reached at office number [   ]
or cellular number [   ]

Above: A November 2006 **FBI memo** referencing Chad Butler.

important factor in putting up big first-week numbers. Without a hit single in heavy rotation, UGK wouldn't be able to maximize this golden opportunity. But they couldn't agree on which record to release as the lead single.

"Man, we need one more record for the album," Bun told Jazze Pha. Jazze sent over "Stop & Go," a track he'd produced for another artist who hadn't come up with the money to pay for it yet.

Bun called Jazze back immediately when he heard the record. There was only problem: it featured a snap beat, a popular Atlanta-based dance craze at the time. "Man, I love the record," Bun told him. "But Pimp is gonna hit the ground if he [hears] that damn snap in that record. Can you go put a clap where the snap is [instead] and then send the record back? I can't let Pimp hear that."

Jazze replaced the snap with a clap and re-sent the record. Even though he volunteered to give them the track for free, Pimp insisted on paying him. "Man, we been doing shit free so long, man," Pimp told him. "We got a nice budget, Jazze. Get you some money off of that … I'm not taking it [for] free."

Even though Pimp liked the record, he didn't think it should be the lead single. But in mid-November, Jive's mixshow department blasted off the Lil Jon-produced "Like That" and Jazze Pha's "Stop & Go," both vast departures from the traditional UGK sound, as the group's new singles. "Jive wants to go pop at all times and I'm going to keep it hard," Pimp complained in *OZONE*.

Concerned that UGK and Jive still weren't seeing eye-to-eye, Bun asked executives, "What do we have to do to make this last album a great album?" Bun asked.

"Just don't make it the last album," came the response.

"Give us a reason for us to want to keep doing business with you," Bun said.

Jive responded by offering a larger advance to extend the contract for one more album; UGK agreed, and on November 29, UGK's contract was extended for a sixth album.

DJ DMD happened to be living near the Galleria in Houston, not far from Chad's high-rise. After a spiritual breakthrough, DMD had made a public declaration that he wanted to rededicate his life to the Lord and arranged to be baptized. He'd put music on the back burner; rap didn't seem that important anymore. "It struck me as funny [that] I used to pray before every show I'd do," he told the *Houston Chronicle*. "Which seems ridiculous now. This big prayer before going onstage to do that foolishness."

DMD spotted Chad in his Bentley one day and waved him down. "Our relationship had gotten strained, and that moment kinda fixed it," says DMD. Chad invited him to come by Cory Mo's studio for a session. As DMD recalls it, Chad said he'd had time to clear his head in prison, and apologized for the way their relationship had ended.

"Man, just make sure you keep good people around you," DMD warned. "People that's gonna really protect you … In this business, we know that you can be around people who just wanna leech you. They don't care, really, about you. They'll let you do whatever you wanna do and not tell you anything, as long as they can hang around … stay away from people like that. Find some people that really love you, that's gonna tell you the truth, that's gonna tell you when you trippin.'"

Since Pimp's return Smoke D had been spending a lot of time in Texas, hoping to relaunch his rap career under the UGK Records umbrella. At a show in Mississippi, Pimp met Larry, an acquaintance of Smoke D's. (Larry still had a case pending from his bizarre 2005 arrest, when he was accused of impersonating a police officer while conspiring to buy pounds of marijuana.)

Larry seemed to have plenty of weed and plenty of money, and was the type of guy who always insisted on paying for everything – group dinners, VIP tables – to show off. "You couldn't pull no money out your pocket [around him]," recalls Smoke.

Larry often stopped by Stax Hip-Hop & Urban Fashion, a small retail store in Jackson which sold t-shirts, mixtapes, and DVDs. He stopped by Stax' shop one day to pick up a few t-shirts. As he was leaving, he told the proprietor Stax, "You know, I got them pints," implying that he was selling codeine. "And I got some weed, too. I'll give you a good number on the shit. I'ma be here for a few days. Here go my number," he added, motioning for Stax to take down his phone number.

Stax wasn't a syrup sipper. "I don't need all that. Just give me something I could smoke," he said, requesting a sample of weed for his own personal use. With a steady, legal source of income already, Stax didn't have time or interest in selling drugs, and didn't believe Larry's posturing.

Larry obliged with a small sample of weed. "Test this out," he said. "I got pounds of this."

Around Jackson, Larry was known by several names. A few years earlier, Larry's right pinky finger had been shot off during a dispute over a half pound of marijuana. Ever since then, people had called him Pinky. Behind his back they called him Lemonhead (due to his yellow-toned complexion and oddly shaped head) or Four-Fingered Larry, a nickname he hated.

Now that he was spending a lot of time in Los Angeles, he'd started going by "L.A." Although codeine cough syrup was popularized by Texas music, those in the know understood that Los Angeles was a key manufacturing and distribution center for the drug, where it was cheap and easily accessible.

Larry seemed eager to paint a picture of himself as a successful drug dealer, bragging that he'd purchased houses in Houston and Los Angeles. He often arrived at Stax' shop in a different car, usually a rental. "He would always make it a point to try to talk like he was some big-time mobster," recalls Stax.

Larry's childhood friends scoffed at his new kingpin persona. Some, like Smoke's friend Antezy, initially didn't even realize this was the same well-behaved classmate he remembered from high school. "He *created* Larry," says Antezy. "Like Rick Ross, he created a person … but it worked for him." Larry's new persona seemed to have a dark aura, a cloud hanging over him, and something told Antezy to keep his distance.

Larry started tagging along with Smoke D on trips to Port Arthur. On one trip, he left a Benz in Port Arthur and gave Smoke the keys. Pimp was suspicious enough to have the car's registration checked to make sure it was legit.

Among Chad's many idiosyncrasies was his belief that birthdays should only be celebrated on the actual day. Since Mama Wes' 60th birthday fell on a Tuesday, Chad insisted that her party be held on Tuesday, even though many attendees would have to rush back to Houston for work the next morning.

The party was still a huge success; Ed barbecued, while guests pinned money on Mama Wes' red Dickies, a Texas tradition. Bun helped her cut the cake. DJ Bird, Mitch, the X-Mob, Mike and Cory Mo, and many others were in attendance as well as Chad and his entire family.

But amidst all the familiar faces was one Mama Wes didn't recognize: Larry, who'd tagged along with Smoke D. Normally, when Mama Wes didn't like someone, she just ignored them, but as the party was winding down, something prompted her to comment.

"That boy gives me a creepy feeling," Mama Wes told Chad, once Larry was out of earshot. Chad nodded. "Mama, we'll talk about it," he said.

Over on the West Coast, Jada was growing increasingly disillusioned with her pimp Jamal. At first, she'd been thrilled by all the attention she was getting from wealthy men. But she'd started to realize that the things which initially enthralled her about "the game" – the cars, the money – were mostly a façade.

While Jada initially believed Jamal was sincere about helping her save up money to launch a legitimate business, she wasn't seeing any progress. There wasn't any money being saved, and a lot of the wealth was an illusion – stolen luxury cars with switched VIN numbers, for example.

After Jamal forced an awkward sexual encounter on her, she started thinking about leaving. While browsing MySpace, she came across a profile titled Da Hood Boss. "I was just being loose," she recalls. "Flirting and stuff." The man pictured, Ocean "O" Fleming, wore layers of jewelry and flaunted stacks of cash, posing in front of expensive luxury cars.

They exchanged messages; Ocean told Jada that he owned an escort service called Glamour Girls. Jada had heard of Glamour Girls, where a popular escort named Stephanie was rumored to be making $2,500 a day. *If he taught her everything she knows, he must be good,* Jada thought.

When Ocean offered to fly her to Las Vegas, Jada told him she was already with Jamal. "Jamal's my homie," Ocean assured her. "Trust me, if you wanted to fuck with me … we can talk to him and everything will be okay."

To Jada's surprise, Jamal readily agreed to let her go. "That's when I realized that I was nothing to Jamal," she says. "I was nothing to him but employee #7 and #52."

Jada told Ocean she wanted two things: a house and breast implants. Ocean promised that if she came to work for him, she could get breast implants in 30 days. She decided to give him a chance and boarded a flight to Las Vegas shortly after Christmas 2006.

She expected Ocean would pick her up in one of the expensive luxury cars pictured on his MySpace page, but instead, he was waiting outside the Las Vegas airport in a chameleon-green old school Impala with TV screens. His MySpace pictures didn't reveal his broken tooth, either. *Okay,* she reasoned. *He's a hood nigga. Every hood nigga has to have an old school, right?*

Jada happened to get a call from a previous client who was in town looking to have a little fun. Ocean's eyes lit up when she returned from the call with $1,200, as if he'd hit the jackpot. It was her first inkling that Ocean didn't really own an escort service. He had no expensive cars or expensive jewelry, and she was his only girl.

Ocean Fleming, born to a prostitute and a pimp on the lucky date of 7/7/77, was once a high-ranking gang member in the Rolling 60s Crips and one of the most feared drug dealers in Las Vegas. He had been sentenced to five years in federal prison on a drug conspiracy charge and landed in a cell alongside an older pimp, who passed the time telling stories of his glory days on the track.

"Eventually I fell in love with a game I was born to do, with a destiny I was born to be," Ocean says. He took a job working valet at The Mirage while he was in a halfway house, where he met plenty of escorts coming in and out of the casino. His high school buddy Bryan Scott owned two escort services, which were located in the same strip mall as Jamal's escort service on Industrial Road.

Even after Jada realized that Ocean wasn't the big baller he'd portrayed himself as on MySpace, she found his personality endearing. She liked riding around the city with him; other men feared him and called him "the Boss." His confident attitude reminded her of the rapper Young Jeezy.

"Ocean was cool," she says. "He made you feel like you had a bodyguard – you were riding around with a mob boss, no one could touch you, and you're bulletproof." Plus, she considered his down-to-earth personality a breath of fresh air after living in Jamal's "weird pimp version of Hugh Hefner land." Jada decided to give him a chance.

Ocean set a quota: Jada needed to bring in $2,500 a day. Eager to please, Jada signed up for four more escort services and started posting ads on Erosguide and Craigslist. Every day she woke up at noon and worked on her own until 4 PM, when she started an eight-hour shift taking calls exclusively from escort services. If she'd hit her quota by midnight she could go home and go to sleep; otherwise, she'd keep working.

For the first week, she was easily hitting her $2,500 daily quota, sometimes even landing $5,000 or $8,000 from one client. She turned over all the money to Ocean. "When I moved to Vegas, the whole lifestyle and the whole city … it puts you in a trance," she explains. "It'll suck you up under the belly of the whale, really, really fast, and you'll think that's the way things are supposed to be. Every girl you meet that looks like she has her shit together – she might drive a Porsche, have diamonds and have houses and have plastic surgery – she has a pimp. *Every* girl has a pimp."

Ocean, who describes Jada as "unforgettable … the best bitch I ever had in my life," considered their meeting a key turning point in his life. "I [was] float[ing] around town living off my name and trying to find away in the game [until] I met [JADA]!" he writes. "She changed my life forever, showed me everything, taught me everything … help[ed] me shed my rough edges [and] my gangbangin' ways, she added swag to my limp and in essence she created a monster."

In escort ads Jada alternately presented herself as a Hawaiian lingerie model, a Swedish and Spanish mix, or a Portuguese woman filled with "pure lust." On Craigslist, "Star" promised to be "your personal sex kitten." Shortly before New Year's, Jada was lounging around lazily smoking weed with a friend when a prospective client called. "Yeah, I'll be there," she promised.

She hung up and laughed. "Fuck naw!" she said. "He's the police."

"You're high and paranoid," her friend told her. "I'll go, bitch."

Jada's instincts were correct. The caller was an investigative reporter for Las Vegas' Channel 8 News. Jada's friend "Cat" agreed to perform oral sex for $350 and was promptly arrested along with a dozen other women. Televised news coverage of the sting featured Jada's pictures from the Craigslist ad. Amused, she forwarded the link to Chad's email, prompting him to begin referring to the site as "Fedslist."*

Meanwhile, UGK was closing out 2006 with a lively New Year's Eve performance at Club Blue in Dallas. Pimp C insisted on keeping his black-and-white striped mink coat on throughout the whole show in the hot, sweaty nightclub.

"Say, check this out," Pimp told the crowd as the DJ shut off the music. "We came to the end of the show, but I wanna thank everybody for comin' out tonight, know what I'm talkin' 'bout? I know some of y'all had a hard time getting in, niggas wanna overcharge at the door, niggas wanna overcharge at valet…"

The crowd yelled in agreement that yes, they had been overcharged.

"Pussy ass niggas ain't even wanna let my people in tonight, but that's alright," he griped of the promoter. "We brought in '07 together … y'all look good out there, man. If y'all got some people out there locked up, put some money on they books on Tuesday when the shit open back up, man. All you hoes in here going home with that nigga and you know your nigga locked up need to put some money on his books, biiitch! Straight bidness!"

"And answer them calls, bitch!" Bun chimed in. "Take the block off the phone!"

"Take that block off the phone! Tell 'em Bun B!" Pimp echoed. "All you niggas that's going home with a nigga gal tonight, you need to give her some money to put on that nigga's books, 'cause that ain't yo' gal, nigga. You borrowing that hoe, mane."

Laughter spread throughout the crowd. "You renting her, 'cause when that nigga come home, he coming to get his gal, mane. But nigga, have fun while you can," Pimp joked. "Hey, I wanna wish everybody a Happy New Year, God bless y'all, everybody get home safe! Let's get some paper this year! UGK for life! *Underground Kingz*, double album, 26 songs, the Pimp and the Bun! We love y'all D-Town! We outta here!"

(*Craigslist defended their controversial erotic services section by saying that they created it to keep escort ads out of the mainstream personals. Craigslist eventually caved in to pressure from law enforcement and closed the section in 2010.)

CHAPTER 44

"You know what I like to do when I get to my video set? I like to just fire all the broads that are already there. I just fire everybody, send 'em all home. Shit, I'll bring my own crew of bitches. I'd rather have a real live prostitute bitch on the set than some bitch that's been fucking the director and got promised a spot in my video ... I've got more respect for a real hoe than a bitch that's out here tryin' to play like she's a hoe." – Pimp C, *OZONE* Magazine

"If I was a real pimp I wouldn't rap about [pimpin']. Why? So I could have my muthafuckin' self charged with crimes?" – Too $hort, *The Source* Magazine

January 2007

Upset that Jive leaked the Lil Jon and Jazze Pha records to lukewarm response, Pimp felt like he had to go into damage control mode by releasing something that sounded more like a traditional UGK track. He took "Game Belongs to Me," the track originally created by Avery in Port Arthur, and asked N.O. Joe to meet him in Los Angeles along with a team of live musicians. The finished product was one Pimp referred to as "a team effort," one of his personal favorites.

On January 11, Jive's mixshow department blasted off the final version of UGK's "Game Belongs To Me" to DJs and media as UGK's next single. The album release date had been pushed back to March. Confident that this might be the right record, with time running short, they rushed to schedule a video shoot.

Even though he'd clashed with Pimp C on the set of "Front, Back" over the use of Chamillionaire's red Biarritz, Dr. Teeth had his heart set on directing a UGK video. He submitted an extravagant treatment, which would feature glistening nighttime shots of UGK rolling through all the key places in the city. Jive shut down the idea, saying they preferred to shoot a simple performance video to keep costs down.

For an artist of UGK's caliber, Dr. Teeth assumed that the budget would be somewhere in the range of $150,000 – $225,000. But Jive informed him that they were only willing to spend $60,000, far below his minimum budget requirement. Dr. Teeth agreed to drop his budget for UGK, viewing it as the chance of a lifetime.

In Las Vegas, since Jada was exceeding her quota every day, Ocean put her up in a two-story four-bedroom house. She was impressed that Ocean put everything in her name after only a week – something Jamal never would've done. ("I didn't realize [it was because] he had fucked up credit," she laughs.) It was still empty and unfurnished, save for an air mattress.

Ocean also gave Jada permission to schedule her breast augmentation. It was an investment; bigger breasts, he believed, would help Jada procure more clients and bring him more money. Ocean also didn't mind spending money at the mall, the tanning salon, hair salon, or nail salon; since Jada was the merchandise, anything that improved her appearance would improve his income. Jada had already done her research and scheduled an appointment for January 27 with Houston doctor Michael Ciaravino, a breast augmentation specialist.

Jada knew that Ocean had once been a big-time drug dealer, but she didn't know about his lengthy history of violence. (A few months before they met, he'd been charged with burglary and battery for punching his prostitute ex-girlfriend repeatedly in front of her four-year-old child. Charges were dropped when the woman refused to cooperate with police.) But the longer she stayed in Las Vegas, it was hard to ignore all the rumors. "Stay away from him," she kept hearing. "I heard he's a gorilla."* *There's no way,* she told herself. *If he was [violent], maybe it was just to her because she was a bitch.*

While there was a long list of rules which women in "the game" were expected to follow, pimps had rules too. For one, pimps weren't supposed to have sex with "square" women, women who weren't paying them.

One day, Ocean brought an overly flirtatious blonde to the house, and Jada felt a tinge of jealousy. "That was against the rules," she remembers. "I was knee deep in the game ... living by the rules and talking by the code ... I was really militant, a pimp's hoe, and ... at the time I was proud to be that."

Jada criticized Ocean for breaking the rules. "Check her, or we're gonna fight," she snapped.

Ocean slapped Jada across the face. Stunned, she blinked through tears.

"After he slapped the shit out of me he [saw] how scared I was, so he had sex with me," she remembers. "It kinda brainwashed me a little and transitioned my feeling of sadness into whatever your body goes into when you have sex ... it clouds your brain."

The "Game Belongs to Me" video shoot was already off to a bad start. Jive set a date and flew down executive Max Nichols to oversee the shoot, but Chad cancelled at the last minute due to a sinus infection. Nichols, skeptical of the excuse, was upset that he'd wasted time and money.

Apparently, Chad had decided that he needed a real prostitute in the video to complete the visual. On "Game Belongs to Me," he rapped:

UGK Records, it's an institution
Know a lot of niggas livin' off of prostitution
Pimpin ain't dead, it just moved to the web
Bitch ain't gotta hit the track, ain't gotta give no tricks no head
Ain't gotta give no tricks no pussy, just cameras and screens
Easiest money you can get, it's the American Dream!

The day after Ocean slapped her, Jada got a call from Chad in the middle of the night. "I need you to come and be beside me in this video shoot," he told her. "I'm gonna make you a video celebrity. A TV superstar."

"Yeah, okay," Jada shrugged. *Why not?*

She wanted to tell him about Ocean hitting her, but decided against it; she didn't know if she was in the wrong, and didn't want him to think she'd been out of pocket.

Unsure how Ocean would react if he knew about her dealings with Pimp C, Jada was afraid to tell him about the video shoot and risk getting slapped again. She told Ocean she had a family emergency and needed to go to Houston a few days early.**

(*A "gorilla" pimp is one who uses physical violence to control his women. Pimp C didn't approve of gorilla pimpin'. "Pimpin' is a non-contact sport," he told WordofSouth.com. "The [only] reason why a man would ever hit a woman is because he ran out of shit to tell her ... That ain't pimpin' right there, that's some muthafuckin' gorilla shit, and a nigga that pimp like that, that pimp from his hand or his dick, he ain't gonna [be able to] keep a woman anyway.")
(**As Ocean remembers it, he knew about the video shoot in advance and had no problem with Jada going to Houston. He and Pimp C had met briefly in the mid-90s and shared a mutual respect. "[Jada] and Chad had some weird type bond which I didn't have a problem with because I understood Chad was married with kids, he was an entertainer," Ocean says. "I believe if he wasn't married he would've made a move on her, but he offered $3,500 for her to be in the video, so I sent her to Houston." Jada denies Ocean's claim, saying that Chad never paid for her appearance in the video.)

Pimp C and **Bun B** reunited outside of the Huntsville Unit in Huntsville, TX, on December 30, 2005.

Photo: Julia Beverly

Above: **Chad** shows his sons **Chad Jr.** and **Corey** a picture an inmate drew of **Bun B wearing a "Free Pimp C" hat** after his release, December 30, 2005.
Photo: Julia Beverly

Below: **Chad** greets his mother after his release as **Bun B** (accompanied by his manager **Red Boy** and his wife **Queenie**) stands by.
Courtesy of Rap-A-Lot Records

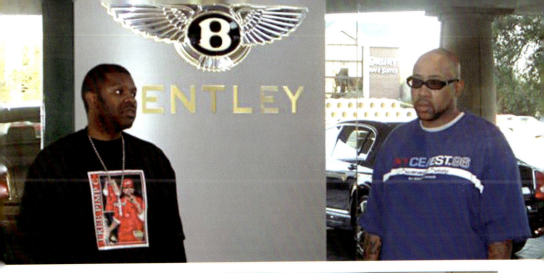

Above: **J. Prince** and **Pimp C** at the Houston Bentley dealership, January 2006.
Right: **Pimp C** and **J. Prince** picking out some jewelry with **Emit** at Exotic Diamonds, January 2006.
Courtesy of Rap-A-Lot Records

Below: **Pimp C** getting settled in his new Bentley at Houston's Studio 7303, January 2006.
Photo: Julia Beverly

Above: **Pimp C** and **T.I.** filming the video for "Front Back" in Houston, January 2006.
Below: The **Cadillac Eldorado Biarritz** Chamillionaire gave to Pimp C.

Photos: Julia Beverly

Above: **Chad** and video director **Mr. Boomtown** *(in the red hat)* survey the damage moments after Chad's car was struck by a vehicle fleeing gunfire in Port Arthur, April 2006.
Below: Chad's bodyguard **JT** being loaded onto a stretcher.
Photos: Jaro Vacek

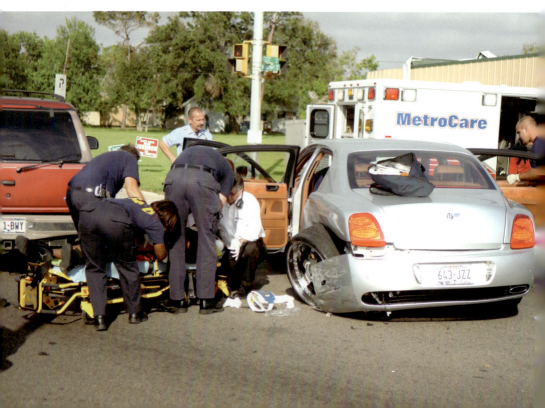

Pimp C and his new red Bentley on the set of "Knockin' Doors Down," October 2006.
Photo: Julia Beverly

Below: **Pimp C,** flanked by his bodyguard **JT**, angrily taps on the mic at the failed UGK reunion show at Bar Rio, February 2006.
Photo: Edgar L. Walker Jr.

Above: **Pimp C** and **J. Prince** on the set of "Knockin' Doors Down."
Left: **Pimp C** and **Mr. 3-2** at the video shoot for Trae Tha Truth's "In The Hood."
Photos: Julia Beverly

Right: Chad's friend **Jada** in an advertisement for Las Vegas escorts.

Above: **Chad** at home in Port Arthur with his three children **Chad Jr., Corey,** and **Christian,** his mother **Mama Wes,** and his grandmother **Bessie Jacob.**
Below: **Chad** and **Angie Crooks** celebrating their son **Corey's** sixth birthday, June 2006.
Photos: Edgar L. Walker Jr.

Chad with his father **Charleston Butler** outside of his childhood home in Port Arthur, 2006.

Photo: Mike Schreiber

Chad and his mother **Weslyn "Mama Wes" Monroe** celebrating her 60th birthday at her home in Port Arthur, December 2006.
Photo: Edgar L. Walker Jr.

Friends and family gather at Mama Wes' home in Port Arthur to celebrate her 60th birthday, December 2006. *Clockwise from below:* **Mama Wes** celebrating; **Heather Johnson, Chad, Mama Wes,** and **Riley Broussard**; **Big Munn** and **Mama Wes**; **Chad Jr., Mama Wes, Chad,** and **Chinara; Mitchell Queen Jr., Mama Wes,** and **DJ Bird; Mitchell Queen Jr., Chinara,** and **Chad**.

Photos: Edgar L. Walker Jr. and Titus Thomas

Friends and family gather at Mama Wes' home in Port Arthur to celebrate her 60th birthday, December 2006.

Clockwise from above: **Bun B, Mitchell Queen Jr.,** and **Chad; Bun B** cutting the cake; **Queenie, Mama Wes, Angie Crooks,** and **Heather Johnson; Mama Wes** celebrating.

Photos: Edgar L. Walker Jr. and Titus Thomas

Smoke D's friend **Larry** lurks in the background as **Chad**, **Mama Wes**, and **VIcious** pose for a picture in Mama Wes' kitchen during her 60th birthday party.
Photo: Edgar L. Walker Jr.

Above: **Pimp C, Cory Mo,** and **Too $hort** at MAD Studios, 2006.
Below: **Mike Mo, Z-Ro,** and **Pimp C** at MAD Studios, 2006.

Below: **Pimp C** and **David Banner** at the
2006 OZONE Awards in Orlando, FL.
Photo: Marcus "@GrandHussle" Jethro

Below: **8Ball, Pimp C,** and **MJG**; **Big Gipp** and **Pimp C** at Atlanta nightclub Primetime, 2006. Photos: Julia Beverly

Above: **Pimp C** and **Bun B** performing together for the first time since Pimp C's release at the OZONE Awards in Orlando, FL, August 2006. Bun was joined by **Young Jeezy** *(below)* for "Get Throwed."
Photos: Ray Tamarra

On the day of the rescheduled shoot Dr. Teeth shot a brief scene with Pimp C at Houston's Studio 7303, with cameos from Slim Thug, Chamillionaire, Webbie, and Mike Jones. Pimp was in a mood, and his quiet demeanor made Dr. Teeth uncomfortable. While the production crew packed up to go to the next location, Pimp left to go pick Jada up from the airport.

With Pimp gone, the production crew spent most of the afternoon and evening shooting Bun B, who arrived promptly at his call time. For the final location, Dr. Teeth had a backdrop arranged for UGK under a bridge with a police car behind them, lights flashing, and a smoke machine blowing for added effect. As the crew set up, Jeff Sledge assured Dr. Teeth that Pimp was on his way back with his Bentley as a prop. "He wants to shoot these girls out on the track, and he pulls up with the car, and he's getting money from these girls," Jeff explained.

Dr. Teeth nodded, but his heart sank. *Oh God,* he thought. *I don't want to do a 'pimping' video.*

"Look, we just need you to make that happen," Jeff Sledge said nervously. Everyone at the label was on edge. Pimp had already backed out once, and they couldn't afford for that to happen again.

"Well, hold on… what if I could shoot…." Dr. Teeth said, thinking out loud. "I can have Pimp in the car, and I can use the high beams, and have it like a spotlight on the wall, and I can have a girl moving and dancing for him seductively, and he's looking at her through the car?"

"No, well, he wants to … he wants to give the chick some money," one of the Jive reps said.

"Alright, fine," Dr. Teeth said, throwing up his hands. "I'll do what you want."

"Okay, well, can you tell him?" came the timid response.

"Why I gotta tell him?" Teeth laughed. No one else laughed. He looked around, Jive staffers exchanging nervous glances.

As the hours passed by, there was no sign of Pimp. They had more than enough footage of Bun but continued shooting just to kill time. It was an unusually chilly January day in Houston and temperatures had dipped down into the low 40s. A light rain started to fall, and as the clock ticked past midnight, the Jive crew and production crew stood shivering in the cold.

Dr. Teeth was nervous; the budget was already small, and they'd gone into overtime hours ago. Jeff Sledge called Chad repeatedly, who assured him he was on the way.

In reality, Chad was lounging at the Icon Hotel, doing absolutely nothing. Jada asked what time they were supposed to be at the video shoot.

"I'll go whenever I feel like going," he responded.

"He was just being an asshole," Jada laughs. "He just wanted to piss people off."

By the time Pimp's red Bentley pulled up past 4 AM, everyone on set was irritated and exhausted. Jeff Sledge's mind flashed back to the great meeting they'd had a year earlier at the Ritz Carlton, when he'd seemed so positive and ready to get back to work. *Damn, back to the same bullshit,* Jeff thought. *I thought he had really changed.*

Jeff squinted through the darkness and could see a woman in the passenger seat. He wondered if she was the reason for the delay. Pimp stayed seated in the vehicle until Bun finally approached to coax him out of the car. Pimp escorted Jada to the wardrobe trailer, where Dr. Teeth's video girls were waiting. Pimp informed everyone that the girl accompanying him would be the one used in the video.

The crew exchanged nervous glances. To some, it was fairly obvious that she was a working girl. "You could tell by her actions and energy [it was] like a pay-for-play type of thing," remembers Jeff Sledge.

Jada could feel everyone staring at her; judging her. She felt awkward and out of place. Wardrobe staff produced an elaborate feathered skirt and bikini top which looked like it was straight off the set of Nelly's "Get Your Eagle On" video. Jada was already afraid of this; she'd brought her own clothes and already gotten her makeup done. She snapped at the on-set makeup artist for trying to touch up her concealer.

The other girls were irritated that they'd waited until 4 AM and now this newcomer was getting special treatment. "Are you a stripper?" one of the video girls asked.

"Are you *his* stripper?" another added condescendingly. Her friend observed that Jada's shoes looked like Gucci knockoffs; they giggled amongst themselves.

Jada went over to UGK's trailer and informed Chad that the video girls were "haters." Furious, he confronted them. "Fuck y'all frontline video hoes," he told them. "You can take your $200 paychecks and go home."

Finally, outfitted in a black mink, Pimp was ready to shoot. "Man, let's do this shit," he said, walking out of the trailer. "Let's get this shit over with."

With Pimp finally ready, the two dozen label reps and production staff still on hand gathered around in a small huddle. "So, look, we don't have a lot of time, so we gonna have to condense this, so Teeth's gonna tell you what we're gonna do," Jeff Sledge said, looking at Dr. Teeth expectantly.

"Alright," Dr. Teeth said. "Well, they said you wanted to come up, bring your cars up, and get out the car and give a girl some money, and -"

Pimp cut him off midsentence. "Wait a minute. First of all, I don't expect you to know nothin' about pimpin'."

"What?!?" Teeth said, embarrassed at the rebuke.

"I don't expect you to know nothing about pimpin', because a pimp don't give a bitch money," Pimp snapped. "A bitch gives a pimp money."

Dr. Teeth felt his face getting hot; he turned defensive as a few hushed snickers rang out in the small crowd. "Well, I'm just saying what they're telling me," he argued. Teeth looked around and realized that everyone was taking Pimp's side.

Pimp started cracking jokes at Dr. Teeth's expense. Teeth was humiliated; he'd never wanted to do the 'pimp' scene at all. He couldn't understand where the animosity was coming from. *I was a fan first,* he thought bitterly. *I dropped my budget to do this.*

Dr. Teeth tried to choose his words carefully. He knew that if he pushed Chad too far, he'd just get back in the Bentley and leave and there would be no video at all. "We didn't agree on this," he said, frustrated. "I wish you had told me before and we would've written something else, but now it's dark and it's cold and we're running out of time. I don't wanna have to pay the crew [more] overtime."

Finally, Pimp conceded. "You know what? Do what you wanna do," he shrugged.

Teeth took a deep breath. "Look, we'll put you in the Bentley. I'll shoot performances around the Bentley. We'll use the girl you want to use."

They rushed through a quick shot with Jada in the Bentley and then spent a substantially longer amount of time shooting another girl that Teeth selected dancing on the car. Pimp didn't find the girl attractive and was irritated because he got the impression she had some kind of relationship with Dr. Teeth.

Cliff Mack, a BET cameraman, pulled Pimp aside for some behind-the-scenes commentary. He asked why people should go buy the new UGK album.

"Why should people go buy the new album?" Pimp repeated, his voice drifting off. He paused. "Everybody might not like the new UGK album, you know? I tell you what: go get the bootleg first, and if it's jammin', then go buy the real one ... that's what I do."

As they continued shooting Pimp C's performance scenes, he was irritable, barking out orders. The crew had already been on the clock for more than 16 hours, putting them in triple overtime. A label rep informed the producer Keith Paschall that they were too far over budget and weren't willing to approve any additional costs. Keith walked over to Dr. Teeth. "Alright, y'all gotta shut it down."

"Whoa, whoa, whoa," Dr. Teeth said, shaking his head. He knew if the video was half-complete, they'd still attach his name to it, even if it wasn't the finished product he'd envisioned. "Yo, I gotta get this last shot. I gotta shoot the car."

"No," Keith ordered. "Shut it down."

Pimp walked over to see what the commotion was. "What's wrong?"

"Yo, man, I need to shoot three scenes to make this thing make sense," Dr. Teeth explained. "I need to shoot this car, I need to shoot the close-ups of you, and another performance."

"Shut it down," Keith insisted.

This time, Pimp came to Dr. Teeth's defense. He shot Keith a look. "Hey, nigga, this *my* shit," he snapped. "Ain't nobody shutting down. *I'm* paying for this shit."

"Look, man, you know, the label ain't paying for it," Keith said.

"Hey, you know what?" Pimp said. "We finna whoop your ass."

Dr. Teeth started laughing, until he realized Pimp was serious. He looked around – all the onlookers and homeboys had long since departed, and the only person from Pimp's crew still on set was his manager Rick Martin. *Who is 'we'?* Teeth wondered.

Keith threw his hands up and turned around. Pimp kept yelling after him as he walked away. "Hey, man, shoot your shit, man. Ain't nobody shutting us down."

By the time they finally wrapped the video and packed up the equipment, the sun was rising. While Jive had been optimistic about the new UGK project, the video shoot was a disappointing turn. Even Jeff Sledge, their most vocal proponent at the label, was discouraged. "It was just a fucked up night … standing out in some desolate part of Houston, freezing your ass off just waiting for Chad to act right," he remembers.

Despite all the drama, everyone was pleased with the finished video, which began with swooping nighttime shots of the downtown Houston skyline. At Pimp's insistence, the only girl who made the finished cut was Jada.

"You know what I like to do when I get to my video set?" he told *OZONE*. "I like to just fire all the broads that are already there. I just fire everybody, send 'em all home. Shit, I'll bring my own crew of bitches. I'd rather have a real live prostitute bitch on the set than some bitch that's been fucking the director and got promised a spot in my video … [I tell them,] 'Bitch, you've been fucking the camera dude, you've been fucking the director, and he promised you all kinds of shit? Bitch, get your funky ass up out the set, man.'"

"[I'd rather] bring some of these real hoes off the track and put some real bitches in [the] video," he finished. "I've got more respect for a real hoe than a bitch that's out here tryin' to play like she's a hoe."

Jada planned to stay in Houston after the video shoot for her breast surgery, but started to get cold feet. She was starting to feel uncomfortable with Ocean after he'd slapped her, and didn't think it was wise to become indebted to him with such a large investment.

She'd been helping to recruit girls for Ocean online, reasoning that bringing others into their makeshift family would lighten her workload and improve their lifestyle. But when she heard that Ocean had flown in one of the girls, she went back to Las Vegas to find out what was going on.

The new arrival, Vanessa, was a tall Native American girl who'd been living in a foster home in Seattle. Vanessa was new to the prostitution game, and Ocean sent her out with Jada to learn the ropes. When Vanessa popped an ecstasy pill and lagged behind, Jada got irritated, told the girl she was going to the restroom, ran to the taxi line and moved on to the next casino.

This went on for several nights; Jada resented Vanessa, whom she considered lazy and unproductive. After being ditched again, Vanessa complained to Ocean that Jada wasn't being a good wife-in-law.* Late that night, Ocean and Jada were going to sleep in Jada's bedroom and

Vanessa, across the hallway in her own room, began crying loudly and dramatically, pouting that she couldn't join them.

"When she gives you some real money, she can sleep in my bed," Jada snapped. She was already irritated, losing respect for Ocean. His life seemed to be out of control and she was upset with his inability to manage. If he was having problems with two girls, how would he ever be able to manage a team?

Ocean told Jada to go get Vanessa and bring her to their bedroom. She refused.

"Oh, you're not gonna do it?" he said.

"Will you just leave me alone?" she brushed him off, irritated.

"You're not gonna listen to me? You're not gonna do whatever I ask you to do!?"

"No! *You* go do it," she snapped.

"WHAT?!" Ocean yelled.

"NO!" she yelled back. "Why should *I* do it?! I didn't do anything wrong! I'm my own woman, I make my own money! You should be grateful for the money I give you! Whatever you and her have going on, you need to take control of that! I don't have anything to do with that! FIGURE THAT SHIT OUT and KEEP ME THE FUCK OUT OF YOUR PROBLEMS!"

Ocean slapped her hard across the face. She fell to the floor, curling up into a fetal position, hiding her face and covering her body.

"GET UP, BITCH!" Ocean demanded.

"NO!" she yelled. Even though she knew she was physically no match for Ocean, she was angry. She'd grown up as a tomboy, wrestling her brothers, and had always been a fighter. *Fuck it,* she thought. *It's me against him.* Besides, how bad could it get?

Jada tried to show no reaction, curled up in silence.

"Oh, you think you're tough?" Ocean snarled. He slapped her a few times.

Afraid, she looked up at him. His eyes glossed over with anger. He took off his belt. "You think you bad?" he demanded. "You think you tough?!"

Gripping the loose end of his leather belt strap, Ocean unleashed on Jada's petite frame, the metal belt buckle stinging her flesh over and over again until her body was covered in welts and bruises. Jada had been trying to keep up a brave front, but it hurt too much – she curled up in a ball, screaming, crying, begging him to stop.

Vanessa, drawn by her cries, peeked through the doorway with a sadistic grin on her face, watching the beating. *Haha, I got you in trouble,* her expression read.

When Ocean finally stopped, Jada was shaking uncontrollably and bleeding from her face and legs. He grabbed her by her hair and dragged her into the bathroom, where he ran cold water and threw her in the tub.

Jada had the surreal sensation of floating above herself, looking down at her battered body writhing in pain. She was almost as surprised as Ocean to hear herself burst out laughing hysterically.

What the fuck? read the expression in Ocean's eyes as he backed away from the tub. *This bitch is really crazy.*

After Jada's maniacal laughter subsided, Ocean dragged her to their air mattress. Exhausted and numb, she drifted off to sleep as Ocean called Vanessa in the room to join them.**

Jada woke up the next morning feeling as if she'd been run over by a semi-truck. Ocean wouldn't let her go to the hospital, so she downed handfuls of pain pills to cope. She stayed home for three days, watching the bruises change color: green to yellow to purple to black.

Ocean kept a close eye on her. Pimps had protocol for situations like this. He talked to her

---

(*Two girls working for the same pimp refer to each other as wife-in-laws.)

(**As Ocean recalls it, Jada never returned after the "Game Belongs to Me" video shoot. He declines to comment when asked if he has ever been violent towards women. Jada says she later learned that Ocean was diagnosed with bipolar disorder. "He was a good person, and then he flipped," she says. "He would turn into a monster, like a demon." Ocean denies that he is bipolar.)

softly, explaining why he needed to punish her. He offered a twisted, manipulative apology, still placing the blame squarely on her. "I'm sorry that I got out of my element, but you know you fucked up, and I had to punish you," he said.

Jada nodded, pretending to agree with his assessment, but knew she had to leave. *This doesn't make sense,* she thought.

By the first of February, about a week after the video shoot, Jada's bruises were starting to heal and Ocean insisted she go back to work. Ocean and her former pimp Jamal both owned recording studios upstairs in the strip mall where the escort services were located, which functioned mostly as a hangout spot for their girls waiting for calls. Ocean planned to start a record label on the side and invest in some rappers.

The women who worked the phones for the escort services were concerned when they saw Jada's condition. Although she put on an upbeat front, she was still reeling from the emotional and physical pain of the beatdown, and the realization that she was working as a prostitute with visible bruises felt like hitting rock bottom.

Ocean had told her in the past almost exactly what her ex-pimp Dre had said – "Don't ever feel like you can't come to me and tell me to my face that things aren't working out. 'Cause if we can't work them out, then I'm gonna make sure you're straight" – but by now, she understood the game. She knew this really translated to: *Let me know before you try to leave so I can manipulate you to stay.*

"That's the game ... allowing them to get a warning sign so they can either fuck the shit out of you and get you to stay, go buy you a purse to get you to stay, or [beat the shit out of you] ... maybe all of the above," Jada says. She knew the only way to leave a pimp was just to leave.

When a few rappers stopped by Ocean's studio and his focus was temporarily distracted, Jada saw her opportunity. Ocean hadn't asked her yet for the money from her last call; she had less than a thousand dollars in her purse, but it was enough to survive. Terrified of what Ocean might do if he caught her leaving, she knew she had to act decisively.

Jada told Ocean she was going to run downstairs to a convenience store and grab some snacks. Ocean ignored her, bobbing his head to the beat. Jada went downstairs and called a taxi, scanning the parking lot. With so many escort services in the building there were always pimps and their enforcers hanging out around the property, but for the moment, the coast looked clear. As soon as she spotted the taxi coming down the street she bolted in heels through the parking lot, jumping in the taxi before the driver could even pull into the parking lot.

Jada fled to a friend's house. Finally safe, the enormity of the ordeal struck her, and she cried for what seemed like an entire day. A few days later, she went back to the house to try to get her clothes, but Ocean had already kicked in the door and cleared the place out. Terrified that Ocean would come looking for her, her fear mounted when she learned he'd spotted one of her friends in traffic and run her off the road.

Not only had Jada taken away Ocean's primary source of income, but she knew how much he enjoyed the pursuit. "He was the type of dude that if [another pimp] called him ... [and said] 'My bitch just left me...,' he would be soooo freakin' excited to get into that street shit with them," she recalls. If a girl left her pimp under bad circumstances, the pimp would blast off a "renegade alert," in which a group of pimps would gang up on her and force her to choose up.*

"[Ocean would help them] find the bitch, or if she chose up with somebody that wasn't reputable, they would all go in a group ... they would pull girls out [of the casino] by their hair, and they would be in a circle to where the [casino] cameras don't see it. Caveman style," Jada

(*To "choose up" is to leave one pimp and begin working for another one. Women working as "renegades" – or "outlaws," as they were known in *The Mack*, were constantly harassed by pimps trying to force them to "choose up." With the rise of social networks like Twitter, "renegade alerts" have gone digital. "#RENEGADEALERT ...RUN IN HER PURSE TILL SHE CHOOSE UP," read one tweet, which included the woman's phone number and Twitter screenname.)

remembers. In some twisted way, these types of attacks sometimes brought the girl back to her original pimp. "In a psycho sense, whenever you're in the game, you think, 'Oh, he cares about me enough to chase me down,'" she explains.

Jada was now faced with a dilemma: Las Vegas was the best place for an escort to make money, but in order to work, she needed to go to the escort services on Industrial – the number one spot to avoid unless she wanted another Ocean beatdown. Other girls, in fear for their own lives, refused to take her on calls because she was now a liability. Going to the casinos and soliciting clients herself was risky on two fronts: even if she managed to avoid Ocean, the casinos were filled with undercover police. Working for an escort service was safer because they acted as a buffer of sorts between the girls and the vice detectives.

Getting out of the game entirely was almost out of the question. Jada was addicted to the money and the lifestyle, plus, even if a woman could escape physically, she often couldn't escape mentally. "Once these young women get caught up in that lifestyle, there are a lot of degrading acts, as you can imagine, and there's also that shame and guilt that goes along with it. They don't value themselves any longer," Lt. Karen Hughes of the Las Vegas Metro Police vice squad told the *Las Vegas Sun*. "Manipulation is huge."

Stuck, Jada turned to Chad for help, asking him to get Ocean off her back. "I need you to call this guy and just tell him that I'm choosing up with you, 'cause I don't know what to do," she begged. "I'm afraid of these other guys. I don't want to have to go to another [pimp]."

"I just need somebody to serve him that he will respect," she explained. "If he respects you, he'll accept the serving. Just call the guy so he'll stop harassing me."*

Chad seemed hesitant to get involved, so Jada turned the pressure up a notch, calling him repeatedly, crying. "WHY CAN'T YOU BE MY PIMP!?" she'd scream dramatically.

It certainly wasn't the first time Pimp C had been approached with such offers. "Man, y'all lucky I ain't pimpin', cause y'all [pimps] would be in trouble," he'd joke.

"Pimp [C] actually did dive in the game once or twice," says Pimpin' Ken. "He wasn't public with it, but he had women all the time trying to give him money ... I think [Too] $hort and Pimp, if they wanted to be in the game, they could have [been] because they understood the principles and they ... cherish and respect the game."

"We weren't trying to pimp hoes, because we didn't have to," Too $hort explains. For a successful rapper like Too $hort or Pimp C, accepting money from prostitutes would be hustling backwards. They were already making more money legally.

"All the pimps that I know are really tryin' to get out of that game and tryin' to get into something legal [just like] the drug dealers that I meet," Pimp told *OZONE*. He added in an interview with WordofSouth.com, "I got too much rap money to be accepting hoe money ... why would I wanna get into a game [that] folks [are] trying to get out of?"

Besides, he didn't need those kind of headaches. "Pimp was getting $25,000 a verse," says Ivory P, a pimp who later became affiliated with UGK Records. "Dealing with a bitch, a bitch [might] run off, she gon' talk shit ... But one thang about that CD on the shelf, it ain't gonna run off, it ain't gonna talk shit, it just gonna sit there 'til it sell."

"He liked the [pimp] image ... but at the same time, I think he was smart enough to realize that it wasn't worth [the] sacrifice," Jada says.

Although Too $hort admitted he'd once "had a couple of hoes who were extremely inadequate" and often fielded offers from women trying to choose up with him (for example, an anonymous woman who handed him $1800 in a nightclub, simply saying, "You're the reason why I got in the game"), he didn't consider himself an active pimp. "If I was a real pimp I

(*When a hoe chooses up with a new pimp, the new pimp "serves" the old pimp, contacting him to give notice that the girl is now working for him.)

wouldn't rap about the shit," he told *The Source*. "Why? So I could have my muthafuckin' self charged with crimes?"

Similarly, Pimp C had the respect of active pimps. "[Pimp C is] one of the Greatest of All Time to ever represent the game and the lifestyle for us," says pimp Good Game. "That's why so many hoes was chasing him."

"Pimps honor different types of principles when it comes to women," explains Milwaukee pimp Paperchase. "The type of value that the average female should put on theyself, a pimp [is] gonna put on himself. Like … my dick is [a] treasure … I'm a king. [And] kings ain't just gonna share theyself [with everyone]. You gotta be part of the kingdom … That's how [Pimp C] was rockin'."

If he were still alive, Iceberg Slim likely would've concluded that Pimp C didn't have it in him to fully embrace the pimp lifestyle: he was too close to his mother. In 1972 Iceberg Slim told the *Los Angeles Free Press* that great pimps had to be "utterly ruthless and brutal without compassion" with "a basic hatred for women."

"The best pimps I know are the pimps that were abandoned by their old ladies – left in garbage cans and in the alleys when they were little, tiny – that never knew any affection or love," Iceberg Slim told journalist Richard Milner in 1969. "These were the fellows that had absolutely no hearts. To be a great pimp, I think you've really got to hate your mother."

In any case, Chad's pimp friends advised him that fraudulently posing as Jada's pimp ("dry serving") would violate the rules of the game. "I can't be a part of that," he told her. "My name can't be a part of that." He suggested she should find someone that would be easy to get rid of. "Just go get someone, you know, a lame, give them a couple dollars and have them do it."

Jada stopped by Las Vegas' Fashion Show Mall to buy some clothes, where she was approached by a man in a Kangol hat who looked vaguely familiar. Normally she would have ignored him, but with Pimp C's words ringing in her head, she lavished him with attention. *This is perfect,* she thought.

In the community of Las Vegas, which Jada says is comprised of nothing but "pimps, hoes, strippers, casino workers, taxi drivers, and police," word had been spreading about a new DVD series. The *Too Real For TV: Cross Country Pimping* documentary, filmed by Michael Maroy, was billed as "The Film That Will Change The Way You View Pimping Forever."

From Jada's perspective, Maroy was pimping the local pimps, offering them the opportunity to appear on the cover of the DVD for $5,000. The idea was that if a pimp appeared high-profile, he would be able to attract more women to his stable and make more money. The downside, of course, was that these activities were illegal and bragging about them on a DVD would inevitably attract the attention of law enforcement.*

"[Admitting you're] doing something illegal on a DVD … [is] some stupid ass shit to do," Pimp told *OZONE*. "You niggas on DVDs talking about they 'pimps.' C'mon, man. Stop it … pimpin' and pandering, you get three of them [charges], you get forty years [in prison]."**

This concept certainly wasn't new. When Iceberg Slim's book *Pimp* became a sensation, the FBI and law enforcement agencies all across the country ordered copies. According to Kool Ace, many of the pimps who appeared on *Too $hort's Gettin' It (Album Number 10)* ended up in prison. "[Too $hort sold] a lot of records, but it also ended up putting these people in jail,

(*As of 2011, Las Vegas vice detectives are required to watch Maroy's *Best of Both Worlds* DVD, featuring Pimp C and Pimpin' Ken, as well as the *American Pimp* and *Pimps Up, Ho's Down* documentaries, to familiarize themselves with "the game." Required reading includes Iceberg Slim's *Pimp*, Pimpin' Ken's *Pimpology: The 48 Laws of the Game*, and *Black Players: The Secret World of Black Pimps*.)
(**Pimp said he didn't respect the rookie pimps promoting themselves on DVDs. "Bunch of these niggas ain't doing nothing but being pedophiles, fucking little girls with no rubber on, mane," he said.)

because when you get on records and say [you're doing] things … [that are] against the law, all you're doing is indicting yourself," says Kool Ace.

Typically, a pimp and hoe would engage in a sort of job interview before they began working together. Jada and the man in the Kangol hat sat down in the food court for an impromptu interview. A lightbulb lit up in Jada's head as she realized that this was Maroy. *Ohhhh, that's the camera guy,* she thought. From what she'd heard, he was harmless. This was exactly what she needed: someone halfway square, who was close enough to the pimp world to serve Ocean.

Maroy asked her a few basic questions: What experience do you have in the game? How many pimps have you had? Jada was unimpressed; she didn't care for his looks or his personality. Normally, if she was serious about choosing a pimp, she'd run through her own list of questions: How many girls do you have? What do you do with your money? – but she decided that for a temporary situation, this would work.

To choose up with a pimp, a hoe was required to pay an upfront choosing fee. When the conversation turned to finances, Jada said she was willing to pay whatever she needed to pay to have Ocean served, but needed a few days to come up with the money since she hadn't been able to work.

"I can sign on with a couple [escort] services and, you just really have to be patient with me because I gotta really tiptoe around everywhere," she explained, showing him a few remnants of her fading bruises. She couldn't risk running into Ocean or his goons. "I'm not [gonna keep] working in Vegas … if you can't serve Ocean," she said. "I don't feel comfortable in the city until he's served."

Maroy agreed to handle the situation with Ocean as soon as she paid his fee. For the rest of the week, he dropped her off to calls in his old white Jaguar, leaving her for the rest of the day to fend for herself and catch taxis around the strip. By the end of the week, she'd given Maroy several thousand dollars and stashed a little bit for herself.

On February 4, 2007, Super Bowl Sunday, an escort service booked Jada for an overnight call at Planet Hollywood. Apparently, someone at the service tipped off Ocean, who showed up at the client's room, pounding on the door incessantly. Security was called and Ocean was escorted off the property.

Jada managed to make it through the night unscathed. When she emerged the next morning with $4,500 cash, Maroy was waiting for her at the Heart Bar downstairs. *He's sooooo thirsty,* she thought. *Fuck.* She'd planned on stashing half of the money, but she had nowhere to hide it.

After handing over the $4,500, Jada calculated that she'd now given Maroy $8,000 and told him it was time to serve Ocean.* She was hoping to get her clothes and personal effects back, too. "When they serve the dude, the pimps are supposed to meet up, get the [girl's] clothes back, have a drink and all that other shit," she explains. "And then after that, they know that you're not a renegade and they leave you alone."

The two drove over to Ocean's studio on Industrial. Maroy walked in the building but was back within seconds. Jada glared at him, irritated. "That's not enough time for a serving," she snapped.

Apparently, Maroy had a healthy fear of Ocean, and was afraid to confront him with the bad news. Maroy suggested they wait a few days. "Let's let things die down," he said. In fact, he was headed to Milwaukee for Pimpin Ken's Player's Ball and asked Jada to come with him. *What does it hurt to go to a party?* she reasoned.

The following weekend Maroy and Jada touched down in Milwaukee, a city blanketed in snow, and headed to meet Pimpin' Ken at a nearby soul food restaurant. Ken told Maroy he rec-

(*Maroy denies Jada's story. "I'm not a pimp, for the record," he says. "I make movies, documentaries… that's all I do." Ocean writes, "I had heard [Maroy] had a thing with [Jada] but he never said shit to me and she never said shit. It's probably true but niggaz in the game know I had let my emotions get involved when it came to her and in Las Vegas I'm that dude so … niggaz was scared so they'd rather keep it a secret.")

ognized Jada from the UGK video shoot. Later that day, Maroy pulled up Jada's MySpace page and saw that Pimp C was in her Top 8. "You didn't tell me you knew him," he commented.

Jada tried to downplay the relationship, making it seem as if they'd only done some work together. Maroy accused her of sleeping with him. "Hot Dick Chad," he said. "I know y'all did it. He does everyone, everywhere."

Jada laughed.

"Did he trick off?" Maroy asked.

"No," Jada said.

Maroy warned her that if she talked to Pimp C again, she'd be out of pocket. He was a heavy drinker, and by the time they arrived back at the Holiday Inn after the Player's Ball, he was very drunk and apparently still bothered by the revelation that Jada knew Pimp C. "Did you have sex with Chad?" he demanded loudly.

"What are you talking about?" Jada snapped. "No, he's cool, we do business together."

Maroy laughed. "He don't do business with hoes."

"What are you talking about?" Jada repeated. "He's a pimp. Pimps talk to hoes."

"He's not a pimp," Maroy scoffed.

"Well, maybe he's not," Jada said. "I don't know his business like that."

"You slept with him!" accused Maroy. "I can tell by the way you're avoiding my questions. You slept with him! Hot Dick Chad sleeps with everybody! He don't fuck with you. He sleeps with everybody. I hope you don't think he likes you."

"What the fuck are you talking about? You sound like you're hopping on his hot dick," Jada yelled. "Get off that nigga's dick!"

Once they got back to Las Vegas and it became clear that Maroy had no real intention of serving Ocean, Jada left him with barely enough money for a chicken sandwich from Carl's Jr. and called a friend to come pick her up.

Jada realized that in one sense, Maroy was right. Chad had gotten inside her head. "Chad was already changing my mind and changing my life. I was so naïve and I [had been] believing in all the wrong things," she says. "[Chad] was making sense to me. He was trying to help me, and I was very trusting of him … because I didn't trust anybody at the time."

As he'd helped open her eyes, Jada was realizing that everything she believed about the game was a lie. "It's all manipulation. It's all bullshit," she says. "That's what C would tell me – he would expose a lot of situations. He gave me a lot of game … [He showed me how it was all designed] to benefit their pockets."

The irony, of course, was that while Chad's alter ego was publicly a vocal proponent of "the game," he privately warned a woman he cared about of its dangers. He described her as a friend to Mama Wes, albeit one who was sometimes a bit "dizzy." He was cautious not to be hypocritical, simply warning her that if she chose to be in the game, she should make sure it was on her terms instead of allowing others to take advantage of her.

Most of all, Jada says, Chad came into her life at a time when she'd given up on God. She'd stopped praying, feeling abandoned, until Chad turned her back in the right direction. "[Pimp C] was an undercover agent of God," says Atlanta pimp Kool Ace. "[To] change people's lives, you gotta be able to get into [the] spots where people need the most help."

The situation with Maroy, however, led to a rift between Jada and Chad. She stayed in Las Vegas over the hectic NBA All Star weekend to make some money and then fled to Los Angeles. Safely out of Ocean's reach, she sent Chad a long email catching him up on all the drama of the past few weeks.

But Maroy had already called Chad with his version of the story, claiming that Jada had called him a trick. Chad cursed Jada out over the phone, calling her a "fake ass bitch" for trying to degrade his character. "If you want to believe that idiot, than believe him!" she screamed into the phone through tears. "Fuck you if you believe him!"

CHAPTER 45

"Once we got [the finished version of 'Int'l Player's Anthem'] we knew it was special." — Bun B, *XXL* Magazine

—————

"['Int'l Player's Anthem'] was one of the best video shoots ever. [Even though] there were so many characters, at the same time, everybody was so real. Everybody put their guards down."
— Anne-Marie Stripling, former Director of Video Promotion, Jive Records

With UGK's April 10 album release date fast approaching, Jive flew the group to New York for a listening party and some other promotional activities. Chad was thrilled when he was recognized by a passerby in Times Square. "They know me in New York!" he told his cousin Ed. "I made it!"

During a long day of media interviews at Sony Music Studios, Chad let Bun do most of the talking, satisfied to pass the time fiddling behind the boards with old UGK tracks like "Pocket Full of Stones." When AllHipHop's Amanda Diva stopped by to do an interview, Chad was quiet and introspective, playing some early UGK tracks on his laptop. "What album was that on?" Chad asked Bun.

"That's *Super Tight*," Bun told him.

Chad shook his head. "I couldn't rap. I couldn't rap. Big Mike and 3-2 taught me how to rap around 1995."

"So you can't listen to it now because you feel like it's not a fair representation of your abilities?" Amanda Diva asked.

"No, I can't listen to it because it's shitty," Chad replied. "We made some shitty records."

"It's funny to me," Bun said. "It's funny to listen to how far you've come, man."

Amanda Diva asked if his rap skills had improved while he was in prison.

"Nah, I was a beast and a Viking right before I left," he said.

"A Viking?" she laughed.

"Yeah, a vicious animal with a simple style that will tear your head right off if you play with me or underestimate me," Chad explained. "Back then, um… I was just a fan of the music. I just wanted to be down. You know, Bun was lyrical from the first record. I think I got a little better as time went on."

Conversation turned to their explicit lyrics and the influence they had on children. "Make no mistake, man," Chad said, his tone growing somber. "I'm not at home answering the phone, 'Whassup, biiiitch!' Shit is entertainment, man."

"Real shit," Bun agreed.

"I cringe when my records come on and my kids are in the room," Chad admitted. "I cut it off like, 'Whoa, whoa…'"

"I'm Pimp C, the character, on records, [but] that's not how I treat people in the streets," Chad explained in *OZONE*. "I'm really a respectful dude, 'til you rub me the wrong way."

"At a certain point we are role models, and the things we say or do have an impression with the youth," he added. "But it's not the rapper's responsibility to raise the children. I'm not letting

Jay-Z raise my four-year-old daughter, *I'm* raisin' her. It's my job to tell my daughter about my life experiences and to let her know what I know about different drugs and what they'll do to her ... I'm gonna lace my daughter up to know the difference between a real dude and a fake. I wanna lace her up and [help her] understand when somebody is tryin' to run some fugazi game on her, and when a person is being genuine with her."

When they arrived at the BET studios to film for *106th & Park*, rapper Juelz Santana was climbing into his Maserati. Eyeing the car, Pimp reached out his fist to give him dap. "I like the way you doing it, lil' nigga," he commented. Normally, Juelz would take offense to being called a "lil' nigga," but coming from Pimp C, he considered it a compliment.*

Jive also arranged for UGK to make an appearance on BET's *Rap City*, but Pimp would only agree on one condition: they had to film in Port Arthur. The group also headed out to Austin for the annual SXSW music festival, where they performed two back-to-back packed shows.

On Monday morning after SXSW, Smoke D appeared in a Louisiana courtroom for his sentencing hearing. Both he and his co-defendant Stan believed that the hefty fees they'd paid their attorneys would guarantee leniency when it came time for sentencing.

While Smoke's case was ongoing, Judge Wendell R. Miller, the only judge in the district, was also on trial. In 2005, the State of Louisiana had paid $50,000 to settle a sexual harassment lawsuit filed by his former secretary Heather Viator. Both were married and met weekly in the judge's chambers for secret sexual rendezvous.

The revelations in the civil lawsuit led to six formal charges. Miller was accused of fathering a child with his secretary and paying her an extra $800 a month in state funds as child support. He issued a divorce decree to separate her from her husband and ordered the man to pay child support for the child.

When his secretary tried to end the affair, she accused Judge Miller of threatening her, stalking her, and displaying increasingly unhinged behavior. After a series of alarming incidents, including one in which he allegedly placed a gun in his mouth in the judge's chambers and threatened to "do it," she walked off the job. Judge Miller responded by telling her ex-husband about their affair and following her home from church.

The salacious details revealed in the lawsuit were widely publicized in local media. Judge Miller issued press releases and gave interviews, openly discussing the scandal. Authorities reprimanded him for "making a media circus" and "inflaming an already bad situation," concluding that he had "permitted a personal obsession to affect his judiciary duties." It was also noted that "a public courthouse is not an appropriate place for a judge to carry on an adulterous affair, especially on a weekly basis ... a public building funded with taxpayer dollars is not intended to provide a secret location for a judge's sexual liaisons." In January 2007, the Supreme Court of Louisiana removed Judge Miller from office.

Thus, at Smoke D's sentencing hearing on March 19, 2007, any arrangement his attorneys had worked out with Judge Miller would be useless, since Miller's former bench was temporarily occupied by the once-retired Judge Anne Simon.

Smoke didn't seem particularly worried, showing up to court in a Rocawear t-shirt and Nike Shox sneakers. He was hoping for a five year sentence. His friend Jaro, who had driven down from Jackson along with Smoke's mother and children to show support, couldn't believe he was dressed so casually. "Dude, you fucking idiot! What the fuck you wearing?" Jaro demanded. Jaro, who was wearing a more appropriate black button-down t-shirt and black dress

(*R&B singer Lloyd was similarly flattered when Pimp C told him he was "a pretty lil' nigga," the first time he wasn't offended by the label. "He always went out of his way to be complimentary," Lloyd says. "Growing up, I would fight anybody who called me 'pretty.' They thought that because I had curly hair that I was soft, or because I had an earring that I was soft, so I had to always defend myself. He was the first person that actually called me 'pretty' and it was cool.")

shoes, insisted that they switch clothes.

Smoke's six children lined up on one of the benches in the courtroom next to his mother; Jaro held the seventh, still a baby, on his lap. Judge Simon, after reading Smoke D's criminal history aloud, sentenced him to 20 years in a Louisiana state prison.

As the family sat outside in the hallway sobbing, the judge, now in plainclothes, walked past them on her way home for the day. The moment struck Jaro as surreal. "It was the craziest thing I ever experienced in my life," he recalls. "The deepest, most nervewracking, crazy thing … just seeing the guy's life disintegrating, slipping away … It was horrible."

Pimp C called Juicy J and DJ Paul of Three 6 Mafia, reminding them of the conversations they'd had while he was in the County Jail. He asked them to send over the instrumental for the song they'd produced for Project Pat. Paul offered to touch it up; make some changes. "Man, I don't wanna touch nothing," Pimp said. "Just send us the track."

Just as he'd been hesitant to record "One Day," Bun initially didn't like the idea of redoing Project Pat's song. "You can't rap to this dude's song," he protested. "His album just came out. It hasn't been out that long."

Pimp recorded his verse at MAD Studios, adapting some lyrics he'd written back in October 2005 in the Terrell Unit ("cuz I'm a choose luva / under cover / never poke wit out my rubber"). Bun decided to trust his partner's judgment and dropped his verse a few days later.

Jive was hesitant to release the song as a single because it wasn't a typical radio record. At Pimp's insistence they included it on a sampler which circulated during All Star weekend in Los Angeles. A copy of the sampler landed in the hands of Big Boi of OutKast, who reached out to Bun. "Yo, I did a little remix verse to this song I heard y'all got with Three 6 Mafia," he said.

UGK had hoped to feature OutKast on a song which sampled Marvin Gaye, but plans were on hold since they were having problems clearing the sample through Gaye's estate. As it turned out, Big Boi's timing was impeccable. Three 6 Mafia had a huge mainstream buzz after winning the Academy Award for "It's Hard out Here for a Pimp," and their record label Sony was determined to capitalize. Sony was preparing to drop a Three 6 Mafia album and refused to clear the group to appear on other features, afraid it would detract from the project.

Sony was willing to clear Three 6 Mafia to appear on UGK's album, but not to appear on the single. Without Sony's clearance for Three 6 Mafia, UGK couldn't shoot a video. DJ Paul apologized that Sony was acting "dumb as hell" and told Pimp there was nothing he could do.

"Man, I'd like to have you on this muthafucker, but bro, I'm finna take y'all verse off and shoot my video," Pimp told him. "Man, y'all niggas' verse gonna be on the album, but I gotta go shoot my video, bro. Get my money now, man. You know how this shit go. It's a 'now' game, this ain't no 'wait later' [game]."

Pimp was getting nervous; they were running out of time and the album release date had already been pushed back He called his friend Big L to vent about the injustice. "Maaan, we finna ship 600,000 records, man, get yo' mind right. I'm not waiting on you niggas to shoot my video man, c'mon!" he complained. "Man, don't no one monkey stop no show! [DJ Paul] my pa'tna, man, but I'm just saying, man! Man, them niggas [at Sony] don't wanna give me single clearance, man. You think I'm not gonna do my record anyway? Man, you crazy. Man, get yo' muthafuckin' ass up outta here!"

"Nigga, I know I got a bonafide hit and you niggas [at Sony] don't wanna do it because you don't want that record to complete with yo' record!?" Pimp yelled. "Nigga, if you was smart and understood, you having two records on the chart is better for *you*!"*

Ever since OutKast's 2003 double album *Speakerboxx/The Love Below*, which sold more

---

(*Juicy J says that when the song became a huge hit without Three 6 Mafia, Sony executives regretted their decision. "People lost their jobs because [of the clearance issue]," says Juicy J. "I didn't [personally] get anybody fired … [but] the head of Sony just felt like it was stupid for us to not be on that record … it was hella stupid.")

than 11 million albums, it was clear that Big Boi and Andre 3000 were headed in two different directions creatively. Andre's half of the album, where he sang on experimental tunes which were a vast departure from OutKast's earlier work, left some fans confused.

But Pimp understood perfectly; he'd called Andre 3000 and told him to ignore the criticism. "Man, fuck all these pussy ass niggas," Pimp told him. "They just scared and don't know what to do with it. That shit y'all doin' is the most gangster … 'cause you doin' what the fuck you wanna do."

The affirmation from an artist he admired convinced Andre 3000 he was doing the right thing. "After that, not that I was hesitant at all, but I knew if Pimp C … understood, then … I'm good," he told *XXL*.

While Big Boi opened Purple Ribbon Records and started working on his solo album, Andre 3000 launched a preppy clothing line and focused on reinventing himself as an actor. Even though Jay-Z lauded him as a "genius" and Eminem called him "the best rapper," Andre had practically retired from rap, only popping up occasionally with memorable verses on DJ Unk's "Walk It Out" remix, John Legend's "Green Light," and Rich Boy's "Throw Some D's" remix.

Even Big Boi hadn't been able to get a feature from his OutKast partner for his solo project, and Jive executives were skeptical when Pimp told them that Andre was going to feature on the record. "Throughout our time in the business, Pimp and Bun have always been true to us," Andre told *XXL* of his decision to drop a verse.

Once Andre heard the beat, he requested a small modification. "I like it, but I want to rap without the drums," he explained. "I want to rap over the loop." Within 24 hours, he returned the song with his verse; friends were shocked at the quick turnaround. *Damn, Dre did a beat overnight?* Big Gipp thought, amazed.

Pimp called his manager Rick Martin after he heard Andre 3000's verse for the first time. "Damn! That nigga right there… boy! I think we got a Grammy for this one!" he yelled.

Big Gipp appreciated the song's double meaning; "choosing" could mean pimpin', or it could mean marriage. "That's why the song came off so great to me, because as much as Pimp was about that goddamn pimpin', Dre was too, but just in the artsy-fartsy way, in the poetic way," Gipp says.

A few days later, Jive sent the record to Big Boi, who initially thought it sounded odd that his partner was rapping his entire verse before the beat came on. *Damn, you gon' keep the beat out the whole damn time like that?* he wondered. *They gon' let him keep the beat out? How they gon' … play this shit in the club if the beat ain't in the muthafucker?**

Big Boi laid his verse and the song was complete; there were no clearance issues with Out-Kast, who were also under the Jive umbrella. The result was a historic moment for Southern rap: UGK and OutKast together over a Three 6 Mafia beat.** "Once we got [the finished version] we knew it was special," Bun told *XXL*. "Everybody knew it was special."

Chad hadn't spoken to Jada ever since their argument over Maroy. According to Jada, in early April, Chad ran into a mutual friend in Dallas who had heard Maroy make similar comments, referring to him as "Hot Dick Chad." Now convinced that Jada was telling the truth, Chad summoned her to Washington D.C. with instructions to "bring me $10,000 and you could be my bitch."

(*Because the verses were essentially cut-and-pasted together, Bun B says careful listeners will be able to detect the song's imperfections. "The music drops in and out at funny places, like, the music don't really come in when the chorus is supposed to come in," he told Madd Hatta in a radio interview.)

(**UGK and OutKast had previously collaborated on "Tough Guys" from the *Shaft* soundtrack in 2000. Some diehard fans were upset that UGK chose to feature OutKast on "Int'l Player's Anthem" instead of a Pimp C beat. "I've never heard [Out-Kast] rap over a Pimp C beat and I imagine it would be a near perfect fit," journalist Andrew Nosnitsky observed, adding, "Still, all things considered, [it's] a fucking UGK & OutKast record. Which means it's better than just about everything in the universe.")

Jada, who was working in Chicago, came up with the money and flew to meet him, but he refused to accept it. "He was slick," she laughs. "He just wanted to see if I could get it ... and if I would do it for him."

Through Pimpin' Ken, Pimp linked up with Ivory Pantallion, a tall, lanky, pimp/aspiring rapper known as Ivory P. As a youth he'd been featured alongside UGK on Rick Royal (a.k.a. Coco Budda)'s record "Let 'Em Have It." After several stints in prison for robbery and selling drugs, Ivory realized he needed to find a new hustle.

He passed the time while incarcerated reading Iceberg Slim and Donald Goines novels and decided to become a pimp. he started collect-calling random phone numbers to brush up on his game, identifying himself only with a hushed whisper ("it's me"). If a woman answered, he'd try to talk her into making a three-way call for him, promising that if she dialed a special code (*72), the collect call charges would be forwarded to the other person's phone. (No such code exists.) He'd praise her "beautiful voice," lavish her with compliments, and eventually convince her to come visit him.

Ivory had always considered himself a ladies' man, and the scheme boosted his confidence. By the time he was paroled in November 2003, he'd convinced himself that he had a profitable future as a pimp. He moved in with one of the women he'd met on a collect call and managed to persuade her to let two prostitutes move in, a living arrangement which only lasted two weeks. Faced with an ultimatum – her or them – he went with the money.

Fresh out of prison, he met Pimpin' Ken at a Houston strip club and the two collaborated on a mixtape called *From the Track to the Trunk*. Ivory, who was really more of a shit-talker than a rapper, had a distinctive voice and a way with words. ("I'm a young, active, and attractive muthafucker ... women go crazy over me every day," Ivory brags, referring to himself as the "crook with good looks.") When Pimp heard it, he was impressed and asked Pimpin' Ken to pass along his number.

When Ivory P called, Pimp was in Beverly Hills in a great mood. "I'm in a suite right next door to Mary J. Blige, mane," he bragged. "Lookin' good than a muthafucker." Pimp told Ivory P that he'd heard his mixtape and wanted to get him involved with UGK Records. "A lot of these other niggas talkin' this pimp shit, but these niggas ain't even sent a bitch to the corner sto' to get a bag of chips," Pimp said.

Ivory P, of course, was on board – he'd heard there was more money in entertainment, anyway. "Really, I'm tryin' to leave this other shit alone," he told Pimp.

A couple weeks later, when Pimp was back in Houston staying at his new high-rise, a condo towering over the Galleria Mall, he called Ivory P, who happened to be riding around with pimp Good Game. They came by the high-rise, where they were met by DJ B-Do and Z-Ro, who had just come home from jail. After a long night working on music and listening to tracks from the upcoming UGK album, the group went to breakfast at IHOP as the sun came up.

As they sat down for breakfast, Good Game got a call from his bottom bitch, giving him an update as she and the rest of the ladies wrapped up a long night's work. He put them on the phone with Pimp C to get acquainted while he ordered them some food.

"Pimp C. expressed his surprise and appreciat[ion] for how 'GOOD' I treated my ladies and the bond we had, because he felt it was rare for a pimp to be so considerate to his prostitutes," Good Game writes. "I believe this is what sparked the idea for him to play that quarterback [role] with me, and me being the wide receiver that I am, I caught everything he threw at me."

In Pimp C's opinion, a real pimp was supposed to be a "manager" and take good care of his product. "If that woman is riskin' her life every day and going out there and doin' this, she should be livin' in a comfortable place, she should have the best clothes money can buy," he told *OZONE*. "Her kids should be in private school, they should be taken care of. If you wearin' mink, she should be wearin' mink, man. And if you ain't learned that part of the game, then you not really in it at all, are you?"

"That's not just a broad that's workin' out there, that's your woman," he added. "You got to treat her as such, and you got to let her know she's your woman, no matter what lifestyle you in … if she don't feel [special], you goin' to blow her."

After watching Good Game treat his women to an expensive dinner at Fogo de Chao, Pimp passed along Jada's phone number.

Jada, who happened to be hanging out with Big Gipp in Los Angeles, was surprised when a call came in from a number she didn't recognize. Good Game, on the other end of the line, sounded straight out of a 1970s Blaxploitation film. Jada hung up on him and asked Gipp, "Who the hell is Good Game?"

Gipp started laughing. "Go look him up on the internet."

"I know Chad had something to do with this," Jada said, after doing a Google image search.

"I'm not trying to play love connection, but you told me to hook you up with a nigga," Chad laughed when Jada called. "I seen how he let his girls just eat a steak dinner with us."

"You're so fucking corny right now," Jada laughed.

"You wanted me to be your pimp," Chad joked. "So if you wanted a pimp so bad, he's a good one."

It was around this time that Maroy's *Best of Both Worlds* DVD was released, a documentary he'd been filming featuring clips of Pimpin' Ken and Pimp C. Billed as the place "where real pimpin' begins, [and] that rap shit ends," it was a companion piece to Pimpin' Ken's book *Pimpology: The 48 Laws of Game*. Maroy had been trailing Pimp at studio sessions and even earned a shout-out on "Heaven," where Pimp rapped, "*Too Real for TV* like Maroy."

But after the incident with Jada, Pimp was having second thoughts about his affiliation with Maroy. There also were some apparent discrepancies with the financial arrangements on the DVD; Pimp felt that he'd helped raise Maroy's profile and given him credibility by doing the DVD, but instead of cash, Maroy shipped him boxes of the DVDs to sell, which sat collecting dust in Mama Wes' game room. Rumor had it that J. Prince wasn't too happy about Maroy selling a DVD off Pimp's name, either, and reached out to arrange a meeting.

Through Pimpin' Ken, Pimp was introduced to Bankroll Jonez, a Michigan-based pimp/rapper. Although admitting he "wasn't the coldest rapper in the world," Bankroll's work ethic was solid, having churned out nine albums in 10 years. He was so inspired by Pimp's opening line on T-Pain's "I'm in Luv (Wit A Stripper)" remix ("I'm a P-I-M-P, trickin' ain't in my pedigree") that he'd used it as the hook of his record "Pedigree."

Bankroll paid Pimp to drop a verse on the record, and for inspiration, Pimp turned to his real-life experiences with Jada. The first two lines were a shot at Jamal and his 50/50 business model, which Pimp didn't consider "real" pimpin':

Niggas say they not trickin' and suckin' them hoes' cocks*
Lettin' them keep half the money, playin' the shortstop
I was quarterbackin', nigga, puttin' the bitch out on the track
Makin' her get down for the grind and bring all the money back

He then took a shot at Maroy:

You got $8,000, bitch, you ain't no P
I get $15,000 for my choosing fee**

(*In the South the slang term "cock" is sometimes used in reference to a woman's genitals instead of a man's.)

(**Maroy denies Jada's version of events, but declines to comment any further. Her allegation that Pimp was dissing Maroy is confirmed by multiple sources. "[On] the 'Pedigree' record that lil slug [Pimp] was shooting in there, that was for Maroy. That's a fact," says Pimpin' Ken's protégé Paperchase.)

"Yeah, man, I got at that boy [Maroy]," Pimp told Pimpin' Ken and his protégé Paperchase after they heard the record. "Pimp felt like, under no circumstances should you downtalk me to anybody, let alone a female," Paperchase explains. "We supposed to be pimps and players ... If you can't knock a bitch ... off of your muthafuckin' reputation or true character ... that ain't the bitch for you."

Over in Dallas, an underground pimp DVD was circulating; everything from the flimsy paper printout of the cover and misspelled names screamed "low budget production." The producer was obviously relying on controversy to move units, announcing, "MISTA SELFISH CALLS OUT PIMP C & DON JUAN" on the cover in large print.

The DVD opened with a shot of a naked woman pressed up flat against a wall of patterned wallpaper, clapping her ass cheeks for the camera. "Mista Selfish," a self-proclaimed pimp from Dallas, was a ridiculous looking character with a small ponytail sporting a white suit several sizes too large for his thin frame, complete with oversized animal-print accented collars.

Sitting on a couch in a dimly lit room, Mista Selfish spat out rapid-fire words so quickly he could barely keep his breath, every sentence punctuated with a "muthafucker." After saying that he and Pimp C had history back "in the muthafuckin' eighties," he claimed that his "bottom bitch Q-T" had once been UGK's road manager.*

"I got the whole scoop on you and Bun B, hey man, y'all need to leave that muthafuckin' pimpin' to a real muthafuckin' pimp," Mista Selfish continued rattling in his high-pitched rapid-fire voice. "And hey, I just seen the new muthafuckin' ['Game Belongs to Me'] video, man, I like that, you understand what I'm saying? Hey, man, but you screaming that pimpin', hey, but for the record – just for the muthafuckin' record – on the low low, Pimp C, you ain't no muthafuckin' pimp, mane."

Someone passed along the DVD to Pimp, who was amused by Mista Selfish's outfit. "The nigga on the tape in a *blouse*," he howled. "Nigga got a blouse on with some goddamn ... zebra around the collar!"

Pimp was also amused by another segment on the DVD, in which a pimp gave his prostitute instructions via speakerphone on how to negotiate a cheap trick up from $15 to $20. "Nigga, you got hoes fuckin' for [$20]?" Pimp laughed. "That ain't even weed money, man. You can't even get no good swisha for that no more, mane. How you pimping crackheads, dawg?"

To vent, Pimp called in to his old friend Bo-Bo Luchiano's radio show in Dallas, Tha Dirty South Block Party. After promising to "come to Dallas and take [Mista Selfish's] whole stable and set 'em free ... he probably ain't got but two funky flatbackers," Pimp inexplicably threatened to "go in your whole bootyhole with my hand, boy!" As Bo-Bo and his radio co-hosts burst into laughter, Pimp added, "I'm gonna have to get my whole hand cut off after I do it, but, yeah."

His interview was peppered with memorable quotables: "If you don't know me, you must have been locked in a bubble with Michael Jackson playing with boys for the last 20 years!" "[People be] talking about, 'Do you remember me?' No, fool! You didn't write me when I was in prison, why am I gonna remember you, funky fool?! ... Remember you for what!?"

And finally: "Guess what! Your gal wanna get with me, boy! That gu'l wanna get with a wild bull between her legs, talkin' 'bout it smells like $200 cologne and ridin' around in a $200,000 car, boy!"

Pimp also took the opportunity to air out his grievances with Skip Cheatham, the program director of Dallas radio station K104. Apparently, Skip had told Greg Street that he wasn't "feeling" the "Int'l Player's Anthem" record.

"How you can't *feel* a UGK and OutKast [record], fool!?" he demanded. "You can't feel that, but can you feel that boy when he going up in your bootyhole with your ankle bracelet on!? ...

(*Mama Wes says that QT was once a dancer for UGK in the early days, but certainly not a road manager. "I didn't go to high school 'til '88," Pimp C pointed out. "How you know me from the 80s? You met me when I was 14?")

You ain't gotta play my record, fool. I'm gonna get money anyway!"

"Our only problem with Skip Cheatham is this: he's very, very powerful, because he's got power in Dallas," Pimp explained later in a calmer interview with *OZONE*. "He's the nigga that gets record played ... and when niggas got that much power, the more power you get, the more humble you have to become. He's not doing that, and he's not supporting the local artists in Dallas ... when you do that, your region can't blow up."

The interview with Bo-Bo ended on a somber note as they reminisced about a popular Dallas DJ who who had recently been killed. "One thing is for sure, Bo-Bo. We was born to die," Pimp concluded. "We gonna die. Everybody die one day. And we gotta live it all up until it's over with. Cowards die over and over again, but men only die one time, Bo-Bo. As long as you got God on your side – I don't care what you call him – you can call him Allah, you can call him Yashua, you can call him Jaja, it don't matter – as long as you pray in the right direction, your prayer gon' get answered, mane. And I know that might sound funny coming from somebody from my type of music background, but hey, I'm real, mane. I ain't finna play with you and act like I don't know."

A few days after Pimp's interview with Bo-Bo, on May 4, Jive sent out an email to DJs plugging UGK's new version of "Int'l Player's Anthem (I Choose You)," featuring OutKast, as their new priority. The album had already been pushed back from April 10 to April 17 to May 8 to July 17, and everyone was getting irritated. Label employees found it impossible to coordinate their promotional activities when the release date kept changing.

"The fans, they get frustrated when they keep hearing new dates," Pimp told the *Houston Chronicle*. "The record companies need to [have more] responsibility and stop dropping these dates before they really know that everything is in line."

Jive's new Director of Video Promotion, Anne-Marie Stripling, flew to Port Arthur along with producer Thomas Gibson to film a DVD highlighting UGK's return. Anne-Marie arrived with with trepidation, expecting to find the "crazy off-the-chain" Pimp who was notorious around the Jive office. Instead, she found the exact opposite: while Bun seemed nervous and edgy, she found Pimp to be charming; sweet, even. She quickly bonded with Mama Wes and loved Edgar the Dog. *God, I love these people,* Anne-Marie caught herself thinking.

Even though Jive was offering more marketing support than they had in the past, Pimp had learned not to rely on the label to promote his products. He hired Roy "Naztradamus" Cross, a friend of Cory Mo's, to tag along and capture footage for a "side hustle" documentary titled *Underground Kingz: The Making of the Album.*

Naztradamus, a longtime UGK fan, felt emotionally connected to many of their records and was thrilled to get the opportunity to work with the group. "[Pimp] was always about the underdogs," says Naztradamus. "He was always about trying to give people a shot."

With the Jive camera crew, DJ Greg Street, Naztradamus, Nancy Byron, and others in tow, Chad sped off in his red Bentley and led the group on a tour of Port Arthur, introducing them to Mitchell Queen and his former choir teacher Marjorie Cole. The interviews helped Jive staffers gain a better understanding of UGK's influence. *Ohhh ... he's the one who kicked it all off,* Anne-Marie realized. *They were the originators.*

After a long day of filming, they ended up at Avery's studio in Port Arthur. Trill Studios, as it was known, didn't look like much from the outside: it was a beat-up two-story house in a rundown part of town which apparently lacked air conditioning. "You wouldn't even know that house was a studio," says local producer Phreeky. "It looked like some bullshit."

At the studio, Chad was met by producer Steve Below to mix down the final version of

"Swishas & Dosha," an experimental track Steve had thrown on a beat CD as filler. "I couldn't imagine anybody rapping on it," Steve Below told HipHopDX. "I [initially] didn't have any intentions of sending it out."

While the cameramen tracked him, sweating, Chad spent a solid two hours layering the hook to "Swishas & Dosha," reciting the same lines over and over. "He was just real meticulous, 'cause he liked to harmonize," recalls Naztradamus. "It was cool to watch the process of how he put it down but … [it took] a long muthafuckin' time, man."

"It was like [seeing] another layer revealed," Anne-Marie says. "Just hearing him in the studio and seeing how he layered the tracks … It was like [meeting] *Pimp*, the artist … That was the moment when it all became clear because I actually saw the talent shining through."

Steve was floored when he learned that "Swishas & Dosha" would be the opening track on *Underground Kingz*. "That showed me what working with true artists like Pimp C and Bun B was like … [somebody who can] see something in the track that [even the producer] couldn't see themselves," he told HipHopDX. "That boosted my confidence and made me want to work harder."

Through Cory Mo, Chad also linked up with Swishahouse DJ OG Ron C to create a bonus CD, *Still Ridin' Dirty*, to be included with the DVD. When Russell Washington heard about the underground CD, he called Mama Wes to inquire about purchasing 250 copies. Even if he harbored resentment towards UGK, he was still a businessman, and any UGK product was always in high demand at Big Tyme Recordz. "Making money overrules the way I feel about you," Russell laughs.

One day at the flea market, Russell was lounging on a couch near the Big Tyme booth when a UGK affiliate dropped off the 250 copies of *Still Ridin' Dirty*. Close behind him was Chad, followed by Hezeleo and a couple other guys. "This is the dude that put me out," Chad told them, introducing Russell. "If it wouldn't be for him, I probably wouldn't even be here."

Although it had been a long time coming, Chad and Russell finally made amends. "Russ, them people divided us to conquer us, because they knew we was gonna take over, man," Chad said.

"The beef had long been gone, as far as C was concerned," explains Mama Wes. "They made their peace … that was something C had been wanting to do for a long time."

"In all honesty and fairness, I can't blame Russell for all the mistakes that he made," Chad told *Scratch* Magazine. "He was young. We were all young."

It took a few weeks to coordinate everyone's busy schedules, but on May 16, 2007, a beautiful, warm day in Los Angeles, UGK and OutKast congregated at Brookins Community A.M.E. Church to shoot the "Int'l Player's Anthem" video. For the first time in their career, UGK secured a six-figure video budget from Jive. (Still, Bun estimates it was less than half of what Jive would normally spend on an OutKast video.)

While Pimp had always taken the lead in UGK's musical direction, film was Bun's baby. He chose director Bryan Barber, a good friend who was also a close friend of Andre 3000, to oversee the project. Barber's participation ensured that Andre would feel comfortable doing the video. "[Andre] understood the historical value of OutKast and UGK being on the screen together," Barber told *XXL*. "I can't really take credit for that. It wasn't like I had to convince him. Dre, he's a huge fan of Pimp and Bun … he's been a fan of UGK before he started really rapping."

While Bun was actively involved in putting together the treatment, he turned over the direction of the video to Barber. Based on Andre's introductory verse, everyone agreed that a wedding was a logical setting for the video. Barber, aiming to "capture the dynamic between men and women at a wedding," decided to stage a mock wedding video.

Despite Sony's refusal to allow Three 6 Mafia clearance to appear on the single, nothing could keep them away from the video shoot. It was a historic moment on set as UGK, OutKast, and Three 6 Mafia gathered in the same room for the first time while Andre filmed his introductory scene. They ad-libbed the intro. "It was [just] what friends might say when their buddy is making that walk [down the aisle]," Andre 3000 told *XXL*. "None of it was scripted."

They were joined by comedian DeRay Davis, who observed, "It felt like somebody's real wedding." A host of other celebrities stopped by: T-Pain gave an elaborate performance as the choir director, backed by Cory Mo and others. Actor Lukas Haas, a close friend of Andre's, played the role of a groomsman.

BET's *Access Granted* cameras were there filming behind-the-scenes; David Banner held up a "Free Smoke D" t-shirt for the MTV News cameras as Bun served as a narrator. Banner had dropped what he was doing and rushed to the set when he got the call. "Those are two of my biggest influences – 'Kast and UGK," Banner told *XXL*. "To even be asked to be part of something so monumental is dope to me."

As the "wedding" scene commenced in the chapel, onlookers and celebrities filtered into the pews. Among them was the flamboyant pimp godfather Bishop Don "Magic" Juan, wearing one of his custom-made green suits, sporting a bejeweled flip phone hanging around his neck, with a blonde girl in tow wearing a matching green dress. (Green and gold was the Bishop's trademark colors: "Green is for the money and gold is for the honey.")

The Bishop, in his mid-50s, offered a business card to a woman sitting on the end of one of the pews, who looked up at him in surprise. The contrast between the flamboyant pimps and the church atmosphere only added to the surreal nature of the day. "That was one of the best video shoots ever," recalls Jive's Anne-Marie Stripling. "[Even though] there were so many characters, at the same time, everybody was so real. Everybody put their guards down."

Bun viewed the shoot as the ultimate realization of the Pimp C persona, the visual evolution which had begun at the "Big Pimpin'" video. "I'm glad we didn't make a Pimp a groomsman," Bun laughs. "I like the fact that he and the pimps were there, kind of looking for girls in the wedding party. We're different personalities … [If] we would have done [a] performance with me and Pimp next to each other, wearing the same kind of suit, that would have looked terrible. I think the video represents [each of us] very well."

As the day passed, the shoot turned into a pimp convention of sorts. An array of pimps flaunting mink coats and bejeweled pimp cups – Pimpsy a.k.a. 619, Pimpin' Ken and his protégé Paperchase, Good Game, Bankroll Jonez – convened in Chad's trailer.* "He wanted the video to have real pimps and players in it [and] give it that authentic [feel]," recalls Don Magic Juan.

Pimp C's scene would take place at the mock wedding reception, in a banquet hall decorated in intricate white, gold, and purple detail. One of the last scenes they filmed, the girl-on-girl food fight, had to be done in one take. The majority of people on set, unaware that the women were actually hired stuntwomen, stood watching with their mouths agape as the women literally threw each other into the four-layered wedding cake. "They was literally making contact [with punches]. For real, for real. Like where you can hear it," Fonzworth Bentley told *XXL* Magazine, adding, "[They] went to the floor still swinging. The whole nine. It was crazy."**

––––––––––

On set, Chad was joined by a few women he'd just met. Among them were Halimah and Ayesha Saafir, two sisters from Dallas who had just relocated to Los Angeles and were making

("Chad had previously dissed Pimpsy – "I heard the nigga say his name was Pimp C on that 'Bossin' Up' movie, but that nigga ain't me," on 8Ball & MJG's record "Whatchu Wanna Do" – before the two were formally introduced by mutual friends. He later shouted him out on an interlude from XVII's *Certified*.)

(**"Int'l Player's Anthem (I Choose You)" won Best Collaboration, Duo or Group at the BET Hip-Hop-Awards in October 2007. It was also nominated for Best Video. When the award was given to Kanye West's "Stronger," Kanye remarked to Busta Rhymes, seated near him, "Definitely UGK should have won this." Kanye refused to accept the award and called director Bryan Barber to the stage to accept the award on behalf of UGK and OutKast, a move which Bun B called "beautiful.")

the rounds in the Hollywood social scene.

Halimah had just enjoyed an innocent flirtation with Andre 3000 as one of the girls on featured in OutKast's video for "Idlewild Blue (Don'tchu Wurry)." But it was her younger sister, 20-year-old freckled and voluptuous Ayesha, who had caught Chad's attention. After a brief encounter at a Los Angeles recording studio, they'd bumped into each again other while going through security at the Los Angeles airport. Ayesha was charmed by Chad, who gave her not one but three phone numbers, and explained that he wasn't going to let her "slip through [his] fingers" again.

During the recording of *Underground Kingz*, Pimp had bumped into an aspiring rapper named Torris "T.O.E." Alpough at Avery's studio in Port Arthur. T.O.E. and his partner, rapper/producer Bradley "DJ B-Do" Davis, wanted to get Pimp on a verse for their record "Grind Hard."

As it turned out, T.O.E. was the nephew of Kim "Infinity" Broussard, the female rapper who sparred with Bun in the early 90s on UGK's "Cramping My Style." When T.O.E. told Pimp he could only afford to pay $2,000 for a feature, Pimp shrugged and agreed to give him the Port Arthur discount. "Come on with it," he nodded.

After hearing the finished version of the song, Pimp liked T.O.E.'s distinct, high-pitched voice so much he invited T.O.E. to come by his house and handed him a stack of cash. "Here, man, this $4,000," Pimp told him. "I want to give you your money back and sign you to my label, UGK Records."

Pimp also wanted to use "Grind Hard" as the introductory record for a group called Da Underdawgz, which would consist of him, DJ B-Do, and T.O.E. "It's a dream to work with them niggas," DJ B-Do told AllHipHop. "I was just surprised I even made it." (DJ B-Do was most recognizable for his acting role as the lead character in Lupe Fiasco's "Hip-Hop Saved My Life" video.)

Pimp was still learning about new computer programs like ProTools, so he considered younger producers like DJ B-Do, who had just graduated from Full Sail's audio engineering school, an asset to help him stay updated. Late one night as they were wrapping up the double album, Pimp called DJ B-Do and told him he wanted to use "Grind Hard" on UGK's project.

"Pimp, stop lying," B-Do laughed. "Nigga, ain't no way you gonna put this on a UGK album."

"Man, we're going to L.A. tomorrow to master it," Pimp said.

"But it's not even mixed," B-Do protested.

"We fly out in the morning." Pimp told him. "How quick can you get to L.A.?"

During the Los Angeles studio session, Pimp played the finished cut of "Swishas and Dosha," on which he rapped, "I know Short Dog, the real Short Dog," referring to Too $hort. B-Do and young Houston rapper Short Dawg happened to be friends.

"Man, why you fuckin' with Short Dawg?" B-Do asked.

"Man, fuck all these rap niggas," Pimp C said. "Man, if that nigga really yo' friend, we gon' call him right now and [if] he'll answer the phone I'ma fly him out there."

B-Do got Short Dawg on the phone. "Pimp wanna holla at you real quick."

"What's up, man," Pimp said. "I had to check you, man. Boys telling me you real, but I had to check you to see where your head is at." He explained that he considered it disrespectful for him to adopt Too $hort's name. "This [is the] O.G.'s call, man," Pimp explained. "Like, Too $hort, I'll wash that nigga's car, y'know what I'm sayin'?"

They went back and forth for a few minutes. Finally, Pimp said, "You know what? I respect it because you got enough nuts to sit here and just not back down. My man B-Do says you're cool, so we'll air the shit out." He invited him to fly out to L.A. so they could talk things over.

Pimp told his manager Rick he was going to go pick up Short Dawg. "Man, that lil' young dude say he want to come by here and meet with me."

Rick was nervous. "Boy, don't you go out there and mess with that lil' boy," he warned. "He might be crazy."

Short Dawg was actually 20, but Pimp was under the impression he was much younger. "That lil' 16-year-old?" he laughed. "He probably had to ask his mama permission [if he] could go out there [to Los Angeles]."

Pimp booked Short Dawg a room at the Beverly Hilton and showed up later that day in a chauffeured Escalade, playing some tracks from the upcoming UGK album. "There was only one thing I said. You ain't gotta worry about hearing nothing else," he laughed, referring to the line on "Swishas and Dosha."

Short Dawg offered Pimp a sip from his Styrofoam cup, just to be polite, but Pimp passed. "Nah, I'm alright."

Pimp nodded his head in approval as he listened to a few of Short Dawg's tracks. "Man, I need you out here representing Texas, man," Pimp told him. "Me and you and Too $hort, we gonna get together and we gonna do some songs. We gonna make everything right."

After a stop at Three 6 Mafia's studio, Pimp dropped Short Dawg back at the hotel and called Too $hort. "$hort, I like the lil' dude," he explained. "I like his rap. I like him. But he can't have your name. I told him he gotta change [it] some kinda way."

Too $hort laughed; he knew all about Chad's rules and regulations. "Anytime anybody ever said anything [bad] about me, whether I was around or not, C got mad," Too $hort says. "He just felt that [way because] he came up listening to me … it's like the way I feel about George Clinton. You could say bad stuff about George Clinton, but you can't say it around me. I've worked with the man, I know the man, and I've admired the man from childhood. Growing up, his music was a part of my life. So you could attempt to assassinate his character, but not around me."

CHAPTER 46

"I Like The Snow Man (Young Jeezie Or Geezie I Can't Spell Shit Yet)! His Shit Is Hot!" – Pimp C letter to Wendy Day, June 2005

———————

"BMF changed [Atlanta]. When [L.A. Reid and Babyface] left our city, it opened the door for people to believe in what BMF stood for. Like, fuck what the music is [about]. We got that *money*." – Big Gipp

With the OutKast collaboration in steady rotation and the timing finally looking right for the album to drop over the summer, Chad hoped to secure a few more high-profile features. Memphitz brought UGK an Akon beat called "Hard As Hell," a departure from the traditional UGK sound. While Chad thought the record was "jammin'," others weren't so enthusiastic, and the record was pulled from the project.*

Although UGK had previously rejected Jive's idea to duplicate "Big Pimpin'" by working with Timbaland and Jay-Z on *Dirty Money*, Chad now thought it was a good idea. Unfortunately, the opportunity had passed with time. When *FADER* asked if they were working with Timbaland, Chad said he didn't know how to contact him, adding, "If you got his numbers, man, I'd love to link him up."

Chad also hoped to feature Jay-Z on "Everybody Wanna Ball," which sampled his verse from "Big Pimpin'," but the feature never materialized. While he publicly stated that he understood Jay's schedule, he privately griped that he didn't even have a direct contact number and had to go through an assistant to get in touch with him. "That's kind of how Jay-Z is ... that's kind of always how he was," Jeff Sledge says. "I could see Chad being upset about that ... but that's just kind of how Jay [operated]."**

While Chad was incarcerated, Bun's collaborations with hot new artists like Young Jeezy had helped him stay relevant and keep the UGK name alive. (Jeezy credited himself with "singlehandedly help[ing] Bun get back on his feet when the [UGK] shit was falling off.") Although Chad hadn't developed the same type of personal relationship with Jeezy, he was a big fan of his music and counted Jeezy among his favorite rappers.

Still, at the "Get Throwed" video shoot when Chad first came home, something about Jeezy's attitude bothered him. Around that time, Chad recorded a remix to Webbie's "Like That" for the *Pimpalation* project, where Webbie and Lil Boosie name-dropped a long list of female celebrities. While Webbie admired rapper Trina's "big fine ass" and wondered if singer Ciara could "shake that ass on this nine-piece," Boosie fantasized about making "a caramel sundae" with socialite Paris Hilton and having singer Fantasia's lips "put [him] to sleep."

But on Pimp C's verse, aside from Prince's lovers Vanity 6 and Apollonia, the only female celebrity he named was Young Jeezy's girlfriend: singer Keyshia Cole. "Tell that gu'l Keyshia Cole she need to give me some pussy / She shoulda cheated with Sweet Jones, 'cause that nigga's a rookie," Pimp rapped, a reference to her 2006 record "I Should Have Cheated." (The only other

———

(*The Akon/UGK record "Hard As Hell" was released later on UGK *4 Life*.)
(**"C would get mad at everybody, but I really don't think ... he had any real issue or beef with Jay," says Mama Wes.)

womens' names he mentioned were hurricanes, offering to "sweep through your pussy like Rita or Katrina.")

Pimp generally avoided name-dropping female celebrities, knowing that it could be misinterpreted. In *OZONE's* annual "sex issue," rappers were asked to envision celebrities of the opposite gender in bed. It was intended to be humorous, and most artists gladly participated for entertainment purposes, but Pimp C declined.

"I don't think that's a good thing to do," he said. "Some of these ladies … might have relationships with guys that I know, which is disrespectful for me to talk in a sexual way about one of my friends' wives or girlfriends." The Keyshia Cole mention seemed too deliberate to be a mere coincidence; that wasn't his style. Chad told his cousin Ed the line was a slight shot at Jeezy, just to see if he'd react.

Chad's real issue with Jeezy was deeper than rap. Jeezy's ascent in the rap game coincided with the rise (and fall) of the Black Mafia Family (BMF), a large-scale cocaine trafficking organization attempting to disguise itself as a legitimate record label.

Led by the charismatic Demetrius "Big Meech" Flenory and his behind-the-scenes brother Terry "Southwest T" Flenory, BMF rose to prominence during Chad's incarceration. Although the brothers had started out hustling in Detroit, their base of operations shifted to Atlanta.

BMF was known for pulling up to Atlanta nightclubs one-hundred deep in a parade of luxury cars, everyone wearing black BMF t-shirts and carrying their own bottle of champagne. Club owners both loved and hated them; they attracted chaos and unnecessary drama, but spent ridiculous amounts of money. "They were too flossy, too loud, everywhere they went they rolled so deep that they caused trouble in clubs, fights would break out, people would get shot … It was just too much shit," recalls Wendy Day.

The federal government had been tracking BMF for nearly a decade. BMF had a fleet of vehicles with hidden compartments transporting cash and cocaine from coast to coast. Between 1996 and 2005, authorities seized more than 200 kilograms of cocaine and nearly $4 million dollars in cash connected to BMF in more than 16 seizures across the country.

BMF was making so much money that losing $4 million didn't even bother them. In fact, their biggest problem was how to clean all their dirty money. They bought and leased luxury vehicles under fake names and laundered cash by buying Michigan lottery winners' tickets. Big Meech became known for his over-the-top flamboyance, holding an extravagant birthday party filled with exotic animals and beautiful women. He rented a Miami mansion for $30,000/month, filming BMF's wild excursions all over South Beach for a DVD.

Meech had his own artist, Bleu Davinci, but was also good friends with Young Jeezy. Meech and the BMF crew promoted Jeezy by tossing hundreds of thousands of dollars in Atlanta-area strip clubs while his records played, giving rise to the infamous term "making it rain."

BMF was moving so much product that suppliers were forced to come down on their prices just to do business with them, and even rival dealers were forced to buy from them. Jeezy started calling himself "Mr. 17.5," implying that his drug suppliers were so well-connected they had kilograms of cocaine for the discounted price of $17,500.

According to Big Meech, Jeezy wasn't lying. "Prices [for a kilogram of cocaine] were $16,500 and $17,500 in Atlanta before BMF got indicted," Big Meech confirms. "Atlanta had prices like we had borders surrounding us."

BMF was so bold they enacted a prominent billboard in downtown Atlanta which read "The World Is Ours," a reference to the cocaine-kingpin movie *Scarface*. It was the beginning of the end. The DEA felt like BMF was taunting them, and began working with the IRS to bring down the organization.

BMF started unraveling when one of their mid-level distributors Omari "O-Dog" McCree ("745s, back to back, me and O-Dog," Jeezy rapped on "Air Forces") was arrested. Eventually, their behind-the-scenes finance whiz William "Doc" Marshall was pressured into cooperating, and authorities managed to get a wiretap on Meech's brother Terry's phone.

In June 2005, authorities seized 250 kilograms of cocaine and $1.8 million cash from a BMF property in California. The party finally came to an end on October 20, 2005, when a federal indictment was filed against Big Meech, Terry, and 25 others in the BMF organization.* Authorities snatched up Terry's luxurious Mulholland Drive home in Los Angeles, Big Meech's Buckhead mansion in Atlanta, eight homes in Michigan, two Bentleys, two BMWs, an Aston Martin, and 13 other vehicles. The federal government estimated BMF's profits at $270 million.

At the height of BMF's reign, in July 2005, Young Jeezy's debut album *Let's Get It: Thug Motivation 101* dropped. Propelled by the street cred he'd obtained through his affiliation with BMF, the album sold two million copies. Critics described it as "endless celebration of Jeezy's drug sales." Bun applauded the fact that his records were "based off reality," telling AllHipHop that you'd have to "damn near be the junkie or be the actual cocaine" to "give more inside information" on the drug game than Jeezy.

But some, like Chad, didn't like the fact that Jeezy was reaping all the benefits of his affiliation with BMF while avoiding all the consequences. Chad and Meech had known each other since the late 90s when Meech was already a well-known figure in Atlanta's underworld, occasionally crossing paths at local strip clubs. (Meech like to joke that his cousin Terrance "Texas Cuz" Short, who bore an uncanny resemblance to Chad, was Pimp C's twin brother.) Although they weren't close friends, they respected each other, and it was more about the principle.

Chad complained that Jeezy was "snitching on records," making money by shining a spotlight on active drug dealers. "[Jeezy was] … rapping about that shit before them [BMF] niggas got locked up," says Young Smitty. "They was still active drug dealers … Jeezy was selling dope, but he wasn't … [on the level of] Meech and them. He was riding their coattails."

———————

Back in the 90s, rap collaborations usually took place between friends. Money was rarely exchanged; instead, they operated on an unspoken barter system: You do a verse for me, I'll do a verse for you. UGK had never attempted to seek out the hottest emcees for features – they simply worked with their friends. "[Back in the day], it was special," says Sleepy Brown. "Back then, Hip-Hop for us was a little more smaller, so it wasn't as hard to get with other artists."

By the time Chad returned to the rap game, the small, community vibe, the musical kinship with fellow comrades like the Dungeon Family, had given way to a multi-billion dollar industry. And the new generation's business model, where everything was filtered through managers and agents and label reps, struck Pimp as fake.

"The artists [now], they just don't give a shit," says the Geto Boys' Willie D. "They don't care about what you've done or who you are. They're like, 'Gimme my money.' Even the producers … [they] come out the gate hitting established artists up [trying to sell tracks]. They don't understand the concept of using certain situations as stepping stones."

Collaborations became less organic, often orchestrated by record label executives. Now that ProTools sessions could be emailed, artists could collaborate by recording their verses in different locations instead of vibing together in the studio. "You need that vibe, with all the complexities that artists bring to the table," adds Willie D.

"The Southern [rap] business always [operated on love] until money [and] greed came along," says producer Mannie Fresh. "[It changed] when we started doing 'big homie business' … [that's] when we started letting somebody else who really didn't even love music – [who] loved money – start controlling shit."

New artists like Jeezy, some felt, were representative of the changes that had taken place while Chad was away. "[The BMF era] really changed [Atlanta]," says Big Gipp. "It opened the

(*A week before his trial was set to begin, Big Meech pled guilty to Continuing Criminal Enterprise and money laundering. He was sentenced to 30 years in federal prison and is scheduled to be released in May 2032.)

door for people to believe in what BMF stood for: like, fuck what the music is [about]. We got that *money* … It destroyed us being a city of music [and we] became 'dope boys in the trap.'"

"I don't know specifically where the change came from … I just remember there being a shift," agrees Gipp's ex-wife Joi Gilliam. "It [used to be] about art and originality and authenticity, and suddenly … everything was based around money."

Jeezy had never been shy about proclaiming his love for UGK. He'd proudly said that "Pocket Full of Stones" was his anthem when he was a young teenager in Macon selling drugs to buy a new pair of Jordans.* When he reached out in 2006 asking UGK to feature on a Shawty Redd-produced track titled "Dickies," Pimp rushed to knock out his verse in time for the song to make Jeezy's second album. He assumed that when the time came, Jeezy would return the favor.

Wendy Day, who had shifted her focus to helping independent labels get off the ground, had relocated to Atlanta to work with Jeezy's label Corporate Thugz Entertainment (CTE). The sense around the CTE office, as Wendy recalls it, was that "Dickies" just wasn't good enough. "It wasn't a hit record," Wendy says. "And [Jeezy] was trying to deliver an album full of hit records."

When Jeezy's album *The Inspiration: Thug Motivation 102* hit stores, the UGK feature wasn't on it. Pimp, feeling a little slighted, tried reaching out to see if they could get "Dickies" back for the UGK album and was told that Jeezy was going to use the song on a mixtape instead. Now Pimp was irritated; he'd done the track for free with the understanding that it would be on the album. "Man, this nigga put that shit on a mixtape," he complained.

Something sparked in Pimp's memory, and he remembered seeing Jeezy in Atlanta back in the late 90s. At the time, Jeezy was just a youngster known as "Lil J," far from the drug kingpin persona he was now portraying. "Man, I *remember* that nigga, man!" Pimp exclaimed. "I remember that nigga, with the backpacks and the pant leg rolled up!"

Even if "Dickies" wasn't an option, Pimp still wanted to get a Jeezy feature on the UGK album. But when he called the number Jeezy had given him, it wasn't Jeezy's number, it was his business partner Demetrius "Kinky B" Ellerbee. Pimp tried calling several other people and kept getting the runaround. When he finally got Jeezy's direct number, he called repeatedly, but there was no answer. He even left a voicemail message, which tugged at his ego. "He took that shit as a direct 'fuck you,'" recalls Hezeleo.

Instead of a call back from Jeezy, Pimp got a call from Jive Records asking why they'd received an invoice from Jeezy's record label for $60,000. Pimp tried to stay calm, assuming it was just a misunderstanding. He called Wendy Day, complaining that he hadn't been able to reach Jeezy. Wendy happened to be at the CTE office, where she saw Jeezy in another room. "Call him right now," she urged quietly. "He's in the office right now. He'll pick up. Just call him."

Pimp did call, and Jeezy sent the call to voicemail. Pimp was livid. Shortly after, Pimp got a call from Jeezy's manager Kevin "Coach K" Lee. Mentioning the invoice, Pimp said there had been some type of misunderstanding.**

"Yeah, it's a mistake, man," Coach K said. "Jeezy said you get the homeboy rate – $50,000."

As soon as they hung up the phone, Pimp went ballistic. "Man, I just did this nigga a feature for *no* money!" he yelled. "I ain't even charge this nigga!" En route from Port Arthur to Houston, he spent the rest of the hour-long drive venting to his passenger Big L.

"That muthafucker … I did something for him for free! We're bigger than he is!" Pimp

(*Jeezy quoted Pimp C's verse from Three 6 Mafia's "Sippin' On Some Syrup" on his infamous diss record aimed at fellow Atlanta rapper Gucci Mane, offering a $10,000 reward to anyone who could bring him Gucci Mane's chain. "You need to take that monkey shit off, you embarrassing us," Jeezy said.)

(**Young Jeezy did not respond to interview requests. Jeezy has since parted ways with his former business partner Kinky B and former manager Coach K, and both filed separate lawsuits against him. Kinky B's lawsuit alleged that Jeezy had "intentionally misappropriated, diverted and/or converted" millions of dollars. Both men declined to be interviewed in light of their pending litigation, but they believe that Jeezy and Pimp did speak directly at some point, and Jeezy personally quoted Pimp a price of $50,000 or more. The invoice was not merely a misunderstanding. "Man, I did four verses for them dudes for free, man," Jeezy told AllHipHop in defense of his fee. It was unclear which songs he was referring to.)

seethed late that night on the phone with Wendy Day. "How is he going to turn around and charge me?! Fuck him!"

Mannie Fresh understood why Pimp would be upset with Jeezy. "Damn, dude, this is the rebirth of UGK," Mannie says. "You don't want to help out with that [even though] you say you been repping them all your life?"

"It wasn't just Jeezy, it was Ludacris too," says Big Gipp. "He felt disrespected." Pimp had been offended when Ludacris' label issued a five-figure invoice after he'd done a verse free of charge for Ludacris' "Do Your Time." ("If you wanna charge Bun B $50,000 for a verse and then try to come back to me and pay me one dollar to get me on your album, guess what you are?! You fake and you garbage!" Pimp complained later in his infamous Hot 107.9 radio interview.)*

Pimp took offense to new artists like Jeezy and Ludacris charging him, when he had helped pave the way for them to be able to command such hefty fees. "Pimp felt like, Goodie Mob, OutKast, UGK, Scarface ... man, we fought the battles for you niggas to be able to be asking for $40,000, $50,000 a verse," says Big Gipp. "And when we ask for a verse y'all hit us with [invoices]? [He felt] like, '[Get the] fuck outta here.'"

———————

Since he came home from prison, Chad had been proud to announce that he was drug free. "At this point in my life I'm really not a drug user, I'm like a square right now," he'd told *OZONE* in February 2007. "I don't see any billionaires getting high. Do you?"

At the same time, he wasn't trying to cover up his past. "A whole bunch of these rappers be hiding in the closet doing a whole bunch of gay things, and all up in the bathroom trying to do some drugs they ashamed of," he added. "Anything I ever did in life, I'm not ashamed of it. [But] that don't mean I'm going to indulge in everything and ... be [like] Tony Montana [in *Scarface*] trying to see how many drugs I can take, 'cause a whole bunch of my friends died taking drugs."

When asked about his line on "Pourin' Up" ("let me snort some white girl up off your titty / you heard me right, we play with our nose"), he explained, "[Cocaine is] the devil. I'm convinced that anybody that deals in coke, sellin' it or using it, is dealin' with the devil. [So] how do I rap about sellin' coke and snortin' powder? I done danced with the devil before. It don't mean I'm dancing with him today. I'm convinced that cocaine is the devil – powder form, rock form, or whatever form they put it in."

He'd had a lengthy conversation with Nitacha after he came home, assuring her that he planned to stay sober for his kids. In *OZONE*, he'd concluded that all "shit [he] had no business doin'" was only "detrimental to [his] success" and "a waste of time and money."

But now that the money was rolling in again, it was easy to forget those lessons. Plus, as he explained to Naztradamus, who was filming him for the *Making of the Album* documentary, he had a lot on his shoulders. "He was like, 'Nobody knew me when I went in ... but when I came back out, everybody knew me,'" remembers Naztradamus. "I don't know if he was ready for that ... [it seemed] like there was a lot of pressure on him that he didn't expect."

Mama Wes still came to some shows, but didn't have the energy to accompany Chad everywhere the road. Concerned that he was "surrounded by a bunch of yes people" who were all "scared of [his] ass," she relied on Heather and Hezeleo to make sure he stayed sober. She was concerned that he had people like DJ B-Do and T.O.E. around, who had access to drugs and wouldn't hesitate to give Chad whatever he wanted.** She'd never liked T.O.E., who didn't "look right" to her. "I had a trust issue with him," she says. "I didn't want C [around] that element."

———————

(*It is not clear which song Pimp was upset over, but Ludacris was featured on "Trill Recognize Trill" from Bun's album Trill and Pimp C was featured on "Do Your Time" from Ludacris' album Release Therapy. Ludacris' manager Chaka Zulu, who was a good friend of Pimp C's, says he was never aware of any problems between Pimp C and Ludacris.)

(**In one unconfirmed story, Jada says she later overheard DJ B-Do and T.O.E. laughing about the time Chad called them asking for some cocaine. Instead of "punching him in the mouth" as he'd previously instructed them to do, they allegedly gave it to him anyway.)

Mama Wes knew about the pact Chad and Heather had made to support each other in their promise to stay cocaine-free, but she also knew that the temptation would always be there. "[Cocaine's trendiness] comes and goes," Chad told *OZONE*. "It surges and then it dies out and then it comes back ... but from what I can see, ain't nobody slowing down with the use."

One warm weekend in early summer, while Chad and Chinara were in Houston, Heather volunteered to take Corey and Christian to go swimming. She laid out tanning while they swam at the pool at her Beaumont apartment, leaving her phone inside. Hours later, she came inside and saw an urgent text from Chad. "I need you to come to me right now," it read. "By yourself."

She called him immediately, apologizing. Chad told her it was okay, but his tone seemed off. Heather couldn't think of anything that would be so urgent – except the promise they'd made to hold each other accountable. She got a sinking feeling in her stomach. Had he slipped?

Chad had always been nocturnal, which his mother always attributed to the fact that he was born around midnight. He called Mama Wes daily between 2 AM and 4:30 AM, and, if he was in town, invited her to come meet him at the Waffle House. She adjusted her schedule to accommodate him, tucking Corey in every evening at 6 PM and retiring herself by 7 PM.

If Mama Wes didn't feel like getting out of bed to meet him at Waffle House, Chad would often call his cousin Ed in the middle of the night and ask him to come over and barbecue. The other option was Happy Donuts, which opened every morning at 4 AM. If Chad had a taste for Bear Claw donuts and the Texas breakfast specialty Bourdain Kolaches, he'd ring the doorbell at T.O.E.'s mom's house. "Man, let's go to Happy Donuts," he'd insist, as T.O.E. stumbled to the door blearly-eyed, mumbling, "You know what time it is?" (T.O.E.'s mother was willing to overlook this after Chad charmed her by promising to make her son rich.)

If it wasn't a school night, he'd take Chad Jr., always amused by his father's "awkward scheduling," for a 5 AM father/son excursion to Happy Donuts. Chad Jr. enjoyed the silent comradery, riding alone with his father in the early morning hours when the city wasn't yet awake.

Chad would call Ronda Forrest at 4 AM just to vent, ignoring her protests about her sleeping husband. ("Tell that nigga shut up," Chad would say.) "To him, 4 AM was just normal time," says Mama Wes' houseguest Travis. "I guess he thought everybody would be up at 4:00 in the morning, 'cause he would just call and say, 'What are you doing?'"

Everyone was accustomed to Chad's nocturnal nature, but over the summer of 2007, his schedule became increasingly erratic and his moods increasingly volatile. Wendy Day remained a confidant and was frequently the recipient of his 4 AM calls when he needed to vent. He complained that Bun had changed; although he loved him like a brother, they couldn't get along, and said Bun had started acting "Hollywood" after he signed with Rap-A-Lot.

But most of his wrath, as Wendy remembers it, was directed at his wife. "He always dogged her to me ... [so] I would just never bring [her] up," says Wendy. "He didn't like her. [He said] she was an anchor around his neck, she didn't understand him, she was too demanding on him ... he [said he] was going to leave her."

When he wasn't calling Wendy at 4 AM to vent, he was calling me.* I was usually still up and found it flattering. Mostly, he talked, and I listened. He complained about rappers sending him invoices when he'd done verses for them for free; he mentioned Ludacris by name, but never told me about the "Dickies" drama with Jeezy. He thought it was hypocritical for Jay-Z to call him his "brother" on stage at shows, but he didn't even have his direct phone number.**

(*He also complained to me about Wendy, saying that she "tells everybody's business." When I mention this during our interview, she laughs. "I do... I absolutely do, it's very true," she agrees. "I'm doing it right now.")
(**On this point, Mama Wes says Chad was "lying his ass off" and it wouldn't have been hard for him to get in touch with Jay-Z directly. Jay-Z frequently called Mama Wes at the Shreveport Ave. house, and had a knack for calling when Chad happened to be there. "That nigga can *smell* me," Chad theorized.)

Over time, his rants became increasingly bizarre. Frequently he talked about Superhead, or a MediaTakeout-sparked rumor that a Houston rapper had HIV. (The rumor was so widespread that Slim Thug mailed his HIV test, proving he was negative, to media outlets.) Chad told me he knew exactly who it was.* Another frequent topic of discussion involved Gloria Velez; he often implied that she had blackmail-worthy information on other rappers.

"We know who getting fucked with the dildos in the ass by the broad," Chad told WordofSouth.com. He bragged to AllHipHop, "I'm plugged in [to] the pimp wire … when these niggas come to town and do some funny ass shit [I hear about it]. The pimp wire don't lie."

But what concerned me most was that he'd started repeating himself. Sometimes he made perfect sense; other times he was telling the same story as the night before. At times, he sounded so amped up that I couldn't help but wonder if he was under the influence of something.

I wasn't well-versed in the telltale indicators of cocaine use, but as a former user herself, Heather knew all the signs. Small things, like the way he sniffed his nose, made her suspicious. Mike Mo didn't see drug use, but did see a noticeable shift in Chad's attitude. "It was uncontrollable," Mike Mo says. "I thought it was just mainly his personality that was getting out of hand."

Since the "Int'l Player's Anthem" video shoot, Chad had been seeing Ayesha occasionally when he was in Los Angeles. He was spending a lot of time in the studio mixing and mastering the album; Ayesha had little interest in the music business, but kept him company while he was in town. She was amused at the contradiction between his pimp persona and real life, in which she considered him "the most romantic guy ever."

When Ayesha came to his hotel room for the first time, Chad kept interrupting the conversation to go to the bathroom. *He has to pee a lot,* Ayesha thought, chalking it up to the fact that they were drinking. But as the night went on, it seemed like something more than alcohol. He was talking unusually fast. *What the hell? What kind of drugs is this dude on?* Ayesha wondered.

Chad again left Ayesha lounging on the bed and went to the bathroom. But this time, the minutes dragged by and he still hadn't returned.

Suddenly, there was a loud crashing sound. Then, silence. Ayesha started to panic and knocked gently on the bathroom door. "Are you okay?" she asked quietly, hoping not to embarrass him.

"Shit…." she heard Chad mumble through the door. *"Fuck."*

Hesitantly, Ayesha reached for the doorknob, which was unlocked, and slowly pushed the door open. Chad was on the ground face-forward, his pants down around his ankles, the jewelry and cash he'd had in his pocket scattered. His glasses, which were out of reach, had fallen off.

"Oh, my God," Ayesha gasped, attempting to help him up, but struggling under his weight. She helped him walk back to the bedroom and lay down, then, once he was comfortable, cleaned up the bathroom and straightened up all the jewelry and cash into a pile on the counter.

Chad was asleep when she returned to bed. She spent the night but barely slept, worried that things would be awkward the next morning.

When Chad woke up, he didn't remember anything that had happened. They finally discussed the incident a week later. According to Ayesha, Chad explained that he'd been using cocaine and when mixed with his prescription medication, it sometimes caused him to lose consciousness. He explained that he'd stopped sipping syrup for the same reason.

He dismissed cocaine as his vice, reasoning that everybody had "they thang." Ayesha's was alcohol, and he suggested they should stop together.

To her embarrassment, Chad dubbed Ayesha "Cocaine" and began introducing her to friends as such. He gave her a shout-out over a David Banner beat which would later become

(*Pimp C mentioned this rapper by name on UGK's "Fly Lady," but the line was censored on the final edit. "Bitch you looking funny, you been fucking with that [name omitted]? / Oh, you burned, fuckin' germs, got that gangsta STD," he rapped. Since this rumor has never been proven to be true, we will not name the rapper.)

"Midnight Hoes":

I got a young yella hamma, call the girl Cocaine
'Cause the pussy like dope, swallow it all don't choke
Got that red pussy hair, nigga, smell it in the air, nigga
She don't wear draws, got them deep pussy walls

———————

Around the end of May, Pimp C did a show in Moss Point, Mississippi, where he exchanged contact info with a local clothing store owner. The owner passed Pimp C's number along to an up-and-coming rapper from nearby Pass Christian, a tiny town on the Gulf Coast.

Craig Isabelle couldn't believe he really had Pimp C's phone number. He'd always idolized UGK and the Geto Boys, trekking to Be-Bop Records in nearby Biloxi to pick up cassette tapes whenever a new release dropped. As a young teenager, he happened across someone selling a stolen 17-shot Glock pistol; he bought it and proudly toted it everywhere. His friends dubbed him "Seventeen." A troublemaker, his parents shipped him off to military school. It was there that he started rapping, using the Roman numerals "XVII" as his rap name.

XVII was comfortable dropping underground projects, moving a few thousand units locally. He spent the rest of his time hustling with his partner Robert "Polo" Anderson. "There ain't nothing to do [in Pass Christian] but sell drugs," says XVII. "We [never] really left home."

It was Hurricane Katrina in 2005 that forced XVII out of his comfort zone. His family left town with nothing but a laundry basket full of clothes, expecting there might be some minor flooding, but when they returned, their home of 24 years was nothing but a concrete slab. "That shit looked like somebody blew up the inside with dynamite," XVII recalls. "The front steps and the front door was still there, but both sides of the house was just *gone*."

XVII and Polo relocated for a year, stepping up their hustle to feed their children. "[Selling drugs] ain't nothing to glorify … [but] we was doing what we had to do," XVII says. Once things were almost back to normal, XVII had enough money flowing to launch his rap career properly. He'd been in Atlanta recording with Yo Gotti and Bohagon and was headed back again to work with Pastor Troy. His album *Certified* was almost complete, and XVII didn't think there was any point in calling Pimp C; he probably wouldn't be able to afford him anyway.

"Call him," Polo urged. "As long as you been listening to Pimp, man, you gotta [try]."

XVII called Pimp, nervous, trying to hide the quiver in his voice, and asked what he would charge for a verse. Pimp asked if he was signed to a label.

"No," XVII said.

"You got a distributor?" Pimp asked.

"Naw, I ain't never did none of that," XVII told him. "I sell my records in the streets."

Pimp threw out a number – $15,000 – sounding as if he expected a counter-offer. His price for features usually depended on who was asking. In Port Arthur, when he was approached by up-and-comers who only had a few thousand dollars, he would often shrug and say, "Let's do it."

XVII was relieved; the price wasn't even as high as he'd expected. "Alright," he said. "When you want to do it? I can email it to you."

Pimp paused. "You ain't got no major behind you and you gonna give me $15,000 to feature on your album?"

"Yeah."

"Fuck that. You need to be in Houston tomorrow."

XVII already had plans to record with Pastor Troy the following day. "Pimp, I gotta go to Atlanta tomorrow," he apologized. "I gotta do this song with Troy."

Pimp thought he was referring to Lil Troy. "Who?! Lil Troy?!" he said, his voice rising. "What the fuck you gonna do something with him for!? That pussy-ass nigga done ran to Atlanta!?"

CHAPTER 47

"If you're gonna go into battle with somebody, you wanna take Pimp C."
— Willie D, FOX News, December 2007

———————

"C *had* to have something controversial. He *had* to have something to fight about. And if he didn't have anything to fight for, then he would get depressed."
— Mama Wes

Thursday, June 17, 1998
Nacogdoches, Texas

Nine years earlier, it was just another routine Thursday morning when narcotics officer Kent Graham pulled in to his usual spot on the grassy median along Interstate 59 north of Houston. It was just past 8 AM when a large green van passing by caught his attention. "It was an incredibly large vehicle for just two people, and I didn't see a bunch of packages or clothes or suitcases or anything like that in the vehicle when it came by," Graham said later. "I thought … that was kind of a waste of a large vehicle just for two people."

On a hunch, thinking it might be stolen, Graham pulled the van over. (He later justified the traffic stop by saying they'd swerved into the next lane.) The driver, Dexter Thomas, produced his driver's license and explained that his passenger, Troy Birklett, a.k.a. "Lil Troy," had rented the vehicle.

Officer Graham skimmed the Avis rental car agreement, which showed that the van was actually rented to a woman named Darlene Murray.* Officer Graham asked Dexter where they were going.

"Shreveport," Dexter replied.

"You going gambling?" Graham asked.

"No, sir," Dexter answered. "We're going to court."

"Is it a criminal or civil case?" Graham asked.

"I'm not sure," Dexter admitted. "It's my little brother."

Graham asked how long they planned to stay in Shreveport; Dexter said they would be returning to Houston right after court.

While Dexter waited at the rear of the vehicle, Officer Graham walked over to the passenger side and asked Lil Troy the same questions. Troy said they were going to court in Shreveport for *his* brother, and planned to stay the night. "Depending on what the lawyers say," he explained, "We might stay at my auntie's."

To Graham, the conflicting statements about the "brother" seemed "highly suspicious," especially since the person who rented the van wasn't there. After confirming that Dexter and Troy were not related and therefore could not have the same brother, Graham patted down both men and asked if he could search the van. Dexter agreed.

When Graham opened the rear hatchback, he caught an immediate whiff of fabric softener.

———

(*Darlene, a girlfriend of Troy's, had actually added Troy to the rental agreement as an additional driver. Officer Graham would later testify that he was never given that part of the agreement and was never told who she was.)

Fabric softener was a popular way for drug smugglers to try to throw off drug-sniffing dogs. During Graham's police training, he'd spent hours learning to distinguish between the smell of air freshener and fabric softener.

Graham climbed into the back of the van, where the scent led to a small storage compartment. Inside was a suspicious-looking bundle which contained 2.5 kilograms of cocaine.

Six days later, Lil Troy's *Sittin' Fat Down South* was released. The compilation album was a cut-and-paste job orchestrated by producer Bruce "Grim" Rhodes using old verses Troy had purchased over the years from various rappers. Troy used unauthorized 10-year-old Scarface vocals on two songs, "Small Time" and "Another Head Put to Rest."

The standout track by far, "Wanna Be A Baller," was led by a catchy hook sung by Big T and featured verses from Troy's artists Yungstar and Lil Will, and Fat Pat's brother Big Hawk of the SUC.* "Wanna Be A Baller" exploded, reaching #6 on the *Billboard* charts.**

In November 1998, federal charges related to the cocaine seizure were filed against Troy. His attorney argued that the traffic stop was unconstitutional. "It appears that Officer Graham [only] became suspicious of this vehicle because two black males were driving a late model vehicle," Troy's attorney wrote. Prosecutors said it didn't matter, since Dexter had given "valid consent" to search the vehicle.

On the day Troy's trial was set to begin in February 1999, an agreement was reached. Under federal sentencing guidelines, someone convicted of possessing 2.5 kilograms of cocaine would be sentenced to 5-40 years. But under the terms of Troy's sealed plea agreement, the cocaine charge would be dismissed. He would only plead guilty to "using a communication device to facilitate the commission of a felony" and serve less than four years.

Between March and September 1999, Lil Troy became a frequent "source of information" for local police. Officers praised him for giving information which proved "to be truthful, credible and reliable in excess of ten (10) occasions."***

When *Sittin' Fat Down South* went gold independently off the strength of "Wanna Be A Baller," Universal Records offered Lil Troy a distribution deal and re-released his album on April 20, 1999. While Lil Troy was collaborating with police, the album would go on to sell nearly two million copies worldwide. Troy loved to brag that he was the first Houston rapper to go platinum, but the ironic truth was that "Wanna Be A Baller" *did not even contain his vocals*. In fact, he only rapped on six of the album's 14 songs. (Scarface actually went platinum first with 1994's *The Diary*.)

As *Sittin' Fat Down South* was selling millions of copies, Lil Troy wasn't sharing the proceeds with his team. Initially, Troy credited producer Grim with the project's success, but when the money came rolling in, Grim claimed Troy hadn't paid him anything towards the agreed 3% producer's royalty.****

Lil Troy had recruited journalist Matt Sonzala to write his biography and other content for his website, then disappeared without paying the paltry $250 fee. With a newborn daughter, Sonzala was struggling to provide for his growing family when Troy finally pulled up to Son-

(*There were several versions of "Wanna Be A Baller." Many sources attribute the hook on "Wanna Be a Baller" to Fat Pat, but this is incorrect.)

(**"Wanna Be A Baller" was so ubiquitous that Pimp C referenced it on Too $hort's 1999 record "Playaz Life," rhyming, "Comin' down on 'em in a candy toy / Livin' like a baller like that nigga Lil Troy." Troy had relatives in Port Arthur who lived next door to DJ Bird's mother, so Pimp and Troy had been acquaintances for years.)

(***This statement is included in an affidavit used to obtain a search warrant for Mark Potts' home. It does not specifically mention Lil Troy's name; the informant is only referred to as the "SOI" or "source of information." Potts allegedly told Scarface that the source was Lil Troy, and both case files corroborate this accusation. On the intro to Scarface's 2008 album *Emeritus*, J. Prince instructs, "Yo 'Face. You know the homie Lil' Potts is still doing twelve years behind this clown, so expose this snitch nigga Lil Troy.")

(****In February 2003, Grim sued Lil Troy for $1.3 million dollars in royalties. A judge granted Grim a $200,000 judgment and Lil Troy filed bankruptcy to avoid paying.)

zala's house in a Mercedes. Troy, wearing a pile of platinum chains and flashy jewelry, puffed on a blunt as he told Sonzala, "*Maaan,* things have just been kinda hard lately. I ain't got the money to pay you right now. I'm sorry, man."

Sonzala stared at the expensive rings on Troy's finger, thinking of his newborn daughter inside who needed diapers and food. *Fuck you,* he thought.

Houston police had been hearing about a major drug supplier who went by the nickname "Mexican." Lil Troy told police that "Mexican" was a man named Mark Potts, and allowed them to record him calling Potts to discuss large cocaine purchases. Police began regular surveillance of Potts' unassuming three-bedroom home in northeast Houston.

On September 8, 1999, Troy stopped by Potts' house and reported to police that there were several kilograms of cocaine in plain sight. Six days later, Troy called Potts to come meet him at a nearby gas station to pick up some money. Police pulled Potts over as he left his house.

With a search warrant obtained with information provided to them by Lil Troy, police searched Potts' house and found 50 kilograms of cocaine in the attic and $118,304 cash in the trunk of a 1969 Chevrolet Camaro in the garage. They also seized two Harley-Davidson motorcycles, a Rolex, a loaded .38 revolver, and a triple beam scale.*

The officer who obtained the search warrant later acknowledged that the informant who led them to Potts was "given judicial consideration for a pending case" in exchange for his cooperation. On September 23, nine days after police raided Potts' home, the federal government filed a 5K1.1 motion in Lil Troy's case, asking the judge to give Troy a lenient sentence. Prosecutors wrote that Troy had "made a good faith effort to provide substantial assistance and has in fact, provided substantial assistance to the United States of America and the State of Texas in the investigation and prosecution of other cocaine dealers in Houston, Texas."

Lil Troy was scheduled to turn himself in on November 8, but a judge granted him a three week extension to do shows. (His attorney argued that he needed the money to pay off his court fees.) After Troy turned himself in on November 29, 1999, Scarface sued him for $500,000 for using his vocals on *Sittin' Fat Down South.* ("You gotta pay! You can't just use my shit for free," says Scarface. "The fuck you think this is!?")

Reluctantly, Lil Troy agreed to pay Scarface $220,000 to settle the lawsuit. "The 'Wanna Be A Baller' song is what sold my album, so he wasn't entitled to trying to rape me for half-million dollars," Troy complained to SOHH.com.

While he was incarcerated in Beaumont, Lil Troy happened to cross paths with Scarface's friend George Simmons and started asking questions about Scarface's involvement in his case. "I never would go into detail about it, so he stopped really asking me," George says.

Lil Troy was released on March 16, 2001 after serving 10 months in a federal prison and six months in a halfway house. "[If you] snitch on your whole city and get a whole bunch of people dads and uncles and brothers locked up so you can get a two year sentence and come home quick, you're a snitch ass nigga," Pimp C told *OZONE.* "The only reason a person would wanna spill the beans on somebody is to destroy them or get theyself out of trouble."

With bad blood already brewing between Scarface and Troy, when "some serious muthafuckers" told Scarface about the Potts situation, he felt obligated to address it on the Geto Boys' 2005 album *The Foundation.*

"We don't talk to police, we don't make a peace bond," was the chorus on "G-Code." Scarface rapped that "real niggas never squeal," adding, "Right here the truth revealed, Troy you a mouse / Yeah you rappin' but the homie Lil' Potts can't get out."

Even though he didn't specifically name "Lil Troy," Houston understood. "A hit dog will

(*Potts was found guilty on federal cocaine charges and sentenced to 13 years in prison. He was released in August 2009 after serving 10 years. He was unable to be reached for comment.)

IN THE UNITED STATES DISTRICT COURT
FILED - CLERK
U.S. DISTRICT COURT

FOR THE EASTERN DISTRICT OF TEXAS

99 SEP 23 AM 9: 57

LUFKIN DIVISION

TX EASTERN LUFKIN

BY_____

UNITED STATES OF AMERICA	*	
VS.	* CRIMINAL NO. 9:98-CR-41	
TROY BIRKLETT	*	

<u>GOVERNMENT'S 5K1.1 MOTION FOR DOWNWARD DEPARTURE</u>

TO THE HONORABLE JUDGE OF SAID COURT:

Now comes the United States of America, by and through the United States Attorney for the

Eastern District of Texas, and files this Motion for the Court to consider a downward departure

pursuant to §5K1.1 of the Federal Sentencing Guidelines.

I.

The District Court pursuant to §5K1.1 of the Federal Sentencing Guidelines and Title 18,

United States Code, Section 3553(e), may downwardly depart from the prescribed sentencing

guidelines to reflect a Defendant's substantial assistance in an investigation and/or prosecution of

other individuals who have committed an offense.

II.

With respect to the Defendant, TROY BIRKLETT, the Government states the following:

1.   The Defendant, TROY BIRKLETT, has made a good faith effort to provide substantial assistance and has in fact, provided substantial assistance to the United States of America and the State of Texas in the investigation and prosecution of other cocaine dealers in Houston, Texas.

2.   More specifically, the Defendant, TROY BIRKLETT, provided a detailed overview of his own involvement in the distribution of cocaine. He identified his main source of supply and agreed to participate in making consensually recorded phone calls to his source of supply and made a surveilled visit to that individuals' residence. He was able to report to the Houston Police Department that the individual had two kilos of cocaine at his residence. Thereafter, the police department executed a search warrant on the residence and discovered fifty kilograms of cocaine and a large amount of U.S. currency. In addition, the officers seized three expensive vehicles at the scene. Finally, the Court should be advised that the individual that Mr. Birklett cooperated against is now cooperating with the authorities. The Government will elaborate more on this operation with testimony during the sentencing hearing.

III.

Without question, the Defendant was deeply involved in cocaine trafficking. However, the

Defendant demonstrated considerable determination in assisting the United States Government and

the State of Texas, and the Government believes that a downward departure would be an appropriate

reward for BIRKLETT.

Above: **Lil Troy's 5K1** filed by the federal government as a reward for his cooperation.
(Editor's Note: This image is the combination of two pages to condense space.)

holler," Scarface shrugs. "Shit … I know a million [people named] Troy."

Media outlets wondered why Scarface even bothered mentioning him. "'Wanna Be A Baller' was 10 years ago; we wouldn't even be talking about Lil Troy still if not for Scarface," pointed out HipHopDX.

"I was [just] standing up for what was right," Scarface says. "What's right is right and what's wrong is wrong. If you gave up any information on any-muthafuckin'-body you wrong as fuck, especially if you was down with it."

When George Simmons' cousin Byron Harris brought Lil Troy a copy of the affidavit from his case which the DEA had tried to use to tie Scarface into the drug conspiracy during their Rap-A-Lot probe, Lil Troy decided to go on the offensive. "Scarface called me a [snitch], I couldn't make no money, he hurt my money for a minute," Troy explained. "So why not hurt his pockets and capitalize at the same time?"

In July 2005, two months after I interviewed Pimp C at the Terrell Unit, I was back in Houston shooting Bun B's *OZONE* cover when I got a call from Lil Troy. I'd never met him and knew nothing about him aside from "Wanna Be A Baller." He told me he had some paperwork to show me, a big story that would be good for *OZONE*, and invited me to come by his house.

Curious, I stopped by. Troy wanted me to interview him about his upcoming album with his 19-year-old son Troy Birklett Jr., a.k.a. "T2." More importantly, though, he wanted to show me the DEA affidavit which he claimed proved Scarface was a snitch.

After reading the affidavit several times, I couldn't understand how it implicated Scarface. It said that he introduced two people who later arranged a drug deal, but there was nothing to indicate that he knew one of the men was an informant, or that he was involved in the deal.

For a second opinion, I asked *OZONE's* attorney, Kyle King, to review the affidavit. "I don't think it would be fair to call [Scarface] a snitch based on the affidavit," King wrote. "There's no information or proof … that Scarface knew the [confidential source Carboni] was a snitch."

I published snippets of the affidavit in *OZONE*, along with a statement from George Simmons. "Lil Troy is using my name and case… to promote a CD or DVD to increase his sales, by falsely accusing one of the best rappers in the rap game and a friend of mine … [of snitching] on me," Simmons wrote. "But now let the truth be told… [Scarface] never did take the stand on me during my trial but my cousin [Byron Harris did]."

After presenting both sides of the story, my article concluded, "Lil Troy … is using [the beef] as a dubious publicity stunt for his upcoming joint album with his son."

Troy used the affidavit as the basis for a DVD titled *Paperwork: The Scarface G-Code Violations*. On it, Lil Troy's mother claimed that she used to feed Scarface and wash his clothes when he stayed at their house. In another scene Troy waved an assault rifle in one hand and the affidavit in the other, saying, "I know this here must be breaking you Scarface fans' hearts, but the truth must be told." He was backed by Byron Harris, who complained, "I did six muthafuckin' years and that bitch [Scarface] ain't do a day."

Such an accusation had the potential to destroy Scarface's life, and he was livid. "If I ever told on anybody, for *anythang*," he emphatically told radio host Combat Jack, "I want my entire fuckin' bloodline to be wiped out, from the oldest person in my family to the youngest person in my family, myself included."

When Scarface performed at Houston's annual Los Magnificos car show in November 2005, Lil Troy passed out promotional flyers for the DVD at the event. It featured a paragraph from the DEA affidavit, and in red block letters: "LOOK WHO'S TALKING 'SCARFACE.'"

Backstage, Scarface told *Hood News DVD*, "Troy, you's a hoe. The biggest hoe. But I got your ass though. Cryin' on the [stand] testifying against my homeboy, nigga. I know about it."*

During his show, Scarface had his DJ shut the music off as he introduced "G-Code." He'd even brought along a copy of the Federal Sentencing Guideline Handbook, which he waved emphatically. (The handbook showed that Troy should have spent a minimum of five years in prison.) "Troy got popped a few times with the work, right? The muthafucker ain't do but nine to ten months," he yelled.**

Scarface led a chant of "Fuck Troy! Fuck Troy! Fuck Troy!" The crowd of teenagers chanted along, mostly unaware of what it was all about.

At the time, Troy was in serious financial trouble. Not only had he been ordered to pay Grim $200,000, but owed the IRS more than $90,000. A few weeks after the car show, Lil Troy filed bankruptcy.

In the spring of 2006, Lil Troy, DEA affidavit in hand, appeared on DJ Whoo Kid's Shade 45 satellite radio show to promote *Paperwork*.*** He gave out Scarface's home address on the air and suggested that listeners mail him copies of the affidavit to be autographed. DJ Whoo Kid sounded hesitant to take sides, saying, "We gotta get Scarface's input on this."

Troy, who brought his attorney with him, complained that he wasn't invited to *The Source's* "Great Day in Houston" cover shoot. "Ain't nobody come talk to me about that," he grumbled. He also complained bitterly about the $220,000 lawsuit settlement he paid Scarface, asking, "When [did] gangsters start suing each other?"

Less than a month later, Lil Troy did exactly that, filing a lawsuit against Scarface over the lyrics on "G-Code." (Troy had listed a "potential claim against [Scarface] for defamation and slander" as an asset on his bankruptcy filing.) When Scarface didn't show up for a court hearing, a judge granted Lil Troy a default judgment against him for $511,000.

After learning that he legally owed Troy six figures, Scarface hired Warren Fitzgerald, an experienced attorney who worked with Rap-A-Lot. (Coincidentally, Fitzgerald was the same attorney who wrote UGK's 1992 contract with Big Tyme Recordz.) Fitzgerald successfully re-opened the case, got the $511,000 judgment overturned, and set out to find evidence of Lil Troy "snitching."

"Legally, truth is a defense to a defamation," explains Fitzgerald. "So if you can prove that what you said is true, then generally speaking – it's not a defamatory statement." Even though Lil Troy's case file was sealed, with a little persistence, Fitzgerald was able to obtain a copy of Lil Troy's 5K1.1 paperwork where prosecutors applauded him for providing "substantial assistance … in the investigation and prosecution of other cocaine dealers."

Scarface and Fitzgerald brought copies of the 5K1.1 to a deposition at Lil Troy's attorney's office. Confronted with the evidence, Lil Troy dropped his lawsuit. "Don't nobody wanna fight a losing battle," Scarface told HipHopDX.

Although Pimp C knew about the beef, he avoided getting involved until Troy posted a video on YouTube attacking Scarface and Rap-A-Lot. "That shit didn't have nothing to do with me until that muthafucker [posted a video saying] that everybody at Rap-A-Lot is fake, so Lil' J must be fake too," Pimp said later. "When he made that statement, he put me in that shit."

"I actually didn't watch Lil Troy's YouTube shit, because I knew that shit was negative," he

---

(*Potts gave up his right to a jury trial so it seems unlikely that Troy actually testified against him in court. Police said that Troy cooperated with them on more than 10 occasions so it is not known if Scarface may have been referring to a different case.)

(**Troy included snippets of Scarface cussing him out at the car show on his *Paperwork* DVD, laughing, "That nigga sound mad as a muthafucker, huh?")

(***It appears that Lil Troy talked his way onto DJ Whoo Kid's show by playing up a rumored, but non-existent, beef between Scarface and 50 Cent. Whoo Kid was 50 Cent's DJ. The rumor originated with the record "Snitch Niggas," which combined some old Scarface vocals with new verses from Bun B and Z-Ro. On Z-Ro's verse he took a few jabs at 50 Cent, accusing him of "dry snitchin' on BET." Z-Ro later clarified that Scarface and Bun weren't talking about 50 Cent, telling MTV News that they were "just doing a song in general about these snitches.")

admitted. "And I knew that if I watched it, it may actually make me angry for real. Once a person gets angry for real, they're at a disadvantage, ya dig?"

Around the same time Lil Troy posted his YouTube video, Mississippi rapper XVII wrapped up his Atlanta studio session with Pastor Troy and flew to Houston. By phone, Pimp had promised XVII that if he was really doing it that big – flying city to city, studio to studio, buying features without the backing of a major label – he would personally pick him up from the airport with a "red-haired bitch with no drawers on."

Sure enough, when Pimp C pulled up in his Bentley at Houston's Bush Intercontinental airport, red-haired Ayesha was riding shotgun in a skimpy green dress (no underwear, XVII assumed). They headed straight for Mike and Cory Mo's MAD Studios, where XVII pulled out $15,000 cash.

"First of all, how you get all that fucking money on the plane?" Pimp asked. "Just give me seven [thousand]."

XVII handed over $7,000, and Pimp laughed, asking, "You thought I was gonna make you pay $15,000 and you ain't got no major behind you?"

"I didn't know."

"I wouldn't make you pay seven, but I gotta pay my granny's bills and my mama's bills," Pimp explained.

XVII pulled up the Heartbeat-produced track "True Story." Now that Dog and Biz were deceased, Pimp decided it was time to relate the soap opera of the Nashville streets. He still kept in touch with his ex-girlfriend Lanika, who now had an eight-year-old son with Askia "Priest" Covington, the Nashville hustler who gave rapper "Young Buck" his name.* ("Me and Priest had the streets on lock," Young Buck rapped on his 2004 record "Bonafide Hustler.")

When Pimp and Lanika first met back in the mid-90s, she was involved with Nashville drug dealer Terrell McMurry. Terrell also dabbled in the rap game with his group First Born and a record label called Totally Independent Productions.

Pimp didn't like Terrell, and took great pleasure in taking both his girlfriend and his Mustang 5.0 convertible. On the record, he referred to Terrell only as "T." ("Pimp C [kept it] g-code; that's why he didn't say full names," says Biz's brother Troy "T-Roy" Hunter.)

Terrell McMurry and his Hispanic partner Tim Booker had been indicted on federal drug conspiracy charges in late 1999. ("I don't trust no hoes, that's how T got popped / He showed a bitch where his stash was, she told it to the cops," Young Buck rapped on "Bonafide Hustler.") Authorities accused them of bringing more than 100 kilograms of cocaine and hundreds of pounds of marijuana to Nashville every year.

Both McMurry and Booker pled guilty and became the government's star witnesses against more than 20 of their former employees. McMurry was sentenced to serve 162 months (13.5 years) in prison and ordered to forfeit $10 million dollars' worth of assets.**

Young Buck had come a long way since he was a skinny teenager tagging along with Dog and Biz, rapping with DJ Bird in Pimp's garage. After three years of waiting at Cash Money, he hopped on Juvenile's tour bus as Juvenile departed the label. In New York, they met unsigned rappers 50 Cent and Lloyd Banks. 50 and Young Buck hit it off, and 50 bought Buck's record "Bloodhounds."

Shortly after that, 50 Cent met Eminem and Dr. Dre. "Bloodhounds" ended up on his debut album *Get Rich or Die Tryin'*, which sold more than 11 million copies. 50 then signed Young Buck to his G-Unit imprint, and Buck's *Straight Outta Ca$hville* debut sold 300,000 copies in the first week.

(*Their teenage son DJ Priest is now the official DJ for T.I.'s son Domani, and Lanika is his proud "momanager.")
(**McMurry was released from a federal prison in July 2010.)

Young Buck and Young Jeezy had become close friends, and Buck's new catchphrase "Nashville Ten-A-Key" implied that he had the best drug connects and cheapest prices. (Buck's record "4 Kings," which also featured T.I. and Young Jeezy, included Pimp singing a modified version of his memorable appearance on Big Mike's "Havin' Thangs" as the hook.) Pimp, who knew the real prices Dog and Biz were paying for kilos back when they were supporting Buck's early rap career, apparently took offense to the claim. He rapped:

> The South is circles and Atlanta is squares
> They're lyin' 'bout their prices, it ain't 17 up there
> I'm down with Young Buck, and Buck down with Pimp C
> But ain't nobody got 'em for 10 in no damn Tennessee
> It might be 27 or it might be 23
> Dog and Biz used to come and get 'em for 16 from me
> They had two niggas that would drive the shit back*
> They were servin' T, I took his bitch and his 'Lac
> His jewelry and his money and his 5.0
> She had a baby from Priest, but that's still my hoe
> She was translating Spanish with the Mexicans
> Tryin' to get a better price, he got fucked in the end
> She a square now, Dog and Biz both dead
> Pussy nigga T got locked in the Feds
> That was his Ferrari in the Juvy video
> The bitch killed Dog 'cause he was fuckin' his hoe
> Same time, T was fuckin' Dog wife
> Shot him in the back, he a bitch for life
> See me in the streets, bitch, better keep steppin'
> 'Cause even on parole, I'm ice cold with the weapon
> So R.I.P. to Big Dog and his mother
> But at least before he died he killed your pussy-ass brother**

Pimp knocked out his verse quickly and looked expectantly at XVII. But now that he was in the studio with his idol, XVII was too nervous to get on the mic. He thought he could just take the ProTools file with Pimp's verse, go home and record his own verse separately.

"What time y'all flight leave in the morning?" Pimp asked. They had an early flight out; Pimp offered to get them a room at the Icon Hotel, where he was staying with Ayesha.

The clerks at the Icon Hotel knew Chad by a variety of names, since he always checked in under a different alias. Mama Wes was on a first-name basis with the night clerk; she'd often call and ask to be connected to his room.

"Look, baby, you know my voice. Hook me up to C," she'd say. "Do you gotta make me go through all these names tonight?"

"Mama, I just like to hear you rattle 'em off," the clerk would chuckle.

She'd try C.L. Butler first, then run through the list: there was Jack Tripper, Percy Mack, James Jones, Tony Snow … eventually Chad started telling his mother in advance who he was going to "be" that night, in case she needed to reach him.

On this particular night, XVII laughed as Chad checked in under the alias "Rick James."

(*On the record Pimp implies that Dog and Biz were using the same couriers as Terrell "T" McMurry's organization. T paid two Mexican couriers, Marco Juarez and Ricky "Playboy" Luna, a $5,000 monthly salary to transport cocaine and money between Nashville and their San Diego-based supplier. Both men were sentenced to more than 17 years.)

(**Lanika would not reveal the identity of any of the men mentioned on this song; that information was obtained through further research. Mama Wes asserts that 95% of the record was indeed a "true story." Chad later emailed Lanika and told her he'd written a song about her. Priest, obviously, did not appreciate the mention.)

Early the next morning, a knock came at XVII's door as a clerk informed him, "Mr. James would like to see you at his room."

"Who?" XVII asked, confused. A few seconds later, it clicked. *Rick James.* XVII started laughing and walked over to Chad's room. Chad instructed him to put his bags in the car so they could head out to Port Arthur. "What you talking about, Pimp? The flight leaves in like an hour," XVII said. "I thought you was gonna take us to the airport."

"No. Y'all going to P.A. with me," Chad said. "I'm fixin' to hear you rap. I've been thinking about it all night. I called my Mama."

XVII agreed to put his bags in the car but wondered why they were leaving so early. Chad explained that he had to check in with his parole officer. "Why I gotta go with you to see your P.O.?" XVII asked.

I can't believe I'm arguing with this nigga, he thought. *My whole life, I idolized this nigga.*

"Just shut up," Chad told him. "We gotta go see my P.O."

After checking in with his parole officer, Chad raced home, XVII and his cousin Dub in tow. When he was pulled over for speeding, Chad apologized to the officer and explained that he was trying to get home in time to see the "Int'l Player's Anthem" video premiering on BET's *106th & Park.* The female officer asked for an autograph and let him go.

At the house, Heather dropped off plates of shrimp from Tracy's Seafood Deli as everyone gathered around the television and Chad instructed XVII to put his bags in the guest room. Later that night they headed out to Avery's studio, where XVII, under Pimp C's watchful eye, kept flubbing his lines.

"Man, why you messing up?" Pimp asked.

"Man, I'm nervous," XVII said.

"What the fuck you nervous for, nigga?" Pimp asked.

After XVII ran through it several times and finally got it right, Pimp enthusiastically bobbed his head in approval.

"Can I go home now?" XVII asked. His cousin Dub laughed.

"No, man, you with me," Pimp told him. "We gonna do this as a '*Pimp C presents... XVII*' thing."

The next day, Pimp dropped XVII and Dub off at the airport. Before hopping on a flight himself to Los Angeles, he called me and said that he wanted to start doing a monthly column in *OZONE.* He had some things he needed to say.

CHAPTER 48

"I ain't scared! 'Cause when you live this life, see, I'm on borrowed time anyway. I'm just blessed to be here. God saved me to tell the truth, and to preach!"
— Pimp C

———————

"Letz be carfull what we put out next month ! U the only media person i talk 2!"
— Text from Pimp C to the author Julia Beverly, July 24, 2007

Sunday, June 10, 2007
Atlanta, Georgia

The next night, I closed out a few last emails on my computer at the *OZONE* office and looked at the clock and sighed. *4:22 AM.* How did it get so late? It was two days before my 26th birthday, but I'd barely even had time to think about celebrating. Instead I was still here at the office at 4 AM on a Saturday night, tallying up nominations for the upcoming OZONE Awards.

Aside from the awards, I still had tight deadlines and a monthly magazine to produce. I'd just returned from a photo shoot in New Orleans and was scheduled to hit the road in the morning for a concert in Tallahassee, and Pimp C was holding me up. I'd marked a page for his monthly column and needed to get it on press ASAP.

I dialed Pimp C's number again twice from the office line and kept getting his voicemail. *OZONE* now had a small staff, but from the beginning, I'd been sort of a one-woman production, multi-tasking as an interviewer/writer/photographer/editor/transcriptionist/designer/ad saleswoman. To save time, I often typed artists' interviews in real-time as I interviewed them by phone. It was convenient but distracting, and could present a problem if I ever had to back up what I'd printed, so I'd started using a recorded phone line for interviews.

I finally gave up and headed home. As I turned the key in the lock at 5:04 AM, Pimp finally called in to the recorded line, announcing himself as *"Piiiiiiiiimp."*

"I just gotta [record] it like this now because people are always talkin' shit in their interviews and then they'll try to say that they didn't say it later," I said apologetically. "So this way I can play it back- "

He interrupted me. "Yeah, well, I ain't gonna say something and then say I didn't say it later." Then, he took a tone with me I'd never heard before: "And for the record mane, if we gonna start airing out muthafuckers, you know, *The Source* Magazine and the *XXL*, when them muthafuckers was small they was, uh, goddamn meek and kind and shit. When you came to my prison and seen me that time and put me on the cover, you was more humble than you is now. You done got successful…"

I laughed, thinking he was joking. He wasn't.

He kept going, his voice rising into a hoarse scream, "…and this shit is changing you too! So what I'ma tell you is, take a note from the rest of these muthafuckers and just stay humble. The more successful you get, the more humble you gotta be, Julia. Y'know what I'm saying? Because the shit will fuck you up too. The game is fucked up."

Okay, he was serious. My mind started racing. What had I done that wasn't humble? I disagreed with his assessment that I was getting arrogant, but I couldn't deny I was changing. Everything was changing. The OZONE Awards had me stressed out; everyone had an angle, everyone wanted something. My phone rang constantly. It was too much. The pressure was overwhelming. He was right, though. The game was fucked up.

"I feel you," I agreed. What else could I say?

"It's full of homosexuals," Pimp C spat. "And look, ain't nothing wrong with gay people, as long as they admit they gay and come out and don't be making passes at people that's not down with that bullshit. But all that ol', fuckin' your manager and then getting out here and trying to mess with the girls too, trying to act like you a straight-up nigga? Man, fuck you in yo' ass, nigga, literally. A nigga like that deserve to get fucked 40 million times. I said it!"

I laughed uneasily. *Homosexuals?* I was accustomed to Pimp C going way off topic, and undercover homosexuals were one of his favorite things to rant about.* I tried to bring the conversation back to his original point. "Damn, so you think I'm getting cocky now or you just talking in general?" I asked.

"Naw, I think you getting cocky now, yeah," he told me. "Bitches done started paying you for the cover and the shit gettin' successful so what I'm saying is, stay humble. Because the more successful UGK gets, the more humble I have to be in the streets with my fans."** Okay, he was right. I made a mental note to be more humble.

"I ain't gotta be humble when I'm airin' these bitch-ass niggas out, though," he finished. "So c'mon, let's go … let's go in on these niggas."

"Aight," I began. "So – "

"The first muthafucker I wanna air out is Lil Troy," he practically spat into the phone. "Lil' bitch-ass Troy. That's who I wanna talk about."

Lil Troy? My face twisted into a confused expression. Lil Troy wasn't even relevant; why would we talk about him?

"This bitch got on the internet and said that every – a direct quote of this bitch – and you could call him and get his quote if you want to, 'cause he a fuck boy," Pimp said, his voice rising. "When I see him, nigga, we can pop it out, stab it out, or box it out, bitch! But we ain't gonna lip-wrassle it out. I ain't no lip-wrassler. I ain't goddamn makin' no records about no niggas. I'm going to a nigga house. Bitch, if you don't like me, don't call Bun B and try to get me off yo' ass, bitch-ass Lil Troy! Nigga, you call *me* to get me off your ass!"

Pimp paused. "Now the truth of the story is this: He put a DVD out – and then I'ma go back to the shit that he said just recently. He put a goddamn DVD out called *Paperwork*, do you know about that?"

"Yeah, talking about Scarface?" I said, recalling my strange stop at Lil Troy's house.

"Did you actually read the paperwork that he says [proves] Scarface was a snitch?" Pimp asked.

"Yeah, I saw it," I replied.

"Did it prove that he's a snitch?" Pimp prompted.

I hesitated. I always refrained from inserting my personal opinions into interviews, feeling that my statements on the record should be neutral and objective. But fuck it, it was Pimp C. "Naw, it was some bullshit," I admitted.

"Okay, it was some bullshit," he agreed. "And while you recording me, you gonna quote yourself too, right?"

(*While Pimp C always clarified that he wasn't into "gay bashing," he was always vocal about his hatred of down-low men. "I'm not a homophobic," he told OZONE. "I never gay-bash, UGK has never bashed anybody gay, [but] just come out and be what you are. How can you do anything that you ashamed of? …[If] I gotta go hide in the closet and do [something]… that mean I don't need to be doing it, right?" He added, "I went to prison for four years and at no time in jail did a nigga's ass look like nothing that I wanted to deal with, you know what I'm sayin'? An ashy man can never be like a woman. He might dress up and look like a woman, but … he ain't no woman.")

(**Since the very first issue, the cover of OZONE, which was distributed at thousands of locations for free in addition to newsstands, was sold as a promotional package to offset printing costs. When Pimp C appeared on the cover in May 2005 it was part of an Asylum advertising package, likewise, UGK's cover appearance was part of a Jive advertising package.)

I laughed. "If I'm quoting myself I'm gonna re-word that."

"Nah, don't re word it, Julia!" he practically screamed. "Why you gotta re-word it! Julia, you said it was some bullshit. Why you gonna re-word yours and you don't want me to re-word mine and we recording the conversation? You said it was some bullshit. It was some bullshit! Don't re-word it, mane! Lil Troy put out some bullshit on Scarface and said he was a snitch!"

Okay, he had a point, but I did 're-word' his interviews slightly, at least to make them flow better. I was still confused where he was going with this. The Lil Troy/Scarface "snitch" accusations were several years old and no one was talking about it anymore. Why bring it up now?

"Well, newsflash!" Pimp yelled. "Lil Troy told on the whole muthafuckin' north side of Houston! He crushed a bunch of people's lives and put a bunch of people's daddies, brothers, uncles, and sons in the penitentiary. The bitch did all his muthafuckin' time in protective custody, right over there off Beaumont, in the goddamn Fed prison like a bitch. He did two years when the shit he got caught up with he was at least supposed to get a double digit [sentence]!"

"And the fuck ass nigga came home and tried to put out another muthafuckin' album, after he fucked everybody on the first [one]," Pimp added, referring to Troy's second attempt *Back to Ballin'* after the artists on his first project said they weren't paid. "If it wasn't for Yungstar [who rapped on 'Wanna Be A Baller'] and them niggas givin' him them songs, he wouldn't have been able to put no record out, 'cause he ain't no muthafuckin' rapper. He a funky bitch. And I said it!"

By this time I'd reached the bed and kicked my shoes off, and exhaustion was taking over. I was laying on my side, eyes closed, BlackBerry resting on my ear, trying to stay into the conversation, but I knew I didn't have to say much to keep it going. A simple "oh?" or "mmhmm" here and there would suffice. Besides, I would have to transcribe, edit, and proof-read this all later, so I'd hear it at least three more times. I started to drift off, but the recorder kept rolling:

And now watch this. This is why I'm getting on his funky ass right now. I been knowing he was a bitch. But I ain't gotta talk about no nigga when everybody know you a bitch. And you hiding, nigga! You don't come out in Houston, bitch! Every time I go to the mall, to the Galleria Mall in Houston, I see Slim Thug comin' in or out the mall and me and him going in and grabbing bags.* Them other bitch ass niggas, we don't never see them. Nigga lookin' like Grover off of muthafuckin' the Muppet Babies.** Shaving they face all bald and wearing v-neck sweaters and Argyle socks. Pussy-ass niggas think they sexy now. Yeah! And all them niggas buying them diamonds over there from [King] Johnny [at Johnny's Custom Jewelry in King's Flea Market] thinking you got them big pieces and that shit look good? Man, news flash – Lil Flip my pa'tna, I respect him, Mike Jones my pa'tna, I respect him – but them big ol' plates they be wearing that look like big dinner plates?!? Nigga, them diamonds is monkey!! You need to take that monkey shit back, 'cause you embarrassing us! If you come to the OZONE Awards with that bullshit on, nigga…

The OZONE Awards reference roused me from my mini-nap. *Shit. You can't be falling asleep during interviews,* I reprimanded myself, trying to quickly think of a question to ask. He started again with no prompting.

"Now," he said, "I just made peace with the lil nigga Short Dawg 'cause … it wasn't his fault. It was ol' dick-in-the-booty-Russell-Simmons' fault for not taking the message back to him and telling him to change his name!"

Oh shit. Fully awake now, I sat straight up in the bed and the BlackBerry fell off my face. I *had* to have heard him wrong.

He read my mind. "Yeah, I said you 'dick-in-the-booty,' nigga! I know what I'm talking about, bitch! I'll air you out too!"

Holy shit. Did he just diss Russell Simmons? Def Jam's co-founder? The "godfather of Hip-Hop"? I barely had time to process what he'd said when he continued on to another topic.

(*"I'm on Westheimer every day, bitch, and the only [rapper] I see every day is Slim Thug!" Pimp would often proclaim. "I'm in Houston ridin' Bentleys by myself and the only nigga I see in the street is Slim Thug. He's the only nigga I see in the streets without no bodyguard. These pussy ass niggas don't come out of the house.")

(**Privately, Pimp liked to say that rapper Mike Jones looked like Grover from Sesame Street.)

"Muthafuckers talking about they got kilos for 17.5. Bitch, ain't no kilos for 17.5 up there, nigga!" he screamed. "You come to Houston to get the muthafuckin' work at them prices, 'cause we right there by San Antonio and we going down there and getting the work!"*

His voice was practically breaking at this point, he was so hoarse from screaming. "And guess what, mane? All you niggas talkin' about y'all selling dope and y'all niggas was some d-boys? I don't *believe* you niggas no more, 'cause I'm seeing you niggas in button-up shirts getting cute and pretty, trying to look sexy. Nigga, fuck you! And nigga, I ain't gotta say your name!"

"Play with me [and] I'll expose the niggas that was wearing backpacks and had they god-damn pant legs rolled up, back there in Atlanta when me and Big Meech used to be off in the club kickin' it, buyin' each other champagne!" he continued. "And they need to free Big Meech! Niggas are cool when it's cool to drop a nigga name, but ain't cool when the muthafuckin' grease gets hot!"

Somewhere in the midst of this I'd done an awkward forward-roll off the bed, clutching the phone to my ear, and stood straight up. *$17.5? Meech?* I was sleepy and slower than usual, but it had finally clicked. *Is he talking about Young Jeezy?*

"Now, let's go back to Lil Troy!" Pimp C shouted. "You ready?"

"Alright, go ahead," I said.

"This bitch got on the internet and said … everybody at Rap-A-Lot is fake, so Lil' J must be fake too. Can you believe this bitch? Then the pussy nigga had the audacity to say [I disrespected] him by not putting his beef and Scarface's beef in my song 'Knockin' Doors Down' … Bitch, you ain't even no rapper, what the fuck [do] I need to talk about you fo'? Nigga, you a has-been. Old-ass nigga about 48 years old out here tryin' to dress like they young. And these young ass niggas that used to be wearing gangsta clothes, wearing v-neck sweaters and Argyle socks looking like Pharrell. What is these niggas, metrosexual, homosexual, or what is they?"

"Are you talking about anybody in particular?" I asked.

"You goddamn right!" he shouted. "Go find the pictures of these hoe-ass nigga dressing all funny!"

I laughed.

"You ain't Fonzworth Bentley, nigga!" Pimp C yelled. "You can't dress like that! You can't wear Argyle socks and v-neck sweaters and get away with it. You ain't Pharrell, nigga! Get yo' fanga out yo' ass! Get off that ol' puss'-ass sexy-ass shit. All these niggas think they sexy. Man, keep yo' damn shirt on! You ain't 50 Cent, nigga! Yo' chest ain't cut up, bitch! Keep yo' mutha-fuckin' shirt on, nigga, in the video!"

"And for the record, most of you niggas *ugly*," he continued. "And ya bitch … if I take the makeup off ya bitch, my skin prettier than all you hoes, 'cause I wear LaMer [moisturizing cream]! I get LaMer from the goddamn sto' – my skin prettier than a muthafucker! My toes is pretty! I'm a young, funky, wild boy and I'm a sexy young muthafucker!"**

During interviews, I had a habit of dwelling on one or two key lines, making a mental note to use them later as pull-quotes (printed in a larger, bold font to draw attention to the article). But there were so many classic one-liners coming out of his mouth I couldn't keep up.

"I ain't out here dressing up tryin' to be sexy, licking my lips all out like ol' gay-ass Ne-Yo!" he yelled. "Lickin' lips at niggas! Pussy dick-in-the-booty-ass nigga, wearing all that goddamn lip gloss at they video shoot and letting niggas put makeup on they face!"

I was stunned. *The superstar R&B singer?* "You said 'Ne-Yo'?" I asked. "Did I hear you correctly?"

"Yeah, I said 'Ne-Yo!' You heard what the fuck I said!" he yelled. "Pussy-ass nigga putting all that lip gloss on they muthafuckin' lips, lookin' like they just been eating a po'k chop

---

(*"Work" in this context refers to cocaine.)

(**Iceberg Slim's daughter Misty Beck recalled her father often donning a wig to impress her and her high school friends, insisting, "I'm pretty! I'm a good-looking muthafucker! I'm a pretty muthafucker!" Chad, who loved to brag about his pretty skin, once saw his manager Rick Martin take his shoes off in the studio. "My feet looked like I walked on ash," Martin told *The Source*. "He talked about my feet for damn near six months.")

sam'wich … wit' no hands! Bitch ass nigga!"

I couldn't help it. He was dead serious, but I laughed out loud.

"I saw that nigga in New York at the muthafuckin' hotel lookin' so faggotty!" he yelled. "Man, get yo' fanga out yo' booty, dawg!"

Faggotty? That wasn't even a word.

"You gon' be a faggot, won't you come out, nigga, and say you a faggot!" Pimp yelled. "Come out the closet, bitch, we wanna know who's who! We don't wanna be guessing and playing them pussy-ass games!"

Wow! I was at a loss for words.

"And now guess what?" Pimp said. "Guess what! A bunch of them New York niggas mad at me about that '[Quit] Hatin' the South' record, right?"

"Mmhmm," I nodded.

"But they don't call me about it. They be calling Bun B, asking him why I'm trippin'," he laughed. "If you pussy ass niggas can get Bun B number, why don't you call me up and ask *me* why I'm trippin', bitch?! You know why I'm trippin', 'cause you pussy-ass niggas got an attitude up there and y'all act like the whole Hip-Hop and rap game belonged to y'all for years! And y'all wouldn't give us a chance, and we were buying y'all records and supporting y'all, and y'all were shitting on us! That's why I'm shitting on you pussy ass niggas!"

I agreed with him.

"If your records ain't selling get your finger out your ass, bitch!" he yelled. "And you bitch ass niggas talking all this ol' '17.5' and all these ol' numbers, these ol' funny-ass dope numbers, how you gonna get it for 17.5 if you ain't come and get it from me for 10, bitch? Come down to the South!"

"I don't give a damn if you niggas get mad at me or not!" he continued, screaming. "I'm working with Sean Paul [of the YoungBloodz], we squashed our beef, I fuck with niggas all over the place. I fuck with niggas [in Atlanta], but Atlanta is not the South! When you go to Atlanta, what yo' clock say?!"

There was a long pause.

"When you go to Atlanta what yo' phone say when you get off?!? What Coast time it say?!?" He paused again, then yelled, "I want you to answer me!"

I'd assumed it was another rhetorical question. "I didn't understand what you said," I stammered. "You said when you come to Atlanta…"

"When you get off the plane from Los Angeles or from Texas and get off the plane in Atlanta, what time do it be over there?" he shouted. "Atlanta on East Coast time!"

"Right, right," I said.

"You niggas ain't in the South!" he yelled.

I laughed. Was he joking? "Alright…" I said. We already had more than enough for the planned one-page column, but it didn't seem like I could stop him even if I tried. "Damn, so you riding on Atlanta or what?" I asked.

"I ain't ridin' on Atlanta, I'm callin' it like I see it!" he spat. "And any one of them bitch-ass niggas don't like what I'm saying, bitch, come on out and let's get it on, 'cause I'ma come to your house, bitch! … Atlanta ain't the South. Ain't no water around Atlanta. How the fuck y'all got kilos for 17.5, when I used to live in Atlanta from 1996 to 2001 and I know kilos in Atlanta [cost] 23 [thousand]? Them niggas ain't getting no good prices! You go up to muthafuckin' goddamn Nashville and the [cost] go up to goddamn 27 [thousand]!"

"So are we talking about…" I began carefully. "The only person I know –"

He interrupted again, as if he knew a Young Jeezy question was coming. "Look, Young Buck is my pa'tna, mane. The people he used to be signed with, [his] name is on my arm," he said, referring to the Big Dog tattoo on his forearm. "Big Dog and Biz, they both dead. The niggas that signed Young Buck first."

"Dawg, it's not Nashville Ten-A-Key when y'all was coming to Houston buyin' em for 16," Pimp yelled. "Dawg, and you my pa'tna, and I love you dawg, and if the war ever popped off I'm on Young Buck's side. And you know what war I'm talking about too, don't you?"

I had no idea what he was talking about. *The North vs. the South?* I wondered.*

"I know what you're talking about," I lied, trying to change the topic and go back to the Jeezy question. He was the only one who consistently referenced "17.5" dope prices. "Well, look, the only rapper I know -"

Pimp cut me off again. "If it ever popped off I'm on Young Buck's side, but it is not Nashville Ten-A-Key. It's Nashville Sixteen-A-Key, if you drive to Texas and buy it and drive it back. It is Nashville Twenty-Seven-A-Key if a nigga bring it up there to ya, and it's gonna be stepped on twice!"**

"You niggas don't know nothing about selling no dope!" Pimp yelled. "I'll give you niggas a pack of cocaine and some baking soda and a goddamn Pyrex and I *bet* you have to go buy a Master P record to get the recipe from C-Murder, bitch, and you niggas still couldn't make it rock up!"***

"Nigga don't even know he could hit the coke with some ammonia and make it rock! George Clinton told me that. And come back and hit it with some goddamn lemon juice and make it go back to powder," he stopped yelling, and then, in a completely calm voice, asked me, "Did you know that?"

I laughed dryly. "Nah, I did not know that."

"You think you a muthafuckin' drug dealer!?" he screamed, still addressing the imaginary drug dealers on our conference call. "I used to take risks up and down the muthafuckin' highway. I paid the cost to say this shit! I was on the goddamn highway I-10, riding up and down that bitch tryin' to get money to go to the studio to put these records out. *I'm* the original d-boy on the records!"

"Fuck all that shit mane!" he screamed. "You niggas ain't *real!* Eazy E was *reeeeeeal!* Lil Eazy *reeeeal!* Bunch of these niggas on the West Coast – I just did two songs with Snoop Dogg – he real! Y'know what I'm talkin' 'bout? A bunch of you niggas be smiling in a nigga face and talkin' down behind a nigga back!"

And on it went, past 6 AM… "I know y'all niggas think I be talking crazy, but I don't be talking crazy! I know what the fuck I be saying, mane!" he yelled. "Whoever don't like what I'm saying, if you get offended, nigga, don't call Bun B no more, nigga! Either call Lil' J or call me direct and come meet us at Governors Circle over there at The Compound. Rap-A-Lot Mafia life! You ain't gotta like it, but you've gotta respect it, bitch!"

"I ain't scared!" he finished. "'Cause when you live this life, see, I'm on borrowed time anyway. I'm just blessed to be here. God saved me to tell the truth, and to preach! Chuuuch tabanacle! Three, four titties and you heard that! I'm gone!"

And with that, he hung up.****

(*Apparently, my assumption was correct. Pimp made similar statements in a later interview with AllHipHop. "If y'all want to start a Civil War it ain't nothing," he said. "If it do pop off between the East and the South … I'm standing side by side with my comrades down here. I'm standing … with Atlanta, with Jeezy, with Ludacris, with Lil' Jon and everybody else. It's one thing for us to have our disagreements down here amongst ourselves [but it's] another thing for some other niggas out of our environment [to] try to say some funny ass shit.")

(**Cocaine has been "stepped on" and is no longer pure when a drug dealer has added other substances to it to double their product.)

(***Pyrex is glass cookingware popular for cooking crack cocaine.)

(****In a later interview, Pimp C told me that Lil Troy's YouTube video was the reason for his rant. "That's where my aggravation came from," he explained. "That night that me and you did that interview, that's what really had me hot.")

CHAPTER 49

"The whole radio system is fake anyway. All these [program directors] want you to do is pay 'em to play your record, and when you won't come to town and do they free concert for 'em, they don't wanna play your record no more."
– Pimp C, radio interview with Bo-Bo Luchiano, May 2007

———————

"Radio has been killed. Every playlist is the same all over the country. It wasn't like that back [in the 90s] ... you could fly on an airplane and go to different places and every city you went to, they had a different song on the charts ... When these two companies bought up all the radio stations and started controlling all the playlists and started putting handcuffs and bracelets on all the DJs, they stopped all that." – Pimp C

mid-June 2007
Los Angeles, CA

Back in Los Angeles, Chad turned his focus towards mixing and mastering the double album, alternating between Westlake and Chalice Recording Studios. UGK studio sessions were mostly serious business, not a wild party atmosphere. "The studio was like, the office," recalls Bun's road manager Bone. "If you were in there, you had to be in there for a purpose."

Still, Chad was always a comedian, turning to David Banner and Young Lo one day at Westlake to ask if they'd ever "thought about fucking a midget." When an intern carried in a fruit tray and Mike Mo incorrectly referred to the honeydew melon as "green cantaloupe," Pimp howled with laughter, joking, "I can't take your country ass nowhere!"

Chad played three recent indie artist features he'd done for DJ B-Do and T.O.E. "Number one sounded better than all of them," T.O.E. said, referring to XVII's record "True Story." DJ B-Do agreed. "I'm thinkin' about letting him be down with us," Chad told them.

Being in Los Angeles suited Chad; he was in the midst of a community of many other rappers and musicians. A young up-and-coming producer named Cavie, who had ties to Goodie Mob, played some tracks for Pimp. The one that stood out was a track T.I. had already paid for, intending to use on his 2006 album *King*. Pimp dropped a verse for it anyway.[*]

One night, Big Gipp brought Pimp by the Hit Factory recording studio to meet rapper Nelly. "Nelly and them was just so mesmerized by him," remembers Big Gipp. "This [is] a nigga [who] embodied that era, and these young niggas ... they can't buy that ... To experience somebody like Pimp at his rawest and when his confidence was at his best ... It's nothing like it."[**]

Sean Paul of the YoungBloodz happened to be recording in the room next door at the Hit Factory. Never the type to hold a grudge, he'd come to consider their brief run-in as a compliment. ("How many folk can say they was beefin' with Pimp C, a legend?" he laughs. "For him to even have my name in his mouth, that was big.")

[*The finished version of this song, "P.I.M.P.," didn't appear until T.I.'s 2012 mixtape *Fuck Da City Up*, with an additional verse from Too $hort.)
[**On XVII's album *Certified* Pimp commended Nelly for his "gangsta style," saying that he only "make[s] friendly records 'cause it pays.")

Pimp poked his head in Sean Paul's session, telling him, "Nelly got this song, man, he want you on it. You might as well go get that check, mane." The finished version was Nelly's record "Cut It Out," featuring Pimp C and Sean Paul.

The process of completing the UGK double album involved hiring live musicians to replay the raw elements of the track. One day in the studio, Pimp, who never remembered the name of any of their songs, instructed Mike Mo to pull up the finished version of "that song [where] Bun is talking about where the car is like a bitch."

"'Candy'?" Mike Mo asked.

"Naw, naw, he talking about that car like it's a hoe, man," Pimp said. "Talkin' about she take a lot of baths."

"'Chrome Plated Woman'?" Mike offered.

"Yeah! Pull that muthafucker there up," Pimp instructed him. "That's a serious son of a bitch, ain't it?"

Pimp turned towards Bun. "I *told* you we was gonna jam with them instruments on it!" he howled. "But Bun be knowing though! He know what I'ma do, man! Bun be knowing what I'ma do to that hoe ass shit!"

Sean Paul came by one of these sessions, hoping to collaborate on some more records. "Truthfully, let me tell you how good of a musician Pimp C really is," Sean Paul says. "He in there with his guitars, his little band [was] playing that funk, that jazz, I'm so damn high I fell asleep … I kept falling asleep every day, 'cause they were so funky. It's just like a baby, when a little baby [listens to] some music, they fall asleep … I was so high I was just falling asleep to this shit every day."

"If Pimp's cooking, you wanna be around," agrees Fonzworth Bentley, an artist signed to Kanye West's G.O.O.D. Music who also stopped by the session. "[Even though] he's cooking for somebody [else] … ain't nothing like Pimp C leftovers." (Fonzworth, who considered himself a Pimp C "fanatic," had introduced himself by phone via Cory Mo by rapping Pimp's verses on "Take It Off" and "Murder" back to back. Pimp dropped a memorable verse on Fonzworth's record "C.O.L.O.U.R.S." alongside Lil Wayne.)

Fonzworth Bentley had spent three years working at a fine dining restaurant in New York, where he'd been fascinated watching the executive chef oversee the line cooks: one on fish, one on meat, one preparing sauces, one prepping the appetizer, another preparing salad, all under the expert direction of the master.

Pimp C's production style reminded Fonzworth of a master chef; he deftly coordinated five or six professional musicians at the same time, creating a delicious audio mix. "Naw, that ain't the funk I want," he told the bass player, pulling up an old funk record to demonstrate the style he wanted. Once he had everyone on the same page, Pimp positioned himself behind the organ.

With the release date already pushed back half a dozen times, the pressure was on to finish mastering the project in time for the official August 7 release date. Mike Mo, who had gone back to Houston, shipped a hard drive with some audio files to Los Angeles. Apparently some key files were missing, and Pimp, irritated, had some choice words for Mike over the phone. "Man, you trying to sabotage the album?" he demanded.

As Mike lay awake that night, unable to sleep, Pimp's pointed insults kept playing back in his mind. Finally, Mike sent him a text, which read simply: "I ain't your hoe."

No response came. It was late, but usually, Pimp would still be awake. Mike, worried that Pimp was really angry, took an early morning flight to Los Angeles. By the time he landed, Pimp had seen the text and called Rick Martin and J. Prince, demanding a new road manager. Prince was somewhat amused by the whole thing. As soon as Mike landed, Rick called, begging him to apologize.

Mike took a deep breath and called Pimp.

"Man, what's ... I didn't call you a whore!" Pimp yelled.

"Look, man, I don't want to fight you, bro. You know I'm not trying to sabotage this album. You said some shit to me on that phone, bro..." Mike said, searching for an analogy. "You know what? Check this out. What if Too $hort said them exact same words to you?"

There was a long pause. "Man, if Too $hort would have said that shit to me, man, I'da cried," Pimp admitted. By the time Mike arrived at the studio, everyone was able to laugh about the whole situation.

The annual BET Awards were held in Los Angeles on June 26, 2007. Pimp, who had Ed drive his Bentley all the way from Port Arthur to Los Angeles for the event, initially planned to make a grand entrance and walk the red carpet.

Things didn't turn out that way, though; it appears that Pimp didn't even attend. Bun performed on the red carpet during a pre-show event with Mike Jones, and apparently Pimp was upset that he wasn't included. He vented to his attorney Craig Wormley, who got the impression there was a growing rift between him and Bun, and complained to XVII that Bun had been "acting like a hoe."

While most of the music industry was in town for the BET Awards, Sony held a UGK meet-and-greet in the courtyard of the Sony building. They flew in the Jive staff, including video promoter Anne-Marie Stripling, who had become one of UGK's biggest advocates at the label alongside Barry Weiss and Jeff Sledge. "UGK [was so] refreshing in the industry when everything had gotten so materialistic and fake," Anne-Marie says.

Anne-Marie had already met Bun's wife Queenie ("the cutest couple I've ever seen!") but had never met Chad's wife. When Chad arrived with Ayesha, Anne-Marie incorrectly assumed it was his wife. Excited to finally meet her, Anne-Marie gushed about what an adorable couple they were, admiring their matching complexion.*

"Y'all look so cute together," she enthused. "Look at your freckles!"

Ayesha hadn't planned on getting involved with a married man, but it was hard to feel guilty when it didn't seem like they were doing anything wrong; they certainly weren't hiding. She felt like she was becoming part of the family.

Pimp was scheduled to fly back to Houston after the BET Awards for a UGK performance at The Box's "Hip-Hop 4 HIV" concert. Houston's HIV statistics were frightening: African-Americans accounted for only 18% of the population but 54% of the HIV cases. Fans between the ages of 15 and 30 years old could get free tickets to the show by getting tested for HIV.

The Box's partner in the Hip-Hop 4 HIV event was Texas State Representative Borris Miles' non-profit organization The Texstars Foundation. Miles was a wealthy businessman and politician who attended a Baptist church on Sundays and gave away free turkeys every Thanksgiving with his smiling wife Cydonii by his side.

But for those who had seen the other side of Borris Miles, the idea of him championing a HIV/AIDS prevention event was laughable at best, considering his penchant for unprotected sex with prostitutes. Miles was rumored to frequent hole-in-the-wall strip joints, where he huddled in dark corners, picking out pretty, petite strippers and paying them extravagantly to lavish attention on him while he snorted cocaine. Strippers and escorts hated his disrespectful, self-entitled attitude, but tolerated him because he paid well.**

(*If you see a rapper with a woman, it's best to assume it is *not* his wife.)
(**In an ironic twist, Borris Miles later became a client of Chad's escort friend Jada; she describes him as "the creepiest guy on earth." He also was the focus of controversy in December 2007, when he was accused of forcibly kissing another man's wife and threatening partygoers with a pistol during a drunken rant at an upscale holiday party. He was also accused of flashing a pistol at a Rockets game at the Toyota Center in an incident not unlike the one that sent Pimp C to prison. Unlike Pimp C, Miles was not charged with Aggravated Assault with a Deadly Weapon. The "deadly conduct" charges against Miles were later reduced to a misdemeanor and he was eventually acquitted.)

In the early 90s, when rap music became popular in Houston, radio had competition: fans could tune in to either Magic 102 or 102 Jamz. In 1994, media conglomerate Clear Channel bought both stations and consolidated them into one. In 2000, Radio One bought The Box.

At the helm of The Box was program director Terri Thomas, a petite white woman who had arrived in Houston around the same time Pimp C was released from prison. In a city which was the proud home of decades of their own music culture, Terri was a Boston-born newcomer now holding one of the most powerful positions in the local Hip-Hop scene.

Terri was the type to recite upbeat yet cliché motivational phrases ("keep God first and follow your dreams!" and "netWORK to increase your netWORTH!") and wrote children's books in her free time. "Since I've been [in Houston], one of the things I've tried to do is make sure the radio stays close to the local community," Terri professed in a 2009 interview posted on her website, but others disagreed, saying that The Box of 2007 was a far cry from Houston's glory days. "The Box turned their back on Houston hard," says Matt Sonzala.

Still, The Box was the only Hip-Hop station in Houston, and had substantial leverage to pressure artists into doing its bidding. It was illegal for an artist (or their label) to pay a radio station for spins ("payola"), so instead, it was common practice for radio stations to expect artists to perform at their shows for free or cheap, so they could make money off ticket sales in exchange for having their records played. "[They're] technically not supposed to do that, but most stations do," says former Box on-air personality Brandi Garcia. "It's an unspoken thing."

"They got some reverse payola shit going on where they try to force you to come and do free concerts for 'em," Pimp told *FADER*. "And if you don't come and do 'em, they freeze you out and don't play your records. They don't actually tell you straight up, 'If you don't come do this free show for us we not gonna play your records,' but they insinuate it."

UGK did have an upcoming album to promote, and it was for a good cause, so Chad agreed to perform at The Box event for free. But when he found out that UGK would be opening for the headliners Lil Wayne and Birdman, he changed his mind. "I'm not going to do no show before [Lil] Wayne in Houston," Chad told his mother. "Because if I went to [New Orleans] he wouldn't come on before me."*

A few days before the scheduled show, Mama Wes spoke with Terri Thomas trying to find a solution. "Let's just let this one slide and we'll do something for you at a different time," Mama Wes suggested, attempting to be diplomatic, but Terri didn't seem interested in negotiating.

When the three of them ended up on a three-way call, Mama Wes was nervous.

"Don't even worry, Mama," Chad had assured her in advance. "I want to have this done right. I can't [go off]. I won't do that. I want to do whatever show I can do to help her and her station and I want her to know that." He aimed to maintain UGK's key relationship with the radio station without compromising his principles.

Once Terri joined the call, Chad began by explaining that when they'd toured with Too $hort in the early days, even if the promoter wanted them to perform after Too $hort, they refused. It was a matter of principle, showing respect for those who had laid the groundwork.

"In C's defense – and it's not often times I can defend C, because he was usually wrong," laughs Mama Wes, "he was trying to be a gentleman and he was trying to explain to her the rules of the game."

Chad referenced an upcoming show with Scarface as an example. The promoter had Scarface before them on the lineup, and Chad didn't feel right about it. They'd only agreed to do it with Scarface's blessing.

Chad continued speaking in a soft voice, very calmly; almost too calmly, thought Mama Wes. He was peppering his speech with "ma'am" and doing his best to keep the conversation

(*It's worth noting that UGK did perform before Lil Wayne at the 2006 OZONE Awards, however, that event was in Orlando, FL, not in Houston. It's also worth noting that half the crowd left after UGK's performance thinking they *were* the headliners.)

cordial. Mama Wes held the phone lightly, looking towards the heavens and silently praying, *Don't let this muthafucker go off, because he's 'bout to blow.* No matter what Chad said, it seemed that Terri wasn't hearing him, needling him with rude and nasty remarks. Chad was notorious for his short-fused temper and Mama Wes felt that Terri was pressing him to get a reaction.

Chad added that he had already spoken to Lil Wayne, who understood. "It's a matter of principle, for *me*," Chad emphasized. "I just *cannot* do it. It's breaking a code."

Terri pointed out that Bun B had agreed to UGK's performance slot.

"Look, Bernard is his own man," Chad responded, carefully referring to Bun by his government name. "And *I* am my own man. If he wants to do it, I really would never have a problem with [it], because we don't always have the same code of ethics. And Bernard is my brother, [so] I'm not saying anything bad about my brother. But I know he understands how I feel."

"Look, ma'am," Chad concluded, frustrated. "I mean, just tell me what [else] you want me to do," adding that he'd be willing to participate in a different station event in the future. "But I *can't*, as a man – and I *can't*, as a rapper – and I *can't*, as an artist – do that [show]. I feel that strongly about it. That's just not right. That's just not the way we do it."

"Are you threatening me?" Terri abruptly demanded.

There was silence on the line, Chad and his mother both completely caught off guard by the accusation.

What just happened? Mama Wes wondered.

Chad was at a loss for words. "What are you talkin' 'bout, lady?" he finally said, repeating the phrase several times, his voice rising. "What are you talkin' 'bout? We not talkin' 'bout threatening nobody! I don't know what you talkin' 'bout, lady. I ain't no gangsta, I'm a musician. Yeah, I've been to jail, but I'm not no gangsta. And anyway, I have better sense than to threaten you!"

"Are you threatening me?" Terri repeated, pausing for emphasis, and then ominously adding a threat of her own: "I'll call your P.O. and have you put back in prison."

"You *got* to be crazy," Chad snapped. "I can't believe you said that."

Mama Wes had been listening silently but couldn't hold back any more. "Now look," she said, interjecting on her son's behalf. "I think you have gone a lil' damn bit too far … he didn't threaten you. And I know my lil' five foot ass didn't."

Chad knew it was no idle threat. "[Being] on parole is serious business," he told *OZONE*. "I've got one foot in [prison] and one foot out. A muthafucker can just [claim] that I said, 'Hey, man I'm gonna kill your muthafuckin' ass,' [and] that's called 'terroristic threats.' If they tell my P.O. and … they can lock me up and hold me 'til they prove if I really said it or I didn't say it, and even if they don't prove I said it, [they] … can send me back to prison."

Mama Wes is adamant that Chad never threatened Terri or cursed at her. "He wasn't doing anything to attack that lady," Mama Wes says firmly. "In my opinion she was … needling him to make him go off. [Her threat] was totally uncalled for."

"*Could* C and *would* C threaten people? *Yes*. But did he do it in that conversation? No," continues Mama Wes. "Matter of fact, I don't know when I had heard him carry on a conversation more intelligently, you know? He was really trying. I think she had her mind made up [already], and she's a vicious bitch. I think she wanted some confusion and I think that she knew C was famous for having a short fuse."

Chad managed to get off the call without losing his temper, and vented to an unidentified friend at The Box on a recorded line.*

(*The conversation with Terri Thomas as described here is based on Chad and Mama Wes' separate descriptions of the call. Terri Thomas did not respond to several requests for comment. Terri Thomas now controls both The Box and Boom92 in Houston, which, ironically, uses a lot of UGK material in its advertisements and promotions. The audio of Chad complaining about Terri Thomas was later released by rapper Trae Tha Truth when he had a similar issue with her.)

"She's a bitch … I'm finna go on a 'Fuck 97.9' spree on that bitch anyway. [I'm just] waiting to see if my spins fall off for not coming to that fuck ass show," he said. "I bet you one thing: If I do print up some 'Fuck 97.9' t-shirts I bet you I get all the local artists to ride with me. Bitch think she holding."*

"[If they stop playing my record] I'm gonna file a lawsuit against every-muthafuckin'-body, 'cause it's reverse payola, bitch," he added. "You can't never think … Young Pimp gonna come somewhere for free and open up for some niggas? You got me fucked all the way up … when you stop playing people's records because they don't do your free shows, that's illegal. That's reverse payola … that's a multi-billion dollar lawsuit … How you think that's gonna sound when that [news] hits the streets? … That the radio stations is forcing niggas into doing shows or they don't play their records?"

It was a valid concern; in fact, The Box had done it before, prior to Terri Thomas' arrival. When scheduling conflicts prevented UGK from performing at a concert for The Box during the *Ridin' Dirty* era, the station stopped playing their music. Now, UGK was practically a Texas institution, and banning them from the airwaves would probably hurt the station more than it would hurt UGK.

"That bitch was gonna call my P.O. and tell her I terroristically threatened her," Chad vented. "That bitch finna send me back to the penitentiary, mane, 'cause I told her I wouldn't open up for Baby and Wayne. Now, I love Baby and Wayne, but do you think that UGK [is] supposed to open up for anybody in the city of Houston, mane?"

"I didn't tell the broad nothin' about doing no bodily harm to her or doing nothing to that woman," he finished. "I ain't got no violence in me. I'm out here trying to take care of my kids. This broad was actually gonna call my P.O. and tell these people I terroristically threatened her. The broad asked me on the phone, 'Are you threatening me?' I said, 'Man, I don't threaten people. I'm not no gangsta, I'm a rapper.' And to send me back to prison 'cause I didn't wanna do her funky ass show is not right, mane."

"Sadly, [Terri Thomas] is still there [at The Box]," says Jammin' Jimmy Olson, The Box's co-founder and namesake. (He was once known as "The Boy in the Box.") While clarifying that he has nothing against Terri personally, Olson says he agrees with Pimp C's description of modern-day radio tactics as "reverse payola."

"It is incredibly sad the way that radio has gotten … It really, really sucks," Olson adds. "It is incredibly sad what goes on at The Box."

"Radio has been killed," Pimp C said on UGK's *Making of the Album* documentary. "Every playlist is the same all over the country … these two companies bought up all the radio stations and started controlling all the playlists and started putting handcuffs and bracelets on all the DJs … It took the fun out the music."

"Everywhere I go they playing the same shit," he grumbled. "I hear the same damn Beyoncé song playing all muthafuckin' day long. It makes a nigga sick to his stomach."

"In 1991-92, if your shit was jamming and people liked it, you got on the radio … Back then, they were playing whatever the people requested. Now, it don't matter what the people say," he told *On Tha Real* Magazine. "All [the radio stations] play is what the [Program Director] says to play. They even fuck with the mix show DJ playlist. It's hard for an independent under-ground artist to get on and shine now like we did back then. In New York, motherfuckers don't know what we like down here and a country ass white man don't know what to play in New York, ya feel me?"

(*In street terms someone who is "holding" has drugs available for sale and therefore has the upper hand in negotiations. Chad likely meant that Terri Thomas was overestimating her power.)

"no mo fkn wit negative people no matter how much i care bout em"
– Pimp C's 2007 New Year's Resolution, *OZONE* Magazine

———————

"Very few people are gonna walk this planet and say everything they wanted to say, to everyone they wanted to say it to, how they wanted to say it. Very few people are gonna walk this planet and do what they wanna do, when they wanna do it. For right or wrong, better or worse, that was why we loved [Pimp C]. And [even though] you loved him, you didn't know if one day you might end up in his radar ... He was so brutally honest ... Pimp was never scared to tell you what he felt about you, but it came out of love, because he didn't feel he could lie to you." – Bun B, radio interview with Madd Hatta, December 2007

Saturday, June 30, 2007

More than 7,500 people streamed into Houston's Reliant Arena on June 30 for the Hip-Hop 4 HIV concert featuring Slim Thug, David Banner, Lil Keke, Kelly Rowland, Mike Jones, and Trae tha Truth. Fans and station employees were completely unaware of the drama behind the scenes that resulted in a solo Bun B set instead of UGK. And finally, the headliner Lil Wayne shut down the arena with a stellar performance.

As concertgoers were being entertained in Houston, Chad was lounging with Ayesha at the unassuming yet sophisticated L'Ermitage Hotel in Beverly Hills. Chad had confided in Ayesha that he was exhausted with managing all the conflict around him in his personal life, and felt trapped in his Rap-A-Lot situation. "He was very unhappy with the way things were going in his life… [his wife and his mother] constantly [fighting]," Ayesha recalls.

Ayesha was a big believer in books like *The Secret* and *Law of Attraction*; she explained that when she was struggling with things in her life, she called upon her sisters, who all dabbled in the psychic world and believed they could channel spirits.

"You think you could do that for me?" Chad asked.

It happened to be Halimah's 25th birthday, but she was flattered when her sister Ayesha called to see if she would give Chad a reading. Halimah had started dabbling in the spirit world after experiencing strange dreams, seeing ghosts, and hearing voices. "I have emerged from the living dead," she announced on her MySpace page, where she regularly posted poems with titles like "Sorcery Bliss," "Mermaid Cocaine," and "Sensual Fury." She'd read a book to learn how to go into a trance, and eventually met her "spirit guide," a gypsy woman whom she considered "a more extreme form" of herself. The more she practiced, the clearer the messages became.

Halimah dimmed the lights at L'Ermitage as her boyfriend settled in on the couch, the décor a comforting array of oranges and browns topped off by crisp white bedsheets and pillows. Chad positioned himself on the bed next to Ayesha, at a safe distance. Halimah chucked to herself; that was normal. "Some people be scared," she explains. "They don't know what's going on, especially people from the South, they think it's gonna be something spooky."

As Halimah began meditating, she spoke in slow, measured tones, dragging out every syllable. Her voice took on a strange tone. "I just soften my body to where it's totally open," she explains. "I connect with my spirit guide, which is my higher self. She uses me to speak [for her]… it's not me [speaking], it's [my spirit guide] connecting with their spirit."

The room was filled with silence, everyone hesitant to make a sound. Halimah asked Chad to select a topic to begin; he chose "business."

"What I see is like a grid with ink spots, sort of, you know, like the paper that you do math on? With plans. But ink spots all over your plans," began Halimah. "You need to keep a more clear focus, and not let others influence your decisions." She told him that he needed to focus on reaching "bigger and higher" and becoming an "international star," beyond racial lines and cultural lines.

"I keep seeing Asian symbols," she added. "Maybe that's a big market for you. I see millions of dollars and I see Asian symbols." Chad had Asian symbols tattooed on his right forearm which roughly translated to "gaining fame and fortune" and an Asian symbol under his ear which meant "King."

"Maybe you want to travel to some unseen foreign lands," Halimah theorized in her low, hypnotic monotone. "You just need a change of direction so you can reach your top. And don't you wanna go much higher so you'll unscrew this top, by exploring new things?"

"Some days, yeah," Chad mumbled, slowly. "Some days I just wanna quit."

Halimah laughed softly. "That's how every human lives, but if you quit, you would get really, really bored," she said, pointedly drawing out the last word.

"I'm under the impression…" Chad said quietly, his voice drifting off. Barely audible, searching for the right words, he continued, "I heard the word 'low energy people…' man… these people the devil. And my question is, is the devil really close to me?"

"Of course," Halimah purred.

"And one of the names is James Prince, the other name is Freddie Southwell," Chad continued slowly, his voice so low it was a near whisper.

"Yes, definitely," agreed Halimah. "He's one of those devils with long fangs. When I see him I see black clouds."

"Which one?" Chad asked.

"The first name," Halimah said. "I see him with long fangs, black clouds around him."* She sighed. "He has a dark energy in certain ways in his life, very low energy in other places. He has a very dark murky spirit, even though he had some light within his soul, because all of us do. But in this lifetime I think he'll always kind of murk in the bottom. So he's one of those kinds of people you don't want to know your real plans, ever. And you know that. So he's one of those kinds of people who you stay sort of at a distance from. You should. Because when people are doing low and dark [things], they don't help you shine more. They kind of will cloud your image. So it's best to get away from these kinds of people."

"The second one, he's not as dark as the first," Halimah said, referring to Freddie Southwell, a.k.a. Smoke D. "He's kind of a follower. He follows behind people. He creates something of himself, an image of himself that he's not. He's very false. Not very honest at all. He's not honest about who he is and he's living behind lies. That is what I see when I see him."

"Neither of these people are very conducive to your success," she concluded. "Some people when you reach the top, sometimes they add to your energy. But these people, they suck from it."

"I think [he] creates glass rooftops…" Chad mumbled, "so niggas won't go no further. I want to know how to protect myself from this person. The second one, he's not a threat. The first

(*It is logical to assume that Halimah, who was from Texas, would likely have heard of Prince's name and feared reputation.)

one is very clever…"*

"He is clever," Halimah agreed.

"…He thinks two and three and four and five years ahead of what's going to happen," Chad finished.

"Let me tell you something about life," Halimah said. "You're never unprotected. You spend a lot of time trying to be protected, but you already are … In life you never have to be a victim of anything. What you must do is decide, and get your mind to believe, that you are fully protected … No one has power unless you give them power, you understand? That's how life is."

"Mmhmm," Chad agreed.

"People spend so much time trying to pound into children's heads all these things to fear, when there's nothing to fear," Halimah elaborated. "Your greatest enemy is your mind … If you give someone too much energy and too much power, they'll stop you. Once you realize that you're bigger than them, they'll just bow to you and go on about their way, controlling someone [else] who believes that they're bigger than them."

"You don't think they'll… attack?" Chad asked, cautiously.

"No," Halimah said. "Of course, you must do things very cleverly, but what you must do is get rid of your ideas of anybody ever being able to harm you … when you give anyone energy or power they can sense it. That's why some very, very small people like him can be – very, very powerful, because it's his belief."

"I know this to be true, and when you say 'small,' you not actually saying 'small' as in a 'small-type' way," Chad said. "His stature is actually small."

"Small in all ways," Halimah said, laughing.

"Small ways are…" Chad started, "When people have small stature they have complexes."

Halimah laughed again softly. "Yes, well, not all of them, but yes – very often, they seek to find power and they try to find people with lots of light and crush their light and suck their energy and use their energy so they can feel big. You understand? That's what he does to you; he tries to suck your energy. He tries to suck lots of entertainers, or people who he knows can be really big and shine, he sucks all their energy so he can feel shiny, because he knows he's a small little fanged beast. But you can really just smush [him] like a cockroach, you understand?"

She warned him not to make any "sudden moves" until he'd formed "new beliefs." She added, "If you still fear and you make a sudden move, then someone can harm you. But once you and [your] energy grow … mountains become anthills. You understand? And instead of you being just regular size, you'll be like a giant. And you just step over a little anthill and you don't even really notice it."

"You understand?" Halimah asked. "It might seem confusing."

"It don't seem confusing at all," he responded. "I understand."

There was a pause.

"Todd Shaw," he said, referring to Too $hort.

Halimah couldn't hear him. "What did you say?"

"The name is Todd Shaw," Chad repeated.

"Todd Shaw? He seems boring," Halimah responded, breaking her hushed tone and laughing, offering everyone relief from the tension of the session. "What kind of name is that?"

They both laughed. "That's a terrible name," she continued. "Isn't it a terrible name? I don't know. You're making me laugh."

Halimah tried to refocus but said she couldn't see anything. "There's some people who, when I say them, you get kinda blank," she explained. "Like, blah energy. And that's the energy that I pick up from this person. They have too much talk, too little work … you need people who build your energy up and he'll never do that. Just kinda suck you. He's trying to take advantage of you in some way. He has some things he can offer you … [but] it's an energy drain, and as

(*Generally, a "glass ceiling" – or "glass rooftop" as Chad said – is used to describe barriers formed by racism or sexism in the workplace. In a broader sense, the phrase refers to "an invisible but real barrier through which the next stage or level of advancement can be seen, but not reached.")

sensitive as you are to people, you don't need a lot of energy drains … I don't know if I've given you any information but that's what I see from him. He's a bore."

Chad didn't agree. "Once upon a time in my life he helped me."

"Yeah," Halimah said. "Everybody helps you once upon a time in your life. But you can have loyalties to people, but … everyone has an expiration date."

"Nah," Chad disagreed.

She continued, "And it comes a time in your life when people no longer benefit you and you no longer benefit them … You're not helping him by having a loyalty to him and he's not really helping you in the ways that you need."

The next person Chad asked about was rapper Snoop Dogg, one of the few "gangsta rappers" who had managed to cross over into the mainstream and achieve multi-platinum success.

"Have you come in contact with Calvin Broadus? I can't figure him out," Chad asked.

"He's kinda sneaky. Is he kinda like a snake?" Halimah asked. "Snakes are good when … you and them have the same goals. I'm not seeing him as a negative person … He just does not trust people very quickly. He has to warm up to them. So he'll act like he's cool but he's all the while trying to figure you out … That's what he has to do sort of to protect himself. He's very wary of people."

"You've heard of him," Chad stated.*

"Yes, definitely," Halimah said. "He's been burnt by people very close to him. Lots of times."

"I'm only gonna ask you about one more person and it's just for fun's sake," Chad said, chuckling. "What is wrong with Don 'Magic' Juan?"

"He's an elf," responded Halimah. "You know what an elf –"

Chad burst out laughing. "An elf!?"

"Next time you look at him, look at him closely," Halimah explained. "You see his eyes glint and they have a little sparkle in them? He plays really stupid but he's not as dumb as he acts. He, um… part of his brain's not very clear, it's very foggy. His brain has a slight fog over it at all times. So he's not very … clear. He's just living life for the ride, he has no real purpose in life anymore … he's going to enjoy whatever he can get. But he's fun. But at every moment he's looking for his next kick. And elves are kinda mischievous, they like to play jokes … They like to make mischief, cause trouble, and bother people, but they're lots of fun. They keep life fun. But he'll – when he gets bored with life he'll just die, 'cause everything he wants to accomplish in life he already did – in his past. And he's just living until he gets bored."

Halimah paused. "Any more people?"

"The thing about traveling abroad makes a lot of sense, and I know where the Japanese connection is," Chad contemplated. "The problem is, I'm on parole [so I can't travel overseas]. I'm in the process of trying to get off parole."

"Okay, let me tell you one thing," Halimah said. She took a deep breath and finally said: "Live life. And don't do this literally, but in your head start to believe that you're like a superhero, k? Make up these crazy ideas that you can be like invincible and start to trick yourself into believing them and your life will speed up and catch up to your new ideas, you understand?"

"Everything you experience is because of the beliefs you have in here," she continued, tapping the side of her head. "And that's how your life is. So as you change beliefs, your life changes … some people; they just never believe that they'll ever go to jail and they never will. You going to jail was an experience that you sort of wanted, even though you might not believe this, but it's something you sort of wanted and you saw it as being part of your environment so naturally you wind up behind the bars, you understand?"

Chad disagreed. "Naw, I prayed for one thing and that went the wrong way."

"But if you pray for..." Halimah said, her voice drifting off before continuing, "Sometimes

(*Halimah says she isn't a rap fan and doesn't watch TV, and the only name Chad mentioned which was familiar to her was Calvin "Snoop Dogg" Broadus. "When [I'm] in a trance, basically you could tell me a name and … the imprint of their spirit, it just shows up for me," she explains. "I usually see … pictures, and then I explain what I see … I'm seeing a visual." Her sister Ayesha adds, "It's more about the energy that you get from [the image]. We're all connected.")

if you don't want something really bad, it happens to you. You understand? Like, if you're really scared you're gonna slip and fall, you'll slip and fall eventually, or sooner than somebody who never worries about slipping and falling … That's how life is … whatever you focus on happens … But you earned more stripes on your belt by [going to prison], and you learn lots of things about yourself and other people there. So, it's something that added to your life even though sometimes you might think it took away from it."

"I figured out [that the prison time] added to my life, but I didn't figure it out until the last minute," Chad agreed.

"You know," he added slowly, "The prayer went like this: 'Don't let me die.' I seen everybody dying around me and it was total destruction, and the only way to save me from death was to hide me. And I didn't figure it out until the last year [of my prison time]. But I turned a negative into a positive."

"Yes," Halimah nodded. "You're good at doing that. And that's a very admirable thing. And all the situations that you're facing now, you can turn negatives into positives."

There was one more thing that was bothering Chad. "I've got a dude named Larry around us…." he began, his voice drifting off slowly.

"Why do you have so many sucky people around you?" Halimah asked.

"You tell me," Chad said.

Halimah laughed. "Um… I really could pick up nothing from him. He just doesn't seem very interesting … Doesn't seem like a very high energy person. Not a very – kind of a mediocre person," she paused. "You know what you want? You want to add people to your team who are like rockets."

"Where do you find them?" Chad asked.

"You need to start changing your perception of how people are in general," Halimah told him. "[Believe] that people are here to help you … When someone appears in your life kinda magically, you're like, 'You're sent to me. You're my blessing,' you know? … It's about your perception of people in general."

She paused. "Do you have any more questions?"

Ayesha, who'd remained silent for most of the session, couldn't resist throwing a name out. Ray J's sex tape with Kim Kardashian had just been released and he was riding the wave of publicity by prepping for his fourth album *All I Feel*. The sisters had partied with him a few days prior at a Hollywood nightclub.

"What about Ray J?" Ayesha asked.

Chad laughed. "He's a joke."

"What was he thinking? He's quite a joke," Halimah laughed. She looked at the silver digital recorder Chad had left running next to her on the desk and added, "You know, if you take this tape and blackmail me I will kill you."

Everyone laughed. Halimah's voice took on a serious tone, adding, "He's just always looking for his next little money-making thing … He's just one of those people who always wanted to be as big as someone else, like his sister."

"Living in the shadows," Chad added.

"Yeah," agreed Halimah, adding, "Ray J is a person who is very fun to play jokes on. So use him for entertainment. Some people are in your life for pure entertainment."

Chad laughed. "Gotta have fun with Ray J."

"[What about] Tupac?" Ayesha asked. "I'm curious."

"Let me tell you something," answered Halimah. "This is what Tupac does. He hasn't left the earth. He's like a ghost, sort of."

Everyone in the room laughed, the tension of the session lifting.

"I'm not lying," Halimah insisted. "Like, some people when you die, you leave the earth. Some people are like, 'Aw, why'd I have to die?' and he's one of those people who was not satisfied when he died, even though he talked his death into existence. He wanted his death, but when he died, he was like, *'Shit.'* So he still lives on the earth."

"Can you channel Tupac?" Ayesha prodded her sister.

"Oh, I don't like doing that," Halimah said.

"Don't do that," Chad agreed. "He used to ride in my car. I knew that shit was real. I believe."

"Ask Snoop has he ever seen Tupac," Halimah suggested. "He's going to look at you like you crazy. But he's seen him too. He just thought he was too high."

"He told me some stuff the other day," Chad admitted. "He told me real low in my ear."

"He's really trying to trust you," said Halimah.

"He said that we've got fifteen years of catching up to do," Chad said.

"That's interesting," Halimah said. "You and him both have a lot to learn from each other."

As the session concluded, Chad pressed "stop" on the digital recorder. He later gave the device to someone he trusted, explaining, "There's something on there I want to keep."

The following Friday, Pimp C headed out to the Midwest to meet up with Bun and the rest of the crew for a three-date mini-tour. On July 6, the first night in Cincinnati, the promoter told UGK he needed them at the venue at 9 PM. Entourages inevitably adopt some of the characteristics of their leader, so Pimp and Bun's dual management was beginning to create complications. While Bun's crew was strictly business, arriving at the scheduled time and following all the rules, Pimp's crew was the exact opposite.

Bun, always on time, arrived promptly at 9 PM and was ushered into a dressing room near the backstage entrance. But the first opening act Big Mike was just getting on stage, and there were still several more acts slated (Devin the Dude and Scarface) before UGK.

Meanwhile, the promoter had been calling Pimp, rushing him to hurry up and get to the venue. When Pimp pulled up out back and learned that they were nowhere near ready for UGK to hit the stage, he blasted the promoter. "You can't rush a pimp!" he yelled. "I don't know why these niggas think they can rush a pimp, mane! I gotta get pretty and I gotta put my cologne on!"

As Pimp kept yelling, making a scene, a crowd gathered as the promoter tried to calm him down. Bun, sitting in the room backstage, heard a loud commotion out back. He tilted his head and looked at his security guard Truck. "Man, that Pimp?" Bun asked.

Everyone in the room fell silent, listening to the muffled yells. "Man, that's Pimp, man," Bun sighed. "Go check on him, see what's going on."

Truck and Bun's road manager Bone ran out back to see what the problem was. Pimp was yelling at the promoter, "Hoe ass nigga rushin' me and shit! Got me takin' hoe baths! I'm a yellow pretty nigga! I gotta take a shower! I gotta wash myself good!"*

Pimp glanced over at Truck and Bone and let on a slight smile. "What I'ma do is – fuck y'all – I'ma go in this muthafucker, I'ma holla at Truck, I'm finna holla at Bunny, we gon' do this show and get this muthafuckin' money!"

Pimp slung his arm around Truck as the whole entourage crowded in through the back door. "Whassup, man!?" Truck asked.

"Man, ain't shit," Pimp laughed. "I just wanna talk shit before I get up here."

He turned towards Bone. "Y'know, Bone, I gotta create a scene."

Chad had grown to love being "Pimp C" as much as Bun had once loved being "Bun B"; the two had almost completely switched roles. "Early in the game, [Chad] didn't like being Pimp C the artist," says Mama Wes. "[But later], C loved [the attention]. He ate it up ... he loved it."

"In the early days of UGK ... I was the person that was more likely to curse you out and fight you ... and Pimp was the more composed, relaxed, chill person," Bun agrees. "I had no responsibilities, I had no wife, I had no kids, I had no girlfriend ... so I just [didn't] care."

(*A hoe bath involves an improvised shower using a sink.)

As Chad had grown increasingly flamboyant, Bun, having left his "crazy years" behind him, grew increasingly withdrawn. He was so lowkey that people sometimes didn't recognize him. He once stopped by a convenience store to pick up some cigars, where the women behind the register were laughing as he approached the counter.

"What y'all laughing about?" he asked.

"[We were] talking about how much you look like Bun B," one chuckled.

"Yeah, right, like Bun B would come in here," he deadpanned. "Every day somebody tells me I look like Bun B."

When Chad got back to Port Arthur, he stopped by his mother's house to catch up on a few things. As they wrapped up the conversation, Chad turned to leave and headed out through the garage door. Edgar the Dog followed him, tail wagging.

Abruptly, Chad stopped and turned back towards the kitchen. "Hey, let me tell you about when I talked to the psychic, Mama. How you feel about that stuff?"

She looked up from what she'd been doing. "C, I don't have time to worry about that kind of shit. I've got too much work to do. You keep a nigga too busy."

"Yeah, well, you know, I had some time on my hands," Chad responded. He looked down at Edgar, whose tongue was hanging out, tail wagging furiously. "What you think about that? Oh yeah?" he asked the dog, pausing for an imaginary response. "Aw, Mama, Ed say that's bullshit."

Mama Wes said she agreed with Edgar.

"Those people kinda know what you want 'em to say, huh?" Chad thought aloud. He said he'd been insulted by Halimah's condescending remarks about Too $hort.

It had been a running joke throughout years of touring that $hort didn't care about anything as long as he got paid – he would perform anywhere, no matter the sound system quality. He never bothered to go to soundcheck, and Chad often joked that if he put the orange plastic record player he'd had as a toddler on stage with Too $hort, he'd still perform. $hort was even known to bootleg his own album before the release date, a fact which Chad found hilarious.*

But no matter how much they joked internally, Chad would never allow an outsider to say anything negative about his friend. ("Too $hort is my OG, and you is never gonna talk bad about Too $hort [around me]," he'd proclaimed during a radio interview with Bo-Bo Luchiano.)

"Mama, I still say, when we were coming up and nobody embraced us, he was the first nigga to embrace us," Chad said.

The following weekend, Pimp C and Bun B were back in Los Angeles on a hot Thursday afternoon for the Zune BBQ. The Zune was a personal MP3 player, Microsoft's attempt to compete with the Apple iPod.** Microsoft had deep pockets, and Bun was in the process of negotiating a corporate sponsorship deal with them.

Perhaps overestimating the attendance, Microsoft had dozens of police officers on hand, even more than the lingering concertgoers. Rows and rows of police cars and bicycle cops were lined up under a nearby freeway overpass.

E-40 hit the stage just after 4 PM, followed by an energetic stage-diving performance by David Banner. Bun and Pimp pulled up separately; Pimp arriving in red Dickies accompanied by Ayesha and Halimah, Ed, and Mike Mo.

DJ Latin Prince, backstage wearing Dickies with the UGK logo, grabbed Bun for a quick on-camera interview. "What does it mean to have Pimp back home, man?" Latin Prince asked.

"It's just like having my right arm back," Bun said. "Imagine what it's like doing everything

---

(*When the *Underground Kingz* double album came out, Chad posted a bulletin on his MySpace which read: "THE NEW ALBUM IS PLATNUM! THANK YALL WHO GOT THE REAL AND IF U GOT THE BOOTLEG U AINT PLAY NOBODY BUT YOSELF CUZ I BOOTLEG MY OWN SHIT!!!!!!!!!! CANT BEAT EM JOIN EM!")

(**The Zune failed to put up strong sales numbers against the iPod and was discontinued in 2011.)

with one hand."

Pimp C was amused by the overabundance of police. Bun came out first, then brought Pimp out to join him for "Int'l Player's Anthem." A street team in the front of the crowd held big cutout posters advertising the upcoming UGK album. After running through older classics like "Pocket Full of Stones," "Akickdoe!" and "Let Me See It," Pimp told the crowd they should spark up a blunt and do whatever they wanted to do despite the heavy police presence. "Fuck the police!" Pimp proclaimed.

"It was just kinda awkward because you got uniformed police officers standing right next to you," recalls Bone.

"Last song, bitch!" Pimp announced, before leading into "Get Throwed." Pimp slung his arm around Bun's shoulder as the two men walked off stage together to the "Game Belongs to Me" instrumental.

A cameraman from Hard Knock TV caught up with Pimp and asked him to spit a "vintage" rhyme. "Or you wanna hear something new?" Pimp asked, then spit a capella:

I had a lot of niggas that was down with me
Or, should I say, a lot of niggas hung around with me
But when I took my fall
I found out I really didn't have many friends at all
When I was out there rollin' in the Benz and ball
My mama used to get a lot of telephone calls
Niggas tryin' to see how it was, I had a buzz
But all that shit stopped when I got stopped by the fuzz
A couple niggas kept the shit true indeed
But not the ones I used to bail out of jail and feed
We used to smoke weed and get drunk off brew
I went to TDC, nigga, I couldn't find you
You couldn't find me, that's what you told yourself
But you couldn't tell that bullshit to nobody else
So when they asked 'em how I was doing, they told 'em I was cool
Knowin' you ain't talked to me since I went to the pen, fool
No pictures, no commissary, no money to eat
And you think it's all good 'cause I'm back on these streets?
I'm back on these beats, you still blowin' in the wind
But these is the niggas that we call "friends"*
And the cold part about it, nigga, I still love you
Nigga, can't you see what all that drank and drugs do?
I wanna help you save your life
But I can't get caught up no more, I already paid the price
Negative is not my forte
Maybe we can get back on the same page one day

"What about your friends?" he asked rhetorically, then walked away from the camera shouting, "*Chuuuuuch!*"

Regardless whether there was any validity to the psychic Halimah's visions, Chad's questions had been revealing within themselves. Clearly, he had doubts about some of the people around him.

(*Pimp C had used this line before on his DJ Screw freestyle over the Whodini "Friends" instrumental. It was a reference to the original line from the Whodini song, "These are the people that we call friends." Snoop Dogg has said that he and Pimp C recorded an unreleased record called "Friends" around this time. It is not known if this is the same record.)

CHAPTER 51

"[Larry] was just a fuck-up ... he was just the type of person to leave a path of destruction and misunderstanding everywhere he went." – Smoke D

"Larry was like the mystery man ... [In Jackson, we were all] wondering what was the connection with him and Pimp. [He] was a guy who was infatuated with Pimp C. He wanted to look like him, he wanted to dress like him, he wanted to live his lifestyle. Everything [Pimp] did, *he* did. [He] wanted to *be* Pimp."
– An acquaintance of Larry's who declined to be named

Even though Chad's feelings on Smoke D had soured after the failed legal intervention at Mama Wes' house, he had publicly maintained their friendship, even proclaiming "Free Smoke D!" on Bo-Bo Luchiano's radio show in early May. But by late June, as evidenced by his psychic session with Halimah, he'd started to wonder if Smoke was "the devil" in disguise.

Security at the Louisiana jail where Smoke and his co-defendant Stan were being held was relatively loose, and contraband like weed and cell phones were easily accessible. Smoke had a cell phone, and used it constantly. He'd been close enough to taste success, meeting with major record labels alongside Pimp C. Watching it all slip away, he became increasingly desperate.

"[Smoke] was just doing too much," recalls his friend Jaro. "He was sitting there on his ass, locked up for several months already ... I can understand he feels powerless and he's trying to help himself and do whatever he can do, so he [was] calling and calling [all the time] ... and micromanaging stuff, like ridiculously."

Ever since the late 90s, when Chad believed – probably correctly – that Merrick Young was trying to set him up, Chad refused to take calls from people in jail. "He didn't talk to people in jail ... He had that in his head: Don't trust nobody in jail, [because] they'll sell your ass out," says Mama Wes. "They'll invent [a story]. Because it had happened before, you know?"

"Nigga, don't call me from jail!" Chad snapped at Smoke. When Chad stopping taking his phone calls, Smoke began texting incessantly. Chad, already paranoid, became convinced that Smoke was trying to set him up. Even a call from Jaro set Pimp off. "Jaro, fuck this code language, man!" he yelled. "I ain't got nothing to hide, man. Let's fuckin' speak straight!"

Smoke wasn't on good terms with Larry anymore, either; they'd fallen out during a trip to Los Angeles prior to his incarceration. (Smoke declines to explain specifics, but it sounds like a drug deal gone bad.) "I was trying to get money for a lawyer and [Larry] was getting in my way," Smoke shrugs. "He was just a fuck up ... he was just the type of person to leave a path of destruction and misunderstanding everywhere he went."

As Pimp became increasingly suspicious of Smoke, Larry seized the opportunity to move into Smoke's position. "[Larry] kind of like poisoned Pimp's mind on Smoke D," says Ed. "The further Smoke got away from Pimp, the closer L.A. got."

When Stan was notified that Smoke D had accepted a plea agreement in exchange for testifying against him, he decided to plead guilty. The state offered a 30-year plea bargain; his attorney negotiated them down to 15.

Someone – likely Larry – informed Pimp that Smoke had agreed to testify. Pimp also heard, incorrectly, that Smoke D's sentence had been reduced from 20 years to five years.

"I'm free, muthafucker, so stop telling the Feds all that ol' lies tryin' to get that time off you, tryin' to get me on Conspiracy [charges] and tryin' to fuck me off and send me to the pen," Pimp told *OZONE*, a comment likely directed at Smoke D. "Nigga, you know who you is. If you got a double-digit number and now they went to a single-digit number … Nigga, your lawyer alright, but he ain't got it like that!"

Although Chad had two Bentleys, a large house, and all the visible trappings of success, he still wasn't in a good position financially. His IRS problems had never really been resolved. "We were afraid that the Feds were gonna pick him up when he got out of jail," Mama Wes recalls.

In late 2006, the IRS filed two tax liens against him, $28,276.87 for his 2000 taxes and a whopping $228,537.27 for 2001. They also placed a $43,098.97 tax lien for the year 2002 on his Oakmont home. Concerned that the IRS was going to take the San Jac house, Chad transferred it into Chinara's father's name. Plus, he still hadn't paid Quanell X the $44,000 he'd agreed to pay within six months of his release.

It had been more than a year and a half since he received the six-figure advance from Jive for the UGK album, and it wasn't likely that he'd be receiving more money from them anytime soon. Chad's attorney Craig Wormley got the impression that he didn't want to go to Prince for more money; the relationship with Rap-A-Lot, at least on a financial level, seemed strained.

When Chad appeared on a record for the group Missez called "Love Song," their label rep Shawn "Tubby" Holiday got a call from J. Prince demanding payment for Pimp C's appearance on the record. Pimp technically wasn't signed to Rap-A-Lot so Interscope wasn't required to pay a clearance, but they cut a check anyway. When Tubby mentioned it to Pimp, Pimp told him he shouldn't have paid Prince. As Tubby recalls it, Prince snapped back saying that if Pimp felt like he owed him some money, he should come to his house and get it.

Although there had been complaints in the past from Rap-A-Lot artists who felt they weren't being fairly compensated, Mama Wes believed Chad was the exception to the rule.
"It's my impression that everything that J and C did – C was either the winner or they broke even. He didn't really fuck C around where money was concerned," says Mama Wes. "He really didn't … [and] I'll be honest with you, I feel like C got some stuff from J he really didn't deserve."

Chad hoped to transition into someone behind the scenes instead of just an artist; he didn't want to still be rapping by the time he turned 40. "Financially, running a label is the smartest thing that anybody could want to do in this business," he told *FADER*. His plan, he told All-HipHop, was to sign some artists and "evolve into [an] executive type" so he wouldn't have to always "be in the spotlight."

He'd initially planned on launching UGK Records with old friends like X-Mob, Smoke D, and female rappers Bo$$ and Suga, but instead, he'd attracted a crop of young hustlers. "I'm fucking with the underdog, because that's the people that's hungry," he told WordofSouth.com.

"We always looking for artists [but] we ain't looking to sign no muthafuckers up [if] we gotta be holding they hand in the studio," he told *Tha Buzz* TV, adding that he was looking for people who could handle their own business and were "self-contained."

Along with T.O.E. and DJ B-Do, there was Mama Wes' artist Hezeleo and fellow Port Arthur native Big Bubb, aspiring rappers who didn't mind filling other roles as needed: selling merchandise, ad-libbing Pimp's vocals on stage, or throwing t-shirts into the crowd.

Pimp decided to bring XVII into the UGK Records camp because he had money to invest in himself and wasn't afraid to spend it. XVII almost had *too much* money; Pimp knew what he was doing to get it, and was afraid that if he didn't help him get out of the streets, he would end up dead or in prison like so many of the friends he'd lost in the past.

After their initial meeting, Pimp invited XVII back to Houston and gave him back $5,000 of the $7,000 he'd paid for the first feature. "I would give you the whole $7,000 back, but I'm a little short right now," he laughed. "Go give this to [TV] Johnny." He'd already asked the jeweler TV Johnny to make UGK Records pieces for his artists.

Pimp explained that constantly being "in character" could be exhausting, and he needed someone else to step up and play the role of the flashy rapper so he could sometimes relax in the background. "When you see Dr. Dre, Dr. Dre don't have to have all that jewelry. Dr. Dre don't have to be in no Bentley," Pimp explained. "Dr. Dre could be in a sweatsuit and you still gonna respect him."

Just as he'd told DJ B-Do and T.O.E., Pimp explained that until he was able to secure a distribution deal, there would be no paperwork; he wanted his artists to be free to pursue other opportunities until he had something more substantial to offer. "I'm not even gonna lie to you," he explained. "I'm not going to sign y'all to no paperwork if I can't pay y'all how y'all should be paid."

XVII became somewhat of a polarizing figure in the UGK Records camp. Many felt that he was trying too hard to emulate Pimp. "XVII actually idolized Pimp to the point where he wanted to sound like him," says engineer Avery Harris.

Plus, everyone knew XVII had gained entrance to the camp by paying Pimp, but so had nearly everyone else. "It's not very many people that was a part of [UGK Records] that didn't really pay their way," observes Pimp's cousin Ed. But XVII was the only one who had an album close to completion. "This is my first round draft pick, 'cause he's raced ahead of all you funky niggas," Pimp would proclaim.

"Man, don't say that shit," XVII told him. "You gonna have them niggas mad at me."

"No, they need to get mad, 'cause they need to put a fire up under they ass," Pimp responded. "Ain't nothing I said a lie."

———————

While incarcerated, Smoke D got a call from a trusted friend in Vicksburg, Mississippi. "Man, you [been] hangin' with a dude that got nine fingers? His name is Larry or L.A. or whatever? Stop hangin' around him," the friend said.

"Why?" Smoke asked.

"Stop hangin' around him," the friend said firmly, hinting that Larry was working with law enforcement.

The more he thought about it – and Smoke had *plenty* of time to think – certain things about Larry just didn't make sense. Smoke had been around the drug game for years, and he knew the qualities of a big-time drug dealer. "[Larry] wasn't moving nothing," Smoke explains. "He was lazy. He didn't have no hustle, he was [passed out] all the time … He was too high to do the hustle or do anything … [I'd] never seen him bust a move."

To Smoke, Larry's laziness made his endless supply of cocaine, codeine, and weed seem all the more unlikely. "[Larry] always had work when ain't nobody had none … he had *everything* all of the time," Smoke says. "That's what spooked me. When ain't nobody have nothing, he had it in abundance."

Smoke knew that Larry had latched on to Pimp C, especially now that he was gone. This new information – coupled with the fact that Smoke had nothing but hours of idle time on his hands, and his mind was going to some strange places – had him convinced that Pimp was in immediate danger.

But when Smoke called Pimp to warn him that he'd heard Larry was an informant, Pimp was pissed. Pimp, notoriously paranoid, was already on edge over Smoke's constant calls and texts. "Well, shit! You the one who brought him to me!" Pimp pointed out, launching into one of his infamous curse-filled rants.

Smoke had known Pimp long enough to know that it was pointless to argue with him.

Instead of reacting, he simply listened as Pimp finished cussing him out.

Later, Smoke sent him a text. "God is gonna show you what I'm tryin' to tell you," it read.*

Pimp, who was down the street from his house in Port Arthur at the gas station with XVII when he got the text, stared at the phone. "He done gone too far this time," he grumbled, showing the text to XVII. Pimp was so infuriated he pulled the battery out of his phone and angrily threw both the phone and the battery in the dumpster. The next stop was Avery's studio, where Pimp recorded a track called "Da Game Been Good to Me."

Wendy Day thought Smoke D's attorneys had worked out a situation with the judge to give him a light sentence. She was shocked when she heard about the 20 years and called Chad to ask what happened.

"Fuck him," Pimp snapped. "Fuck that nigga."

Throughout all the drama with Smoke D, Larry was always around, lurking in the background. Lowkey and nondescript, he had a strange knack for blending in; even people who had met him couldn't remember what he looked like. Pimp's crew considered him a "mystery man," a "phantom figure" who rarely held a conversation with anyone besides Pimp.

Smoke wasn't the only one who heard that Larry was working with authorities; rumors of Larry's police cooperation were rampant in Jackson. The rumor wasn't completely unfounded: Larry was still facing 20 years in prison for his 2005 marijuana arrest. His trial had been delayed several times while his attorney negotiated a plea agreement with prosecutors.

Prosecutors were at a disadvantage because they could not locate Larry's co-defendant Daniel Hernandez, an illegal alien who had apparently fled back to Mexico. Without his testimony, it would be difficult to convict Larry of conspiracy. They agreed to a plea agreement in which Larry would only serve five years of probation.**

Pimp, who likely didn't know that Larry was facing drug charges back in Mississippi, kept him around for one reason: "That boy got money," he told Ayesha, explaining that he planned to help Larry clean his dirty money.***

Big Bubb, who sometimes acted as security, recalls seeing large cash transactions between Larry and Pimp on more than one occasion. According to Big Bubb, Pimp told him that Larry was investing $200,000 into UGK Records. "[Larry] put some money down to be a part owner of UGK. That was my understanding from Pimp's mouth," says Big Bubb. Pimp allegedly told Bubb that Larry had robbed a drug courier of a large six-figure sum, and that was the reason for his strange, evasive behavior.

Although it isn't clear where that alleged six figures went, it was around this time that Pimp paid off his loan with Quanell X, gifting him with a Bentley that was later exchanged for a more low-profile vehicle. "I've never talked about any of this publicly," Quanell X cautions, declining

---

(*According to Smoke D, this was the last text he sent to Pimp C. XVII doesn't recall what the text said, but believes it was something different which seemed to be referencing a previous drug transaction. XVII agreed with Pimp that the series of text messages sounded suspicious. According to XVII, the texts were so blatant that Pimp believed Smoke was either trying to warn him that authorities were investigating him, or really trying to set him up. "I feel like [Pimp] misread that," says Smoke's codefendant Stan. "As far as [Smoke] setting him up, I can't see it.")

(**Larry's attorney Sam Martin says that Larry's plea agreement didn't involve any cooperation with law enforcement. Although there isn't any evidence to support the idea that Larry was working with authorities, it seems clear that authorities were at least keeping tabs on him. Larry often shipped pints of codeine through regular USPS and UPS shipments back to a friend in Jackson, and authorities eventually caught onto their scheme. The friend, who asked not to be identified, was arrested in Jackson in 2011 and charged with possession with intent to distribute codeine. He refused to identify Larry as his supplier and served 16 months in a state prison.)

(***Pimp name-dropped Larry on the Jazze Pha-produced "Fly Lady," apparently because he needed something to rhyme with a line about "hairy" pussy. Pimp raps, "You'll never trick me, bitch, and bitch I bet you never trick that Larry." The record was later released on *Naked Soul of Sweet Jones*.)

to discuss the details of their financial transaction. "[But] Pimp C was a man of his word. He did not burn me. In fact, he blessed me tremendously."

Pimp never discussed the alleged $200,000 buy-in with other key members of his team, but he did begin referring to Larry as his business partner. Most people couldn't understand how he was a partner if he didn't *do* anything.

Larry's involvement with UGK Records was discussed in a few meetings Chad held with his business manager Rick Martin and his attorney Craig Wormley. Wormley, who perceived Larry as a "very mysterious guy" with a lot of money to blow, didn't think it was a good idea and got the impression that Rick felt threatened by Larry's involvement.

Mama Wes had no idea what Larry's purpose was either, and since she'd first caught a bad vibe from him, she mostly ignored him. "You know, Mama, nobody can change your mind when you don't like somebody," Chad commented. "But what is it that does that?"

"It's the creepy feeling," Mama Wes told her son, struggling to find the right words. "He just gives me a creepy feeling."

J. Prince, who encountered Larry at an event, also caught the "creepy feeling," turning to Mama Wes and asking, "Whassup with that dude?"

"Something don't smell right?" Mama Wes smiled, quoting one of Prince's favorite phrases.

"Yeah," Prince nodded. "Yeah, that's it."

As Larry got closer to Pimp, friends back home in Jackson watched as he slowly morphed into a near caricature of the rapper, wearing mink coats and slurring his voice into an exaggerated Southern drawl. "[We were all] wondering what was the connection with him and Pimp," admits an acquaintance of Larry's who asked not to be identified. "[He became] infatuated with Pimp C. He wanted to look like him, he wanted to dress like him, he wanted to live his lifestyle. Everything [Pimp] did, *he* did. [He] wanted to *be* Pimp."

Larry told anyone who would listen that he was half owner of UGK Records. Most weren't sure whether to believe him, and to people close to the situation, the claim seemed ludicrous, since UGK Records wasn't even incorporated as an actual entity.

Larry pulled up to Stax' clothing store in Jackson one day wearing a mink coat, a cigar hanging from his mouth and a new chain hanging around his neck. "You gonna let him smoke that in here?" someone asked Stax as Larry approached the door.

"Aw, be quiet," Stax said. Larry was a good customer who spent several hundred dollars every time he stopped by.

"UGK Records, we 'bout to start doing some thangs," Larry bragged, holding up a UGK diamond pendant with his initials "L.A." above it. He held the piece up close for Stax to get a good look at it. "I'm co-president. We gonna start signing some artists."

What the fuck is a co-president? Stax thought, maintaining a poker face.

Stax was usually unimpressed by the local hustlers who stopped through to tell exaggerated tales of their conquests. He wondered what possible value Pimp C saw in someone like Larry. *Must be breaking bread or doing some dirty work for him, taking penitentiary chances,* Stax mused. He considered Larry nothing but a male groupie and assumed he was paying Pimp in some form for the opportunity to hang around; anything to have more stories to tell, to increase his perceived importance or relevance.

"When he'd come in, I'd humor him … you wanna tell some lies or whatever, [it's cool]," Stax explains. "I ain't have no problem with [Larry] because the lying and dickriding doesn't offend me. It's humor and entertainment to me." Stax knew Larry's type and exactly how to cater to them; he'd make them feel important to entice them into spending money. "Them some nice shoes you got on," or "that's a bad ass coat," he'd offer, throwing out half-hearted compliments.

"Damn, nice piece," Stax told him.

"Yeah, Emit got me right!" Larry said enthusiastically. He'd gone to Pimp's jeweler in Houston to get the UGK piece. Clearly enjoying the attention, Larry turned and skimmed the rows of Stax' Blockwear t-shirts lining the walls.

"Give me *everythaaang* in a 5," he pronounced, waving his arm grandly towards the wall full of t-shirts, drawing out each syllable in an exaggerated Southern accent. *This nigga is tryna be Pimp,* Stax laughed to himself as he walked into the back stockroom to package up all the 5X t-shirts.

When Stax returned with the merchandise, Larry pulled out his cell phone. "I want you to hear something," he said. Larry played a clip of "Da Game Been Good To Me" and rapped along with Pimp C's verse to make sure Stax and the handful of other men hanging out in the store could understand the words:*

You got caught with that work on 10
Made a deal with the state to turn your fall partner in
But he took 15, befo' you could tell
*He ain't witchu no mo', hoe, you got 20 in a cell***
I sent you a lawyer, you ain't listened that time
*Ain't no appeal, but they dropped it to five?****
Who you had to fuck to give back that time?
Textin' me from a cell phone, bitch, you lost yo' fuckin mind?
How dare you tryna get me on Conspiracy, jack?
If the Feds hit me, I'ma hit yo' ass back!
You fight wit' yo' tongue, I'll send them killas
Transcript writer, I'll kill you, nigga!

"Ooh wee wee!" Larry yelled when the verse ended, imitating Chad's new catchphrase, his face lighting up.**** "I *told* y'all [Smoke D was a snitch]!" he shouted. "I been *tellin'* y'all 'bout that boy!!"

(*This song was later released on UGK's *4 Life.*)
(**"Fall partner" is slang for an inmate's co-defendant. Smoke had agreed to testify against Stan. When Stan learned that Smoke planned to testify against him, he agreed to a plea bargain and was sentenced to 15 years. Smoke had already accepted a plea bargain and was sentenced to 20 years.)
(***Pimp believed that Smoke's sentence had been reduced from 20 years to five years, which was incorrect. "Pimp's information was kinda wrong," says Stan. According to Smoke D, Stan's mother, who is a U.S. Marshal, was able to get his sentence reduced to 15 years. "I like [Stan's] mom. I respect his mom. Because of [her] my situation is not as bad as [it could be]," Smoke D says.)
(****"Trademark – ooh wee wee!" Pimp C ad-libs on "Down 4 Mine.")

CHAPTER 52

"People cared about Pimp because *Pimp* cared ... Pimp C, whether you agreed with him or not, was passionate about what he did. He gave a damn about what he did." – Bun B, The *Village Voice*, March 2008

———————

"Chad had real values ... he *stood* for something ... [People] liked his music, but what they all [loved] about that boy [was that] he had a big heart, and people saw that. No matter how [much] he would blow up at people, at the end of the day he would hug you. And mean it." – Rambro

Monday, July 23, 2007
Atlanta, Georgia

Six long weeks after my bizarre 5 AM interview with Pimp C, I was walking through Atlanta's Cumberland Mall when I got a text from Todd1, a radio producer for the local Hip-Hop station Hot 107.9, asking if the Pimp C interview was real. I was slightly offended; of course it was *real*. Why would we print a fake interview?

I smiled remembering the call; it was a distant memory at this point, but of course his wild statements about Ne-Yo and Russell Simmons were hard to forget. With only a few slight edits, I'd transcribed the first 15 minutes as the first installment of his monthly column, titled "The Chronicles of Pimp C." Due to space constraints, the piece ended with his observations about Atlanta being on "East Coast time." I planned to use the second half of the audio for next month's column.

I hadn't been to the office yet, but I'd heard that the shipment of magazines had just been delivered and distribution had begun to some key places around the city, like recording studios and radio stations.

I called Pimp, the phone tight to my ear to block out the noise of the shopping mall. After making arrangements for him to call in to the station for an interview on the Durtty Boyz' show with ET and J-Nicks, I texted him the call-in number and stopped by Jason's Deli to grab a sandwich, having no idea that I'd just set in motion what would become one of the most epic Hip-Hop radio interviews of all time.

"Hot 107-niiiiiine ATL!" the radio host announced. "I know y'all done heard about all the stuff in the *OZONE* Magazine, asking about Pimp C, what's he talking about, is he talking about the ATL? Pimp C, we got Pimp C on the phone right now. Pimp C!"

"Yo, what's up?" came Pimp's voice on the other end of the line.*

"What up, Pimp C? Talk to me homeboy?" the host demanded. "What's going on with this stuff in the *OZONE* Magazine, man? A-Town is kind of furious!"

ATL wasn't really furious – not the general public, at least. The magazine wasn't even available yet in stores, but apparently the boxes we'd dropped off at the radio stations and recording

———

(*Reading this interview in print, and all other Pimp C quotes contained in this book, simply doesn't have the same effect. Google "Pimp C Hot 107.9 interview" and listen to the audio for maximum impact.)

studios had reached some key people.

"You tell me how you took it, and I'ma tell you what I meant," Pimp C responded.

"Okay, let me tell you what the A-Town is saying," the host explained. "The A-Town's basically saying – they think you dissing Atlanta, talking about, 'Atlanta is not the South.'"

"Okay, well first of all, listen to this. I used to *live* in Atlanta from '96 'til 2001, okay? That's the first thing," Pimp began. "The second thing is this. When I get off the airplane in Atlanta, what time is it?"

"It's whatever time it is out here, homie," the host responded, sounding as confused as I was when Pimp asked me the question.

"It's Eastern Standard Time," Pimp said.

"But it's still on the South side of the map," the host argued.

"Okay, but it's Eastern Standard Time, ain't it?" Pimp asked.

Neither of them was willing to back down. "On the South side of the map, yeah," the host answered.

"Answer my question!" Pimp C spat. "Is it Eastern Standard Time?!?"

"Yeah it is, on the South side of the map," the host repeated.

"Alright, after saying that, listen to this. All my statements are my statements, that's how I feel. And feelings is like booty holes, anybody can have they own feelings. That's my feelings, that ain't got nothing to do with Bun B," Pimp said. "That's the first thing, so let's separate Pimp C's statements from UGK and Bun B."

No one had mentioned Bun B, but apparently there was already some tension brewing. "That's how *I* feel!" Pimp continued, his voice rising. "You want to get mad at me for the way *I* feel, then go on and get mad at me. And a fight go with that, you feel me?"

"But, Pimp C," the show's co-host protested, "Why are you so mad? It just seems like you real angry."

"You wanna know why I'm mad? Let me tell you why I'm mad!" Pimp yelled. "I'm mad because everybody [is] on these records lying! Everybody lying! Everybody's this big d-boy, everybody these hardcore gangsters, everybody going to do 'this' to each other when they see each other. And the truth be told, we too blessed and we having too much money in this rap game to be going to war with each other! Truth be told, nobody want to fight nobody in this rap game, 'cause 98% of these dudes is cowards!"

"You got any specific artists you referring that to?" the host asked.

"I'm not dissing nobody, man!" Pimp yelled. "I'm just telling you if we don't clean it up, we gonna lose everything we fought to get, mane. Don't you see that the game is finna leave the South and go somewhere else if we don't straighten up?"

"Yeah, we see that. I know what's going on," the host agreed.

"If we don't clean out our own closet, who going to clean it for us?" demanded Pimp C.

"By you saying that, what do you think needs to be done?" the host asked.

Pimp sounded as if he'd been waiting for the question. "This what I think needs to be done, man," he said. "Come on man, at the end of these records we listen to, we don't get nothing out of them no more, man. We don't get no social commentary, we ain't getting no kind of knowledge out of these records. Everybody just talking about how many chains they got on and how much dope they sold, but the truth of the matter is this: *I don't believe you.* 'Cause I *know* you dudes and I *know* you didn't sell no dope!"

"Say man, I'm from Texas, mane. I'm *from* the [dope] game," he added. "Them [cocaine] prices that them boys talking about, man, them boys ain't got no prices like that in no Atlanta! And if you do, right now, bring some to where my people at. We'll buy it and flush it down the toilet, because we don't support drugs, but show it to me, mane!"

"I know who was wearing them backpacks, I know who had they pants rolled up with Timberland boots in 1998 and [now] they acting like they some big time drug dealers," he sneered, taking a dig at Young Jeezy. Knowing Jeezy had a relationship with his partner, he added, "[And] if y'all want to get mad, get mad at the Pimp. Don't get mad at the Bun, and don't put the UGK on it … this [is] *my* opinon. Me! I'm talking like a man, and I'll stand up [for my opinion]!"

He changed topics. "Anytime an artist in Atlanta makes crunk music … they need to shout out Three 6 Mafia, because y'all *know* that's where that music started at, mane," Pimp said. "[And] y'all know for a fact that UGK started the word 'Trill.'"*

"Everybody in Atlanta feels like … you dissed them," the co-host said.

"If they would read in between the lines and hear what I'm telling them, I ain't dissing them, but we got to check ourselves 'fore someone else checks us," Pimp said. "'Cause this would hurt a whole lot more coming from somebody from the East Coast or from the West Coast, than coming from one of our forefathers down here."

"[But] you're saying that we're not even from the South, like Atlanta ain't the South," the co-host protested. "It's a lot of UGK fans that got their feelings hurt today, because they really love you."

"Here's the truth of the matter: I love them too, but we got to straighten out the game," he responded. "If the statement was made in the wrong context, I apologize about that. But I meant what I was saying. Now, maybe it was heard the wrong kind of way."

"Everybody running around basically telling Jeezy – 'cause the magazine hasn't hit the stands – that you were pointing him out with the [17.5 comment]," the co-host said.

"And the Meech talk," the other host added. "The magazine's making it seem like you pointing out Jeezy with the 17.5 talk, and it had something about Meech."

"Everybody's blowing up Jeezy phone, saying that … it's about to be some beef between you and him," the female co-host added. "That's just the talk in Atlanta."

"There's a whole bunch of people lying [on records about dope prices]," responded Pimp C. "If I was going to diss Young Jeezy, I would have came right out [and] said his name and dissed him. I ain't scared of no man!"

"They *need* to free Big Meech, because it's all circumstantial evidence [against him] … Everybody was down … with BMF before they got busted," Pimp continued. "Everybody wanted to be down with [BMF] 'til they [got] busted, and when it went sour, didn't nobody want to fly the flag no more. Am I lying or telling the truth!?" he demanded.**

"I think it's 'cause they ain't wanna go to jail, though," the co-host said, stating the obvious.

"When the party was going on and everybody was throwing money in the club, everybody was still down!" Pimp C said. "You gotta be down in the good times and the bad times! When I went to prison, Bun stayed down with me in the bad times. So when your pa'tna go to prison, you gotta stay down in the bad times and the good times. If you was Black Mafia Family in the streets when they was spending all that money in the strip clubs, you need to be Black Mafia Family right now while everybody getting indicted!"

"Let me say it again," he reiterated. "If I was gonna diss somebody, I'ma say they name, to they face, and a fight go with that! So naw, I ain't diss Young Jeezy, 'cause Young Jeezy ain't the only one spitting fake dope prices! I'm dissing everybody lying about selling drugs, and ain't touched a ne'er drug."

"Aight," the host said. "What's up with the Russell Simmons comment?"

"What about it?" Pimp shot back.

"I mean, it's basically saying…" the host sounded uncomfortable. "You saying he's, uh… a faggot."

(*DJ Paul appreciated Pimp C speaking out on their behalf, but he says Three 6 Mafia wasn't mad at the new artists who adopted the 'crunk' movement. "Some say we created crunk music [and] … a lot of people thought we didn't get recognized for it," he acknowledges. "But we won plenty awards, we made tons of money … We had two TV shows, produced three movies … [and] it's been going on for 20 years, so, I think Three 6 Mafia got what [we] deserved.")

(**Rumor held that there was a growing beef between Jeezy and Meech. "[Pimp's] beef with Jeezy … really wasn't a beef," writes Big Meech. "It was more about 'Loyalty' to the BMF family that ignited Jeezy career. That's why Pimp said 'if you was BMFin' in the clubs when they was throwing money then you should be 'BMFin' when they got indited, but that's a whole other book within itself.")

There was a pause. "Okay," Pimp responded, with a chuckle in his voice.

Everyone burst out laughing.

"That's kinda self-explanatory," the co-host joked "But, Pimp, Mister Pimp C… Do you think that your comments are going to ruin some of [the] relationships that Bun B made [while you were in prison] since you guys are a group?"

"If these is real people, they won't let my statements affect they relationships with Bun," Pimp said. "Bun got a lot of relationships with a lot of people I don't respect, I don't like, [and] I don't wanna work with 'em."

"When I get ready to do my album, and I'm calling and calling you and calling you, and you don't call me back, then that means you're not down with helping me get my thang together," he continued, taking another subtle shot at Jeezy. "But when it's time to do your album, and you call me, and I have the record back within 24 hours, that means I'm being a real *what*?"

"Nucca…" the hosts answered, censoring the word for radio.

"Exactly," said Pimp C, satisfied that his point had been made. "So now, guess what! If you wanna charge Bun B $50,000 for a verse and then try to come back to me and pay me one dollar to get me on your album, guess what you are?" he said, referring to Ludacris. "You fake, and you garbage! If you was a cartoon character on your first album, then you need to be a cartoon character on your last one!"*

"That's why I'm calling in, to let it be known [that] the things I say don't need to reflect on my brother [Bun B]," Pimp said. "He can have relationships with them dudes all he want to, 'cause truth of the matter is if you fake … and we go to a club somewhere and somebody jump on me, you ain't going to help me fight no way. You gon' run, and I don't need to be friends with you."

"And the next thing is this," Pimp continued, referring to Jay-Z. "If I ain't never had a personal phone number on you, [if] I gotta call your personal assistant to get to you, news flash: you ain't my friend in the first place."

"I'm down with OutKast, the Goodie Mob, the whole Dungeon Family, I'm down with Jazze Pha," he said, listing his Atlanta friends. "I'm down with Lil Jon. I'm down with people that get back in touch with me after I call them, mane! If I'm *calling you, calling you, calling you* to do some work, and you don't get back with me, then you a *broad*! All you gotta do is call me and tell me you don't want to get on the record with me, and that's cool!"

The co-host tried to change the topic. "Hey, Pimp … I have heard people say … [that] since you were a part of the old game, that you don't respect the newer rappers on the scene."

"I coulda swore I was on T.I.'s album explaining what the King of the South was, wasn't I?" Pimp asked. "I coulda swore I just did a song with Young Jeezy called the 'Dickies' song that didn't come out, and every time he called me to do something I did it for free and never charged him no money. I coulda swore that after Crime Mob took my freestyle off the lil chick [Diamond's] mixtape and put it on they album I didn't even sue 'em or do nothing to 'em … Show me one place where I talked down on [these new rappers like] Yung Joc … [or said] they not supposed to be in this game and they not supposed to be getting money."**

"My thang is this," Pimp continued, finally getting around to his point. "I want us to continue getting money for the next 15 years instead of falling off and letting it go back to the West or to the East because we're not putting no social commentary into the records. Truth be told, if you started being a gangbanger after your first or second album, you a busta! And these kids out here listening to us and looking up to us because a lot of them don't have no father figure in

---

(*Ludacris' 1999 debut, *Incognegro*, featured a cartoon-like illustration of himself on the cover.)

(**The feature Pimp C originally did for Diamond was a gift to her free of charge because he liked her work, intending for it to be used on her mixtape. "At the time, everything I recorded, the label had rights to, because I was signed to them," says Diamond, admitting that she was young and inexperienced and didn't understand the music business. Diamond says her record label, BME/Warner Bros., used the Pimp C vocals for "Go To War" on Crime Mob's second album *Hated On Mostly* without consulting her. Apparently, no one at the label bothered to check and see if Pimp C's verse had been cleared or if it was okay to use his vocals on the album.)

they house, and every record you get on, you lying about some dope!"

"Get off the boo-boo!" Pimp insisted. "Get off of it, mane! 'Cause if you gonna talk about some squares and talk about the drug game, you need to talk about the bad side of the drug game, too. What about when you get busted and you go to jail? What about [when] your mama and your wife and your kids is crying because they at home and you in prison in a cell? What about that part of the dope game!?"

Pimp said he was exhausted with the same repetitive songs. "Everybody talking about how many cars they got and how many jewels they gonna buy and how many squares coming off, but ain't nobody talking about the other side of it. If you gonna talk about that, you gotta talk about both sides. And I'ma say it again: if you a cartoon character on your first album, you need to be a cartoon character on yo' last. 'Cause the way we start is the way we gon' finish."

Pimp had completely taken over the radio show, reducing the hosts to ad-libbers on their own program. "Can't do nothing but respect that, homeboy," the host agreed.

"Now," Pimp said forcefully. "You go back to that *OZONE* article, and you read every statement I made in there, and if you find a place in there where I lied about somebody, you research it. Y'all give me a call back and I'll clarify what I meant … Now, I want it to be clear. I'm not *apologizing* for what I said. I'm *clarifying what I meant* by what I said. We all know Atlanta the South. But we gotta start acting like it's the South. And we gotta start having some pride like it's the South!"

After a brief digression in which Pimp launched into another rant against closeted homosexuals (referring to a rumor about rapper Ma$e being caught in a Range Rover with a transsexual), he concluded, "I'm proud of all the rappers in the South, I'm proud of everybody selling records in Atlanta. But everybody ain't my friend, and I don't like all y'all records. Now if you wanna diss me and get on with me, go on and do it. But the difference between me and them other dudes is this: You gon' diss me and I'm gon' come see you, jack! You gonna diss them other dudes, they gon' play lip-wrassle with you … Leave Bun out of it, and we gonna see in the end, 'cause you gonna smell my cologne! Issey Miyake or some Bond No. 9, 'cause I do not play!"

The host laughed. "That's the same cologne I wear."

"All the real street people in Atlanta and all the hardcore UGK fans, I hope I have clarified what I meant by that statement," Pimp concluded. "Anybody else that don't like me or wanna hate on me, come on with it!"

"I think all in all, your fans in Atlanta just still wanted to know that you love them, that's all," the co-host chimed in.

"Hey, man, guess what," Pimp said. "I used to live in Atlanta. If I wasn't on parole, I would still live in Atlanta, and I still would've made them statements. And I'm coming back to Atlanta as soon as somebody book me a ticket to come there and do a show!"

"We tried to get you to come last night!" the co-host pointed out, referring to a scheduled date he'd just missed at Primetime Nightclub.

"I had a blowout in the rain and had to change the tire myself," Pimp explained. "If you have a blowout and you got both yo' kids in the backseat and yo' wife driving, is you gonna jump in another car and leave them on the side of the road to go catch the airplane?"

"Hell no," the host said.

"I didn't think you would," Pimp nodded. "So you know what? When that rain was coming down and we had that blowout in that Lexus and both my babies was in the backseat, I had to get out and change that myself. I didn't have time to call nobody else to do it, and I was not going to leave my family on the side of the road. Anybody [who] don't like that can eat seven thousand wee-wees and die!"

"There it is," the host agreed.

"So if you don't like that and you don't understand that, then you don't have no understanding about life," said Pimp. "And anybody that puts this rap game or they job or anything ahead of they family – well, you know what – shame on you. And guess what – part two of my article is coming out next month in *OZONE*, so get ready to get your jaws tight again!"

"Can we expect to hear from you again next issue?" the host asked.

"You can hear from me anytime you want to," Pimp promised. "But let me tell you this, mane. We need to stop with the boo-boo, mane. We need to stop promoting negative thangs. UGK started off talking about drugs and thangs, but now we on the records talking about the other side of the drugs and what happens when you get off into negative thangs. We need to stop promoting the wrong thangs."

By the end of the interview, Pimp seemed to have swayed even the radio hosts to agree with him. "Somebody gotta step up and make it happen," the co-host agreed. "I'm with you on that."

"Somebody gotta do it," Pimp repeated. "Don't nobody like medicine. It don't taste good … Everybody licking each other booty and being cowards. Well, guess what! I'm taking a stance against the cowards, I'm taking a stance against the lies, and I'm telling you we need to stop doing all this ol' negative stuff."

"Alright, Pimp. Man, we appreciate you checking in," the host concluded.

"Anybody got something to say about me, just make a list of they names and tell 'em, look, you could come see me," Pimp said. "I'll give you my address. We can box it out, stab it out, pop it out, or talk it out."

Todd1 emailed me the audio file of the interview, which I forwarded to Pimp at his request. Filled with Pimp's entertaining quotables, the interview quickly was posted on dozens of blog sites, spawning debates over whether Pimp C was either the most honest rapper alive or just a crazy drug addict.

Blogger Byron Crawford posted it as evidence that Pimp C was "clearly batshit" and "smoked one sherm stick too many," while others proclaimed it the "greatest… interview… ever." *XXL* Magazine speculated on the "Top 10 reasons why Pimp C is so mad" ("ran out of sizzurp," "too many outta pocket strippers in the A, shawty").

"It's a shame that most people can't really understand what that man is saying," noted a commenter named BMAN. "He is trying to save you drowning fools, and save our community."

In Houston, the Rap-A-Lot team crowded around a computer in Red Boy's office to listen to the radio interview. Reactions were mixed. "That's Pimp," one shrugged matter-of-factly. Another looked displeased, shaking his head and announcing, "Okay, we need to do some damage control."

Pimp's publicist Nancy Byron laughed off the idea of damage control. "I don't think there was such a thing as 'damage control' with him," she says.

Houston journalist Matt Sonzala listened to the Hot 107.9 interview, shaking his head in disbelief at the pointed Russell Simmons insult. Rumors about Simmons' sexuality had persisted for years, but he was still a powerful man who deserved respect. Sonzala thought Pimp was being reckless. Too reckless.

That dude's gonna get fuckin' killed, he thought.

CHAPTER 53

"UGK's moment to become crossover stars has long since passed with their appearance on Jay-Z's 2000 hit 'Big Pimpin'.' But on *Underground Kingz*, Pimp and Bun seem content with their standing, because they've finally got what they've been seeking all along: respect."
– Brendan Frederick, *XXL* Magazine, March 2007

"I think [Pimp C] had an epiphany ... in terms of what he was willing to promote and not promote. I don't think it was a personal thing against Jeezy ... it was that Pimp saw the effects of the drug war, having been in the penitentiary and seeing thousands of young black men that were in there for nonviolent drug offenses ... I think [his] anger was at that, and less about Jeezy." – Killer Mike

Over at Jive, a few staffers were entertained by the drama, but most were irritated. This wasn't the type of promotion they had in mind for the double album, dropping in just two short weeks. The label was already nervous because "Game Belongs to Me" had been slow picking up radio spins, and they needed radio spins to put up big first week sales numbers. "He's fucking up the project," staffers grumbled.

Usually, questions about Pimp were directed at Jeff Sledge: "Yo, what's up with your boy?" Jeff would shrug and say, "Dude, I've heard these conversations for 15 years." The radio interview, he felt, was tame compared to Chad's usual rants.

A radio promotional run Jive was putting together was scrapped. "Everybody had set up a whole bunch of shit around [the album's release date, and] … things [started] getting shut down," says Anne-Marie Stripling. "[His radio interview] left a bad taste in everybody's mouth." Other promotional activities and appearances were cancelled. "We could never get Bun and Pimp together at the same time," recalls Ron Stewart.

"It became very frustrating," agrees Jeff Sledge. "We did want to promote them to be a bigger group, 'cause they were so dope and they were so talented, but Chad made it hard … We wanted to do more videos and … radio promo tours … but Chad made that almost impossible."

Confronting Chad about his inconsistency never worked, either. "He could always come up with a reason," says Jeff Sledge. "He would always kind of concoct a story … to [justify] why he didn't do what he said he was gonna do. He was very persuasive."

Pimp had been in preliminary conversations with Def Jam executive Shakir Stewart about signing a solo deal with Def Jam, where Jay-Z was now President of the label. There was also the possibility of doing a deal for UGK at Def Jam after finishing their last Jive album. But after the interview (in which Pimp disrespected Russell Simmons, Def Jam's co-founder), plans for Pimp to meet with executive Steve Bartells to move forward with the deal were scrapped.

Some people felt like Pimp was being hypocritical; in interviews, he'd previously cited Jeezy as one of his favorite new rappers. Wasn't he the same guy in the "Get Throwed" video with Jeezy more than a year earlier, who was wearing a "17.5" t-shirt? If it wasn't an issue then, why was it an issue now? And just a few months ago, he'd been preaching unity. "When he first came out of jail, [it] was like, 'Our savior's home,' and then … [he started] calling people out [and] turning up as the king of controversy," says Paul Wall.

Besides, how was Pimp C in a position to criticize new rappers for their emphasis on drugs, money, and hoes when UGK's own catalogue included records like "Pocket Full of Stones" and "Big Pimpin'"? Still, others agreed with Chad's assessment that Hip-Hop needed to re-awaken its conscience. UGK's vulnerability and honesty had always been one of things that set them apart.

"The difference between a UGK 'Pocket Full of Stones' and today's [trap rap] is that at the time, it was needed," says David Banner. "To a Southern cat, Pimp C was like Jay-Z [is] to a New Yorker. [Rappers like] UGK and the Geto Boys did for the South what N.W.A did for the West Coast. They told the story of what was really happening in the South at that time."

The real point Pimp wanted to get across was his desire to hear more substance in the music. Everyone might not have agreed with his approach, but on that point, no one could argue that he was wrong. "The trend right now is … candy cars, and we gonna all talk about how much weed we smokin', and we gonna all just 'party party party' and we all rich … but hey man, in reality, it ain't like that on the streets," Pimp told *HipHop2Nite* TV.

"These rappers are very intelligent … they just scared to go against the grain," he added. "Can't you see they all confused? They keep making the same beat over and over again? … Everybody's confused about where the music is going and what the sound is gonna be … 'cause they didn't make the sound up theyselves. They imitating something they heard someone else doing. And when you don't know where something started, it's hard to take it to the next level."

It certainly wasn't the first time Pimp had made outrageous, controversial statements, but in the past, his comments hadn't reached the mainstream. Just two months earlier, during his Dallas radio interview with Bo-Bo Luchiano, he'd instructed Oprah Winfrey ("with her fat self") to "stop being a lame up there with that faggot Stedman … [who likes] to take it in the butt" and stop telling black youth that rap wasn't a good career aspiration. ("Rap music saved my life," he explained.)

Pimp felt like he was only sharing knowledge with the younger generation, the same way others had done before him. "[Folks] like Too $hort and Ice-T … they look at me like their little brother, like they raised me," he said. "They really did raise me out here on the road, taught me what to say and what not to do, checked me when I needed to be checked, patted me on the back when I needed my back patted on, you know what I mean?"

Still, Chad knew that he'd made a mistake. Mama Wes hadn't yet heard about the growing uproar from the radio interview until Chad called her late that night and told her he'd taken shots at Young Jeezy.

"Oh my God," she gasped. "Why did you do that? That wasn't smart."

"I know, Mama," he sighed.

She got the impression it had something to do with a verse. When Chad started to explain, she cut him off. "That's crazy," she told him. She already knew the things that would spark Chad's temper.

"Anything could trigger him," she explains. "He had so many triggers." An artist failing to return his phone call, an artist sending him a track that he felt was inferior to their previous work, anything he perceived as disrespectful could send him into a tailspin. "If [an artist] was going to do something and he didn't … feel like he gave it his best [shot], it would set him off," she says.

But if there was one thing Mama Wes understood about her son, it was his passion, because he'd gotten it from her. "C *had* to have something controversial," she explains. "He had to have something to fight about. And if he didn't have anything to fight for, then he would get depressed."

As the radio interview spread, Chad started reaching out to his Atlanta friends like Goodie

Mob and the Dungeon Family to make sure they weren't offended. He texted Kool Ace, assuring him, "I ain't talkin' about you." When Sleepy Brown called, Pimp picked up the phone and apologized without even saying hello. "Sleepy, I'm sorry," he began, launching into a lengthy explanation.

Most weren't offended; in fact, they supported him wholeheartedly. "Way to fuckin' go!" Killer Mike called to congratulate him, laughing and applauding him for his courage. "Pimp, you need to have a freakin' radio show," Fonzworth Bentley told him.

Most were willing to overlook Pimp's "Atlanta is not the South" statement; Jazze Pha felt that he was experiencing "culture shock" since the Atlanta of 2007 was far from the Atlanta of the 90s. Killer Mike felt like the city needed someone to check them, and it came from a place of love, not malice.

"How you gonna get offended by your uncle checking you?" Killer Mike asks rhetorically. "He had more history in Atlanta than the people he was talking to [on the radio] and that's no disrespect to them … but shit, Pimp C lived here before any of y'all … How can you be mad at someone who taught you [how] to be cool?"

"You've gotta take the emotion out of it when you're listening to Pimp C," agrees David Banner. "The dude really had some [intelligent] shit to say."

Chad's old friend Mia X heard the radio interview, and although she agreed with him, she understood how others might take it the wrong way. She called Chad and encouraged him to think things through before he spoke publicly. "You're so smart," she told him. "I want people to get the opportunity to know Chad the man, not just Pimp C the rapper and Pimp C the producer and Pimp C the guy with the slick mouth that could come off the top of his head with the funniest insults."

"Well, you a gu'l," Chad told Mia X. "You gonna make it a little softer, you gonna make it a little pretty. I ain't here to make it pretty for nobody."

"It's a different game now," Mia told him. "People are far more sensitive."

"I don't give a *fuuuuuck*," Chad drawled. "I had to get some things off my chest."

"You can't handle everybody the same way," she reminded him. Although they eventually had to agree to disagree, Chad appreciated her concern, and was impressed that she'd grown into such a peacemaker.

Another person who reached out with concern was Bobby "Tre9" Herring, a Houston-area rapper who considered himself a "Hip-Hop missionary." He viewed himself as a conduit between the Christian Hip-Hop community and secular artists, hoping to minister without being judgmental. Tre9 produced a weekly event called Hip-Hop Hope Tuesdays and helped organize community events with J. Prince's wife.

Tre9 had gotten Pimp C's phone number already, planning to reach out on behalf of Bushwick Bill, who was recording a gospel album. As Tre9 read some of the violent, hate-filled comments on the blogs about Pimp's radio interview, he sent Pimp a text with a Bible verse and some words of encouragement.

"Who is this?" Pimp responded.

Tre9 texted back explaining who he was and was surprised when Pimp called a few minutes later. Tre9 told Pimp that he thought he was onto something important, but he was missing part of the message. He'd hit the nail on the head as far as the dope game but he was still taking shots at people. "You're saying put God first," Tre9 argued. "The Lord said, 'vengeance is mine.' You're to be a peacemaker."

"Yeah, that's true," Pimp agreed. "But I have a right as a man, under God, to defend my family if someone is trying to take food off my plate."

"Let's say you get involved, you retaliate, and you go to jail? Let's say you get involved and you get shot? What happens to your family then?" Tre9 asked.

"Yeah, that's the other side of the game," Pimp laughed.

Even if Bun didn't agree with Pimp's position, he couldn't help but admire his boldness. "He wanted to be as honest with people as he could – almost to a fault," Bun told MTV News later, adding, "Everything he loved – everyone he loved – he loved hard and embraced it fully. He was very passionate [and] if he felt a certain way about things; he couldn't hold it in, he couldn't filter himself, he couldn't be politically correct. It just wasn't in him to not say what he felt ... He spoke from his heart."

"Even if you didn't agree with him, you have to give him credit and respect the fact he was willing to stand by what he said," Bun noted. "So many people can be wishy-washy ... [but he] just wanted everyone to be their best ... he wanted Southern Hip-Hop to be the best. He wanted everybody involved to be the best. He never looked down on anybody. He never made anybody feel small. He tried to uplift ... And that's why, even though if I [didn't agree with] how he felt, I couldn't tell him to not speak from his heart."

Still, Pimp C's statements were obviously putting a strain on Bun's relationship with Jeezy. Bun always tried to stay on good terms with everyone, but it was hard to do that when his partner insisted on being at war.

Bun felt like forcing fans to choose between UGK and Jeezy would be bad for business; they shared the same fan base. In fact, this was exactly why Bun had served as the group's spokesman for so long. "When he did decide to do interviews, he was always so controversial, which is why he didn't do 'em too much," Bun told Jeff Sledge. "[We'd decided] it might not be the best for him to talk all the time ... He had no internal filter, so he was just basically gonna say what he felt like saying at the time and deal with the repercussions later."

Aside from the Jeezy issue, Bun felt that Pimp made some valid points, but the timing was terrible. "He never would pick the right time to say things ... he was really on point with many of those things," Bun said. "But I think the way he said things and the way he addressed situations sometimes could be a little bit off-putting for people because he was a very direct person. A lot of times people don't wanna deal with issues head-on ... they'd rather deal with it behind closed doors."

———————

UGK was selected as one of the first Southern acts to perform at four of the 15 scheduled stops (Atlanta, Miami, Dallas, and Houston) of the Rock the Bells Festival series, along with other acts like Wu-Tang, Nas, Cypress Hill, David Banner, Mos Def, and Talib Kweli.

Bun was already concerned that Pimp's "fuck the police!" rant at the Zune BBQ had strained his relationship with Microsoft, and after the radio interview, he could already see where this was headed.

In a way, Bun understood, because for years he had been the one out getting drunk and smoking weed while Pimp was the introvert, the professional at home focused on the music. But now, the opportunities were far bigger, and there was far more money on the line.

Rock the Bells was funded by Coca Cola's Monster Energy Drink; and Bun didn't want to ruin this opportunity. Bun wished he could tell Pimp, "Man, you could feel how you wanna feel, but just keep it to yourself for 45 minutes to an hour. Let's do this lil' show, then you can go and cuss out whoever you want to cuss out," but he knew that wouldn't work. Nobody was going to tell Pimp C to be quiet.

Instead, Bun decided he had to take a drastic step to get Pimp's attention. "[It was] too much personal business getting involved with the professional side of it, and I always felt like those things gotta be separated," Bun explained on the Breakfast Club radio show. "[Pimp] had every intention on going on that stage every night and cussing people out and talking crazy about people, and I just couldn't let him do it to himself ... [I felt like it was] better to pull out and step away from the situation than get on this kind of a platform with this kind of exposure and misrepresent yourself."

Bun informed Rock the Bells that UGK was pulling out of the festival, and had his manager call Pimp's manager to tell him that they weren't going to be doing the tour.* (Publicly, Bun did not offer a reason for UGK's cancellation.) Pimp was pissed when he got the phone call. "If you don't wanna do a show with me then we're not really in a group," he complained to Ayesha.

The day after the controversial radio interview, I was on and off the phone with Pimp frequently. At one point, I connected him and Bun on a three-way call. I thought nothing of it, assuming they talked all the time.

After we hung up, Pimp texted me, "Letz be carfull what we put out next month ! U the only media person i talk 2! Thank u again for bringing me and my brother together! J Prince say whatever them atl niggaz wana do he riding wit me! Itz ugk 4 life nomatter what! Chuuch."

"Im not perfect ! But i dont lie!," he added a few minutes later. "Me and bun ok! We got alot 2 work on but we ugk 4 life!"

'*Thank u again for bringing me and my brother together?*' *Wow*, I thought. What did that mean?

Bun and Pimp weren't even on speaking terms. Big Gipp or Bun's wife Queenie often served as the go-between, relaying messages between the two. "I got Pimp on one [phone line] like, 'Man, I'ma go to war with all these niggas,' and I got Bun [on the other line] like, 'Yo, man, tell him to chill … he gon' fuck up the money,'" Gipp remembers.

Pimp heard rumors that Jeezy was getting ready to drop a diss record, and indirectly communicated with Jeezy through Young Buck. "I told Buck … you better tell Potato Head that if he drop that [diss record] it's gonna be World War 3," he told me.**

Late that night, Pimp called Bun's bodyguard Truck, talking about the reaction to the controversial interview. "70% down with me, man," he said. "[The other] 30%, y'know, man, them niggas think I'm goin' crazy. But I'm tellin' the truth though, Truck."

The real reason for Pimp's call, it seemed, was to gauge the temperature of things over in Bun's camp. "Bunny know I love him, mane," Pimp said. "This ain't the first [time] … you know, friends gon' go through some shit, y'know. We gonna be alright, Truck."

Truck had seven brothers, so he understood the dynamic of brotherly relationships. He and his brothers didn't always get along, either; hell, he'd nearly gotten in a shootout with one of them. Still, he'd just heard that the Rock the Bells tour dates were cancelled, and Truck reminded Pimp that a lot of people depended on UGK to pay the bills.

"Whatever the fuck goin' on, y'all need to get it together," Truck said. "Man, we gotta do some more shows. This how a nigga get paid, y'know? You fucking up the money … we gotta get these shows." Truck pointed out that at least Pimp's crew had something to sell – he'd seen Hezeleo and Big Bubb out hustling UGK DVDs, but Bun's crew relied on show money. Without it, he'd be forced to return to his illegal side hustles.

Pimp agreed, offering to meet up with Truck at the Galleria to bring him some DVDs.

Even when they weren't speaking, Bun and Pimp publicly presented an image of solidarity. Bun insisted their differing opinions were a "non-issue," telling *XXL*, "He made it clear that his views were not UGK's views 'cause UGK is bigger than Bun B and Pimp C. The people own

---

(*The Houston Rock the Bells Festival date ended up being cancelled anyway with less than 1,000 tickets sold. Matt Sonzala, who was hired to help promote the event, attributed the low ticket sales to the lineup. He couldn't understand why Wu-Tang would be slated as the headliner when their founder and producer RZA had just been quoted in *URB* saying, "How has the South dominated Hip-Hop for the last four, five years without lyrics, without Hip-Hop culture really in their blood? Those brothers came out representing more of a stereotype of how black people are, and I think the media [would] rather see us as ignorant, crazy motherfuckers than seeing us as intelligent young men." As Sonzala pointed out to the *Houston Press*, "Wu-Tang [has acted] like ignorant, crazy motherfuckers [too]." New Orleans-bred rapper Jay Electronica shot back at RZA's "ridiculously stupid, ignorant" comments during an interview with TheMostInfluential.com, saying that Southern emcees like Bun B and Andre 3000 were more lyrically skilled than some East Coast rappers.)

(**Pimp believed Jeezy had recorded a diss song, but Jeezy's former business partner Kinky B says he doesn't believe one ever existed. Internally, the general sense in Jeezy's camp was that he didn't have enough ammunition to diss a legend like Pimp C and it would be a bad decision to go to war with UGK.)

UGK. I have a right to feel how I wanna feel and Pimp C has a right to feel how he wanna feel."

Likewise, Pimp focused on the positive in an *OZONE* interview, explaining that he and Bun worked separately so they could expand the group's reach. "When we separate we can cover more ground than we can being together," he reasoned. "If there's a certain amount of promotion that has to be done, it's easier for Bun to fly to the East Coast and me to go to the West Coast … a lot of times, that's why you see me and him in different places at different times."

"It's still UGK for life," Pimp assured fans. "We've just figured out ways to go and promote our thing where we can cover more ground … He works good on his own, he's got a real good mouthpiece and I'm doing good on my own," he paused and added with a chuckle, "When I can control my tongue."

When I published the article I hadn't known that Pimp actually *was* dissing Jeezy, and was angry at myself for not having the foresight to see how this chain of events would backfire. Now, only two weeks away from the second OZONE Awards, I'd unintentionally sparked a beef between two of the biggest Southern rappers. Emails flew between our publicity team and production staff debating if the Pimp C interview would create a problem at the awards.

With tension in the air, both sides were preparing for war. I had a habit of pacing as I talked on the phone, especially for intense conversations, so I spent most of the day in the parking lot in front of my office, alternating calls between J. Prince and Jeezy's partner Kinky B, attempting to negotiate some type of truce.

There was an unsettling feeling gnawing at me that maybe I'd gotten *too* involved. I was supposed to be an observer, not a participant. Had I caused a glitch in the matrix by unintentionally setting this whole thing in motion? Worse, what if something catastrophic happened as a result: would I be at fault? I'd always viewed myself as a historian documenting the culture, not an active participant altering the outcome. I came to the sinking realization that I'd helped put something terrible in motion and now was powerless to stop it.

I cautioned Pimp, explaining that I wanted peace at the OZONE Awards. "No blood! I promise!" he texted me after we got off the phone. "Im not trying 2 fk up yo thing! As long as nobody attackz me wit they eyez mouth or handz we good!"

No blood? I covered my face with my hands. What had I gotten myself into?

I called Bun, too, trying to get a handle on things. "He's going back to the old Pimp," Bun sighed before we hung up the phone.

The comment lingered. Having never known the pre-prison Pimp, I had no basis for comparison and wondered what exactly he meant.

This, in fact, was exactly what Bun was afraid would happen. "We're at a crucial point in our career where we could really take this South shit to another level, so we're not tryin' to get caught up in no dumb shit," he'd told me a few months prior. "My whole thing is to try to keep my eyes open and see problems coming from afar and try to move that shit out the way."

Bun hadn't seen this one coming in time. He was hoping things weren't going to boil over, relaying a message to Pimp asking him not to "shoot first." He understood that if Pimp dissed Jeezy first, Jeezy would have no choice but to defend himself. "[Jeezy's] whole reputation is built around his street credibility," Bun said later on the Breakfast Club. "And Pimp [was] attacking his credibility."

Just like the Master P beef back in the 90s, the Jeezy tension seemed to spark Pimp's creativity. Rapper Kanye West, who apparently had terrible timing, had just requested a Pimp C verse for his "Can't Tell Me Nothing" remix. Coincidentally, it also featured Kanye's Def Jam labelmate Young Jeezy. Pimp used the opportunity to take shots, rapping:

I'm on this track like white on rice
Mr. Potato Head tryin' to make me Christ
I'm sorry, Atlanta, Georgia really is the South

But too many boys got them thangs in they mouth
I ain't talkin' good grills mane
I'm talkin' 'bout that Angus beef with that big ol' vein
Gipp say they lookin' like Sisqo
The Chocolate City is the new San Francisco
[…] This is for the busters and the suckers
And the fake drug dealers and the internet cluckers
Need to stop lyin' to the kids, for real
Ain't have no Benz until you signed your first record deal

Pimp also redid the chorus:
Naaah, naaah naah, bitch I been had my money right
I'm Rap-A-Lot in this Mafia life
Excuse me, do you really wanna go to war?
Say something I'll leave your brains on your mini bar
I think they bluffin' and they frontin'
I'm Pimp C, you can't tell me nothin'*

Next, he pulled up a track J. Prince wanted him to drop a verse for, alongside Louisiana teenager Hurricane Chris. Hurricane Chris had landed a major record deal with Polo Grounds/J Records off the strength of his Top 10 record "A Bay Bay," but J. Prince had managed to obtain material he recorded prior to signing with a major and was rushing to drop an album first.

Pimp didn't like the beat to the Hurricane Chris track, "Get Out Yo' Mind," which he thought was corny. He improvised the verse without writing anything down:
Might not be the best but I'm as real as they come
You ain't got no blow, if you do, bitch go get me some
I got my $17.5, I ain't seen no bricks yet
Rap-A-Lot Mafia life, you wanna get wet?
J. [Prince] told me to gut him, Bun told me to chill out
Drop that song, I cut your belly, let it spill out
On the concrete, steaming guts on the streets
$50,000 for your verse? I sent you mine for free!
That's a sign of disrespect, you saying "Fuck me!"

Now that he was in a mood, Pimp also recorded a remix to T.I.'s "Big Shit Poppin' (Do It),"	taking shots at Lil Troy.** He also forwarded me a snippet of another unreleased song, where he rapped, "Ya' read the OZONE and wanna *kiiiill* me, but you a faker from Macon, you ain't no reeeeal G," dragging out every syllable for extra emphasis.***

Worried that things were getting out of control, especially with the upcoming OZONE Awards, I continued pleading with him to calm down. "Whoever against me im getting on they ass!" Pimp texted me. "U already n the middle so n joy the murder show! This aint a record war itz a street war! So letz c how gangster these cowards iz!"

I sighed. *Enjoy the murder show?*

"If that bitch drop a dis song itz on sight!" Pimp added. "War no talkin no playing no handz just u know what! We trying 2 touch the bitch b4 yo show! The street war is on!"

(*This version of "Can't Tell Me Nothin'" was never released; the official remix only featured Young Jeezy. Kanye asked Pimp to redo the verse. "I done vowed I'm not gonna drop that shit, because Kanye told me that the song is a prayer," Pimp told me. "I'm finna go back and [redo it] and treat it as such, and treat it with respect, like I'm talking to the Lord. I'm not gonna invite no man to my dick on no muthafuckin' song … when I'm supposed to be praying. So I'm gonna go clean that up." If Pimp did do a second, cleaner version of the remix, it was never released.)
(**T.I. apparently never released this version of the record.)
(***Pimp often criticized Jeezy because he represented the city of Atlanta but was actually from rural Hawkinsville, south of Macon, Georgia.)

Late that Saturday night, he posted a semi-apology on his Myspace blog: "To all my Atlanta fans and friends, I want to say I apologize for my statement in the Ozone magazine about Atlanta not being the south!! That was a bullshit statement!! Atlanta is and has always been the dirty mthfkn South!! But the rest of what I said about them pussy ass niggaz is and always will be the truth!"

He also asked Nancy Byron to email it out as a press release. "She got everybody's email address in the world," he told me.

Knowing it would be futile to argue with him, Nancy emailed the statement to media outlets exactly as written. While several Hip-Hop outlets like HipHopDX posted it, some mainstream press found it offensive. Nancy copied and pasted the same reply to them all: "Pimp C is not rated E for Everyone."

On Monday, July 30, one week after the Hot 107.9 interview, Pimp was back on the radio in Atlanta, this time on Greg Street's show on V103. Greg, who had been part of the UGK family for more than a decade, was a little upset at Pimp for doing an interview with his competitor.

"You got a lot of people around the A-Town upset, and you know you my family," Greg Street cautioned. "[You] got me in the middle of all this, mane. First of all, I gotta tell you, mane, you gotta really, really, really watch who you interviewing with and who you talking to."

Pimp was far more contrite than he had been in the previous interview, repeating his apology and somewhat retracting his statements about Russell Simmons' sexual preference. "My apology is sincere ... ain't nobody force me to do this," Pimp concluded. "I ain't scared of nothing, I ain't scared of nobody, and I don't bow down to nobody but God. I'm only gonna die one time in this life [but] you cowards die every day."

While Pimp was doing damage control, Lil Troy was filming another YouTube video, challenging Pimp to come to the south side of Houston. "I'm ready to take one of them fuckin' Bentleys," Troy threatened, complaining that Pimp had "aired out all his dirty laundry to the white bitch."

"White bitch Beverly don't love no muthafuckin' body," Troy claimed. "She could give a goddamn if we kill each other, hurt each other, if one of us die she wouldn't give a fuck, she gon' cover it and put it in her magazine so she could get some fuckin' ratings. She don't give a fuck about us."

Around midnight, Troy blasted off a press release attacking both of us and plugging his *Paperwork* DVD. I forwarded it to Pimp, who replied, "J WANA KNOW WHATZ HIS ADDRESS SO WE CAN GO C HIM ON THE SOUTHSIDE!!!!!!!!!!!!!!!!!"

"Shit leave me out of it but he shouldn't be hard to find," I responded.

"WE GOIN FIND HIM," Pimp responded.

Lil Troy told *XXL* Magazine that Pimp was only coming after him because he'd "exposed" Scarface as a snitch. "Pimp ain't even no gangster," Troy added. "I went to jail on drug charges. He got locked up for pulling a gun on a woman in a mall. Is that gangster? You can't compare your rap sheet to mine."

Inspired, Pimp headed to Avery's studio in Port Arthur, where he addressed Lil Troy's YouTube video on the XVII record "Massacre," rapping:

I wish a muthafucker would try to run up on me
Pussy ass rat, tryin' come up on me
You say you gon' take my Bentley? Which one, pussy nigga?
Got a silver and a red, bust your spleen and your liver
[...] I'ma come to your hood in both of my Bentleys
And a 'Lac and a Phantom, bringin' Fifth Ward with me
I know your number and your address too

I know your son and your fat bitch too
You on the run like a fat snitch do
And if you ridin' with that nigga, you a rat bitch too
Bitch, I knew DJ Screw, the south side with me
Knew the real Fat Pat, Hawk and Don Keke
I know Klondike Kat and that boy Dope-E*
Smoked dip with Ganksta N-I-P, you niggas is a trip
You think I'm ridin' for 'Face? That ain't the case
I'm ridin' 'cause you said the whole Rap-A-Lot fake
So then J. Prince must be fake too
Talkin' shit on YouTube, throw your brains on the roof

"Eat my dick," Pimp instructed Lil Troy on the outro. "Pussy ass nigga, we ain't say your name 'cause you like to take niggas to court and sue a nigga."** He continued, taunting, "I thought you was a gangsta, bitch? Why you hiding, bitch? Hey, man. I'm on Westheimer, in somethin' foreign."

"We are going look for lil troy n the southside of houston! Me J and bout 500 gangsterz!" Pimp emailed me. "Wit a camara !"

On another shit-talking interlude for XVII's album, Pimp addressed Jeezy. "You know, Bun B told me, 'Don't shoot first,'" he said. "But Potato Head, I heard through the grapevine, got a muthafuckin' diss song on me!"

He laughed dryly, adding, "*Biiiitch*! [If you] fuck with me, I'ma tell where you're really from! Nigga, I got pictures of you from the 90's, dressed funny with that backpack and your muthafuckin' pant leg rolled up and them Timberland boots on!"

Pimp ran through a colorful roll-call of all his folks across the country – WC, Nelly and the St. Lunatics, Minister Seamore and Bishop Don "Magic" Juan, T.I., the Dungeon Family and Organized Noize collective, and DJ Kay Slay – before concluding, "Guess what, nigga? You surrounded, bitch! Yeah, [don't] make me do it, nigga, I'ma cut out your muthafuckin' guts, nigga. J. Prince told me to gut you like a fish! Go on and drop that [diss] record, bitch! I dare you!"

As the buzz grew, everyone wanted one of Pimp C's classic interviews. *XXL* Magazine editor Bonsu Thompson reached out to Nancy to schedule a Q&A with Pimp for their monthly "8Ball" column, eight questions on a specific topic.

"I don't know if [Russell Simmons] likes Martians, squirrels or whatever, so I ain't gonna speak on something that I didn't see," Pimp told Bonsu. "It's no gay-bashing with me. It's just, be proud of what you are, instead of hidin' in the closet. And if ya fuck boys in the ass, then don't be tryna fuck with the girls, too, poisoning the pussy population wit' ya shitty ol' dirty-ass dick."

'Poisoning the pussy population'?!? Bonsu thought. *That was awesome. That's a pull quote like a muthafucker.*

"Do you ever feel any compassion for Bun B, for being in a group with a man like yourself, who is unfiltered and can be bullheaded in his ways?" Bonsu asked.

"You been programmed to think I'm bullheaded. I just know what the fuck goin' on," Pimp argued. "I know who's a faggot, I know who lettin' them girls fuck 'em in the ass with them dildos, I know who really sold dope, I know who didn't. The only nigga I see [in Houston] goin' to the mall by himself is Slim Thug. Other niggas, when I see 'em, they got bodyguards around 'em. How you gonna be scared of the neighborhood you supposed to be reppin'?"

"So the only Houston rapper you're acknowledging is Slim Thug?" Bonsu asked.

"I didn't say that!" Pimp protested. "I said, *again*, 'the only nigga I see at the mall by himself is Slim Thug.' You magazine muthafuckers need to have more responsibility for what you write!"

(*Klondike Kat and Dope-E were popular underground rappers from the south side of Houson.)
(**When an early leak of "Massacre" was posted on YouTube under the unofficial title "Pussy Nigga Anthem," AllHipHop asked Pimp if it was a Lil Troy diss. "Who's that?" Pimp deadpanned. "I don't even know who that is.")

As I had previously, Bonsu tried to ask Pimp if his 17.5 reference was a diss towards Jeezy. And just as he had previously, Pimp evaded the question, even complimenting Jeezy as "a cold muthafucker with a microphone."

"Don't single out Jeezy, because he ain't the only one that's kickin' numbers that don't match!" Pimp yelled. Then, he switched his tone up abruptly, casually asking Bonsu, "Yo, you ever sell drugs?"

Bonsu, caught off guard, was at a loss for words. "Excuse me?" he finally managed.

"Well, you do know there's no water around Atlanta. So all the drugs in Atlanta either come from Miami or Texas," Pimp explained. "Ain't no way those prices match up. If work in Texas is $15,000 to $16,000 a ki, you gotta pay a muthafucker $2,000 to $2,500 a bird to bring it back to your city. How you gonna sell it for lower than you got it? A muthafucker might be cold and go down to San Antonio to buy it straight from the muthafuckers that get it across the border for $10,000. But news flash: I know you muthafuckers ain't comin down here to get it, 'cause we woulda saw ya."

On Tuesday, August 7, 2007, UGK's album *Underground Kingz* finally dropped, a light shining amidst Pimp's dark brewing battles. The double disc sold nearly 160,000 copies the first week, earning UGK their first #1 album.*

Pimp was excited about the possibility of going platinum. "For me to get my first number one, it made me feel blessed. I never had a number one album before," he told AllHipHop. "It showed that if you take your time and you work hard anything can happen. We put a lot of time and money into this project. I couldn't have done it without the man upstairs or the people at Jive [Records]. It was a team effort."

"It's really vindication for the fans, for the cats who were fighting for years telling anyone who would listen that UGK was the shit," Bun told MTV News. "It's really vindication for them."

The limited-edition version featured the bonus DVD that Anne-Marie Stripling had helped put together featuring Big Boi of OutKast, T.I., David Banner, Rick Ross, Three 6 Mafia, and (ironically) Jeezy discussing UGK's influence.

Underground Kingz was praised by music reviewers all over the country, even New York outlets which previously hadn't paid them much attention. "Even when they were scrappy new-comers from a town no one in rap cared about, UGK's Bun B and Pimp C sounded like wiz-ened old veterans," wrote Tom Breihan for *Pitchfork*, adding, "Fifteen years later, the Texas duo sound like eternal, immovable features on rap's landscape, and their style has hardened into a blueprint; an album like T.I.'s *Trap Muzik*, say, would've been near-unthinkable without UGK's precedent."

"The kingdom they laid claim to nearly 20 years ago can hardly be called the 'underground' in 2007," noted *XXL* Magazine. "Southern-fried d-boy rap is now the easy road to success, but the *Underground Kingz* aren't interested in treading the same, beaten path."

While critics panned the inclusion of tracks like Lil Jon's "Like That," most agreed that the highlights were the tracks produced by Pimp C. "The album really hits its stride … when Pimp takes over the controls and brings back the sad, heavy country-rap that he does better than anyone else," Tim Breihan wrote in *Pitchfork*, citing "The Game Belongs to Me" and "How Long Can It Last" as other standouts.

For the most part, the first half got good reviews, while the second half was described as "hit or miss." HipHopDX called it "a flawed, bloated masterpiece," saying that if they'd cut it in half, it would've been a classic. "Plenty of fat could easily have been trimmed," added *Pitchfork*. "Nobody needs another two tinny synth-beast from Jazze Pha." *Rolling Stone* gave it a 3.5 out of 5 stars, saying it was "one monster comeback album" but "two discs are about one too many."

(*The album went on to sell nearly 500,000 copies.)

"I heard a little bit of criticism [of the album] from magazines that don't understand our type of music," Pimp told me later. "But all the magazines that do understand our type of music like yo' book [OZONE] ... I ain't hear nobody complaining about how long the record was. I heard people complain about how long the record was in books like *Rolling Stone* and *Spin Magazine*, muthafuckers that don't know too much about our music in the first place, but hey, man, fuck them. We ain't makin' it for them. We're making it for our fans."

"UGK's moment to become crossover stars has long since passed with their appearance on Jay-Z's 2000 hit 'Big Pimpin'," concluded *XXL* Magazine's Brendan Frederick. "But on *Underground Kingz*, Pimp and Bun seem content with their standing, because they've finally got what they've been seeking all along: respect."*

The double album also impressed UGK's most important critic: Mama Wes. "I heard so much maturity in C and in Bun [on *Underground Kingz*]," she says. "It's not about music, actually, it's about what my saw in my babies and [their] level of maturity."

On Friday, August 10, Pimp posted a bulletin on his MySpace page: *WE DID IT ONCE AGAIN!!!!!!!!! THANK ALL YALL FOR GOIN OUT AND GETTING THE NEW UGK DOUBLE ALBUM UNDERGROUND KINGZ!!!!!!! ... WE COULDNT HAVE DONE IT WITHOUT YALL!!!!! THE STREETZ SAY CLASSIC! AND THE STREETZ DONT LIE!!!!!!!!!!CHUUCH!!!!! RIGHT ON 2 THE TRILL AND DEATH 2 THE FAKE!!!!!!!!!!!!!!!!!!!!!!!!!!*

Amidst the OZONE Awards preparation, I'd never made it to Best Buy to purchase UGK's album and show support on the day of its release. On my way home well past midnight, I stopped in a 24-hour Wal-Mart to pick up the double CD.

The store, nearly empty, only had one register open. The clerk, a chubby black guy wearing Wal-Mart's standard navy blue polo and tan khakis, looked at the CD and then eyed me, the white girl, as he swiped the bar code at the cash register.**

"What you know about UGK?" he smirked.

Wendy Day, still working at the CTE office, was concerned that things were going to come to a head at the OZONE Awards and begged Pimp not to attend. "Everybody was [preparing for war]," she recalls. "Both sides were ... it was just crazy. I was afraid that it was going to be another Tupac/Biggie situation."

I had my hands full juggling dozens of other artists and their entourages and coordinating a variety of logistics for the show. J. Prince told me he needed 100 tickets; Jeezy told me he wasn't coming unless he could get 80 tickets. Everyone in Pimp's camp was pressuring him not to attend, reminding him that he was still on parole.

In the end, the OZONE Awards took place in Miami without incident. Jeezy performed, but Pimp was not in attendance. Late that night after the show was over and I was back in my hotel room overlooking downtown Miami, I finally saw the text he'd sent hours earlier.

"If patato head say one thing funny tonight at that ozone awards im gona gut that bitch!" Pimp wrote. "They talkin fly n the croud ! They 1OO deep! I called his man last week and told em we wasnt goin! So they safe tonight! God bless em if he slip! Chuuch!"

(*The *XXL* review was actually published in March 2007, when the album was originally scheduled to drop.)
(**I didn't know that Wal-Mart only stocked the clean version of rap CDs. The clean version of a UGK CD, needless to say, just doesn't have the same effect.)

CHAPTER 54

"My apology is sincere ... ain't nobody force me to do this. I ain't scared of nothing, I ain't scared of nobody, and I don't bow down to nobody but God. I'm only gonna die one time in this life [but] you cowards die every day."
– Pimp C, radio interview with Greg Street, July 2007

"I'm trying to be more of a leader than a nigga who cause problems ... I realize [my mouth] is like a tommy gun. I can shoot to kill, I can shoot to start wars and I can shoot to stop wars. I don't think it's right for Pimp C and UGK to start wars with niggas right now." – Pimp C, AllHipHop, October 2007

Late August 2007

With their son Corey, Chad and Angie were generally able to peacefully co-parent, but as the school year approached, one thing they couldn't agree on was where he was going to start the first grade. Corey had been staying in Port Arthur over the summer. Chad wanted him to stay in Port Arthur, and offered to pay for him to attend a private school near Mama Wes' house. Angie wanted him to come back to Houston and go to a public school.

"[I wanted] to keep him grounded," says Angie. "I never wanted him to feel like he was better than anyone else [and get] that big head syndrome ... I never wanted that for my kids." They agreed on a compromise: Corey would go to a public school but stay in Port Arthur, so Chad would still be able to spend time with him.

According to Mama Wes, Chinara was often lax about making sure that Christian got up in the mornings on time, and her "old fashioned grandma side" was concerned that Corey wouldn't always make it to school if he continued living at the Oakmont house. She offered that Corey could come stay with her; Angie dropped off a garbage bag of his clothes.

Chad wanted all his children to have his initials, C.L.B., and planned to change the boy's name from his given name (Dahcorey Turner) to Corey Butler. It became a point of contention with Chinara, who once told Chad during an argument that he should get a DNA test. As Mama Wes recalls it, Chad was livid at the suggestion. "He said he didn't need nobody to tell him who his children were," Mama Wes says. "He didn't feel that DNA was necessary."

But rather than easing his wife's apparent insecurities, Chad overcompensated, instead showing favoritism and often proclaiming Corey his "best child" just to piss off his in-laws. Once, Mama Wes called him to the side after she'd heard him make such a statement. "Stop doing that!" she whispered. "Don't do that, C, you're being ugly now."

Chad just chucked, flashing a devilish grin. "Heh heh," he chuckled. "I got 'em, didn't I?"

Chad believed that Corey had inherited his rap skills, and called his mother one day after he'd seen the child rapping to himself in the bathroom. "You ever heard that lil' nigga spit?" he asked Mama Wes.

"Yeah, he knows all your stuff, and he knows how to make it clean, too," Mama Wes said. Corey would omit the cuss words when reciting his father's raps.

Chad laughed. "I'ma use him on the next album to do the clean lyrics."

"Well, that'll be good training for him," she joked.

"Mama, I'm serious," he said. "I saw him this morning when I came downstairs. He didn't see me. And he had that brush … that was his mic, and man, Mama, he was goin' off, and he got some talent, too."

"He likes it," she agreed.

"Yeah, but you know, I don't want him to be a child rapper," Chad said thoughtfully. "'Cause I don't want him to be 'lil' somebody. I don't want him to be a full-fledged rapper until he's 16. Then he won't be a 'lil' nobody."

"Well, he'll still be 'Lil C,'" Mama pointed out.

"*Yeaaaah*, that's so cute, Mama," Chad said, exaggerating his thick Southern drawl. "Man, I got a *lil'* offspring."

Chad was generous with all of his children, and trying to make up for lost time ever since he'd come home from prison. Mama Wes warned that he was spoiling them to death.

"Mama, I'm just doing to them what you did to me," he said. "You used to wear old shoes so I could have a new suit to go to the football game."

Mama Wes nodded. "I did do that," she said. "I think that's the way you oughta do it."

Chad slipped easily out of the "Pimp C" persona when it came time to be a father, which his children appreciated. "He kept us away from [the rap game] a lot," says Chad Jr. "Any time I was near some rappers, it was either at a concert or maybe in the studio, but … home time was just normal."

Chad Jr., shy and introverted, preferred it that way. He was embarrassed when his father picked him up from school in the Bentley and was swarmed by kids requesting autographs. But sometimes, his father's celebrity status did come in handy. Chad Jr. was an avid gamer and had his heart set on the Xbox 360 video game *Bioshock*. His father took him on a shopping spree to celebrate his 14th birthday on August 21, the same day *Bioshock* was released.

Unfortunately, Game Stop was sold out, except for one remaining copy on hold for another customer. Chad negotiated a deal with the clerk, who didn't have the heart to turn down Pimp C (or his extra cash).

But when Chad came to pick up his son a few days later for a weekend birthday trip to Dallas, Nitacha sensed that something was off.

"Man, what the fuck are you on?" she demanded; inspecting him carefully.

Chad denied he was on anything.

"I'm not a fool," Nitacha snapped back. "Chad, come on, man. You talking to *me*."

Nitacha believed that the drama between Chad's wife and mother had driven him back into drug use. "When Chinara and [Mama Wes] started hating each other, and there was so much conflict to [the point] where they couldn't even have a holiday sit-down as a family, I think that pushed him to want to be back on the road more [and] party, so he don't have to hear any shit coming from his mama, or hear any shit coming from his wife," Nitacha says. "That man had no peace. So he turned to other things to catch his peace."

In any case, Chad took Chinara and all three of his kids to Dallas at the end of August, where he made a surprise guest appearance at a Soulja Boy back-to-school concert with K104. Although East Coast rappers often pointed to Soulja Boy as the posterchild for everything that was wrong with Southern rap, Pimp was quick to defend him.

""A lot of people attack music like Soulja Boy, but hey man, my kids love that," Pimp told *OZONE*. "We need fun records. We gotta have dance music. We gotta have club music. We gotta have kids' music … We need those types of records to balance out all the other shit."

But Nitacha wasn't the only one concerned. Chad's hyper moods, erratic behavior, irritability, and bizarre scheduling had his inner circle convinced that he'd been using cocaine again. "I could just tell … I just knew it in my heart," says Heather Johnson. "He was slippin'."

When Heather tried to confront him, he shut down the conversation. Security guard Big Munn, whose father was a cocaine user, was very familiar with all the signs. But as soon as Munn told him he needed to "chill out with that bullshit," he didn't get a call to work the next show.

"I think he's doing something, Mama," Heather confided in Mama Wes.

"Let's just give it a little time," Mama Wes suggested.

Mama Wes, in fact, was the only person who wasn't convinced. "I don't think the cocaine became a major issue," she says. "I think that C was just doing a lot of shit. He was wrassling with a lot of stuff, and he wasn't good at that."

Even if it wasn't a "major issue," he was certainly doing *something*. Chad's drug of choice had always been marijuana, but he was still on parole. Cocaine and codeine had the benefit of dissipating from his system faster than marijuana. With an upcoming parole meeting, Chad asked Mike Mo to run out and get him some niacin pills to flush out his system.

Mike was already out on a "drank mission" accompanied by one of MAD Studio's new engineers, Ghost. Ghost told Mike a story about the time he'd taken niacin pills in high school to pass a drug test for probation. Ignoring the suggested dosage, he'd taken too many pills and ended up with puffy eyes, red skin, and an itchy sensation all over his body.

When they pulled up to the high-rise in Houston to deliver the niacin pills, Chad came downstairs and strolled out of the building, belly protruding, one hand in front holding up his baggy jeans in lieu of a belt. "Hey, Ghost, man, tell Pimp the story about the niacin pills," Mike prompted.

"My face swelled up, man," Ghost told Chad, relaying his bad experience. "You better be careful with them."

Chad looked at the bottle of pills. "Mike Mo, man, what the fuck you tryin' to do, mane!?" he yelled. "You tryin' to *KILL* me!? C'mon man, I don't wanna *DIE!*"

During one conversation with XVII, Chad mentioned Mama Wes' promise that she would turn him in if she found out he was using drugs again. "My mama would never give me up, no matter what," XVII said.

Chad laughed and said, "You don't know my Mama."

When Wendy Day passed through Port Arthur on September 5 on a promo run with a group she was working with, the TMI Boyz, she made plans to meet with Chad. He didn't show up but called an hour later, apologizing. They made plans to meet later that night in Houston, but Chad was again a no-show. Wendy, already fed up with his late-night phone calls, deleted his number from her cell phone. *Fuck him,* she thought. *I can't deal with this.*

The Hot 107.9 interview gained so much notoriety that some enterprising comedian created a hand puppet resembling Pimp C and posted a video of it ranting on YouTube, which Pimp proclaimed "the funniest shit I've [ever] seen in my life." Less amusing was a rumor someone spread in internet forums claiming that "UGK frontman Pimp C" had never made it to his Arkansas show "after being arrested by cops for possession of crack cocaine."

In our next *OZONE* interview, Pimp laughed off the rumor as something invented by "one of them ol' internet gangsta ass sites where them ol' faggot ass niggas be watching each other like they gon' suck each other's dick."

"I don't understand that internet shit anyway," he complained. "I don't be on that shit every day like these niggas. I'm in the streets trying to get money but you got some faggot ass niggas and bitch ass niggas that all they do all day is [watch] YouTube and read that bullshit."

———————

Chad's relationship with JT had soured after the Bentley accident. JT still told people he was Chad's bodyguard, though, and apparently after a late night fry smoking session, became convinced that someone was going to harm Chad. At 4 AM on Monday, September 17, 2007, JT called 911 reporting that someone was going to hurt Chad Butler. Police officers responded, quickly arriving at Chad's gated Oakmont home.

Awakened by the commotion outside, Chad came outside to find the 7'1" JT trying to climb over the gate.

"What the fuck are you doing!?" Chad demanded, livid, especially since his three children were asleep inside. JT was reeking of fry.

"They're coming to get you, man!" JT yelled at Chad, his eyes wide. "They're gonna kill you! You gotta watch your back, dawg. They're coming to get you!"

"Man, get the fuck outta here!" Chad yelled. "What are you talking about?" He tried to calm JT down and get him to leave peacefully, not wanting to cause a loud disturbance and wake his neighbors in the middle of the night. Everyone in town knew the large corner lot across from the golf course was "where the rapper stays," and being new to the area, he didn't want to cause problems.

Chad asked police to allow JT to leave, but instead, they searched his vehicle and found stacks of cash, 2.7 grams of cocaine, two weapons, and illegal ammunition. JT was already a convicted felon with a previous robbery conviction, and Port Arthur police were very familiar with him. "Pistol Pete," as they called him, was already under investigation for a local incident in which he was accused of pulling a gun on someone at a clothing store. Police arrested JT and turned the case over to federal authorities, who charged him for being a felon in possession of a firearm.

Chad called his friend Big L. "Man, guess what this fool just did? Man, this fool just tried to jump the gate at my house, man, talkin' about he had a dream somebody finna kill me! Maaan, you better leave them drugs alone, fool!"

The general belief was that JT must have smoked a bad batch of fry or was just plain crazy. "He had major mental issues," says Heather Johnson. "He was insane. Literally insane, like, he has lost his mind. His brain does not work anymore."

JT's brain worked well enough to understand that he was in serious trouble. His public defender began negotiating a plea agreement on his behalf. During a meeting with police at the federal holding facility in Beaumont, JT told detectives that he could provide damaging information about Pimp C if it would help him receive a reduced sentence.* Among other things, JT claimed that Pimp was selling 15 kilograms of cocaine a week.

Port Arthur Police Detective Marcelo Molfino thought JT's information resembled something from a childhood game of "telephone," having passed through several sets of ears before it emerged as something unrecognizable. Skeptical, he pressed for specifics, and JT listed several dates when he claimed Pimp had been in El Paso picking up large drug shipments.

"Some of the stories he came up with, the accusations he made, you could tell weren't true," says Molfino. "There was just no way that things could [have] happened the way he was saying."

On dates that JT claimed Pimp had been in El Paso picking up massive quantities of cocaine, Detective Molfino was easily able to confirm that Pimp had been in other parts of the

(*JT pled guilty to being a convicted felon with a firearm as part of a sealed plea agreement. In October 2008 he was sentenced to 57 months in prison. He was released from federal custody in November 2011.)

country performing or doing video shoots or other verifiable appearances. Detective Molfino dismissed JT's information as pure fiction, but notes that in the hands of less scrupulous authorities, the situation could have caused serious problems for Chad.

"All it takes is somebody like [JT] to bring you down," observes Detective Molfino.

––––––––––––

"Mama, you better get some insurance on me. These niggas tryin' to kill me," Chad remarked one day on the phone.

While Mama Wes didn't take his statements lightly, she also didn't press him for details. "You need to be careful what you say sometimes," she advised.

In late September, Jeezy finally addressed the beef rumors in an interview with AllHipHop. "If he ain't referring to me he ain't referring to me," Jeezy said. "Me personally, I think niggas was getting way too emotional. If you a G, you'll reach out. I got a phone, you got a phone, whatever, and you'll holla like men. You don't get in a magazine and say nothing crazy and think a nigga ain't going to take it personal."

In a follow-up interview, Pimp appeared to back down, even commending Jeezy for his response. "I liked how Jeezy handled himself in [your] interview," he told AllHipHop. "He could have went crazy and … said a whole bunch of reckless shit."

"I'm trying to be more of a leader than a nigga who cause problems," Pimp explained of his change of heart. "I'm trying to create a situation where we come together a little bit more. I realize this thing on my face [my mouth] is like a tommy gun. I can shoot to kill, I can shoot to start wars and I can shoot to stop wars. I don't think it's right for Pimp C and UGK to start wars with niggas right now."

Others also applauded Jeezy for the way he'd handled the situation. "I think [Pimp] had an epiphany … in terms of what he was willing to promote and not promote," says Killer Mike. "I don't think it was a personal thing against Jeezy … it was that Pimp saw the effects of the drug war, having been in the penitentiary and seeing thousands of young black men that were in there for nonviolent drug offenses … I think [his] anger was at that, and less about Jeezy."

Killer Mike felt that Jeezy, being the #1 rapper at the forefront of the trap music movement which appeared to glorify the lifestyle of major drug dealers, was just the easiest target. "I think Jeezy understood that, and I wanna applaud Jeezy for handling that shit in a very grown up, very G'd up kinda way," says Killer Mike. "A lot of lesser men with bigger egos would've felt more disrespected and challenged, and in turn disrespected an idol. So I've always thought Jeezy deserved admiration and recognition for that and never quite got it."

––––––––––––

As he prepared for a show in Hattiesburg, Mississippi, Pimp suggested that XVII should organize a UGK Records signing party in nearby Gulfport to let his hometown know it was official. As they left the party at the Boiler Room, XVII's partner Polo discreetly pointed out two cars in the parking lot which he suspected were undercover agents following him. Pimp nodded and pointed at a Dodge Durango. "There's another one right there," he said.

Convinced that XVII's life of crime would soon catch up with him if he didn't get out of Mississippi, Pimp insisted that XVII come stay with him at the high-rise in Houston. When XVII returned to Gulfport, Pimp had Mama Wes call XVII's mother and have a talk with her.

XVII panicked when his mother called at 2 AM, sure something was wrong. He rushed home to find her on the phone with Pimp C. She handed him the phone. "Just put some drawers in the trunk and come on," Pimp demanded. "Ain't nobody gonna let you stay down there."

"Pimp basically was trying to save XVII's life," says Bankroll Jonez, the Midwest pimp who had relocated to Houston after the "Int'l Player's Anthem" video shoot. "I think Pimp saw a lot of himself in XVII. Not just the fact that they both high yellow [skin tone] and got hotheads and tempers and attitudes."*

XVII was also pushing Pimp to bring Bankroll Jonez into the UGK Records fold. For pimps and drug dealers looking for a legit hustle, rap was attractive for several reasons. There was no barrier to entry, virtually no education needed, potential for a large payoff, and they'd still enjoy the same perks – women and a flashy lifestyle. Plus, it was one of the few legitimate careers where their criminal background would be an asset, not a liability. "What he really wanted more than anything was for all his artists to be able to get a big music check [so] they could leave the fuckin' streets alone and focus on music full-time," Bankroll Jonez says.

"Every nigga I know that's really out here moving some work is really trying to get them another career and trying to find a way up out the game," Pimp said thoughtfully on the *Will Hustle* DVD. "Every pimp I meet that's a real P.I. cross country is really trying to take that money, mane, and figure out a way to get out of that and get off into this music shit."

Since the argument with Terri Thomas, Pimp had kept his distance from The Box. The night before the annual Los Magnificos car show and concert, sponsored by the radio station, Cory Mo called to ask if he was coming to the car show.

"Man, what car show?" Pimp asked.

"Everybody gonna be there," Cory Mo told him. "Slim, Cham, Paul, man, everybody. You gotta go and show up."

"Man, fuck that car show, I ain't going to that shit," Pimp said.

Cory tried to convince him. "C'mon, man, you owe that to the city. Just go and show your face, everybody will trip out if they see you."

Pimp thought about it; by the next morning, he'd concluded that a surprise performance at the car show might be a good way to show that he was at peace: with Bun, with The Box, with the city. "Man, where that shit at?" he texted Cory Mo.

Pimp C pulled up to the car show in his red Bentley, dressed in all black. The place was packed with more than 20,000 people. He was hyper, talking rapidly instead of his usual laid-back twang. "I just decided about four this morning I was gonna come jump out here and come do a couple of these ol' hits, mane," he told a camera backstage. "I just got so many, mane, I don't know how many they're gonna let me do. I'm just gonna rap 'til they cut the mic off."

He spotted J. Prince walking in flanked by a Rap-A-Lot entourage. The two men embraced, then shook hands. "Somebody said they're gonna take my Bentley," Pimp commented to a camera nearby, waving the key to his Bentley and issuing a challenge to Lil Troy. "Now, I got both of 'em outside, and I got a BMW and J. Prince got about 50 cars over here too. I'm lookin' for a lil' boy … I think I got more fans on the Southside than lil' boy ever had in his life."

The Box's morning show co-host Nnete pulled Pimp aside for an obligatory interview with the station. She asked if he'd read his mother's article in *OZONE*; the newest issue profiled Mama Wes in a section called "Family Business."

"Mom is on point," Pimp said. "I get it from my Mama."

Unusually amped up and hyper, Pimp peppered another backstage interview with outbursts like "chuuuuch taba'nacle sanctuary!" and "alligator soufflé!" and inexplicably wiggled his tongue at the camera. He was also overly animated in an interview with young host J. Xavier for Music Choice TV, asking how old he was.

"I'm 15, sir," J. Xavier said.

(*Unlike XVII, Polo couldn't just pick up and leave Mississippi on a whim – he was married with three children. Pimp's instincts were correct. In January 2008, Polo was arrested when he brought $180,000 cash to a Gulfport truck stop to purchase 10 kilograms of cocaine from a federal informant posing as a supplier. In August 2008 he was sentenced to 10 years in federal prison. Polo was released in April 2014. XVII says he likely would have met the same fate. "If it wasn't for [Pimp] I probably wouldn't even still be here," XVII reflects. "He took me away from all that.")

"I made my first record when I was 16 years old," Pimp C told him. "Let me tell you something, man. Don't let nobody tell you [that] you can't chase your dream and go do what you wanna do. It's out there for you to get it, mane."

Bun, just as surprised as everyone else at Pimp's impromptu appearance, was prepping for his performance with The Box's morning show host Madd Hatta when Pimp approached. "Man, what y'all wanna do?" he asked.

Bun and Madd Hatta both looked at each other; then, back at Pimp. "*Shiiiit*, man, let's get on stage," Pimp suggested. "Let's do something."

Nearby, a couple Houston artists posed in front of the 97.9 The Box backdrop for pictures. A few more jumped in, then a few more; by the time Bun and Pimp jumped in the memorable shot, even J. Prince had joined in, alongside Lil Flip, Slim Thug, Mike Jones, Trae, Lil Keke, and Paul Wall and Chamillionaire, who were peacefully coexisting for the first time in months.

As the crowd dispersed, Pimp C noticed that Chamillionaire had a diamond missing from one of his rings. "I'm gonna let you know what to do if you missing a diamond," Pimp said. "You just put some tissue paper in there … nobody's gonna know you're missing a diamond."

Chamillionaire, laughing, stuck out his pinky and pointed at the large diamond in the center of his pinky ring. "What about this big diamond right there? What if you missing that?"

When Chad finally joined Bun on stage in front of the hometown crowd, the crowd roared their appreciation, rapping along with "Get Throwed" and "Int'l Player's Anthem."

"That was a touching moment," says Cory Mo. "When they hit that damn stage, they rocked it. And there was no one that could get up on the stage [after them]," agrees Brandi Garcia, a radio personality for The Box at the time. "I'll never forget that show."

J. Prince came out to Port Arthur for an informal meeting with Chad over plates of gumbo at Mama Wes' house. Their plan to form Wood Wheel Records as a joint venture had been derailed by Chad's four-year vacation, but Prince wanted to revisit the idea.

Prince was also trying to convince Chad to release his solo album through Rap-A-Lot. Chad had always been blunt about his reasons for not wanting to be a Rap-A-Lot artist; he didn't feel that the label spent enough money to promote their projects. In interviews, Chad was always careful to clarify that he wasn't signed to Rap-A-Lot Records, but that he was affiliated with J. Prince "for life."

Mama Wes warned Prince that it was useless to try to change his mind. "You're not gonna convince him," she told him, "and I'm not either, 'cause you know once it's in that big head…"

"…It ain't comin' out," Prince laughed, finishing her sentence.

Over dinner, Chad reiterated his plan to release his solo album on Jive, but it was agreed that they would compromise by releasing a *Pimpalation* compilation every year on Rap-A-Lot.

"Mama, that's the only nigga I couldn't even get mad at for not doing it my way," Prince sighed after Chad left.

A few days later, Chad happened to stop by his mother's house when she was meeting with her insurance broker. "I been telling Mama she need to take [out] this policy on me," Chad said.

The woman agreed that was a good idea, explaining that since he was so young, he could get a policy at a good rate. "At your age, you know, we wouldn't even need to take your blood pressure," she explained.

"Yeah, she told me she took a policy, $250,000 on her for me," Chad said. "I don't want that, I want the other way around."

"Yeah, we really do need to get that done," Mama Wes nodded.

"First of the year, right Mama?" Chad said. They planned to convene at the beginning of 2008 to get organized and handle everything that had fallen in disarray while he was in prison.

"First of the year," Mama Wes echoed.

On the set of "Int'l Player's Anthem" in Los Angeles *(right, top to bottom)*: Onlookers watch as **Bun B** and **David Banner** film a scene; **Pimp C** greets **Bishop Don "Magic" Juan**; **Pimp C** gathers the pimps for his scene.

Photos: Julia Beverly

On the set of "Int'l Player's Anthem" in Los Angeles *(clockwise from below)*: **David Banner** and **Bun B** telling MTV News to "Free Smoke D"; **Fonzworth Bentley** helps adjust **Pimp C's** wardrobe as **Bishop Don "Magic" Juan** looks on; **Andre 3000** accompanied by **Big Boi** in his wedding scene while **T-Pain** leads the choir; **Andre 3000** departing his "wedding" with **Big Boi** and **Khujo** and **Big Gipp** of the **Goodie Mob**.
Photos: Julia Beverly

Over the summer of 2007, Chad was often accompanied by **Ayesha Saafir** *(below, right)* and her sister **Halimah Saafir** *(pictured above with Andre 3000 on the set of "Idlewild Blue").*

Pimp C claimed that **Terri Thomas** *(right)*, program director for Houston radio station The Box, threatened to lie to his parole officer and send him back to prison when he refused to perform for free at their **Hip-Hop 4 HIV concert** *(above)*. Instead, he spent the day at **L'Ermitage in Beverly Hills** *(below left)*, getting a psychic reading with the **Saafir sisters** *(below right with Ray J)*.

Pimp C's "fuck the police" proclamation during UGK's performance at the **Microsoft Zune BBQ** in Los Angeles *(left)* caused a rift between him and Bun.

Clockwise from above: Jada's pimp **Ocean "O" Fleming** and filmmaker **Michael Maroy** of *Too Real For TV;* Maroy's ***Best of Both Worlds* DVD** with Pimp C and Pimpin' Ken; **Jada's** appearance in UGK's "Game Belongs to Me" video; **Jada's bruises and blood-spattered clothing** from her altercation with Ocean following the video shoot.

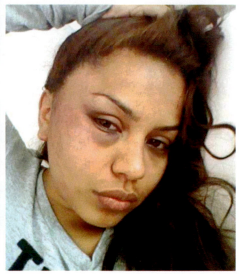

Pimp C took issue with young Texas rapper **Short Dawg** using his mentor **Too $hort's** nickname *(above)*, but they later squashed their beef *(below, with Three 6 Mafia)*.

Photo above: Julia Beverly

Right: **Pimp C** performing in Baton Rouge in October 2007.

Photo: King Yella

At the 2006 OZONE Awards, **Young Jeezy** presented **UGK** with the Living Legend Award *(above)*, but in 2007, the relationship between Pimp and Jeezy soured. Photo: Ray Tamarra

Pimp also took shots at Houston rapper **Lil Troy** *(below)*. Troy is pictured holding a DEA affidavit he attempted to use to cast doubt on rapper **Scarface's** credibility, and vinyl he released on the then-unknown rapper in the late 1980s. Photo: Julia Beverly

CHAPTER 55

"My mama told me a rapper is only as good as his last show." – Pimp C

———

"One thing is for sure: We was born to die. And we gotta live it all up until it's over with. Cowards die over and over again, but men only die one time. And as long as you got God on your side – I don't care what you call him, you can call him Allah, you can call him Yahshua, you can call him Jah, it don't matter – as long as you pray in the right direction, your prayer gon' get answered."
– Pimp C, radio interview with Bo-Bo Luchiano, May 2007

November 2007

Despite their public display of solidarity at the car show, the relationship between Bun and Pimp was still strained. And regardless of all the disclaimers Pimp issued that his opinion was only *his* opinion, he still expected Bun to back him up on the Jeezy situation. Bun professed that "there was never a question what side I was riding on," but it didn't seem that way to Pimp.

"From what I gathered … he was more hurt [with] Bun [than Jeezy]," says Pimp's friend Big L. "He really felt like Bun shoulda rolled with him on that situation."

Bun's method of handling problems was simply to avoid the issue. "There was certain shit we wouldn't agree on … but we wouldn't talk about that shit," Bun told *Murder Dog*. "We only had three arguments in a 15-year career and an 18-year friendship."

This non-confrontational approach didn't work for Pimp, who needed an outlet to express his frustration. Often, Mama Wes was the listening ear. The issues had always been there, but since Chad came home from prison, he'd become more outspoken. Chad had always contributed more than Bun musically, and was starting to feel that he deserved more recognition. He also resented the fact that Bun's personality wasn't as strong as his, complaining that his partner had "the backbone of a jellyfish."

"That's the way it always was," Mama Wes reminded him. "So why are you upset about it now? You always ran the show. And you gonna have to accept that and keep it moving."

Pimp had been overheard snapping at Bun over the phone, telling him he could come to Port Arthur to talk – if he could remember how to get there. The fact that Bun seemed to represent Houston more than Port Arthur was another of Chad's frequent complaints. ("I don't like P.A. either," his mother would tell him. "I just stay here for you.")

Those who knew Chad knew not to take his statements too seriously. "Everybody knows Chad had this conflicting personality of 'fuck you,' 'I love you.' He did with everybody," says Too $hort. Chad would complain to Wendy Day that David Banner was an opportunist who always wanted something from him, and then call her the next day with Banner on three-way, asking advice on a project they were working on together.

"Me and C would fight [too]… he fired me about five times," nods Mama Wes, adding with a laugh, "C would fall out with everybody every other day. I loved C and C loved me, but sometimes I could just strangle that nigga."

Most people in the inner circle understood that Bun and Chad's issues were a brotherly disagreement and family business stayed private. Those who had known the group from the beginning knew this wasn't the first time they'd been at odds.* And even though Pimp's emotions sometimes got the best of him, he'd always stayed true to their promise. "We took an oath back when we were teenagers that this is 'UGK for life' and we even went as far as to put that shit in our skin," he told *OZONE*. "This shit is for life."

Chad stopped by his mother's house on the morning of November 21, 2007, the day before Thanksgiving, with some things on his mind. He'd been thinking about the first day he came home from prison, when Edgar the Dog had nearly attacked Bun when he came in the house.

"Mama, why didn't you tell me [he had never been there]?" Chad asked.

"Well, you know," she sighed. "That's like going to see somebody in ICU and telling them who else just died. I mean, that ain't nothing I'm going to tell you."

"I guess Queenie wouldn't let him come," he said quietly.

"That ain't your business," Mama reminded him.

It all came pouring out: how betrayed he felt when Bun didn't write him or visit. How hurt he was by the belief that Bun had profited financially from the "Free Pimp C" movement and never shared the proceeds with him while he was sitting in a prison cell, unable to make money to feed his family. But most of all, he was hurt because Bun hadn't *been* there; not for him, not for his kids, and not for his mother.

Mama Wes frequently came to Bun's defense, partly because she knew her son. "C was my child, [and even] I wouldn't have put up with that nigga 15 minutes," she laughs. "As a woman, I couldn't have been nothing to C – his girlfriend, his woman, his wife – I'd have killed that nigga. I mean, C was hard to deal with. And I think Bun had finally come to the realization that [the only way to deal with him was] to just let him go do what the fuck he wanna do."

Mama Wes' house on Shreveport Ave. had always been a magnet for a strange assortment of people who needed a mother, a foster home of sorts. Along with Pops, Mama Wes, and seven-year-old Corey, Mama's assistants Travis and Heather were also living there, along with Chad's cousin Ed and engineer Marlan Rico Lee.

After Chad vented to his mother about Bun, conversation turned to religion as one of Ed's Masonic brothers stopped by. Ed was a 32nd Degree Mason, a fraternal organization which believes in the Bible. Chad expressed interest in the organization, and Ed's friend encouraged him to read Psalms 133.

Chad was still solidifying his spiritual beliefs, but it was evident he was searching for something. A few days earlier he'd joined Antioch Missionary Baptist Church in Beaumont. "I know for a fact that there's a higher power, but I don't always know what that higher power's name is," he told *OZONE*. "I read a lot of books [about different religions]. When you pray and your heart is in the right place and you ask for forgiveness, I know he's listening."

As Ed and Chad packed their bags to head out to Dallas, Chad grabbed a Bible. He spent most of the five-hour drive committing Psalms 133 to memory. ("Behold, how good and pleasant it is for brethren to dwell in unity," it begins.)

Accompanying them to Dallas was the rest of the crew, including Cory Mo and Mike Mo, Byron Amos, Ivory P, Bankroll Jonez, Big Bubb, Hezeleo, TOE, and XVII. They hit a literal bump in the road when Chad's red Bentley with low-profile tires caught a flat en route, as it often did. Unconcerned, Chad left the Bentley on the side of the road and hopped in another vehicle.

Chad had just spent several thousand dollars getting customized Dickies and t-shirts made to match the color of all of his shoes. He'd invited Teresa from SF2 to stop by the high-rise

---

(*"I would like to see the [UGK] story always be told on some love shit between [Pimp] and Bun, but, they had issues," says Born 2wice. "Brothers go through that … I prefer that they always be remembered as brothers. I can't be mad at you for telling the complete truth [in the book] … but if you tell the complete truth, it's gonna hurt the fans. Houston pride always wants me to [protect them because] they're superheroes now.")

and browse his walk-in closet, filled with black mink shoes, pink gators, Air Forces, Jordans, and old-school FILAs, taking pictures of all his shoes to create matching outfits. (The Dickies included embroidered stitching so Pimp could switch clothes depending on his mood: "Tony Snow," "Sweet James Jones," "Mackeal Jordan," "Jack Tripper," and so on.)

Morale was high as the rest of the UGK posse tried on their own customized Dickies. XVII's *Certified* and Bankroll Jonez' *Skroll Muzik* were circulating in the streets, and even though UGK Records was still an informal entity, the crew was excited to be seeing some progress.

Bun arrived at the Dallas nightclub with the MDDL FNGZ, who didn't mix and mingle much with the UGK Records posse. Bun had never even met most of Pimp's crew. The way Bun saw it, their entourages had always been separate for a reason. "We don't hang around the same [types] of people, so my friends are not going to really get along with your friends," Bun says. "It's just going to be a big room of a bunch of people that just kind of sit around looking at each other."

Bun had always distanced himself from UGK Records, which he describes as "a totally Pimp C creation," because he had no interest in running a record label. "I never wanted the responsibility of artists," he explains. "I know how temperamental artists can be, so I didn't want to be in control of artists' [careers]."

The use of the name wasn't an issue. "It was already understood that UGK was going to be [an] umbrella [to branch off into other things] … UGK was Pimp's baby, [so] UGK Records was Pimp's baby," Bun says. "I was just always a person that would help him manifest his dreams to reality."

Still, some of Bun's crew weren't so sure that the talent on the UGK Records roster would live up to UGK quality standards. Pimp had assembled a team based more on their hustle and drive than their rap skills, perhaps reasoning that with his production backing them, their talent could be developed. But some were concerned that subpar rappers releasing mediocre material could dilute the UGK brand.

When the show began, Bun and Pimp's chemistry was intact. Their set included a lively performance of "Let Me See It" and "Draped Up," and they were joined on stage by Chamillionaire during "Knockin' Doors Down." Fans peered down from the crowded balcony onto the colorfully lit stage.

But as they departed the show and went their separate ways, Chad sank into the car seat on the verge of tears. "Man, this nigga ain't even acknowledge my crew!" he complained. "I went over and hollered at them Double Knuckle niggas, you know, I show them love," he added, referring to Bun's MDDL FNGZ crew.

"Fuck it," Chad muttered bitterly. "There ain't no more UGK. There ain't no more UGK…"

The crew sat in silence, knowing that he was only speaking out of pain. "He loved that boy [Bun]," says XVII. "He might have been mad at him … but he loved that nigga … [The problem was,] Pimp loved people more than they loved him. It wasn't just Bun, it was a lot of people. I feel like he loved them more than they loved him. And he *knew* that."

Chad's pain turned to anger; he called UGK's old friend Rick Royal, now a radio personality in Dallas, to vent. "Pimp was talking real reckless, and I was really trying to calm him down," Rick remembers. "I [was trying to] be the voice of reason instead of being the gasoline or the cooking oil on the fire."

By the time they got back to the hotel past 3 AM, Chad called Mama Wes, furious. "He was just so mad at Bun because he wanted the UGK organization to be more … classy?" remembers Mama Wes. Chad was angry that he had spent money out of his pocket to make customized UGK Dickies and t-shirts for all the UGK posse members and brought them all to the show, and Bun didn't seem to care how his crew presented themselves.

"That's not Bun," his mother reminded him gently. "Bun is not gonna dress and look like you because that's not Bun. You are all individuals, and he's gotta be him and you've gotta be you."

"Yeah, Mama you right," Chad said, calming down. "Hell, it's been this long."

Still, he repeated his declaration that it was time for UGK to come to an end. And as she often did, Mama Wes came to Bun's defense.

"Stop it," she told him. "Just stop it, because you all are never gonna separate. You know it, and I know it too."

"How you know?" Chad asked.

"Because I know you. If I were Bun, I would've been left your monkey ass alone," she said. "'Cause I wouldn't have put up with you, C, for 15 minutes. But he's not gonna leave you and you're not gonna leave him."

Chad chuckled. "You're right."

"So stop already," said Mama Wes.

The next morning, Thanksgiving Day, UGK Records affiliate Ivory P came downstairs at the hotel to find Pimp purchasing a six-ounce bottle of codeine-promethazine from the local "drank man." Pimp downed the six ounce bottle straight.

"Goddamn, man," Ivory said. "You gonna be alright?"

"Hey, man, I'm finna go to sleep," Pimp said, climbing into one of the vehicles headed back to Houston.

When Hezeleo got in the car, he could tell Pimp was under the influence of something. A reformed drug user himself, Hezeleo didn't even smoke weed anymore. He could hear Mama Wes' instructions ringing in his mind: "Keep my baby out of trouble," she'd told him. "I need my baby here. That's my only child."

Hezeleo didn't understand why others in the crew didn't seem concerned with keeping Pimp sober, since Pimp was the leader of the organization. If he violated parole or something happened to him, none of them would have a job.

Still, talking to Pimp wasn't always easy. Hezeleo had tried the tactful approach once before. "Look how long you been gone, you know? You on [parole]," he'd reminded Pimp. "I feel like you need to approach all that shit with a clear head, the best you can, and make sure the niggas around you is doing they job so you won't have to stress so much."

Pimp had responded by telling a story. Back when he was a young up-and-comer and found himself in the studio with George Clinton, he was shocked to see Clinton take a hit from a crack pipe.

"Come on, man, you one of my muthafuckin' funk idols, and you sitting up here consuming some bullshit?" Pimp had chided him.

Clinton simply looked at him and replied, "Nigga, I'm George Clinton!"

Hezeleo got the message loud and clear: *Nigga, I'm Pimp C! Mind your business.*

Pimp passed out the rest of the drive back to Houston. As they reached the city, they stopped at Whataburger for Thanksgiving dinner. Pimp's security guard Byron Amos had just heard that "Young Jeezy's ThugsGiving" concert would be held the following day at Bar Rio.

"Jeezy got a show tomorrow," Byron joked as they ate. "Let's go to the show."

Pimp was still sluggish when they arrived back at the high-rise, needing assistance to get out of the car. Upstairs, Chinara was making sweet potato pies, his second favorite food after barbecue ribs. "Y'all can eat all them muthafuckers except for two," he instructed the crew. "You got to save me one and you got to save my wife one."

The next evening, Pimp strolled into the living room where the crew was lounging around watching television and announced, "I'm going to the Jeezy show. Who's coming with me?"

Someone laughed. "Man, you crazy," another one said.

"Yeah, I'm going to Jeezy's show," Pimp said. "I'm gonna be jammin' to Jeezy."

He turned around and went back in his room. Everyone exchanged glances, unsure if he was serious.

Pimp called Teresa from SF2 and asked her to bring a pair of shoes he'd had her order as a gift to J. Prince to Bar Rio. At the back entrance to the club, as Teresa filed in with Pimp and his large entourage, she asked who they were there to see.

"Mr. Potato Head," Pimp responded. Everyone laughed.

Security had just cleared the back door, anticipating Jeezy's imminent arrival. Pimp banged on the door. "It's Pimp C, muthafucker, you better open this goddamn door," he demanded. "We coming in there."

Finally, the door cracked open and Pimp and his entourage pushed their way in. As they poured into the dark, crowded club, the first person they encountered was DJ Drama, who was serving as Jeezy's DJ. The color drained from his face.

"That nigga looked like he was gonna just faint," recalls XVII. "He stood absolutely still."

Pimp gave Drama a slight smile. *You ain't gotta worry,* his expression read. Pimp and his crew headed upstairs to his VIP section next to J. Prince as Jeezy and his CTE crew climbed out of a fleet of Escalades out back. Pimp gave Prince the shoes, and Prince had something to show him, too: a copy of Lil Troy's 5K1.1 paperwork.

Pimp, wearing all white, positioned himself in a visible spot directly above the stage. A sense of excitement hung in the air; everyone was on edge, wondering what was going to happen. Pimp's camp largely felt invincible. Houston, especially Bar Rio, was Rap-A-Lot territory. If anything did happen, Jeezy was clearly the outsider, outnumbered and at a disadvantage.

With Prince and Pimp watching from the balcony, Jeezy emerged on stage in a hoodie to the tune of Bonecrusher's "Neva Scared." He dropped his hoodie and looked up at the balcony. "Big shout out to Rap-A-Lot," Jeezy said, then proclaimed, "Seventeen-five, damn right I said it." Pimp sipped slowly from a glass, showing no reaction.

Although most concertgoers in the packed nightclub weren't fully aware of the situation unfolding around them, those who did know were more amused than afraid. "They were sending subliminal shots at each other," recalls Byron Amos. "That night was comical. It really was."

The climax of the Pimp C vs. Jeezy beef ended without incident; clearly, neither side really wanted war. As Bun B tumbled out into the parking lot after the show with the rest of the crowd, he was relieved that "cooler minds [had] prevailed" and the potentially explosive situation was fizzling out.

Bun was political as always when asked about the Bar Rio show, telling Matt Sonzala, "[Pimp] wanted to go there and let it be seen that he had nothing against Jeezy and that he enjoyed Jeezy's music."

Pimp's recap of the night was a bit different. "Did u here I went 2 jeezy show n houston the other night!" he emailed me later. "I went n peace but he coulda left n peacez if he woulda sead the wrong thing! That nigga a hoe!"

I replied joking that he should have taken a picture with Jeezy. "It wasnt friendly between me and jeezy!" he responded. "we went there n peace but he coulda left n peacez had he sead or done the wrong thing! he came out wit that 17 5 i sead it and i ment it bullshit! but lil daddy was shook! and he scrached off b4 we got down from vip! played a song like he was gona do one last song and ran out the club ! ... by the way we got the real lil troy paperwork with discriptionz of how he helped the lawz! it was a document asking for less time ... j showed it 2 me at the jeezy show! that bitch jeezy tried 2 meen mug me for 2 seconds! i smiled at him! i saw drama face 2 face he looked like he was gona shit on hisself! smiled at him 2!"

After the Jeezy show, everyone congregated at Chad's high-rise.* The high-rise functioned as sort of a frat house/meeting place for the UGK Records crew, but also was home to Chad's wife and kids when they were in Houston. Chad had set up a small studio in the living room, and the closet of the kids' bedroom was rigged with a professional microphone and soundproof padding.

Mama Wes' assistant Travis was sound asleep at 3 AM when Chad called, announcing himself as "Young *Piiiiiimp*" and insisting that he drive 45 minutes across town to bring him the "Front, Back & Side to Side" instrumental. Chad had been impressed by a CD compilation Travis put together of all his verses, and told Mama Wes he planned to hire him.

"I need it *now!*" Chad insisted. "I need to record to that shit *right now.*"

Bankroll Jonez summoned his engineer Jeffrey "Ghost" Nations, a young graduate of Full Sail audio engineering school who also worked at Mike Mo's studio. (Ghost was Hispanic but looked white, and Chad's reaction the first time seeing him at the studio had been, "Who the fuck is this white boy? Y'all got the laws in here? What the fuck goin' on?")

Bankroll had a handful of girls working at strip clubs and taking outcalls off Craigslist and had initially tried to barter their services for Ghost's engineering services. Ghost declined and they settled on $20 an hour, which Bankroll paid out around 5 or 6 in the morning when his girls returned from the strip club. What Bankroll Jonez lacked in rap skills he made up for in work ethic, keeping Ghost busy recording one or two songs every day.

Chad had decided that rather than pushing one individual artist, they would release a UGK Posse project and let the fans decide who stood out. "This is the reason I got you niggas here," he announced to the men assembled at the high-rise. "You niggas is the UGK Posse."

He told them he wanted them to take the initiative to get their own projects off the ground, using UGK Records as a springboard from which they could move on to bigger opportunities. "If y'all pop off, y'all pop off. If y'all don't, we'll keep it moving," he explained. "If Def Jam wants to come sign y'all, hey, go to Def Jam."

Chad threw on the "Take It Off" instrumental, which he planned to redo as "Break It Off." He bobbed his head enthusiastically with the beat. "Man, this is the best shit I ever produced," he proclaimed. "If I could make a beat better than this, I would quit producing."

"Nah, man," somebody chimed in, saying that "Murder" was the best beat he'd ever done.

"Man, I was so fucked up during [the recording of] *Ridin' Dirty*," Chad said. "I was in a zone."

A friendly debate ensued, with Big Bubb, Ivory P, and the rest of the crew tossing out other song titles. What about Crooked Lettaz' "Get Crunk," or Master P's "Break 'Em Off"?

"That's just some bullshit, I sold that shit to P!" Chad said. "You know he recorded that shit in my bathroom?"

By the time the engineer Ghost arrived, the track in progress was called "Pusherman," a Curtis Mayfield sample on which Pimp C urged, "Have some coke, have some weed." He recorded the hook quietly, barely above a whisper, and then had Ghost increase the volume. Pimp hovered behind him, doling out rapid-fire engineering instructions.

Throughout the night, Pimp became increasingly animated and hyper, taking frequent breaks to go to the bedroom. Ghost tried to pass him a blunt, asking, "Pimp, you wanna hit this?"

Pimp declined. "Hey man, I don't smoke weed! I do *coke!*"

(*Some members of the UGK Posse believe this recording session took place the night before the Jeezy concert, while others believe it was after the Jeezy concert. It is possible it was a combination of both.)

Whatever he was doing, it was pretty evident to everyone on hand that Chad wasn't sober; plus, he was pissed off, which was a bad combination. As the night wore on, he started venting his frustrations, enjoying the opportunity to talk shit in front of audience.

"I kept screamin' [to Jeezy], 'I'm here, muthafucker! Here I go!' and he's just looking away!" Chad laughed. He also was upset with Bun. "That muthafucker left with Jeezy! I'm tired of him pickin' sides. When [Master] P put me in the hospital, he was still doing songs with him, and he calls me his brother! Why are you standing on stage with the muthafucker that just put your so-called brother in the hospital?"

"I let that shit slide!" Chad continued ranting. "And I didn't ask Bun to get involved in shit. But why are you leaving with your tail between your legs with Jeezy?"

"Fuck UGK!" Chad yelled. "Bun is out. I'ma get somebody else."

Bankroll occasionally had to take breaks during recording to give his prostitutes some stern instructions by phone. After he hung up, Chad yelled, "See mane, that's what the fuck I'm talkin' 'bout, mane! That's real, muthafuckin', live pimpin!"

By 4:30 AM, their numbers were dwindling. Ivory P had sipped too much drank and passed out. Ed and Byron Amos were asleep at opposite ends of the couch and XVII had retreated to one of the bedrooms.

Chad glanced at the clock. "I'm late calling my Mama," he said to nobody in particular. "She's probably worried."

All night, Ghost had been trying to contain his excitement, not wanting to appear too star-struck. But as they wrapped things up, he had to tell Pimp, "Man, you a muthafuckin' legend in my book. I been jammin' you since I was a little kid, man."

Chad complimented him on his engineering style. "Say, jack," Chad said. "I need your business card. How much Mike Mo pay you [to work at MAD Studios], man?"

"Shit, $10 an hour," Ghost answered.

"Fuck that shit, Ghost!" Chad yelled. "It's $25 around this bitch!"

Chad gave him $300 and told him he needed him to start working with the UGK posse. "I just put this ol' computer shit in my house and I need an engineer, mane," Chad told him. "Mike Mo be bullshitting, man, once it gets past 12:00 at night he don't wanna work no more. I need an engineer that's ready to work all night!"

Ghost handed over his business card and pulled out his cell phone, putting in a number for "Pimp C."

"Nah, man! Fuck that shit! *Tony Snow!*" Chad corrected him.

The session drew to a close when Chinara arrived around 7 AM. The next day, with UGK Posse members sprawled around the high-rise passed out, Chad emerged from the bedroom in high spirits, dancing a funny jig. His security guard Byron Amos had planned to accompany him to Los Angeles, but Chad said he'd decided not to go. Byron headed back to Atlanta with *Behold a Pale Horse*, one of Chad's favorite books, as a parting gift.

Ghost was back at his apartment, enthusiastically recapping his crazy night with Pimp C. "I smoked a whole ounce of weed at Pimp C's place, made $300, I'm full, he gave me all the beer I wanted in the world..." Ghost bragged to his roommates, who looked at him skeptically.

"I got his number, man!" Ghost insisted, pulling out his phone to show them *Tony Snow's* phone number.

Later that day, Chad called Mama Wes, in high spirits. "My lil' Mama!" he exclaimed. "What are you doing?"

"What do you want?" she laughed.

"Aye, Mama. Why you gotta say I want something?"

"When you start the conversation with 'my lil mama,' you want something. Now what is it you want?" she said.

Chad laughed and responded with something absurd.

"You lyin' like a muthafucker," cracked Mama Wes.

"Mama! That ain't the way mamas talk to their lil baby boys," he said, his voice dropping to a soft childish tone. But this was the transition he'd been looking for. "But, by the way, I have been lying about something."

"Well, I knew that," she responded. She suspected her son had been using drugs, but he'd continued to deny it.

"I've been lying, about doing… stuff," he admitted. "But I'm ready to get it straight."

Two days later, Bun attended Radio One's Dirty Awards in Atlanta to accept UGK's award for Best Rap Group. Backstage, he had a brief conversation with Jeezy, who assured him that he "wasn't trippin'."

Securing a distribution deal for UGK Records had been one of Chad's primary goals ever since he came home. ("It's UGK Records, right now we need distribution," he rapped within weeks of his release on the remix to Trae tha Truth's "Swang.") Over the summer of 2007, prior to their falling out, he'd asked Wendy Day to help secure a deal with Select-O-Hits to release XVII's *Certified*.

While Wendy considered Chad a friend, she also considered him "a nightmare on the business tip" and decided there wasn't "enough money in this world" to justify working with him again. She also considered Rick Martin "a fucking idiot" and couldn't understand why Chad had hired him as management. "Rick was about *Rick*," Wendy says. "Rick was about making money for Rick, not about building UGK as a brand."

Jeff Sledge also felt that Rick was a part of the problem amidst the growing division in UGK. "Rick was trying to throw a big wedge between Pimp and Bun," says Jeff. "He was definitely trying to find a way to push Chad to the forefront and make it like it was 'Chad's group.'"

Rick Martin was in talks with Los Angeles-based Fontana Distribution about a possible deal for UGK Records. Since Fontana was a distribution company, not a record label, UGK Records would have creative control over their own projects but also have the responsibility of marketing and promoting the albums. Fontana would give them an advance and charge a fee to distribute their records.

Ron Spaulding, a 25-year veteran of the music industry and close friend of J. Prince, had just joined the company and was interested in closing the deal. But he had one firm policy: "[If] I haven't met, spoken to, sat across the table from you… [I can't] make sure that we'll be good business partners," Spaulding explains. Rick made arrangements for Chad to meet with Spaulding on the afternoon of Friday, November 30, to finalize the deal.

"Why you gotta go to Fontana, can't [your partner] Larry do it?" XVII said sarcastically.

Chad shot him a withering look. "That nigga can't get no money on my behalf. I gotta go."

Larry had been using his "UGK Records co-president" title a bit too much, trying to make decisions on behalf of the company, and the UGK Records crew got the impression that Chad was planning to cut him loose.

Chad spent his last few days in Houston recording, putting together new material to present to Fontana. When he passed by MAD Studios, Bankroll Jonez was recording to a beat which sampled Bobby Womack's "Across 110th Street." Inspired, Chad jumped in the booth and laid the hook, improvised from an old Billie Holiday record: "Mama may have, Papa may have, but

God bless the child that's got his own."

On Wednesday, November 28, the posse gathered again for a late night recording session at the high-rise. Everyone got a turn to spit on "Believe In Me," which featured a few bars each from Cory Mo, Hezeleo, Big Bubb, Bankroll Jonez, and Da Underdawgz DJ B-Do and T.O.E.

Ivory P, whom Pimp had christened the UGK Records "official intro man," blessed the beginning of the track with some pimp game, proclaiming himself "something very young, active, and attractive." Pimp cooed on the hook, wooing a female ("If you gon' believe in something, why not believe in me?") and quoted a Master P line from "Playaz From the South" ("If there was a muthafuckin' band, I'd be a baritone"). The standout was T.O.E., who, like Pimp, made up for what he lacked in lyricism ("take notes from this pimp shit / but don't choke when my dick in your throat, bitch") with his distinctive voice and flow.

As dawn broke on Thursday, November 29, Chad and Chinara headed to the airport to catch a flight to Los Angeles.* Overall, Chad was pleased with the material he'd gathered to present to Fontana and was also optimistic about the coming year. He'd spent most of 2006 and 2007 playing catch-up, making up for lost time, but was brimming with ideas for 2008.

He'd instructed me to look at the Chrysler website and pick out which make and model car I wanted; he was in the midst of negotiating a deal with Chrysler and planned to give cars to his whole crew. There was a cologne deal in the works and talks of filming a reality show pilot for MTV. He planned to team up with comedian Lil Duval to do a satellite radio show and drop vocals for an episode of David Banner's Adult Swim cartoon *That Crook'd 'Sipp*. His own cartoon would be titled *Pimp Stick*, which was also the name of the clothing line he planned to produce with Teresa from SF2. He'd sketched out a dozen ideas for the line, such as a t-shirt with the Cadillac logo and the inscription "Never Let Hoe Ass Niggas Ride." Rick Martin was working on potential film-scoring deals, and Chad planned to "grab [his] nuts about doing that ol' acting shit" and seek out some advice from Ice-T about breaking into Hollywood.

Aside from all those side projects, he still had his hands full on the music side. In 2008 he planned to release a second *Pimpalation* project with Rap-A-Lot, another UGK album with Jive, and most importantly, his first real solo album. He hoped to achieve absolute perfection on the album, which he envisioned as half-singing, half-rapping. He'd already recorded "Down For Mine," a revamped version of "I'm A Hustler," for the project.

With Rick Martin's assistance, Chad had been shopping around for a solo deal, taking meetings with Sylvia Rhone at Universal Motown and Barry Weiss at Jive. "The [proposed] solo deal was always convoluted because of James Prince and Rap-A-Lot," says a perplexed Barry Weiss. "He was always telling us that he wasn't signed to Rap-A-Lot, but then they would always keep putting [his] records out. So it was all a little bit strange, to be honest."

Although he'd had his issues with Jive in the past, Chad was pleased with the direction they were headed. Plus, he'd come to realize that signing with another label might come with a whole new set of problems. Mama Wes advised that it was better to deal with the devil he knew rather than the one he didn't know. "Jive doesn't really fuck with you, you know?" she pointed out. "They kinda let you do what you wanna do, for the most part. And you know pretty much how to get what you want. But you would have to learn that all over again if you went [somewhere else]."

"Since we already know all of their quirks, we know how to get around 'em," Chad agreed.

"The grass always looks greener on the other side of the fence, but you can't see the bugs underneath," Mama Wes nodded.

Chad anticipated a seven-figure advance from Jive for his solo project and dreamed of investing the money in an apartment complex or a hotel. The same way Pimp believed that a

---

(*Some reports stated that he flew to Los Angeles on Wednesday, November 28.)

man should be married by age 30, he firmly believed that a man shouldn't be rapping past age 40. After releasing his solo album, he hoped to transition into being a full-time producer.

"The day that I make a serious solo album and produce all of the songs myself … it'll be my last album," he told AllHipHop. "When you hear that one, you'll know that there will never be another one after that."

Along with his longstanding plans to do the Broad Playaz group album with Too $hort, he wanted to do a joint album with Willie D, an album with C-Bo ("Cowboy and Young Pimp, that's gonna really fuck 'em up!"), Da Underdawgz project with DJ B-Do and T.O.E., a "Pimp C presents … Pastor Troy" album through Select-O-Hits, and an R&B album with Z-Ro titled *Young Pimp and the King*.

He planned to get more involved with Trill Entertainment and was shopping around for a deal for the V12 Boyz project ("we jumping out of cars with big motors and all that," Pimp explained of the name) with Lil Boosie and Webbie. So far, he wasn't happy with the low numbers that record labels had offered for the V12 Boyz, and told Webbie they weren't going to settle "for no muthafuckin' pennies."

After securing a distribution deal for UGK Records, he planned to help Houston underground acts like Street Military shop around for a distribution deal, to "take these boys nationwide, the way it should've been done 15 years ago." There were talks of re-releasing *The Southern Way* on CD. He also wanted to work with Ovadose, one of his original Port Arthur acts, whose plans had been sidetracked when he went to prison.

He was mentoring a team of up-and-coming producers, to be called the 808 Boyz (DJ B-Do, Averexx, Steve Below, and Cory Mo), and planned to bring some OGs like Sleepy Brown and Leo Nocentelli into the fold. "Mister Leo" was awakened by Pimp calling at 5 AM to ask if he wanted some money, "about a million or close to it upfront," to be a part of the production deal.

But the most important item on Chad's agenda for 2008 was to lose weight. Since childhood, his health had always been a serious concern. He'd lost both his great-grandmother and his grandfather at an early age of heart-related conditions and was concerned that it might be hereditary.

Since he'd come home from prison a hundred pounds heavier, he'd not only endured teasing (his bodyguard Big Munn, tipping the scales at several hundred pounds himself, liked to tease him about "looking like a lil' rolly polly") but noticed the negative effects on his health. He spent hours in the car driving to shows with his entourage, and concerns had been raised about his irregular sleeping habits; he sometimes appeared to stop breathing in his sleep.

After Mama Wes and Ed also became concerned about Chad's irregular sleep habits at home, he visited his doctor Dr. Barlow for a check-up. Dr. Barlow, an ear, nose, and throat specialist, often treated Chad for sinus and allergy problems. Chad had been through surgery twice to remove his adenoids, a patch of tissue behind his nose, and Dr. Barlow recommended he go to a sleep clinic to determine whether sleep apnea or scar tissue from his adenoids was causing his sleep problems.

Losing weight was the most effective way to cure sleep apnea, so Dr. Barlow recommended exercise. Chad agreed to start swimming on a regular basis, the only athletic activity he enjoyed. He was considering moving to Los Angeles, where he could swim year-round.

Scarface, an avid golfer, had been trying to get Chad out on the golf course, even offering to buy him some golf shoes. ("I'm not going nowhere and hitting no lil' white ball, and then pick that lil' bitch up and hit it again," Chad told his mother. "That shit don't make sense.") Chad finally relented, agreeing to meet Scarface on the golf course for some light exercise.

He also called David Banner for some advice; Banner had recently lost a significant amount of weight due to similar health concerns. "Banner, mane, I hear all these girls talkin' about you and all that weight you lost," Chad told him. "I need to get in the gym with you."

Banner, who had relocated to Los Angeles, offered to pick Pimp up from the airport when he learned he was headed to town. He'd come to view Pimp as a mentor, someone who'd talked him down off the proverbial ledge when things in his career weren't going the way he'd planned. "Banner, niggas will never be satisfied," Pimp advised him. "[Just] do you."

Chad still kept in touch with his childhood friend from Crowley, NcGai. The friendship seemed to be a connection to his youth, a throwback to the days when he was just Chad, without the pressure of balancing the Pimp C persona and all the complications of adulthood and fame.

Like Chad, NcGai had also gained weight as an adult. A relative expressed concern when he'd noticed NcGai stop breathing in his sleep. His problem had become so severe that he'd caught himself dozing off at red lights, exhausted from sleepless nights. NcGai spent a night surrounded by cameras at a sleep clinic in Baton Rouge, where concerned doctors informed him that he had severe sleep apnea and could potentially die from the condition.*

There were only two options to treat sleep apnea: surgery or a CPAP machine. Taking sedatives like cough medicines and sleeping pills were actually dangerous for people suffering from sleep apnea, because they could interfere with the body's natural ability to resume breathing.

NcGai opted for the CPAP, a device worn over the mouth which releases pressurized air. Patients sometimes described the CPAP as having a "tornado" in their nose; the high flow of air could sometimes lead to sinus congestion or runny noses. Chad had tried the CPAP and found it irritating and uncomfortable.

But when NcGai and Chad spoke in late November 2007, their conversation revolved around Chad's grandmother. The topic of sleep apnea never came up.

"I need to go visit your grandmother," NcGai said. "How's she been doing?"

"Granny's getting old," Chad sighed. "She's lived a long life."

"Yeah, she has," agreed NcGai, visions of childhood afternoons at the park across from Miss Bessie's house passing through his mind.

"I don't know how much longer it's gonna be," Chad said quietly, expressing the very real possibility that his 91-year-old grandmother would soon pass.

The two friends agreed it'd been way too long since they'd seen each other. Chad said he planned to visit Louisiana after he returned from Los Angeles. He needed to visit his granny and his aunt, plus, he planned to record with Vicious and check out some of Dolby D's new beats.

"Man, we've gotta make sure that the next time we see each other, it's not at a funeral," Chad said before he hung up.

(*Studies have shown that people with untreated sleep apnea are 3-4 times more likely to die than those who are treated for sleep apnea, although statistics can be misleading because many people with sleep apnea are older, obese males who are more likely to have other health issues. Sleep apnea was such a widespread, yet underdiagnosed problem that former NBA player Shaquille O'Neal, who suffered from the condition, appeared in a sleep apnea infomercial for Harvard Medical School.)

CHAPTER 56

"There was a bigger man there than what the world had the opportunity to see ... and that's the tragedy to me. Just like 'Pac. Our people get taken away from us before they're able to blossom into what they actually are or what they have the capacity to become." – David Banner, *OZONE* Magazine, January 2008

"I said everything I needed to say to Pimp. No regrets about anything. The last time I saw him, I hugged him and I told him I loved him. [That's] what I did every time I saw him, because you never know how life is gonna work out. That's one regret that I won't have ... We can argue, cuss, fuss, and fight all day long, but we gon' say 'I love you' when it's over." – Bun B, radio interview with Madd Hatta

Thursday, November 29, 2007
Los Angeles, California

"Man, I'm ready to work!" Chad's voice came through on the other end of the line. DJ Paul of Three 6 Mafia, lounging at home in the Hollywood Hills, glanced at the clock and laughed. It was past 3 AM. "Man, you was supposed to be here at six," DJ Paul said.

Chad apologized; he'd checked into his room at the Mondrian and fallen asleep, and he didn't have transportation. With a poor sense of direction and bad eyesight, he rarely rented cars in unfamiliar territory.

"Alright, Pimp," DJ Paul sighed. "I'm fixin' to come and get you, man… stay woke until I get there."

Since their "Sippin' On Some Syrup" collaboration with UGK, Three 6 Mafia had come a long way. In 2006 their song "It's Hard Out Here For a Pimp" from the film *Hustle & Flow* won the Academy Award for Best Original Song, catapulting them to a whole new level of mainstream success.

Now preparing to release their ninth studio album *Last 2 Walk*, they were disappointed at the response to their first single "Doe Boy Fresh." They wanted to have Pimp C feature on the album, plus, they had already been working on several records for a joint UGK/Three 6 Mafia album to be titled *Underground Mafia*.

Three 6 Mafia was once a six-member group, but over the years it had been whittled down to just DJ Paul and Juicy J, two of the founding members. Drug use had always played prominently in Three 6 Mafia's music, and some didn't know their limits. "A lot of them was on drugs badly," admits Three 6 Mafia affiliate Project Pat. "We all did [drugs], but some maintained and some didn't. They overdid it … A lot of what messed Three 6 Mafia over was the drugs and drug addiction."

Even though "Sippin' on Some Syrup" had been their first breakthrough hit, DJ Paul had never been a big syrup sipper. And after seeing too many friends in the hospital with "messed up livers and pancreases" he had sworn off syrup entirely. Liquor was his only vice. "I drink alcohol every fucking day," he laughs. "I don't really need too much else."

Chad had a vision for a record that could be the lead single for the Underground Mafia project, and once they got to DJ Paul's house, they got right to work. Three 6 Mafia and Pimp C studio sessions were generally more like a comedy routine; they'd tell stories, joke around, and eventually a record would develop organically.

The result of this session, "On Sum Chrome," was an odd combination of "Pocket Full of Stones" with the Christmas melody "Carol of the Bells." Chad, energized and in good spirits after a long nap, outlasted DJ Paul. Struggling with a hoarse voice, Chad only laid the vocals for six bars, which began:

First day I got out of the slave plantation
My niggas and my bitches gave me a donation
J. [Prince] bought a [Bentley Flying] Spur, silver not black
Chamillionaire gave me his candy red 'Lac

DJ Paul passed out in the studio. When he roused himself near daybreak on Friday morning, Chad was still awake, intently hovering over the console fine-tuning the record.

"*Maaan*, you still working?" DJ Paul asked drowsily.

They made their way to the kitchen, where Paul's 11-year-old son was sitting at the table eating breakfast. Paul reminded him to take the trash out before he went to school.

"You don't have to do that. I'm gonna take the garbage out," Chad told the boy, offering to do his chores for him. "Go on and finish eating breakfast."

After the boy left, they resumed things in the studio, finally wrapping up "On Sum Chrome" around 11 AM. DJ Paul, slightly drunk and too sleepy to drive, asked his driver to drop Pimp off at the Mondrian.

The driver returned with a copy of XVII's *Certified*, saying, "Pimp left a CD in your car."

Later that afternoon, Pimp called Ron Spaulding at Fontana to apologize; he was running several hours behind and would be late for their meeting. Spaulding had a tight schedule and suggested they could reschedule their meeting for Monday afternoon. Pimp agreed and left a message for his parole officer, asking to reschedule his Monday morning check-in for Tuesday.

At the Jive offices in New York, Rico Wade and his Organized Noize production partners Sleepy Brown and Ray Murray were meeting with Barry Weiss about the soundtrack for Out-Kast's movie *Idlewild* when Rico got a call from Pimp C. Pimp was humming out a tune, an unfinished track Rico had been working on for TLC in the late 90s.

Rico was amazed that he still remembered it. "We ain't use it," Rico told him.

"Ooooh, I want that, Ric," Pimp C said, adding that he also wanted to redo the slept-on Dungeon Family record, Lil Will and Cool Breeze's "Looking For Nikki," for his solo project with Jive. Rico put Pimp on speakerphone so he could explain to Barry Weiss the importance of getting some Organized Noize tracks for his upcoming album.

Meanwhile, Bun was en route to Seattle for a Zune promotional event alongside producer Swizz Beatz. His relationship with Microsoft was still intact, despite Pimp's "fuck the police" rant at the Zune BBQ.

In Chicago, Pimp C was scheduled to receive the "Don Juan Lifetime Achievement Award" at Bishop Don "Magic" Juan's annual Player's Ball. Pimp shot a text message to their mutual pimp friends Pimpsy (a.k.a. "619") and Good Game, apologizing for his absence and asking them to relay his birthday wishes to the Bishop.

On Saturday morning, Pimp called DJ B-Do and asked him to send over the files from the songs they'd recorded at the high-rise. His voice was still hoarse and raspy from the Three 6

Mafia studio session.

"What's wrong with your voice?" B-Do asked.

Pimp brushed it off. "Nothing, really."

Warren G, out on the football field with Snoop Dogg's youth football league, relayed a conversation he'd had with Pimp the night before. Pimp had customized UGK Dickies for Snoop in grey and blue (Crip colors) and plans to hit the studio with Warren G on Sunday night. "I talked to Pimp C, he said he got a jacket for you," Warren G told Snoop. "I'ma call him so we could go link up with him. He out here."

On Saturday afternoon, Chad was on the phone with his mother when he put her on hold to take an incoming call. He came back on the line, angry. "Maaan, they 'bout to tow my damn car," he complained. "This bitch done parked my car in a no-parking zone."*

Apparently, Chinara had parked the silver Bentley illegally at the airport. The customized rims Chad had put on the Bentley meant that it constantly got flat tires, and the last time it had been towed, there had been costly damage to the undercarriage. Chad, already irritated with Chinara, told her to go back to Houston and move the car so it wouldn't be towed again.

While Chinara was en route to the airport, Chad called XVII to make arrangements for he or Ed to pick her up in Houston after she moved the Bentley to an appropriate parking space.

XVII reminded Chad that Ed had an extra key for the Bentley and could move the car for him.

"She don't need to know everything," Chad told him.

Chad called his mother back, explaining that he'd been doing a lot of thinking about all the things in his life he needed to fix. For one, he planned to start seeing a therapist again.

"I think you should," she agreed. "Because we bumping heads too often."

"Oh Mama, you know how it is," he sighed. "We always gonna bump heads, 'cause you know you're a stubborn lil' ol' lady."

"Like you not a stubborn big head nigga," she laughed.

According to Mama Wes, Chad was fed up with Chinara and planned to file for divorce. Although Mama Wes didn't like Chinara, she didn't blame her, she blamed her son's short attention span.

He wanted to clean house not only in his personal life, but in his professional life as well. Things had been falling through the cracks with Mike Mo as the road manager, a detail-oriented position which didn't suit him. Chad planned to bring in several new crew members, including a new road manager, and keep Mike Mo on board as a studio engineer.

"Wendy Day crossed my mind the other day," Mama Wes said.

Chad hadn't spoken to Wendy since his no-show at their scheduled meeting in September, and he wanted to make things right. "You got a number on her?" he asked.

"I think I do, darling," she replied.

Conversation turned to Young Jeezy. "I just wish that had never happened," Chad admitted.

"I wish you hadn't done that," his mother agreed, reminding him that it was his fault. The incident felt distant enough that they could share a laugh over it.

Chad said he planned to reach out to Jeezy and squash things. "I'm gonna fix it. I'm gonna fix it, Mama," he promised.

He'd been swimming, and felt that it was helping his sleep problems. "I think it's getting better," he told his mother. Mama Wes and Heather had been researching a sleep clinic in Los Angeles, which wanted him to set aside four or five days to come in for testing. But right now, four or five days was a long time – he had too many commitments. Plus, he wanted to be free to

(*Chad had four phones. According to Mama Wes, the call from the airport came in on his "hotline," a number reserved for emergencies which was only accessible to her, Chinara, and Chad's parole officer. The implication is unclear.)

do shows over the holidays, when promoters would be willing to pay a premium price.

"If these niggas don't want to do shows over the holidays I'm going to clean up," he reasoned. "I'm gonna get that paper." He asked his mother to schedule the sleep clinic appointment for January 3.

While he was in the mood to fix things, there was one more person Chad needed to call. He'd changed his phone number after his last heated exchange with Bun and finally decided it was time to call and patch things up. The two had what Bun would later recall as a "very long, serious talk."

———————

That evening, Pimp walked next door to the House of Blues on the Sunset Strip, where Too $hort was scheduled to perform in front of a sold-out crowd. As the show got underway, Too $hort ambled towards the center of the stage wearing all black, the House of Blues logo prominently displayed behind him. The crowd cheered as they recognized the familiar instrumental of "I'm a Player" coming through the speakers.

"Got my nigga Pimp C in the house, he's a real playa," $hort announced, gesturing to his left. "Shout out to a real player." Near the rear of the stage amidst a small crowd, Pimp C, wearing a black mink coat, bobbed his head to the beat and pointed back at $hort, acknowledging his friend.

"You see I made up my mind when I was 17," Too $hort rapped. "I ain't wit' no marriage or a wedding ring."

Chad bobbed his head to the beat, rapping along with the song.

"It's some real players up in this muthafucker!" Too $hort announced as the song ended, wiping beads of sweat off his forehead with a small towel. "You think we come up here tryin' to get some pussy? We up here tryin' to get some muthafuckin' money, biiiitch!"

Pimp C stepped to the front of the stage and leaned in towards $hort. "Give me a mic," he whispered. "I'm gonna be your hype man tonight." A stage attendant rushed over and handed him a microphone as the instrumental to Too $hort's "Gettin' It" pumped through the speakers.

"If you believe in making money, say 'Hell yeah!'" $hort instructed the crowd. "It's been a long time since I first got down," he rapped.

"First got down," echoed Pimp C.

"But I still keep," $hort rapped.

"Makin' these funky sounds," finished Pimp C.

"Touch that shit, man," $hort said, stepping back and motioning for Pimp to take center stage. "Talk to 'em, Pimp!"

"Hey, man, something young, active and attractive, know what I'm talkin' about?" Pimp said, repeating one of Ivory P's favorite lines. "Had to come out and represent for my OG Too $hort. He let me drive my first Benz, know what I'm talkin' about? Now I wreck them hoes, of course."

Pimp C swayed with the beat, holding up a Styrofoam cup in his left hand.* "You should be gettin' it, gettin' it while the gettin' is good!" he sang, finishing out the track with some melodic vocals as Too $hort gave shout outs to the Bay Area.

"Texas always in the house," Too $hort announced. "Pimp C!" The crowd cheered.

After the show, everyone gathered in Too $hort's dressing room upstairs, where Pimp C had everybody laughing. "He was his normal self, like a lot of celebrities are," Too $hort recalls. "We shine in the room with other people, and he shined that night."

(*Despite the connotation, Too $hort is adamant that Pimp C wasn't high. "I have never seen Pimp C do syrup. Ever," he says. "I don't do that shit so when he's around me he was never sippin' on no syrup. The nigga was not loaded at the House of Blues. He was not doing drugs around us … he wasn't getting high.")

"Can you tell me the secret to having this kind of longevity?" a cameraman asked Pimp C.

"I just follow what Too $hort told me," Pimp said. "He told me, 'Don't stop rappin'. I just kept on making the kind of records that the people down where I live at like. I feel like, if you could make your own lil' town rock, and if you can make the people in your neighborhood jam, you could make anybody love it. We just stayed true to it, even when everybody else was doing some different thangs. That's all. Just stay true to what you do."*

Further down the Sunset Strip, the sisters Ayesha and Halimah were partying at a Hollywood nightclub where they ran into Ray J. Ray J pulled them into his VIP section and ordered more bottles of champagne. "Where Pimp at?" he asked.

Ayesha and Chad had parted ways several months earlier on bad terms. "I don't know," Ayesha admitted. "We don't really talk anymore."

At the Too $hort show, Pimp was accompanied by Larry and his girlfriend Mel. For unknown reasons, Pimp had dubbed Mel, who was from the Bay Area, "Wee-Bey."** They made another stop before driving back to the Mondrian, and when Larry stepped out of his vehicle, Mel heard Pimp muttering to himself in the backseat and asked what he was talking about.

Pimp replied that he was talking to Tupac.

By the time he got back to the room around 2 AM, Chad's voice was almost completely gone. He called XVII, who was asleep at the high-rise in Houston, two hours ahead of Los Angeles. "I was just Too $hort's hype man," Chad bragged, excitedly recapping the night. "Man, I was just playing your shit for DJ Paul and them."

XVII, half asleep, mumbled, "Man, call me tomorrow and tell me tomorrow."

"Hey! Did you hear what I said!? I said DJ Paul and Juicy J liked your music!" Chad yelled.

"Call me tomorrow," XVII mumbled again.

Chad told XVII he was going to cuss him out when he got back to Houston. "I'm out here working for *you!*"

Still amped up, Chad called Z-Ro to "make sure his foot wasn't in nobody's ass." Z-Ro had been spending enough time around Pimp to distinguish between his different personalities, and he knew this amped-up, crunk voice on the other end of the line was Jack Tripper.

"Mane, I'm finna sign this solo deal with Jive," Jack Tripper informed Z-Ro. "I'm comin' back with a million muthafuckin' dollars, jack. While J. [Prince] getting your shit together I'm finna put some bread in yo' pocket."

Pimp hung up the phone abruptly, leaving Z-Ro staring at the phone with his mouth wide open. *Man, that nigga there wild,* Z-Ro thought.

Over in Pasadena, 30 minutes away from Hollywood, a woman named Bianca was surprised to see her phone light up past 2 AM with Chad's number.*** His voice was hoarse and raspier than usual; she assumed he was in the midst of a late-night studio session.

"What are you doing?" she laughed. "It's 2 AM!"

"I'm here in L.A.!" he said, inviting her to come meet him at the Mondrian.

Bianca had been waiting months for this call. *Finally,* she thought. "Aw, hell no! I'm on my way!" she told him. Slightly upset to learn that she wasn't invited to the Too $hort show, she quickly put on a sexy-but-comfortable Jordache jumpsuit, threw together an overnight bag, and called for a towncar.

Chad had met Bianca through UGK Records' artist Big Bubb at a Dallas nightclub more

(*This YouTube video is billed as "Pimp C's Last Interview Before Death" but it is not known where and when it was actually recorded.)

(**Wee-Bey is a character on the TV show *The Wire*. Larry's girlfriend declined to be interviewed.)

(***"Bianca" is an alias.)

than a year earlier. She and Big Bubb were friends, sometimes more. According to Bianca, Chad wasn't bothered by the fact that she'd already slept with three members of his entourage.

Still, Bianca carried herself with class. She was a little older than Chad and had dated other high-profile men, but prided herself on discretion, striving to stay out of the spotlight. She didn't want to be categorized as a groupie, considering herself a notch above the Superheads of the world. "I don't need to make a name laying on my back, I'm too educated for that," she says. A professional painter, she took pride in her work and also held a master's degree in education.

Bianca and Chad had been talking for several months, and she considered him a muse. Their connection inspired her to create. "He was a little cookoo for coco puffs," she admits. "But he was just a musical genius … I just found it so amazing, and I think that's what really attracted me to him. [Since] I'm an artist also, I've always been attracted to musicians or someone in music because it just sparks my creativity also, just feeding off of them and vibing off of them."

Bianca had recently relocated to the Los Angeles area to care for her cancer-stricken mother. A previous liaison with Chad at the Four Seasons hotel ended abruptly when Chinara arrived unexpectedly. "My girl came in," he'd told her apologetically. Bianca thought he was referring to a girlfriend, not a wife, and was still eager for some one-on-one time with him.

It was nearly 4 AM by the time Bianca's towncar dropped her off at the Mondrian, where Chad had left a key under her name at the front desk. Expecting a private late-night rendezvous, she was surprised when she slid open the door to the one-bedroom suite in room 618 and saw a man she didn't recognize sitting on the couch.

The man, wearing sunglasses, merely nodded as Chad introduced him as "L.A." The Hispanic-looking woman seated beside him didn't speak, either. Bianca had met most of Chad's entourage but didn't recognize either one of them. Based on the man's appearance and standoffish demeanor, she assumed he was some kind of bodyguard.

First of all, who is this bitch, and who is this nigga? Bianca thought. She didn't say anything until they were alone in the bedroom, motioning with her eyes towards the living room and quietly asking, "Chad, who -"

"That's my boy L.A.," he responded, vaguely. "Sometimes he works with me."

She wasn't satisfied with his answer, but didn't want to cause drama and ruin their first night together. Still, the strangers' presence made Bianca uncomfortable. She suggested they should get something to eat. While Larry and his girlfriend stayed in the room, Chad and Bianca walked a few blocks down Sunset to Mel's Diner, a popular retro-themed 24-hour restaurant, and cozied up next to each other in a booth over breakfast.

After hearing some of his wild "Pimp C" interviews, Bianca was struck by Chad's soft-spoken, shy demeanor. He told her about his plans to get a condo in L.A.; Bianca hoped they'd be able to spend more time together. But when the conversation turned towards their future, Chad finally came clean.

"Well," he admitted slowly, "I do have a wife."

"Where's your girl?" Bianca was confused.

"Well…" there was a long pause. "My girl is my wife."

Bianca wasn't worried about a girlfriend, but a wife was something different entirely. She couldn't believe he'd omitted this fact during the past eight or nine months they'd been talking. Still, she felt like her heart was already invested and it was too late to break away. She didn't mind being his woman on the side. After all, his wife lived in Texas.

Chad was a fan of Bianca's paintings and wanted to find a way to help her promote her art. He'd picked out a piece of her work, titled "Contemplation," that he wanted to get framed. As Bianca recalls it, he suggested that maybe he could find a way for her and Chinara to get along. "Oh yeah, that'll be something," she laughed. "You big pimpin' now, huh?"

After they got back from the diner, Chad and Bianca retreated to the bedroom while Larry and his girlfriend slept on a pull-out bed in the living room.

Ayesha, who had spent the rest of the night in Ray J's VIP section drinking, couldn't stop thinking about Chad and how badly things had ended. She called him, drunk, and the short conversation deteriorated into an argument. "I hate you," she bawled, through drunken tears.

Bianca could vaguely hear a woman's voice, screaming on the other end of the line. "Fuck you, bitch," Chad snapped, before hanging up the phone. Bianca knew better than to ask too many questions, but she assumed his wife had learned he was with another woman.

The next morning, as they lounged in bed talking, Chad took Bianca's fingers in his hand and looked them over. He'd always been meticulous about his hygiene. (Even while incarcerated, he filed his fingernails and toenails almost daily, to the amusement of his cellmates.) "You need some maintenance," he told her, suggesting they should spend the day getting manicures. "Your hands are everything."

"Baby, I'm about to go right back and dip in this paint," she laughed. "They're about to be all messy all over again."

While Bianca showered, Chad called his mother. Mama Wes was surprised he was up so early. "Where's Coro?" Chad asked, referring to his pet name for Corey.

"Baby, I think he's riding outside, just like he was riding the day you left," she told him.

"He like that damn bicycle, don't he," Chad observed.

"Yeah, he does," she agreed.

"You know what, Mama? I was thinking about featuring him – not on the next album but the next one," Chad told her.

"I thought you said you didn't want him to be a rapper until he was 16? He won't be 16 by that time. Unless you follow your usual pattern," she joked, "and it's five years between the next album."

Chad laughed. "But you see Mama, that would give me a chance to introduce him."

"Are you changing your mind about that?" she asked, referring to the 'no-rap-til-you're-16' rule he'd previously laid down.

"Well, I was talking to Snoop, and we were talking about that," Chad began.

An interruption brought the conversation to a halt. Mama Wes wanted to bring up some of the serious topics they'd discussed the previous day, but she got the impression he had other people around, and the timing didn't seem right.

Around 2 PM, Chad called Red Boy to arrange for a barber to come give him and Larry a cut. As the barber cut his hair, he asked Larry, "Man, you said you were gonna give me some stuff to wear?" Larry handed over some Blockwear t-shirts from Stax' shop in Jackson. Chad selected one, dark green with white lettering, and asked Bianca to iron it for him.

As the barber finished up his cut, Mama Wes called Chad again, expecting his phone would go straight to voicemail. She was uncomfortable with him being in Los Angeles alone, without his usual crew, and urged him to come back to Texas.

"C, quit answering this fuckin' phone," she told him. "It oughta be off, C, because you oughta be in the air."

He laughed and said he was getting his hair cut.

"Just go to the airport," she insisted. "C, you can fly out of L.A. to Houston at any hour. Don't play with me. Just go to the airport … You won't have to sit longer than one hour, you know that you can fly out of L.A. anytime. Find a damn airline and fly the fuck up out of there."

"Mama, you paranoid," he told her.

"Well, you made me paranoid," she said.

He laughed. "That's alright, Mama. I still love you."

Bianca was uncomfortable with Larry and Mel's presence. Neither of them spoke or made eye contact with her. Bianca, who had spent time in the Army and was trained to be observant, wondered why Larry wore his sunglasses inside. *Why won't this fool take them off?* she wondered.

After the barber left, Larry produced an unmarked bottle of codeine-promethazine and a two-liter bottle of 7-Up on the counter of the kitchenette area. He mixed it up, poured a glass, and handed it to Bianca, who was sitting out on the sofa.

Out of respect, Bianca leaned to pass the first glass to Chad, but Larry stopped her. "No, that one is yours," he snapped.

Larry handed a different glass to Chad. Bianca wondered why Larry hadn't poured a glass for himself.

After Larry and Mel packed their bags, Larry began cleaning the room thoroughly. *Who cleans up a room at a hotel?* Bianca wondered. Larry washed the glasses, wiped the rims, dried them, and put them back on the kitchen counter, replacing the hotel's paper lids on top. He emptied the trash can, tossing in the liter of 7-Up as he left the room with the trash bag.

Chad told Bianca he was headed out to handle some business and would call her after he finished so they could go get their nails done. She got the impression he planned to stay with her another night and fly out on Sunday. She was confused by a cryptic exchange between him and Larry, implying that they were about to meet with someone. ("Is ol' boy straight?" Chad asked Larry. "You sho' that nigga good?")

Bianca wondered why Larry was leaving if Chad still had business to handle in Los Angeles. The whole situation struck her as odd enough that when she finally left around 4 PM, she hesitated outside the room, pressing her ear up against the door, trying to figure out what Chad and Larry had planned. She couldn't hear anything but muffled voices inside.

That evening, Chad had tentative plans to meet Shawn "Tubby" Holiday, the Interscope executive who had arranged the Missez feature, for dinner. He wasn't thrilled about Tubby's suggestion to meet at a sushi bar called Katana ("I'm from Texas, mane, we don't eat sushi").

When their plans never solidified, Chad reached out to Too $hort to see if he wanted to meet for dinner. $hort assumed they would go "sit at a fly ass restaurant and order shrimp and lobster and [all the expensive] shit off the menu and run the bill up hella high and pay for it" like they always did when they were in the same city. They tossed around names of a few restaurants.

But $hort had some errands to run first, and by late afternoon, he realized he wasn't going to have time. "Man, I ain't gonna make it. Let's get up tomorrow," he texted Chad.

Shortly after 11 PM, someone in room 618 at the Mondrian ordered room service. Chad's phone continued ringing throughout the night – Warren G asking what time he wanted to be picked up for their scheduled studio session, Ed awaiting a response on what time Chad would need to be picked up from the airport in the morning.

At 2:30 AM in Port Arthur, two hours ahead of Los Angeles, Mama Wes awoke abruptly and looked at the clock. She hadn't talked to Chad since noon, and it was odd that he hadn't called yet. She called, but there was no answer.

CHAPTER 57

"Pimp was larger than life. I honestly thought he would live forever."
– Nancy Byron, *The Source*, February 2008

———————

"The worst thing about death is just the void, knowing that he's not there any-more, period. And there's absolutely no choice [of] getting any of that extra en-ergy and talent that he possessed." – Willie D, *Houston Press*, December 2007

Monday, December 3, 2007
Hollywood, California

On Monday morning, a Mondrian housekeeper slid open the door to room 618, then left abruptly when she saw luggage and reported that someone was still in the room. Since the oc-cupant was high-profile, management decided to extend the room another night.

At the high-rise in Houston, Ed and XVII were worried. They didn't find it unusual that Chinara hadn't heard from Chad, since they'd been arguing. But the fact that he hadn't called anyone to come pick him up from the airport was alarming; he never missed his parole meet-ings. Ed pulled up his flight confirmation number to see if the flight had been changed; it hadn't.

Too $hort got a call from Mama Wes on Monday afternoon. As many times as they'd talked over the years, $hort had never heard her voice sound this strained. "$hort, are you there in L.A.?" she asked. "Something is going on. I haven't talked to Chad since Sunday at noon, and I'm calling and not getting any response. A whole day has passed, and I haven't talked to him."
Whoa, $hort thought, remembering their cancelled dinner plans.

Over at Fontana Distribution, the time marked in Ron Spaulding's schedule came and went without a word from Pimp C, but Spaulding wasn't concerned. "I've been in the urban entertain-ment business for a long time," he chuckles. "Time sometimes moves at a different pace [with rappers] than it does for some other businesses … so I was used to things being rearranged." He assumed some other pressing business had come up.

Bianca didn't wake up until late Monday afternoon, feeling groggy. She didn't realize a whole day had passed, and her mother was worried about her near-comatose state. "You slept a whole damn day!" she remarked.

When Chinara learned that Chad had rescheduled his parole meeting for Tuesday morn-ing, everyone at the high-rise was relieved. XVII reasoned that he was probably nervous about the possibility of being drug tested. *He's giving himself time to clear his system out,* XVII thought.
But as night fell and no one had heard from Chad, Mike Mo, DJ B-Do, and an engineer named J. Walker drove over to the airport to see if Pimp's Bentley was still there. It was. "I was at the high-rise in Houston, and I kept calling," Chinara told *XXL*. "He was supposed to be home,

and that was odd. We text everything. And this is weird. Chad hasn't texted me on anything. And I just felt like something was so wrong."

Mama Wes had been calling Chad's hotline repeatedly. Even if he didn't answer the regular phone, he would *always* answer the hotline, which was reserved for emergencies, like the time Corey was rushed to the hospital with an asthma attack.

By midnight, Mama Wes *knew*, in only the way a mother could know. She took a deep breath and verbalized what she'd been thinking all day. "He's gone," she said out loud, to no one in particular. "Chad is gone."

She called his phone incessantly throughout the night. "I knew he wasn't gonna answer," she recalls. "That was the weirdest night of my life … Every time he didn't answer, I was just going crazy."

After a terrible, sleepless night, Mama Wes was convinced that her son was either dead or missing. It was unprecedented for him to go two nights without calling. At daybreak in Los Angeles on Tuesday morning, December 4, she called Rick Martin.*

"Rick. Head over to that damn hotel," she insisted. "Now."

Rick knew Chad hadn't arrived in Houston on Monday morning as planned, but he wasn't in panic mode yet, and was hesitant to interrupt Chad at such an early hour. He assumed he'd probably just overslept or was preoccupied with a female visitor.

"Rick, I'm trying to be nice about this," Mama Wes said firmly. "There's something seriously wrong, and you need to get your monkey ass over there now."

"Okay," he sighed. "I'm gonna take a quick shower."

"Rick, baby, just go. Nobody's really out to smell your funk right now," she urged.

Rick seemed to think she was being overdramatic. "You need to stay positive," Rick told her. "When I get there, I'm going to call you."

Mama Wes woke Heather, saying, "Baby, I need you to come to the kitchen and sit down and we need to talk." Surprised at the unusual request, Heather sleepily dragged herself into the kitchen.

"I think C is dead," Mama Wes told her.

"What!? What are you talking about?" Heather asked. "No, no. What are you talking about?"

"I think he's dead," Mama Wes repeated.

Heather started panicking. "What do you mean, you *think*?!? What are you talking about?"

At the high-rise, Chinara was starting to panic too. "Give the hotel a call … [you can] have them go check the room," Ed suggested. Chinara called the hotel and became irritated when they put her on a lengthy hold. XVII was awakened by Chinara screaming into the phone, "Somebody go check on my fucking husband!!"

At 9:20 AM in Los Angeles, the Mondrian's security director Marvin Sweetwood used a master key to enter room 618. Chad's body, lying on his right side on top of the sheets in the middle of the bed, was already in the early stages of decomposition. Clad in a black t-shirt, white boxer briefs and white boxers under black Polo sleep pants, he was still wearing his glasses, his watch, earrings, a ring, and a bracelet. Sweetwood checked for a pulse but found nothing.

Three minutes later, a female clerk at the Mondrian picked up the phone for what TMZ would later dub "The Calmest 911 Call Ever Made."

"What's going on there?" the 911 operator asked.

(*Rick Martin declined to be interviewed. His statements and actions as described in this chapter are from other people's recollections, or statements he made to other media outlets.)

"Security says there's a – it's a guy in the room who's not responding to anything," the clerk answered.

"Is he awake and breathing?"

"I don't know if he's breathing, but he's not awake."

"Do you know how old he is?"

"I have no idea."

"Okay, just to verify with you, that's 8550 West Sunset Blvd., room number 618, in West Hollywood."

"Correct."

At the 911 operator's request, the hotel clerk radioed security on a handheld walkie-talkie. "Do you know if the guy in the room is breathing?" she asked.

"No. Negative," came the staticky response.

A sheriff's deputy and a fire truck arrived within minutes. At 9:38 AM, Chad Butler was pronounced dead.

Big Munn, who was driving an 18-wheeler, got a call from a friend in Los Angeles. "Check on your people," his friend told him. "I got a homegirl [who] works at the muthafuckin' [Mondrian] hotel, she sayin' ya' pa'tna Pimp dead."

Munn called Mama Wes. "Say mane, my pa'tna in L.A. talkin' about 'Pimp C dead,'" he chuckled. "I know that's some bullshit."

He was expecting a laugh back, but instead, there was an extended silence on the other end of the line. "Baby, I think so," Mama Wes finally managed.

"What!? *Maaan*, stop playing, Mama," Munn said.

"Baby, I think so," she repeated, explaining that she hadn't heard from him in several days. Munn knew that was serious. "That nigga, no matter what the fuck was goin' on – high, drunk, whatever – he was gonna call his Mama," Munn explains. "Always."

Munn called Bun, who was busy packing. He, Queenie, and her two children were preparing to move into a new house in Pearland on the south side of Houston. "Say, Bun, see if you can get Pimp on the phone," Munn said, without elaborating.

Next Munn called Mike Mo, whose phone had been blowing up all morning. "Man, what the fuck is going on with Pimp?"

Mike Mo called Rick. "Rick, what the fuck is going on, man? We getting all these crazy ass calls. Is Pimp alright?"

"Oh God, I don't know," Rick told him. "I'm on my way to the hotel."

December 4, 2007, marked the release date for Scarface's *Made,* and MAD Studios' engineer Steve-O's first stop was Best Buy to pick up the album. Knowing that Mike Mo had worked on the project, Steve-O texted him to tell him he was buying a copy.

"Cool, get me one too, then come to the house," Mike Mo texted back. "They can't find Pimp."

'They can't find Pimp?' What the fuck does that mean? Steve-O wondered.

Shortly after 10 AM, Rick Martin got a call from Marvin Sweetwood at the Mondrian. "We need you to come up here [to the hotel]," he said. "We have a… situation."

Rick was already en route. "What is the situation?" he asked hesitantly.

"Just ask for security when you get here," he was told.

That couldn't be good. Rick called DJ Paul of Three 6 Mafia, who was still in bed, to see if he'd talked to Pimp. "Man, don't start no rumors, but I think it might be something wrong with Pimp," Rick told him.

By this time, homicide detective Daniel Dyer was at the hotel doing a preliminary investigation. He poked through a duffle bag full of CDs and noted that the ironing board was still up, but everything looked fairly normal. Dyer concluded that "there were no visible signs of trauma... [or] criminal activity."

When Rick Martin pulled within eyesight of the Mondrian, he was alarmed to see police cars and ambulances surrounding the hotel. He was on the phone with Mama Wes. "I might not be able to get up in here," he told her as he pulled up to the entrance shortly before 11 AM. "Looks like something else has happened."

"Rick, C is dead," Mama Wes said firmly.

"No, don't say that! Don't say that," Rick insisted.

Rick was greeted by a police officer who asked if he could identify a deceased person. Rick's legs buckled.

After security escorted him to the room, Rick was faced with the grim task of calling everyone back in Texas. At the high-rise Ed passed the phone to Chinara, who dropped it after hearing the news. In Port Arthur, Mama Wes and Heather broke down in tears when Rick called to confirm their worst fears.

Mama Wes was irritated that Chinara had caused such a scene that hotel security had gone into the room first. "That's what I *didn't* want," she says. "I wanted Rick to get there first."

TMZ and other media outlets quickly arrived on the scene and were corralled by Ed Winter, the media spokesman from the coroner's office. Dozens of news outlets picked up on TMZ's story, reporting that Pimp C had been found dead in a hotel room.

Calls started coming in from everywhere; Heather was so upset she could barely keep her composure, so Mama Wes fielded most of the calls. Mama Wes also called Nitacha's parents, the Broussards, who owned a home health agency in nearby Nederland. Nitacha's father left to go get Chad Jr. from school, and Nitacha's mother pulled her into a private office. "I've got to tell you something," she said. "It's about Chad."

Nitacha thought her son was in trouble at school. "What did he do?" she asked.

"No..." her mother said slowly. "It's about big Chad."

He got arrested again. I knew it, Nitacha thought angrily. She hadn't seen him since their argument on Chad Jr.'s birthday, but knew he was slipping back into his old habits. *He's gonna be in there for a while.*

"He back in prison?" she asked.

Her mother led her outside to her car before dropping the bomb. "Chad's dead."

Fourteen-year-old Chad Jr. was practicing his typing skills in computer class when an office administrator came in the classroom to inform him, "Your grandpa is here to pick you up early."

Getting picked up from school early couldn't be good. *Am I in trouble?* Chad Jr. wondered.

His grandfather was waiting in the hallway. "What's up, Grandpa? What's going on?" Chad asked, trying to figure out what this was all about.

"Uh, nothing much, man," Grandpa replied in a somber tone. A friend passed by as they exited the building. "Hey, man, sorry to hear about your-" the friend began sympathetically, cut short by a warning glance from Grandpa.

Once they'd driven off the school property, Grandpa shared the news. Chad Jr. was silent in disbelief, struggling to process the information.

Nitacha pulled up to Mama Wes' house in a daze; she felt like she was dying. Her father arrived around the same time with Chad Jr. Nitacha's phone never stopped ringing, friends and acquaintances calling to ask if it was true. Fed up, she snapped on one of them, "Call muthafuckin' Channel 5 news and ask them muthafuckers if it's true. I ain't no muthafuckin' reporter!" In the back of her mind, she still hoped it would turn out to be a bad dream.

Corey's mom Angie had the day off work and was at home asleep when a call from Queenie woke her up. She'd seen something online saying that Pimp C was dead. Angie put Queenie on hold and tried calling Chad's phone several times, but there was no answer. She called Mama Wes to ask what was going on.

"Where are you, are you at work?" Mama Wes asked.

"No, I'm at home," Angie responded.

"Well, are you alone?" Mama Wes wanted to know.

"No," Angie said.

"Okay. Well, he's gone," said Mama Wes.

"Gone where?" Angie asked.

There was a lengthy silence, the implication finally starting to sink in.

"You okay?" Mama Wes asked.

"Yeah," Angie said, fighting back tears. "Mama, hold on. Hold on."

She clicked in Queenie on three-way. "Mama, this is Queenie," Angie blurted out. "Queenie, she say he gone!"

Queenie started screaming hysterically; Angie could hear Bun in the background echoing Queenie's grief.

"I wish I could sit here and describe it, the overwhelming wash that comes over you," Bun told *XXL* of that moment. "I don't know. It's really hard to explain it. To say that the person is dead. You know, you cry or whatever. It's just a very deep, deep, deep pain that you feel."

Bun called his mother sobbing. "He gone," he said through tears.

———————

Wendy Day was walking from her Atlanta office to a nearby restaurant when she got a call from *XXL* Magazine editor Vanessa Satten, who had just seen the TMZ story. "Oh my God, Pimp C is dead!" Vanessa exclaimed.

"No, he's not," Wendy responded dryly, in her standard monotone. *Couldn't be.*

Wendy hadn't talked to Chad since their last falling-out, and didn't want to call his mom with such a depressing question. She turned to her assistant Ace, who also worked with DJ Greg Street, and asked him to get Greg on the line.

"Is Pimp C dead?" Wendy asked Greg.

Greg laughed. "Naw, he's like Keith Richards. He's gonna live forever."

Wendy tried calling Chad's cell phone, which went to voicemail. She was momentarily relieved. *There's room on the voicemail, so he's not dead. 'Cause if he was dead, everybody would be calling him, right?* she reasoned. She left a message.

I was in high spirits as my taxi pulled up to the curb around 2:30 PM at New York's JFK airport. It had been an extremely productive trip, and I'd just received a phone call with the best news of my professional career. As I pulled out cash for the cab driver, my phone rang. *Wendy Day?* Wendy *never* called me. We always emailed; this must be important.

"Hey!" I answered, as the driver pulled my luggage from the trunk. "What's up?"

"It's not true, is it?" she exclaimed.

"What?" I was lost. "What's true?"

"Pimp C died!" she said.

"Uh, I doubt it," I said. "But I'll find out."

This *had* to be a rumor, I thought. Lil Boosie had "died" so many times in the past few months I was weary of calling his manager to confirm it wasn't true. Celebrity death rumors were so rampant that artists sometimes sent out press releases to assure fans they were alive and well, like E-40 had a few months earlier when he "died" during All Star weekend in Las Vegas. Too $hort had been battling rumors about his "death" for so long he'd even written a song about it ("Dead or Alive").

I called Pimp's phone twice as I printed out my boarding pass at the kiosk, but there was no answer. Come to think of it, I'd tried calling him twice last night with no response.

"Hey, u good?" I texted him.

I called Bun B. No answer.

Hmm. Surely Pimp C was alive and well, but who else could I call to confirm? The rumor, Wendy said, was that he'd passed away in Los Angeles. As far as I knew, he was home in Texas. I texted Too $hort and asked if Pimp C was in California.

He answered immediately. "Yep. He was at my show on Saturday."

Oh, shit. Pimp *was* in L.A. I started to get a sinking feeling in my stomach.

"Have u talked to him today?" I replied. "Can u try calling him & make sure he's good?"

As $hort and I exchanged a few more messages, we both started getting emails, texts, and phone calls from all over and realized this was too big to be just a rumor. I sat in the terminal at JFK in stunned silence, without realizing that my flight had already departed. I felt disconnected from the world around me.

"Pimp – please say that aint so?" Rahman Dukes from MTV News emailed me.

"oh my god, please tell me its not true about pimp c," came an email from Hot 97's Miss Info, followed by "What happened? Was it bc of lean?"

I stopped answering the phone. People sounded too... *excited.*

Some 20 miles away in Manhattan, it was business as usual at Def Jam Records, where Jive's Jeff Sledge was absorbed in a meeting with A&R Jay Brown. Jeff happened to glance at his BlackBerry and noticed an explosion of texts and emails coming through. *Fuck, oh fuck, fuck, oh fuck,* he thought as he skimmed through them.

The rest of the day was a nightmare. Jeff could barely remember how he'd gotten back to his office at Jive, but there he was, surrounded by people who wanted information. "There wasn't no remorseful shit," Jeff remembers. "Like, nobody was coming to our office *sad*. Maybe a couple people did, but a lot of them came in like, 'Yo, you heard the news?' almost like it was a hot new blog or something … Like, I've known this guy since '92 … I was talking to [Mama] Wes and Bun [B] and it was just – it was just terrible. It was very terrible. Yeah, it was terrible."

Over in New Orleans, Mannie Fresh was still reeling from the sudden death of his sister Angela "Nina" Bryant a week earlier when a flood of text messages started coming through on his cell phone. "Say a prayer for Pimp C's family," one read. "Another soldier gone too soon," said another.

Mannie shook his head. *Niggas play too much,* he thought.

Mannie's manager DJ Wop was on the phone with Mia X reminiscing about the good ol' days, when the two of them, along with Mannie and his sister Nina, were often a foursome hitting the New Orleans nightclubs. Mia X and Mannie Fresh had formed one of New Orleans' first rap duos in the 1980s.

Wop clicked over to take another call. When he returned, he said apologetically, "Mia, I gotta call you back. Somebody on my line sayin' Pimp C is dead."

Mia's knees buckled; she grabbed a nearby countertop for support.

Wop's next call was from Mannie. "Yeah, dude," Wop sighed in his thick New Orleans accent. "That shit real."

In Baton Rouge, producer KLC was just pulling up to the studio and flipping through radio stations. He caught the tail end of UGK's "One Day" before the station went to a commercial break. His mother called to ask if he knew a rapper named Chad.

Chamillionaire, in the studio fine-tuning some Pimp C vocals, was writing a verse about Hawk, Moe, and other fallen Houston rappers. When someone in the studio told him Pimp C had passed, he didn't believe it, but called Bun B to be sure. The unsteadiness in Bun's voice told him everything he needed to know. Shaken, Chamillionaire cancelled the session and sat in his car outside in disbelief. He emailed Nancy Byron: "Pimp C has passed this morning."

Nancy stared at the computer screen, feeling numb. Chamillionaire wasn't the type to spread unverified gossip.

In another Houston recording studio, Willie D heard the rumors and called J. Prince, expecting him to shoot them down. He didn't. Trae called J. Prince about some other business and could tell from the tone of Prince's voice that something was terribly wrong. "I cannot believe the boy dead," Prince murmured repeatedly. *"Fuck."*

Scarface was so unconcerned with first week sales of his new album that he was spending the release day on the golf course. He was irritated when his phone rang, interrupting his concentration on the putting green.

"You heard about Pimp C, huh?" his driver Freeway asked.

Scarface shook his head, figuring Pimp had gotten into some beef over one of his controversial interviews. "Damn, man, I gotta go fuck some people up behind Chad? Somebody done jumped on Chad or something?" he asked.

NBA player Stephen Jackson was already en route to a funeral; he was scheduled to speak at the service for teammate Matt Barnes' mother, who had passed suddenly of cancer. His cousin reached to turn up the radio. "Breaking news," came the radio announcer's voice. "Pimp C just passed. Chad Butler from UGK was found dead in a hotel."

Jackson's mouth dropped; he called Bun, his voice breaking: "Tell me this isn't true…"

Calls were pouring in at Mama Wes' house: Mitch, Bundy and Vicious of the X-Mob, T.O.E., Hezeleo, even the librarian Chad worked with at the Terrell Unit. Mama Wes skipped the formalities, she'd simply pick up the phone and tell them all the same thing: "He gone, baby."

Over in Dallas, Bo-Bo Luchiano had been going through a rough time caring for his mother, who had just been diagnosed with Alzheimer's. He'd been forced to give up his radio show, too; he felt like he was losing everything. Chad was his last remaining confidant. They'd talked a few days ago about Scarface's album. "Man, that Scarface is bangin'," he'd texted Chad on Sunday night, but no reply came. *He must be in the studio,* Bo-Bo had thought.

When he got the call saying Chad had died, he thought surely it was a rumor. He called Mama Wes. "Yeah, baby, he gone," she told him. Bo-Bo broke down sobbing.

For Rick Royal, the news was a wakeup call. His mind flashed back to all the times Chad had invited him to the studio and he'd flaked. He'd not only passed up the opportunity to oversee the *Ridin' Dirty* album, but missed studio sessions for an embarrassingly long list of UGK classics. "My ass is lazy sometimes," Rick admits. "The [things] Pimp actually was asking of me – I really wish I had listened to him … I just didn't see what he saw in me."

At a telemarketing center in Beaumont, Alonzo Cartier, an aspiring young rapper who'd met Pimp at Avery's studio, was crushed when he saw the news on SOHH.com. Alonzo ripped off his headset and threw it down angrily. *My dream is over,* he thought. *Fuck this.*

For young men from Port Arthur, Pimp C was their only tangible link to the entertainment world. They viewed him as their only opportunity, and his accessibility gave them hope. "My nephew's working in the same studio as Chad Butler," Alonzo's uncle liked to brag. Now, Alonzo felt, it was all over.

Bun and Red Boy drove over to the high-rise and dropped off Ed, Chinara, and XVII to meet Mike Mo and his wife at the airport for the next flight out.

Shortly before 1 PM in Los Angeles, homicide detective Steve Lankford arrived at the Mondrian. He'd been informed that the person found deceased in the hotel room was noteworthy enough to attract media attention. Laid back and soft-spoken, Lankford wasn't much of a rap fan and had no idea who "Pimp C" was.

Lankford inspected the room, finding no signs of forced entry.* He quickly concluded it was a "non-criminal death" since there appeared to be no sign of foul play. "His eyeglasses were still on … other than the bed being unkempt, as far as the sheets and stuff like that, there wasn't anything tipped over in the room," Lankford recalls. "There was absolutely no indication that there was any type of a struggle."

Lankford summoned Deputy Steve Thomas to take some photos of the room, but didn't call out a full investigative team since he didn't consider it a crime scene. He reviewed a copy of the door log entry and room billing information provided by hotel security.** In the room he found a half-empty pint-sized bottle of codeine-promethazine with no label.

Lankford interviewed Rick Martin; he was under the impression that Rick had been staying in the room next door. Rick said he'd last spoken to Chad around 3 PM on Sunday afternoon and he seemed to be in good spirits. Lankford asked if Chad had ever threatened to commit suicide. Rick said no, but admitted that Chad was bipolar and had a history of depression.

Rick quietly explained that Chad likely had some female visitors, but since he had a wife back home in Houston, it would be best if they could keep that quiet.

According to Mama Wes, J. Prince told her he was sending a team to Los Angeles to retrieve the hotel's surveillance footage. When Chinara, Ed, and XVII touched down in Los Angeles, they spotted Rap-A-Lot affiliates aboard their flight.

Apparently afraid of Rap-A-Lot, Chinara called Rick Martin and asked him to remove Chad's jewelry and his laptop with unreleased music before the Rap-A-Lot crew could get there. XVII knew two bodyguards in L.A., 6'4" twin brothers Calvin and Melvin Tenner, and Rick insisted that he call them for protection.***

Also on a flight from Houston to Los Angeles was Chad's attorney friend Craig Wormley. Wormley summoned a private investigator named Chuck Steeno to meet him at the hotel.

Detective Lankford left the body undisturbed until the coroner's investigator Jerry McKibben arrived shortly before 2 PM. For the coroner's office, it was just one of 18,000 calls they receive every year. On average, nearly 20% of those cases reveal drugs in the bloodstream.

When Wormley arrived, he felt that detectives had already reached their conclusion. "I got the impression that … they didn't really know who he was, and they just thought it was just an OD or something," Wormley says. "They weren't gonna spend a lot of time on it."

Rick handed over the jewelry and laptop to Wormley and Steeno for safekeeping before the Rap-A-Lot crew arrived at the hotel. Prince, who didn't know that Chinara had confiscated it, told Mama Wes that Chad's jewelry was missing.****

(*Lankford doesn't recall if he ever viewed the hotel's surveillance footage. "Either the cameras weren't working or [hotel security] had reviewed it and didn't see anything [unusual]," he says.)
(**The Los Angeles Sheriff's Department would only release three pages of a 19-page report related to this incident. They either could not locate or would not release the door log.)
(***Calvin Tenner, also an actor, appeared as a warehouse worker on NBC's hit series *The Office*.)
(****What actually happened to the jewelry and laptop – possibly two laptops – has been the subject of much debate. "There have been a thousand different rumors about that jewelry and the laptop," says Mama Wes. It is believed that Chinara left with the laptop, and Wormley's investigator Chuck Steeno put the jewelry in a safe deposit box. Detective Lankford says that the jewelry on Chad's body was inventoried by the coroner's office and then released to Chinara as his next of kin.)

Wormley started doing his own investigation, hoping to provide some helpful information to the coroner's investigator McKibben. First of all, he was surprised to meet Chinara, since he and his wife had recently gone on a double date with Chad and a different woman. Chinara put Wormley in touch with the doctor who had treated Chad's sinus problems. McKibben reached out to request medical records, which indicated he had sleep apnea.*

Ed was suspicious as soon as he walked in the room. To him, it was too clean – Chad would normally have socks, clothes, underwear, and other miscellaneous items scattered everywhere. He never picked up after himself – that task fell to Mama, Ed, or Bird. To Ed, it seemed obvious that someone had cleaned the room.**

Chad had a habit of burning candles on the road to freshen the smell of stale hotel rooms, and he'd always lectured Ed about forgetting to blow his out. Ed noted that Chad's candle was burned all the way down.

Chinara, hysterical, tried to get close enough to see the body, but others in the room tried to keep her away. "His wife was just a mess," recalls Mike Mo. "She was in pieces. My wife [was] trying to help her, and [we were trying to] handle business ... it was just [one] blow after another. Either you're gonna break down or you've got to handle his business for him. It was kind of tough."

After Chad's body was transported to the Los Angeles Forensic Science Center around 4:30 PM, Ed pulled back the covers from the bed; both pillows and the mattress beneath were completely soaked with blood. To everyone except the coroner and Detective Lankford, the amount of blood and bodily fluids seemed excessive. "It seemed unusual to us, but I'm not a doctor," says Craig Wormley. "I don't really know. But it just seemed like it was too much, you know?"

Chinara, XVII, Ed, Mike Mo and his wife piled in Rick's car to head over to the Forensic Science Center for the grim task of identifying the body. Rick and J. Prince had never liked or trusted each other, and Rick seemed convinced that Rap-A-Lot was involved in Chad's death. Rick was so tense that when Ed's iPhone alarm went off unexpectedly, Rick jumped with a start.

While the rest of the group went inside, Rick stayed in the car doing a phone interview with *The Source*, a fact which bothered some. But they couldn't deny this was Chad's body; it was all there: the "TRILL ASS NIGGAZ" and "GET PAID!" tattoos on his left arm next to "R.I.P. DJ SCREW," and beneath it, "UGK FOE LIFE," "RIDIN' DIRTY" across his stomach, the UGK Records shield, and "Pimpin' Ain't Dead" on the back of his right arm.

As XVII recalls it, Chinara had been livid all afternoon that Larry wasn't answering anyone's calls or texts. It wasn't until after they'd viewed the body that Rick received a text from Larry, indicating that he would be willing to talk after he consulted with an attorney. Rick called again, but Larry didn't answer.

For Bun back in Houston, the rest of the day felt surreal. He was almost glad to have to pack, to have a project to keep his mind occupied, but every few minutes another phone call or text would remind him that this was really happening.

As the scene unfolded at the Mondrian, Paul Wall was backstage at an Amsterdam nightclub, nine hours ahead of Los Angeles. His phone was off to avoid international roaming charges. The concert promoter poked his head in the dressing room. "You heard about Pimp C, right?" he asked.

___

(*Wormley also told McKibben that "an associate of [Chad's] ... indicated that [Chad] had obtained some cocaine on the evening of December 2," an interesting notation since Chad had implied to Heather that Wormley himself "liked to party," a.k.a., use cocaine. Wormley says he doesn't recall making this statement, but surmises that he might have been referring to Larry.)

(**Opinions on the room varied. Wormley thought it "looked like there had been a party in there" and Detective Lankford considered it "cluttered" but to Ed and others who had traveled with Chad, it appeared abnormally neat.)

"No, heard what?" Paul asked.

"Yeah, man, Pimp C died," the promoter told them.

Paul looked at his road manager and his cousin Gu. They all laughed. *Yeah, right.* Paul had been the subject of several unfounded text message rumors. "Shit, I died about 13 times already," Paul joked.

"No, it's real," the promoter insisted. "It's on the internet. He died."

Paul called home; his wife Crystal said she'd heard the rumors but wasn't sure if it was true. It didn't really hit him until he stepped out on stage and spotted a resourceful fan who was already wearing a homemade "Rest In Peace Pimp C" t-shirt.

The date also happened to be Jay-Z's birthday; the rap mogul was reported to be staying in a luxurious hotel suite in Paris, attending a cabaret show with his R&B superstar girlfriend Beyoncé.

At the Terrell Unit in Rosharon, where Chad spent the last year of his prison sentence, Smit-D was lifting weights on the rec yard when a friend brought him some bad news. "Say mane, you know your boy Pimp gone?"

"Go on, man," Smit-D scoffed. *Pimp C can't be dead.*

SUC rapper Dat Boy Grace was on his 70th day of solitary confinement at a federal prison in Mississippi. His career had been continually cut short due to his legal troubles and multiple arrests for small quantities of cocaine. When he was caught carrying a weapon, which he argued was necessary to protect his recording studio after a robbery attempt, he was sentenced to more than 5 years. He'd been sent to the hole when he was accused of being the ringleader of a violent race-related riot. Chad had often called a mutual friend, Dominique, to meet him at a Shell gas station on Westheimer, handing over a letter or cash for her to send Grace.

He was doing some push-ups when a fellow inmate beat on the door to his cell. "Hey, Grace, man, they talkin' about your pa'tna gone. Turn your radio on." Speculation around the prison yard was that it had something to do with drank, but Grace had never known Chad to indulge any more than anyone else.

In a Louisiana prison, Smoke D heard the news on television. He hadn't talked to Chad since their heated argument and cryptic text message exchange. "I just remember crying a whole lot," he sighs. "I remember crying, and I remember thinking that I had to change. [But I knew] it was just God's will … none of us ain't in control anyway."

With media outlets like TMZ, the *Los Angeles Times*, and the *Houston Chronicle* clamoring for information, the coroner's representative Ed Winter told them it did not appear anyone else had been in the room at the time of Chad's death. "There's no signs of foul play," he reported. "It appears to be possibly natural, but pending autopsy and toxicology [which will take six to eight weeks] we can't say the cause. There were no signs of trauma, no signs of drug paraphernalia."

Celebrities like Snoop Dogg, David Banner, DJ Khaled, Juelz Santana, Yung Joc, Gorilla Zoe, Slim Thug, and LeToya Luckett called in to Houston's The Box, offering their condolences. "I grew up on 'em," Ludacris said. "If it wasn't for UGK, Ludacris probably wouldn't even be here … [We need to] celebrate that man's life and his music, man. I'm telling you, go get the whole catalog, 'cause them boys set the foundation for Hip-Hop music in the South – or, as he would say – country rap tunes."

Lil Wayne said he considered Pimp C a mentor, one had taught him "a whole lot of things mentally, physically, and spiritually" and "helped me be who I am." MTV News had trouble getting quotes, since many of the people they contacted were "too distraught to comment." "I'm just sitting here seeing this happen and wishing Pimp would just wake up," Slim Thug told them.

As rapper Jadakiss once dryly noted, dead rappers get better promotion, and with Pimp C's death he began getting the mainstream recognition that had eluded him throughout much of his career. The *New York Times* called him "the rapper who helped define Southern Hip-Hop," while the *LA Weekly* lauded him as "one of Hip-Hop's most influential figures." New York-based newspaper The *Village Voice* praised him as "one of the greatest producers in rap history," a "musical visionary … a kid who translated years of musical training into rap beats, sliding mournful organs and slippery blues guitars under slow-thumping drums, creating a fuller, more expansive sound than just about anyone else in rap."

With the next issue of *OZONE* about to go on press, I felt terrible calling some of his friends for comment. Some, like Big Gipp and Cory Mo, were on the verge of tears, their voices breaking. "Everybody wants to give praise and buy records and play songs and play videos [now that he's dead]," David Banner noted. "Pimp C is finally now getting what he deserves … Everybody's playing his videos on all the channels. Everybody's playing his music now. I remember when they wouldn't play [UGK records] and now they're gonna do it when he's dead? Why can't we see [the success] while we're alive?"

"The worst thing about death is the void … knowing that he's not there anymore, period," Willie D told the *Houston Press*. "And there's absolutely no chance in getting any of that extra energy and talent that he possessed. That's over."

Port Arthur's KFDM Channel 6 sent a camera crew over to Mama Wes' house, where Pastor John Morgan explained to viewers that despite his name, "Pimp C" wasn't just some misogynistic gangsta rapper but a "wonderful, loving, kind guy."

"This is a terrible shock," Mama Wes added, her face framed by a large picture of Chad in the background. "Mama's just a little tougher than most, but I break too."

Some were still having a hard time believing it. "That nigga ain't dead," Z-Ro overheard someone say. "That nigga's spirit was too big to be in a body anyways … [he's probably] in here with us right now."

Ayesha Saafir asked her sister Halimah to do a psychic reading to connect with Chad's soul and find out why he had "chosen" to leave earth. "That reading was really interesting," Halimah says. "He wanted to do something different with his life, [but] he felt stuck being Pimp C and he just couldn't disappoint his fans."*

On Wednesday, XVII, Ed, and Chinara returned to Houston, where they were joined by Big Bubb and DJ B-Do at the high-rise. Chinara announced her intention to start a new record label called Smoke Somethin' Records. Everyone knew she didn't get along with Mama Wes, and she told the four men they were going to have to choose. "You gotta make a decision, 'cause there is no more UGK Records," she told them.

DJ B-Do had always been closer to Chinara than Mama Wes, but the other three men exchanged glances. XVII couldn't believe this was even a topic of conversation when they'd barely even returned from viewing his body. "That decision was real fucking easy for me," says XVII. "It was common sense … anybody [who] knew Pimp knows how much he loved his Mama. He'll kill you over his Mama. He wasn't gonna kill you over Chinara."

There was already a mad rush in progress to collect Pimp's music. "Niggas got dispatched like Navy Seals," joked one observer. Mama Wes explains, "I think that people thought that C had way more [unreleased material] than he probably actually did."

Mike Mo sent Bankroll Jonez to Port Arthur on a mission – which Bankroll referred to as "Mission Impossible" – to retrieve Pimp's music from Avery's studio. When Rap-A-Lot caught

(*During our interview, Halimah offered to connect me to Chad's spirit so I could interview him. I declined.)

wind of this, one of their associates appeared at MAD Studios with a pistol, demanding the hard drives with all of Pimp's material. Mike Mo insisted he didn't have any unreleased masters.

"I was being sweated for his music from the time I got the phone call [that he died]," sighs Mike Mo. After consulting with his attorney, he turned over the masters that he did have to Chinara. "I did the right thing," Mike says. "I didn't do the emotional thing or the heartfelt thing, I did the legal right thing … A lot of people wasn't happy, but they had to respect me … I don't really care if they don't like me. I know I did right by my friend."

J. Prince drove over from Houston to visit Mama Wes on Wednesday night. Convinced her son could not have died of natural causes, Mama Wes was struck by the disturbing possibility that anyone in his life could have been involved in his death. Like everyone else, she knew of Prince's feared reputation and was well aware of the whispers theorizing of his involvement.

Even though Mama Wes knew her son feared Prince, she believed they also truly loved each other. As Prince settled on her living room couch, Mama Wes scanned the eyes of the man she considered a mentor and close friend. *Did you have anything to do with this?* she wondered.

In his eyes, she detected nothing but genuine sorrow and fatigue, not even a trace of betrayal. *Nah, I don't see that in those eyes right now,* she concluded. *That's not what I'm seeing.* Satisfied with her intuition, Mama Wes eliminated Prince from her mental rolodex of "persons of interest."

Besides, Mama Wes reasoned, Chad's death didn't serve Prince's best interest. "C was more valuable to him alive," she says. "[Prince] likes to win, okay? He's *gotta* win. And with that boy [Chad], he hadn't won yet … He wanted [Chad] for certain things, and he didn't have that yet. And you see, J. is a winner … J. has *got* to win, and he wasn't finished with [Chad] yet."

Over in Houston, Matt Sonzala's Damage Control Radio show kicked off on KPFT at midnight. They aired an annual tribute to DJ Screw every November, but with the recent passing of SUC rapper Big Moe, they'd been talking about doing a tribute show for all of Houston's fallen soldiers.* Now, the idea seemed especially poignant. "UGK shaped Southern rap," Sonzala told listeners. "They were the backbone of all this, and Pimp C, man, we love you and miss you. I can't believe – I don't believe it yet."

Pimp's publicist Nancy Byron called in, saying she'd just been through the "hardest two days of [her] life." She'd been flooded with inquiries from media outlets like BET and *Rolling Stone*. Most disturbing was the automatic assumption that Pimp's death was drug-related. She'd issued a statement on behalf of Rick Martin, asking "that everyone please respect his family and those close to him at this time and refrain from rumors and innuendo."

"I'm saddened by the suddenness and the quickness that people have and are just so willing to dump on the negative, the drug use," Nancy said. "I don't understand why people can't wait for facts to come out before they start running their mouths."

"If you don't listen to this music and you only hear it as a passerby … Houston artists do wear that codeine stuff in their music to the ground," Sonzala admitted, adding that he frequently received calls from mainstream journalists asking about this whole Houston "lean" thing.

Still, it wasn't just the media making that assumption. Most people assumed Pimp had been using drugs prior to his death, especially if he'd been recording with Three 6 Mafia. "I don't think it's any big secret that Three 6 Mafia does drugs," Nancy Byron agrees. But despite people's assumptions, DJ Paul firmly states that wasn't the case. "It wasn't no codeine or none of that shit around when we was together," he says.

(*Houston rapper Kenneth "Big Moe" Moore, a member of DJ Screw's Screwed Up Click, had a heart attack at age 33 and died on October 14, 2007. Moe was morbidly obese, but excessive syrup-sippin' may have also played a role in his death. His biggest hit "Purple Stuff" was an ode to codeine cough syrup, followed by "Leave Drank Alone," a solemn admission that he was addicted to the drug. "Maybe his death tells us it's time for everyone to put their cup down," local radio personality Crisco Kidd told the *Houston Chronicle* in response to Moe's passing.)

Too $hort, too, was insistent that Chad wasn't using drugs at the House of Blues. "He was the one who had everybody laughing, cracking jokes," Too $hort told *The Source*. "He was very much alive and kicking over the weekend."

Pimp's "last show with Too $hort" was cited in many media reports, and $hort quickly grew weary of the barrage of questions from journalists, acquaintances, or even strangers passing by: *"What was Pimp C like just before he died?"*

"I wish that shit didn't happen on *my* time, when *I* was in the area, when *I* was with him, you know? I didn't want [that] burden," Too Short sighs. "I don't want to make a novelty of my homie's memory. I'm the wrong guy to ask some personal shit like that: *'What was he doing in his last moment?'* Man, I wouldn't tell nobody what the fuck we did in our private time ... That shit is irritating to me to be asked what he was like in his last minutes ... I wasn't there in his last minutes. I was there at the Too $hort show, when we were in a good fuckin' mood. A whole 'nother day went by; another night went by. I don't know what the fuck happened."

On Thursday morning, while the medical examiner Dr. Raffi S. Djabourin was reviewing photos from the scene and preparing to conduct the autopsy, Larry called Mama Wes' house. He told Heather, who answered the phone, the story of his girlfriend overhearing Chad's conversation with "Tupac."

Larry told Mama Wes that he'd last seen Chad when he dropped him off at the hotel. "You know, they might be investigating this thing," Larry said. "You think I should get a lawyer?"

Mama Wes was taken aback by the unexpected question. *Now why do you need a fuckin' lawyer if you ain't done nothing?* she wondered.

"Why would you need a lawyer?" she responded sharply.

"Oh, well..." Larry's voice drifted off. "I don't know what I was thinking about."

Yeah, nigga, you knew what you was thinking about. You knew exactly what you were thinking about, she muttered to herself as she hung up the phone, now doubly suspicious of a man she'd never liked or trusted. *Why would you be all of a sudden thinking 'I need a lawyer'?*

Bianca's mind wasn't on hiring an attorney, but she was expecting that there would be a thorough investigation. Meticulous by nature, she carefully took notes, documenting everything she could remember about that night while it was still fresh in her mind. Mike Mo told her they'd been speaking with detectives, so she assumed they would be contacting her.

Bianca realized she hadn't been paying close attention when Larry mixed the lean, and thought aloud that he might've slipped something in Chad's drink. "I think someone tried to kill you, too," her mom remarked. "You slept a whole damn day!"

Still in shock, Bianca skimmed news articles about Chad's death. On an AOL message board, a fan posted a question: "I know the police aren't saying anything till all the tests are over, but does anyone know how he died?" Most respondents theorized that drugs were involved, but there was one comment that caught Bianca's attention.

The commenter, under the handle "pimp5life," wrote: "...Pimp didnt seem to be the type to be alone in a room first of all,i think he was with some female or chilling with some playa partners,and we all know how we do it,it aint no military secret,we get our freak on.to make a short story shorter it could have been anything from syrup to viagra.or natural. im just glad who ever left him there cleaned the place up and tried to give the PIMP some respect ang dignity,that how playas do it."

Bianca was stunned. How could anyone know that the room was cleaned – besides Larry?

Bun had been holed up in his house for two days, unprepared to face the public. On Thursday afternoon, he did an interview by phone with *VIBE* Magazine. "When was the last time you saw [Pimp]?" writer Linda Hobbs asked.

"We attended the Young Jeezy concert together [on] Thanksgiving. And that was the last time I physically saw him," Bun said. "We met, we hugged, said we loved each other. When we separate we always make sure we hug and say we love each other."

That same afternoon, nominations for the 50th Annual Grammy Awards were announced, which included UGK and OutKast's "Int'l Players Anthem (I Choose You)" for Best Rap Performance by a Duo or Group. In a press statement, Bun described it as "bittersweet" that Chad's "lifelong dream" of going to the Grammys was only recognized after his death. "In all honesty, this is what he wanted … [to] put a Grammy on his Mama's shelf," he told MTV News.*

On Friday morning, while Chad's body was en route back to Texas, Bun sat down with Madd Hatta's morning show on Houston's The Box for an emotional 90 minute interview. "So many people were starting to speculate [on the cause of death]," Madd Hatta said, carefully dancing around the 'how did he die' question. "You've seen a lot of news reports throw all kinds of innuendo in the air. We did receive a report that they said it was natural causes…"

"Nobody knows anything, including the coroner, and everybody's just making assumptions … the hard truth of the matter is that the brother's gone," Bun said.

"Did you say everything you needed to say [to Pimp]?" Madd Hatta asked.

"I said everything I needed to say to Pimp. No regrets about anything," Bun said. "I know the last time I saw him, I hugged him, and I told him I loved him, which is what I did every time I saw him, because you never know how … life is gonna work out. That's one regret I won't have."

Acknowledging that their relationship hadn't always been smooth, Bun continued, "We can argue, cuss, fuss and fight all day long, but we gon' say 'I love you' when it's over. I may not *like* you when it's over. But I *love* you, and you're gonna know that. I don't go to sleep angry … I always told my boy I loved him, he always told me he loved me, and as men, we were never ashamed to say that."

Madd Hatta verbalized what many people were thinking: this was terrible timing. Things were finally on the upswing. Pimp had made it through four years in prison and UGK had finally topped the charts just months earlier. "Do you feel like you did all that work to no avail?" Madd Hatta asked.

"Not at all. Never. Not at all," Bun said. "It's no regrets … Rapping wasn't really my dream … it was a hobby … [but] music was all Pimp ever wanted to do. And UGK was more his dream than mine, and I'm just happy that it came true for him."

Jada was half-asleep napping on her bunk in a Houston jail. She'd been arrested in Chicago on prostitution-related charges, a violation of her parole on previous drug charges, and extradited back to Texas. She drifted in and out of consciousness as UGK records streamed through a small speaker radio. *Must be an early morning old school mix,* she thought. It wasn't until Bun B's sorrowful voice came through the speakers that she realized something terrible had happened.

During a break, The Box played "One Of These Days," a Pimp C tribute just recorded by Lil Flip and D-Redd. The phone lines lit up with dozens of callers hoping to offer their condolences or share a time when Pimp C had touched their lives.

"Anytime you met Pimp C there was a story," Bun told Matt Sonzala later. "If you met him three times, you had three stories to tell. Literally, that's no joke. That's just how hard he was on people's minds. He was just un-fuckin'-deniable. You was gonna know he was in the room."

Bun called the whole experience "surreal," explaining, "I've likened it to trying to hold onto a bowling ball with silk gloves on, it's the only way I can explain the process of how I'm trying to wrap my head around this. It doesn't process in the normal sense that things logically process."

(*Although "Big Pimpin'" had previously been nominated, this was UGK's first nomination for their own work. Bun and Chinara attended the Grammy Awards on UGK's behalf in February 2008, where the big winners were Kanye West and Amy Winehouse. The Best Rap Performance by a Duo or Group award, which was not televised, went to Common and Kanye West's "Southside.")

On the *Houston Chronicle's* website, a memorial guestbook was flooded with hundreds of entries by people whose lives had been touched by Pimp C. Commenters included his high school bandmates, DJ DMD, Donny Young, and his former bodyguard JT's mother Mama Farr, who described her son as "devastated."

"The value of one's life cannot be determined based upon the number of years that he has lived, but moreso what he does with the years that he is given," wrote Chloe Crater of Little Rock. Judging from the comments, Pimp had done a lot: fans credited UGK's music with everything from introducing them to their spouse to helping them overcome homelessness. Many described Pimp C as father figure. "When my father wasn't [there] I learned ALOT from you and Bun," wrote A.D. Washington of Louisiana.

Baronica Tarrance of Mississippi thanked Pimp for "dedicat[ing] most of your life to us" while AJ Smith of Texas applauded him for "always taking up for the South when nobody else would!"

"You are truly missed. Ain't no other cat dat will ever slur those country words into rap like you," wrote Polennium Cash Hawka of Dallas. "All I can say is that when Pimp died, he took a piece of me with him," agreed Chad Carmouche of Louisiana.

With the initial shock wearing off, friends were forced to analyze everything they'd done, or *hadn't* done. Mike Mo regretted not heading out to L.A. But even if he'd gone, would he have been able to alter the outcome?

While many in Texas chastised themselves for not being there, Chad's friends in California were struck by the fact that they *were* there and hadn't been able to help him. Too $hort regretted not following through with their dinner plans for Sunday. "I was just so close to my man right before he went that you just wish you could've *known*," he told the *Raw Report* DVD. "It would've been a different encounter if I had known – like, that's the last time I'm ever gonna see my homie."

"He was in the same city I was in," Snoop Dogg agrees. "Like, damn. Why'd it have to happen where I'm from? We just started to bond and become really good friends. Could I have done something to prevent this or what?" Big Gipp, Warren G, David Banner, and DJ Paul were all struggling with similar questions.

Even Ron Spaulding at Fontana was struck with a strange sense of guilt. What if he had cancelled his other meeting on Friday evening instead of rescheduling for Monday? "Not that… [it would have] changed God's plan," he says. "You can't ever blame yourself for tragedy, right? Because … those life decisions are not typically in our hands." Still, he couldn't help but wonder if he shared some responsibility.

David Banner took it as a sobering lesson. "We're getting blatant signs every day that there's something else we're supposed to be doing with this time we've got here on earth," he told *OZONE*. "Pimp C's passing is a sign to me to keep my health up and keep myself out of bullshit and unnecessary drama."

"We don't know if we got time to speak or call somebody back or get back with them later," Banner added on *The Final Chapter DVD*. "Take this opportunity to call somebody and let 'em know that you care about 'em."

Most of all, Banner regretted the fact that most people would never get to know the real Chad Butler. "There was a bigger man there than what the world had the opportunity to see. I hope that people can dig just a little bit deeper and see what I saw," he told *OZONE*. "It was more than the jewelry and the mink coat. The nigga was *smart* … It was so much bigger than pimpin' and hoes … and that's the tragedy to me. Just like 'Pac. Our people get taken away from us before they're able to blossom into what they actually are or what they have the capacity to become."

CHAPTER 58

"I had 33 years – almost 34 – with C and I have no regrets. Everything I did I would do it again. If I had a request I would've asked God for 33 more years. I didn't get that, but I am so grateful for the 33 that I was granted. And I would never ever turn back the hands of time and do it any differently. I love him as much today as I did the day he was born."
– Mama Wes, Damage Control Radio, December 2008

"Everybody was trying to console [Mama Wes], but she was stronger than all of us." – Larry "NcGai" Wiltz

Monday, December 10, 2007
New York City, New York

Less than a week after Chad's body was found, Chinara and Rick Martin were on a couch in Barry Weiss' New York office, sitting uncomfortably close. Rick wrapped his arm around Chinara, holding her tightly.

Jive staffers like Jeff Sledge, who had spent 15 years dealing with Mama Wes for everything UGK-related, were not only in a state of shock over Chad's death but baffled by the sudden appearance of a wife they'd never even known existed. Jeff stared at Rick and Chinara cuddling on the couch; their intimate embrace struck him as sexual, not one of compassion, and he didn't know how to react to the awkward moment. *What the fuck am I looking at right now? This shit is crazy,* Jeff thought.

The purpose of their visit was clearly financial: Chinara seemed primarily concerned with collecting all the monies due her husband. "She had all these demands she was making, and [Rick] was puppeteering the whole shit," Jeff recalls. "[Chinara] was non-existent through the whole UGK career, and then she comes in, and because she was the wife, legally, she started making all these demands … It was all fucked up."

The fact that Chinara was even in New York while everyone else was grieving in Texas struck some as odd. Heather Johnson considered it "suspicious," especially because of Rick Martin's involvement; she'd always considered him "a snake ass muthafucker."

Mama Wes was convinced her son was murdered. Her informally adopted son Tim Hampton had booked a flight from Tampa as soon as he heard the news. Mama Wes escorted him and his suitcase to a bedroom. "Tim, he was killed," she said firmly. "But we not gonna discuss that now. We got a lot of business to take care of."

Tension had long simmered between Chinara and Mama Wes, and things came to a head in the weeks following Chad's death. "I don't think she ever liked me," says Mama Wes. "But she couldn't show it [when C was alive]."

Mama Wes wanted to hold the funeral on December 12, her 61st birthday, but Chinara overruled her, setting services for December 13. They disagreed on several other key points. Mama Wes, whose father had owned a funeral home, says she was embarrassed by the "cheap ass casket" Chinara selected. Secondly, Mama Wes was horrified to learn that Chinara planned to bury her son in the ground. She didn't believe in ground burial, but guaranteeing his spot in the mausoleum would cost an extra $4,000.

Jive Records was covering most of the funeral costs, but Mama Wes was $1,700 short of the $4,000 mausoleum fee. According to Tim Hampton, he chipped in the remaining balance. The reason was simple. "[Chad] gave me something that nobody could give me: He shared his mom with me," Tim says. "And I'm forever in his debt for that."

With Chad no longer there to keep the peace, some felt that Chinara was taking advantage of her newfound power. "I know now [that Chinara was only nice to me while C was alive] because she didn't have a choice," says XVII. "You gotta understand, when Pimp was here, she had to sit down and shut the fuck up ... If you had to sit down and shut the fuck up all that time, and then the person that was the reason you had to sit down and shut the fuck up is gone ... you can jump up and act like you run shit now."

Many of Chad's relatives considered Chinara an outsider and didn't like the fact that she wasn't even taking Mama Wes' input into consideration. "I think she wanted to show that she was in control and it was going to be her way ... [anything Mama] Wes suggested, she didn't want it," says Chad's godmother Brenda Harmon.

Brenda knew the mothers of Chad's sons and some of the "ones that wanted to be baby mamas," but had never even met Chinara. "[There was] a feeling that ... although legally she was the wife, she wasn't the [best] person to make decisions that were going to write the final episode of his life," Brenda says. "She really didn't *know* him. We felt like *we* knew him."

The week passed by in a blur; the phones never stopped ringing at Mama Wes' house. With the chaos unfolding around him, Chad Jr. struggled to come to terms with the idea of his father being *gone*. The only possible silver lining was that he didn't have to go to school. But without schoolwork to occupy his time, he spent hours lost in thought. Entire days passed by and he didn't even utter a word. He thought about the future, wondering if he could have done anything to change the outcome. He pondered the heavy questions of life, the intricacies of cause and effect. *What do you have to do to change how things are gonna happen?* he wondered.

It was a challenge to pull himself out of his thoughts and rejoin reality; communication was difficult. His silence concerned the family. "Of course your family wants to know what you're thinking, what's on your mind, what state of mind you're in, and I didn't really have anything to tell them, 'cause *I* don't even know what state of mind I'm in," Chad Jr. explains. "They're worrying because I'm not telling them how I feel, [but] *I* don't even know how I feel, you know?"

The task of handling many of the funeral details fell to Nancy Byron and Rick Martin. "If it wasn't for Rick Martin, a lot of things with the funeral probably wouldn't have gotten done. Nobody else really initially was prepared to do it," says Ed.

Nancy helped put together the obituary, almost grateful to "have a task to throw [herself] into where there is no room for emotion." Still in shock, she told *The Source*, "Pimp was larger than life. I honestly thought he would live forever." For the cover of the funeral booklet, she used a picture Ed took of Pimp in his red Trill hat at the failed Bar Rio show, tapping on the mic. Inside, a colorful collage featured images of Chad with all his rap friends and collaborators – Bun B, Rick Ross, Too $hort, Jazze Pha, Sleepy Brown, E-40, David Banner, Slim Thug, Chamillionaire – and notes from Chinara and the kids.

While Chad's friends and family were in mourning, the city of Port Arthur was simultaneously grieving the death of its idol and buzzing with anticipation. Nothing ever happened in Port Arthur, and the possibility of celebrities coming to town for Chad's funeral had everyone excited. The *Port Arthur News* theorized that Chad's "entertainment friends" like Snoop Dogg and Beyoncé would be in attendance. "I would not be surprised to see Jay-Z," the police chief told the *Beaumont Enterprise.*

"I'm not willing to confirm any of the rumors of the celebrities who will be at the funeral," Nancy Byron dryly responded. "This is a funeral, I'm not trying to build hype for this. It's not the Grammy's." For that very reason, some celebrities decided not to attend, afraid it would turn into a media circus. Snoop Dogg was worried that his presence would be a distraction. "I wanted it to be about him, not me," he explains.*

Chad's obituary ran in the *Port Arthur News* on December 12. "Chad knew, as early as nine years old, HIS DESTINY," it read, continuing with a brief recap of his career. "Music was his JOY. He was doing what he loved. He never had a job, just another SHOW."

The same day, an "URGENT REPORT" was issued from the FBI's Houston division to their command center in Washington D.C., informing them that Chad Butler's funeral was a "MATTER GENERATING SIGNIFICANT MEDIA ATTENTION." It read, in part:

Some local officials have estimated that 5,000 individuals may try to attend the funeral along with prominent celebrities. Only 2,500 people will be granted entry. This event is anticipated to draw national media attention and has prompted local media personnel to contact the Beaumont resident agency (BMTRA) inquiring as to what will be the FBI's response.

BUTLER, more commonly known as "Pimp C," is referenced in various FBI reporting in connection to narcotics transactions, money laundering, and violent disputes between other musicians. BMTRA has received information that individuals may try to disrupt the service in retaliation.

Meanwhile, there was drama unfolding at Mama Wes' house. Several members of the UGK posse, hanging out in the driveway smoking weed, were laughing reminiscing on a time they'd seen Chad passed out, incapacitated, presumably from drug use. Mama Wes overheard enough to catch the gist of the conversation and was furious, primarily with DJ B-Do and T.O.E. "They thought it was a damn big joke," she says. "I could've killed 'em. Literally."

Mama Wes didn't confront them, but Tim Hampton, disgusted by the behavior of Chad's "flunkies, his do-boys," was angry. "Y'all laughing and joking and talking about how he was all fucked up, laying on the floor in the bathroom?" he said angrily. "If y'all love him, man, y'all would have chastised him right then and there."

Either because of Heather's extremely emotional response to Chad's passing, or perhaps the fact that Chinara now had access to Chad's cell phones and text messages, Chinara believed her husband had been carrying on an affair with Mama Wes' assistant Heather. She blamed Mama Wes, holding her responsible for concealing their illicit relationship.**

The night before the funeral, Mama Wes, Heather, and a handful of others were gathered in the kitchen on Shreveport Ave. when Chinara called. She instructed Mama Wes that Heather was not to attend the private funeral in the morning. Several men in the kitchen exchanged glances. "She doesn't want Heather there? What's she going to do about the other 250 [of Chad's women] who'll be there?" one asked.***

Another one of the many people staying at Mama Wes' house that night was Bianca, who had flown in straight from her grandfather's funeral in Nebraska. Most of Chad's friends were at least vaguely aware of her relationship with Chad, and some knew that she'd been with him the

(*A few other celebrities were unable to attend for legal reasons. C-Murder and T.I., who were both on house arrest awaiting trial, requested permission from their respective judges to attend the funeral but were denied. T.I. posted a video over the Christmas holidays apologizing for missing the service.)

(**Heather describes Chad as her "best friend" and says they had "a soul connection." Mama Wes explains, "I really didn't know that they had an affair going on, because he had lots of female friends. [Heather] had a hard time after C died. She really cared a lot for C … but I think that was the beginning of the end with me and Chinara. Because I honestly did not know … but [even if I had,] I don't believe in explaining myself, 'cause I really don't give a fuck. [Chinara] likes to say [that his alleged affair with Heather is] why she had problems with me. That ain't the real reason.")

(***"That place was packed with hoes. C's hoes," Mama Wes jokes of the funeral.)

FBI URGENT REPORT

Precedence: IMMEDIATE   Date: 12/12/2007

To: Director
      SIOC

From: Houston
         Contact: [   ]
                                                              b6
Approved By: ASAC [   ] *illegible*   b7C
Drafted By: [   ] jtp *illegible*

Subject/Title/Case ID #:804B-HO-67588-MISC
                         CRIMINAL INTELLIGENCE ANALYSIS;
                         MISCELLANEOUS;
                         BEAUMONT RA

Purpose/Synopsis: MATTER GENERATING SIGNIFICANT MEDIA ATTENTION

INITIAL
URGENT REPORT

Chad BUTLER (DOB 12/29/1973), a musician from Port Arthur, Texas, died unexpectedly on 12/04/2007 in West Hollywood, California. A private unannounced funeral will take place at 7 a.m. for family members at a local church in Beaumont, Texas. A public funeral is scheduled to be held at 11 a.m. on 12/13/2007 at the Robert A. "Bob" Bowers Civic Center located at 3401 Cultural Center Drive, Port Arthur, Texas 77642. Some local officials have estimated that 5,000 individuals may try to attend the funeral along with prominent celebrities. Only 2,500 people will be granted entry. This event is anticipated to draw national media attention and has prompted local media personnel to contact the Beaumont resident agency (BMTRA) inquiring as to what will be the FBI's response.

BUTLER, more commonly known as "Pimp C," is referenced in various FBI reporting in connection to narcotics transactions, money laundering, and violent disputes between other musicians. BMTRA has received information that individuals may try to disrupt the service in retaliation.

The BMTRA's Southeast Texas Safe Streets Taskforce will be present during the event [   ]
[   ] The Port Arthur Police Department (PAPD) SWAT team will be deployed at the civic center. The Jefferson County SWAT team will be deployed at the burial site in Groves, Texas. PAPD's Special Response Team, trained to respond to riots, will be present providing perimeter control. Security personnel will screen the attendees for prohibited items.

Above: An **FBI internal memo** in preparation for Chad's funeral.

night prior to his death.

Like Heather, Bianca was extremely emotional. Tensions in the house were already high, and Heather quickly grew tired of Bianca's tearful reminiscing about her "baby."

"Bitch, you and a hundred other bitches," Heather finally snapped at her. "Do you know how many hoes he got? Like, stop it. You are not special."

In Houston, Teresa and her crew at SF2 had been working around the clock. Before Chad's passing, he had ordered 50 more customized Dickies for his crew. In light of the sad circumstances, she'd been flooded with new requests to create shirts for Chad Jr., Corey, and others for the funeral. Everyone had special requests for the embroidering, like "R.I.P" or "Trill Niggas Don't Die," which could take up to four hours each shirt.

At daybreak on Thursday, December 13, Bun and Queenie, Chad Jr. and Nitacha, and other friends and family – even Chad's parole officer – gathered at Mama Wes' house. Scarface picked up Too $hort from the airport in Houston and the two rode in silence to Port Arthur for the funeral. Also en route from Houston was J. Prince and a large Rap-A-Lot entourage.

Mama Wes climbed into a limo with Chad Jr., Corey, and Nitacha. Behind them was J. Prince's limo, followed by a long procession of other cars. They met the hearse at the appointed time a few blocks from Chad's Oakmont home. Waiting there was Chinara and about 30 other vehicles with members of her side of the family.

The funeral director Anthony Kay signaled for the hearse to head straight down 9th Avenue towards the funeral home. Chinara's vehicle pulled off directly behind the hearse. To Mama Wes' surprise, Kay held her vehicle in place, directing the other vehicles in Chinara's procession to go first.

When they arrived at the funeral home, Mama Wes asked Kay why he had deliberately placed her in the back of the funeral procession. Kay replied that he was acting on Mrs. Butler's instructions. J. Prince leaned in towards Kay. "I don't suggest you make that mistake again," he said, in a tone that implied it was not a *suggestion* at all.

Close to 200 friends and family members gathered inside the chapel. For many, the reality of the situation hadn't hit home until the saw Chad's body in the casket, outfitted in a red baseball cap and some red Dickies covered in the UGK shield with five stars stitched on each shoulder, like a five-star general.* "That's when it got real," remembers NcGai. "It's really him."

Too $hort stared at the casket. *I just saw this muthafucker two weeks ago,* he thought in disbelief. *That cannot be Chad. I can't believe it.*

"That was a terrible feeling to see Chad in that damn casket," says Scarface. "I wish I never would have seen him like that. I don't want people to see me like that. I want people to remember me the way I was."

"That's how I know that God breathes breath into you," he reflects. "And that he can take it away from you when it's time to go. That soul leaves."

Bianca, sitting in the front row, broke down sobbing. "What the fuck is this bitch doing here?" she overheard Chinara remark. (Bianca assumed that Chinara recognized her from nude photos on Chad's laptop.) Too $hort was shocked to learn for the first time that his friend was married; Big Gipp, who thought Sonji was Chad's wife, was also stunned to meet Chinara.

NcGai, who had driven over from Louisiana hoping to console Mama Wes, quickly found

---

(*The outfit was put together by Teresa at SF2, at Chinara's request. Although Dickies were certainly a staple of Pimp C's wardrobe, some friends like Big L felt the look didn't accurately represent a man who "lived a life of flamboyance." He adds, "I felt like they shoulda put dude away in his mink coats, his mink hats, and his jewels, you know?")

that it was the other way around. "Everybody [was] trying to console her [but] she [was] stronger than all of us," he recalls.

Mama Wes, who didn't believe in open-casket services, was sitting in the back and trying not to look at her son's lifeless body. As family members streamed out of the funeral home, Mama Wes requested that the casket be closed so she could have "just a few minutes alone with my baby." Kay, who was well aware of Prince's powerful status in the community, followed his instructions as the procession departed the funeral home: this time, the hearse was followed by Mama Wes' vehicle, with Chinara trailing behind her.

Over at the Robert A. "Bob" Bowers Civic Center, just three miles down Highway 73 from Mama Wes' house, fans had been lining up since 5 AM, forming two lines snaking through the parking lot. A light rain had been falling all morning, the gloomy skies overhead capturing the mood. Scattered colorful umbrellas in the parking lot contrasted with the grey clouds. One SUV in the overflowing parking lot was decorated with "R.I.P. Pimp Much Love" and "UGK 4 Life" painted in white lettering across the windows.

As Chamillionaire dressed for the funeral, he'd reached for his pinky ring and was stunned to see the big diamond, the one he'd pointed out to Pimp C at the car show just a few weeks earlier, missing. A chill ran up his spine. He left the ring at home.

Many of the roads surrounding the Civic Center were barricaded. As Chamillionaire and his crew tried to pull into the parking lot, they found the entrance blocked by two Port Arthur police cars. Behind the police cars, federal agents were unloading from large vans. "Look at these niggas in the blue vans, son!" exclaimed one of the occupants of Chamillionaire's vehicle. "These niggas in, like, full body armor," murmured another. "C'mon, man, these niggas got full body armor on, G!"

Thanks to the FBI memo, there were more than 80 police officers and several dozen federal agents on hand. At least three snipers were not-so-discreetly positioned on the rooftop of the nearby library. Wendy Day had decided to make an exception to her "no-funerals" rule for her tumultuous relationship with Chad. As she walked through the parking lot with Michael Watts, a federal agent wearing an "FBI" jacket zoomed in on them with a powerful zoom lens and snapped pictures.

Many, like David Banner, found the federal agents' presence "very disrespectful." The security precautions seemed like "overkill" even to security professionals like Hashim Nzinga. "Texas is a [big] state that likes to intimidate people," Hashim says. "They got them big budgets and all them [law enforcement officers] that got nothing to do."

"Who [did they think] was gonna fight at the funeral? [They thought] all the rappers was gonna get together and duke it out, and bring machetes and uzis and nine [mms]?" asks Mama Wes. "I don't know [why the FBI was there]. It was stupid. That was a total waste of money."*

The *Port Arthur News* dryly noted that the only purpose served by the excessive law enforcement seemed to be as the "fashion police," turning away about 50 people who didn't fit the dress code: no caps, du-rags, hoodies, or low-hanging jeans.**

Mike Jones, wearing a blue "R.I.P. Pimp C" t-shirt covered by his Ice Age chain and a brown du-rag, was waved inside, but police stopped Webbie, who was wearing a bright, colorful leather jacket topped with his giant Trill Entertainment chain. "I just got off the plane from New York, I ain't even had time to go change clothes, but they saying we ain't dressed right. I'm out here to come see Pimp C funeral and come show my respects, but *them* muthafuckers," Webbie told a camera, gesturing angrily towards the police, "they don't even *know* Pimp."

(*With a smile, Mama Wes adds that she did have her 9mm, just in case.)
(**"I was furious when I heard that people were turned away from his funeral," Chinara later wrote in a statement published by the *Port Arthur News*, although the dress code was enforced at her request. "These people came out to show their love for my husband, [and] he would have wanted them all there.")

Too $hort and **Pimp C** on the Sunset Strip in Hollywood, August 2006.
Photo: Alexander Sibaja

Above and Left: **UGK** at one of their last performances during 97.9 The Box's car show in Houston, November 2007.

Photos: Edgar L. Walker Jr.

Below: The crowd at The Box car show.

Photo: Julia Beverly

Above: The **House of Blues** and the **Mondrian** on the Sunset Strip in Hollywood, where Chad spent his last weekend, pictured in 2014.

Photo: Julia Beverly

Clockwise from left: **Edgar Walker Jr.** and **XVII**; Chad's friend **Bianca**; in what was likely his last photo, **Pimp C** poses for **Excel Beats** at the House of Blues in Hollywood; Chad's manager **Rick Martin**.

Edgar Walker and XVII photo courtesy of Hezeleo
Pimp C photo courtesy of Brian "Excel Beats" Whittaker
Rick Martin photo by Julia Beverly

Above: **Chad Jr.** and **Bun B** enter the civic center for Chad's funeral on December 13, 2007.
Below: Decorated vehicles in the parking lot.

Photos: Johnny Hanson/©Houston Chronicle. Used with permission.

Right: A federal agent snaps a photo of **Bishop Don "Magic" Juan.**

Above: **Mama Wes** is escorted by supporters as she leaves Chad's funeral on December 13, 2007.
Below: **Bun B** and **J. Prince** embrace after the services, as **Jeff Sledge** and **Anzel "Red Boy" Jennings** look on.
Photos: Johnny Hanson/©Houston Chronicle. Used with permission.

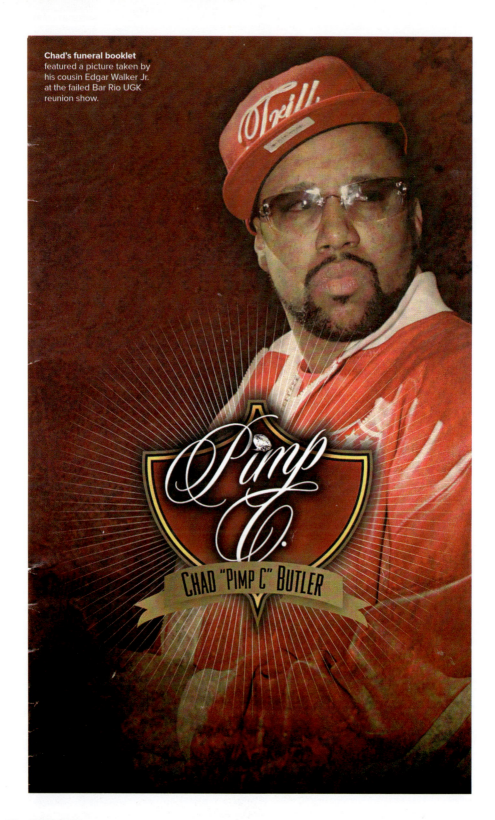

Chad's funeral booklet featured a picture taken by his cousin Edgar Walker Jr. at the failed Bar Rio UGK reunion show.

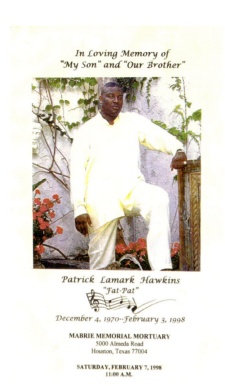

In Loving Memory of
"My Son" and "Our Brother"

Patrick Lamark Hawkins
"Fat-Pat"

December 4, 1970--February 3, 1998

MABRIE MEMORIAL MORTUARY
5000 Almeda Road
Houston, Texas 77004

SATURDAY, FEBRUARY 7, 1998
11:00 A.M.

Celebrating the Life of:
John Edward "Big Hawk" Hawkins

Born:
Nov. 15, 1969

Departed:
May 1, 2006

Tuesday, May 9, 2006
11:00 a.m.

Mabrie Memorial Mortuary
5000 Almeda Road ◆ Houston, TX 77004

Bishop James W. E. Dixon, II, Officiant

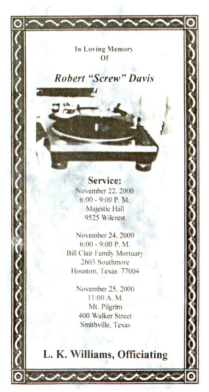

In Loving Memory
Of

Robert "Screw" Davis

Service:
November 22, 2000
6:00 - 9:00 P. M.
Majestic Hall
9525 Wilcrest

November 24, 2000
6:00 - 9:00 P. M.
Bill Clair Family Mortuary
2603 Southmore
Houston, Texas 77004

November 25, 2000
11:00 A. M.
Mt. Pilgrim
400 Walker Street
Smithville, Texas

L. K. Williams, Officiating

Sadly, Chad "Pimp C" Butler joined a long list of Texas rappers who passed away at a young age. Others include *(clockwise from below)* **Kenneth "Big Moe" Moore, Robert "DJ Screw" Davis Jr.**, and brothers **Patrick "Fat Pat" Hawkins** and **John "Big Hawk" Hawkins.**

Courtesy of the University of Houston Library Special Collections

A Service of Remembrance
Honoring the Life of

Kenneth D. Moore
"Big Moe"

Alpha: August 20, 1974

Omega: October 14, 2007

Chad "Pimp C" Butler was laid to rest in a mausoleum on the northeast corner of Greenlawn Memorial Park in Groves, Texas.   Photos: Julia Beverly

Webbie protested and was eventually allowed inside to pay his respects. But Big Tyme's Russell Washington, turned away at the door because he was wearing a t-shirt, readily accepted defeat and drove back to Houston. It felt like an ironically appropriate ending to his 15-year saga with UGK. He'd watched it all from a distance, admiring the "Big Pimpin'" and "Int'l Players Anthem" videos, wishing he'd been invited to the shoot.

"It was kind of like the final scar," he reflects, his voice tinged with regret. "I was on the outside looking in for so many years, I might as well be on the outside on that day, too."

Shortly before 11 AM, the black hearse pulled into the parking lot, followed by the caravan of limousines. Media outlets gathered along the barricade at the side entrance as rappers like Trae, Willie D, and Bun B entered the building.

Mama Wes climbed in J. Prince's limo. Since their initial conversation, Prince hadn't mentioned if he'd retrieved the surveillance footage from the Mondrian. Mama Wes had been so numb she hadn't even thought to ask. Regardless, whatever information Prince had gathered prompted him to ask if "L.A." would be at the funeral. Mama Wes shook her head; she hadn't talked to Larry since he asked if he should hire an attorney. "I haven't heard from him," she said.

They continued talking beneath the privacy of the dark tinted windows as people streamed past the vehicle. Prince thumbed through a copy of the funeral booklet slowly, expressing concern that Mama Wes was planning to speak at her only child's funeral. "You're gonna be alright? You're gonna do this?" he asked. "You're on this program, you didn't tell me that."

"Look, I can do this," Mama Wes insisted. "I can do this. I gotta do this. Don't worry about me. I'm gonna do this for my baby. I'm gonna -"

She stopped abruptly mid-sentence, distracted by a man walking past the car. It was something about his stride that captured her attention. The man appeared to be heavily disguised. To Mama Wes, he looked unnatural.

Prince followed her gaze. "Mama. That ain't that nigga, is it?" he asked.

Not wanting any drama to mar her son's funeral, especially with dozens of FBI agents in the vicinity, Mama Wes brushed it off. "Naw, baby. Nah," she said.

Although she hadn't gotten a good look, she would remain convinced that the man was Larry.

Big Bubb, seated inside, glanced at the back of the auditorium as people filtered in. The opening notes of the instrumental for "One Day," playing softly in the background, caused at least one woman to break down in tears. Bubb saw DJ Paul and Juicy J walking through the doorway, but it was a man behind them in the foyer that momentarily captured his attention. The man wore glasses, a hat, and a wig, but there was something about his face that clicked in Big Bubb's memory. He couldn't place it. The doors swung shut and reopened momentarily as more people streamed into the auditorium; the man was gone.

Four men in suits unloaded the hearse and rolled the shiny silver coffin inside. Mama Wes and her entourage, wearing UGK t-shirts and Dickies, walked in through the side entrance, immediately followed by J. Prince and the Rap-A-Lot crew.

Inside, nearly 2,000 people were seated in rows along the floor of the main hall and scattered among the bleachers on the side. Flower bouquets lined the front, including one arrangement with a giant Rap-A-Lot logo. Producer Steve Below, watching the crowd, truly got the sense that he'd been a part of something big. "It was almost feeling like the end of some type of era," he remembers. "The end of something epic."

While a prayer was read, the pallbearers – Bun, Mitch, DJ Bird, Chad Jr., Bo-Bo Luchiano, Ed, XVII, and T.O.E., most wearing personalized red or black UGK Dickies – slowly carried the casket to the front of the stage. In the audience, DJ Paul of Three 6 Mafia broke down, sobbing uncontrollably. He sank down in his chair as Nancy Byron, seated next to him, rubbed her hand softly against his back to comfort him. Behind them, Wendy Day clung to Michael Watts, gripping his hand tightly. *I'm not gonna cry, I'm not gonna cry,* she told herself repeatedly. In the front, Bun and Mitch were also struggling to maintain their composure.

After a few words from Port Arthur's Mayor Deloris "Bobbie" Prince, Jeff Sledge approached the podium. He'd been asked to speak on Jive's behalf for Barry Weiss, who wasn't able to break away from pressing business in Europe. While he considered it an honor, he also felt pressure to deliver. As a native New Yorker with a sharp East Coast accent, Jeff felt out of his element and was worried that he might not be able to connect with the audience.

Jeff rose to the challenge, delivering a poignant speech filled with the right mix of somber moments and laughs. He recounted the story of Chad's last-minute demand for a publishing advance to buy the new Benz for the "Big Pimpin'" video shoot, and recalled how amazed he'd been by Chad's "inner calm" after his release from prison.

"He had the most passion and most integrity of anybody I worked with," Jeff said. "Maybe some will equal but no one will surpass. He loved what he did with a passion. He loved Texas with a passion. He loved it – every record, every album, he mentioned it. He's a hometown hero, as you see by the turnout today. He put this town on the map."

In closing, Jeff mentioned Jimmie Johnson Blvd., a local thoroughfare named after the popular Dallas Cowboys' coach who hailed from Port Arthur. "Mayor, I don't want to put pressure on you," he finished, turning towards the Mayor. "But the next time I drive down here, I hope I can drive down Chad Butler Blvd."*

The suggestion brought the crowd to its feet for a standing ovation. They continued clapping as Mama Wes approached the stage. A hush fell over the large room as she stood silently for a moment, surveying the crowd.

A few people exchanged nervous glances. Was it normal for a mother to speak after the death of her only child? Everyone was already on the verge of tears – what if she broke down crying?

Mama Wes wasn't concerned; she'd never been one for emotional outbursts. "I very rarely cry in public," she said later. "And I was in too much shock to cry."

As the first words came out of her mouth – her voice bold and steady with no hesitation – the audience visibly relaxed. "I attempted about 87 times to write something, but C said, 'Go 'head and wing it, Mama,' so that's what I'll do," she began.

"From the bottom of my heart, *I'm* alright. *You're* alright. 'Cause *he's* alright. My C is celebrating today," she announced with all the confidence and gusto of a seasoned preacher. "He's happy to see you, because Jesus is alright. He's alright. He got there to heaven and told them, 'The *Sauuuuuth* is here!'"

Smiles and chuckles broke out throughout the audience at her spot-on imitation of her son's Southern drawl. As she wrapped up her brief speech, she asked rhetorically, "You say he was your friend? He's got three children. Holla at 'em. Take 'em under your wing."

"Thank you," she finished. "You've done my baby right. *Chuuuuch!*"

Attendees were impressed with Mama Wes' fortitude. "I couldn't believe she held it together and didn't even show no signs of weakness," says Willie D. "[She's] a phenomenal woman. I mean, I'm [just] his homie and I couldn't have [spoken at his funeral] … I was very impressed with her being able to hold her composure. Calling her a 'strong woman' is an understatement … She's really one of the strongest people I know, period."

(*Mama Wes did reach out to the mayor to discuss the possibility of having the two-mile stretch of Savannah Street, between 19th Street and Procter, renamed Chad Butler Blvd. The most direct route between Chad's father Charleston's house on 13th Street and Mama Wes' house on Shreveport Ave., it also held significance because it contained several locations mentioned on UGK songs like Troy's, BJ's, and McDonald's. Bun name-dropped BJ's and Savannah Street on "Family Affair" and rapped, "I saw a fiend chase ya from BJ's up to Mickey D's" on "Tell Me Something Good." "I'm 'bout to hit Gulfway, just past Troy's," Pimp rapped on "Front, Back & Side to Side.")

Mama Wes' composure had a profound effect on her grandsons, who watched her for guidance on how to handle the loss. "[Prior to that] I thought being strong was shutting down your feelings," Chad Jr. said. "It was unearthly to me how she could be so strong and still have such strong feelings … My granny taught me you could still love your family and have emotions and be strong."

Finally, Pastor John R. Adolph stepped to the podium to deliver the eulogy. A hush again fell over the audience, expecting quiet reflections, perhaps a Bible verse.

Instead, he boldly declared, "It's hard out here for a pimp!"

The unexpected opening drew laughter and a few raised eyebrows.

Adolph explained that Chad had just joined his church in Beaumont, and he'd struggled with the idea of how to properly eulogize a man with the nickname "Pimp C."

"I didn't know how to handle this, this pimpin' business," he explained, adding, "I remember when the word 'crack' was a hole in the sidewalk; when 'weed' was something you had to pull up; when a 'hoe' was a garden tool and when 'sugar daddy' was a piece of candy … I remember when pimps were in the red zone in town, brothers dressed up with scantily clad women."

With a little research, he'd come to understand that the meaning of the word "pimp" had changed. Referencing Xzibit's popular MTV show *Pimp My Ride*, where rundown cars were transformed into something extraordinary, he said that for Pimp C, 'pimping' was about aspiring towards greatness. "It's not about having some sister out on the corner. It's about a way to live large," Adolph said.

While Pastor Adolph was speaking, FBI agents in the parking lot were snapping away at the sight of Bishop Don "Magic" Juan, adorned in a large jewel-encrusted cape and gold crown, carrying a gold pimp cup. Once inside, the Bishop made a beeline down the center of the aisle, accompanied by two girls.

Some of Chad's pimp friends, like Good Game and Pimpin' Ken, were already in the building, but Bishop Don "Magic" Juan was impossible to miss. Everyone's head turned towards the distraction, a rumble spreading throughout the crowd. *What is that?* Mama Wes thought, wondering who had invited a clown.

The Bishop headed straight for the front row, where he leaned down towards Mama Wes to give her an awkward hug. "Mama C," he said. "I wanna say a few words."

She looked right at him and firmly said, "No."

Many were horrified at the disruption; Willie D, seated next to Mama Wes, was furious, trying to restrain himself from causing a scene in the midst of the service.

"Pimp C joined my church November 18," Pastor Adolph continued. "He never had the chance to see December 18. Lord, it may be hard out there for a pimp, but there is hope in here for those who believe."

"It's hard in here," Adolph said, looking towards the casket. "This man was 33 years old, he leaves a wife and three kids. His mama just came up here and said it's alright, but it's not. But there is hope in here. God is a God who will pardon your past."

Adolph asked the audience to gather around the closed casket. Some raised their hands, while others bowed their heads while the pastor offered up a prayer. Chad Jr. pulled his hat low as tears poured from his eyes.

At the conclusion of the service, the pallbearers gathered to lift Chad's casket, covered in red flowers. "Damn, nigga, you heavy," Bun quipped, straining under the weight.

While some of the pallbearers didn't mind Bun's insensitive joke, Chad Jr. was offended by the comment and confided in Mama Wes that the callous remark made him look at Bun in a different light. "People react different ways to different things," Mama Wes told him gently.

As they loaded the casket into the waiting hearse outside, Bun caught the eye of a *Raw Report* DVD cameraman capturing the somber finality of the moment. "It's *still* UGK for life, nigga," he told the camera, twisting his arm to show his UGK tattoo.

Nitacha, who had ridden over in Mama Wes' limo, was still angry over the funeral procession slight and confronted Chinara after the service. "That was fucked up," she said, heated. "That's that man's mama. You don't do some shit like that. You don't put your family before us."

According to Nitacha, Chinara gave a half-hearted apology, mentioning the situation with Heather by way of explanation. *All this over a broad?* Nitacha thought.

You don't let the world know our business!" Nitacha snapped. "You don't like Ms. Monroe, Ms. Monroe don't like you, [but] we are a family unit, we've got kids in this [situation]!"

Nitacha wasn't happy that Bianca, whom she considered "one of his little tricks from California," was in the building either, but says she'd learned to accept Chad for who he was. "You knew what the fuck you was getting into when you married this man," she snapped. "What, did you really think that your pussy was lined in 24-karat gold?"

To outsiders, though, the family bond appeared intact. Reporter Shaheem Reid, who covered the funeral for MTV News, was impressed with Mama Wes' strength as he saw her exit the funeral home. "They were all together interlocking arms, almost like a march," he observed. "There was [a] feeling [of] unification in the family."

Hoping to avoid a media frenzy, Nancy Byron had granted exclusive rights to film the funeral to Houston television station CW39, who serviced approved snippets to other media outlets. With attendees streaming out of the civic center, reporters stood along the barricades hoping to snag a celebrity for a quick soundbite.

"There's been a lot of Houston rappers that's passed. How big is Pimp's passing?" one excited *Rolling Out* reporter asked Chamillionaire, as if it were a new album release. "Pimp C was like one of the creators or the godfathers of this whole scene," Chamillionaire said. "A lot of us got our whole style and swagger from Pimp."

Bishop Don "Magic" Juan emerged, raising his pimp cup for the cameras. "We had a great funeral. It was great!" he proclaimed.

Exiting shortly behind the Bishop was a far more somber J. Prince, wearing all black and dark sunglasses. "I think the pastor summed it up well. He said, 'It's hard out here for a pimp, but I got hope in Christ.' So I've got that hope today … I think the family [is] gonna move on and I think we're all gonna be great, but it was a stunning loss," Prince told the *Houston Chronicle*. "Pimp helped lay the foundation that we stand on where Southern Hip-Hop music is concerned … Everybody that's rapping today is imitating Pimp."

The Houston Chronicle also spoke with Webbie, who told them, "Last time I talked to him we was talking about getting money off this rap shit, we wasn't talking about dying, so know that was a surprise to him just like it was to me."

"He supported me at a time when I was really in need and I'm gonna be here for [his family] in his time of need," Trae tha Truth somberly told Nasircle TV. "Being a child growing up in the streets, [you learn] not to really question God, you know?"

The funeral procession headed towards Chad's gravesite at Greenlawn Memorial Park, ironically located across the street from one of his favorite spots, Happy Donuts.

Willie D pulled Bishop Don "Magic" Juan to the side and explained that he – and many others – had been offended by his grand entrance. "I definitely wasn't trying to offend nobody, man," the Bishop responded. "You know, I had just got there, I came in from out of town … I was just trying to get here [and] I was just caught up in the moment."

Reports of Bishop Don "Magic" Juan "disrupting" Pimp C's funeral later circulated online, and he took offense at the label, saying that his actions had been misinterpreted. "I would do no such thing," he protests. "I made it my business to huff and puff to get there, because I know he would have wanted me to be there … I didn't come all the way [to Port Arthur] to make a commotion. I'm just a controversial guy, and that's the way it is … I was there for Pimp C."

Some viewed it as exactly what Pimp would've wanted. "You can't be upset – that's Pimp's friends," says Bundy of the X-Mob. "You love Pimp for [his] music. You can't love him and choose his friends."

Friends and family congregated at Mama Wes' home after the interment, feasting on overflowing plates of food delivered by thoughtful friends and neighbors. The solemn mood was lightened by seven-year-old Corey, who used the opportunity to hustle the extra copies of his father's *Best of Both Worlds* DVD sitting in the game room for $5 apiece.

As Bishop Don "Magic" Juan paraded up the driveway, Corey commented matter-of-factly, "I didn't know my daddy knew Flavor Flav." He had mistaken the pimp for the Public Enemy hypeman starring in the VH1 reality dating show *Flavor of Love*.*

Bun collapsed to the floor in a fit of laughter, falling into Edgar the Dog's bowl and scattering dog food all over the kitchen. "Me and my dad used to watch you on TV all the time!" Corey told the Bishop as he entered, then ran throughout the house yelling, "FLAVOR FLAV!"

After everyone had a good laugh, Mama Wes turned towards the Bishop. "So you the one who [had] him always saying '*Chuuuch*,' huh?" she asked.

"Yes ma'am, I am the Chuuuch," he pronounced grandly.

Mama Wes had mostly been amused when her son adopted Bishop's "chuuuch!" "tabanacle!" lingo, but some found it offensive. "Y'all take a positive thing and try to make it a negative," Bishop Don "Magic" Juan says. "I beg to differ … we got gangsters, rappers, [and] millionaires all fellowshipping together saying, 'Chuuuch!' It means to fellowship and to come together … it means love, not hate."

"People got to understand that pimps, players, hustlers, and nightlifers, they're spiritual [too], they believe in God," he adds. "They're God-fearing creatures. Pimp C was a God-fearing man … that's why he was so blessed. He lived a short life, but he lived long enough to do what his job was on this earth."

A few friends like Killer Mike, Mr. 3-2, and Mia X had chosen not to attend, preferring to hold onto their warm memories instead of seeing him "in a box." Chad's ex-girlfriend Kristi Floyd, who'd been afraid to "see him like that," had second thoughts after she skipped the funeral. She called Mama Wes' house to see how she was holding up, but the call went to voicemail, where she was greeted by Chad's familiar voice thanking her for calling UGK Records. Kristi collapsed in tears at the sound of his voice.

For many, the day passed in a surreal blur. "I recall very little [from the funeral]," says Bun's road manager Bone. "A lot of people was just like robots that day, just going through the motions."

Mama Wes, who remembered virtually every interaction she'd had with her son over nearly 34 years in vivid detail, had absolutely no recollection of the funeral. The only thing that stuck in her mind was the sting of her placement in the back of the funeral procession. It was a slight that would help push the rift between her and Chinara into a growing chasm.

"I was very angry with [Chinara] when C passed away," Mama Wes said several years later. "I'm not even angry at her anymore, [but] I will never, *ever* forget the things she did."

(*Corey wasn't the only one; Chad's attorney friend Craig Wormley had also assumed that the "guy [who] showed up in a costume" during the pastor's eulogy was Flavor Flav.)

CHAPTER 59

"Whoever released the [official cause of death] just came up with a story that would sound good ... [the coroner] had to give the public a reason, because it would sound stupid to say, 'We don't know.'" – Mama Wes

———————

"[Larry] made it sound like ... something else happened in that [hotel] room."
– Craig Wormley

As the weeks passed by with no word from the coroner, grief and sorrow gave way to disbelief and suspicion. Most of Chad's friends and family members found it impossible to think he could have passed from natural causes at 33 years old. And for those who suspected foul play, there was no shortage of potential suspects. Not only was he having problems with Bun, his wife, and others who were close to him prior to his death, but as Nancy Byron succinctly states, "Pimp has a lot of people in his life that are scary."

Although Mama Wes had already eliminated the possibility of J. Prince's involvement in her mind, others were suspicious of him, due to his reputation for being cold, calculating, and ruthless, and the fact that he had a financial stake in Chad's career. "[The rap game] is such a cutthroat business that people honestly feel like you are worth more dead than you are alive," Nitacha says.

But Prince had another suspect in mind. Three weeks after Chad's death, a Rap-A-Lot affiliate allegedly spotted Larry landing at a Texas airport and trailed him to Chinara's house in Port Arthur. It was reported back to Mama Wes that Larry spent several nights at Chinara's house over the Christmas holidays.

Mama Wes couldn't understand why Larry and Chinara would be spending the holidays together – were they closer than they wanted people to believe? XVII too thought it was strange that Chinara would be on such friendly terms with Larry when just a few weeks earlier, she'd been fuming that he wouldn't answer the phone in Los Angeles. "We were like, *what the fuck?*" recalls XVII. "It didn't make no sense."

Larry, who had met Craig Wormley several times through Chad, called Wormley to inquire about hiring him as a defense attorney.* Wormley believed Larry was seeking representation because police were trying to interview him, but there is no indication that detectives were even aware of Larry's existence or ever sought him for questioning.

When pressed for specifics, Larry was extremely vague and said he didn't want to go into details on the phone. "He kinda made it sound like he knew something," Wormley recalls. "He made it sound like ... something else happened in that room."

Larry also hinted that there was another reason he needed an attorney. "He felt that his life was in danger," remembers Wormley. "And it might not have had anything to do with Chad ... He made it sound like ... he was in [bad] with the wrong group, maybe even a cartel ... he was scared. I got the impression that it was something completely outside of [Chad's death] that he

(*Larry also contacted his attorney back home in Jackson, Sam Martin, expressing concern that he might be under suspicion because he was the last person to see Chad alive. Larry struck Martin as "genuinely distraught and upset" over Chad's death.)

wanted to talk to me about [also, because] he wanted to confide in a lawyer."*

Intrigued, Wormley made several unsuccessful attempts to meet with Larry. They arranged to meet at a Los Angeles restaurant, but Larry was again a no-show. Wormley found him to be such a "dodgeball" that he eventually gave up, and the two lost contact.

Detective Lankford had already concluded that Chad's death was "non-criminal" and had not made any attempt to find out who else was there when he died. There is no indication that authorities ever contacted Larry, his girlfriend, or Bianca.

Bianca, expecting a call, had written down everything she remembered from that night and constantly replayed it over and over again in her mind. Why did Larry have a glass specifically prepared for Chad? She could clearly see him wiping the rims of each glass, neatly replacing the little paper lids. And the one thought she couldn't shake: *Why did he take the trash out?*

Craig Wormley's investigator Chuck Steeno eventually reached out to Bianca and asked her a few cursory questions. She didn't volunteer any information about Larry, codeine, or any other drug use, and he didn't ask.**

On January 8, the medical examiner Dr. Djabourian received the toxicology report, which was inconclusive, and requested additional testing. By late January, nine weeks had passed and the media was getting restless. "The L.A. Coroner's Office admits [it's taking] longer than usual for a death investigation," the *Beaumont Enterprise* reported.

Around this time, Mama Wes received the call from the coroner's office informing her that they didn't know why Chad had died. The only information she was given was that the body appeared to have been deceased for nearly two days, so Chad likely had died on Sunday. ("[A homicide detective's work] is not like how you see on TV [shows like CSI]," explains Detective Lankford. "You know, 'This guy took his last breath at 3:05 PM.' It's really never that simple.")

In Mama Wes' mind, the lack of information solidified her suspicion that her son was murdered. But when she called Bun to share her suspicions, the conversation deteriorated into an argument. He didn't like her suggestion that there was foul play involved.

"Well, that's my baby, and if that's the way I feel, I got a right to say it," she said firmly. "I think somebody killed my son."

A few days after the inconclusive call from the coroner, Mama Wes was shocked to receive the February 4th copy of the *Port Arthur News*, which reported that Pimp C had "died from a combination of promethazine with codeine and sleep apnea." The paper quoted Ed Winter of the coroner's office, explaining that the death was the result of "a combination of sleep apnea and congestion medication that slowed down his breathing ability."

Ed Winter? Mama Wes thought, confused. *That's not the person I spoke to.****

On the carefully-worded autopsy report, the medical examiner Dr. Djabourian listed the death as accidental, with "promethazine/codeine effects and other unestablished factors" as contributing factors. Sleep apnea (which was not detectable in the autopsy, but mentioned in Chad's medical history) was described as a "condition contributing [to] but not related to the immediate cause of death."

(*Larry declined to be interviewed. Based solely on rumors and speculation, there are two possible explanations for this. Larry might have been referring to his fear of J. Prince, who allegedly wanted to speak with him about Chad's death, or he could have been referring to the cartel or organization from whom he had supposedly bragged of stealing more than $200,000 in a botched drug deal.)

(**Craig Wormley turned over Chuck Steeno's report to the authorities, but says that they didn't uncover anything notable. "I didn't see anything that looked like it was out of place or foul play," Steeno says. "It seemed to me that the coroner pretty much did his job." Steeno, who no longer works as an investigator, was not able to locate his records related to Chad's death.)

(***Ed Winter also handled media inquiries in the 2009 death of Michael Jackson and 2012 death of Whitney Houston. The Los Angeles coroner's office, no stranger to high-profile celebrity deaths, is the only coroner's office in the world that has a gift shop.)

In a more detailed explanation, the medical examiner clarified that this conclusion was an educated guess. "It appears the most likely cause for this death is effects of multiple drug intake, with promethazine and codeine having the greatest effect," he wrote. "Though levels were not in the usual lethal ranges, in combination with sleep apnea, the drug effects in our opinion were factors in his death."

He added, "Additional factors in the death cannot be excluded due to decomposition."

Mama Wes dismissed the official story as "boo-boo." "Whoever released that shit just came up with a story that would sound good," she says. "I think that [the coroner's media spokesman] Ed Winter would've had to give [the public] a reason, because it would sound stupid to say, 'We don't know.'"

When speaking with media outlets, Winter was careful to clarify that although they believed promethazine and codeine were contributing factors, Chad did not overdose. "It wasn't an overdose," he told MTV News. "We think it was a result of taking the cough medication with his sleeping problems."

But on the same day Winter stressed to MTV News, the *Port Arthur News,* and *LA Weekly* that Pimp C *did not* overdose, the *Houston Chronicle* reported that "an overdose of cough syrup and a pre-existing sleep apnea condition killed Chad Butler." *XXL* Magazine also reported that it was an overdose. Both articles quoted Winter explaining, "[With] sleep apnea, you stop breathing … Coupled with a medication that suppresses your respiratory abilities, you end up with an accidental death."

Fans, noting the contradiction, were just as confused as Mama Wes. Journalist Andrew Nosnitsky posted an article on CocaineBlunts.com describing Pimp C's death as accidental, followed by an update which read, "Now the *Houston Chronicle* is reporting that it was, in fact, an overdose. And citing the same coroner's office representative… WTF?"

"Call it what you want, this doesn't appear to be definitive closure," noted one commenter named SukedowN. Another commenter named Chulo added, "It seems da coroners r confused. Was this a homicide or an accident? I think this case needs to be investigated a lil deeper, we really need 2 know the truth."

The *Houston Chronicle* posted another conflicting account the following day, February 5, saying it was "an overdose of cough syrup," then adding, "The coroner was careful to say that Pimp C did not die from ingesting too much cough syrup."

"Drugs Killed Pimp C," blared the headline in the *New York Times* on February 6, attributing his death to "an overdose of drugs celebrated by Three 6 Mafia and the Pimp C group Underground Kingz in the 2000 single 'Sippin' on Some Syrup.'"

Rumors spread in the Jackson area that J. Prince was looking for Larry. Stax hadn't seen Larry in several months when he popped up one quiet afternoon at the clothing store. Without prompting, Larry bragged that he'd been in Los Angeles with Pimp when he died. "Shit, when he died, he had on one of yo' shirts," Larry volunteered, adding, "No lie." He pointed out one of Stax' Blockwear designs, a popular syrup-themed t-shirt.

Stax knew Larry well enough to take the comment with a grain of salt. "He lies a lot, and you have to filter it because it'll have some merit to it – it'll have some truth – but he tells a lot of lies around it," Stax explains.

Smoke D's friend Jaro was also back in Jackson for a brief visit. He'd missed so many classes at Jackson State traveling back and forth to Port Arthur that his student visa wasn't renewed, and had been living in his native Czech Republic when Pimp C died.

The rumors of Larry's involvement with Pimp C's death didn't surprise Jaro at all. He'd always considered Larry "a shiesty dude," but they knew each other fairly well. He'd even had his first (and only) experience sipping lean from Larry's cup. Jaro arranged to meet with Larry,

AUTOPSY REPORT

No.

2007-08785

I performed an autopsy on the body of ➡ BUTLER, CHAD LAMONT

at _____ the DEPARTMENT OF CORONER

Los Angeles, California _____ on _____ DECEMBER 6, 2007 @ 0825 HOURS

(Date)   (Time)

From the anatomic findings and pertinent history I ascribe the death to:

(A)   PROMETHAZINE/CODEINE EFFECTS AND OTHER UNESTABLISHED FACTORS
DUE TO, OR AS A CONSEQUENCE OF

(B)
DUE TO, OR AS A CONSEQUENCE OF

(C)
DUE TO, OR AS A CONSEQUENCE OF

(D)
OTHER CONDITIONS CONTRIBUTING BUT NOT RELATED TO THE IMMEDIATE CAUSE OF DEATH.

   SPLEEP APNEA (BY HISTORY)

Based on the available medical history, autopsy, and toxicological
findings, it appears the most likely cause for this death is
effects of multiple drug intake, with promethazine and codeine
having the greatest effect. Though levels were not in the usual
lethal ranges, in combination with sleep apnea, the drug effects
in our opinion were factors in his death. Additional factors in
the death cannot be excluded due to decomposition, as microscopic
exam is suboptimal and metabolic abnormalities cannot be evaluated.
Due to the drug effects, the manner is accident.

_____   2/21/08
RAFFI S. DJABOURIAN, M.D.   DATE
DEPUTY MEDICAL EXAMINER

RSD:rs:f/c
D-12/06/07 @ 1125
T-01/10/08

76A890M—Rev. 8/94

Above: A portion of **Chad Butler's autopsy report.**

(Editor's note: The image above is actually the combination of two different pages, due to space constraints.)

asking him to explain what had happened with Pimp.

As Jaro recalls it, Larry said they'd simply overdone it one night. He implied that he'd been staying somewhere else; he'd felt sick when he woke up the next morning and called Pimp to check on him, but there was no answer.

While Jaro didn't find Larry's version of events wholly believable, one thing was clear: Larry *really* liked telling the story. He showed Jaro where he'd added "R.I.P. Pimp C" to his "UGK 4 Life" tattoo. "He seemed to be proud of the situation," recalls Jaro. "He was really getting off on the [Pimp C] affiliation, all his tattoos and shit."

Most of all, Jaro was struck by Larry's apparent lack of remorse. His tone wasn't one of regret or sorrow. His thoughts weren't on Chad's family and friends, or what Pimp's death meant to the music industry, but seemed to revolve around himself and his perceived link to greatness. His proximity to Pimp C had been his claim to fame around town, and he appeared pleased – giddy, even – that his reputation was now solidified as *the guy who was there when Pimp C died*.

Larry told similar tales all over the country. He liked to tell people that Pimp was having a conversation with "Tupac" in the backseat of his car right before he died. "Pimp was kinda on some other shit," he'd say. He was overheard in a nightclub bragging that he'd cleaned up the room after Pimp C died. In some versions of the story, he'd left to take his girlfriend home and when he came back, Pimp was napping in the same position he'd been when he left. In other versions of the story, the last time he'd seen Pimp was when he'd dropped him off at The Mondrian after Too $hort's show.

The coroner's conclusion made sense to Ed, who had witnessed Chad's sleep apnea struggles firsthand. "It's like [he was] holding his breath, and [then] he would gasp for air to catch his breath," Ed recalls. "It makes sense because codeine slows down everything, and it's gonna make it harder for you to catch your breath [because] it relaxes your muscles."

By all accounts, Chad had put his body through a lot during the week prior to his death, abusing both depressants and stimulants without getting much sleep. It was feasible that his body might have been more susceptible than usual. Still, many had a hard time comprehending it. "Sleep apnea" sounded foreign to Too $hort. "I can't picture Chad fully dressed, laying down on the bed and just *dying*," he says. "I can't accept that Chad just laid down and died."

While she acknowledges that Chad had severe sleep apnea and "a multitude of health issues," Mama Wes says she is "absolutely sure that C did not die of natural causes." She lists six reasons why she believes her son was murdered:

1. He was in fear for his life. Based on their conversations, she believed he sensed imminent danger from unspecified sources.

2. The autopsy was inconclusive. Mama Wes believes that the promethazine/codeine/sleep apnea story was just a plausible theory invented for the media.

3. He did not die of a drug overdose. Despite the fact that that Chad's death has been widely reported as an "overdose," both the coroner and the autopsy report confirm that it was not an overdose.

4. There was too much blood. Mama Wes believed that he could not have died from sleep apnea because of the excessive amount of blood. Ed, extremely disturbed by what he'd seen when he pulled back the covers at the Mondrian, consulted with medical professionals for their opinion. "[Some of them said] that could be normal … because of the amount of time he had probably been there," he says. "When you pass, all your bodily fluids drain."

5. Someone else was in his hotel room. Although Mama Wes did not view the room herself, Ed and others who did were convinced it was too neat to be Chad's room. Mama Wes believes someone was there when he died and cleaned up after him.

6. He had too many plans for the future. The idea that Chad could possibly have committed suicide, as was suggested, struck Mama Wes as "the craziest, most stupid thing" she had ever heard. "He did not have any designs on dying," she says firmly.

With a steady stream of guests coming through Mama Wes' house, she couldn't be sure who had left this anonymous note in her game room, the handwritten words scrawled across notebook paper erratically as if the writer had been in a hurry:

I don't know but whoever that girl was that was in Calif. With Chanara I feel had to do with what happened to "C." I've been getting all kinds of feed back stating that they might have not left L.A. until after he had pass. I've been under security every since I've talk to a few people all of a sudden there's a guy here that live's across the street from J's baby mama house. If for some reason you have to read this I've found out to much and it has been found necessary to have me eliminated. But "C" was put out. Somebody did him. It was not accidental *

Mama Wes didn't take the bizarre anonymous note too seriously, but it did bother her because it wasn't the first time she'd heard that Chinara had another woman with her in Los Angeles. Still, she didn't suspect Chinara of involvement. "I don't like the girl, but I don't feel like she would be that vicious," says Mama Wes, adding, "I really don't think she has enough sense. [But] I think she may know who [did] it."

Relations between Bun and the rest of Chad's camp, especially the UGK Posse, were especially strained after his death. Many resented the fact that Bun was perceived by the public as Chad's spokesman yet kept his distance from the rest of the camp. Some even suspect him of being involved in Chad's death.

Although Mama Wes didn't share these sentiments, she understood why those who "knew that there were major differences between C and Bun at the time of C's death" might be suspicious. While Bun publicly acknowledged that they had "went through a rough patch," some felt that he was downplaying the seriousness of their issues. Mama Wes also understood why some people found Bun's behavior after Chad's death odd. "He was a different kind of strange," she says. "I know we were all strange after that happened, but he was a different kind of strange."

"Pimp was in Los Angeles when he was found dead. Were you with him?" *VIBE* Magazine had asked Bun two days after Chad's body was found.

"No. He was [there] doing some recording with Three 6 Mafia and performing with Too $hort," Bun answered.

Mama Wes says she later learned from a "factual" source that Bun actually *was* in Los Angeles, a fact which she found disturbing. (She cannot recall the source of information but believed it to be credible.) "I feel confident that Bun was there," says Mama Wes. "He lied about being there. Why would he lie about being there? … I never understood why he lied about that."

Swizz Beatz, who was at the Microsoft Zune event in Seattle with Bun on Friday before Chad's death, somewhat corroborated this idea in an MTV interview. "[Bun and I] was just vibing [in Seattle] and I was like, 'Where C at?'" he recalled. "He was like, 'Oh, he in L.A. chillin'.' I think he was about to go out there, like, after our show."**

"I wouldn't wanna believe that [Bun could have anything to do with it]," says Mama Wes. "But *could* he do it? Hell yeah. *Could* he pull it off? Hell yeah … Bun is an excellent actor." If Bun actually *was* in Los Angeles when Chad died, clearly, that would create far more questions than answers.

But while many in the UGK Posse are suspicious of Bun, others feel that *they* were the ones partly to blame. "[No one] was signed to UGK [Records], because there were no contracts," says Tim Hampton. "But they wore the UGK shirts everywhere and go in the club and always throwing up Chad's name … what did you really bring to the table? You watched Chad fall [back into drug use]. All you did was ride his coattail … Chad just had the wrong people around him, and

(*Chinara was with Ed and XVII at the high-rise on Sunday morning, so the allegation that she didn't leave "L.A. until after he had pass" could not be true.)

(**Bun performed in Seattle on Friday night and was in Houston when Chad's body was found on Tuesday morning. He did not comment when asked if he was in Los Angeles at any point between Friday night and Tuesday morning.)

he was trying to help these dudes."

Mama Wes believes that Chad was poisoned with a substance such as cyanide. Cyanide, which has legitimate uses in pesticides and chemical research labs, is not sold at retail outlets in the United States but is available from industrial sources. Cyanide looks similar to salt or sugar and dissolves quickly in liquid; ingesting just one tablespoon would likely lead to death within 2-6 hours.

Cyanide deprives the body of oxygen, so some thought it was logical that cyanide poisoning could've been misdiagnosed. "Sleep apnea is when you stop breathing in your sleep," says Tim Hampton. "[Cyanide] attacks your body's ability to properly use oxygen. The same thing."

Cyanide poisoning is rare and extremely difficult to diagnose. Because it dissipates quickly in the bloodstream, it is difficult to detect after the body begins decomposing. Current toxicology tests can only detect the presence of cyanide within a few hours of death, or up to two days at the most. Chad's body wasn't found for about two days, so it is possible that even if cyanide had been used, it wouldn't have been detected.

"Many people think, with [cyanide] poisoning being rare and something that may not be [detected], that this would be a murder someone could get away with," Dr. Robert Geller, medical director of the Georgia Poison Center, told CNN in 2013.

Because cyanide is so rare, standard toxicology tests don't look for it unless the medical examiner suspects it.* "The harder you want to find something, the more expensive it is, and this country's forensic labs run on a shoestring budget," Dr. Geller added.

Even though cyanide dissipates quickly, it does often leave behind other signs. The body of a cyanide poisoning victim may have patchy cherry-red discolorations on the skin or blue-tinted blood. The odor of bitter almonds is sometimes present. Ingesting cyanide would leave the stomach lining damaged and blood-stained; however, if the cyanide was diluted in liquid, damage to the stomach might be minimal. None of these symptoms appear to be present in Chad's autopsy.

Mama Wes believed authorities simply didn't care enough to research any further. "I really think that they didn't dig deep enough, because [they thought], *Why do it*?" she says. "Michael Jackson, he wasn't."

"They could have found out how C died," she adds. "What I think was that it would've taken more time and money, and that lil' rap nigga just wasn't worth it."

Dr. Benjamin, a forensic toxicology expert asked to review the autopsy report to give a second opinion for this book, doesn't see any indication of poisoning or foul play, although with the small toxicology screening he believes it would be "hard to tell about the drug levels when the body was decomposed."

Dr. Benjamin agrees with the coroner's conclusion that it was an accidental or natural death. He confirms that the amount of codeine/promethazine in the bloodstream was "not in the toxic to lethal range for a healthy man" and finds it "reasonable" to conclude that sleep apnea combined with codeine caused his death.

Because the tip of Chad's tongue was clenched between his teeth, Dr. Benjamin offers a similar theory: "I think he had a seizure, stopped breathing due to a combo of the drugs and the lack of oxygen during the seizure, probably caused by the sleep apnea."

Bianca, after replaying the scene in her head a thousand times, firmly believes that Larry

---

(*In one high-profile case, when a 46-year-old Illinois lottery winner died suddenly in 2012, it was determined that he had died of natural causes. At the objection of relatives, more extensive toxicology tests revealed that he had been poisoned by cyanide.)

slipped something in Chad's drink. When asked if it was possible that Chad could have been poisoned, Detective Lankford shrugs. "I mean, is it possible that he could've had some people over and they could've purposely drugged his drinks or whatever?" he wonders aloud. "Yeah, I guess so."

If Larry was involved, there remains one important unanswered question: *why?* What could possibly be his motive for killing a man he idolized? "I really have not [figured] that one [out] yet," sighs Mama Wes. "And really, I've given that a lot of thought."

Even for those who didn't trust Larry, a motive appears elusive. Most agree that he wouldn't have any reason to hurt Pimp and wouldn't gain anything from his death. Most believe Larry was only guilty of enabling Pimp's drug use. "I think that if it happened that way ... he was trying to kiss Pimp ass, y'know, giving him everything he want," Smoke D theorizes.*

"[Larry] drank a lot ... lean, alcohol ... he went hard," says Larry's friend Korleon. "That's why [some] people would say that he was responsible for what occurred with Pimp ... But at the end of the day, [Pimp] can either choose to partake or not partake."

The only possible motive seems to be the idea that Chad was about to cut ties with his "co-president." If Larry had indeed injected a large amount of cash into UGK Records, could he have been so devastated at losing his money and position that he would resort to drastic measures?

Another theory held that Chad might have died naturally while Larry was still in the room, and Larry panicked, cleared the room out, and left without alerting authorities. To Bianca, this theory seems illogical, since Larry had cleaned the room in advance.

The idea of a powerful figure or entity paying Larry to poison his idol seems unlikely, although not impossible. "Why would someone go to such an extreme to do that?" Bianca wonders aloud. "I don't know. It's just weird."

Vague conspiracy theories abounded, mostly because of Chad's over-the-top interviews prior to his death. Some thought he'd pissed off the wrong person. YouTube videos flashing 666 signs theorized that Pimp C had been killed by the Illuminati for exposing Russell Simmons and Ne-Yo as homosexuals.

Matt Sonzala, a conspiracy theorist by nature, thoroughly analyzed Pimp's Hot 107.9 interview for clues. "I think he was murdered. Pimp was murdered. Pimp did not die of fucking codeine and sleep apnea," he says flatly. "It's very obvious that something was gonna happen to him with all the shit he was talking, in my opinion."

Aside from pointing fingers at alleged homosexuals, Sonzala believes that Pimp's unfiltered rants were "putting a lot of people in jeopardy"; he was ranting about cocaine prices during BMF's federal trial and bragging about the Rap-A-Lot Mafia while J. Prince was facing off with Studio 7303 owner Ronald Bookman in court over an alleged assault. "A lot of stuff he said made a lot of sense," Sonzala says. "[But] he was so reckless he was dumb."

"In my opinion, he was exposing a lot of people, and he was about to expose a lot of people that were close to him. And they knew that," XVII says, adding, "It benefited [some] people to make him be quiet."

Not everybody believes the conspiracy theories. "It's not a mystery," says Nancy Byron. "I think Pimp was fat and high, [with] sleep apnea. Not a good combination."

"Everybody got a theory," sighs Big Munn. "I just know my homeboy is dead ... That's the hard truth of it."

Even though Chad didn't die of a drug overdose, it seems clear that drugs did play a role in his death, and many lamented the fact that he didn't have a strong support system. "Unfortunately, you've gotta blame it on the people around him," says Ice-T. "But it's hard – when you're

(*Even if Larry unintentionally caused Chad's death, legally, authorities could possibly have charged him with involuntary manslaughter. People in California have been charged with involuntary manslaughter for failing to call 911 while a person was dying. In the most famous example of California's involuntary manslaughter law, Dr. Conrad Murray was convicted and sentenced to four years for administering the lethal dose of propofol which killed Michael Jackson.)

a boss, who can really tell you that what you're doing is wrong?"

"Rap is like rock & roll, and if you get kinda caught up into the lifestyle, it could take you out," Ice-T adds. "You've gotta have a little squareness in you to stay focused, because there's too much temptation … it's kinda based in negativity. The more craziness you do, the more props you get … the more publicity you get."

Ice-T says there's a lesson to be learned in Pimp C's tragedy. "Certain people [have to] pass away to send out a message: 'Don't go down that route,'" he says. "I've seen 'Pac die, seen Big die, seen C die … [and I realized], *I can't let that happen to me.* I can't get caught up in this shit. That's why my life is totally different [now]. If I was [living] the same [as I was before], I'd be dead."

In retrospect, it would be easy to wonder: what if Chad had never gone to prison? Maybe he wouldn't have gained so much weight; maybe he wouldn't have developed sleep apnea? Could a better attorney or a more sympathetic judge have indirectly prevented his death? On the other hand, if he had come home from Los Angeles as planned for his parole meeting, what if he had failed a drug test and been sent back to prison to serve out the remainder of his eight-year sentence, to the collective sigh of the Hip-Hop community?

At the end of the day, some say the circumstances of his death and the "what if"s are irrelevant. "He's dead and gone, y'know?" Smoke D says sadly. "You could theorize whatever … [but] at the end of the day, the devil's plot is just a part of God's plan."

———————

The idea that Pimp C died of a drug overdose – completely invented by irresponsible media, directly contradicting the coroner's own statements – has been repeated so many times over the years that many fans have come to believe it is a fact. (To this, Pimp likely would have quoted Franklin Roosevelt: "Repetition does not transform a lie into the truth.")

Complex Magazine has repeatedly stated that Pimp C died "of a drug overdose" after "a long and unsuccessful bout with his infatuation with the codeine and sprite mixture known as lean." In a 2014 profile on Bun B, *Texas Monthly* attributed his partner's death to an overdose of cough syrup.

In *XXL* Magazine, the story has changed over the years. In 2008 they reported that Pimp C died "after complications from a sleep apnea condition combined with a large dose of Promethazine/Codeine." Three years later it was an "accidental overdose"; by 2012 they were calling his death "an overdose of promethazine/codeine syrup," adding that "his lack of self-control ended up costing him his life."

Only a few, like MTV News and the *Port Arthur News,* have consistently reported the coroner's conclusion accurately as "a deadly combination of syrup and his sleep apnea condition."

The incorrect reports irritated Mama Wes. Of course, no mother would ever want to believe that their child died from drug-related causes: essentially a preventable, self-inflicted death. But even subtracting emotion and motherly love from the equation, there are valid reasons to suspect that there was more to Chad Butler's death than the information that has been made publicly available.

"I haven't figured it all out yet … [but] I'll tell you one thing: Do I think [his murder will] be solved? Yes. I think it will," she says.

"It always perturbs me when I hear something about C on a television show or radio show and they give him all these accolades and then say, 'He died of a drug overdose.' C did not die of a drug overdose … I don't have a problem with the truth. I really don't. But I do have a problem with slanderous allegations," Mama Wes told *B.R.E.A.D.* Magazine in 2013. "The fact is – he *is* gone. We all know that. It's been over five years now, but the pain is still as deep as it ever was, and it doesn't make me feel any better when people continuously say things like that. It was *not* an overdose. I repeat: *my son did not die of an overdose* … I will be screaming it until the day that y'all roll me down the aisle."

CHAPTER 60

"Just like [when] I was young and I watched Michael Jordan [play in] Game 6 [and] it made me wanna go right into my driveway and shoot around, well … I listened to Pimp C and [when] they said 'we drinking that lean,' it made *me* wanna drink the lean. So I picked the cup up." – Lil Wayne, 2011

"We been rapping about sipping drank for fifteen years … niggas had to catch up with us." – Pimp C, *Tha Buzz* TV, 2007

Pimp C's passing, incorrectly reported by many media outlets as a codeine overdose, would become inextricably linked to other codeine-related deaths like DJ Screw and Big Moe. Somehow, it only made the drug seem more alluring to a whole new generation of syrup sippers.

Some people didn't believe that codeine had actually killed Pimp and DJ Screw, because it seemed like *everyone* was sipping it. "I can't say that Pimp C and [DJ] Screw were no more addicted than anybody else," ponders Lil Keke. "The whole culture … It [was] all about how much you consumed."

Some had been sipping it so long they practically felt invincible. "When you've been drankin' some shit [for] like 20 years and ain't shit happen to you [yet] … you ain't really thinking about [the dangers]," says Z-Ro.

"I sipped more than Pimp, to be honest with you. That's why I'm so skeptical when people say drank killed him," adds SUC rapper Lil O. "[Hearing] of someone dying because of a codeine overdose [is] very uncommon. I been in these streets since I was 15 [and] the only people I have ever heard [of] dying from drank [are rappers]."

"You know what they say about the young lion?" asks Big Mike. "The young lion don't fear nothing, you know what I mean? The young lion thinks he's invincible." The man who once smoked fry with Pimp C is now clean and sober and avoids glorifying drugs in his music. "[Kids are] just doing it because everybody else does it," Big Mike adds. "The way they pour it up with the soda is very deceptive."

Cough syrup abuse became so widespread that the Office of National Drug Control Policy ran a PSA during the 2008 Super Bowl, a few months after Pimp C's death, which depicted a street drug dealer complaining that all his good clients had started getting high off of substances from their medicine cabinet instead. "Seems like half my customers don't need me anymore," he complained. "They're getting high for free."

Actually, *everybody* wasn't doing it. Most of the OGs who had once glorified the drug in their music – like Bun and DJ Paul of Three 6 Mafia – had long since given it up. "The shit fucked with my stomach," Bun told Rhapsody.com. He'd never considered himself a serious sipper, only going through about four ounces a month, but in the summer of 2007 he'd given it up for good. He still had a few vices – weed and liquor – but was trying to leave his immature habits in the past and learn to "deal with reality" rather than use drugs to escape from it.

At the time of Pimp's death, Bun had already recorded a song for *II Trill* which included a verse about sippin' lean, but decided it would be in "poor taste" and scrapped the verse. "While it wasn't solely the cause of his death, we have to be very real about the consequences to some of these things," he told My Fox Houston in a television interview.

On December 4, 2008, the anniversary of Chad's passing, Bun happened to stop at the mall and was approached by a few teenagers asking to take a picture with him.

"Bun B, where the drank at?" one of them asked.

"You 15. Don't even talk to me like that," Bun snapped. "Matter of fact, unless you got something real to say to me, don't even talk to me, man, because you think that's what you supposed to say … [but] that's not what it's about, homie. And today, of all days, you ought not to be talking to me 'bout no punch."

Occasionally, Bun reached out to friends like Killer Mike when he saw them "going too hard" to suggest they should slow down. He was willing to admit that records like "Sippin' on Some Syrup" looked different in retrospect. "If everyone judged themselves at 28 on what they said or did at 18 I don't think anybody would be happy with themselves," he told HipHopDX. "You get older, you learn different things, you go through life experiences … People change at their own rate."

Still, Bun stopped short of becoming an anti-syrup advocate. "That ain't my place … I'm not finna tell people to stop doing shit," he told *Raw Report DVD*. His verse on Glasses Malone's "Certified" remix ("RIP to the Pimp 'til the day I expire … sippin' on syrup") raised some eyebrows. He was also criticized for posting a picture wearing a "Purple Sprite" t-shirt on Instagram. ("How you gone wear a shirt with the same product that killed your brother?" asked one commenter.)*

"All the younger cats that you see with their Styrofoam cups walking around with their Sprite bottles and shit, I've done that," shrugs 8Ball. "I've seen all the repercussions … It really ain't no good except [for] the muthafucker selling it."

Not only does codeine wreak havoc on the intestinal tract, leading to constipation, but also slows the user's metabolism. The combination of laziness brought on by the drug, Texas-sized appetites, unhealthy eating habits, and slow metabolism leads to what Texans call "barre belly." Many syrup sippers saw their weight ballooning, leading to countless other health problems.

"Y'all would think after three felony cases I would leave drank alone," Z-Ro rapped on "I Can't Leave Drank Alone," reminiscing on pouring up a pint with DJ Screw on his 22nd birthday. Z-Ro finally did quit, once he hit 285 pounds and realized that he was so addicted to the drug it was affecting every aspect of his daily routine. Plus, he was wasting all his show money, estimating he was spending more than $20,000 a month just to get "fucked up."

Texas rapper Killa Kyleon also decided to quit syrup after he'd gained a hundred pounds and found himself spending several thousand dollars a week on his vice. Irritability was another undesirable side effect. "It gives you the worst fuckin' attitude in the world," he says.

Paul Wall had packed on over a hundred pounds partly because of his abuse of codeine and other prescription drugs like Vicodin and Xanax. In a 2010 *OZONE* interview, he said he'd quit to improve his health and his relationship with his family. Growing up, he'd spent years in drug treatment programs to cope with being abandoned by his heroin-addicted father. "As I saw myself turning into my dad, being addicted to a drug is kinda scary," he said. "It really made me just want to get better and be a better father to my kids."

Today's syrup-sippers who mix the drug with soda are actually experiencing a less potent version than the syrup sippers of the early 90s, who drank cough syrup straight out of the bottle or mixed it with Boone's Farm Wine.

To some OGs, syrup's newfound trendiness is comical. "This shit so old we don't even do it no more," laughs Lil Keke. "Like, it's done played out. And [new rappers are] on it like it came out yesterday … People used to laugh [at us for] drinking codeine. [And] this is the biggest thing

(*Similarly, in 2014, Chinara announced a Pimp C signature line as a collaboration with clothing line Black Scale. One of the featured designs, a Styrofoam cup with purple drank sloshing out of the top, prompted writer Andrew Nosnitsky to sarcastically tweet that they should also offer a "Kurt Cobain collection" with a "needle and a sawed off" in remembrance of the heroin-addicted Nirvana frontman who committed suicide in 1994.)

in the game right now; everybody talking about these Styrofoam cups and double cups."

"Back [in the mid-90s] when I was sipping it, nobody else was sipping it … people used to look at me crazy," agrees Bun.

"It's funny now [that] it's the popular thing to do with everybody," Beanie Sigel told Nahright.com. "I was talking about that on my first album, that lean. Now everybody's double-cupped up, with the dirty Sprites and all that."

And for out-of-towners who come to Houston thinking it's fashionable to carry around a Styrofoam cup, Lil Keke says they may be in for an unpleasant surprise. "You going to the penitentiary down here for that shit," he reminds visitors. Texas police now carry a straw-sized device which can detect the presence of codeine, and having a Styrofoam cup is probable cause to be detained.

Although lean was most closely affiliated with Texas, no one was more influential than New Orleans rapper Lil Wayne in bringing the trend to the mainstream. His music over the years had been peppered with codeine references, memorably rapping "I like my Sprite Easter-pink" on DJ Khaled's "We Takin' Over" and dreaming of "jumpin' off a mountain into a sea of codeine" on the haunting "I Feel Like Dying."

He later explained in a video PSA that he'd started sippin' out of respect for the culture of Southern rap. "I started drinking [codeine/promethazine] because I'm from the South," he said. "We grew up on UGK and the Geto Boys … I mean, I'm human. Just like I was young and I watched Michael Jordan [in] Game 6 [and] it made me wanna go right into my driveway and shoot around, well, I was also young and I listened to Pimp C, and [when he] said, 'we drinkin' that lean,' it made *me* wanna drink the lean. So I picked the cup up."

After Pimp C's death, Lil Wayne found his drug use under a microscope. (He was also arrested for drug possession in Arizona in the summer of 2007.) During a February 2008 performance in Newark, NJ, he took a break between songs to vent, telling the crowd he was tired of friends and family members urging him to slow down.

After the show, Wayne was frustrated when MTV News asked if Bun B had talked to him about cutting back on his syrup consumption. "No, he hasn't talked to me," he said. "But I'm going through that same shit with my friends, with my mom. Everybody wants me to stop all this and all that. It ain't that easy."

Codeine, essentially liquid heroin, is derived from the opium poppy seed. Withdrawal symptoms include severe nausea and vomiting, achy muscles, breaking out in a sweat, and shivering with the chills. "It's like [having] the worst kind of flu in the world," clinical psychiatrist Dr. Gerald Busch told *Complex*.

"It pissed me off 'cause I couldn't get off it," Lil Wayne told journalist Benjamin Meadows-Ingram. "That pissed me the fuck off … [those withdrawal symptoms] wasn't pain I could take." Although a doctor prescribed him medication to help him quit, he instead opted to try to wean himself off codeine slowly by limiting his intake. "I tell niggas to pour it for me instead of me pouring it … I be patient," he said.

"[The media] can't force Lil Wayne to stop sipping drank," Bun told Rhapsody. "That's going to be a personal choice … The kid said he would love to stop, but the withdrawal symptoms are too intense for him."

In 2011, Lil Wayne's album *Tha Carter IV* sold nearly a million copies in one week. Shortly after that, he released a video PSA announcing that he was no longer a syrup sipper, telling young fans that the drug wasn't "something to do [just] because it's cool."

"I can't blame the kids," he said. "I blame you adults. See, it's okay for a kid to look at somebody [like me or Pimp C] and see something and wanna be just like [them]. It's only right. It's only human nature … I don't do this to be cool."

"I *did* this," he finished, correcting himself with the past tense, "because I was sick." He told MTV's Sway he didn't want to be the "poster boy" for the drug. "I did it 'cause Pimp C did it, flat out," he said. "All I listen to all day is UGK."

CHAPTER 61

"C was so complex, why should we expect his death to be anything less? People want his death to be clean and straightforward, but that wasn't him. So you should expect a little turmoil and chaos in the aftermath." – Byron Amos

---

"[Chinara] stole a lot of money from those children. [And now] it's nothing left."
– Mama Wes

Chad Butler died without a will. Nitacha and Angie gave their blessing on behalf of their sons, 15-year-old Chad Jr. and seven-year-old Corey, to allow Chinara to manage his finances and serve as Administrator of his Estate. In theory, 50% of any funds received on his behalf would go to his wife, with the remaining 50% being divided equally among his three children.

But in the 16 months following Chad's death, more than $615,000 in publishing royalties and advances passed through the Estate, of which only a paltry $4,889 each was set aside for his sons.* (Revenue included a $275,000 publishing deal with Bug Music, a $75,000 advance from Rap-A-Lot for a Pimp C solo album, and a $125,000 advance from Jive/Sony for the final UGK album.) In 2010 a judge removed Chinara from her position as the Administrator of the Estate, citing "gross negligence" in her handling of the Estate's finances.

"[Chinara] stole a lot of money from those children," Mama Wes alleges. "[And now] it's nothing left. She did away with it all. And she lied and told people she was splitting it up."

Part of the problem was Byron Hill, who ran up the Estate's legal fees with an aggressive campaign trying to collect $5,173,642.47.** The figure included the $3 million dollar judgment he had managed to preserve by strategically filing bankruptcy the day before the 2003 hearing, even after a judge had declared it invalid, plus interest of nearly $900 a day since April 2001.

Less than a week after Chad's burial, Byron Hill was at the Fulton County courthouse in Atlanta obtaining a certified copy of the judgment. He had remained intent on collecting money from UGK over the years, occasionally calling Jeff Sledge with threats to sue Jive. When Chad purchased the home on Oakmont Drive, Byron registered the ominously-named corporation Shrevemont Enterprises. The purpose of the entity was unclear, but the name was apparently a combination of Mama Wes' home on Shreveport Ave. and Chad's home on Oakmont.

The six-week hiatus Chad intended to take after his return from prison to handle unfinished business had never happened. He'd expressed an interest in reaching out to Byron Hill to put their beef "to bed" but had never gotten around to making the call. "Once he came home, things were moving so fast," Mama Wes remembers. "The whole time, from the time C got [arrested] that day at that damn mall, it was just such a nightmare. It was like a rollercoaster ... it never stopped until C passed away."

(*An additional $3,919 per child is being held in the Registry of the Court in Jefferson County.)
(***Chinara's attorney Craig Schexnaider received $48,070 from the Estate in 2011, and an additional $15,830 also went towards attorneys working with Schexnaider. Schexnaider did not pay taxes on the income and was the subject of an IRS criminal investigation. In April 2013 he pled guilty to tax violations in a federal courtroom, admitting that he had not filed income tax returns since 2006. In February 2015 he turned himself in to a federal prison to begin serving 12 months.)

Byron also filed a lawsuit against Bun, who was unsure how they had ended up legally owing more than $5 million. He also sued Rap A Lot and Jive's new owner Sony, obtaining an order for them to garnish Bun's royalties. When Bun launched a tour in support of his second solo album *II Trill* at the SXSW Music Festival in Austin, Byron sued SXSW (Artists are not paid to perform at SXSW, unless they are paid by a corporate sponsor) and sent a deputy to serve Bun while he was making an appearance at the Boys and Girls Club of Austin. (The deputy reported "placing the citation in between [Bun's] forearm and body as [he] was attempting to evade service… [he then allowed] the paperwork to fall to the ground as he exited the building.")

Attempts to reopen the case in Atlanta and have the judgment overturned were unsuccessful; UGK's attorney Tanya Mitchell Graham argued that the case was "a travesty of justice." (If UGK had fought the case when it was initially filed, they could have likely argued that the contract was invalid: one, Bun and Chad were residents of Texas, not Georgia where the lawsuit was filed, and had never been served with the lawsuit. Also, Byron's contract was between Bun and a company called Nomad, Inc., which didn't exist at the time of the filing.)

To get rid of Byron Hill, Bun reluctantly paid him $100,000 out of his Jive advance for the sixth and final UGK album. Oddly, their settlement agreement included no provision releasing Chad's liability from the judgment, and it appears that no one from Bun's camp bothered to tell anyone in Chad's camp about the settlement. "I don't know what happened with [Chad's] Estate working it out with [Byron]," Bun admits, wincing at the mere mention of Byron Hill's name.

Even after collecting $100,000 from Bun, Byron continued pursuing a $5 million dollar claim against Chad's Estate, sending process servers to Chinara's house six times over the 2008 Christmas holidays.* "[Chinara] never comes to the door and whoever is present tells the officer that [Chinara] is not there," he complained in court paperwork.

The court was already irritated with Chinara for her failure to turn in required documents, complaining that her procrastination "has delayed the orderly work of the Court's staff." When Chinara didn't respond, Byron sued Jive, Zomba, Sony, Sony/BMG, ASCAP, Universal Music Publishing, Bug Music and Rap-A-Lot, attempting to garnish all funds owed to the Estate.

"My number one concern is the well-being and livelihood of his family who are the ones most deeply affected by this loss. All efforts will be made to ensure that they are properly cared for in this tragic time and beyond," Rick Martin claimed in the hours following Chad's death.

Court records tell a different story. In the 16 months following Chad's death, Rick Martin pocketed $382,874, more than 62% of the Estate's revenue, with Chinara's full approval. Included in that figure was $171,021.50 for unspecified "performance commissions" and "guest appearance commissions." (Mama Wes still handled most Pimp C show bookings and it is unclear if Rick Martin was entitled to commission for shows and features. Some have claimed that Rick did not even have a written contract with Chad.)

Rick Martin also received a hefty commission for the Bug Music publishing deal. According to producer Avery Harris, the terms of the deal, which had already been in motion at the time of Chad's death, were changed significantly. "Rick switched the [publishing] deal after Chad died from what [Chad] wanted to happen to what would benefit *Rick*," Avery alleges. "He only allowed people to make money if it was gonna benefit him."

(*The Estate was also being pursued, albeit less aggressively, by Nashville promoter Hans Niknejad of Twin Entertainment. He had obtained a $64,128 judgment against UGK because they did not file an answer in his lawsuit relating to the failed UGK show in Atlanta. He claimed he was owed $91,558.09, including interest. He had attempted to garnish UGK's publishing checks through Jive/Sony, but failed because he referred to them as UGK, Inc., an entity which does not exist. Mama Wes says she was never aware of the Tennessee lawsuit. If UGK had been aware of the lawsuit and hired an attorney, it seems they would have two valid arguments – Niknejad himself was in breach of contract because he had not paid their full fee. Secondly, UGK arrived at the venue prepared to perform and fulfill their obligations, but apparently due to Niknejad's failure to properly promote the show, both parties agreed to cancel the show and rebook it at a later time. UGK's contract also stated that it was governed by Texas law, so they could have easily disputed Niknejad's Tennessee-based lawsuit.)

Naztradamus says that Rick similarly cut him out of revenues for the *Underground Kingz: Making of the Album* DVD after Chad died. "Pimp was about helping people," Naztradamus says. "[But] Rick was not about that shit. Rick was an asshole."

After cashing in, Rick Martin promptly disappeared. "I haven't heard from that fucker since August 2008," Mama Wes says.

———————

After several years passed and Chinara still had not filed an answer to Byron's claim, he was able to convince the Court to force her to turn over the Estate's financial documents and eventually requested that she be removed as the Administrator of the Estate. Byron complained that Chinara had authorized the $171,021 payment to Rick Martin with no documentation, saying, "There is no apparent reason for the retention of a personal manager for an artist who is deceased." It was also noted that Nancy Byron had received $21,912 for publicity services. (Nancy, who was managed by Provident Financial, the same financial management firm as the Estate, says the check was for publicity services performed prior to Chad's death.)

Another point of contention was the fact that the $150,000 in jewelry which Chinara listed as an Estate asset on her initial financial filings had apparently disappeared. When confronted by Nitacha, Chinara claimed the jewelry had been stolen. When she returned to Los Angeles to retrieve Chad's jewelry from the safe deposit box where Craig Wormley's investigator Chuck Steeno had placed it for safekeeping, Chinara claimed the jewelry had either gone missing or been replaced by worthless imitations.

The judge agreed with Byron, ruling that Chinara had "misapplied, or … is about to misapply … the [Estate's] property committed to her care." The Court ruled that Chinara "does not fully understand the duties and responsibilities required of [her]," "cannot account for certain estate assets," "cannot recall the names of the law firms she used," "cannot identify assets which belong to the estate," and "filed conflicting and ambiguous documents with the Court."

"The actions and inactions of Chinara Butler comprise both negligence and gross negligence concerning proper administration of the estate," the judge concluded, removing her as the Estate's Administrator in 2010.*

"The truth is, she's in way over her head," observed Mama Wes. "[Chinara] really shoulda left that shit alone."

Chinara was also in danger of losing the Oakmont house, the Estate's biggest asset. (The leased silver Bentley was returned promptly after Chad's death, and Nitacha claims the red Bentley was given to Rick Martin.) The property was scheduled for a foreclosure auction six times after Chad's death, but the bank was unable to foreclose through traditional methods because the mortgage was listed in Chad's name only. Legal proceedings on the property are still ongoing. (In 2013, the mortgage company claimed Chinara had not paid the monthly $1,643.79 payment in five years. "That's probably right, she don't pay nobody," quips Mama Wes.)

The $75,000 Rap-A-Lot advance Chinara accepted in 2008 gave them exclusive ownership of all Pimp C solo records he had recorded since October 2000. She also agreed to turn over 10 masters to Rap-A-Lot. When the label leaked "Grippin' on the Wood" in the summer of 2011 to build up a buzz for Pimp C's second posthumous solo album *Still Pimpin'*, Chinara told AllHipHop she wasn't "feeling" the record and alleged she hadn't been paid.*

On June 16, 2011, Chinara's attorney Craig Schexnaider faxed Rap-A-Lot a letter ordering

———

(*Chinara was later reinstated as the Estate's Administrator after posting a bond.)
(**"Grippin On The Wood" featured Bun and Big K.R.I.T., who told *XXL*, "I never would have dreamed in a million years [I'd be on a record with UGK]. To be influenced by them so much, to actually have a record, an unheard Pimp C verse, and to be able to be on it? It's crazy, man." The beat and hook of Scarface's popular 1998 record "Fuck Faces" was recycled for "Finer Things" featuring Slim Thug and Brooke Valentine. Smoke D, Paul Wall, Da Underdawgz, Too $hort, Lil Keke, Killa Kyleon, Cory Mo, Hezeleo, Vicious, and C-Bo were also featured on the album, which overall got mediocre reviews.)

9   Chinara Butler, as Independent Administratrix of the Estate of Chad Lamont Butler, Deceased, misapplied, lost and/or caused to be lost and/or misapplied jewelry belonging to the estate which had a stated value of $150,000 00

10   Chinara Butler negligently allowed Provident Financial Management to become manager of financial affairs of the estate assets and was negligent in overseeing the activities of Provident Financial Management concerning the financial affairs of the estate

11   Chinara Butler, as Independent Administratrix of the Estate of Chad Lamont Butler, Deceased, negligently caused Provident Financial Management to be engaged as appraiser of the Estate of Chad Lamont Butler, Deceased

12   Chinara Butler, as Independent Administratrix of the Estate of Chad Lamont Butler, Deceased, negligently engaged FM2 Radio, Inc , to serve as agent for the Estate of Chad Lamont Butler, Deceased

13   Chinara Butler, as Independent Administratrix of the Estate of Chad Lamont Butler, Deceased, negligently executed a note in the amount of $171,021 50, payable to FM2 Radio, L L C , for unproven and undocumented monies due for unpaid artists performance commission and unpaid artist guest appearance commissions

14   Chinara Butler does not fully understand the duties and responsibilities required of an Independent Administratrix

15   Chinara Butler cannot account for certain estate assets while she served as the Independent Administratrix of the estate

16   Chinara Butler cannot recall the names of the law firms she used while serving as Independent Administratrix of the estate

17   Chinara Butler cannot identify assets which belong to the estate

18   Chinara Butler filed conflicting and ambiguous documents with the Court while serving as Independent Administratrix of the estate

19   The actions and inactions of Chinara Butler comprise both negligence and gross negligence concerning proper administration of the estate while serving as Independent Administratrix of the estate

Above: **Court documents** citing the reasons for Chinara's removal as Administrator of the Estate in 2010.

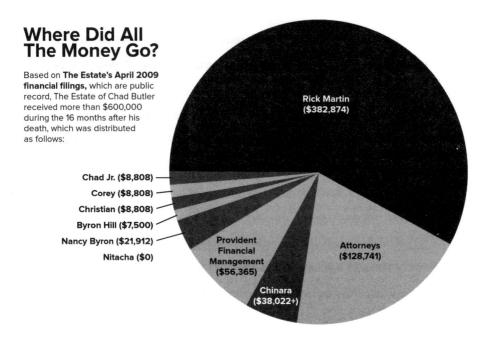

Where Did All The Money Go?

Based on **The Estate's April 2009 financial filings,** which are public record, The Estate of Chad Butler received more than $600,000 during the 16 months after his death, which was distributed as follows:

Rick Martin ($382,874)

Chad Jr. ($8,808)
Corey ($8,808)
Christian ($8,808)
Byron Hill ($7,500)
Nancy Byron ($21,912)
Nitacha ($0)

Provident Financial Management ($56,365)

Attorneys ($128,741)

Chinara ($38,022+)

Chinara Butler makes all the business decisions for the heirs of Chad L. Butler, (a/k/a Pimp C). Pimp C passed away in 2007. I represent Chinara Butler.

There is a contract between Rap-A-Lot and Chinara Butler. The contract names Pimp C Enterprises as the responsible party for Pimp C's music. Pimp C Enterprises no longer exists and Chinara Butler has no affiliation with Pimp C Enterprises, LLC.

Chinara Butler is the person that can and will contract regarding all of Pimp C's music, likeness, writings, photographs, etc.

You had a contract signed by Chinara Butler. You have failed to perform your contractual obligations under that contract. **As of today, you are to stop, cease and desist any activities with respect to Pimp C.** This includes any releases, any publication, any advertisements, any sales and anything else regarding Pimp C.

According to the internet, you are releasing music which has never been released. You have not conferred with Chinara Butler on this release. You have not paid Chinara Butler for a previous release. In fact, you have not paid Chinara Butler in a long time and it does not appear as if you have ever intended to do so. You have not paid engineers and production people with respect to Pimp C productions. As such, you have voided your contract with Chinara Butler.

You are to stop all activities related to Pimp C as of today, June 16, 2011.

Thank you for your cooperation in this matter.

Yours very truly,

Craig J. Schexnaider

CJS/ksb

Above: **A 2011 letter from Chinara's attorney to Rap-A-Lot.** Rap-A-Lot responded by filing a lawsuit.

them to "stop, cease and desist any activities with respect to Pimp C." "According to the internet, you are releasing music which has never been released," it said. "You have not conferred with Chinara Butler on this release. You have not paid Chinara Butler for a previous release. In fact, you have not paid Chinara Butler in a long time and it does not appear as if you have ever intended to do so."

Rap-A-Lot promptly filed a lawsuit against Chinara, claiming she was withholding masters that they contractually owned. "I'm being sued when you are putting out a project and I haven't even received my money or anything from?" she told AllHipHop, adding, "I just think it's sad."

Bun kept his distance from the whole situation, while Mama Wes found the idea of Chinara waging war against J. Prince in a courtroom hilarious. "You're not gonna win the lawsuit against [Rap-A-Lot] in Houston, so you might as well go and sit down somewhere," she chuckles.*

The Byron Hill saga finally came to an end in July 2011. His attorneys had long since withdrawn from the case, but Byron pressed forward pro se. A settlement was finally reached in which he would receive $7,500 from the Estate in exchange for the return of "certain [Pimp C] memorabilia" and dismissal of the judgment.

Since then, it appears that Chinara still receives Pimp C-related revenue from a variety of sources. Publishing checks come from ASCAP, Universal Music Publishing, AARC, Sony BMG, and other entities. (In 2008, the Estate's accounting firm Provident Financial estimated that the Estate would receive $274,316 a year for the next eight years, although this estimate was based on *4 Life* selling more than it actually did. From ASCAP alone the Estate has received more than $50,000 since Chad's death.) Chinara also has licensed Pimp C's name and image for a variety of other products including air fresheners and vaporizers. Her "Pimp C Forever" t-shirts, she told the *Port Arthur News*, would benefit the "Children of Chad Butler Trust Fund."**

Many well-intentioned rappers announced publicly that they were donating money to Pimp C's children. Fonzworth Bentley donated the publishing from his record "C.O.L.O.U.R.S." to Chinara and joked that the only thing he wanted in return was the chance to try on one of Pimp C's mink coats. Jazze Pha donated several records; T.I. announced he was donating proceeds from his "P.I.M.P." record to the family. Pimp C verses have appeared on high-profile projects from artists like Juicy J, Jay-Z, and A$AP Rocky, presumably for a hefty fee.

Bun publicly commended Chinara for being "strong" enough to "take charge after her husband passed away, honestly with an occupation that she knew nothing about" by handling Pimp's rap career. Others felt that those tasks should have been handed to Mama Wes.

Chinara frequently contacted Jeff Sledge asking questions about UGK publishing checks and other sources of income. (UGK, indebted to Jive more than $4.4 million at the time of Chad's death, doesn't receive royalty checks.) Jeff, already irritated at the way Chinara had tried to bully them after Chad's death, didn't like her approach. "She was very money-hungry," Jeff says. "It was more about money for her ... she didn't care about the UGK legacy. She just wanted some bread. And she made things very difficult."

"When Pimp C died I bought the car back from his family," Chamillionaire said in a radio interview. "You know why I bought it? Because I wanted to do something for his family." This transaction was not reflected in the Estate's financial filings, prompting Nitacha to confront Chinara about the money from the car. (According to Nitacha, Chinara said she had merely given the car to Chamillionaire for "safekeeping" and had not received any money for it.)

(*Chinara never filed a response and the lawsuit was dismissed in December 2011.)
(**According to Mama Wes, Chinara doesn't have custody of her daughter Christian, who has been in the care of her grandmother since a complaint was filed with CPS. "[Chinara's mother Normia] wanted that child, and what Normia wants, Normia gets," says Mama Wes. Shari Pulliam, a media spokeswoman for the Texas DFPS/CPS, was unable to confirm if there had been complaints lodged against Chinara, citing confidentiality concerns. If Christian is indeed living with a family member such as Chinara's mother, this would mean that CPS did not take custody. "When I searched the name to see if we had taken custody there was no match," Pulliam explains. "But, that does not mean [CPS] weren't involved at all. If we ... investigated a case without taking custody that information is confidential.")

Financial filings for the Estate don't reflect income from any of these side projects, and if there is money being set aside somewhere for Chad's sons, no one seems to know where it is.

"I think that the kids deserve to profit way more than they are," says Mama Wes, who is left in the dark when it comes to the financial dealings of the Estate. "They oughta be the ones to get [those funds]. They're his kids, and they're growing up, and they have needs. It's as simple as that … I have no doubt in my mind that C would want his kids to be taken care of properly. When he was here … he spoiled them to death."

By all accounts, Chad was generous with his children and always made sure they were cared for properly. But legally, he hadn't been making child support payments since he went to prison and owed Nitacha nearly $119,189.

Nitacha filed a claim twice with the Estate hoping to collect a portion of the back child support and grew frustrated when her claim was denied twice with no explanation. Nitacha says she has never received financial statements, and conference calls with Chinara, Rick Martin, and Chinara's attorney didn't help resolve the situation. "How did the Estate get fucked over as far as the money?" Nitacha wonders aloud. "Why is it not there? Where are the royalties?"

"I trusted [that] when [Chad] died, [Chinara] was fighting to make sure that the kids were straight," Nitacha says. "I would [have] loved to have funds set up for [Chad Jr.] for him to continue [his education]. That's money his daddy worked for. Why shouldn't he get his share?"

Chad Jr. graduated from high school in June 2011, a proud moment for everyone in his family. "I never got to see C do it, so I've been waiting for this for 17 years," Mama Wes excitedly gushed before his graduation.

Five months later, just before Thanksgiving, 18-year-old Chad and his high school sweetheart Crishonda "Cre" Valsin showed up at Mama Wes' house on Shreveport Ave., both struggling to suppress smiles, and announced that they had some big news. "From that grin I'm looking at on your faces, I don't know whether I wanna hear this," Mama Wes said.

"Well, she ain't pregnant," said Chad Jr., pausing for dramatic effect before continuing, "But we got married." The two had chosen the lucky date of 11/11/11 for their surprise nuptials and elected to tell Mama Wes first, as the "only young old person" they knew.

After the initial shock wore off, Mama Wes wondered aloud how the elder Chad would have taken the news. "Like you, Granny," Chad Jr. theorized. "He would've probably said, 'Nigga, why didn't you tell me?' but then he would've been okay. He would've said, 'Well, it's yo' thang.'"

Passionate about technology, Chad Jr. builds computers as a hobby and his mother Nitacha considers him "a beast with any technical gadget." He's a talented guitar and piano player and has dabbled in music production, but was sent back to the drawing board when Mama Wes declared his early production attempts as "boo-boo." "Think about the things your dad did," she advised him. "You don't want to imitate him, but you want your music to be [just] as rich."

He's considered the possibility of working behind-the-scenes in some capacity in the music business, but rapping isn't in Chad Jr.'s future –unless he can invent a character like his father did. "I'm an inward person. I don't like to be in the spotlight too much … If I [had to be] in the spotlight, [that person] might not be me," says Chad Jr. "I'd probably have to turn into somebody else, like my dad used to do. [Pimp C] was basically a persona … just another side of him, a little part of him that he didn't always use. I could see him instantly switch back and forth."

With his father gone too soon, Chad Jr. feels great responsibility not only towards the family he's building with his new wife, but the father figure role he's inherited for his two younger siblings. "I constantly think about how I can better myself to help the rest of my family," he says. "I just want to have a successful life, [so] I can support myself and the closest members of my family. That's all I really want to do; I don't think too much about anything else anymore."

Corey continued living with Mama Wes after Chad passed. "Having a piece of Chad … is better than nothing at all," she says. "He might be bad as hell, but he's mine."

Even as a child, Corey was very conscious of the void his father left behind. "He just thinks if he was here, things would be different," his mother Angie sighs. "I tried as hard as I can … you can never make him not miss him, but we go overboard – I think everyone does – trying to [help], but we could never do the things C did."

While Chad Jr. avoids social media and has little interest in the music industry, Corey's Instagram tagline reads, "I'll be famous one day." Chad always envisioned Chad Jr. becoming a producer and Corey becoming a rapper. As Mama Wes sees it, Chad's sons inherited his different personalities. "Chaddyboo is strictly Chad, maybe a touch of C, but Corey is all those [other characters]," she says. "Corey is *Pimp C's* son. Chaddyboo is *Chad's* son."

Relatives marvel at Corey's mannerisms, which they say remind them of Chad. "If there ever was [such a thing as] tripolar, Corey would have it," jokes Chad's godmother Brenda's daughter Janeen Harmon. "He's got a little bit of Chad, Corey, Pimp C, and a couple other people mixed into one."

"That nigga's just like C, and it's not just because he hangs around me," laughs Mama Wes.*

Although Corey showed an interest in rap, Mama Wes was initially firm in her decision to not allow him to rap until he was 16. In 2010, Chad's former neighbor Ronda Forrest moved back to Port Arthur. Her son Travione was Corey's age and the two boys hit it off immediately. Tra had already been bitten by the rap bug, wearing a gold dookie rope everywhere and adopting the nickname "Iceman."

When Tra got a last-minute opportunity to open up for Diggy Simmons at the nearby Montagne Center, Mama Wes didn't have the heart to stop Corey from joining his friend on stage. On the ride home, the boys told Ronda they'd decided to form a group: the underground kidz, or UGKidz.

A few weeks later, with Snoop Dogg coming to town, Ronda arranged for the boys to be one of the opening acts. Mama Wes still wasn't sold on the idea. "He can go with [Tra to] the lil' shows, y'know, he can be the little hype man, but I really don't want him doing too much with it," she told Ronda.

Before Snoop went on stage, Mama Wes was invited on his tour bus. Snoop had already seen video footage of the boys' performance. "[That boy] got his swagger," Snoop told her. "Y'know, [Pimp and I] had talked about that, and … he told me he didn't want [his son] to be a child rapper."

"That's exactly the words he used with me," Mama Wes smiled.

"I was telling him to let him get [ready] if he thought he had any talent," Snoop said. He began laughing. "It's just like my kids," he said, referencing his sons Cordé and Cordell, who were around the same age as Chad Jr. and Corey. "We had talked about that, and I think – C said he was gonna talk to you about that. Because he thought that [Corey] should be groomed now."

"It's really strange that you would bring that up, because I'm right at that crossroads right now," Mama Wes said thoughtfully. "On one side, I'm hearing C say, 'I don't want him to be a child rapper,' and then I'm looking at him – who wants to get involved. Frankly, I don't give a damn what anybody else thinks."

"I think C had moved over to that side," Snoop nodded.

"After a very intimate and beautiful and wonderful conversation with Snoop … I made the decision to go ahead and let them hook up and [become the] underground kidz," Mama Wes told *B.R.E.A.D.* Magazine.

With the help of Ronda's brother Ron "Crumz" Forrest and their cousin David "D-A" Frost,

---

(*Mama Wes believes that because of Chad's favoritism towards Corey, Chinara holds a grudge against the child. "Chinara never questioned [Corey's paternity] as long as [Chad] was living, but as soon as he died, *she* started [questioning his paternity]," says Mama Wes. In 2014 Chinara "executive produced" a 75-page digital book called *King of Trill*, a purported Pimp C biography riddled with inconsistencies and typos, which implied that Chad only had two children and seemed to deliberately omit any mention of Corey.)

the boys released several records over the summer of 2012, trying to stay kid-friendly with themes like "Sugar Crash" ("belly full of junk, I ain't even eatin' lunch").

———————————

"To my knowledge Bun B is the only person I really know that's actually went above and beyond for [Pimp's] family ... Everybody else that screamed 'Pimp C,' I didn't see anybody else doing nothing," Chamillionaire said in a radio interview shortly after Pimp's death.

Mama Wes disagrees with the statement, saying that Bun has largely been absent from the boys' lives. Instead, Paul Wall, Slim Thug, Trae, and 2 Chainz are among those who have built a relationship with the boys, giving generously of both their time and money.

While Bun is widely revered in the rap world, his relationship with Chad's sons is just as strained as it was with Chad in the months prior to his death. As the most visible representative of Pimp C, Bun received the bulk of condolences from the public. It was an outpouring of love which he himself sometimes tried to deflect, but some in Chad's life resented him for it.

Nitacha was especially offended when Bun appeared on *The Mo'Nique Show* on BET in March 2011. After Bun plugged Pimp C's posthumous album *The Naked Soul of Sweet James Jones*, Mo'Nique asked, "With his new CD that's out right now, will his family benefit?"

"Absolutely, his family's already benefiting from it through the record label, of course, Rap-A-Lot Records," Bun responded. "J. Prince is a very good person, he's a very fair person, and the family has been compensated financially."

"All you Pimp C fans out there, make sure you go out and support that brother, because it will benefit his wife and his babies!" gushed Mo'Nique. "Even though he's passed on, baby, let's make sure his family is gonna be okay!"

It all sounded great on television, but it wasn't actually true – of the $75,000 Rap-A-Lot advance for the project, Chinara had signed most of it over to Rick Martin. None of it benefited Chad's "babies," at least not his sons.

"I don't have too much respect for [Bun or J. Prince] or any of them," says Nitacha. "[Bun] does this in every interview, and it pisses me off ... he claims in every interview [that] he's taking care of the kids... [that he and] J. Prince [are] making sure the kids are doing great ... Are you fucking kidding me?"

Tensions between Bun and Corey, who is more outspoken than his brother, came to a head at Stephen Jackson's August 2012 Back to School concert in Port Arthur. Bun commented disapprovingly on Corey's venture into the rap world, telling him he should be playing somewhere and "having fun" like a kid.

Hurt at "Uncle Bun's" comment, Corey snapped back. "I *am* having fun," he said. "This is what we do for fun ... and we play basketball and eat Granny's food, too."

Mama Wes feels that Bun's "preachy approach" when he attempts to fill in as a father figure doesn't work well with Corey. "I don't think [Bun] understands," she says. "I really don't think he means any harm."

While Chad Jr. is laid back and amicable, preferring not to be involved in any drama, his mother Nitacha is angry at the people in the music industry whom she believes use him when it's convenient but don't put in the time or effort to build a real relationship with him. Bun, she says, is absent from birthday parties and graduations. "I wish [they'd] either love him or leave him alone," Nitacha says. "Either be in his life or stay the fuck out of his life ... If he needed anything, he couldn't [even] call Bun. He don't have Bun's number."

"This is the same nigga that used to sleep at [Mama Wes] house and eat all her food, you know what I'm saying?" says XVII. "[Bun] don't fuck with them kids ... [It's] not no beef shit, it's just the truth ... [and] I know it would hurt Pimp."

"We're all supposed to be family," Corey's mom Angie sighs. "I don't know."

CHAPTER 62

"[UGK is] in the center of so many things in Hip-Hop, so many branches, [they're] damn near [the] trunk of the fuckin' tree. In a hundred years we'll look at [their legacy] and we'll see it all. They'll look cool in black and white."
— Curren$y, *Sama'an Ashrawi's All Star Tribute to UGK* documentary

"UGK's legacy is gonna be both sides of the equation. You've got the ignorant part [of their music] – I guess some people could see it that way – but [on] the other side of the equation, [their music] shows you the consequences and how doing wrong affects the soul and it affects the people around you. That's what I've always got from them."
— Dizzee Rascal, *Sama'an Ashrawi's All Star Tribute to UGK* documentary

On December 29, 2007, which would have been Chad's 34th birthday, Mama Wes and Bun B hosted a party at the Venecian in Houston. Mama Wes arrived in a white stretch SUV with Chad Jr. and Corey, all wearing red Dickies.

"He's here tonight," Mama Wes told the crowd. "He was gonna be in the house tonight in the flesh, but he's here in spirit … I admire all of you for coming out to say Happy Birthday to my precious angel baby. He is an angel now, and he's just walking around heavy, all day. I know he is. I talk to him every day, and some of you may hear from him."

"If you loved him, if you respected him … I want you to give that love to my Bun B, because he's gonna carry it on. He's gonna do what he got to do, and we gonna keep on moving," she said. "Give all that love! I want you to say it right now: 'I give all that love'..."

"*I give all that love!*" the crowd shouted.

"To Bun B!"

"*To Bun B!*"

"All I had for Pimp C, I give it to Bun B!" Mama Wes said. "Because he's gonna carry on the legacy. UGK will never die! Pimp C is not dead, he's just a little bit absent right now. And I respect you, I love you, I love all of you for coming out. Pray for us!"

Bun turned down hefty show offers for Christmas and New Year's Eve, worried that he wasn't emotionally prepared to perform. It wasn't until February 8, 2008, that he took the stage in front of a diverse crowd at Warehouse Live for the first show after Pimp C's death. He brought out Slim Thug for "3 Kings," Mike Jones for "My '64," and Z-Ro for "Get Throwed" before launching into a set of UGK classics.

"It was probably the first time I cried on stage," Bun told journalist Jesse Serwer. "It was just real. But there wasn't many dry eyes in the room. I'm not the only person that loves Pimp C, and I know it."

The show even generated coverage in the *New York Times*: "Houston's Hip-Hop Scene Picks Up the Pieces After Yet Another Death," it reported, running through the requisite mentions of DJ Screw and Big Moe's syrup-related deaths. "It's a cardinal rule of tribute concerts and memorial services and newspaper articles about great musicians who die too young: You're supposed to emphasize the good, saying something comforting about a spirit living on, forever unforgotten," observed writer Kalefa Sanneh. "And it's true: Pimp C's brash voice will echo for a long time … But on Friday night it was hard not to be overwhelmed by what's gone. Houston's sad roll call keeps getting longer."

It was tough for Bun to get back in the studio after Chad's passing, but with his second solo album *II Trill* scheduled to drop in May 2008, he didn't have a choice. (Pimp was featured on the album along with Chamillionaire on "Underground Thang.") Highlights included the Mr. Lee-produced "You're Everything," with Rick Ross, David Banner, and 8Ball & MJG, and the uptempo "Pop It 4 Pimp" from Trill Entertainment's producer Mouse.

One of the last songs Bun recorded for the album was "Angel in the Sky," a dedication track to Pimp with a hook sung by Razah. "I guess I just assumed we had more time / For us to make more music and write more rhymes," Bun rapped, reminiscing on the times back when "it all began on Shreveport Ave., sittin' off in the den."

At the BET Awards the following month, UGK won Best Group and Video of the Year for "Int'l Player's Anthem." It's hard to do this with my brother not being here," Bun, accompanied by Chinara, said during his acceptance speech. "We want to thank y'all for supporting UGK all these years."

On the evening of August 10, 2008, while Mama Wes was in Houston attending events surrounding the OZONE Awards, she got a call informing her that her mother had passed away. The obituary for Chad's Grandma Bessie saluted her "92 years, 6 months, 18 hours, and 50 minutes of trials, tribulations, sunshine and rain."

Later that night, Jeezy brought Bun out for a special guest performance during his concert at Houston's Arena Place. "I got some shit on my mind. Don't go nowhere, my nigga," Jeezy told Bun before he stepped off stage.

"I'm right here, baby," Bun responded.

Jeezy, wearing a black leather vest with the United States flag on the back, launched into "My President is Black," his anthem in support of presidential candidate Barack Obama. He rapped a capella:

It's all love, Bun, I'm forgiving you, Pimp C
You know how the Pimp be, that nigga gon' speak his mind
If he could speak down from heaven, he'd tell me stay on my grind

The highlight of the OZONE Awards the following night at Houston's George R. Brown Convention Center was a Pimp C tribute set featuring rappers covering Pimp's verses on "Big Pimpin'" (Too $hort), "Int'l Player's Anthem" (David Banner, joined by Big Boi of OutKast), "Pocket Full of Stones" (Hezeleo and 8Ball), "One Day" (Webbie, Lil Boosie, and singer Billy Cook).

During the grand finale, which featured Bun performing "Angel in the Sky" backed by a live choir, the family emerged on stage behind him holding hands. "That night was kinda emotional," remembers Corey's mom Angie. "That song, Bun's song … it put a little jagged edge in there. It was sad."

The only family members absent from the stage were Chinara and her daughter Christian, who remained backstage. Chinara frequently sought to distance herself from the rest of the family. "It was just drama, drama from the beginning of that day," remembers Angie.

On December 4, 2008, the one year anniversary of Pimp's death, Matt Sonzala's Damage Control Radio aired an emotional three-hour tribute show, which featured call-ins from Mama Wes and J. Prince. They also premiered a few unreleased UGK tracks from the 90s, like "Weed Weed."

"One thing about Pimp, you know, UGK was his dream," Bun said. "UGK was something that he sat in his bedroom at 5048 Shreveport … and that's what he prayed for, to visualize, to actually come true … It may seem like it came out of nowhere, man, but that was a grand vision."

"It's a lot of people that say they 'bout they music and they 'bout they movement," Bun added. "But I have yet to meet a man that lived and breathed what he talked about more than [Pimp C], and [not just] in music. I don't know a boxer that loved boxing the way Pimp loved this Southern music, man. I don't know a football player that loved being on the field or a basketball player that loved being on the court or a baseball player on the diamond … I never met anybody who's passion for what they were doing exceeded Chad Butler's. *Never.*"

The last caller of the night was Smit-D, who had been released on parole two months earlier and reminisced on his emotional conversation with Chad at the Darrington Unit. "God put it on my heart to call," Smit began. "I really, really need everybody to know that Chad had God first. Chad is in *Heaven*, man. You know? Chad is in Heaven. When you lose somebody, sometimes you wonder if he really went to Heaven. You know, 'Pac hollered, 'Is there Heaven for a G?' … Well, the gates opened up for Chad Butler, man. The gates opened up for him and he's in Heaven resting with the Father up there, man. I want everybody to know that … Chad had a real relationship with God, y'know?"

With Bun's solo album in stores, focus turned to the UGK album. Jive again offered Bun the option to replace Pimp and bring in another group member, but since this was the sixth and final album to complete their contract, he felt it was only fitting to put UGK to rest with the final album *4 Life*. "We kind of knew what we had to do, because … in a sense, we had done it before," Bun said, realizing that Pimp's incarceration had been sort of a test run.

Bun and Pimp had been in such a creative groove while recording *Underground Kingz* that they'd continued recording even after filling two discs. Since they had several extra songs and had already developed themes and concepts prior to Pimp's passing, the task was more challenging emotionally than musically. Recording sessions often turned into sorrowful reminiscing. The first sessions at Mike and Cory Mo's studio were the hardest; they ended up reminiscing and laughing, and eventually crying with the realization that Chad would never be there again.

During one session, when Bun and Cory Mo were going through some unused vocals from one of Pimp's first recording sessions when he came home from prison, Pimp proclaimed he was "back from the dead!" They looked at each other. "Damn, man, we gotta make that the intro," Cory Mo said.

"Muthafuckers all up in [the studio] crying and shit," Bun recalled in an *OZONE* interview. "It took a while to get all of that out and get to business." Since Pimp had already been grooming a new collective of producers, like Avery, DJ B-Do, Steve Below, and Cory Mo, it was only natural that they handle the bulk of the production. "[Working with them was] the best chance I had of trying to keep the UGK sound intact," Bun told *Pitchfork*.

They were up for the challenge, but at the same time, knew they wouldn't be able to replace Pimp. "There's no use in trying to duplicate what he did, because I won't be able to do it, and there's no use fooling myself into thinking that I can," Steve Below told the *Houston Chronicle*. Cory Mo's technique was to imagine Pimp sitting next to him, giving him instructions.

When artists like Pharrell and Lil Wayne reached out wanting to be a part of the final UGK album, Bun had to make a tough decision: stay true to their original fanbase or try to reach the mainstream? In the end, he decided to do what he believed Pimp would've done: stick with longtime friends of UGK like Too $hort, Sleepy Brown, E-40, Big Gipp, and Lil Boosie and Webbie.

"There were extreme amounts of resources available to me for this UGK album," he explained. "I can't think of an artist in the industry that didn't want to be a part of this album in some form or fashion. But it would be far too easy to put the Lil Wayne's, Kanye's and Jay-Z's of the world on the album for exploitive purposes."

For the lead single, they went with "Da Game Been Good to Me," the track Avery produced which Pimp had recorded in frustration after his heated phone call with Smoke D. They removed Pimp's Jeezy disses from Da Underdawgz record "Used to Be" and gave it a new beat. Another unreleased track which ended up on *4 Life* was Akon's "Hard As Hell," which had been cut from the double album.

In the vault Bun pulled up the Mannie Fresh track "Here We Go Again," one of the first songs they'd recorded together after Pimp's return. It was retitled "The Pimp & The Bun," with Ronald Isley singing the hook. Also from the vaults came "The Southern Sound," an unfinished *Ridin' Dirty* leftover, which was modified to create the "7th St." and "Texas Ave." interludes.

"She Luv It," the Cory Mo-produced track which was pulled from the double album due to an issue with clearing the R. Kelly sample, was also repurposed. Cory called on one of Pimp's favorite guitar players, Rick Marcel, for assistance, experimenting with three or four different beats before settling on the perfect track to go with the vocals. "It's hard as hell to [build a song backwards] like that," he says. "I'd never done that before." The remixed version of "She Luv It" still had open space for another verse, and Bun gave the opportunity to locals Slim Thug and Killa Kyleon.

Overall, the recording process went much smoother with Jive on *4 Life* than it ever had in the past. Bun credited this to the "very human side of Barry Weiss" being "very understanding with the circumstances." (It probably also had something to do with the absence of Pimp's temperamental personality.)

The album was turned over to producer/engineer Mike Dean (whom Bun B called "the best hands you can get touching music") for mixing and mastering. It was a process which he described as "extremely emotional," given his long-standing friendship with Pimp. Dean laughed when asked by MTV News if there would be any Auto-Tune on the project. "He would've come up from the dead and given me a bitch slap!" Dean joked.

When it was released on March 31, 2009, UGK's *4 Life* hit #1 on the *Billboard* rap charts. Music critics considered it unusually good for a posthumous rap album, normally "the most vile of Hip-Hop banalities." HipHopDX called it "a gift to UGK purists," concluding, "Bun and company have done a remarkable job of synthesizing Pimp's vision given the circumstances. UGK *4 Life* needs no formal Pimp C tribute because the album itself is a grand testament to his legacy."

"It would have been tempting (and easy) to fill the disc with somber tributes and memories," agreed the *Houston Chronicle*. "But … Pimp C remains very much alive throughout the 16 tracks built around vocals he left behind."

"This is the last album as far as UGK is concerned," Bun told the *Houston Chronicle*, adding, "The [posthumous] music doesn't really matter to me. I'd give it all back if I could have my friend back."

———————

Mainstream media had always embraced Bun as the articulate, political half of UGK, and his partner's passing only solidified Bun's image as what the *Houston Press* called "Hip-Hop's grieving widower, the guy for whom you want to leave a pot roast on the front steps." MTV News worshiped Bun as "one of our favorite people ever in the history of this rap game."

Still, journalist Andrew Nosnitsky felt that the common perception of Bun as the "ideal interview subject" and Pimp as the disgruntled, difficult one was somewhat misguided. "Folks don't realize [that] Pimp was every bit as friendly … [and] as happy to talk to me about music as I was to him," he wrote on CocaineBlunts.com, explaining, "[As a music journalist] you really learn to appreciate the occasions where you're made to feel like a human being and not just a receptacle for release dates … Pimp was probably the first 'celebrity' rapper to treat me as such."

He also expressed disappointment in the direction of Bun's music was going since Pimp's passing. In response to the leak of the DJ Premier-produced "Let 'Em Know" in July 2010 from Bun's third solo album *Trill OG* (trilogy, get it?), Nosnitsky criticized Bun's "phoned-in" verse and Premier's "generic" beat, accusing both of lazily "resting on their laurels" instead of pushing forward to greater levels of creativity.*

In Nosnitsky's opinion, Bun and Premier were merely being praised for their "inherited martyrdom" after the loss of their partners. (Like Bun, DJ Premier was also a rap widower after the death of his rap partner Keith "Guru" Elam in April 2010.) "Not to sound callous, but … the friends of dead rappers get better promotion too," he wrote. With no Pimp C to challenge him creatively, and not many rappers on his level to push him, he wondered if Bun was falling off into mediocrity, adding:

The boost in career attention that [Bun] has seen in recent years has coincided with a rapidly decreasing technical ability. Some of this comes with age but mostly I think he's been spreading himself too thin. As a guest rapper he remains in high demand, offering tokenism to See I Always Liked The South Northerners, "lyrical" legitimacy to half assed rappers, mentorship to up and comers, reverence to his predecessors and a selling point to his former peers. But very rarely does he give any of them a great verse in the process … his rhymes are uniformly predictable … for a rap veteran of his stature.

He often gets away with it because … a lot of the people who propped him up in the first place aren't fully aware of or personally invested into the heights he once reached. And the rest are so blinded by his significance that they wouldn't dare criticize him. This is an unfortunate turn of events because, as Bun would probably tell you himself, being a lyrical monster was his primary contribution to UGK while emotions and ideas were more Pimp's domain. In his prime Bun was the Black Thought of the South. Strip him of his technical superiority and he's basically Mike Jones with a legacy.

He will remind you of this legacy too. Constantly. This is noble, to an extent, the whole UGK 4 Life battle cry in the absence of the Pimp but it also is limiting from a creative perspective and can become exhausting to listeners. But then again these days it's likely that nine out of ten of Bun's human interactions involve him being told how important he is. So then what's left for him to rap about but how important he is? It's not like he's selling dope anymore.

Of course, a big part of the reason Bun and Preem have been able to sustain their legacies so effectively is that, well, they're really nice guys. Both are outstanding conversationalists. Bun is literally the friendliest and most accessible rapper I've ever dealt with, almost disconcertingly so … But it would be nice if either of these artists made even the smallest effort to meet or exceed their earlier accomplishments.

"Bun's songs [today] are not the same Bun B," agrees producer Mannie Fresh, adding, "[He's a] phenomenal emcee, but the [spark] that was in his eye when I first met him, I can't say it's there no more." But Mannie understood, in a way. It had been a struggle to go back, creatively, to the old "Mannie Fresh that people want" after his sister died.

"When [you lose someone] it takes away from you, it takes your spirit, it takes everything that moves you," Mannie says. "[And] the world [is] not forgiving … People don't think that you should go through shit. They're just like, 'Bounce back, nigga, make some songs.' [But] I'm human, just like you."

Other journalists obviously disagreed with Nosnitsky's assessment; *The Source* (although not as revered as they were in the 90s) awarded *Trill OG* its coveted five-mic rating when it dropped in August 2010, the first album in five years to receive this honor.

Although people had been calling Bun an O.G. for years, it had taken him years to embrace the term. "[People] calling you O.G., nine times out of ten, is really just calling you 'old,' you know," he joked with The Breakfast Club. "But I've come to take it as a term of affection."

Bun described *Trill OG* as the first time he'd been able to put together a cohesive album with no pressure and get back to the foundation of making music. "*Trill* had incredible songs [but] I don't necessarily think I made a cohesive album," he admitted, adding, "[*II Trill* was] a

(*Bun likely would disagree with this assessment. "Every rhyme I write is meant to be the best of me, so I don't phone nothing in," he told The Breakfast Club radio show in 2013.)

cohesive album, but some of the songs could have been better. I still was a little bit shaken up with Pimp C's passing away."

Trill OG included a lot of high-profile guest features, like Drake, T-Pain, Young Jeezy, and Gucci Mane. On the hook of "Put It Down," Drake rhymed on the hook, "Just bought a car / The nigga Pimp owned it," adding on the verse, "I got 100 girls in each phone / Drizzy Drake, mane, Young Sweet Jones."* Chad Jr. appeared in the video as a stand-in for his father.

Some diehard UGK fans were critical of the moniker, but Drake was dismissive. "I'm a huge Pimp supporter," he told MTV News. "I'm a huge Pimp fan. I feel like I'm extended UGK family. Bun and Pimp are like uncles, dads to me. They're G's ... I never meant any disrespect [by using the nickname] Young Sweet Jones."

It wasn't the last time Drake, a half-Jewish Canadian, would be criticized for his connection to Texas music. "Sometimes I feel guilty for how much I love Screw and the SUC," Drake admitted in an email to The *Guardian*. "I feel like Houston must look at me as someone who is just latching on to a movement. But I just can't express how that shit makes me feel. That brand of music is just everything to me. It's Hip-Hop, it's sexy, it's relaxing. I live for those emotions."**

Bun said he endorsed Drake because he saw something of himself in Drake's hunger and passion. "It reminds me of when I was coming in the game and how hungry I was and how ready I was to just attack and be heard and be seen and be known and let people realize my movement," Bun told *VIBE*, adding, "I understand that kind of intensity. I see it in his eyes and I remember that look when I used to ... [look] in the mirror in the morning."

One highlight on *Trill OG* was set in motion when singer Lloyd came across the impromptu verse Pimp C had done for the Tupac tribute album back in 2006 and offered the session to Bun. Tupac's vocals were from the 90s, Pimp's vocals were from 2006, and Bun recorded a 2010 verse for a song which now effectively spanned three decades. Bun turned the vocals over to producer Steve Below, who accepted the challenge to create the track. Once the beat was finished, singer Trey Songz took a break from rehearsals for Jay-Z's *Blueprint 3* tour to lay a hook for the record, "Right Now."***

Left on the cutting room floor was a record J. Cole produced and sent over called "Bun B For President," which Bun was afraid would come off as "too cocky," but the track later leaked out online. "That's one of the greatest regrets in my life [that the song didn't make the album]," J Cole told filmmaker Sama'an Ashrawi. "He shoulda did something with that ... [but] I still vote for you, man. For President. For real."

In October 2010, Rap-A-Lot released Pimp C's posthumous solo project *The Naked Soul of Sweet Jones* through their new distribution deal with Fontana/Universal. (The title was a play off of Iceberg Slim's fourth book *The Naked Soul of Iceberg Slim*, which he described as "a position paper.") Overseeing the project were a number of producers and engineers Chad worked with prior to his death. "When I heard Mike Dean and [Steve] Below and DJ B-Do was over the project I rested a little bit better," Mike Mo told KeepItTrill.com.

The album kicked off with "Down 4 Mine" (originally produced by Scarface, with a revamped beat by Cory Mo), probably the closest indication of the direction Chad was going with

(*Although the lyric was an exaggeration, there was some truth to it. Drake had attempted to buy Pimp's red drop-top Cadillac Biarritz. Cee-Lo Goodie and T-Pain had also made offers, hoping to add the car to their collections. "[The car] is preserved right now," Bun told *VIBE*. "They put it up. It's really a show car not to be driven.")
(**Drake's connection to Houston was also related to the fact that he was discovered by J. Prince's son, Jas Prince, who introduced him to Lil Wayne and helped facilitate his record deal with Young Money. J. Prince was an executive producer on his first album.)
(***During the *Blueprint 3* tour stop in Houston, Jay-Z brought Bun B to the stage to perform "Big Pimpin'" and the crowd rapped along with every word of Pimp C's verse. "That nigga fought tooth and nail not to get on that song, and when the song plays right now [or] when Jay-Z does that fuckin' song [in concert] ... everybody sings that nigga's part. Like, fuckin' word for word," laughs Big Munn.)

his solo album. (Cory Mo's partner Naztradamus produced an unofficial video for the song, featuring a video montage of old Pimp C footage.) The Too $hort collaboration "Made 4" gave fans a taste of the intended Broad Playaz album.

The rest of the album was compiled from revamped leftover tracks Chad had been working on prior to his death. Some, like "Dickies" with Young Jeezy (with a revamped beat by DJ B-Do) and the Lil Troy diss "Massacre" (originally included on XVII's *Certified* album) had already been circulating for several years. "Hit the Parking Lot" was originally a mixtape track by the V12 Boyz (Pimp, Lil Boosie, and Webbie) titled "Swerve Pt. 2."

Other features included "Since the 90s" with E-40 and Gator Mane, and "Midnight Hoes," the track Pimp recorded over the summer of 2007 mentioning Ayesha with additional verses from Rick Ross and Slim Thug. Some members of the UGK posse were upset that their vocals were removed from "Believe In Me" and "Colors," the last two songs recorded at the high-rise. "This was some shit my nigga was doing for his team of niggas he was fucking with, but that shit got swiped away from us," says Hezeleo.

The most controversial track on the album was "What Up," featuring Drake.* (Drake, arguably a pop star, was known for his emotional rhymes about women, the exact opposite of Pimp C's "pimpin'" persona on records.) Diehard UGK fans viewed Drake's inclusion as blasphemous; critics panned the collaboration as "aural gonorrhoea."

"There's no way you can convince me that if the Pimp was still with us that he would have [Drake] on his lead single with production from Boi-1da," wrote blogger HaZe on Dirty-Glove. com, announcing plans to "just delete this [track] and pretend it never happened."

"Fuck [producer] Boi-1da AND [Drake]," agreed a blogger from TheTrillConnection.com. "Whatever they wanna do with their hoe ass, dick-in-the-booty ass, teeny bopper garbage music is their own damn business. But keep it far, far away from my country rap tunes."

"C reacted to different people differently," Mama Wes' assistant Travis points out. "[People say] he wouldn't have wanted to work with Drake, [but] you don't know that. C was unpredictable. Half the time I don't think C know what he fuck he was gonna do until he did it."

Mama Wes refused to listen to the album. "It wasn't the right time for me to [be] hearing what I thought would probably be boo-boo, and I didn't wanna hear C's shit done like that," she says. In the years following Chad's death, Mama Wes says she was emotionally unprepared to even consider releasing any music. In 2011, she finally reached out to Chad's former engineer Rambro to talk about collaborating on a project to be titled *Legends*. A compilation of sorts, *Legends* would feature remixed versions of some Pimp C songs with features from other artists like Spice 1 and members of the UGK Posse like XVII and Hezeleo.

One of the planned records was a remake of "Big Pimpin'" which Chad and Rambro had been working on. "Until the day C died, he didn't like 'Big Pimpin'," says Mama Wes.

"He always wanted to do the beat for that song," Rambro says. "[This album has] all the things that he dreamed about, all the orchestration ... that's what we're setting out to do, is fulfill his dreams on this record ... We [want to] make this *Legends* album the album that he wanted to make, the way he wanted to make it."

"I miss [Pimp] so much," Rambro adds. "He had a lot of plans that, wow – if he had lived

---

(*The Pimp C verse that was used on "What Up" first appeared on a song titled "Stackin' Money" by Do-Boy, which also was included on Vol. 3 of the *Pitch Control Mixtape* DVD series as "Stack Money," credited to Ju-Boy and D.O. The song was later released by a group calling themselves Da G Kamp. After Pimp died, Do-Boy donated the verse and footage from the video shoot to Chinara. Since then, the song has gone through several transformations. DJ B-Do created a beat for a track which featured Pimp, Lil Wayne, and Bun. The same beat was also used for T-Pain's mixtape track "Let's Talk Money," on which Lil Wayne rapped, "That nigga Pimp called me before he left this bitch, told me, 'Keep doing your thing and don't tell 50 [Cent] shit," of their brewing beef, and, "Everybody know what I drink so a nigga never coughs / And a nigga forever rich / But pussy never cost 'cause a nigga forever pimps / 'Cause we were better taught by a nigga named Pimp / And Bun B from Port Art." The session eventually was turned over to Drake's team, who redid the beat and replaced Lil Wayne's verse with Drake for the album version of "What Up." In DJ B-Do's opinion, "What Up" was the only questionable track on the album. "I think ['What Up' would've] been more appropriate without Drake, but it's all politics," says DJ B-Do, adding, "But C's album pretty much sounded how he wanted it to sound.")

... he wanted to always push the level, the envelope, and that's why – right now today – when I end up doing Hip-Hop sessions, everybody still copies off of him."

In November 2012, film school graduate Sama'an Ashrawi, who had been adopted by Bun as his videographer and a "Trill Gladiator," released an *All-Star Tribute to UGK* documentary on the 20th anniversary of *Too Hard to Swallow*. The following month, UGK was officially inducted into the Gulf Coast Museum's Music Hall of Fame in downtown Port Arthur.

At the induction ceremony, Mayor Deloris "Bobbie" Prince proclaimed December 2nd the Underground Kingz Day in the city of Port Arthur. "I know what it's like growing up in this area, looking for inspiration, looking for someone to look up to," Bun, outfitted in a black suit, told the crowd of more than 350 people. "Hopefully with our 20 year musical legacy, myself and Pimp C have been able to be that for people in this area ... [for] future generations."

After Mama Wes and Chad Jr. were presented with the induction certificate on behalf of Pimp C, Mama Wes, in her trademark red Dickies, took to the stage. "Even though he's not with us here physically today, Bun and I know he's here with us spiritually," she said, smiling as she gestured toward the sky, "Matter of fact, I thought I saw him flying around a few minutes ago."

As he accepted his certificate of induction, Bun thanked Mama Wes and Chinara, his mother, father, wife, kids, and granddaughter, and other people who'd played key roles in the UGK movement like DJ Bird, Mitchell Queen, Steve Below, and Bo-Bo Luchiano, who were all in attendance. "I never woulda thought, sitting in my mama's bedroom on 15th Street, that [my work] would be in a place like this," Bun said. "I never thought, sitting in Chad's bedroom on Shreveport Avenue, that we would be in a place like this."

After the ceremony and a short performance by the UGKidz Corey a.k.a. "Lil C" and his partner Tra a.k.a. "Ice 7000," the crowd headed upstairs for the unveiling of the permanent UGK exhibit. (Other notable names honored in the Gulf Coast Museum include former Dallas Cowboys coach Jimmy Johnson, NBA players Stephen Jackson and Kendrick Perkins, and rock band ZZ Top. The centerpiece of the music department is a large Janis Joplin display, featuring a replica of her handpainted car, a poster from Woodstock, and a vinyl copy of Janis Joplin's *Greatest Hits*.)*

The exhibit, mostly featuring items donated by Bun and Pimp's families, has been expand-ed significantly since the initial unveiling and includes BET Awards, OZONE Awards, Dirty Awards, copies of UGK CDs, a "Free Pimp C" hat, a "Trill" hat, "RIP Pimp C" shoes, UGK-embroidered Dickies, a vinyl copy of UGK's "Pimpin' Ain't No Illusion," and a 2001 letter from the Grammy committee congratulating them their nomination for "Big Pimpin'."**

For Mama Wes, the proud yet bittersweet moment was only soured when she reached to put her arm around her granddaughter Christian as the family posed in front of the exhibit and felt the girl trembling in fear. *Damn, y'all gonna pay for that,* Mama Wes thought, believing that Chinara had turned her granddaughter against her. *That's really ugly.*

"I don't get to see her, but I love that kid," Mama Wes says. "[What] bothers me [is that] she thinks I'm some kind of ogre, because when she stood next to me, the child was shaking like I was gonna do something [to her] ... I'd never do anything to that kid. I love that kid, but I guess they've told her these horror stories about this horrible person that I am... she's so scared of me."

(*Despite being born and raised in Port Arthur, Janis Joplin was not nearly as complimentary of the city as UGK. "I just had to get out of Texas, baby, it was bringin' me down ... I've been all around the world but Port Arthur is the worst place that I've ever found," she sang on her 1970 record "Ego Rock." "[Port Arthur] treated her like shit," Bun B told journalist Nardwuar. "People really were against her because she was trying to do soul music, collaborating with black artists, and [Port Arthur] in those days was very racist ... she left and went out in the world and ... came back as a legend," he further explained in an interview with NPR.)

(**Information about visiting the Gulf Coast Museum can be found on museumofthegulfcoast.org.)

"I just wish that [my father] was here to get [these accolades] himself, I wish me and my brother didn't have to [get] it for him … but other than that … it's a great thing. I'm proud to be here," Chad Jr. told local media on hand for the event, adding, "I hope to be able to visit this with my kids someday and say, 'That was your grandfather.'"

Bun told *Texas Monthly* that he was most proud of the fact that UGK had done things on their own terms. "We didn't schmooze, we didn't politic, we didn't kiss music-industry butt," he noted. "And we're still recognized by people who don't necessarily understand what we do, but acknowledge that we're making a difference."

Since 2009, Chinara has teamed up with the CCM Foundation to hold an annual "Chad 'Pimp C' Butler Hip-Hop Health & Wellness Fair" every December in her late husband's memory. The goal, reported MTV News, was to "raise awareness among young people about the importance of their own personal health, which includes HIV and STD testing, drug prevention and regular physical exams." Chinara describes the annual festival as a day of "peaceful fellowship."

Mama Wes put on a good face and came the first year, but ceased participating as the relationship between her and Chinara further deteriorated over the years. Celebrity attendees have included Bun B, Chamillionaire, Paul and Crystal Wall, Trae, Big KRIT, Tami Roman, Slim Thug, Devin the Dude, Chingo Bling, and DJ Michael Watts, and Z-Ro, who performed "I'm a Gangsta" and encouraged people to get tested ("It's gangsta to know your status, know what I'm talkin' 'bout?"). "I come through every time [Chinara needs me] because of what Pimp C and Bun B and UGK mean to me," Chamillionaire told *3rd Ward* TV.

Chamillionaire often brings his red Cadillac Biarritz to the event, along with local car aficionado Saul Gonzalez, who's customized "RIP Pimp C" 1984 Cadillac Eldorado was featured in Houston's 2012 Los Magnificos car show.

The main attraction is the Pimp C memorabilia display. Included in the display is a framed case with a Bentley car key and a pair of Chad's sunglasses, the mink coat he wore in the "Int'l Players Anthem" video, his gold *Menace II Society* plaque and his platinum plaque for Scarface's *My Homies*. Until 2011, the display included Pimp C's gold plaque for UGK's *Ridin' Dirty*, when Chinara auctioned it off and announced that the proceeds would be used to establish the Chad "Pimp C" Butler Scholarship Foundation.

Over the years, attendance has been light (one year, a video was released announcing that the event was a success because 32 people were tested for syphilis). The event has emphasized STD testing, cold and flu immunizations, and well as glucose screening and BMI screening to put an emphasis on combating obesity.

Curiously absent is any discussion of the health effects of syrup sippin'. One year, Chinara posed next to an Algierz cut-out cartoon of Pimp C alongside DJ B-Do and T.O.E., both holding their omnipresent Styrofoam cups. "We don't want to play up the drug and the codeine and all the negative stuff, because the cause of his death was sleep apnea," Chinara told Urban Life Entertainment. "He died in his sleep, so we also want to clear up that misconception and keep Chad's name going in a positive manner."

Also absent from the event is any mention of Chad's sons. In 2013, Chinara did an interview about the event with *Mass Appeal*, in which she never mentioned his sons but spoke at length about her dream for Christian to be the one carrying on her father's legacy.

"The long term goal is that one day my daughter Christian will be organizing the 50th Annual Pimp C Hip-Hop, Health & Wellness Festival," she said. "I'd like Christian to not feel pressured into keeping her father's legacy alive through music only. This will give her another outlet to keep the legacy going."

Chinara also formed an unlikely alliance with The Box's Terri Thomas, the same woman who allegedly threatened to send her late husband back to prison. "Terri has always celebrated Chad's legacy in music with tributes annually on his birthday and on the day of his untimely passing, so ... she was fully cooperative," Chinara told *Mass Appeal*. "The Box truly cares about the health and wellness of its listeners."

———————

In interviews, Bun has repeatedly emphasized the fact that he doesn't have any unreleased Pimp C music. "I don't control the music. I don't have the Pimp C catalogue," he told *Pitchfork*. "The Estate owns, controls, and chooses how to distribute everything."

Even outside of the Estate, there's still some unreleased Pimp C verses in the vaults. Former Beats by the Pound producer KLC treasures his unreleased Pimp C verse so much he doesn't even keep a copy of it at his studio, lest it fall into the wrong hands. A planned Pimp C collaboration called "Naked Lady" intended for Chamillionaire's album *Venom* was left in limbo during his bitter departure from Universal Records. (According to some reports, Chamillionaire gave the verse back to Chinara so it could be used elsewhere.)

Jazze Pha says he turned over an unreleased Too $hort and Pimp C record, "Single Life," to J. Prince. Disappointed with all the politics between Pimp C's family and Rap-A-Lot after his death, other producers like Mannie Fresh and Mr. Lee have decided to steer clear of any drama and simply keep their unreleased Pimp C material under wraps.

Likewise, Killer Mike and Z-Ro don't plan to release their treasured Pimp C collaborations. "I'm in no way gonna capitalize on no man's death and try to put it out there now. It's all about the musical integrity to me," Killer Mike told HipHopDX.

"I'ma keep the song to myself," agrees Z-Ro. "I ain't gonna try to make no money off it. You know how niggas do, man ... Everybody wants to try to find a way to get some bread off of your demise."

Occasionally, a "new" Pimp C verse makes its way to the mainstream, such as Big Boi's 2013 record "Gossip" which used an unreleased Pimp C verse originally recorded for Dungeon Family artist Lil Will. "UGK is one of my favorite groups ever, and having Big K.R.I.T. and Bun and Pimp C on the record over an Organized Noize track is a dream come true," Big Boi told HipHopDX.

While Jay-Z was recording his 12th studio album *Magna Carta Holy Grail* in 2013, he recruited Rick Ross to come by the studio and lay a verse on "FuckWithMeYouKnowIGotIt." Ross was impressed as Jay-Z premiered some records from the album, but had one complaint.

"I just ain't hear that *Southern* one," Ross told Jay-Z. "You know, that *one* record ... I ain't felt that one since Pimp C and Bun B on 'Big Pimpin.'" At Ross' suggestion, Jay-Z added a vocal interlude from Pimp C at the beginning of the record, which was pulled from an interview posted on YouTube as "Pimp C Last Interview Before Death."

"A little over a year ago I was in bondage," Pimp had said. "Now I'm back out here reaping the blessings and getting the benefits that go along with everything that's out here for kings like us. The reason why we like this jewelry and this diamonds and stuff and they don't understand is because we really from Africa and that's where all this stuff come from. We originate from kings ... so don't look down on the youngsters 'cause they wanna have shiny things. It's in our genes ... we just don't all know our history."

Jay-Z also released a remix of his *Magna Carta Holy Grail* track "Tom Ford" on December 4, 2013 (Jay-Z's 44th birthday and the six-year anniversary of Pimp's passing) featuring an unreleased Pimp C verse.

Big L released an album called *Udigg Records Presents: The Final Compilation* on iTunes which featured several verses that he'd paid Pimp C for after their initial transaction in Miami. On "Final Freestyle," Pimp bragged that "they pay me $30,000 just to breathe on the mic" and rapped, "I'm a flirt but I ain't Kelly, I don't piss on no bitches / Get my paper up front, 'cause my dick is delicious / Fresh and clean like a Subway salad / Gettin' sucked doin' 90 but my license is valid."

Big L was upset when he heard the same verse re-used on the remix to Juicy J's 2013 record

"Show Out." When asked by *FUSE* TV how he had obtained the verse, Juicy J laughed, "It's a secret, man. That's the #1 question [I get] … It's a blessing to get it." Juicy had apparently obtained the vocals from Chinara, and since she didn't have the original ProTools session for the verse, he admitted to *FUSE*, "[The audio was] a little distorted. We had to take it and chop it up and remix it and get the voice to sound right."

Juicy J, based on his relationship with Chinara, is one of the few artists who has access to Pimp C vocals. Juicy's 2013 solo album *Stay Trippy* featured Pimp C on "Smokin' Rollin'." (In August 2014, the exclusive version of Wiz Khalifa's album *Blacc Hollywood* included "Word On The Town," featuring Pimp C and Juicy J.) In August 2013 Juicy J announced that he was producing a new Pimp C album to be released on Nas' new label Mass Appeal Records with distribution through Sony RED. (It was later clarified that the project would be an EP, not a full-length LP.)

"I'm just there to lend a helping hand in whatever way, whatever capacity [Chinara] wants me to be involved," Bun told The Breakfast Club of the upcoming project. "This is something that she feels she needs to do for her husband to maintain his legacy and I stand behind her 100%. I would want people to stand by and support my wife – whether or not they agreed with her – if she felt this is what she needed to do to maintain my integrity."

J. Prince was tight-lipped when asked about the project on The Breakfast Club. "Most of all, Pimp C kids is what's important," he said. "As long as they don't get cheated."

"Nobody knows the full amount of dumb shit I've done in my life," Bun admitted to *Texas Monthly* in 2014. But, in a testament to his intelligence and versatility, Bun has grown far beyond the reckless youth who was once smoking fry, transporting cocaine and selling dime bags of weed along with soul food dinners. Bun, now in his 40s, is a loving grandfather, a college professor, performing with the local symphony and collaborating on children's books (*Bun B's Rap Coloring and Activity Book* with Shea Serrano). The Bun B of 2015 is either an incredible transformation or a man who has turned his back on his hometown, depending on your perspective.

While some in the rap game wondered if Bun was losing his edge, he was gaining respect in other communities. As his reputation as an intelligent, humble rapper with mainstream appeal spread, it wasn't unusual for him to make guest appearances speaking at high schools and middle schools. In 2010, Rice University humanities professor Dr. Anthony Pinn invited Bun to speak to his class about moral codes in Hip-Hop. Dr. Pinn was so impressed with Bun's "thoughtful, very clever, very compelling" speech that he invited him to co-teach the course with him for a semester.

Pinn's class on Religion and Hip-Hop Culture takes a broad look at the concept of "religion," which he summarizes as human attempts to answer the big questions in life – who are we and why are we here? – and how Hip-Hop culture has attempted to answer those questions. While Pinn himself had caused a bit of a ripple when he "came out" as an atheist in 2011, Bun was a Southern Baptist who professed that "reconnecting with God" was the only way he'd been able to cope with the loss of Pimp C. "My partner is only gone physically," he told *The Source*. "I'm a God-fearing Christian so I believe his spirit still walks with me."

Bun's mother had always been upset with him for not going to college, but in March 2011, he did her one better: Bun officially became a professor at Rice University. He and Dr. Pinn's Religion and Hip-Hop Culture course immediately became one of the most popular on campus, with 250 students gathering twice a week in one of the largest auditoriums on campus. (The course is now available for free online at edX.org.)

Although Bun insisted on being called "Professor Freeman" on campus (sometimes he would accept "Professor Trill") to differentiate from his rap persona, he still used his connections to bring celebrities like Russell Simmons, Talib Kweli, and Lupe Fiasco as guest speakers. He took his role as a professor seriously, spending several hours preparing for each class.

The *Beaumont Enterprise* asked Bun how he explained the perceived conflict between Hip-Hop and religion; how could he justify rappers wearing cross necklaces while rapping about drugs and misogyny?

"All Hip-Hop does is really expose the rawer side of the world that society chooses to basically forget even exists," Bun said. "The story's a reflection of the struggle of real people. There are real people in this world who sell drugs [but are] still religious. Just because they don't carry the doctrines of their religion every day doesn't necessarily mean that they don't have a ... religious foundation and they don't concern themselves with ... the afterlife [or] the consequences of your actions."

Bun wasn't the first rapper to transition into the world of higher education (Public Enemy's Chuck D has lectured at universities, and producer 9th Wonder has taught classes on African-American studies at Duke University in North Carolina), but certainly one of the most high profile. Many viewed it as a victory for Hip-Hop.

"Bun B is just fascinating because he has grown," says *XXL* Magazine's Vanessa Satten. "He has managed to age with Hip-Hop so unbelievably well, because he realized the role he plays ... He hasn't gotten old, he hasn't gotten out of touch."

While admitting that he still feels "slightly fucked up about" not going to college, Bun says his mother is a lot more understanding these days of his decision to pursue rap. "A new car will do that for you," he jokes.

As Bun himself embarks on a career in education, Joi Gilliam suggests that UGK should be the focus of a college course. "I could *personally* teach a class on the relevance of UGK [in] American music history," she says. "You cannot have a conversation about the greats of Hip-Hop and not include UGK. You cannot speak about well-crafted Hip-Hop tracks, where cats were actually creating their own melodies ... not relying on samples exclusively. You cannot have that conversation and *not* talk about UGK. You just can't. They *have* to be included in that conversation of the greats."

In the years following his appointment at Rice University and approaching his 40s, Bun continued to grow and expand into the mainstream. Exactly 17 years after *Super Tight* was released, Houston Mayor Annise Parker proclaimed August 30, 2011 as Bun B Day.

Bun, who had always been considered the unofficial mayor of Houston, has a good relationship with the real Mayor, inviting her to watch the Houston Rockets playoff games from his suite and referring to her on Twitter as the "Best. Mayor. Ever." The *Houston Press* half-jokingly suggested that once Mayor Parker moved on to bigger and better things, Bun B should run. ("Vote Bun B for Mayor and Keep Houston Trill as Fuck," one commenter suggested as a campaign slogan.)

Initially, Bun laughed off the suggestion, saying he had "too many skeletons in the closet," like his possession of a controlled substance with intent to distribute charge. (On the Breakfast Club radio show he acknowledged that since "the mayor of Toronto [Rob Ford] is literally smoking crack like, right now, in office" his drug charge might not be as big of an obstacle as he thought.) Many have encouraged Bun to seriously consider the suggestion.

"Sadly, there's also one big, unfortunate reality of politics: it's boring," noted writer Chris Gray in the *Houston Press*. "If people are already calling Bun Houston's unofficial mayor ... why mess with a good thing?"

"I mean, he [already] is the mayor to us," upstart Houston rapper Kirko Bangz told *Texas Monthly*. "I don't even know what the real mayor looks like, you know what I'm saying?"

Beyond music, Bun has branched off into a wide variety of ventures in clothing and fashion (he's a serious sneakerhead), performing at culinary events and launching a foodie blog, driving around the world with car aficionados in the Gumball 3000 road race, and despite his initial hesitation to join Twitter, has become a social networking all-star. Chamillionaire lauds him as the rapper with the "widest Rolodex."

He's nearly omnipresent in Houston, appearing on anti-texting-while-driving public service announcements, tossing out the first pitch at Houston Astros games, even appearing on a tourism billboard at Houston's Bush Intercontinental airport. (The only thing he turned down, it seems, was an offer to appear on the Houston installment of VH1's controversial reality show series *Love & Hip-Hop*.) *Texas Monthly* magazine dubbed him a "one-man chamber of commerce."

Bun told NPR Music that he views himself as the Indiana Jones of his neighborhood, an ambassador of sorts. "Most of [the people in Port Arthur] never have the opportunity to leave that small town and go out into the world and see things," he told NPR. "So I feel kind of obligated to go out and explore the world for their sake."

But the further Bun has grown in the world, some in his hometown of Port Arthur perceive him to be getting further and further away. Some old friends, like Donny Young, respect his intelligence but have come to consider him "an arrogant muthafucker."

A 2014 exchange in a Facebook page dedicated to UGK summarized the way some Port Arthur natives feel about Bun.

"[Bun is] so sensitive about Chad & how folks perceive him," Mitchell Queen noted.

"Seems like [Port Arthur] has a grudge against him cuz he's doing a lot for Houston but never here," chimed in UGK fan Rob Reyes. "If he would just touch base more often it might be different."

"He's a celebrity," added Boonie, of the old DMI crew. "Chad was a person."

Bun is very aware of the way some people back home view him. In 2013, he posted a picture of the Port Arthur seawall on Instagram. "Lots of memories here," he wrote. "Sometime[s] I drive down and stand here just to chill and reflect. People think I don't be in PA. I'm here way more than you know." Often, those trips include a trip to his mother's house, or a stop at Chad's gravesite.

He can understand why some people perceive him to be standoffish, admitting that he's a "moody fuck" and needs to try to be "more personable," but says that change was necessary. "[When people] see me nowadays, it's, you know, 'Bun's a little different,'" he says. "But, it was necessary. Everybody has to change at some point."

"Some of the criticism that Bun gets [in Port Arthur] is unwarranted because he can't *make* you a fuckin' star," says Mama Wes, who sometimes jokingly referred to Chad as the Great Red Hope. "I think he should do a little better with entertaining it, because C would entertain it. That's why they loved C."

"Every nigga of that era from P.A. – other than C and Bun – feel like they was overlooked," she adds. "Let me tell you something: Nobody in this little city had any aspirations to be anything in the music industry until C and Bun came along."

"Even if it seemed like the music wasn't right or the presentation wasn't together or the lyrics wasn't [good], Pimp would never tell nobody they couldn't do it, because *he* did it," Bun added on Damage Control Radio.

Short Texas as Pimp C knew it no longer exists. The corner of 7th Street & Texas Ave is now the nearly abandoned intersection of Rev. Dr. Ransom Howard & Freeman Ave. (7th Street was renamed after Rev. Dr. Ransom Howard, a beloved local Baptist pastor. It is not known if the renaming of Texas Ave. as Freeman Ave. had anything to do with Bernard "Bun B" Freeman.)

Bun hired a Houston graffiti artist named Dez Woods to paint a UGK mural on a nearby downtown Port Arthur building. (Sadly, the building has since been demolished.) He owns the trademark on the word "Trill" and has grown weary of being asked to define it in interviews. "Being trill really just means being true to who you are," he told NPR. "'Trill' does not mean keeping it 'hood, keeping it gangster, or anything like that."

All things considered, when Bun looks back on everything UGK accomplished, starting with his 1991 decision to pursue rap for one year, it still feels surreal. "There [was] no blueprint," he told the *Houston Chronicle*. "None at all. This [shit] wasn't supposed to go this far. We figured we'd give it a try and see what happens and then get back to the real world. It just kept going."

Like Bun, some have concluded that at the end of the day, all the drama UGK endured is ultimately a part of their success. "I think the trials and tribulations of UGK are a part of the story for sure," says journalist Matt Sonzala. "All the fucked up shit that an artist can go through in the [music] industry, they went through it … they lived it."

"I don't think C would've ever disbanded UGK, and I don't think Bun would've done that either. I think C would've gone on to have a successful solo career, which is what he wanted, but he would never have disbanded UGK," says Mama Wes. "And honestly, no matter how mad he ever got with Bun, I still think C honestly loved Bun. I really do."

Beyond UGK, friends theorize that Chad would have become a great blues singer in his later years. "[Hip-Hop music] was just his vehicle," says Mama Wes. "He didn't intend to do it for very much longer … That was his way of getting in and doing what he wanted to do, [but] he never intended to stick with it. He used to say he was going to do R&B when he got to be old. When he got to be 50, he was going to be a blues artist … His love was really just making the music [but] he felt like he would get it faster with rap."

Even though he didn't intend to stick with rap forever, he left behind a lasting impact in the rap game. "I think it's kinda impossible [to forget Pimp C]," Bun said on Damage Control Radio. "You really gotta catch amnesia or get diagnosed with short-term memory loss to forget a dynamic person like a Pimp C; people who are more alive in your memories than you are right here in real life. You'll be like, 'Man, they took him too early,' and then at the same time, 'Man, you did it *all*.' You know what I'm saying?"

Many would agree that his passing marked the end of a definitive era in music history. "People really don't know what we lost when we lost Pimp C," Big Gipp says. "What UGK did with that [Southern] music, Pimp was the nucleus of that shit … niggas can only copy that shit."

"It's amazing to me how some of the greatest rappers of our generation pay homage to [Pimp C] almost on a daily [basis]," says singer Lloyd. "Lil Wayne, Drake, I see [his influence] in all of them," agrees Sleepy Brown. "I see a piece of Pimp C in all of 'em. I truly do."

Not only are today's artists influenced by Pimp C's sound, but *literally* using his sounds. "This shit you're hearing on the radio now, that's my drums," Pimp had told *XXL* in 2006.

"I still use [Pimp C's drum sounds] to this day," producer KLC nods in 2013.

As evidence of Pimp's influence, many point to Mississippi rapper/producer Big K.R.I.T., described by journalist Andrew Nosnitsky as "like Pimp C but with none of the anger." The problem, Nosnitsky wrote, was that the younger generation almost idolized Pimp C *too* much, explaining in a 2009 opinion piece:

"*[Artists like Big K.R.I.T.] make music for a certain type of fan – ones who either grew up on UGK/OutKast/Ball&G or ones that wish that they did … [they] have studied their predecessors closely, who have the intellectual capacity and skill level to follow their formula, but have thus far been too wrapped up in those standards to evolve beyond them … they are able to synthesize just about everything but the flair (dare I say swagger?) of their rap heroes. Their personalities don't engage on the level of an Andre 3000 or Pimp C. And I'm sure if you were to ask them, they'd tell you of course not, those are the greats. They, like their audience, put their predecessors on an unattainable pedestal, which is a self limiting standard.*"

"The shit these youngsters doing, mane, we designed this game," Pimp said in 2007, during one of his last interviews with *Tha Buzz* TV. "A nigga that's copying this shit, he don't actually know where to take it no more because he don't have the prototype. See, I got the blueprint to this shit because I *made* it, you know?"

Above: **UGK mural** by Dez Woods in downtown Port Arthur. (The building was later demolished.) Photo: Keadron Smith
Below: **Bun B** with the **MDDL FNGZ** and **UGK Records posse** shortly after Chad's death *(L-R):* **Kilo, Bankroll Jonez, Edgar Walker Jr., Bad Ass Bam, Bandit, Hezeleo, Vicious, Big Bubb, XVII, DJ B-Do,** and **T.O.E.** Photo: Mike Frost

Bun B performs at Warehouse Live in Houston, February 2008. *Clockwise from above:* **Mama Wes** embraces **Bun B** backstage; **Mama Wes** and **J. Prince** dressed appropriately; **Hezeleo, Mama Wes,** the author **Julia Beverly, XVII,** and **Bankroll Jonez; DJ Bird, Bun B,** and **Mitchell Queen Jr.**
Photos by Julia Beverly and Keadron Smith

The **Pimp C Tribute at the 2008 OZONE Awards** in Houston, featuring *(clockwise from below)*: **Billy Cook**, **Webbie**, and **Lil Boosie**; **David Banner**; **Too $hort**; and **Big Boi** of OutKast.
Photos by King Yella and J Lash

Left: **Mama Wes, Corey, Christian,** and **Chinara.** *Above:* **Bun B** closes out the set backed by **Mama Wes, Chad Jr., Nitacha, Queenie** and her daughter **Breneshia,** and **Angie Crooks.**
Photos by Ben Rose/www.benrosephotography.com

Chinara Butler *(clockwise from above)*: with **T.O.E.** and **DJ B-Do** at the health fair; with **Bun B** at the 2008 Grammy Awards; with **Mama Wes** at the health fair; with her daughter **Christian** at the health fair; **Pimp C's outfit from the "Int'l Player's Anthem" video** displayed at the health fair.

Grammy photo by Frazer Harrison/Getty
Health Fair photos via KeepItTrill.com

Clockwise from above: **Rick Ross** and **Bun B** remembering Pimp C at a Houston nightclub; **Bun B** and his wife **Queenie**; **Bun B** and the mayor of Houston **Annise Parker**; **Lupe Fiasco** speaking on a panel during **Professor Freeman's** Hip-Hop and Religion course; Pimp C lives on in **Mama Wes' living room**; **Mama Wes** and **Trae tha Truth**; **Mama Wes** and **Red Boy**; **2 Chainz** debuting his tribute song "Pimp C Back" for **Mama Wes** at Trae Day.

Bun B and Queenie
photo by Ben Rose

Annise Parker, Lupe
Fiasco, and Mama
Wes' living room pho-
tos by Julia Beverly

Above: The **UGK exhibit** at the Gulf Coast Museum's Music Hall of Fame. Photo: Julia Beverly
Below: **Bun B, Mama Wes,** and Chad's sons **Corey** and **Chad Jr.** at the UGK Induction Ceremony
Bun B and Mama Wes photos via the Beaumont Enterprise

'UGK for life'

Port Arthur rap duo inducted into music hall of fame

By Brooke Crum
The News staff writer

Bernard "Bun B" Freeman makes it a habit to come back to Port Arthur to see his mother, but he said coming back Sunday to be inducted into the Museum of the Gulf Coast Music Hall of Fame was different.

"Who would've thunk?" Freeman said as he accepted his certificate of induction.

The other half of the hip-hop/rap duo, Chad "Pimp C" Butler, died in December 2007 at the age of 33. His death was ruled an accident caused by sleep apnea aggravated by the use of prescription cough medicine. More than 3,000 people attended his funeral at the Robert A. "Bob" Bowers Civic Center.

But Sunday was about remembering UGK's accomplishments and honoring those memories as the Port Arthur Historical Society inducted the rap duo, Underground Kings, into the Music Hall of Fame. The induction came almost five years to the day after Butler's death.

"Chad and I walked the same streets as everybody else," Freeman said. "We had no more advantage than anybody else."

But being from Port Arthur was an advantage in itself, he said. The streets and school days that shaped them in Southeast Texas propelled the hip-hop duo to find a way to achieve what they had dreamed. Freeman advised anyone else aspiring to fulfill what may seem like a lofty dream not to give up or give in to intimidation.

"Don't let anyone tell you that just because you're from a small town that you can't make it," he said.

Obviously, Butler and Freeman did not let anyone tell them that, and

Sunday was a testament to that fact. Chad Butler's mother, Weslyn "Mama Wes" Butler, and his sons, Chad Butler Jr. and Corey Butler, accepted the hall of fame honor on his behalf.

"Even though he's not with us here physically today, Bun and I know he's here with us spiritually," Mama Wes said. "Matter of fact, I thought I saw him flying around a few minutes ago."

Sam Monroe, president of the Port Arthur Historical Society and Lamar State College-Port Arthur, explained to the

See 'UGK,' page A4

Bernard "Bun B" Freeman, center, of the rap duo UGK, reacts to the unveiling of an exhibit in the Music Hall of Fame at the Museum of the Gulf Coast on Sunday. Joining in the unveiling ceremony are "Mama" Weslyn Butler, left, the mother of Chad "Pimp C" Butler the other member of UGK; Sam Monroe, president of the Port Arthur Historical Society, which owns the museum and family members.

"Mama" Weslyn Butler (left) photo the mother of the late Chad "Pimp C" addressed a packed audience at the museum. Chad Butler Jr., center, and Corey Butler join their grandmother on the stage. The Norwood (at left in photo on right), also known as Ice TOGG, nephew of Chad "Pimp C" Butler, and Corey Butler, perform at the induction ceremony of the rap duo UGK. The younger generation rappers are known as the UnderGround Kids.

Above: **Mama Wes, Lil Wayne,** and **J. Prince** at Houston's Bar Rio for Bun B's *II Trill* album release party, 2008.
Below: **Too $hort** and **Snoop Dogg** wearing their UGK customized Dickies.

Photos: Julia Beverly and Keadron Smith

Left: Killa Kyleon's **Pimp C tattoo.** Photo: Julia Beverly
Below: **Pimp C fan tribute tattoos.**

Above: **Chad Jr.** and his mother **Nitacha** after his high school graduation, 2011. Photo: Julia Beverly
Clockwise from below: **Chad Jr.** and **Mama Wes; Corey, Wiz Khalifa** and **Chad Jr.; Chad Jr.** and **Jay-Z.**

Chad's teenage son **Corey** is embarking on his own rap career with his group **UGKidz**. *(Clockwise from below):* with **Trae tha Truth** and his UGKidz rap partner **Tra**; with **Tra** and **Too $hort**; with **Tra**, **2 Chainz**, and **Mama Wes**; with **Tra** and Tra's mother/manager **Ronda Forrest**; at his 5th grade graduation with **Mama Wes** and **Jada**; with **Bun B** and his siblings **Christian** and **Chad Jr.**; on **Snoop Dogg's** tour bus.

"Short Texas," 2013
Photo: Julia Beverly

Clockwise from below:
2013 photos of Chad's
childhood home on **13th
St.**; the **Oakmont** house;
and the **San Jac** house,
which has sustained
significant hurricane
damage in recent years.
Photos: Julia Beverly

Chad's father **Charleston** and son **Corey** in Port Arthur on Easter Sunday, 2015.
Photo: Angie Crooks

$ir
$weet
Jone$

"One thing that I believe – whatever your dream is, you should pursue it. I've seen too many people in my age bracket [who] had dreams that they did not pursue, and now they can't. And they'll never know whether they ever could [have]. So whatever it is, even if you fail at it, you tried. But if you never try, you'll never know." – Mama Wes, *Trill Spill* TV

"Every day, at the end of the day, you should be able to say that you've done something useful. Don't waste time, because time is not promised to you. This could be the last interview I ever do, and I'm well aware of that ... I think that we should live every day like it might be your last."
– Mama Wes, *B.R.E.A.D* Magazine, April 2013

Most of the interviews for this project were done between the fall of 2010 and the summer of 2013 with Mama Wes' invaluable input and assistance. In total, we recorded nearly 40 hours of audio right there in her kitchen on Shreveport Ave., where it all began. She outlined all of the key moments in her son's life and gave me crucial (and often comical) insight on the credibility of other people I interviewed.

I was originally optimistic about shopping this project, but after months of persistence, I'd received nothing but blank stares and rejection letters from book publishers and agents. I knew there was an audience that wanted to know the real story of Pimp C, of UGK, but no one was seeing my vision.

Finally, in a moment of discouragement, I asked myself: *What would Pimp C do?*

The answer came easily: he would tell 'em to get off the boo-boo, and he'd do the project himself. When New York record labels didn't understand his music, he'd followed his heart and created his own genre. I'd followed a similar ethos when launching *OZONE*. The trailblazing attitude had worked well for both of us. Why stop now?

So, unable to find anyone willing to fund this endeavor, I embarked on it as a labor of love and worked on it whenever I could find the time. I did interviews amidst other adventures like hiking the Grand Canyon, climbing a glacier in Iceland, running a half-marathon on the Great Wall of China (without permission, but that's a story for another day) and filming rappers everywhere from St. Tropez to Alaska.

As my research progressed, I became more and more curious about the mysterious "Larry." Mama Wes had never considered him relevant or important enough to save his number. I knew most of Pimp's entourage and was surprised I'd never met him before. Most of Pimp's crew barely remembered him, and no one knew anything about him beyond his first name. (Judging from his cryptic psychic session, Pimp didn't even know Larry's last name.) Finally, Jackson rapper Korleon gave me a phone number. The outgoing voicemail message was for "A&A Roofing & Construction," a company registered to a man named Larry Adams.

I finally got in touch with Larry and asked to interview him. I found him to be extremely evasive. We spoke a handful of times, making plans to meet in Los Angeles, but as soon as I arrived, he'd say he was somewhere else or send me to voicemail. In one brief conversation we agreed to meet in Atlanta, but he dodged me again. I called daily for several weeks with no response.

"You ain't gonna find that nigga," Mama Wes told me.

Korleon showed me Larry's cameo in an unreleased 2012 music video for a record called "Northside" (to the beat of the Big Tymers' "#1 Stunna"). Now, the descriptions of Larry as a "phantom figure," a "mystery man," took on new clarity. Skimming through pictures from UGK photo shoot, Mama Wes' birthday party, and even pictures I myself had taken at the UGK Bar Rio event – there was Larry popping up everywhere, in the background just staring at the camera. I *had* seen him before and didn't even know it.

On the morning of June 1, 2013, I headed back out to Texas. In the sweltering summer humidity I found Mama Wes traipsing across the huge Free Press Festival grounds in downtown Houston along with Corey, Tra, and Ronda to appear on stage with 2Chainz, one of her "babies."

I'd dragged a portable scanner in my carry-on (TSA was not amused) and spent most of the following week in Port Arthur with Mama Wes. She pulled out old photo albums from family vacations, even some of Chad's school paperwork and mementos dating back more than 25 years, giving me material to scan for the book.

On June 4, Mama Wes rescheduled our interview, saying she had a doctor's appointment which was taking far longer than expected. I used the day to ride around the city taking pictures of key spots discussed in the book. I'd been to Port Arthur nearly a dozen times but this trip, despite the suffocating heat, was the first time I truly saw the beauty in the city.

I visited the UGK exhibit at the Gulf Coast Museum; passed by the San Jac house and the hospital where Chad was born and tried to snap photos through the car window without looking like a creep. I grabbed a plate of soul food for lunch from Bun's old employer RBJ's and drove over to the seawall, where clouds danced along the horizon. I took pictures at Chad's gravesite; as I framed the first shot, a gust of wind blew abruptly, moving the vase of flowers from left to right. I couldn't help but smile, knowing he was up there somewhere.

Back at Mama Wes' house later that week, she asked Pops to dig up something that had been sitting untouched for nearly eight years: Chad's red mesh commissary bag, which contained all the paperwork from 2002-2005 he considered important enough to save. In the context of researching for this book, it was a goldmine.

There were plenty of gems in that bag, but my favorite was one I nearly overlooked. On the back of a yellow envelope containing a card from his old friend Bo$$, he'd sketched out in pencil the idea for (I assume) an album titled "$WEET JONE$ the Pimp: Pimp C's Trill Life Story." I scratched my original title for the book and used his.

I told Mama Wes I was scheduled to fly out on June 8. "You never leave when you're supposed to leave," she laughed. She was right. Instead of boarding my flight, I filmed a Bun B and Too $hort show in Houston. Afterwards, I spent two more productive days in Port Arthur digging deep into Mama Wes' memory banks. By the end of another long day, I'd crossed off nearly all of the follow-up questions from our initial set of interviews spanning Pimp C's life. We were finally *done*.

Mama Wes read a few snippets of the book I'd printed out and said she was impressed by the thorough research. As a former librarian herself, she appreciated that I was taking the time to do it right.

Previously, I hadn't told her about the struggle to find a publisher. I mentioned I'd been briefly discouraged with the project and slacked off for a few months. She eyed me curiously. "That doesn't sound like you," she said.

––––––––––––

n I initially approached Mama Wes (and Chinara and Bun) with the idea to do a book on Pimp C back in 2010, all three gave verbal approval.* Over the course of our interviews, I'd come to understand why Mama Wes so readily entrusted me with the task of telling her son's life story. "[Chad] admired you a lot … because he saw you as a very strong woman," she told me. "The term he used was 'a little spitfire.'"

She told me that I'd even been considered as Pimp's potential manager. "[Rick Martin] couldn't do that job … the [only] person who could have worked with C on that level, other than me, would've been you … he admired what you had done with [OZONE] Magazine," she said. "He had a lot of respect for your abilities, and not just your abilities, but your tenacity."

I was at first shocked by this suggestion, but in going through my old interviews, was reminded of Pimp asking me to help set up a meeting with Interscope about a distribution deal, asking me to help coordinate a tour with Houston artists, and wished I'd been paying more attention. If he'd had more honest people working with him, could he have been spared the Byron Hills and Eddie Floyds?

Plus, writing this book had given me a certain level of sympathy for him, especially with his legal situation, where it seemed that a relatively minor incident had been blown completely out of proportion. Even for me, with the benefit of hindsight, digging through hundreds of pages of his case-related paperwork and legal terminology was incredibly confusing and difficult to unravel. It was easy to see how Chad – and so many others who got caught up in the system – would find it hard to navigate while caught up in it.

Not only did I have a newfound sympathy for Pimp C, but as I wrote, my anger grew towards all the injustice he had suffered at the hands of people he'd trusted. How could his manager walk away after his death with 62% of his money while his kids received .05%? Why didn't he have more people in his life looking out for his best interests? He fought everyone else's battles, why was no one else fighting for him?

I began to see the things he'd said – which had once sounded like bizarre rants – in a new light. His 4 AM phone calls, even the Hot 107.9 radio interview, now that I understood them in context, weren't crazy at all: he was telling the absolute truth.

Most of all, Mama Wes told me, she believed in me because her son felt I had what they called "stickability," the dogged persistence often required to see a project through to the end. "C liked to see people who just wouldn't quit … who would just push and push and push until they got it done," she'd told me once. "[He] knew a little bit about the history of OZONE, and you, too. You had a rough time getting that thing [going]; you had to push to get it off the ground … C had a lot of respect for anybody who would persevere."

A year earlier, she had eloquently summarized the concept of "stickability" for a crowd of aspiring artists at SF2's Kickback Sundays.

"I wanna give you a little advice, straight from Mama Pimp and Pimp up [in Heaven]: don't quit. If there's anything that's gonna get you going [and] keep you going, it's 'stickability,'" she'd told them, adding, "When it gets rough, that means something good is gonna happen. You gotta believe that. If you don't believe in yourself … If you don't believe in what you doing, you damn sure not gonna be able to convince me and nobody else … There is no magic bullet, [just] a lot of hard work. You can do it … Go everywhere [and] see everybody, because you never know when your magic moment is. That's all you gotta do – you gotta be in the right place at the right time."

I assured her I had "stickability" and had moved past the minor setback. The next step was to send her a rough draft; we made plans to film her on camera next time telling some of her favorite Pimp C stories. We embraced and said our goodbyes.

Our interviews during that trip were sometimes interrupted by terrible fits of coughing which I privately felt sounded alarming, but knowing she was an elderly woman who routinely

---

(*Chinara initially agreed to the terms of the book deal but never signed the paperwork and ceased communication for no apparent reason. The book was completed without her participation.)

mentioned doctor's visits, thought it would be inappropriate to voice any of my uninformed opinions about her health.

I finally left Houston on Tuesday, June 11, truly inspired, armed with all the information I needed to finish the book. As my flight taxied down the runway, I didn't know that 400 miles away, Larry "L.A." Adams was also boarding a plane in Jackson, Mississippi.

Loss had become a constant in Larry's life. In six years he'd lost his grandmother, his father, and his older brother Rod to a construction-related accident. Even though he had reasons to be optimistic about the future (he and his fiancé had just set a wedding date), his codeine use had become constant. He'd been depressed and gained weight, ballooning to 300 pounds.

When he landed that evening in Fresno, California, his godmother's cousin Sheree Hammond rented a room for him at the nearby Piccadilly Inn. Two days later, Larry called his mother back home in Jackson, sounding depressed. Later that night, he got a portrait of his brother's face tattooed on his right arm and texted a picture of it to his mother.

A friend in Fresno, Lloyd Edwards, picked him up and they stopped at Carl's Jr for some chicken fingers. Larry had been sluggish all day; when Lloyd dropped him off at the hotel late that night, he was concerned enough to offer to stay with him. Larry declined.

At 8 AM the next morning, Sheree, also concerned about Larry's depressed demeanor, stopped by the Piccadilly Inn. She found his body face-up on the floor of Room 159, lifeless and stiff with a blue-purplish hue, clear foam pouring abundantly from his mouth.*

Larry Adams, just 30 years old, was pronounced dead at 9:27 AM on June 14, 2013. In his room, Fresno firemen found five empty prescription bottles of promethazine-codeine, totaling roughly four pints.

On the other side of the country, I got a text: "Four-fingered Larry died today."

Initially, the rumor in Jackson was that Larry had been found at the same hotel as Pimp C. Some thought he'd idolized Pimp so much he even wanted to die like him. This part was proven inaccurate, but a few days later, when his obituary appeared in the Jackson newspaper, I took a deep breath and called Mama Wes.

"I'm not sure whether this is good news or bad news…" I started, unsure how to even begin the conversation.

She sounded upset at the news of Larry's passing, blurting out, "Oh, no. Now Corey will never know the truth."

The comment struck me as odd. Didn't *she* want to know, too?

The Fresno County Coroner would later conclude that Larry Adams committed suicide by overdosing on codeine. Toxicology showed that Larry's blood contained 585 ng/mL of codeine and 622 ng/mL of morphine; codeine turns into morphine when it passes through the liver, and too much of it can cause the heart and lungs to stop functioning.**

The main "person of interest" in Chad's possible murder being found dead alone in a hotel room struck many of Chad's friends as ironic. It could be viewed as karma, a very strange coincidence, or just another in a long list of codeine cautionary tales.

"Well," reflected XVII, "Sounds like that situation worked itself out."

"Somebody must have got him too," DJ Bird whispered conspiratorially.

Although I regretted never being able to speak with Larry, it struck me that from a writer's standpoint, it was a very appropriate ending for the book. What better way to end the story?

(*Curiously, Larry also had three abrasions on the left side of his forehead. "It is unknown how he sustained these injuries," the police report stated. The report listed his occupation as "Rapper.")
(**More than 500 ng/mL of codeine or 200 ng/ML of morphine in the bloodstream is toxic.)

Sadly, I was wrong. The story wasn't over yet.

———

Two months after Larry's death, I got a call from Ronda Forrest saying that Mama Wes was back in the hospital. I knew she'd recently had a bout with pneumonia and was unable to attend Trae Day 2013. (When Mama joked that she was "doing time," Jada sent a flower arrangement to the hospital with a note quoting Pimp C's "Free": "Do your time. Don't let your time do you.") When I asked how serious it was, there was a long pause. "Between you and me," Ronda confided, "She has stage four lung cancer."

I froze. *Lung cancer?!?* Mama Wes lit up a cigarette occasionally at the house and talked freely in our interviews of smoking since she started teaching in the 1960s, but it still came as a shock. How long had she known? Why hadn't she told anyone?[*]

When Mama Wes started smoking, 42% of American adults were smokers. The health hazards wouldn't become widespread public knowledge until some 20 years later. And even though smoking has been the leading cause of preventable deaths in the country for decades, killing nearly half a million Americans every year, I never imagined it'd happen to *her*. She seemed larger than life, somehow; like her son.[**]

Skimming the results of a Google search for "stage four lung cancer and pneumonia" was terrifying. Pages upon pages of results said the combination of pneumonia and lung cancer was a sure sign that the patient was near death. *Death??? But this is Mama Wes; she's a fighter!* I thought. This couldn't be the end. Not yet. If anybody was strong enough to fight, it was her.

As I sat numbly on the flight to Houston the next day, everything we'd talked about during our last visits came flashing back. Without realizing it, I'd been documenting the last words of a woman who felt death upon her. She'd even hinted at it. Shortly before one of our last interviews, she'd gotten an unexpected call from Byron Hill. Years of heavy drinking had taken a toll on him, and after not one but *two* liver transplants, he'd reached out to her just to talk about his brush with death. "That kind of thing tends to put different things on your mind," she'd said, recalling her near-fatal car accident. "I know 'cause I had that brush."

By the time I reached Port Arthur, Mama Wes was already sedated and unable to communicate. 2 Chainz, who was in nearby Austin for a performance on Lil Wayne's America's Most Wanted tour, had rushed to her bedside and was the last person to see her before one of her lungs collapsed and doctors were forced to put her in a breathing incubator.

The hours rolled into Saturday morning, the sun rising on a tense and tearful day as Mama Wes' grandsons, family members, close friends, Bun and Queenie, Trae, and many others congregated for hours in the waiting room at The Medical Center of Southeast Texas. (There were even a few not-so-welcome guests – like the male groupie type with fake dreadlocks who had to be escorted out of ICU as he insisted that Mama Wes had authorized him to pick up Corey to attend Lil Wayne's concert.)

The contrasting aspects of Pimp C's sons' personalities emerged there, too. As Chad Jr. exhibited a calm demeanor and stepped up to make tough decisions on behalf of the family, Corey was the class clown, making bets to collect dollar bills from the friends and family gathered, and playing basketball in the waiting room with packets of ketchup and hot sauce (an activity in

(*According to Pops, he had long suspected lung cancer, but Mama Wes insisted her nagging cough was just allergies. It appears the cancer grew at an extremely accelerated rate because of an unexpected heart procedure she had in late June, shortly after our last interview, in which a coronary stent was installed to alleviate chest pain. She was diagnosed with lung cancer in early August 2013, about a week before she was rushed back to the hospital. The lung cancer death rate in the Beaumont/Port Arthur area is nearly 50% higher than the rest of the country, likely because of the smog and air pollution emitted by the refineries, several of which are located around the corner from Mama Wes' home of nearly 40 years.)

(**Chad didn't smoke cigarettes and had never approved of his mother's only vice. In a 2007 *OZONE* interview, he said he considered cigarettes and alcohol even more dangerous than PCP. "Just because it's sold in the store don't make that shit safe," he said. "It shouldn't be socially acceptable just because these muthafuckers will sell it to you in a pretty package. Beware of the pretty package, you know?")

which I may or may not have participated).

Between ICU visiting hours, the group gathered at Mama Wes' home on Shreveport Ave just a few miles away and offered words of support to Pops. Thoughtful neighbors dropped by with dishes of food prepared, a small token of gratitude for Mama Wes' meals they'd surely enjoyed over the years. Thirteen-year-old Corey declared that the gumbo was good, but not as good as Granny's.

When the group headed back to the hospital that Saturday afternoon, there had been no improvement. Pastor John Morgan led everyone in prayer, holding hands around her bedside, asking God for a miracle. Corey's mom Angie, a registered nurse, tried to keep hope alive, but knew the situation was dire. Doctors said she could hear and understand voices, but the immobile, unresponsive body wasn't the Mama Wes I knew; not the entertaining, uplifting woman I wanted to remember.

Although Mama Wes was sedated, nurses occasionally revived her for brief moments with Pops and her grandsons. The attending nurse said he'd never seen such a large group visiting an ICU patient. Mama Wes may have only had one biological son, but she was *everyone's* informally adopted mother, as evidenced by the diverse crowd on hand.

Only a few people, like Big Munn, had been able to maintain relationships with both Chinara and Mama Wes. Big Munn, who had always considered their feud "corny," was one of many who stopped by the hospital on Saturday. He called Chinara from the ICU waiting room, his booming voice drawing strange looks from some seated nearby.

"Say mane, you need to bring that girl up here so she could see her grandmother," Big Munn said.

Chinara had already declined Angie's offer to bring Christian to the hospital. "Munn, I don't wanna…" Chinara began.

"Chinara, listen to me," Munn urged. "We not dealing with *if* she make it. We dealing with *when* she die."

"It's that serious?" she asked.

"*Maaan,* I wouldn't be calling you if it wasn't fuckin' that serious," Munn snapped.

Chinara knew her presence at the hospital wouldn't be welcomed by those who knew the history between her and Mama Wes. "I don't need no niggas…" she argued.

Munn interrupted. "It ain't about what 'them niggas' want. It ain't about that shit, Chinara. What would that boy [Chad] want you to do? Fuck them niggas."

Doctors summoned the family back to the hospital before daybreak on Sunday morning, telling them it was only a matter of time. Chinara and her mother Normia brought 11-year-old Christian to the hospital as the sun rose Sunday morning. Some considered Chinara's presence vengeful, while others interpreted it as reconciliatory – yet too little, too late. It was only the third time Christian had seen her grandmother since Chad died.

"I made my peace [with Chinara]," Mama Wes had told me back in 2010. "I doubt whether she ever will." Her only regret, she said, was not getting to be a part of her granddaughter's life. The Easter basket Mama Wes had bought for the girl was still resting on the fireplace mantel at Shreveport Ave.

"I hated that they never did work out their differences, 'cause it could've been a totally different turn-out," sighs Big Munn. "[Pimp has] a good legacy, but it could've been a whole lot fuckin' better with them two working together."

As for me, I did what I always do to cope when life gets too heavy: I laced up my running shoes, looping six miles on a dirt path, sweating in the humidity and trying to mentally prepare myself for the inevitable.

As a journalist I'd always taken pride in being objective enough to separate my emotions from the task at hand, and until now, had never considered how much losing Mama Wes might affect me personally. But as I'd stood there at her bedside, holding hands with the family as John Morgan said a prayer, a tear escaping from his eye and finding its way slowly down his cheek, my heart ached too.

But it wasn't just sorrow washing over me, there was something else there, too: unity, comradery, the sense that everything was going to be okay because we weren't in it alone. I'd become part of the family. As with her son, I'd started out intending to cover the story and become part of the story. And I'd finally realized that the story I was writing wasn't about rap. It was about family: a boy and his mother who took over the world together, both in triumph and in tragedy, with a bit of comedy along the way.

Any other Sunday at 11:00 AM, Mama Wes would be in her Dickies playing the tambourine as services began at United Christian Fellowship Church, but this week, God had other plans. At 11:01 AM on the morning of Sunday, August 18, 2013, she passed away surrounded with love, after 66 years of a full life. "I think Mama just gave up," Pops sighs. "She just gave up and wanted to go. She wanted to be with C."

Silence reigned for a few hours; everyone lost in their own grief. Finally, Bun B issued a touching eulogy via Instagram: "Thanks to everyone that has sent prayers and condolences. She was a great woman. Nurture us from boys to men and made us strong enough to handle this industry. She was the one that kept us going when we didn't wanna go anymore. She was the backbone of UGK, the definition of loyalty, the personification of unconditional love and the essence of what being Trill really meant. She's finally reunited with her son. God bless you both. RIP Mama Wes. You gave everything to make us Underground Kings." //

"I would not give up those years, darling, for anything in the world. Because I lived a life that [few] people get a chance to live."

– Mama Wes, Damage Control Radio, December 2008

Above: **Mama Wes' funeral booklet**, which cleverly incorporated the UGK logo.
Design: Kevin "Mr. Soul" Harp

Above: In one of her last public appearances, **2 Chainz** brought **Mama Wes** out on stage at Houston's Free Press Summer Festival on June 1, 2013. She was accompanied by the **UGKidz** *(below)* **Tra** and her grandson **Corey**. Photos: Julia Beverly

Less than three months later, 2 Chainz was one of the last people to see Mama Wes at a Port Arthur hospital before she passed. His touching flower bouquet *(right)* at her funeral read, "I tried to find a heart bigger than yours, and I could not."

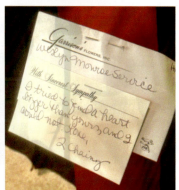

Clockwise from above: **Larry Adams**, pictured in a 2012 music video sporting a "UGK 4 Life" tattoo, UGK Records chain, and double-cupped Styrofoam; the **tattoo of his brother Rod** that Larry got the night before he died; Larry's **UGK Records chain** with "L.A." at the top.

Courtesy of Korleon

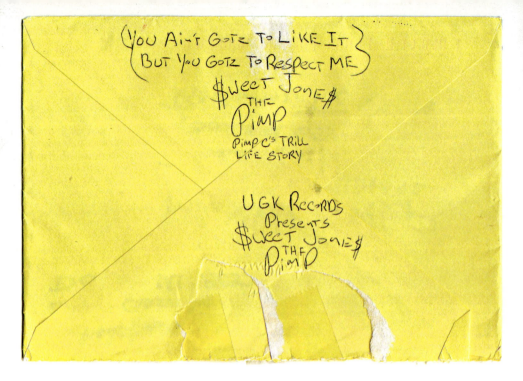

Above: Paperwork from Chad's years behind bars.

Courtesy of Weslyn Monroe

Below: **Mama Wes' interment** at Greenlawn Memorial Park on August 23, 2013.

Photo: James "FLX" Smith

Below: Pallbearers **Bun B, Trae tha Truth, Ron Forrest, DJ Bird, Edgar Walker, Byron Amos, Hezeleo, XVII,** and others carry Mama Wes home.

Photos: Julia Beverly

Above: **Weslyn "Mama Wes" Monroe** and **Chad "Pimp C" Butler's** final resting place at Greenlawn Memorial Park in Groves, Texas.

Photo: Julia Beverly

Above: After Mama Wes' funeral, dozens of friends and family members gathered at her home on Shreveport Ave. **A rainbow and angelic cloud** hovered above the house after a sudden but brief thunderstorm doused the neighborhood.

Photo: Benjamin "Benzo" Thomas

ACKNOWLEDGMENTS

No doubt about it, God is the real publisher of this book, because there's no way this project could have come together as perfectly as it did without somebody above coordinating everything.

This book also would not have been possible without Mama Wes, who was an invaluable resource when piecing together the events described in this book. She's a master storyteller, and nearly everyone I interviewed did their best impression of her son's one-of-a-kind voice while reminiscing, but naturally, she's the only one who can nail it. I spent countless hours in her kitchen listening to her stories, indulging in her famous homecooked meals, and trying to wrestle my iPad back from Corey.

Mama Wes was remarkably strong even when discussing her son's death. The only time I ever saw her get choked up was when discarding the "99,000" pairs of Chad's Dickies gathering dust in her game room. She's also unusually open-minded for a woman in her 60s, and to Bun B's dismay, she'll name "I Left It Wet For You, Nigga" as one of her all-time favorite UGK songs (Bun B: "Now that's just wrong"). I can only hope to be as cool as her one day when I grow up.

Thanks to Bun B for encouraging me to be as honest as possible and trusting me to tell Pimp C's story, and in turn UGK's story, accurately.

Thanks to J. Prince, one of the smartest men I've ever met and the closest thing I've ever had to a mentor. I truly appreciate the times you allowed me to come around and soak up some game. I wouldn't be qualified to write a book on Southern rap otherwise.

Thanks to the original Pappadeaux seafood restaurant on Westheimer, a.k.a. My Houston Office. In truth, this project was just an excuse to spend a lot of time there eating conducting interviews.

BBB, I erased everything sappy I wrote here, but you played a role in all this, and for that I thank you. Here's that pimpin' book you always swore I was writing. Hope Daddy likes it.

Thanks to Lil Wayne and Cortez Bryant, Eddie Lance, Rick Ross, and Dollah Dae; Chad Jr., Corey, Angie, Nitacha, Pops, Ronda, and Tara; Maurice Garland, Andrew Cencini and Debbie Warnock, Ebonee Thompson, Matt Sonzala, Candace Primeaux, kris ex, and Tamara Palmer. Thanks to the H-Town crew Devi and Duane, Slim Thugga, and Scarface for always making me feel at home. Thanks to Mr. Soul for helping bring the visuals to life. Thanks to King Yella, Korleon, Ronda Forrest, Pookie, Tambra Cooper, Aaron Cole, Maurlon Banks, Curtis Daniel III, Naztradamus, and everyone else who went the extra mile to assist with my research.

God bless Google, ExpressScribe, and whoever designed PACER and the Harris County District Clerk's website. Thanks to all my friends and family for being so understanding through this process even though I've been neglecting you lately. Apologies to anyone I didn't mention by name. And finally, thanks to everyone who took the time out to do an interview for this book:

Langston Adams
Phalon "Jazze Pha" Alexander
Jeremy "Mouse" Allen
Torris "T.O.E." Alpough
Byron Amos
Lalionee Anderson
Michael "Big Mike" Barnett
Robert Barnett a.k.a. "T-Mo Goodie"
Chris "Mr. 3-2" Barriere
Paul Beauregard a.k.a. "DJ Paul"
Steve Below
Madison "Korleon" Blackmon
Anthony "Boz" Boswell
Anthony "B.A.N.D.I.T." Bowser
Calvin "Snoop Dogg" Broadus
Kim "Infinity" Broussard-Small

Nitacha Broussard
Riley "Scoobie" Broussard
Cheryl Brown-Marks
Nicholas "Truck" Brown
Patrick "Sleepy" Brown
Ricardo "Kurupt" Brown
R. Scott Budge
Sylvester "Vesto" Bullard
Darrell "Pharoah" Burton
Chad Butler Jr.
Nancy Byron
Evander "Boonie" Cade
Bobby Caillier
Travis "Mugz" Cains
Donald Campbell a.k.a. "Bishop Don 'Magic' Juan"
Brittany "Diamond" Carpentero

Danny "Kartel" Castillo
Demetrius "DJ Dolby D" Charles
Imani Chyle a.k.a. "MC Bytch"
Marjorie Cole
Ronald "OG Ron C" Coleman
Devin "the Dude" Copeland
Wanda Coriano
Angela Crooks
Roy "Naztradamus" Cross
Lavell "David Banner" Crump
Johnny "TV Johnny" Dang
Curtis Daniel III
Bradley "DJ B-Do" Davis
Charleston "Short Dawg" Davis
Wendy Day
Willie Dennis a.k.a. "Willie D"
Dwayne Diamond

Dorie "DJ DMD" Dorsey
DeJuan Durisseau a.k.a. "D Stone"
Kehinde "KD" Durisseau
Marcus "Lil Keke" Edwards
Anthony "Ace Deuce" Elder
Quanell "X" Evans
Quincy Evans
Warren Fitzgerald
Brian "Kool Ace" Fleming
Ocean "O" Fleming
Demetrius "Big Meech" Flenory
Kristi Floyd
Ron "Crumz" Forrest
Ronda Forrest
Steve Fournier
Brad "Kamikaze" Franklin
Bernard "Bun B" Freeman
David "D-A" Frost
Joi Gilliam
Reginald "Point Blank" Gilliland
Cameron Gipp a.k.a. "Big Gipp"
Marlon "MJG" Goodman
Stephanie Gowdy
Charles "Dat Boy" Grace
Webster "Webbie" Gradney Jr.
Yakeen Green a.k.a. "Lil Green"
Warren Griffin III a.k.a. "Warren G"
Michael "Big Munn" Grisby
Lowell "Young Lo" Grissom
Daniel "DJ Bird" Grogan
Robert Guillerman
Tim Hampton
Lee "Master" Harmason
Brenda Harmon
Janeen Harmon
Avery "Averexx" Harris
Cleveland "Captain Jack" Harris
Darrell "D-Solo" Harris
Pam Harris
Patrick "Wink Dawg" Harris
Christopher "King Yella" Hawkins
Bobby "Tre9" Herring
Shawn "Tubby" Holiday
Jordan "Juicy J" Houston
Troy "T-Roy" Hunter
Craig "XVII" Isabelle
"Pimpin" Ken Ivy
Jelon Jackson
Stephen "Stak5" Jackson
Wesley Jacob Jr.
Eric "Vicious" Johnson
Fredrick "Freddy" Johnson
Heather Johnson
Joseph "N.O. Joe" Johnson
Nahala "Mr. Boomtown" Johnson
Vee Johnson
Mike Jones
Richard "Fiend" Jones
Brad "Scarface" Jordan
Sean Paul Joseph
Herbert "Superb Herb" Keller
Elliott "Bo-Bo Luchiano" Kennedy
Isreal "Bluelite" Kight
Doug King
Willie "Khujo Goodie" Knighton Jr.
Detective Steve Lankford
Lichelle "Bo$$" Laws
Craig "KLC" Lawson

Marlan Rico Lee
Desmond Louis
Lonnie "Big L" Love
Pierre "Born 2wice" Maddox
Ore "Lil O" Magnus-Lawson
Pam Malek
Michael Maroy
Sam Martin
Kenneth "KB Da Kidnappa" McGee
Joseph "Z-Ro" McVey
John "Stax" Miller
Percy "Master P" Miller
Detective Marcelo Molfino
Weslyn "Mama Wes" Monroe
Charles Moore Jr. a.k.a. "Mike Mo"
Cory Moore a.k.a. "Cory Mo"
Carlos "Lo" Moreland
Pastor John Morgan
Ashlei Morrison
Tracy "Ice-T" Morrow
Herbert "Hezeleo" Mouton
Ray Murray
Jeffrey "Ghost" Nations
Faith Newman
Dawn Nico
Leo Nocentelli
Hashim Nzinga
"Jammin" Jimmy Olson
Ivory Pantallion a.k.a. "Ivory P"
Pearce Pegross
Eric Perrin
Charles Pettiway
Lloyd Polite
Greg "Street" Polk
Raymond "Mo B. Dick" Poole
Roland "Lil Duval" Powell
Kawan "KP" Prather
Mitchell Queen Jr.
Dale "Rambro" Ramsey
Shaheem Reid
Michael "Killer Mike" Render
Rob Reyes
Winston "Tela" Rogers
Millard "Pops" Roher
Brandi Rook a.k.a. "Brandi Garcia"
Ricardo "Rick" Royal
Ayesha Saafir
Halimah Saafir
Ariel "REL" Santschi
Vanessa Satten
Mike Schreiber
Justin "Big K.R.I.T." Scott
Malik Zulu Shabazz
Richard "Bushwick Bill" Shaw
Todd "Too $hort" Shaw
David "Mr. DJ" Sheats
Stan "Hot Boy" Shepherd
George "G" Simmons
John "Baz" Singleton
Paul Slayton a.k.a. "Paul Wall"
Jeff Sledge
Brodrick "Young Smitty" Smith
Courtney "C-Note" Smith
Premro "8Ball" Smith
Roderick "Smit-D" Smith
Matt Sonzala
Freddie "Smoke D" Southwell

Ron Spaulding
Selena Starring
Stephanie Starring
Stephen Starring
Tara Starring
Chuck Steeno
Earl "E-40" Stevens
Ron Stewart
Kavin Stokes
Corey "Funkafangez" Stoot
Anne-Marie Stripling
Roger Tausz
Byron "Mannie Fresh" Thomas
Daniel "Lil Dan" Thomas
Dewayne Thomas
Joe Thomas
Shawn "C-Bo" Thomas
Stayve "Slim Thug" Thomas
Matthew "Knowledge Born" Thompkins
Bonsu Thompson
Frazier "Trae" Thompson
Stephan "Steve-O" Townsend
Micah "Pastor" Troy
John "Dr. Teeth" Tucker
Jaro Vacek
Rico Wade
Teresa Waldon
Edgar Walker Jr.
J. Walker
Zachary "Big Zack" Wallace
Russell Washington
Derrick "Fonzworth Bentley" Watkins
Barry Weiss
Wesley "Lil Flip" Weston Jr.
Edward "Big Bubb" Williams
Dr. Kirk Williams
Rowdy "Ganksta N-I-P" Williams
Charlie Wilson
Larry "NcGai" Wiltz
Calvin "Good Game" Winbush
Ed Winter
Craig Wormley
Mickey "MempHitz" Wright, Jr.
Adrian "Donny" Young
Charles "Pep C" Young
Merrick Young
Mia Young a.k.a. "Mia X"
Eric "Bone" York
Bankroll Jonez
Bianca*
Bundy G
DJ Chill
DJ C-Wiz
DJ Funky
Greedy Ent.
Jada*
KayK
Kep
Killa Kyleon
Kilo
Kiwi
Lanika
Mean Green
Paperchase
Travis*
Troy D
Wickett Crickett

(*Three names were changed at the participants' request.)

Texas Monthly: "Looking back on over twenty years of
being an artist, what are you most proud of?"
Bun B: "Probably the fact that my partner in all of it
was Pimp C. Nobody else can say that."

BARRY WEISS & JIVE RECORDS:

In 2008, Weiss got a promotion, taking over for Clive Davis overseeing the RCA/Jive division of Sony BMG. In April 2011, he departed Sony for their chief competitor, Universal Music Group. Based in New York, he now serves as the Chairman and CEO of Island Def Jam, Motown, and Republic Records.

In October 2011, Jive Records – as well as Clive Davis' Arista and J Records – folded into their parent company, RCA Records. Most of the artists were released, and some were absorbed into RCA.

In 2013, *Complex* Magazine named Barry Weiss the "Best A&R in Hip-Hop History," noting that he'd "built the most powerful and lasting roster of Hip-Hop and Hip-Hop-influenced R&B and pop music in history" during his tenure as CEO of Jive Records.

In addition to being an early believer in UGK, *Complex* writer Dan Charnas cited Weiss' investment in then-unknown artists like A Tribe Called Quest, Too $hort, E-40, KRS-One, DJ Jazzy Jeff & The Fresh Prince (Will Smith), R. Kelly, Aaliyah, T-Pain, and Chris Brown – as well as multi-platinum international pop stars like The Backstreet Boys, N'Sync and Justin Timberlake, and Britney Spears – as undeniable evidence of his talent-scouting abilities.

Although he was ahead of the curve on the Texas rap movement, Weiss says he can't call it when asked for a prediction on the future of the rap game. "Oh God, I don't know," he laughs. "I can't really say. I don't have any pearls of wisdom."

BYRON AMOS:

Mama Wes' only complaint about Byron Amos is that he's "too nice to be in this raggedy-ass [music] business." In 2011, Amos, who had worked as a community organizer in Atlanta for more than 20 years in addition to his work with UGK, ran for the Atlanta school board. But his campaign didn't come without controversy.

After learning that he'd previously been Vice President of UGK Records, an influential teachers' union pulled their support. "For him to actually want to run for the board and say that he cares about children, when what he's doing is using this [rap] music to do the worst for our children," complained Shawnna Hayes Tavarez, president of the union. "It's like robbing them and killing them. It's like cheating for them."

"He insists we should understand that it was just a job for him to be outside of a nightclub promoting gangster rap music that calls my nieces, and your daughters, [a vulgar term]," the former chairman of the school board, Khaatim S. El, agreed.

Nevertheless, Amos won the election and was appointed Vice Chairman of the Atlanta Board of Education in December 2011. He has been recognized by WATL 36 as an "Unsung Hero" and an "Outstanding Atlantan" for his work developing new housing and reducing crime in the Atlanta neighborhood where he lives with his wife and four children.

BYRON HILL:

Oddly, Mama Wes' passing indirectly brought me face-to-face with the man Bun had once predicted I'd never find: the elusive Byron Hill. Ronda Forrest called the number for "Byron" in Mama Wes' phone – which she assumed to be Byron Amos – to make arrangements to meet with him when the UGKidz visited Atlanta for the 2013 BET Hip-Hop Awards. But the man on the other end of the line was Byron Hill.

When I reached out to him, he agreed to be interviewed, but our meeting at an Atlanta area Pizza Hut can only be described as bizarre. He appeared disheveled, paranoid and combative, his eyes darting over his sunglasses scanning the parking lot as we spoke. He changed his mind about being interviewed and refused to allow me to record the conversation.

Byron expressed sorrow at Mama Wes' passing, saying that he'd taught her everything she knew about the music business. Byron seems to view his brief involvement with UGK as the sole reason for their success. It was a tale Mama Wes had told me she'd heard "35,000 times" before.

"I know [Byron Hill's] story … he really feels like he's totally responsible for their success," Mama Wes had told me several years earlier. "There was a time that I thought he was just bullshitting, but … I really and truly believe that somewhere in his delusional mind he believes that. [But] he didn't put in the legwork. He didn't put in the long hours. And I don't know how he can honestly think he's responsible."

In Mama Wes' opinion, Byron's contribution to the group's success was minimal. "I think he taught 'em about getting screwed," she laughs. "He taught 'em a real good lesson."

Up until her death, Mama Wes had been one of the few people who still kept in touch with Byron, calling him once in a while just "to see if he's still alive." Most of his former associates are surprised, and somewhat upset, to learn that he is. "[He's] probably dead," Russell Washington shrugs. "I wouldn't care."

"I'm surprised he doesn't have a bullet in his head," agrees Doug King.

CHARLESTON BUTLER:
Chad's father Charleston Butler still lives on 13th Street in Port Arthur and recently retired from Gulf Oil after 40 years with the company.

DJ BIRD:
DJ Bird, who works for the Port Arthur school district, says he still misses the good ol' days on the road with Chad. "I seen some wild shit. Boy, it was fun at times. I had fun," he smiles. "If C was still alive, I'd be with him right now, on the road, making big money."

DJ DMD:
DMD was once viewed as the mastermind of Port Arthur's Hip-Hop scene, but today, to say that he is disliked by his former peers would be an understatement. If there is one thing that unites Port Arthur rappers, it appears to be their mutual disdain for DMD. (Some say he was "exiled" from the city.)

Although Pimp C and Isreal Kight squashed their differences, the small community never quite forgave DMD for allegedly instigating the drama, an accusation which DMD brushes off. "[As] time goes on [and] we all get older, we realize how stupid that stuff was," he says.

DMD's transition into gospel music was widely met with skepticism. "DMD is a bitch," says former Inner Soul artist Boonie. "[He's only] acting like he's into God real heavy so niggas won't kill his ass."

"Once a snake always a snake, but GOD CAN TAKE OUT THE VENOM, leaving the snake worthless!" Mitchell Queen writes of DJ DMD.

"Cats used to run my name in the mud," DMD acknowledges. "But as you see, all of them ain't doing nothing but sitting around getting high. One of the reasons why I had to leave."

"To this day, nobody in Port Arthur understands why I made the decision I did," DMD told the *Houston Chronicle*. DMD says he no longer listens to secular rap. When rock band ZZ Top covered "25 Lighters" in 2012, DMD used his royalty check to establish E5 Entertainment (after the Biblical book of Ephesians) and released a remix of "25 Lighters" called "25 Bibles."

DMD says he is discouraged by the direction of today's Hip-Hop music. "Hip-Hop was music for people to get away from their problems, to have fun," he told the *Houston Chronicle*. "We got away from that and started making cookie-cutter music about chasing the dollar. People say, 'It's just music.' But it's not just music. We have a choice about what we do. There's power in our words."

Despite the rough spots in their relationship, DMD says he has nothing but fond memories of Chad Butler. "[Chad] was a pioneer in music [and a] good dude with a sweet spirit," says DMD. "I still just remember the jheri-curl trumpet player with glasses in my garage. That's how I like to remember him."

DJ SCREW:
Today, grey Screw tapes are cherished like trophies. One of them is on display at the University of Houston's M.D. Anderson Library, which also houses DJ Screw's record collection. (Screw tapes are now available on CDs and can be purchased online at www.screweduprecords.com.)

"I wanna Screw the whole world," DJ Screw had told *The Source* back in July 1995. In the decade following his death, that dream has become a reality. Not only did Screw music inspire an entire generation of rappers, but even pop singers like Justin Timberlake, Ciara, and Chris Brown have used elements of the style in their records. "Kelly Rowland, Fantasia, everybody got a lil' Screw in the hook, everything kinda chopped and slurred," notes Lil Keke.

As for Houston, the city's underground scene remains strong, but has fallen out of the national spotlight. "The Houston artists didn't take advantage of opportunities," J. Prince told The Breakfast Club. "They didn't apply their hustle aggressively when the spotlight was on the city. I mean, a lot of 'em got comfortable … they was going everywhere *but* the studio."

In Bun's opinion, Houston rappers relied too heavily on DJ Screw's legacy. "A lot of people got in the game based on being affiliated with Screw or Michael Watts … [but now] we're gonna have to be able to stand on our own laurels as artists and as men and put our lives out there on record," Bun told *OZONE*.

Today, creating "Screwed and chopped" versions of songs is easier than ever with computer software like Logic, Audacity, and Frooty Loops. Listeners worldwide of all ages have been exposed to Screw's music, but SUC members say no one will ever top the original. "The reason Screw is the king is based on timing," Lil Keke told *VICE*. "[He was the king] when being the king meant something."

"Screw was a good person, that's why we represent him," Bun told journalist Maurice Garland. "Screw could've been more famous than he was. He was very modest and selfless, that's why we all miss him to this day."

HEATHER JOHNSON:

Mama Wes' former assistant Heather Johnson is one of many who credits Chad with saving her life. "I know God sent him into my life … If it wasn't for him, honestly, there ain't no telling where I would be," she says. "It was just a matter of time before I would've slipped back into the old lifestyle."

HEZELEO:

In Bun B's opinion, UGK Records representative Hezeleo is underappreciated. "[Hezeleo has] really been the shoulder for Mama Wes to cry on … when her son left," Bun said on Damage Control Radio. "[He] needs to get credit on a larger scale … not just on the music side but as a homie and as a friend and as a supporter and as a member of this UGK family."

JADA:

When she was released from a Texas prison in November 2008, Jada discovered an unopened email from Chad in her inbox, which he'd sent on Halloween before he died. She christened her dog "Tony Snow" in his memory.

Jada says she has retired from her days as a Las Vegas escort, but jokes, "I still suck dick on the side." Jada believes she is suffering from PTSD (post-traumatic stress disorder, a condition most frequently found in military veterans) from her years in "the game." A scar on her leg from Ocean's belt buckle is a constant reminder to avoid pimps. She now views pimping as "modern day slavery" and hopes to one day start a foundation to help women who have been exploited. "Chad changed my life," she says.

JELON JACKSON:

Jelon Jackson, otherwise known as Big Jack, owns a barbershop in Port Arthur. He says that friends don't believe he was once a part of the Underground Kingz and jokingly call him the Unseen King.

KENNETH "WEASEL" WATSON:

Watson was never formally tried for the murder of Fat Pat, but DJ Screw said he had faith that karma would come around. "He killed him. He gonna get what's comin' to him," Screw told *Murder Dog* in 1999.

Watson didn't appear in court to face the murder charge and fled the state; after he was sentenced to eight years for Bail Jumping, authorities apparently decided not to pursue the case any further. By February 2006, just eight years after Fat Pat's death, Watson was back on the streets, making weekly trips to Houston to buy kilos of cocaine to sell in the Killeen/Ft. Hood area.

On June 26, 2006, a police officer attempted to pull over Watson's Chevy Avalanche for a traffic violation on the outskirts of Killeen. Watson refused to pull over, setting off a high-speed chase. When his tire blew out, Watson crashed into a ditch. He fled on foot through a quiet residential neighborhood and stashed several duffle bags at a nearby church, presumably hoping to return for them later. Police got to them first and found two pounds of marijuana, nearly a kilogram of cocaine, mail addressed to Watson, an assault rifle and a 9mm pistol.

In the following weeks, Killeen Police raided *eight* properties attempting to find Watson. He was hiding out at a girlfriend's house in Houston, where he remained a fugitive for nearly 10 months. HPD finally arrested Watson on April 19, 2007, in a raid which also turned up two semi-automatic pistols, $36,610 cash, more than three pounds of marijuana, 128 ounces of codeine, and a kilogram of cocaine.

Watson pled guilty to federal drugs and weapons charges and was sentenced to 35 years. In a lengthy and somewhat combative letter from a federal penitentiary in Atlanta, Watson declines to comment on Fat Pat's death. He is scheduled to be released in January 2040.

MARJORIE COLE:

Chad's high school choir teacher Marjorie Cole inspired many other students throughout her career. In 2006 Cole was one of 25 honorees selected by St. Paul's United Methodist Church to be featured in their book *Who's Who Among Black Port Arthurans*. She has also been honored by the NAACP and Who's Who Among America's Teachers.

An accomplished pianist and singer herself, Cole once considered abandoning teaching to pursue a career in classical music. But she doesn't regret her decision to stay. "If I had gone pro I would have missed all of this," Cole told the *Port Arthur News* in 2006, gesturing to her classroom full of harmonizing students. "The Lord puts us where he wants us."

MITCHELL QUEEN JR.:

"People may never really understand how much of a contribution Mitchell Queen has made to UGK," Bun said on Damage Control Radio. Although Mitch is used to people reminding him what "might" have happened if he had stuck with rapping instead of going off to college, he says he's happy with the role he played. "It was supposed to happen the way it happened, man," he said on Damage Control Radio. "Everything happens for a reason."

Mitch says he has plans to release the early material he and Chad recorded prior to *The Southern Way*, as well as previously unreleased songs like "Weed Weed." "Mitch is a real music connoisseur," Chad explained on *The Final Chapter* DVD. "I never was that organized, I was moving too fast." Mitch still raps under the name Big Smokin' Mitch and his albums *Big Mitch iz Still Smokin'* and *Big Mitch iz the Foundation* are available on iTunes. "If [my music] is an extension of [UGK's legacy], you know I'm not gonna put out no bullshit," he says.

OCEAN "O" FLEMING:

After Jada's "30 days of hell" with Ocean in early 2007, he spent several profitable years as a pimp on the streets of Las Vegas. His violent history was sometimes useful in his new line of work. One of his girls, a 17-year-old working with a fake ID, was sent by an escort service to visit a client who allegedly raped her and held her against her will. "I really wanted to find [the client]," Ocean writes. "I guess he crossed somebody else because before I caught up with him somebody else did ... Word on the streets is that he got pinned down, raped with a broomstick, and beaten to a bloody [pulp], then left in the middle of the street asshole naked with shit runnin' down his legs. I don't think he'll be a problem to no females no more!!"

Although likely unaware of the broomstick incident, Las Vegas vice detectives were already investigating Ocean. "He brought his violence with him [to the pimp game] from the gang side, and that's why he was such an important target for us," Detective Chris Baughman told *FOX5 News*.

Police caught a break on September 28, 2011, when one of Ocean's prostitutes, April Millard, fled after a severe beating. Sobbing uncontrollably, she happened across a woman named Sivon Kadosh who was pulling out of her home and asked for help. Ocean blocked the woman's car and threatened to throw a rock through the window. The driver panicked as April, sobbing, called 911.

Ocean dragged April from the car, took her back to the home they shared, and beat her with a metal belt buckle for "snitching." Police found her several days later at a friend's house covered in bruises. Ocean was soon arrested, held on a million dollar cash bond, and charged with 27 felonies including first degree kidnapping, battery, and assault with a deadly weapon.

Police presented pictures from Ocean's cell phone ("HOE DOE" spelled out in stacks of hundred-dollar bills, for example) as evidence; four of his former prostitutes testified against him and recounted vicious beatings. "He just had this look... he wasn't even looking at me, he was like, looking past me," one recalled. "He just had a blank stare, like he was blacked out ... I had never seen anybody that angry."

A jury found Ocean guilty on all counts. At his sentencing hearing, he accused the prosecution of being "malicious and overaggressive" and referred to himself as a "sacrificial lamb" in Las Vegas' authorities' war against sex trafficking, but the court was not moved. "You need to blame yourself," the judge said. "Your arrogance got you in this mess. You preyed upon women with low self-esteem; you manipulated them."

Ocean was sentenced to life in prison and will not be eligible for parole until 2026. He plans to use his time behind bars to write two books, ½ *Man* ½ *Ape: The Memoirs of Gorilla Ocean* and the follow-up, *H.O.P.E.: Hookers Owe Pimpin' Everything.* "This is what I signed up for, and I understood he consequences when I put my gators on," Ocean writes. "Crying about what's done is not an option so instead I choose to keep toasting to this beautiful game that I love and respect so much!" He adds, "[Pimpin' is] in my D.N.A. I gave my life up for it and if they were to let me out today I'd do it again!"

RUSSELL WASHINGTON:

After a successful eight-year run, Russell shut down his record label, but the original Big Tyme Recordz shop remains. "I will always regret that they split," Mama Wes says. "In the long run, Russ got cheated out of the fame, the glitz, and the glamour. He didn't get to share in that ... I really and truly did like Russell and I will always appreciate what he did for those boys. 'Cause he gave them that first push."

Most of all, Russell mourns the loss of a friendship which never fully materialized. "I thought we all would've been friends a lot longer," he sighs. "I won't [sign] any more artists ... Even when I hear something good, I know the headache [that] comes after. With [any] artist, if I make you a million dollars, the first thing that's gonna come to your mind is how much *I* made ... They're all excited, they're hungry at first when nobody can get them there, but the minute you get them in the door ... you're the enemy. It's weird."

Over the years, even when they were at odds, Russell remained a diehard UGK fan. "I have every UGK record, even the one where they're dissing me," he says. "I still jam them." Unfortunately, Russell tossed most of his early UGK memorabilia, and is sad to report that he doesn't even have one copy of the original *The Southern Way* cassette. But if nothing else, he'll always have a place in rap history. "If there was no Big Tyme, I believe there would have been no UGK," he says. "Who knows if it would've been the same?"

SMOKE D:

Smoke D, currently in a Louisiana halfway house and scheduled for an August 2015 release, says he's come to view his time in prison as a blessing in disguise. "If I hadn't went [to prison], I would be dead," Smoke says. "This is a blessing for me [even though] I didn't see it at first."

Chad's fear that Smoke was cooperating with authorities appears unfounded, especially since Smoke's co-defendant was released several years before him. "He making himself look like a smothered pork chop sandwich right now, 'cause the streets ain't stupid," Smoke says. "If I'm such a big [snitch, then] why am I still in jail and you've been out five years?"

In the end, Smoke asserts that the real "crooks" were his attorneys. In fact, of the four attorneys involved with his case, three were already under investigation for various ethical and illegal violations and have since been disbarred.

Eddie Austin Jr. was already under investigation at the time he took Smoke's case for allegedly pocketing a six-figure sum entrusted to him by an elderly woman. After being narrowly cleared of the charges by the Supreme Court of Louisiana, he was sued by another former client who claimed he could not account for $1.2 million of their funds. He filed bankruptcy to halt the lawsuit but was eventually disbarred for "converting client funds to his own use." The following year he and his wife were sued by the Securities and Exchange Commission for a penny stock scam in which they had allegedly stolen $174,471 from investors by posing as owners of a fake solar power company claiming to have multi-million dollar worldwide contracts.

Eddie Austin Jr.'s law partner Greg Lyons, who represented Stan, had a longstanding gambling problem and was arrested after racking up more than $20,000 in unpaid gambling debts at a Las Vegas casino. He admitted he'd been so distracted with his personal problems that he'd been simply taking money from clients and never handling their cases. Lyons was permanently disbarred and sentenced to five years of probation for theft. He was ordered to pay $192,000 in restitution and attend Gamblers Anonymous meetings.

As for Craig Wormley, the State Bar of California had restricted his practice before he even met Chad. In September 2007 he was accused of passing off his legal responsibilities to people who weren't properly trained and ordered to stop practicing law in the state of California. He was reinstated in 2009 and then suspended again 2011 for "ethical violations" which included "not refunding or promptly refunding unearned fees, not competently performing legal services… charging unconscionable or illegal fees, noncompliance with a court order and failing to communicate." Wormley was permanently disbarred in March 2014.

TARA STARRING:

Tara Starring's plans to move to Port Arthur and start working with Pimp C and UGK Records were derailed both by Pimp's untimely passing and her own legal troubles. At 18 years old, she was indicted on federal drug charges for acting as a receptionist for her drug-dealer/gangbanger boyfriend Lyric "Half Dead" Greaves.

Tara's attorneys emphasized her "minimal involvement" in Greaves' drug-dealing activities, alleging that she had no "knowledge or understanding of the scope and structure of the enterprise" and had not "gained financially" from the sales. Tara admitted she'd been "naïve," describing herself in a letter to the judge as "a girl who had fallen for the wrong guy." She was sentenced to three years of probation and 100 hours of community service.

After Tara completed her community service and graduated from culinary arts school, she wrote a letter to the judge asking to be released from probation so she could move to Texas. "A very successful family member of mine has offered me an opportunity of a life time … to travel and record music as a career," she wrote. "My Aunt Wes has a very well known management company in the music industry. Her son was in one of the most famous rap groups … She is willing to mold me as an artist/musician."

Unfortunately, it wasn't until Mama Wes' funeral in August 2013 that Tara finally made it down to Texas. She has since relocated to the Houston area and continues to pursue her music career. She hopes to make sure the UGK Records brand lives on. "Pimp C is gone [and now] Mama's gone," she sighs. "Usually when that happens … everything fades out. I would personally like to make sure that it doesn't fade out."

YOUNG SMITTY:

Young Smitty now works in real estate in the Dallas/Ft. Worth area and says he's okay with the fact that his rap career never really took off. He's realized that he's lucky to have a calmer lifestyle and time to spend with his children. While some only saw Pimp C as the belligerent, shit-talking rapper, in Smitty's mind, Chad is just the friend who cried with him when he learned that his grandmother was dying. "That's the real Chad," he says. "That's the Chad with the heart."

December 12, 1946 – Weslyn Jacob is born in Crowley, Louisiana

December 1966 – Charleston Butler is drafted
May 13, 1967 – Charleston Butler and Weslyn Jacob marry in Crowley, Louisiana
May 20, 1967 – Charleston Butler departs for Vietnam
December 10, 1967 – Otis Redding and the Bar-Kays die in an airplane crash in Wisconsin
January 1968 – Weslyn Butler graduates from USL with a Bachelor of Arts degree in English Liberal Arts

Fall 1972 – Weslyn Butler begins teaching in Port Arthur
March 19, 1973 – Bernard Freeman is born in Houston, Texas
March 22, 1973 – Charleston and Weslyn Butler buy their first house on 13th Street in Port Arthur
November 25, 1973 – A baby shower is thrown for Weslyn Butler in Crowley, Louisiana
December 29, 1973 – Chad Lamont Butler is born at St. Mary Hospital in Port Arthur, Texas
September 1974 – Weslyn's father Wesley Jacob dies
December 26, 1974 – Charleston and Weslyn Butler buy land on Shreveport Ave. in Port Arthur, Texas
1977 – Weslyn Butler gets her Master's degree in Library Science from Lamar University
January 12, 1979 – Shortly after Chad's fifth birthday, the Butler family moves to Shreveport Ave.

July 24, 1981 – Charleston and Weslyn Butler divorce
June 3, 1982 – Norward and Mable Monroe divorce
December 1983 – Ten-year-old Chad hears Run-DMC's album and decides to become a rapper
1984 – Weslyn marries Norward Monroe
Summer 1984 – Bernard Freeman moves to Port Arthur with his mother
1987 – James Prince starts Rap-A-Lot Records
February 27, 1987 – A vehicle registered to J. Prince's dealership is discovered with 76 kilograms of cocaine
November 17, 1988 – Tim Hampton's mother Russell Jean DeJohn Hampton is killed
Fall 1989 – Bernard "Bun B" Freeman starts attending the Summit Program at Lincoln High School

April 7-11, 1990 – Chad and selected students from the Lincoln High School choir sing at Carnegie Hall in New York
Summer 1990 – Chad produces the first version of "Tell Me Something Good"

May 1991 – Chad meets Russell Washington at Big Tyme Recordz
May 28, 1991 – Mitchell Queen Jr. and Bun B graduate from high school

January 1992 – "Tell Me Something Good" debuts on Houston radio
Early 1992 – Chad drops out of high school
February 11, 1992 – UGK's first project, *The Southern Way* EP, is released through Big Tyme Recordz
April 14, 1992 – UGK officially signs a record contract with Big Tyme Recordz
April 29, 1992 – Rodney King is acquitted; rioting breaks out in Los Angeles
May 1, 1992 – UGK signs with Jive Records
May 1992 – J. Prince is arrested by Houston Police for alleged weapons charges which are later dropped
May 23, 1992 – UGK performs at the Memorial Weekend Jam in Port Arthur
May 27, 1992 – Chad's former classmates at Lincoln graduate from high school
July 1992 – UGK shoots the video for "Tell Me Something Good" in Dallas
July 16, 1992 – Chad buys a house on San Jacinto in Port Arthur
August 1, 1992 – UGK's *Banned* EP is released on Big Tyme Recordz
August 20, 1992 – Chad and Bun sign a management agreement with Byron Hill
September 21 – October 30, 1992 – Eddie Floyd allegedly embezzles money from his employer, Leschaco
November 10, 1992 – UGK's major label debut *Too Hard to Swallow* is released on Jive Records
December 1992 – UGK shoots the video for "Use Me Up" in Port Arthur
December 29, 1992 – Nitacha, a senior in high school, learns she is pregnant on Chad's 19th birthday

January 10, 1993 – J. Prince is arrested and accuses police of planting drugs on him
February 21, 1993 – UGK rides in D-Ray's car in the first Port Arthur Mardi Gras parade
February 23, 1993 – Johnnie Remo is convicted of killing a man on Short Texas and sentenced to 10 years
February 28, 1993 – Chad's stepfather Monroe falls ill and is admitted to the hospital
March 11, 1993 – Norward Monroe dies on the same day Chad receives the masters for the "Pocket Full of Stones" remix
March 19, 1993 – The Geto Boys' *Till Death Do Us Part*, featuring J. Prince speaking out against the IRS and DEA on the intro, is released
Spring 1993 – Mama Wes is forced to retire due to a foot injury
April 20, 1993 – The DEA and IRS raid an auto dealership affiliated with J. Prince
May 25, 1993 – The *Menace II Society* soundtrack is released, featuring UGK's "Pocket Full of Stones" remix
May 30, 1993 – Mama Wes is involved in a serious car accident
August 21, 1993 – Chad and Nitacha's son Chad Jr. is born
October 11, 1993 – UGK's road manager Drake Jolivette turns himself in to a federal prison
October 1993 – Mama Wes takes over as road manager for UGK's show at the Bomb Factory in Dallas
December 1993 – UGK renegotiates their deal with Jive and cuts out Big Tyme Recordz

January 13, 1994 – Big Tyme Recordz files a lawsuit against UGK
April 22-23, 1994 – UGK films the video for "Supposed to Bubble" during Freaknik in Atlanta
June 18, 1994 – Smoke D kills two people in Jackson, Mississippi, claiming self-defense
July 7, 1994 – DEA Agent Jack Schumacher shoots a suspected drug dealer in Houston, the sixth person he has killed in the line of duty
August 30, 1994 – UGK's *Super Tight* is released on Jive
October 22, 1994 – Smit-D allegedly murders DJ Peace, then attends a UGK show during TSU homecoming
November 1994 – Lakita Hulett is arrested for theft

February 15, 1995 – UGK files a countersuit against Big Tyme Recordz
March 1995 – Dawn Nico's son Aaron is born
April 13, 1995 – Mike Mo is arrested with pounds of marijuana in Anahuac
June 12, 1995 – Smoke D is sentenced to 20 years in Mississippi
August 1995 – Mama Wes meets Millard "Pops" Roher
August 3, 1995 – Andre 3000 of OutKast gives a memorable acceptance speech at The Source Awards
Fall 1995 – Jive informs Byron Hill that he is no longer UGK's manager
October 31, 1995 – No Limit's *Down South Hustlers* compilation is released featuring UGK
December 4, 1995 – DJ Screw and Pimp C are arrested together for misdemeanor marijuana possession
December 8, 1995 – Bo-Bo Luchiano's son Luke dies in a Dallas house fire

Early 1996 – UGK and Master P record "Break 'Em Off Something"
Early 1996 – Chad moves to a garage apartment in the Atlanta suburb of College Park
March 18, 1996 – Smit-D is convicted of the murder of DJ Peace and sentenced to 25 years
April 10, 1996 – Big Tyme Recordz files a second lawsuit against UGK
July 10, 1996 – Lakita Hulett is arrested for theft
July 30, 1996 – UGK's *Ridin' Dirty* released on Jive
September 13, 1996 – Tupac Shakur dies in Las Vegas
November 21, 1996 – Rap-A-Lot's James Smith officially changes his name to James Prince
Late 1996 – Chad moves to Mableton, Georgia

March 9, 1997 – Christopher Wallace a.k.a. "Notorious B.I.G." dies in Los Angeles
May 14, 1997 – Merrick "Money" Young is indicted on federal drug charges in Louisiana
September 10, 1997 – Ronald Carboni is indicted on federal drug charges in Michigan
September 30, 1997 – Donald "D-Ray" Graham is killed in Port Arthur
November 1997 – Federal authorities raid a car dealership affiliated with Rap-A-Lot
December 5, 1997 – Bun B is arrested in Killeen, Texas on misdemeanor marijuana charges

Early 1998 – Chad moves to Stone Mountain, Georgia
January 12, 1998 – Lakita Hulett is arrested for theft
January 30, 1998 – Chad and Bun announce plans to file bankruptcy to avoid a trial with Big Tyme Recordz
February 3, 1998 – Fat Pat is killed in Houston
February 19, 1998 – Big Mike tries to burn down a Rap-A-Lot recording studio
April 2, 1998 – FBI agents speak with a confidential informant, likely Merrick Young, who claims Pimp C is a drug trafficker
May 7, 1998 – Ronald Carboni accepts a federal plea agreement
June 8, 1998 – Phyllis Conner is arrested with two kilograms of cocaine by DEA Agents in New Orleans
June 15, 1998 – Waymond "Big Dog" Fletcher is killed in Nashville
June 18, 1998 – Lil Troy is pulled over with 2.5 kilograms of cocaine in Nacogdoches, Texas
June 23, 1998 – Lil Troy's album *Sittin' Fat Down South* is released
July 1-3, 1998 – Pimp C records "Get Crunk" with Crooked Lettaz in Atlanta
July 23, 1998 – Bun B appears in court in Killeen to face marijuana charges
July 30, 1998 – Big Tyme Recordz' second lawsuit is dismissed
August 1998 – DEA Agent Jack Schumacher takes over the Rap-A-Lot investigation
September 5, 1998 – The New Black Panther Party's Million Youth March is held New York City
September 29, 1998 – Chad is ordered to pay child support to Nitacha for Chad Jr.
October 29, 1998 – Ronald Carboni is sentenced in Detroit

January 6, 1999 – Phyllis Conner appears in a federal courtroom in Louisiana for a pretrial hearing
January 7, 1999 – Rap-A-Lot's Edward "Spook" Russell and "Cash" McCarter arrested in a DEA sting operation
January 14, 1999 – Phyllis Conner agrees to a plea bargain
January 17, 1999 – DEA agents pull over a Rap-A-Lot wrapped van and allegedly assault three employees
February 10, 1999 – Lil Troy accepts a federal plea bargain
February 22, 1999 – Scarface introduces George Simmons to Ronald Carboni, who is accompanied by an undercover officer
March 3 & 12, 1999 – George Simmons' cousin Byron Harris sells crack to the undercover officer Rodney Glendening
Spring 1999 – Jive erroneously reports to the IRS that Chad made $10 million dollars in 1998
April 1999 – Beats by the Pound leaves No Limit
April 12, 1999 – Pimp C meets engineer Rambro at Patchwerk Recording Studios in Atlanta
April 20, 1999 – Crooked Lettaz' debut album *Grey Skies* is released
April 20, 1999 – Lil Troy's album *Sittin' Fat Down South* is re-released by Universal Music Group
April 26, 1999 – Byron Harris again sells crack to undercover officer Glendening and is arrested; Scarface is arrested for
    misdemeanor marijuana possession
June 1999 – J. Prince is pulled over by DEA Agents near a McDonald's
June 15, 1999 – Ronald Carboni turns himself in to serve federal time
July 2, 1999 – The Cash Money Block 2 Block Tour, featuring UGK, begins in Houston
July 8-14, 1999 – J. Prince and Jack Schumacher come face to face during the Cash/Spook trial. Both men are convicted and
    sentenced to 20 years
July 10, 1999 – Pimp C disses Master P on the Birmingham stop of the Cash Money tour
July 29, 1999 – Cash's conviction is overturned
August 1999 – Chad moves out of the Stone Mountain house and moves his studio equipment to Houston
August 13, 1999 – Eddie Floyd goes to jail for violating probation on his 1992 theft charge
August 16, 1999 – George Simmons is sentenced to 20 years in federal prison
August 19, 1999 – Congresswoman Maxine Waters contacts Janet Reno on J. Prince's behalf
August 22, 1999 – UGK performs at the Dallas Hot Fest with Too $hort and Scarface
August 24, 1999 – J. Prince is interviewed by DEA internal investigators in Congresswoman Waters' office
August 30, 1999 – Darryl Austin pays Greg Glass to visit Eddie Floyd in jail
September 8, 1999 – Lil Troy cooperates with authorities; visits Mark Potts' house while wearing a wire
September 15, 1999 – Authorities raid Mark Potts' house and find 50 kilograms of cocaine
September 20, 1999 – DEA Houston director Howard shuts down the Rap-A-Lot investigation
September 23, 1999 – U.S. prosecutors file a motion to decrease Lil Troy's sentence for his cooperation
October 27, 1999 – Master P is waived by the Toronto Raptors
October 1999 – UGK records "Wood Wheel" for Rap-A-Lot's *RNDS* compilation
October 31, 1999 – Chad records his vocals for "Big Pimpin'" at Patchwerk Recording Studios in Atlanta
November 1999 – Chad moves to Alpharetta, Georgia
November 29, 1999 – Lil Troy turns himself in to a federal prison to serve 18 months
December 2, 1999 – Jay-Z allegedly stabs Lance "Un" Rivera

January 26, 2000 – Byron Hill files a lawsuit against UGK in Atlanta
January 30, 2000 – The Super Bowl is held in Atlanta during an ice storm; Three 6 Mafia visits and records "Sippin' On
    Sizzurp" at the Alpharetta house
February 4, 2000 – Byron Hill registers the corporation Nomad, Inc.
February 28, 2000 – Byron Hill attempts to have serve UGK with paperwork at Park Avenue in Dallas
March 6-7, 2000 – Jay-Z and Bun B film the "Big Pimpin'" video during Trinidad's Carnival
March 9-10, 2000 – At a DEA conference, management agree to remove Schumacher from the Rap-A-Lot case
March 12, 2000 – Vice President Al Gore attends services at J. Prince's church in Houston
March 15, 2000 – DEA Agent Jack Schumacher is reassigned to a desk job
Mid-March 2000 – Pimp C films his part for the "Big Pimpin'" video in Miami
April 2000 – Three 6 Mafia and UGK film the "Sippin' on Some Syrup" video in Miami
April 15, 2000 – Pimp C's bodyguard Byron Amos is arrested at the Atrium in Atlanta on weapons charges
May 23, 2000 – Byron Hill is granted a default judgment against UGK
May 25, 2000 – Mark Potts is sentenced to 151 months in federal prison
June 2000 – UGK performs "Big Pimpin'" with Jay-Z at Hot 97's Summer Jam in New York
June 15, 2000 – Chad and Angie's son Corey is born
July 2000 – Master P and four men attack Pimp C at a Houston hotel
September 14, 2000 – Byron Hill's judgment against UGK is overturned and the case is dismissed

September 28, 2000 – DJ Screw is arrested for possession of PCP
September 30, 2000 – Jay-Z films his episode of *MTV Diary* while riding around Brooklyn listening to UGK
October 23, 2000 – Beats by the Pound files a lawsuit against No Limit
October 24, 2000 – J. Prince and Chad Butler sign an agreement to form a joint record label
October 25, 2000 – Byron Hill tries to serve UGK with a new lawsuit at N.O. Joe's recording studio in Houston
October 29, 2000 – UGK performs with Jay-Z at the annual Los Magnificos car show in Houston
November 1, 2000 – The Inspector General opens an investigation into the DEA's investigation of Rap-A-Lot
November 2000 – Darryl Austin introduces Mama Wes to Eddie Floyd
November 7, 2000 – Chad signs a co-management agreement with J. Prince and Mama Wes
November 16, 2000 – DJ Screw is found dead in the bathroom of his recording studio
November 22, 2000 – DJ Screw's funeral is held in Smithville, Texas
December 6-7, 2000 – Congressional hearings are held regarding the DEA's Rap-A-Lot investigation
Mid-December 2000 – Chad moves back to Houston
December 16, 2000 – Chad is arrested at Sharpstown Mall and charged with Aggravated Assault

January 12, 2001 – Byron Amos packs up the Alpharetta house and drives to Houston with Chad's belongings
January 13, 2001 – The Alpharetta house explodes and burns to the ground
February 17, 2001 – New Black Panther Party leader Dr. Khallid Muhammad dies in Atlanta
February 21, 2002 – The Grammy Awards are held in Los Angeles; Jay-Z and UGK's "Big Pimpin'" is nominated
February 28, 2001 – Chad misses his court date and an arrest warrant is issued
March 1, 2001 – Chad meets with Port Arthur psychiatrist Victor M. Fermo Jr., M.D., for an evaluation
March 8, 2001 – Chad is booked at the Harris County Jail
March 13, 2001 – Chad appears in court with attorney Greg Glass
March 16, 2001 – Lil Troy is released from federal custody
Mid-March 2001 – NBPP members Hashim Nzinga and Malik Zulu Shabazz visit Chad at the County Jail
March 20, 2001 – Harris County Sheriff's department notifies the FBI of Chad's visit from the NBPP members; Chad gets a
    visit from "special prosecutors"
March 27, 2001 – Chad appears in court with attorney Greg Glass and posts bond; is released
April 25, 2001 – Chad appears in court and agrees to a plea bargain; receives four years probation
May 3, 2001 – UGK signs a modified contract with Jive
May 24, 2001 – Chad is reported absent from probation due to an apparent clerical error
June 28, 2001 – Chad fails a drug test
July 19, 2001 – Chad fails a drug test
September 6, 2001 – Chad's probation is revoked
September 25, 2001 – Chad returns to the county jail; Eddie Floyd bonds him out the following morning
September 28, 2001 – Lakita Hulett is arrested for theft
October 12, 2001 – Chad is sentenced to serve 30 days in Harris County Jail
October 17, 2001 – Lakita Hulett is sentenced to serve 30 days in Harris County Jail
October 19, 2001 – Chad turns himself in to the Harris County Jail
November 7, 2001 – The IRS files a $7 million dollar tax lien against Chad
November 13, 2001 – UGK's *Dirty Money* is released on Jive
November 18, 2001 – Chad is released from Harris County Jail
November 21, 2001 – Chad is late for a probation visit in Baytown
December 13, 2001 – Chad meets with his probation officer and is given new community service assignment
December 15, 2001 – Chad and Chinara's daughter Christian is born; Chad doesn't do his community service
December 21, 2001 – Smoke D is released from prison in Mississippi

January 16, 2002 – A second probation violation against Chad is filed
January 25, 2002 – Chad goes to court; is returned to Harris County Jail with no bond
March 13, 2002 – Darrell "Pharoah" Burton arrives at Harris County Jail for attacking a woman while under the influence of PCP
March 28, 2002 – At a hearing, Chad's probation is reinstated on the condition that he attend SAFP
April 2, 2002 – Chad writes a letter to the judge asking to withdraw his plea
April 10, 2002 – Antron "Big Lurch" Singleton kills a woman in California while under the influence of PCP
May 24, 2002 – Chad's probation is revoked for the third time because of his refusal to attend SAFP
June 7, 2002 – Brian "Biz" Hunter is killed in Nashville
June 24, 2002 – Mama Wes marries Millard "Pops" Roher
July 11, 2002 – Lakita Hulett sues Genesco, the owner of Jarman Shoe Store in the Sharpstown Mall
August 5, 2002 – Chad appears in court with attorney Ross Lavin and Judge Jeannine Barr sentences him to 8 years in prison
August 21, 2002 – Bun B notifies Jive of his intent to replace Pimp C with another member in UGK
August 22, 2002 – Bun B signs a solo record deal with Rap-A-Lot Records
September 4, 2002 – Chad's attorney Ross Lavin files a motion for a new trial
September 17, 2002 – Sylvester "Don Vesto" Bullard is arrested and arrives at the Harris County Jail
September 24, 2002 – Jive releases the UGK *Side Hustles* album
October 1, 2002 – DJ DMD leaves Port Arthur
October 18, 2002 – Judge Barr denies Chad's motion for a new trial
November 26, 2002 – Pharoah is sentenced to 50 years
December 19, 2002 – Chad departs the Harris County Jail and arrives at Garza West in Beeville, Texas
December 20, 2002 – Ronald Carboni is released from federal custody

February 3, 2003 – Southwest Wholesale officially ceases operations
February 3, 2003 – Byron Hill files bankruptcy the day before a hearing, preserving his $3,000,000 judgment against UGK
February 17, 2003 – DJ DMD's business partner, Inner Soul co-owner John "J-Will" Williams III, is found dead
March 15, 2003 – Bun B marries Chalvalier "Queenie" Caldwell on his 30th birthday
April 2003 – Chad marries Chinara Jackson
Summer 2003 – Chad is transferred to the Dominguez Unit in San Antonio
November 4, 2003 – Byron Hill is arrested in Atlanta for domestic violence
December 2003 – Darryl Austin hires a CPA firm to investigate Eddie Floyd
December 12, 2003 – Chad signs a modified agreement with Jive that will allow him to release a side project with Rap-A-Lot

January 27, 2004 – Bun B files a lawsuit against Jive on UGK's behalf
March 26, 2004 – Pimp C's underground album *Live from the Harris County Jail* is released
June 2004 – Chad gets his GED
June 19, 2004 – T.I. disses Lil Flip at Hot 107.9's annual Birthday Bash concert in Atlanta
July 7, 2004 – Jive and UGK sign a settlement agreement; Bun B dismisses his lawsuit
July 14, 2004 – Attorney Troy J. Wilson files an appeal on Chad's behalf
July 25, 2004 – Darryl Austin asks Chad to sign a management agreement
August 17, 2004 – Heather Johnson is sent to SAFP after violating her probation
November 14, 2004 – Chad is transferred to the Darrington Unit in Rosharon, Texas, for the weekend
November 17, 2004 – Chad is transferred to the Byrd Unit in Huntsville, Texas, for processing
December 2004 – UGK appears on the cover of *XXL* Magazine
December 7, 2004 – Jive releases *UGK – Chopped & Screwed*
Mid-December 2004 – Chad is transferred to the C.T. Terrell Unit in Rosharon, Texas
December 21, 2004 – Rap-A-Lot issues a press release for the upcoming album *The Sweet James Jones Stories*

March 1, 2005 – Pimp C's album *The Sweet James Jones Stories* is released through Rap-A-Lot/Asylum
March 20-21, 2005 – Pimp C does interviews with multiple media outlets at the Terrell Unit in support of his album
May 17, 2005 – Smoke D and Stan are arrested in Louisiana on drugs and weapons charges
July 2005 – Bun visits Pimp C in prison for the first time since 2002
July 27, 2005 – Chamillionaire films his video for "Turn It Up," featuring a red Cadillac Biarritz
July 28, 2005 – The author meets Lil Troy and interviews him about his beef with Scarface
September 21, 2005 – Chad and other inmates are evacuated from the Terrell Unit as Hurricane Rita approaches
September 2005 – Chad is interviewed for parole
October 18, 2005 – Bun B's first solo album *Trill* is released through Rap-A-Lot/Asylum
October 20, 2005 – Big Meech and the BMF family are indicted on federal drug charges
November 2005 – Scarface and Lil Troy face off at the Los Magnificos car show over the *Paperwork* DVD
November 2005 – Chad's mother and wife meet with the parole board
November 19, 2005 – Lil Troy files for bankruptcy
November 30, 2005 – The Texas Board of Pardons and Paroles votes to release Chad Butler
December 14, 2005 – Lakita Hulett is arrested for theft
December 29, 2005 – Chad is transferred to the Huntsville Unit in Huntsville, Texas, on his 32nd birthday
December 30, 2005 – Chad is released from the Huntsville Unit

January 27-28, 2006 – Pimp C and Bun B film the "Get Throwed" video and hold a release party for Pimp C at Club Blue
January 29, 2006 – UGK appears in T.I.'s "Front Back" video, shot in Houston
February 19, 2006 – A planned UGK reunion show at Bar Rio in Houston during All-Star Weekend is abruptly cancelled
February 20, 2006 – *The Source* Magazine shoots their "Don't Mess With Texas" cover photo at J. Prince's ranch
March 20, 2006 – Lil Troy sues Scarface for defamation
March 25, 2006 – Pimp C appears in T-Pain's "In Luv With A Stripper (remix)" video, shot in Miami
April 3, 2006 – Pimp C shoots the "Pourin' Up" video with Mike Jones in Houston
April 19, 2006 – Pimp C shoots the "Pourin' Up" video with Mike Jones in Port Arthur; his Bentley is involved in an accident while leaving the shoot
April 21, 2006 – Pimp C appears in the video for Brooke Valentine's "D-Girl," shot in Houston
May 1, 2006 – Big Hawk is killed in Houston
May 4, 2006 – Pimp C signs a modified recording agreement with Rap-A-Lot
May 14, 2006 – Pimp C records with Ludacris in Atlanta; a scheduled UGK show is cancelled
May 21, 2006 – Smoke D's co-defendant Stan is arrested in Anahuac, Texas
May 23, 2006 – A listening party is held in New York for Pimp C's *Pimpalation*
May 25, 2006 – Smoke D's co-defendant Stan is arrested again in Louisiana
June 16, 2006 – Chad celebrates his son Corey's sixth birthday in Port Arthur
June 17, 2006 – Pimp C performs at Hot 107.9's Birthday Bash 11 at Phillips Arena in Atlanta
June 23-24, 2006 – Pimp C visits Milwaukee for Pimpin' Ken's birthday weekend
June 26, 2006 – Smoke D pleads no contest to drugs and weapons charges in a Louisiana courtroom
July 11, 2006 – Pimp C's *Pimpalation* is released through Rap-A-Lot/Asylum
July 19-22, 2006 – UGK begins working on their next project at Patchwerk Recording Studios in Atlanta
July 29, 2006 – Pimp C is honored at the 3rd Coast Crunkfest Music Awards in Louisiana
August 6, 2006 – UGK performs for the first time since Chad's release at the OZONE Awards in Orlando
August 14, 2006 – Chad buys a new house on Oakmont in Port Arthur
August 15, 2006 – Pimp C appears on BET's *Rap City*
August 23, 2006 – Pimp C attends a Too $hort show at The Roxy in Los Angeles
August 30, 2006 – Ronald Robinson commits suicide in Dallas
October 16-17, 2006 – Pimp C shoots the video for "Knockin' Doors Down" in Houston
October 24, 2006 – Pimp C attends Trae tha Truth's "In The Hood" video shoot in Houston
November 2, 2006 – Ronald Robinson's suicide is aired on A&E reality show *SWAT*
November 16, 2006 – Port Arthur police meet with the FBI to discuss collaborating on an ongoing investigation of Chad and his associates for suspected drug trafficking
November 16, 2006 – Byron Hill registers a corporation titled Shrevemont Enterprises, a combination of the street names where Chad and Mama Wes lived
November 22, 2006 – UGK performs "Big Pimpin'" with Jay-Z on BET's *106th & Jay* special
December 12, 2006 – Chad gathers with friends and family to celebrate Mama Wes' 60th birthday at her home in Port Arthur

Late January 2007 – UGK shoots the "Game Belongs to Me" video in Houston
January 30, 2007 – Jada is beaten by her pimp Ocean in Las Vegas after the "Game Belongs to Me" video shoot
February 10, 2007 – Maroy and Jada attend Pimpin' Ken's Player's Ball in Milwaukee
March 15-16, 2007 – UGK performs at SXSW
March 19, 2007 – Smoke D is sentenced to 20 years in prison in Louisiana
April 13, 2007 – UGK appears on BET's *Rap City*
May 16, 2007 – UGK and OutKast shoot the video for "Int'l Player's Anthem (I Choose You)" in Los Angeles
June 10, 2007 – Pimp C records his first "Chronicles of Pimp C" for *OZONE* Magazine
June 26, 2007 – Bun B performs on the red carpet of the 2007 BET Awards with Mike Jones
Late June 2007 – Pimp C has a verbal altercation with Houston radio program director Terri Thomas
June 30, 2007 – Pimp C does a psychic session with Halimah Saafir in Beverly Hills; meanwhile, in Houston, Bun B performs solo during The Box's Hip-Hop 4 HIV concert
July 12, 2007 – UGK performs at the Zune Live at the BBQ concert in Los Angeles
July 24, 2007 – Pimp C does a classic radio interview with Atlanta's Hot 107.9
July 30, 2007 – Pimp C does a radio interview with Greg Street on V103 in Atlanta
August 2007 – UGK pulls out of the Rock The Bells Festival
August 7, 2007 – UGK's self-titled double album *Underground Kingz* is released on Jive Records
Late August 2007 – Chad takes his family to a Soulja Boy concert in Dallas to celebrate Chad Jr.'s 14th birthday
September 17, 2007 – JT shows up unexpectedly at Chad's house at 4 AM; is arrested on weapons charges
October 8, 2007 – Pimp C films the video for G Kamp's "Stack Money" in Port Arthur with Mr. Boomtown
October 13, 2007 – UGK wins the BET Hip-Hop Award for Best Collaboration for "Int'l Player's Anthem (I Choose You)"
October 22, 2007 – Larry Adams is sentenced to five years of probation in Mississippi for marijuana charges
November 3, 2007 – Pimp joins Bun on stage at The Box's annual Los Magnificos car show in Houston
November 18, 2007 – Chad joins Antioch Baptist Missionary Church in Beaumont, Texas
November 21, 2007 – UGK performs in Dallas the day before Thanksgiving
November 23, 2007 – Chad attends Young Jeezy's performance at Bar Rio in Houston
November 26, 2007 – Bun B and Young Jeezy both attend the Dirty Awards in Atlanta
November 29, 2007 – Chad arrives in Los Angeles, checks into the Mondrian hotel in Hollywood
November 30, 2007 – Chad records with Three 6 Mafia in Los Angeles; Bun B performs in Seattle
December 1, 2007 – Pimp C attends Too $hort's show at the House of Blues in Hollywood
December 4, 2007 – Chad's body is discovered at the Mondrian in Hollywood; he was 33 years old
December 6, 2007 – UGK is nominated for a Grammy for "Int'l Player's Anthem (I Choose You)"
December 13, 2007 – Chad's funeral is held in Port Arthur

February 4, 2008 – The Los Angeles coroner's office announces the cause of death
February 8, 2008 – Bun B performs at Warehouse Live in Houston
February 10, 2008 – Bun B and Chad's wife Chinara attend the Grammy Awards in Los Angeles
March 13, 2008 – Byron Hill serves Bun B with a lawsuit during an appearance at an Austin Boys & Girls Club

May 20, 2008 – Bun B's *Il Trill* is released on Rap-A-Lot/Asylum Records
June 3, 2008 – *Pimp C's Greatest Hits* is released on Rap-A-Lot/Asylum Records
June 24, 2008 – UGK wins Best Group and Video of the Year at the BET Awards
July 1, 2008 – Chinara signs an amended agreement with Rap-A-Lot regarding Pimp C's music
August 10, 2008 – Chad's grandmother Bessie Jacob dies in Louisiana
August 10, 2008 – Young Jeezy remembers Pimp C during a performance at the Arena Theatre during the OZONE Awards
August 11, 2008 – Pimp C is honored with a tribute performance by Bun B, Too $hort, David Banner, Big Boi of OutKast, 8Ball, Hezeleo, Lil Boosie, Webbie, Billy Cook, and more at the OZONE Awards in Houston
September 11, 2008 – Bun B settles his lawsuit with Byron Hill for $100,000
December 12, 2008 – The Chad "Pimp C" Butler Hip-Hop Health & Wellness Festival is held in Port Arthur

March 31, 2009 – *UGK 4 Life* is released on Jive Records
April 30, 2009 – Shawn Jones is sentenced to 70 years for the shooting which wrecked Pimp C's silver Bentley

October 5, 2010 – Pimp C's *The Naked Soul of Sweet Jones* is released on Rap-A-Lot/Asylum
December 11, 2010 – The second Chad "Pimp C" Butler Hip-Hop Health & Wellness Festival is held in Houston

June 1, 2011 – Chad Butler Jr. graduates from high school
June 16, 2011 – Chinara threatens to sue Rap-A-Lot over the release of his music
June 17, 2011 – Rap-A-Lot files a lawsuit against Chinara
July 12, 2011 – Pimp C's *Still Pimping* is released on Rap-A-Lot
August 16, 2011 – UGK's *The Big Tyme Way* is released on RBC Records
November 4, 2011 – The Estate of Chad Butler settles Byron Hill's lawsuit for $7,500
December 10, 2011 – The 3rd Annual Chad "Pimp C" Butler Hip-Hop Health & Wellness Festival is held in Houston

December 2, 2012 – The Mayor of Port Arthur proclaims December 2 "UGK Day"; UGK is honored by the Museum of the Gulf Coast's Music Hall of Fame with a permanent exhibit
December 29, 2012 – The 4th Annual Chad "Pimp C" Butler Hip-Hop Health & Wellness Festival is held in Houston

June 14, 2013 – Larry Adams dies in Fresno, California
August 18, 2013 – Mama Wes dies in Port Arthur, Texas
August 23, 2013 – Mama Wes' funeral is held in Port Arthur, Texas
December 28, 2013 – The 5th Annual Chad "Pimp C" Butler "Hip-Hop Health & Wellness Festival is held in Houston

"We're so serious about our music that we never got to have a good time making music. I've never had a fun album in my career; everything was like giving birth to a baby – painstaking and such." – Pimp C, AllHipHop, August 2006

"Every UGK album is a concept album ... A lot of people don't realize how in-depth Pimp and I would go into making these albums. We were very serious." – Bun B, The *Village Voice*, March 2008

[DEMOS]

DMI – *Rap In It's Rawest Form* (1988)
Side A:
1. "Here's A Story" – DJ DMD
2. "Mission Impossible" – MQJ & MC C
3. "DMI's On A Mission" – DJ DMD, MC C, & MQJ
4. "Outrage" – MC C & MQJ
5. "Boogie Down" – MC C, MQJ, DJ DMD
6. "Rockin' Music" – MQJ
7. "Da Giggle" – Q-Tip
8. "Serious" – DJ DMD & Lee Master
9. "U Got A Problem" – Q-Tip
10. "Y It Always Gotta Be Hip-Hop" – DJ DMD
11. "Just A Gangsta" – MQJ
Side B:
1. "No-Z Girl (Remix)" – Boomer Schooner
2. "Gangsta Time Theatre" – MC Bash a.k.a. Boonie Feel Good
3. "DMI's In Full Effect" – DJ DMD
4. "Daydreamin' (About You)" – MC C & MQJ
5. "Business" – MC C
6. "Business iz Business" – MC Bash a.k.a. Boonie Feel Good
7. "My Blazer (Remix)" – Hardy Boys
8. "Get Off Da Wall" – Boomer Schooner
9. "Supa Soul Sista" – KLC
10. "The Boom Iz Back" – Boomer Schooner
11. "Get On Up" – MC C

Underground Kingz demo (1989)
1. "Underground King" – Pimp C & MQJ
2. "My Place" – Pimp C & MQJ
3. "Funky Connection" – Pimp C & MQJ
4. "Hard Motherfucker" – Pimp C
5. "Boogie Down (Remix)" – MQJ
6. "Break It Down 4 Ya" – MQJ
7. "Nowhere 2 Hide" – MQJ
8. "How We Feel" – PA Militia (Bun B & Jelon Jackson a.k.a. Die Hard)
9. "Dick Suckers (Rudy Ray Moore Mix)" – Pimp C
10. "Cum Inside (Remix)" – Pimp C & MQJ
11. "Turn Down The Lights" – Pimp C
12. "Jenny" – Pimp C
13. "Tell Me Something Good (1st version)" – Pimp C, MQJ, & Bun B

4BM demo (1990)
1. "Dicks Hang Low (When The 4 Stand Stout)"
2. "Shit On My Toe"
3. "Mission Impossible" – MQJ & Pimp C
4. "Tell Me Something Good (1st version)" – Pimp C, MQJ, & Bun B

[ALBUMS]

UGK – *The Southern Way* EP (Big Tyme, 1992)
1. "Cocaine in the Back of the Ride"
2. "Short Texas" featuring Bluelite
3. "Something Good" produced by Pimp C
4. "Trill Ass Nigga"
5. "976-BUN-B"
6. "Use Me Up" produced by Pimp C

7. Bonus Cut: "Something Good (Radio Version)"

UGK – *Too Hard to Swallow* **(Big Tyme/Jive, 1992)**
1. "Something Good (Extended Mix)" produced by Bernie Bismark & Shetoro Henderson
2. "Use Me Up" produced by Pimp C
3. "Pocket Full Of Stones" produced by Pimp C*
4. "Short Texas" featuring Bluelite, produced by Pimp C
5. "Cocaine In The Back Of The Ride" produced by Pimp C, Bernie Bismark & Shetoro Henderson
6. "It's Too Hard To Swallow" produced by Bun B, Bernie Bismark & Shetoro Henderson
7. "Cramping My Style" featuring Infinity, produced by Bun B, Bernie Bismark & Shetoro Henderson
8. "Feel Like I'm The One Doing Dope" produced by Pimp C
9. "I'm So Bad" produced by Pimp C
10. "Trill Ass Nigga" produced by Bun B, Bernie Bismark & Shetoro Henderson
11. "976-BUN-B" produced by Bernie Bismark & Shetoro Henderson
12. "Something Good (Pimp C's Remix)" produced by Pimp C
*The "Pocket Full Of Stones (Remix)" also appeared on the *Menace II Society* soundtrack.

UGK – *Banned* **(Big Tyme, 1992)**
1. Bun B Intro
2. "Pregnant Pussy"
3. "Pusi Mental"
4. "Muthafucka Ain't Mine"
5. "Muthafucka Ain't Mine (Instrumental)"

UGK – *Super Tight* **(Jive, 1994)**
1. "Return" produced by Pimp C
2. "Underground" produced by Pimp C
3. "It's Supposed To Bubble" produced by Pimp C & DJ DMD
4. "I Left It Wet For You" produced by Pimp C
5. "Feds In Town" produced by Pimp C
6. "Pocket Full Of Stones, Pt. 2" produced by Pimp C
7. "Front, Back & Side To Side" featuring Smoke D, produced by Pimp C*
8. "Protect And Serve" produced by Pimp C
9. "Stoned Junkee" featuring Mr. 3-2, produced by Pimp C
10. "Pussy Got Me Dizzy" featuring Mr. 3-2, produced by Pimp C
11. "Three Sixteens" featuring DJ DMD, produced by Pimp C & DJ DMD
*"Front, Back & Side To Side" also appeared on the soundtrack to *A Low Down Dirty Shame*.

UGK – *Ridin' Dirty* **(Jive, 1996)***
1. "Intro" produced by Pimp C
2. "One Day" featuring Mr. 3-2 & Ronnie Spencer, produced by Pimp C
3. "Murder" produced by Pimp C
4. "Pinky Ring" produced by Pimp C
5. "Diamonds & Wood" produced by Pimp C
6. "3 in the Mornin'" produced by Sergio
7. "Touched" featuring Mr. 3-2, produced by N.O. Joe
8. "Fuck My Car" produced by N.O. Joe**
9. "That's Why I Carry" featuring N.O. Joe, produced by N.O. Joe
10. "Hi-Life" produced by Pimp C & N.O. Joe
11. "Good Stuff" produced by Sergio
12. "Ridin' Dirty" produced by Pimp C
13. "Outro" produced by Pimp C
*The cassette version of Ridin' Dirty contained an additional bonus track, "You Don't Know Me."
**The clean version of "Fuck My Car" was called "Ride My Car."

UGK – *Dirty Money* **(Jive, 2001)**
1. "Let Me See It" produced by Pimp C
2. "Choppin' Blades" produced by Pimp C & N.O. Joe
3. "Look At Me" produced by Pimp C
4. "Ain't That A Bitch (Ask Yourself)" featuring Devin the Dude, produced by N.O. Joe
5. "Gold Grill" featuring 8Ball & MJG, produced by N.O. Joe
6. "PA Nigga" produced by N.O. Joe
7. "Holdin' Na" featuring C-Note, produced by N.O. Joe
8. "Don't Say Shit" featuring Big Gipp, produced by Pimp C
9. "Dirty Money" produced by N.O. Joe
10. "Like A Pimp" featuring DJ Paul & Juicy J, produced by Pimp C
11. "Pimpin' Ain't No Illusion" featuring Kool Ace & Too $hort, produced by Pimp C
12. "Take It Off" produced by Pimp C*
13. "Wood Wheel" produced by Pimp C & John Bido**
14. "Money, Hoes & Power" featuring Jermaine Dupri, produced by Bryan-Michael Cox & Jermaine Dupri***
*"Take It Off" was also featured on *The Corruptor* soundtrack.
***"Wood Wheel" was not included on the edited version of *Dirty Money*. It originally appeared on the 1999 Rap-A-Lot compilation *J Prince Presents R.N.D.S. (Realest Niggas Down South)*.
****"Money, Hoes & Power" was also featured on Jermaine Dupri's *Instructions*.

Pimp C – *Sweet James Jones: Live From the Harris County Jail* **(Pimp C Family Entertainment, 2004)***
1. "Comin' Up"
2. "Got A Thang"
3. "Sixteen Five"
4. "Hustler"
5. "So Excited"
6. "Sweet James"
7. "Get My $ Bitch" featuring Pimpin' Ken
8. "I Want A Prostitute"
9. "Very Thin Line" featuring Cory Mo
10. "U Belong To Me"
11. "Pimpin Ain't Dead"
Bonus Tracks:
12. "Rude Boy Gangsta"

13. "Where the Dollas At (In My Pocket, You Bitch)" featuring Lil Boosie**
14. "My Angel (Tribute to Momma)"

*A bonus Chopped & Screwed CD was included with the first eleven tracks.
**A previous version of "Where the Dollas At" appeared as "In My Pocket" on Lil Boosie and Webbie's 2003 album *Ghetto Stories*.

Pimp C – *The Sweet James Jones Stories* (Rap-A-Lot/Asylum, 2005)
1. "Hogg In The Game" produced by Pimp C & Mr. Lee
2. "Swang Down / 10 A Key" produced by John Bido
3. "I'm A Hustler" produced by D. Stone & Mike Dean
4. "Comin' Up" featuring Lil Flip & Z-Ro, produced by DJ DMD
5. "I'sa Playa" featuring Bun B, Twista, & Z-Ro, produced by N.O. Joe*
6. "I Know U Strapped" produced by Mr. Lee**
7. "I Gotta Thang" produced by Dani Kartel & Mike Dean
8. "Slow Down" featuring Cory Mo, produced by Cory Mo, T-Gray, & Mike Dean***
9. "Get My Money" produced by Dani Kartel
10. "Young Prostitute" produced by Mike Dean
11. "Everytime" featuring Devin the Dude, produced by Dani Kartel
12. "A Thin Line" produced by Cory Mo & Dani Kartel
13. "My Angel" produced by Cory Mo & Mike Dean
14. "Young Ghetto Stars" featuring Trae & Z-Ro, produced by DJ DMD

*A previous version of "I'sa Playa" appeared as "Time" on Twista's 2000 album *Adrenaline Rush 2000*.
**A previous version of "I Know U Strapped" appeared as "Play Hard" on Lil Boosie and Webbie's 2003 album *Ghetto Stories*.
***A previous version of "Slow Down" appeared on Vicious of the X-Mob's 2002 solo project *I Ball Like Kobe*.

Pimp C – *Pimpalation* (Wood Wheel/Rap-A-Lot/Asylum, 2006)*
1. "The Pimp Is Free!" featuring J. Prince, produced by Mike Dean
2. "I'm Free!" produced by Int'l Red & Beatmaster Clay D
3. "Knockin' Doorz Down" featuring Lil' Keke & P.O.P., produced by Myke Diesel
4. "Rock 4 Rock" featuring Bun B, Scarface, & Willie D, produced by Mr. Lee
5. "Pourin' Up" featuring Bun B & Mike Jones, produced by Salih
6. "The Honey" featuring Tela, Jazze Pha, & Jody Breeze, produced by Jazze Pha
7. "Gitcha Mind Right" featuring Cory Mo, produced by Mr. Lee
8. "I Don't Fuck Wit U" featuring Smoke D & Vicious, produced by Cory Mo
9. "Working The Wheel" featuring Slim Thug & Pimpin Ken, produced by Mike Dean
10. "Bobby & Whitney" featuring 8Ball & MJG, produced by Mr. Lee
11. "Like That (Remix)" featuring Lil' Boosie & Webbie, produced by Mouse
12. "Cheat On Yo Man" featuring Mannie Fresh & Suga, produced by Mannie Fresh
13. "Havin' Thangs '06" featuring Big Mike, produced by Pimp C
14. "Overstand Me" featuring Chamillionaire & Trae, produced by Mr. Lee
15. "On Your Mind" featuring Ali & Gipp, Big Zak, & Jagged Edge, produced by Jazze Pha
16. "I Miss U" featuring Z-Ro, produced by Beatmaster Clay D, Donald Brown II, & Kendall Jackson
17. "Outro" produced by Pimp C

*A bonus Chopped & Screwed disc by Michael "5000" Watts was included.

UGK – *Underground Kingz* (Jive, 2007)
Disc One:
1. "Swisha and Dosha" produced by Steve Below & Pimp C
2. "Int'l Players Anthem (I Choose U)" featuring OutKast, produced by Three 6 Mafia
3. "Chrome Plated Woman" produced by Pimp C
4. "Life Is 2009" featuring Too $hort, produced by Scarface
5. "The Game Belongs To Me" produced by Averexx, N.O. Joe, & Pimp C
6. "Like That (Remix)" produced by Steve Below & Pimp C
7. "Gravy" produced by Averexx & Pimp C
8. "Underground Kingz" produced by Pimp C
9. "Grind Hard" featuring Young T.O.E., produced by DJ B-Do & Pimp C
10. "Take Tha Hood Back" featuring MDDL FNGZ, Slim Thug, & Vicious, produced by The Runners
11. "Quit Hatin' The South" featuring Willie D & Charlie Wilson, produced by Pimp C
12. "Heaven" produced by Pimp C & N.O. Joe
13. "Trill Niggas Don't Die" featuring Z-Ro, produced by Joe Traxx, John Bido, Yung Fyngas, & Pimp C
Disc Two:
1. "How Long Can It Last" featuring Charlie Wilson, produced by Pimp C
2. "Still Ridin' Dirty" featuring Scarface, produced by Scarface
3. "Stop-N-Go" featuring Jazze Pha, produced by Jazze Pha
4. "Cocaine" featuring Rick Ross, produced by N.O. Joe & Pimp C
5. "Two Type of Bitches" featuring Dizzee Rascal & Pimpin' Ken, produced by MoMo & Pimp C
6. "Real Women" featuring Talib Kweli & Raheem DeVaughn, produced by Pimp C
7. "Candy" produced by Scarface & Bigg Tyme
8. "Tell Me How You Feel" produced by Jazze Pha
9. "Shattered Dreams" produced by Pimp C
10. "Like That" produced by Lil' Jon
11. "Next Up" featuring Big Daddy Kane & Kool G Rap, produced by Marley Marl
12. "Living This Life" produced by N.O. Joe
13. "Outro" produced by Cory Mo
14. "Int'l Players Anthem (I Choose You)" Chopped & Screwed by OG Ron C, featuring Three 6 Mafia, produced by Three 6 Mafia
15. "Int'l Players Anthem (I Choose You)" featuring Three 6 Mafia, produced by Three 6 Mafia
16. "Hit The Block" featuring T.I., produced by Swizz Beatz

UGK – *4 Life* (Jive, 2009)
1. "Intro" produced by Cory Mo
2. "Still On The Grind" featuring Raheem DeVaughn, produced by Steve Below
3. "Everybody Wanna Ball" produced by Cory Mo
4. "Feelin' You" produced by Steve Below
5. "The Pimp & The Bun" featuring Ronald Isley, produced by Mannie Fresh
6. "She Luv It" produced by Cory Mo
7. "7th Street Interlude" produced by Pimp C & Mike Dean
8. "Swishas & Erb" featuring Sleepy Brown, produced by Pimp C & Averexx
9. "Purse Come First" featuring Big Gipp, produced by DJ B-Do
10. "Harry Asshole" featuring Lil Boosie & Webbie, produced by Cory Mo

11. "Used To Be" featuring B-Legit, E-40, & 8Ball & MJG, produced by Pimp C & DJ B-Do*
12. "Steal Your Mind" featuring Snoop Dogg & Too $hort, produced by Steve Below
13. "Texas Ave Interlude" produced by Pimp C & Mike Dean
14. "Hard As Hell" featuring Akon & Giorgio Tuinfort
15. "Da Game Been Good To Me" produced by Pimp C & Averexx
16. "Outro" produced by Cory Mo

*An earlier version of "Used to Be" appeared on Da Underdawgz' mixtape *Ridin' Filthy*.

Pimp C – *The Naked Soul of Sweet Jones* (Rap-A-Lot/Fontana, 2010)
1. "Down 4 Mine" produced by Cory Mo
2. "What Up?" featuring Bun B & Drake, produced by Boi-1da, DJ B-Do & Nick Bongers
3. "Love 2 Ball" featuring Chamillionaire, produced by Steve Below
4. "Fly Lady" featuring Jazze Pha, produced by Jazze Pha
5. "Since The 90's" featuring E-40 & Gator Main, produced by Big E
6. "Dickies" featuring Bun B & Young Jeezy, produced by DJ B-Do
7. "Made 4" featuring Too $hort, produced by Big E & Mike Dean
8. "Midnight" featuring Rick Ross & Slim Thug, produced by David Banner
9. "Believe In Me" featuring Bankroll Jonez, Big Bubb, Cory Mo, T.O.E., DJ B-Do, Hezeleo, & Ivory P, produced by Cory Mo*
10. "Hit The Parking Lot" featuring Lil Boosie & Webbie, produced by Mouse**
11. "Colors" featuring Da Underdawgz, produced by DJ B-Do*
12. "Go 2 War" featuring Bun B & J-Dawg, produced by Steve Below
13. "Massacre" produced by V-Man***

*"Believe In Me" and "Colors" also appear on Da Underdawgz' 2011 mixtape *The 1st One Is For Pimp*.
**"Hit The Parking Lot" also appeared on Webbie's 2011 mixtape *Savage or Die*.
***An earlier version of "Massacre" appeared on XVII's *Certified*.

Pimp C – *Still Pimping* (Rap-A-Lot, 2011)
1. "Pimptro"
2. "Watch The Reaction" featuring Killa Kyleon & Lil' Keke, produced by Steve Below
3. "Grippin' On The Wood" featuring Big K.R.I.T. & Bun B, produced by Beat Masta Wes
4. "Finer Thangs" featuring Brooke Valentine & Slim Thug, produced by Deja The Great
5. "I'm So Proud Of Ya" featuring Cory Mo & Hezeleo, produced by Cory Mo
6. "Get Down" featuring Smoke D, produced by Steve Below
7. "Bread Up" featuring DJ B-Do & Paul Wall, produced by Mike Dean & V-Man
8. "Fuck Boy" featuring Too $hort, produced by Steve Below
9. "What You Workin' With" featuring Bun B & Slim Thug, produced by Big E
10. "Notes on Leases" featuring Da Underdawgz, produced by DJ B-Do
11. "Like Us" featuring C-Bo, Smoke D, & Vicious, produced by Steve Below
12. "Hold Up" featuring Bun B & Paul Wall, produced by Mr. Lee
13. "Gorillaz" featuring Bun B & Da Underdawgz, produced by DJ B-Do

[MIXTAPES, COMPILATIONS, AND UNDERGROUND RELEASES]

DJ Screw – *Chapter 182: Ridin Dirty* (1996)*
SIDE A:
1. Pimp C & Bun B freestyle over UGK's "Fuck My Car" / Bun B freestyle over Total's "No One Else"
2. Dat Boy Grace & Pimp C freestyle over Kris Kross' "Live and Die For Hip-Hop" / Bun B freestyle over Mack 10's "Fo' Life"
3. Bun B freestyle over WC's "The One"
4. Dat Boy Grace & Pimp C freestyle over MC Lyte's "Keepin' On"
5. Pimp C freestyle over the Twinz' "4 Eyes 2 Heads" / Bun B freestyle over Tha Dogg Pound's "Let's Play House"
6. Ant Banks' "Money Don't Make the Man"
7. Dat Boy Grace & Bun B freestyle over Ice Cube's "Check Yo' Self"
8. Bun B freestyle over "It's Goin' On"
9. Bun B freestyle over The Conscious Daughters' "Funky Expedition"
10. Pimp C freestyle
11. Pimp C freestyle over The Lady of Rage's "Afro Puffs"
12. Pimp C freestyle over the Notorious B.I.G.'s "Juicy"
13. Bun B freestyle over Lords of Lyrics' "Wanna B Free"
14. Pimp C freestyle over Dogg Pound's "Reality" / Pimp C freestyle over Too $hort's "Top Down"

*Originally titled just *Ridin' Dirty*, this double disc is available at screweduprecords.com. Side B does not contain any UGK.

UGK & DJ C-Wiz – *Trill Azz Mixez* (1999)
1. UGK "Pocket Full Of Stones" b/w 2Pac "Hail Mary"
2. C-Murder "Ackickdoe!" b/w 5th Ward Boyz "P.W.A. (Pussy, Weed, & Alcohol)"
3. UGK – "Front, Back & Side 2 Side" b/w 5th Ward Boyz "P.W.A. (Pussy, Weed, & Alcohol)"
4. UGK – "I Left It Wet For You" b/w Too $hort "Freaky Tales"
5. Meen Green "Deep In The Game" b/w 3re Tha Hardaway "Top Notch Hoes"*
6. Scarface "2 Real" b/w UGK "Diamonds & Wood"
7. UGK "Diamonds & Wood" b/w Scarface "2 Real"
8. Master P "Playaz From The South" b/w UGK "One Day"
9. UGK "Something Good" b/w Bone Thugs N Harmony "Thug Luv"
10. UGK "Murder" b/w Lil Keke "Southside"
11. Master P "Break 'Em Off Something" b/w Lil Keke "Southside"
12. Lil Sin "Free" b/w Scarface "Homies & Thugs"
13. UGK – "One Day (Remix)"

Side Hustles featuring UGK (Jive, 2002)
1. UGK featuring Smitty & Sonji – "Belts To Match" produced by Organized Noize*
2. Rob Jackson featuring Bun B – "Breakin' Sketti" produced by Melvin Coleman
3. Scarface featuring UGK – "They Down With Us" produced by Scarface
4. Mil featuring UGK – "Dirty Dirty (Remix)" produced by Gavin Marchand & Ty Fyffe**
5. E-40, B-Legit & UGK – "The Corruptor's Execution" produced by Pimp C***
6. Celly Cel featuring UGK – "Pop The Trunk" produced by Studio Ton
7. UGK, KB, Too $hort & 8Ball – "Cigarette" produced by Byrd****
8. Q of ESC featuring Bun B & Marquaze – "We Big Mane" produced by Barry Adams
9. Too $hort & Pimp C – "All About It" produced by Colin Wolfe*****
10. Mil featuring Bun B – "The Game" produced by Franklin "Livin' Proof" Crum
11. UGK – "Pocket Full Of Stones (Pimp C Remix)" produced by Pimp C

*"Belts To Match" also appeared on *The Wood* soundtrack (Jive, 1999).

***"Dirty Dirty" appeared on Mil's album *Street Scriptures* (Jive, 2001).
****"The Corruptor's Execution" also appeared on *The Corruptor* soundtrack (Jive, 1999).
*****"Cigarette" also appeared on Too $hort's *Nationwide 2 Ghetto Pass: The Compilation* (Up All Nite, 2000).
******"All About It" also appeared on Too $hort's *Nationwide: Independence Day* compilation (Short/Jive, 1998)

Jive Records Presents: UGK Chopped & Screwed (Jive, 2004)
1. "One Day"
2. "Diamonds & Wood"
3. "Something Good"
4. "Pimpin' Ain't No Illusion" featuring Kool Ace & Too $hort
5. "Front, Back & Side to Side"
6. "Pocket Full of Stones (Pimp C Remix)"
7. "Let Me See It"
8. "Choppin' Blades"
9. "Take It Off"
10. "Belts to Match" featuring Smitty & Sonji
11. "Fuck My Car" featuring 3-2
12. "Pinky Ring"

UGK – *Still Ridin Dirty (Chopped Up & Not Slopped Up)* by OG Ron C (2007)
1. "Quit Hatin The South" featuring Willie D & Charlie Wilson
2. "Top Drop Dyne" featuring Cory Mo
3. "Stop & Go"
4. "Cocaine" featuring Rick Ross
5. "Still Riding Dirty"
6. "She Love It"
7. "International Players Anthem" featuring Three 6 Mafia
8. "Hit The Block" featuring T.I.
9. "Next Up" featuring Big Daddy Kane & Kool G Rap
10. "Like That"
11. "Game Belongs To Me"
12. "Outro"
13. "International Players Anthem (Clean)" featuring OutKast

Pimp C – *Greatest Hits* (Rap-A-Lot/Asylum, 2008)
1. "Knockin' Doors Down – Intro"
2. "Knockin' Doors Down" featuring Lil Keke & P.O.P.
3. "Pop It 4 Pimp" featuring Juvenile & Webbie
4. "Hogg In The Game – Skit"
5. "Hogg In The Game"
6. "I's A Playa – Skit"
7. "I's A Playa" featuring Bun B, Twista, & Z-Ro
8. "The Honey – Skit"
9. "The Honey" featuring Jazze Pha, Jody Breeze, & Tela
10. "Wood Wheel – Skit"
11. "Wood Wheel"
12. "Pourin Up" featuring Bun B & Mike Jones
13. "My Angel"
14. "Swang Down"
15. "16.5 – Skit"
16. "16.5"
17. "Free"
18. "Comin' Up" featuring Lil' Flip & Z-Ro
19. "Bobby & Whitney – Skit"
20. "Bobby & Whitney" featuring 8Ball & MJG
21. "I'ma Hustler"
22. "Get Cha Mind Right" featuring Cory Mo
23. "Mom and Bun – Skit"
24. "I Miss You" featuring Z-Ro

UGK – *The Big Tyme Way* (RBC Records, 2011)
1. "Like Yesterday"
2. "Cut U N ½"
3. Banned Intro
4. "Pregnant Pussy"
5. "Mutha Ain't Mine"
6. "Mr. Playa"
7. "Something Good (DJ Screw Mix)"
8. "Short Texas (DJ Screw Mix)"
9. "Pregnant Pussy (DJ Screw Mix)"
10. "Like Yesterday (DJ Screw Mix)"
11. "Mutha Ain't Mine (Instrumental)"
12. "What Up My Boy"
13. "Satisfied"
14. "7 Executioners" – Bun B & Big Born 2wice

[FEATURES & PRODUCTION]

1992:
UGK featuring DJ Bird, Ganksta C, & Ron C – "Texas" (Big Tyme/Jive)
Point Blank featuring UGK – "Cut U 'N 1/2" from *Prone to Bad Dreams* (Big Tyme) produced by Pimp C

1993:
Born 2wice featuring UGK – "7 Executioners" from *U Have The Right 2 Remain Violent* (Bigga Records)
UGK – "'93 Mac" from the *Super Tight* sessions (unreleased)
UGK – "Here They Come" from the *Super Tight* sessions (unreleased)
UGK – "How Long Can It Last?" from the *Super Tight* sessions (unreleased)
UGK – "Menage A Trois" from the *Super Tight* sessions (unreleased)
UGK – "Mr. High (Outro)" from the *Super Tight* sessions (unreleased)

UGK – "Rat-Tat-Tat" from the *Super Tight* sessions (unreleased)
UGK – "Smooth Slangin'" from the *Super Tight* sessions (unreleased)
UGK featuring 3-2 & Mitchell Queen, "Weed Weed" from the *Super Tight* sessions (unreleased)
UGK featuring Bo-Bo Luchiano, Big Mike, & N.O. Joe – "High 'Til I Die" from the *Super Tight* sessions (unreleased)
UGK featuring DJ DMD – "Supertight" from the *Super Tight* sessions (unreleased)
UGK featuring Tim Smooth – "Mack The Knife" from the *Super Tight* sessions (unreleased)

1994:
Big Mike featuring Pimp C – "Havin' Thangs" from *Somethin Serious* (Rap-A-Lot) produced by Pimp C (also appeared on the *Dangerous Minds* soundtrack)

1995:
5th Ward Boyz featuring UGK – "Swing Wide" from *Rated G* (Underground/Rap-A-Lot) produced by Pimp C
Kottonmouth featuring Pimp C – "Satisfied" from *100% Kottonmouth* (Youngsta) produced by DJ Snake
UGK, Master P, & Silkk The Shocker – "Playaz From the South" from *Down South Hustlers – Bouncin' And Swingin'* compilation (No Limit/Priority) produced by Mo B. Dick & Pimp C
X-Mob featuring Pimp C – "Watcha Gone Do" from *Ghetto Mail* (Par-Le) produced by Pimp C

1996:
3-2 featuring UGK – "You Wanna Ride" from *The Wicked Buddah Baby* (Noo Trybe/Rap-A-Lot) produced by Swift
DJ DMD featuring Pimp C – "Candy (The 'Introducing Percy Mack' Mix)" from *Eleven* (Inner Soul) produced by DJ DMD
Kilo G featuring Pimp C – "Release Me" (New Orleans, LA) from *The Bloody City* (Cash Money) produced by Mannie Fresh
Master P featuring UGK – "Break 'Em Off Somethin'" from *Ice Cream Man* (No Limit/Priority) produced by Pimp C
Pimp C & Poppy – Whodini's "Friends" Freestyle from *DJ Screw's Chapter 190: 3-4 Action*
UGK featuring Lord Jamar, CoCo Budda, & Keith Murray – "Live Wires Connect" from *Don't Be A Menace To South Central While Drinking Your Juice In The Hood* soundtrack (Island) produced by Lord Jamar

1997:
Critical Condition – "Hood Card" from *CC Water Bound* (Starvin' Artists) produced by Pimp C
Critical Condition – "Playa Haters" from *CC Water Bound* (Starvin' Artists) produced by Pimp C
Critical Condition featuring Aldon X & Shorty – "4 Real Nigga Posse" from *CC Water Bound* (Starvin' Artists) produced by Pimp C
Critical Condition featuring Pimp C – "Creepin'" from *CC Water Bound* (Starvin' Artists) produced by Pimp C
Critical Condition featuring UGK – "Bout 2 Go Down" from *CC Water Bound* (Starvin' Artists) produced by Pimp C
D'Meka featuring UGK – "Money Stacks" from *Now... Feel Me* (All Net) produced by Pimp C
Master P featuring 8Ball & MJG & UGK – "Meal Ticket" from *I'm 'Bout It* soundtrack (No Limit/Priority) produced by Mo B. Dick
Master P featuring Pimp C & Silkk the Shocker – "I Miss My Homies" from *Ghetto D* (No Limit/Priority) produced by Mo B. Dick
PSK-13 featuring UGK – "Like Yesterday" (Houston, TX) from *Born Bad?* (Big Tyme/Priority) produced by Pimp C
Too $hort & UGK – "It's Alright" from the *Dangerous Ground* soundtrack (Jive)
UGK – "HiSide" from E-40 & B-Legit's *Southwest Riders* compilation (Sick Wid' It/Jive) produced by Pimp C
X-Mob featuring Pimp C – "Good Times" from *Paper Chasing* (Par-Le) produced by Pimp C
X-Mob featuring Pimp C – "Mob or Die" from *Paper Chasing* (Par-Le) produced by Pimp C

1998:
Baby Drew featuring Pimp C – "20 Inches & 4 Nickels" from *The Hand That Rocks the Cradle* EP (Ground Hawg)
Celly Cel featuring UGK – "Pop The Trunk" from *The G Filez* (Sick Wid It/Jive) produced by Studio Ton
C-Murder featuring UGK & Master P – "Akickdoe!" from *Life or Death* (No Limit) produced by Pimp C & KLC/Beats By The Pound
DJ DMD featuring Lee Masta & Pimp C – "The Trill Connection" from *Twenty-Two: P.A. World Wide* (Inner Soul) produced by DJ DMD
Fiend featuring UGK & Master P – "Slangin'" from *There's One in Every Family* (No Limit/Priority) produced by KLC
Lil' Sin – "Watch For Tha Slip" from *Who Got Yo Back* (BLVD) produced by Pimp C
Lil' Sin featuring King 13 – "Rollin Stone" from *Who Got Yo Back* (BLVD) produced by Pimp C
Lil' Sin featuring Pimp C – "Mrs. Good Pussy" from *Who Got Yo Back* (BLVD) produced by Pimp C
Lil' Sin featuring UGK – "Free" from *Who Got Yo Back* (BLVD) produced by Pimp C (later re-released on his 2000 Premier album *Livin In Sin*, and his 2006 S.U.C. project *The Greatest Flames*)
Lil' Will featuring Cool Breeze & Pimp C – "Low, Low" from *Better Days* advance CD (Organized Noize/Interscope)
Mafioso Click featuring Pimp C – "Feel My Choppa" from *Feel My Choppa* (Mafioso)
Master P featuring UGK – "Ghetto Life" from *MP Da Last Don* (No Limit/Priority) produced by Mo B. Dick
Meen Green featuring Pimp C – "Deep In The Game" from *The Smoking Section* (Patchwerk) produced by Pimp C
Parental Advisory featuring Big Gipp, Noreaga, & Pimp C – "Dope Stories (Remix)" from *Straight No Chase* (DreamWorks)
Scarface featuring 3-2 & UGK – "2 Real" from *My Homies* (Rap-A-Lot) produced by Mr. Lee & Scarface
Scarface featuring Juvenile, Petey Pablo, Pimp C, & Z-Ro – "Pimp Hard" from *My Homies Part 2* (Rap-A-Lot) produced by Mr. Lee
Sho featuring Pimp C – "Blind and Can't See" from *The Return* (Sho-Nuf-Jammin' Records)
Sleepy's Theme – "Can't Let Go" (Atlanta, GA) from *The Vinyl Room* (Bang II) produced by Pimp C & Organized Noize
Sleepy's Theme – "Simply Beautiful" from *The Vinyl Room* (Bang II) produced by Pimp C
Sleepy's Theme – "Fallin' in Love Again" from *The Vinyl Room* (Bang II) produced by Pimp C & Organized Noize
UGK featuring N.O. Joe – "Bump and Grill" from the *I Got the Hook-up!* soundtrack (No Limit/Priority) produced by N.O. Joe
UGK featuring Smitty – "Tossed Up" from *Mean Green Presents: Major Players Compilation* (No Limit/Priority) produced by Pimp C
Young Bleed featuring Master P & Mystikal – "Bring The Noise" from *My Balls And My Word* (No Limit) produced by Pimp C

1999:
One Gud Cide featuring UGK – "Down Here" from *Contradictions* (Scarred 4 Life) produced by Pimp C
3re Tha Hardaway – "Headcrack" from *Undaconstruction* (Dead Serious) produced by Pimp C (also appeared on their 2001 album *D.S. Foundation*)
3re Tha Hardaway – "Spooked" from *Undaconstruction* (Dead Serious) produced by Pimp C
3re Tha Hardaway featuring Bun B & Lil' Jamal – "Affiliation" from *Undaconstruction* (Dead Serious) produced by Pimp C
3re Tha Hardaway featuring Pimp C – "Top Notch Hoes" from *Undaconstruction* (Dead Serious)
Adamshame featuring Too $hort & UGK – "The Game Ain't Rated" (Atlanta, GA) from *Revelations: The Beginning of the End* (Trump Tight) produced by Pimp C (also re-released as "We Got Game" with a new beat on their 2000 album *Dirty Game*)
Bush featuring Meka B, Pimp C – "All in the Game" from *No More Worries* (Keep It Wicked) produced by Micah Otis
CoCo Budda featuring UGK, Bo$$, & Ivory P – "Let 'Em Have It" from *In Real Life* (On The Rise Records)
Crooked Lettaz featuring Pimp C – "Get Crunk" from *Grey Skies* (Penalty) produced by Pimp C
Klas One featuring UGK – "Peep Yo Gal" from *Once In A Blue Moon* (Kross Road) produced by K-Tron
MC Breed featuring Pimp C & Kurupt – "Rule No. 1" from *It's All Good* (Power/Roadrunner) produced by Jazze Pha
Silky Slim featuring Pimp C – "You Ain't Gonna Be Down" from *Ole Superstar* (Swamp Farm) produced by Dolby D

2000:
5th Ward Boyz featuring UGK – "Mind on Money" from *Recognize the Mob* (Underground/Rap-A-Lot) produced by E-Rock
Ace Deuce featuring UGK – "Grippin' Graine" from *Southern Gutta Butta* (BackWoodz) (also re-released with a different beat on his 2001 album *Raw & Uncut*)
Big Blac featuring Pimp C – "Pimp Walk" single (Tony Mercedes)

Big Boom & The Big Bizness Click featuring Pimp C – "Mr. Playa Hata" from *Paperchase 2000* (Double L Records)
Bun B & MDDL FNGZ featuring Pimp C – "Pay My Bitch" from *Live! From Da Manjah* (Perfecto) produced by Grizz
Camron featuring Ludacris, Juelz Santana, Trina, & UGK – "What Means the World to You (Remix)" single (Epic) produced by Trackmasters
Captain Save 'Em featuring Pimp C – "Representin' Southwest" from *My Cape is in the Cleaner's* (T.W.D.Y.) [2]
E-40 featuring Pastor Troy, Al Kapone, Too $hort, & Pimp C – "Doin' the Fool" from *Loyalty and Betrayal* (Sick Wid It/Jive) produced by SMK
Jahari featuring Pimp C – "BigShots" from *BigShotz* (Success)
Jay-Z featuring UGK – "Big Pimpin'" from *Vol. 3... Life and Times of S. Carter* (Roc-A-Fella/Def Jam) produced by Timbaland
La Chat, Project Pat, & UGK "Lookin' 4 Da Chewin'" from Three 6 Mafia's *We Never Sleep, Volume 2* compilation
Ludacris featuring UGK – "Stick 'Em Up" from *Back for the First Time* (Disturbing Tha Peace/Def Jam) produced by Bangladesh
Mafia Style featuring Pimp C – "No Cheese" from *Unpredictable, Vol. 1: Working With Something* (Mafia Style) produced by Gambino
MDDL FNGZ featuring UGK – "My Bitch" from *Trouble* (Perfecto) produced by Pimp C
OutKast featuring UGK – "Tough Guy" from the *Shaft* soundtrack (Arista) produced by Earthtone III
Profound, Ltd. featuring Dolby D & Pimp C – "What U Wanna Hear" from *Possession with Intent to Distribute* (Red Boy) produced by Groove
Scarface featuring UGK – "They Down With Us" from *The Last of a Dying Breed* (Rap-A-Lot) produced by Scarface, Mr. Lee, & N.O. Joe
Spice-1 featuring Pimp C – "Thug Thang Y2G" from *The Last Dance* (Mobb Status/Thug World) produced by G-Man Stan [2]
Spice-1 featuring Pimp C – "Murder Man Dance" from *The Last Dance* (Mobb Status/Thug World) produced by Al Eaton & Pimp C
Tela featuring UGK – "Sho Nuff 2000" from *The World Ain't Enuff* (Rap-A-Lot) produced by Slice Tee
Three 6 Mafia featuring UGK & Project Pat – "Sippin on Some Syrup" from *When the Smoke Clears: Sixty 6, Sixty 1* (Loud) produced by Three 6 Mafia
Too $hort featuring LeVitti & Pimp C – "Playa'z Life" from *M.V.P.'z: Most Valuable Playaz* soundtrack (Certified) (also appeared under the title "Jus' A Playa" on the *Obstacles* soundtrack.)
UGK – "Family Affair" from the *Baller Blockin'* soundtrack (Cash Money) produced by Pimp C
Willie D featuring Pimp C – "Freaky Deaky" from *Loved by Few, Hated by Many* (Rap-A-Lot/Virgin)
Wreckshop Family featuring Big Moe, D-Gotti, Dirty $, & Pimp C – "4's Recline Tops" (Wreckshop Records)
X-Con featuring UGK – "Mighty Dollar" from the unreleased album *Dirty Life* (First String/Elektra)

2001:
3re Tha Hardaway featuring Precious Red – "Miami Timez" from *D.S. Foundation* (Dead Serious) produced by Pimp C
3re Tha Hardaway featuring Woozac & Daz Dillinger – "Affilation II" from *D.S. Foundation* (Dead Serious) produced by Pimp C
918 featuring UGK & Ronnie Spencer – "I Don't Owe U" from *Reincarnated* (Smugglin' Records) produced by Mike Mosley
Bo-Bo Luchiano featuring UGK – "Get Up Off Me" from *Enemy of Tha MF State* (Roggish Life) produced by Pimp C
Bowtie featuring Pimp C & Polarbear – "Filthy Child (Remix)" from *Son of a Junkie* (Flight Risk) produced by Pimp C
DJ DMD featuring Pimp C – "The Trill Connection II (Breakin' Niggaz Off)" from *Thirty-Three: Live from Hiroshima* (Inner Soul) produced by DJ DMD
Kiotti featuring Mr. 3-2 & Pimp C – "Texas Boys" from *Jag in The Jungle* (Maddvibes)
Lil Derrick featuring Pimp C – "Cop Yo' Drop" from *Done Didit* (Smoked Outt) produced by Pimp C
UGK – "Country Star" from Greg Street's compilation *Six O'Clock, Vol. 1* (Slip-N-Slide/Atlantic) produced by Pimp C
Young Smitty featuring 3re Da Hardaway, PSK-13, & UGK – "What Up My Boy" from *Takin' Over* (Imperial) produced by Steve Below
Yukmouth featuring Pimp C – "Southwest" from *Platinum Thugs: Straight Ghetto* compilation (Zereh) [2]

2002:
D.O.W.N. featuring UGK – "What U Slang?" from *Southern Slang* (4 Sho Records) produced by Lou
E600 featuring Pimp C – "Bitch Nigga" from the *Texas Boys* soundtrack (One Tyme) produced by D.L.P. [3]
Too $hort featuring Lil' Jon & The East Side Boyz & Pimp C – "Quit Hatin' Pt. 2" from *What's My Favorite Word?* (Jive) produced by Lil' Jon
Vicious featuring Pimp C – "Slow Down" from *I Ball Like Kobe* (Par-La) produced by Cory Mo

2003:
Lil Boosie & Webbie featuring Pimp C – "Finger Fuckin'" from *Ghetto Stories* (Trill/Asylum) produced by Steve Below [1]
Lil Keke Presents 1 Da Boy featuring Lil Flip & Pimp C – "Down South Texan" from *Down South Texan* (Avarice) [2]
Sambow featuring Pimp C – "Bitch Nigga" from *Sambow* (Heavy Hitta) produced by D.L.P. [3]
Sambow featuring UGK – "Time to Ball" from *Sambow* (Heavy Hitta)
The Big Boys featuring Pimp C – "Dirty South Shit (Bump 'Dis)" from *Too Big for That* (4712 Music/Yaa Bigg South) [2]

2004:
I-10 Connection featuring Pimp C – "Down With Me" (High Grade Records)
Sir T featuring Pimp C – "Under My Rug" from *Black Grove 401 Records Compilation Vol. 1* (Black Grove 401)
The Boss Pimps featuring UGK – "Diamonds On" from *Pimpin' Off Top* (Boss Play) produced by Steve Below [1]
Young Muhammad featuring Magno, Pimp C, & Thira – "Greenboy" from *Get the Green Boy... By All Means Boy!* (Starvin') [5]

2005:
Bun B featuring Jay-Z, Pimp C, Young Jeezy, & Z-Ro – "Get Throwed" from *Trill* (Rap-A-Lot) produced by Mr. Lee
Dirty Red featuring Pimp C & Six-Two – "Get the Greenboy" from *Gift of Gab* (Mob Muzic) [5]
DJ Dolby Devious featuring Pimp C – "Ain't No Nigga" from DJ Dolby Devious' *Choppin' Up Da Slab II* (Trill Entertainment) produced by Pimp C
Lee Master featuring C-Bo, Laboo, Pimp C, & Yung Ro – "Get Real" from OG Ron C & Bro. Wood's *Real Recognize Real*

2006:
Bone Crusher featuring Pimp C & Too $hort – "Can't Get No Lower" single (So So Def)
Bow Wow featuring Lil Scrappy, Pimp C, Short Dawg, & Lil Wayne – "4 Corner" from *The Price of Fame* (LBW Entertainment/Sony BMG/Columbia) produced by Jermaine Dupri, LRoc, & No I.D.
Brooke Valentine featuring Pimp C – "D-Girl (DopeGirl)" single (Virgin Records) produced by Deja The Great
Don Fetti featuring Pimp C – "Let's Get Em" single
E-40 featuring Bun B, Pimp C & Juelz Santana – "White Gurl" from *My Ghetto Report Card* (Sick Wid' It/BME/Reprise) produced by Lil' Jon
Hezeleo featuring Pimp C & Hardtime – "Bought a Cadillac" from *Block Starz* (UGK Records)
KLC featuring UGK & Fiend – "Down South" (unreleased) produced by KLC
Lil Boosie featuring Pimp C & Webbie – "Fuck You" from *Bad Azz* (Trill/Asylum) produced by Mouse
Lil Flip featuring Pimp C "You'z A Trick (Remix)" single (Clover G/Oarfin)
Lil Keke featuring Paul Wall & UGK – "Chunk Up The Deuce" from DJ Drama's *Minor Setback For The Major Comeback* mixtape
Lil O featuring UGK – "Who Snitchin'?" from *My Struggle My Hustle/The Lost Tapes* (Bar None Entertainment)
Ludacris featuring Beanie Sigel, Pimp C, & C-Murder – "Do Your Time" from *Release Therapy* (Disturbing tha Peace/Def Jam) produced by The Trak Starz

Missez featuring Pimp C – "Love Song" single (Geffen) produced by Tyrice Jones & Dorian Carter for N Key Productions
Mr. Marcelo featuring Pimp C & Prince Bugsy – "Dat Good" from *Son of Magnolia* (Ball or Fall) produced by Avery Jones
Nephew featuring Pimp C – "I's a Playa" single (Lethal)
Project Pat featuring Pimp C – "Cause I'm A Playa" from *Crook By Da Book: The Fed Story* (Sony BMG) produced by Three 6 Mafia
Ray Cash featuring Pimp C & Project Pat – "Bumpin' My Music (Remix)" (Ghet-O-Vision/Columbia)
T.I. featuring UGK – "Front Back" from *King* (Grand Hustle/Atlantic) produced by Mannie Fresh
Too $hort featuring Pimp C & Rick Ross – "Money Maker" from *Blow the Whistle* (Jive) produced by Lil' Jon
T-Pain featuring R. Kelly, Pimp C, Too $hort, MJG, Twista, & Paul Wall – "I'm N Luv (Wit A Stripper) 2 – Tha Remix" single (Jive)
Trae featuring Pimp C & Big Hawk – "Swang" from *Restless* (Rap-A-Lot) produced by Mr. Rogers
Young Buck featuring Pimp C & 615 – "Make It Home" from DJ Drama's *Welcome To The Traphouse* mixtape (G-Unit South)
Young Buck featuring T.I., Young Jeezy, & Pimp C – "4 Kings" single (G-Unit/Interscope) produced by Jazze Pha

2007:
8Ball & MJG featuring Pimp C – "Whatchu Gonna Do" from *Ridin' High* (Bad Boy) produced by Midnight Black
Ali & Gipp featuring Pimp C & Nelly – "Hood" from *Kinfolk* (Derrty/Universal Motown) produced by Stee & T-Wayne
Baby Drew featuring Pimp C – "Gimme Ya Love" from *Free* (Oarfin)
Baby Drew featuring Pimp C – "Hogz 'N' Tha House" from *Free* (Oarfin)
Bo-Bo Luchiano featuring UGK – "Stop Playin With Yo-Self" from *Chamillionaire: Houston's Hardest Artist* (Hip-Hop Village)
C-Note featuring Pimp C – "Holla At Botany" from *Andrew Jackson*
Chamillionaire featuring Bun B, Lil Flip, Lil Keke, Mike Jones, Paul Wall, Pimp C, Scarface, Slim Thug, Trae, & Z-Ro "I Won't Let U Down (Texas Takeover Remix)" from *Ultimate Victory* (Universal)
Chamillionaire featuring Pimp C – "Welcome to the South" from *Ultimate Victory* (Chamillitary/Universal) produced by Kane Beatz
Codaq featuring Pimp C – "Back That Thang Up (The Sweatshop)" single (Sweatshop Records)
Crime Mob featuring Lil Scrappy & Pimp C – "Go To War" from *Hated On Mostly* (Crunk/BME/Reprise)
Dizzee Rascal featuring UGK – "Where's Da G's" from *Maths+English* (XL/Dirtee Stank) produced by Dizzee Rascal & Cage
Fonzworth Bentley featuring Lil Wayne & Pimp C – "C.O.L.O.U.R.S." single (F.J. Bentley Productions)
Foxx featuring UGK – "Wipe Me Down (remix)" single (Trill)
Gucci Mane featuring Pimp C, Rich Boy, & Blaze-1 – "I Know Why" single (Asylum/Atlantic) produced by Butter, Rio, & Polow da Don
Hurricane Chris featuring Pimp C & Hollywood Bay Bay – "Get Out Yo Mind" from *You Hear Me?* (Rap-A-Lot 4 Life)
Ice Water featuring Pimp C & Raekwon – "Knuckle Up" from *Polluted Water* (Babygrande) produced by Triflyn
Kanye West featuring Pimp C – "Can't Tell Me Nothing (Remix)" (unreleased)
Pimp C & Snoop Dogg – "Friends" (unreleased)
Project Pat featuring Pimp C – "Talkin' Smart" from *Walkin' Bank Roll* (Koch) produced by Three 6 Mafia
Three Kings featuring Pimp C – "Stackin' Money" (Upfront Records) [7]
Young Stally featuring Pimp C – "Diamond Grill" from *Young and Flashy* (U Digg Records) [4]
Z-Ro featuring Pimp C, Spice 1, & Vicious – "Murder'ra" from *King of tha Ghetto: Power* (King of the Ghetto/Rap-A-Lot 4 Life)

2008:
Bankroll Jonez featuring Pimp C – "Pedigree" from *Skroll Music* (UGK Records)
Bun B featuring Pimp C & Chamillionaire – "Underground Thang" from *II Trill* (Rap-A-Lot) produced by Cory Mo
Chamillionaire featuring Pimp C – "Naked Lady" (unreleased)
David Banner featuring UGK & Kandi – "Suicide Doors" from *The Greatest Story Ever Told* (SRC/Universal) produced by David Banner
Lil Scrappy featuring Pimp C – "Niggas Do"
Nelly featuring Pimp C & Sean P – "Cut It Out" single (Derrty/Universal Motown) produced by Pi Productions
Three 6 Mafia featuring Pimp C & Project Pat – "I Got" from *Last 2 Walk* (Hypnotize Minds/Columbia) produced by Three 6 Mafia
Three 6 Mafia featuring UGK – "On Some Chrome" from *Last 2 Walk* (Hypnotize Minds/Columbia) produced by Three 6 Mafia
Vicious & Husaholic featuring Pimp C – "I Betcha Dat (Remix)" from *Am I My Brother's Keeper* (1008 Grams)
Webbie featuring Foxx & Pimp C – "Fly As An Eagle" from *Savage Life 2* (Trill/Asylum/Atlantic) produced by Savage & BJ
Z-Ro featuring Pimp C – "Top Notch" from *Crack* (Rap-A-Lot) produced by Mr. Lee

2009:
Da G Kamp featuring Pimp C – "Stack Money" from *Against All Oddz* (UpFront) [7]
Lil Boosie featuring Pimp C – "Life Of Crime" from *Trappin Hard Servin Fenes* mixtape produced by Pimp C
Method Man & Redman featuring UGK – "City Lights" from *Blackout! 2* (Def Jam) produced by Nasty Kutt
Pimp C featuring Cory Mo – "She Love It" from XVII's *Certified* (UGK/Major) produced by Cory Mo
Lil Wayne featuring Pimp C & T-Pain – "Let's Talk Money" [7]
Project Pat featuring Pimp C – "Smokin' Weed Sellin' Pills" from Dutty Laundry & The Senate DJs' *Back 2 Da Hood* mixtape
Slim Thug featuring UGK – "Leanin'" from *Boss of All Bosses* (Boss Hogg Outlawz/E1 Music) produced by Mr. Lee
XVII featuring Pimp C – "Mack On" from *Certified* (UGK/Major) produced by HeartBeatz
XVII featuring Pimp C – "True Story" from *Certified* (UGK/Major) produced by HeartBeatz
XVII featuring Pimp C & Too $hort – "Where It's At" from *The Reason* (UGK/Major)
Xxzotic featuring Pimp C – "Caught Up (Remix)" from the *Death Before Dishonor* compilation (Nextpage Entertainment)

2010:
Bun B featuring 2Pac, Pimp C, & Trey Songz – "Right Now" from *Trill OG* (Rap-A-Lot) produced by Steve Below
Bun B featuring Pimp C & Lil Boosie – "I Got Cake" from *No Mixtape* (Rap-A-Lot)
Playa D featuring Pimp C – "Like Dat" from *Crossroads* (Santiboti)
Smit-D featuring Pimp C & N.O. Capo – "Ass On Leather" produced by D. Berry
T-Hud featuring UGK & Static Major – "Never Thought (Good Weather Music)" from *Good Weather Music* (Gracie)
Webbie – "Straighten It Out" produced by Pimp C from the *Savage or Die* mixtape

2011:
2meezy a.k.a. 2much featuring UGK – "Cake Up" from *Bottles & Models* mixtape (Danotch Music)
Cory Mo featuring UGK & David Banner – "Ain't Nobody Trippin' (Money Already Made)" from *Country Rap Tunez Compilation, Vol. 1* (C Mozart Muzik) produced by Cory Mo
Da Underdawgz featuring Pimp C – "Grind Hard 2011" from *The 1st One Is For Pimp* mixtape
Da Underdawgz featuring Pimp C & Yung Messiah – "Bring It Back" from *The 1st One Is For Pimp* mixtape
Hezeleo featuring XVII, Pimp C, & Roach Killa – "U Ain't Gotta Lie" from *Kangs Amongst Kangs* mixtape
Webbie featuring Lil Phat & Pimp C – "Money Getting Taller" from *Savage or Die* mixtape

2012:
Big Boi featuring UGK & Big KRIT –"Gossip" from *Vicious Lies & Dangerous Rumors* (Purple Ribbon/Def Jam) produced by Organized Noize
C-Bo featuring Pimp C –"Everybody Wants to Bang" single
LE$ featuring Pimp C & Slim Thug – "Wanna Choose" from the *Playa Potna* mixtape (Boss Hogg Outlawz) produced by Mr. Lee
T.I. featuring Pimp C & Too $hort – "P.I.M.P.S." from *Fuck Da City Up* mixtape (Grand Hustle) produced by Cavi
XVII featuring Lil Boosie, David Banner, & Pimp C from *Kang Amongst Kangs, Vol. 2* (Smoke Cleared) (UGK)

2013:
Born 2wice featuring Pimp C – "Excellent Pimp"
Jay-Z featuring Pimp C – "Tom Ford (remix)" single (Roc-A-Fella/Roc Nation/Universal)
Juicy J featuring Pimp C & T.I. – "Show Out" remix single (Taylor Gang/Kemosabe/Columbia) [4]
Juicy J featuring Pimp C "Smokin' Rollin'" from *Stay Trippy* (Taylor Gang/Kemosabe/Columbia) produced by Crazy Mike & Juicy J
Pimp C – "Final Freestyle" from *Udigg Records Presents... the Final Compilation* (UDigg Records)
Pimp C – "Fresh Clean Candy Thing" from *Udigg Records Presents... the Final Compilation* (UDigg Records)

2014:
Wiz Khalifa featuring Pimp C & Juicy J – "Word On The Town" from *Blacc Hollywood* (Rostrum/Atlantic)

2015:
A$AP Rocky featuring Juicy & UGK –"Wavybone" from *At.Long.Last.A$AP* (RCA)

[VIDEOS]

UGK – "Tell Me Something Good" directed by R. Scott Budge (1992)
UGK – "Use Me Up" (1992)
Big Mike featuring Pimp C – "Havin' Thangs" (1994)
UGK – "It's Supposed to Bubble" (1994)
UGK – "Take It Off" directed by Brian Luvar (1999)
UGK – "Wood Wheel" (1999)
Jay-Z featuring UGK – "Big Pimpin'" directed by Hype Williams (2000)
Three 6 Mafia featuring UGK – "Sippin' On Some Syrup" (2000)
Willie D featuring Pimp C – "Freaky Deaky" (2000)
Bun B featuring Pimp C, Z-Ro & Young Jeezy – "Get Throwed" (2006)
T.I. featuring UGK – "Front, Back" directed by Dr. Teeth (2006)
Pimp C – "Pourin' Up" directed by Mr. Boomtown (2006)
Brooke Valentine featuring Pimp C – "Dope Girl" (2006)
Missez featuring Pimp C – "Love Song" (2006)
Nephew featuring Pimp C – "I's a Playa" directed by Mr. Boomtown (2006)
Pimp C featuring P.O.P. – "Knockin' Doors Down" directed by Benny Mathews (2006)
UGK – "The Game Belongs to Me" directed by Dr. Teeth (2007)
UGK featuring OutKast – "Int'l Player's Anthem (I Choose You)" directed by Bryan Barber (2007)
Codaq featuring Pimp C – "The Sweat Shop" (2007)
Three Kings featuring Pimp C – "Stackin' Money" directed by Mr. Boomtown (2007)

[DOCUMENTARIES]

Pimpalation: Return of the Trill, directed by Ariel Santschi (Rap-A-Lot, 2006)
Underground Kingz Official DVD: The Making of the Album, directed by Roy "Naztradamus" Cross (Hustle Brothaz, 2007)
Underground Kingz (Bonus DVD) (Jive, 2007)
The Final Chapter, directed by Ariel Santschi (Rap-A-Lot, 2008)

[AWARDS]

BET Awards
2008, nominated for Video of the Year for "Int'l Player's Anthem (I Choose You)" with OutKast
2008, won "Best Group"

BET Hip-Hop Awards
2007, won Video of the Year for "Int'l Player's Anthem (I Choose You)" with OutKast

GRAMMY Awards
2001, nominated for Best Rap Performance By a Duo or Group for "Big Pimpin'" with Jay-Z
2008, nominated for Best Rap Performance By a Duo or Group for "Int'l Players Anthem (I Choose You)" with OutKast

OZONE Awards
2006, won the Living Legends Award
2008, won Best Rap Group
2008, nominated for Best Rap Album for *Underground Kingz*
2008, won Best Video for "Int'l Player's Anthem (I Choose You)" with OutKast

[1] These two tracks are essentially the same.
[2] The same Pimp C verse appears on five different songs. It is unclear which version was the original.
[3] These two tracks are essentially the same.
[4] The Pimp C verse from the Young Stally record was later reused on the Juicy J remix.
[5] The same Pimp C verse and hook is used on these two records. It is unclear which was the original.
[6] These songs feature the same Pimp C verse as "What Up" on *The Naked Soul of Sweet Jones*.

To conserve space, the full http link (which may be outdated) to many online sources is not included here. A full listing of all sources with web links is posted at **http://www.pimpcbook.com/appendix**

The following sources are referenced in four or more chapters throughout the book:
"20 Essential Southern Albums," OZONE Magazine, Issue #46, June 2006
"a few UGK little known facts," WordOfSouth.com forums, 01/12/2007
"A Song For You," by Adam Matthews, XXL Magazine, Issue #101, April 2008
"AllHipHop's Pimp C Tribute," http://www.youtube.com/watch?v=_ShqypiSoVE
"AM I MY BROTHER'S KEEPER? The Untold Story of the Dungeon Family," by Linda Hobbs, VIBE Magazine, January 2010
"Austin Surreal: Pimp C Tribute: The 3 hour and 20 minute show + a bonus UGK mix from Dolby D, here!" by Matt Sonzala,
    Damage Control Radio, AustinSurreal.blogspot.com, 12/04/2008
"Beat Drop: Pimp C," by buhizzle, MetalLungies.com, 12/04/2008
"Big Gipp remembers Pimp C," as told to Julia Beverly, OZONE Magazine, Issue #63, January 2008
"Big Mike: Still Serious," by Andrew Noz, HipHopDX.com, 11/21/2008
"Bun B – Shop Talk With Jeff Sledge," http://www.youtube.com/watch?&v=xJ-J62f7pV8
Bun B – UGK 4 Life, The Raw Report DVD
"Bun B Interview at Breakfast Club Power 105.1 (11/15/2013)," https://www.youtube.com/watch?v=8b3aGnzI3eA
Bun B interview by Jon Caramanica, Believer Magazine, June/July 2006
Bun B interview by Julia Beverly, OZONE Magazine, Issue #53, February 2007
Bun B interview by Matt Sonzala, HoustonSoReal.blogspot.com, June 2005
Bun B interview by Matt Sonzala, HoustonSoReal.blogspot.com, December 2007
"Bun B Interview," DankAndDrank.blogspot.com, 10/18/2011
Bun B Interview, Texas Monthly, 01/01/2011
"Bun B On Janis Joplin, UGK's Label Struggles And His Voice," by Frannie Kelley and Ali Shaheed Muhammad, NPR Music,
    11/25/2013
Bun B Speaks on the Hip-Hop Scene When He first Started Rapping on Sway in the Morning," Sway in the Morning, Sirius Radio,
    Shade 45, http://www.youtube.com/watch?v=q3xfuElP7lc
"Bun B Talks About the Final UGK Album," by Tom Breihan, Pitchfork, 03/13/2009
Bun B/UGK interview by Black Dog Bone, Murder Dog Magazine, Volume 6 Number 4, 1999
Bun B/UGK interview by Matt Sonzala, Murder Dog Magazine, Volume 16 Number 1
"Bun B, OutKast and More Remember the 'International Player's Anthem' Video Five Years Later," XXL Magazine, 06/10/2012
"Bun B, OutKast's Big Boi, Swizz Beatz Remember 'Real Honorable, Real Cool, Really Respected' Pimp C," by Shaheem Reid and
    Jayson Rodriguez, MTV.com, 12/05/2007
"Bun B: Long Time Coming, 09/04/2007," XXL Magazine, 09/04/2007
"Bun B: Madd Hatta Interview," KBXX 97.9 The Box, HipHopDX.com, 12/07/2007
"Bun B: Remaining Trill," by Hugo Lunny, MVRemix Urban, September 2005
Chad L. Butler vs. The State of Texas, Court of Appeals, First District of Texas, Case #01-02-01126-CR, 02/26/2004
"Chamillionaire Tells All: How His Label Universal Records Did Him Dirty, Stealing The Idea Of His Biggest Song 'Ridin Dirty'
    From Pimp C & Bun B, Why Its Taking Him So Long To Drop Another Album, Giving Back To Pimp C's Family & More!,"
    UStream, 06/10/2010
"Cheddar DVD 5 – Pimp C," http://www.youtube.com/watch?v=k3krnTmPrdc
Cocaine Blunts, www.cocaineblunts.com
"Cover Story: Bun B starts over: With Pimp C gone, the remaining member of UGK contemplates the next step in his career," by
    Andrew Dansby, Houston Chronicle, 02/03/2008
"David Banner remembers Pimp C," as told to Julia Beverly, OZONE Magazine, Issue #63, January 2008
"Diamond in the Rough," by Roy S. Johnson, Fortune Magazine, 09/27/1999
"DJ DMD from 25 Lighters to 25 Bibles," http://www.youtube.com/watch?v=IR0m_GM-nPg
"Don't Mess With Texas: Why Houston's Reign Won't Stop," by Matt Sonzala, The Source Magazine, Issue #198, April 2006
"Dwayne Diamond interviews Pimp C from the group UGK," In The Spotlight with Dwayne Diamond,
    http://www.veoh.com/watch/v326546mafebt2r
Estate of Chad Lamont Butler, Probate Court of Jefferson County, Case #96118, 01/29/2008
"Exclusive: Bun B Q&A, Part One," by Toshitaka Kondo, Rhapsody.com, 03/05/2008
Facebook group "keep u.g.k. music alive.(r.i.p. pimp c)," www.facebook.com/groups/r.i.p.pimpc
"FADER 40: Unpublished Pimp C Interview," The FADER, 01/08/2008
"Family Business," by DeVaughn Douglas, OZONE Magazine, Issue #61, November 2007
FBI case files referencing Chad Butler, obtained through a FOIA request
"FEATURE: UGK, Encore," by Anslem Samuel, XXL Magazine, 04/01/2009
"Fraternal Bond: Remembering The Pimp," by J. Tinsley, TheSmokingSection.com, 12/04/2009
"Hard time helps rapper get focused," by Thor Christensen, Dallas Morning News, 02/17/2006
"Hard to Follow," by Maurice G. Garland, OZONE Magazine, Issue #75, March 2009
Houston Rap, by Peter Beste and Lance Scott Walker, Sinecure Books, 2013
"Interview: Wendy Day," by JB, ABCDrDuson.com, 09/06/2011
"It's So Hard," by Carlton Wade, The Source Magazine, February 2008
King of Trill, by Calvin Stovall, Carlton Wade & Arleen Culpepper
"Kingz of PA," by Rachel Stone, Beaumont Enterprise, 11/25/2005
"Lean & Mean," by Jesse Washington, Houston Press, 04/26/2001
"Legendary Pimp C Interview – Will Hustle TV, Vol. 3 (DVD)," http://www.youtube.com/watch?v=P-HzYYaknxs
Letter from Chad Butler to Wendy Day, 06/30/2005
"Locked & Loaded," by Matt Sonzaia, The Source Magazine, July 2005
Los Angeles County, Department of Coroner, Autopsy Report #2007-08785, Chad Lamont Butler, 12/06/2007
"Man About Town," by Katy Vine, Texas Monthly, May 2014
"Money in the Making," by Joe Nick Patoski, Texas Monthly, August 1998
"Murder Dog Interview with Pimp C of UGK," by Black Dog Bone, Murder Dog Magazine, Volume 8 Number 5, 2001
"Nardwuar vs. Bun B," 05/05/2014, http://www.youtube.com/watch?v=ZD36R6tNLJA
Pimp C interview by Andrew Nosnitsky, CocaineBlunts.com, December 2006
Pimp C interview by Bo-Bo Luchiano, Dirty South Block Party show on 89.3 FM Dallas/Ft. Worth, May 2007
Pimp C interview by Greg Street, Atlanta's WVEE V103, 07/30/2007, audio courtesy of Trill South
Pimp C Interview by Julia Beverly, OZONE Magazine, Issue #34, May 2005
Pimp C Interview by Julia Beverly, OZONE Magazine, Issue #44, April 2006
Pimp C Interview by Julia Beverly, OZONE Magazine, Issue #53, February 2007
Pimp C Interview by Julia Beverly, OZONE Magazine, Issue #54, March 2007
Pimp C Interview by JWood and Karl Orts, On Tha Real Magazine, April 2005
Pimp C Interview by Matt Sonzala, HoustonSoReal.blogspot.com, March 2005
"Pimp C Interview for Rapz.de (funny)," by Jaro Vacek, Rapz.de, http://www.youtube.com/watch?v=vJPcrGxYeD0
Pimp C interview, Murder Dog Magazine, Volume 15 Number 1, 2008
"PIMP C LAST INTERVIEW (R.I.P.)," Tha Buzz, http://www.youtube.com/watch?v=xTFXvd551J8
"Pimp C protégé, Steve Below (The Unheard Legend)," by Edward "Pookie" Hall, OzoneMag.com, 05/28/2010
Pimp C Tribute, Damage Control Radio, Houston's KPFT 90.1, 12/04/2007
"Pimp C tribute Video as seen on Cross Country Pimping Pt.3 R.I.P. Pimp C," Too Real For TV DVD,
    http://www.youtube.com/watch?v=X5tiHYFNvcw
"Pimp C UGK part 3 – EP2 Part5," HipHop2Nite, June 2006, http://www.youtube.com/watch?v=lNO1783uk6M
"Pimp C- Behind the Scenes !!! RATE VIDEO!!!," RollingOutTV, http://www.youtube.com/watch?v=dj97R2VZ6j0
"Pimp C: I Kept It Real For You," by Omar Burgess, AllHipHop.com, 08/21/2006

"Pimp C: My Way Home," *XXL* Magazine, 03/03/2006
"Pimp C's Funeral – Port Arthur, TX," RollingOut.com, http://www.youtube.com/watch?v=HslnDF8LUls
Pimp C's prison letters and other paperwork, courtesy of Weslyn "Mama Wes" Monroe
Pimpulation: Return of the Trill DVD, directed by Ariel "REL" Santschi
"Pimping The Game: Pimp C," by KJ Armour, WordofSouth.com, 2006
"Port Arthur's native son, Pimp C, found dead at 33," by Merecal McKenzie, the *Port Arthur News*, 12/05/2007
"Producer's Corner: Cory Mo & Steve Below," by William E. Ketchum III, HipHopDX.com, 10/06/2010
"Reflections: Bun B Talks Legacy, Marriage, Jay-Z Lessons, 'Big Pimpin' Fail & more," by Clover Hope, *VIBE* Magazine, 09/07/2010
"R.I.P. DJ Screw: *Chapter 182-Ridin' Dirty* Screwtape," by Maurice Garland, MauriceGarland.com, 11/16/2010
Ronald Bookman vs. James Prince et al, District Court of Harris County, Cause #2007-22081, 04/12/2007
Russell Washington vs. Chad Butler et al, District Court of Harris County, Cause #94-01842, 01/13/1994
Russell Washington vs. Chad Butler et al, District Court of Harris County, Cause #96-18012, 04/10/1996
"Sama'an Ashrawi's All-Star Tribute to UGK, Part 2," http://www.youtube.com/watch?v=iBBPOa9ckoo
"Scarface Breaks Down His 25 Most Essential Songs," by Insanul Ahmed, *Complex* Magazine, 01/31/2013
"Scarface: Diary," by Akwanza, *Rap Pages* Magazine, November 1993
"South Coast Live Kimberly Ms. MTV: Pimp C Part 2," http://www.youtube.com/watch?v=e7TVziYwA4o
"Status Ain't Hood Interviews Bun B," by Tom Breihan, The *Village Voice*, 03/04/2008
"Streets is Talking: Pimp C," by Martin A. Berrios, AllHipHop.com, 10/12/2007
"TEN SCREW TAPES," by Dylan K, GovernmentNames.Blogspot.com, 06/04/2005
Texts, emails, and letters from Pimp C to the author Julia Beverly
"The Chronicles of Pimp C," as told to Julia Beverly, *OZONE* Magazine, Issue #58, August 2007
"The Chronicles of Pimp C," as told to Julia Beverly, *OZONE* Magazine, Issue #59, September 2007
"The Chronicles of Pimp C," as told to Julia Beverly, *OZONE* Magazine, Issue #60, October 2007
"The Chronicles of Pimp C," as told to Julia Beverly, *OZONE* Magazine, Issue #61, November 2007
"The Chronicles of Pimp C," as told to Julia Beverly, *OZONE* Magazine, Issue #62, December 2007
"The Chronicles of Pimp C," as told to Julia Beverly, *OZONE* Magazine, Issue #63, January 2008
The Final Chapter DVD, directed by Ariel "REL" Santschi
"'The Golden Boy of Screw': A Conversation With Lil Keke," by Douglas Doneson, *VICE*, 12/31/2013
"The Grind Date," by Jon Caramanica, *XXL* Magazine, Issue #65, December 2004
"The man behind the rap," *Houston Chronicle*, 05/30/1993
"The Oral History of Freaknik," by Angel Elliott, *Complex* Magazine, 04/12/2013
"The Slow Life and Fast Death of DJ Screw," by Michael Hall, *Texas Monthly*, 04/01/2001
The State of Texas vs. Chad Butler, District Court of Harris County, Cause #0863827, 12/17/2000
The State of Texas vs. Chad Butler, District Court of Harris County, Cause #0863828, 12/17/2000
The State of Texas vs. Roderick James Smith, District Court of Fort Bend County, Case #94-DCR-026312, 11/28/1994
The Trill Connection, http://trillconnection.blogspot.com/
The Trill Connection, www.thetrillconnection.com
"The Value Of A Pimp ~ Trill Talk With Pimp C," *Too Real For TV* DVD, https://www.youtube.com/watch?v=b_WiCplvsEo
T.I. interview by Pimp C, *OZONE* Magazine, Issue #45, May 2006
"Too Short Breaks Down His 25 Most Essential Songs," by Willy Staley, *Complex* Magazine, 02/24/2012
"TOO SHORT & SWAY Remembering PIMP C On Shade45," http://www.youtube.com/watch?v=V5jQHlx6DU8
"TOP 5 DEAD OR ALIVE: Bun B," by Alvin "Aqua" Blanco, AllHipHop.com, 03/16/2009
"Trill Spill Tv & Supastarsmag.com Part 1 interview with UGK's Pimp C Mama Wes,"
     http://www.youtube.com/watch?v=XtkNOS4f_gQ
UGK cover story, *Thick* Magazine
UGK Records interview by Ms. Rivercity, *OZONE* Magazine, Issue #65, March 2008
UGK, "Underground Kingz," CD Review by Brendan Frederick, *XXL* Magazine, Issue #89, March 2007
"UGK: Free at Last & Still Trill," by Carlton Wade, *The Source* Magazine, March 2006
"UGK: Underground Kingz In Exile," by Shaheem Reid and Sway Calloway, MTV News, 05/11/2005
"UGK's Bun B Remembers Pimp C," by Jayson Rodriguez and Joseph Patel, MTV News, 12/07/2007
Underground Kingz (Bonus DVD), Jive
Underground Kingz Official DVD: The Making of the Album, directed by Roy "Naztradamus" Cross
"Underground Kingz website," http://web.archive.org/web/20010428040710/http://www.geocities.com/countryraptunes/
"Underground Legend Releases Prison Album," Yahoo.com, 03/31/2005
"Unreleased Pimp C Interview With Pimpin Ken! Speaks About Jay-Z, J-Prince," HipHopNews24-7.com,
     http://www.youtube.com/watch?v=nN-XgM_8rug
"Weslyn 'Mama Wes' Monroe (Mother of Pimp C) B.R.E.A.D. Interview," by Real B of *B.R.E.A.D.* Magazine,
     http://www.youtube.com/watch?v=yr-V-bpInGl
"Weslyn 'Mama Wes' Monroe, mother of late Port Arthur rapper Chad 'Pimp C' Butler, laid to rest," by Erinn Callahan, The
     Port Arthur News, 08/23/2013
XVII interview by Charlie Braxton, *Murder Dog* Magazine, November 2008
"Zro tells Pimp C Secrets and gives Rapalot a Hard Time," HoodBoxOffice, http://www.youtube.com/watch?v=HO-dOFk35gk

Research references included the following:
Davidson County Criminal Court Clerk, http://ccc.nashville.gov
DeKalb County Online Judicial System, http://www.ojs.dekalbga.org
Federal Bureau of Prisons Inmate Locator, http://www.bop.gov/inmateloc/
Georgia Secretary of State, https://cgov.sos.state.ga.us
Harris County Clerk, http://www.cclerk.hctx.net
Harris County District Clerk, http://www.hcdistrictclerk.com
Jefferson County Clerk, https://jeffersontxclerk.manatron.com/
PACER, http://www.pacer.gov
Patchwerk Recording Studios' Session Reports & Materials Log
Port Arthur News Obituaries, www.pap.lib.tx.us/obits/pap_panews-main.htm
Social Security Death Master File, http://ssdmf.info/
Texas Comptroller of Public Accounts, https://mycpa.cpa.state.tx.us/coa
Texas Department of Public Safety, https://records.txdps.state.tx.us
TexasMarriageRecords.org
The Portal to Texas History, http://texashistory.unt.edu/
Wolfram Alpha, www.wolframalpha.com

IN ADDITION TO THE SOURCES LISTED ABOVE, SOURCES FOR EACH CHAPTER ARE AS FOLLOWS:

THE INTRO references the author's interviews with Anne-Marie Stripling, Joi Gilliam, Lloyd, Sleepy Brown, and Too $hort. Additional sources include:
"Ice Berg Slim: Portrait of a Pimp" interview with Ice T and Jorge Hinojosa, Collider.com, 09/12/2012
Pitbull interview by Julia Beverly, *OZONE* Magazine, Issue #19, January 2004
You'll See It When You Believe It: The Way to Your Personal Transformation, by Wayne W. Dwyer, William Morrow Paperbacks, 2001

CHAPTER 1 references the author's interviews with Brenda Harmon, Bun B, Bundy, Connie Butler, Janeen Harmon, Langston Adams, Mama Wes, and Wesley Jacob Jr. Additional sources include:
"Bad Air Days," by Jim Atkinson, *Texas Monthly*, August 2003
"Bessie Jacob," *Teche Today*, 08/14/2008
"L.A. authorities investigating rapper Pimp C's death," by Joey Guerra and Peggy O'Hare, *Houston Chronicle*, 12/05/2007
"PIMP C'S MOTHER 'MAMA PIMP C' TALKS ABOUT ENJOYING WEBBIE MUSIC & ABOUT HER SONS EARLY MUSIC," 89.5
     FM, http://www.youtube.com/watch?v=zkIGZlFoY1o
"Stork Shower Hostesses," *Crowley Post-Herald*, November 1973
"The Cancer Belt," by Harry III, *Texas Monthly*, May 1981

CHAPTER 2 references the author's interviews with Boonie, Bun B, Connie Butler, DJ DMD, Donny Young, Edgar Walker Jr., Freddy Johnson, Langston Adams, Lil Dan, Mama Wes, Marjorie Cole, Mitchell Queen Jr., Mr. Boomtown, NcGai, Pimp C, Pops, Riley Broussard, Ron Forrest, Ronda Forrest, Superb Herb, Tim Hampton, and Wink Dawg. Additional sources include:
"10-Year-Old Suspected In Shooting of School Bus Driver," Associated Press, 11/04/1988
"Bus driver shot twice," by James Castillo, the *Port Arthur News*, 11/17/1988
"Community mourns Hip-Hop artist," by Mary Meaux and Amy Moore, the *Port Arthur News*, 12/04/2007
"Discman," by Craig D. Lindsey, *Houston Press*, 06/10/1999
"DJ DMD Interview (August 2001)," by Charlie Braxton, Down-South.com, August 2001
"DJ DMD: Remaking a song, remaking a life," by Andrew Dansby, *Houston Chronicle*, 10/21/2012
"Family Tree: Pimp C," by Edwin "Stats" Houghton, The *FADER*, 12/07/2007
"School Bus Driver Shot in Head by Boy, 10," *Los Angeles Times*, 11/03/1988
"Student, 10, Shoots School Bus Driver," *Los Angeles Times*, 11/04/1988
"The Apple of Her Eye: Pimp C's Sixth Grade Social Studies Teacher Remembers Chad Butler," by Keith Plocek/John Nova Lomax, *Houston Press*, 12/05/2007
"U.G.K. Hall of Fame Induction Interviews with Bun B and Chad Butler Jr.," http://www.youtube.com/watch?v=2qyMg3dVI-k

CHAPTER 3 references the author's interviews with Averexx, Boonie, Born 2wice, Bun B, Bundy, D Stone, David Frost, Dewayne Thomas, DJ Bird, DJ DMD, Donny Young, Doug King, Freddy Johnson, Imani "MC Bytch" Chyle, Isreal Kight, KD Durisseau, Lil Dan, Mama Wes, Marjorie Cole, Matt Sonzala, Maurlon Banks, Mitchell Queen Jr., Mr. Boomtown, NcGai, OG Ron C, Pearce Pegross, Riley Broussard, Ron Forrest, Ronda Forrest, Steve Fournier, Wickett Crickett, Wink Dawg, and Young Smitty. Additional sources include:
Buppies, B-Boys, Baps & Bohos: Notes on Post-Soul Black Culture, by Nelson George, 07/12/2001
"DJ Ready Red Explains Absence From Geto Boys Reunions," by Jake Paine, HipHopDX.com, 07/30/2013
"DJ Ready Red: The Ultimate Transforming... The Original Geto Boy," by Dynasty Williams, AllHipHop.com, 05/20/2008
"DJ WHOO KID INTERVIEWS LIL TROY Part 1," Sirius Radio SHADE 45, http://www.youtube.com/watch?v=8NO9z39oRF0
"Excerpt: Dirty South: OutKast, Lil Wayne, Soulja Boy, And The Southern Rappers Who Reinvented Hip-Hop, Wherein Scarface Recalls His Mental-Health-Ward Days," by Ben Westhoff, The *Village Voice*, 03/18/2011
Hip-Hop in Houston: The Origin and the Legacy, by Maco L. Faniel, The History Press, July 2013
"Hip-Hop Memories," *The Source* Magazine, November 1993
"Interview with Scarface, HoustonSoReal.blogspot.com, 12/31/2004
"'It Was Like Flies To Honey': 25 Years Of Rap-A-Lot Records," by Andrew Noz, NPR, 02/10/2012
James Andre Smith vs. Non-Adversary (Change of Name), Harris County District Court, Cause #199659146-7, 11/21/1996
"J Prince Interview With The Breakfast Club Power 105.1," www.youtube.com/watch?v=T8NwDi9ok_w
"J Prince Talks About The Rise Of Rap-A-Lot Records," by Rob Kenner, *Complex* Magazine, 12/04/2011
"Mr. Scarface for himself," by Rick Mitchell, *Houston Chronicle*, 10/10/1993
"No Country For Old (Rap) Men: Hip-Hop Legends Deserving of Their Own Dilla Day-Style Dedications," by Robbie Ettelson, *Acclaim* Magazine, 02/13/2014
"Off Tha Wall — Bun B Keeps It Texas Trill," *Mass Appeal*, http://www.youtube.com/watch?v=hgsMjyjwAh8
"Paper Chasers J. Prince Interview," *Paper Chasers Vol. 1* documentary, http://www.youtube.com/watch?v=6SCqkpt0t6A
"Rap Mag Bows in Texas," *Billboard* Magazine, 03/01/1986
"Rap zooms to No. 1 on the charts," by Rick Mitchell, *Houston Chronicle*, 01/20/1991
"Ready Red Comin' Atcha — Still Holdin' His Ground Like a Motherfuckin' Stacha," by Matt Sonzala, HoustonSoReal.blogspot.com, 01/09/2005
"R.I.P. Pimp C," by John Nova Lomax, *Houston Press*, 12/13/2007
"Stephen Jackson talks rap, loyalty & life," by Chris Palmer, ESPN, 12/07/2012
"Thelton Ben Polk," http://www.penpalfriends.org/thelton-ben-polk.html
Thelton Ben Polk vs. Douglas Dretke, United States District Court, Southern District of Texas (Houston), Case #04-cv-03815, 09/22/2004
"UGK on BET RapCity in Port Arthur," http://www.youtube.com/watch?v=vMpmJJ6ENWg

CHAPTER 4 references the author's interviews with Boonie, Bun B, D Stone, David Frost, Dewayne Thomas, Donny Young, Freddy Johnson, Hezeleo, Isreal Kight, KD Durisseau, Kristi Floyd, Lil Dan, Mama Wes, Marjorie Cole, Mitchell Queen Jr., Mr. Boomtown, NcGai, Nitacha Broussard, Pearce Pegross, Pimp C, Ron Forrest, Ronda Forrest, Scarface, Tim Hampton, and Young Smitty. Additional sources include:
"A Clean Look," by Ric Bucher, ESPN, 02/13/2008
"Bun B then talks Pimp C 'At First..We Didn't Like Each Other,'" Thisis50.com, http://www.youtube.com/watch?v=un9L7rnYbGw
"J. Xavier Interviews Pimp C," http://www.youtube.com/watch?v=zkvCuTl37xg, 11/17/2007
"Kids ready for NY," by Susan Walker, the *Port Arthur News*, 04/07/1990
"Man identifies Remo as killer," the *Port Arthur News*, 02/23/1993
"Manslaughter nets 10 years, $10,000," the *Port Arthur News*, 02/24/1993
"Off Tha Wall — Bun B Keeps It Texas Trill," *Mass Appeal*, http://www.youtube.com/watch?v=hgsMjyjwAh8
"PA's Cole a mentor to many," by Mary Meaux, the *Port Arthur News*, 10/08/2006
"Stephen Jackson Speaks on His Rap Career," *XXL* Magazine, 08/16/2012
"UGK: How We Live," *XXL* Magazine, Issue #90, April 2007

CHAPTER 5 references the author's interviews with Big Munn, Bo-Bo Luchiano, Boonie, Born 2wice, Bun B, Captain Jack, Cheryl Brown-Marks, Desmond Louis, DJ Bird, Donny Young, Doug King, Edgar Walker Jr., Freddy Johnson, Ganksta N-I-P, Isreal Kight, Jimmy Olson, Mama Wes, Matt Sonzala, Maurlon Banks, MC Bytch, Mean Green, Mitchell Queen Jr., NcGai, OG Ron C, Paul Wall, Pimp C, Ron Forrest, Ronda Forrest, Russell Washington, Slim Thug, Steve Fournier, Tim Hampton, and Z-Ro. Additional sources include:
"Best of 1991," *Rap Sheet* Magazine, 1991
Bun B interview by David A. Herron, *Texas Monthly*, March 2008
Bun B interview by Scott Bejda, *Murder Dog* Magazine, Volume 15 Number 1, 2008
"Conference Puts Houston Hip-Hop in Scholarly Setting," by Andrew Dansby, *Houston Chronicle,* 03/28/2012
"DJ Screw: from cough syrup to full-blown fever," by Jesse Serwer, The *Guardian*, 11/11/2010
"DJ Screw Interview," by Daika Bray, *Murder Dog* Magazine, 1999
"Excerpt: Dirty South: OutKast, Lil Wayne, Soulja Boy, And The Southern Rappers Who Reinvented Hip-Hop, Wherein Scarface Recalls His Mental-Health-Ward Days," by Ben Westhoff, The *Village Voice*, 03/18/2011
"Graduation Ceremonies," the *Port Arthur News*, 05/29/1991
Houston Police Department Incident Report #001772392, 01/05/1992
"Houston Static," by Hobart Rowland, The *Houston Press*, 12/04/1997
Imani Chyle's bio, http://www.myspace.com/officialimanichyle/blog
"NFL Dreams, Collegiate Reality," by Andy Hilton, Recruit757.com 03/04/2014
"Q&A: Ice-T on Pimping and the Pope," by Eric Spitznagel, *Esquire*, 07/19/2013
"Turn The Beat Around," by Jesse Washington, *Houston Press*, 01/18/2001
"UGK and Big Tyme Records," *Murder Dog* Magazine, Volume 9 Number 1
"What Is The Best Pimp C Verse Of All Time?" by Shea Serrano, *Houston Press*, 09/07/2010
"YO!," by T.C. Bandit, *Houston Chronicle*, 09/30/1992

CHAPTER 6 references the author's interviews with Avery Harris, Barry Weiss, Big Mike, Bo-Bo Luchiano, Brenda Harmon, Bun B, Cheryl Brown-Marks, Dawn Nico, DJ Bird, DJ C-Wiz, D Stone, Donny Young, Freddy Johnson, Jeff Sledge, KD Durisseau, Kurupt, Lalionee Anderson, Langston Adams, Mama Wes, Mia X, Mitchell Queen Jr., Mr. 3-2, Mr. Boomtown, NcGai, Nitacha Broussard, Riley Broussard, Robert Guillerman, Ronda Forrest, Russell Washington, Snoop Dogg, Sophia Chang, Tim Hampton, Too $hort, Travis, Wanda Coriano, Warren Fitzgerald, Warren G, Wendy Day, and Wesley Jacob. Additional sources include:
"A Sony Executive Joins Universal Music," by Ben Sisario, the *New York Times*, 12/07/2010
Bernard Freeman vs. Zomba, United States District Court, Southern District of New York (Foley Square), Case #04-cv-00621, 01/27/2004

"From the Ashes: Former Geto Boy Big Mike," by Ben Westhoff, *Houston Press*, 03/03/2010
"Galveston's Beach Party Weekend may be a thing of the past," by Ian White, KHOU, 04/15/2010
"Hip-Hop artist Mia X weaves family recipes and personal tales into cookbook," The *Times-Picayune*, 09/02/2012
Hyman Weiss Obituary, Telegraph.co.uk, 04/05/2007
"Local rap thriving on independent labels," by Rick Mitchell, *Houston Chronicle*, 07/25/1993
"Radio & Records Isn't Just Statistics; It's An Industry Bible," by Dan Kening, *Chicago Tribune*, 07/13/1993
"Record profits," by Laura Elder, *Houston Business Journal*, 08/31/1997
"Slump stops the music at Southwest Wholesale," by David Kaplan, *Houston Chronicle*, 02/05/2003
"Snoop: It's A Dogg's Life," by Paul Ablett, *Hip-Hop Connection*, #62, April 1994
"UGK and Big Tyme Records," *Murder Dog* Magazine, Volume 9 Number 1
"Worst college football teams of all time," ESPN, http://espn.go.com/page2/s/list/colfootball/teams/worst.html

CHAPTER 7 references the author's interviews with Averexx, Barry Weiss, Big Munn, Bobby Caillier, Bo-Bo Luchiano, Bun B, Captain Jack, D Stone, DJ Bird, Doug King, Dwayne Diamond, E-40, Freddy Johnson, Hezeleo, Imani "MC Bytch" Chile, Isreal Kight, Jeff Sledge, Jimmy Olson, Joe Thomas, Juicy J, Kim Broussard-Small, Lil Dan, Mama Wes, Mia X, Mitchell Queen Jr., Mugz, Nitacha Broussard, Paul Wall, Pimp C, R. Scott Budge, Robert Guillerman, Roger Tausz, Ron Forrest, Ronda Forrest, Royce Starring, Russell Washington, Smoke D, Sophia Chang, Steve Fournier, Stokes, Tim Hampton, Too $hort, Wendy Day, and Young Smitty. Additional sources include:
"Bo-Bo Luchiano – An Interview with Urban South Entertainment," Pegasus News, 11/09/2006
Byron Hill vs. Chad Butler et al, United States District Court, Northern District of Georgia (Atlanta), Case #2000-CV-00202, 01/26/2000
Bun B interview, *The Source* Magazine, Issue #221, May 2008
"Download: Pimp C, 1973 – 2007," by Keith Plocek," *Houston Press*, 12/07/2007
"Interview with Scarface," by Matt Sonzala, HoustonSoReal.blogspot.com, 12/31/2004
"Local rap thriving on independent labels," by Rick Mitchell, *Houston Chronicle*, 07/25/1993
"Pimp C's Mother Responds To Tragedy," *XXL* Magazine, 12/05/2007
"Single of the Year , 1991: Geto Boys," by James Bernard, *The Source* Magazine, January 1992
"Some bad rap from Houston's Geto Boys," by Jon Pareles, *Dallas Morning News*, 09/04/1990
"The 25 Greatest Rap-A-Lot Songs Of All Time," by Brendan Frederick, *Complex* Magazine, 05/21/2010

CHAPTER 8 references the author's interviews with Born 2wice, Bun B, Dawn Nico, Desmond Louis, DJ Bird, Donny Young, Khujo Goodie, Killer Mike, Kristi Floyd, Mama Wes, Mannie Fresh, Marlan Rico Lee, Merrick Young, Mitchell Queen Jr., Nitacha Broussard, Pearce Pegross, Rob Reyes, Robert Guillerman, Ron Forrest, Ronda Forrest, Russell Washington, Scarface, and Tim Hampton. Additional sources include:
"All-Star Tribute to UGK [Mini-Documentary]," http://www.youtube.com/watch?v=Dw4VYMcKpg8
"Big Boi talks UGK with Sama'an Ashrawi," http://www.youtube.com/watch?v=WZAW2FQKrZg
"Killer Mike talks UGK with Sama'an Ashrawi," http://www.youtube.com/watch?v=35nUmkLKqjs
"Local rap thriving on independent labels," by Rick Mitchell, *Houston Chronicle*, 07/25/1993
"Rethinking drug sentences comes too late for some," by Matt Smith, CNN, 08/20/2013
"The greatest Bun B interview," KLRU, http://www.youtube.com/watch?v=0LBazktPezg
"UGK Documentary Clip 'The First Time I Heard UGK,'" http://www.youtube.com/watch?v=ZAzTjubGWc4
"'We're on cloud nine': Mardi Gras officials applaud PA, residents for successful festival," the *Port Arthur News*, 02/23/1993

CHAPTER 9 references the author's interviews with 8Ball, Bandit, Big Gipp, Big Mike, Big Munn, Boonie, Born 2wice, Bo$$, Bun B, D Stone, Dawn Nico, Desmond Louis, DJ Bird, DJ DMD, Donny Young, Freddy Johnson, Kep, Killa Kyleon, Lee Master, Leo Nocentelli, Lil Dan, Lil Flip, Mama Wes, Matt Sonzala, Mitchell Queen Jr., Mr. 3-2, Mugz, Nitacha Broussard, Pearce Pegross, Pep C, Rick Royal, Riley Broussard, Ron Forrest, Ronda Forrest, Russell Washington, Scarface, Smit-D, Smoke D, Superb Herb, Tim Hampton, Travis, Wink Dawg, Young Smitty, and Z-Ro. Additional sources include:
"Codeine Country," by John Nova Lomax, *Houston Press*, 05/05/2005
Erowid Experience Vaults, http://www.erowid.org/experiences
"Houston Hip-Hop News Mama Wes clears up Pimp C didn't die over Promethazine Codeine Syrup or any drug," https://www.youtube.com/watch?v=CS04E1N0pGI
"Lean With It: Rap's Deadly Dance With Syrup," by Rob Kenner, *Complex* Magazine, 03/20/2013
"Leaning on Syrup: The misuse of opioid cough syrup in Houston," by William N. Elwood, Ph.D., Texas Commission on Alcohol and Drug Abuse, 1999
"New drug 'fry' starting to sizzle in popularity," by Joe Stinebaker, *Houston Chronicle*, 12/05/1994
"Pimp C: Never Die," by Dave Bry, *XXL* Magazine, 12/04/2012
"Pressure on cocaine traffic pushes abusers to a new high – Dopers said to be smoking pot laced with embalming fluid," by T.J.
"Straight Talk From the Boss," by Dennis Hunt, The *Los Angeles Times*, 08/22/1993
"TCADA Research Brief: 'Fry:' A Study of Adolescents' Use of Embalming Fluid with Marijuana and Tobacco," by William N. Elwood, Ph.D., Behavioral Research Group, NOVA Research Company, University of Texas School of Public Health
"The 25 Greatest Rap-A-Lot Songs Of All Time," by Brendan Frederick, *Complex* Magazine, 05/21/2010
"The Pimp C Production Thread (RARE/UNDERGROUND ALBUMS)," WordOfSouth.com forums
Underground Kingz (UGK) "Front, Back & Side To Side" review, *The Source* Magazine, December 1994

CHAPTER 10 references the author's interviews with Bo-Bo Luchiano, Boonie, Dawn Nico, DJ Bird, DJ Dolby D, DJ Greg Street, Doug King, Kristi Floyd, Mama Wes, MC Bytch, Mitchell Queen Jr., NcGai, Stokes, Too $hort, Willie D, and Young Smitty. Additional sources include:
"Hip-Hop rap duo to be inducted into Museum of Gulf Coast Music Hall of Fame," by Mary Meaux, the *Port Arthur News*, 11/13/2012
United States of America vs. Farice Daigle, Jr., 08/07/1995, www.leagle.com/decision/19951896894FSupp1002_11755
United States of America vs. John Drake Jolivette et al, United States District Court, Western District of Louisiana (Lafayette), Case #92-cr-60032, 08/07/1992

CHAPTER 11 references the author's interviews with Averexx, Big Mike, Bo-Bo Luchiano, Boonie, Captain Jack, Cheryl Brown-Marks, C-Note, David Frost, Devin the Dude, Dewayne Thomas, DJ Bird, DJ Chill, DJ DMD, DJ GT, Donny Young, Edgar Walker Jr., Freddy Johnson, Hezeleo, Isreal Kight, Jaro Vacek, Jeff Sledge, Joe Thomas, Kim Broussard-Small, Lee Master, Lil D, Mama Wes, Matt Sonzala, Point Blank, Riley Broussard, Ron Forrest, Ronda Forrest, Russell Washington, Smoke D, Sophia Chang, Superb Herb, Vee Johnson, Young Smitty, and Wink Dawg. Additional sources include:
"4 killed in double shootings," by Tara Milligan and Jay Hughes, *Jackson Clarion-Ledger*, 06/19/1994
"Defendant Sentenced," *Jackson Clarion-Ledger*, 06/13/1995
"Hancock Trial Defendant Pleads Guilty," *Biloxi Sun Herald*, 05/28/1995
"Houston's Hip-Hop Scene Picks Up the Pieces After Yet Another Death," by Kalefa Sanneh, the *New York Times*, 02/11/2008
"If This IS Not One Of Your Favorite Albums," WordOfSouth.com forums
"Man, 22, held in Saturday's double slaying," by Jay Hughes, *Jackson Clarion-Ledger*, 06/20/1994
"Off Tha Wall – Bun B Keeps It Texas Trill," *Mass Appeal*, http://www.youtube.com/watch?v=hgsMjyjwAh8
"Rap music acts looking forward to weekend," by Sonia Murray, *Atlanta Journal-Constitution*, 04/21/1994
"Record Report," *The Source* Magazine, October 1994
The State of Mississippi vs. Freddie D. Southwell, Hinds County, Cause #94-3-087-02, 06/12/1995
Underground King'z, "Supertight" album review by J-Mill, *The Source* Magazine, October 1994

CHAPTER 12 references the author's interviews with Bandit, Big Gipp, Big Munn, Bo-Bo Luchiano, Bun B, Bushwick Bill, Dawn Nico, DJ Bird, DJ Dolby D, Donny Young, D-Solo, Jeff Sledge, Khujo Goodie, Killer Mike, Lord Jamar, Mama Wes, Matt Sonzala, Mike Mo, MJG, NcGai, Nitacha Broussard, Pam Harris, Pep C, Pimp C, Ray Murray, Rick Royal, Rico Wade, Scarface, Sleepy Brown, Smit-D, Sophia Chang, Stokes, Too $hort, Willie D, Young Smitty, and Z-Ro. Additional sources include:
"10 Things We Learned At The Awready! Houston Hip-Hop Conference," by Marco Torres, *Houston Press*, 03/29/2012
ATL Rise documentary, VH1, September 2014
"Big Mike Talks 'Bayou Classic,' Forgiving J. Prince, And Rick Ross' Respect," HipHopDX.com, 12/24/2011

"Bun B Rap City Freestyle," http://www.youtube.com/watch?v=brSPoKzB0Jk
Darin J. Black vs. Percy Miller, et. al, United States District Court, Central District of California (Western Division – Los Angeles), Case #01-cv-00989, 02/01/2001
"New drug 'fry' starting to sizzle in popularity," by Joe Stinebaker, *Houston Chronicle*, 12/05/1994
"Number One Spot," by Justin Monroe, *XXL* Magazine, Issue #79, April 2006
"*OZONE* Exclusive: Scarface Feels 'Slighted' By VH1's 'Disrespectful' Dirty South Hip-Hop Honors, Will Not Attend," by Julia Beverly, *OZONE* Magazine, May 2010
"Reginald C. Dennis interview (Source magazine)," Rap Research Archive via HipHopDX.com, 04/04/2010
"The Making of UGK's 'International Player's Anthem (I Choose You),'" *XXL* Magazine, 06/06/2012
"Today In Hip-Hop: OutKast Releases '*Southernplayalisticadillacmusik*'," *XXL* Magazine, 04/26/2013

CHAPTER 13 references the author's interviews with Bo-Bo Luchiano, Bun B, Bundy, DJ Bird, Doug King, Imani "MC Bytch" Chyle, Joe Thomas, KLC, Kristi Floyd, Mama Wes, Merrick Young, Mia X, Mike Mo, Mitchell Queen Jr., Mo B. Dick, Point Blank, Pops, Russell Washington, Smoke D, Stokes, Vicious, and Young Smitty. Additional sources include:
"Funeral set for 'Mama Wes,'" by Mary Meaux, the *Port Arthur News*, 08/22/2013
"KLC of Beats by The Pound," by Black Dog Bone, *Murder Dog*, Volume 5 Number 3
The Psychopathy Checklist, by Dr. Robert Hare

CHAPTER 14 references the author's interviews with Bo-Bo Luchiano, Bun B, Cheryl Brown-Marks, C-Note, Dat Boy Grace, DJ Bird, Donny Young, Isreal Kight, KayK, Killa Kyleon, Kiwi, Lil Flip, Lil Keke, Mama Wes, Mr. 3-2, Robert Guillerman, Ronda Forrest, Russell Washington, Selena Starring, Slim Thug, Stephanie Starring, Stephen Jackson, Steve Fournier, Superb Herb, Travis, Wickett Crickett, and Z-Ro. Additional sources include:
"4 children die in Dallas house fire," by Robert Ingrassia and Jody Sowell, *Dallas Morning News*, 12/9/1995
"10 Things We Learned At The Awready! Houston Hip-Hop Conference," by Marco Torres, *Houston Press*, 3/29/2012
"Big Tyme Makin Big Moves," *Murder Dog* Magazine, 1997
"Conference Puts Houston Hip-Hop in Scholarly Setting," by Andrew Dansby, *Houston Chronicle*, 03/28/2012
DJ Screw Interview by Daika Bray, *Murder Dog* Magazine, 1999
"DJ SCREW – AUSTIN CONCERT," by Dylan K, GovernmentNames.Blogspot.com, 08/24/2005
Fat Pat – *Ghetto Dreams* Documentary
"Flashing Back to the Heyday of DJ Screw," by Mike Giglio, *Houston Press*, 07/23/2009
"Have You Been Screwed Lately?" by Cheryl Smith, *The Source* Magazine, July 1995
Houston Police Department Incident Report #139395795, 12/04/1995
"Interview: Z-Ro on DJ Screw and the S.U.C.," by Jesse Serwer, 11/16/2010
"Leaning on Syrup: The misuse of opioid cough syrup in Houston," by William N. Elwood, Ph.D., Texas Commission on Alcohol and Drug Abuse, 1999
"*OZONE* Exclusive: Scarface Feels 'Slighted' By VH1's 'Disrespectful' Dirty South Hip-Hop Honors, Will Not Attend," by Julia Beverly, *OZONE* Magazine, May 2010
"Panelists discuss the 'Screwed Up' Hip-Hop history of Houston," by Alex Pechacek, TheDailyCougar.com, 04/02/2012
"Paying respect to Screw," by Lance Scott Walker, *Houston Chronicle*, 07/20/2006
"Seeping Out of Houston, Slowly," by Jon Caramanica, the *New York Times*, 11/04/2010
"Services set for 4 children killed in fire," *Dallas Morning News*, 12/13/1995
"The Notorious P.A.T.," by Andrae Linzy, The *Examiner*, 10/28/2011
The State of Texas vs. Chad Lamont Butler, Cause #9552057, Harris County District Court, 12/05/1995
The State of Texas vs. Robert Earl Davis, Cause #9552055, Harris County District Court, 12/05/1995
"Tree on hearth cited in fire that killed 4 children," by Nora Lopez, *Dallas Morning News*, 12/10/1995
United States of America vs. Charles Grace, United States District Court, Southern District of Texas (Houston), Case #05-cr-00043-1, 01/31/2005
"Why Houston?" by Shaheem Reid, Joseph Patel, and Sway Calloway, MTV News, 05/02/2005

CHAPTER 15 references the author's interviews with Angie Crooks, Big Munn, Bo-Bo Luchiano, Born 2wice, Bun B, Bundy, Cheryl Brown-Marks, C-Note, Cory Mo, D Stone, DJ Bird, DJ C-Wiz, DJ Dolby D, Donny Young, Dr. Teeth, Edgar Walker Jr., Freddy Johnson, Funkafangez, Ice-T, Jeff Sledge, KD Durisseau, Joe Thomas, Kristi Floyd, Lee Master, Mama Wes, Marlan Rico Lee, Merrick Young, Mia X, Mo B. Dick, Mr. Boomtown, N.O. Joe, NcGai, Nitacha Broussard, Pearce Pegross, Pep C, Pimp C, Rambro, Rick Royal, Roger Tausz, Smoke D, Sophia Chang, Superb Herb, Too $hort, Travis, Troy Hunter, Vicious, and Young Smitty. Additional sources include:
"A Too Lively Crew at 'Jack the Rapper' Confab," by David Adelson, *Los Angeles Times*, 08/29/1993
"Bun B Describes Relationship With 2Pac," by Jake Paine, HipHopDX.com, 08/19/2010
"It's All Good," by Carter Harris, *The Source* Magazine, February 1994
"Jack the Rapper's family affair gives aspiring artists a boost," by Sonia Murray, *Atlanta Journal-Constitution*, 08/13/1992
"Official vows to press drug probe," by Lee Hancock, *Dallas Morning News*, 11/04/2000
"Pimp C reviews 'Mr. Scarface,'" *OZONE* Magazine, Issue #46, May 2006
"Top HITS," *Houston Chronicle*, 08/15/1996
"U.G.K. Bonus Track from Ridin Dirty: You Don't Know Me," WordOfSouth.com forums
"Will Family Affair be back? Marriott not sure," by Steve Dollar & Sonia Murray, *Atlanta Journal-Constitution*, 08/20/1993

CHAPTER 16 references the author's interviews with Big Gipp, Big Munn, Big Zak, Byron Amos, Captain Jack, Carlos Moreland, Charles Pettiway, DJ Bird, Edgar Walker Jr., Good Game, Hashim Nzinga, Jazze Pha, Joi Gilliam, Kool Ace, Lanika, Mama Wes, Mr. Soul, Pimp C, Pops, Ray Murray, Rico Wade, Royce Starring, Sleepy Brown, Vee Johnson, and Young Smitty. Additional sources include:
"Dr. Khallid Abdul Muhammad remembered," *Amsterdam News*, 03/20/2014
"Muhammad Case Suspect Has a Record of Violence," by Andrea Ford and Mark Arax, The *Los Angeles Times*, 06/01/1994
"Sonji Mickey Audition for Too Fat For Fame," https://www.youtube.com/watch?v=WjYSfhRwaBk
"The Hunt for Khallid Abdul Muhammad," by Peter Noel, The *Village Voice*, 10/13/1998
United States of America vs. Calvin "Good Game" Winbush, United States District Court for the Eastern District of Virginia, Case #12-mj-00052, 02/08/2012
"Who Assassinated Brother Khallid Abdul Muhammad?", AssaNitachakur.org forums

CHAPTER 17 references the author's interviews with Big Mike, Big Munn, DJ Bird, DJ Marly Marl, Donny Young, Doug King, Dr. Teeth, Edgar Walker Jr., Fiend, Freddy Johnson, Ganksta N-I-P, KayK, Killa Kyleon, KLC, Mama Wes, Matt Sonzala, Merrick Young, Mo B. Dick, Mr. DJ, NcGai, Pimp C, Pops, Rambro, Robert Guillerman, Russell Washington, Smoke D, T-Mo Goodie, Troy Hunter, and Young Smitty. Additional sources include:
"4 men plead guilty to roles in drug ring," by Angela Simoneaux, The *Baton Rouge Advocate*, 02/11/1998
"4 'Operation Rap Crack' defendants sentenced," by Angela Simoneaux, The *Baton Rouge Advocate*, 08/11/1998
"5 convicted, 1 acquitted in drug trial," by Angela Simoneaux, The *Baton Rouge Advocate*, 11/03/1998
"9 more indicted in probe of Acadiana crack ring," by Angela Simoneaux, The *Baton Rouge Advocate*, 08/19/1998
"Bun B, Young Jeezy And Scarface Remember Pimp C," by Marvin Brandon, *XXL* Magazine, 12/04/2008
Damon Giron vs. The State of Texas, Court of Appeals of Texas (Beaumont), Case #09-99-192CR, 06/21/2000
"DJ Screw and the Rise of Houston Hip-Hop," University of Houston Libraries
    http://info.lib.uh.edu/about/campus-libraries-collections/special-collections/library-exhibits/djscrew-and-houston-Hip-Hop
"DJ SCREW – AUSTIN CONCERT," by Dylan K, GovernmentNames.com, 08/24/2005
"DJ Screw Interview," by Daika Bray, *Murder Dog* Magazine, 1999
"Donald Ray Graham, Sr." http://www.findagrave.com/cgi-bin/fg.cgi?page=gr&GRid=43163711
Draper, Inc. vs. South Texas Wholesale Records & Tapes, Inc., Case #2003-09148, District Court of Harris County, Texas
"Federal indictment names 15 for roles in south La. cocaine ring," by Angela Simoneaux, The *Baton Rouge Advocate*, 08/20/1997
"Federal Drug Trial Ends With 3 Guilty Verdicts," http://www.usdoj.gov/usao/law/pressrel.html
"Five indicted in cocaine case," by Angela Simoneaux, The *Baton Rouge Advocate*, 01/15/2000
"From the Ashes: Former Geto Boy Big Mike," by Ben Westhoff, *Houston Press*, 03/03/2010
Houston Arson Bureau, Fire Investigation Report, Case #980277, 02/19/1998

"Houston gun violence incidents reports from 1998," Texans for Gun Safety, http://home.earthlink.net/~lsiemers/houston98.htm
"Lafayette man gets 14 years in prison on cocaine charge," by Angela Simoneaux, The *Baton Rouge Advocate*, 12/03/1998
"Man arrested in shooting," the *Port Arthur News*, 10/02/1997
Merrick Young's biograpy, http://www.merrickyoung.com
Metropolitan Police Department of Nashville Incident Report #98-287592, 06/15/1998
"Mother, son sentenced in drug case," by Angela Simoneaux, The *Baton Rouge Advocate*, 10/15/1999
"Paying respect to Screw," by Lance Scott Walker, *Houston Chronicle*, 07/20/2006
Port Arthur Police Department Offense Report, Case #37064-97, 10/01/1997
"Record profits," by Laura Elder, *Houston Business Journal*, 08/31/1997
"SCARFACE 'Last of a Dying Breed' Rap-A-Lot," By Richard Harrington, The *Washington Post*, 11/24/2000
"Sentence cut for aid in drug investigation," The *Baton Rouge Advocate*, 01/08/1999
"Six more indicted in crack case, 'Operation Rap Crack' investigation continues," by Angela Simoneaux, The *Baton Rouge Advocate*, 09/12/1998
South Texas Wholesale Records and Tapes Inc., United States Bankruptcy Court, Southern District of Texas, Case #03-48096, 12/26/2003
"That's the Breaks," by Craig D. Lindsey, *Houston Press*, 02/11/1999
"The Notorious P.A.T.," by Andrae Linzy, The *Examiner*, 10/28/2011
The State of Texas vs. Kenneth Eric Watson, Harris County, Cause #774591, 02/04/1998
The State of Texas vs. Kenneth Eric Watson, Harris County, Cause #872239, 01/30/2001
"the SUC question thread," TexasTakeover.com forums
The United States of America vs. Corey Blount et al, United States District Court, Western District of Louisiana (Lake Charles), Case #98-cr-20058, 06/11/1998
The United States of America vs. Kenneth Eric Watson, United States District Court, Western District of Texas (Austin), Case #93-cr-00132, 08/12/1993
The United States of America vs. Merrick Young et al, United States District Court, Western District of Louisiana (Lafayette), Case #97-cr-60022, 05/14/1997
The United States of America vs. Otis Charles Jackson et al, Appeals from the United States District Court for the Western District of Louisiana, Case #05-30252, 11/20/2007
"Two Rayne men sentenced in crack cocaine distribution," by Angela Simoneaux, The *Baton Rouge Advocate*, 03/26/1999
"Young Buck," *Nashville Scene*, 09/02/2004

CHAPTER 18 references the author's interviews with 8Ball, Big Munn, Big Zak, Bo-Bo Luchiano, Brenda Harmon, Bundy, Carlos Moreland, Connie Butler, Curtis Daniel III, David Banner, DJ Bird, DJ Funky, Duprano, Edgar Walker, Hashim Nzinga, Kamikaze, Lee Master, Lil O, Mama Wes, Pimp C, Quanell X, Russell Washington, Too $hort, and Young Smitty. Additional sources include:
"Abner Louima," http://en.wikipedia.org/wiki/Abner_Louima
"Crooked Lettaz: Grey Skies," by Steve "Flash" Juon, 05/13/1999, RapReviews.com
"David Banner Interview (December 2002)," by Charlie Braxton, Down-South.com, December 2002
"David Banner Interview (July 2003)," by Mista B-Low, Down-South.com, July 2003
Email from Bill Quinn, Doppler Studios, 08/29/2013
"Five Obscure UGK Features," by Shea Serrano, *Houston Press*, 03/12/2010
"Houston police say 2 shooters killed Bentley driver in ambush," by Craig Hlavaty, *Houston Chronicle*, 10/21/2013
"Interview: Too Short," by David Drake, *FADER*, 02/29/2012
"Kamakaze," by Black Dog Bone, *Murder Dog* Magazine, Volume 9 No. 4
Phillip Andrew Liase obituary, *Longview News-Journal*, 10/25/2013
"That's the Breaks," by Craig D. Lindsey, *Houston Press*, 02/11/1999
"The Hunt for Khallid Abdul Muhammad," by Peter Noel, The *Village Voice*, 10/13/1998
"The Notorious B.I.G.: From the Basement to the Boardroom," *Represent* Magazine
"The Pimp C Production Thread (RARE/UNDERGROUND ALBUMS)," WordOfSouth.com forums
"Too $hort – Shop Talk with Jeff Sledge," http://www.youtube.com/watch?v=PR-Z4LBHfi4
"Truest Shit We Ever Spoke," *OZONE* Magazine, Issue #45, May 2006
"UGK and Big Tyme Records," *Murder Dog* Magazine, Volume 9 Number 1
"Unsigned Hype: David Banner And Kamikaze," by Selwyn Seyfu Hinds, *The Source* Magazine, Issue 81, June 1996
"Unsigned Hype Update," by Matty C, *The Source* Magazine, January 1993
"When All Hell Breaks Loose," by Darryl James, *Rap Sheet* Magazine, December 1994

CHAPTER 19 references the author's interviews with Barry Weiss, Bo-Bo Luchiano, Bun B, Cheryl Brown-Marks, DJ Bird, DJ C-Wiz, Dr. Teeth, Vanessa Satten, E-40, Jeff Sledge, Joe Thomas, Joi Gilliam, Mama Wes, Matt Sonzala, Mia X, Mr. Boomtown, Pam Harris, Pimp C, Rambro, Rico Wade, Ron Stewart, Sleepy Brown, Tela, Too $hort, Wendy Day, and Young Smitty. Additional sources include:
"A Sony Executive Joins Universal Music," by Ben Sisario, the *New York Times*, 12/07/2010
"Lost & Sound: UGK-Trill Azz Mixez," by Maurice Garland, MauriceGarland.blogspot.com, 05/19/2009
"South Coast Live Kimberly Ms. MTV: Pimp C," South Coast Live, http://www.youtube.com/watch?v=aRGW8ouBR18
"The Education of Too $hort," by Lee Hildebrand, *San Francisco Chronicle*, 7/30/2006
"The Pimp C Production Thread (RARE/UNDERGROUND ALBUMS)," WordOfSouth.com forums
"Too $hort: The game Belongs To Me," *XXL* Magazine, 08/28/2007
Too $hort Interview by Keita Jones, *Murder Dog* Volume 15 Issue 1, February 2008
"U.G.K. Bonus Track from Ridin Dirty: You Don't Know Me," WordOfSouth.com forums

CHAPTER 20 references the author's interviews with Big Gipp, Big Munn, Bo-Bo Luchiano, Boz, Bun B, Byron Amos, Captain Jack, Carlos Moreland, C-Note, Chad Butler Jr., Curtis Daniel III, DJ Bird, DJ Dolby D, Fiend, Hashim Nzinga, King Yella, KLC, Kool Ace, Lee Masta, Leo Nocentelli, Lil Keke, Mama Wes, Mannie Fresh, Merrick Young, Mitchell Queen Jr., Mo B. Dick, Mr. Soul, Pastor Troy, Pops, Rambro, Rico Wade, Riley Broussard, Wendy Day, and Young Smitty. Additional sources include:
"B.G. Talks Tour With Juvenile, Mutual Respect," MTV News, 07/09/1999
"Birdman Reacts to Pimp C, Production Deal In Place," by Jake Paine, HipHopDX.com, 12/06/2007
"Charlotte waives rapper Master P," The *Baton Rouge Advocate*, 02/02/1999
Craig Bazile et al vs. Boutit Inc. et al, United States District Court, Central District of California (Western Division – Los Angeles), Case #04-cv-04134, 06/09/2004
Craig Bazile et al vs. Boutit Inc. et al, United States District Court, Middle District of Louisiana (Baton Rouge), Case #00-cv-00803, 10/23/2000
Craig Lawson vs. Percy Miller, United States District Court, Middle District of Louisiana (Baton Rouge), Case #02-cv-00256, 03/12/2002
Darin J. Black vs. Percy Miller, et. al, United States District Court, Central District of California (Western Division – Los Angeles), Case #01-cv-00989, 02/01/2001
"Falcons flock to music industry," by Sonia Murray, *Atlanta Journal-Constitution*, 09/07/1994
"Hot Boys Interview," by Black Dog Bone, *Murder Dog*, Volume 6 Number 4, 1999
"Hot Fest offers showcase for fledgling rap talent," by Matt Weitz, *Dallas Morning News*, 8/22/1999
"JT Money Ready For Summer Tour With Juvenile, Cash Money," MTV News, 06/24/1999
"Kevin 'Mr. Soul' Harp, Creative With a Conscience," by Maurice G. Garland, Myspace.com Artist of the Day, 07/09/2013
"KLC Interview (January 2002)," by Charlie Braxton, Down-South.com, January 2002
"Master P-oint guard?" The *Baton Rouge Advocate*, 01/24/1999
"Master P waived," The *Baton Rouge Advocate*, 10/28/1999
"Master P, Snoop Dogg, Other No Limit Artists Set Ensemble Tour," MTV News, 07/15/1999
"Mr. Serv-On Recalls The Phone Conversation That Broke Up No Limit Records," by Jake Paine, HipHopDX.com, 05/03/2013
"Too $hort And Bun B Remember UGK's Early Days," by Shaheem Reid, MTV News, 07/27/2009
"Whitfield spins change of tune," by Matt Winkeljohn, *Atlanta Journal-Constitution*, 01/05/1999

CHAPTER 21 references the author's interviews with Angie Crooks, Barry Weiss, Big Gipp, Big Munn, Bo-Bo Luchiano, Byron Amos, Captain Jack, Carlos Moreland, Curtis Daniel III, DJ Bird, D-Solo, E-40, Fiend, Fonzworth Bentley, Greg Street, Hashim

Nzinga, Ivory P, Jazze Pha, Jeff Sledge, Joe Thomas, Kilo, Lanika, Lil Keke, Malik Zulu Shabazz, Mama Wes, Matt Sonzala, Mitchell Queen Jr., Mr. Boomtown, Mr. Soul, Pam Harris, Pep C, Pimp C, Rambro, Slim Thug, Steve Below, Stokes, Tim Hampton, Too $hort, Wendy Day, XVII, and Young Smitty. Additional sources include:

"Bun B Talks Humor In Pimp Cs Reluctance To Do Jay-Zs Hit Big Pimpin," by Houston Williams, AllHipHop.com, 04/13/2008
"Bun B's Interview With Vibe Magazine, Says Pimp C Passed On Jay-Z's 'A Week Ago,'" KeepItTrill.com, 5/29/2009
"David Banner Interview (July 2003)," by Mista B-Low, Down-South.com, 2003
"DGB Throwbacks: Pimp C Produced Lil' Boosie Tracks," Dirty-Glove.com, 01/03/2010
"I Smoke Blunts," WordofSouth.com forums
"Los Angeles County Coroner, 2007 Annual Report," http://coroner.lacounty.gov/Docs/2007%20Annual%20Report_FINAL.pdf
"Rapper Lil' Flip records song in honor of Pimp C," by Andrew Dansby, Houston Chronicle, 12/07/2007
"The 25 Greatest Rap-A-Lot Songs Of All Time," by Brendan Frederick, Complex Magazine, 05/21/2010
"Too $hort Explains His Stance During East/West Beef," http://www.youtube.com/watch?v=1jPkF9uswTY
"Trill Execs Plead Guilty To Battery Over The Shooting Of Rapper 'Beelow,'" by Mike Winslow, AllHipHop.com, 11/03/2011
"UGK: How We Live," XXL Magazine, Issue #90, April 2007
"Unreleased Pimp C Interview Reveals UGK Was Uncredited For "Big Pimpin,'" by Steven C. Horowitz, HipHopDX.com, 05/12/2011
"Who Assassinated Brother Khallid Abdul Muhammad?", Assata Shakur forums

CHAPTER 22 references the author's interviews with 8Ball, Barry Weiss, Big Gipp, Big Munn, Bo-Bo Luchiano, Bone, Bun B, Carlos Moreland, Chad Butler Jr., Diamond, DJ Bird, DJ Dolby D, DJ Paul, Dr. Teeth, D-Solo, Hashim Nzinga, Jeff Sledge, Juicy J, Kep, Lee Master, Lil Flip, Lil O, Mama Wes, Mike Mo, Mr. Boomtown, Mr. Soul, Pam Harris, Pimp C, Pops, Rambro, Rick Royal, Riley Broussard, Sleepy Brown, Too $hort, T-Roy, Vesto, and Young Smitty. Additional sources include:

Byron Hill vs. Chad Butler et al, United States District Court, Northern District of Georgia (Atlanta), Case #2000-CV-00202, 01/26/2000
"Fairy tale's happy ending," by Steve Hummer, Atlanta Journal-Constitution, 01/31/2000
"Fight shaping up over bar closing hours," by Julie B. Hairston, Atlanta Journal-Constitution, 04/18/2000
"Ice storm aftermath," by Joshua B. Goo & Stacy Shelton, Atlanta Journal-Constitution, 01/25/2000
"Orange Chair with DJ Paul: Best Pimp C Story Ever," KarmaloopTV, http://www.youtube.com/watch?v=gkNKmltVRng
"Ray Lewis' Atlanta legacy not so storied," by Bill Rankin and Bill Torpy, Atlanta Journal-Constitution, 02/03/2013
"Sonji Mickey Audition for Too Fat For Fame," https://www.youtube.com/watch?v=WjYSfhRwaBk
"The Super Bowl (XXXIV) that froze Atlanta," Atlanta Journal-Constitution, January 2000
"Warmer weather at last," by Paul Donsky, Atlanta Journal-Constitution, 01/31/2000

CHAPTER 23 references the author's interviews with Angie Crooks, Barry Weiss, Big Gipp, Big Mike, Bun B, Byron Amos, Carlos Moreland, Curtis Daniel III, DJ Bird, DJ Dolby D, DJ Funky, DJ Paul, Greg Street, Hashim Nzinga, Jazze Pha, Jeff Sledge, Kawan Prather, Khujo Goodie, Knowledge, Kool Ace, Lord Jamar, Mama Wes, Mannie Fresh, Marlan Rico Lee, Matt Sonzala, Mike Mo, Mr. Boomtown, Mr. Soul, Pastor Troy, Pimpin' Ken, Rambro, Rico Wade, Sean Paul, Sleepy Brown, Tim Hampton, T-Mo Goodie, T-Roy, Vanessa Satten, Wendy Day, and Young Smitty. Additional sources include:

American Pimp documentary
"Anything Goes," by David Shaftel, VICE Magazine, 2001
ATL Rise documentary, VH1, September 2014
"City a few thousand short of a Freaknik," by John McCosh, Atlanta Journal-Constitution, 04/15/2000
"Pimp C & Pimpin' Ken Team Up for New DVD, Best of Both Worlds," XXL Magazine, 09/12/2007
"Pimp C performs 'murder' & speaks on Hip-Hop LIVE," Curb Music, http://www.youtube.com/watch?v=nGUhW0AOIUo
"Talib Kweli talks UGK with Sama'an Ashrawi," http://www.youtube.com/watch?v=EgpkTg9bfBA
"Unreleased Pimp C Interview Reveals UGK Was Uncredited For "Big Pimpin,'" by Steven C. Horowitz, HipHopDX.com, 05/12/2011

CHAPTER 24 references the author's interviews with Angie Crooks, Big Gipp, Bobby Caillier, Bo-Bo Luchiano, Boz, Bun B, Byron Amos, Carlos Moreland, C-Note, David Banner, DJ Bird, DJ Dolby D, Fiend, Hashim Nzinga, Kamikaze, Killa Kyleon, King Yella, Mama Wes, Master P, Mia X, Mr. 3-2, Nitacha Broussard, N.O. Joe, Pops, Rambro, Tela, Wendy Day, Wickett Crickett, and Young Smitty. Additional sources include:

Byron Hill vs. Chad Butler et al, United States District Court, Northern District of Georgia (Atlanta), Case #2000-CV-00202, 01/26/2000
"Hip-Hop kings keep the big hall shaking," by Joshunda Sanders, Houston Chronicle, 10/31/2000
"Master P, Kane & Abel and Cash Money Records," by Karen Cortello, OffBeat, 02/01/1997
"Master P, Snoop Dogg, Other No Limit Artists Set Ensemble Tour," MTV News, 07/15/1999
"Mr. Scarface for himself," by Rick Mitchell, Houston Chronicle, 10/10/1993
Rap-A-Lot 2K Records vs. Chinara Butler, District Court of Harris County, Cause #2011-36404, 06/17/2011
"South Coast Live Kimberly Ms. MTV: Pimp C," South Coast Live, http://www.youtube.com/watch?v=7sv9mlqv-K4
"Teen Cribs > MTV Cribs, Top Celeb Teens Countdown," http://www.mtv.com/videos/misc/332831/lil-romeo.jhtml
"The Diary of Jay-Z," MTV, October 2000, www.mtv.com/videos/news/118844/diary-a-day-in-the-life-10-11.jhtml
"The Most Ridiculous Houston Rap Rumors Ever," by Shea Serrano, Houston Press, 07/28/2011

The majority of CHAPTER 25 is a direct transcription of Chad's recorded session with psychic Halimah Saafir on June 30, 2007. It also references the author's interviews with Boonie, Byron Amos, Cory Mo, Dat Boy Grace, DJ B-Do, DJ Bird, DJ DMD, Donny Young, Isreal Kight, KayK, Killa Kyleon, Lee Master, Lil O, Mama Wes, Marlan Rico Lee, Matt Sonzala, Mike Mo, Paul Wall, Pimp C, Riley Broussard, Ron Forrest, Ronda Forrest, Russell Washington, and Superb Herb. Additional sources include:

"Bun B Interview," DrankandDank.blogspot.com, 10/18/2011
"Codeine Overdose Killed DJ Screw, Medical Examiner Says," by Eric Demby, MTV News, 01/11/2001
"Cory Mo remembers Pimp C," as told to Julia Beverly, OZONE Magazine, Issue #63, January 2008
"Covered by ZZ Top, inspired by JC," by Amos Morale III, Beaumont Enterprise, 08/25/2012
"Discman," by Craig D. Lindsey, Houston Press, 06/10/1999
"DJ DMD: Remaking a song, remaking a life," by Andrew Dansby, Houston Chronicle, 10/21/2012
"DJ Screw and the Rise of Houston Hip-Hop," University of Houston Libraries,
    http://info.lib.uh.edu/about/campus-libraries-collections/special-collections/library-exhibits/djscrew-and-houston-hip-hop
"DJ Screw Interview," by Daika Bray, Murder Dog Magazine, 1999
"DJ Screw: from cough syrup to full-blown fever," by Jesse Serwer, The Guardian, 11/11/2010
"Innovators put Houston Hip-Hop on national map," by Michael D. Clark, Houston Chronicle, 06/19/2005
Paul Wall interview by Julia Beverly, OZONE Magazine, Issue #85, April 2010
Robert Earl Davis Jr. Autopsy Report, Office of the Medical Examiner of Harris County, Case #2000-3224, 11/17/2000
The State of Texas vs. Robert Earl Davis, Harris County, Case #865950, 09/28/2000

CHAPTER 26 references the author's interviews with Bo-Bo Luchiano, Born 2wice, DJ Bird, Mama Wes, Mike Mo, Mr. Soul, Pimp C, Pops, TV Johnny, and Vesto. Additional sources include:

"Hip-Hop Behind Bars: Pimp C," by Terence Harris, The Source Magazine, Issue #174, March 2004
Houston Police Department Incident Reports #164691200, #005436498, and #089251896
Letter from Chad Butler to Kevin "Mr. Soul" Harp, 10/02/2003
Letter from Chad Butler to Pierre "Born 2wice" Maddox, 11/25/2005

CHAPTER 27 references the author's interviews with Big Gipp, Byron Amos, DJ Bird, DJ Paul, Hashim Nzinga, Kep, Lil Keke, Mama Wes, Mike Mo, Pimp C, Pops, Rambro, Riley Broussard, and Scarface. Additional sources include:

"10 Things I've Learned," by Pimp C, VIBE Magazine, July 2006
"Collins takes one day at a time after VitaPro acquittal," by Clay Robison, Houston Chronicle, 05/04/2008
"Dr. Khallid Abdul Muhammad remembered," Amsterdam News, 03/20/2014
"Getting Smart on Crime," by Charles M. Blow, the New York Times, 08/14/2009
"New Black Panther Party," Southern Poverty Law Center,
    http://www.splcenter.org/get-informed/intelligence-files/groups/new-black-panther-party
"New Vera report: 'The Price of Prisons: What Incarceration Costs Taxpayers,'" Vera.org, 01/26/2012
State of Texas Criminal Justice Uniform Cost Report Fiscal Years 2003-2004, http://www.lbb.state.tx.us

Texas Tough: The Rise of America's Prison Empire, by Robert Perkinson, Metropolitan Books, 2010
"Texas Tough?: An Analysis of Incarceration and Crime Trends in the Lone Star State," by Justice Policy Institute, October 2000
"The High Budgetary Cost of Incarceration," Center for Economic and Policy Research, by John Schmitt, Kris Warner, and Sarika Gupta, June 2010
Texas Prison Issues, http://brokenchains.us/tdcj/prison-issues/
"The Caging of America," by Adam Gopnik, The *New Yorker*, 01/30/2012
"The Great Texas Prison Mess," by Robert Draper, *Texas Monthly*, May 1996
The Left, The Right, and The State, by Llewellyn H. Rockwell Jr.
"The United States has more people in prison than any other country," Kaleem Omar, *The News International*, 06/18/2009
"The wrong people decide who goes to prison," by Mark Bennett and Mark Osler, CNN, 12/03/2013
"There's No Justice in the War on Drugs," by Milton Friedman, *New York Times*, 01/11/1998
"Who Assassinated Brother Khallid Abdul Muhammad?", AssaNitachakur.org forums

CHAPTER 28 is based largely on a transcription of the Congressional hearings before the Committee on Government Reform held December 6-7, 2000, titled "The Drug Enforcement Administration: Were Criminal Investigations Swayed by Political Considerations?" It also references the author's interviews with Doug King, George Simmons, Matt Green, Pimp C, Scarface, Steve Fournier. Additional sources include:
"2001 Federal Sentencing Guideline Manual," http://www.ussc.gov/Guidelines/2001_guidelines/Manual/5k1_1.htm
"Agent Cited 'Political Pressure' In Shutdown of DEA Investigation," by Rita Cosby, FOX News, 02/02/2001
"Attorney blasts DEA agent's transfer / Congresswoman's intervention 'smells'," by Jo Ann Zuniga, *Houston Chronicle*, 10/06/2000
"Best Black-and-White Soap Opera – 2001: Rap-A-Lot Records and the Drug Enforcement Administration," *Houston Press*
"Burning Down The House," by Dave Marsh
"Court restores conviction in Rap-A-Lot case," by Alan Bernstein, *Houston Chronicle*, 03/02/2001
"DEA again slammed in Rap-A-Lot case," by Kelly Pedersen, *Houston Chronicle*, 11/02/2000
"DEA agent grilled in Rap-A-Lot case," by Jo Ann Zuniga, *Houston Chronicle*, 12/07/2000
"DEA agent shoots suspect to death in drug sting," by Joe Stinebaker, *Houston Chronicle*, 07/08/1994
"DEA chief denies halting task force," by Jo Ann Zuniga, *Houston Chronicle*, 12/08/2000
Dirty South: OutKast, Lil Wayne, Soulja Boy, and the Southern Rappers who Reinvented Hip-Hop, by Ben Westhoff, Chicago Review Press, 2011
"Distributor Withdraws Rap Album Over Lyrics," by Jon Pareles, the *New York Times*, 08/28/1990
"Drug case inquiry revamped," by Lee Hancock, *Dallas Morning News*, 11/03/2000
Email from Mike Spitzer, 10/28/2000, http://www.mail-archive.com/ctrl@listserv.aol.com/msg53731.html
FNV Newsletter, 04/07/2000, http://www.daveyd.com/fnvnov27.html
"Geto Boys – Till Death Do Us Part" CD Review by Matt Jost, RapReviews.com, 04/06/2010
"Hip-Hop Fridays: Rap COINTELPRO Part IV: Congress Holds Hearings On DEA Rap-A-Lot Investigation," by Cedric Muhammad, Black Electorate, 12/08/2000
"House Committee To Probe Halting Of Rap-A-Lot Investigation," by Eric Schumacher-Rasmussen, MTV News, 11/27/2000
"Houston Static," by Hobart Rowland, *The Houston Press*, 12/04/1997
James Andre Smith vs. Non-Adversary (Change of Name), Harris County District Court, Cause #199659146-7, 11/21/1996
"J Prince Interview With The Breakfast Club Power 105.1," www.youtube.com/watch?v=T8NwDi9ok_w
"J Prince Talks About The Rise Of Rap-A-Lot Records," by Rob Kenner, *Complex* Magazine, 12/04/2011
"Kerosene Maxine to Tea Party: 'Go to Hell!'" by Larry Elder, Real Clear Politics, 08/25/2011
Labyrinth: A Detective Investigates the Murders of Tupac Shakur and Notorious B.I.G., the Implication of Death Row Records' Suge Knight, and the Origins of the Los Angeles Police Scandal, by Randall Sullivan, Grove/Atlantic Inc., 2003
"Lawmaker Intervened On Inquiry Into Rapper And Label, Records Show," by Lee Hancock, *Dallas Morning News*, 10/02/2000
"Lawmaker says DEA unhelpful," by Lee Hancock, *Dallas Morning News*, 11/02/2000
Letter from George "Spooney G" Simmons, 08/17/2005
"Live from the Geto," by Frank "P-Frank" Williams, *The Source* Magazine, June 1996
"Mr. Scarface for himself," by Rick Mitchell, *Houston Chronicle*, 10/10/1993
"Music promoter suggests bad 'rap,'" by Stephen Johnson, *Houston Chronicle*, 01/19/1993
"Official vows to press drug probe," by Lee Hancock, *Dallas Morning News*, 11/04/2000
"Panel questions possible donations," by Lee Hancock, *Dallas Morning News*, 10/28/2000
"Paper Chasers J. Prince Interview," *Paper Chasers Vol. 1* documentary, http://www.youtube.com/watch?v=6SCqkpt0t6A
"*PAPERWORK* BY LIL TROY," http://www.youtube.com/watch?v=tVjBmLIuN6o
"Probe of Rap Label Looks at Entrepreneur Behind Bars," by Chuck Philips, *Los Angeles Times*, 09/01/1997
"Rap case suspension wrong, DEA chief says," by Lee Hancock, *Dallas Morning News*, 12/08/2000
"Rap exec, authorities at odds since 1980s," by Lee Hancock, *Dallas Morning News*, 10/02/2000
"Rap figure alleges harassment by DEA," by Lee Hancock, *Dallas Morning News*, 10/05/2000
"Rap records head says grudge resulted in arrest," by Jennifer Liebrum, *Houston Chronicle*, 01/13/1993
"Record label releases rap album attacking DEA after drug probe," by Mary Lee Grant, *The Associated Press*, 10/03/2000
"Reno sets investigation of aborted drug probe," by Jerry Seper, The *Washington Times*, 11/03/2000
"Scarface Album Blasts DEA's Rap-A-Lot Investigation," by Eric Schumacher-Rasmussen, MTV News, 10/04/2000
"SCARFACE 'Last of a Dying Breed' Rap-A-Lot," By Richard Harrington, The *Washington Post*, 11/24/2000
"Smit D Interview," by funkrhythms, 12/13/2010
"Some bad rap from Houston's Geto Boys," by Jon Pareles, *Dallas Morning News*, 09/04/1990
"That Voodoo that You Do So Well," by Scott Henson, GritsForBreakfast.blogspot.com, 08/09/2006
"The Best Little Checkpoint in Texas," by Al Reinert, *Texas Monthly*, August 2013
The State of Texas vs. Stevon McCarter, District Court of Harris County, Cause #821203, 08/09/1999
The State of Texas vs. Stevon McCarter, District Court of Harris County, Cause #820284, 08/06/1999
The State of Texas vs. Brad Jordan, District Court of Harris County, Cause #9917789, 04/26/1999
"The Stimulant Stimulus," by Tina Rosenberg, *New York* Magazine, 07/10/2011
"There's No Justice in the War on Drugs," by Milton Friedman, *New York Times*, 01/11/1998
United States of America vs. Andre Erell Barnes, United States District Court, Southern District of Texas (Houston), Case #00-cr-00834, 11/28/2000
United States of America vs. Byron Keith Harris, United States District Court, Southern District of Texas (Houston), Case #99-cr-00300, 03/09/2007
United States of America vs. Cedrick Rodgers, United States District Court, Southern District of Texas (Houston), Case #01-cv-02105, 06/25/2001
United States of America vs. Edward Dewayne Russell, United States District Court, Southern District of Texas (Houston), Case #99-cr-0037, 02/01/1999
United States of America vs. George Washington Simmons, United States District Court, Southern District of Texas (Houston), Case #99-cr-0030, 05/19/1999
United States of America vs. Phyllis Conner, United States District Court, Eastern District of Louisiana (New Orleans), Case #98-cr-00251, 09/24/1998
United States of America vs. Ronald Carboni et al, United States District Court, Eastern District of Michigan (Detroit), Case #97-cr-81492, 09/10/1997
United States of America vs. Stevon McCarter et al, United States District Court, Southern District of Texas (Houston), Case #99-cr-00737, 12/20/1999
United States of America vs. Stevon McCarter, United States Court of Appeals, Fifth Circuit, Case #01-21203, 12/26/2002

CHAPTER 29 references the author's interviews with Big Munn, Bo-Bo Luchiano, DJ C-Wiz, Mama Wes, Pimp C, Rambro, Smoke D, Warren Fitzgerald, and Wendy Day. Additional sources include:
"Adults on probation in the United States, 1977-2010," Bureau of Justice Statistics, 11/21/2011, http://www.bjs.gov/content/data/corpop11.csv
CD Reviews, *Murder Dog* Magazine, Volume 8 Number 5, 2001
CourthouseForum.com reviews of Judge Jeannine Barr, 11/21/2005
"Galveston County Jail battles recluse spiders," Associated Press, 01/25/2000, http://amarillo.com/stories/2000/01/25/tex_LD0643.001.shtml

"Judge Jeannine Barr, 182nd Criminal District Court," http://www.harriscountygop.com/judges/BioJudgeJBarr.htm
"Lawmaker says DEA unhelpful," by Lee Hancock, *Dallas Morning News*, 11/02/2000
Leschaco, Inc. vs. American Federal Financial Services et al, District Court of Harris County, Case No. 93-02879, 01/25/1993
Letter from Chad Butler to Tim Hampton, 12/05/2004
Letter from Chad Butler to Kevin "Mr. Soul" Harp, 10/02/2003
TheScrewShop.com archives, http://web.archive.org/web/20000511185057/http://thescrewshop.com/main.html
The State of Texas vs. Eddie Floyd, District Court of Harris County, Cause #0657394, 02/17/1993
The State of Texas vs. Lakita Hulett, District Court of Harris County, Cause #0876858, 05/09/2001

CHAPTER 30 references the author's interviews with Angie Crooks, Big Gipp, Big Munn, Bo-Bo Luchiano, Bun B, Captain Jack, Chad Butler Jr., Cory Mo, Desmond Louis, DJ Bird, DJ Dolby D, DJ Paul, D-Solo, Edgar Walker Jr., Freddy Johnson, Jeff Sledge, Juicy J, KB Da Kidnappa, Kep, Mama Wes, Matt Sonzala, Mike Mo, Mr. Soul, Nitacha Broussard, Pam Harris, Pharoah, Pimpin' Ken, Pops, Rob Reyes, Sleepy Brown, Steve Below, Vesto, Wendy Day, and Young Smitty. Additional sources include:
"Aspiring Texas Rapper to Stand Trial in Death of L.A. Woman," by Jennifer Sinco Kelleher, *Los Angeles Times*, 05/30/2002
"Big Lurch Faces Trial For Torture and Murder," by Chuck "Jigsaw" Creekmur, BET.com, 07/12/2002,
"Big Lurch Interview – *Rhyme And Punishment*," http://www.youtube.com/watch?v=AoB6YMX7uc0
"Big Lurch on News," http://www.youtube.com/watch?v=y-tVvjVi2m8
Carlos Hardy vs. Bruce Westbrooks, United States District Court, Middle District of Tennessee (Nashville), Case #10-cv-01049, 11/08/2010
"Fragile Gavel Award," http://www.gracelaw.org/FragileGavel.html
"Free Pimp C!", *VICE* Magazine, December 2004
"Interview: Project Pat Talks Staying Relevant, the Album With Pimp C That Never Was, and Advice for Chief Keef," by David Drake, *Complex* Magazine, 03/10/2013
"Judge Barr removed from bench," 02/15/1998, http://www.texnews.com/1998/texas/barr0215.html
"Judicial Q&A: Judge Jeannine Barr," by David Jennings, BigJolly.com, 08/26/2010
Lakita Hulett vs. Genesco Inc., District Court of Harris County, Cause #200235175-7, 07/11/2002
"Letters From the Women of SAFPF," *Austin Chronicle*, 12/12/2008
"Man Gets Life for Woman's Murder," by Eric Malnic, *Los Angeles Times*, 11/08/2003
Metropolitan Police Department of Nashville Incident Report #02-238966, 06/07/2002
"More litigation over summer heat in Texas prisons: Wrongful death suit filed," by Scott Hanson, GritsForBreakfast.blogspot.com, 06/27/2012
"Negligence, Death Expose Ugly Jail Problems," by Scott Hanson, GritsForBreakfast.blogspot.com, 11/18/2004
"Order of the Supreme Court of Texas, Misc Docket No 97-9226, Order of Suspension,"
    http://www.supreme.courts.state.tx.us/miscdocket/97/97-9226.pdf
"Pimp C Remembered In Bun B's First Interview After Tragedy," by Billy Johnson, Jr., Yahoo.com, 12/07/2007
"Project Pat Out Of Prison, 'Taking It One Day At A Time,'" by Corey Moss, MTV News, 08/03/2005
"Rapper Charged with Murder After Human Flesh Found In Stomach," by Chuck "Jigsaw" Creekmur, BET.com, 06/07/2002
"Rehabilitation or Torture? – Substance Abuse Felony Punishment Facilities," by Patricia J. Ruland, *Austin Chronicle*, 06/17/2008
"Review Tribunal, Appointed by the Supreme Court," IN RE: James L. "Jim" BARR,
    http://caselaw.findlaw.com/tx-review-tribunal/1299059.html
"Substance Abuse Felony Punishment (SAFP) beds now vacant," The *Prosecutor*, July/August 2010
"Texas not adequately monitoring SAFP program," by Scott Hanson, GritsForBreakfast.blogspot.com, 12/11/2008
Texas Prison Issues, http://brokenchains.us/tdcj/prison-issues/
"The Caging of America," by Adam Gopnik, The *New Yorker*, 01/30/2012
"The Great Texas Prison Mess," by Robert Draper, *Texas Monthly*, May 1996
"The Insider," by Tim Fleck, *Houston Press*, 03/20/1997
"The Making of UGK's 'International Player's Anthem (I Choose You),'" *XXL* Magazine, 06/06/2012
The State of Tennessee vs. Carlos Hardy and Atlanta Hardy, Appeal from the Criminal Court for Davidson County, No. 2002-D-1927, 02/10/2006
The State of Texas vs. Darrell Burton, District Court of Harris County, Cause #905436, 03/13/2002
"The Year of Magical Thinking: How Bun B dealt with Pimp C's death," by Ben Westhoff, *Houston Press*, 07/28/2010
United States of America vs. Charles Tyrone Carter, United States District Court, Middle District of Tennessee (Nashville), Case #07-cr-00008-1, 01/10/2007
"Whitmire: Substance Abuse Program Is Doing Fine," by Patricia J. Ruland, *Austin Chronicle*, 12/12/2008
"Will 'Safe-P' and TDCJ Be Held Accountable?," by Patricia J. Ruland, *Austin Chronicle*, 07/18/2008

CHAPTER 31 references the author's interviews with Bun B, DJ Bird, DJ DMD, Isreal Kight, KD Durisseau, Lee Master, Mama Wes, Marlan Rico Lee, Mike Mo, Pearce Pegross, Pharoah, Pimpin' Ken, Vesto, and Wickett Crickett, Additional sources include:
"Bun B Talks About Rap-A-Lot/J. Prince's Influence On UGK," by Jake Paine, HipHopDX.com, 04/02/2010
Elijah Dwayne Joubert v. Texas, Court of Criminal Appeals of Texas, Supreme Court of the United States,
    http://www.supremecourt.gov/Search.aspx?FileName=/docketfiles/07-7830.htm
"Jail time for rapper might not hurt sales," by Thomas Conner, *Chicago Sun-Times*, 10/17/2012
"The Year of Magical Thinking: How Bun B dealt with Pimp C's death," by Ben Westhoff, *Houston Press*, 07/28/2010
"The greatest Bun B interview," KLRU, http://www.youtube.com/watch?v=0LBazktPezg
The State of Texas vs. Darrell Burton, District Court of Harris County, Cause #905436, 03/13/2002
The State of Texas vs. Sylvester Bullard, District Court of Harris County, Cause #0765266, 10/08/1997
The State of Texas vs. Sylvester Bullard, District Court of Harris County, Cause #1033133, 11/30/2000
The State of Texas vs. Sylvester Bullard, District Court of Harris County, Cause #1077595, 09/11/2001
The State of Texas vs. Sylvester Bullard, District Court of Harris County, Cause #0924535, 09/18/2002
The United States of America vs. Chandrea Celestine, United States District Court, Eastern District of Texas (Beaumont), Case #97-cr-00097, 07/22/1997
"Three Days Too Many," by George Flynn, *Houston Press*, 02/17/2005
"Truth and Consequences," by George Flynn, *Houston Press*, 08/26/2004
"UGK Have Bigger Pimpin', Better Hustles Planned," by Soren Baker, MTV News, 10/14/2002

CHAPTER 32 references the author's interviews with Angie Crooks, Big Munn, Born 2wice, Bun B, David Banner, DJ DMD, Gank-sta N-I-P, Heather Johnson, Ivory P, Jeff Sledge, Kamikaze, Lanika, Lee Master, Lil Flip, Lil Green, Mama Wes, Marlan Rico Lee, Matt Sonzala, Mean Green, Mike Mo, Mr. Soul, Pharoah, Pimp C, Point Blank, Pops, Quanell X, Riley Broussard, Robert Guillerman, Nitacha Broussard, Tim Hampton, Travis, Wendy Day, and Z-Ro. Additional sources include:
Bernard Freeman vs. Zomba, United States District Court, Southern District of New York (Foley Square), Case #04-cv-00621, 01/27/2004
Byron C. Hill, United States Bankruptcy Court, Northern District of Georgia (Atlanta), Case #03-61756, 02/03/2003
Byron C. Hill, United States Bankruptcy Court, Northern District of Georgia (Atlanta), Case #04-90891, 02/03/2004
"Coolers installed in seven Texas prisons in summer-heat test," by Mike Ward, *Houston Chronicle*, 06/18/2014
"Declarations Of Independents," by Chris Morris, *Billboard* Magazine, 02/08/2003
"DJ DMD: Remaking a song, remaking a life," by Andrew Dansby, *Houston Chronicle*, 10/21/2012
"Family Sues TDCJ Over Heat-Related Death," by Emily Foxhall, The *Texas Tribune*, 06/26/2012
"Free Pimp C!", *VICE* Magazine, December 2004
"Gateway," Texas Prisoners Network Support, http://brokenchains.us/Gateway-To-Hell/gateway.html
"Hip-Hop Behind Bars: Pimp C," by Terence Harris, *The Source* Magazine, Issue #174, March 2004
"Hip-Hop Outlaw (Industry Version)," by Samantha M. Shapiro, the *New York Times*, 02/18/2007
"Inmate escapes jail while rap video filmed," *USA Today*, 06/18/2004
"KHOU 11 News I-Team investigates Quanell X," by Jeremy Rogalski, KHOU.com, 11/10/2011
"Lack of AC chilling for TDCJ staffing efforts," by Scott Hanson, Gritsforbreakfast.blogspot.com, 07/06/2009
Letter from Chad Butler to Kevin "Mr. Soul" Harp, 10/02/2003
Letter from Chad Butler to Tim Hampton, 12/05/2004
Letter from Chad Butler to Wendy Day, 01/26/2005
"Letters From the Women of SAFPF," *Austin Chronicle*, 12/12/2008

"Merchants & Marketing," *Billboard* Magazine, 01/27/2001
"More litigation over summer heat in Texas prisons: Wrongful death suit filed," by Scott Hanson, GritsforBreakfast.blogspot.com, 06/27/2012
"NY Times: Heat a death sentence for ten Texas prisoners last summer," by Scott Hanson, GritsforBreakfast.blogspot.com, 07/28/2012
"Pair of companies to relocate operations to Bayou City," by Jenna Colley, *Houston Business Journal*, 02/03/2002
"Part 2: Activist Quanell X failed to file proper IRS forms," by Jeremy Rogalski, KHOU, 11/11/2011
"Record profits," by Laura Elder, *Houston Business Journal*, 08/31/1997
"Rehabilitation or Torture? – Substance Abuse Felony Punishment Facilities," by Patricia J. Ruland, *Austin Chronicle*, 06/17/2008
"Retail Track," by Ed Christman, *Billboard* Magazine, 10/20/2001
"Slump stops the music at Southwest Wholesale," by David Kaplan, *Houston Chronicle*, 02/05/2003
South Texas Wholesale Records and Tapes Inc., United States Bankruptcy Court, Southern District of Texas, Case #03-48096, 12/26/2003
"Texas not adequately monitoring SAFP program," by Scott Hanson, GritsForBreakfast.blogspot.com, 12/11/2008
"The Hunt for Khaliid Abdul Muhammad," by Peter Noel, The *Village Voice*, 10/13/1998
The State of Georgia vs. Byron Claude Hill, District Court of Fulton County, Cause #03SC10490, 11/14/2003
The State of Texas vs. Eddie Floyd, District Court of Harris County, Cause #0657394, 02/17/1993
The State of Texas vs. Yakeen Demond Green, District Court of Harris County, Cause #0940569, 02/26/2003
"T.I. Dissin' Lil' Flip Birthday Bash 9," http://www.youtube.com/watch?v=Gi2LLRiGQiM
"T.I. Live Freestyle Lil' Flip Diss," http://www.youtube.com/watch?v=-spIAT-FwJk
"Two Lawsuits Challenge the Lack of Air-Conditioning in Texas Prisons," by Manny Fernandez, the *New York Times*, 06/26/2012
"Whitmire: Substance Abuse Program Is Doing Fine," by Patricia J. Ruland, *Austin Chronicle*, 12/12/2008
"Will 'Safe-P' and TDCJ Be Held Accountable?," by Patricia J. Ruland, *Austin Chronicle*, 07/18/2008
"With no AC, inmates forced to sweat it out in prisons," by Allan Turner, *Houston Chronicle*, 07/03/2009

CHAPTER 33 references the author's interviews with Bandit, Baz, Big Munn, Donny Young, Mama Wes, Pimp C, Rick Royal, and Smit-D. Additional sources include:
"Free Pimp C!", *VICE* Magazine, December 2004
"Terrell Unit searched, administration changed," 05/08/2008, http://www.topix.com/forum/city/rosharon-tx/T54PMB3GGCA3JUOL6
The State of Texas vs. John Henry Singleton, District Court of Harris County, Cause #0525072, 03/11/1989

CHAPTER 34 references the author's interviews with 8Ball, Baz, Bun B, KayK, Lil Keke, Mama Wes, Mannie Fresh, Mike Mo, Naztradamus, OG Ron C, Paul Wall, Pimp C, Slim Thug, Steve Below, Tim Hampton, Vesto, and Willie D. Additional sources include:
"A Gospel-Tinged Goodbye and Hip-Hop in Slow Motion," the *New York Times*, 01/16/2005
"Author Tim Hampton to Expose *Fake* Rappers," by Trill Chris, KeepItTrill.com, 07/22/2008
"Cold-Blooded," by Carlton Wade, *The Source* Magazine, Issue #198, April 2006
"FEATURE: Bun B, Life After Death," by Slav Kandyba, *XXL* Magazine, 11/06/2009
"Houston Hip-Hop," by Roni Sarig, *Houston Press*, 03/22/2007
"Innovators put Houston Hip-Hop on national map," by Michael D. Clark, *Houston Chronicle*, 06/19/2005
Letter from Chad Butler to Tim Hampton, 12/05/2004
Letter from Chad Butler to Tim Hampton, 12/14/2004
Letter from Chad Butler to Wendy Day, 01/26/2005
Paul Wall Interview by Julia Beverly, *OZONE* Magazine, Issue #85, April 2010
"Pimp C UGK part 2," HipHop2Nite, June 2006, http://www.youtube.com/watch?v=_l0wVNOprnk
"Prison and Jail Deaths in Custody, 2000-2009 – Statistical Tables," U.S. Department of Justice, Office of Justice Programs, Bureau of Justice Statistics, http://www.bjs.gov/content/pub/pdf/pjdc0009st.pdf
"$hort Stories: Remembering The Pimp," by Too $hort, *OZONE* Magazine, Issue #63, January 2008
"Show & Prove: Lil Boosie & Webbie," by Brendan Frederick, *XXL* Magazine, Issue #65, December 2004
"Straight Path," *XXL* Magazine, Issue #71, July 2005
"Sweet Revenge" by Jycorri Robinson, *The Source* Magazine, Issue #198, April 2006
Terrell Unit, The Texas Tribune, http://www.texastribune.org/library/data/texas-prisons/units/terrell/
"TOP 30 BUN B FEATURES OF THE YEAR," by Dylan K, GovernmentNames.blogspot.com, 12/30/2004
"Trill Execs Plead Guilty To Battery Over The Shooting Of Rapper 'Beelow,'" by Mike Winslow, AllHipHop.com, 11/03/2011
"UGK slows down hits on 'Dirty South'," by Brent Snyder, *Beaumont Enterprise*, 01/14/2005
"UGK's Pimp C, Remembered By Sway Calloway," MTV News, 12/05/2007
"Why Houston?" by Shaheem Reid, Joseph Patel, & Sway Calloway, MTV News, 05/02/2005

CHAPTER 35 references the author's interviews with Antezy, Big Munn, Born 2wice, Bun B, D Stone, Danny Kartel, DJ DMD, Donny Young, Jaro Vacek, KD Durisseau, Killer Mike, Korleon, Lee Master, Mama Wes, Mannie Fresh, Matt Sonzala, Mia X, Mike Mo, Mitchell Queen Jr., Nitacha Broussard, N.O. Joe, Paul Wall, Pearce Pegross, Pimp C, Rambro, Riley Broussard, Royce Starring, Russell Washington, Smoke D, Stan Shepherd, Steve Below, Tim Hampton, Too $hort, Vanessa Satten, Wendy Day, and Young Smitty. Additional sources include:
"Bun B Reveals Proudest Pimp C Verse, Production," by Jake Paine, HipHopDX.com, 03/09/2009
"C-Murder Shoots Video Behind Bars," *Billboard*, 02/24/2005
CD Review, Pimp C "The Sweet James Jones Stories," by Carlton Wade, *The Source* Magazine, May 2005
"Gretna jury convicts C-Murder in killing," The *Baton Rouge Advocate*, 10/01/2003
"Houston Hip-Hop," by Roni Sarig, *Houston Press*, 03/22/2007
"Isiah Carey Interviews Pimp C Behind Bars!," http://www.youtube.com/watch?v=KO2EO6kww58
Letter from Chad Butler to Wendy Day, 01/26/2005
Letter from Chad Butler to Wendy Day, 04/05/2005
"Pimp C – Sweet James Jones Stories" review by Toshitaka Kondo, *VIBE* Magazine
"Show & Prove: Lil Boosie & Webbie," by Brendan Frederick, *XXL* Magazine, Issue #65, December 2004
"Straight Path," *XXL* Magazine, Issue #71, July 2005
"Sway talks To Pimp C In Prison In 2005," MTV News, 12/04/2007
"Sweet Revenge" by Jycorri Robinson, *The Source* Magazine, Issue #198, April 2006
"UGK's Pimp C, Remembered By Sway Calloway," MTV News, 12/05/2007

CHAPTER 36 references the author's interviews with Bandit, Born 2wice, Bo$$, Bun B, Chad Butler Jr., Donny Young, Heather Johnson, Ivory P, Kilo, Langston Adams, Lil Green, Lil Keke, Mama Wes, Mr. Lee, Nitacha Broussard, Paul Wall, Pimp C, Russell Washington, Sam Martin, Teresa Waldon, Tim Hampton, Travis, Wendy Day, and Z-Ro. Additional sources include:
"50 Cent and Robert Greene CNBC Interview About The 50th Law Book," http://www.youtube.com/watch?v=EBkk6gEtX-Q
"5,000 inmates evacuated by bus," by Cindy Horswell, *Houston Chronicle*, 09/22/2005
Bun B interview by Julia Beverly, *OZONE* Magazine, Issue #44, April 2006
"Critics' Choice: New CD's," by Kelefa Sanneh, the *New York Times*, 10/17/2005
"Evacuations get an early start," *Houston Chronicle*, 09/21/2005
"Hancock Trial Defendant Pleads Guilty," *Biloxi Sun Herald*, 05/28/1995
Houston Police Department Incident Report #188380405, 12/14/2005
"INTERVIEW: Bun B discusses his legacy, UGK, DJ Screw and keeping things trill," by Marcus K. Dowling, TheCouchSessions.com, 10/26/2011
"Interview: Z-Ro on DJ Screw and the S.U.C.," by Jesse Serwer, JesseSerwer.com, 11/16/2010
Letter from Chad Butler to Born 2wice, 11/25/2005
Letter from Chad Butler to Paul Wall, 08/18/2005
Letter from Chad Butler to Paul Wall, 10/08/2005
Letter from Chad Butler to Wendy Day, 07/21/2005
Letter from Pimp C to *OZONE* Magazine, 09/20/2005
"Miami Comedian Larry Dogg Street Dogg Throwback (Pimp C Interview)," http://www.youtube.com/watch?v=HmC6DA49EUM
Pearl Police Department Incident Report #2005091397, 09/28/2005
"PIMP C FREEEEE!!!!!!!," by Matt Sonzala, HoustonSoReal.blogspot.com, 12/02/2005

"Pimp C: Never Die," by Dave Bry, *XXL* Magazine, 12/04/2012
"Rapper Pimp C Released From Prison," Associated Press, 12/30/2005
"Rapper Pimp C set for release from prison," MSNBC, 12/05/2005
"(Slightly) higher Texas parole rates helping reduce overincarceration," by Scott Hanson, GritsForBreakfast.blogspot.com, December 2009
"Straight Path," *XXL* Magazine, Issue #71, July 2005
"Terrell Unit searched, administration changed," 05/08/2008, http://www.topix.com/forum/city/rosharon-tx/T54PMB3GGCA3JUOL6
Texas Board of Pardons and Paroles, Annual Report FY 2007, http://www.tdcj.state.tx.us/bpp/publications/BPP%20AR%202007.pdf
"Texas city: A ghost of past glory," by Karen Aho, MSN Money, 08/14/2012
"The Legacy of Pimp C and the Hip-Hop, Health & Wellness Festival," *Mass Appeal*, 12/27/2013
"UGK Have Bigger Pimpin', Better Hustles Planned," by Soren Baker, MTV News, 10/14/2002
"UGK's Pimp C To Be Released From Prison Within A Month," by Chris Harris, MTV News, 12/06/2005
United States of America vs. Kenneth Blockett, Appeal from the United States District Court, Northern District of Mississippi, Case #06-cr-00149, 05/06/2009
United States of America vs. Milton Tutwiler et al, United States District Court, Northern District of Mississippi, Case #06-cr-00149, 10/24/2006

CHAPTER 37 references the author's interviews with Angie Crooks, Barry Weiss, Big Gipp, Bo-Bo Luchiano, Bone, Brandi Garcia, Bun B, Bushwick Bill, Chad Butler Jr., Cory Mo, Edgar Walker Jr., Heather Johnson, Jeff Sledge, Kristi Floyd, Lil Green, Mama Wes, Mean Green, Memphitz, Nitacha Broussard, Paul Wall, Pimp C, REL, Riley Broussard, Scarface, Sean Paul, Stax, Tim Hampton, T-Mo Goodie, Travis, Wendy Day, Willie D, and Young Lo. Additional sources include:
Bun B interview by Julia Beverly, *OZONE* Magazine, Issue #44, April 2006
"EXCLUSIVE: Bun B's First Interview Since Pimp C's Passing," by Linda Hobbs, *VIBE* Magazine, 12/08/2007
"Ex-Con Pimp C Juiced For UGK Album, Says He Has Lessons To Teach," by Jayson Rodriguez, MTV News, 11/13/2006
"Favorite Pimp C moments," *OZONE* Magazine, Issue #63, January 2008
"Innovators put Houston Hip-Hop on national map," by Michael D. Clark, *Houston Chronicle*, 06/19/2005
"'It turned out just the way he would have wanted it ... because of the love'," by Rose Ybarra, *Beaumont Enterprise*, 12/14/2007
Letter from Chad Butler to Born 2wice, 11/25/2005
"Pimp C Airs Out Russell Simmons, Ne-Yo, Atlanta and MUCH More!," by Shake, HipHopDX.com, 07/25/2007
"Pimp c being released from prison and getting back to work," *TRILL* DVD, http://www.youtube.com/watch?v=7VO8IA0EQUE
"PIMP C Interview by Trix N the hat /Donna Garza," http://www.youtube.com/watch?v=L9BFuvt9JUs
"Pimp C UGK part 2," HipHop2Nite, June 2006, http://www.youtube.com/watch?v=_l0wVNOprnk
"Rapper Pimp C Released From Prison," Associated Press, 12/30/2005
"Rapper Pimp C released from prison," *USA Today*, 12/30/2005
"The Great Texas Prison Mess," by Robert Draper, *Texas Monthly*, May 1996
"UGK: How We Live," *XXL* Magazine, Issue #90, April 2007

CHAPTER 38 references the author's interviews with 8Ball, Antezy, Ashlei Morrison, Big Gipp, Big L, Big Munn, Bone, Boonie, Brenda Harmon, Bundy, Cory Mo, Craig Wormley, D Stone, DJ B-Do, DJ Bird, DJ Dolby D, Dr. Teeth, D-Solo, E-40, Edgar Walker Jr., Fiend, Ghost, Heather Johnson, Hezeleo, Isreal Kight, Janeen Harmon, Jaro Vacek, Jazze Pha, Kavin Stokes, KD Durisseau, Killa Kyeon, Killer Mike, King Yella, KLC, KP, Lanika, Lil Flip, Lil Keke, Mama Wes, Mannie Fresh, Marlan Rico Lee, Matt Sonzala, Memphitz, Mike Mo, Mike Schreiber, MJG, Mugz, Nancy Byron, Naztradamus, NcGai, Pam Harris, Paperchase, Paul Wall, Pimp C, Pimpin' Ken, Rambro, REL, Riley Broussard, Ron Forrest, Ronda Forrest, Scarface, Shaheem Reid, Slim Thug, Smoke D, Steve Below, Steve-O, T-Mo Goodie, Teresa Waldon, Too $hort, Trae tha Truth, Travis, Truck, TV Johnny, Vicious, Wendy Day, Willie D, Young Smitty, and Z-Ro. Additional sources include:
"10 Things I've Learned," by Pimp C, *VIBE* Magazine, July 2006
"A Valentine for H-Town: With nothing but love for her hometown, sexy R&B star hits Third Ward streets to shoot a video," by Joey Guerra, *Houston Chronicle*, 6/22/2006
"Bun B Goes In On Byron Crawford on Combat Jack Radio," ShaBooty.com, 01/05/2012
"Bun B Quit Yer Bitchin'," by Byron Crawford, XXLMag.com, 04/05/2006
"Chad Butler's Blog," http://www.myspace.com/pimpcofugk/blog/
"Cold-Blooded," by Carlton Wade, *The Source* Magazine, Issue #198, April 2006
"Cold Cuts: Bun B vs. Byron Crawford," by John Nova Lomax, *Houston Press*, 04/20/2006
County of Los Angeles Sheriff's Department Incident Report #007-07729-0987-496, 12/04/2007
"FEATURE: Bun B, Life After Death," by Slav Kandyba, *XXL* Magazine, 11/06/2009
"Interview: Project Pat Talks Staying Relevant, the Album With Pimp C That Never Was, and Advice for Chief Keef," by David Drake, *Complex* Magazine, 03/10/2013
"J Prince Talks About The Rise Of Rap-A-Lot Records," by Rob Kenner, *Complex* Magazine, 12/04/2011
Jimmie L. Keller Jr. obituary, *New Orleans Times-Picayune*, 01/06/2006
"Legendary Pimp C, T.I., Slim Thug, Bun B, Sway from MTV Throwback," *CHEDDAR* DVD, http://www.youtube.com/watch?v=6YTFDWtZ29o
"Love & Happiness," *JET* Magazine, 02/21/2005
"Master P vs C-Murder (R.I.P Pimp C)," BET Rap City, http://www.youtube.com/watch?v=OKuk0ZIerL8
"Miami Comedian Larry Dogg Street Dogg Throwback (Pimp C Interview)," http://www.youtube.com/watch?v=HmC6DA49EUM
"Miami Heat: Pimp C. Disses Smitty," 305HipHop.com, 05/01/2006
"Paul Wall Remembers Pimp C Calling Him A 'Square'," KeepItTrill.com, 12/04/2011
"PIMP C Interview by Trix N the hat /Donna Garza," http://www.youtube.com/watch?v=L9BFuvt9JUs
"Pimp C Interviewed about Beef," http://www.youtube.com/watch?v=rcHlVOc7lf0
"Pimp C on Being a Man (w Bun B) from *Beef IV* – REAL TALK!," *Beef IV* DVD, http://www.youtube.com/watch?v=Mu5RhOqSU80
"Pimp C: Legendary Shermhead," by Byron Crawford, XXLMag.com, 04/11/2006
"Pimp C: Tell 'Em I Said That," *XXL* Magazine, Issue #96, October 2007
"Pimp C's Rules of the Game," RollingOut.com, http://www.youtube.com/watch?v=IW0rbgCXVfY
"Scarface remembers Pimp C," as told to Julia Beverly, *OZONE* Magazine, Issue #63, January 2008
"$ir $weet Jone$" Myspace page, http://www.myspace.com/pimpchad6
"Southerners Quit Yer Bitchin'," by Byron Crawford, XXLMag.com, 04/03/2006
"Stephen Jackson talks rap, loyalty & life," by Chris Palmer, ESPN, 07/02/2012
"Sweet Revenge" by Jycorri Robinson, *The Source* Magazine, Issue #198, April 2006
"Talib Kweli talks UGK with Sama'an Ashrawi," http://www.youtube.com/watch?v=EgpkTg9bfBA
"The Mad Blogger," by Ben Westhoff, *Riverfront Times*, 11/02/2009
The State of Texas vs. Brad Jordan, District Court of Harris County, Case #9917789, 04/26/1999
The State of Texas vs. Charles Michael Moore Jr., District Court of Chambers County, Case #9405, 04/13/1995
"UGK Reunite After Pimp C's Release From Prison," MTV News, http://www.mtv.com/videos/news/193515/ugk-reunite-after-pimp-cs-release-from-prison.jhtml#id=1575713
"UGK's Pimp C, Remembered By Sway Calloway," MTV News, 12/05/2007

CHAPTER 39 references the author's interviews with Alonzo Cartier, Ashlei Morrison, Averexx, Big Munn, Bone, Cory Mo, D Stone, Dawn Nico, Detective Marcelo Molfino, DJ Bird, Donny Young, Dwayne Diamond, Edgar Walker Jr., Jaro Vacek, KD Durriseau, Langston Adams, Lil Keke, Mama Wes, Matt Sonzala, Mike Jones, Mitchell Queen Jr., Mr. Boomtown, Naztradamus, Pearce Pegross, Pimp C, Pimpin' Ken, REL, Riley Broussard, Slim Thug, Stax, Too $hort, Travis, Truck, Wendy Day, Young Smitty, and Z-Ro. Additional sources include:
"A Valentine for H-Town: With nothing but love for her hometown, sexy R&B star hits Third Ward streets to shoot a video," by Joey Guerra, *Houston Chronicle*, 6/22/2006
"Bad Air Days," by Jim Atkinson, *Texas Monthly*, August 2003
"Conference Puts Houston Hip-Hop in Scholarly Setting," by Andrew Dansby, *Houston Chronicle*, 03/28/2012
"DJ Screw and the Rise of Houston Hip-Hop," University of Houston Libraries, http://info.lib.uh.edu/about/campus-libraries-collections/special-collections/library-exhibits/djscrew-and-houston-hip-hop
"Natural cause likely in Pimp C's death," *Houston Chronicle*, 12/06/2007
"PA man sentenced to 70 years over assault rifle attack," the *Port Arthur News*, 05/01/2009

"Performer chooses town where he grew up to film part of video," by Christine Rappleye, *Beaumont Enterprise*, 04/20/2006
"Police: Few clues in Houston rapper's slaying," by Michael D. Clark, *Houston Chronicle*, 05/02/2006
"Rap Deaths: John Edward Hawkins," CBS News, http://www.cbsnews.com/2316-100_162-1496696-3.html
"Rapper's bodyguard still in hospital," by Christine Rappleye, *Beaumont Enterprise*, 04/21/2006
Shawn Donell Jones vs. The State of Texas et al, United States District Court, Eastern District of Texas (Beaumont), Case #95-cv-01097, 12/07/1995
"Short Stories: Remembering The Pimp," by Too Short, *OZONE* Magazine, Issue #63, January 2008

CHAPTER 40 references the author's interviews with Angie Crooks, Big Mike, Big Munn, Big Zak, Bo$$, Byron Amos, Cory Mo, Curtis Daniel III, Detective Marcelo Molfino, Diamond, DJ B-Do, Edgar Walker Jr., Funkafangez, Heather Johnson, Hezeleo, Jaro Vacek, Jeff Sledge, Kavin Stokes, Killer Mike, Lloyd, Mama Wes, Maroy, Matt Sonzala, Mike Mo, Mr. Lee, Mr. Soul, Nancy Byron, Pimp C, Pimpin' Ken, Rambro, REL, Riley Broussard, Short Dawg, Smoke D, Stan Shepherd, Tara Starring, Too $hort, Travis, Truck, and Wendy Day. Additional sources include the following:
"Big Mike Talks 'Bayou Classic,' Forgiving J. Prince, And Rick Ross' Respect," HipHopDX.com, 12/24/2011
"Birthday Bash 11 – Pimp C HD," 06/17/2006, http://www.youtube.com/watch?v=KzknYP5V25o
"Family Tree: Pimp C," by Edwin "Stats" Houghton, The *FADER*, 12/07/2007
"Favorite Pimp C moments," *OZONE* Magazine, Issue #63, January 2008
"Friends, family pay tribute to Pimp C," by Kristie Rieken, *USA Today*, 12/13/2007
"From the Ashes: Former Geto Boy Big Mike," by Ben Westhoff, *Houston Press*, 03/03/2010
Hans Niknejad d/b/a Twin Entertainment vs. UGK, Inc., Circuit Court for Williamson County, Case #06665, 11/15/2006
Heather C. Viator vs. Wendell Miller, United States District Court, Western District of Louisiana (Lake Charles), Case #CV03-1273, 07/03/2003
"Killer Mike talks UGK with Sama'an Ashrawi," http://www.youtube.com/watch?v=35nUmkLKqjs
"Killer Mike: Pledge Of Allegiance," by Paul W. Arnold, HipHopDX.com, 01/18/2008
"Paying respect to Screw," by Lance Scott Walker, *Houston Chronicle*, 07/20/2006
"Pimp C album release at Greenspoint mall in HOUSTON," Orbits World TV, http://www.youtube.com/watch?v=ri5GGZfkguo
"Pimp C The Pimpalation (Return of the Trill)" CD review by Paul Cantor, *XXL* Magazine, 06/26/2006
"Pimp C – Pimpalation Review," by SOHH Rizoh, SOHH.com, 07/10/2006
Rap-A-Lot 2K Records vs. Chinara Butler, District Court of Harris County, Cause #2011-36404, 06/17/2011
"Short Dawg: Little Brother," by Paine, AllHipHop.com, 09/26/2006
"The High Budgetary Cost of Incarceration," by John Schmitt, Kris Warner, and Sarika Gupta, Center for Economic and Policy Research, June 2010
"The Pimp Is Free – Pimp C 'Pimpalation'," TheSmokingSection.net, 02/23/2007
The State of Texas vs. Stanley Monte Shepherd, District Court of Chambers County, Case #14035, 05/21/2006
United States of America vs. Tara Starring, United States District Court, District of Massachusetts (Boston), Case #07-cr-10230, 07/24/2007

CHAPTER 41 references the author's interviews with Big L, Bobby Caillier, Bone, Brenda Harmon, Bun B, Connie Butler, Cory Mo, DJ Dolby D, Edgar Walker Jr., Fiend, Ghost, Hezeleo, Jada, Janeen Harmon, Jaro Vacek, Jeff Sledge, Kamikaze, Mama Wes, Mannie Fresh, Mike Mo, Pastor John Morgan, Paul Wall, Pimp C, Pops, Travis, and Truck. Additional sources include:
"7th Annual Crunkfest (Return Of Kingz)," groups.yahoo.com/neo/groups/dabizness/conversations/messages/1141
"Bun B Interview," by Scott Bejda, *Murder Dog* Magazine, Volume 15 Number 1, 2008
Bun B interview by Julia Beverly, *OZONE* Magazine, Issue #44, April 2006
"Pimp C Crib ...pic inside," WordofSouth.com forums
"RapCity – Pimp C – Draped Up Freestyle," http://www.youtube.com/watch?v=DpL09pGK_xE
"Trill Tribute The Legacy of Pimp C," ReppinDaSouth, https://vimeo.com/72807932
"UGK: Underground Kingz" review by Tom Breihan, *Pitchfork*, 08/17/2007
"Underground Kingz's Pimp C, Hip-Hop pioneer," by Ryan Pearson, The *Boston Globe*, 12/06/2007

CHAPTER 42 references the author's interviews with Big Munn, Bone, Jada, Jaro Vacek, Joi Gilliam, Mama Wes, Paperchase, Pimp C, Rico Wade, and XVII. Additional sources include:
American Pimp documentary
"Board rejects man's exotic animals request after neighbors complain," by Conor Shine, *Las Vegas Sun*, 08/10/2011
"FBI raids rapper Mally Mall's Las Vegas home, business," by Jeff German and Mike Blasky, *Las Vegas Review-Journal*, 09/29/2014
"Pimp subculture filled with money, manipulation, violence," by Tovin Lapan, *Las Vegas Sun*, 03/11/2013
"Six arrested in alleged sex ring case," 08/25/2006, http://abc13.com/archive/6982058/
The State of Nevada vs. Ocean Fleming, District Court of Clark County, Case #C-11-276866-1, 10/14/2011
"The Psychology of the Pimp: Iceberg Slim Reveals the Reality," by Kalamu ya Salaam, *The Black Collegian*, January/February 1975
United States of America vs. Andre McDaniels et al, United States District Court, Southern District of Texas (Houston), Case # H-09-453, 08/04/2009
United States of America vs. Andre McDaniels, United States District Court, Southern District of Texas (Houston), Case #12-cr-00167, 03/22/2012
VIPTianna4u.com, http://web.archive.org/web/20100501232852/http://viptianna4u.com/

CHAPTER 43 references the author's interviews with 8Ball, Alonzo Cartier, Anne-Marie Stripling, Antezy, Averexx, Bo-Bo Luchiano, Bone, Bun B, Cory Mo, Detective Marcelo Molfino, Devin the Dude, DJ DMD, Jada, Jaro Vacek, Jazze Pha, Jeff Sledge, Korleon, Lil Flip, Lil O, Mama Wes, Mannie Fresh, Mr. 3-2, Ocean Fleming, Paul Wall, Pimp C, Pimpin' Ken, Ron Stewart, Smoke D, Stax, Teresa Waldon, Trae Tha Truth, Travis, Vicious, Wanda Coriano, Willie D, and three friends of Larry Adams' who declined to be named. Additional sources include:
"Dallas man apparently shoots self, officer in standoff," *Houston Chronicle*, 08/31/2006
Dallas SWAT, Season 1: Episode 17, 11/02/2006, www.aetv.com/swat/video/episode-17
"Ex-Con Pimp C Juiced For UGK Album, Says He Has Lessons To Teach," by Jayson Rodriguez, MTV News, 11/13/2006
Fresno Police Department, Law Enforcement Report Form, Event #13AW1656, 06/14/2013
"Gunman wounds officer, hostage at Dallas hotel," by Robert Tharp and Jason Trahan, *Dallas Morning News*, 08/31/2006
"He Left On A Major Legacy," MTV News, 12/05/2007
"He Was Definitely A Dope Dude," MTV News, 12/05/2007
"I-Team Investigation: Selling Sex Online," by Colleen McCarty, KLAS-TV 8 news NOW Las Vegas
"Industry 101: Memphitz," by Brian Sims, HipHopDX.com, 01/26/2008
"Jay Z featuring UGK – Big Pimpin' Live Performance," http://www.youtube.com/watch?v=dF70pvl4c3l
"L.A. authorities investigating rapper Pimp C's death," by Joey Guerra and Peggy O'Hare, *Houston Chronicle*, 12/05/2007
"No regrets for wounded Dallas officer," by Holly Yan, *Dallas Morning News*, 09/02/2006
Paul Wall interview by Julia Beverly, *OZONE* Magazine, Issue #85, April 2010
"PIMP C Interview by Trix N the hat /Donna Garza," http://www.youtube.com/watch?v=L9BFuvt9JUs
"Pimp C's Rules of the Game," RollingOut.com, http://www.youtube.com/watch?v=IW0rbgCXVfY
"Rapper Lil' Flip records song in honor of Pimp C," by Andrew Dansby, *Houston Chronicle*, 12/07/2007
"REAL PIMP TALK (ONE ON ONE)," http://www.youtube.com/watch?v=MfFsSEBZI7M
"Record labels take the rap," by Joey Guerra, *Houston Chronicle*, 08/08/2007
"Rhymes & reasons," by Sarah Moore, *Beaumont Enterprise*, 12/14/2007
The State of Nevada vs. Ocean Fleming, District Court of Clark County, Case #C-11-276866-1, 10/14/2011
"UGK at Los Magnificos Car Show," by DJ Brandi Garcia, www.youtube.com/watch?v=IdGWJkvGIZU
United States of America vs. Ocean Fleming et al, Case #98-cr-00292, United States District Court, District of Nevada (Las Vegas), 08/12/1998

CHAPTER 44 references the author's interviews with Ashlei Morrison, Bankroll Jonez, Dr. Teeth, Good Game, Ivory P, Jada, Jeff Sledge, Kool Ace, Mama Wes, Maroy, Memphitz, Nancy Byron, Naztradamus, N.O. Joe, Ocean Fleming, Paperchase, Pimp C, Pimpin' Ken, Ron Stewart, Steve Below, Too $hort, and Young Smitty. Additional sources include:

"America's No. 1 Pimp Tells It Like It Is!," by Richard B. Milner, *Rogue* Magazine, Issue #18, June 1969
American Pimp documentary
Iceberg Slim: The Lost Interviews, by Ian Whitaker, Infinite Dreams Publishing, 2009
"It's All Good," by Carter Harris, *The Source* Magazine, February 1994
"Pimp subculture filled with money, manipulation, violence," by Tovin Lapan, *Las Vegas Sun*, 03/11/2013
"Portrait of a Pimp," by Helen Koblin, *Los Angeles Free Press*, Volume 9 No. 8 Issue 397, 02/25/1972
"$ir $weet Jone$'s Blog," http://www.myspace.com/pimpchad6/blog
"Still Fly," by Thomas Golianopoulos, *XXL* Magazine, Issue #85, October 2006
The State of Nevada vs. Ocean Fleming, District Court of Clark County, Case #C-11-276866-1, 10/14/2011
The United States of America vs. Ocean Fleming, et al, Case #98-cr-00292, United States District Court, District of Nevada
    (Las Vegas), 08/12/1998
"What It Means to UGK," http://www.youtube.com/watch?v=cl9Rp1HehQI

CHAPTER 45 references the author's interviews with 8Ball, Anne-Marie Stripling, Antezy, Ashlei Morrison, Averexx, Ayesha Saafir, Bankroll Jonez, Big Gipp, Big L, Bishop Don "Magic" Juan, Bo-Bo Luchiano, Bone, Bun B, Cory Mo, Craig Wormley, DJ B-Do, DJ Greg Street, DJ Paul, Edgar Walker Jr., Eric Perrin, Good Game, Halimah Saafir, Ivory P, Jada, Jaro Vacek, Jeff Sledge, Juicy J, KB Da Kidnappa, Kilo, Lee Master, Lloyd, Mama Wes, Maroy, Memphitz, Naztradamus, OG Ron C, Paperchase, Pimp C, Pimpin' Ken, Rick Royal, Rico Wade, Ron Stewart, Russell Washington, Short Dawg, Smoke D, Snoop Dogg, Stan Shepherd, Steve Below, Superb Herb, T.O.E., Too $hort, Wendy Day, Willie D, and Z-Ro. Additional sources include:
American Pimp documentary
"Anything Goes," by David Shaftel, *VICE* Magazine, 2001
"Bishop Don Magic Juan: P.I.M.P. Part One," by Martin A. Berrios, AllHipHop.com
"Bo-Bo Luchiano – An Interview with Urban South Entertainment," Pegasus News, 11/09/2006
"Bun B Rap City Freestyle," http://www.youtube.com/watch?v=brSPoKzB0Jk
Halimah Saafir's Myspace page, http://www.myspace.com/halimahsaafir
Heather C. Viator vs. Wendell Miller, United States District Court, Western District of Louisiana (Lake Charles Division),
    Case #CV03-1273, 07/03/2003
Michael Joseph Viator vs. Wendell R. Miller, Louisiana Third Circuit Court of Appeals, 04/27/2005
"MISSISSIPPI DA MOVEMENT PT. 3 PIMP C, LIVE FROM CLUB ROLEX, PORT GIBSON,"
    http://www.youtube.com/watch?v=XcSFPSyjxDg
"Orange Chair with DJ Paul: Best Pimp C Story Ever," KarmaloopTV, http://www.youtube.com/watch?v=gkNKmltVRng
"Pimp C and Pimpin' Ken Team Up for New DVD, Best of Both Worlds," *XXL* Magazine, 09/12/2007
"Pimp C and Pimpin Ken: Best Of Both Worlds," *Too Real For TV* DVD, http://www.youtube.com/watch?v=SPJheSmQK6c
"PIMP C and PIMPIN KEN(live) pimp diss ATL an speaks his mind," http://www.youtube.com/watch?v=DAzxMCpxTRQ
"Pimp C Exposes Undercover Homo Thugs," *Down South Hustler* DVD, http://www.youtube.com/watch?v=2xr9nkO39K8
"Pimp C: A Portrait Of An Artist," by Jake Paine, HipHopDX.com, 12/09/2007
"PIMP C : TRILL NGGZ DON'T DIE! R.I.P. Chad Butler," http://www.youtube.com/watch?v=emqD0MXFAzE
"Pimpin' is hard work," by Denise Downling, Salon.com, 01/29/2000
"Record labels take the rap," by Joey Guerra, *Houston Chronicle*, 08/08/2007
"Snippet of Mista Selfish from *Real Pimps: The Movie*", http://www.youtube.com/watch?v=W5gSKGNi3cU
"Some game from Pimp C," http://www.youtube.com/watch?v=7lE63vtVUkw
"South by Southwest 2007," by John Nova Lomax, *Houston Press*, 03/22/2007
"Supreme Court boots judge over 'notorious' sexual affair," Legalnewsline.com, 02/19/2007
Supreme Court of Louisiana, Re: Judge Wendell R. Miller, 01/26/2007
"The BET Awards," by Richard L. Eldridge and Sonia Murray, *Atlanta Journal-Constitution*, 10/14/2007
"The Happy Hustler," by Dave Hoekstra, *Chicago Reader*, 12/14/2000
"The Making of UGK's 'International Player's Anthem (I Choose You),'" *XXL* Magazine, 06/06/2012
The State of Texas vs. Ivory Pantallion, District Court of Harris County, Cause #876916, 05/10/2001
"Trill Tribute The Legacy of Pimp C," ReppinDaSouth, https://vimeo.com/72807932
"UGK concert 1 during SXSW," http://www.youtube.com/watch?v=RhjqwlTkr5E
"UGK/Crime Mob SXSW Show 2," http://www.youtube.com/watch?v=mlL-JWEZgbk
"UGK live Austin @ sxsw 2007 RIP PIMP C," http://www.youtube.com/user/d2nwo
"UGK on BET RapCity in Port Arthur," http://www.youtube.com/watch?v=vMpmJJ6ENWg

CHAPTER 46 references the author's interviews with Ayesha Saafir, Big Gipp, Big L, Big Meech, Big Munn, Bo-Bo Luchiano, Bone, Bun B, Chad Jr., Cory Mo, David Banner, DJ C-Wiz, Ed Walker, Greg Street, Heather Johnson, Hezeleo, Jada, Jeff Sledge, Joi Gilliam, KLC, Mama Wes, Mannie Fresh, Mean Green, Memphitz, Mia X, Mike Mo, Naztradamus, Nitacha Broussard, Paper-chase, Pimp C, Pimpin' Ken, Ron Stewart, Ronda Forrest, Shawn Holiday, Sleepy Brown, Slim Thug, Teresa Waldon, T.O.E., Travis, TV Johnny, Wendy Day, Willie D, XVII, and Young Smitty. Additional sources include:
ATL Rise documentary
"'Best Friend' Wants Half of Young Jeezy," by Nick McCann, *Courthouse News*, 08/22/2012
BMF: The Rise And Fall Of A Hip-Hop Drug Empire documentary
"Bun B, Young Jeezy And Scarface Remember Pimp C," by Marvin Brandon, *XXL* Magazine, 12/04/2008
Demetrius Ellerbee vs. Jay Jenkins et al, Superior Court of Fulton County, Case #2012CV020124, 08/17/2012
"Interview with Bun-B," by Devil, *Murder Dog* Magazine, Volume 6 Number 2
"'It turned out just the way he would have wanted it ... because of the love'," by Rose Ybarra, *Beaumont Enterprise*, 12/14/2007
Pimp C interview on Hot 107.9 WHTA, Atlanta, GA, 07/23/2007
"Pimp C is Dead," by Tom Breihan, The *Village Voice*, 12/04/2007
"Streets Is Talking: Young Jeezy," by Aqua, 09/25/2007, AllHipHop.com
"The Quarterly Report: Status Ain't Hood's Favorite Albums Since July," by Tom Breihan, The *Village Voice*, 10/04/2005
The United States of America vs. Demetrius Flenory et al, United States District Court, Eastern District of Michigan,
    Case #05-80955, 10/28/2005

CHAPTER 47 references the author's interviews with Chad Butler Jr., DJ Bird, George Simmons, Hezeleo, Lanika, Mama Wes, Matt Sonzala, Pearce Pegross, Pimp C, Scarface, T-Roy, XVII and Warren Fitzgerald. Additional sources include:
Bruce Rhodes vs. Troy Birklett, Harris County District Court, Cause #2003-09741, 02/25/2003
"Bun B Interview Lil Troy," Short Stop TV, http://www.youtube.com/watch?v=S4BpxMxBVrs
"BUN B TALKS ABOUT THE DEATH OF PIMP C ON FOX NEWS!," http://www.youtube.com/watch?v=Qbw8IkRmjXg
"Chart News: BET 106 & Park," http://atrl.net/forums/archive/index.php/t-31995-p-7.html
"DJ WHOO KID INTERVIEWS LIL TROY Part 1," Sirius Radio SHADE 45, http://www.youtube.com/watch?v=8NO9z39oRF0
"DJ WHOO KID INTERVIEWS LIL TROY Part 2," Sirius Radio SHADE 45, http://www.youtube.com/watch?v=kxRfHpBrCC8
"Flipside: Lil Troy vs. Scarface," by Julia Beverly, *OZONE* Magazine, Issue #39, November 2005
"Ja Rule Aims At Eminem, But Scarface Wasn't Aiming At 50," by Shaheem Reid, MTV News, 04/01/2003
"Lil' Troy, Free From Prison, Is Back To Ballin'," by Soren Baker, MTV News, 10/08/2001
"Never Surrender," by Anthony Mariani, The *Village Voice*, 10/16/2001
Paperwork: Scarface G-Code Violations DVD, Short Stop Records, 2006
"Rapper offers message of hope," by Patrick Reynolds, *Houston Chronicle*, 08/23/2011
"Scarface: The Grand Finale," by Paul W. Arnold, HipHopDX.com, 11/30/2008
"Stop Snitchin': Lil Troy Fingers Scarface As The 'Real Snitch'," CrazyPellas.net
Terrell McMurry vs. Constance Reese, United States District Court, Southern District of Mississippi, 09/04/2007
The State of Texas vs. Troy Birklett Jr., Harris County District Court, Cause #1024220, 12/22/2005
The United States of America vs. Jose Ruiz Solorio et al, United States Court of Appeals, Sixth Circuit, case #01-5602,
    04/29/2003
The United States of America vs. Mark Potts, United States District Court, Southern District of Texas (Houston),
    Case #99-cr-00585, 10/12/1999
The United States of America vs. Terrell McMurry et al, United States District Court, Middle District of Tennessee (Nashville),
    Case #99-cr-00120-1, 07/28/1999
The United States of America vs. Troy Birklett, United States District Court, Eastern District of Texas (Lufkin), Case #98-cr-00041,

11/12/1998
Troy Birklett vs. Brad Jordan, Harris County District Court, Cause #2006-18021, 03/20/2006
Troy Birklett, United States Bankruptcy Court, Southern Division of Texas (Houston), Case #05-93889, 11/19/2005
"Video: Scarface on The Combat Jack Show (Ep. 3)," Nahright.com, 05/16/2013
"Young Buck," Nashville Scene, 09/02/2004

The majority of **CHAPTER 48** is a direct transcription of the author's interview with Pimp C on June 10, 2007. Additional sources include:
Iceberg Slim: The Lost Interviews, by Ian Whitaker, Infinite Dreams Publishing, 2009
"PIMP C and PIMPIN KEN(live) pimp diss ATL an speaks his mind," http://www.youtube.com/watch?v=DAzxMCpxTRQ
"Pimp C Exposes Undercover Homo Thugs," *Down South Hustler* DVD, http://www.youtube.com/watch?v=2xr9nkO39K8

CHAPTER 49 references the author's interviews with Anne-Marie Stripling, Ayesha Saafir, Big Gipp, Bone, Brandi Garcia, Craig Wormley, DJ B-Do, Jada, Jimmy Olson, Mama Wes, Matt Sonzala, Mike Mo, Mr. DJ, Pimp C, Ron Stewart, Sean Paul, Steve Below, Teresa Waldon, TOE, XVII, and Young Lo. Additional sources include:
"10 Questions with Terri Thomas, AllAccess.com, 01/25/2011
"BORRIS MILES FEEDS THE COMMUNITY!," IsiahFactor.com, 11/22/2010
"Fonzworth Bentley remembers Pimp C," as told to Julia Beverly, *OZONE* Magazine, Issue #63, January 2008
"Fonzworth Bentley To Donate Publishing To Pimp C's Kids," DJSmallz.com, http://www.youtube.com/watch?v=a7ijcpfozDl
"Former rep Miles found not guilty of deadly conduct," by Brian Rogers, *Houston Chronicle,* 01/15/2009
"Hip-Hop 4 HIV – Know Your Status" press release, http://www.industryhotel.com/hotellobby.html
"Photograph from party helps exonerate ex-Rep. Miles," by Brian Rogers, *Houston Chronicle,* 01/15/2009
"PIMP C EXPOSING THE TRUTH BOUT 97.9," http://www.youtube.com/watch?v=nN9any3KI5M
"Pimp C was Threatened With Prison For Not Doing 97.9 The Box Concert, Audio Reveals," TexasTakeover.com
"Secrets To Success," by Terri Thomas, 09/29/2009, http://territhomas.com/blog/?p=27
"Singled Out: Cavie," SOHH.com, 01/10/2012
"State Rep. Miles to surrender after deadly conduct indictment," by Brian Rogers, *Houston Chronicle,* 04/14/2008
"Terri Thomas – Jamming the Box," by Michele Fling, *Rolling Out,* 09/09/2009
"Trae Tha Truth Talks Threats Made To Pimp C & Lack Of Support From Houston Artists (pt 2)," KeepItTrill.com, http://www.youtube.com/watch?v=s7pOJEn8XIl
"Willie-D Interview," by Matt Sonzala, *Murder Dog* Magazine, Volume 10 Number 2

The majority of **CHAPTER 50** is a direct transcription from an audio recording of Chad's psychic session with Halimah Saafir, and also references the author's interviews with Ayesha Saafir, Bishop Don "Magic" Juan, Bone, Brandi Garcia, Bun B, E-40, Edgar Walker Jr., Halimah Saafir, Hezeleo, Mama Wes, Mike Mo, Mitchell Queen Jr., Snoop Dogg, and Truck. Additional sources include:
"David Banner Live @ The Zune Barbeque: Like A Pimp," https://www.youtube.com/watch?v=ySNo3RB3mpw
Halimah Saafir's Myspace page, http://www.myspace.com/halimahsaafir
"HIP HOP 4 HIV CONCERT," http://www.youtube.com/watch?v=fu5Er60AWiU
"Live at the BBQ Zune Concerts," http://www.zunescene.com/live-at-the-bbq-zune-concert/
"Pimp C Hard Knock TV Exclusive 'What About Your Friends?!' freestyle," http://www.youtube.com/watch?v=UblA3_iLCM0
"Rap show slated for fairgrounds this week," *Indianapolis Star,* 07/03/2007
"Too Short And Bun B Remember UGK's Early Days," by Shaheem Reid, MTV News, 07/27/2009
"UGK Bun B & Pimp C @ Zune 'Live at the BBQ' LA DUBCNN," https://www.youtube.com/watch?v=LPaO7wIEFic
"Zune Presents Live At The BBQ: Los Angeles 07/12/07," http://laist.com/2007/07/13/zune_presents_l.php
"Zune Live at the BBQ with Bun-B," Mix Revolution TV, http://www.youtube.com/watch?v=S3SUe4ZBXco

CHAPTER 51 references the author's interviews with Antezy, Ayesha Saafir, Bankroll Jonez, Big Bubb, Big Munn, Byron Amos, Craig Wormley, DJ B-Do, Ed Walker, Heather Johnson, Hezeleo, Ivory P, Jaro Vacek, Killer Mike, Korleon, Langston Adams, Lee Master, Mama Wes, Mike Mo, Pimp C, Quanell X, Riley Broussard, Sam Martin, Shawn Holiday, Smoke D, Stan Shepherd, Stax, Tim Hampton, T.O.E., Vicious, Wendy Day, XVII and Young Lo. Additional sources include:
"Hezeleo releases first album on Pimp C's label," by Robert Lopez, *Beaumont Enterprise,* 09/22/2006
"MISSISSIPPI DA MOVEMENT PT. 3 PIMP C, LIVE FROM CLUB ROLEX, PORT GIBSON," http://www.youtube.com/watch?v=XcSFPSyjxDg
Pearl Police Department Incident Report #2005091397, 09/28/2005
United States of America vs. Milton Tutwiler et al, United States District Court, Northern District of Mississippi, Case #06-cr-00149, 10/24/2006

CHAPTER 52 & 53 contains a direct transcription of Pimp C's radio interview with Hot 107.9 WHTA in Atlanta, GA, on 07/23/2007, and also references the author's interviews with Anne-Marie Stripling, Ashlei Morrison, Ayesha Saafir, Big Gipp, Big Meech, Big Vee, Bonsu Thompson, Brandi Garcia, Curtis Daniel III, David Banner, Diamond, DJ Funky, DJ Paul, Fonzworth Bentley, Ganksta N-I-P, Jazze Pha, Jeff Sledge, Khujo Goodie, Killer Mike, Kool Ace, Lil Duval, Mama Wes, Matt Sonzala, Mia X, Mike Mo, Nancy Byron, Paul Wall, Pimp C, Rambro, Rico Wade, Ron Stewart, Sleepy Brown, Tre9, Truck, Vanessa Satten, Wendy Day, XVII, and Young Smitty. Additional sources include:
"Chad Butler's Blog," http://www.myspace.com/pimpcofugk/blog
"Fonzworth Bentley remembers Pimp C," as told to Julia Beverly, *OZONE* Magazine, Issue #63, January 2008
"Houstonian sees hope in Hip-Hop," by Kent Matthews, *Houston Chronicle,* 07/31/2009
"Houston's Lil Troy Responds to Pimp C's Tirade; Claims, 'Pimp ain't even no gangster," *XXL* Magazine, 07/30/2007
"Killer Mike: Pledge Of Allegiance," by Paul W. Arnold, HipHopDX.com, 01/18/2008
"Last respects," by Fred Davis, *Beaumont Enterprise,* 12/13/2007
"Lil Troy dissing Pimp C of UGK.," Short Stop TV, http://www.youtube.com/watch?v=QLAct24srgo
"Pimp C Apologizes To Atlanta But Nobody Else," by Anthony Springer, Jr., HipHopDX.com, 08/01/2007
"Pimp C = clearly batshit," by Byron Crawford, ByronCrawford.com, 07/25/2007
"Pimp C UGK released from prison," HipHop2Nite, June 2006, http://www.youtube.com/watch?v=PDGjtvV8zAw
"Pimp C: Tell 'Em I Said That," *XXL* Magazine, Issue #96, October 2007
"RZA Addresses Comments About The South That Offended Jay Electronica," by Shaheem Reid, MTV News, 06/02/2010
"Still Here, By Being Stubborn, Not Mellow," by Kelefa Sanneh, the *New York Times,* 08/07/2007
"Tell 'Em Why U Madd," XXLmag.com, 07/25/2007
"This Just In: Rock the Bells Canceled," by Keith Plocek, *Houston Press,* 08/07/2007
"UGK On Topping The Charts: 'It Feels Good!' – For Now...," by Shaheem Reid and Joseph Patel, 08/17/2007, MTV News
"UGK: Underground Kingz," review by Jason Roberts, HipHopDX.com, 08/13/2007
"UGK: Underground Kingz" review by Tom Breihan, *Pitchfork,* 08/17/2007
"Wu-Tang: Widdling Down Infinity," *URB* Magazine, 07/23/2007
"XVII of UGK – Pimp C [Speaks]," http://www.youtube.com/watch?v=_3YGo4plAj4

CHAPTER 54 references the author's interviews with Bankroll Jonez, Big Bubb, Big L, Big Munn, Brandi Garcia, Byron Amos, Chad Butler Jr., Connie Butler, Dat Boy Grace, Detective Marcelo Molfino, DJ B-Do, DJ GT, Edgar Walker Jr., Ghost, Heather Johnson, Jada, Killer Mike, King Yella, Lil Duval, Lil O, Mama Wes, Marian Rico Lee, Matt Sonzala, Mr. 3-2, Mr. Boomtown, Nancy Byron, Nitacha Broussard, Paperchase, Paul Wall, Pimp C, Point Blank, Ronda Forrest, Stokes, Tim Hampton, T.O.E., Trae, Truck, Vesto, Wendy Day, XVII, and Z-Ro. Additional sources include:
"97.9 the Box – Car Show – Pimp C Interview," http://www.youtube.com/watch?v=NblHn5iwQAU
"Artist was on verge of busting out big," by Eyder Peralta, *Houston Chronicle,* 10/15/2007
"Bun B Backstage at 97.9 The Box Car Show," http://www.youtube.com/watch?v=LnpXzw-94Tk
"Cory Mo remembers Pimp C," as told to Julia Beverly, *OZONE* Magazine, Issue #63, January 2008
"Houston rappers remember Big Moe, dead at 33," by Eyder Peralta, *Houston Chronicle,* 10/15/2007
"J. Xavier Interviews Pimp C," 11/17/07, http://www.youtube.com/watch?v=zkvCuTl37xg
"Mother to keep Pimp C promise," by Robert Lopez, *Beaumont Enterprise,* 02/10/2008
"NNETE W/ PIMP C....AND A FIGHT COME WIT DAT!!!," http://www.youtube.com/watch?v=o71XRz06R_U
"PIMP C and PIMPIN KEN(live) pimp diss ATL an speaks his mind," http://www.youtube.com/watch?v=DAzxMCpxTRQ

Pimp C interview by Greg Street, V103 WVEE Atlanta, 07/30/2007
"Pimp C Last Interview/Tribute," Yippi.com, 11/04/2007, http://www.youtube.com/watch?v=hTaQDZXpILk
"Pimp C performs 'murder' & speaks on Hip-Hop LIVE," Curb Music, http://www.youtube.com/watch?v=nGUhW0AOIUo
Port Arthur Police Department Offense Report, Case #58829-07, 09/17/2007
"Streets Is Talking: Young Jeezy," by Aqua, AllHipHop.com, 09/25/2007
Texas Prison Issues, http://brokenchains.us/tdcj/prison-issues/
The United States of America vs. Johnathon Travis Pete, United States District Court, Eastern District of Texas (Beaumont),
    Case #07-cr-00189, 09/19/2007
The United States of America vs. Robert L. Anderson, United States District Court, Southern District of Mississippi, Case
    #08-00016-WJG-JMR, 02/05/2008

CHAPTER 55 references the author's interviews with Bandit, Bankroll Jonez, Barry Weiss, Big Bubb, Big L, Big Munn, Born 2wice,
Bun B, Byron Amos, Craig Wormley, David Banner, DJ B-Do, DJ Dolby D, Don Vesto, D-Solo, Edgar Walker Jr., Ghost, Heather
Johnson, Hezeleo, Ivory P, Jazze Pha, Jeff Sledge, KB Da Kidnappa, Kep of Ovadose, Leo Nocentelli, Lil Duval, Mama Wes, Man-
nie Fresh, Marlan Rico Lee, Mia X, Mike Mo, Nancy Byron, NcGai, Pastor Troy, Pimp C, Rick Royal, Riley Broussard, Ron Spaulding,
Ronda Forrest, Sleepy Brown, Stax, Teresa Waldon, Tim Hampton, T.O.E., Too $hort, Travis, Truck, TV Johnny, Vesto, Vicious,
Wendy Day, Willie D, XVII, and Z-Ro. Additional sources include:
"Coroner: Pimp C died of natural causes," by Ashley Sanders, the *Port Arthur News*, 12/05/2007
"Fonzworth Bentley remembers Pimp C," as told to Julia Beverly, *OZONE* Magazine, Issue #63, January 2008
"Mannie Fresh's Sister Reportedly Murdered In Her New Orleans House," by Kurt Orzeck, MTV News, 11/30/2007
"New sleep lab at Christus detects problems of sleep apnea," by Sharon Kerr, *Beaumont Enterprise*, 02/13/2008
"Obstructive Sleep Apnea: An Expert Interview With Christopher Lettieri, MD," by Nancy Otto, *Medscape News*, 09/23/2009
"Opening a Passage to Better Sleep," by Gerald Secor Couzens, the *New York Times*, 08/29/2007
"PIMP C, BUN B & Chamillionaire On Stage last month," Chamillionaire TV, http://www.youtube.com/watch?v=8lYNU3MVp-Q
"Pimp C Last Interview/Tribute," Yippi.com, 11/04/2007, http://www.youtube.com/watch?v=hTaQDZXpILk
"Rappers talk about Pimp C," by Lindsay Meeks, *Houston Chronicle*, 12/13/2007
"Shaq Attacks Sleep Apnea," Harvard Medical School, 05/05/2011
"The Last Ugk Show," by Edgar Walker Jr., http://www.youtube.com/watch?v=ItO71jRaRLg
"T.I., Busta Rhymes, Bun B Honor Pimp C On Twitter," by Mawuse Ziegbe, MTV News, 12/04/2010
"Webbie Memorializes Pimp C on the Anniversary of His Death," *XXL* Magazine, 12/04/2009
"Webbie x VIBE.com," *VIBE* Magazine, http://www.youtube.com/watch?v=u1rZG2wK76o
"Young Jeezy's Thugs Giving," http://www.flavorus.com/event/YOUNG-JEEZY-S-THUGS-GIVING/47755
"Zune Live at the BBQ with Bun-B," Mix Revolution TV, http://www.youtube.com/watch?v=S3SUe4ZBXco

CHAPTER 56 references the author's interviews with Antezy, Ayesha Saafir, Bianca, Big Bubb, Bishop Don "Magic" Juan, Detec-
tive Steve Lankford, DJ B-Do, DJ Paul, Edgar Walker Jr., Greedy, Heather Johnson, Mama Wes, Nitacha Broussard, Ray Murray,
Rico Wade, Ron Spaulding, Shawn Holiday, Snoop Dogg, Teresa Waldon, Too $hort, Warren G, XVII, and Z-Ro. Additional sources
include:
"He Was Definitely A Dope Dude," MTV News, 12/05/2007
"Interview: Project Pat Talks Staying Relevant, the Album With Pimp C That Never Was, and Advice for Chief Keef," by David
    Drake, *Complex* Magazine, 03/10/2013
"Pimp C – Last Interview Before Death," http://www.youtube.com/watch?v=JK3HLJk8iMY
"Pimp C Last Show With Too Short @ House of Blues," http://www.youtube.com/watch?v=vkwwCFjLno4
"*Pimpology* with Gangsta Brown, Too Short and Pimpin Ken," http://www.youtube.com/watch?NR=1&v=RvNanBcqgl4
"The Last Days of Pimp C," *VIBE* Magazine, 12/08/2007
"THE REAL MOB TV – Z-Ro Interview: Working With Pimp C," *MOB TV, Vol. 3: MAAB Edition* DVD
"Three 6 Mafia Speak On The Realities of Sizzurp In Hip-Hop," by Paul W. Arnold, HipHopDX.com, 04/25/2008
"TOO $HORT, PIMP C AND GREEDY ENTERTAINMENT," http://www.youtube.com/watch?v=oSmploMeRQA
"Tuned In: Zune Takover (Seattle, WA)," by DJ B-Mello, AllHipHop.com, 12/04/2007
"Zune concert – Bun B – Part 2," https://www.youtube.com/watch?v=qJq0zjY6qaw

CHAPTER 57 references the author's interviews with Alonzo Cartier, Angie Crooks, Ayesha Saafir, Bianca, Big Bubb, Big Gipp,
Big L, Big Munn, Bo-Bo Luchiano, Bone, Bundy, Chad Butler Jr., Chuck Steeno, Craig Wormley, Dat Boy Grace, David Banner,
Detective Steve Lankford, DJ Bird, DJ Paul, Edgar Walker, Ghost, Halimah Saafir, Heather Johnson, Hezeleo, Ice-T, J. Walker, Jada,
Jeff Sledge, KLC, Mama Wes, Mannie Fresh, Mean Green, Mia X, Mike Mo, Nancy Byron, Naztradamus, Nitacha Broussard, Paul
Wall, Rick Royal, Riley Broussard, Royce Starring, Scarface, Smit-D, Smoke D, Snoop Dogg, Stax, Stephen Jack-
son, T.O.E., Too $hort, Trae tha Truth, Vanessa Satten, Wendy Day, Willie D, Wink Dawg, and XVII. Additional sources include:
"Cause of Death: Pimp C Found Dead," http://aolanswers.com/questions/cause_death_pimp_c_dead_rap_
    music_3506591619414/true_niggas_hear_believe_bullshit_518115943776642
"Chad Butler Condolences," *Houston Chronicle*,
    http://www.legacy.com/guestbooks/houstonchronicle/guestbook-entry-print.aspx?n=chad-butler&pid=99446736
"Coroner: Pimp C May Have Died of Natural Causes," TMZ, 12/04/2007
County of Los Angeles Sheriff's Department Incident Report #007-07729-0987-496, 12/04/2007
"EXCLUSIVE: Bun B's First Interview Since Pimp C's Passing," by Linda Hobbs, *VIBE* Magazine, 12/08/2007
"Fallen rapper's funeral planned for this weekend," by Ashley Sanders and Mary Meaux, the *Port Arthur News*, 12/06/2007
"First Grammy nomination for UGK comes two days after rapper's death," by Robert Lopez, *Beaumont Enterprise*, 12/07/2007
"Friends and family say goodbye to Pimp C," Associated Press, 12/13/2007
"Grammy's golden night," by Andrew Dansby, *Houston Chronicle*, 02/10/2008
"Hip-Hop star dies in hotel room," by David Pierson and Richard Winton, *Los Angeles Times*, 12/05/2007
"L.A. authorities investigating rapper Pimp C's death," by Joey Guerra and Peggy O'Hare, *Houston Chronicle*, 12/05/2007
"Lil' Flip Mourns Comrade Pimp C," by Chris Gray, *Houston Press*, 12/05/2007
"Lil Wayne Speaks about PIMP C. Death – EXCLUSIVE," Chamillionaire TV, http://www.youtube.com/watch?v=BV61_VQTRYI
"Los Angeles County Coroner, 2007 Annual Report," http://coroner.lacounty.gov/Docs/2007%20Annual%20Report_FINAL.pdf
"Natural cause likely in Pimp C's death," *Houston Chronicle*, 12/06/2007
"No Grammy for UGK, only memories," by Randall Roberts, *Beaumont Enterprise*, 02/11/2008
"Official: Pimp C likely died in sleep," by Fred Davis, *Beaumont Enterprise*, 12/07/2007
"Pimp C Died From Accidental Cough-Medicine Overdose, Sleep Condition: Autopsy," by Jayson Rodriguez, MTV News,
    02/04/2008
"Pimp C is Dead," by Tom Breihan, The *Village Voice*, 12/04/2007
"Pimp C Nominated for Grammy Two Days After Death," HipHop-Elements.com, 12/06/2007
"Pimp C, Southern Hip-Hop Rapper, Dies at 33," by Kalefa Sanneh, the *New York Times*, 12/05/2007
"Pimp C – The Calmest 911 Call Ever Made," TMZ, 12/07/2007
"Rapper Pimp C's Death Ruled An Accident," by Christine Pelisek, *LA Weekly*, 02/04/2008
"Report on Pimp C's passing," KFDM TV,
    http://www.dailymotion.com/video/x3ofrq_report-on-pimp-c-s-passing_music?search_algo=2#.US0hINs265w
"R.I.P. Pimp C," by John Nova Lomax, *Houston Press*, 12/13/2007
"Scarface: Guess Who's Back?" by Paul W. Arnold, HipHopDX.com, 11/18/2007
"The Last Days of Pimp C," *VIBE* Magazine, 12/08/2007
"The life & death of Pimp C," by Sarah Moore, *Beaumont Enterprise*, 12/05/2007
"THE REAL MOB TV – Z-Ro Interview: Working With Pimp C," *MOB TV, Vol. 3: MAAB Edition* DVD,
    http://www.youtube.com/watch?v=qjrvtxAHGDM
The United States of America vs. Charles Grace, Case #05-cr-00043-1, United States District Court, Southern District of Texas
    (Houston), 01/31/2005
"UGK's Pimp C: An Underground Legend Who Defied The Mainstream," by Shaheem Reid, MTV News, 12/04/2007
"Unlabeled cough syrup found in Pimp C's hotel," by Kristie Rieken, Associated Press, 02/06/2008
"Willie D Remembers Pimp C," by Keith Plocek, *Houston Press*, 12/05/2007

CHAPTER 58 references the author's interviews with Angie Crooks, Bianca, Big Bubb, Big L, Bishop Don "Magic" Juan, Bone,

Brandi Garcia, Brenda Harmon, Bundy, Byron Amos, Chad Butler Jr., Craig Wormley, David Banner, Dr. Teeth, Edgar Walker, Hashim Nzinga, Heather Johnson, Hezeleo, Ivory P., Janeen Harmon, Jeff Sledge, Killer Mike, Kristi Floyd, Langston Adams, Lanika, Lil O, Mama Wes, Mean Green, Merrick Young, Mia X, MJG, Mr. Lee, Mr. Soul, Nancy Byron, NcGai, Pimpin' Ken, Quanell X, Russell Washington, Scarface, Shaheem Reid, Snoop Dogg, Stephanie Starring, Stephen Starring, Steve Below, Nitacha Broussard, Teresa Waldon, Tim Hampton, T.O.E., Too $hort, Trae tha Truth, Travis, Wendy Day, Willie D, and XVII. Additional sources include:

"Butler remembered with love," by Mary Meaux, the *Port Arthur News*, 12/13/2007
"Fallen rapper's funeral planned for this weekend," by Ashley Sanders and Mary Meaux, the *Port Arthur News*, 12/06/2007
"FANS AND FRIENDS SAY GOODBYE TO PIMP C," http://www.youtube.com/watch?v=etCi2ZIWTHQ
"Fans turn out to bid Butler farewell," the *Port Arthur News*, 12/13/2007
"Friends, family and fans pay respects to Pimp C," by Joey Guerra, *Houston Chronicle*, 12/13/2007
"Interview with Scarface," by Matt Sonzala, HoustonSoReal.blogspot.com, 12/31/2004
"'It turned out just the way he would have wanted it ... because of the love'," by Rose Ybarra, *Beaumont Enterprise*, 12/14/2007
"Judge Denies C-Murder's Request to Attend Pimp C's Funeral," *XXL Magazine*, 12/12/2007
"Lil Wayne Speaks about PIMP C. DEATH – EXCLUSIVE," Chamillionaire TV, http://www.youtube.com/watch?v=BV61_VQTRYI
"Memphitz is the man with the plan," by Andria Lisle, The *Commercial Appeal*, 04/04/2008
"Pimp C Funeral Service," Nasircle Production," http://www.youtube.com/watch?v=GBrVjYsgkNw
"Pimp C Is Given Uplifting, Heartfelt Farewell At Funeral," by Shaheem Reid, MTV News, 12/13/2007
"Pimp C shirts aim to keep legacy alive," by Merecal McKenzie, the *Port Arthur News*, 01/25/2008
"Pimp C's Final farewell R.I.P.," http://www.youtube.com/watch?v=YeLYGlpCx4
"Rapper's funeral brings out big names in Hip-Hop," by Amy Moore, the *Port Arthur News*, 12/12/2007
"Rappers talk about Pimp C," by Lindsay Meeks, *Houston Chronicle*, 12/13/2007
"Remembering UGK's Pimp C," MTV News,
      http://www.mtv.com/videos/news/195557/pimp-cs-funeral-we-lost-a-homie.jhtml#id=1575713
"Rhymes & reasons," by Sarah Moore, *Beaumont Enterprise*, 12/14/2007
"The burden of burial," by Fred Davis, *Beaumont Enterprise*, 12/08/2007
"Thousands attend Chad 'Pimp C' Butler's funeral," the *Port Arthur News*, 12/13/2007
"T.I. Apologizes For Missing Pimp C's Funeral In Christmas Message," HipHop-Elements.com, 12/28/2007
"Ugk Rapper Pimp C's Funeral," KFDM, http://www.youtube.com/watch?v=XgAR4O3crlk

CHAPTER 59 references the author's interviews with Antezy, Ayesha Saafir, Bianca, Big Bubb, Big Munn, Boonie, Byron Amos, Chuck Steeno, Craig Wormley, Detective Steve Lankford, DJ Bird, DJ Dolby D, Dr. David Benjamin, Edgar Walker Jr., Heather Johnson, Ice-T, Jaro Vacek, Korleon, Mama Wes, Matt Sonzala, Mike Mo, Nancy Byron, Sam Martin, Shaheem Reid, Smoke D, Stax, Nitacha Broussard, Tim Hampton, Too $hort, and XVII. Additional sources include:
"Bun B To Produce Pimp C Tribute For Ozone Awards," by Anthony Thomas, *XXL Magazine*, 08/06/
"Butler 'Pimp C's' death ruled accidental," by Mary Meaux, the *Port Arthur News*, 02/04/2008
"California's Involuntary Manslaughter Law," http://www.shouselaw.com/involuntary_manslaughter.html
"Cause of death: Coroner's report on Pimp C due this week," The *Beaumont Enterprise*, 02/04/2008
"ChemNote: Cyanide Poisoning," by Dr. A.J. Attar,"
      http://chemsee.com/poison-detection/poison-detection-resources/cyanide-poisoning/
"Coroner Still Testing For Pimp C's Cause Of Death," 01/28/2008, AllHipHop.com
"Cyanide Poisoning: Autopsy Finding," http://cyanidepoisoning.blogspot.com/2004/10/autopsy-finding.html
"Drugs Killed Pimp C," the *New York Times*, 02/06/2008
"EXCLUSIVE: Bun B's First Interview Since Pimp C's Passing," by Linda Hobbs, *VIBE* Magazine, 12/08/2007
"Forensic Research Extends Detection Of Cyanide Poisoning," 01/09/2012,
      http://www.shsu.edu/~pin_www/T@S/2012/cyanideresearch.html
"He Was Definitely A Dope Dude," MTV News, 12/05/2007
"Illuminati Killed Pimp C," http://www.youtube.com/watch?v=Yjps7jY80fc
"Lil Wayne On Syrup: 'Everybody Wants Me To Stop ... It Ain't That Easy," by Shaheem Reid, MTV News, 02/28/2008
"Lil Wayne Won't Take Full Credit For 'Double Cup' Trend," by Maurice Bobb, MTV RapFix, 11/24/2012
"Lottery winner exhumed; cyanide deaths rare, experts say," by Jen Christensen, CNN, 01/18/2013
"Pimp C Died from Overdose, Sleep Condition," *XXL Magazine*, 02/04/2008
"Pimp C: Never Die," by Dave Bry, *XXL Magazine*, 12/04/2012
"Pimp C's death caused by overdose and sleep condition," by Andrew Dansby, *Houston Chronicle*, 02/04/2008
"Pimp C Died From Accidental Cough-Medicine Overdose, Sleep Condition: Autopsy," by Jayson Rodriguez, MTV News, 02/04/2008
"Pimp C's Mother, Weslyn 'Mama Wes' Monroe, Was Laid to Rest This Weekend," by Dharmic X, *Complex* Magazine, 08/25/2013
"Pimp C's Widow Wages War With Rap-A-Lot Records Over Masters," by Martin Spasov, *XXL Magazine*, 06/21/2011
"Rapper Pimp C's Death Ruled An Accident," by Christine Pelisek, *LA Weekly*, 02/04/2008
"Toxicological Investigation of Acute Cyanide Poisoning of a 29-year-old Man: A Case Report," 11/28/2012, *Iranian Journal of Toxicology*, Volume 7, No 20, Spring 2013
"UGK enshrined in hometown museum," by Brooke Crum, the *Port Arthur News*, 12/02/2012

CHAPTER 60 references the author's interviews with 8Ball, Big Mike, Big Munn, Bun B, KayK, Killa Kyleon, Killer Mike, Lil O, Mr. 3-2, Paul Wall, Pimp C, Short Dawg, XVII, and Z-Ro. Additional sources include:
"Actavis Reportedly Pulls Cough Syrup After Musicians Cast Product In Bad Light," by Jason MacNeil, The *Huffington Post Canada*, 04/23/2014
"Bun B: Trill Recognize Trill," by Aliya Ewing, HipHopDX.com, 03/10/2008
"Bun B Comments on Lil Wayne's Syrup Addiction," by William E. Ketchum III, HipHopDX.com, 03/06/2008
"Cough Syrup Abuse Worries: From Rapper's Death to Super Bowl Ads and Study," by Mike Nizza, the *New York Times*, 02/05/2008
"Lean With It: Rap's Deadly Dance With Syrup," by Rob Kenner, *Complex* Magazine, 03/20/2013
"Lil Boosie: Lean Has 'F***ed Up' Rap Culture," TMZ, 04/24/2014
"Lil Keke Calls Lean Use 'The Saddest Thing In The Game,'" by Danielle Harling, HipHopDX.com, 05/27/2014
"Lil Wayne: I Drank Sizzurp 'Because I Was Sick,'" TMZ.com, http://www.tmz.com/videos/1_1zqn8urq/
"Lil Wayne On Syrup: 'Everybody Wants Me To Stop ... It Ain't That Easy," by Shaheem Reid, MTV News, 02/28/2008
"Lil' Wayne Won't Put Down The Lean, 'I Pour It Up For Pimp C,'" SOHH.com, 03/20/3008
"Lil Wayne Won't Take Full Credit For 'Double Cup' Trend," by Maurice Bobb, MTV RapFix, 11/24/2012
"Much Ado About Sizzurp," by Jeff Deeney, *The Atlantic*, 03/19/2013
The State of Texas vs. Charleston Davis, District Court of Harris County, Case #1198559, 01/11/2009
"Video: Beanie Sigel talks About Lean," Nahright.com, 08/30/2012
"What's 'sizzurp'? A dangerous way for kids to get high," by Jeff Rossen and Josh Davis, *TODAY*, 01/23/2014

CHAPTER 61 references the author's interviews with Angie Crooks, Averexx, Brenda Harmon, Bun B, Byron Amos, Chad Butler Jr., Chuck Steeno, Connie Butler, Craig Wormley, DJ B-Do, Edgar Walker Jr., Fonzworth Bentley, Hezeleo, Janeen Harmon, Jazze Pha, Jeff Sledge, Mama Wes, Matt Sonzala, Nancy Byron, Naztradamus, NcGai, Ron Forrest, Ronda Forrest, Nitacha Broussard, T.O.E., Vicious, Wendy Day, and XVII. Additional sources include:
"Beaumont, Texas, Attorney Pleads Guilty to Tax Violation," 04/15/2014, www.justice.gov/usao/law/news/wdla20140414f.html
"Big K.R.I.T. Reflects on Recording With UGK," by Adam Fleischer, *XXL Magazine*, 07/21/2011
Byron Hill vs. Bernard Freeman, District Court of Harris County, Cause #2007-77221, 12/21/2007
Dirty Glove Bastard, http://www.dirty-glove.com/
Hans Niknejad d/b/a Twin Entertainment vs. UGK, Inc., Circuit Court for Williamson County, Case #06665, 11/15/2006
"Houston's Hip-Hop Scene Picks Up the Pieces After Yet Another Death," by Kalefa Sanneh, the *New York Times*, 02/11/2008
"Juicy J Says He's Producing Posthumous Pimp C Album," by Yohance Kyles, AllHipHop.com, 08/13/2013
"OFFICIAL STATEMENT FROM PIMP C'S MANAGER REGARDING HIS UNTIMELY DEATH," email from Nancy Byron, 12/04/2007
"Pimp C shirts aim to keep legacy alive," by Merecal McKenzie, the *Port Arthur News*, 01/25/2008
"Pimp C: Still Pimping," review by Emanuel Wallace, RapReviews.com, 07/19/2011
"Pimp C's Mother & Son On Stage To Remember Pimp C! + Fans Throw Money TO The Family!,"

http://www.youtube.com/watch?v=yWG1P1rBX_E
"Pimp C's Widow Wages War With Rap-A-Lot Records Over Masters," by Martin Spasov, *XXL* Magazine, 06/21/2011
"Pimp C's Wife Responds To Rap-A-Lot Lawsuit Over Masters," AllHipHop.com, 07/11/2011
Rap-A-Lot 2K Records vs. Chinara Butler, District Court of Harris County, Cause #2011-36404, 06/17/2011
"Singled Out: Cavie," SOHH.com, 01/10/2012
"The Mo'Nique Show Guest Rewind: Bun B on Moving On," BET.com, 03/01/2011

CHAPTER 62 references the author's interviews with Angie Crooks, Averexx, Bandit, Bankroll Jonez, Big Gipp, Big K.R.I.T., Big L, Big Munn, Bone, Boonie, Bun B, Carlos Moreland, Cory Mo, DJ B-Do, Donny Young, E-40, Edgar Walker Jr., Hezeleo, Joi Gilliam, Kamikaze, Killa Kyleon, Killer Mike, KLC, Lloyd, Mama Wes, Mannie Fresh, Mitchell Queen Jr., Mr. Lee, Naztradamus, Rambro, Sleepy Brown, Smit-D, Tim Hampton, Too $hort, Travis, Truck, and Vanessa Satten. Additional sources include:
"2nd Annual Chad 'Pimp C' Butler Hip-Hop, Health & Wellness Festival," http://www.youtube.com/watch?v=_NgQ85kBop4
"3rd Annual Chad 'Pimp C' Butler's Hip-Hop Health & Wellness Festival," http://www.youtube.com/watch?v=2rXARr6Y81o
"A Tribute to Pimp C of UGK," Urban Life Entertainment, http://www.youtube.com/watch?v=HU3Ytn_xS9E
"ASAP Rocky Talks UGK with Sama'an Ashrawi," http://www.youtube.com/watch?v=_C0PdB69wPM
"Audio: Pimp C Ft. Bun B & Aubrey — What Up," Dirty-Glove.com, 08/28/2010
"Bessie Jacob," *Teche Today*, 08/14/2008
"Big Boi Praises Dr. Dre's "The Chronic," Explains How He Got A Pimp C Verse," by Steven J. Horowitz, HipHopDX.com, 01/21/2013
"Bun B briefly trades recording studio for classroom," *Beaumont Enterprise*, 03/14/2011
"Bun B Brings 'Em Out at II Trill Listening Session in NYC," by Jayson Rodriguez, MTV News, 03/05/2008
"Bun B Comments on Lil Wayne's Syrup Addiction," by William E. Ketchum III, HipHopDX.com, 03/06/2008
"Bun B Explains Why J. Cole's 'Bun B For President' Didn't Make Album," *VIBE* Magazine, 08/11/2010
"Bun B For Mayor: Could This Ever Be a Thing?" by Chris Gray, *Houston Press*, 11/13/2013
"'Bun B' Freeman returns to PA for food drive," by Mary Meaux, the *Port Arthur News*, 11/26/2009
"Bun B Helps Pimp C's Wife Spread HIV Awareness In Houston," by Trill Chris, KeepItTrill.com, 12/12/2011
Bun B interview, *The Source* Magazine, Issue #221, May 2008
"Bun B Interview at Breakfast Club Power 105.1 (11/15/2013)," https://www.youtube.com/watch?v=8b3aGnzl3eA
Bun B interview by David A. Herron, *Texas Monthly*, March 2008
Bun B interview by Randy Roper, *OZONE* Magazine, Issue #85, April 2010
"Bun B Receives Own Day in Houston," by Elan Mancini, *XXL* Magazine, 08/29/2011
"Bun B Reveals Details On New Drake Video," *VIBE* Magazine, 11/12/2010
"Bun B Reveals Proudest Pimp C Verse, Production," by Jake Paine, HipHopDX.com, 03/09/2009
"Bun B Talks Pimp C Tribute With Jay-Z," by Shaheem Reid, MTV News, 02/26/2010
"Bun B Talks Tupac Collaboration & Drake's First Week Numbers," by Insanul "Incilin" Ahmed, *Complex* Magazine, 06/24/2010
"Bun B To Produce Pimp C Tribute For Ozone Awards," by Anthony Thomas, *XXL* Magazine, 08/06/2008
"Bun B To Release One Last UGK Album To Honor His Late Partner, Pimp C," by Jayson Rodriguez, MTV News, 01/23/2009
"Bun B's Answer Key," by Teresa Mioli, *Beaumont Enterprise*, 03/15/2011
"Bun B: Trill Recognize Trill," by Aliya Ewing, HipHopDX.com, 03/10/2008
"Bun B's album tops the charts," by Rose Ybarra and Christine Rappleye, *Beaumont Enterprise*, 05/31/2008
"Bun B Interview talks Pimp C 'At First..We Didn't Like Each Other,'" Thisis50.com, http://www.youtube.com/watch?v=un9L7rnYbGw
"BUN B REMEMBERS PIMP C: SHARES HIS FAVORITE MEMORIES & PIMP C LYRICS!," by Devi Dev, 97.9 The Box,
    http://www.youtube.com/watch?v=6bg__ffHORI
"Chad 'Pimp C' Butler Health & Awareness Festival Next Saturday," by Trill Chris, KeepItTrill.com, 12/03/2010
"Chamillionaire * DEE 1 504 @ Pimp C Butler Hip-Hop Health & Wellness 2012 #3RDWARDTV,"
    http://www.youtube.com/watch?v=GHVeo68gvsg
"Coroner: Pimp C died of natural causes," by Ashley Sanders, the *Port Arthur News*, 12/05/2007
"DJ Screw: from cough syrup to full-blown fever," by Jesse Serwer, The *Guardian*, 11/11/2010
"Drake Says 'Young Sweet Jones' Reference Pays Tribute To Pimp C," by Shaheem Reid and Sway Calloway, MTV News,
    09/21/2010
"Expect long lines, large crowd Sunday at UGK museum induction," by Brooke Crum, the *Port Arthur News*, 11/30/2012
"FEATURE: Bun B, Life After Death," by Slav Kandyba, *XXL* Magazine, 11/06/2009
"Fitting farewell from UGK," by Joey Guerra, *Houston Chronicle*, 03/29/2009
"Freddie Gibbs talks UGK with Sama'an Ashrawi," http://www.youtube.com/watch?v=XhLG3XQOgD8
"Health fair in rapper Pimp C's memory," *Beaumont Enterprise*, 12/02/2009
"Hip-Hop rap duo to be inducted into Museum of Gulf Coast Music Hall of Fame," by Mary Meaux, the *Port Arthur News*,
    11/13/2012
"Houston Rapper Bun B Given His Own Day In The City Of Houston!," by Isiah Carey, IsiahFactor.com, 08/31/2011
"Houston's Hip-Hop Scene Picks Up the Pieces After Yet Another Death," by Kalefa Sanneh, the *New York Times*, 02/11/2008
"Jay Z Releases 'Tom Ford' Remix To Honor Death Of Pimp C," *Huffington Post*, 12/05/2013
"J Prince Interview With The Breakfast Club Power 105.1," www.youtube.com/watch?v=T8NwDi9ok_w
"Jeezy's Tribute to Pimp C," MTV News, 08/18/2008
"Juicy J Explains Pimp C's Appearance On The 'Show out Remix'," by Jake Paine, HipHopDX.com, 06/11/2013
"Juicy J on 'Stay Trippy,' Sippin' Lean & Pimp C," FUSE TV, http://www.youtube.com/watch?v=z1ZpwnVFVNQ
"Juicy J Says He's Producing Posthumous Pimp C Album," by Yohance Kyles, AllHipHop.com, 08/13/2013
"Killer Mike: Pledge Of Allegiance," by Paul W. Arnold, HipHopDX.com, 01/18/2008
"Lil' Wayne Won't Put Down The Lean, 'I Pour It Up For Pimp C,'" SOHH.com, 03/20/3008
"Long live the Kingz: UGK wins BET awards," by Rose Ybarra, *Beaumont Enterprise*, 06/26/2008
"Memorialized," by Sarah Moore, *Beaumont Enterprise*, 12/03/2012
"Nas to Record On Mass Appeal Records; Will Release 'Lost Tapes 2' & Posthumous Pimp C Album," by Reggie Ugwu, *Billboard*,
    05/16/2014
"No More Baubles: Onetime Procurer Iceberg Slim Turns to Prose — and Still Sells," by Monroe Anderson, *The National Observer*,
    12/04/1971
"PIMP C LAST INTERVIEW (R.I.P.)," Tha Buzz, http://www.youtube.com/watch?v=xTFXvd551J8
"Pimp C Remembered By Bun B, Chamillionaire, More On First Anniversary Of His Death," by Steven Roberts and Shaheem Reid,
    MTV News, 12/04/2008
"Pimp C's Legacy Carried On Through Hip-Hop Health Fair," by Kyle Anderson and Rahman Dukes, MTV News, 12/04/2009
"Pimp C's Wife Launches Chad Butler Hip-Hop Wellness Expo," by Nolan Strong, AllHipHop.com, 11/24/2009
"Pimp C's Wife Launches Scholarship Fund," AllHipHop.com, 09/11/2011
"Pimp C – Last Interview Before Death," http://www.youtube.com/watch?v=JK3HLJk8iMY
"Port Arthur rapper Bun B ready to lecture at Rice," *Beaumont Enterprise*, 10/22/2010
"Port Arthur rapper Bun B releases third album," *Beaumont Enterprise*, 08/03/2010
"Port Arthur's Bun B releases rap coloring book," by Maggie Galehouse, *Beaumont Enterprise*, 09/10/2013
"RAP ROYALTY: The one and only UGK Bun B hopes duo's final album leaves fans with a Pimp C legacy," by Joey Guerra,
    Houston Chronicle, 03/31/2009
"Rap-A-Lot Gives Pimp C's 'Naked Soul' Album A Release Date," KeepItTrill.com, 07/02/2010
"Remembering Mama Wes, Pimp C's Mother," Channel 6 KFDM, 08/18/2013
"#RIPPimpC — Two Christian rap songs that sample the UGK legend," by Sketch the Journalist, *Houston Chronicle*, 12/04/2012
"Rollin' again," by Christine Rappleye, *Beaumont Enterprise*, 03/26/2008
"Sixty Four Dollar Cologne, Bitch!" CocaineBlunts.com, 12/04/2008
"Still Trill," by Jesse Serwer, *XLR8R* Magazine, Issue #116, April 2008
"Texas Rappers United To Honor Pimp C. During Charity Event," by Nolan Strong and Grouchy Greg Watkins, AllHipHop.com,
    12/04/2010
"The greatest Bun B interview," KLRU, http://www.youtube.com/watch?v=0LBazktPezg
"The Legacy of Pimp C and the Hip-Hop, Health & Wellness Festival," *Mass Appeal*, 12/27/2013
"The Making Of Pimp C's Naked Soul of Sweet Jones Album (KeepItTrill Exclusive!),"
    http://www.youtube.com/watch?v=jDTGWRdhZKk
"The Year of Magical Thinking: How Bun B dealt with Pimp C's death," by Ben Westhoff, *Houston Press*, 07/28/2010
"Today In Hip-Hop: Bun B Celebrates His 40th Birthday," by Sean Ryon, *XXL* Magazine, 03/19/2013

"Too Short And Bun B Remember UGK's Early Days," by Shaheem Reid, MTV News, 07/27/2009
"Two Nights Ago: Bun B and Other Members of the UGK Family," by Shea Serrano, *Houston Press*, 02/10/2008
"UGK enshrined in hometown museum," by Brooke Crum, the *Port Arthur News*, 12/02/2012
"UGK fans must wait in line or watch Sunday exhibit induction online," the *Port Arthur News*, 11/29/2012
"UGK: UGK 4 Life" CD Review by Andrew Noz, HipHopDX.com, 03/30/2009
"UGK's Last Album An 'Emotional Experience' After Pimp C's Death," by Kim Stolz, MTV News, 03/02/2009
"U.G.K. Hall of Fame Induction Interviews with Bun B and Chad Butler Jr.," http://www.youtube.com/watch?v=2qyMg3dVl-k
"Video magic happens in Port Arthur," by Mary Meaux, the *Port Arthur News*, 03/26/2008
"Where religion and rap collide," by Jason Bellini, *Houston Chronicle*, 02/10/2011
"Young Jeezy at LIVE NATION Houston Texas," http://www.youtube.com/watch?v=pYYcWzrXuyl

The **AFTERWORD** references the author's interviews with Big Munn, DJ Bird, Korleon, Mama Wes, Pimp C, Pops, XVII, and several of Larry Adams' friends who declined to be named. Additional sources include:
Fresno County Coroner, Larry Adams, Case #13-06.133, 06/14/2013
Fresno Police Department Law Enforcement Report Form, Event #13AW1656, 06/14/2013
"Houston Hip-Hop News Mama Wes clears up Pimp C didn't die over Promethazine Codeine Syrup or any drug," https://www.youtube.com/watch?v=CS04E1N0pGl
"Kickback Sunday Ft Mama Wes," http://www.youtube.com/watch?v=-gZYJg6i0d0
Larry Adams obituary, *Jackson Clarion-Ledger*, 06/22/2013
Lucille Davis obituary, *Natchez Democrat*, 01/16/2007
"mama wes," Colby Savage's M.O.E. documentary, http://www.youtube.com/watch?v=Ee07cDbohho
"Report on Pimp C's passing," KFDM TV,
    http://www.dailymotion.com/video/x3ofrq_report-on-pimp-c-s-passing_music?search_algo=2#.US0hlNs265w
Roderick Adams obituary, *Jackson Clarion-Ledger*, 01/29/2011
"We know it can kill us: Why people still smoke," by Jen Christensen, CNN, 01/13/2014

The **BACK COVER** references the author's interviews with Barry Weiss and Scarface. Additional sources include:
"RAP ROYALTY: The one and only UGK Bun B hopes duo's final album leaves fans with a Pimp C legacy," by Joey Guerra,
    Houston Chronicle, 03/31/2009

Julia Beverly solidified her position in the male-dominated urban music industry as the CEO and Editor-in-Chief of *OZONE* Magazine, which she founded in 2002. Tagged as "your favorite rapper's favorite magazine," *OZONE* carved out a unique niche with its raw and uncensored journalism style and gained a solid following in the crowded urban marketplace. *OZONE* was instrumental in introducing Southern rap's biggest names, such as Pitbull, Young Jeezy, Rick Ross, Lil Wayne and more, to the mainstream.

In 2006, Beverly extended the OZONE brand to include a star-studded award ceremony. In addition to freelance photography and journalism for *VIBE*, *The Source*, *URB* Magazine, and the *Miami New Times*, Beverly herself has been featured in publications like *Businessweek* and the *Orlando Sentinel*. Her work with *OZONE* has generated press in the *New York Times,* the *New York Daily News*, the *New York Post*, the *Miami Herald*, the *Houston Chronicle* and more.

In 2008, Beverly launched another successful venture, Agency Twelve, a booking agency which secures artists for concerts and appearances all the way from Hong Kong to the remote regions of Alaska. In addition to her work as a booking agent, Beverly has toured internationally with many artists and served as pop star Flo Rida's videographer. An avid distance runner, she has run races everywhere from the cold streets of Iceland to the Great Wall of China and aims to spark renewed interest in fitness among the Hip-Hop community.

For interview requests and other business inquiries, contact jb@ozonemag.com.

Above: **Pimp C** and **Julia Beverly** at the 2006 OZONE Awards in Orlando, FL; **Julia Beverly** and **Pimp C** in Milwaukee, 2006.
Below: **Julia Beverly** taking pictures of **Pimp C** outside the Huntsville Unit when he was released from prison; **Julia Beverly, Mama Wes,** and **J. Prince** at the 2008 OZONE Awards in Houston.